The **Rough Guide** to

Morocco

written and researched by

Mark Ellingham, Daniel Jacobs, Hamish Brown and Shaun McVeigh

with additional contributions by
Darren Humphrys, Daniel Lund and James Stewart

ROUGH GUIDES

NEW YORK · LONDON · DELHI

www.roughguides.com

Contents

Moroccan architecture
colour section following
p.312

Crafts and souvenirs
colour section following
p.456

Festivals and music
colour section following
p.552

3

◄◄ Mosquée Hassan II, Casablanca ◄ Tanneries, Fes

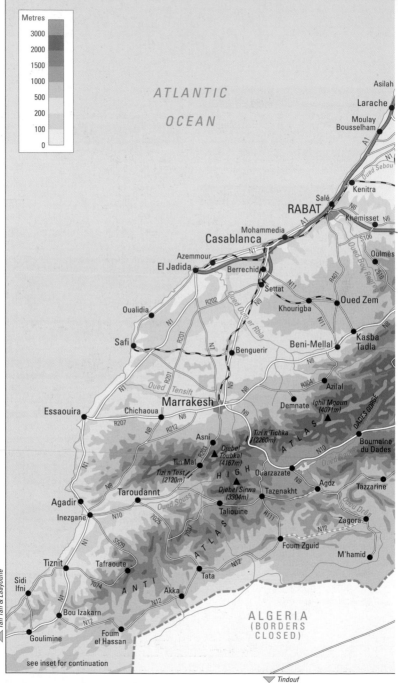

Metres
3000
2000
1500
1000
500
200
100
0

ATLANTIC

OCEAN

Asilah

Larache

Moulay
Bousselham

Oued Sebou

A1

N1

Salé   Kenitra

RABAT   N6

Khemisset   N6

S106

Mohammedia

Casablanca   Oulmès

Azemmour   Oued Bou Regreg

El Jadida   Berrechid   R401   R416

Settat   N11

N1   N9   Khouribga   Oued Zem

Oualidia   R202   N11   N8

R201   Kasba
Tadla

Safi   N7   Beni-Mellal   N8

Benguerir   R304   Azilal

Oued Tensift   N8   Demnate   Ighil Mgoun
(4071m)   DADES GORGE

Essaouira   Chichaoua   Marrakesh   N9

R207   N8   R212   N8   Tizi n'Tichka
(2260m)   ATLAS   N10   Boumalne
du Dades

Asni   R203   Oued Dadès

Tin Mal   Djebel
Toubkal
(4167m)   Ouarzazate   N9   Agdz   Tazzarine

Tizi n'Test
(2120m)   HIGH   Tazenakht

N1   N8   Taroudannt   Djebel Sirwa
(3304m)   Oued Drâa

Agadir   N10   Oued Souss   Taliouine   R111   Zagora

Inezgane   N12

T025   ATLAS   N12   Foum Zguid   M'hamid

Tiznit   Tafraoute   N1   Tata

Sidi   7074   ALGERIA
Ifni   ANTI   Akka   (BORDERS
CLOSED)

Bou Izakarn   N12

N12

Goulimine   Foum
el Hassan

see inset for continuation   Tindouf

Tan Tan & Laayoune

4

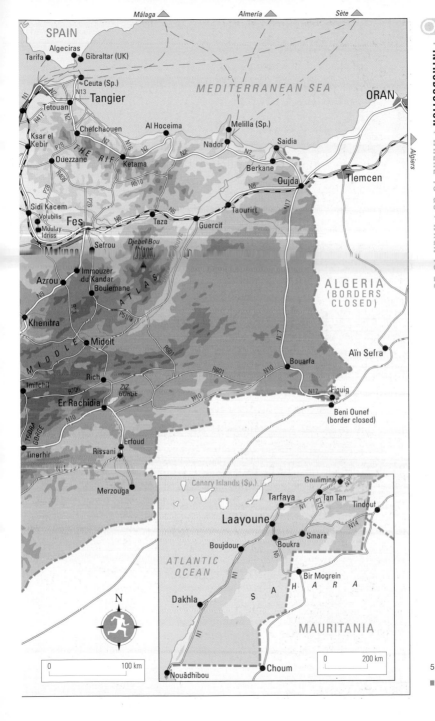

SPAIN

Málaga

Almería

Sète

Algeciras

Tarifa

Gibraltar (UK)

Ceuta (Sp.)

N13

Tangier

MEDITERRANEAN SEA

ORAN

Tetouan

N2

R417

Chefchaouen

Al Hoceima

Melilla (Sp.)

Ksar el
Kebir

Nador

Saidia

P28

THE RIF

N16

N2

Ouezzane

Ketama

R406

Berkane

R510

N6

Oujda

Tlemcen

Sidi Kacem

Volubilis

Taourirt

Fes

Taza

Guercif

N17

Moulay
Idriss

Sefrou

Djebel Bou
Iblane

Malinga

Immouzer
du Kandar

ALGERIA
(BORDERS
CLOSED)

Azrou

Boulemane

ATLAS

Khenifra

Midelt

Bouarfa

Aïn Sefra

MIDDLE

P5106

R601

Imilchil

Rich

R706

ZIZ
GORGE

N10

Figuig

N17

Er Rachidia

M10

Beni Ounef
(border closed)

TODRA
GORGE

Tinerhir

Rissani

Erfoud

Merzouga

Canary Islands (Sp.)

Goulimine

Tarfaya

Tan Tan

Tindouf

N1

N14

Laayoune

Smara

Boujdour

Boukra

ATLANTIC
OCEAN

N5

Bir Mogrein

Dakhla

S A H A R A

MAURITANIA

N

N1

Nouâdhibou

Choum

0   100 km

0   200 km

Algiers

Introduction to

Morocco

For Westerners, Morocco holds an immediate and enduring fascination. Though just an hour's ride on the ferry from Spain, it seems at once very far from Europe, with a culture – Islamic and deeply traditional – that is almost wholly unfamiliar. Throughout the country, despite the years of French and Spanish colonial rule and the presence of modern and cosmopolitan cities like Rabat and Casablanca, a more distant past constantly makes its presence felt. Fes, perhaps the most beautiful of all Arab cities, maintains a life still rooted in medieval times, when a Moroccan empire stretched from Senegal to northern Spain, while in the mountains of the Atlas and the Rif, it's still possible to draw up tribal maps of the Berber population. As a backdrop to all this, the country's physical make-up is also extraordinary: from a Mediterranean coast, through four mountain ranges, to the empty sand and scrub of the Sahara.

All of which makes Morocco an intense and rewarding experience, and a country that is ideally suited to independent (or, for activities, small-group) travel. If you have time enough, you can cover a whole range of experiences – hike in the Atlas, drive through the southern oases, relax at the laidback Atlantic resorts like Asilah or Essaouira, and lose yourself wandering the old streets of Fes or Marrakesh. It can be hard at times to come to terms with the privilege

▲ Dyers' souk, Marrakesh

of your position as a tourist in a country with severe poverty, and there is, too, occasional hassle from unofficial guides. But Morocco is essentially a safe and politically stable country to visit: the death in 1999 of King Hassan II, the Arab world's longest-serving leader, was followed by an easy transition to his son, Mohammed VI. And your enduring impressions are likely to be overwhelmingly positive, shaped by encounters with Morocco's powerful tradition of hospitality, generosity and openness. This is a country people return to again and again.

> **With a powerful tradition of hospitality, generosity and openness, this is a country people return to again and again**

Fact file

• Morocco's area of 446,550 square kilometres (722,550 sq km including the Western Sahara) makes it slightly smaller than France or Spain, slightly larger than California. The population of just over 30 million compares with just eight million at independence in 1956.

• Nearly 99 percent of Moroccans are Muslim, with tiny minorities of Christians and Jews. The literacy rate is 51.7 percent (64.1 percent for men, 39.4 percent for women).

• The main languages are Arabic, Berber and French. English is increasingly spoken by young people, especially in tourist areas.

• Morocco gained independence from French and Spanish rule on March 2, 1956. The head of state is King Mohammed VI, who succeeded his father Hassan II on July 30, 1999. The government is chosen from an elected legislature and is currently a coalition of six political parties under prime minister Driss Jettou of the USFP ("Socialist Union of Popular Forces"). The other main party is the Istiqlal (Independence) Party, also in theory socialist. The main opposition is the moderate Islamist PJD (Party of Justice and Developmentt). All legal political parties operate within a political consensus, and are not allowed, for example, to oppose the monarchy.

• Morocco's principal legal exports are clothing, fish (notably sardines), phosphates, fruit and vegetables. Cannabis, though illegal, is also an important export. Morocco's main trading partners are France and Spain.

Where to go

Geographically, the country divides into four basic zones: the **coast**, Mediterranean and Atlantic; the great cities of the **plains**; the **Rif** and **Atlas** mountains; and the oases and desert of the pre- and fully fledged **Sahara**. With two or three weeks – even two or three months – you can't expect to cover all of this, though it's easy enough (and highly recommended) to take in something of each aspect.

You are unlikely to miss the **mountains**, in any case. The three ranges of the Atlas, with the Rif a kind of extension in the north, cut right across the interior – physical and historical barriers, and inhabited for the most part by the indigenous Moroccan **Berbers**. Contrary to general preconceptions, it is actually the Berbers who make up most of the population (only around ten percent of Moroccans are "pure" Arabs) although with the shift to the industrialized cities, such distinctions are becoming less and less significant.

A more current distinction, perhaps, is the legacy of Morocco's colonial occupation over the fifty-odd years before it reasserted its independence in 1956. The colonized country was divided into **Spanish** and **French** zones – the former contained Tetouan and the Rif, the Mediterranean

▲ Camels, Erg Chebbi Dunes, Merzouga

Arabs and Berbers

The Berbers were Morocco's original inhabitants. The Arabs arrived at the end of the seventh century, after sweeping across North Africa and the Middle East in the name of their new revolutionary ideology, Islam. Eventually, nearly all the Berbers converted to the new religion and were immediately accepted as fellow Muslims by the Arabs. When Muslim armies invaded the Iberian peninsula from Morocco, the bulk of the troops were Berbers, and the two ethnic groups pretty much assimilated. Today, most Moroccans can claim both Arab and Berber ancestors, though a few (especially Shereefs, who trace their ancestry

back to the Prophet Mohammed, and have the title "Moulay") claim to be pure Arabs. But in the Rif and Atlas mountains, and in the Souss Valley, groups of pure Berbers remain, and retain their ancient languages (Tarfit, spoken by about 1.5m people in the Rif; Tamazight, spoken by over 3m people in the Atlas; and Teshalhit, spoken by 3–4m people in the Souss Valley region). Recently, there has been a resurgence in Berber pride (often symbolized by the Berber letter ⵣ) TV programmes are now broadcast in Berber languages, and they are even taught in schools, but the country's majority language remains Arabic.

and the northern Atlantic coasts, and parts of the Western Sahara; the latter comprised the plains and the main cities (Fes, Marrakesh, Casablanca and Rabat), as well as the Atlas. It was the French, who ruled their "protectorate" more closely, who had the most lasting effect on Moroccan culture, Europeanizing the cities to a strong degree and firmly imposing their language, which is spoken today by all educated Moroccans (after Moroccan Arabic or one of the three local Berber languages).

> **Fes and Marrakesh are almost unique in the Arab world for city life which remains in large part medieval**

Broadly speaking, **the coast** is best enjoyed in the north at **Tangier**, beautiful and still shaped by its old "international" port status, **Asilah** and **Larache**, and in the south at **El Jadida**, at **Essaouira**, perhaps the most easy-going resort, or at remote **Sidi Ifni**. **Agadir**, the main package tour resort, is less worthwhile – but a functional enough base for exploration.

Inland, where the real interest of Morocco lies, the outstanding cities are **Fes** and **Marrakesh**. The great imperial capitals of the country's various dynasties, they are almost unique in the Arab world for the chance they offer to witness some city life which, in patterns and appearance, remains in large part medieval. For monuments, Fes is the highlight, though Marrakesh, the "beginning of the south", is for most visitors the more enjoyable and exciting.

Hammams

"Hammam" means bath or bathroom, but in particular a traditional bathhouse, or "Turkish bath". Actually the North African steam bath dates back to Roman times, and the principle of a hammam is the same as that of a Roman bath. There is a hot room where you gather around you all the buckets of hot and cold water that you need, clean a space for yourself on the floor, and then lie down on it and sweat out all the dirt. Then you, or a friend, or the hammam attendant, scrub your skin with a rough glove called a kissa, or with a loofah. For men and women alike, the hammam is a place to socialize, and for female travellers, it's a great place to meet Moroccan women. For men, the big time to visit the hammam is before Friday prayers. When you've sweated it all out and rubbed it all off, you emerge glowing and also very relaxed. Ideally, you then rest in the changing room a while before heading for home (women) or a café (men) to enjoy a nice cup of mint tea.

Travel in the **south** – roughly beyond a line drawn between Casablanca and Meknes – is, on the whole, easier and more relaxing than in the sometimes frenetic north. This is certainly true of the **mountain ranges**, where the **Rif** can feel disturbingly anarchic, while the southerly **Atlas ranges** (Middle, High and Anti) are beautiful and accessible.

Hiking in the **High Atlas**, especially around North Africa's highest peak, **Djebel Toubkal**, is in fact something of a growth industry. Even if you are no more than a casual walker, it's worth considering, with summer treks possible at all levels of experience and altitude. And, despite inroads made by commercialization, it remains essentially "undiscovered" – like the Alps must have been in the nineteenth century.

Equally exploratory in mood are the great **southern routes** beyond – and across – the Atlas, amid the **oases** of the pre Sahara. Major routes here can be travelled by bus, minor ones by rented car or local taxi, the really remote ones by four-wheel-drive vehicles or by getting lifts on local camions (lorries), sharing space with the market produce and livestock.

The oases, around **Tinerhir**, **Zagora** and **Erfoud**, or (for the committed) **Tata** or **Figuig**, are classic images of the Arab world, vast palmeries stretching into desert horizons. Equally

Tajines

Like paella or casserole, the word tajine strictly refers to a vessel rather than to the food cooked in it. A tajine is a heavy ceramic plate covered with a conical lid of the same material. The prettiest tajines, decorated in all sorts of colours and designs, come from Safi (see p.404), but the best tajines for actual use are plain reddish-brown in colour, and come from Salé (see p.364). The food in a tajine is arranged with the meat in the middle and the vegetables piled up around it. Then the lid is put on, and the tajine is left to cook slowly over a low light, or better still, over a charcoal stove (kanoun), usually one made specifically for the tajine and sold with it. The classic tajines combine meat with fruit and spices. Chicken is traditionally cooked in a tajine with green olives and lemons preserved in brine. Lamb or beef are often cooked with prunes and almonds. When eating a tajine, you start on the outside with the vegetables, and work your way to the meat at the heart of the dish, scooping up the food with bread.

memorable is the architecture that they share with the Atlas – bizarre and fabulous pisé (mud) **kasbahs** and **ksour**, with Gothic-looking turrets and multi-patterned walls.

Further south, you can follow a route through the **Western Sahara** all the way down to Dakhla, just 20km short of the Tropic of Cancer, where the weather is scorching even in midwinter.

When to go

As far as the **climate** goes, it is better to visit the south – or at least the desert routes – outside **midsummer**, when for most of the day it's far too hot for casual exploration, especially if you're dependent on public transport. But July and August, the hottest months, can be wonderful on the coast, while in the mountains there are no set rules.

Spring, which comes late by European standards (around April to May), is perhaps the best overall time, with a summer climate in the south and in the mountains, as well as on the Mediterranean and Atlantic coasts. **Winter** can be perfect by day in the south, though desert nights can get very cold – a major consideration if you're staying in the cheaper hotels, which rarely have heating. If you're planning to **hike** in the **mountains**, it's best to keep to the months from April to October unless you have some experience of snow conditions.

◄ El Jadida

Weather conditions apart, the **Islamic religious calendar** and its related festivals will have the most seasonal effect on your travel. The most important factor is **Ramadan**, the month of daytime fasting; this can be a problem for transport, and especially hiking, though the festive evenings do much to compensate. See p.61 for details of its timing, as well as that of other festivals.

Morocco's climate

	Jan	Apr	July	Oct
Agadir				
Daily max/min (°C)	21/7	24/13	27/18	26/15
No. of days rain	6	3	0	3
Casablanca				
Daily max/min (°C)	17/7	21/11	26/18	24/14
No. of days rain	8	7	6	6
Dakhla				
Daily max/min (°C)	26/12	27/14	27/18	30/16
No. of days rain	0	0	0	1
Er Rachidia				
Daily max/min (°C)	17/1	25/8	38/20	27/12
No. of days rain	2	1	1	3
Fes				
Daily max/min (°C)	16/4	23/9	36/18	25/13
No. of days rain	8	9	1	7
Marrakesh				
Daily max/min (°C)	18/4	26/11	38/19	28/14
No. of days rain	7	6	1	4
Tangier				
Daily max/min (°C)	16/8	18/11	27/18	22/15
No. of days rain	10	8	0	8

35

things not to miss

It's not possible to see everything that Morocco has to offer in one trip – and we don't suggest you try. What follows is a selective and subjective taste of the country's highlights, in no particular order: outstanding natural features, spectacular cities, history, culture and beautiful architecture. They're arranged in five colour-coded categories to help you find the very best things to see, do and experience. All entries have a page reference to take you straight into the Guide, where you can find out more.

01 **Kasbah Glaoui, Telouet** Page **515** • An evocative relic of the time when the Glaoui clan ruled over the Atlas and Marrakesh.

02 Chefchaouen Page **160** • Simply the most beautiful small town in Morocco, with its blue-washed walls.

03 Majorelle Gardens, Marrakesh Page **466** • A lovely, mature botanical garden, maintained by Yves Saint Laurent.

04 Fes Page **250** • The most complete medieval city in the Arab world, Fes's labyrinthine streets hide away monuments and medersas (Islamic colleges), such as the Bou Inania Medersa.

05 Windsurfing Page **417** • The Atlantic coast, around Agadir and especially Essaouira, is one of the world's great destinations for windsurfing, as well as kitesurfing and parasailing.

06 Painted Rocks Page **659** • Just outside Tafraoute, in the Anti-Atlas, are these huge rocks, painted by a Belgian artist and a team of Moroccan firemen.

07 Barbary apes Page **310** • Troupes of apes populate the cedar forests of the Middle Atlas.

16

08 Atlas passes Pages **506** & **514** • The stunning Tizi n'Test pass and the higher Tizi n'Tichka lead over the Atlas mountains providing breathtaking views.

09 Koutoubia Mosque Page **444** • The symbol of Marrakesh, the Koutoubia's twelfth-century minaret is visible for miles around the city.

10 Skiing at Oukaïmeden Page **491** • Not many skiers can list north Africa – but this is a reliable, low-key resort.

11 Music see *Festivals and music colour section* • Music is integral to Moroccan life – and ever present at festivals and markets.

12 Casablanca Page 372 •
Casa's colonial architecture, such as the cathedral, incorporates traditional Moroccan designs into French Art Deco, creating a style known as Mauresque.

13 Crafts see *Crafts and souvenirs colour section* •
From carpets and leatherwork to pottery, Morocco's craft tradition is extraordinarily vibrant, and entirely on show in its souks.

14 Essaouira Page 409 •
Relax by the sea at this laid-back Atlantic resort.

15 Cascades d'Ouzoud Page 327 •
The most dramatic of the country's waterfalls, with overhanging cafés, and pools to plunge into.

16 **Route of the Kasbahs** Page **537** • Morocco's southern oases are dotted with mud-built kasbahs, like these at Aït Benhaddou.

17 **Tea** Page **59** • *Whisky Maroccain*, they call mint tea – the accompaniment to any discussion or transaction.

18 **Tin Mal Mosque** Page **511** • This great Almohad building, built in 1153–54, stands isolated in an Atlas river valley.

19 Todra Gorge Page **571** • Take a walk in the majestic Todra Gorge, with its 300-metre canyon walls.

20 Desert roads Page **674** • The Sahara proper begins on the road to Tan Tan, south of Agadir.

21 Goats climbing Argan trees Page **621** • One of the stranger sights of the Souss valley, near Agadir.

22 Asilah Page **132** • This relaxed northern seaside town hosts an international festival in August, celebrated in music, art and murals.

23 **Berber transport** Page **43** • Up in the Atlas, Berber trucks offer public transport on market days for people ... and animals.

24 **Imilchil Wedding Festival** Page **577** • Catch a Moroccan festival if you can – particularly in the Atlas.

25 **Prehistoric carvings** Page **491** • The Atlas and indeed the Sahara were rich in wild animals, as depicted in countless rock carvings.

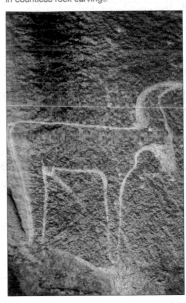

21

26 **Trekking in the Atlas** Page **498** • The Atlas mountains offer fantastic trekking opportunities, from day walks to long expeditions.

27 **Tangier** Page **101** • The old "International Port", sometime home of Bowles and Burroughs, has a seedy charm of its own.

28 **Riads** Page **53** • Stay a few nights in a riad hotel – a renovated old mansion centred on a patio.

29 **Camel trekking** Page 543 •
Try at least a day's camel trek from
Zagora, though, according to the sign, it
takes 52 days to reach Timbuktu.

30 **Birdwatching** Page 733 •
Morocco offers much to birdwatchers,
from storks nesting on minarets to desert
bustards.

31 **Bab Oudaïa, Rabat** Page 352
• Perhaps the most beautiful gate of
the medieval Moorish world.

32 **Djemaa el Fna, Marrakesh** Page 442 • Musicians, acrobats and
storytellers converge each night on the city's great square.

33 Sidi Ifni Page **662** • This old Spanish colonial town retains a seductive array of Art Deco buildings.

34 Henna Page **444** • While away an hour having your hands or feet decorated with henna.

35 Volubilis Page **243** • Volubilis was the chief city of Roman Morocco, and is today a beautiful, extensive ruin.

Basics

Basics

Getting there

The simplest way to get to Morocco is, of course, to fly, but it is also possible to get there from Europe by land and ferry. As an alternative to a direct flight, therefore, you could fly to France, Spain or Gibraltar and pick up a ferry there; indeed, from Britain or Ireland, you could go all the way by land and sea.

Regardless of where you buy your ticket, fares will depend on **season**, with the highest being at Christmas and the New Year, and at the height of summer in July and August, when fares can double, and seats become hard to find. Note also that flying at weekends can sometimes add as much as £50/$100 to the round-trip fare.

You can often cut costs by going through a **specialist flight agent**. Some agents, such as STA Travel and Travel Cuts, specialize in the student/youth market, but they offer low-cost fares to all travellers, irrespective of age or student status. Price ranges quoted on pp.28–29 include tax and assume midweek travel. Many of them will be subject to restrictions such as fixed dates, and some may require advance purchase.

Some agents specialize in **charter flights**, which may be cheaper than anything available on a scheduled flight, but again departure dates are fixed and withdrawal penalties are high. For Agadir and even Marrakesh, you may even find it cheaper to pick up a bargain **package deal** from one of the tour operators listed on pp.34–38; you could then find your own accommodation when you get there, but an advantage of using a tour operator is that they can get good value deals on flight plus resort accommodation. Upmarket operators can also offer excellent rates on stays at top hotels like the *Mamounia* in Marrakesh, *El Minzah* in Tangier, and *Palais Jamaï* in Fes.

If you're interested in visiting Morocco as part of a much wider journey, note that it is unlikely to feature on the itineraries of the cheaper Round The World flight tickets, but can be visited on custom tickets issued by the airline consortia Star Alliance (Ⓦwww.staralliance.com) and One World Alliance (Ⓦwww.oneworld.com).

Alternatively, try the online build-your-own itineraries offered by companies like Airtreks (Ⓦwww.airtreks.com).

Finally, when choosing an airline, be aware that if your **baggage goes astray** in transit, you cannot have it delivered to your hotel in Morocco, but will have to go back to the airport to pick it up in person when it does arrive. If arriving on an indirect flight, tight connections make baggage loss more likely.

Flights from the UK and Ireland

Both BA (through its franchisee, GB Airways) and Royal Air Maroc run direct **scheduled flights** from London Heathrow to Casablanca (3hr 15min); RAM also fly from London Gatwick to Marrakesh, which is served by BA from both Heathrow and Gatwick (3hr 30min). In addition, BA fly seasonally (twice weekly June–Sept) from Heathrow to Tangier (2hr 50min).

Rather more cheaply, Marrakesh is now served by a handful of **no-frills airlines**: EasyJet (from Gatwick), Atlas Blue (from Gatwick), ThomsonFly (from Luton and Manchester) and Ryanair (from Luton). Ryanair also fly three times a week from Luton to Fes. There are **charter flights** (run by tour operators such as First Choice, Panorama and Airtours) from other British airports, particularly to Agadir, and sometimes to Marrakesh, but these do not necessarily fly all year, and they are not especially cheaper than scheduled services; they may also limit you to a two-week stay.

In **Ireland**, Sunway offer charter flights from Dublin (and sometimes other airports) to Agadir. Panorama have operated charter flights to Morocco in the past but do not currently do so.

Otherwise, you can get an indirect flight to Morocco from most British or Irish airports via London or a European city such as Paris or Amsterdam. Connecting flights from Casablanca reach most other Moroccan airports. The Spanish enclave of Melilla is served by Iberia via Madrid.

A return flight from London to Casablanca with BA will **cost** around £275 in summer, £225 in winter (prices quoted include tax); with RAM you can expect to pay £185–400 year-round, depending on the specific flight. Fares on flights with the no-frills airlines depend on demand, and can vary from as little as £75 up to £275 for the round trip. A charter flight from Ireland will cost around €450–560 return, while an indirect scheduled flight will set you back €375–605 depending on the time of year and the popularity of the flight.

Looking for a charter fare, it is worth keeping an eye out for full **package holidays**, which may work out at little more than a flight-only option, and sometimes even less. See pp.34–38 for details of tour operators.

It is also possible, and often a lot cheaper, to take a **flight to Jerez, or to Malaga or Gibraltar**, where you can either get a ferry directly across the Straits, or take a bus to Algeciras for more frequent ferries from there (see p.32). Airlines such as EasyJet and Ryanair run low-cost flights to Malaga from several British and Irish airports. From Gibraltar you'd have to walk across the border to La Linea for the bus; from Malaga airport, it's usually easier to change buses at Marbella than in Malaga itself. A pricier but more exciting alternative is Helisureste's helicopter service direct from Malaga airport to Ceuta (☎+34/965 663 835, ⦿www .helisureste.com), four times daily weekdays, once on Saturdays, twice on Sundays, costing €130.90.

Flights from the US and Canada

Morocco's national airline, **Royal Air Maroc (RAM)**, operates nonstop flights to Casablanca from New York and Montreal (flight time 7hr). The alternative is to take an **indirect flight** with a European carrier, changing planes at their European hub.

Those serving Morocco include British Airways (to Casablanca, Marrakesh and Tangier), Air France (to Casablanca, Marrakesh and Rabat), Iberia (to Casablanca, Tangier and the Spanish enclave of Melilla), or Alitalia or Lufthansa (both to Casablanca only). If you intend to fly via London, note that, though there are Marrakesh flights from both Heathrow and Gatwick, Casablanca and Tangier flights leave from Heathrow only, so ease of transfer may well depend on which airport you fly into. Another possibility is to take a connecting flight to New York or Montreal and continue from there on RAM (Delta codeshare the New York flight, so they should be able to sell you a through ticket without much trouble), or to buy a through ticket via Europe with an airline such as American, Continental, Delta or United in conjunction with a European carrier.

From New York, you can expect to pay (including tax) US$1250 in high season, or $780 in low season, for a fixed-date direct flight with RAM. From Montreal, the fare will be C$1500/1050 in high/low season. You may be able to save a little on these fares by buying your ticket from an online or discount travel agent such as those listed on pp.34 and 000, though this may involve taking an indirect flight. Getting to Morocco from the West Coast will obviously cost more: expect to pay upwards of US$1650/970 to Casablanca from LA in high/low season, or C$1850/1350 from Vancouver.

Flights from Australia, New Zealand and South Africa

There are no direct flights from Australia, New Zealand or South Africa to Morocco. **From Australasia**, you will need to change planes in Europe or the Middle East. Emirates are usually the most convenient airline, and offer a decent choice of Australian and New Zealand airports to depart from, but you can also fly with a European airline such as British Airways, Lufthansa or Air France, or buy a through ticket with Qantas or Air New Zealand in conjunction with their partners in Europe, which has the advantage of offering a wider choice of departure airports.

Fly less – stay longer! Travel and climate change

Climate change is a serious threat to the ecosystems that humans rely upon, and air travel is among the fastest-growing contributors to the problem. Rough Guides regard travel, overall, as a global benefit, and feel strongly that the advantages to developing economies are important, as is the opportunity of greater contact and awareness among peoples. But we all have a responsibility to limit our personal impact on global warming, and that means giving thought to how often we fly, and what we can do to redress the harm that our trips create.

Flying and climate change

Pretty much every form of motorized travel generates CO_2 – the main cause of human-induced climate change – but planes also generate climate-warming contrails and cirrus clouds and emit oxides of nitrogen, which create ozone (another greenhouse gas) at flight levels. Furthermore, flying simply allows us to travel much further than we otherwise would do. The figures are frightening: one person taking a return flight between Europe and California produces the equivalent impact of 2.5 tonnes of CO_2 – similar to the yearly output of the average UK car.

Fuel-cell and other less harmful types of plane may emerge eventually. But until then, there are really just two options for concerned travellers: to reduce the amount we travel by air (take fewer trips – stay for longer!), and to make the trips we do take "climate neutral" via a carbon offset scheme.

Carbon offset schemes

Offset schemes run by ⓦwww.climatecare.org, ⓦwww.carbonneutral.com and others allow you to make up for some or all of the greenhouse gases that you are responsible for releasing. To do this, they provide "carbon calculators" for working out the global-warming contribution of a specific flight (or even your entire existence), and then let you contribute an appropriate amount of money to fund offsetting measures. These include rainforest reforestation and initiatives to reduce future energy demand – often run in conjunction with sustainable development schemes.

Rough Guides, together with Lonely Planet and other concerned partners in the travel industry, are supporting a **carbon offset scheme** run by climatecare.org. Please take the time to view our website and see how you can help to make your trip climate neutral.

ⓦ**www.roughguides.com/climatechange**

For the cheapest through ticket in high/low season, you can expect to **pay** A$2900/2610 from Australia, or NZ$2700 year-round from New Zealand.

Flying **from South Africa**, you could again fly with an operator such as Emirates via Dubai or Air France via Paris, even BA via London, though it's something of a long detour. The most direct route, however, is to fly SAA to Dakar, changing there onto a Royal Air Maroc flight to Casablanca (Air Senegal International operate a code-share with the respective airlines on both sectors of this route). Expect to **pay** upwards of R9480/9250 from Johannesburg to Casablanca in high/low season.

By rail from the UK and Ireland

London to Morocco by train and ferry takes a good two days at full pelt, but it's worthwhile if you have the time to stop en route and take in something of France and Spain. In particular, Cordoba's Great Mosque and Granada's Alhambra are arguably the two finest achievements of medieval Moorish architecture, and a visit to these classic Andalusian cities would fit very well with a trip to Morocco. However, you will certainly pay more to travel by train than you would for a flight.

The cheapest train departures (to Europe by ferry) are from London's **Charing Cross**

B

Station, with faster but pricier services available via the Channel Tunnel from Waterloo. **Through rail tickets** from London to Morocco are no longer available, but tickets to Algeciras (where you can take a ferry to Morocco) are available from International Rail, RailEurope or Trainseurope (see p.38 for contact details), though it may well be cheaper to buy it in stages (London–Paris, Paris–Madrid, Madrid–Algeciras). The entire journey from London to Algeciras costs £150–250, and details of the journey and the fares for each stage can be found on the Man in Seat 61 website at ⓦwww.seat61.com/Morocco.htm. Tickets for the London to Paris stage are available on line from Eurostar (ⓦwww.eurostar.com), for Paris–Madrid from the French railway SNCF (ⓦwww.sncf.fr), and for Madrid to Algeciras from the Spanish railway RENFE (ⓦwww.renfe.es); be aware that seat reservation is compulsory, and if you do not buy your ticket in advance, your connecting train may be fully booked when you arrive in Paris or Madrid, in which case you will not be allowed to get a ticket.

It is also possible to buy an InterRail pass (see ⓦwww.interrailnet.com for details), which supposedly allows unlimited travel within a certain period on trains across Europe, but not in your country of residence; Morocco was previously among the countries covered by the InterRail pass, but it no longer is. The pass will only be useful if you intend to spend a while getting down to Morocco, stopping in various countries en route. On most of the trains you will actually want to use, supplements or special fares are in any case payable, so the promise of unlimited travel proves to be something of a sham. It may be worthwhile if you are travelling from Ireland, but is much less likely to be if you are travelling from Britain. In theory, to buy an InterRail pass, you must have been resident in a participating country for at least six months; agents may not ask, but you should not count on that.

By bus from the UK and Ireland

There are regular bus services to Morocco from London (Victoria Coach Station), changing vehicles in Paris and travelling via the Algeciras–Tangier ferry. It is a 36-and-a-half-hour journey to Algeciras, and a total of 58 hours to Marrakesh, including a four-and-a-half-hour wait between buses in Paris – all in all, quite an endurance test. Transport from Tangier onwards is with the Moroccan bus company CTM (see p.40). Fares from London to Algeciras start at £96 one-way (£87 if you are under 26 or over fifty), £167 (£151) return. To Marrakesh, the through fare is £113–143 (£102–132) one-way, or £193–248 (£174–229) return, depending on the season. It is possible to get through tickets from other parts of Britain – a ticket from Edinburgh, for example, will cost around £15 more each way – but such a journey would involve a lot of time waiting in London and possibly elsewhere in Britain as well as in Paris and even elsewhere in Europe en route. Through fares are available from Ireland too (€185 from Dublin to Algeciras, €202 to Marrakesh), but not always from Northern Ireland, where you may have to buy one ticket to London and another from there; this is best done on line as prices are sometimes higher if you do not buy your ticket at least four days in advance.

By car from the UK and Ireland

If you plan to **drive down to Morocco through Spain and France**, it's a good idea to allow a minimum of four days for the journey from London or southern England, five days from Scotland or Ireland. The buses detailed above cover the route to Algeciras in 48 hours but they are more or less nonstop, with two drivers and just a few short meal breaks.

There are **car ferries** across to Morocco from Spain at **Almería** (to Melilla, Nador and Al Hoceima) at **Malaga** (to Melilla), at **Algeciras** (to Ceuta or Tangier), at **Tarifa** (to Tangier) and at **Gibraltar** (to Tangier but only twice weekly). Ferries also sail from **Sète** in France to Tangier and Nador (June–Sept). The Algeciras–Ceuta crossing is the shortest. For more details, see pp.32–33.

Driving routes

Driving down from Britain allows you to see some of the Moorish architecture of

Andalusia, which of course compliments that of Morocco. The most direct **route** is: London–Channel Tunnel–Calais–Paris–Tours–Bordeaux–Bayonne–San Sebastián (Donostia)–Madrid–Granada–Malaga–Algeciras. French and Spanish motorways charge hefty tolls, but routes which avoid them are much slower.

A cheaper but slower alternative to the Channel Tunnel (whose vehicle shuttle service is operated by Eurotunnel ☎0870/535 3535, ⓦwww.eurotunnel.com) is to take a cross-Channel ferry from southern England to France (for routes and operators see ⓦwww.routesinternational.com/ferrybooking.htm or ⓦwww.aferry.to). From Scotland, it's possible to avoid the drive through England by taking a ferry from Rosyth to Zeebrugge with Superfast Ferries. From Ireland, you can cut out Great Britain by taking a direct ferry to France with Brittany Ferries or Irish Ferries. From England, you can cut out the French section of the route by taking a direct ferry to northern Spain with Brittany Ferries or P&O. It is also possible to drive south through France to Sète and take a ferry to Morocco from there. You could even load your car onto a motorail train for part of the journey (Calais to Avignon or Narbonne for example – for further details, contact RailEurope).

Entering Morocco by ferry

Leaving Europe for Morocco proper (not Ceuta or Melilla), you have to go through passport control before boarding the ferry. Once on board, you have to obtain a **disembarkation form** from the purser's office, fill it in, and submit it with your passport for stamping to a **Moroccan immigration** official on the boat. Announcements to this effect are not always made in English, but if you don't have a stamp, you'll have to wait until everyone else has cleared frontier and customs controls before being attended to. When disembarking, show your newly acquired stamp to a Moroccan policeman at the exit.

Returning from Morocco to Spain, you need to collect an embarkation form and departure card and have these stamped by the port police prior to boarding your ferry.

Entering Morocco through the Spanish enclaves of Ceuta or Melilla (the most economic crossings for vehicles), try to avoid arriving at the weekend. If there are any problems, you may well be sent back to Ceuta or Melilla to wait until the Monday to sort them out. Some visitors choose to tip at the frontier, leaving a note in their passport to get them through more quickly.

Vehicle red tape

Taking a vehicle to Morocco you must take out **Green Card Insurance**; some insurance companies don't cover Morocco, so you may need to shop around; it speeds things up if the reference to Morocco is prominent and in French.

Entering Morocco, you will need to present the card, along with your vehicle registration document – which must be in your name or accompanied by a letter from the registered owner. Trailer caravans, as well as the vehicle itself, need **temporary importation documents**, which are obtainable at the frontier (or on the ferry, if not travelling to Ceuta or Melilla) for no charge. For information on driving in Morocco, see pp.44–47. For legal requirements, see box, p.44.

Airlines, agents and operators

Online booking

ⓦwww.expedia.co.uk (in UK), ⓦwww.expedia.com (in US), ⓦwww.expedia.ca (in Canada).
ⓦwww.lastminute.com (in UK).
ⓦwww.opodo.co.uk (in UK).
ⓦwww.orbitz.com (in US).
ⓦwww.travelocity.co.uk (in UK), ⓦwww.travelocity.com (in US), ⓦwww.travelocity.ca (in Canada)
ⓦwww.zuji.com.au (in Australia), ⓦwww.zuji.co.nz (in New Zealand).

Airlines

Aer Lingus Republic of Ireland ☎0818/365 000, Northern Ireland ☎0870/876 5000, ⓦwww.aerlingus.com.
Air Canada Canada ☎1-888/247-2262, ⓦwww.aircanada.com.
Air France UK ☎0870/142 4343, Ireland ☎01/605 0383, US ☎1-800/237-2747, Canada

Ferry routes and agents

Fares quoted below (mainly in euros, €1 being roughly 68p or US$1.35) are the cheapest adult passenger fares (steerage if available, shared cabin if not), the lowest car fares (usually for a vehicle up to 2.5m long), and lowest motorcycle fares (usually up to 250cc, but 125cc on Comanav), with seasonal variations shown. Children (up to 12 years) normally pay half fare. Most lines offer discounts (usually 20 percent) to holders of youth and student cards, some to senior citizens too. Trasmediterranea, Buquebus and EuroFerrys do not normally charge for bicycles, but Nautas, FRS and Comanav do charge, though this is inconsistently applied and you can usually avoid it if you take your bike apart, pack it up and carry it on as baggage Certain firms (Comanav for example) may refuse to take women over six months pregnant. All departures are subject to **weather conditions**, especially out of Algeciras, Tarifa and Gibraltar. For detailed schedules and prices, contact the operators, or **Southern Ferries**, 30 Churton St, London SW1V 2LP ☎ 0870/499 1305, 🌐 www.southernferries.co.uk, the UK agents for Trasmediterranea and Comanav. Most passenger tickets can be bought at boat stations on departure, but for vehicles, especially at times of high demand, and for departures out of Sète, it is best to book in advance – for vehicles on ferries out of Sète, make that *well* in advance. Also note that the routes listed below (especially those out of Tarifa, Gibraltar, Almería, Sète and Genoa) are subject to change and should always be checked before departure.

Algeciras

Tickets can be bought in Algeciras from any travel agent (there are dozens along the seafront and on the approach roads to the town) or at the boat station itself. Ticket prices are standard, wherever you buy them. Boats regularly depart thirty minutes to an hour late, and that the next to leave may not necessarily be the first to arrive, since fast ferries quite frequently overtake slow boats on the crossing. On some Ceuta services, if travelling with a vehicle, it may be cheaper to buy a return rather than a one-way ticket.

Algeciras–Ceuta catamaran Trasmediterranea, Nautas, Buquebus and EuroFerrys. 16–20 crossings daily (35min). Passenger €34.10, car €44.50, motorbike €26.20, bicycle free or €5.

Algeciras–Tangier ferry Jointly operated by the Spanish companies Trasmediterranea, EuroFerrys and Lineas Maritimas Europeas, and the Moroccan companies Comanav, Limadet, IMTC and Comarit. Up to 24 crossings daily in summer, depending on demand; 11–12 daily in winter (2hr 30min). Passenger €36, car €99, motorbike or bicycle €34.

Algeciras–Tangier fast ferry Trasmediterranea. 34 daily (1hr). Passenger €37, car €97, motorbike or bicycle €33.

Algeciras–Tangier fast ferry Nautas. 3–4 daily (1hr 30min). Passenger €35, car €97, motorbike or bicycle €34.

Tarifa

Tarifa–Tangier catamaran FRS (free bus from Algeciras). 6–8 daily (35min). Passenger €29, car €80, motorbike €29, bicycle €25.

Gibraltar

Gibraltar–Tangier catamaran FRS. 2 weekly (1hr 20min). Passenger £23, car £60, motorbike £15, bicycle £8.

Malaga

Malaga–Melilla ferry Trasmediterranea. 1 daily (7hr). Passenger €34, car €128, motorbike €37, bicycle free.

Almería

Almería–Melilla ferry Trasmediterranea. 6 weekly (6hr–7hr 30min). Passenger €34, car €128, motorbike €37, bicycle free.

Almería–Nador ferry Comarit. 1 daily (7hr). Passenger €43, car €189, motorbike €70, bicycle €70.

Almería–Nador ferry Ferrimaroc. 1 daily (7hr). Passenger €43.35, car €109.40, motorbike €68.80, bicycle free.

Almería–Nador ferry Trasmediterranea. 1 daily (7hr). Passenger €44, car €182.40, motorbike €68.80, bicycle free.

Almería–Nador ferry Euroferrys. 5 weekly (7hr). Passenger €43.35, Car €182,

motorbike or bicycle €68.80.
Almería–Nador ferry Comanav. 1–2 daily
(6hr). Passenger €43, car €186, motorbike
€77, bicycle €35.

Sète

Booking well in advance is essential for Sète
ferries – Comanav's central offices for
reservations from abroad are those in
Casablanca and Sète, or you can book
through Southern Ferries in London (see
opposite).
Sète–Tangier ferry Comanav. Every 2–4

Genoa

Genoa–Tangier ferry Comanav. 1 weekly
(48hr). Passenger €39–230, car €230–345,

Ferry operators

Buquebus ⓦ www.buquebus.es; Estación
Maritima, Local C-8, Algeciras ⓣ 902 41 42
42; 8 Rue Youssoufia, Immeuble Youssoufia,
Entre-Sol Apt. 9B, Tangier ⓣ 039 34 23 84;
Estación Maritima, Local EB-5, Ceuta ⓣ 956
50 77 80. *Algeciras to Ceuta.*
**Comanav (Compagnie Marocaine de
Navigation)** ⓦ www.comanav.co.ma; 7 Bd
de la Résistance, Casablanca ⓣ 022 30 24
12, ⓕ 022 30 07 90; c/o Transbull, Paseo de
la Conferencia 13, 2nd floor, Algeciras ⓣ 956
57 04 20; c/o SNCM, 4 Quai d'Alger, Sète
ⓣ 04/6746 6800; c/o AMU, 2/82 Via Dante,
Genoa ⓣ 010/570 4420; 43 Av Abdou el Alâa
el Maâri, Tangier ⓣ 039 93 40 96; c/o
Transbull, Muelle de Rivera, Almería ⓣ 950
28 11 43; Entrée du Port, Beni Enzar (Nador
port) ⓣ 036 60 86 28; c/o Southern Ferries
(see opposite) in London. *Algeciras and
Genoa to Tangier, Almería to Tangier, Nador
and (in summer) Al Hoceima; Sète to Tangier
and Nador.*
Comarit ⓦ www.comarit.es; 3 Av Virgen del
Carmen, first floor, Algeciras ⓣ 956 66 84
62; Estación Maritima, Almería ⓣ 950 62 03
03; Résidence Hasnae, Av Mohammed VI,
Tangier ⓣ 039 32 00 32. *Algeciras to
Tangier; Almería to Nador.*
EuroFerrys ⓦ www.euroferrys.com; Av Virgen
del Carmen 1, 5th floor ⓣ 956 65 23 24; Avda
Muelle Cañonero Dato, Ceuta ⓣ 956 50 70
70; Port, Tangier ⓣ 039 94 81 99. *Algeciras to
Tangier and Ceuta; Almería to Nador.*
Ferrimaroc ⓦ www.ferrimaroc.com; BP 96,
Beni Enzar (Nador port) ⓣ 036 34 81 00;
Muelle de Ribera, Almería ⓣ 950 27 48 00.

Almería– Al Hoceima ferry Comanav.
1–2 daily, summer only (6hr). Passenger
€43, car €186, motorbike €77, bicycle
€35.

days (36hr). Passenger €35–45, car
€190–230, motorbike under 125cc or
bicycle €104.
Sète–Nador ferry Comanav. Irregular, but
usually every four days (34hr). Passenger
€103–179, car €169–288, motorbike under
125cc or bicycle €70–100.

motorbike under 125cc or bicycle €85–120.

Almería to Nador.
FRS (Ferrys Rápidos del Sur) ⓦ www.frs
.es; Estación Maritima, Tarifa ⓣ 956 68 18
30; Paseo Maritimo, Algeciras ⓣ 956 62 72
87; c/o Turner & Co, 65–67 Irish Town,
Gibraltar ⓣ +350/50828; 18 Rue el Farabi,
Tangier ⓣ 039 94 26 12. *Tarifa, Gibraltar and
(in summer) Algeciras to Tangier.*
**IMTC (International Maritime Transport
Corporation)** 50 Av Pasteur, Casablanca
ⓣ 022 43 76 20; Port, Tangier ⓣ 039 37 09
83; c/o Vapores Suardiaz, 15 Av Virgen del
Carmen, ninth floor, left, Algeciras ⓣ 956 66
23 00. *Algeciras to Tangier.*
Limadet (Lignes Maritimes du Détroit) 13
Rue Prince Moulay Abdallah, Tangier ⓣ 039
93 36 21; Recinto del Puerto, Algeciras
ⓣ 956 66 96 13. *Algeciras to Tangier.*
Lineas Maritimas Europeas ⓦ www.
lineasme.com; 3 Av Virgen del Carmen, first
floor, Algeciras ⓣ 956 66 83 08; c/o Comarit
(see above) in Tangier. *Algeciras to Tangier.*
Nautas ⓦ www.nautasferry.com; Estación
Maritima, Locales F-4 & F-23, Algeciras
ⓣ 956 58 95 30; Estación Maritima, Ceuta
ⓣ 856 20 51 90; Port, Tangier ⓣ 039 93 44
63. *Algeciras to Tangier and Ceuta.*
Trasmediterranea ⓦ www.trasmediterranea
.es, all telephone enquiries in Spain ⓣ 902 45
46 45; Recinto del Puerto, Algeciras; Estación
Maritima, Local E-1, Malaga; Estación
Maritima, Almería; Avda Muelle Cañonero
Dato, Ceuta; General Marina 1, Melilla; c/o
Southern Ferries (see opposite) in London.
*Algeciras to Ceuta and Tangier; Malaga to
Melilla; Almería to Melilla and Nador.*

☎1-800/667-2747, Australia ☎1300/390 190, South Africa ☎0861/340 340, ⓦwww.airfrance.com.

Air New Zealand Australia ☎13/2476, ⓦwww.airnz.com.au, NZ ☎0800/737 000, ⓦwww.airnz.co.nz.

Air Senegal International South Africa ☎011/886 9232, ⓦwww.air-senegal -international.com.

Alitalia UK ☎0870/544 8259, Ireland ☎01/677 5171, US ☎1-800/223-5730, Canada ☎1-800/361-8336, ⓦwww.alitalia.com.

American Airlines US & Canada ☎1-800/433-7300, ⓦwww.aa.com.

British Airways UK ☎0870/850 9850, Ireland ☎1890/626 747, US & Canada ☎1-800/AIRWAYS, Australia ☎1300/767 177, New Zealand ☎09/966 9777, ⓦwww.ba.com.

Continental US & Canada ☎1-800/523-3273, ⓦwww.continental.com.

Delta US & Canada ☎1-800/221-1212, ⓦwww.delta.com.

EasyJet UK ☎0905/821 0905, ⓦwww.easyjet.com.

Emirates Australia ☎02/9290 9700, New Zealand ☎09/968 2200, South Africa ☎0861/364 728, ⓦwww.emirates.com.

Iberia UK ☎0845/601 2854, Ireland ☎01/407 3017, US ☎1-800/772-4642, ⓦwww.iberia.com.

Lufthansa UK ☎0870/837 7747, Ireland ☎01/844 5544, US ☎1-800/645-3880, Canada ☎1-800/563-5954, Australia ☎1300/655 727, New Zealand ☎0800/945 220, ⓦwww.lufthansa.com.

Qantas Australia ☎13/1313, NZ ☎0800/808 767 or 09/357 8900, ⓦwww.qantas.com.

Royal Air Maroc UK ☎020/7439 4361, US & Canada ☎1-800/344-6726, ⓦwww.royalairmaroc.com.

Ryanair UK ☎0871/246 0000, Ireland ☎0818/303 3030, ⓦwww.ryanair.com.

SN Brussels Airlines UK ☎0870/735 2345, US ☎1-516-740-5200, Canada ☎1-866/308-2230, ⓦwww.brusselsairlines.com.

ThomsonFly UK ☎0870/190 0737, ⓦwww.thomsonfly.com.

Charter flights

Airtours UK ☎0871/664 7988, ⓦwww.airtours .co.uk. Gatwick, Birmingham and Manchester to Agadir.

First Choice UK ☎0870/850 3999, ⓦwww.firstchoice.co.uk. Gatwick, Birmingham and Manchester to Agadir.

Sunway Travel Ireland ☎01/288 6828, ⓦwww.sunway.ie. Dublin to Agadir.

Discount agents

ebookers UK ☎0800/082 3000, ⓦwww.ebookers.com, Ireland ☎01/488 3507, ⓦwww.ebookers.ie. Low fares on an extensive selection of scheduled flights and package deals.

North South Travel UK ☎01245/608 291, ⓦwww.northsouthtravel.co.uk. Friendly, competitive travel agency, offering discounted fares worldwide. Profits are used to support projects in the developing world, especially the promotion of sustainable tourism.

Trailfinders UK ☎0845/058 5858, Ireland ☎01/677 7888, Australia ☎1300/780 212, ⓦwww.trailfinders.com. One of the best-informed and most efficient agents for independent travellers.

Travel Cuts Canada ☎1-866/246-9762, US ☎1-800/592-2887, ⓦwww.travelcuts.com. Canadian youth and student travel firm.

STA Travel UK ☎0870/163 0026, ⓦwww.statravel.co.uk, US ☎1-800/781-4040, ⓦwww.statravel.com, Australia ☎1300/733 035, ⓦwww.statravel.com.au, NZ ☎0508/782 872, ⓦwww.statravel.co.nz, South Africa ☎0861/781 781, ⓦwww.statravel.co.za. Specialists in independent travel; also student IDs, travel insurance, and more. Good discounts for students and under-26s.

USIT Republic of Ireland ☎01/602 1904, Northern Ireland ☎028/9032 7111, ⓦwww.usit.ie. Ireland's main student and youth travel specialists.

Tour operators

Many of these, particularly the adventure and specialist operators, can sell packages (online, for example) to customers from outside the countries they are based in.

Mainstream

Abercrombie & Kent UK ☎0845/070 0612, ⓦwww.abercrombiekent.co.uk, US ☎1-800/554-7016, ⓦwww.abercrombiekent.com, Australia ☎1300/851 800, ⓦwww.abercrombiekent .com.au, New Zealand ☎0800/441 638. Upscale operator with a strong reputation, and a selection of tailor-made and bespoke tours, including nine days in Rabat, Fes and Marrakesh, or ten days in Marrakesh, Essaouira and the Atlas.

Absolute Travel US ☎1-800/736-8187, ⓦwww .absolutetravel.com. A range of luxury Morocco tours, concentrating on Fes, Marrakesh and Casablanca.

Best of Morocco UK ☎0845/026 4585, ⓦwww .morocco-travel.com. One of the leading Moroccan specialists, with accommodation in quality hotels and riads, and upmarket "designer" trekking in the High Atlas and Djebel Sarhro.

Blue Men of Morocco ☏ +34/952 46 75 62, ⓦ www.bluemenofmorocco.com. Malaga-based firm run by a Moroccan–American couple, offering Andalusia/Morocco combination packages as well as tours of just Morocco.

Cadogan Holidays UK ☏ 0845/615 4390, ⓦ www.cadoganholidays.com. Reliable, relatively upscale operator offering holidays in Marrakesh, Agadir, Essaouira, Tangier, Fes, Rabat, Casablanca, Taroudannt and Ouarzazate.

CLM ("Morocco Made to Measure") UK ☏ 020/7235 0123, ⓦ www.clmleisure.co.uk. Reliable and flexible agency, offering tailor-made holidays, and accommodation at top hotels, riads and out-of-the-way *auberges*.

CVTravel UK ☏ 020/7384 5870, US ☏ 1-866/587-9395, ⓦ www.cvtravel.net. Upmarket and often extraordinary villa rentals in Marrakesh, Ouarzazate and Tangier.

Goway Travel Experiences US & Canada ☏ 1-800/665-4432, Australia ☏ 1800/227 268 or 02/9262 4755, ⓦ www.goway.com. Options include city stays in Marrakesh, Casablanca or Agadir, a seven-day Imperial Cities tour of Casablanca, Rabat, Fes and Marrakesh, or a thirteen-day "Magical Kingdom" tour of those places plus Erfoud, Rissani and Ouarzazate.

Homeric Tours US ☏ 1-800/223-5570, ⓦ www.homerictours.com. Several Morocco packages including city breaks in Marrakesh and Agadir, a 4x4 tour of the southern kasbahs, or a twelve-day "Discovery of Morocco" tour.

Journeys International US ☏ 1-800/255-8735, ⓦ www.journeys-intl.com. Prestigious, award-winning operator focusing on ecotourism and small-group trips worldwide, with eight- or twelve-day Morocco tours, and combinations with other North African countries.

Kuoni Travel UK ☏ 01306/747 002, ⓦ www.kuoni.co.uk. Tour operator running flexible package holidays to Fes, Marrakesh, Agadir, Essaouira, Tangier, Casablanca and Rabat, plus a variety of tours and multi-centre holidays.

Panorama UK ☏ 0871/664 7984, ⓦ www.panoramaholidays.co.uk, Ireland ☏ 0818/202 020, ⓦ www.panoramaholidays.ie. Family package holidays, particularly at Agadir.

Peregrine Adventures UK ☏ 0844/736 0170, Australia ☏ 1300/854 444 or 03/8601 4444, ⓦ www.peregrine.net.au. A neat little range of eight- to fourteen-day Morocco tours. Their budget tour brand, Gecko's (ⓦ www.geckosadventures.com), offers adventure tours.

Prestige UK ☏ 01425/480 400, ⓦ www .prestigeholidays.co.uk. One- or two-centre holidays in Fes, Marrakesh, Essaouira, Taroudannt and Ourigane.

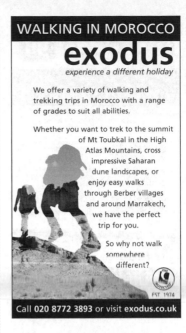
Tribes Travel UK ☏ 01728/685 971, ⓦ www.tribes.co.uk. A "fair trade" company and past winner of Tourism Concern's award for "most responsible tour operator" offering Atlas treks, imperial cities tours and Marrakesh weekend breaks among other options.

The Ultimate Travel Company UK ☏ 020/7386 4646, ⓦ www.ultimatetravelcompany.co.uk. Fairly upmarket operator offering tailor-made tours, treks and safaris, plus stays in top hotels and riads.

Wilderness Travel US ☏ 1-800/368-2794, ⓦ www.wildernesstravel.com.Ten- to fifteen-day Atlas, Sahara and imperial cities tours

Ya'lla Tours US ☏ 1-800/644-1595, ⓦ www.yallatours.com. Five different Morocco tours, from a seven-day Imperial Cities tour to a fourteen day "Glory of Morocco" tour.

Trekking, hiking and adventure

Acacia Adventure Holidays UK ☏ 020/7706 4700, Ireland c/o USIT ☏ 01/602 1904, Canada c/o Travel Cuts ☏ 1-866/246-9762, Australia c/o Adventure World ☏ 02/8913 0700, New Zealand c/o Adventure World ☏ 09/524 5118, South Africa ☏ 021/556 1157, ⓦ www.acacia-africa.com. Africa specialists offering eight- to fifteen-day Moroccan adventure tours.

Adventure Center US ☏ 1-800/228-8747 or 1-510/654-1879, ⓦ www.adventurecenter.com.

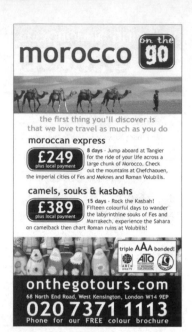
Hiking and "soft adventure" specialist with a big
range of eight- to fifteen-day tours in the Atlas, the
Anti-Atlas, the Sahara and the imperial cities of Fes,
Meknes, Marrakesh and Rabat.

AMIS (Atlas Mountain Interactive Services)
UK ☎01592/873 546, ℱ01592/741 774. Small
agency and consultancy run by Hamish Brown, author
of the High Atlas chapter in this book. Most years
there are a few places on exploratory treks and other
one-off ventures and tours, or can help independent
travellers to find local contacts.

Backroads US ☎1-800/GO-ACTIVE,
ⓦwww.backroads.com. Adventure vacations
including six-day biking and walking tour in
Marrakesh, Essaouira and the Atlas.

Biotrek Adventure Travels US & Canada
☎1-866/BIOTREK, ⓦwww.biotrektours.com.
A fifteen-day small-group adventure tour (max 10
people) focusing on culture and environment, and
led by a professional photographer who is on hand to
advise on better snapping.

Classic Journeys US ☎1-800/200-3887 or
1-858/454-5004, ⓦwww.classicjourneys.com. A
nine-day cultural adventure tour visiting Fes, Erfoud,
Ouarzazate and Marrakesh.

Discover UK ☎01883/744 392, ⓦwww.discover
.ltd.uk. Tailor-made Morocco tours and educational
field trips. Discover also own and run the Kasbah du
Toubkal (see p.495).

Exodus UK ☎0870/240 5550, Ireland c/o Abbey
Travel ☎01/804 7153, US and Canada c/o GAP
☎1-800/708-7761, Australia and New Zealand
c/o Peregrine (see p.35), South Africa c/o Mask
Expeditions ☎011/807 3333, ⓦwww.exodus
.co.uk. A variety of High Atlas, Anti-Atlas, Djebel
Sarhro and Sahara treks, from five days in Marrakesh
and the Ouirgane Valley to a 21-day "Atlas Grand
Traverse", plus mountain-biking tours, an eight-day
ascent of Djebel Toubkal (summer only), and a series
of discovery truck tours.

Explore Worldwide UK ☎0870/333 4001,
Ireland c/o Maxwells Tours ☎01/677 9479, US
c/o Adventure Center ☎1-800/227-8747, Canada
c/o Trek Holidays ☎1-888/456-3522, Australia
c/o Adventure World ☎02/8913 0700, New
Zealand c/o Adventure World ☎09/524 5118,
South Africa c/o Shiralee Travel ☎028/313 0526,
ⓦwww.explore.co.uk. An imaginative range of
treks including fourteen days in the High Atlas or
Djebel Sarhro, as well as desert and Imperial City
truck tours.

Far Frontiers UK ☎01285/851 921,
ⓦwww.farfrontiers.com. Treks, weekend breaks,
or tailor-made Atlas Explorer and self-drive Fes-to-
Coast trips.

GAP Adventures Canada & US ☎1-800/708-
7761, UK ☎0870/999 0144; Australia ☎1300/853
325, ⓦwww.gapadventures.com. Adventure travel
and ecotourism firm whose Moroccan options include
a fourteen-day "Highlights of Morocco" tour, and an
eight-day Atlas "Hike & Bike" tour.

Geographic Expeditions US ☎1-800/777-8183
or 1-415/922-0448, ⓦwww.geoex.com. Adventure
travel and cultural tours including a seventeen-day
Casablanca to Marrakesh tour, or a 22-day tour taking
in Morocco plus assorted places in West, Central and
southern Africa too.

Guerba UK ☎01373/826 611, ⓦwww.guerba
.com. A fifteen-day cycle Morocco tour, a nine-day
family adventure or an eight-day Djebel Toubkal climb
are among the options offered by this longstanding
overland firm.

Headwater UK ☎01606/720 033, Ireland
c/o Leopardstown Tours ☎01/295 8901, US
c/o Breakaway Adventures ☎1-800/567-6286,
Australia c/o Adventure World ☎02/8913 0700,
New Zealand c/o Adventure World ☎09/524 5118,
ⓦwww.headwater.com. Easy walking trips based in
Marrakesh and Ouarzazate.

The Imaginative Traveller UK ☎020/8742
8612, ⓦwww.imaginative-traveller.com. A "soft"
adventure operator, offering thirteen different
Morocco tours.

Kumuka Expeditions UK ☎0800/389 2328,
Ireland ☎1800/946 843, US ☎1-800/517-0867,

Canada c/o Skylink Holidays ☎1-800/262-6818, Australia ☎1300/667 274, New Zealand ☎0800/440 499, South Africa ☎0800/991 503, ⓦwww.kumuka.com. Adventure tours taking in Tangier, Rabat, Casablanca, Essaouira, Marrakesh, Ouarzazate, the desert, Fes and Chefchaouen, all in two weeks (phew!).

Mountain Travel Sobek US ☎1-888/MTSOBEK or 1-510/594-6000, ⓦwww.mtsobek.com. Well-established mountain wilderness and adventure operator with a fourteen-day winter "Camel Trek".

Overseas Adventure Travel US ☎1-800/493-6824, ⓦwww.oattravel.com. Fifteen-day "Morocco Sahara Odyssey" for small groups (max 16 people) includes a tour of the Imperial Cities and three nights under canvas in the desert, with optional extensions in Marrakesh, or Casablanca and Essaouira.

Ramblers Holidays UK ☎01707/331 133, ⓦwww.ramblersholidays.co.uk. A long-established operator offering hiking rather than trekking holidays, including Marrakesh and the Ourika Valley (eight days), a Djebel Toubkal climb (thirteen days), or fifteen-day tours of southern or western Morocco.

Sherpa Expeditions UK ☎020/8577 2717, ⓦwww.sherpaexpeditions.com. Two-week High Atlas tours (Djebel Toubkal or Djebel Sarhro), or a week-long self-guided trip from Asni to Setti Fatma.

Travel Bag Adventures UK ☎01420/541 007, ⓦwww.travelbag-adventures.co.uk. Small groups, mostly off the beaten track, with a variety of tours including family holiday options with kids in mind, easy hikes or demanding treks.

Walks Worldwide UK ☎01524/242 657, ⓦwww.walksworldwide.com. Atlas and Rif treks, or a week in Marrakesh with a short Atlas trek, and all with the option of a seaside extension in Essaouira.

Wilder Places (Nomadic Morocco) Ireland ☎087/261 5463, ⓦhttp://wilderplaces.com. Trekking, climbing and snowshoeing in the Atlas.

Biking, riding, surfing and other sports

Golf specialists are listed on p.60.

Equitour UK ☎0800/043 7942, ⓦwww.equitour.co.uk. Horseriding holidays based at Agadir or Ouarzazate.

Greenslades UK ☎01823/332 226, ⓦwww.greenslades.co.uk. Windsurfing holidays in Essaouira, with surfing, kitesurfing and quad biking options, and tuition if needed.

H–C Travel UK ☎01256/770 775, ⓦwww.hctravel.com. Seven- and ten-day off-road motorcycle tours (bikes provided, previous off-road experience necessary).

Moto Aventures ☎+376/738110, ⓦwww.motoaventures.com. Andorra-based company running seven- or nine-day off-road motorcycle tours (bikes provided, previous off-road experience necessary).

Pure Vacations UK ☎01227/281 700, ⓦwww.purevacations.com. Surfing holidays north of Agadir, with tuition if required, or golfing holidays in Marrakesh.

Rock & Sun UK ☎0871/871 6782 or 078 8077 3786, ⓦwww.rockandsun.com. Rock climbing in Todra gorge (experience necessary).

Surf Maroc UK ☎01794/322 709, ⓦwww.surfmaroc.co.uk. Surfing holidays based near Taghazout, including lessons for beginners and more advanced surfers.

Water by Nature UK ☎01226/740 444, US & Canada ☎1-303/988-5037, ⓦwww.waterbynature.com. Canoeing and kayaking holidays.

Welsh Airsports UK ☎01873/854 090, ⓦwww.welshairsports.com. Paragliding, hang gliding and paramotoring around Legzira and Tafraoute, including training courses with qualified instructors.

Wildcat Adventures UK ☎01786/816 160, ⓦwww.wildcat-adventures.co.uk. On-road and off-road mountain-biking and motorcycle tours.

Special interest

Birdquest UK ☎01254/826 317, ⓦwww.birdquest.co.uk. Upmarket birdwatching tours in Morocco run once or twice per year.

Equatorial Travel UK ☎01335/348 770, ⓦwww.equatorialtravel.co.uk. Fair-trade small-group ecotours including walking tours, an arts and crafts tour and a music tour.

Heritage Tours US ☎1-800/378-4555 or 1-212/206 8400, ⓦwww.heritagetoursonline.com. Customized tours and packages exploring the 2500-year Jewish experience and the tradition of Muslim/Jewish coexistence in Morocco.

Martin Randall Travel UK ☎020/8742 3355, ⓦwww.martinrandall.com. Small-group cultural tours, focusing on art, architecture, archeology and music, with expert lecturers and one or two trips to Morocco every year.

Naturally Morocco Ltd UK ☎0845/345 7195 or 01239/654 466, ⓦwww.naturallymorocco.co.uk. Ecologically oriented tours of Morocco based at Taroudannt, with vegetarian or vegan food if desired and a variety of special services available, including Arabic, Berber or French tuition and even Moroccan cookery lessons.

Naturetrek UK ☎01962/733 051, ⓦwww.naturetrek.co.uk. Natural history holidays led by expert naturalists, including ten days birdwatching in southern Morocco, a five-day bald ibis break at the

Souss–Massa National Park, or an eight-day birds and butterflies High Atlas tour.

Prospect Music and Art Tours UK ☎01227/773 545, ⓦwww.prospecttours.com. An eight-day Imperial Cities cultural tour for art lovers, visiting Fes, Meknes, Rabat and Marrakesh.

Rhode School of Cuisine UK ☎01252/790 222, US ☎1-888/254-1070, ⓦwww .rhodeschoolofcuisine.com. Spring and autumn Moroccan cookery courses in Marrakesh.

Rail contacts

European Rail UK ☎020/7387 0444, ⓦwww .europeanrail.com.

International Rail UK ☎0870/084 1410, ⓦwww.international-rail.com.
Irish Rail International Ireland ☎01/703 1885, ⓦwww.irishrail.ie.
RailEurope (SNCF French Railways) UK ☎0870/830 6050, ⓦwww.raileurope.co.uk.
Trainseurope UK ☎0871/700 7722, ⓦwww.trainseurope.co.uk.

Bus contacts

Eurolines UK ☎0870/514 3219, ⓦwww.nationalexpress.com/eurolines, Ireland ☎01/836 6111, ⓦwww.eurolines.ie.

Getting around

Moroccan public transport is, on the whole, pretty good. There is an efficient rail network linking the main towns of the north, the coast and Marrakesh, and elsewhere you can travel easily enough by bus or collective taxi. In the mountains and over the more remote desert routes, where roads are often just dirt tracks (*pistes*), local people maintain a network of market-day lorries – uncomfortable but fun.

Renting a car can be a good idea, at least for a part of your trip, opening up routes that are time-consuming or difficult on local transport. Most major companies allow you to rent a car in one city and return it to another.

By air

Royal Air Maroc (RAM) operates **domestic flights** from its Casablanca hub to major cities nationwide, as does domestic rival **Regional Air Lines**. Between any other two points, however, you will usually have to change planes at Casablanca, unless both points are stops on a single Casa-bound flight (Dakhla to Agadir, for example). In general, flying is not really worthwhile except for long-distance routes such as to Laayoune or Dakhla in the Western Sahara, when they can save you a lot of time. A 21-day advance-purchase round trip from Casablanca to Laayoune (which costs less

than half the full one-way fare) would set you back 999dh (£60/$120) and take an hour and a half each way (plus journey time to the airport, check-in time and delays), compared to nineteen hours each way by bus. Casa to Dakhla (1089dh advance-purchase return), would take you two hours and ten minutes each way by air compared to 28 hours by bus. You can usually get a reduced fare if you buy three days in advance, and promotional round-trip fares are sometimes available. If you're very pressed for time, you might want to use the services between Casablanca and places like Agadir or even Oujda. On shorter routes, the speed of a flight is counterbalanced by factors such as the price, the time taken travelling between airports and town centres, the relative infrequency of flights compared to buses, and the fact that domestic flights are very often subject to long delays, which may well make your total journey time more than by bus.

Police checks on travel

Police checks take place on travellers throughout the country. They come in three forms. One is a check on local transport; European cars, or rental cars, are usually waved through. Buses (other than CTM services) are much more likely to be stopped, but usually only briefly. The second kind of police check is a routine but simple passport check – most often polite and friendly, with the only delay due to a desire to relieve boredom with a chat. Nonetheless, you should always have your passport with you if travelling between towns – even on day-trips.

The third kind of check – usually found only in the Western Sahara – is more prolonged and involves being stopped by police stationed at more or less permanent points on the roads, who will conduct a fairly detailed inquisition into all nonresident travellers, with a considerable amount of form-filling and delay. For further details, and suggestions on how to save time at these checks, see box, p.679.

In the **Rif mountains**, especially around the cannabis-producing region of Ketama, you may also come across police checks – concerned, obviously enough, with just the one substance. Buses are usually delayed more than grands taxis at such checkpoints. There are also several and sometimes lengthy checks for duty-free contraband on buses from Nador to Fes.

A summary of flights available is given in the "Travel Details" section at the end of each chapter of this book, along with details of train and bus services. Information on Morocco's airports, including daily departure lists for some of them, can be found on the website of the Office National des Aéroports at @www.onda.org.ma. RAM offices are detailed in the "Listings" or "Practicalities" sections for each major town. The airlines can also be contacted through their head office and reservation centres at Casablanca airport (RAM ⊕090 00 08 00; Regional Air Lines ⊕082 00 00 82), or their websites (RAM @www.royalairmaroc.com; Regional Air Lines @www.regionalmaroc.com). You must always confirm flights 72 hours before departure. **Student** and under-26 youth **discounts** of 25 percent are available on RAM domestic flights, but only if the ticket is bought in advance from one of its offices.

By rail

Trains cover a limited network of routes, but for travel between the major cities they are easily the best option – reliable, comfortable, efficient and fairly fast.

The **map** at the beginning of this book shows all the passenger train routes in the country, and services are summarized in the "Travel Details" at the end of each chapter. There are basically two lines which carry passengers: from Tangier in the north down to Marrakesh, and from Oujda in the northeast, also to Marrakesh, joining with the Tangier line at Sidi Kacem. Branch lines serve El Jadida, Safi, Oued Zem and Casablanca airport. There are plans to extend the railway south to Agadir, and on to Laayoune in the Western Sahara, but it's anyone's guess when that project will reach fruition. Schedules change very little from year to year, but it's wise to check times in advance at stations. **Timetables**, printed by ONCF, the national railway company, are usually available at major train stations and tourist offices – if they don't have a full timetable at the station, they'll print you off a mini-timetable of services between any two stations. You can also check schedules (*horaires*) and fares (*tarifs*) on the ONCF website at @www.oncf.ma, though you cannot buy tickets online.

There are two **classes** of tickets – first and second. **Costs** for a second-class ticket are slightly more than what you'd pay for buses; on certain "express" services ("express" refers to the level of comfort rather than the speed), they are around thirty percent higher. In addition, there are **couchettes** (160dh extra) available on the Tangier–Marrakesh and Casablanca–Oujda night trains – worth the money for both the comfort and the security, as couchette passengers are in

Distance chart (kilometres by road)

	Ag	Al H	Casa	Dakh	Er Rach	Ess	Fes	Figuig
Agadir	–	1037	511	1208	773	173	756	1151
Al Hoceima	1037	–	570	2245	637	940	281	773
Casablanca	511	570	–	1719	557	351	289	935
Dakhla	1208	2245	1719	–	1981	1381	1964	2359
Er Rachidia	773	637	557	1981	–	676	350	378
Essaouira	173	940	351	1381	676	–	640	1054
Fes	756	281	289	1964	350	640	–	706
Figuig	1151	773	935	2359	378	1054	706	–
Laayoune	694	1731	1205	514	1467	867	1450	1845
Marrakesh	273	764	238	1481	500	176	483	878
Meknes	740	341	229	1948	328	580	60	706
Nador	1063	280	596	2271	554	947	307	525
Oujda	1076	397	609	2284	564	960	320	386
Ouarzazate	375	927	442	1483	296	380	646	674
Rabat	602	479	91	1810	466	442	198	1199
Tangier	880	323	341	2088	595	692	303	1457
Tetouan	873	273	362	2081	595	713	276	1478

their own locked carriage with a guard. Most of the **stations** are located reasonably close to the modern city centres, in the French-built quarters – the Villes Nouvelles. They generally have **left-luggage** depots, though these accept only luggage that can be locked (effectively excluding rucksacks). An alternative may be provided by nearby cafés, where staff will often agree to look after your luggage for a small tip.

By bus

Bus travel is generally only marginally cheaper than taking a grand taxi, and there are far more **regular routes**. Travelling on public transport for any length of time in Morocco, you are likely to make considerable use of the various networks.

Grands taxis are likely to do a journey in about two-thirds of the time a bus would take (though CTM now runs a few non-stop express buses). Buses, on the other hand are safer and more comfortable, though on some older buses leg room is extremely limited and long journeys can be rather an endurance test for anyone approaching six feet or more in height. In summer, it can be worthwhile taking **night buses** on the longer journeys. Though still not very comfortable,

many long-distance buses run at night when they are both quicker and cooler. Although most buses are fitted with reading lights these are invariably turned off, so you will not be able to read on buses after dark. Also note that the rate of accidents involving night buses is quite high, especially on busy routes, and most of all on the N8 between Marrakesh and Agadir.

When travelling during the day, especially in summer, it pays to sit on the side away from **the sun**. Travelling from north to south, this means sitting on the right in the morning, on the left in the afternoon, vice versa if going the other way. Travelling from east to west, sit on the right, or on the left if going from west to east. Note too, especially on rural services, that some passengers may be unused to road travel, resulting in travel sickness and vomiting.

CTM and private lines

There are a variety of bus services and companies. In all sizeable towns, you will generally find both CTM (the national company) and a number of other companies, privately owned and operated.

The **CTM buses** are faster and more reliable, with numbered seats and fixed

Laay	Mar	Mek	Nad	Ouj	Ouarz	Rab	Tan	Tet
694	273	740	1063	1076	375	602	880	873
1731	764	341	280	397	927	479	323	273
1205	238	229	596	609	442	91	341	362
514	1481	1948	2271	2284	1483	1810	2088	2081
1467	500	328	554	564	296	466	595	595
867	176	580	947	960	380	442	692	713
1450	483	60	307	320	646	198	303	276
1845	878	706	525	386	674	1199	1457	1478
–	967	1434	1757	1770	1069	1296	1574	1567
967	–	467	790	803	204	321	579	600
1434	467	–	363	380	652	138	267	267
1757	790	363	–	139	840	501	597	547
1770	803	380	139	–	850	518	714	664
1069	204	652	840	850	–	528	783	804
1296	321	138	501	518	528	–	250	271
1574	579	267	597	714	783	250	–	58
1567	600	267	547	664	804	271	58	–

departure schedules. Schedules, fares and seat availability can usually be checked on their website at ⓦ www.ctm.co.ma. The CTM services are often referred to as the "rapide", and buses come equipped with videos on the longer routes. They usually have reading lights too, though you may have to ask the driver to turn those on. Some of the **larger private company** buses, such as SATAS (which operates widely in the south) and Trans Ghazala (which runs in the north) are of a similar standard. By contrast, many other private companies are tiny outfits, with a single bus which leaves only when the driver considers it sufficiently full. On the other hand, such private buses are much more likely to stop for you if you flag them down on the open road, whereas CTM services will only pick up and set down at official stops.

Bus terminals

Most towns have a main **bus station** (gare routière), often on the edge of town. CTM buses usually leave from the company's office, which may be quite a way from the main bus station, though in several places CTM and the private companies share a single terminal, and in some cases the CTM bus will call at the main bus station when departing a city, though not when arriving.

Bus stations usually have a number of ticket windows, one for each of the companies operating out of it. There is often a departures board, but it may be in Arabic only, and it may be out of date anyhow, so you should always check departure times at the appropriate window. Bus conductors or ticket sellers may be calling out destinations in the bus station in any case, or may greet you as you come in by asking where you want to go. On the more popular trips (and especially with CTM services, which are often just once a day in the south), it is worth trying to buy **tickets in advance**; this may not always be possible on smaller private-line services, but it's worth enquiring about.

You can sometimes experience problems getting tickets at **small towns** along major routes, where buses can arrive and leave already full. It's sometimes possible to get round this problem by taking a local bus or a grand taxi for the next section of the trip (until the bus you want empties a little), or by waiting for a bus that actually starts from the town you're in. Overall, the best policy is simply to arrive at a bus station early in the day (ideally 5.30–6am).

Fares

Fares for train, bus and grand taxi journeys follow a reasonably consistent pattern. For **bus** journeys, reckon on around 1.50–2.50dh for each 10km, or 2.50–3.50dh on CTM, Supratours or SATAS.

For **trains**, expect to pay around 3.50dh per 10km in second class, 5dh in first.

Collective **grands taxis** charge 2–4dh per place for each 10km. Fares tend to be lower for more popular routes, and higher for routes where the taxi needs to wait longer for passengers before setting off.

For **comparison**, between Casablanca and Marrakesh, a train will take three hours and cost 84dh in second class, 125dh in first. A CTM bus will cost 90dh and take three hours, while an ordinary bus will cost 45–55dh and take around four hours. A shared grand taxi will cost 100dh and take two and a half hours (though on most routes in fact the difference between the grand taxi and ordinary bus fare is a good deal less). For the forty-minute plane journey, you would pay 1370dh for a full-fare economy-class ticket, but 21-day advance-purchase round-trip tickets are available for 599–699dh.

On private-line buses, you generally have to pay for your **baggage** to be loaded into the hold (or onto the roof). The standard fee is 5dh, but this may be foregone on short hops. Note that you only pay to have your baggage loaded, not to have it unloaded on arrival, whatever anybody may say. On CTM, SATAS and Supratours buses your luggage is weighed and you are issued with a receipt for the baggage charge (usually about 10dh, depending on weight and distance – allow time for this procedure). On arrival, porters with wheeled box-carts (*chariots*) may offer their services, but always agree a price before engaging one.

Supratours buses

An additional service, on certain major routes, is the **Supratours express buses** run by the train company, **ONCF**. These are fast and very comfortable, and run from Nador, from Tetouan, and from Essaouira, Agadir and the Western Sahara to connect with rail services at, respectively, Taourirt on the line from Oujda to Fes and Casablanca, Tnine Sidi Lyamani on the Tangier–Casablanca line near Asilah, and Marrakesh for train services northwards. Timetables and fares for Supratours buses can be found along with those for trains on the ONCF website (🌐 www.oncf.ma). ONCF/Supratours services are more expensive than regular buses and compare, both in terms of time and cost, with CTM buses. They do not use the main bus stations, but depart from outside their own town-centre offices (detailed in the text). Through tickets to and from connecting rail stations are available (Nador through to Fes, for example), and travellers with rail tickets for connecting services have priority. It's best to book tickets in advance if possible.

By grand taxi

Collective **grands taxis** are one of the best features of Moroccan transport. They operate on a wide variety of routes, are much quicker than buses (usually quicker than trains, too), and fares are very reasonable. They are also a good way of meeting people and having impromptu Arabic lessons.

The taxis are usually big Peugeot or Mercedes cars carrying six passengers (Peugeots are less common but have a slightly less cramped seating arrangement). Most business is along specific routes, and the most popular routes have more or less continuous departures throughout the day. You just show up at the terminal (locations are detailed, city by city, in the guide) and ask for a place to a specific destination. The best time to arrive is early morning (5–7am), when a lot of people are travelling and taxis fill up quickly; lunchtime, on the other hand, is a bad time to turn up, as fewer people will be travelling, and the taxi will take longer to fill up. As soon as six (or, if you're willing to pay extra, four or five) people are assembled, the taxi sets off. Make sure, when asking about grands taxis, that it is clear you only want a place (*une place* in French, *plassa* in Arabic, or hold up one finger) in a shared collective taxi (*taxi collectif*), as drivers often "presume" that a tourist will want to charter the whole taxi (see below), which means paying for all six places.

Most collective grands taxis run over a fairly short route, from one large town to the next. If you want to travel further, you will have to change taxis from time to time. Sometimes a route may be covered in **stages**, in which case drivers will generally assist you in finding a connecting taxi. Picking up a grand taxi on the road is much more problematic, since they will only stop if they have a place free (if a passenger has already alighted in other words). When trying to hail a taxi on the open road, hold up one, two or more fingers to indicate how many places you need.

Fares for set routes are fixed, and drivers do not usually try to overcharge tourists for a place (though occasionally they try to charge for baggage, which usually travels free of charge). If you think that you are being overcharged, ask the other passengers, or check the price with your hotel before leaving – or, as a general guideline, consult the "Fares" box opposite. Occasionally, five passengers may agree to split the cost of the last place to hasten departure, or one passenger may agree to pay for two places. You will normally be expected to pay the full fare for the journey even if travelling only part of the way.

If you want to take a **nonstandard route**, or an excursion, or just to have the taxi to yourself, it is possible to charter a whole grand taxi (*une course* in French, *corsa* in Arabic). In theory this should be exactly six times the price of a place in a shared taxi if the route has a set fare, but you'll often have to bargain hard to get that. Hotels can sometimes be useful in helping to charter grands taxis.

Some people consider grands taxis **dangerous**. It is certainly true that they are prone to practices such as speeding, and overtaking on blind curves or the brows of hills, and that they have more than their fair

share of accidents. Drivers may work all day and into the night, and it seems a large number of accidents involve them falling asleep at the wheel while driving at night, so you may wish to avoid using them for night-time journeys, especially on busy roads (the N8 between Marrakesh and Agadir is the worst). Note also that with the seating arrangements, it is not usually possible to wear a seat belt.

Trucks and hitching

In the countryside, where buses may be sporadic or even nonexistent, it is standard practice for **vans** and **lorries** (*camions*), **pick-up trucks** (*camionettes*) and **transit-vans** (*transits*) to carry and charge passengers. You may be asked to pay a little more than the locals, and you may be expected to bargain over the price – but it's straightforward enough.

In parts of the **Atlas**, local people run more or less scheduled truck or transit services, generally to coincide with the pattern of local souks. If you plan on traversing any of the more ambitious Atlas *pistes*, you'll probably be dependent on these vehicles, unless you walk.

Driving requirements

The **minimum age** for driving in Morocco is 21 years. EU, North American and Australasian **driving licences** are recognized and valid in Morocco, though an **International Driving Licence**, with its French translations (available from the AA or equivalent motoring organizations) is a worthwhile investment, especially if your domestic licence does not have a photograph on it (Moroccan police will find that strange). You must **carry your driving licence and passport** at all times.

You **drive on the right**.

Hitching

Hitchhiking is not very big in Morocco. Most people, if they own any form of transport at all, have mopeds – which are said to outnumber cars by something like five hundred to one. However, it is often easy to get rides from other **tourists**, particularly if you ask around at the campsites, and for **women travellers** this can be an effective and positive option for getting around – or at least a useful respite from the generally male preserves of buses and grands taxis.

Out on the road, it's inevitably a different matter – and hitching is definitely not advisable for women travelling alone. We have heard of (Moroccan) hitchhikers being robbed on the N12 Tata–Bou Izakarn road, and it probably happens elsewhere too. Hitchers should also not be surprised to be asked to pay for a ride if picked up by country Moroccans. Local rides can operate in much the same way as truck taxis (see p.43).

By car

There are few real problems driving in Morocco, but be aware that **accident rates** are high – in large part because much of the population is not yet tuned in to looking out for motorized vehicles, but also because motorists routinely ignore traffic regulations, and most people get their licence by paying baksheesh rather than passing a test fairly. The N8 between Marrakesh and Agadir is a particular accident blackspot. Do not expect other drivers to indicate or observe lane discipline, beware when coming up to blind curves or hills where vehicles coming in the other direction may be trying to overtake without full view of the road ahead, treat all pedestrians with the suspicion that they will cross in front of you, and all cyclists with the idea that they may well swerve into the middle of the road. All this makes driving a particularly hair-raising experience in towns.

However, with those caveats in mind, daytime and certainly long-distance driving can be as good as anywhere. Good road surfaces, long straight roads, and little traffic between inhabited areas allow for high average speeds. The usual **speed limit** outside towns is 100km per hour (62mph), which is difficult to keep down to in desert areas, where perceptions of speed change. On motorways, you can drive at up to 120km per hour (75mph). In built-up areas, the speed limit is generally 40km per hour (25mph). Signs indicate speed limits other than those. There are on-the-spot fines of 300dh upwards for speeding offences, and oncoming motorists flashing their headlights at you may well be warning you to slow down for a police check ahead (radar speed traps are common). The French rule of giving priority to traffic from the right is observed at roundabouts and junctions – meaning that cars coming onto a roundabout have priority over those already on it.

Be very wary about driving **after dark**. It is legal to drive without lights at up to 20km per hour, which allows all cyclists and mopeds to wander at will; donkeys, goats and sheep do not carry lights, either.

By law, drivers and passengers are required to wear **seatbelts**. Almost no one does, but if you follow suit and are stopped by the police, you may have a small fine (possibly unofficial) extracted. Given Morocco's high road-accident rate, it is foolhardy not to wear a seat belt anyway.

It is of course difficult to generalize, but for the purposes of planning a journey, you can expect to make an average **headway** of

50km per hour driving on major routes, more on the motorways (currently Asilah–Rabat, Rabat–El Jadida, Rabat–Fes and Casablanca–Settat, though the network is gradually being extended), but less in the south, where roads are narrower and less well maintained. Trunk roads are designated N or RN for "Route Nationale", and will have one or occasionally two lanes in each direction. Less major routes are designated R ("Route Régionale"). Smaller routes than this will have a four-digit number, sometimes prefixed with a P (for "Route Provinciale"). Motorways (*autoroutes*) are designated A, and carry a toll (20dh, for example, from Rabat to Casablanca in an ordinary car).

Piste driving

On the *pistes* (rough, unpaved tracks in the mountains or desert), there are special problems. Here you do need a good deal of driving and mechanical confidence – and if you don't feel your car is up to it, don't drive on these routes. Obviously, a 4x4 vehicle is best suited to the *pistes*, but most *pistes* are passable, with care, in an ordinary small car, though it's worth asking local advice first. On mountain roads, beware of gravel, which can be a real danger on the frequent hairpin bends, and, in spring, flash floods caused by melting snow. The four-volume series, *Pistes du Maroc* (Gandini), are invaluable guides for anyone planning on driving *pistes*; they are available in the main Moroccan bookshops. Roaming Yak (@www.roamingyak.org) have invaluable information about ten desert *piste* routes on their website, and produce an accompanying DVD.

Land Rover exploring

This can be an exciting way of exploring the mountains and desert, off *goudron* (tarmac/ hard top) or even off *piste* (dirt track). Companies lay on vehicles, driver and mess tent, organize food and cooking and will go wherever requested, in whatever style required – criss crossing the mountains or wandering into the desert, climbing peaks in remote areas, looking at wildlife, botanizing, coast exploring or anything else. For economical and practical reasons groups should number five or eleven, so you'll probably find yourself exploring with strangers. UK-based AMIS (see p.36) specializes in this field or you can, more expensively, contact hotels or ONMT (tourist office).

Car rental

Car rental is expensive, from around 2200dh (£135/$270) per week or 350dh (£21/$42) a day (there's usually a three-day minimum) for a basic car, usually a Fiat Uno, with unlimited mileage. You will be expected to leave a large deposit, and petrol prices are high too (see p.46). However, having a car does pay obvious dividends if you are pushed for time, allowing you to explore unusual routes and take in much more in a lot less time. This is especially true in the **south**, where getting around can be quite an effort if you have to rely on local buses.

Many visitors rent a car in Casablanca, Marrakesh or Agadir expressly for the southern routes. If you're organized, however, it may work out cheaper to **arrange car rental in advance** through the travel agent who arranges your flight. If you have problems, try one of the Morocco specialists detailed on pp.34–35. Major international firms such as Hertz, Budget, Europcar, National and Avis have facilities for booking from home on toll-free or cheap-rate numbers or via the Internet (see p.46).

Details of **car rental companies in Morocco** are given where relevant in city listings in the guide. The best-value places are mostly in Casablanca and Agadir. Deals to go for are unlimited mileage and daily/ weekly rates; paying by the kilometre invariably works out more expensive. Local firms have the advantage that the price is more likely to be negotiable, though the condition of the vehicle should be well checked. Many hotels can also arrange car rental, often at very reasonable rates. If you can't or don't want to drive yourself, car rental companies can often arrange a **driver** for around 300dh (£18/$36) a day.

Before making a booking, be sure to find out if you can pick the car up in one city and return it to another. Most companies will allow this if they have more than one office. Check also, if booking in Morocco, whether you will be charged extra for payment with a credit card; there is often a (negotiable) six percent fee for this. Before setting out, make sure the car comes with spare tyre, tool kit and full documentation – including insurance cover, which is compulsory issue with all rentals. It's a good idea to get full insurance to avoid charges for bumps and scratches. Most car rental agreements prohibit use of the car on unsurfaced roads, and you will be liable for any damage sustained if you do drive off-tarmac.

International car rental agencies

Avis UK ☎0870/606 0100, 🖳www.avis.co.uk; Ireland ☎021/428 1111, 🖳www.avis.ie; US ☎1-800/230-4898, 🖳www.avis.com; Canada ☎1-800/272-5871, 🖳www.avis.com; Australia ☎13/6333 or 02/9353 9000, 🖳www.avis.com.au; New Zealand ☎09/526 2847 or 0800/655 111, 🖳www.avis.co.nz; South Africa ☎0861/113 748, 🖳www.avis.co.za.

Budget UK ☎0870/156 5656, 🖳www.budget.co.uk; Ireland ☎0903/27711, 🖳www.budget.ie; US ☎1-800/472-3355, 🖳www.budget.com; Canada ☎1-800/268-8900, 🖳www.budget.ca; Australia ☎1300/362 848, 🖳www.budget.com.au; New Zealand ☎0800/283 438, 🖳www.budget.co.nz; South Africa ☎011/398 0123, 🖳www.budget.co.za.

Europcar UK ☎0870/607 5000, 🖳www.europcar.co.uk; Ireland ☎01/614 2800, 🖳www.europcar.ie; US & Canada ☎1-877/940-6900, 🖳www.europcar.com; Australia ☎1300/131 390, 🖳www.europcar.com.au; New Zealand ☎0800/800 115, 🖳www.europcar.co.nz; South Africa ☎0860/011 344, 🖳www.europcar.co.za.

Hertz UK ☎020/7026 0077, 🖳www.hertz.co.uk; Ireland ☎01/870 5777, 🖳www.hertz.ie; US & Canada ☎1-800/654-3131, 🖳www.hertz.com; Australia ☎13/3039 or 03/9698 2555, 🖳www.hertz.com.au; New Zealand ☎0800/654 321, 🖳www.hertz.co.nz; South Africa ☎021/935 4800, 🖳www.hertz.co.za.

National UK ☎0870/400 4581, 🖳www.nationalcar.co.uk; Ireland ☎021/432 0755, www.carhire.ie; US & Canada ☎1-800/227-7368, 🖳www.nationalcar.com; New Zealand ☎0800/800 115, 🖳www.nationalcar.co.nz; South Africa ☎0861/011 323, 🖳www.nationalcar.co.za.

Equipment

Whether you rent a car or drive your own, always make sure you're carrying a spare tyre in good condition (plus a jack and tools).

Flat tyres occur very frequently, even on fairly major roads, and you can often be in for a long wait until someone drives along with a possible replacement.

Carrying an emergency windscreen is also useful, especially if you are driving your own car for a long period of time. There are lots of loose stones on the hard shoulders of single-lane roads and they can fly all over the place.

If you're not mechanically minded, be sure to bring a car maintenance manual with you – a useful item, too, for anyone planning to rent a vehicle.

Fuel and breakdowns

Petrol stations are to be found in towns of any size but can be few and far between in rural areas: always fill your tank to the limit. Premium is the standard brand for cars; unleaded is available at larger stations, including most of the Afriquia branches, but it's always worth filling up when you have the chance as supplies can be sporadic. Fuel prices are generally lower than in Western Europe, at 10.25dh (62p/$1.25) a litre for leaded petrol (*super*) or unleaded, and 7.22dh (44p/88¢) for diesel (*gasoil*). Fuel costs for a Fiat Uno work out at around 7dh per 10km. In the Saharan provinces (basically the Western Sahara), fuel is subsidized, and costs about half as much, but unleaded petrol is all but unobtainable. Fuel is duty-free in the Spanish enclaves of Ceuta and Melilla, and around 25 percent cheaper than it is on the Spanish mainland, but it still costs the same or more than it does in Morocco, at €0.92 (62p/$1.25) per litre for *súper*, €0.86 (58p/$1.17) for unleaded (*sin plomo*), and €0.76 (52p/$1.03) for diesel (*gasóleo*).

Moroccan mechanics are usually excellent at coping with breakdowns and all medium-sized towns have garages (most with an extensive range of spare parts for most French cars, and usually for Fiats too). However, if you break down miles from anywhere you'll probably end up paying a fortune to get a lorry to tow you back.

If you are driving your own vehicle, there is also the problem of having to re-export any car that you bring into the country (even a wreck). You can't just write off a car: you'll have to take it out of Morocco with you.

Vehicle insurance

Insurance must by law be sold along with all rental agreements. Driving your own vehicle, you should obtain Green Card cover from your insurers. If you don't have it on arrival, you can buy it from Assurance Frontière for 880dh (£53/$107) a month for a car, 2470dh (£150/$300) for a caravan or camper, at Tangier port (☎039 94 90 92), Nador port (☎056 60 37 07), or the land frontiers at Ceuta and Melilla; to renew it, the main AF office is at 59 Bd Bordeaux, Casablanca (☎022 48 41 56 or 57).

Parking: gardiens and hotels

In almost every town of at least moderate size, you will find a *gardien de voitures* makes an appearance. *Gardiens* are often licensed by local authorities to look after cars, claiming a couple of dirhams by way of parking fees. Alternatively, most of the larger hotels in the Ville Nouvelle quarters of cities have parking spaces (and occasionally garaging). It's always worth paying for a *gardien* or parking in a garage, as new or well-looked-after cars attract a certain level of vandalism. Red and white striped kerbs mean no parking is allowed.

By motorbike

Each year an increasing number of **motorcyclists** travel to Morocco and find that it has all the major attractions sought by the enthusiast. The first choice to make when planning a trip is between going with an escorted group or on an independent journey. If you have never taken a bike abroad before and want to go to Morocco, seriously consider the group option. H-C Travel in the UK (see p.37), Moto Adventures in Andorra (see p.37) and Wilderness Wheels in Ouarzazate (see p.536) offer off-road and trailbiking packages. For those on their own, the following are some practical tips to help organize a trip. Read the comments on driving on pp.44–45 too, particularly in relation to the absence of lights at night.

Renting a motorbike

There is a fair bit of bureaucracy involved in taking a motorbike to Morocco. One way of getting around the hassles is to **rent a motorbike** there (see p.478, p.536 & p.618).

If you take your own motorbike, you will need **special insurance**. Most companies, especially those based outside Europe, will not cover motorcycling as part of a holiday overseas, particularly when off-road riding is contemplated or inevitable (as it often is in Morocco). You'll have to shop around and remember to take the policy with you, together with your bike registration certificate, biker's licence and International Driving Permit.

Even large insurance companies don't give clear answers about "**Green Cards**" for motorcycling in Morocco and do not understand that you may encounter up to a dozen police roadblocks a day.

When **entering Morocco**, try to arrive as early in the day as possible. If you are a lone traveller and speak neither Arabic nor French, you may be left queuing until those without queries have been dealt with. If the office then closes, you may have to return the next morning. In these circumstances, it might be worth investing in a tout who, for a fee, will take your papers to a friendly officer. It's also worth picking up a couple of (free) extra immigration forms for the return journey.

What to take and when to go

Don't take a model of bike likely to be unfamiliar in Morocco. Previous bikers recommend that you take all cables and levers, inner tubes, puncture repair kit, tyre levers, pump, fuses, plugs, chain, washable air filter, cable ties, good tape and tool kit. For riding off-road, take knobbly tyres and rim locks, brush guards, metal number plate and bashplate. In winter, take tough fabric outer clothing. In summer, carry lighterweight clothing, wool pullovers and waterproofs. Drying out leathers takes a long time. In the south, the heat in summer can be overwhelming, making travelling a far from enjoyable experience.

For further information, see Chris Scott's *The Adventure Motorbiking Handbook* (Compass Star), which claims to be the first world guide to overlanding on two wheels.

Cycling

Cycling – and particularly **mountain biking** – is becoming an increasingly popular pursuit for Western travellers to Morocco. The country's regular roads are well maintained and by European standards very quiet, while the extensive network of **pistes** – dirt tracks – makes for exciting mountain-bike terrain, leading you into areas otherwise accessible only to trekkers or four-wheel drive expeditions.

One nuisance in the countryside is **local kids**, who for some reason have developed a fondness for **throwing stones** at cyclists. You need to keep your wits about you, wherever you cycle, and your eyes wide open. The heat and the long stretches of dead straight road across arid, featureless plains – the main routes to (or beyond) the mountain ranges – can all too easily drain your energy. Additionally, public **water** is very rare – there are very few roadside watering places such as are found in Europe – and towns and villages are often a long way apart.

Regular roads are generally surfaced (*goudronné* or *revêtue*) but narrow, and you will often have to get off the tarmac to make way for traffic. Beware also of open land-drains close to the roadsides, and loose gravel on the bends.

Cycling on the **pistes**, mountain bikes come into their own with their "tractor" tyres and wide, stabilizing handlebars. There are few *pistes* that could be recommended on a regular tourer. By contrast, some intrepid mountain bikers cover footpaths in the High Atlas, though for the less than super-fit this is extremely heavy going. Better, on the whole, to stick to established *pistes* – many of which are covered by local trucks, which you can pay for a ride if your legs (or your bike) give out.

Getting your bike to Morocco

Most **airlines** – even charters – carry bikes free of charge, so long as they don't push your baggage allowance over the weight limit. When buying a ticket, register your intention of taking your bike and check out the airline's conditions. They will generally require you to invert the handlebars, remove the pedals, and deflate the tyres; some (like

KLM) provide/sell a cardboard **box** to enclose the bike, as protection for other passengers' luggage as much as for the bike; you are, however, unlikely to be offered a box for the return journey. A useful alternative, offering little protection but at least ensuring nothing gets lost, is to customize an industrial nylon sack, adding a drawstring at the neck.

If you plan to cross over **by ferry to Morocco**, things couldn't be simpler. You ride on with the motor vehicles (thus avoiding the long queues of foot passengers) and the bike is secure during the voyage. At time of writing, bicycles travel for free on Trasmediterranea ferries from Algeciras to Ceuta or Tangier, and Malaga or Almería to Melilla but not on Comanav services from Sète to Tangier or Nador.

Cycles and local transport

Cycling around Morocco, you can make use of local transport to supplement your own wheels. **Buses** will generally carry cycles on the roof. CTM usually charges around 10dh per bike – make sure you get a ticket. On other lines it's very much up to you to negotiate with the driver and/or baggage porter (who will probably expect at least 5dh). If you're riding and exhausted, you can usually flag down private-line buses (but not usually CTM services) on the road.

Some **grands taxis** also agree to carry cycles, if they have space on a rack. You may well have to pay for this, but of course you can haggle. In mountain or desert areas, you can have your bike carried with you on **truck or transit services** (see p.43). Prices for this are highly negotiable, but should not exceed your own passenger fare.

Cycles are carried on **trains** for a modest handling fee, though it's not really worth the hassle. Bikes have to be registered in advance as baggage and won't necessarily travel on the same train as you (though they will usually turn up within a day).

Accommodation

Accommodation doesn't present any special problems. The cheaper **hotels** will almost always let you keep your bike in your room – and others will find a disused basement or office for storage. It's almost essential to do this, as much to deter unwelcome tampering as theft, especially if you have a curiosity-inviting mountain bike. At **campsites**, there's usually a *gardien* on hand to keep an eye on your bike, or stow it away in his chalet.

Routes

Rewarding areas for biking include:
Tizi n'Test (High Atlas): Asni to Ijoukak, and an excursion to Tin Mal.
Asni to Setti Fatma (High Atlas: Ourika Valley) and beyond if you have a mountain bike.
Northern and Western Middle Atlas (well-watered side).
Djebel Sarhro and Djebel Bani: a choice of good east–west Anti-Atlas routes.
In summer it wouldn't be a good idea to go much beyond the Atlas, though given cooler winter temperatures, rewarding long routes exist in the **southern oasis routes**, such as Ouarzazate to Zagora or Ouarzazate to Tinerhir, and the desert routes down to El Rachidia, Erfoud and Rissani.

See box, pp.500–503 for more on mountain biking in the High Atlas.

Repairs

Most towns reveal a wealth of **general repair shops** in their Medina quarters, well used to servicing local bikes and mopeds. Though they are most unlikely to have the correct spare parts for your make of bike, they can usually sort out some kind of temporary solution.

It is worth bringing with you **spare spokes** (and tool), plus **brake blocks** and **cable**, as the mountain descents can take it out on a bike.

Tyres and tubes can generally be found for tourers, though if you have anything fancy, best bring at least one spare, too.

Obviously, before setting out, you should make sure that your brakes are in good order, renew bearings, etc, and ensure that you have decent quality (and condition) tyres.

Problems and rewards

All over Morocco, and particularly in rural areas, there are stray, wild and semi-cared-for **dogs**. A cyclist pedalling past with feet and wheels spinning seems to send at least half of them into a frenzied state. Normally, cycling in an equally frenzied state is the best defence, but on steep ascents and off-road

Addresses

Arabic names – Derb, Zankat, etc – are gradually replacing French ones. The main street or square of any town, though, is still invariably Avenue or Place Hassan II (the last king) or Mohammed V (his father). Older street signs are usually in French and Arabic lettering; new ones are often Arabic only.

this isn't always possible. In these situations, keep the bike between you and the dog, and use your pump or a shower from your water bottle as defence. If you do get bitten, a rabies inoculation is advisable.

Another factor to be prepared for is your susceptibility to the unwanted attentions of local people. Small **children** will often stand in the road to hinder your progress, or even chase after you in gangs. This is normally good-natured but it can become intimidating if they start throwing stones. Your attitude is important: be friendly, smile, and maintain strong eye contact. On no account attempt to mete out your own discipline: small children always have big brothers.

Despite all this, cycling in Morocco can be an extremely rewarding experience; as one of our correspondents put it: "I felt an extra intimacy with the country by staying close to it, rather than viewing it from car or bus windows. And I experienced unrivalled generosity, from cups of tea offered by policemen at roadside checkpoints to a full-blown breakfast banquet from a farming family whose dog had savaged my leg. People went out of their way to give me advice, food, drink and lifts, and not once did I feel seriously threatened. Lastly, the exhilaration I felt on some of the mountain descents, above all the Tizi n'Test in the High Atlas, will remain with me forever. I was not an experienced cycle tourer when I arrived in Morocco, but the grandeur of the scenery helped carry me over the passes."

Further information

In the UK, the British Cycle Touring Club (☏0870/873 0060, ⊛www.ctc.org.uk), keeps members' reports on past tours in

Morocco, which are available to other members, who can also get good-value insurance among other services from the club. In the US, Adventure Cycling (℡1-800/755-2453 or 406/721-1776, ⓦwww.adventurecycling.org), can help find general information about biking, and produces the Cyclist Yellow Pages, which offers listings of all sorts of bike-related information (suppliers, tour operators) but no specific information about Morocco tours.

Inspiration for mountain bikers can be found in Nick Crane's **book**, *Atlas Biker* (Oxford Illustrated Press, UK, 1990), an adventurous account of a traverse of the High Atlas on – or at times carrying – mountain bikes. For general advice on equipment and clothing, a useful source is *Bicycle Expeditions* by Paul Vickers, which is now out of print (it was published in 1990) but can be downloaded as a PDF file from ⓦwww.rgs.org/eacpubs, or ordered as a printout for £5 from the Expedition Advisory Service, Royal Geographical Society, 1 Kensington Gore, London SW7 2AR, UK (℡020/7591 3000).

City transport

You'll spend most time exploring Moroccan cities on foot. The alleys of the old Medina quarters, where the sights and souks are, will rarely accommodate more than a donkey. In the newer quarters, you may want to make use of city taxis and occasionally a bus. In the new city quarters, you should be aware that pedestrian crossings don't count for very much, except perhaps at junctions "controlled" by traffic lights. And even then, cycles and mopeds pay scant attention to traffic lights showing red.

Petits taxis, usually Fiats or Simcas, carry up to three passengers and (unlike grands taxis) can only operate within city limits. All petits taxis should have meters, and you should insist that they use them. Failing that, you will need to bargain for a price – either before you get in (wise to start off with) or by simply presenting the regular fare when you get out. If you are a lone passenger, your taxi driver may pick up one or two additional passengers en route, each of whom will pay the full fare for their journey, as of course will you. This is standard practice.

Don't be afraid to argue with the driver if you feel you're being unreasonably overcharged. During the daytime, you should pay what is on the meter. After 8pm, standard fares rise by fifty percent. Tips are not expected, but of course always appreciated. Taxis from airports run at fixed rates, which should be on display at the airport taxi rank.

Accommodation

Hotels in Morocco are cheap, good value, and usually pretty easy to find. There can be a shortage of places in the major cities and resorts (Tangier, Fes, Marrakesh and Agadir) in August, and in Rabat or Casablanca when there's a big conference on. Other times, you should be able to pick from a wide range.

The most important distinction among Moroccan hotels is between **classified hotels** (which are given star-ratings by the tourist board) and **unclassified hotels** (which are not). The latter tend to be cheap places, with few facilities, in the old Medina quarters. For any level of comfort, you'll want a classified hotel.

If you're on a limited budget, a good course is to **alternate between the extremes**, spending most nights in basic Medina hotels but going for the occasional blast of grandeur. At any rate don't limit yourself to the middle categories – these are mostly dull, and staying all the time in the Villes Nouvelles will cut you off from the

Accommodation price codes

Our hotel price codes are based on the rate for the cheapest double room in high season (June– Sept).

Hotels in the lower price categories generally have rooms with just a washbasin – you always pay extra for en-suite shower and WC – and double rooms can generally be converted into triples/family rooms, with extra beds, for a modest extra charge. Single occupancy usually costs about two-thirds the price of a double, though in some places a single person will pay the same rate for a room as two people sharing, and in other places exactly half as much. Prices quoted are for bed only, without breakfast (unless specified in the text), but including local taxes.

For places that offer **dorm beds**, rates per person are given in dirhams, and in the Spanish enclaves of **Ceuta** and **Melilla**, current euro prices for the cheapest high-season double are given.

❶ under 100dh
(under £6/$12/€9)

❷ 100–150dh
(£6–9/$12–18/€9–13.50)

❸ 150–200dh
(£9–12/$18–24/€13.50–18)

❹ 200–300dh
(£12–18/$24–36/€18–27)

❺ 300–500dh
(£18–30/$36–60/€27–45)

❻ 500–800dh
(£30–49/$60–96/€45–72)

❼ 800–1500dh
(£49–91/$96–182/€72–134)

❽ 1500dh or over
(over £91/$182/€134)

---

most interesting aspects of traditional Moroccan life.

In winter, one thing worth checking for in a hotel is **heating** – nights can get cold, even in the south (and especially in the desert), and since bedding is not always adequate, a hotel with heating can be a boon.

Unclassified hotels

Unclassified (*non-classé*) **hotels**, (price codes ❶ and ❷), are mainly to be found in the older, Arab-built parts of cities – the **Medinas** – and are almost always the cheapest accommodation options. They offer the additional advantage of being at the heart of things: where you'll want to spend most of your time, and where all the sights and markets are concentrated. The disadvantages are that the Medinas can at first appear daunting – with their mazes of narrow lanes and blind alleys – and that the hotels themselves can be, at worst, dirty flea traps with tiny, windowless cells and half-washed sheets. At their best, they're fine: traditional "*caravanserai*" buildings with whitewashed rooms round a central patio.

One other minus point for unclassified Medina hotels is that they sometimes have a problem with **water**. Most of the Medinas

remain substantially unmodernized, and some cheap hotels are without hot water, with squat toilets that can be pretty disgusting. On the plus side, there is usually a hammam (Turkish bath – see box, p.53) nearby.

Unclassified hotel **rates** fluctuate widely, depending on their location, sometimes varying with season, and being more or less negotiable depending on demand. The cost of a double room in high season ranges from 40dh (£2.50/$4.50) to 200dh (£12/$22).

Classified hotels

Classified (*classé*) **hotels** are most likely to be found in a town's **Ville Nouvelle** – the "new" or administrative quarters, built by the French and usually set slightly apart from the old Medina quarters.

Classified hotels are allowed, regardless of **star-rating**, to set their own prices – and to vary them according to season and depending on demand. Prices and ratings should be on display at reception and behind the bedroom door, but if in doubt about value for money, don't hesitate to ask to see the room in question; indeed, you will normally be invited to do so.

At the bottom end of the scale – a **one-star hotel** (price codes ❷ to ❹) – a basic

...Hipmarrakech.com...

A selection of English-speaking riads in Marrakech

We offer a wide selection of high quality traditional and modern riads or villas in Marrakech. We are open 7 days per week, and respond to enquiries quickly. Availability of rooms can be checked on-line.

www.hipmarrakech.com +44 208 816 7065

double room with a washbasin will cost around £10/$20 a night, with a shower and WC around £12/$25. Moving into **two- and three-star hotels** (price codes ❸ to ❺), you will be paying around £25/$50 for a double with shower and WC, at the top end of the scale. You get a fair bit more comfort for your money and there are a scattering of elegant, old hotels in these categories – places which used to be the grand hotel in town but have since declined. At the top end of the mid-range, the *Ibis Moussafir* chain (🌐www.ibishotel.com) offers reliable hotels always located next to train stations – though rather characterless and almost identical in every town, they're comfortable, efficient and good value.

For Western-style standards of comfort, you need to look, on the whole, at **four-star hotels**. These are used by most foreign tour operators and charge around £40–75/$80–150 (price codes ❻ to ❼) for a double, though often a lot less if you get them as part of a package tour. If you can afford the upper end of this scale, you'll be moving into real style, with rooms looking out onto palm-shaded pools and gardens – at their best in buildings that have been converted from old palace residences. But even here, you are advised to check what's on offer. The plumbing, heating and lighting are sometimes unreliable; restaurants are often closed and swimming pools empty. Hotels in this price category are particularly likely to offer discounted and promotional rates off-season.

Hotels accorded the **five-star-luxury rating**, (invariably price code ❽) can be very stylish, often in a historic conversion (most famously the *Hôtel Mamounia* in Marrakesh and the *Palais Jamaï* in Fes) or in a modern building with a splendid pool and all the international creature comforts, but even in a five-star hotel, service is frequently amateurish by Western standards, and staff ill-trained and unprofessional; this is especially the case in establishments that cater mainly for tour groups.

In the Spanish enclaves of **Ceuta and Melilla**, accommodation at the lower end of the spectrum costs about twice as much as it does in Morocco proper, with a double room in the cheapest *pensiones* at €25–30. At the top end of the scale, prices tend to be much the same as they are in Morocco, with four-star hotels charging around €70–100.

Riads

Morocco's trendiest accommodation option is in a **riad** or **maison d'hôte**. Strictly speaking, a riad is a house built around a patio garden – in fact, the word *riad* correctly refers to the garden rather than the house – while *maison d'hôte* is French for "guest house". The two terms are both used, to some extent interchangeably, for a residential house done up to rent out to tourists, but a riad is generally more stylish and expensive,

while a *maison d'hôte* is likely to be less chic and more homely. In a riad, it is often possible to rent the whole house.

The riad craze started in Marrakesh, where it took off big-time, and quickly spread to Fes and Essaouira. Since then it has gone nationwide and almost every town with tourists now has riads too. Even the Atlas mountains and the southern oases are dotted with them, and there appears to be no shortage of takers.

Hammams

The absence of hot showers in some of the cheapest Medina hotels is not such a disaster. Throughout all the Medina quarters, you'll find local **hammams**. A hammam is a Turkish-style steam bath, with a succession of rooms from cool to hot, and endless supplies of hot and cold water, which you fetch in buckets. The usual procedure is to find a piece of floor space in the hot room, surround it with as many buckets of water as you feel you need, and lie in the heat to sweat out the dirt from your pores before scrubbing it off. A plastic bowl is useful for scooping the water from the buckets to wash with. You can also order a massage, in which you will be allowed to sweat, pulled about a bit to relax your muscles, and then rigorously scrubbed with a rough flannel glove (*kiis*). Alternatively, buy a *kiis* and do it yourself. For many Moroccan women, who would not drink in a café or bar, the hammam is a social gathering place, in which tourists are made very welcome too. Indeed, hammams turn out to be a highlight for many women travellers, and an excellent way to make contact with Moroccan women.

Several hammams are detailed in the text, but the best way of finding one is always to ask at the hotel where you're staying. You will often, in fact, need to be led to a hammam, since they are usually unmarked and can be hard to find. In some towns, you find a separate hammam for women and men; at others the same establishment offers different hours for each sex – usually mornings and evenings for men, afternoons (typically noon to 6pm) for women.

For both sexes, there's more modesty than you might perhaps expect: it's customary for men (always) and women (generally, though bare breasts are acceptable) to bathe in swimming costume (or underwear), and to undress facing the wall. Women may be also surprised to find their Moroccan counterparts completely shaven and may (in good humour) be offered this service; there's no embarrassment in declining.

As part of the Islamic tradition of cleanliness and ablutions, hammams sometimes have a religious element, and non-Muslims may not be welcome (or allowed in) to those built alongside mosques, particularly on Thursday evenings, before the main weekly service on Friday. On the whole, though, there are no restrictions against *Nisara* ("Nazarenes", or Christians).

Finally, don't forget to bring soap and shampoo (though these are sometimes sold at hammams), and a towel (these are sometimes rented, but can be a bit dubious). Moroccans often bring a plastic mat to sit on, too, as the floors can get a bit clogged. Mats can be bought easily enough in any town. Most Moroccans use a pasty, olive oil-based soap (*sabon bildi*), sold by weight in Medina shops. On sale at the same shops, you'll find *kiis* flannel gloves, a fine mud (*ghasoul*), used by some instead of shampoo, pumice stones (*hazra*) for removing dead skin, and alum (*chebba*), used as an antiperspirant and to stop shaving cuts from bleeding.

Most riads are eighteenth- or nineteenth-century **Medina town-houses** which have been bought and refurbished by Europeans or prosperous Moroccans (often Moroccans who have been living in Europe). They tend to have a standard interior-design look, and you'll frequently find interior design magazines lying about in their salons, indicating the source of the owner's inspiration. Most of them have roof terraces, some have plunge pools or Jacuzzis, pretty much all offer en-suite rooms, and breakfast is usually included in the room price.

However, the sudden popularity of riads has attracted a fair few amateur property developers, some of whom invest minimum money in the hope of maximum returns. Before you take a riad therefore, even more than with a hotel, it is always best to give it a preliminary once-over. Riads are usually substantially more expensive than hotels with a similar level of comfort, but at the top of the market, they can be a lot classier than a run-of-the-mill five-star hotel. In the mid range, however, despite the popularity of riads, and their undoubted charm, it is worth bearing in mind that hotels are likely to offer better value for money.

Hostels

Morocco has fourteen *Auberges de Jeunesse*. Most are clean and reasonably well run, and charges vary from 30dh (£1.80/$3.60) to 60dh (£3.65/$7.30) per person per night in a dorm; most have private rooms too. Hostelling International (HI) membership cards are not required but you may have to pay a little extra if you do not have one. The hostels are located at Asni (High Atlas), Azrou (Middle Atlas), Casablanca, Chefchaouen, Fes, Goulmima, Laayoune, Marrakesh, Mehdiya, Meknes, Rabat, Rissani, Tangier and Tinerhir. Addresses and details are given for all of these in the relevant sections of the guide; those at Casablanca, Marrakesh and Tangier recommend booking in advance. One general attraction is the opportunity for meeting other travellers, including young Moroccans on holiday. Further information on Moroccan youth hostels can be found on the Hostelling International website at ⓦwww.iyhf.org or in the *International Youth Hostels Guide* (£9.99), often available in public libraries. Alternatively, contact the *Fédération Royale Marocaine des Auberges de Jeunesse*, Parc de la Ligue Arabe, BP No 15998, Casa Principale, Casablanca 21000 ⓣ022 47 09 52.

Youth hostel associations

Australia ⓣ02/9565 1699, ⓦwww.yha.com.au.
Canada ⓣ1-800/663-5777, ⓦwww.hihostels.ca.
England & Wales ⓣ0870/770 8868, ⓦwww.yha.org.uk.
Ireland (Republic) ⓣ01/830 4555, ⓦwww.irelandyha.org.
New Zealand ⓣ0800/278 299 or 03/379 9970, ⓦwww.yha.co.nz.
Northern Ireland ⓣ028/9032 4733, ⓦwww.hini.org.uk.
Scotland ⓣ01786/891 400, ⓦwww.syha.org.uk.
South Africa ⓣ021/788 2301, ⓦwww.hisa.org.za.
USA ⓣ301/495-1240, ⓦwww.hiayh.org.

Refuges and gîtes d'étape

In the Djebel Toubkal area of the High Atlas mountains, the Club Alpin Français (CAF; 50 Bd Moulay Abderrahmane, Beauséjour, Casablanca ⓣ022 99 01 41) maintain five huts, or refuges (at Imlil, Oukaïmeden, Tachdirt, Tararht and Toubkal) equipped for mountaineers and trekkers. These provide bunks or bedshelves for sleeping at 60–95dh (£3.70–£5.85/$7.30–11.60) per person, with discounts for members of CAF or its affiliates, and for HI youth hostel cardholders. Some refuges can provide meals and/or cooking facilities. They are detailed in the relevant sections.

Also in trekking areas, a number of locals offer rooms in their houses: an informal scheme which the Moroccan tourist authorities have begun promoting as **gîtes d'étape**. Lists of these *gîtes* are to be found in the ONMT (tourist office) pamphlet *La Grande Traversée des Atlas Marocains*. Current charges are around 60–80dh per person per night, with breakfast for around 30dh and an evening meal for 60dh.

Camping

Campsites are to be found at intervals along most of the developed Moroccan coast and in most towns or cities of any size. They are inexpensive and often quite informal and makeshift, advertised from season to season on roadside signs. Most sites are very cheap, at around 10dh (65p/$1.10) per person, plus a similar charge for a tent or a car, and 20dh (£1.30/$2.20) for a motorcaravan or campervan; they usually have basic (and sometimes very basic) washing and toilet facilities. A few more upmarket places, in Meknes or Fes, for example, offer swimming pools and better facilities at around double the cost – sometimes more. Details and addresses are given in relevant sections of the guide. Comprehensive, and often highly critical reviews of Morocco's campsites, in French, can be found in Jacques Gandini's *Campings du Maroc et de Mauritanie: Guide Critique* (Broché, France), which should be available at better Moroccan bookshops, such as Marrakesh's Librairie Chatr (see p.470).

Campsites don't tend to provide much security, and you should never leave valuables unattended. Camping outside official sites, this obviously applies even more, and if you want to do this, it's wise to ask at a house if you can pitch your tent alongside – you'll usually get a hospitable response. If you're trekking in the Atlas, it is often possible to pay someone to act as a *gardien* for your tent. In the south especially, and particularly in the winter, campsites are not much used by backpackers with tents, but rather by retired Europeans in campervans seeking the sun.

If travelling in a campervan, you can often park up somewhere with a *gardien*, who will keep an eye on things for a small tip (usually 20dh per night). Failing that, you may be able to park outside a police station (*commissariat*). In the north of the country, at Larache, Kenitra and Malabata (near Tangier), there are *Aires de Repose*, which are rest areas for tourist coaches, with toilets, showers, a restaurant and *gardien*. There's no fee for parking your camper here or using the facilities, but it is usual to pay a contribution of around 20dh to the *gardien* if you stay overnight.

Food and drink

Like accommodation, food in Morocco falls into two basic categories: ordinary Moroccan meals served in the Medina cafés (or bought from stalls), and French-influenced tourist menus in most of the hotels and Ville Nouvelle restaurants. There are exceptions – cheap local cafés in the new cities and occasional palace-style places in the Medina. Whatever your budget, don't be afraid to try both options. The Medina places are mostly cleaner than they look and their food is usually fresh and tasty.

Basic café food

Basic Moroccan meals may begin with a thick, very filling soup – most often the spicy, bean and pasta **harira** (which is a meal in itself, and eaten as such to break the Ramadan fast). Alternatively, you might start with a **salad** (often very finely chopped), or have this as a side dish with your main course, typically a plateful of **kebabs** (either *brochettes* – small pieces of lamb on a skewer – or *kefta*, made from minced lamb). Some small places also offer fried fish, a stew of beans (*loobia*), or a plate or kebab of offal such as liver or brain, which many Western tourists prefer to avoid, though in fact it can be very tasty. A few hole-in-the-wall places specialize in soup, which they sell by the bowlful all day long – such places are usually indicated by a pile of soup bowls at the front. As well as *harira*, and

55

especially for breakfast, some places sell a thick pea soup called *bisara*, topped with full-flavoured green olive oil.

Alternatively, you could go for a **tajine**, which is essentially a stew, steam-cooked slowly in an earthenware dish, with a conical earthenware lid over a charcoal fire. Like "casserole", the term "tajine" actually refers to the dish and lid rather than the food cooked in it. Classic tajines include lamb/mutton with prunes and almonds, or chicken with olives and lemon. Less often, you may get a tajine of fish or just vegetables. A popular alternative is *kefta*, a tasty tajine of meatballs topped with eggs. A tajine is to Moroccan cuisine what a curry is to Indian, and you'll find a whole variety of different ones on offer at Moroccan eateries through from the very cheapest to the most expensive place in town. Mopped up with bread, they can be unbelievably delicious.

Kebabs or a tajine usually cost little more than 30dh (£2/$4) at one of the hole-in-the-wall places in the Medina, with their two or three tables. You are not expected to bargain for cooked food, but prices can be lower in such places if you enquire how much things cost before you start eating. There is often no menu – or a board written in Arabic only.

If you're looking for **breakfast or a snack**, you can buy a half-**baguette** – plus butter and jam, cheese or eggs, if you want – from many bread or grocery stores, and take it into a café to order a coffee. Many cafés, even those which serve no other food, may offer a breakfast of bread, butter and jam (which is also what you'll get in most hotels), or maybe an omelette. Some places also offer soup, such as *harira*, with bread, and others have stalls outside selling by weight traditional griddle breads such as *harsha* (quite heavy with a gritty crust), *melaoui* or *msimmen* (sprinkled with oil, rolled out thin, folded over and rolled out again several times, like an Indian *paratha*) and *baghira* (full of holes like a very thin English crumpet). If that is not sufficient, supplementary foods you could buy include dates or olives, yoghurt, or soft white cheese (*ejben*).

Restaurant meals

More expensive dishes, available in some of the Medina cafés as well as in the dearer restaurants, include **fish**, particularly on the coast, and **chicken** (*poulet*), either spit-roasted (*rôti*) or in a tajine with lemon and olives (*poulet aux olives et citron*).

You will sometimes find **pastilla**, too, a succulent pigeon pie (in cheaper versions chicken may be used), prepared with filo pastry dusted with sugar and cinnamon; it is a particular speciality of Fes.

And, of course, there is **couscous**, perhaps the most famous Moroccan dish, Berber in origin and based on a huge bowl of steamed semolina piled high with vegetables and mutton, chicken, or occasionally fish. Restaurant couscous, however, tends to be disappointing. There is no real tradition of going out to eat in Morocco, and this is a dish that's traditionally prepared at home for a special occasion (on Friday, the holy day, in richer households; perhaps for a festival in poorer ones). Often, you'll need to give two or three hours' notice for it to be cooked in a restaurant. In the home, remember that every Moroccan's mum cooks the finest couscous in the kingdom.

At festivals, which are always good for interesting food, and at the most expensive tourist restaurants, you may also come across **mechoui** – roast lamb, which may even take the form of a whole sheep roasted on a spit. In Marrakesh particularly, another speciality is **tanjia**, which is jugged beef or lamb, cooked very slowly in the embers of a hammam furnace (see p.471).

To supplement these standard offerings, most tourist restaurants add a few **French dishes** – steak, liver, various fish and fowl, etc – and the ubiquitous **salade marocaine**, actually very different from the Moroccan idea of salad, since it's based on a few tomatoes, cucumbers and other greens. You'll also probably have the choice of fruit, yoghurt, or sometimes even crème caramel for dessert.

Restaurants are typically open noon–3pm for lunch, and 7–11pm for dinner, though cheaper places may be open in the morning and between times too. In the text we have indicated what kind of **price range** a restaurant falls into. At restaurants described as "cheap", a typical meal (starter, main course, dessert and drink) will cost less than 80dh (£5/$10). At places described as "moderate",

© M.OSMONT · LIC.075950346

Small, charming, quiet, authentic

COME UNWIND AT LA VILLA NOMADE

Tucked in Bab Taghzout, next to the medina, our ryad has been renovated in the pure and authentic moroccan style. After having mastered the art of haggling in the souks, you may feel the need to relax in the spa or the pool, sip a cocktail on the rooftop terrasse and then enjoy a fine dinner at our gourmet restaurant. The choice is all yours !

TEL. 00 212 24 38 50 10 | villanomade@menara.ma

www.lavillanomade.com

Villa *Nomade*

MARRAKECH | MAROC

you can expect to pay 80–150dh (£5–9/$10–18), while anywhere likely to cost over 150dh (£9/$18) is described as "expensive". Places that don't display prices are likely to overcharge you big-time unless you check the price before ordering – the maxim that where prices are not shown they must be too high is worth bearing in mind.

Eating Moroccan style

Eating in local cafés, or if **invited to a home**, you may find yourself using your hands rather than a knife and fork. Muslims eat only with the **right hand** (the left is used for the toilet), and you should do likewise. Hold the bread between the fingers and use your thumb as a scoop; it's often easier to discard the soft centre of the bread and to use the crust only – as you will see many Moroccans do.

Eating from a **communal plate** at someone's home, it is polite to take only what is immediately in front of you, unless specifically offered a piece of meat by the host.

Vegetarian eating

Moroccan cuisine presents distinctly limited options for **vegetarians** – a preference that will meet with little comprehension in most of Morocco, though restaurants in some places are becoming more aware that tourists may be vegetarian. Tajines can be requested without meat (and, with some difficulty, without meat stock), but beyond these vegetarian casseroles, and ubiquitous omelettes and sandwiches, the menus don't present very obvious choices. *Bisara* (pea soup), a common breakfast dish, should be meat-free, but *harira* (bean soup) may or may not be made with meat stock, while most foods are cooked in animal fats. In cafés and restaurants, asking for a dish *sans viande ou poisson* (without meat or fish) can still result in your being served chicken or lamb, so you'll need to take the trouble to explain matters very clearly.

If you are a very strict vegetarian or vegan, it may be worth bringing some basic provisions (such as yeast extract, peanut butter and veggie stock cubes) and a small Camping Gaz stove and pan – canisters are cheap and readily available, and in some cheap hotels, Moroccan guests may well cook in their rooms.

Locally, there are plenty of beans, grains, seeds and pulses available, basic cheeses, excellent yoghurts, and a great selection of fruit and nuts; dates, figs, almonds and pistachio nuts can all enliven dishes. In the countryside, you may find fresh fruit and vegetables hard to obtain except during the weekly souk.

The most difficult situations are those in which you are invited to eat at someone's house. You may find people give you meat when you have specifically asked for vegetables because they think you can't afford it: a scenario in which you might decide that it's more important not to offend someone showing you kindness than to be strict about your principles. Picking out vegetables from a meat tajine won't offend your hosts; declining the dish altogether, on the other hand, may end up with the mother/sister/ wife in the kitchen getting the flak. One possible way to avoid offence when invited to a home (or to explain your needs in a restaurant) is to say that vegetarianism is part of your religion (this is normal in Hinduism and Buddhism for example), a concept that most Moroccans should have no problems with.

Cakes, desserts and fruit

Cakes and desserts are available in some Moroccan café-restaurants, though you'll find them more often at pastry shops or street stalls. They can be excellent, not generally too sickly and often made with nuts, especially almonds; there are infinite variations, like *m'hencha* (almond-filled pastry coils which sometimes appear covered in honey) and *cornes de gazelles* (banana-shaped pastries filled with a kind of marzipan).

Yoghurt (*yaourt* or *rayeb*) is also delicious, and Morocco is surprisingly rich in seasonal **fruits**. In addition to the various kinds of **dates** – sold all year but at their best fresh from the October harvests – there are grapes, melons, strawberries, peaches and figs, all advisably washed before eaten. Or for a real thirst-quencher (and a good cure for a bad stomach), you can have quantities of **prickly pear**, cactus fruit, peeled for you in the street for a couple of dirhams in season.

Tea, coffee and soft drinks

The national drink is **mint tea** (*atay deeyal naanaa* in Arabic, *thé à la menthe* in French, "Whisky Marocain" as locals boast), Chinese gunpowder green tea flavoured with sprigs of mint (*naanaa* in Arabic: the gift of Allah) and sweetened with a minimum of four cubes of sugar per cup, or four lumps knocked off a sugar loaf – something you won't find nowadays in many other parts of the world. It tastes a little sickly at first (you can ask for it with little or no sugar – *shweeya soukar* or *ble soukar*) but is worth getting used to. It's perfect in the summer heat and a ritual if you're invited into anyone's home or if you're doing any serious bargaining in a shop. In cafés, it is usually cheaper to ask for a pot (*une théière*) for two or three people.

In winter, Moroccans often add wormwood (*chiba* in Arabic, *absinthe* in French) to their tea "to keep out the cold". You can also get black tea (*atal ahmar* in Arabic, *the rouge* in French, literally meaning "red tea") – inevitably made with the ubiquitous Lipton's tea bags, a brand fondly believed by Moroccans to be typically English. **Herbal Infusions** include aniseed (*anis*) and verbena (*verveine*).

Also common at cafés and street stalls are a range of wonderful fresh-squeezed **juices**: orange juice (*jus d'orange* in French, *'asir burtuqal* in Arabic – if you don't want sugar in it, remember to say so), almond milk (*jus d'amande* or *'asir louze*), banana "juice", meaning milk shake (*jus des bananes* or *'asir mooz*) and apple milk-shake (*jus de pomme* or *'asir tufah*). Also common is *'asir panaché*, a mixed fruit milkshake often featuring raisins. *Leben* – soured milk – is tastier than it sounds, and does wonders for an upset stomach.

Other soft drinks inevitably include Coke, Fanta and other fizzy soda pops – all pretty inexpensive and sold in large bottles. Mineral water is usually referred to by brand name, ubiquitously the still Sidi Harazem or Sidi Ali (some people claim to be able to tell one from the other), or the naturally sparkling Oulmès. The Coca-Cola company is marketing filtered, processed non-mineral water in bottles under the brand name *Ciel*.

Coffee (*café*) is best in French-style cafés – either *noir* (black), *cassé* (with a drop of milk), or *au lait* (with a lot of milk). Instant coffee is known, like teabag tea, after its brand – in this case Nescafé.

Lastly, do not take risks with **milk**: buy it fresh and drink it fresh. If it smells remotely off, don't touch it.

Wine and beer

As an Islamic nation, Morocco gives **drinking alcohol** a low profile. It is in fact not generally possible to buy any alcohol at all in the Medinas, and for beer or wine you always have to go to a tourist restaurant or hotel, or a bar in the Ville Nouvelle. Outside of tourist hotels, **bars** – which are often called **brasseries**, though they serve no food – are very much **all-male preserves**, in which women travellers may feel uneasy (bartenders may occasionally be female, but female Moroccan customers are likely to be on the game). On the drinks front, Moroccan **wines** can be palatable enough, if a little heavy for drinking without a meal. The best to be found is the pinkish red *Clairet de Meknès*, made purposefully light in French claret style. *Beauvallon* is another good one, but usually reserved for export. Other varieties worth trying include the strong red *Cabernet*, and *Ksar*, *Guerrouane* and *Siraoua*, which are also red, the rosé *Gris de Boulaoune* and the dry white *Spécial Coquillages*.

Those Moroccans who drink in bars tend to stick to **beer**, usually the local *Stork* or *Flag*. *Flag* from Fes is held by many to be superior to the version brewed in Casablanca (the label will tell you which it is). The most popular foreign brand is *Heineken*, which is made under licence in Morocco.

The media

A selection of European newspapers (usually including some British dailies) and the *International Herald Tribune* are available in all the main cities. The British *Guardian Weekly* is also usually available, as occasionally is *USA Today*, and more commonly *Time*, *Newsweek* and *The Economist*. Also often available, though of limited value as a serious source of news, is the *Saudi Gazette*, whose content is, needless to say, slavishly favourable to the Saudi regime. Failing that, you can always log onto the website of your favourite newspaper from home (or from anywhere else come to that).

Newspapers and magazines

The **Moroccan press** encompasses a reasonable range of papers, published in French and Arabic. Their news coverage, and coverage of international news in particular, however, is pretty weak. Of the **French-language** papers, the most accessible is the official – and somewhat rigorously pro-government – daily, *Le Matin du Sahara* (Ⓦwww.lematin.ma). Others include *L'Opinion* (Istiqlal party; Ⓦwww.lopinion.ma), *Maroc Soir* (independent; website supposedly under construction at Ⓦwww.marocsoir.ma), *L'Economiste*, (independent; Ⓦwww.leconomiste.com), and *Al Bayane* (communist; Ⓦwww.albayane.ma). Periodicals include *Maroc-Hebdo* (Ⓦwww.maroc-hebdo.press.ma), *La Vie Eco* (Ⓦwww.lavieeco.com), and the Time/Newsweek-style news magazine *Tel-Quel* (Ⓦwww.telquel-online.com).

Arabic daily newspapers include *El Alam*, which supports the Istiqlal party, and *El Ittihad el Ichtiraki*, which supports the nominally socialist USFP party.

In addition to these, Morocco has a number of football magazines, women's magazines and other publications in French that are often worth a peruse, as well as the excellent Francophone African news magazine, *Jeune Afrique* (Ⓦwww.jeuneafrique.com). Also of possible interest is the English-language online magazine *Tingis* (Ⓦwww.tingismagazine.com), billed as "an American-Moroccan magazine of ideas and culture".

Radio

If you have a short-wave radio, you can pick up the **BBC World Service**, which is broadcast on various frequencies through the day. The most consistent reception is generally on 12,095 and 15,485 KHz (25m and 19m bands) during the daytime, or 6195 and 9410 and 12,095 KHz (49m and 31m bands) after dark; programme listings can be found online at Ⓦwww.bbc.co.uk/worldservice. You can also pick up **Voice of America** during the day on 15,195 or 17,895 KHz, at night on 1593 KHz – see Ⓦwww.voa.gov for full frequency and programme listings.

Television

Most of the pricier hotels receive **satellite TV** – CNN, the French TV5, and occasionally the UK Sky channels. In the north of the country you can also get Spanish TV stations and, in Tangier, the English-language **Gibraltar** TV and radio broadcasts. The independent Qatari news channel Al Jazeera is a major source of news for people in Morocco (many cafés show it), and you may even be able to get it in English if you have access to cable or satellite, but it is unfortunately not obtainable on terrestrial TV.

Morocco's own two TV channels broadcast in Arabic, but include some French programmes – plus news bulletins in Arabic, French, Spanish and, more recently, Berber.

Festivals

If the popular image of Islam is somewhat puritanical and ascetic, Morocco's festivals – the moussems and amouggars – do their best to contradict it. The country abounds in holidays and festivals of all kinds, both national and local, and coming across one can be the most enjoyable experience of travel in Morocco – with the chance to witness music and dance, as well as special regional foods and market souks.

Perhaps surprisingly, there are rewards, too, in coinciding with one of the major Islamic celebrations – above all Ramadan, when all Muslims (which means almost all Moroccans) observe a total fast from sunrise to sunset for a month. This can pose some problems for travelling but the celebratory evenings are again good times to hear music and to share in hospitality.

Ramadan

Ramadan, in its observance, parallels the traditional Christian Lent. The ninth month of the Islamic calendar, it commemorates the time in which the Koran was revealed to Muhammad. In contrast to the Christian West, the Muslim world observes the fast rigorously – indeed Moroccans are forbidden by law from "private disrespect" of the fast, and a few are jailed for this each year.

Ramadan and Islamic holidays

Islamic religious holidays are calculated on the **lunar calendar**, so their dates rotate throughout the seasons (as does Ramadan's), losing about eleven days a year against the Western (Gregorian) calendar. Exact dates in the lunar calendar are impossible to predict – they are set by the Islamic authorities in Fes – but approximate dates for the next few years are:

	2007	2008	2009	2010	2011	2012
Aïd el Kebir	20 Dec	8 Dec	27 Nov	16 Nov	6 Nov	26 Oct
Moharem	20 Jan	10 Jan & 29 Dec	18 Dec	7 Dec	26 Nov	15 Nov
Mouloud	31 Mar	20 Mar	9 Mar	26 Feb	15 Feb	4 Feb
1st Ramadan	13 Sept	1 Sept	22 Aug	11 Aug	1 Aug	20 July
Aïd es Seghir	13 Oct	2 Oct	21 Sept	10 Sept	30 Aug	20 Aug

Fêtes nationales

Secular *fêtes nationales*, all celebrated to some extent, are tied to Western calendar dates:

January 1	New Year's Day
January 11	Anniversary of Istiqlal Manifesto (see p.786)
May 1	Labour Day
July 30	Feast of the Throne
August 14	Allegiance Day
August 21	King's Birthday and Youth Day
November 6	Anniversary of the Marche Verte (see p.684)
November 18	Independence Day

The **Feast of the Throne** is the largest secular holiday, a colourful affair, celebrated throughout Morocco, over two to three days, with fireworks, parades and music.

The Ramadan fast involves abstention from food, drink, smoking and sex during daylight hours throughout the month. With most local cafés and restaurants closing during the day (indeed, many restaurants close up altogether and take a month's holiday), and smokers in particular getting edgy towards the month's end, it is in some respects an unsatisfactory time to travel: efficiency drops, drivers fall asleep at the wheel (hence airline pilots are excused fasting), and guides and muleteers are unwilling to go off on treks. The month-long closure of so many eating places can also make life difficult if you are dependent on restaurants to eat.

But there is compensation in witnessing and becoming absorbed into the pattern of the fast. At sunset, signalled by the sounding of a siren and the lighting of lamps on the minarets, and in some places by a cannon shot, an amazing calm and sense of wellbeing fall on the streets. The fast is traditionally broken with a bowl of *harira* and some dates, a combination provided by many cafés and restaurants exactly at sunset. You will also see almsgiving (*zakat*) extended to offering *harira* to the poor and homeless.

After breaking their fast, everyone – in the cities at least – gets down to a night of celebration and **entertainment**. This takes different forms. If you can spend some time in Marrakesh during the month, you'll find the Djemaa el Fna square at its most active, with troupes of musicians, dancers and acrobats coming into the city for the occasion. In Rabat and Fes, there seem to be continuous promenades, with cafés and stalls staying open until 3am. Urban cafés provide venues for live music and singing, too, and in the southern towns and Berber villages you will often come across the ritualized *ahouaches* and *haidus* – circular, trance-like dances often involving whole communities.

If you are a **non-Muslim** outsider you are not expected to observe Ramadan, but you should be sensitive about breaking the fast (particularly smoking) in public. In fact, the best way to experience Ramadan – and to benefit from its naturally purifying rhythms – is to enter into it. You may lack the faith to go without an occasional glass of water, and you'll probably have breakfast later than

Mouloud moussems

Meknes: Ben Aissa moussem

The largest of all the moussems, this includes a spectacular **fantasia** (a charge of horses with riders firing guns at full gallop) if weather conditions permit, held near Place el Hedim. With this, the enormous conical tents, and crowds of country people in white *djellabahs* beneath the city walls, it has the appearance of a medieval tournament. At least, that is, until you see the adjoining fairground, which is itself fun, with its illusionists and riders of death.

In the past, this moussem was the principal gathering of the **Aissoua** brotherhood, and the occasion for them to display their extraordinary powers of endurance under trance – cutting themselves with daggers, swallowing glass and the like. Their activities today are more subdued, though they still include going into trance, and of course playing music. Their focus is the *marabout* tomb of Ben Aissa, near the road in from Rabat.

Accommodation in Meknes is a problem at this time unless you arrive two or three days in advance. However, you could quite easily visit on a day-trip from Fes.

Salé: Wax Candle moussem

As the name suggests, this festival centres on a procession of wax candles – enormous lantern-like creations, carried from Bab el Rih to the Grand Mosque on the eve of the *Mouloud*. The candle bearers (a hereditary position) are followed by various brotherhoods, dancing and playing music.

The **procession** starts about 3pm and goes on for three or four hours; the best place to see it is at Bab Bou Hadja, where the candles are presented to local dignitaries.

sunrise (it's often wise to buy supplies the night before), but it is worth an attempt.

Other Islamic holidays

At the end of Ramadan comes the feast of **Aïd es Seghir** or **Aïd el Fitr**, a climax to the festivities in Marrakesh, though observed more privately in most communities. Equally important to the Muslim calendar is **Aïd el Kebir**, which celebrates the willingness of Abraham to obey God and to sacrifice Isaac. Aïd el Kebir is followed, about two months later, by **Moharem**, the Muslim new year.

Both *aïds* are traditional family gatherings. At the Aïd el Kebir every household that can afford it will slaughter a sheep. You see them tethered everywhere, often on rooftops, for weeks prior to the event; after the feast, their skins can be seen being cured on the streets. On both *aïd* days, shops and restaurants close and buses don't run; on the following day, all transport is packed as people return to the cities from their family homes.

The fourth main religious holiday is the **Mouloud**, the Prophet's birthday. This is widely observed, with a large number of moussems (see boxes opposite and overleaf) timed to take place in the weeks around it. There is also a music festival, **Ashorou**, which is held thirty days after Aïd el Kebir, when people gather to play whatever traditional instrument they feel capable of wielding, and the streets are full of music.

Public holidays

Nowadays each of the big **religious feasts** is usually marked by **two days off**. These are announced or ratified by the king, each time, on TV and radio the preceding day.

On these public holidays, and on the secular *fêtes nationales* (see box, p.61), all banks, post offices and most shops are closed; transport is reduced, too, but never stops completely.

Moussems and ammougars

Moussems – or ammougars – are held in honour of saints or *marabouts*. They are basically local, and predominantly rural, affairs. Besides the Aïd es Seghir and Aïd el Kebir, however, they form the main religious and social celebrations of the year for most Moroccans, especially for the country Berbers.

Some of the smaller moussems amount to no more than a market day with religious overtones; others are essentially harvest festivals, celebrating a pause in agricultural labour after a crop has been successfully brought in. A number, however, have developed into substantial occasions – akin to Spanish fiestas – and a few have acquired national significance. If you are lucky enough to be here for one of the major events, you'll get the chance to witness Moroccan popular culture at its richest, with horse-riding, music, singing and dancing, and of course eating and drinking.

Aims and functions

The ostensible aim of the moussem is religious: to obtain blessing, or *baraka*, from the saint and/or to thank God for the harvest. But the social and cultural dimensions are equally important. Moussems provide an opportunity for country people to escape the monotony of their hard working lives in several days of festivities. They may provide the year's single opportunity for friends or families from different villages to meet. Harvest and farming problems are discussed, as well as family matters – marriage in particular – as people get the chance to sing, dance, eat and pray together.

Music and singing are always major components of a moussem and locals will often bring tape recorders to provide sounds for the rest of the year. The different religious brotherhoods, some of whom may be present at larger moussems, each have their own distinct styles of music, dancing and dress.

Moussems also operate as **fairs**, or markets, with artisans offering their produce to a wider market than is available at the weekly souk. Buyers in turn can inform themselves about new products and regional price differences, as the moussem attracts people from a much wider area than the souk. There is a welcome injection of cash into the local economy, too, with traders and entertainers doing good business, and householders renting out rooms.

At the **spiritual level**, people seek to

Other popular moussems

February	**Tafraoute** Moussem to celebrate the almond harvest.
March	**Beni Mellal** Cotton harvest moussem.
May	**Moulay Bousselham** moussem of Sidi Ahmed Ben Mansour.
	Berkane Harvest moussem for clementines.
	El Kelâa des Mgouna Rose festival to celebrate the new crop.
June	**Goulimine** Traditionally a camel traders' fair, elements of which remain.
	Tan Tan Moussem of Sidi Mohammed Ma el Ainin. Large-scale religious and commercial moussem. Saharan "Guedra" dance may be performed.
July	**Tetouan** Moussem of Moulay Abdessalem. A very religious, traditional occasion with a big turnout of local tribesmen. Impressive location on a flat mountain top south of the town.
	Sefrou Festival to celebrate the cherry harvest.
	Al Hoceima Festival to celebrate the bounty of the sea.
August	**Setti Fatma** Large and popular moussem in the Ourika valley, southeast of Marrakesh.
	Sefrou Moussem of Sidi Lahcen el Youssi, a seventeenth-century saint.
	El Jadida Moussem of Moulay Abdallah. Located about 9km west of the city at a village named after the saint. Features displays of horse-riding, or fantasias.
	Tiznit Moussem of Sidi Ahmed ou Moussa. Primarily religious.
	Immouzer du Kandar Harvest moussem for apples and pears.
	Immouzer des Ida Outanane Week-long honey moussem.
September	**Chefchaouen** Moussem of Sidi Allal al Hadh. Located in the hills out of town.
	Moulay Idriss Zerhoun Moussem of Moulay Idriss. The largest religious moussem, but visitable only for the day as a non-Muslim. Impressive display by brotherhoods, and a highly charged procession of gifts to the saint's tomb. Also a large fantasia above town.
	Imilchil Marriage moussem. Set in the heart of the Atlas mountains, this is the most celebrated Berber moussem – traditionally the occasion of all marriages in the region, though today also a tourist event. In fact there now seem to be two moussems, with one laid on specifically for package tours from Marrakesh and Agadir; the real event is held in the last week in September or the first in October.
	Fes Moussem of Moulay Idriss II. The largest of the moussems held inside a major city, and involving a long procession to the saint's tomb. The Medina is packed out, however, and you will have a better view if you stand at Dar Batha or Place Boujeloud before the procession enters the Medina proper.
November	**Erfoud** Three-day date harvest festival.
December	**Rafsaï** Olive harvest moussem.

improve their standing with God through prayer, as well as the less orthodox channels of popular belief. Central to this is *baraka*, good fortune, which can be obtained by intercession of the saint. Financial contributions are made and these are used to buy a gift, or *hedia*, usually a large carpet, which is then taken in procession to the saint's tomb; it is deposited there for the local *shereefian* families, the descendants of the saint, to dispose of as they wish. Country people may seek to obtain *baraka* by attaching a garment or tissue to the saint's tomb and leaving it overnight to take home after the festival.

The procession taking the gift to the tomb is the high point of the more **religious** moussems, such as that of **Moulay Idriss**, where an enormous carpet is carried above the heads of the religious **brotherhoods**. Each of these brotherhoods will be playing its own music, hypnotic in its rhythms; spectators and participants may go into a trance, giving themselves up to the music. If you witness such events, it is best to keep a low profile (and certainly don't take photographs); the presence of foreigners or non-Muslims at these times is sometimes considered to impede trance.

Release through trance probably has a therapeutic aspect, and indeed some moussems are specifically concerned with **cures** of physical and psychiatric disorders. The saint's tomb is usually located near a freshwater spring, and the cure can simply be bathing in and drinking the water. Those suffering from physical ailments may also be treated at the moussem with herbal remedies, or by recitation of verses from the Koran. Koranic verses may also be written and placed in tiny receptacles fastened near the affected parts. The whole is reminiscent of the popular remedies found at European pilgrimage centres like Lourdes.

Practicalities

There are enormous numbers of moussems. An idea of quite how many can be gathered from the frequency with which,

travelling about the countryside, you see *koubbas* – the square, white-domed buildings covering a saint's tomb. Each of these is a potential focal point of a moussem, and any one region or town may have twenty to thirty separate annual moussems. Establishing when they take place, however, can be difficult for outsiders; most local people find out by word of mouth at the weekly souks.

Many moussems are held around religious occasions such as the **Mouloud**, which change date each year according to the lunar calendar (see box, p.61). Others, concerned with celebrating the **harvest**, have their date decided at a local level according to when the harvest is ready. Moussems of this type are obviously more difficult to plan a visit around than those which occur at points in the Islamic year. **August** and **September** are the most promising months overall, with dozens of moussems held after the grain harvest when there is a lull in the agricultural year before sowing starts prior to the first rains in October or November.

The **lists** on p.62 and opposite give an approximate idea (sometimes an exact one) of when the moussems are, but you will generally need to ask at a local level for information. Sometimes tourist offices may be able to help, though often not.

The **accommodation** situation will depend on whether the moussem is in the town or countryside. In the country, the simplest solution is to take a tent and camp – there is no real objection to anyone camping wherever they please during a moussem. In small towns there may be hotels – and locals will rent out rooms in their houses. **Food** is never a problem, with dozens of traders setting up stalls, though it is perhaps best to stick to the grills, as stalls may not have access to running water for cleaning.

Sports and outdoor activities

Morocco is doing much to keep up with the increasing interest in activity and sporting holidays. In addition to its magnificent trekking opportunities, the country offers impressive golf and tennis facilities, a couple of ski resorts (plus some adventurous off-piste skiing) and excellent fishing. The national sporting obsession, however, is football; enthusiasts can join in any number of beach kick-about games, or watch local league and cup matches.

Trekking

Trekking is one of the very best things Morocco has to offer. In the High Atlas, the country boasts one of the most rewarding mountain ranges in the world – and one of the least spoilt. If you are used to the Pyrenees or Alps, here you will feel you are moving a century or so back in time.

A number of **long-distance Atlas routes** can be followed – even a "Grand Traverse" of the full range. Most people, however, limit themselves to **shorter treks** round the **Djebel Toubkal** area (best in spring or autumn; conditions can be treacherous in winter). Other promising areas include the **Djebel Sirwa**, **Western High Atlas**, or in winter the **Djebel Sarhro** and **Tafraoute** region of the Anti-Atlas. The **Middle Atlas** has much attractive walking too, from such places as **Tazzeka** (Taza), the **Djebel Iblane** range, **Kerrouchen** and **Azrou**.

Each of these areas is featured in some detail in this guide. For further information, check the **trekking books** detailed on p.89. And if you haven't had much experience or feel a little daunted by the lack of organized facilities, try one of the **specialist trekking companies** offering Moroccan trips (see pp.35–37).

For general **trekking practicalities**, see pp.498–499. For information about survey-style **maps**, see p.88.

Skiing

Morocco doesn't immediately spring to mind as a skiing destination, but the High Atlas mountains are reliably snow-covered from late January to early April, and occasionally the Middle Atlas, too, has sufficient snows for the sport.

In the High Atlas, the only resort is **Oukaïmeden** (see p.491), two hours' drive from Marrakesh. It is quiet, well appointed and inexpensive, with pleasant chalet hotels, seven *piste* runs, a ski lift, local instructors, and equipment rental. In the Middle Atlas, **Mischliffen** (see p.306) – in a volcanic crater – has rather limited facilities, with three lifts, a shorter and unreliable season, and very old-fashioned equipment for rent. A third prospective ski centre is at **Djebel Bou Iblane** in the eastern Middle Atlas (see p.301), which offers little more than an approach road (often blocked by snow) and a single ski lift.

Off-piste skiing is popular in the High Atlas, particularly in the **Toubkal massif**, where the Toubkal Refuge (see p.501) is often full of groups. Most off-*piste* activity is ski mountaineering, but skinny skis (*langlauf*) are good in the Middle Atlas if there is snow, in which case the Azilal–Bou Goumez–Ighil Mgoun area is possible. Experienced off-*piste* skiers may relish the challenge of trekking to remote peaks. **Snowboarding** is also gaining in popularity at Moroccan resorts. For further information on skiing and mountaineering, contact the Fédération Royale Marocaine du Ski et du Montagnisme (FRMSM), Parc de la Ligue Arabe, BP 15899, Casablanca (☎022 22 47 49, ✆frmsn@hotmail.com).

Riding

The established base for **riding holidays** is *Résidence de la Roseraie* at **Ouirgane** on the Tizi n'Test road (see p.507). The hotel runs trekking tours into the **High Atlas**, offering anything from one-day excursions to extended trips staying at villages en route. You should bring your own helmet. Another stable offering horseriding is REHA near Agadir (see p.622). UK-based travel firm Equitours (see p.37) offers horseriding packages, and Best of Morocco (see p.34) is among operators offering stays and packages at *La Roseraie*, as well as **camel treks**.

Those with an interest in horse breeding might also want to visit the **Haras de Meknes** (see p.234), Morocco's largest National Stud Farm, which is open to the public.

Fishing

French visitors to Morocco have long appreciated the possibilities for fishing. The country offers an immense Atlantic (and small Mediterranean) **coastline**, with opportunities to arrange boat trips at Safi, Essaouira, Moulay Bousselham (near Asilah), and elsewhere.

Inland, the **Middle Atlas** shelters beautiful **lakes** and **rivers**, many of them well stocked with trout. Good bases include **Azrou** (near the Aghmas lakes), **Ifrane** (near Zerrrouka), **Khenifra** (the Oum er Rbia River) and **Ouirgane** (the Nfis River). Pike are also to be found in some Middle Atlas lakes (such as Aguelmame Azigza, near Khenifra), and a few of the huge artificial **barrages**, like **Bin el Ouidaine** (near Beni Mellal), are said to contain enormous bass.

For the really determined and adventurous, the most exciting Moroccan fishing is along the coast of the **Western Sahara**, where catches weigh in regularly at 20–30 kilos. The best places to make enquiries about this

are the fishing ports of Dakhla, Boujdour and the territory's capital, Laayoune.

For all fishing in the country, you need to take your own **equipment**. For coarse or fly fishing you need a **permit** from the Administration des Eaux et Forêts at: 11 Rue Moulay Abdelaziz, Rabat ☎037 76 26 94; 25 Bd Roudani, Casablanca ☎022 27 15 98; or any regional office. For trout fishing, you are limited to the hours between 6am and noon; the season starts on March 31.

Water sports and swimming

Agadir has **sailing**, **yachting**, **windsurfing** and **diving** on offer. Taghazoute, just north of the resort, has evolved into something of a **surfing** village, with board rental available, and board repair shops on hand. It's a paradise for right footed surfers thanks to its cluster of excellent right-hand point breaks. Banana Beach, a few kilometres south, has a mellower right break, suitable for less experienced surfers. There are lesser surfing centres at Sidi Ifni, Mirhleft (north of Sidi Ifni), Konitra, Bouznika Plage (between Rabat and Casablanca), El Jadida, Safi, and even Rabat. With your own transport, you could scout out remote places all the way down the coast. When they're working, all breaks can be busy in peak season (Oct–Feb), when deep lows come barrelling east across the mid-Atlantic. **Etiquette** is therefore important, and you should observe the rules and respect local surfers. Wetsuit-wise, a good 3mm will cover winter months (although a thermal rash vest keeps things snug in

---

Animal welfare

Animals – and especially pack animals – have a tough life in Morocco. **The Society for the Protection of Animals Abroad** (SPANA; ⊛www.spana.org.uk) works throughout North Africa to improve conditions, replacing painful, old-style bits on donkeys and horses, employing vets, and running animal clinics and refuges. It has centres in Tangier, Rabat, Casablanca, Marrakesh, Khémisset, Khenifra, Midelt, Had Ouled Frej (near El Jadida) and Chémaia (near Marrakesh) – all of which can be contacted if you are are concerned about animals you've come across, or if you are interested in the Society's work and would like to visit. The best initial contact address in Morocco is SPANA's administrative office in Temara, 14km south of Rabat (☎037 74 72 09, ⊛www.spana.org.ma). There's also a British office (14 John St, London WC1N 2EB; ☎020/7831 3999), which can provide details of the Moroccan centres listed above.

January) and it's also worth bringing booties, unless you enjoy digging urchin spines out of your feet.

For **windsurfing**, the prime destination is **Essaouira**, north of Taghazoute and west of Marrakesh, which draws devotees year round. Online **weather information** for surfers and windsurfers can be found at ⓦwww.windguru.com/int.

Anywhere on the Atlantic coast, surfers, windsurfers and **swimmers** alike should beware of strong undertows. The Atlantic can be very exposed, with crashing waves, and you'll often see Moroccan bathers venturing rather timidly into the water in formation.

Inland, most towns of any size have a municipal **swimming pool** – they're always very cheap and addresses are given in the guide, but women especially should note that they tend to be the preserve of adolescent males. In the south, you'll be dependent on campsite pools or on those at the luxury hotels (which often allow outsiders to swim, either for a charge or if you buy drinks or a meal).

The High and Middle Atlas have also become a popular destination for **whitewater rafting** and **kayaking** enthusiasts. One holiday firm specializing in these sports is Water by Nature (see p.37).

Golf

The British opened a golf course in Tangier as far back as 1917 – a rather more refined alternative to their then-favoured sport of pig-sticking. Today the country has an international-level course at **Rabat** (Dar-Es-Salam Royal Golf; see p.363), and eighteen-hole courses at **Mohammedia** (Royal Golf; see p.370), **Marrakesh** (Amelkis, Palmeraie Golf, Royal Golf; see p.479), **Tangier** (Tangier Royal Golf; see p.126), **El Jadida** (Royal Golf; see p.396); and nine-hole courses at **Casablanca** (Royal Anfa; see p.392), **Agadir** (Royal Golf, plus three each at the Dunes Golf Club and Golf du Soleil; see p.619), **Fes** (Royal Golf; see p.295), **Cabo Negro** (Royal Golf; see p.126), **Ben Slimane** (Royal Golf, Avenue des FAR, BP 83, Ben Slimane ☎033 32 87 93), and **Meknes** (Royal Golf; see p.241). Further information on golf in Morocco can be found online at ⓦwww.tafilalet.net/tourism/golf.

Tour operators offering golfing holidays in Morocco include: Best of Morocco (see p.34), Whole World Golf Travel (UK ☎0800/026 9987, US ☎1-770/928-1980, ⓦwww.golf.uk.com), Exclusive Golf Tours (UK ☎0870/870 4700, ⓦwww.exclusivegolf .co.uk), the Golf Holiday Co (UK ☎0870/112 1314, ⓦwww.golfholidaycompany.com), and 3D Golf (UK ☎0870/122 5050, ⓦwww.3dgolf.com).

Football (soccer)

Football is important in Morocco and the country is a growing force. The national side has made the World Cup finals on four occasions, and were the first African team to reach the finals (in 1970), and the first to progress beyond the group stage (in 1986). Morocco has won the African Nations Cup only once (in 1976), but reached the final in 2004. Moroccan teams have in the past been very successful in African club competitions, though the last Moroccan side to win the Champions League was Raja Casablanca, back in 1999. More recently, FAR Rabat won the Confederation Cup (equivalent to Europe's UEFA Cup) in 2005, and Raja won its predecessor, the CAF Cup in 2003.

Moroccan clubs compete in an annual **league** and the (knockout) **Throne Cup**. For a long time there was just one full-time professional team, **FAR** (the army), but the 1990s saw the introduction of sponsorship and a number of semi-professional sides, the best of which are **Wydad** (WAC) and **Raja**, the two big Casablanca teams, plus **MAS** from Fes and **Hassania** from Agadir. The result is a fairly high standard of skill in the Moroccan league, but unfortunately Moroccan clubs are unable to afford the money commanded by top players in Europe, with the result that the best Moroccan players are to be found playing for clubs in France, Belgium, the Netherlands, Spain and England.

One negative aspect of Moroccan league games is a tendency towards defensive play (the former system of giving two out of three possible points for a draw encouraged this), but there is always the potential for displays of individual dynamism and inspiration – a parallel, so Moroccans would have it, with the Brazilian style of play.

Brazilian comparisons could certainly be made with the social background of Moroccan football, players developing their game in unstructured **kick-arounds** on the beach, street or patches of wasteland. The lack of a team strip in these games (and hence easy recognition of team mates) discourages long balls and intricate passing, and encourages individual possession and quick one-twos. The same conditions produced Pelé and Maradona.

Other sports

The Marrakesh International **Marathon** (ⓦwww.marathon-marrakech.com) takes place every year on the third or fourth Sunday in January. It starts on Place Djemaa el Fna, passes through the Hivernage, encircles the Palmeraie and finishes a couple of hours later back at the Djemaa el Fna. The Marrakesh Marathon is not to be confused with the (even more gruelling) Marathon des Sables, the world's toughest race, covering 240km on the edge of the Moroccan Sahara (see p.547).

There are **tennis** courts at most four-star and five-star hotels, especially in Agadir (which now has a total of over 120 courts) and Marrakesh. Tennis equipment can often be loaned from hotels but it is not often up to much and you'd be advised to bring your own rackets and balls.

Paragliding is increasingly popular in the south of Morocco, around Tafraoute and Sidi Ifni in particular. Paragliding, hang-gliding and paramotoring trips, with instructors, are offered by Welsh Airsports (see p.37).

Also popular in the south is **rock climbing**, particularly in the region around Tafraoute, and at Todra Gorge. For anyone planning a climb in the region, Claude Davies's comprehensive *Climbing in the Moroccan Anti-Atlas: Tafroute and Jebel El Kest* (Cicerone Press, UK) is invaluable, with marked-up photos and detailed descriptions of each ascent. Wilder Places and Rock & Sun (see p.37) are among the operators offering climbing packages.

Culture and etiquette

Moroccans are extremely hospitable and very tolerant. Though most people are religious, they are generally easy-going, and most young Moroccan women don't wear a veil, though they may well wear a headscarf. Nonetheless, you should try not to affront the religious beliefs especially of older, more conservative people by, for example, wearing skimpy clothes, kissing and cuddling in public, or eating or smoking in the street during Ramadan.

Clothes are particularly important: many Moroccans, especially in rural areas, may well take exception to (or get the wrong idea from) clothes that do not fully cover parts of the body considered "private". That may include both legs and shoulders, especially for women. It is true that in cities Moroccan women wear short-sleeved tops and knee-length skirts (and may suffer more harassment as a result), and men may wear sleeveless T-shirts and above-the-knee shorts. However, the Muslim idea of

"modest dress" (such as would be acceptable in a mosque for example) requires women to be covered from wrist to ankle, and men from over the shoulder to below the knee. In rural areas at least, it is a good idea to follow these codes, and definitely a bad idea for women to wear shorts or skirts above the knee, or for members of either sex to wear sleeveless T-shirts or very short shorts. Even ordinary T-shirts may be regarded as underwear, particularly in rural mountain areas. The best guide is to note how Moroccans dress locally – and not how other tourists choose to.

When **invited to a home**, you normally take your shoes off before entering the reception rooms – follow your host's lead on that. It is customary to take a gift: sweet pastries or tea and sugar are always acceptable, and you might even take meat (by arrangement – a chicken from the countryside for example, still alive of course) to a poorer home.

Tipping

You're expected to **tip** – among others – waiters in cafés (1dh per person) and restaurants (5dh or so); museum and monument curators (3dh); *gardiens de voitures* (4–5dh; see p.47); petrol pump attendants (2–3dh); and porters who load your baggage onto buses (5dh). Taxi drivers do not expect a tip, but always appreciate one.

Mosques

Without a doubt, one of the major disappointments of travelling in Morocco if you are not Muslim is not being allowed into its mosques – as is permitted in many other Muslim countries. In Morocco, all non-Muslims are excluded and the rule is strictly observed. The only exceptions are the partially restored Almohad structure of Tin Mal in the High Atlas (see p.512), the similarly disused Great Mosque at Smara in the Western Sahara (see p.681), the courtyard of the sanctuary-mosque of Moulay Ismail in Meknes (see p.232) and the Mosquée Hassan II in Casablanca (see p.385). Elsewhere, if you are not a believer, you'll have to be content with an occasional glimpse through open doors, and even in this you should be sensitive: people don't seem to mind tourists peering into the Kairaouine Mosque in Fes (the country's most important religious building), but in the country you should never approach a shrine too closely.

This rule applies equally to the numerous whitewashed **koubbas** – the tombs of *marabouts*, or local saints (usually domed: *koubba* actually means "dome") – and the "monastic" **zaouias** of the various Sufi brotherhoods. It is a good idea, too, to avoid walking through **graveyards**, as these also are regarded as sacred places.

Sex and gender issues

There is no doubt that, for women especially, travelling in Morocco is a very different experience from travelling in a Western country. One of the reasons for this is that the separate roles of the sexes are much more defined than they are in the West, and sexual mores much stricter. In villages and small towns, and even in the Medinas of large cities, many women still wear the veil and the street is strictly the man's domain. Most Moroccan men still expect to marry a virgin, and most women would never smoke a cigarette or drink in a bar, the general presumption being that only prostitutes do such things.

It should be said, however, that such ideas are gradually disappearing among the urban youth, and you will nowadays find some Moroccan women drinking in the more sophisticated bars, and even more often in cafés, until quite recently an all-male preserve. In the Villes Nouvelles of large cities, and especially in the Casa–Rabat–El Jadida area on the coast, and in Marrakesh, you'll see most women without a veil or even a headscarf. You'll also see young people of both sexes hanging out together, though you can be sure that opportunities for pre-marital sex are kept to a minimum. Even in traditional Moroccan societies, mountain Berber women, who do most of the hard work, play a much more open role in society, and rarely use a veil.

Sexual harassment

Different women seem to have vastly different experiences of **sexual harassment** in Morocco. Some travellers find it persistent and bothersome, while others have little or no trouble with it at all. Many women compare Morocco favourably with Spain and other parts of southern Europe, but there is no doubt that, in general, harassment of tourists here is more persistent than it is in northern Europe or the English-speaking world.

Harassment will usually consist of men simply trying to chat you up or even asking directly for sex, and it can be constant and sometimes intimidating. In part this is to do with Moroccan men's misunderstanding of

Western culture and sexual attitudes, and the fact that some think they can get away with taking liberties with tourists that no Moroccan woman would tolerate.

The obvious **strategies** for getting rid of unwanted attention are the same ones that you would use at home: appear confident and assured and you will avoid a lot of trouble. Making it clear that you have the same standards as your Moroccan counter-parts will usually deter all but the most insistent of men. No Moroccan woman would tolerate being groped in the street for example, though they may often have to put up with cat-calls and unwanted comments. Traditionally, Moroccan women are coy and aloof, and uninhibited friendliness – especially any kind of physical contact between sexes – may be seen as a come-on, so being polite but formal when talking to men will diminish the chances of misinterpretation. The negative side to this approach is that it can also make it harder for you to get to know people, but after you've been in the country for a while, you will probably develop a feel for the sort of men with whom this tactic is necessary. It is also wise not to **smoke** in public, as some men still seem to think this indicates that you are available for sex.

How you **dress** is another thing that may reduce harassment. Wearing "modest" clothes (long sleeves, long skirts, baggy rather than tight clothes) will give an impression of respectability. Wearing a headscarf to cover your hair and ears will give this impression even more. One reader, agreeing with this advice, wrote to say that she felt a headscarf was "the single most important item of dress", and added that you can pull it over your face as a veil if unwanted male attention makes you feel uncomfortable. Indeed, Western liberals often forget that the purpose of wearing a veil is to protect women rather than to oppress them. However, you will notice that many Moroccan women totally ignore the traditional dress code, and do not suffer excessive harassment as a result. As for immodestly dressed women being taken for prostitutes, the fact is that actual sex workers in Morocco are often veiled from head to foot, as much to disguise their identities as anything else, and they most definitely do not go around in miniskirts, smoking cigarettes.

Other strategies to steer clear of trouble include avoiding eye contact, mentioning a husband who is nearby, and, if travelling with a boyfriend or just with a male friend, giving the impression that he is your husband. You should also avoid physical contact with Moroccan men, even in a manner that would not be considered sexual at home, since it could easily be misunderstood. If a Moroccan man touches *you*, on the other hand, he has definitely crossed the line, and you should not be afraid to **make a scene**. Shouting "*Shooma!*" ("Shame on you!") is likely to result in bystanders intervening on your behalf, and a very uncomfortable situation for your assailant.

It is often said that women are second-class citizens in Morocco and other Islamic countries, though educated Muslim women are usually keen to point out that this is a misinterpretation of Islam. It is certainly true that feminism and sexual equality have a long way to go in Morocco, but in some ways, at least in theory, the sexes are not as unequal as they seem. Men traditionally rule in the street, which is their domain, the woman's being the home. One result of this is that Moroccan women will receive their friends at home rather than meet them in, say, a café (although this is slowly changing) and this can make it difficult for you to get to know Moroccan women. One place where you *can* meet up with them easily is the hammam (see p.53). It may also be that if you are travelling with a man, Moroccan men will address him rather than you – but this is in fact out of respect for you, not disrespect, and you will not be ignored if you join in the conversation. In any case, however interpreted, Islam most certainly does not condone sexual harassment, and nor do any respectable Moroccans. Being aware of that fact will make it seem a lot less threatening.

Gay attitudes

As a result of sexual segregation, **male homosexuality** is relatively common in Morocco, although attitudes towards it are a little schizophrenic, not unlike those inside a Western prison. Few Moroccans will declare themselves gay – which has connotations of femininity and weakness; the idea of being a passive partner is virtually taboo, while a dominant partner may well not consider himself to be indulging in a homosexual act. Private realities, however, are rather different from public show (on which subject, note that Moroccan men of all ages often walk hand-in-hand in public – a habit that has nothing to do with homosexuality and is simply a sign of friendship).

If you are visiting Morocco specifically as a "gay destination" be warned that the legendary Joe Orton days of Tangier as a gay resort are long gone. Gay sex is, of course, still available, and men travelling alone or together may be propositioned, but gay sex between men is **illegal** under Moroccan law. Article 489 of the Moroccan penal code prohibits any "shameless or unnatural act" with a person of the same sex and allows for imprisonment of six months to three years, plus a fine. There are also various provisions in the penal code for more serious offences, with correspondingly higher penalties in cases involving, for example, corruption of minors.

A certain amount of information on the male gay scene in Morocco (gay bars, meeting places and cruising spots) can be found in the annual *Spartacus Gay Guide*, available in bookshops at home. A tourist-oriented gay scene does seem to be emerging, very discreetly, in Marrakesh (see p.479), and to a lesser extent Agadir (see p.617), but pressure from religious fundamentalists makes it difficult for the authorities to ease up, even if they wanted to, and there have been one or two arrests of tourists for having gay sex in recent years.

There is no public perception of **lesbianism** in Morocco, and as a Western visitor, your chances of making contact with any Moroccan lesbians are very small indeed. Moroccan women are under extreme pressure to marry and bear children, and anyone resisting such pressure is likely to have a very hard time of it.

One website which posts up-to-date information on gay rights in Morocco is Behind the Mask at ⓦwww.mask.org.za. There is also an information exchange for gay and lesbian Moroccans at ⓦhttp://gaymorocco .tripod.com, but it is probably best to avoid accessing this site within Morocco.

Shopping

Souks (markets) are a major feature of Moroccan life, and among the country's greatest attractions. They are to be found everywhere: every town has a souk area, large cities like Fes and Marrakesh have labyrinths of individual souks (each filling a street or square and devoted to one particular craft), and in the countryside there are hundreds of weekly souks, on a different day in each village of the region.

When buying souvenirs in Morocco, it's worth considering how you are going to get them home: many Moroccan goods – ceramics, for example – break all too easily, and you aren't going to find any bubble wrap to protect them. If they're in your baggage in the hold of a plane, they are very likely to get damaged in transit, especially if you have to change planes on your way home. It's also not worth taking too literally the claims of shopkeepers about their goods, especially if they tell you that something is "very old" or an antique – *trafika* (phoney merchandise) abounds, and there are all sorts of imitation fossils and antiques about.

Souk days

Some villages are named after **their market days**, so it's easy to see when they're held.

Clothing and shoe sizes

Women's dresses and skirts

American	4	6	8	10	12	14	16	18
British	8	10	12	14	16	18	20	22
Continental	38	40	42	44	46	48	50	52

Women's blouses and sweaters

American	6	8	10	12	14	16	18
British	30	32	34	36	38	40	42
Continental	40	42	44	46	48	50	52

Women's shoes

American	5	6	7	8	9	10	11
British	3	4	5	6	7	8	9
Continental	36	37	38	39	40	41	42

Men's suits

American	34	36	38	40	42	44	46	48
British	34	36	38	40	42	44	46	48
Continental	44	46	48	50	52	54	56	58

Men's shirts

American	14	15	15.5	16	16.5	17	17.5	18
British	14	15	15.5	16	16.5	17	17.5	18
Continental	36	38	39	41	42	43	44	45

Men's shoes

American	7	7.5	8	8.5	9.5	10	10.5	11	11.5
British	6	7	7.5	8	9	9.5	10	11	12
Continental	39	40	41	42	43	44	44	45	46

The souk days are:

Souk el Had – Sunday (literally, "first market")
Souk el Tnine – Monday market
Souk el Tleta – Tuesday market
Souk el Arba – Wednesday market
Souk el Khamees – Thursday market
Souk es Sebt – Saturday market

There are very few village markets on **Friday** (el Djemaa – the "assembly", when the main prayers are held in the mosques), and even in the cities, souks are largely closed on Friday mornings and very subdued for the rest of the day.

In general, village souks begin on the afternoon preceding the souk day, as people travel from all over the region; those who live nearer set out early in the morning of the souk day. As a consequence, the souk itself is usually over by noon and people disperse in the afternoon. You should therefore arrange to arrive by mid-morning at the latest.

Craft traditions

Moroccan **craft** traditions are still highly active, and even goods mass-produced for tourists are surprisingly untacky. To find pieces of real quality, however, is not that easy – some crafts have become dulled by centuries of repetition and others have been corrupted by modern techniques and chemical dyes.

In general, if you're planning on buying anything, it's always worth getting as close to the source of the goods as possible, and to steer clear of the main tourist centres. **Fes** might have the richest traditions, but you can often find better work at much cheaper prices elsewhere; **Tangier** and **Agadir**, neither of which has imaginative workshops of its own, are generally poor bets. As stressed throughout the guide, the best way to get an idea of standards and quality is to visit the various **traditional crafts museums** spread round the country: there are good ones in Fes, Meknes, Tangier, Rabat and Marrakesh.

For more on crafts and shopping see the *Crafts and Souvenirs* colour section.

Foodstuffs

You'll find quite a variety of **food products** in Morocco that you would be hard pressed to find at home, and which make excellent and inexpensive gifts or souvenirs (assuming your country's customs allow their importation). Locally produced **olive oil** can be excellent, with a distinctive strong flavour, and in the Souss Valley there's delicious sweet **argan oil** too (see p.621), with a number of cooperatives springing up in the region to produce it. Olives themselves come in numerous varieties, and there are also almonds, walnuts and spices available, notably **saffron**, which is grown in the area east of Taliouine (see p.637). A jar of lemons preserved in brine is useful if you want to try your hand at making a tajine back home.

Cakes, sweets and biscuits are tempting but won't keep for long, while Moroccan wines are generally mediocre at best compared to those produced in California, Australia or Europe. Of more everyday **groceries** not easily available at home, cans of spiced sardines are worth considering, as is Knorr's surprisingly good instant fish soup.

For those with transport, **hypermarkets** run by the French firms Macro and Marjane are located on major approach roads at the edge of most big cities, offering a wide choice of Moroccan and imported foods and other goods at discount prices.

Bargaining

Whatever you buy, other than groceries, you will want (and be expected) to **bargain**. There are no hard and fast rules – it is really a question of paying what something is worth to you – but there are a few general points to keep in mind.

First, **bargaining is entirely natural** in Morocco. If you ask the price in a market, the answer, as likely as not, will come in one breath – "Twenty; how much will you pay?"

Second, don't pay any attention to **initial prices**. These are simply a device to test the limits of a particular deal or situation. Don't think, for example, in terms of paying one-third of the asking price (as some guides suggest) – it might well turn out to be a tenth or even a twentieth. Equally, though, it might not – some sellers actually start near the price they have in mind and will bustle you out of their shop for offering an "insulting" price. Don't feel intimidated by either tactic; if you return the following day for some coveted item, you will most likely be welcomed as an old friend. Take your chances, but have in mind a figure that you want to pay, and a maximum above which you will not go. If your maximum and the shopkeeper's minimum don't meet, then you don't have a deal, but it's no problem.

Third, **don't ever let a figure pass your lips** that you aren't prepared to pay – nor start bargaining for something you have absolutely no intention of buying – there's no better way to create bad feelings.

Fourth, **take your time**. If the deal is a serious one (for a rug, say), you'll probably want to sit down over tea with the vendor, and for two cups you'll talk about anything but the rug and the price. If negotiations do not seem to be going well, it often helps to have a friend on hand who seems – and may well be – less interested in the purchase than you and can assist in extricating you from a particularly hard sell.

Fifth, remember that even if you're **paying more than local people**, it doesn't necessarily mean you're being "ripped off". As a Westerner, your earning power is well above that of most Moroccans and it's rather mean to force traders down to their lowest possible price just for the sake of it.

The final and most golden rule of all is never to go shopping with a **guide** or a hustler. Any shop that a guide steers you into will pay them a commission, added to your bill of course, while hustlers often pick up tourists with the specific aim of leading you to places that (even if you've agreed to go in "just to look") will subject you to a lengthy high-pressure hard-sell.

An approximate idea of what you should be paying for handicrafts can be gained from checking the **fixed prices** in the state- or cooperative-run Ensembles Artisanals, which are slightly higher than could be bargained for elsewhere.

Travelling with children

Moroccans love kids, and travelling with small children, you may well find that people will frequently come up to admire them, to compliment you on them and to caress them, which may be uncomfortable for shyer offspring. Children are very important, and numerous, in Moroccan society, and people are not really considered complete adults until they have at least one child. In Moroccan families, children stay up late until they fall asleep and are spoiled rotten by older family members. The streets are pretty safe and even quite small children walk to school unaccompanied or play in the street unsupervised.

As a parent however, you will encounter one or two difficulties. For example, you won't find baby changing rooms in airports, hotels or restaurants, and will have to be discreet if breastfeeding – find a quiet corner and shield infant and breast from view with a light cloth over your shoulder. Beach resort and package tour hotels may have facilities such as playgrounds, children's pools and a babysitting service, but mid-range city hotels are far less likely to cater specifically for children. Many hotels do, however, allow children to share their parents' room for free.

You may want to try a holiday with Club Med (Wwww.clubmed.com), whose purpose-built holiday resorts at Agadir and Marrakesh feature kids' club, entertainment and sports facilities on site. Panorama (see p.35) specialize in child-friendly family holidays, and Travel Bag Adventures (see p.37) run treks that are suitable for families with children. Attractions that should appeal to small people include Oasiria in Marrakesh (see p.480) and the tourist train in Agadir (see p.612).

Disposable nappies are available at larger supermarkets, and sometimes city pharmacies, at prices similar to what you pay at home, but off the beaten track, you may need to stock up, or take washables. You may want to take along some dried baby food; any café can supply hot water. Wet wipes are also very handy, if only for wiping small hands before eating when you aren't too sure where they've been.

On public transport, children small enough to share your seat will usually travel free, but older kids pay the full adult fare on buses and grands taxis. On trains, travel is free for under-fours, and half price for four- to eleven-year-olds.

Among hazards that you'll need to bear in mind are traffic and stray animals. Dogs can be fierce in Morocco, and can also carry rabies, and there are a lot of feral cats and dogs about. Children (especially young ones) are also more susceptible than adults to heatstroke and dehydration, and should always wear a sunhat, and have high-factor sunscreen applied to exposed skin. If swimming at a beach resort, they should do so in a T-shirt, certainly for the first few days. The other thing that children are very susceptible to is an upset tummy. Bear in mind that antidiarrhoeal drugs should generally not be given to young children; read the literature provided with the medication or consult a doctor for guidance on child dosages.

Travel essentials

Costs

Costs for food, accommodation and travel in Morocco are low by European or North American standards. If you stay in the cheaper hotels (or camp out), eat local food, and share expenses and rooms with another person, £100/$200 each a week would be enough to survive on. On £200/$400 each you could live pretty well, while with £500–750/$1000–1500 a week between two people you would be approaching luxury.

Accommodation costs range from £5/$10 a night – sometimes even less – for a double room in a basic hotel to as much as £250/$500 a night in a very top luxury hotel or riad (see pp.51–54). The price of a **meal** reflects a similar span, ranging from £2/$4 to around £7.50/$15 a meal (see pp.56–58). **Alcohol** is really the only thing that compares unfavourably with Western prices: a bottle of Moroccan wine costs upwards of £4/$8, a can of local beer about 50p/$1 in the shops, 90p/$1.80 in a normal bar, or £2/$4 in hotel bars and discos.

Beyond accommodation and food, your major outlay will be for **transport** – expensive if you're renting a car (prices start at around £135/$270 a week plus petrol), but very reasonable if you use the local trains, buses and shared taxis (see box, p.42 for sample fares).

Regional variations

To some extent, all of these costs are affected by where you are and when. Inevitably, **resorts** and larger **cities** (Rabat and Casablanca especially) are more expensive, with bottom-line hotel prices from around £7/$14 a night for a basic double. In **remote parts** of the country, too, where all goods have to be brought in from some distance and where transport (often only lorries or Land Rovers) has to be negotiated, prices can be steep. This is particularly true of the popular trekking region of Djebel Toubkal in the High Atlas.

In the Spanish enclaves of Ceuta and Melilla, prices for most things are the same as they are in mainland Spain, except that there is no duty on alcohol, tobacco and electronic goods. For everything else, Ceuta and Melilla are around twice as expensive as Morocco proper. In the Saharan provinces of the far south (roughly the Western Sahara), petrol is cheap as it is subsidized by the state.

Hidden costs

Hidden costs in Morocco are twofold. The most obvious is that you'll almost certainly end up buying a few **souvenirs**. Moroccan crafts are very much a part of the fabric of the towns and cities, with their labyrinthine areas of souks (markets). Rugs, carpets, leather, woodwork, pottery and jewellery are all outstanding – and few travellers leave without at least one of these items.

A harder aspect to come to terms with is that you'll be confronting real **poverty**. As a tourist, you're not going to solve any problems, but with a labourer's wages at little more than 5dh (30p/60¢) an hour, an unemployment rate of nearly twenty percent in urban areas, and nearly one in five people living below the poverty line, even a small **tip** to a guide can make a lot of difference to individual family life. For Moroccans, giving alms is a natural function – and a requirement of Islam, especially since there is no social security here. For tourists, rich by definition, local poverty demands at least some response. Do not, however, dispense money indiscriminately to **children**, which simply promotes a dependence on begging.

Youth and student discounts

The various official and quasi-official **youth/student ID cards** can save you a small amount of money in Morocco. Student cards entitle you to cheaper entry at some museums and other sights, and a small discount on some ferry tickets. They're not worth going out of your way to get, but if you have one you might as well bring it along.

Full-time students are eligible for the **International Student ID Card** (ISIC, ⓦwww .isiccard.com). An alternative available to anyone under 26 is the **International Youth Travel Card**, which carries the same benefits. Teachers qualify for the **International Teacher Card**. All of these are available from youth travel specialists such as STA Travel and Travel Cuts, and from Hostelling International.

Crime and personal safety

Keeping your luggage and money secure is an important consideration in Morocco. For all the tales, the situation is probably no worse than in Spain or Italy, but it is obviously unwise to carry large sums of cash or valuables on your person – especially in Casablanca and Tangier, and to a lesser extent Fès and Marrakesh. Mugging as such is pretty rare, however, and those who fall victim to theft usually have things taken by stealth, or are subject to some kind of scam (see p.79 for more on these).

Hotels, generally, are secure and useful for depositing money before setting out to explore; larger ones will keep valuables at reception and some will have safes. **Campsites** are considerably less secure, and many campers advise using a **money belt** – to be worn even while sleeping. If you do decide on a money belt (and many people spend time quite happily without), leather or cotton materials are preferable to nylon, which can irritate in the heat.

If you are **driving**, it almost goes without saying, you should not leave anything you cannot afford to lose visible or accessible in your car.

The police

There are two main types of Moroccan **police**: the *Gendarmerie* (who wear grey uniforms and man the checkpoints on main roads, at junctions and the entry to towns), and the *Police* (*Sûreté*), who wear navy blue uniforms or plain clothes. Either force may demand to see your passport (and/or driving papers). The carrying of ID cards or passports is obligatory, though you should not have any problems if you leave yours in a hotel safe while wandering around town, especially if you carry a photocopy of the important pages.

The *gendarmes* have jurisdiction outside built-up areas, but you will find their prominent headquarters in, or on the edge of, most towns; they are generally better educated and more polite than the police. You can report any kind of crime to them – or turn to them if you need help.

The **police**, who operate within towns, are usually polite and helpful to visitors, although they are more concerned with public order and petty crime in the towns. There is now a *Brigade Touristique* in cities such as Marrakesh and Fès, specifically set up to protect tourists, though there have been reports that the *Brigade Touristique* in Fès will turn a blind eye to the activities of pickpockets, who pay them off for the favour.

In addition to these, there is a green-uniformed *Force Auxiliaire*, who wear berets and look more like the army. Their role is as a back up to the regular police and *gendarmes*, and you are unlikely to have any contact with them.

If you do need to **report a theft**, try to take along a fluent French- or Arabic-speaker if your own French and Arabic are not too hot. You may only be given a scrap of paper with an official stamp to show your insurance company, who then have to apply themselves to a particular police station for a report (in Arabic). If you cannot prove that a theft has taken place, the police may decline to make any report, especially if the theft is of money only. They will always give you a report, however, if you have lost any official document (passport, driving licence, etc.)

The police emergency number is ⓣ19.

Kif and hashish

The smoking of **kif** (marijuana) and hashish (cannabis resin) has for a long time been a regular pastime of Moroccans and tourists alike. Indeed, in the 1960s and 1970s (or further back, in the 1930s), its ready availability, good quality and low cost made *kif* a major tourist attraction. It is, however, illegal, or, as the ONMT puts it:

Guides, hustlers, conmen and kids

Armed with this book, you shouldn't need a guide, but some people like to hire one to negotiate the Medinas of larger cities. In addition to the guides authorized by the local Délégation du Tourisme, you may be importuned by young Moroccans offering their services. These "unofficial guides" are not strictly speaking legal, and police clampdowns have largely removed them from the streets of main cities, though they still operate in some smaller towns.

With all guides, official or otherwise, it is important to establish at the outset what you want to see, and what you don't. Do not be pushed into a tour of the craft stores or you will see nothing else. If you do want to visit shops, make it clear what kind of goods you are interested in seeing, and equally clear that you do not want to purchase on an initial visit. Any purchase you make with a guide in tow will add to the price since commission is added, especially in the case of official guides, who can demand 40 percent or more.

Would-be guides, moreover, are not the only people who will be on your case in Morocco. You are also likely to be accosted by hustlers of various sorts, often posing as potential guides. Police clampdowns have removed a lot of these people from the streets, and the problem is nothing like as bad as it once was, especially in places like Tangier, Fes and Marrakesh, but you will still meet the odd few. Hustlers include outright thieves, confidence tricksters and dope dealers, but by far the majority are hoping for a commission by steering you (sometimes with the most amazing deviousness) into shops that will pay them a commission, most commonly carpet shops where you will be subjected to hours of hard-sell. Many people who approach you, on the other hand, are not hustlers at all, but simply trying to be friendly – they may want to help you, or to practise their English, or think that you are able to get them a visa to work abroad and if you want to make contact with local people, it's important not to treat every Moroccan who approaches you as a hustler.

Official guides

Official guides, engaged through tourist offices (or some of the larger hotels), are paid at a fixed rate of 180dh for half a day, 350dh for a full day, plus sustenance. The rate is for the guide's time, and can be shared by a group of people – though the latter would be expected to make some additional tip.

Taking an introductory tour of a new city with an official guide can arguably be useful for orientation – especially in the vast Medinas (old quarters) of Fes and Marrakesh. Your guide may well be an interesting and entertaining presence, too. Some are highly knowledgeable. Official guides can identify themselves by a large, brass "sheriff's badge".

Unofficial guides and hustlers

Unofficial guides may approach you in the street in some towns, offering to find you a hotel, show you the sights, or perhaps, if you look a likely customer, sell you some *kif* or hashish. Your task is to distinguish between offers, to accept (perhaps limited) services from those who seem friendly and enjoyable company, and to decline others politely but firmly.

In general, don't agree to a guide showing you to a **hotel**; they will only take you to those which pay them a commission, meaning not only a higher bill for you, but also that the hotels you are being taken to are more likely to be dodgy. Letting someone guide you to a **café** or **restaurant** won't increase the price of a meal (although waiters will generally make a small tip to the guide).

If you do decide to hire an unofficial guide, be sure to **fix the rate**, as well as the **itinerary**, in advance. You should make it clear that you know the official rates for guides and should agree on these as a maximum. Many unofficial guides will attempt to charge a rate per person.

Friendships

Following clampdowns on "unofficial guides", there are laws in effect that can make relationships with Moroccans problematic. In theory, any Moroccan – without a guide's permit – seen "accompanying" a tourist can be arrested and imprisoned. In practice this is rarely enforced but friendships, especially with young Moroccans in tourist cities like Tangier, Agadir, Fes or Marrakesh, should be discreet. On the whole, once invited to a home, and having met a family, you are unlikely to encounter problems, and your hosts will deal effectively with any enquiries from curious local policemen.

Conmen and scams

Hustlers and conmen are a distinct minority in Morocco, but tourists are an obvious target for them. In recent years, they have been largely cleaned off the streets by police action, and those who remain are less persistent. Many seem to have moved on to smaller places rather than remain in the classic hustler cities – Tangier, Tetouan, Fes or Marrakesh. However, forewarned is forearmed, so a few notes on the **most common scams** follow:

● All guides (not least official ones) have an interest in getting you into craft shops, where they can earn commission of thirty to fifty percent. Even if you say you're not interested, they may suggest taking tea with a cousin who owns a shop. Don't be afraid to insist on keeping to your agreed itinerary and going where *you* want to go.

● A favourite line is that there is a Berber market taking place – and this is the only day of the week to see it. This is rarely true. You will probably visit everyday shops and souks.

● Some of the more exploitative hustlers will guide you into the Medinas, then, when you have no idea where you are, charge a large fee to take you back out and to your hotel. If this happens to you, don't be afraid to appeal to people in the street; your hustler will not want attention. If you feel genuinely threatened or harassed, don't hesitate to threaten or indeed to go to the police: hustlers tend to vanish fast at the prospect of police involvement.

● A few tales are told each year of people approaching visitors with a letter or package to mail to the USA or Europe when you leave Morocco. Never agree to this; you may be involving yourself in a drugs plant.

● Many more hustlers will simply use the excuse of a letter ("Could you help translate or write one?") as a means of attaching themselves to you; it's best to decline assistance.

● Another favourite way for hustlers to introduce themselves is by pretending to be someone you have met but forgotten, so if someone you don't remember says, "Hey, remember me?" it's probably a hustler trying to lure you into a carpet shop or practise some scam on you.

● A common line from hustlers if you don't want to engage their services is that you must be paranoid or racist. They are appealing quite cynically here to the guilty conscience of the Western liberal.

● On trains, especially at Tangier, hustlers sometimes pose as porters or railway staff, demanding an extortionate fee for carrying baggage or payment of supplements. Genuine rail staff wear beige overalls and have ID cards, which, if suspicious, you should ask to see.

● Drivers should beware of hitchhiking hustlers, who spend all day hitching between a pair of towns and can get highly obnoxious in their demands for money when you approach one or other destination. Alternatively, they may wish to thank you for the lift by taking you home for a cup of tea – except that "home" turns out to be a carpet shop, where you are then subjected to hours of hard-sell. We've even heard of people who seem to have broken down on the road flagging down passing tourists and asking them to take a note to a "mechanic", who turns out to be a carpet salesman. This one is particularly common on the N9 (formerly P31) between Marrakesh, Ouarzazate and Zagora, and the N10 (formerly P32) between Ouarzazate and Tinerhir.

● In the south, especially Goulimine, be wary of offers to meet "Blue Men" (desert Touareg nomads) in the "desert". The "nomads" are almost invariably rogues.

● In a number of towns, con merchants have been posing as students, working alone or in couples, befriending tourists, and then, after a day or two, telling some sad tale about needing money for getting a passport off a corrupt official, or to look after sick relatives, or some such. You may feel a little foolish if you give money and then meet six other travellers with identical tales to tell.

● Heading for the beach, especially in Tangier, leave most of your money back at your hotel. Keep your eyes open for petty theft and pickpocketing, particularly in the Medinas and by juveniles; mugging is rare but not unheard of, especially in Tangier and Casablanca.

Dealing with children

In the countryside, and especially along the major southern routes, you will find fewer hustlers and guides, but many more children, eager in their demands for a dirham, *un cadeau* (present) or *un stylo* (a pen/pencil). Working out your own strategy is all part of the game, but, whatever else you do, be sure to keep a good humour: smile and laugh, or kids can make your life hell. Faced with **begging from children**, we strongly recommend not obliging, as this ties them to a begging mentality, and encourages them to harass other visitors.

"Tourists coming to Morocco are warned that the first article in the Dahir of April 24th 1954 prohibits the POSSESSION, the OFFER, the DISTRIBUTION, the PURCHASE, the SALE and the TRANSPORTATION as well as the EXPORTATION of CANNABIS IN WHATEVER FORM. The Dahir allows for a penalty of IMPRISONMENT from three months to five years and a fine of 2400 to 240,000 dirhams, or only one of these. Moreover the law court may ordain the SEIZURE of the means of transport and the things used to cover up the smuggling as well as the toxic products themselves."

In practice, there is no real effort to stop Moroccans from using *kif*, but as a tourist you are rather more vulnerable. Large fines (plus prison sentences for substantial amounts) do get levied for possession, though you should be aware if arrested for cannabis that the police normally expect to be paid off, and that this should be done as quickly as possible while the minimum number of officers are involved (but offer it discreetly, and never refer to it as a bribe or even a *cadeau*).

What can you do to avoid all this trouble? Most obviously, keep well clear – above all, of the *kif*-growing region of **Ketama** in the Rif mountains – and always reply to hustlers by saying you don't smoke. If you are going to indulge, be very careful who you buy it from (definitely do not buy it from touts or hustlers, especially in Tangier or Tetouan), and above all **do not try to take any out** of the country, even to Spain (where attitudes to possession are relaxed but there's nearly always a prison sentence for importing). Searches at Algeciras and Malaga can be very thorough, with sniffer dogs, and you'll get sometimes as many as four checks if travelling through Ceuta or Melilla.

If you do get in trouble there are **consulates** for most nationalities in Rabat, Casablanca and, to a lesser extent, in Tangier and Agadir (see lists on p.126, p.362, p.391 and p.478). All of the consulates are notoriously unsympathetic to drug offenders, but they can help with technical problems and find you legal representation. For more on *kif* traditions and the hash industry in the Rif, see box, pp.180–181.

Disabled travellers

Facilities for people with disabilities are little developed in Morocco, and, although families are usually very supportive, many disabled Moroccans are reduced to begging. Despite this, able-bodied Moroccans are, in general, far more used to mixing with disabled people than their Western counterparts, and are much more likely to offer help without embarrassment if you need it.

Blindness is more common than in the West, and sighted Moroccans are generally used to helping blind and visually impaired people find their way around and get on and off public transport at the right stop.

Wheelchairs, though often ancient, do exist, but there is little in the way of wheelchair access to most premises. In the street, the Ville Nouvelle districts are generally easier to negotiate than the often crowded Medinas, but don't expect kerb ramps at road crossings or other such concessions to wheelchair users. Medina areas in cities like Rabat and even Marrakesh should not be too hard to negotiate at quiet times of day, but in Fes and Tangier, where the streets are steep and interspersed with steps, you would need at least one helper and a well-planned route to get around.

Bus and train **travel** will be difficult because of the steps that have to be negotiated, but grands taxis are a more feasible mode of transport if you can stake a claim on the front seat (maybe paying for two places to get the whole of it) – if you don't have a helper travelling with you, and you require assistance, the driver or other passengers will almost certainly be happy to help you get in and out.

You're likely to find travelling on a **package tour** much easier than fully independent travel, but all the same you should contact any tour operator in advance and inform them of your exact needs before making a booking. It's also important to ensure you are covered by any **insurance** policy you take out.

Accommodation at the lower end of the market is unlikely to be very accessible. Cheap city hotels tend to have small doorways and steep, narrow staircases, and often no lift or elevator, though many will have ground-floor rooms. Beach hotels are more able to cater for visitors with mobility difficulties. Some package hotels, especially in Agadir, make an attempt to cater for wheelchair-users, with ramps, for example, but no accessible toilets. It is at the very top end of the market, however, that real changes are being made: new five-star hotels almost always have a couple of rooms specifically adapted for wheelchairs. Obviously this needs to be booked well in advance, and it also confines you to very expensive places, but it is at least a start.

Hotels that have rooms specially adapted for wheelchair users include the *Mövenpick* in Tangier (see p.110), the *Transatlantique* in Meknes (see p.230), the *Palais Jamaï* in Fes (see p.261), the *Sheraton* and *Hyatt Regency* in Casablanca (see p.379 & p.380), the *Sofitel* in Essaouira (see p.417), and the *Atlas Modina*, *Meridien N'Fis*, *Ryad Mogador Menara* and *Sofitel* in Marrakesh (see p.110). Other hotels, such as the *Royal Mirage* in Fes (see p.202), the *Hilton* in Rabat (see p.349) and the *Agadir Beach Club* and *Amadil Beach* in Agadir (see p.611 & p.612), claim to be accessible, and to cater for wheelchair users, but do not have any specially adapted rooms. Obviously, you should always call ahead to check whether any particular hotel can meet your specific needs.

Electricity

Most of the country runs on 220v but some towns still have 110v sockets and you'll sometimes even find both in the same building. Electric shavers work OK on any voltage, but heat-producing items like hairdryers need converters to function properly if they're designed to run on a different voltage.

Entry requirements

If you hold a full passport from the UK, Ireland, the US, Canada, Australia, New Zealand or any EU country, you require no visa to enter Morocco as a tourist for up to ninety days. However, your passport must be valid for at least six months beyond your date of entry, and always double check your visa requirements before departure as the situation can change. South African citizens are among those who need a visa; applica-

tions should be made to the nearest Moroccan embassy or consulate (see pp.82–83), with three passport photos, and a form that you can download at Ⓦwww.maec.gov.ma/fr/consulaires/visa.pdf

When **entering the country**, formalities are fairly straightforward, though you will have to fill in a form stating personal details, purpose of visit and your **profession**. In the past, Moroccan authorities have shown an occasional reluctance to allow in those who categorize themselves as "journalist"; an alternative profession on the form might be wise. See p.31 for more on red tape if arriving by ferry.

Items such as **electronic equipment and video cameras** may occasionally be entered on your passport. If you lose them during your visit, they will be assumed "sold" when you come to leave and (unless you have police documentation of theft) you will have to pay 100 percent duty. All goods entered on your passport should be "cleared" when leaving to prevent problems on future trips. Vehicles need a Green Card (see p.31).

It is in theory obligatory in Morocco to carry official ID at all times. In practice, a photocopy of the important pages of your passport will do, so long as the real thing is in your hotel in the same town. When travelling between towns, you should always have your passport on you.

Visa extensions

To **extend your stay** in Morocco you should – officially – apply to the Bureau des Étrangers in the nearest main town for a residence permit (see p.82). This is, however, a very complicated procedure and it is usually possible to get round the bureaucracy by simply leaving the country for a brief time when your three months are up. If you decide to do this – and it is not foolproof – it is best to make a trip of at least a few days outside Morocco. Spain is the obvious choice and some people just go to the enclave of Ceuta; the more cautious re-enter the country at a different post. If you are very unlucky, you may be turned back and asked to obtain a **re-entry visa** prior to your return. These can be obtained from any Moroccan consulate abroad (see pp.82–83).

Duty-free allowances

You can bring in, without charge: one litre of liquor (wine or spirits); 200 cigarettes, 25 cigars or 250g of tobacco; 150ml of perfume or 250ml of toilet water; jewellery, a camera and a laptop for personal use; gifts worth up to 2000dh (£120/$240). Prohibited goods include arms and ammunition, controlled drugs, and "books, printed matter, audio and video cassettes and any immoral items liable to cause a breach of the peace".

Extending a stay officially involves opening a bank account in Morocco (a couple of days' procedure in itself) and obtaining an *Attestation de Résidence* from your hotel, campsite or landlord. You will need a minimum of 20,000dh (£1210/$2420) deposited in your bank account before making an application.

Once you have got through these two stages, you need to go to the **Bureau des Étrangers** in the central police station of a large town, at least fifteen days before your time is up, equipped with: your passport and a photocopy of its main pages; four passport photos; two copies of the *Attestation de Résidence*; and two copies of your bank statement (*Compte de Banque*). If the police are not too busy they'll give you a form to fill out in duplicate and, some weeks later, you should receive a plastic-coated permit with your photo laminated in.

For anyone contemplating this labyrinthine operation, the Bureau des Étrangers in **Agadir** is one of the simplest to approach, since a number of expatriates live in the city and banking facilities there (try the Banque Populaire) are fairly efficient. The Bureau is located at the Préfecture de Police on Rue du 18 Novembre.

Foreign embassies and consulates in Morocco

Foreign embassies and consulates in Morocco are detailed in the "Listings" sections for Rabat (see p.362), Casablanca (see p.391), Tangier (see p.126), Marrakesh (see p.478), Agadir (see p.618) and Oujda (see p.213). Foreign representation in Morocco is detailed on the Moroccan Foreign Ministry's website at ⓦ www.maec.gov.ma (click on "Diplomatic & Consular Corps Accredited in Morocco" under "Diplomatic Network" in the English-language section of the site).

Ireland has a consulate in Casablanca (see p.391), but not in Rabat. New Zealanders are covered by their embassy in Madrid, Spain (Pl de la Lealtad 2–3o, 28014 Madrid; ☏ 00-34/91 523 0226), but can use UK consular facilities while in Morocco. Australians have their nearest diplomatic representation in France (4 Rue Jean Rey, 75015 Paris; ☏ 00-33-1/4059 3300), but can use Canadian consular facilities in Morocco.

Moroccan embassies and consulates abroad

A complete up-to-date list of Moroccan diplomatic missions around the world can be found on the Moroccan Foreign Ministry's website at ⓦ www.maec.gov.ma (click on "Moroccan Embassies & Consulates abroad" under "Diplomatic Network" in the English-language section of the site).

Algeria 12 Rue Branly, al-Mouradia, 12070 Algiers ☏ 021/69 70 94, ✉ consgenmaroc@wissal.dz; 26 Av Cheikh Larbi Tebessi, 31000 Oran ☏ 041/41 16 26 or 27, ✉ consulatmaroc.oran@eepad.dz; 5 Av De l'A.N.P., Sidi Bel Abbes ☏ 048/54 34 70, ✉ benali9000@hotmail.com.

Australia 2/11 West St, North Sydney, NSW 2060 ☏ 02/9922 4999; 17 Terrigal Crescent, O'Malley, Canberra, ACT 2606 ☏ 02/6290 0755, ✉ sifmacan@bigpond.com.

Canada 38 Range Rd, Suite 1510, Ottawa, ON K1N 8J4 ☏ 1-613/236-7391, ✉ sifamaot@bellnet .ca; 1010 Sherbrooke St W, Suite 1510, Montreal, PQ H3A 2R7 ☏ 1-514/288-8750, ⓦ www .consulatdumaroc.ca.

Ireland 39 Raglan Rd, Ballsbridge, Dublin 4 ☏ 01/660 9449, ✉ sifamdub@indigo.ie.

Mauritania Av Général de Gaulle, Tevragh Zeina 634, BP621, Nouakchott ☏ 525 1411, ✉ sifmanktt @mauritel.mr; Av Maritime, Nouadhibou ☏ 574 5384, ✉ consu.ndh@maec.gov.ma; formalities for entering Morocco (by car, for example) can only be completed in Nouakchott, not Nouadhibou.

Spain c/Leizarán 31, 28002 Madrid ☏ 91 210 9300, ⓦ www.embajada-marruecos.es; c/Diputació 91, 08015 Barcelona ☏ 93 289 2530, ⓦ www .marocconsuladobcn.org; c/Teniente Maroto 2, first

Children on parents' passports

If travelling as a family, note that **children travelling on their parents' passports** must have their photographs affixed to the passport. If this is not done, it is possible that you will be refused entry to Morocco. This is not just a piece of paper bureaucracy: families are sometimes refused entry for failing to comply.

floor, 11201 Algeciras ℡ 95 666 1803, Ⓔ cg.algesiras@hotmail.com; c/Soldado Español 14, 04004 Almería ℡ 95 028 0202, Ⓔ consalme @consalme.es; Pabellon de la Naturaleza 4, Camino de los Descubrimientos, Isla de la Cartuja, 41092 Seville ℡ 95 408 1044, Ⓔ consumarsevilla @supercable.es; Edificio Britania, c/Pelayo 14, 35010 Las Palmas, Gran Canaria ℡ 92 826 2859, Ⓔ cosul@cosuladomarruecoslp.com; also in Valencia, Alicante, Bilbao and Burgos (see Ⓦ www .embajada-marruecos.es, "Consulados" under "Guia Consular", for full details).

South Africa 799 Schoeman St (cnr Farenden), Arcadia, Pretoria 001 ℡ 012/343 0230 Ⓔ sifmapre@mwebbiz.co.za.

UK 97–99 Diamond House, Praed St, London W2 1NT ℡ 020/7724 0719, Ⓔ moroccanconsulate .uk@pop3.hiway.co.uk.

USA 1601 21st St NW, Washington DC 20009 ℡ 1-202/462-7979, Ⓔ embassy@moroccous .com; 10 E 40th St, 24th Floor, New York, NY 10016 ℡ 1-212/758-2625.

Health

For minor health complaints, a visit to a **pharmacy** is likely to be sufficient. Moroccan pharmacists are well trained and dispense a wide range of drugs, including many available only on prescription in the West. If pharmacists feel you need a full diagnosis, they can recommend a doctor – sometimes working on the premises. Addresses of English- and French-speaking doctors can also be obtained from consulates and large hotels.

If you need **hospital treatment**, contact your consulate at once and follow its advice. If you are near a major city, reasonable treatment may be available locally. State hospitals are usually OK for minor injuries, but for anything serious, a private clinic is generally preferable. Morocco, however, is no country in which to fall seriously ill, and depending on your condition, repatriation may be the best course of action.

The latest advice on health in Morocco can be found on the US government's travel health website at Ⓦ www.cdc.gov/travel /nafrica.htm.

Inoculations

There are no **inoculations** officially required of travellers, although you should always be up to date with polio and tetanus. Jabs against hepatitis A and typhoid are worthwhile, too. Those intending to stay a long time in the country, especially if working with animals or in the healthcare field, are also advised to consider vaccinations against TB, hepatitis B, diphtheria and rabies, though these are not worth your while if just going on holiday.

Moroccan authorities deny the existence of **malaria** anywhere on Moroccan territory, including the Western Sahara, but other authorities report occasional cases between May and October in the region to the north of Beni Mellal and Khenifra, in the area between Chefchaouen and Larache, and in the province of Taza. Local strains of malaria are not life-threatening and malaria pills are not normally considered necessary unless you actually fall ill with it (in which case they are easy enough to get at any pharmacy), but if you really want to be on the safe side, you could take a course of chloroquine (brands include Resochin, Nivaquin and Avlaclor). Note that chloroquine should not be taken if pregnant, and is best not taken for stretches of more than six months at a time. The dose is two tablets weekly for adults, to be taken from a week before entering a malarial zone until four weeks after leaving it. More importantly, avoid bites; use mosquito repellent on all exposed areas of skin, especially feet, and especially around dusk. Repellents using DEET are usually recommended for adults. Alternatives include citronella oil, though it is only effective for a few hours, not all night. Electric mosquito repellent scent diffusers are also effective indoors. Mosquito "buzzers" are useless.

If you haven't had a typhoid jab then buy some Intétrix capsules (available from any pharmacy in Morocco). These are excellent antibacterial medication – useful for diarrhoea as well as typhoid prevention – and some doctors consider them more effective than inoculation. They are certainly valuable if you are travelling for any length of time in the south.

Water and health hazards

The **tap water** in most of Morocco is generally safe to drink (in Chefchaouen, for example, it is pumped straight from a well), though in the far south and Western Sahara it's best to stick to bottled mineral water.

A more serious problem in the south is that many of the **river valleys and oases** are infected with **bilharzia**, also known as **schistosomiasis**, caused by a tiny fluke worm that lives part of its life cycle in a freshwater snail, and the other part in the blood and internal organs of a human or other mammal which bathes in or drinks the water. The snails only live in stagnant water, but the flukes may be swept downstream. Staying clear of slow-flowing rivers and oasis water is the best way to avoid it. If infected while bathing, you'll probably get a slightly itchy rash an hour or two later where the flukes have entered the skin. Later symptoms may take several months to appear, and are typified by abdominal pains, and blood in faeces or even urine. If you suspect that you might have it, seek medical help. Bilharzia is easily cured, but can cause permanent intestinal damage if untreated. Care should be taken, too, in drinking water from **mountain streams**. In areas where there is livestock upstream **giardiasis** may be prevalent and is a common cause of travellers' diarrhoea. Other symptoms include nausea, weight loss and fatigue which usually last no more than two weeks and settle without treatment. If they continue for longer, then a course of **metronidazole** (Flagyl) generally leads to effective eradication, but always finish the course, even after symptoms have gone, and even though this antibiotic will probably make you feel nauseous and precludes consumption of alcohol. Using iodine water purification tablets, or boiling any drinking or cooking water (remember that you'll have to boil it for longer at high altitudes, where the boiling point is lower) is the simplest way to avoid putting yourself at risk from either of these illnesses.

Diarrhoea

At some stage in your Moroccan travels, it is likely that you will get **diarrhoea**. As a first stage of treatment it's best simply to adapt your diet. Plain boiled rice is your safest bet, while yoghurt is an effective stomach settler and prickly pears (widely available in summer) are good too, as are bananas, but other fruit is best avoided, along with greasy food, dairy products, (except yoghurt), caffeine and alcohol. It's important if you have diarrhoea to replace the body fluids and salts lost through dehydration (this is especially the case with children) and dissolving **oral rehydration salts** (*sels de réhydratation orale* in French) in water will help. These are available at any pharmacy, but if you can't get any, then a teaspoon of salt plus eight of sugar per litre of water makes a reasonable substitute. Water (at least two litres per adult daily) should be drunk constantly throughout the day, rather than all in one go.

If this doesn't shake it off in a couple of days, you could obtain **carboxylate capsules** (such as Carbosylane) from a pharmacist. If symptoms persist for several days – especially if you get painful cramps, or if blood or mucus appear in your stools – you could have something more serious (see previous column) and should seek medical advice.

Other hazards

There are few natural hazards in northern Morocco, where wildlife is not very different from that of Mediterranean Europe. If you venture into the Sahara however, be aware of the very real dangers of a bite from a **snake, palm rat** or **scorpion**. Several of the Saharan snakes are deadly, as is the palm rat. Bites should be treated as medical emergencies.

Certain scorpions (see opposite) are very dangerous; their sting can be fatal if not treated. Avoid going barefoot or in flip-flops (thongs) in the bush, or turning over stones. In the desert, shake out your shoes before putting them on in the morning. Most snakes are nonvenomous, and few are life-threatening, but one or two species can be dangerous, most notably the horned viper. All scorpions sting, which can be extremely painful, especially if you are allergic, but again, not many are life-threatening. If you do get bitten by a snake or stung by a scorpion, don't panic – even in the case of life-threatening species, actual fatalities are rare, and you should be in no danger if treated in a reasonable time. Sucking out the poison only works in movies, and tourniquets are dangerous and ill-advised. The important thing is to relax, try not to move the affected part of your body, and seek medical help as quickly as possible. Try to remember what the creature looked like and if it's possible to kill or catch it without danger, then do so, so that you can show it to doctors or paramedics. Most scorpion-sting fatalities are caused by one species, the fat-tailed scorpion (*Androctonus australis*), 4–10cm long and pale yellow with a darker tail tip, which is typically found under stones and in cracks and crevices. Other dangerous species are the death stalker, (*Leiurus quinquestriatus*), the blacktip scorpion (*Buthus occitanus*), the black fat-tailed scorpion (*Androctonus bicolor*), and two other fat-tailed scorpions (the thin-clawed *Androctonus Mauretanicu* and the *Androctonus amoreuxi*). Photographs of all of these, plus much information and sound advice can be found on the Scorpion Venom website at Ⓦ web.singnet .com.sg/~chuaeecc/venom/venom.htm.

Never underestimate Morocco's **heat**, especially in the south. A hat – preferably light in both weight and colour – is an essential precaution and, especially if you have very fair skin, you should also consider taking a sunblock cream with a very high screening factor, as the sun really is higher (and therefore stronger) in Morocco than in northern latitudes. Resulting problems include **dehydration** – make sure that you're drinking enough (irregular urination such as only once a day is a danger sign) – and **heatstroke**, which

is potentially fatal. Signs of heatstroke are a very high body temperature without a feeling of fever, but accompanied by headaches, nausea and/or disorientation. Lowering body temperature, with a tepid shower or bath, for example, is the first step in treatment, after which medical help should be sought.

Contraceptives and tampons

Poor quality and rather unreliable condoms (*préservatifs*) can be bought in most pharmacies, and so can the pill (officially by prescription, but this isn't essential).

Tampons can be bought at general stores, not pharmacies, in most Moroccan cities. Don't expect to find them in country or mountain areas.

Medical resources for travellers

CDC US ☎1-877/394-8747, Ⓦwww.cdc.gov /travel. Official US government travel health site.
Canadian Society for International Health Ⓦ www.csih.org/en/travelhealth/index.asp. Extensive list of travel health centres in Canada.
International Society for Travel Medicine US ☎1-770/736-7060, Ⓦwww.istm.org. Their website has a list of travel health clinics worldwide.
Travellers Abroad UK ☎0113/238 7575, Ⓦwww .masta.org. Clinics throughout Britain; call or check online for the nearest one to you.
Travellers' Medical and Vaccination Centre Australia ☎1300/658 844, Ⓦwww.tmvc.com .au. Lists travel clinics in Australia, New Zealand and South Africa.
Tropical Medical Bureau Ireland ☎1850/487 674, Ⓦwww.tmb.ie. Has a list of clinics in the Republic of Ireland.

Insurance

Wherever you're leaving from, it's frankly reckless to travel without insurance cover. Before paying for a new policy, however, it's worth checking whether you are already covered: some all-risks home insurance policies may cover your possessions when overseas, and many private medical schemes include cover when abroad. In Canada, provincial health plans usually provide partial cover for medical mishaps overseas, while holders of official student/ teacher/youth cards in Canada and the US are entitled to meagre accident coverage and hospital in-patient benefits. Students will often find that their student health coverage extends during the vacations and for one term beyond the date of last enrolment.

After exhausting the possibilities above, you might want to contact a specialist travel insurance company, or consider the travel insurance deal we offer (see below). A typical travel insurance policy usually provides cover for the loss of baggage, tickets and – up to a certain limit – cash or cheques, as well as cancellation or curtailment of your journey. Most of them exclude so-called dangerous sports unless an extra premium is paid: in Morocco this could include mountaineering, skiing, water rafting or paragliding. Read the small print and benefits tables of prospective policies carefully; coverage can vary wildly for roughly similar premiums. Many policies can be chopped and changed to exclude coverage you don't need – for example, sickness and accident benefits can often be excluded or included at will. If you do take medical coverage, ascertain whether benefits will be paid as treatment proceeds or only after returning home, and whether there is a 24-hour medical emergency number. When securing baggage cover, make sure that the per-article limit – typically under £500/$1000 – will cover your most valuable possession. If you need to make a claim, you should keep receipts for medicines and medical treatment, and in the event you have anything stolen, you must obtain an official statement from the police (called a *papier de déclaration*). Bank and credit cards often have certain levels of medical or other insurance included and you may automatically get travel insurance if you use a major credit card to pay for your trip.

Most insurance policies work by **reimbursing** you once you return home, so be sure to keep all your receipts from doctors and pharmacists. If you have had to undergo serious medical treatment in Morocco, and incur major hospital bills, contact your consulate. They will normally be able to arrange for an insurance company, or possibly relatives, to cover the fees, pending a claim.

Rough Guides has teamed up with Columbus Direct to offer **travel insurance** that can be tailored to suit your needs.

Products include a low-cost **backpacker** option for long stays, a **short break** option for city getaways, a typical **holiday package** option, and others. There are also annual **multi-trip** policies for those who travel regularly. Different sports and activities (trekking, skiing, etc) can usually be covered if required. See our website (Ⓦwww .roughguidesinsurance.com) for eligibility and purchasing options. Alternatively, UK residents can call ☎0870/033 9988; Australians can call ☎1300/669 999 and New Zealanders can call ☎0800/559 911. All other nationalities can call ☎+44 870/890 2843.

Internet

Cybercafés and Internet stations are widespread in Morocco, where few people have home computers, and you should have no trouble accessing the Internet in pretty much any town (the most convenient offices are listed in the "Practicalities" or "Listings" sections of places in this book). However, most Internet offices in Morocco tend to overload their bandwidth with terminals, which means slow connections when all are in use (7–8pm is a peak period) – for that reason it's best to use them at quiet times, such as late at night, early in the morning, or when everybody is having lunch or supper. Connections tend to be faster in remote towns in the far south and the Western Sahara than in Marrakesh or the north. Expect to pay around 5dh per hour to use the internet, though some places charge double that, and hotels with internet services often charge even more; conversely, some places in small towns in the south charge as little as 3dh per hour.

Laundry

In the larger towns, laundries exist that will take in clothes and wash them overnight, but you'll usually find it easier to ask at hotels – even in cheap hotels without an official laundry service, the cleaning lady will almost certainly be glad to make a few extra dirhams by taking in a bit of washing.

Left luggage

You can deposit baggage at most train stations, but it will have to be locked or padlocked (so unlockable rucksacks for example will not be accepted); if you are catching a late train, make sure that the office will be open on your return. There are similar facilities at the main bus stations, CTM offices and ferry stations (Tangier, Ceuta, Melilla). Where no left luggage facilities are available, café proprietors will generally agree to look after baggage for you, sometimes for a small fee, more often for free in out-of-the-way places.

Living in Morocco

Your only chance of paid work in Morocco is **teaching English**. For information, try the following schools: The British Council (ⓦwww.britishcouncil.org/morocco) in Rabat, 36 Rue de Tanger (☎037 76 08 36, ⓔbc@britishcouncil.org.ma) or Casablanca, 87 Boulevard Nador, Polo (☎022 52 09 90, ⓔcasa.info@britishcouncil.org.ma); The American Language Centre, 1 Pl de la Fraternité, Casablanca (☎022 27 77 65, ⓦhttp://.casablanca.aca.org.ma), and in Agadir, Fes, Kenitra, Marrakesh, Meknes, Mohammedia, Rabat, Tangier and Tetouan – for contact details see ⓦhttp://.marrakesh.aca.org.ma/contactalc.html; or the American School in Rabat, 1 bis Rue el Amir Abdelkader, Agdal (☎037 67 14 76, ⓦwww.ras.ma), Casablanca, Route de la Mecque, Lotissement Ougoug, Quartier Californie (☎022 21 41 15, ⓦwww.cas.ac.ma), Marrakesh, BP 6195, Route de Ouarzazate (☎024 32 98 60 or 61, ⓦwww.as m.org) or Tangier, 49 Rue Christophe Colombe (☎039 93 98 27 or 28, ⓦwww.as-t.org). Reasonable spoken French and an EFL qualification are normally required, and they usually do their recruiting at home, but they may be able to direct you to smaller schools in Casablanca, Rabat and other Moroccan towns.

It is also possible to **volunteer** to take part in a work camp. Experiment in International Living (EIL; ⓦwww.experiment .org/programs.htm; US ☎1-802/258-3467 or 1-310/450-4624, Canada c/o Friends Student Exchange ☎604/886-3783, UK c/o EIL ☎01684/562 577, Ireland c/o EIL ☎021/455 1535, New Zealand c/o NZIIU ☎09/279 9371, South Africa c/o SASTS ☎021/418 3794) runs voluntary work placements with Moroccan

NGOs, preceded by a four-week intensive language course in Rabat. Another organization that recruits workcamp volunteers is SCI/IVS (ⓦwww.sci-ivs.org; US & Canada ☎1-206/350-6585 or 1-413/528 3401, Canada ☎416/216-0914, south England ☎01206/298 215, north England & Wales ☎01132/304 600, Scotland ☎0131/226 6722, Republic of Ireland ☎01/855 1011, Northern Ireland ☎028/9023 8147, Australia ☎02/9699 1129). In the US, Volunteers for Peace (1034 Tiffany Rd, Belmont, VT 05730–0202; ☎1-802/259-2759, ⓦwww.vfp.org) recruits volunteers for a variety of projects that are detailed on its website. Alternatively, there are Moroccan organizations you can approach direct: Les Amis des Chantiers Internationaux de Meknès (ACIM) (BP 8, 50001 Meknès ☎035 51 18 29, ⓔacim@hotmail .com), whose projects generally involve agricultural or construction work around Meknes – three weeks in July and August, accommodation and food provided; Chantiers Jeunesse Maroc (BP 1351, 10001 Rabat ☎037 72 21 40 ⓔcjm@mtds .com); Chantiers Sociaux Marocains (BP 456, 10001 Rabat ☎037 29 71 84, ⓔcsm @planete.co.ma); Association Chantiers de Jeunesse (ACJ), BP 171, CCP 4469 H, 11000 Salé ☎037 85 53 50, ⓔacj.org .maroc@hotmail.com; and Chantiers des Jeunes Volontaires (CJV) (BP 558, Batha, 30200 Fès ☎035 70 02 58, ⓔcjv1962 @yahoo.fr). Most of the work camps are open to all-comers over eighteen years of age; travel costs have to be paid by the participant, but you generally receive free accommodation (take a sleeping bag) and meals.

Mail

Letters between Morocco and Western Europe generally take around a week to ten days, around two weeks for North America or Australasia. There are postboxes at every post office (*La Poste*) and on the wayside; they seem to get emptied fairly efficiently, even in out-of-the-way places.

Stamps can sometimes be bought alongside postcards, or from some *tabacs* as well as at the PTT, where there is often a dedicated counter (labelled *timbres*), and where stamps may also be sold in the phone section, if there is one. A postcard or simple letter costs 7.50dh to Europe or the British Isles, 9.60dh to South Africa, 10.10dh to North America, 10.80dh to Australasia.

At major post offices, there is a separate window for **parcels**, where the officials will want to examine the goods you are sending. Always take them unwrapped; alongside the parcels counter, there is usually someone (on a franchise) to supply wrapping paper, string and all the trimmings, or wrap your parcel, if you want.

Post office hours are typically Monday to Friday, 8am–4.30pm. Central post offices in big cities will be open longer hours (typically Mon–Fri 8am–6.30pm, Sat 8am–noon), for sale of stamps and money transfer services, but the same hours as small offices for parcels and poste restante. During Ramadan, offices open Monday to Friday 9am–3.30pm, larger ones also Saturday 9am–noon.

Poste restante

Receiving letters **poste restante** (general delivery) can be a bit of a lottery, as Moroccan post office workers don't always file letters under the name you might expect. Ask for all your initials to be checked (including *M* for Mr or Ms, etc) and, if you're half-expecting anything, suggest other letters as well.

To pick up your mail you need your passport. To have mail sent to you, it should be addressed (preferably with your surname underlined) to Poste Restante at the central post office of any major city.

Alternatives to sending poste restante to post offices are to pick a big **hotel** (anything with three or more stars should be reliable) or have things sent **c/o American Express** – represented in Morocco by Voyages Schwartz in Tangier, Casablanca and Marrakesh (see p.126, p.390 & p.478 for addresses), though this service is really only for Amex card- or cheque-holders.

Maps

The **maps of Moroccan towns** in this book should be sufficient for most needs. Local commercial ones exist but add little to those we've printed; the most authoritative local series, the **Plan-Guides** published by Editions Gauthey, look impressive but are next to useless in trying to find your way round the twists and turns of a Medina. They may, however, be useful if you need to find places way out on the edge of town.

One thing you will probably want, though, is a **road map**. Reasonable ones are sometimes available at ONMT tourist offices, and these are adequate if you are not driving or going far off the beaten track. Should you wish to buy one, we recommend our own Rough Guide Map on a scale of 1:1,000,000, which shows roads, contours and geographical features clearly, and is printed on waterproof, tear-proof plastic. Among the alternatives, a good choice is GeoCenter's 1:800,000 map, with the Western Sahara on a 1:2,500,000 inset. Also good is Michelin's Morocco map (#959), on a scale of 1:1,000,000 with 1:600,000 insets of the Casa–Rabat area, the Fes–Meknes–Rif area, the Marrakesh area and the Middle Atlas, though much of the Western Sahara is only on a 1:4,000,000 inset.

Note that maps (or guidebooks) which do not show the Western Sahara as part of Morocco are banned and liable to confiscation. Even maps showing a reduced-scale version of the territory, such as Michelin's, are frowned upon.

Trekking maps

At present, the vital **topographical maps** needed by trekkers, climbers, skiers, etc (1:50,000 and 1:100,000) are very difficult to find in Morocco. You have to go in person to the *Division de la Cartographie*, Avenue Hassan II, km4, Rabat ☎037 29 50 34 (near Rabat bus station), show your passport, and submit an order which *may* then be available for collection several days later – if the request is approved, which is far from certain. The only exceptions are the maps of Toubkal (both scales) which will be served over the counter. These are also sporadically available at the *Hôtel Ali*, Marrakesh, or in Imlil, the trailhead for treks in the area. However, if you are planning to go trekking, it is best to try and get maps through a **specialist map outlet** before you leave home. Look for 1:100,000 (and if you're lucky 1:50,000) maps of the Atlas and other mountain areas. In Britain, Stanfords (ⓦwww.stanfords.co.uk) does a good pack of four maps covering the Djebel Toubkal area.

AMIS (see p.36) produces brief **map-guides** to the Asni-Toubkal, Western High Atlas (Taroudannt) and Sirwa (Taliouine), Anti-Atlas (Tafraoute), Aklim (Igherm) and Djebel Bou Iblane/Bou Naceur (Middle Atlas) areas. Written by our High Atlas contributor, Hamish Brown, these are useful complements to the coverage in this guide. AMIS do mail order worldwide, and are definitely the best place to try for Moroccan maps that you cannot obtain elsewhere.

More **detailed trekking guidebooks** are also available in both English and French. The most useful are Michael Peyron's *Grand Atlas Traverse* (West Col, UK; 2 vols), Robin Collomb's *Atlas Mountains* (West Col, UK), Richard Knight's *Trekking in the Moroccan Atlas* (Trailblazer Publications, UK) and Karl Smith's *Atlas Mountains: A Walker's Guide* (Cicerone Press, UK). Also available from West Col, in English, is a map guide to the Mgoun Massif at 1:100,000, which is useful for a wide region, second only to Toubkal in popularity. For climbing, a modern reproduction of the 1942 Dresch–Lépiney *Le Massif du Toubkal*, available at some bookshops, is useful. To find these in Morocco, Rabat has some good bookshops, but Marrakesh's Librairie Chatr (see p.478) has the best selection. Guidebooks are also on sale at the *CAF Refuge* at Oukaïmeden. One useful publication available in Morocco is *Randonées Pedestre dans le Massif du Mgoun*, which has routes shown on a 1.100,000 scale.

If you pass through London en route to Morocco, you might also want to consult some of the Expedition Reports at the **Royal Geographical Society** (1 Kensington Gore, London SW7 2AR). To find out what they have, you can search their database online, by country, at ⓦwww.rgs.org/expeditionreports, and the RGS's **Expedition Advisory Centre** (☏020/7591 3030) can help locate relevant material, maps and reports. The **Alpine Club** (55–56 Charlotte Rd, London EC2A 3QF ☏020/7613 0755 ⓦwww.alpine-club.org.uk) has a library that can be used by appointment (no fee, but donations invited), with a good collection of guidebooks and maps.

Money

Though the easiest way to carry your money in Morocco is in the form of plastic, it is a good idea to also carry at least a couple of days' survival money in cash, and maybe some travellers' cheques as an emergency back-up.

Morocco's basic unit of **currency** is the **dirham** (dh). The dirham is not quoted on international money markets, a rate being set instead by the Moroccan government. The present rates are approximately **16dh to £1, 8dh to US$1, 11dh to €1**. As with all currencies there are fluctuations, but the dirham has roughly held its own against Western currencies over the last few years. The dirham is divided into 100 **centimes**, and you may find prices written or expressed in centimes rather than dirhams. Confusingly, centimes may also be referred to as **francs** or, in former Spanish zones of the country, as **pesetas**. You may also hear prices quoted in **rials**, or *roales*. In most parts of the country a dirham is considered to be twenty rials, though in Tangier and the Rif there are just two rials to the dirham. These are forms of expression only: there are no actual physical Moroccan rials. Coins of 5, 10, 20 and 50 centimes, and 1, 5 and 10 dirhams are in circulation, along with notes of 20, 50, 100 and 200 dirhams.

In Algeciras, you can buy dirhams at poor rates from travel agents opposite the port entrance, and at slightly better rates from those inside the lorry terminal. You can also buy dirhams at similar rates from agents near the ferry terminals in Ceuta and Melilla. In Gibraltar, moneychangers will usually give you a very slightly better rate than in Morocco itself. When you're nearing the end of your stay, it's best to get down to as little Moroccan money as possible. You can change back dirhams at the airport on departure (you can't use them in duty-free shops), but you may be asked to produce bank exchange receipts – and you can change back only fifty percent of sums detailed on these. You'll probably be offered re-exchange into euros only. You can also change dirhams (at bad rates) into euros in

Ceuta, Melilla and Algeciras, and into sterling in Gibraltar.

Banks and exchange

English pounds and US and Canadian dollars can all be changed at banks, large hotels and some travel agents and tourist shops, but by far the mostly widely accepted foreign currency is the **euro**, which many people will accept in lieu of dirhams, currently at the (bad) rate of €1=10dh. Gibraltarian banknotes are accepted for exchange at a very slightly lower rate than English ones, but Scottish and Northern Irish notes are not negotiable in Morocco, and nor are Australian and New Zealand dollars or South African rand. If entering from Algeria or Mauritania, don't bother bringing any dinars or ouguiya with you either (though you should be able to change CFAs). Note too that Moroccan bank clerks may baulk at changing banknotes with numbers scrawled on them by their counterparts abroad, so change any such notes for clean ones before leaving home.

For exchange purposes, by far the most useful and efficient chain of **banks** is the BMCE (Banque Marocaine du Commerce Extérieur). There is at least one BMCE in all major cities and they are dotted about in smaller towns (see Listings sections in the text of the guide). They handle cash or travellers' cheques with the minimum of hassle, and give cash advances on Visa and Mastercard, as well as currency exchange. The Banque Crédit du Maroc (BCM) also handles **Visa and Mastercard**, as do larger branches of Banque Populaire. Most other banks don't tend to have facilities for credit card transactions, despite the stickers in their windows, though they will exchange cash and travellers' cheques. In the far south, you may find that Banque Populaire and BMCE are your only choices.

Standard **banking hours** for most of the year are Monday to Friday 8.15am–3.45pm. During Ramadan (see p.61), banks open 9am–2pm. In major resorts there is usually one or more bank that keeps extended hours on bureau de change transactions to meet tourist demand, and BMCE and Attijariwafa Bank sometimes have a separate bureau de change open longer hours and at weekends. In some places you may find travel agents with exchange facilities, and most large hotels will also change money for nonresidents out of banking hours.

In most **exchange transactions** at banks, customers fill in forms at one desk, then join a second queue for the cashier. You'll usually need to show your passport as proof of identity. Cheque/cash transactions usually get dealt with in ten to fifteen minutes, but it's wise to allow up to an hour if you need to draw cash on a credit card. Obviously, if you can change money at a hotel or travel agent, or a bureau de change, the whole procedure will be quicker and easier.

There is a **black market** for currency in Morocco, especially in Casablanca and Rabat (black-market moneychangers in Rabat may hang about outside the BMCE bureau de change on Avenue Mohammed V out of hours; in Casa you may be approached on Boulevard de Paris east of Place Mohammed V), but you are not recommended to use it: changing money on the street is illegal and, of course, subject to all the usual scams, and in any case the rate is not particularly preferential. If you do change money on the street, never hand over your currency until you have the dirhams in your hand and have counted them out yourself first. Abort the deal immediately if the dealers start trying to distract you or rush you, such as by talking about the police approaching.

Plastic

Credit and debit cards belonging to the Visa, Mastercard, Cirrus and Plus networks can be used to withdraw cash from **ATMs** at most branches of Morocco's main banks, but not the ones outside post offices. You'd have to be somewhere pretty small for there not to be a bank in town with an ATM, and many banks (BMCE, BCM and Banque Populaire for example) advance cash against Visa or Mastercard anyway. By carrying plastic and using it in ATMs, you get trade exchange rates, which are somewhat better than those charged by banks for changing cash, but your card issuer may well add a foreign transaction fee. This is usually lower than the banks' commissions, but it's worth checking before you leave, as the more rapacious banks, especially in the US, do charge quite high fees, sometimes as much as five percent, occasionally even $5 for each withdrawal.

You can pay directly with plastic (usually with Mastercard, Visa or American Express, though the latter cannot be used in ATMs) in upmarket hotels, restaurants and tourist shops. However, there is usually a weekly limit on credit and debit card cash withdrawals, typically around 5000dh/per week.

Travellers' cheques

Travellers' cheques are as secure as plastic but nothing like as convenient. Though they are accepted at the more upmarket hotels, travel agencies and tourist shops, some banks won't change them, and staff seem to dislike changing travellers' cheques, often finding spurious reasons not to do so: they may well demand to see the original receipt for the cheques, though of course you are not supposed to carry that and the cheques together (if you do show it, don't let the bank keep it), or even other, non-existent documentation that you will certainly not have. Thomas Cook, Visa and American Express are the best-known and most widely accepted cheques, whether in euros, dollars or sterling. In the event that your cheques are lost or stolen, the issuing company will expect you to report the theft to them and to local police immediately. Most companies claim to replace lost or stolen cheques within 24 hours, though they may drag their feet if they suspect fraud. Visa and American Express offer pre-paid cards that you can load up with credit before you leave home and use in ATMs like a debit card – effectively travellers' cheques in plastic form.

American Express

American Express is represented by branches of Voyages Schwartz and S'Tours in Tangier (see p.126), Casablanca (see p.390) and Marrakesh (see p.478). Note that these are only agents, and not every American Express service is available at their offices. Staff can issue Amex travellers' cheques (but often won't cash them), and hold clients' mail, but they cannot cash personal cheques or receive wired money.

Emergency cash

Despite travellers' tales, very few people lose (or are conned out of) all their money in Morocco – but it does happen. Access to an **emergency source** of money – whether it be a credit card or an arrangement with your bank or family to wire you money after a phone call – is reassuring and may prove invaluable.

The quickest and easiest way to wire money is via **MoneyGram** (ⓦ www .moneygram.com) or **Western Union** (ⓦ www.westernunion.com). Transfer is pretty well instantaneous. Western Union is the more convenient of the two since money can be received at most post offices and branches of WAFA Bank. MoneyGram's local agent will usually be a branch of Crédit du Maroc.

Opening hours

Opening hours follow a reasonably consistent pattern: banks (Mon–Fri 8.15am–3.45pm); medersas (daily 9am–6pm); museums (daily except Tues 9am–12.15pm & 3–6.15pm); offices (Mon–Thurs 8.30am–noon & 2.30–6.30pm; Fri 8.30–11.30am & 3–6.30pm); Ville Nouvelle shops (Mon–Sat 8.30am–noon & 2–6.30pm); Medina shops (Sat–Thurs 9am–8pm, Fri 9am–1pm). These hours will vary during Ramadan, when banks, for example, open 9am–2pm, and certainly nothing will be open at nightfall, when those observing the fast – which is to say, nearly everybody – has to stop and eat.

Phones

The easiest way to call within Morocco or abroad is to use a public phone booth (*cabine*), which takes a **phone card** (*télécarte*) issued by Maroc Télécom. The cards are available from some newsagents and *tabacs*, and from post offices, and come in denominations of 18dh, 30dh, 60dh and 99dh – the higher denomination cards give you more units per dirham. Cardphones are now widespread throughout the country, and you can usually find a number of them by a town's main post office if nowhere else. Unfortunately, they are not very well maintained, and often don't work. Not infrequently, they dock a unit or two from your

Emergency numbers

Fire ☎15
Police (in towns) ☎19
Gendarmes (police force with
jurisdiction outside towns) ☎177

card and fail to connect you, but they are still the best and most convenient way to make calls.

An alternative is to use a **téléboutique**, which you'll find in abundance in all towns, great and small. You can dial abroad from almost all of these. Some use coins – 5dh and 10dh coins are best for foreign calls (you'll probably need at least 20dh) – others give you a card and charge you for the units used. Alternatively, you can make calls through a hotel. Even fairly small places will normally do this; however, it'll cost you, so be sure to ask in advance both about possible surcharges and the chargeable rate. Note that international calls from a hotel are usually charged for each three-minute period. If you go one second over, you're charged for the next period.

Some *téléboutiques* will send a **fax** for you – and, by arrangement, receive one for you. A few also have a **photocopier**, but they are not well maintained and you may have to visit several to find one which works well. Newsagents, stationers and bookshops may also do photocopies.

Mobile phones can be used from most places in Morocco (the country now has about 90 percent coverage), and populated areas of the Western Sahara, but note that prepaid cards from abroad cannot be charged up or replaced in Morocco, so

remember to bring enough credit with you. One or other of the Moroccan mobile service providers, Maroc Télécom and Méditel, will probably have a roaming agreement with your provider at home, but calls are expensive, and you pay to receive them as well as to make them. Depending on how long you are spending in Morocco therefore, it may be worth your while to sign up with one of the Moroccan firms, using their SIM cards and a Moroccan number for your handset.

Instead of a dialling tone, Moroccan phones have a voice telling you in French and Arabic to dial the number. When calling a Moroccan number, the **ringing tone** consists of one-and-a-half-second bursts of tone, separated by a three-and-a-half-second silence. The **engaged tone** is a series of short tones (pip-pip-pip-pip), as in most other parts of the world. A short series of very rapid pips may also indicate that your call is being connected.

Phone numbers

All **Moroccan phone numbers** are now nine-digit beginning with zero, and all nine digits must be dialled, even locally. Landline numbers have been changed a couple of times in the last few years, and all now begin with 03 (in the north) or 02 (in the south) – see opposite for details on how to convert old phone numbers to new ones.

The Spanish enclaves of **Ceuta and Melilla** also now have nine-digit numbers, and the former area codes (956 for Ceuta, 952 for Melilla) are now part of the number itself and must be dialled even locally. To call from mainland Spain, you will only need to dial the nine-digit number. Calling Ceuta or

International dialling codes

	From Morocco, Ceuta or Melilla	To Morocco	To Ceuta or Melilla
UK	☎00 44	☎00 212	☎00 34
Ireland	☎00 353	☎00 212	☎00 34
US and Canada	☎001	☎011 212	☎011 34
Australia	☎00 61	☎0011 212	☎0011 34
New Zealand	☎00 64	☎00 212	☎00 34
South Africa	☎00 27	☎09 212	☎09 34

Melilla from abroad, or from Morocco proper, dial the international access code (00 from Morocco), then 34, then the whole nine-digit number. To call Morocco from Ceuta or Melilla, dial 00-212, then the last eight digits of the number, omitting the initial zero.

All post-2002 Moroccan numbers beginning 04 have changed to 02, and those beginning 05 have changed to 03. If you have an older (pre-2002) six-digit number with a two-digit area code, here's how to convert it:

Mobiles that were ☏01/xx xx xx are now ☏061 xx xx xx.

Numbers that were ☏02/xx xx xx (Casablanca region) are now ☏022 xx xx xx.

Numbers that were ☏03/xx xx xx (El Jadida region) are now ☏023 xx xx xx.

Numbers that were ☏04/xx xx xx (Marrakesh region), and subsequently ☏044 xx xx xx, are now ☏024 xx xx xx.

Numbers that were ☏05/xx xx xx (Fes/Meknes region), and subsequently ☏055 xx xx xx, are now ☏035 xx xx xx.

Numbers that were ☏06/xx xx xx (Oujda region), and subsequently ☏056 xx xx xx, are now ☏036 xx xx xx.

Numbers that were ☏07/xx xx xx (Rabat region) are now ☏037 xx xx xx.

Numbers that were ☏08/xx xx xx (Agadir region), and subsequently ☏048 xx xx xx, are now ☏028 xx xx xx.

Numbers that were ☏09/xx xx xx (Tangier region) are now ☏039 xx xx xx.

International calls

To **call Morocco from abroad**, you dial the international access code (00 from Britain, Ireland, Spain, the Netherlands and New Zealand; 0011 from Australia; 011 from the USA and most of Canada), then the country code (212), then the last eight digits of the number, omitting the initial zero. To **call Ceuta or Melilla**, dial the international access code, then 34, then all nine digits of the number, beginning with 956 for Ceuta, 952 for Melilla.

For an **international call** from Morocco, Ceuta or Melilla, dial the international access code **00**, followed by the **country code** (1 for North America, 44 for the UK, etc), the area code (omitting the initial zero which prefixes area code in most counties outside of North America) and the subscriber number.

There is a twenty percent discount on international call rates from midnight to 8am weekdays, and all day at weekends. To reverse call charges, a good policy is to phone someone briefly and get them to ring you back, as collect (reverse charge) calls are hard to arrange. **Home country direct** services to the British Isles and North America are available from most phones, and charge cards from your phone company at home can also be used in Morocco.

Photography

Photography needs to be undertaken with care. If you are obviously taking a photograph of someone, ask their permission – especially in the more remote, rural regions where you can cause genuine offence. In Marrakesh's Djemaa el Fna, taking even quite general shots of the scene may cause somebody in the shot to demand money from you, sometimes quite aggressively. Also note that it is illegal to take photographs of anything considered strategic, such as an airport or a police station, so be careful where you point your camera – if in doubt, ask. On a more positive front, taking a photograph of someone you've struck up a friendship with and sending it on to them, or exchanging photographs, is often greatly appreciated. In fact, while in Morocco, you may be surprised to find yourself dragged off by new friends or acquaintances to a street or studio photographer for a photo session. This is quite common practice and has no untoward ends.

Time

Morocco keeps Greenwich Mean Time the whole year. Ceuta and Melilla keep Spanish time, which is GMT+1 in winter and GMT+2 in summer. The difference – two hours in summertime – is something to keep in mind when coming from Morocco to catch ferries out of Ceuta or Melilla, or trains out of Algeciras. Morocco is on the same time as Britain, Ireland and the Canary Islands in winter, an hour behind in summer. It's five hours ahead of the US east coast (EST) and eight ahead of the west coast (PST), an hour less in summer; and it's eight hours behind Western Australia, ten hours behind eastern Australia, and twelve hours behind New

Zealand, an hour more if daylight saving time is in operation in those places. Morocco is two hours behind South Africa year-round.

Tourist information

Morocco's national tourist board, the **Office National Marocain de Tourisme** (ONMT; Ⓦ www.tourisme-marocain.com) maintains general information offices in several Western capitals, where you can pick up pamphlets on the main Moroccan cities and resorts, and a few items on cultural themes.

In Morocco itself, you'll find an **ONMT** office or **Syndicat d'Initiative** bureau in all towns of any size or interest – often both; their addresses are detailed in the relevant sections of the Guide. Occasionally, these offices can supply you with particular local information sheets – lists of hotels, riads, campsites, upmarket restaurants, car rental firms, and sometimes local transport timings – and they can of course try to help out with specific questions. But don't expect too much from them; their main function, from their point of view, is to gather statistics and to put you in touch with an officially recognized guide.

In addition, there is quite a bit of information available online, and plenty of books on Morocco (see our booklist on pp.768–780). British residents may be interested in the British Moroccan Society (35 Westminster Bridge Rd, London SE1 7JB

Ⓣ020/7401 8146), which organizes various Moroccan-oriented events and discussions, usually in London. The Maghreb Society, based at the Maghreb Bookshop, 45 Burton St, London WC1H 9AL Ⓣ020/7388 1840, Ⓦ www.maghrebreview.com, publishes the *Maghreb Review*, the most important English-language journal on the Maghrebian countries, and members get a discount on books sold at the bookshop.

ONMT offices abroad

Australia 11 West St, North Sydney, NSW 2060 Ⓣ02/9922 4999.
Canada PI Montréal Trust, 1800 Rue McGill College, Suite 2450, Montreal, PQ H3A 2A6 Ⓣ1-514/842-8111.
Spain c/Ventura Rodriguez 24, first floor, left, Madrid Ⓣ91 542 7431.
UK 205 Regent St, London W1R 7DE Ⓣ020/7437 0073, Ⓔmnto@btconnect.com.
USA 20 E 46th St, Suite 1201, New York, NY 10017 Ⓣ1-212/557-2520; PO Box 2263, Lake Buena Vista, Orlando, FL 38230 Ⓣ1-407/827-5335.

Travel advice

Australian Department of Foreign Affairs Ⓦ www.smartraveller.gov.au.
British Foreign & Commonwealth Office Ⓦ www.fco.gov.uk.
Canadian Department of Foreign Affairs Ⓦ www.voyage.gc.ca.
US State Department Ⓦ www.travel.state.gov.

Guide

Guide

Tangier, Tetouan and the northwest

CHAPTER 1 # Highlights

✻ **Tangier's Petit Socco**
Watch the low-life from the
very cafés where Burroughs
and Bowles looked out.
See p.116

✻ **Café Halfa** Sip a mint tea at
this clifftop café while gazing
at Europe across the Straits
of Gibraltar. See p.120

✻ **The Caves of Hercules** Look
out to sea from this grotto
in the cliffs, through a cave
window shaped like Africa.
See p.130

✻ **Asilah** A laidback beach
resort with a clean and tidy
Medina, an arts festival, and
the palace of an old bandit
chief. See p.132

✻ **Lixus** Extensive Roman ruins
in a fine setting, which you'll
have pretty much to yourself
to explore. See p.140

✻ **Moulay Bousselham** Take
a boat ride out to see the
flamingos on this lagoon.
See p.142

✻ **Ceuta** A Spanish enclave with
a couple of forts and no less
than three army museums
– not to mention good beer,
tapas, and shops full of duty-
free booze. See p.145

✻ **Chefchaouen** One of the
prettiest and friendliest
towns in Morocco, up in the
Rif mountains, with a Medina
full of pastel blue houses.
See p.160

△ Asilah's Medina

Tangier, Tetouan and the northwest

The northwest can be an intense introduction to Morocco, encompassing the two Moroccan cities – Tangier and Tetouan – that are most notorious as blackspots for hustlers and unofficial guides preying on first-time travellers, along with long stretches of coast on both Atlantic and Mediterranean. **Tangier**, hybridized and slightly seedy from its long European contact, has a culture distinct from any other Moroccan city, a setting and skyline the equal of any Mediterranean resort, and an age-old role as meeting point of Europe and Africa. In recent years the town's reputation has improved as the majority of hustlers and con artists have been cleared out and various renovation projects begun. Tangier has an international airport at Ibn Batouta (previously known as Boukhalef), and ferry connections with Algeciras, Gibraltar, Tarifa, the French port of Sète and the Italian port of Genoa. Unless you are bringing a car over from Spain, it's a better point of arrival than Ceuta: both for the town's own attractions, and for the convenience of moving straight on into Morocco.

Heading south from Tangier along the **Atlantic coast** towards Rabat, the best places to get acclimatized are the seaside resorts of Asilah and Larache. **Asilah** is a low-key, though growing, tourist resort, and in August hosts an **International Festival**, northern Morocco's major cultural event. **Larache** is less well known, but no less enjoyable, with a relaxed feel, fine beach and proximity to the ancient Carthaginian-Roman site of **Lixus**. A more distinctively Moroccan resort is **Moulay Bousselham**, south of Larache and accessible by bus or grand taxi via Ksar el Kebir or Souk el Arba du Rharb.

The Spanish enclave of **Ceuta** is a slightly frustrating port of entry. Although in Africa, you are not yet in Morocco, and you must make your way to the border at Fnideq, then on from there to **Tetouan**, the first Moroccan town. In the shadow of the wild Rif mountains, Tetouan feels more Moroccan than Tangier – its Medina a glorious labyrinth, dotted with squares, souks and buildings from its fifteenth-century founding by Muslim refugees from Andalusia in southern Spain. Most easily reached via Tetouan is the popular mountain town of **Chefchaouen** – a small-scale and enjoyably laidback place to come to terms with being in Morocco.

The Mediterranean coast between **Fnideq** and **Martil**, Tetouan's home beach, has been developed over the past ten years, its sands colonized by large

TANGIER, TETOUAN & THE NORTHWEST

hotels, a golf course at Cabo Negro, a couple of marinas and a clutch of tourist complexes. **Mdiq** and **Martil** are the only resorts here with much charm, though **Oued Laou**, in the shadow of the Rif, remains a "travellers' resort", with basic facilities. All are easily reached from Tetouan.

The main southern Rif town of **Ouezzane**, historically significant because of its strategic location between northwestern Morocco and Fes and Meknes, as well as an important place of pilgrimage for both Muslims and Jews, is a nice enough place to stroll around for a couple of hours should you be waiting for ongoing transport.

International zones

Northern Morocco has an especially quirky **colonial history**, having been divided into three separate zones. Tetouan was the administrative capital of the **Spanish zone**, which encompassed Chefchaouen and the Rif, spreading south through Asilah and Larache – itself a provincial centre. The **French zone** began at Souk el Arba du Rharb, the edge of rich agricultural plains sprawling south towards the French Protectorate's capital, Rabat. **Tangier**, meanwhile, experienced **International Rule** under a group of foreign legations. The Spanish enclave of Ceuta (see p.145) is, along with Melilla (see p.192), a peculiar legacy of this colonial past.

One modern consequence of this past is that, although French is the official second **language** (after Arabic) throughout Morocco, older people in much of the northwest are equally, or more, fluent in **Spanish** – a basic knowledge of which can prove extremely useful. Adding to and perpetuating the colonial legacy is the fact that Spanish TV and radio can be received (and attract enthusiastic audiences) throughout much of northern Morocco.

Tangier (Tanja, Tanger) and around

For the first half of the twentieth century **TANGIER** was one of the stylish resorts of the Mediterranean – an international city with its own laws and administration, plus an eclectic community of exiles, expatriates and refugees. It was home, at various times, to Spanish and Central European refugees, Moroccan nationalists and – drawn by loose tax laws and free-port status – to over seventy banks and 4000 companies, many of them dealing in currency transactions forbidden in their own countries. Writers were also attracted to the city. **Paul Bowles**, the American novelist who knew Tangier in the 1930s and called it his "dream city", settled here after 1945. **William Burroughs**, in whose books Tangier appears as "Interzone", spent most of the 1950s here, and most of the Beats – Jack Kerouac, Allen Ginsberg, Brion Gysin and the rest – passed through. Tangier was also the world's first and most famous **gay resort** – favoured by the likes of Tennessee Williams, Joe Orton and Kenneth Williams – a role it maintains to a lesser degree today.

The ghosts of these times left a slight air of decay about the city, still tangible in the older hotels and bars. Until recently Tangier's tourism future didn't look

Illicit trade

As well as tourism and trade from the port, Tangier has two other sources of wealth, neither of which appears in official statistics. **Cannabis** is widely cultivated in the Rif and, until an alternative cash crop is found, will continue to be so; you'll certainly see (and smell) plenty of it being smoked around town, increasingly in joints rather than the traditional *sebsi* pipe.

There is also a lucrative business in ferrying would-be **immigrants** across the Straits to Spain, with money made in these ways being invested in apartments and other speculative ventures. You may well meet people from West and even Central Africa waiting for an opportunity to break through Europe's ever-stronger immigration barriers. Crossing the Straits illegally is an expensive and dangerous operation, with passengers fleeced by unscrupulous people-smugglers, and frequently killed as small boats – used to evade the attention of coastguards on both sides – fall victim to bad weather. Probably hundreds of people die in this way every year.

too rosy, as it had gained a reputation as somewhere to avoid or, at best, only as a transit point for onward travel. King Mohammed VI, however, seems to have a soft spot for the city and he has provided much of the impetus for Tangier to re-invent itself under a flurry of renovation and building projects, such as the clean up of the seafront avenues d'Espagne and des FAR (now both renamed as Av King Mohammed VI) and the Grand Socco. Foreign, mainly Spanish, investment has increased and a small invasion of European hoteliers and restaurateurs is also under way. Although Tangier is never likely to become a major mainstream tourist destination it is becoming increasingly popular with holidaying Moroccans and day-tripping Spanish.

Tangier's port, recently re-named Tanger-Ville and ranked second only to Casablanca, is central to its economic future. The now constant stream of ferries arriving daily – nearly around the clock during the August holidays – has prompted the construction of another, goods-only port, Tanger Méditerranée, 20km from Ceuta on the Atlantic coast and financed by the private sector, which will eventually leave Tanger-Ville a passenger-only port.

Finally, despite the clear-out of most of its hustlers, Tangier is still a tricky place for first-time arrivals – hustling and mugging stories here should not be discounted and the characters you run into at the port are as objectionable as any you'll find in Morocco – but once you get the hang of it, Tangier is lively and very likeable, highly individual and with an enduring eccentricity.

The **Bay of Tangier** curves around to a pair of capes: Spartel to the west, with the picturesque Caves of Hercules; and Malabata to the east, which has the better beaches. Either makes a pleasant detour or afternoon's trip from Tangier, if you have a day to fill waiting for a ferry or flight.

Some history

According to legend, **Tangier** was founded by Sophax, son of the Greek demi-god **Hercules** and of **Tingis**, widow of a giant by the name of Antaeus. Hercules had married her after slaying her husband (hewing Europe and Africa asunder in the process), and when Sophax later founded a city here, he named it after his dear old mum. So much for the legend: the truth is that Tingis is Amazigh (Berber) for a marsh, betraying the site's Berber origins, though it was colonized around the seventh century BC by the **Phoenicians**, a seafaring people from what is now Lebanon. In 42 AD, the **Romans** made Tingis the capital of their newly created province of Mauretania Tingitania (roughly the north of modern Morocco). The main street of Roman Tingis probably followed the course of Rue es Siaghin from the main gate, on what is now the Grand Socco, down to the forum (probably where the Petit Socco is today), and on down Rue de la Marine to a sea gate, probably in roughly the same place as today's Bab el Marsa. With the collapse of the Roman Empire's western half, Tangier was taken in 429AD by the Vandals, and its history then becomes a bit hazy. It seems to have been regained a century or so later by the Roman Empire's resurgent eastern half in the form of the **Byzantines**, before falling to Spain's rulers, the **Visigoths**, in the early seventh century.

In 707, Tangier was taken by the **Arabs**, who used it as a base for their invasion of the Iberian peninsula. With the Christian reconquest of Spain and Portugal however, Tangier was itself vulnerable to attack from across the Straits, and fell to the **Portuguese** in 1471. In 1661, they gave it to the **British** (along with Bombay) as part of Princess Catherine of Braganza's dowry on her wedding to Charles II. Tangier's Portuguese residents, accusing British troops of looting and rape, abandoned the town, but new settlers arrived, many of them Jewish refugees from Spain, and Britain granted the city a charter guaranteeing

Tangier's hustlers

Faux guides ("false guides") are petty crooks who attach themselves to new-in-town tourists, usually claiming to be "guiding" you and therefore due payment, or just steering you into hotels or shops where they receive a commission (added to your bill, naturally). At one time, Tangier's *faux guides* were particularly heavy, leading foreigners into dark alleys and mugging them, or simply refusing to leave them alone. Nowadays they have largely been cleaned out of town thanks to a nationwide police crackdown, and those who remain do so because they work for tourist craft shops in the Medina able to pay off the police (the *faux guides* themselves also have to pay protection money).

Generally speaking, *faux guides* now limit their activities to steering you into the shops that employ them – though if they can hustle you into a hotel that will pay them commission, they will do that too.

There are several favourite ambush points in town: the port exit, obviously, where arrivals laden with luggage are prime targets; the corner of Avenue Mohammed VI (formerly Avenue d'Espagne) and Rue Marco Polo on the seafront by the *Hôtel Marco Polo*; the corner of Boulevard Pasteur and Boulevard Mohammed V in the centre of town; the Belvedere; and both entrances to the kasbah at the top of the Medina. They may also be on hand in the Medina to misdirect you to their employers' shops, no matter where it is you are actually trying to get.

Faux guides have a number of approaches you will soon learn to recognize: a favourite is trying to guess your nationality or asking "Are you lost?" or "What are you looking for?" If you ignore them or turn down their advances, they will typically accuse you of being angry or "paranoid". The best way to get rid of them is to ignore them completely, or explain politely (while never slackening your pace) that you are all right and don't need any help. As a last resort – and it should not come to this – bear in mind that local residents, not to mention the law, are on your side, and you can dive into a café or even threaten to go to the police if necessary (the *Brigade Touristique* are based in the former Gare de Ville train station by the port, and there is also a police post in the kasbah).

---

freedom of religion, trade and immigration. The British also introduced tea, now Morocco's national drink. Under virtually constant siege however, they found Tangier an expensive and unrewarding possession: "an excrescence of the earth", according to the diarist **Samuel Pepys**, who came here in 1683 as treasurer of a special commission. Pepys, who regarded the townswomen as "generally whores", records in his diary how he and his chaplain spent an evening having "a great deal of discourse upon the viciousness of this place and its being time for God Almighty to destroy it". **Moulay Ismail** laid siege to the city in 1678, and in 1680, England's parliament refused any further funding to defend it. Four years later, unable to withstand the siege any longer, the British abandoned Tangier, destroying its fortifications as they left. Moulay Ismail had them rebuilt, and the city then remained in Moroccan hands until the twentieth century, growing in importance as a port – one of its exports, mandarins, even took their name from the city, being known in Europe as **tangerines**.

Tangier's strategic position made it a coveted prize for all the colonial powers at the end of the nineteenth century. European representatives started insinuating themselves into the administration of the city, taking control of postal communications, sanitation and other vital parts of the infrastructure, and when France and Spain decided to carve up Morocco between them, Britain insisted that Tangier should become an **International Zone**, with all Western powers having an equal measure of control. This was agreed as early as 1905, and

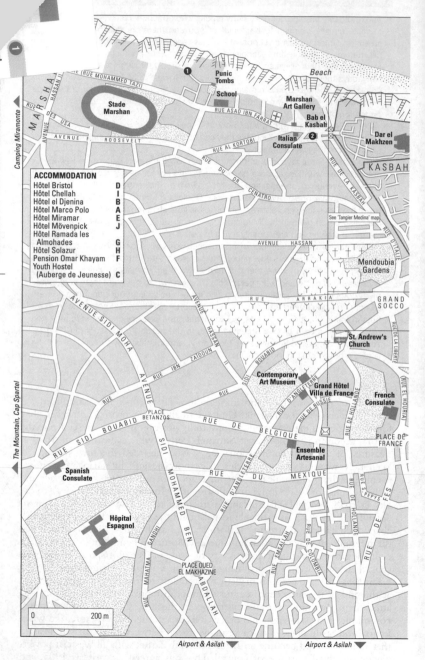

Camping Miramonte ▲

The Mountain, Cap Spartel ▲

Beach

❶ Punic Tombs

School

Marshan Art Gallery

RUE (RUE MOHAMMED TAZI)

RUE DES USA

AVENUE HASSAN II

AVENUE F. ROOSEVELT

Stade Marshan

RUE ASAD IBN FARRAT

Bab el Kasbah

❷

Italian Consulate

RUE AL KORTOBI

Dar el Makhzen

KASBAH

RUE DU DR CENATRO

RUE DE LA KASBAH

RUE D'ITALIE

See 'Tangier Medina' map

AVENUE HASSAN

Mendoubia Gardens

ACCOMMODATION

Hôtel Bristol	D
Hôtel Chellah	I
Hôtel el Djenina	B
Hôtel Marco Polo	A
Hôtel Miramar	E
Hôtel Mövenpick	J
Hôtel Ramada les Almohades	G
Hôtel Solazur	H
Pension Omar Khayam	F
Youth Hostel (Auberge de Jeunesse)	C

AVENUE SIDI MOHA

AVENUE HASSAN II

RUE IBN ZAIDOUN

RUE ARRAKIA

GRAND SOCCO

RUE DE LA LIBERTE

St. Andrew's Church

RUE SIDI BOUABID

RUE

Contemporary Art Museum

RUE D'ANGLETERRE

RUE DE RUSSIE

Grand Hôtel Villa de France

RUE DE HOLLANDE

French Consulate

RUE EL MOURJ

RUE SIDI BOUABID

PLACE BETANZOS

RUE DE BELGIQUE

PLACE DE FRANCE

Ensemble Artesanal

SIDI MOHAMMED BEN

RUE D'ANGLETERRE

RUE DU MEXIQUE

RUE DE PEPYS

RUE DE FES

Spanish Consulate

RUE EMSALLAH

RUE DE COLOMBIA

RUE DE HOLLANDE

GANDHI

MAHATMA

ABDALLAH

Hôpital Espagnol

PLACE OUED EL MAKHAZINE

0   200 m

Airport & Asilah ▼   Airport & Asilah ▼

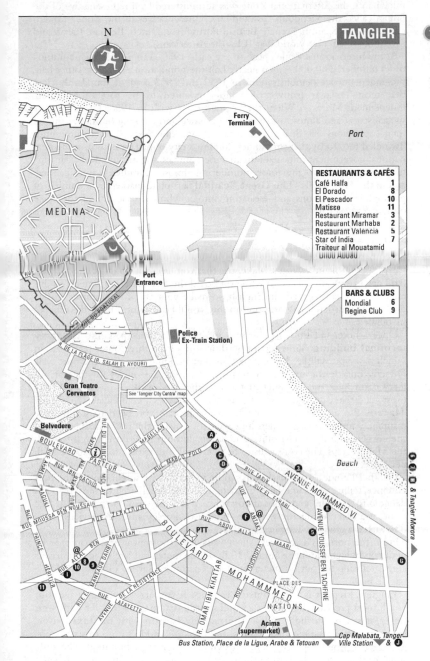

TANGIER

RESTAURANTS & CAFÉS
Café Halfa	1
El Dorado	8
El Pescador	10
Matisse	11
Restaurant Miramar	3
Restaurant Marhaba	2
Restaurant Valencia	5
Star of India	7
Traiteur al Mouatamid	4

BARS & CLUBS
Mondial	6
Regine Club	9

Ferry Terminal

Port

MEDINA

PETIT

Port Entrance

Police (Ex-Train Station)

Gran Teatro Cervantes

See 'Tangier City Centre' map

Belvedere

BOULEVARD PASTEUR

RUE DU PRINCE

RUE MARCO POLO

RUE MSELLAH

AVENUE MOHAMMED VI

Beach

RUE TARIK

RUE EL FARABI

AVENUE YOUSSEF BEN TACHFINE

RUE ABOU ALLA EL MAARI

BOULEVARD MOHAMMED V

PTT

RUE ALTAI BEN ABDALLAH

RUE MANSOUR DAHBI

RUE EL FARABI

RUE ZERKTOUNI

PLACE DES NATIONS

RUE DE LA RESISTANCE

AVENUE LAFAYETTE

Acima (supermarket)

Bus Station, Place de la Ligue, Arabe & Tetouan

Cap Malabata, Tanger Ville Station &

finalized by treaty in 1923. An area of 380 square kilometres, with some 150,000 inhabitants, the International Zone was administered by a representative of the Sultan called the Mendoub, "assisted" by representatives of the Zone's foreign communities (Spanish, French, British, Portuguese, Dutch, Belgian, Italian and Swedish, joined after World War II by the Americans).

At the International Zone's peak in the early 1950s, Tangier's foreign communities numbered 60,000 – then nearly half the population. As for the other half, pro-independence demonstrations in 1952 and 1953 made it abundantly clear that most Tanjawis (natives of Tangier) wanted to be part of a united, independent Morocco. When they gained their wish in 1956, Tangier lost its special status, and almost overnight, the finance and banking businesses shifted their operations to Spain and Switzerland. The expatriate communities dwindled too (today there are under 2000 in a city of half a million), as the new national government imposed bureaucratic controls and instituted a "clean-up" of the city. Brothels – previously numbering almost a hundred – were banned, and in the early 1960s "**The Great Scandal**" erupted, sparked by a number of paedophile convictions and escalating into a wholesale closure of the once outrageous gay bars.

Arrival

Disembarking by **ferry** at Tangier can be a slow process, with long queues for passport control and customs. Make sure that you have your **passport stamped** (and departure card collected) while on board the ferry; announcements to this effect are not always made in English, so make your way to the purser's office during the journey. If you miss out on this, you'll be left until last by the officials in Tangier.

Once ashore, and through customs, most ferry arrivals pass into the **ferry terminal building**. Some ferries berth at one of the three outer terminals, in which case you will be directed to a smaller building alongside the port wall. Directly outside the main ferry terminal building are offices for the various ferry companies and branches of most of the local banks (some with ATM); most sell dirhams at regular rates but they don't always accept traveller's cheques. There is also an Assurance Frontière office in case you need to sort vehicle insurance, and a **consigne** (left luggage) just outside the port entrance, round the corner from the CTM office and about 20m up Rue du Portugal towards the Medina steps. The cost seems to be negotiable but expect to pay about 10dh per piece.

Unofficial guides – or **hustlers** – can be incredibly persistent around the port entrance, telling you some fairly amazing tales: the hotels are full, the Medina is dangerous, the trains and buses are on strike. Don't take too much of this at face value, and don't feel in any way duty-bound to employ anyone's services – you don't need a guide in Tangier.

From the port, it's a relatively short walk into the centre or a short ride by petit taxi (which should be around 10dh on the meter, but lately the taxi drivers are all refusing to "put on meter" and are charging a set fee of around 50dh – haggle hard).

Tangier's **airport** is 15km outside the city. If you arrive on a package tour you'll most probably be met by a hotel shuttle (try to get a transfer with your ticket, if you're on flight only). Alternatively bargain with the **taxi** drivers lined up outside the terminal, who should charge 120dh for up to six passengers (get a group together before leaving the terminal building). The only other option is to walk 2km to the main road, where you can pick up bus #9, which goes to Rue de Fes in town. There are currently (at the time of writing a newer, bigger terminal was being built) two **banks** at the airport which are usually open to meet incoming flights; one of them will cash travellers' cheques and they also have ATMs. There is also a **post office**, British Airways and Royal Air Maroc desks as well as desks for most of the international **car rental** firms.

Trains arrive and depart from a new station to the east, **Tanger Ville**, 3km from the port, and around 15dh from the centre by petit taxi. It is served by bus #16, which will get you as far as the bus station (see below), but does not run into the city centre. Tanger Ville is relatively handy for hotels at the eastern end of the beach such as the *Almohades* or the *Solazur*, but for the city centre you may prefer to get off at the penultimate stop, **Tanger Morora**, where you can take bus #13 into town.

Bus services from most towns generally arrive at **Tangier Gare Routière** (bus station), south of the Ville Nouvelle. **CTM** has buses from Rabat, Casablanca, Fes, Marrakesh and the other major cities, some of which continue on from the *gare routière* to the port entrance. It's about a fifteen-minute walk into town from the *gare routière*, or around 10dh by petit taxi.

Orientation and information

After the initial confusion of an unfamiliar Arab city, Tangier is surprisingly easy to find your way around. As with all the larger Moroccan cities, it's made up of two parts: the **Medina**, the original Moroccan town, and the **Ville Nouvelle**, built by its several European colonizers. Inside the Medina, a classic web of alleyways and stepped passages, is the old citadel or **kasbah**, with the former Sultanate's palace at its centre.

Together with the **beach** and the seafront **Avenue Mohammed VI** (formerly **Avenue d'Espagne**), the easiest reference points are the city's three main squares – the Grand Socco, Petit Socco and Place de France. **Place de France** is a conventional, French-looking square at the heart of the Ville Nouvelle,

---

Street name confusions

Spanish and French colonial names are still in use alongside their Arabicized successors. In addition, both *Rue* and *Calle* are sometimes replaced by *Zankat*, and *Avenue* and *Boulevard* by *Charih*.

Local maps tend to use the new Arabic versions, though not all of the street signs have been changed. In the text and maps of this guide, we have used new names only when firmly established. Among the main street name changes, note:

Main squares
Place de France – Place de Faro
Grand Socco – Place du 9 Avril 1947
Petit Socco – Place Souk Dakhil

Medina
Rue des Chrétiens – Rue des Almouahidines
Rue de la Marine – Rue Djemaa Kebir
Rue des Postes – Rue Mokhtar Ahardane

Beach
Avenue d'Espagne – Avenue Mohammed VI
Avenues des FAR – Avenue Mohammed VI

flanked by kerbside cafés and a **terrace-belvedere** looking out over the Straits to Spain with the small port of Tarifa usually visible almost directly opposite. From here, **Boulevard Pasteur** (the main city street) leads off past the fairly useless ONMT **tourist office** at no. 29 (Mon–Thurs 8.30am–noon & 2.30–6.30pm, Fri 8.30–11.30am & 3–6.30pm; sometimes open lunch and weekends in July & Aug; ☏039 94 80 50), towards the main PTT (post office).

North from Place de France, **Rue de la Liberté** runs to the **Grand Socco**, a popular open space in front of the Medina. The north side of the square opens onto the Medina's principal street, **Rue es Siaghin**, which culminates in the **Petit Socco**, a tiny square of old cafés and cheap hotels.

City transport

Grands taxis (large cream/beige Mercedes) are permitted to carry up to six passengers. The price for a ride should be fixed in advance – 15–20dh per person is standard for any trip within the city, including tip. Two fixed-fare shared runs from the Grand Socco are of possible interest: to the flea market at Casa Barata, and to Ziyatin, where you can change for an onward taxi to the Caves of Hercules.

Small blue/green **petits taxis** (which carry just three passengers) can be flagged down around the town. Most of these are metered – a typical rate for a city trip is 10dh per person – make sure the driver starts his meter from zero. On the streets you can **hail a taxi**, whether it has passengers or not; if it is going in your direction it will generally take you. If you join a taxi with passengers, you pay the full fare, as if it were empty. **After 8pm** both grand and petit taxi rates increase by fifty percent.

City buses are not tremendously useful to tourists. The most useful route is #2, which runs from St Andrew's Church in the Grand Socco to Ziyatin and on to the village of Jabila, not far from the Caves of Hercules. At weekends in summer, it runs to the caves themselves; other times, you can get a grand taxi from Ziyatin. Route #9 goes from Rue de Fes along the Rabat road to the airport turn-off, some 2km from the airport. Route #16 connects the train station and the bus station, and runs on to Cape Malabata, but does not serve the city centre.

Accommodation

Tangier has dozens of **hotels and pensions**, and finding a room is rarely much of a problem: if the first place you try is full, most hotels will be happy to phone and reserve you a place elsewhere. The city does, however, get crowded during July and August, when many Moroccan families holiday here, or spend a few days en route to and from Europe. Cheaper hotels and pensions hike up their prices at this time of year, and you'll often get a better deal at one of the mid-range hotels.

As always, there is a choice between the **Medina** or **Ville Nouvelle**. If it's your first time in Tangier, you will probably prefer the easier, more familiar feel (and greater comforts) of the Ville Nouvelle places.

Should you not wish to stay in, but remain close to, Tangier – perhaps for an early or late ferry connection – the *Hôtel Ibis Moussafir*, 2km south of the airport and 12km from the port on the N1 (formerly the P2) (☏039 39 39 30, ⓦwww .ibishotel.com; ❸), is a functional and comfortable place with restaurant, bar, swimming pool and, perhaps the main reason why you would stop here, ample secure parking. They even allow pets to stay over.

Tangier also has two **campsites**, *Camping Miramonte*, also known as *Camping Marshan* (☏039 93 71 33), and *Camping Tingis* (☏039 32 30 65); both are some distance from the town centre, have dubious security, and often seem to be closed for no apparent reason. Better are *Camping Ashakar* (☏064 80 13 25), 16km from town and 5km south of the Cap Spartel lighthouse, and close to the Caves of Hercules and several beaches (see p.131), or the well-maintained campsites on the northern edge of **Asilah**, 35km from Tangier (see p.134).

Seafront hotels

All the places below are along or just off the seafront **Avenue Mohammed VI** (formerly **Avenue d'Espagne** and its continuation **Avenue des FAR**). Several hotels are on Rue Magellan, which is easy to miss: it zigzags up from the seafront alongside the *Hôtel Biarritz* towards Boulevard Pasteur in the Ville Nouvelle. A number of others are on Rue Salah Eddine el Ayoubi (Rue de la Plage), which runs uphill from the port to the Grand Socco and is lined with small pensions.

On the whole, the seafront places get pricier and fancier as you move around the bay away from the port, though you may find some closed for renovation or lack of tourists. All those listed below are within walking distance of the port, though you may prefer to take a petit taxi to the further ones.

Cheap

All these hotels are marked on the Tangier City Centre map on p.112, except where stated.

Hôtel Exclesior 17 Rue Magellan, straight up from *Hôtel Biarritz* ☏012 08 91 11. This 23-roomed hotel has seen better days but is good value for the price. Large, airy rooms, some with small balconies and views. Shared showers and toilets. Hot showers 10dh. ❷

Hôtel L'Marsa 92 Av Mohammed VI (formerly Av d'Espagne) ☏039 93 23 39. Located above its own pavement restaurant with a range of rooms available, some of them with balcony and ocean views. Shared showers and toilets. ❷

Hôtel el Muniria 1 Rue Magellan ☏039 93 53 37 or 010 04 72 27. This is where William Burroughs wrote *The Naked Lunch* (in room 9, no longer available), and Jack Kerouac and Allen Ginsberg stayed here too when they came to visit him. Nowadays it's a clean and quiet family-run *pension*, with the sole remnant of its Beat history the adjoining *Tanger Inn* bar (see p.124), but it's still a favourite and consistently gets good reports. En-suite showers, but hot water mornings and evenings only. ❹

Pension Atou 45 Rue Salah Eddine el Ayoubi (no phone). Basic, with no showers (there are public

ones just down the street), but very cheap, especially for singles, with a great rooftop terrace overlooking the Jewish cemetery and the port. ❶

Pension Madrid 140 Rue Salah Eddine el Ayoubi ☏039 93 16 93. One of several old Spanish town-houses now turned into *pensions* – and this is one of the most popular. ❷

Pension Miami 126 Rue Salah Eddine el Ayoubi ☏039 93 29 00. Beautifully tiled old Spanish town-house said to be over one hundred years old. Pleasant rooms, and bathrooms on each corridor. ❶

Pension Omar Khayam 28 Rue el Antaki; see map pp.104–105 (no phone). A strange mix of musty old corridors, recently decorated lobby and bathrooms, and reasonably clean and decent rooms. ❹

Youth Hostel (Auberge de Jeunesse) 8 Rue el Antaki; see map pp.104–105 ☏039 94 61 27. Ahmed Laroussi, the current warden, is maintaining the high reputation of this well-established hostel. Sixty beds (40dh with YHA card, 45dh without; breakfast not included; hot showers 5dh). Open 8–10am, noon–3pm & 6–11pm (midnight in summer).

Moderate to expensive

All these hotels are marked on the Tangier map on pp.104–105, except where stated.

Hôtel Biarritz 104 Av Mohammed VI (formerly Av d'Espagne); see map p.112 ☏039 93 24 73. An old hotel with comfortable rooms, all en suite, and a fair bit of charm. Reductions for long stays. ❹

Hôtel Bristol 14 Rue el Antaki ☏039 94 29 14, ☏039 34 30 94. A good bet, 100m uphill from the beach, with large en-suite rooms with TVs, plus a bar and restaurant (you may be obliged to have half board in midsummer). A 1950s lift (accommodating two people with luggage at a squeeze) still operates and saves climbing the stairs. ❹

Hôtel el Djenina 8 Rue el Antaki ☏039 94 22 44, ⨍039 94 22 46. Though the rooms are a little on the small side, it's immaculate and an excellent choice. ❺

Hôtel Marco Polo Corner of Av Mohammed VI (formerly Av d'Espagne) & Rue el Antaki ☏039 94 11 24, ⨍039 94 22 76. Recently refurbished and very efficiently run, with a dozen comfortable rooms, popular restaurant and lively bar (both open to nonresidents). Discounts In winter. ❺

Hôtel Miramar 168 Av Mohammed VI (formerly Av des FAR) ☏039 94 17 15, ⨍039 94 63 46. An old place, and a little shabby, but friendly, with a bar and restaurant. ❹

Hôtel Mövenpick Route de Malabata; off map ☏039 32 93 00, ⊛www.moevenpick-hotels.com.

One of Tangier's most deluxe hotels, 4km east of town on the road to Malabata, with three restaurants, a pool, health club, sauna and casino, with some rooms adapted for wheelchair users. ❽

Hôtel Nabil 11 Rue Magellan; see map p.112 ☏039 37 54 07. A refurbished warehouse converted into a first-class hotel. All rooms are en suite, and there are stunning views from the front top-floor rooms. Good parking. ❹

Hôtel Ramada les Almohades 43 Av Mohammed VI (formerly Av des FAR) ☏039 94 07 55, ⊛www .ramada.com. A luxury hotel towards the eastern end of the town beach, with 138 rooms, four restaurants, nightclub, sauna and pool. ❽

Hôtel Solazur Av Mohammed VI (formerly Av des FAR), on the next block after Av Yacoub el Mansour ☏039 32 07 59, ⧉ag@kasbah.net.ma. One of the older beach hotels, which, despite attempts at modernization, seems stuck in a 1970s time-warp. ❻

Central Ville Nouvelle hotels

Most of these recommendations are within a few blocks of Place de France/Place de Faro and the central Boulevard Pasteur; coming up from the port, if you've got much luggage, a taxi can be useful as it's a steep climb. All these hotels are marked on the Tangier City Centre map on p.112, except where stated.

Hôtel Atlas 50 Rue Moussa Ben Noussair ☏039 93 64 35, ⨍039 93 30 95. A bit out of the way but value for money, with good-size rooms and a 1930s feel. ❺

Hôtel Chellah 47–49 Rue Allal Ben Abdellah; see map pp.104–105 ☏039 32 44 57, ⨍039 32 09 98. A clean but soulless package-tour hotel, with a swimming pool and garden. Ask for a room on the swimming pool and garden side, away from the nearby mosque's early morning call. ❺

Hôtel Dawliz Complex Dawliz, 42 Rue de Hollande ☏039 33 33 77, ⊛www.ledawliz.com. Facing the once-elegant but now-ruined *Grand Hôtel Villa de France*, this four-star establishment has a pool and all mod cons (satellite TV, a/c, heating and so on). Breakfast included. ❼

Hôtel el Minzah 85 Rue el Houria (Rue de la Liberté) ☏039 93 58 85, toll-free within Morocco ☏080 00 37 34, ⊛www.elminzah.com. Built in 1931, this remains Tangier's most prestigious hotel, with a wonderful garden, a pool overlooking the sea and town, elegant (if pricey) bar, and a new

wellness centre with hammam. Past guests have included Cecil Beaton, Jean Genet and Mick Jagger, and tradition has it that it was from here that World War II Allied agents spied on their German counterparts at the *Hôtel Rif*. ❽

Hôtel de Paris 42 Bd Pasteur ☏039 93 18 77, ⨍039 93 81 26. Central hotel with spacious and spotless rooms, good breakfasts, a few Art Deco touches in the public areas, some interesting old photos in the lobby and very helpful staff. Breakfast included. ❺

Pension Hollande 139 Rue de Hollande ☏039 93 78 38, ⨍039 93 78 38. Behind the French Consulate, this large, airy house, shaded by trees, offers simple, but good-value rooms. ❸

Rembrandt Hôtel Corner of bds Pasteur and Mohammed V ☏039 33 33 14, ⨍039 93 04 43. A reasonably stylish hotel with bar and pool, but getting a bit shabby now. ❻

Tanjah Flandria Hôtel 6 Bd Mohammed V ☏039 93 32 79, ⧉hotelflandria@hotmail.com. Better-than-average modern package-tour hotel, with a pool on the roof, disco and sauna. ❼

Medina hotels

Since around 2000, Tangier's Medina has been experiencing a mini–renaissance and this is evident in the number of Moroccan and European investors who are

transforming rundown residences into chic **riads**. They are still i[n]
– there are about 35 hotels in the Medina and most of them are fa[r]
and aren't cheap, but generally they have a style and charm that you wo[uld]
in the hotels, and are safe enough as long as you have the initial confidenc[e]
the area. To reach the Medina from the port, either walk up Rue du Portug[al]
to the Grand Socco, or go up the steps behind the port entrance, round to the
Grand Mosque and the junction of Rue des Postes/Rue Dar el Baroud. All
these places are marked on the Tangier Medina map on p.116.

Dar Nour 20 Rue Gourna, in the kasbah, off Rue Sidi Ahmed Boukouja ☏062 11 27 24, ⓦwww.darnour.com. There are sweeping views of both the Medina and the Straits from the whitewashed rooftop terrace of these two joined houses, with seven individually styled suites, all en suite and some with private terrace and sitting room. Sumptuous breakfast included. ❻

Hôtel Continental 36 Rue Dar el Baroud ☏039 93 10 24, ⓔhcontinental@iam.net.ma. By far the best hotel in the Medina, the Continental was founded in 1865, with Queen Victoria's son Alfred its first official guest, and other notables including Degas and Churchill. Today, the hotel has a somewhat ragged feel and, despite renovations, is showing its age. However, nothing can detract from the unrivalled view of the port from its terrace – captured in Bertolucci's film of Paul Bowles' novel *The Sheltering Sky*. Taking a taxi is the easiest way to get to the hotel, or, if on foot, make your way from Petit Socco along Rue Jemaa Kebir, past the Grand Mosque, and then along Rue Dar el Baroud (both part of what was Rue de la Marine) to the hotel gates. ❻

Hôtel du Grand Socco (*Hôtel Taïeb*) Grand Socco, entrance round the back on Rue Imam Layti ☏039 93 31 26. The oldest hotel in Tangier, in Jewish hands until the Spanish arrived in 1912. It's seen better days, but the large rooms are reasonable value if shared by three to five people, and the café has a great vista over the Grand Socco. No showers, but public ones less than 50m away. ❷

Hôtel Mamora 19 Rue des Postes ☏039 93 41 05. Centrally located in the heart of the Medina, with clean, pleasant rooms, all with showers – though there's only hot water in the mornings. ❹

Hôtel Olid 12 Rue des Postes ☏039 93 13 10. Tatty, ramshackle and eccentrically decorated, but still reasonable value for money. Some rooms are en suite. Hot showers 10dh. ❷

Pension Fuentes 9 Petit Socco, at the heart of the Medina ☏039 93 46 69. One of the first hotels in Tangier, and boasting, over the years, the likes of Saint-Saëns and the Beat people; it's still a friendly and atmospheric dive, though there is little residual glamour and the café below can be noisy. ❸

Pension Mauretania 2 Rue des Chrétiens (Rue des Almouahidines), just off the Petit Socco ☏039 93 46 77. Fairly well kept and cheap, but with only cold showers. ❶

Pension Palace 2 Rue des Postes ☏039 93 61 28. A touch of past splendours – balconies and a central court with fountain – led Bertolucci to shoot part of *The Sheltering Sky* here. Some rooms are quite pleasant, including a few en-suite ones. ❸

Riad Tanja 2 Rue Amar Alilech, turn off Rue de Portugal near the Old American Legation ☏039 33 35 38, ☏039 33 30 54. Less than two years old and already known for exemplary service and a warm, understated character. Six rooms decorated in zellij tiling, all en suite and come with their own sitting room complete with satellite TV. Parking available near the American Steps. Breakfast included. ❼

The beach and Ville Nouvelle

Tangier's interest and attraction lies in the city as a whole: its café life, beach, and the tumbling streets of the Medina. The handful of "monuments", with the notable exception of the Dar el Makhzen palace, are best viewed as adding direction to your wanderings, rather than as unmissable sights.

The town beach

It was the beach and mild climate which drew in Tangier's first expatriates, the Victorian British, who used to amuse themselves with afternoon rides along the sands and weekends of "pig-sticking" in the wooded hills behind. Today's

...e more packaged on the **town beach**, with camel rides,
...ing of club-like beach bars. It's no Acapulco, nor even an
...e sands are diverting and fun, with Moroccans entertaining
...batics and football.

...nd some say compulsory to change in a cabin, so when
...beach you might like to attach yourself to one of the
...of which offer showers and deck chairs, as well as food
...one of the main areas of development in Tangier at the
...eems that a new bar or restaurant opens up every few
months... the institutions from the city's past glory days, like *Emma's*
BBC Bar and *The Windmill* – where Joe Orton hung out – are either gone

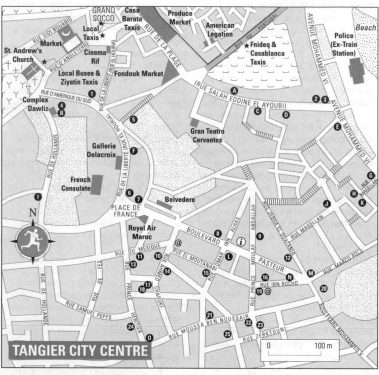

TANGIER CITY CENTRE

0 ——— 100 m

ACCOMMODATION		RESTAURANTS & CAFÉS				BARS & CLUBS	
Hôtel Atlas	O	Café Metropole	8	Restaurant Marrakech	21	Atlas Bar	24
Hôtel Biarritz	G	Café de Paris	6	Restaurant Number One	20	Borsalino	22
Hôtel Dawliz	B	Casa España	12	Restaurant Pagode	18	Caïd's Bar	F
Hôtel Excelsior	H	Cristal Palace	11	Restaurant Populaire		Carrousel Bar	17
Hôtel L'Marsa	E	L'Horizon Restaurant	4	Saveur Mediterannée	5	Dean's Bar	1
Hôtel el Minzah	F	El Korsan	F	Restaurant Raihani	10	Morocco Palace	9
Hôtel el Muniria	J	L'Marsa	E	Restaurant San Remo	14	The Pub	25
Hôtel Nabil	K	Porte	19	Relais de Paris	4	Radio Club	22
Hôtel de Paris	L	Rahmouni	23	Rubis Grill	16	Scott's	15
Pension Atou	A	Restaurant Africa	3			Tanger Inn	J
Pension Hollande	I	Restaurant Agadir	13				
Pension Madrid	C	Restaurant le Coeur					
Pension Miami	D	de Tanger	7				
Rembrandt Hôtel	M	Restaurant Hassi					
Tanjah Flandria Hôtel	N	Baida	2				

△ Tangier's town beach

or have been seriously renovated and lost their individuality. *The Sun Beach*, where Tennessee Williams wrote a first draft of *Cat on a Hot Tin Roof*, is the exception and still manages to tick away all year with a regular flow of clientele. *Mondial* and *Miramar* are two of the better recent additions, and *Miami*, with its gardens to laze around in, is one of the most pleasant. However, the favourites change each year, so look around and take your pick. Some close in the colder months.

By day, don't leave anything on the beach unattended. By night, limit your exploration to the beach bars as the beach itself, although floodlit, can still be unsafe and you may become a target for unsavoury types.

The Grand Socco and Place de France

The **Grand Socco** (or Zoco Grande) is the obvious place to start a ramble around the town. Its name, like so many in Tangier, is a French–Spanish hybrid, proclaiming its origins as the main market square. The markets have long gone, but the square remains a meeting place and its cafés are good points to sit around and absorb the city's life. Recently, largely thanks to King Mohammed VI's interest, it has had a substantial facelift. The main centrepiece is now a large marble fountain encircled by walkways, park benches – great spots for people watching – palm trees and new streetlights. The Grand Socco's official but little-used name, **Place du 9 Avril 1947**, commemorates the visit of Sultan Mohammed V to the city on that date – an occasion when, for the first time and at some personal risk, he identified himself with the struggle for Moroccan independence.

A memorial to this event (in Arabic) is to be found amid the **Mendoubia gardens**, flanking the square. These enclose the former offices of the Mendoub – the Sultan's representative during the international years – and were receiving a makeover at the time of writing. A spectacular banyan tree, said to be over 800 years old, will remain part of the revamped gardens. The old **markets** of the Grand Socco were moved out in the 1970s, onto the Rue de Portugal (running down to the port) and to some cramped terraces beside the Rue d'Angleterre, southwest of the square. More interesting, however, is the little **Fondouk Market**, which is to be found by following **Rue de la Liberté** from the Grand Socco towards Place de France, then turning left down a series of steps, past the *El Minzah* hotel. The stalls here offer everything from pottery to spectacle repairs, from fruit and vegetables to bric-a-brac and plain old junk.

Over in the **Place de France**, the cafés are the main attraction – and at their best in the late afternoon and early evening, when an interesting mix of local and expatriate regulars turn out to watch and be watched. The seats to choose are outside the *Café Paris*, a legendary rendezvous throughout the years of the International Zone. During World War II, this was notorious as a centre of deal making and intrigue between agents from Britain, America, Germany, Italy and Japan; later the emphasis shifted to Morocco's own politics: the first nationalist paper, *La Voix du Maroc*, surfaced at the café, and the nationalist leader Allal el Fassi, exiled in Tangier from the French-occupied zone, set up his Istiqlal party headquarters nearby.

St Andrew's Church and the Musée d'Art Contemporain

Just south of the Grand Socco, on Rue d'Angleterre, is the nineteenth-century Anglican **Church of St Andrew**, one of the city's odder sights in its fusion of Moorish decoration, English country churchyard and flapping Scottish flag – the cross of St Andrew, to whom the church is dedicated (though, being an English church, they sometimes fly the cross of St George instead). The regular congregation has fallen considerably but the church is still used for Sunday morning services (8.30am & 11am), when the numbers are swollen by worshippers from West African countries, particularly Nigeria, en route (hopefully) to a better life in Europe. On weekdays (9.30am–12.30pm & 2.30–6pm) the caretaker, Mustapha Cherqui, is generally on hand to show off the church, whose interior is notable for its rendition of the Lord's Prayer in Arabic script around the chancel arch.

In the strangely serene graveyard, among the laments of early deaths from malaria, you come upon the tomb of **Walter Harris** (see p.769), the most brilliant of the chroniclers of "Old Morocco" in the closing decades of the nineteenth century and the beginning of the twentieth. Also buried here is **Dean** of *Dean's Bar* ("Missed by all and sundry"), a former London cocaine dealer (real name Don Kimfull) who left Britain after being implicated in a scandal surrounding the death by overdose of a young actress in 1919 – he tended bar in Germany, France and the *El Minzah* hotel before opening his own bar in 1937, and worked as a spy for British intelligence in Tangier during World War II. Other graves reveal epitaphs to **Caid Sir Harry Maclean**, the Scottish military adviser to Sultan Moulay Abd el Aziz at the turn of the twentieth century; and to a number of Allied aircrew who died over the Straits in the last days of World War II. Inside the church another Briton, **Emily Keane**, is commemorated. A contemporary of Harris, she lived a very different life, marrying in 1873 the Shereef of Ouezzane – at the time one of the most holy towns of the country (see p.168). One of the more recent graves is that of **David Herbert**, second son of the Earl of Pembroke and a notable eccentric and keen churchgoer. His tombstone reads simply "He loved Morocco" and its position by the south porch is so that, as he threatened, he could check on latecomers for the morning service.

A little further along Rue d'Angleterre is a large white-walled villa, ᴉᴄ the British Consulate and now the **Musée d'Art Contemporain de la V.** **de Tanger** (closed for refurbishment at the time of writing), devoted to contemporary Moroccan artists. Opposite, the now sadly derelict remains of the **Grand Hôtel Villa de France** belie its place in art history: the French painters Eugène Delacroix and Henri Matisse both stayed here, and Matisse painted one of his best works through his room window.

The American Legation and Gran Teatro Cervantes

If you follow Rue de la Plage out of the Grand Socco, then turn left down towards the port on the Rue du Portugal, you come to a small gate in the Medina wall on the left; climb the steps to the gate and, just through it, is the **Old American Legation** (Mon–Thurs 10am–1pm & 3–5pm, Fri 10am–noon & 3–5pm, other times by appointment; free; ☎039 93 53 17, Ⓦwww.legation .org), a former palace given to the US government by the Sultan Moulay Slimane, and preserved today as an American Historic Landmark. Morocco was the first overseas power to recognize an independent United States and this was the first American ambassadorial residence, established in 1777. A fascinating three-storey palace, bridging an alleyway (the Rue d'Amérique) below, it houses excellent exhibits on the city's history – including the correspondence between Sultan Moulay Ben Abdallah and George Washington – and has displays of paintings by in the main, Moroccan resident American artists. Downstairs, by the library (Sat 3–5pm, Sun 10am–1pm, though it's best to call beforehand), a room dedicated to Paul Bowles features photographs of Bowles and his contemporaries, including a shot of him by Beat poet Allen Ginsberg.

Over to the southeast of the Grand Socco, off the Rue de la Plage, is another interesting relic of Tangier's international past, the **Gran Teatro Cervantes** – the old Spanish theatre. Located on a side street still labelled in Spanish as Calle Esperanza Orellana (the wife of its architect), it is an unmistakeable building, with its tiled, Art Nouveau front and impressive glass dome. The facade was restored with the help of EU and Spanish funds, though it is starting to show signs of wear again and sadly the interior remains derelict.

The Medina

The Grand Socco offers the most straightforward **approach to the Medina**. The arch at the northwest corner of the square (probably on the site of a Roman gate) opens onto **Rue d'Italie**, which becomes Rue de la Kasbah, the northern entrance to the kasbah quarter. To the right, there is an opening onto Rue Semarine which leads onto Rue es Siaghin, off which are most of the souks and at the end of which is the Petit Socco, the Medina's principal landmark and little square. An alternative approach to the Medina is from the seafront: follow the steps up, walk round by the Grand Mosque, and Rue des Postes (Rue Mokhtar Ahardane) will lead you into the Petit Socco.

Rue es Siaghin

Rue es Siaghin – Silversmiths' Street – follows the course of a Roman street, and was Tangier's main thoroughfare into the 1930s. It remains an active one today, with a series of fruit, grain and cloth markets opening off to its sides. Halfway along from the Grand Socco (on the right), locked and decaying, is the **old Spanish Cathedral** and **Mission**. The area behind here was formerly the **Mellah**, or Jewish quarter, centred around Rue des Synagogues. Moroccan Jews traditionally controlled the silver and jewellery trade – the "Siaghin" of the

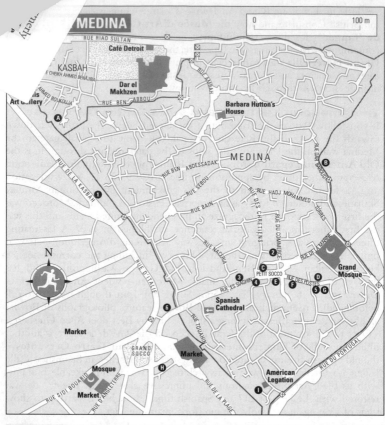

ACCOMMODATION				RESTAURANTS			
Dar Nour		Hôtel Olid	G	RESTAURANTS			
Hôtel Continental	A	Pension Fuentes	E	Chez Hammadi	1	Restaurant Andaluz	2
Hôtel du Grand Socco	B	Pension Mauretania	C	Chez Hassan	3	Ray Charly	4
Hôtel Mamora	H	Pension Palace	F	Mamounia Palace	6	Riad Tanja	I
	D	Riad Tanja	I	Restaurant Ahlen	5		

street name – but few remain in Tangier, having left at Moroccan independence in 1956 for Gibraltar, France and Israel, and the street itself has long been taken over by tourist stalls.

The Petit Socco

The **Petit Socco**, or Zoco Chico, (Little Market) seems too small ever to have served such a purpose, though in Roman times this was probably the site of the forum. Nineteenth-century photographs show the square almost twice its present size, and it was only at the beginning of the twentieth century that the hotels and cafés were built. These, however, give the place its atmosphere: very seedy and rather conspiratorial, and the location for many of the Moroccan stories of Mohammed Mrabet.

In the heyday of the "International City", with easily exploited Arab and Spanish sexuality a major attraction, it was in the alleys behind the Socco that

A café in the Petit Socco

the straight and gay brothels were concentrated. William Burroughs used to hang out around the square: "I get averages of ten very attractive propositions a day," he wrote to Allen Ginsberg, ". . . no stasis horrors here." The Socco cafés (the recently renovated *Central* was the prime Beat location) lost much of their allure at independence, when the sale of alcohol was banned in the Medina, but they remain diverting places to sit around, people-watch, talk and get some measure of the town. Today the reek of hashish pervades the square, but foreigners are strongly advised not to smoke it in any of the Petit Socco's cafés – police informers abound, and a bust could cost you dear. The fact that Moroccans all seem to be smoking it does not make it safe.

The area around the Petit Socco has an important place in Morocco's **postal history**, and one of the streets off the square was even called Rue des Poste. During the days of the International Zone, Britain, Spain, France and – until World War I – Germany all had post offices in Tangier. Spain's was at no. 3 in the square itself, Britain's at 23 Rue de la Marine. A few doors towards the square, 37 Rue de la Marine was the office of Morocco's first ever postal service back in the nineteenth century, a pony-express like horseback relay service between Tangier and Fes. Number 76, opposite, was the site of Morocco's first national bank.

Towards the kasbah

It is beyond the Petit Socco that the Medina proper seems to start, "its topography", to quote Paul Bowles, "rich in prototypal dream scenes: covered streets like corridors with doors opening into rooms on either side, hidden terraces high above the sea, streets consisting only of steps, dark impasses, small squares built on sloping terrain so that they looked like ballet sets designed in false perspective, with alleys leading off in several directions; as well as the classical dream equipment of tunnels, ramparts, ruins, dungeons and cliffs".

Walking up from the Petit Socco, you can follow **Rue des Chrétiens** (Rue des Almouahidines) and its continuation **Rue Ben Raisouli** and emerge, with luck, around the lower gate to the kasbah. Heading past the Socco towards the sea walls are two small streets straddled by the Grand Mosque. If you want to get out and down to the beach, follow **Rue des Postes** and you'll hit the flight of steps (known as the "American Steps") down to the port. If you feel like wandering, take the other one, **Rue de la Marine**, which curls into **Rue Dar el Baroud** and the entrance to the old *Hôtel Continental* – another fine place to sit and drink tea. From here it's relatively simple to find your way across to the square below the Kasbah Gate.

The **Grand Mosque** itself is screened from public view – and, as throughout Morocco, entrance is strictly forbidden to non-Muslims. Enlarged in the early nineteenth century, the mosque was originally built on the site of a church by the Sultan Moulay Ismail in celebration of the return of Tangier to Moroccan control in 1685. Prior to this, the city had seen some two centuries of European rule: Portuguese, then Spanish, then British (see pp.102–103). It was the Brits who destroyed the city's medieval fortifications, including a great upper castle which covered the entire site of the present-day kasbah.

The kasbah and beyond

The **kasbah**, walled off from the Medina on the highest rise of the coast, has been the palace and administrative quarter since Roman times. It is a strange, somewhat sparse area of walled compounds, occasional colonnades, and a number of luxurious villas built in the 1920s, when this became one of the Mediterranean's most chic residential sites. Richard Hughes, author of *A High Wind in Jamaica* (and of a book of Moroccan tales), was the first European to take a house here – his address fabulously titled "Numéro Zéro, La Kasbah, Tangier".

Among those who followed was the eccentric Woolworths heiress, Barbara Hutton, who reputedly outbid General Franco for her mini-palace, Sidi Hosni. Her parties were legendary – including a ball where thirty Reguibat racing camels and their drivers were brought 1000 miles from the Sahara to form a guard of honour.

Local guides point with some pride to these locations, but the main point of interest here is the former **Sultanate Palace**, or **Dar el Makhzen**, now converted to an excellent **museum of crafts and antiquities** (Mon, Wed, Thurs & Sun 9am–12.30pm & 3–5.30pm, Fri 9–11.30am; 10dh; ☏039 93 20 97, ⓦwww.maroc.net/museums). It stands near the main gateway to the Medina, the **Bab el Assa**, to the rear of a formal court, or *mechouar*, where the town's pashas held public audience and gave judgement well into the twentieth century. The entrance to the palace, a modest-looking porch, is in the left-hand corner of the court as you enter from the Medina – scores of children will probably direct you.

Just before the entrance to the palace, you pass (on your left) the ramshackle clubhouse of the Orquesta Andalusi de Tanger, a fine group of musicians who play Andalous music with a lot of swing. If they're around practising, they may well invite you in to watch them play.

The Dar el Makhzen and Café Detroit

The **Dar el Makhzen** – built, like the Grand Mosque, by Moulay Ismail – last saw royal use in 1912, with the residence of the Sultan Moulay Hafid, who was exiled to Tangier after his forced abdication by the French. The extraordinary negotiations which then took place are chronicled in Walter Harris's *Morocco That Was*. According to Harris, the ex-Sultan found the building "uncomfortable, out-of-date, and out-of-repair and by no means a satisfactory place of residence, for it was not easy to install 168 people within its crumbling walls with any comfort or pleasure". Most of this extended entourage seem to have been members of the royal harem and well able to defend their limited privileges. Moulay Hafid himself ended up with "only a couple of very shabby rooms over the entrance", where he apologetically received visitors and played bridge with a small circle of Americans and Europeans.

However out of date and uncomfortable the palace may have been, it is by no means a poor example of Moroccan craftsmanship and architecture. The design is centred on two interior courtyards, each with rich arabesques, painted wooden ceilings and marble fountains. Some of the flanking columns are of Roman origin, particularly well suited to the small display of **mosaics and finds from Volubilis** (see p.243). The main part of the museum, however, is devoted to **Moroccan arts**, laid out according to region and including an exceptional collection of ceramics from Meknes and Fes.

At the entrance to the main part of the palace is the **Bit el Mal**, the old treasury, and adjoining is a small private **mosque**, near to which is the entrance to the herb- and shrub-lined palace **gardens**, shaded by jacaranda trees. If you leave this way, along Rue Riad Sultan, you will pass under the **Café Detroit** (entered via the first doorway on your left). *Détroit* is French for "strait", which is why so many places here have that name (and also why the city of Detroit in Michigan is so called). The café was set up in the early 1960s by Beat writer Brion Gysin, partly as a venue for the **Master Musicians of Jajouka**, drummers and pipe-players from a village in the foothills of the Rif who

Malcolm Forbes: Tangier's last tycoon

The American publishing tycoon **Malcolm Forbes** bought the **Palais du Mendoub** in 1970. His reason, ostensibly at least, was the acquisition of a base for launching and publishing an Arab-language version of *Forbes Magazine* – the "millionaires' journal". For the next two decades, until his death in 1990, he was a regular visitor to the city, and it was at the Tangier palace that he decided to host his last great extravagance, his **seventieth birthday party**, in 1989.

This was the grandest social occasion Tangier had seen since the days of Woolworths heiress Barbara Hutton (see opposite), whose scale and spectacle Forbes presumably intended to emulate and exceed. Spending an estimated $2.5m, he brought in his friend Elizabeth Taylor as co-host and chartered a 747, a DC-8 and Concorde to fly in eight hundred of the world's rich and famous from New York and London. The party entertainment was on an equally imperial scale, including six hundred drummers, acrobats and dancers, and a *fantasia* – a cavalry charge which ends with the firing of muskets into the air – by three hundred Berber horsemen.

In the media, Malcolm's party was a mixed public relations exercise, with even the gossip press feeling qualms about such a display of American affluence in a country like Morocco, and, despite Liz Taylor's presence at Forbes' side, using the choice of location to hint at the tycoon's sexual preferences (a story that broke in full cry after Forbes' death). However, Forbes most likely considered the party a success, for his guests included not just the celebrity rich – Gianni Agnelli, Robert Maxwell, Barbara Walters, Henry Kissinger – but half a dozen US state governors and the chief executives or presidents of scores of multinational corporations likely to advertise in his magazine. And, of course, it was tax deductible.

His former home on Rue Mohammed Tazi, used in the 1990s to house personal guests of King Hassan II, is now a museum (daily 10am–4pm; free; ☎039 93 36 06) displaying Forbes' collection of 120,000 military miniatures, depicting various famous battles of the past.

achieved cult fame when they worked with Rolling Stone Brian Jones, a friend of Gysin's (see p.747 for more). The café has been closed for refurbishment for several years, and whether it will reopen is uncertain. Affording perhaps a little compensation for this is a small archway in the wall, just before the café, which opens out to a vacant piece of land with fantastic views over the Straits of Gibraltar.

Café Halfa, Palais du Mendoub and Jews' Beach

Leaving the Medina by Bab Kasbah, a ten- to fifteen-minute stroll along Rue Asad Ibn Farrat and then Rue Mohammed Tazi, will bring you to the quarter known as *La Marshan*, an exclusive residential quarter with a rich spread of villas, consulates and royal properties. You will pass on your right the small Marchan Art Gallery (10am–1pm & 3–6pm daily except Fri) owned by local artist Rachid Alaoui, who is usually on hand to comment on the various pieces on display. After the grand **Italian Consulate**, and just before the sports stadium, a rock on a pedestal and a series of columns on the north side of the street lead down to a group of **Punic rock-tombs**, not very exciting in themselves, but a lovely spot where Tanjawis come to smoke a pipe of *kif*, or just admire the view across the Straits to the Spanish town of Tarifa. On a clear day, you can also see the Rock of Gibraltar over to the right. The next turning, bearing left down a narrow lane, leads to the rustic **Café Halfa**. The steep hillside is terraced and from the café, shaded by shrubs and trees, there are stunning views over the straits. Serving coffee, mint tea, sandwiches and cakes, this is just the place to spend the late afternoon – as was the habit of Paul Bowles and his friends, Tennessee Williams, Truman Capote and Jack Kerouac.

Going along Rue Mohammed Tazi you come to the **Palais du Mendoub** on the right. From the 1920s, this was the residence of the Mendoub, the sultan's representative during the international years, and more recently was owned by Malcolm Forbes (see box, p.119). Continuing past the palace for a further 1km, you reach *Camping Miramonte*, and a track down to the **Jews' Beach** – so called from its role as the landing stage for Spanish Jews fleeing the Inquisition. There is a pleasant little **beach café** open here in summer.

Gardens on the mountain

The two most prestigious addresses in Tangier are **La Marshan**, the area west of the Palais du Mendoub, and **La Montagne**, the "Mountain" behind the Spanish Consulate, on the inland route to Cap Spartel (see p.130). The Mountain, less imposing than its name suggests, was a rebel base against the British and Portuguese occupations of Tangier, but is now thoroughly tamed. Its cork and pine woods shield two vast royal palaces: one, built by the Victorian British consul Sir John Hay, was (until her death in 1992), the residence of King Hassan's mother; the other, heavily guarded, among the numerous retreats of the Saudi royal family. It is also peppered with villas, many of which have beautiful gardens with stunning views of the bay, and several of which are owned by expats who are prepared to show serious garden-lovers around. One such is Anne Lambton, Villa Palma, La Vielle Montagne (℡039 93 13 93), who asks only for a donation to SPANA, the animal welfare charity. Like many who live on the Mountain, Anne is an artist and occasionally exhibits at the Lawrence Arnott Art Gallery (see p.125).

To reach La Montagne you'll need to drive or take a taxi. From Place de France take Rue Belgique to its end, where it becomes the Rue de la Montagne and begins winding its way up. If you want to make a day-trip of it, you can continue over the mountain towards the Caves of Hercules (see p.130).

Eating, drinking and nightlife

Tangier is not really a night-time city, and if you're looking for international resort-style action, or the Tangier of sin-city legend, you'll be disappointed. Over the last few years, however, the local **restaurant** scene has been rejuvenated and there is now a broad choice of quality eateries, ranging from inexpensive to top end, scattered around the city centre. The possibilities for films, theatre, the occasional concert and, at the right time of year, festivals are also surprisingly varied. The same can't really be said for most of the **bars** and **discos** which seem to be either stuck in a time warp or grossly expensive.

Restaurants

As with most Moroccan cities, the cheapest places to eat are in the **Medina**, though alcohol is not served in this quarter. For fancier meals – and drinks – you'll need to try the **Ville Nouvelle** or the **seafront**; for late-night snacks, several of the cafés around the Grand Socco stay open all night. You'll need a car to get to all of the **out-of-town** recommendations.

Medina

All these restaurants are shown on the Tangier Medina map on p.116, unless otherwise stated.

Ohaa Hammaul 2 Rue de la Kasbah ⊕039 93 45 14. Just outside the west wall of the Medina, this is a rather kitsch salon, where traditional Moroccan dishes – and good pastilla – are served to entertainment from a worthwhile band of Andalous musicians. Moderate.

Chez Hassan 22 Rue es Siaghin. Small, unpretentious restaurant (with Arabic/English name sign up high) on the main street of the Medina, not far from the Petit Socco. Cheap.

Mamounia Palace 4 Rue es Siaghin. A nicely done-out place, not quite achieving the palatial style it aspires to, but laidback, with comfortable seating, unobtrusive musicians and decent food. The only options are two set menus, at 115dh each.

Ray Charly Corner of Petit Socco. A hole-in-the wall diner – just a counter and a row of seats – serving burgers, chicken, egg and chips. One disadvantage of this place is that beggars sometimes come and hassle you while you're eating. (Very) cheap.

Restaurant Ahlen 8 Rue des Postes. Simple but well-cooked food – roast chicken, grilled beef, *harira* – and a warm welcome. Cheap.

Restaurant Andaluz 7 Rue du Commerce. In the first alley to the left off Rue de la Marine (the street running from the Petit Socco to the Grand Mosque). With a trio of tables, it is about as simple as it's possible to be – and excellent, serving impeccably fried swordfish steaks and grilled brochettes. Cheap.

Restaurant Marhaba 26 Palais Ahannar, off Rue de la Kasbah at no. 67, just outside the Medina; see map pp.104–105 ⊕039 93 79 27. A splendid old palace, stacked with antiques, and with music and good food. Set menus for 150dh and 190dh. Open lunch and dinner. Moderate to expensive.

Riad Tanja 2 Rue Amar Alilech, turn off Rue de Portugal near the Old American Legation ⊕039 33 35 38, ℗039 33 30 54. Small and intimate restaurant, stylishly and simply decorated, whose signature *nouvelle cuisine Marocaine* includes light vegetable salads, fish *tajine* and caramelized fruit dessert. Open to nonresidents. Lunch and dinner; closed Mon. Reservation recommended. Expensive.

Ville Nouvelle

All these restaurants are shown on the Tangier City Centre map on p.112, unless otherwise stated.

Casa España 11 Rue Jebha el Ouatania, by the *Rembrandt Hôtel*. Tangier's Spanish club, with a twenty-percent surcharge for nonmembers, but still reasonably good value with three different paellas (Valencian, seafood and vegetarian), plus such Iberian standards as kidneys in sherry, tortilla and, in season, Andalusian gazpacho. Moderate.

El Dorado 21 Rue Allal Ben Abdallah, near the *Hôtel Chellah*; see map p.104–105. Dependable

Moroccan–Spanish cooking, with couscous on Fridays and paella on Sundays. Moderate.

L'Horizon Restaurant Complex Dawliz, 42 Rue de Hollande ☎039 33 33 77. Mainly French cuisine with 80dh and 150dh set menus and a 65dh couscous menu on Fridays. Not as intimate as *Relais de Paris* next door, but with fantastic sea views. Moderate to expensive.

El Korsan in the *Hôtel el Minzah*, 85 Rue de la Liberté ☎039 93 58 85. The hotel's Moroccan restaurant has a reputation as one of the country's best, serving authentic and traditional specialities to the accompaniment of a group of musicians. However, it has the occasional lapse and if you want classic Moroccan cooking you may feel your money is better spent at *Raihani's* (see next column). Expensive.

El Pescador 39 Rue Allal Ben Abdallah; see map p.105. Similar in style and menu to the nearby *El Dorado*, but with the added attraction of an inviting tapas bar at the rear and a takeaway service. Lunch and dinner, closed Sun. Moderate to expensive.

Restaurant Africa 83 Rue Salah Eddine el Ayoubi (Rue de la Plage), at the bottom of the hill, opposite *Hôtel Valencia* ☎039 93 54 36. Best of the many restaurants on this street, which leads down from the Grand Socco. Formerly a Spanish town-house though now rather more simply decorated, it serves regular Moroccan dishes, well prepared, and there's beer and wine. Moderate.

Restaurant Agadir 21 Rue Prince Héritier, off Place de France. This small and friendly restaurant, run by a Tafraouti, with accomplished French and Moroccan cooking, is a particular favourite. Licensed. Moderate, with a 70dh set menu.

Restaurant le Coeur de Tanger 1 Rue Annoual, off Place de France (it's above the *Café Paris*, though the entrance is on a side street). Moroccan dishes served in some style. Set menus of 140dh. Moderate to expensive.

Restaurant Hassi Baida 83 Rue Salah Eddine el Ayoubi (Rue de la Plage) ☎061 58 83 85. Bright, tiled restaurant serving fish, couscous, tajine and pizza. Moderate, with a 45dh set menu.

Restaurant Marrakech 22 Rue Moussa Ben Noussair. Small and popular with freshly grilled fresh fish, paella, couscous and tajines. Open noon 'til late, closed Sunday. Cheap, clean and well prepared.

Restaurant Number One 1 Bd Mohammed V, across the side street from the *Rembrandt Hôtel* ☎039 94 16 74. A restaurant and cocktail bar, with a well-cooked French–Moroccan menu, which attracts a business crowd at lunchtime (noon–3pm) and tends to be fairly quiet in the evenings (6.30–11pm). Expensive.

Restaurant Pagode Rue el Boussiri, just off Rue Prince Héritier ☎039 93 80 86. The best Chinese food in Tangier, though the service is pretty joyless. Expensive.

Restaurant Populaire Saveur Mediterannée On the steps leading down from Rue de la Liberté to the Fondouk Market. A small and popular diner specializing in fish. Closed Fri. Cheap.

Restaurant Raihani 10 Rue Ahmed Chaouki, a side street opposite the terrace-belvedere on Bd Pasteur ☎039 93 48 66. This is an excellent restaurant, serving traditional Moroccan food – it's worth at least one visit for the superb couscous and pastilla – as well as a decent French-based menu. Open lunch and dinner. Moderate, with a 100dh set menu.

Restaurant San Remo 15 Rue Ahmed Chaouki, see *Raihani's* above. Credible, good-value Spanish, French and Italian cooking, and with a cheaper pizzeria across the road. Moderate.

Relais de Paris Complex Dawliz, 42 Rue de Hollande ☎039 33 18 19, ⊛www.relaisdeparis .com. The current meeting place of choice for Tangier's wheelers and dealers. Fine French cuisine including succulent grills and a set menu of 110dh. The Medina and sea views may make the expense worthwhile, although the cheaper *l'Horizon* is right next door. Open lunch and dinner but a reservation is recommended. Expensive.

Rubis Grill 3 Rue Ibn Rochd, off Av Prince Moulay Abdallah. Long established, serving Spanish and other European dishes; the candle-lit hacienda decor is a bit over the top, but the food and service are exemplary. Moderate.

Seafront

The restaurants facing the former Gare de Ville across Avenue Mohammed VI (formerly Avenue d'Espagne) all serve very cheap *harira*, but their food can be a bit hit and miss, so you're better off popping round the corner to the *Africa* or the *Hassi Baida*. All restaurants are marked on the map on pp.104–105 unless otherwise stated.

Hôtel Biarritz 104 Av Mohammed VI (formerly Av d'Espagne; map p.112). One of the nicer hotel

restaurants, with old-style service and a limited but reliable menu. Moderate.

Hôtel Marco Polo corner of Av Mohammed VI (formerly Av d'Espagne) & Rue el Antaki. Very noisy ground-floor bar, with restaurant on the first and top floors, and views of the bay. Limited menu but generous helpings, and cheerful, swift service. Moderate.

L'Marsa *Hôtel L'Marsa*, 92 Av Mohammed VI (formerly Av d'Espagne; map p.112). Superb pizzas and spaghetti, with home-made ice cream to follow, served (slowly) on a roof terrace, patio or inside. Moderate, with an 80dh set menu.

Restaurant Miramar Av Mohammed VI (formerly Av des FAR), opposite the *Hôtel Rif* ☎039 94 40 33. Overlooking the beach, this new restaurant has a varied menu of Moroccan, Spanish and seafood dishes. Noon–midnight. There's a separate tapas bar at the rear. Moderate to expensive.

Restaurant Valencia 6 Av Youssef Ben Tachfine ☎039 94 51 46. A simply furnished fish restaurant, very popular with locals and tourists. Closed Tues. Moderate.

Star of India Av Mohammed VI (formerly Av des FAR), on the beach opposite the *Hôtel Solazur* ☎039 94 48 66 or 94 49 02. Tangier's only curry house, with Indian dishes for vegetarians and meat-eaters, as well as a pretty good chicken tikka masala. Expensive.

Out of town

Chez Abdou 17km out of town, on the coast road leading south towards Asilah, in the so-called Forêt Diplomatique. Recommended for seafood. Expensive

Club Le Mirage near the Caves of Hercules (see p.131) in the area known as Ashakar, 5km south of the Cap Spartol lighthouse ☎039 33 33 32, ⓦwww.lemirage-tanger.com. An international-style restaurant located within a long-established and popular resort. The food is excellent – saffron-flavoured *soupe de poisson* and curried langoustine brochettes are amongst the signature dishes – and so are the views. Expensive.

Le Riad Restaurant 7km along the Malabata road, amid the trees to the right. A pleasant lunchtime stop. Moderate.

Villa Joséphine 231 Rue de la Montagne, Sidi Masmoudi, Cap Malabata ☎039 33 45 35, ⓦwww .villajosephine-tanger.com. Former residence of Pasha el Glaoui (see p.456) and Walter Harris (see p.769) with fantastic Straits views from the outdoor terrace, and serving up some of the best French and Moroccan cuisine in Tangier. There are 11 opulent guest rooms, each with their own fireplace and balcony, starting from 2500dh per double. Expensive

Cafés

Like all Moroccan towns, Tangier has many cafés, each with its particular clientele and daily rhythm, some good for breakfast, others popular late morning or evening. There are also some excellent take-out **patisseries**, among which three in particular are rated by the cognoscenti: *Matisse* at Rue Allal Ben Abdallah (near *Hôtel Chellah*; map pp.104–105), which is the poshest; *Rahmouni*, at 35 Rue du Prince Moulay Abdallah (map p.112), which is the oldest; and the upstart *Traiteur al Mouatamid Bnou Abbad*, at 16 Rue al Mouatamid Ibn Abadd (map pp.104–105). All the following are shown on the Tangier City Centre map on p.112, unless otherwise stated.

Café Halfa Marshan; see map pp.104–105. This cliff-top café is the perfect late-afternoon locale to gaze across the Straits and write your postcards. For help finding it, see p.120.

Café Metropole 27 Bd Pasteur, next to the synagogue. This serves the best *café au lait* in town and pastries can be bought across the road at *Pâtisserie Le Petit Prince* and consumed at your table.

Café de Paris Place de France. Tangier's most famous café, from its conspiratorial past, is a little dull these days, though still an institution for expats.

Cristal Palace 5 Rue Mexique. A good place for breakfast, with various different breads, eggs, and toast with honey or jam on the menu, this rather classy café is decorated with mirrors featuring interior and exterior views of London's nineteenth-century Crystal Palace.

Porte 23 Rue Prince Moulay Abdallah. A very grand café-patisserie, set up by a Frenchwoman, Madame Porte, in the days of the International Zone. Just the spot for a pot of tea and a pastry if you're feeling refined.

Bars

Tangier's **bars** are much depleted from past glories and most of those that do survive have fallen into a not very interesting seediness. The better options are in or alongside the older hotels, supplemented in summer by the beach bars, which stay open till 1am or so (though take care in this area after dark). All these are shown on the Tangier City Centre map on p.112, unless otherwise stated.

Atlas Bar 30 Rue Prince Héritier, across the road from the *Hôtel Atlas*. Small and friendly tapas pub open nightly. Proudly boasts it opened for business in 1928.

Caid's Bar in the *Hôtel Minzah*, 85 Rue de la Liberté. Long the chi-chi place to meet – ritzy decor and very pricey drinks. Over the bar is a grand painting of Caid Harry Aubrey Maclean, former commander in chief of the sultan's army (see p.114).

Carrousel Bar 6 Rue Khalil Metrane, off Rue Prince Héritier. Comfortable British-run wine bar, which has been around since 1936.

Dean's Bar Rue d'Amérique du Sud. The closest bar to the Medina – a tiny shop-room that was once the haunt of people like Tennessee Williams, Francis Bacon and Ian Fleming. It is now frequented more or less exclusively by Moroccans although tourists are welcomed. For more on Dean himself, see p.114.

Hôtel Marco Polo Av Mohammed VI (formerly Av d'Espagne). The ground floor is popular with tourists, especially hard-drinking Scandinavians and Germans getting through its range of European beers.

Mondial 52 Av Mohammed VI (formerly Av des FAR), on the beach opposite the *Hôtel Solazur*; see map pp.104–105. New beachside bar with a separate entry from the adjoining nightclub. Tapas and sports TV with a not-so-intimidating feel for women travellers, though the drinks are expensive. Noon–midnight.

The Pub 4 Rue Sorolla. A British-themed pub, with hunting scenes on the walls and bar food but it's not quite the real thing. Daily 9pm–1am.

Tanger Inn 16 Rue Magellan, below the *Hôtel Muniria* (see p.109). One of Tangier's last surviving International Zone relics, with photos on the wall of Burroughs, Ginsberg and Kerouac while they were staying at the hotel above. Daily 9pm–2am, but liveliest Thurs, Fri and Sat nights.

Discos and clubs

The principal area for **discos** is a grid of streets off Place de France, in particular Rue Sanlucar (Zankat Moutanabi), Rue du Mexique and Rue du Prince Moulay Abdallah (off Boulevard Pasteur). Admission is usually 100dh, drinks are two or three times regular bar prices and take care if leaving late at night as the streets hereabouts are none too safe; the best idea is to tip the doorman 5dh to call you up a taxi.

All these venues are shown on the Tangier City Centre map on p.112, unless otherwise stated.

Borsalino 30 Rue du Prince Moulay Abdallah. A small and usually quite lively disco, with a mixed crowd, screened by the doorman.

Mondial 52 Av Mohammed VI (formerly Av des FAR), on the beach opposite the *Hôtel Solazur*; see map pp.104–105. Brand new player on the scene catering to a young, modern crowd of twenty-something Moroccans and weekender Europeans. Two resident DJs and regular guest DJs. Open nightly 11pm–5am.

Morocco Palace 13 Rue du Prince Moulay Abdallah. A clear winner among Tangier's night-spots, this strange, sometimes slightly manic place puts on traditional Moroccan music and dance (plus a couple of Egyptian belly-dancing sets) each night from around 9pm until 4am. Customers are predominantly Moroccan and expect – and get – a good show.

Radio Club 30 Rue du Prince Moulay Abdallah. Attractively sleazy club sometimes featuring Moroccan bands.

Regine Club Rue el Mansour Dahbi (opposite the Roxy Cinema); see map pp.104–105. Mainstream disco, larger and a little cheaper than most. Open from 10pm.

Scott's Rue el Moutanabi (Rue Sanlucar). Traditionally (though not exclusively) a gay disco, this is worth a look if only for its very particular choice of paintings – Berber boys in Highland military uniform. It's usually very quiet until after midnight.

Concerts and films

Music concerts – traditional and popular – are sporadic events in Tangier. The old Spanish bullring, out beyond the bus station in the Ville Nouvelle, has had a major refurbishment as an open-air concert hall, so it might be worth asking about events there. Cultural events are also hosted by the **Old American Legation** (see p.115) and the **Institut Français de Tangier**; the latter organizes the Tangier Music Festival (see Listings, p.126). You can pick up a programme for Institut Français events from Galerie Delacroix (see below).

One of only a few **cinemas** still operating in Tangier is the Cinéma Rif (ⓦ www.cinemathequedetanger.com), on the Grand Socco, which has been renovated and reborn thanks to the not-for-profit organization Cinémathèque de Tanger, the dream of Moroccan-born photographer and artist Yto Barrada. The cinema aims to become the focal point for cinema culture for all of north Africa. Currently there are weekly showings of new releases, documentaries and classics, and there are plans for free open-air showings in the Socco and live theatre in the future.

Up-to-date **information** on local events can be found in the weekly *Les Nouvelles du Nord*, available in cafés and hotel receptions on Friday or Saturday.

Galleries, shops and stalls

The **Galerie Delacroix**, 86 Rue de la Liberté (Tues–Sun 11am–1pm & 4–8pm), usually has an interesting exhibition on by contemporary artists. Two other **galleries** are also worth a look for work by local artists: the Lawrence Arnott Art Gallery, 68 Rue Omar Ibn Alhas, near *Hôtel Chellah* (Mon–Fri 10am–12.30pm & 4–7pm, Sat 10am–12.30pm), and the Volubilis Art Gallery, 6 Sidi Boukouja (in the kasbah, Tues–Sun 10.30am–1pm & 3.30–7pm), under the very friendly management of Mohamed and Karla Raiss el Fenni, who also manage the Volubilis Boutique below.

Many of the Tangier **market stalls and stores** are eminently avoidable, geared to selling tourist goods that wouldn't pass muster elsewhere. But a few are worthwhile, unique, or both; a half-hour preliminary browse at the more "fixed price" outlets on Boulevard Pasteur is useful for establishing roughly what you should pay for things.

There are fruit and vegetable stalls in a couple of central locations. One is the **Fondouk Market** at the bottom of the steps beyond the *Hôtel el Minzah* (see p.114). Another is the **Fes Market**, between Rue de Fes and Rue de Hollande in the Ville Nouvelle, where you can also buy groceries. **Beer and wine** is sold in supermarkets in the Ville Nouvelle. The **Sidi Bouabid Market** behind the police post on the Grand Socco sells mainly clothes and electronic goods, while there's a massive flea market (daily, but best on Sundays), out of town at **Casa Barata**, reached by shared grand taxi from the Grand Socco or bus #16 from the bus and train stations. For supermarkets see Listings on p.126.

Crafts and souvenirs

Bazaar Tindouf 64 Rue de la Liberté, opposite the *Hôtel el Minzah*. One of the better-quality junk-antique shops, with a good array of cushion-carpets and old postcards. Bargaining is difficult but essential.

Ensemble Artisanal Rue Belgique (left-hand side, going up from the Place de France). Modern Moroccan crafts are displayed in this small government-run store, as in other major cities. They are rarely the best or the cheapest available but prices are (more or less) fixed, so this can be a useful first call to get an idea of quality and costs before bargaining elsewhere. Open daily except Fri 9am–1pm & 3–7pm.

Marrakech la Rouge 50 Rue Siaghin. Large and not-too-pushy bazaar selling rugs, jewellery, pottery, antique weaponry and leather, wood and metal crafts. Open daily.

Parfumerie Madini 14 Rue Sebou, in the Medina, and at 12 Bd Pasteur, opposite the Belvedere. Madini makes inspired copies of brand-name perfumes from natural oils, which he sells at a fraction of the "real" price, as well as musk and traditional fragrances. Given a couple of days and a sample, he will reproduce any scent you like. Closed 1–4pm and Friday.

Rue Touahin first right off Rue Siaghin, entering the Medina from the Grand Socco. This line of jewellery stalls may turn up something appealing, though don't take silver, gold or most stones at face value: judge on aesthetics.

Volubilis Boutique 15 Place Petit Socco. A usually interesting mix of traditional Moroccan and Western fashion.

Listings

Airlines Royal Air Maroc, 1 Place de France ☏039 93 47 22. Air France ☏039 93 64 77; KLM ☏039 93 89 26 and Lufthansa ☏039 93 13 27 all have offices at 7 Rue du Mexique.

American Express c/o Voyages Schwartz, Hôtel Intercontinental, Park Brooks, Bd de Paris ☏039 93 60 28.

Banks Most are grouped along Bd Pasteur/Bd Mohammed V. BMCE has branches at 21 Bd Pasteur and in the Grand Socco, both with ATMs. SGMB also has a Grand Socco branch with ATM. WAFA Bank has a *bureau de change* at 22 Bd Pasteur, (Mon–Fri 8am–6pm, Sat 9am–1pm). WAFA also represents Western Union, as does the Post Office. Most banks in Tangier will cash traveller's cheques, a service not widely offered in many other parts of the country.

Books The long-established Librairie des Colonnes at 54 Bd Pasteur (Mon–Sat 9.30am–1pm & 4.30–7pm) has some good French books on Tangier and Morocco, and a small selection of English-language books.

Car rental Most of the big companies have offices along Bd Pasteur/Bd Mohammed V. Avis, 54 Bd Pasteur ☏039 93 46 46, ☏039 33 06 24; Budget, 7 Rue du Prince Moulay Abdallah ☏039 94 80 60, ☏039 33 62 28; Europcar, 87 Bd Mohammed V ☏039 94 19 38, ☏039 34 03 94; Hertz, 36 Bd Mohammed V ☏039 32 21 65, ☏039 94 58 30. Avis, Budget, Europcar and Hertz also have desks at the airport. A local agency, offering a more personal service, is Harris Rent-a-Car, 1 Rue Zerktouni, off Bd Mohammed V (☏039 94 21 58, ☏039 94 55 74).

Car repairs Most repairs can be undertaken – or arranged – by Garage Lafayette, 27 Rue Mohammed Abdou (☏039 93 28 87).

Consulates Spain, 85 Av Président Habib Bourghiba ☏039 93 70 00; Sweden, Immeuble Beethoven II, appt 80, third floor, Place Roudani ☏039 94 59 82; UK, Trafalgar House, 9 Rue Amerique du Sud ☏039 93 69 39 (Mon–Fri 8.30am–1pm; emergency number ☏061 16 43 35). There is no US consulate in Tangier (nearest US diplomatic representation is in Rabat).

Ferry companies You can buy ferry tickets from any travel agent (see opposite) and also from the ferry companies themselves: Comanav, 43 Av Abou Aala el Maari ☏039 94 04 88 (to Algeciras, Sète and sometimes Genoa); Comarit, Av des FAR, corner of Rue de Marseille ☏039 32 00 32 (to Algeciras and Sète); EuroFerrys, 31 Av de la Résistance ☏039 32 22 53 (to Algeciras); FRS, 18 Rue el Farabi ☏039 94 26 12 (to Algeciras, Tarifa and Gibraltar); IMTC, 2 Bd Pasteur ☏039 33 60 02 (to Algeciras); Limadet, 13 Rue Prince Moulay Abdallah ☏039 93 36 21 (to Algeciras); LME c/o Comarit (to Algeciras); Nautas, in the port ☏039 93 44 63 (to Algeciras); Trasmediterranea c/o Limadet (to Algeciras).

Festivals Tanjazz Festival features more than 100 international artists for a week every May; see ⓦwww.tanjazz.com. Les Nuits de la Méditerranée is a three-week festival in June and July, organized by the Institut Français de Tangier, and featuring music from Morocco and abroad. For further details, check the Institut's website at ⓦwww.iftanger.ma.

Golf Tangier Royal Golf Club, BP 41, Tangier ☏039 94 44 84, ☏039 94 54 50 (18 holes); and Cabo Negro Royal Golf, BP 696 G Tetouan ☏039 97 83 03, ☏039 97 83 05 (9 holes). A new eighteen-hole course in Asilah, with surrounding property development, should be open sometime during 2007.

Hammam The *Hôtel el Minzah*'s Wellness Centre is open to non residents. For 150dh you get a traditional wash and scrub from an attendant and can indulge yourself in steam and soap all day long.

Hospitals Clinique Assalam, 10 Av de la Paix (☏039 32 25 58), is regarded as the best private clinic in Tangier for medical emergencies. Also recommended is Clinique Bennis (☏039 34 07 47), on the Tangier–Tetouan road. The government-run Hospital Mohammed V (☏039 93 80 56) is on the road to the airport. For a private ambulance, call ☏039 95 40 40 or ☏039 94 69 76.

Internet access Cybercafé Adam, 4 Rue Ibn Rochd (off Bd Pasteur); Euronet, 5 Rue Ahmed Chaouki (off Bd Pasteur); Club Internet 3000, 27

Rue el Antaki (also sells computer accessories); ViaWeb, 48 Rue Allal ben Abdallah, in a téléboutique opposite the *Hôtel Chellah*.

Newspapers English-language newspapers are sold outside the post office, in various stores along Bd Pasteur or Av Mohammed VI (formerly Av d'Espagne), and by vendors around the *Café Paris*.

Pharmacies There are several English-speaking pharmacies in the Place de France (try the Pharmacie Pasteur, next door to the *Café Paris*, or the Pharmacie de Paris opposite) and along Bd Pasteur. A roster of all-night and weekend pharmacies is displayed in every *pharmacie* window. Pharmacists are happy to recommend local doctors.

Photographic equipment and developing Studio Flash, 79 Rue de la Liberté.

Police The Brigade Touristique has its HQ at the former train station by the port (☎039 93 11 29). There are smaller police stations at 22 Rue Mountanabi and on the Grand Socco, and a police post in the kasbah. Emergency ☎19.

Post The main PTT is at 33 Bd Mohammed V and has a *poste restante* service (Mon–Fri 8am–6pm & Sat 8am–noon).

Supermarkets There is a brand new Acima with a liquor outlet on Rue al Hariri (off Place des Nations) open daily 9am–9pm. Marjane Hypermarket, selling everything from groceries (including bacon) and alcohol to clothing and household goods, is on the edge of the city on the N1 road to the airport and Asilah.

Travel agencies There are many travel agents, particularly along the seafront, which handle ferry and flight bookings and most will advise on – and book – travel and hotels in Morocco. Two reliable agents are: Voyages Marco Polo, 72 Av Mohammed VI (formerly Av d'Espagne), by the *Hôtel Valencia* ☎039 93 43 45; and Koutoubia, 112 bis Av Mohammed VI (formerly Av d'Espagne) ☎039 93 55 40. American Express is represented by Voyages Schwartz, 54 Bd Pasteur ☎039 37 48 37, ℗039 93 01 59 (Mon–Fri 9am–5pm).

Moving on

Travelling on **into Morocco** from Tangier is simplest either by **train** (the lines run to Meknes–Fes–Oujda or to Rabat–Casablanca–Marrakesh; all trains stop at Asilah en route), or, if you are heading east to Tetouan, by **bus** or shared **grand taxi**. Leaving the country, **ferries** run to Algeciras, Gibraltar, Tarifa, Genoa (Italy) and Sète (France). Note that Tarifa is not an international port and therefore only accepts passengers holding EU passports.

By train

Tangier has a new train station, **Tanger Ville**, 2km east of town on the continuation of Boulevard Mohammed V, and only 300m or so off the eastern end of the beach. Services inside the station include an ATM, Budget car rental desk, small bookshop and a café. The best way to get to it is by petit taxi (15dh or so); it is also served by bus #16 from the bus station but not by any buses from the city centre. Alternatively, bus #13 from the port goes to Tangier's second station, **Tanger Morora**, 4km down the Tetouan road, which is served by all trains out of Tanger Ville.

The best train service from Tangier by far is the **night train to Marrakesh**, with very comfortable couchettes – a great way to arrive refreshed the next morning. There are also three trains a day to both Casablanca and Sidi Kacem, most of which connect with onward services to Marrakesh, or with trains to Meknes, Fes and Oujda (which also get one direct train a day). For further information on journey times see "Travel Details", p.169.

By bus and grand taxi

CTM long-distance buses leave from the port entrance (see map, p.105), including those for Tetouan and Chefchaouen. If you have missed their daily (noon) direct bus to Chefchaouen but still want to push on, an alternative is to go to Tetouan and then find a bus or grand taxi going to Chefchaouen. All other long-distance services start from the **gare routière**, 2km from the centre of town, by the large, modern Syrian Mosque (*Masjid Suri* – funded by a group of Syrian emigrés who made their fortune in real estate here in the 1970s). It's easiest to take a petit taxi (around 15dh on the meter) but if on foot, from the seafront, take Avenue Youssef Ben Tachfine, cross Boulevard Mohammed V and continue a further 400m to the *gare routière*. Useful departures include, again, Tetouan and Chefchaouen (the latter doesn't involve a change of bus, though you stop in Tetouan for twenty minutes; don't pay extra to hustlers there who might just suggest your ticket covers only a "reservation fare" for the Chefchaouen stage).

Grands taxis also mostly leave from the *gare routière*. Regular shared runs (ask for a *plassa*) are to Asilah, Tetouan and Fnideq. This last is a particularly scenic route, passing over Djebel Moussa, with vistas across the Straits to Algeciras and Gibraltar, and great views of Ceuta as you descend into Fnideq. Occasionally you may find a taxi direct to the Ceuta border, 2km beyond Fnideq. Shared grands taxis to Fnideq also depart from Rue du Portugal off Rue de la Plage at the southernmost corner of the Medina, as do those for Casablanca and Ksar es Seghir.

For destinations in the immediate **vicinity of Tangier**, you may need to charter a grand taxi at the rank on the Grand Socco, though it's possible to get to places like the Caves of Hercules or Cap Malabata by shared grand taxi or city bus (see p.108).

By ferry and hydrofoil

Although **ferries** often depart an hour or so late, you should **check in** at the port at least one hour before official sailing time to get through the chaos of official business. **Hydrofoil** departures, on the other hand, are usually on time.

At the ferry and hydrofoil terminal (Gare Maritime Ouest), you have to get an embarkation card and departure card from the *départ* desk of the ferry companies. These should be readily available – if not, you can get them from the ferry company offices located along the driveway at the terminal entrance/exit. Arrival and departure information is displayed on screens in the terminal building. Should your ferry or hydrofoil depart from terminals 1 or 2, present your cards, along with your passport, to the *Controle Police et Douane* (immigration and customs police) at the far end of the building. If you are departing from terminals 3, 4 or 5 you need to present yourself at a separate, smaller immigration and customs building located about 50m outside, alongside the port wall. Arrive later than an hour before official departure time and you may find the visa police have knocked off – which means waiting for the next ferry. There is a **café and restaurant** on the ground floor of the main terminal building.

Two **periods to avoid** the ferries from Tangier are the end of the **Easter week** (Semana Santa) holiday, and the **last week of August**, when the ferries can be full for days on end with Moroccan workers returning to northern Europe. If it's not possible to avoid travelling during this period, reservations are essential.

Details of **ferry and hydrofoil routes** are to be found in the "Basics" section of this book (see pp.32–33). **Tickets and timetables** can be obtained from any travel agent in Tangier or from the ferry company's agents (listed on p.33).

By air

Tangier's **airport** at Ibn Batouta (previously Boukhalef), is 15km west of the city (information ☎039 93 51 29). Some hotels will organize a transfer for you, otherwise the best way to reach the airport is by grand taxi from the Grand Socco (120dh is the standard rate, though you may need to bargain hard to get it). It's possible to get to the airport turn-off on the Asilah road on bus #9 from

Rue de Fes, but then it's a two-kilometre walk to the airport itself. The two bureaux de change at the airport claim to exchange dirham notes back to Euros and US dollars if you can show an original exchange receipt. A new airport terminal was being built at the time of writing so perhaps the solitary café will be joined by other eateries and shops in the near future. Currently all domestic flights from Tangier fly via Casablanca.

West of Tangier: the Caves of Hercules and around

The **Caves of Hercules** (Grottes d'Hercule) are something of a symbol for Tangier, with their strange sea window, shaped like a map of Africa. The name, like Hercules' legendary founding of Tangier, is purely fanciful, but the caves,

△ The Caves of Hercules

16km outside the city and above the "Atlantic Beach", make an attractive excursion, together with the minor Roman site of Cotta. If you feel like staying for a few days by the sea, the beach can be a pleasant base, too; outside of July and August only stray groups of visitors share the long surf beaches. Take care with currents, however, which can be very dangerous even near the shore.

Cap Spartel and the Caves

The most interesting route to the caves and Cap Spartel runs around and above the coast via the quarter known as La Montagne (see box, p.120). Follow this road for around 14km and you'll reach a short turn-off to the lighthouse at Africa's most north-westerly promontory, **Cap Spartel**, a dramatic and fertile point, known to the Greeks and Romans as the "Cape of the Vines". The lighthouse, which you can visit and sometimes, if the keeper is around, climb, was built in 1864 by Sultan Mohammed III, who then persuaded Britain, France, Italy and Spain to pay for its maintenance; they did, until Moroccan independence in 1956. There is a pleasant restaurant here (open summer only) with ocean views.

To the south of Cap Spartel begins the vast and wild "Atlantic Beach", known locally as **Robinson Plage**. It is broken only by a rocky spit – 5km from the Cape – and then rambles off for as far as you can see. On the spit are located the **Caves of Hercules**. Natural formations, occupied in prehistoric times, they are most striking for a man-made addition – thousands of disc-shaped erosions created by centuries of quarrying for millstones. There were still people cutting stones here for a living until the 1920s, but by that time their place was beginning to be taken by professional guides and discreet sex hustlers; it must have made an exotic brothel. Today, there's a standard admission charge of 5dh (9am–sunset), and you'll probably get some would-be guide attaching themselves to you in the hope of payment too. There are usually a few restaurants open surrounding the car park, serving grilled fish caught on the rocks below.

Ancient Cotta

Five minutes' walk past the caves, a track turns inland from the beach and leads you to the rather scant ruins of **Ancient Cotta**, a small Roman town, founded in the second century AD and occupied for two hundred years or so. Like Lixus to the south (see p.140), the town produced *garum* (a kind of fish sauce) for export. Parts of the factory, and of a temple and baths complex, can be made out, while nearby have been found the ruins of several Roman farms which cultivated olives for oil. Even before the Romans, and certainly afterwards, this was a well-populated and prosperous area.

The most remarkable feature, these days, is the modern factory plant you see just beyond the site, with its tall, thin red-and-white chimneys discharging hot air and flames. This is the point where the **Maghreb–Europe Gazodue pipeline**, carrying natural gas from Hassi Rimel in Algeria and across Morocco, goes under the Straits of Gibraltar to Spain and beyond. The 45km submarine section was a unique challenge, given that the strait has a rocky, mountainous seabed, and strong currents, often in three layers, with the top and bottom flowing in one direction, the middle in the opposite direction.

Practicalities

If you have your own **transport**, you can head out to the caves via La Montagne and make a round trip by continuing along the coast road, and then taking either the minor road through Jabila or the faster main road

(N1, formerly P2) back to Tangier. If you don't, it shouldn't cost you more than 100dh including waiting time to charter a **grand taxi** from the Grand Socco. Alternatively, the #2 **bus**, from St Andrew's Church by the Grand Socco, goes there on summer weekends only; at other times it stops at the nearby village of Jabila, a long walk from the caves – but you're better off alighting before then, at Ziyatin on the old airport road, from where there are connecting taxis to the caves. You can also get to Ziyatin on shared grands taxis from St Andrew's Church.

Close by the caves, on the same rocky spit, are two **hotels**: the *Hôtel Robinson* (☎039 33 81 52, @www.robinson-tanger.com; ❻), a pleasant old-established place with spacious bungalow-type rooms, large balconies and sea views; and the *Club Le Mirage* (☎039 33 33 32, @www.lemirage-tanger.com; ❽), an upmarket cliff-top complex of 27 bungalows with full facilities including swimming pool and satellite TV. The restaurant and piano bar are open to non-residents and is a very pleasant, albeit expensive, lunch stop if you are on a day's outing from Tangier. On the landward side of the hotels there is the **campsite**, *Camping Ashakar* (☎064 80 13 25), a pleasant, well-wooded site with showers, café, restaurant and small shop, but really only for those with transport.

East of Tangier: Cap Malabata and Ksar es Seghir

The best beaches in the immediate vicinity of Tangier are to be found at **Cap Malabata**, where much wealthy villa development has been taking place. Beyond here, **Ksar es Seghir** offers a pleasant day by the sea, or a stop on the recently resurfaced and much improved coast road to Ceuta, if you have your own transport to get there.

Cap Malabata and Villa Joséphine

The bay east of Tangier is flanked by a gritty strip of beach and a chain of elderly villas and new apartment blocks until you reach the "*complexe touristique*" of **Cap Malabata**, which has a couple of intermittently open hotels. Its buildings encompass the splendid turn-of-the-twentieth-century **Villa Joséphine** (also known as Villa Harris) and its gardens, built by the writer Walter Harris (see p.769) and given by him to the people of Tangier. Harris's wife decently cited his obsession with the garden (rather than his predilection for boys) in her case for divorce. The villa is now a top-end *maison d'hôte* (see p.123) and the whole estate is in impeccable condition, retaining the Mediterranean, Arab and African influences from its original owner. There is a restaurant and bar as well as an outdoor terrace with fantastic views of both the Straits of Gibraltar and Bay of Tangier and is worth a stop if you're passing through. It's open all year round.

You can get to Cap Malabata on bus #15 or #16, or by petit taxi. Between here and Ceuta, the only real development taking place is of the industrial kind. The Port Tanger Méditerranée is being constructed near the village of Dalia, 20km from Ceuta. The port is for commercial container ships only and, together with the road and rail network to accommodate the anticipated traffic, is a mammoth project considering the ruggedness of the terrain. The positive consequence for road users will be the proposed double-lane highway from Ceuta to Tangier.

Inspired by the success of the Gazodue pipeline (see opposite), and perhaps by the Channel Tunnel between Britain and France, Spain and Morocco agreed in 1996 to explore the possibility of building a rail tunnel between Cap Malabata and Punta Paloma in Spain – not the narrowest point on the Strait, but the shallowest, only 300m deep compared to 900m further east. Engineering tests are now under way, and a decision is expected in 2008, when construction will begin if the go-ahead is given.

Ksar es Seghir and Djebel Moussa

KSAR ES SEGHIR, halfway to Ceuta, makes a pleasant stop, and can be reached by shared grand taxi from Rue de Portugal in Tangier, or on any bus running between Tangier and Fnideq. The picturesque little fishing port attracts a fair number of Moroccan beach campers in summer, but few Europeans. The centre of town is the junction where the roads to Tangier, Tetouan and Fnideq all meet, and where grands taxis from Tangier will drop you. Just across the river from the junction lie the remains of a fort and associated buildings dating from Portuguese times (there's a plan of the site posted up by the west side of the bridge), and legend has it that Tariq Ibn Ziyad invaded Spain from here in 711. The *Café-Restaurant Diamant Bleu* (open summer only) has **rooms** overlooking the sea, and there's a campsite (also summer only) by the beach just east of the ruins. Otherwise, you may be able to rent rooms from local residents. More upmarket accommodation can be found 12km before the town at the *Hôtel Tarifa*. There are a few café-restaurants by the beach, but the best places in town to **eat** are the *Restaurant La Achiri* by the taxi station, *Restaurant el Ghoroub* just up the hill and the recently opened *Restaurant Borj Wad Ghalala* on the eastern edge of town overlooking the beach. Banque Populaire is the only **bank** in town and has an ATM.

From Ksar es Seghir the road to Fnideq climbs around the windy **Djebel Moussa** – the mountain that, with Gibraltar, forms the so-called Pillars of Hercules. According to legend, Hercules separated Europe from Africa with a blow of his sword during his fight with the giant Antaeus (see p.102), and seen from a plane Gibraltar and Djebel Moussa really do look like two pillars. They also produce remarkable thermal currents, speeding passage for **migratory birds** at this, the shortest crossing between Africa and Europe. A spring or autumn visit should ensure sightings, as up to two hundred species make their way across the Straits, as well as providing sightings of a new addition to the landscape of Djebel Moussa, a line of 35-metre-high wind machines producing electricity for the area.

Asilah and around

The first town south of Tangier – and first stop on the train line – **ASILAH** is one of the most elegant of the old Portuguese Atlantic ports, ranking with El Jadida and Essaouira to the south of Casablanca, and is small, easy to manage, and exceptionally clean. First impressions are of wonderful square stone ramparts, flanked by palms, and an outstanding beach – an immense sweep of sand stretching to the north halfway to Tangier. Further exploration reveals the Medina, which is one of the most attractive in the country, colourwashed at every turn, and with a series of murals painted for the town's **International Festival**. The first festival was in 1978 and it has been held most years since. It always takes place in August and runs for three to four weeks, with a programme usually including art, dance, film, music and poetry, attracting performers from around the world.

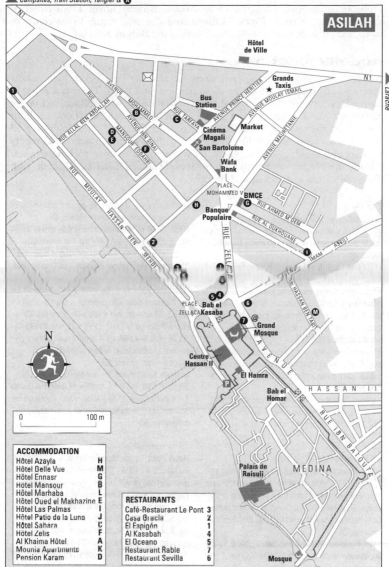

ASILAH

Hôtel de Ville

Grands Taxis
★ AVENUE MOULAY ISMAIL

Bus Station

Market

Cinéma Magali

San Bartolome

Wafa Bank

PLACE MOHAMMED V

BMCE

Banque Populaire

RUE AHMED M'DEM
RUE AL OUKHOUANE

PLACE ZELLACA **Bab el Kasaba**

@ Grand Mosque

Centre Hassan II

El Hamra

Bab el Homar

HASSAN II

Palais de Raisuli

MEDINA

Mosque

0   100 m

ACCOMMODATION

Hôtel Azayla	H
Hôtel Belle Vue	M
Hôtel Ennasr	G
Hôtel Mansour	B
Hôtel Marhaba	L
Hôtel Oued el Makhazine	E
Hôtel Las Palmas	I
Hôtel Patio de la Luna	J
Hôtel Sahara	C
Hôtel Zelis	F
Al Khaima Hôtel	A
Mounia Apartments	K
Pension Karam	D

RESTAURANTS

Café-Restaurant Le Pont	3
Casa Gracia	2
El Espigón	1
Al Kasabah	4
El Oceano	5
Restaurant Rable	7
Restaurant Sevilla	6

Arrival

The **train station** is 2km north of the town; there is occasionally a taxi to meet arrivals but don't count on it. It's an easy enough walk into town, so long as you're not weighed down with bags. **Buses** arrive at the *gare routière* on Avenue Prince Héritier, while coming from Tangier or Larache by **grand taxi**, you'll probably be dropped a block over on Avenue Moulay Ismail. From either of these, it's a short walk to **Place Mohammed V**, a small square in the centre of town, a short walk from the Medina's main gate, **Bab el Kasaba**.

Accommodation

Asilah can be packed during its festival but at other times, even high season, there's usually space in the dozen or so pensions and hotels. There is a string of **campsites** between the town and the train station, of which *Camping Echrigui* (℡039 41 71 82; open all year) is one of the closest and best. Located about 400m from the town, it is well maintained, with thatched "bungalows" as well as pitches for tents, and has hot showers, a small shop and a cafeteria. Camper-vans are also usually allowed to park for the night in an open parking area just outside the Medina wall at the end of Rue Moulay Hassan Ben Mehdi – tip the *gardien* 10dh and you should be right.

Cheap

Hôtel Belle Vue Rue Hassan Ben Tabit ℡ & ℻039 41 77 47. A well-located hotel with slightly bizarre decor, but reasonably priced, with clean, en-suite rooms. ❸

Hôtel Ennasr 3 Rue Ahmed M'dem (no phone). Basic with quite simple rooms around a courtyard; a last resort if everywhere else is full. ❷

Hôtel Marhaba 9 Rue Zellaca ℡039 41 71 44. A friendly place, close by the town gate, with small, simple rooms but good value for money. ❷

Hôtel Sahara 9 Rue Tarfaya ℡039 41 71 85. A little way from the action, behind the Cinéma Magali, and not all rooms have external windows, but it's quiet, clean and comfortable. Hot showers 5dh extra. ❷

Pension Karam 40 Rue Mansour Eddahbi ℡039 41 76 26. A small *pension* close to the seafront (and behind the prominent *Hôtel Oued el Makhazine*). ❹

Moderate

Hôtel Azayla 20 Rue Ibn Rochd ℡039 41 67 17, ℻039 41 76 00. The newest hotel in town and just a short stroll from the Medina or the beach. Good-value bright, clean rooms, and some extra large rooms with a sitting area. Breakfast included. ❺

Hôtel Mansour 49 Av Mohammed V ℡039 41 73 90, ⓦwww.hotelmansour.fr.fm. Has long been one of the better mid-range hotels in town, with immaculate rooms and an English-speaking owner who also runs a handy travel agency, Jaouharat el

Haram Voyages. There's a 25 percent discount after the second night. Breakfast included. ❺

Hôtel Oued el Makhazine Av Melilla ℡039 41 70 90, ℻039 41 75 00. A pleasant and comfortable hotel, it may not be the most exciting in town, but it's close to the seafront and has a swimming pool and bar. ❺

Hôtel Las Palmas 7 Rue Imam Assili ℡039 41 76 94. A decent hotel with cheerful, if slightly small rooms, all en suite and some with balconies. ❹

Hôtel Patio de la Luna 12 Rue Zellaca ℡039 41 60 74, ℻039 41 65 40. A small house, beautifully converted into a hotel, with a small patio and garden – very central. ❺

Mounia Apartments 14 Rue Moulay Hassan Ben Mehdi ℡039 41 78 15. A range of apartments with kitchenettes, next to *Restaurant Casa Garcia* on the promenade. The owner has other apartments elsewhere. ❺

Expensive

Hôtel Zelis 10 Rue Mansour Eddahbi ℡039 41 70 29, ℻039 41 70 98. Still one of the better hotels in town but can be a bit up and down. Bright, airy rooms, some with ocean views. Has a swimming pool, café and Internet. The restaurant, however, is not recommended. Breakfast included. ❻

Al Khaima Hôtel Route de Tanger, 1km north of town on the Tanger road ℡039 41 74 28, ℻039 41 75 66. This efficient, modern hotel is built around a pool and has always had very positive reports. It has a pleasant bar, open to all-comers, which can be a little noisy in high season. ❻

The Town

Before the tourists and the International Festival, Asilah was just a small fishing port, quietly stagnating after the indifference of Spanish colonial administration. Whitewashed and cleaned up, it now has a prosperous feeling to it: the Grand

Mosque, for example, has been rebuilt and doubled in size, there's a new paved seaside promenade and property developments, including a marina and golf course estate, are popping up either side of the town.

The ramparts and Medina

The Medina's circuit of **towers and ramparts** – built by the Portuguese military architect Botacca in the sixteenth century – are pleasant to wander around. They include two main gates: **Bab el Homar**, on Avenue Hassan II, and **Bab el Kasaba**. If you enter by the latter, you pass the **Grand Mosque** and the **Centre Hassan II des Rencontres Internationales**, a venue and accommodation centre for the festival, with a cool open courtyard.

Further on is a small square overlooked by the "red tower", **El Hamra**. This is used for exhibitions, particularly during the festival. Turn right past here, along a tiny network of streets, and down towards the platform overlooking the sea, and you'll come upon at least a half-dozen **murals** painted (and subsequently repainted) during the festivals; they form an intriguing mix of fantasy-representational art and geometric designs. In turn, these offset the whitewashed walls of the houses, with their doors and windows picked out in cool pastel shades. It's quite an entrancing quarter, as can be seen from the number of houses displaying "Not For Sale" signs.

Palais de Raisuli

The town's focal sight – stretching over the sea at the heart of the Medina – is the **Palais de Raisuli**, built in 1909 with forced tribal labour by one Er Raisuli, a local bandit. One of the strangest figures to emerge from what was a bizarre period of Moroccan government, he began his career as a cattle rustler, achieved notoriety with a series of kidnappings and ransoms (including the British writer Walter Harris and a Greek-American millionaire, Perdicaris, who was bailed out by Teddy Roosevelt), and was eventually appointed governor over practically all the tribes of northwest Morocco. Harris described his captivity in *Morocco That Was* as an "anxious time", made more so by being confined in a small room with a headless corpse. Despite this, captor and captive formed a friendship, Harris finding Raisuli a "mysterious personage, half-saint, half-blackguard", and often entertaining him later in Tangier.

Another British writer, Rosita Forbes, visited Raisuli at his palace in 1924, later writing his biography. She described the rooms, today mostly bare, as hung with rugs "of violent colours, embroidered with tinsel", their walls lined with cushions stuffed with small potatoes. The decoration seems logical enough – the palace today still looks more like a glittering Hollywood set than anything real. The great reception room, a long glass terrace above the sea, even has dialogue to match: Raisuli told Forbes that he made murderers walk to their death from its windows – a 27m drop to the rocks. One man, he said, had turned back to him, saying, "Thy justice is great, Sidi, but these stones are more merciful."

The palace overhangs the sea ramparts towards the far end of the Medina (away from the beach). It is not officially open to visitors but if you're interested – and the interior is worth seeing – knock or enlist the help of a local and you may strike lucky with the caretaker. If you are really determined you could visit the Hôtel de Ville (the town hall) beforehand and ask them to give you a note in Arabic for the caretaker.

The beaches and the harbour

As with Tangier, the **beach** is the main focus of life in summer. The most popular stretches are to the north of the town, out towards the campsites.

For more isolated strands, walk south, past the Medina ramparts, for about fifteen minutes.

For some years there have been plans to extend the small **harbour**, to provide anchorage for fishing boats and a marina for yachts. In 1995 there was even extensive advertising of the new facilities and adjoining apartment blocks, but a subsequent change of plan will now see separate provision for commercial and leisure craft. At the time of writing, though the sea walls are there, they are incomplete and the apartment block which had been built has been demolished.

Church of San Bartolome and around

At the junction of Avenue Mohammed V and Avenue Prince Héritier, is the **Church of San Bartolome**, built by Franciscan priests from Galicia, in northwest Spain. The cool and airy colonial-Spanish-style interior is complemented by the nuns' own small chapel in Moorish style, with prayers common to Islam and Christianity carved in Arabic. One of the few church bells allowed to be used in Morocco is rung for Mass at 11am on Sundays and the sisters, from a teaching order founded by Mary Ward in Yorkshire in 1585, train local girls in dressmaking, embroidery and literacy. Visitors are welcome at any time – ring the bell by the door alongside the church.

The **Hôtel de Ville** is inland on the Tangier–Rabat road as it bypasses Asilah. Nearby is a modern, massive **monument** commemorating the passage of Mohammed V on his way to Tangier in April 1947, when he identified himself with the struggle for Moroccan independence.

There's a villagers' **market**, at its liveliest on Thursday and Sunday, held on the near side of the Tangier–Rabat road.

Restaurants, cafés, discos and baths

The town's most prominent **restaurants** are *El Oceano* (also called *Casa Pepe*) and *Al Kasabah*, side by side in the Place Zellaca, just outside the ramparts. Both have outdoor tables and Spanish-style fish and seafood dishes. Further north along the seafront are *Casa Gracia*, *Café-Restaurant Le Pont* and *El Espigón*, again specializing in fish and seafood. In the town, the *Restaurant Sevilla*, near the *Hôtel Las Palmas* at 18 Av Imam Assili, serves generous helpings of Spanish-style dishes, and there is a string of small eateries, including *Restaurant Rabie,* on Avenue Hassan II opposite the Grand Mosque, with tables outside under the shade of large eucalyptus trees.

In summer, there are **discos** at the *Hôtel al Khaima* and at several of the campsites. **Internet access** is available on Avenue Hassan II opposite the al fresco eateries. Finally, ask directions to the town's small **hammam**, tucked down an alleyway in the north of the Medina. Unusually, the keeper charges Westerners a group rate and gives you the place to yourselves.

Mzoura

If you have an interest in ancient sites, you might devote a half-day to explore the prehistoric **stone circle of Mzoura**, south of Asilah. The site, whose name means "Holy Place" in Arabic, originally comprised a tumulus, assumed to be the tomb of some early Mauritanian king, enclosed by an elliptical circle of some 167 standing stones. It was excavated in 1935 and the mound is now reduced to a series of watery hollows. To the north of the circle, there still stands a tall, upright stone known as El Uted, where, legend has it, Sebastian, the young king of Portugal, lunched on his way from Asilah, where he had landed, to his death the following day at the cataclysmic Battle of the Three Kings near Ksar el Kebir. There are photographs of Mzoura, pre-excavation, in the archaeological museum in Tetouan.

To reach Mzoura, follow the N1 (formerly P2) south of Asilah for 16km, then turn left along the R417 (formerly P37) towards Tetouan. After crossing the railway line, and 4km from the junction with the N1, turn left by the Somepi petrol station and onto a side road signposted El Yamini (Tnine Sidi Lyamani). From here the site is 5km northeast, across a confusing network of sandy tracks; it's a good idea to enlist a guide at El Yamini.

Larache and around

LARACHE is a relaxed, easy-going town, its summer visitors primarily Moroccan tourists who come to enjoy the beaches to the north of the estuary of the River Loukos. You'll see as many women around as men – a reassuring feeling for women travellers looking for a low-key spot to bathe. Nearby, and accessible, are the ruins of **ancient Lixus**, legendary site of the Gardens of the Hesperides.

Physically, the town looks like an amalgam of Tangier and Tetouan; an attractive place, if not spectacularly so. It was the main port of the northern Spanish zone and, though the central Plaza de España has since become Place de la Liberation, it still bears much of its former stamp. There are faded old Spanish

RESTAURANTS & CAFÉS		ACCOMMODATION	
Balcon Atlantique	1	Hôtel Cervantes	A
Café Triana	B	Hotel España	B
Estrella del Mar	4	Hôtel Essalam	E
Restaurant Commercial	2	Hôtel Riad	F
Restaurant al Khozama	5	Pension Amal	D
Restaurant Larache	3	Pension Essalama	C

Ksar el Kebir (H1) ▼   ▼ Lixus & Asilah (H1)

hotels, Spanish-run restaurants and Spanish bars, even an active Spanish cathedral (Mass Sat 7pm, Sun 11am) for the small colony who still work at the docks. In its heyday it was quite a metropolis, publishing its own Spanish newspaper and journal, and drawing a cosmopolitan population that included the French writer Jean Genet, who spent the last decade of his life here and is buried in the old Spanish cemetery.

Before its colonization in 1911, Larache was a small trading port, its activities limited by dangerous offshore sand bars. Without these, it might have rivalled Tangier, for it is better positioned as a trade route to Fes. Instead, it eked out a living by building pirate ships made of wood from the nearby Forest of Mamora for the "Barbary Corsairs" of Salé and Rabat.

The town and beach

The town's circular main square, **Place de la Libération** (originally Plaza de España) is a striking piece of Spanish colonial architecture, set just back from the sea and a straightforward 400-metre walk from the bus station and grand taxi stand.

A high archway, **Bab el Khemis**, at the centre of the square leads into the **Medina**, a surprisingly compact wedge of alleys and stairways leading down towards the port. It is now the poorest area of Larache – better-off families have moved out to the new parts of town, leaving their houses here to the elderly – but it doesn't seem so bad a place to live, artfully shaded and airy in its design. The colonnaded market square, just inside the archway, was again built by the seventeenth-century Spanish.

If you carry on through the Medina, you can reach the small Place de Makhzen, below the **Château de la Cigogne** (Castle of the Stork), a hulking, three-sided fortress from the original Spanish occupation. Standing back from here, to the right, is a palace, built by the Spanish in 1915 and now used as a music school. Opposite, overlooking the Oued Loukos and across to Lixus, is a fine esplanade and a small **archeological museum** (daily except Mon 9am–noon & 3–6pm; 10dh), converted from a prison and containing a few Roman coins and other relics from Lixus.

The beach and coastline

If you walk from the Place de la Libération, directly to the seafront, you find yourself on another and longer promenade, Avenue Moulay Ismail. The shore below here is wild and rocky, but cross the estuary of the Oued Loukos and there are miles of fine sandy **beach** sheltered by trees and flanked by a handful of café-restaurants. You can get there by bus (#4 from the port, every 20min – some buses start from the square), a circuitous seven-kilometre route, or, more fun, from the port in a flotilla of small **fishing boats** (5–15dh per person depending on whether you haggle), which shuttle across leaving from the base of a flight of stone steps. From the square, the quickest route down to the **port** is along the promenade and under the crumbling ruins of the **Fort Kebibat** (Little Domes), built by Portuguese merchants in the sixteenth century.

In summer, an oddity on the beach is the variety of foreign languages you hear – yet with so few foreigners around. The explanation is the number of migrant families, scattered about Europe, who return to the town for their holidays. As well as being part of communities in Barcelona, Naples and Paris, people from Larache make up a big part of the Moroccan community in London, and on the beach you're likely to come upon kids with disarming English accents.

For an alternative walk, head southwest of the town, **along the cliffs** towards the jail and the **lighthouse**. Before you reach the jail, you will pass the neglected Spanish Christian cemetery where **Jean Genet** is buried; the gravestone, regularly whitewashed, is marked by a small handwritten card.

Larache also has a link with **Thor Heyerdahl** of Kon-Tiki expedition fame. Planning to cross the Atlantic in a vessel made of papyrus reeds, re-creating voyages believed to have been undertaken by ancient Egyptian mariners, Heyerdahl was intrigued to hear about similar craft being used in Larache. He visited the town in 1969 to find out more about the **reed boats**, known as *madia*, which he knew had been in use as recently as 1913 on the Oued Loukos. Anticipation turned to disappointment however, when local fishermen told him "You've come a generation too late. Here we can show you only boats of plastic." For more information on Heyerdahl's trip, see p.404.

Practicalities

Long-distance **buses**, including CTM, use the town bus station, just off Avenue Hassan II. There are a few **banks** around Place de la Libération with ATMs, but no tourist office.

Accommodation

Larache has some decent accommodation, but there's not a lot of choice. In summer, it's a good idea to book ahead. For caravans or campervans there's a free site, *Centre d'Acceuil* or *Aire de Repos* (☎039 52 10 69), on the N1 road towards Ksar el Kebir (the main road into town coming from the toll road) where you can park up (tip the *gardien* 20dh or so), with showers, toilets and a restaurant.

Hôtel Cervantes 3 Rue Tarik Ibnou Ziad, off Pl de la Libération ☎039 91 08 74. Don't be put off by the unappealing paintwork – this is a friendly little place, with comfortable enough rooms and shared hot showers. ❸

Hôtel España Pl de la Libération/entrance at 6 Av Hassan II ☎039 91 31 95, ☎039 91 56 28. *The Grand Hôtel* in Spanish days –now much decayed but retaining a touch of elegance. It has a range of rooms (with and without bathrooms) and prices. ❹

Hôtel Essalam 9 Av Hassan II ☎039 91 68 22, ☎039 91 68 22. One of our readers described this place as "the best budget hotel in Morocco", and we'd be hard-pressed to disagree: the rooms, some of which are en suite, are spacious and immaculate, with constant hot water and even a TV. ❸

Hôtel Riad Av Moulay Mohammed Ben Abdallah ☎039 91 26 26, ☎039 91 26 29. The former mansion of the Duchesse de Guise, mother of the current pretender to the French throne, and supposedly the best hotel in town, with gardens, tennis courts, swimming pool, a restaurant and café. It's getting rather shabby, though, and there's hot water mornings and evenings only. Breakfast included. ❻

Pension Amal 10 Rue Abdallah Ben Yasin ☎039 91 27 88. Basic, with simple but decent rooms, this is signposted – off to the left down an alleyway on the street from the bus station to Place de la Libération. Hot showers 6dh extra and there is a public shower in the same little side street. ❶

Pension Essalama 50 Av Moulay Mohammed Ben Abdallah ☎076 99 47 47. Welcoming, refurbished hotel – though the plumbing is a problem. Hot showers 10dh. ❶

Eating

Meals in Larache, except at the Medina cafés, or the **sardine grills** down by the port, remain resolutely Spanish. The cheapest **cafés** are in Place de la Libération around Bab el Khemis, the entrance archway of the Medina. The *Restaurant Commercial* here serves fine paella, fish and chicken tajine.

A little more upmarket, and worth trying for seafood, are *Restaurant Larache* at 18 Av Moulay Mohammed Ben Abdallah, and the *Estrella del Mar* at 68 Av Mohammed Zerktouni (the other end from Place de la Libération). Take a look, too, at the *Restaurant al Khozama* at 114 Av Mohammed V, in a pavillion between the PTT and the Château de la Cigogne.

Larache is well endowed with **tea rooms**, including the *Balcon Atlantique* overlooking the sea on Rue de Casablanca, which has pizzas, and the *Café Triana* next to the *Hôtel España*, which is good for breakfast.

Ancient Lixus

Ancient Lixus is one of the oldest – and most continuously – inhabited sites in Morocco. It had been settled in prehistoric times, long before the arrival of Phoenician colonists around 1000 BC, under whom it is thought to have become the first trading post of North Africa. Later, it was in turn an important Carthaginian and Roman city, and was deserted only in the fifth century AD, two hundred years after Diocletian had withdrawn the empire's patronage. There are remains of a church from this period, and Arabic coins have also been found.

As an archeological site, then, Lixus is certainly significant, and its legendary associations with Hercules (see box below), are rich soil for the imagination. The ruins lie upon and below the summit of a low hill on the far side of the Oued Loukos estuary, at the crossroads of the main Larache–Tangier road and the narrow lane to Larache beach. A track wends up to the amphitheatre area, where there are mosaics, which is worth climbing for the panoramic view alone. The ruins are interesting rather than impressive, and only around a quarter of the site has been excavated. Even so, if you're spending any amount of time in Larache, or passing through by car, the Lixus ruins are good for an hour or two's exploration.

It's a four- to five-kilometre walk to the ruins from either the beach or town, or you can use bus #6 which runs between the two or bus #5 from town; alternatively, for about 100dh you could charter one of the boats to row you over from Larache, wait an hour or so, and then row you back to the town or beach. The site is not effectively enclosed, so there are no real opening hours.

The site

A notice by the roadside at the entrance explains the site with a useful map board. The site's Lower Town, spreading back from the modern road, consists largely of the ruins of factories for the production of salt – still being panned nearby – and, as at Cotta, *garum* fish sauce. The factories seem to have been developed in the early years of the first century AD and they remained in operation until the Roman withdrawal.

Lixus and Hercules

The legendary associations of Lixus – and the site's mystique – centre on the Labours of Hercules. For here, on an island in the estuary, Pliny and Strabo record reports of the palace of the "Libyan" (by which they meant African) King Antaeus. Behind the palace stretched the Garden of the Hesperides, to which Hercules, as his penultimate labour, was dispatched.

In the object of Hercules' quest – the Golden Apples – it is not difficult to imagine the tangerines of northern Morocco, raised to legendary status by travellers' tales. The site, too, seems to offer reinforcement to conjectures of a mythic pre-Phoenician past. Megalithic stones have been found on the Acropolis – they may have been linked astronomically with those of Mzoura (see p.136) – and the site was known to the Phoenicians as Makom Shemesh (City of the Sun).

A track, some 100m down the road to Tangier, leads up to the Acropolis (upper town), passing on its way eight rows of the Roman **theatre** and **amphitheatre**, unusually combined into a single structure. Its deep, circular arena was adapted for circus games and the gladiatorial slaughter of animals. Morocco, which Herodotus knew as "the wild-beast country", was the major source for these Roman *venationes*, and local colonists must have grown rich from the trade. Until 1998, the **baths** built into the side of the theatre featured a remarkable **mosaic** depicting Neptune's head on the body of a lobster; unfortunately, the mosaic was irreparably damaged when the *gardien*'s son tried to dig it up to sell, and just about a third of it remains.

Climbing above the baths and theatre, you pass through ramparts to the main fortifications of the **Acropolis** – a somewhat confused network of walls and foundations – and **temple sanctuaries**, including an early **Christian basilica** and a number of **pre-Roman buildings**. The most considerable of the sanctuaries, with their underground cisterns and porticoed priests' quarters, were apparently rebuilt in the first century AD, but even then retained Phoenician elements in their design.

South from Larache

Heading south from Larache, the main road and most of the buses bypass **Ksar el Kebir** on their way towards Meknes, Fes or Kenitra/Rabat. You'll probably do likewise, though the town does have one of the largest weekly markets in the region (on Sundays). Just past here, you cross the old border between Spanish and French colonial zones. Beyond, Roman enthusiasts may want to explore the minor sites at **Banasa** and **Thamusidia**, while bird-watchers should head for the lagoon and local bathing resort of **Moulay Bousselham**.

Ksar el Kebir

As its name – in Arabic, "the Great Enclosure" – suggests, **KSAR EL KEBIR**, 36km southeast of Larache, was once a place of some importance. Founded in the eleventh century, it became an early Arab power base and was enlarged and endowed by both Almohads and Merenids, and perennially coveted by the Spanish and Portuguese of Asilah and Larache. It was about 12km north of here where, in August 1578, the Portuguese fought the disastrous **Battle of the Three Kings**, the most dramatic and devastating in their nation's history – a power struggle disguised as a crusade, which saw the death or capture of virtually the entire nobility. For the Moroccans, it resulted in the fortuitous accession to power of Ahmed el Mansour, the greatest of all Saadian sultans. The Portuguese were not so lucky: their sovereign's death in the battle left Spain's Felipe II as next-in-line to the throne, and Portugal fell under Spanish rule for 62 years before it was able to break free.

The town fell into decline in the seventeenth century, after a local chief incurred the wrath of Moulay Ismail, causing him to destroy the walls. Neglect followed, although its fortunes revived to some extent under the Spanish protectorate, when it served as a major barracks.

The **Sunday souk** is held right by the *gare routière* and Moulay el Mehdi station. On any morning of the week, however, there are lively **souks** around the main **kissaria** (covered market) of the old town – in the quarter known as Bab el Oued (Gate of the River). There is also an active **tannery** on the south side of the Medina and a handful of minor Islamic monuments scattered about. It doesn't amount to much, but if you've time to spare you might get a local to show you around – especially the souks.

Practicalities

The easiest way to get to Ksar el Kebir is by train, but for the town centre get off at Moulay el Mehdi station, one stop south of Ksar el Kebir station, which is way out on the northern edge of town. As the motorway bypasses the town, few long-distance buses come here, though cheaper bus companies still pass through (stopping at the *gare routière* just opposite Moulay el Mehdi train station); grands taxis from Larache operate to and from a station just across the tracks from the *gare routière*, and those from Ouezzane and Souk el Arba du Rharb operate from one 500m further south.

Hôtel Ksar al Yamama, 8 Bd Hassan II (℡039 90 79 60, ℻039 90 38 38; ❷), is good value, with nice, large, airy rooms, some en suite with a tub, and some with balconies overlooking a town square. There's also a *salon de thé* downstairs. To get to it, head south from the Moulay el Mehdi station and turn right after 300m. There's a trio of cheaper and more basic hotels just across the square on Boulevard Mohammed V. For **meals**, there isn't much, but try *Restaurant La Vie*, opposite *Hôtel Ksar al Yamama*.

Arbaoua and Souk el Arba du Rharb

Beyond Ksar el Kebir, a decaying customs post at **ARBAOUA** marks the old colonial frontier between the Spanish and French zones. There is a row of worthwhile **pottery stalls** at the border post, while the village itself is 4km south and then 1.5km west from the main road, with accommodation at the *Hostellerie Route de France* (no phone; ❸).

South again, **SOUK EL ARBA DU RHARB** is the first settlement of any size, though it is little more than its name suggests (Wednesday Market of the Plain), a roadside sprawl of market stalls, with some grill-cafés and a few **hotels**, the best of which is the *Gharb Hôtel* (℡065 04 35 11; ❷). The *Hôtel Adil* opposite (℡037 90 22 87; ❷) is cheaper but more basic, and less than 100m north is the *Grand Hôtel* (℡037 90 20 20; ❷), with a popular bar on the ground floor. The town is not a very compelling place to stay, though it is a minor transport interchange point, with buses passing through (if avoiding the motorway tolls) between Tangier or Tetouan and Rabat or Meknes. Grands taxis from here reach Rabat, Meknes and Fes as well as Ksar el Kebir and Moulay Bousselham (to which regular grands taxis take 30min; local buses, if they stop at all villages en route, up to two hours). There's a BMCE **bank** with ATM by the *Grand Hôtel*.

From Souk el Arba Du Rharb you can visit **Basra**, the summer retreat of Idriss II, son and successor of the sultan who created Fes. To get there, head north on the N1 towards Ksar el Kebir, turning right after 9km on the R408 towards Ouezzane, and, after another 12km, you arrive at a village with the ruins of Basra standing on hills above it. The tenth-century walls were demolished in the sixteenth century, but can still be traced, along with the town gates. Now it's a pleasant viewpoint and a great place for a picnic.

Moulay Bousselham

MOULAY BOUSSELHAM, 55km from Ksar el Kebir, is a very low-key resort, popular almost exclusively with Moroccans. It comprises little more than a single street, crowded with grill-cafés and sloping down to the sea at the side

Wetland wildlife

Adjoining the Moulay Bousselham lagoon is a large wetland area – recently given protected wildlife status – known as **Merdja Zerga** ("Blue Lake"). This open barren space is used for grazing by nomadic herds of sheep, cattle and goats, while around the periphery are lines of dwarf palm and the giant succulent agave.

This diversity of habitat, and the huge extent of the site, ensures rewarding **birdwatching** at all times of year. There are large numbers of waders, including a large colony of flamingos, plus little ringed plovers, black-winged stilts and black-tailed godwits. These can be seen most easily by taking a boat trip – though at 150dh an hour this can be expensive, and make sure that you arrange to set off at least an hour before high tide or you will run aground a tantalizing distance from the birds.

For serious bird-watchers, it is the **gulls and terns** that roost on the central islands which are worthy of the closest inspection, as, among the flocks of lesser black-backed gull and black tern, it is possible to find rarer species such as **Caspian tern**. However, the campsite at Moulay Bousselham is probably the best place in Morocco to see pairs of North African **marsh owl** which usually appear hunting over the adjacent grassland ten to fifteen minutes after sunset, and the same vantage point is also a good spot for seeing **Barbary partridge**. One bird you'll certainly see wintering here, usually around cattle (and sometimes sitting on their backs), is the **cattle egret**.

The Café Milano in Moulay Bousselham keeps a bird log and will put you in touch with a local bird guide if you wish. For rarity-spotters, the grail is the **slender-billed curlew**, an endangered species, spotted once or twice in recent years; it is smaller than the European curlew with distinct spade-like markings on its flanks.

of a broad lagoon and wetland area, known as **Merdja Zerga**. This is one of northern Morocco's prime **bird-watching** locations (see box above), and any foreign visitor will be accosted by the growing number of resident guides to see the lagoon's flamingo and other bird colonies in one of the locals' fishing boats. The **beach** itself is sheltered by cliffs – rare along the Atlantic – and has an abrupt drop-off, which creates a continual crash of breaking waves. While a lot of fun for swimming, the currents can be highly dangerous and the beach is strictly patrolled by lifeguards. Take care.

For Moroccans, the village is part summer resort, part pilgrimage centre. The saint from whom the village takes its name, the **Marabout Moulay Bousselham**, was a tenth-century Egyptian, whose remains are housed in a *koubba* prominently positioned above the settlement. In July this sees one of the largest **moussems** in the region.

Practicalities

Moulay Bousselham has two **campsites**: the ageing *Camping Caravanning International* (☎037 77 72 36), 500m east of town on the lagoon and consequently plagued by mosquitoes; and the nearby curiously named *Flamants Loisirs*, or "spare flamingos" (☎037 43 25 39) which is in slightly better condition but open in summer only. **Accommodation** includes the *Villa Nora* (☎037 43 20 71; ❺), a family-run villa on the coast road at the northern end of town, about 1.5km from the centre. Overlooking the beach and the Atlantic rollers, it's an attractive place, with an English owner, Jean Oliver, who is knowledgeable on local birdlife and in summer exhibits works of Moroccan art. Down by the lagoon is ⚜ *La Maison des Oiseaux*, "the house of the birds" (☎061 30 10 67, ☎037 43 25 43; ❺), a whitewashed villa run by a Moroccan/French couple, with a choice of rooms including some family suites that sleep up to four adults. They also organize week-long themed courses such as cooking, painting and yoga. On the town's main road and with fantastic views over the lagoon is the new *Hôtel Le Lagoon* (☎037 43 26 50, ℻037 43 26 49; ❺) with comfortable rooms and a restaurant. The *Hôtel Mirimar* (no phone; ❷), in the middle of town and overlooking the beach, has very basic rooms with separate showers and toilets at the back of a busy café.

Most of the **grill-cafés** will fix you a mixed platter of fish – served in copious amounts and at very reasonable prices. For **restaurants**, *Firdaous, Normandie* and *Restaurant Milano*, all on the main street, are good bets. The *Milano* is a good place to contact local ornithologist Hassan Dalil (☎068 43 41 10), who comes highly recommended as a guide to the area and its birdlife.

Moulay Bousselham has a **post office** (east of town on the Souk el Arba road), branches of the **banks** Banque de Populaire and Credit Agricolè, the latter with an ATM, and a **téléboutique**.

Banasa and Thamusida

This pair of minor Roman sites is really of specialist interest only – and for those with transport. **Banasa** lies south of Souk el Arba du Rharb, and **Thamusida** just west of the main N1 road to Kenitra.

Banasa

BANASA was settled from around 250 BC, but later enlarged by Octavian (the future Emperor Augustus) as a colony for veterans. It was linked by both land and water with Lixus (see p.140) and prospered into the second and third centuries AD, the period from which most of the visible ruins date. Within the traces of the city walls, the central feature is a forum, around which stood the capitol, a basilica (or law courts) and municipal buildings. In the town, among the houses and shops, were two public baths.

The custodian, who lives nearby, will probably notice your arrival and add a little life to the stones. He can point out a few mosaics, though most, he claims, have been removed to museums.

The site is easy to find. Leave Souk el Arba by the main road (N1) to Kenitra, then, just after Souk Tleta, turn left onto a minor road, crossing the Oued Sebou by a bridge. After 2km you reach a T-junction: turn left and, after another 2km, look for a track on the left (better signposted coming the other way, from Mechra Ben Ksiri). This leads to the ruins, which are overlooked by a marabout dedicated to Sidi Ali Boujnoun.

Thamusida

THAMUSIDA is more or less contemporary with Banasa, some 45km to the north. A Roman camp and small town, it was occupied from around 200 BC, fortified fifty years later, and abandoned by 250 AD, after fire damage. You can trace the walls of the camp and barracks, and make out a temple and baths, though the site as a whole is less extensive – and less interesting – than Banasa; its setting, however, closer to the Oued Sebou, is impressive.

There are several possible approaches to the site, which is quite tricky to find, and it's probably best to ask the help of a local. If you enquire at **Sidi Aïche** on the main road (N1), someone will be able to direct you.

Near the site there is a prominent *koubba*, dedicated to Sidi Ali Ben Ahmed, and a favourite picnic spot for locals. The site lies between this *koubba* and the river.

Ceuta (Sebta)

A Spanish enclave since the sixteenth century, **CEUTA** (Sebta in Arabic) is a curious political anomaly. Along with Melilla, east along the coast, it was retained by Spain after Moroccan independence in 1956 and today functions largely as a military base, its economy bolstered by a limited duty-free status. It has been an autonomous city, with a large measure of internal self-government for its 80,000 inhabitants, since 1995. The Spanish government apparently sees no irony whatsoever in its occupation of Ceuta, while objecting to Britain's occupation of Gibraltar, clearly visible just across the straits. Even if they wanted to, the Spanish would find it hard politically to return Ceuta to Morocco, and in reality, nobody is much interested in their so doing. Stand-offs over sovereignty do occur, however. In July 2002, a dozen Moroccan border guards in a rowing boat attempted to reclaim an uninhabited islet, **Parsley Island** (Isla de Perejil, known in Arabic as Leila), which lies just 200m off the Moroccan coast to the west of the Ceuta border. Parsley is considered by Spain to be part of its territory, though its only residents seem to be Moroccan goats. Amid much bluster on the part of Spain and Morocco, and general amusement from the rest of the world, Spain's deputy prime minister called the invasion "an act of hostility", and Spanish forces reoccupied it a few days later. The confrontation and flag-waving no doubt roused support for nationalist politicians in both countries, but Ceuta's position was never really under serious challenge: large numbers of Moroccans live and/or work in Ceuta; the local police and taxi drivers are fluent in both Spanish and Arabic, with both euros and dirhams accepted in many shops and restaurants, (though dirhams can't be used on buses, so when travelling into Ceuta from the frontier you need €0.62, or €0.67 on Sundays).

Border trade: people and drugs

Until recently, the economies on both sides of the border seemed to benefit from the enclave, spurred by Ceuta's duty-free status, but there has been growing political friction of late, aggravated by Spain's membership of the European Union (EU). The border here is the frontier between Africa and Europe and the EU is increasingly concerned about traffic in drugs and illegal immigrants, financing a £15m ($22m) hi-tech "wall" with closed circuit TV and sensors along the eight-kilometre boundary.

The money to be made from outflanking these defences has attracted equally hi-tech smugglers, trading in hash, hard drugs, disadvantaged Moroccans, and refugees from as far south as Liberia and Rwanda. The more affluent refugees are sent over to Spain nightly, often in small boats unsuited to the short but difficult crossing. The more desperate try to swim across to Ceuta from Fnideq's beach or scale the six-metre high border fence. During one week in October 2005 at least 500 people, almost exclusively of sub-Saharan nationality, tried to scale the fence in an organized "assault" during which at least five died from aggressive action taken by both Moroccan and Spanish border guards. Human rights groups have been pushing for public investigations into these deaths and the subsequent mass deportation of hundreds of immigrants to Morocco's desert regions near the borders of Algeria and Mauritania.

The Moroccan government, keen to gain some form of member status in the EU itself, has made efforts to stamp out the trade in both people and drugs. In the past few years, numbers of customs and police officers have been arrested and jailed. The trade, however, continues little affected.

▲ Algeciras

CEUTA

ACCOMMODATION
Hostal Real   G
Hôtel Atalaya   A
Hôtel Tryp   C
Gran Hotel Ulises   F
Parador de Ceuta   B
Pensión la Bohemia   D
Pensión Charito   E

RESTAURANTS & CAFÉS
La Campana   6
China Town   1
Club Nautico   2
Gran Muralla   4
Hollywood Café   5
Restaurante Marina   3

Monte Acho ▶

Note that Ceuta works to Spanish time, which is one hour (in winter) and two hours (in summer) ahead of Morocco. When **phoning Ceuta** from Morocco (or anywhere else outside Spain), you must prefix phone numbers with the international code (℡00 34). Dialling numbers within Ceuta you must include the old local code 956 as part of the new nine-digit number. To **phone Morocco from Ceuta**, you need to dial ℡00 212, followed by the local code (minus the initial zero) and number.

The Town

Ceuta has a long and eventful history, with occupation by Phoenicians, Romans, Visigoths and Byzantines, prior to the Moors, who from the eighth century onwards used it as a springboard for invasions of Andalusia. The Europeans only regained pre-eminence in the fifteenth century, with Portugal first taking control, and ownership passing to Spain in 1580. In 1936, the port and airstrip were used by General Franco to launch his invasion of the Iberian peninsula at the beginning of the Spanish Civil War.

All of this notwithstanding, there's not a great deal to see – or do. The town is modern, functional and provincial in the lacklustre Spanish manner, and its most attractive part is within several hundred metres of the new ferry dock, where the **Plaza de Africa** is flanked by a pair of Baroque churches, **Nuestra Señora de Africa** (Our Lady of Africa – open most days) and the **cathedral** (usually locked). Bordering the square, to the west, are the most impressive remainders of the city walls – the walled moat of **Foso de San Felipe** and the adjacent **Muralla Real**, (daily 10am–2pm & 4–8pm; free). The oldest fortifications here were built by the Byzantines, but additions were made under Portuguese and Spanish rule in the sixteenth, seventeenth and eighteenth centuries. Notice the artillery emplacements are at different heights, enabling cannons to fire over each other and engage attackers at various distances.

Crossing the border at Ceuta

Since the Algeciras–Ceuta ferries and hydrofoils are quicker than those to Tangier (and the ferries significantly cheaper for cars or motorbikes), Ceuta is a popular **point of entry and exit**. Coming over on a first visit to Morocco, however, try to arrive early in the day so that you have plenty of time to move on to Tetouan – and possibly beyond. There is no customs/passport check at the port as you don't officially enter Morocco until the border, 3km out of town. This can be reached by local bus #7 from the centre of Ceuta (turn left as you come off the ferry or hydrofoil and it is about 800m away, in Plaza de la Constitución). Coming from the Moroccan side, most buses and grands taxis drop you off in **Fnideq**, 2km short of the border (see p.159). If so, just head down to the coastal highway, where you can pick up a grand taxi to the border post for 5dh or you can simply walk.

At the border, formalities are brief on the **Spanish side** – at least, if you are leaving Spain: searches are common for those coming back, and there are often tailbacks of cars on Sunday evenings, though the main customs check (complete with dogs and X-ray machines) is across the Straits at Algeciras. On the **Moroccan side**, the procedure can be time-consuming, especially for drivers. You need a registration form (yellow or photocopied white) for yourself, and, if you have a car, an additional green form; these are available – if you ask for them – from the security *chefs* outside the frontier post. The car form requires inconvenient details such as chassis number and date of registration. If you despair of getting a form and having it processed, you can always enlist an official porter (they have badges – ask to see it) for a 10dh tip; try and avoid unofficial touts (and ignore touts trying to charge you for immigration forms, which are free). The whole business can take ten minutes on a good day, an hour or two on a bad one, and the noise and chaos can be a bit unsettling. Just try to keep a steady head and if you are in doubt as to where and what you should do, ask one of the (sometimes over-stressed) officials for assistance or directions.

Once across and into Morocco proper, you can take a shared **grand taxi** to Fnideq, 2km away (5dh per place), where you'll find connecting services to **Tetouan** (15dh) or **Tangier** (30dh); buses also run from Fnideq to both towns. More recently there also seem to be direct grands taxis from the border post but expect to pay considerably more for the convenience (100dh to Tangier, for example). Coming into Ceuta, local bus #7 departs directly from the border post (€0.62 or €0.67 on Sundays) as do metered taxis (€2.90 to the town centre).

On the Moroccan side of the border there are branches of BMCE and Banque Populaire, which accept cash and travellers' cheques, and on the Spanish side there are a couple of travel agencies that will change Moroccan dirhams for you.

Drivers should note that **petrol** in Ceuta is about forty percent cheaper than in mainland Spain, so stock up as best you can. It is tempting to fill up spare tanks too, but be aware that Spanish customs officers at Algeciras could sting you for duty if you do.

To the east of Plaza de la Constitución, an oldish quarter rambles up from the bottom of the long **Paseo del Revellin**. There's an interesting little municipal museum here, the **Museo de Ceuta** (June–Aug Mon–Fri 10am–2pm & 6–9pm, Sat 10am–2pm; Sept–May Mon–Fri 10am–2pm & 5–8pm, Sat 10am–2pm; free), displaying archeological finds from Stone Age and Roman times through to the Islamic era, well laid out and with good explanations, but in Spanish only. To the south of here, the **Museo de la Legión** (Mon–Sat 10am–1.30pm; free), on the Paseo de Colón, offers a glimpse of Spanish–African military history, crammed with uniforms, weapons and paraphernalia of the infamous Spanish Foreign Legion.

From the museum, if you have a couple of hours to spare, you can continue along a round circuit of the peninsula by heading east on Recinto Sur. As the buildings, three to a dozen blocks in width, gradually disappear from view, the land swells into a rounded, pine-covered slope, known as **Monte Acho**, crowned by a Byantine-era fort offering fine views out to the Rock of Gibraltar. Around midway, signs direct you to the **Ermita de San Antonio**, an old convent rebuilt during the 1960s and dominated by a monument to Franco. At the very eastern end of the peninsula is another military museum, the **Museo del Desnarigado**, (Sat & Sun 11am–2pm & 4–6pm; free), housed in a fort that is mainly nineteenth-century though with remnants from the sixteenth and seventeenth centuries.

Other Ceuta attractions include a **town beach**, 1km southwest of the moat, and a seafront leisure and amusement complex, the Parque Maritime del Mediterráneo (daily 11am–8pm; closed Thurs in winter; €5, children €3), complete with swimming pools and a casino.

The duty-free status of the port draws many Tangier expats on day-trips to buy cheap spirits, and Spanish day-trippers to buy radios and cameras, but these aren't very compelling pursuits for casual visitors. If you want a cheap bottle, stop at either of the Supersol or Aliprox supermarkets just outside the ferry terminal on Avenida Muelle Cañonero Dato.

Practicalities

There are two **tourist information kiosks** in Ceuta: the main one on Avenida Alcalde Sanchez Prado at Plaza de la Constitución (daily 8am–9pm in theory, but often closed; ℡956 52 81 46 or 47, ⓦwww.turiceuta.com), and another in a box-like building on Avenida Cañonero Dato coming into town from the ferry terminal (same hours, but even more frequently closed; ℡956 50 14 10), plus a better than average desk in the ferry terminal itself. You can get more reliable information at the excellent Flandria **travel agency**, at Calle de la Independéncia 1 (Mon–Sat 9am–2pm & 4.30–8.30pm; ℡956 51 20 74), which also sells ferry tickets. **Shipping companies** represented at the ferry terminal include Acciona Trasmediterránea (℡956 52 22 15), Balearia Nautus (℡956 20 51 90), Buquebus (℡956 50 11 13) and Euroferrys (℡956 52 15 29). The Spanish train company RENFE is also represented in Ceuta, at 11 Plaza Rafael Gilbert (℡956 51 13 17).

Accommodation

If you plan to stay overnight in Ceuta, book ahead; with its large garrison and its consumer goods, the town has a constant flow of Spanish families. Accommodation problems are compounded at **festival times**, the main events being Carnival (February), Holy Week, the Fiesta de Nuestra Señora de Monte Carmel (July 16), and the Fiesta de Nuestra Señora de Africa on August 5.

Most of the dozen or so hotels and *hostales*, and cheaper *pensiones*, *casas de huespedes* and *fondas* are to be found along the main thoroughfare, Paseo del Revellín, or its extensions, Calle Camoens and Calle Real. Some of the cheaper places are easy to miss, distinguished only by their blue and white signs (H for *Hostal*; P for *Pension*; CH for *Casa de Huespedes*; F for *Fonda*). There is at present no town **campsite** – ignore signs for *Camping Marguerita*, which has been closed for some time; the nearest campsite is over the border and 15km south at Alfrata.

Hostal Real c/Real 1, third floor ☎ & ⓕ 956 51 14 49. A pleasant, comfortable little *pension*, a cut above the usual, though most rooms lack outside windows. €33

Hotel Atalaya (*Hotel-Residencia Skol*) Avda Reyes Catolicos 6 ☎ 956 50 41 61. A quiet two-star hotel on the way into town from the border, on bus route #7. All rooms are en suite. €47

Hotel Tryp Gran Via 2 ☎ 956 51 12 00, ⓦ www .solmelia.com. A new four-star hotel with a gleaming white atrium and quite luxurious rooms. €90 midweek, with special offers at weekends.

Gran Hotel Ulises c/Camoens 5 ☎ 956 51 45 40 ⓦ www.hotelceuta.com. A recently refurbished and respectable four-star business hotel on a pedestrian mall. Breakfast included. €85

Parador de Ceuta (*Gran Hôtel La Muralla*) Pl de Africa 15 ☎ 956 51 49 40, ⓦ www.parador.es. Ceuta's characterful old *parador* remains the prime choice if you can afford it. €110

Pensión la Bohemia Paseo del Revellín 12, first floor ☎ 956 51 06 15. Best deal among the cheapies, clean and comfortable though most rooms lack outside windows. €30

Pensión Charito c/Arrabal 5 ☎ 956 51 39 82. One of the best and most welcoming among a number of small, cheap lodgings in this area (ask to be directed elsewhere if it is full). Located above *Límite* bar and café. Cold showers. €66

Eating and drinking

Ceuta's main concentration of restaurants is around the Plaza de la Constitución.

La Campana c/Real 13 ☎ 956 51 80 05. A smoke-filled bar café with a reasonable €6 set menu (though no choice for non-pork eaters), plus tapas, spaghetti, sandwiches, beer and wine from the barrel. The hilariously grumpy service makes it worth the visit alone. It also has a great patisserie next door. Cheap.

China Town Marina Club ☎ 956 50 90 53. A cheerful and busy Chinese restaurant by the ferry terminal. Cheap to moderate.

Club Nautico c/Edrissis ☎ 956 51 44 00. A small fish restaurant, just off Paseo de las Palmeras and overlooking the fishing harbour within the town's boat club. Open Mon–Sat 9am–3pm & 5pm–midnight, Sun 10am–3pm. Moderate.

Gran Muralla Plaza de la Constitución 4 ☎ 956 51 76 25. A popular, long-established Chinese restaurant with extensive menu and sweeping views over the harbour, located up the steps from the square. Moderate.

Hollywood Café c/Padilla 4 ☎ 956 51 08 95. Very friendly, family-run café with toasted sandwiches, paella and other Spanish dishes. Daily 10am–9pm. Cheap.

Restaurante Marina c/Alferez Bayton, between the Paseo del Revellín and Paseo de la Marina Española. Good place for coffee and *tostadas* to start the day, or for full meals later on. Moderate to expensive, with a €7 set menu. Closed Tues.

Moving on

Leaving Ceuta **by ferry** for Algeciras, you can normally turn up at the port, buy tickets, and board a ferry within a couple of hours, though you can only travel with the company from which you have purchased your tickets. The two periods to avoid, as at Tangier, are the end of the **Easter week** (Semana Santa) holiday and the **last week of August**, when the ferries can be full for days on end with Moroccan workers and their families returning to northern Europe.

If you plan to use the quicker **hydrofoil service** to Algeciras, it's best to book the previous day – though you should be fine outside the high season; details and tickets are available from the agents in town, from desks in the ferry terminal, or from an office nearby at Muelle Cañonero Dato 6 (☎956 51 60 41).

Services inside the ferry terminal include an ATM, tourist information desk, numerous travel agencies and a couple of café-bars.

For details of ferry services, see p.32. Be aware that all arrivals from Ceuta need to go through customs at Algeciras, where searches of suspected drug-runners can be extremely thorough.

Tetouan

If you are new to Morocco, coming from Ceuta, **TETOUAN** will be your first experience of a Moroccan city with its crowded streets and noisy souks. The Medina here seems – initially – overwhelming and totally unfamiliar, and there may be some hustlers. On the positive side, the city boasts a new university, albeit based at Martil, 11km to the east, on the coast, so young people you meet may well be genuine students. Nonetheless, you do need to keep your wits about you for the first few hours, especially arriving with full baggage at the bus station, where pickpockets and con men await.

Approaching Tetouan from the landward side it looks strikingly beautiful, poised atop the slope of an enormous valley against a dark mass of rock. Its name (pronounced *Tet-tá-wan*) means "open your eyes" in Berber, an apparent reference to the town's hasty construction by Andalusian refugees in the fifteenth century. The refugees, both Muslims and Jews, brought with them the most refined sophistication of Moorish Andalusia – an aristocratic tradition that is still reflected in the architecture of the Medina. Their houses, full of extravagant detail, are quite unlike those of other Moroccan towns; indeed, with their tiled lintels and wrought-iron balconies, they seem much more akin to the old Arab quarters of Cordoba and Seville.

The Spanish connection was reinforced by colonization in the early years of the twentieth century, Tetouan becoming a provincial capital of the Spanish northern protectorate, encompassing the Rif Mountains. Spanish is still the second language of older Tetouanis and there are many other reminders of mainland Spain, particularly in the cuisine and in *el paseo* – the summer evening stroll.

Arrival, orientation and information

Tetouan is not too hard a city in which to get your bearings – or to negotiate your own way around. Arriving by bus, or by grand taxi, you'll find yourself on the edge of the **Ville Nouvelle** at the *gare routière*. Built by the Spanish in the 1920s, this quarter of town follows a straightforward grid. At its centre is **Place Moulay el Mehdi**, with the Spanish consulate, post office and main banks. From there the pedestrianized Boulevard Mohammed V runs east **to Place Hassan II** and the **Royal Palace**, beyond which lies the Medina, still partially walled and entered through the Bab er Rouah gateway.

The **Medina** is not as large as it appears and, by day at least, you won't get lost for long without coming to an outer wall or gate – beyond which you can loop back to the Ville Nouvelle. If this is your first foray into Morocco you might want to consider arranging an **official guide** at the helpful

tourist office (Mon–Thurs 8.30am–4.30pm, Fri 8.30–noon & 1-4.30pm; ⓣ039 57 78 00, ⓕ039 57 90 02), a few metres from Place Moulay el Mehdi at 30 Bd Mohammed V.

Accommodation

Ignore all offers from touts and head for one of the recommendations below. You're likely to get the best deal at the **hotels**, as most of the thirty-or-so **pensions** (including the few we've listed) raise their prices well above basic rates in summer. The high pension prices are partly because newly arrived tourists will pay whatever they're asked, but also reflect demand. With its excellent local beaches, Tetouan is a popular Moroccan resort and rooms in July or August can be in short supply. If at all possible, phone ahead and make a booking.

The nearest **campsites** are on the beach or nearby at **Martil**, 11km out (see p.157 for transport details), which can be useful fallbacks if you have problems finding a room.

Cheap

Hôtel Dilbao 7 Bd Mohammed V (no phone). This is one of the cheapest *pensions* but is centrally placed, and it's reasonably clean, with cold showers in the rooms. ❶

Hôtel National 8 Rue Mohammed Ben Larbi Torres (no phone). Reasonable, old-fashioned hotel with a café and restaurant. Go for a room with smooth floor tiles if possible, as those with grooved tiles can get a bit grimy, even though they are cleaned daily. Though most rooms have en-suite showers or baths, there are no communal facilities for those that do not. ❸

Hôtel Principe 20 Av Youssef Ben Tachfine ⓣ066 55 38 20. Midway from the bus station to Place Moulay el Mehdi, just off the pedestrianized strip of Bd Mohammed V. A decent cheapie but with gloomy rooms, some boasting a shower. There's a ground-floor café for breakfast and snacks. ❷

Hôtel Regina 8 Rue Sidi Mandri ⓣ039 96 21 13. A small hotel with en-suite rooms, cheaper and rather better value than the *Oumaima* and the *Paris*. A small café serves breakfast. ❷

Hôtel Rio Jana 2 Av 10 Mai (no phone). One of a trio of centrally located cheapies (pensions *Florida* and *Bienvenida* are opposite) with drab rooms, shared bathroom facilities and a rather old-fashioned feel. Hot showers 10dh. ❸

Hôtel Trebol 3 Av Yacoub el Mansour (no phone). Right behind the bus station, so very noisy if you get a room at the front; still, it's safe, clean and cheap (especially for single rooms), but has no showers at all. ❶

Hôtel Victoria 23 Av Mohammed V ⓣ039 96 50 15. Good-value, clean and very cheap with shared bathroom facilities. ❷

Pension Iberia 5 Pl Moulay el Mehdi, third floor ⓣ000 00 00 T3. Above the BMCE bank, this place is central and clean, but the beds are rather soft, and hot showers cost extra (10dh). ❶

Moderate to expensive

Hôtel Chams Rue Abdelkhaleq Torres ⓣ039 99 09 01, ⓕ039 99 09 07. Still one of Tetouan's best offerings, 3km out of town on the road to Martil. Comfortable – with a pool, a/c and satellite TV – but hardly worth the out-of-town inconvenience. ❻

Hôtel Oumaima Av 10 Mai ⓣ039 96 34 73. Central and functional, with small rooms, each with a TV, and a ground-floor café for breakfast. ❹

Paris Hôtel 31 Rue Chkil Arssalane ⓣ039 96 67 50, ⓕ039 71 26 54. Not dissimilar to the *Oumaima* (even the price was identical at last check), with slightly nicer rooms, those at the back being quietest. The restaurant is open in summer only. ❹

🏃 **El Reducto** 38 Zankat Zawya, in a lane off Bd Mohammed V ⓣ039 96 81 20, ⓦwww .riadtetouan.com. Recommended by readers and with good reason. Tetouan's newest and most upmarket accommodation, this small riad used to be the home of the Spanish governor and has been lovingly brought back to life by the current owner. There are four individually furnished suites looking down onto a central courtyard and restaurant. Price includes half board. ❼

The Medina

Two cities rose and fell in the vicinity of Tetouan before the present-day city was built. Tamuda, the scant ruins of which can still be seen on the

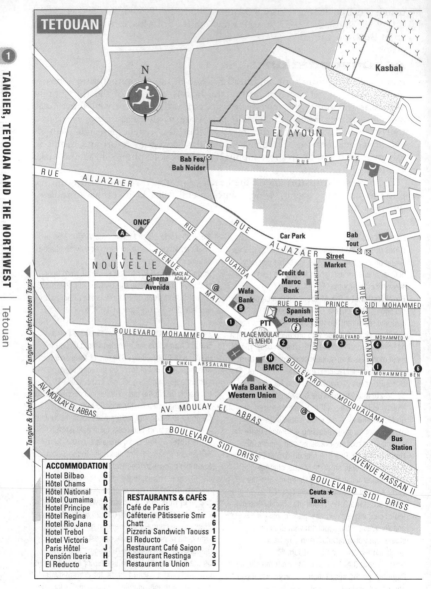

ACCOMMODATION

Hotel Bilbao	G
Hôtel Chams	D
Hôtel National	I
Hôtel Oumaima	A
Hotel Principe	K
Hôtel Regina	C
Hotel Rio Jana	B
Hotel Trebol	L
Hotel Victoria	F
Paris Hôtel	J
Pensión Iberia	H
El Reducto	E

RESTAURANTS & CAFÉS

Café de Paris	2
Caféterie Pâtisserie Smir	4
Chatt	6
Pizzeria Sandwich Taouss	1
El Reducto	E
Restaurant Café Saigon	7
Restaurant Restinga	3
Restaurant la Union	5

south side of Oued Martil 4km southeast of town, was founded by the Berber Mauritanians in the third century BC, and razed by the Romans in 42 AD; and the original Tetouan, built by the Merenids in 1307, on the same site as today's Medina, was destroyed by a Castilian raiding party in 1399. The present town was established in 1484 by Muslims and Jews fleeing the Christian reconquest of Andalusia in southern Spain. Jewish

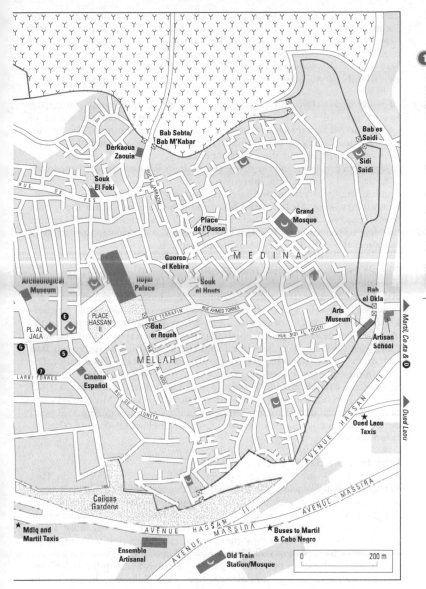

Bab Sebta/
Bab M'Kabar

Bab es
Saidi

Derkaoua
Zaouia

Sidi
Saidi

Souk
El Foki

Grand
Mosque

Place
de l'Oussa

MEDINA

Guoroa
el Kebira

Archeological
Museum

Royal
Palace

Souk
el Houts

Rah
el Okla

PLACE
HASSAN
II

RUE TERRAFIN

RUE AHMED TORRES

Arts
Museum

PL. AL
JALA

Bab
er Rouah

RUE SIDI EL YOUSTI

Artisan
School

MELLAH

LARBI TORRES

Cinema
Español

RUE DE LA LUNETA

Oued Laou
Taxis

Cajigas
Gardens

AVENUE HASSAN II

AVENUE MASSIRA

Mdiq and
Martil Taxis

AVENUE HASSAN II

AVENUE MASSIRA

Buses to Martil
& Cabo Negro

Ensemble
Artisanal

Old Train
Station/Mosque

0   200 m

▶ Martil, Ce.ta & ⓓ

▶ Oued Laou

merchants – able to pass relatively freely between Muslim North Africa and
Christian Europe – brought prosperity to the city, and ramparts were put
up in the seventeenth century under Moulay Ismail.

Tetouan has since been occupied twice by the Spanish. It was seized briefly,
as a supposed threat to Ceuta, from 1859 to 1862, a period which saw the
Medina converted to a town of almost European appearance, complete with

street lighting. Then in 1913 a more serious, colonial occupation began. Tetouan served first as a military garrison for the subjugation of the Rif, later as the capital of the **Spanish Protectorate Zone**. As such it almost doubled in size to handle the region's trade and administration, and it was here in 1936 that **General Franco** declared his military coup against Spain's elected Liberal–Socialist coalition government, thus igniting the Spanish Civil War.

For Tetouan's Moroccan population, there was little progress during the Spanish colonial period. "Native tradition" was respected to the extent of leaving the Medina intact, and even restoring its finer mansions, but Spanish administration retained a purely military character and only a handful of schools were opened throughout the entire zone. This legacy had effects well beyond independence in 1956, and the town, alongside its Rif hinterland, adapted with difficulty to the new nation, dominated by the old French zone. It was at the centre of anti-government rioting as recently as 1984. Aware of this undercurrent, the new king, **Mohammed VI**, made it his business to visit the former Spanish protectorate almost as soon as he ascended the throne in 1999, a gesture that has helped to give Tetouan and its region a much stronger sense of belonging than it had under the previous monarch.

Place Hassan II and the Mellah

To explore Tetouan, the place to start is **Place Hassan II**, the old meeting place and former market square. Completely remodelled in 1988, this is a squeaky-clean public square, with a shiny pavement of Islamic motifs, minaret-like floodlights at each corner and a brand-new Royal Palace – replacing the old Spanish consulate and incorporating parts of a nineteenth-century Caliphal Palace that stood beside it. The usual approach to the Medina is through **Bab er Rouah** (Gate of the Winds), the archway just south of the Royal Palace. The lane on the right, just before the archway, opens on to Rue al Qods, the main street of the **Mellah**, the old Jewish quarter. This was created as late as 1807, when the Jews were moved from an area around the Grand Mosque. Very few of the population remain today, although if you ask around someone will point out the old synagogues, the oldest of which, the eighteenth-century **Yitzhak Benoualid**, remains in use.

Into the Medina: the souks

Entering the Medina proper, at Bab er Rouah, you find yourself on **Rue Terrafin**, a relatively wide lane that (with its continuations) cuts straight across to the east gate, Bab el Okla. Along the way a series of alleys give access to most of the town's food and craft souks. The **Souk el Houts**, a small shaded square directly behind the grounds of the Royal Palace, is one of the most active: devoted to fish in the mornings, meat in the afternoons, and with an all-day smattering of local pottery stalls.

From the north side of the Souk el Houts, two lanes wind up through a mass of alleys, souks and passageways towards Bab Sebta. Following the one on the right (east) for about twenty metres, you'll see an opening to another small square. This is the **Guersa el Kebira**, essentially a cloth and textile souk, where a number of stalls sell the town's highly characteristic *foutahs* – strong and brilliantly striped lengths of rug-like cotton, worn as a cloak and skirt by the Djebali and Riffian women.

Leaving the Guersa at its top right-hand corner, you should emerge more or less on **Place de l'Oussa**, another beautiful little square, easily recognized by an ornate, tiled fountain and trellis of vines. Along one of its sides is an imposing nineteenth-century **Xharia**, or almshouse; on another is an artesania shop, elegantly tiled and with good views over the quarter from its roof.

Beyond the square, still heading up towards Bab Sebta, are most of the specific **craft souks** – among them copper and brass workers, renowned makers of *babouches* (pointed leather slippers), and carpenters specializing in elaborately carved and painted wood. Most of the shops along the central lane here – **Rue el Jarrazin** – focus on the tourist trade, but this goes much less for the souks themselves.

So, too, with the nearby souks around **Rue de Fes**, which is reached most easily by following the lane beside the Royal Palace from Place Hassan II. This is the main thoroughfare of a much more mundane area selling ordinary everyday goods, with the occasional villagers' **Joutia**, or flea market. At its main intersection – just to the right as you come out onto the lane up from Place Hassan II – is **Souk el Foki**, once the town's main business sector, though it's little more than a wide alleyway. Following this past a small perfume souk and two sizeable mosques, you meet up with Rue el Jarrazin just below **Bab Sebta** (also known as Bab M'Kabar).

Walk out this way, passing (on your left) the superb portal of the **Derkaoua Zaouia** (no admission to non-Muslims), headquarters of the local Derkaoua brotherhood, and you enter a huge **cemetery**, in use since at least the fifteenth century and containing unusually elaborate Andalusian tombs. Fridays excluded, non-Muslims are tolerated in most Moroccan cemeteries, and walking here you get illuminating views over the Medina and across the valley to the Rif.

Proceeding east from Place Hassan II instead, along the roofed main drag of Rue Terrafin/Rue Ahmed Torres/Rue Sidi el Yousti, you reach the eastern edge of the Medina at **Bab el Okla**. The quarter to the north of here, below the Grand Mosque, was the Medina's most exclusive residential area and contains some of its finest mansions. Walking towards the gate you see signs for a *Palais*, one of the best of the buildings, but converted into a carpet and crafts warehouse aimed at tourists.

On the west side of the Medina, and most easily accessed from the Ville Nouvelle, there is a regular **street market** by Bab Tout, spilling out of the gates and along Rue Aljazaer. This is well worth a stroll and is only a couple of blocks north of Boulevard Mohammed V.

The Moroccan Arts Museum and Artisan School

Considerably more authentic than tourist emporiums such as the *Palais*, and an interesting comparison for quality, is the **Moroccan Arts Museum** (Mon–Fri 9am–4pm, 10dh), the entrance to which is just inside Bab el Okla (entering the gate, turn left and it's just round to the left). A former arms bastion, the museum has one of the more impressive collections around of traditional crafts and ethnographic objects. Take a look particularly at the zellij – enamelled tile mosaics – and then head across the road to the **Artisan School** (Ecole des Métiers; Mon–Thurs & Sat 8am–noon & 2.30–5.30pm; closed Aug; 10dh), where you can see craftsmen working at new designs in the old ways, essentially unmodified since the fourteenth century. Perhaps owing to its Andalusian heritage, Tetouan actually has a slightly different zellij technique to other Moroccan cities – the tiles are cut before rather than after being fired. A slightly easier process, it is frowned upon by the craftsmen of Fes, whose own pieces are more brittle but brighter in colour and closer fitting.

The Ensemble Artisanal and Archeological Museum

Outside the Medina the most interesting sight is the **Ensemble Artisanal** (Mon–Sat 9.30am–1pm & 3.30–7pm) on the main road below the town. The regular exhibits on the ground floor are well worth a check if you're planning to make purchases in the souks and want to assess prices and quality first. But where the Ensemble scores most highly is in the displays of craftworking. Go up the stairs, at either the front or back of the main building, and you come to a fascinating array of carpet and embroidery workshops, while outside the building there are metalwork, basketry and musical instrument artisans at work. This is really a great opportunity to get up close to the craftsmen and women and their work without feeling pressured into buying anything. Nearby is the **Old Train Station**, a singular building, which looks like an Oriental palace and was in use when a narrow-gauge line connected Tetouan with Ceuta and Martil. It closed when the Spanish left, and is now a mosque with a little café beside it.

The **Archeological Museum** (Mon–Fri 8am–noon & 1–4pm; 10dh) is off Place al Jala at the eastern end of Boulevard Mohammed V. It was founded during the Spanish protectorate, so it features exhibits from throughout their zone, including rock carvings from the Western Sahara. Highlights, as so often in North Africa, are the Roman mosaics, mostly gathered from Lixus and the oft-plundered Volubilis.

Other than these, the most interesting exhibits are concerned with the stone circle at Mzoura (see p.136), including a model and aerial photographs.

Eating and drinking

Tetouan is not exactly a gourmet's paradise. There are a couple of reasonable restaurants and a slew of snack bars, some cafés, and a few dive-like bars (mostly around Place el Adala on Av 10 Mai), but really nowhere worth going out of your way for. As ever, the cheapest food is to be found in the **Medina**, particularly the stalls inside Bab er Rouah and along Rue de la Luneta in the old Mellah quarter. For variety, try one of the many places on or around Boulevard Mohammed V or Rue Mohammed Ben Larbi Torres in the **Ville Nouvelle**.

Restaurants

El Reducto 38 Zankat Zawya, in a lane off Bd Mohammed V ☎039 96 81 20, ⊛www .riadtetouan.com. This recently opened riad and restaurant is open to nonresidents daily 9am–late. The menu is mainly Moroccan with some Spanish and seafood dishes, all very reasonably priced. No alcohol. Moderate.

Restaurant Café Saigon 2 Rue Mohammed Ben Larbi Torres. Mainstream Spanish-Moroccan cooking, despite the name. A popular place that serves a reasonable paella. Open daily 11am– 11.30pm. Moderate.

Restaurant Restinga 21 Bd Mohammed V. Eat indoors or in a courtyard at this very pleasant restaurant that's been serving tajine, couscous and fried fish twelve hours a day (11.30am–11.30pm) since 1968. Beer available with meals. Moderate.

Restaurant la Union (formerly known as *Restaurant Moderno*), 1 Pasaje Achaach, off Rue

Mohammed Ben Larbi Torres – to find it, go through the arcades opposite Cinema Español. Popular with locals, this budget eatery serves up standard Moroccan fare, including *harira*, brochettes and a reasonable meat tajine, though the service can be a bit erratic. Open daily noon–9.30pm. Cheap.

Cafés and snack bars

Café de Paris Place Moulay el Mehdi. A large café on the main square, which has become quite a fashionable and relatively female-friendly hangout.

Cafétérie Patisserie Smir 17 Bd Mohammed V. Rich gateaux, sweets and soft drinks. Daily 11am–11.30pm.

Chatt Rue Mourakah Annual. Popular spot with pretty much everything you'd need for breakfast, plus tea, coffee, burgers, omelettes and snacks. Daily; opens early and closes very late.

Pizzeria Sandwich Taouss 3 Rue 10 Mai. Pizzas, sandwiches and snacks to eat in or take out.

Entertainment

The Orquesta Andalusi de Tetouan is one of the best-known groups playing Moroccan-Andalous music, a seductive style awash with Oriental strings. It was founded, and is still conducted, by Abdessadaq Chekana, and his brother Abdellah leads on lute. The orchestra has recorded with Spanish flamenco singer Juan Peña Lebrijano and has toured with British composer Michael Nyman (best known for his soundtracks for Peter Greenaway's films – and for *The Piano*). Despite such collaborations, none of them reads music; everything is committed to memory. They often play in Tetouan and you may be able to catch them locally at an official reception, or at a wedding or festival; ask at the tourist office, where staff may be able to help.

Two good **cinemas** are the Avenida, on Place al Adala (off Av 10 Mai) and the Monumental, near the *Hôtel Principe*. The Español, near the *Restaurant La Union*, mainly shows "*l'histoire et la géographie*" (a double bill of Bollywood and kung fu).

Moving on

From the main **bus station** there are regular departures to Chefchaouen, Meknes, Fes and Tangier; ask around for times at the various windows, as both CTM and private companies operate on all of these routes (if it's convenient, best take the CTM). Beware of con men at the station, tales abound of touts posing as bus officials and demanding "supplements" or "booking fees" on top of your ticket – often on the bus itself; resist and, if needs be, appeal to your fellow passengers.

Heading for Tangier, Chefchaouen, Ceuta or the nearby coast resorts, it's easiest to travel by **grand taxi**; these are routine runs – just go along to the ranks and get a place. Collective grands taxis for Tangier and Chefchaouen leave from Avenue Khaled Ibnou el Oualid, west of town, a twenty-minute walk or 15dh petit taxi ride. For the Ceuta border at Fnideq, they leave from Boulevard Sidi Driss, below the bus station. Grands taxis to Mdiq, Martil and Cabo Negro leave from the junction of Boulevard Sidi Driss with Avenue Hassan II, southeast of the bus station; those for Oued Laou leave from the beginning of Avenue Ksar el Kebir, which is the Oued Laou turn-off from Avenue Hassan II, not far from Bab el Okla.

An ONCF office (Mon–Fri 8am–1pm & 3–7pm, Sat & Sun 9.30am–noon & 3–5.30pm; ☎039 96 75 59) on Avenue 10 Mai, opposite the *Hôtel Oumaima*, sells through **train tickets** to Fes, Meknes, Rabat, Casablanca, Marrakesh and beyond, including a connecting Supratours bus service to the station of Tnine Sidi Lyamani, just south of Asilah. The bus leaves from outside the ONCF office at 8.15am & 4.50pm (but times change, so check) and is often full, so it's worth booking in advance if possible.

The Tetouan beaches: Mdiq to Oued Laou

Despite the numbers of tourists passing through, Tetouan is above all a resort for Moroccans, rich and poor alike – a character very much in evidence on the extensive beaches to the east of the town. Throughout the summer whole villages of family tents appear at **Martil**, **Mdiq** and, particularly, around **Restinga-Smir**, further north. At **Oued Laou** by contrast, 40km southeast of

Tetouan, a younger and slightly "alternative" crowd does turn up in summer to use its small hotel and excellent campsite. All these places are accessible by bus and shared grand taxi from Tetouan (see p.157).

Martil and the coast north

MARTIL, essentially Tetouan's city beach, was its port as well until the river between the two silted up. From the fifteenth to eighteenth centuries, it maintained an active corsair fleet, twice provoking Spanish raids to block the harbour. Today it is a small semi-active fishing village with a slightly ramshackle appearance, owing to unmade roads and the rows of tourist huts along the seafront. The beach, stretching all the way around to the headland of Cabo Negro, is superb – an eight-kilometre stretch of fine, yellow sand that is long enough to remain uncrowded, despite its summer popularity and colonization by *Club Med* and other tourist complexes.

There are various options for **accommodation**. Arriving from Tetouan, there is a small hotel on the right, *Hôtel Los Mares* (℡039 68 80 10; ❸), a little bit down-at-heel, but adequate for the price, as is *Hostal Nouzha* (no phone; ❷), at the southern end of Avenue Moulay Rachid, the main road in town running parrallel to the seafront road. Somewhat more expensive, but good value for money, is the *Hôtel Etoile de la Mer* (℡& ℻039 97 92 76; ❺; closed in winter), on the seafront by the grand taxi stand; known locally as the *Nejma el Bahr*, it has a popular café and restaurant.

Of the **campsites**, *Camping Martil*, on the town beach, was closed and being redeveloped at the time of writing. *Camping al Boustane*, a kilometre north (℡039 68 88 22), is well maintained and friendly, with plenty of shade, decent facilities, quite a classy restaurant and a pool. A third site, *Camping Oued el Maleh*, is further out to the north (signposted from town), reached along a riverbank. It's a dusty site but safe enough and has some shade and a useful shop; the beach is just 200m away, through a wood.

There are many **cafés and restaurants**, though the majority are closed during the winter; recommended for seafood are *Restaurant Rio Martil*, on Avenue Prince Héritier nearly opposite *Hôtel Etoile de la Mer*, and *Café Restaurant Avenida*, 102 Av Mohammed V. Five kilometres towards Mdiq is the *Restaurant La Lampe Magique* (℡039 97 08 22), an extraordinary place complete with cupolas, one of which is made up of nine thousand Heineken bottles and illuminated at night. For pasta and pizza, try the friendly and popular *Aux Vitamins de la Mer*, 9 Av Moulay Rachid, next door to *Hostal Nouzha*.

Mdiq

MDIQ is a lovely coastal village and fishing port, which can be approached via Martil or direct from Tetouan (18km on the N13). Though it is getting a little overdeveloped, a popular promenade has been constructed overlooking its superb beach and there are some nice places to stay. The best hotel is the *Golden Beach* (℡039 97 51 37, ℻039 97 50 96; ❼), a four-star beach holiday hotel with nightclub, swimming pool and all mod cons. The town's only budget option is the *Narjiss* opposite the police station on Avenue Lalla Nazha, the main road to Martil (℡068 24 80 95; ❹). There is no campsite but campervans are usually allowed to stay overnight in the car park next to the promenade.

Restinga-Smir and Fnideq

RESTINGA-SMIR is more a collective name for a length of beach than for an actual place or village: an attractive strip of the Mediterranean, dominated by package hotels and holiday villages. Many Moroccan families still camp in the woods between here and Fnideq. The rather spartan but inexpensive *Al Fraja* **campsite**, opposite the *El Andalouz* tourist complex and 15km from Fnideq, makes a good first or last stop in the country in summer; in winter it's closed.

In addition, there are several **hotels** in **FNIDEQ** (formerly called Castillejos), just 2km from the Ceuta border. The best of these is the *Hôtel Ceuta* (T 039 97 61 40, F 039 67 58 31; ❸), on the main street, Avenue Mohammed V and the *Ibis Moussafir* (T 039 67 77 77, W www.ibishotel.com; ❺) at the edge of town 200m from the border post. Fnideq, however, has little to recommend it, except a busy market for cheap Spanish goods; Moroccans from Tetouan and even Tangier come here regularly for household items and clothes.

Southeast: in the shadow of the Rif

Southeast of Tetouan the coastline almost immediately changes. For a few kilometres, the road (N16, formerly S608) follows the sea and the still more-or-less continuous beach, dotted in summer with communities of tents. Very soon, however, it begins to climb into the foothills of the Rif, a first taste of the zigzagging Moroccan mountain roads, though in this case always with the sea down below, and including the occasional swoop down to cross the estuary of a mountain stream dry in summer but often destructive in winter – watch out for diversions around broken bridges. Alongside the beach, near Cap Mazari, is the nicely shaded *Camping Azla* (14km from Tetouan; open summer only) with a small café/shop.

Oued Laou

Tetouan is connected to **Oued Laou**, 44km away, by local **bus** and **grand taxi**, and when you finally arrive, you're unlikely to want to return immediately. A stay, in any case, is a positive option. Oued Laou is not an especially pretty place – Riffian villages tend to look spread out and lack any core. However, it has a near-deserted beach, which extends for miles on each side, particularly to the southeast, where the river has created a wide, fertile bay down to Kâascras, 8km distant. Equally important, Oued Laou is a very easy-going sort of place and one of the best parts of the Rif to meet and talk with local people. Hustlers have nothing to hustle except *kif* and rooms, and aren't too bothered about either.

There is one **hotel** and a campsite in the area. The friendly *Hôtel-Restaurant Oued Laou* (T 039 67 08 54; ❹) is open all year round (with massive reductions off-season) with hot water and clean, sunny rooms. It's one block from the beach on Boulevard Massira and if it's full, or you want to pay less, the staff can find you **rooms** elsewhere – everyone knows everyone here. *Camping Oued Laou* (T & F 039 67 08 95), alongside the municipal building, is a secure site, shaded with olive trees, and very well kept, with newly refurbished hot showers and washing facilities (built with aid from the autonomous government of Andalusia), a small shop and a café. Camping fees are reasonable and there are three two-bedroom bungalows (150dh a night) that will comfortably house four adults or a family. The town's mosque has an unusual octagonal minaret. On Saturdays, there is a **souk**, held 3km inland from Oued Laou, which draws villagers from all over the valley; look for the terracotta pottery, fired locally.

Kâaseras, El Jebha and the roads to Chefchaouen

Heading east from Oued Laou is complicated without your own transport. The coast road is sealed all the way to El Jebha, but only one bus a day, leaving

Tetouan at 7am, travels the full six-hour-plus, 137km, route, via Oued Laou, Kâaseras, Targha and Bou Hamed.

It's no problem getting a taxi as far as **KÂASERAS**, twenty minutes from Oued Laou – and in similar mould. A tiny resort, it is geared towards Moroccans camping on the beach, though there are usually a few rooms available, if you ask around. If heading from Oued Laou to Chefchaouen, it's possible to drive along the minor road up the Oued Laou valley – which includes some impressive peaks and gorges – but it's not advisable when the road is wet, and never on a motorbike. At present, a bus from Kâaseras leaves for Chefchaouen at 6am, and returns in the afternoon, leaving Chefchaouen at 5pm.

It's also possible to keep to the coast and make a circuit to Chefchaouen via **Bou Hamed** (38km from Oued Laou) or, further on, via **El Jebha** (93km from Oued Laou). Bou Hamed is a largish village on a broad alluvial plain. The road from here into the Rif calls for a Fiat Uno or better still a 4x4. The Rif road (8310) from El Jebha is easier and shorter but El Jebha itself is not the most appealing of destinations – a shabby sort of place, with little beyond a lighthouse and a few fishermen's cottages.

Chefchaouen (Chaouen, Xaouen) and around

Shut in by a fold of mountains, **CHEFCHAOUEN** (pronounced "shef-**sha**-wen", sometimes abbreviated to Chaouen) becomes visible only once you have arrived – a dramatic approach to a town that, until the arrival of Spanish troops in 1920, had been visited by just three Westerners. Two of these were missionary explorers: Charles de Foucauld, a Frenchman who spent just an hour in the town, disguised as a rabbi, in 1883, and William Summers, an American who was poisoned by the townsfolk here in 1892. The third, in 1889, was the British journalist Walter Harris (see p.769), whose main impulse, as described in his book, *Land of an African Sultan*, was "the very fact that there existed within thirty hours' ride of Tangier a city in which it was considered an utter impossibility for a Christian to enter".

This impossibility – and Harris very nearly lost his life when the town was alerted to the presence of "a Christian dog" – had its origins in the foundation of the town in 1471. The region hereabouts was already sacred to Muslims due to the presence of the tomb of Moulay Abdessalam Ben Mchich – patron saint of the Djebali tribesmen and one of the "four poles of Islam" – and over the centuries acquired a considerable reputation for pilgrimage and *marabouts* – "saints", believed to hold supernatural powers. The town was actually established by one of Moulay Abdessalam's *shereefian* (descendant of the Prophet) followers, Moulay Rachid, as a secret base from which to attack the Portuguese in Ceuta and Ksar es Seghir. In the ensuing decades, as the population was boosted by Muslim and Jewish refugees from Spain, Chefchaouen grew increasingly anti-European and autonomous. For a time, it was the centre of a semi-independent Emirate, exerting control over much of the northwest, in alliance with the Wattasid sultans of Fes. Later, however, it became an almost completely isolated backwater. When the Spanish arrived in 1920, they were astonished to find the Jews here speaking, and in some cases writing, a medieval form of Castilian extinct in Spain for nearly four hundred years.

△Chefchaouen

These days, Chefchaouen is well established on the excursion routes but it retains a certain individuality. There are the inevitable souks and stalls for tourists and a major hotel disfigures the twin peaks (*ech-Chaoua*: the horns) from which the town takes its name, but local attitudes towards visitors are generally relaxed, the Medina *pensions* are among the friendliest and cheapest around, and staying here a few days and walking in the hills remains one of the best possible introductions to Morocco.

As the centre of so much *maraboutism*, Chefchaouen and its neighbouring villages have a particularly large number of **moussems**. The big events are those in Moulay Abdessalam Ben Mchich (40km away: usually in May) and Sidi Allal el Hadj (in August). There are dozens of others, however – ask around and you should come upon something.

Arrival, orientation and information

With a population of around 42,000 – a tenth of Tetouan's – Chefchaouen is more like a large village in size and feel, and confusing only on arrival. **Buses** drop you at the new *gare routière*, 15dh by petit taxi to Place Outa el Hammam or twenty to thirty minutes' walk to the town centre: take Avenue Mohammed Abdou eastward (and upward) for 300m to the next main junction, where you turn left up Avenue Mohammed V, which leads into the centre of town. **Grands taxis** from Tetouan and Ouezzane drop much more centrally, close to the *Hôtel Sevilla*. The marketplace and a straggle of modern buildings are in the Ville Nouvelle alongside Avenue Hassan II, which is dominated by the Ben Rachid mosque. There's a **PTT** here, plus Wafa, BMCE and Banque Populaire **banks**, all with ATMs. Banque Populaire also has a bureau de change, open daily, up in Place Outa el Hammam. **Internet access** is available at outahammam.com (daily 9am–10pm, later in summer), located between Place Outa el Hammam and Place el Makhzen, and upstairs by *Café Mondial* (same hours) on Avenue Hassan II, nearly opposite Bab el Ain.

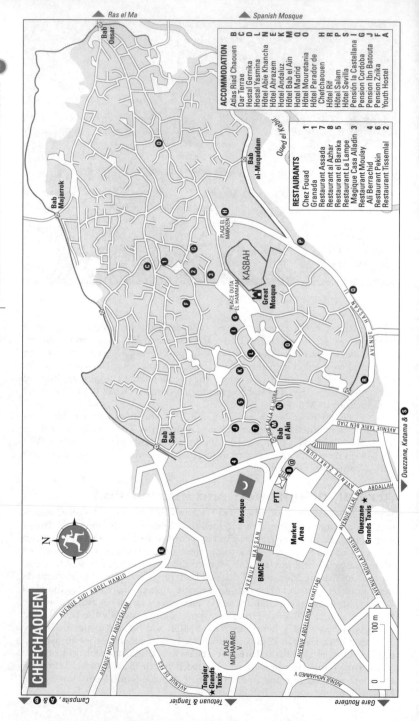

CHEFCHAOUEN

ACCOMMODATION

Atlas Riad Chaouen	B
Dar Terrae	C
Hostal Gernika	D
Hostal Yasmina	L
Hôtel Abie Khancha	N
Hôtel Ahrazem	E
Hôtel Andaluz	K
Hôtel Bab el Ain	M
Hôtel Madrid	O
Hôtel Mouretania	H
Hôtel Parador de Chefchaouen	R
Hôtel Rif	P
Hôtel Salam	S
Hôtel Sevilla	I
Pensión la Castellana	G
Pension Cordoba	J
Pension Ibn Batouta	F
Pension Znika	A
Youth Hostel	

RESTAURANTS

Chez Fouad	1
Granada	1
Restaurant Assada	7
Restaurant al Azhar	8
Restaurant el Baraka	5
Restaurant La Lampe Magique Casa Aladdin	3
Restaurant Moulay Ali Berrachid	4
Restaurant Pekin	6
Restaurant Tissemlal	2

KASBAH

Great Mosque

PLACE EL MAKHZEN

PLACE OUTA EL HAMMAM

Market Area

PLACE MOHAMMED V

Mosque

BMCE

PTT

AVENUE HASSAN II

AVENUE SIDI ABDEL HAMID

AVENUE MOULAY ABDESSALAM

AVENUE DES FES

AVENUE ABDELKRIM EL KHATTABI

AVENUE MOULAY DRISS

AVENUE ALLAL BEN ABDALLAH

AVENUE TARIK BEN ZIAD

AVENUE ZERKTOUN

AVENUE MOHAMMED V

AVENUE HASSAN I

RUE LALLA EL HORA

Bab Suk

Bab el Ain

Bab al-Muqaddam

Bab Majarrok

Bab Omar

Ras el Ma

Spanish Mosque

Oued el Kebir

Tangier Grands Taxis

Ouezzane Grands Taxis

Campsite, A & B

Tetouan & Tangier

Ouezzane, Ketama & S

Gare Routière

N

100 m

0

The main gateway to the Medina, Bab el Ain, is a tiny arched entrance at the junction of Avenue Hassan II with Rue Moulay Ali Ben Rachid. Through the gate a clearly dominant lane winds up through the town to the main square, **Place Outa el Hammam** (flanked by the gardens and towers of the **kasbah**) and, beyond, to a second, smaller square, **Place el Makhzen**.

Accommodation

Along and around the main route in the Medina there are a number of small **pensions**, most of them converted from private houses; rooms can be a bit cell-like, but most are exceptionally clean and remarkably inexpensive. For more comfort (and less "community life"), several of the **hotels** in the Ville Nouvelle are good value, too, and there's also an old Spanish parador in the heart of the Medina.

Chefchaouen's **campsite**, *Camping Azilan* (℡039 98 69 79), is on the hill above the town, by the *Atlas Riad Chaouen* (see p.164), whose signs you can follow along the road; on foot, there is a shortcut through the cemetery. It is shaded and inexpensive, with a café and small shop, but can be crowded in summer, and with *pensions* so cheap it hardly seems worth the 2km climb.

Alongside the campsite is the very basic **youth hostel** (℡066 90 84 42, ✉arjikamal@yahoo.fr; 20dh per person per night, bedding not provided). The warden works in the *Maison de la Jeunesse* in town – if he is not around, wait at the campsite until he arrives. The hostel has no hot water, but you can use the showers at the campsite for 10dh.

Cheap

The recommendations below are in the Medina or just outside. Chefchaouen can get bitterly cold during winter and all of those listed proclaim to have hot water, though few have en-suite bathrooms. This lack is to some extent mitigated by the presence of the local **hammams**. The town, unusually, has separate hammams for men and women. The male one is next door to the *Pensión La Castellana*, off Place Outa el Hammam; the one for women, which is older and much more elaborate, is in the quarter of the souks – ask someone to show you the way because it totally defies written directions. In recent years, entrance to the hammams for tourists has been limited, and sometimes refused unless you have a group and book the hammam together. Ask your *pension/hotel* for advice, or for someone to accompany you.

Hostal Gernika 49 Onsar ℡039 98 74 34. This old house has been superbly converted by its female Spanish owner and deserves a look. It's in the higher quarter of the Medina, going up towards Bab Onsar. Some rooms are en suite. ❸

Hostal Yasmina 12 Rue Lalla el Hora ℡039 88 31 18, ℻039 98 73 29. Small, bright and clean with only six rooms, but very conveniently located, just off the Medina's main square, modern in style, and a very pleasant little place to stay. Hot showers 10dh. ❷

Hôtel Abie Khancha 57 Rue Lalla el Hora ℡039 98 68 79. Conveniently situated, 30m up on the right from the Bab el Ain, this is a rather basic place with small rooms, but it has an open courtyard, a salon, a high terrace, and shared showers. ❶

Hôtel Ahrazom 76 Rue Sidi Abdelhamid ①039 98 73 84. Just outside the Medina, not far from Bab el Souk, this friendly and well-kept little place is run by Dr Agrazem. ❷

Hotel Andaluz 1 Rue Sidi Salem ℡039 98 60 34. Small, functional *pension*, whose rooms face an inner courtyard – not too airy, but otherwise fine, and with a friendly management, shared showers and a kitchen. It is signposted off to the left at the near end of Place Outa el Hammam. ❷

Hôtel Bab el Ain 77 Rue Lalla el Hora ℡039 98 69 35. A well-maintained modern conversion, just inside the Bab el Ain on the right. It charges a bit more than most of the *pensions* but the rooms are comfortable with en-suite showers and toilets, and the price includes breakfast. ❷

Hôtel Mouretania 15 Hadi Alami ☏ 039 98 61 84, ℻ 039 98 61 84. Signposted from halfway up Rue Lalla el Hora, with small, basic rooms around a covered patio, quite homely decor, and shared bathroom. ❶

Hôtel Salam 39 Av Hassan II ☏ 039 98 62 39. A friendly place just below Bab el Hammam, and long a favourite with individuals and groups. Back rooms and a shady roof terrace overlook the valley. Bathrooms are shared and meals are served in a salon or on the terrace, which can get a bit crowded at times. ❷

Pensión la Castellana 4 Rue Bouhali ☏ 039 98 62 95. Just to the left at the near end of Place Outa el Hammam – follow the signs. Aficionados return loyally to the *Castellana* each year, creating a distinctly laidback and youthful atmosphere; others take one look at the poky rooms and leave. The key is the manager, Mohammed

Nebrhout, who arranges communal meals and excursions on request. There's also a hammam right next door. ❸

Pension Cordoba Rue Garnata ☏ 066 64 10 10. Lovely rooms and tasteful decor in a charming old Andalusian-style house, beautifully done out. Not quite a riad, but a lot cheaper than one. Breakfast included. ❹

Pension Ibn Batouta 31 Rue Abie Khancha ☏ 039 98 60 44. One of the quietest of the *pensions*, with less of a "travellers' hangout" feel; located in an alley to the left, about 70m along from Bab el Ain, beyond the *Restaurant Assada*. Rooms are very cheap if a little dingy, bathrooms shared (hot showers 5dh). ❶

Pension Znika 14 Rue Znika ☏ 039 98 66 24. An excellent-value *pension*, well kept and quiet with welcoming management and a panoramic terrace; shared bathrooms. ❷

Moderate to expensive

There is more comfort in the Ville Nouvelle's purpose-built hotels and a few of them have the character to match the Medina *pensions*. None is far from the Medina, except for the hilltop *Atlas Riad Chaouen*, which frankly is not worth the climb.

Atlas Riad Chaouen (formerly *Hôtel Asmaa*) on the hill above town ☏ 039 98 60 02, ℯ riadchaouen @menara.ma. An ugly modern building on the site of an old fort, half an hour's walk away. The views of the town and valley, and a swimming pool, are its best features. Comfortable rooms geared for package trade but not a very welcoming place, though it has recently changed ownership. Breakfast included. ❻

Dar Terrae Av Hassan I ☏ 039 98 75 98 or 070 46 53 70. Chefchaouen's first riad, in a charming old Andalusian-style house. There's a homely atmosphere and though not all rooms are en suite, each is different and comes with a fireplace, and there are three roof terraces. Breakfast included. ❺

Hôtel Madrid Av Hassan II ☏ 039 98 74 96, ℻ 039 98 74 98. Tastefully decorated, with a fine panoramic rooftop breakfast terrace and most rooms en suite, though the hot water supply can be erratic. Breakfast included. ❹

Hôtel Parador de Chefchaouen Place el Makhzen ☏ 039 98 61 36, ℯ parador@iam.net .ma). The former Spanish "grand hotel", once part of the Parador chain, now reconstructed for the package trade. The bar and swimming pool help justify the expense and there are stunning views from the terrace. However, if you're only having an occasional splurge, this isn't special enough. ❻

Hôtel Rif 29 Av Hassan II ☏ 039 98 69 82, ℻ 039 98 69 82. A popular hotel for some years, now under new and rather better management, with perfectly adequate – if slightly dreary and sometimes eccentrically furnished – en-suite rooms. Breakfast included. ❹

Hotel Sevilla Av Allal Ben Abdellah ☏ 039 98 72 44. A well-run place with cosy, comfortable rooms, most en suite, and a café downstairs serving excellent breakfasts. ❸

The town and river

Like Tetouan, Chefchaouen's architecture has a strong Andalusian character: less elaborate (and less grand), perhaps, but often equally inventive. It is a town of extraordinary light and colour, its whitewash tinted with blue and edged by soft, golden, stone walls – and it is a place which, for all its present popularity, still seems redolent of the years of isolation. The roofs of its houses, tiled and with eaves, are an obvious physical assertion, in contrast to the flat ones found everywhere else in Morocco. But it is something you can sense about life in general here, even about the people themselves – inbred over many generations.

The souks and Mellah

Since the Medina is so small, it is more than ever a place to explore at random: the things which draw your attention are not so much "sights" as unexpected strands of detail. At some point, though, head for the two main squares, and for the **souks** – just below Place Outa el Hammam.

There are basic town souks held on Mondays and Thursdays in the market square, and these, to some degree, have been set up for, or at least geared to, the tourist industry. But both the quality and the variety are surprising. When the Spanish arrived in 1920 Chefchaouen craftsmen were still working leather in the manner of twelfth-century Cordoba, tanning with bark, and hammering silver to old Andalusian designs. Although you won't see any of this today, the town's carpet and weaving workshops remain active and many of their designs unchanged. Vendors are well used to haggling with travellers, and if you're staying for a few days, prices can fall dramatically.

It's interesting, too, to observe the contrasts in feel between the main, Arab part of Chefchaouen and the still modestly populated Jewish quarter of the **Mellah**. This is to be found behind the jewellers' souk, between the Bab el Ain and the kasbah.

Place Outa el Hammam and the kasbah

The elongated pedestrian-only **Place Outa el Hammam** is where most of the town's evening life, and a fair whack of the daily tourist traffic, takes place. It's a pretty square, with its cafés overhung by upper rooms (mostly the preserve of *kif* smokers) and is great for a spot of people watching. On the northern end, on Zankat el Targui, in amongst the run-of-the-mill tourist stalls are a few **souvenir shops** that typify the place's relaxed feel. At the beginning of Zankat el Targui is Aladin, a small, two-story treasure chest of spices, aromatic oils and soaps, candles and crystals. They'll gladly explain the characteristics and benefits of many of the concoctions on display. Further up, at 75 Rue Adarve Chabu, also known as Rue Granada, is the Hatman. So small you'd struggle to swing a mouse, this shop is well known in the village for the distinctive woollen beanies, berets and leg-warmers for sale.

On one side of the square is the town's **kasbah** (daily except Tues 9am–1pm & 3–6pm; 10dh), a quiet ruin with shady gardens and a little museum of crafts and old photos. The kasbah was built, like so many others in northern Morocco, by Moulay Ismail. Inside, and immediately to the right, in the first of its compounds, are the old town prison cells, where Abd el Krim (see pp.178–179) was imprisoned after his surrender in nearby Targuist in 1926. Five years earlier, he had driven the Spanish from the town, a retreat that saw the loss of several thousand of their troops. Next to the kasbah is the Great Mosque, with a fifteenth-century octagonal tower.

The *place* was once the main market square, and off to its sides are a number of small **fondouks**; one of the more visible is at the beginning of the lane opposite the kasbah. The local Djebala tribesmen, who form most of the town's population, have a particular tradition of homosexuality, and there were boy markets held here until as recently as 1937, when they were officially banned by the Spanish administration.

Place el Makhzen and Ras el Ma

Place el Makhzen – the old "government square" – is nowadays more of a continuation of the marketplace, an elegant clearing with an old fountain and more souvenir stalls.

If you leave the Medina at this point, it's possible to follow **the river**, the Oued el Kebir, around the outside of the walls, with Bab Onsar up to your left. Here, past a couple of traditional flour-mills, **Ras el Ma** (head of the water) lies outside the top, eastern side of the town, where water (tapped for the town's supply) comes out of the gorge wall in a cascade so clear and cold that, in the local parlance, "it knocks your teeth out to drink it". It has long been a favourite picnic spot, and is to an extent a holy place, due to the nearby *marabout's* tomb of Sidi Abdallah Habti. To stop here and watch the local women going about their daily laundry chores is a rewarding – and inexpensive – treat.

Over to the southeast of the town, an enjoyable, half-hour walk brings you to the ruined "**Spanish Mosque**". It is set on a hilltop, with exterior patterned brickwork and an interior giving a good sense of the layout of a mosque – normally off-limits in Morocco.

Into the hills

Alongside the path to the Spanish Mosque are some spectacular rock-climbing pitches, frequented by European climbers; and in the limestone hills behind there are active cave systems – the source of local springs.

Further afield, a good **day's hike** is to head east, up over the mountains behind Chefchaouen. As you look at the "two horns" from town, there is a path winding along the side of the mountain on your left. A four-hour (or more) hike will take you up to the other side, where a vast valley opens up, and if you walk further, you'll see the sea. The valley, as even casual exploration will show, is full of small farms cultivating *kif* – as they have done for years. Walking here, you may occasionally be stopped by the military, who are cracking down on foreign involvement in the crop. For more ambitious hikes – and there are some wonderful paths in the area – ask at the *pensions* about hiring a **guide**. Someone knowledgeable can usually be found to accompany you, for around 150dh a day; the harder the climb, the more it costs.

Eating

Most of Chefchaouen's better **restaurants** are in the back streets of the Medina. **Place Outa el Hammam** is one of the prime spots for a meal, and the restaurants giving onto it are surprisingly cheap, though not all of them are that great to eat at – be particularly wary of those which have ready-fried fish lying out in their kitchens to serve rather than cooking it fresh for each customer (some of those at the northern end of the square are particularly guilty of this).

Medina

Chez Fouad Rue Adarve Chabu. A poky little place known for its tajines and fish kebabs. Cheap.

Granada opposite *Chez Fouad* on Rue Adarve Chabu. Extremely cheap, with quite reasonable food (chicken and chips, tajines), but nothing tremendously exciting.

Restaurant Assada on a nameless lane just north of Bab el Ain, opposite the *Hôtel Bab el Ain*. This has long been a favourite and has recently extended across the lane and above to an open terrace. Very friendly, and serves food all day from breakfast through to tajine or couscous at dinner. Cheap.

Restaurant el Baraka near *Hôtel Andaluz* on Rue Sidi Salem. This is a great little place: a beautiful 150-year-old house, built for a judge, and sensitively, though slightly eccentrically, converted; the food's good, too. Cheap.

Restaurant La Lampe Magique Casa Alladin Zenkat el Targui. A reasonable tourist restaurant just off Place Outa el Hammam, with vegetarian tajine and couscous on offer.

Restaurant Pekin Place Outa el Hammam The middle of three restaurants (the other two are *Morisco* and *Bab Kasba*) in a row on the square, directly opposite the kasbah. All three serve fairly standard Moroccan food and are open from breakfast 'til late. Moderate.

Restaurant Tissemlal Zenkat el Targui ☏ 039 98 61 53. A beautifully decorated old house with French-Moroccan set menu (60dh). There are a few rooms here, too; a double room with half-board (**⑤**).

Restaurant al Azhar At the bottom of the steps on Av Moulay Idriss. Popular local eatery with good food and friendly and efficient service. Cheap.

Restaurant Moulay Ali Berrachid Rue Moulay Ali Ben Rachid – just up from Bab el Ain. A popular restaurant, specializing in fresh fish. Cheap.

Moving on

The **gare routière** is a fifteen-minute walk southwest from the town centre – head south from Place Mohammed V down Avenue Mohammed V, cross Avenue Abdelkrim el Kattabi, and turn right after 200m down Avenue Mohammed Abdou (no street sign at the junction). A petit taxi from Bab el Ain shouldn't cost much more than 15dh.

Unfortunately, CTM and most other lines start their Chefchaouen routes elsewhere so that buses can (despite promises) arrive full, with no available space. The best advice is to visit the bus station the evening before you plan to leave and, if possible, book a ticket in advance.

Availability tends to be best on the routes to Tetouan, Tangier or Fnideq – indeed, Tetouan has at least one departure every hour between 6am and 6pm, and sometimes as many as four. Services to Fes and Meknes are more likely to be full, and you may have to take a grand taxi to Ouezzane and another to join to pick up onward transport there.

Grands taxis for Ouezzane and Bab Berred (connecting there for Issaguen and points east) leave from around the junction of Avenue Allal Ben Abdallah with Avenue Zerktouni near the market. For Tangier and Tetouan, they leave from Avenue Jamal Dine el Afghani, off the west side of Place Mohammed V. To reach Fes or Meknes, you can change vehicles at Ouezzane and again at Jorf (where, be warned, grands taxis to Fes and Meknes are sparse, and you'll probably end up having to wait for a bus) or travel in style by chartering a grand taxi – you'll need to bargain hard, but the trip should cost around 450dh for up to six passengers.

Dardara

The tiny rural hamlet of **DARDARA** lies 11km from Chefchaouen at the junction of the N2 to Al Hoceima and the P28 to Ouezzane. Here you will find ⅔ *Auberge Dardara* (☏039 88 39 19, ⓦ www.dardara.com, compulsory half-board ⓰), which has been welcoming guests, including King Mohammed VI, to experience its unique blend of rustic getaway and agri-tourism since 2001. The brainchild of local man El Hababi Jaber ("call me Jabba"), the auberge has twelve comfortably furnished rooms – each named after an influential woman in Jabba's life – and focuses on environmentally friendly practices and community involvement. The **restaurant** serves fresh, hearty food – the aptly named "mountain breakfast" is highly recommended – and is open all day to nonresidents. Fresh, in-season supplies are sourced daily through a local co-operative, and guests can visit some of these surrounding farms to see various products such as olive oil and goats' cheese being made. The range around the village is popular with hikers, and Jabba has accompanied the King hiking on numerous occasions.

Dardara village can be reached by any bus or grand taxi plying the route between Chefchaouen and Ouezzane or by grands taxis travelling between Chefchaouen and Bab Taza or Issaguen (Ketama). *Auberge Dardara* is 300m east of the junction, on the road to Bab Taza.

Ouezzane (Wazzan)

OUEZZANE, 60km southwest of Chefchaouen, has a fine, mountainous site, looping around an outreach of the Djebala mountains. It stands virtually at the edge of the Rif and formed the traditional border between the *Bled es-Makhzen* (the governed territories) and the *Bled es-Siba* (those of the lawless tribes). As such, the town was an important power base, and particularly so under the last nineteenth-century sultans, when its local sheikhs became among the most powerful in Morocco.

The sheikhs – the *Ouezzani* – were the spiritual leaders of the influential **Tabiya brotherhood**. They were *shereefs* (descendants of the Prophet) and came in a direct line from the Idrissids, the first and founding dynasty of Morocco. This, however, seems to have given them little significance until the eighteenth century, when Moulay Abdallah es-Shereef established a *zaouia* at Ouezzane. This religious centre acquired a huge following, becoming one of the great places of pilgrimage and an inviolable sanctuary.

Unlike Chefchaouen, the town that grew up around this centre was not itself sacred, but until the beginning of the twentieth century Jews and Christians were allowed to take only temporary residence in one of the *fondouks* set aside for this purpose. Walter Harris, who became a close friend of the Ouezzani *shereefs* in the late nineteenth century, found the town "the most fanatical that Europeans may visit" and the *zaouia* a virtually autonomous religious court. Strange to relate, however, an Englishwoman, Emily Keane, married in 1877 the principal *shereef*, Si Abdesslem, whom she had met while out riding. For several decades she lived in the town, openly as a Christian, dispensing medical care to the locals. Her *Life Story*, published in 1911 after her husband's death, ends with the balanced summing up: "I do not advise anyone to follow in my footsteps, at the same time I have not a single regret." She is commemorated in the Anglican church in Tangier.

Ouezzane is also a place of pilgrimage for Moroccan Jews, who come here twice a year (April & Sept) to visit the tomb of Rabbi Amrane ben Diwane, an eighteenth-century Jewish *marabout* buried in a Jewish cemetery north of town.

The Town

The **Zaouia**, distinguished by an unusual octagonal minaret, is the most striking building in the town, and though the Tabiya brotherhood now maintain their main base elsewhere, it continues to function and is the site of a lively spring **moussem**, or pilgrimage festival. (As in the rest of Morocco, entrance to the *zaouia* area is forbidden to non-Muslims.)

The older quarters of Ouezzane – many of their buildings tiled, gabled and sporting elaborate doors – enclose and rise above the *zaouia*, newer suburbs sprawling into the hills on each side. There is a grandeur in the site, though with the *zaouia* off limits, little of specific interest.

The main **souks** climb up from an archway on the main square, Place de l'Indépendance, by the *Grand Hôtel*. Ouezzane has a local reputation for its woollen rugs – most evident in the weavers' souk, around Place Rouida near the top end of the town. Also rewarding is the metalworkers' souk, a covered lane under the Mosque of Moulay Abdallah Shereef; to find it, ask directions for the pleasant (and adjacent) *Café Bellevue*. The town has an Ensemble Artisanal on Place de l'Indépendance, and there is a large Thursday souk down the hill from Place de l'Indépendance, near the bus station.

Practicalities

Few tourists stay in Ouezzane, as it is only a couple of hours out of Chefchaouen, but there are worse places to be stranded. The bus and grand taxi terminal is about 50m below the **Place de l'Indépendance**, where you'll also find four small **hotels**. The best of these, though it's by no means deluxe, is the *Grand* (no phone; ❷). The *Marhaba*, *Horloge* and *El Elam* (all ❶) are more basic, with little to choose between them, except that the *Horloge* is the cheapest. The only relatively upmarket option is the new *Motel Rif*, 4km out on the Fes road (☎037 90 71 72). There is a **hammam** on Avenue Mohammed V and **grill-cafés** on the square.

Ouezzane provides a useful link if you're travelling by **public transport** (bus or grand taxi) between Chefchaouen and the Atlantic coast. There are also a fair number of **buses** to Meknes and Fes, but if you're stopping or staying, buy onward tickets in advance; as with Chefchaouen it's not unusual for them to arrive and leave full. Grands taxis occasionally run direct to Fes, but usually you have to take one to the truck-stop village of Jorf and pick up onward transport there. If you arrive early in the day, you should find grands taxis from Jorf to Fes, but otherwise, and for Meknes, you will have to take a bus.

Travel details

Trains

Tangier to: Asilah (6 daily; 40min); Casablanca Voyageurs (3 direct & 3 connecting daily; 5hr 15min); Fes (1 direct & 5 connecting daily; 5hr 10min); Marrakesh (1 direct & 5 connecting daily; 9hr 40min); Meknes (1 direct & 5 connecting daily; 4hr 15min); Oujda (1 direct & 2 connecting daily; 11hr 40min); Rabat (3 direct & 3 connecting daily; 4hr 15min); Souk el Arba (5 daily; 2hr); Taza (1 direct & 3 connecting daily; 7hr 50min).

Buses

Asilah to: Larache (25 daily; 1hr); Tangier (25 daily; 40min).
Chefchaouen to: Al Hoceima (1 CTM daily; 4hr 30min); Casablanca (3 daily; 9hr); Fes (3 CTM and 8 others daily; 5hr); Fnideq (4 daily; 2hr 30min); Meknes (4 daily; 5hr 30min); Rabat (5 daily; 8hr); Tangier (1 CTM and 9 others daily; 3hr 30min); Tetouan (2 CTM daily & others at least hourly 6am–6pm; 2hr).
Larache to: Asilah (3 CTM & 22 others daily; 1hr); Ksar el Kebir (8 daily; 40min); Meknes (2 daily; 5hr 30min); Rabat (20 daily; 3hr 30min); Souk el Arba (8 daily; 1hr).
Ouezzane to: Chefchaouen (4 daily; 2hr); Fes (3 daily; 5hr 30min); Meknes (2 daily; 4hr); Tangier (1 daily; 5hr).
Souk el Arba to: Moulay Bousselham (5 daily; 35min); Ouezzane (3 daily; 1hr 30min).

Tangier to: Agadir (1 CTM & 1 other daily; 16hr); Al Hoceima (7 daily; 6hr); Asilah (3 CTM & 22 others daily; 40min); Casablanca (4 CTM & 35 others daily; 6hr 30min); Chefchaouen (1 CTM & 9 others daily; 4hr 30min); Fes (3 CTM & 9 others daily; 5hr 45min); Fnideq (for Ceuta) (13 daily; 1hr); Larache (3 CTM & 22 others daily; 1hr 30min); Marrakesh (1 CTM & 6 others daily; 10hr); Meknes (3 CTM & 9 others daily; 7hr); Nador (6 daily; 12hr); Rabat (5 CTM and 35 others daily; 5hr); Tetouan (2 CTM and over 50 others daily; 1hr 30min).
Tetouan to: Agadir (1 CTM bus daily; 15hr); Al Hoceima (2 CTM and 9 others daily; 5hr 30min); Casablanca (2 CTM & 23 others daily; 6hr); Chefchaouen (2 CTM & 20 others daily; 1hr 30min); Fes (3 CTM & 4 others daily; 5hr 20min); Fnideq (for Ceuta) (12 daily; 1hr); Larache (6 daily; 3hr); Marrakesh (1 CTM & 7 others daily; 10hr); Meknes (2 CTM & 5 others daily; 6hr); Nador (1 CTM & 7 others daily; 9hr 30min); Oued Laou (5 daily; 1hr 30min); Rabat (2 CTM & 18 others daily; 5hr); Tangier (1 CTM & some 50 others daily; 1hr 30min).

Grands taxis

Asilah to: Larache (40min); Tangier (40min).
Chefchaouen to: Bab Berred (50min); Ouezzane (1hr 15min); Tangier (2hr); Tetouan (1hr).
Fnideq to: Ceuta border (10min); Mdiq (20min); Tangier (1hr); Tetouan (20min).
Ksar el Kebir to: Larache (30min); Ouezzane (1hr); Souk el Arba (30min).

Larache to: Asilah (40min); Ksar el Kebir (30min).
Mdiq to: Fnideq (for Ceuta) (30min); Martil (15min); Tetouan (20min).
Ouezzane to: Chefchaouen (1hr 15min); Jorf (change for Fes) (45min); Ksar el Kebir (1hr); Souk el Arba (1hr).
Souk el Arba to: Ksar el Kebir (30min); Moulay Bousselham (30min); Ouezzane (1hr).
Tangier to: Asilah (40min); Chefchaouen (2hr); Fnideq (for Ceuta) (1hr); Ksar es Seghir (30min); Tetouan (1hr).
Tetouan to: Chefchaouen (1hr); Fnideq (for Ceuta) (20min); Martil (15min); Mdiq (20min); Oued Laou (1hr); Tangier (1hr).

Ferries

Ceuta to: Algeciras (12–30 daily; 45min–1hr 30min).
Tangier to: Algeciras (12–22 daily; 1hr 30min–2hr 30min); Genoa (1 weekly; 48hrs); Gibraltar (1 weekly; 1hr 20min); Sète (1–2 weekly; 36hr); Tarifa, passage for EU passport holders only (4–10 daily; 35min).

Flights

Tangier to: Casablanca (3–5 daily on RAM & Regional Air Lines; 55min).

The Mediterranean coast and the Rif

CHAPTER 2 # Highlights

✻ **Chefchaouen to Al Hoceima** The scenic and sometimes vertiginous drive along the northern slopes of the Rif is spectacular, and more relaxed than it used to be. See p.175

✻ **Mar Chica, Nador** A mint tea and cake at sundown in the seafront café here is the perfect end to a day's bird-watching by the dunes and lagoons. See p.189

✻ **Melilla** The Spanish enclave boasts a wealth of Art Nouveau buildings, perfect for touring after tapas. See p.192

✻ **Grotte du Chameau** Explore this cavern of stalactites, and take a walk in the nearby Zegzel Gorge. See p.198

✻ **Saïdia** Close to the Algerian border, this enjoyable beach resort comes alive in summer, hosting a Raï music and popular arts festival in August. See p.199

✻ **Cirque du Djebel** This classic car-driver's route crosses between the Rif and Middle Atlas, and passes by the massive Friouato Cave. See p.208

△ Art Nouveau building, Melilla

The Mediterranean coast and the Rif

Morocco's Mediterranean coast extends for nearly 500km – from the Spanish enclave of Ceuta east to Saïdia on the Algerian border. The westerly reaches around Tetouan, described in the previous chapter (see pp.157–159), shelter the only established resorts. Beyond Tetouan you enter the shadow of the Rif Mountains, which restrict access to the sea to a very few points. Such beaches as there are here remain almost entirely undeveloped and for a seaside stop you really need to head east to the fishing harbour and small-time resort of Al Hoceima, or to Saïdia, beach playground for the city of Oujda, at the end of the road. Neither is much visited by foreigners, though this may change in Saïdia with the completion of two European-financed residential golf resorts just west of the town. If you're making a loop east of the Rif, you'll find Oujda a pleasant, relaxed city, with a scenic side-trip through the Zegzel gorges, and further gorges, cutting into the Middle Atlas, at Taza, on the Fes–Oujda road.

Between Al Hoceima and Oujda is a second Spanish enclave, **Melilla**, which with its flights and ferries to various cities on "the mainland" sees a fair bit of traffic. Though pleasant and interesting in its way, Melilla will not tempt many for a detour if not travelling through other than bird-watchers, as the dunes and lagoons spreading around nearby **Nador** are among the richest sites in Morocco.

The **Rif Mountains** themselves are even less on the tourist trail than the coast – and with some reason. This is wild, isolated country, and always has been, with a tradition of dissent from central government and little relationship with the authorities. A vast, limestone mass, over 300km long and up to 2500m in height, the Rif is in fact the natural boundary between Europe and Africa, and with the Sahara it cuts off central Morocco from Algeria and the rest of the Maghreb. In the past this was a powerful barrier – it took the first recorded European traveller three months to travel from Al Hoceima to Melilla – and even today there is no other part of Morocco where you feel so completely incidental to ordinary local life. That is, unless you happen to be involved in smuggling. For the Riffian economy, these days, is based very largely on cannabis, and the sale of its dried leaves to smoke as **kif** or of its resin, compressed into browny-black blocks, as **hashish**. Even where uncultivated, the plants grow wild around the stony slopes, and with prices bringing growers five

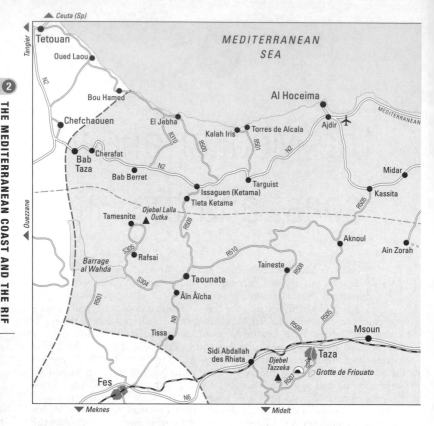

times that of other cereal crops, it is not surprising that it has taken over so much of the farmland. The cultivation itself is legal, but Moroccan laws forbid its sale, purchase and even possession outside the region (see p.80). These laws are enforced on occasion with some vigour, so don't be seduced by the locals: police roadblocks are frequent, informers common. Cannabis in the Rif is big business and not for casual visitors to get mixed up in; there are enough Westerners already in jail in Morocco for hash.

If you want a look at some dramatic Riffian scenery, there's nothing to stop you taking a bus or grand taxi between Chefchaouen and Fes, via **Ketama**, or Al Hoceima or Nador and Taza, via **Aknoul**. For many years it was considered unwise to **drive** through Ketama, especially in a foreign-registered or rented vehicle, as local gangsters frequently forced such cars off the road, pressurizing the drivers into buying large amounts of low-grade hash or simply robbing them at knifepoint. According to locals and some resident ex-pats, however, such incidents are very rare these days, and the N2 (formerly P39), which passes through Ketama and contours the northern slopes of the Rif, feels reasonably secure and busy, at least during the day. Moreover, if you drive on a **souk** day – and there is virtually no weekday when there isn't a market somewhere around Ketama – you are unlikely to be the only car on the road for any length of time. However, common sense applies, and you should on no

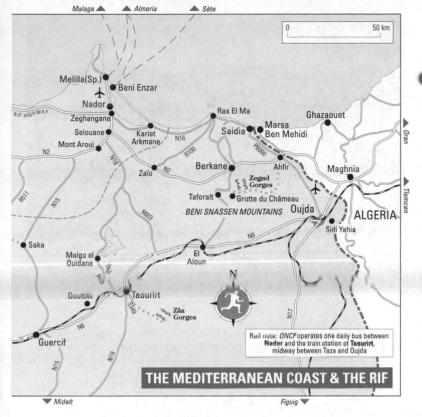

Rail note: *ONCF* operates one daily bus between **Nador** and the train station at **Taourirt**, midway between Taza and Oujda

THE MEDITERRANEAN COAST & THE RIF

account stop for hitchhikers or people who appear to be asking for help and never stop if a car pulls over to the side of your vehicle to offer you some hash "on the go". As an alternative, you can opt to drive between Fes and Al Hoceima or Melilla using the main road (N6, formerly P1) via Taza and cross over the Rif via Aknoul (R505, formerly S312) or make a detour further east via Guercif and Saka (N15). Between Fes and Chefchaouen go via Ouezzane (N4/N13; formerly P26/P28); and between Chefchaouen and Al Hoceima, you could take the long way round via Ouezzane, Fes, Taza and Aknoul (N13/N4/N6/R505/N2).

On top of the Rif: the road from Chefchaouen to Ketama and Al Hoceima

There are very few journeys in Morocco as spectacular as that from **Chefchaouen** (see p.160) **to Al Hoceima**. The road precisely – and perversely – follows the backbone of the Western Rif, the highest peaks in the north of the country. You can look down on one side to the Mediterranean coast, and on the other across the southern range; "big mountains and more

175

△ Rif mountains

big mountains" – as Paul Bowles put it in a wonderful travel piece, "The Rif, to Music", in *Their Heads are Green* – "mountains covered with olive trees, with oak trees, with bushes, and finally with giant cedars". This is not a route to be undertaken by inexperienced drivers; although in good condition, it seems constructed entirely of zigzags and hairpin turns. Just beyond Chefchaouen, an excellent first stop is the hamlet of Dardara, and its eco-friendly auberge (see p.167).

Bab Taza, Bab Berret and Ketama

BAB TAZA, 23km out of Chefchaouen, is the first village of any size – an attractive place surrounded by rolling, green, flower-strewn countryside and outcrops of claret thyme. It has a Wednesday souk, a petrol station and a branch of Banque Populaire (foreign exchange available). Ten kilometres further on is **Cherafat**, a little village with a noted spring and a small waterfall which rushes under the road. A set of stone steps 25m beyond the bridge at the entrance to the village leads up to the spring, from where there are breathtaking views of the valleys below. If you feel adventurous you can scramble further into the mountain following the obvious route up the gorge. Like Bab Taza, Cherafat has no hotel, although cafés and grill-bars line the main road, as buses travelling through to Al Hoceima, Nador and Oujda make a stopover here. Fifteen kilometres further east is **Khamis Medik**, where an inviting Thursday souk attracts a multitude of Berber villagers – locally known as *Djebala* – from the surrounding areas.

Once beyond Khamis Medik, you wind around the tops of ridges with sheer drops on either side to gorges and isolated valleys. The road is particularly scenic on the approach to **BAB BERRET**, a smallish market village and former Spanish administrative centre. It's always busy with traffic, not least during the Monday souk, and several basic **hotels** (all ❶) on both sides of the main road, all with communal toilets and cold showers, cater mainly for passing Moroccan tradespeople. The *Barcelona* and *Etoile* are at the western end of the main road; the *Sahara* and *Rif* are near the grand taxi stand; and the *Dakhla*, the best of the lot, is 200m beyond. The CTM **bus** to Al Hoceima passes through at 8.30am on its way to Nador (50dh). Non-CTM buses leave for Fes at 9am and 10am (60dh). The village also signals the real beginning of *kif* country – it is surrounded, in fact, by the plants from March to August (during the winter months only wheat is grown) and the expensive and isolated villas that dot the landscape are testimony to the wealth generated by the illegal trade. At **ISSAGUEN** (usually marked on maps simply as "Ketama"), 30km to the east, where the N2 from Chefchaouen to Al Hoceima meets the R509 (formerly S302) Route de l'Unité, you arrive at the epicentre of the *kif* region.

The region, **KETAMA**, even in transit, is an initiation because absolutely everybody seems to be involved in "Business". If you get off the bus at Issaguen you might well be immediately offered large amounts of hash – and few locals will believe that you are here for any other purpose. Anywhere in Morocco, if people introduce themselves as "from Ketama", there is no ambiguity about what they are offering. Small-time dealers or growers here may invite you to stay at their farms – not to be recommended, even if you've got an insatiable appetite and curiosity for *kif* production travellers tend to leave parted from their money and possessions. Apart from a hectic Thursday souk, and the three-hour trek up nearby **Djebel Tidighine** there is no particular reason to stay, and indeed both Issaguen, and the region's main village – **TLETA KETAMA**, 8km down the road to Fes – are probably best avoided. If travelling by grand taxi from Fes or Chefchaouen to Al Hoceima, or vice-versa, you will probably have to change vehicles at Issaguen; if that happens, make sure you arrive early enough to be certain of getting a vehicle out. Grands taxis for Chefchaouen and for Targuist and Al Hoceima leave from, respectively, just west and just east of the road junction, which is where buses also stop; grands taxis for Taounate, where you change for Fes, leave 300m south of the junction. Just walking that 300m or waiting for a connecting vehicle, you are sure to be accosted by several unpleasant "hello my friend" types wanting to sell you hash. Even if you want to buy some, this is not the place to do it, and these are not the people to buy it from. There are a couple of cheap and fairly run-down hotels, the *Warda* (❶) and the slightly better *Saada* (☎039 81 30 61; ❶) south of the N2/R509 junction near the Taounate taxi stand. The old Spanish *parador*, the *Hôtel Tidighine*, just south of the junction, where once upon a time tourists stayed to ski or hunt wild boar on Djebel Tidighine, lies vacant, still awaiting a multi-million dirham investment which will reportedly restore the town's landmark to its former glory.

Roads to the coast lead off 23km before and 12km beyond Issaguen, cutting through the mountains to El Jebha (see p.160). This is a memorable trip but there are much better resorts at Torres de Alcala and Kalah Iris, accessible from the next junction (see p.178).

Continuing east from Ketama, with the cedar forests giving way to barren, stony slopes, you reach the town of **TARGUIST**, Abd el Krim's HQ and last stronghold (see box, pp.178–179) and the site of his surrender to the French. Paul Bowles described the place, almost forty years ago, in "The Rif, to Music", as "a monstrous excrescence with long dirty streets, the wind blowing along them, whipping clouds of dust and filth against the face, stinging the skin". It has not improved and, despite a trio of **small hotels** (all ❶), would

Abd el Krim and the Republic of the Rif

Until the establishment of the Spanish protectorate in 1912, the **tribes of the Rif** existed outside government control – a northern heartland of the *Bled es Siba*. They were subdued temporarily by *harkas*, the burning raids with which sultans asserted their authority, and for a longer period under Moulay Ismail; but for the most part, bore out their own name of *Imazighen*, or "Free Ones".

Closed to outside influence, the tribes developed an isolated and self-contained way of life. The Riffian soil, stony and infertile, produced constant problems with food supplies, and it was only through a complex system of alliances (*liffs*) that outright wars were avoided. Blood feuds, however, were endemic, and a major contributor to maintaining a viably small population. Unique in Morocco, the Riffian villages are scattered communities, their houses hedged and set apart, and where each family maintained a pillbox tower to spy on and fight off enemies. They were different, too, in their religion: the *salat*, the prayers said five times daily – one of the central tenets of Islam – was not observed. *Djinns*, supernatural fire spirits, were widely accredited, and great reliance was placed on the intercession of local *marabouts*.

It was an unlikely ground for significant and organized rebellion, yet for over five years (1921–27) the tribes forced the Spanish to withdraw from the mountains. Several times they defeated whole Spanish armies, first and most memorably at **Annoual** in 1921 (see p.186), which with later disasters led to General Primo de Rivera becoming – with the king's blessing – the virtual dictator of Spain. It was only through the intervention of France, and the joint commitment of nearly half a million troops, that the Europeans won eventual victory.

In the intervening years, **Abd el Krim el Khattabi**, the leader of the revolt, was able to declare a **Republic of the Rif** and to establish much of the apparatus of a modern state. Well educated, and confident of the Rif's mineral reserves, he and his brother, Mohammed, manipulated the *liff* system to forge an extraordinary unity among the tribes, negotiated mining rights in return for arms with Germany and South America, and even set up a Riffian State Bank. Still more impressive, the brothers managed to impose a series of social reforms – including the destruction of family pillboxes and the banning of *kif* – which allowed the operation of a fairly broad administrative system. In their success, however, was the inevitability of defeat. It was the first nationalist movement in colonial North Africa, and although the Spanish were ready to quit the zone in 1925, it was politically impossible for the French to allow that. Intervention by French troops tipped the balance against the rebels.

be a perverse place to stay. For much of the year most of the newly built houses in town stand empty, waiting for their Moroccan owners, working in Europe, to come back for their yearly holiday. As a result the place has a desolate feel which only lifts during the summer months. It does, however, have a lively **Saturday souk**, which draws villagers from the dozens of tiny communities in the neighbouring hills.

Back on the main road, 2km beyond the junction to Targuist and alongside the Shell petrol station, there is a good, modest **restaurant**, the *Targuist*, favoured by long-distance buses.

Torres de Alcala and Kalah Iris

A pair of temptingly low-key beach resorts, **Torres de Alcala** and **Kalah Iris** are accessible via a broken road (signposted Beni Boufrah and Torres de Alcala) 5km west of Targuist, and can be reached by grand taxi from Targuist or Al Hoceima. The single-lane road winds up terraced slopes peppered with prickly pear cacti, almond trees and giant, mushroom-shaped haystacks.

Defeat for the Riffians – and the capture of Abd el Krim at Targuist – brought a virtual halt to social progress and reform. **The Spanish** took over the administration en bloc, governing through local *caids* (district administrators), and although they exploited some mineral deposits there was no road-building programme nor any of the other "civilizing benefits" introduced in the French zone. There were, however, two important changes: migration of labour (particularly to French Algeria) replaced the blood feud as a form of population control, and the Riffian warriors were recruited into Spain's own armies. The latter had immense consequences, allowing General Franco to build up a power base in Morocco. It was with **Riffian troops** that he invaded Andalusia in 1936, and it was probably their contribution that ensured the Fascist victory in the Spanish Civil War.

Abd el Krim was a powerful inspiration to later nationalists, and the Riffians themselves played an important guerrilla role in the 1955–56 **struggle for independence**. When, in April 1957, the Spanish finally surrendered their protectorate, however, the Berbers of the former Spanish zone found themselves largely excluded from government. Administrators were imposed on them from Fes and Casablanca, and in October 1958, the Rif's most important tribe, the Beni Urriaguel, rose in open **rebellion**. The mutiny was soon put down, but necessitated the landing at Al Hoceima of then-Crown Prince Hassan and some two-thirds of the Moroccan army.

Half a century later, the Rif is still perhaps the most unstable part of Morocco, remaining conscious of its under-representation in government and its historical underdevelopment. King Mohammed VI seems sympathetic to this situation and in recent years the region has witnessed substantial school-building programmes, improved road, air and ferry accessibility, a large, new, agricultural project in the plains south of Nador and Al Hoceima and massive tourism developments near the Algerian border. Labour **emigration**, too, remains high – with Western Europe replacing Algeria as the main market – and (as in the rest of Morocco) there is widespread resentment at the difficulty of obtaining a passport and then a visa for this outlet. With the growth of more sophisticated government systems, further tribal dissidence now seems unlikely, though there has recently been public displays of dissent, near the Riffian town of Al Hoceima, directed at the national government over its delayed assistance to some victims of the fatal earthquake that rocked the area in 2004.

Nearer the sea the road periodically disappears under the debris of flash floods as it crosses and recrosses the *oued* beyond the hamlet of Beni Boufrah. In fact, Torres de Alcala is located at the edge of an alluvial plain, and is subject to the mixed blessings of the fertile sediments the *oued* brings and the high soil erosion it also causes.

Torres de Alcala

TORRES DE ALCALA is a simple, whitewashed hamlet, 250m from a small, pebbly beach. Cliffs frame its beach and on the western headland is a deserted fort, probably Spanish, with stunning views along the Mediterranean coast. A local man, Abdelhouaid Elhamdi (⊕039 80 89 63), has grouped together some fellow locals to form the Yellich Association, which offers bungalow **accommodation** (❺) along with some camping sites and homestays. Other than that, there's just a bakery and the smallest of shops.

Along a rocky cliff-path, 5km to the east, are the **ruins of Badis**, which from the fourteenth to the early sixteenth century was the main port of Fes,

Kif in Morocco – then and now

The traditions of kif . . .

Smoking *kif* or consuming hashish is an age-old tradition in the Rif and northern Morocco. Its effects were enthusiastically described by James Grey Jackson in *An Account of the Empire of Marocco*, published in 1809:

> The plant called Hashisha is the African hemp plant; it grows in all the gardens and is reared in the plains of Marocco for the manufacture of string, but in most parts of the country it is cultivated for the extraordinary and pleasing voluptuous vacuity of mind which it produces in those who smoke it; unlike the intoxication from wine, a fascinating stupour pervades the mind, and the dreams are agreeable. The Kief, which is the flower and seeds of the plant, is the strongest, and a pipe of it half the size of a common English tobacco pipe, is sufficient to intoxicate. The infatuation of those who use it is such that they cannot exist without it.

> The Kief is usually pounded, and mixed with an invigorating confection which is sold at an enormous price; a piece of this as big as a walnut will for a time entirely deprive a man of all reason and intellect: they prefer it to opium from the voluptuous sensations which it never fails to produce. Wine or brandy, they say, does not stand in competition with it.

> The Hashisha, or leaves of the plant, are dried and cut like tobacco, and are smoked in very small pipes, but when the person wishes to indulge in the sensual stupour it occasions, he smokes the Hashisha pure, and in less than half an hour it operates: the person under its influence is said to experience pleasing images: he fancies himself in company with beautiful women; he dreams that he is an emperor, or a bashaw, and that the world is at his nod.

. . . and the modern industry

Although many of the Riffian tribes in the mountains had always smoked *kif*, it was the Spanish who really encouraged its cultivation – probably as an effort to keep the peace. This situation was apparently accepted when Mohammed V came to power, though the reasons for his doing so are obscure. There is a story, probably

and used for trade with the western Mediterranean states, in particular Venice. A once-considerable caravan route ran across the Rif, following the course of the modern R509 road, the so-called Route de l'Unité (see p.201).

Offshore from Badis is a small island, the **Peñon de Velez de la Gomera**, which – like the islands off Al Hoceima, and Chafarinas further east – remains Spanish territory. It was this that caused the port's decline. The Spaniards occupied it in 1508, then in 1522 it passed to the Turks, who used it as a base for raids along the Spanish coast. Felipe II of Spain tried to regain it, failed to do so, but destroyed Badis in the process. Subsequently, the island was used by Turkish and other pirates before, in the twentieth century, the Spanish took possession, using it until recent years as a penitentiary.

Kalah Iris

At **KALAH IRIS**, 4km west of Torres de Alcala along a paved road, there's a longer beach, with a natural breakwater, formed by a sandspit that runs out to one of two islets in the bay. There is no village as such here but few facilities: a good **campsite** (☎039 80 87 27; June–Aug), plus a restaurant, café and a shop with fresh food. It is not totally undiscovered, with excursions being offered to European holidaymakers in Al Hoceima, but it's still a delightful spot.

apocryphal, that when he visited Ketama in 1957, he accepted a bouquet of cannabis as a symbolic gift.

Whatever, Ketama continued to supply the bulk of the country's cannabis, and in the early 1970s it became the centre of a significant drug industry, exporting to Europe and America. This sudden growth was accounted for by the introduction, by an American dealer, of techniques for producing hash resin. Overnight, the Riffians had access to a compact and easily exportable product, as well as a burgeoning world market for dope. Inevitably, big business was quick to follow and over a quarter of a century on, Morocco is reckoned to be the world's leading producer of cannabis, supplying the vast majority of Europe's demand, and contributing an estimated US$2bn (£1.2bn) to the Moroccan economy. Even bigger money, however, is made by the dealers – mainly British, Dutch, Spanish, and Italians – who organize the shipments and sell the hash on the streets at prices fifty times higher than those paid to the Riffian growers.

The Moroccan authorities are caught between a rock and a hard place over the cannabis industry. They are pressured by Western European governments – and the UN – to take action against growers and dealers, and, given their aspirations to join the EU, have made efforts to cooperate. But the cultivation and sale of cannabis are important items in the local economy. Short of radically diversifying the agriculture of the Rif, and paying large subsidies to the local farms, little can be done to limit the cultivation. Hassan II actually announced such a scheme as long ago as 1994 promising to devote US$9.8 billion in the economy of the Rif in a programme developed with the European Union.

The EU, through its MEDA programme, allocated a budget of €5.4 billion for Morocco for the period 2000–2006. These funds included grants to improve the north's infrastructure and to support integrated rural development in the Rif region. Cannabis cultivation had expanded well beyond the Ketama region, causing a fall in quality and prices, but under UN and EU pressure, the government clamped down in 2006, confining cultivation to Ketama once again. Its stated aim was to eradicate the crop completely by 2008.

Al Hoceima and on to Nador

Coming from the Rif, **AL HOCEIMA** can be a bit of a shock. It may not be quite the "exclusive international resort" the tourist board claims, but it is truly Mediterranean and has developed enough to have little in common with the farming hamlets and tribal markets of the mountains around.

If you're travelling through the Rif, you will probably want to stop here and rest a couple of days – maybe longer. It is a relaxing place, with none of the hassle of Tangier or Fes or Tetouan, and the cafés and streets full of people going about their business or pleasure. In late spring, or September, when the beaches are quiet, it's near idyllic. In midsummer, though, the town and its beaches get pretty crowded under the weight of Moroccan families and French and German tourists, and rooms can be difficult to find. It is, after all, a small town and not geared to tourism on the scale of, say, Tangier or Agadir.

The peaceful atmosphere of the town was tragically disturbed, not for the first time, in the early hours of February 24, 2004, by an earthquake measuring 6.5 on the Richter scale. Although most of the buildings in town are built to withstand earthquakes, it was the smaller communities around Al Hoceima, particularly Imzouren and Aït Kamra, that were badly hit by the quake. The final death toll was 572. Al Hoceima was also very near the epicentre of Morocco's

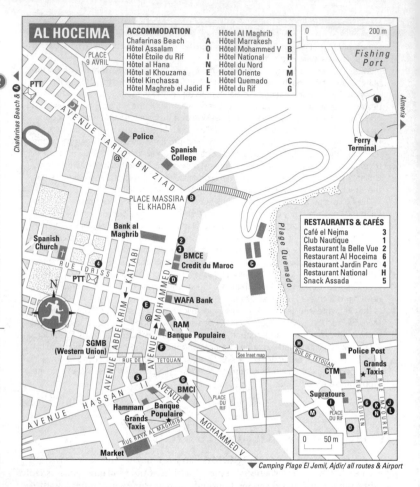

Chafarinas Beach & ◀

AL HOCEIMA

ACCOMMODATION

Chafarinas Beach	A	Hôtel Al Maghrib	K
Hôtel Assalam	O	Hôtel Marrakesh	D
Hôtel Étoile du Rif	I	Hôtel Mohammed V	B
Hôtel al Hana	N	Hôtel National	H
Hôtel al Khouzama	E	Hôtel du Nord	J
Hôtel Kinchassa	L	Hotel Oriente	M
Hôtel Maghreb el Jadid	F	Hôtel Quemado	C
		Hôtel du Rif	G

RESTAURANTS & CAFÉS

Café el Nejma	3
Club Nautique	1
Restaurant la Belle Vue	2
Restaurant Al Hoceima	6
Restaurant Jardin Parc	4
Restaurant National	H
Snack Assada	5

▼ *Camping Plage El Jemil, Ajdir/ all routes & Airport*

previous big earthquake in 1990. Physical evidence of either quake, in Al Hoceima at least, is minimal. There are reports, however, that some of the more remote villages affected by the most recent quake haven't yet received any significant assistance, resulting in sporadic protests and confrontations with the local *gendarmerie*.

The Town

Al Hoceima's compact size is one of its charms. Until the 1950s, it consisted of just a small fishing port to the north of the bay, and a fringe of white houses atop the barren cliffs to the south. At the heart of this older quarter is the **Place du Rif**, enclosed by café-restaurants and *pensions*, and the terminal for CTM and private-line buses.

The newer part of town, with its neat grid of boulevards and occasional palms, occupies the land sloping down to the cliffs above the town beach, **Plage Quemado** – between the harbour and the original village – and at every turn you can see either the wooded hills behind the town, or the sea. If this quarter can be said to have a heart, it is the **Place Massira el Khadra**, a squeaky-clean square on the cliff top, at the upper end of **Avenue Mohammed V**, the principal boulevard.

From some vantage points, you get a view of the **Peñon de Alhucemas**, another of the Spanish-owned islands off this coast (and another former penitentiary), over in the bay to the east of town. It's a pretty focal point, topped with sugar-white houses, a church and tower. The Spanish took it in 1673 and have held it ever since – a perennial source of dispute between Morocco and Spain. Some Moroccan patriots refer to it as the *Ile de N'Kor*, after the Oued Nekor, which flows into the bay.

There seems, however, no lobby for a change of name for Al Hoceima itself, which was developed by the Spanish after their counter-offensive in the Rif in 1925 (see pp.178–179), and was known by them as **Villa Sanjuro**. The name commemorated the Spanish General José Sanjuro, who landed in the bay, under the cover of Spanish and French warships, with an expeditionary force – and it is still occasionally used for the old part of town around the Place du Rif. Coincidentally, it was at Al Hoceima, too, that the then Crown Prince Hassan led Moroccan forces to quell the Riffians' revolt in 1958, following independence.

Names aside, the Spanish left little to distinguish their occupation. The only notable architectural feature is the **Spanish College**, the Colegio Español de Alhucemia, which, until 1956, was the provincial headquarters of the *Mición Cultural Española* in Morocco. It is the custard cream and chocolate building, with blue and white *azulejos* tiles, on the north edge of town, beyond the main square. At the college Moroccan children are given the opportunity to study a Spanish academic programme, taught by Spanish teachers, that leads to A-level/Baccalaureate-standard qualifications; then they can opt to go to Granada to pursue a higher degree at the university.

Beaches

Swimming – and walking in the olive-groved hills if you want a change – is the main attraction of Al Hoceima. If you wake early enough it is worth going down to **Plage Quemado**, the town beach, to watch the *lamparo* fishermen coming in; they work at night using powerful electric lamps to attract and dazzle the fish.

Besides Quemado, there is a less crowded beach at **Asfiha**, a kilometre southeast of town, along the Ajdir road (a cheap petit taxi ride, if you don't fancy walking). This stretches right round the bay to Djebel Hadid, the headland to the east. Four kilometres west of town from Place Massira el Khadra is **Plage Tala Youssef**, best known by the name of the exclusive and expensive resort *Chafarinas Beach* (see p.184) at its far end. You can walk the distance in about one hour – otherwise it's a rather steep 70dh by grand taxi. Both of these are better choices than Quemado, which gets very busy in high season.

There are beaches further west at Torres de Alcala and Kalah Iris (see p.179 & p.180), which, although 60km away, are nevertheless thought of as Al Hoceima beaches. They can be reached along a minor inland road by grand taxi.

Practicalities

All **buses** arrive in Al Hoceima at Place du Rif from where it is very easy to locate food and lodgings situated around the square or on Avenue Mohammed V, a short stroll away. If you are arriving by **grand taxi** from Nador, Oujda or Taza you will be dropped off just east of Place du Rif on Rue Alouien. Those arriving from other destinations such as Issaguen and Kalah Iris alight west of Avenue Mohammed V on Rue Raya al Maghriba.

At the time of writing the **tourist office** on Avenue Tariq Ibn Ziad, 300m northwest of Place Massira el Khadra had been demolished with no apparent temporary location until a new one is built. A well-known tour operator in town, ✈ Chafarinas Tours at 109 Bd Mohammed V (☎039 84 02 02, ⓦhttp://rifitours.tripod.com), has taken on the role of pseudo-tourism office. The staff are very helpful and will give you any assistance they can. They also organize **walking tours** and **pony trekking** in the Rif mountains, the logistics for which typically include accommodation in rural Berber houses and luggage relay either by 4x4, or mules in more rugged terrain.

There are plenty of **banks** with ATMs in town, including the Banque Populaire, BMCE and Crédit du Maroc all on Avenue Mohammed V. Numerous hotels and travel agents, however, will change money faster, at the same rates, and at times when banks are closed (the *Hôtel Étoile du Rif* and *Hôtel al Khouzama* for example). For **Internet** access, there is Cybercafé Aouragh on Avenue Tariq Ibn Ziad (open late afternoon until late evening) and Cyberclub On-line on Avenue Mohammed V (10am–2pm & 4pm–midnight). There are several **pharmacies** around town, mainly along Avenue Mohammed V, and a very handy one with helpful staff at the northeast corner of Place Massira (8.30am–12.30pm & 3–7.30pm).

The most convenient **hammam** is at 12 Rue Azzalaga, parallel with Avenue Hassan II behind the Banque Populaire. It's near the centre and easy to find (women daily 9am–5pm, men daily 5–9pm & Sat 5–9am) – a picture hung outside tells you which sex is in occupation.

Accommodation

Most of the cheaper, reasonable if basic *pensions* are grouped in and around the Place du Rif; there are also a couple of more upmarket options. There's a small, friendly **campsite**, *Camping Plage el Jamil* (also called *Camping Cala Bonita*), 500m east of town along the Ajdir road (☎039 98 40 26). Open year-round, it backs onto a stony beach, with a bar and restaurant and, in summer, a café, grocery store, water-skiing and pedalos.

Cheap

Hôtel Assalam 10 Pl du Rif ☎039 98 14 13. A larger *pension* than most, with a café on the ground floor. Some rooms have balconies and some have showers, which are cold, though hot common ones are available. ❷

Hôtel Étoile du Rif 40 Pl du Rif ☎039 84 08 47, ⑤039 98 56 96. The former *Hôtel Florido*, an ornate Spanish building in the middle of the square, with a lively café downstairs. Now refurbished, this is still the best-value hotel in town, with bright, clean, en-suite rooms, the best ones overlooking the square. ❸

Hôtel al Hana 17 Rue Imzouren ☎039 98 16 42. A decent place with simple but clean rooms. ❷

Hôtel Kinchassa next to *Hôtel du Nord* on Rue Imzouren. Cheapest of the budget hotels but very spartan. No French spoken. ❶

Hôtel Al Maghrib 23 Rue Imzouren (no phone). Brand new with large, tiled rooms, though none en suite. ❷

Hôtel Marrakesh 2 Rue Abdallah Hammou ☎039 98 30 25, ⑤039 98 10 58. A small hotel, whose clean, comfortable rooms are all en suite, with reliable hot water; all in all, good value for money. ❸

Hôtel du Nord 20 Rue Imzouren ☎039 98 30 79. Cleaner than a lot of the cheapies. Some rooms have balconies and hot showers are available (10dh). ❷

Hôtel Oriente Pl du Rif (no phone). Not all rooms have external windows, but some that do also have balconies. Probably a last resort if everywhere else is fully booked. ❷

Hôtel du Rif 13 Rue Moulay Youssef ☎039 98 22 68, ⑤039 98 02 20. Quite a large place, off the Place du Rif, in the jewellers' quarter. Simple but clean rooms with showers (10dh) on the corridor. ❶

Moderate to expensive

✈ **Chafarinas Beach** Plage Tala Youssef (Plage Chafarinas) ☎039 84 16 01,

Ⓟ039 84 16 05. If you are after upmarket accommodation and a peaceful setting, this is the obvious choice. Five kilometres from town, the far-reaching views over the Mediterranean from the magnificent reception hall and adjacent restaurant – open to nonresidents – are unmatched by any hotel in town, and these same views can be enjoyed from the twenty apartments dotted on the cliff slopes above the main building. Shuttle service to and from town. Breakfast included. **❼**

Hôtel al Khouzama Rue al Andalous ☎039 98 56 69, Ⓟ039 98 56 96. A modern hotel, with en-suite rooms and a lively café on the first floor. Rooms with windows facing onto the street are much brighter than those facing into a light well. **❺**

Hôtel Maghreb el Jadid 56 Av Mohammed V ☎039 98 49 14, Ⓟ039 98 25 05. The best upmarket choice in town: a central hotel, with a top-floor restaurant and bar. Clean and spacious

modernized en-suite rooms overlooking the main road. Discounts in winter. **❺**

Hôtel Mohammed V Pl Massira el Khadra ☎039 98 22 33 or 34, Ⓟ039 98 33 14. The old state-run grand hotel, privatized and reopened in 1997, with all mod cons, great beach views, and a terrace restaurant to enjoy them from over breakfast. **❻**

Hôtel National 23 Rue de Tetouan ☎039 98 21 41, Ⓟ039 98 26 81. A central location, close to buses in Place du Rif, ensures the popularity of this oldish hotel, with a/c and heating in all rooms, and TV in some. **❺**

Hôtel Quemado Plage Quemado ☎039 98 33 15. Same management as *Hôtel Mohammed V* but only open in summer. Four ugly apartment blocks plus thirty bungalows and chalets constitute this package hotel, the only hotel on the beach. It is used by tour groups, so book ahead. Includes a bar, restaurant and disco. **❻**

Eating and nightlife

Al Hoceima has quite a lot of good, cheap eateries, though nothing very upmarket, nor much in the way of nightlife, beyond the *Hôtel Quemado*'s Jupiter **disco** at the main beach (open year-round, 11pm–3am or later) or discreet **bars** on the top floors of the hotels *Quemado* and *Maghreb el Jadid*. **Cafés** offering omelettes, croissants or bread and jam for breakfast include the *Hôtel Etoile du Rif* in Place du Rif and the *Café el Nejma*, next door to the *Belle Vue* (see below) on Avenue Mohammed V by Place Massira el Khadra. There are some good **patisseries** in town; one of the best is on Avenue Mohammed V across from *Hôtel Maghreb el Jadid*.

Club Nautique by the fishing port ☎039 98 16 41. The best place in town to tuck into freshly landed, freshly cooked fish and seafood of various sorts. Licensed; closed during Ramadan. Daily 2pm–1am. Moderate.

Hôtel Chafarinas Beach Plage Tala Youssef (Plage Chafarinas) ☎039 84 16 01. Unbeatable sea views, gourmet cuisine and prices to match. Reservations necessary for both lunchtime and evening meals. Expensive.

Hôtel Maghreb el Jadid 56 Av Mohammed V ☎039 98 25 04. This hotel's top-floor licensed restaurant is a good choice for upmarket eating. Daily noon–3pm & 7–10pm. Moderate.

Restaurant la Belle Vue Av Mohammed V by Pl Massira el Khadra. A café all year, and a fully fledged restaurant in summer, with fish, meat,

tajines and paella, plus great views. Daily 6am–midnight. Cheap.

Restaurant Al Hoceima Rue Alouien. A reliable place for inexpensive food at any time – mainly brochettes and tajines. Open 24hr. Cheap.

Restaurant Jardin Parc 3 Mars, opposite the PTT. Relaxing spot with outdoor tables on the southeast corner of the square. Basic but well-cooked tajine and chicken dishes. Daily 7.30am–midnight. Cheap.

Restaurant National next to *Hôtel National* on Rue de Tetouan. Friendly French- and Spanish-speaking owner, serving most Moroccan staples – good hearty fare delivered to your table without delay. Daily 10am–11pm. Cheap.

Snack Assada 24 Av Hassan II. A small place but with a good selection of snacks or basic meals. Daily 10am–10pm. Cheap.

Moving on

Buses tend to leave Al Hoceima early, especially heading eastwards. All depart from Place du Rif, where CTM and various other companies have offices. All Oujda buses leave in the morning, plus a very late CTM one at 12.30am, while the last bus for Nador currently leaves at 3.30pm. Some of the Nador buses continue to the Melilla border. For Targuist, Ketama, Chefchaouen, Tetouan and Tangier, there are departures both morning and evening, while there's just one daily bus to Casablanca, currently leaving at 8pm and calling at Fes, Meknes and Rabat en route. **Grands taxis** bound for Nador, Oujda and Taza gather in Rue Alouien, just east of Place du Rif, while those with destinations like Targuist, Issaguen, Beni Ahdiba and Kalah Iris are to be found in Rue Raya al Maghribia, off Avenue Mohammed V by the *Paris* restaurant. For Chefchaouen, you have to change at Issaguen, a place that you can avoid if travelling to Fes by going via Taza instead, though the latter is the less scenic route.

The local **airport**, Aeroport Charif al Idrissi, is 17km east of Al Hoceima on the Nador road (N2), just before the village of Imzouren (☎039 98 20 63). It caters largely for charter flights from France and Germany – used as much by Moroccan workers as tourists – although RAM has a weekly flight to Amsterdam.

A small passenger **ferry** terminal, catering for the annual summer onslaught of holidaying Riffians returning from their European work bases, has recently been built between Plage Quemado and the fishing harbour. The twice daily crossings to the Spanish port of Almería operate from June to September only.

East to Nador and Melilla

There are now two separate highways heading east from Al Hoceima to Nador. The 164km **inland route** (N2) via Selouane has little of interest whereas the recently completed **Rif Mediterranean Highway** is a spectacular, yet desolate, drive that for the most part hugs the coastline before joining the main road into Nador (P39) at the village of Zeghangane, 6km south of Nador.

Al Hoceima to Selouane

The N2 from Al Hoceima climbs inland alongside the Oued Nekor, crossing a high pass before arriving at **KASSITA** (60km), and the friendly *Hôtel-Restaurant Andalous* (❷). This was the territory of Abd el Krim's first, dramatic rising – the so-called **Rout of Annoual** – of July–August 1921. In those two months, the Spanish were forced back to Melilla, losing over 18,000 of their troops along the way.

Here you can take the R505 south to Taza, via Aknoul. Heading east towards Nador, if you drive into the hills north of the road, at Midar or Driouch, there is still the occasional lookout post and barracks to be seen from the Rif War.

At **MONT ARAOUI**, where the road crosses the Oued Moulouya, there is a large and wonderful **Sunday souk**, plus several café-restaurants and a spotless **hotel**, the *Hassan* (☎036 26 24 33; ❷), with a choice of cheaper ordinary rooms, or pricier ones with en-suite bathrooms.

SELOUANE, 9km further east (and 11km short of Nador), stands at a rather complex junction of the roads to Al Hoceima and Oujda. It hosts a Saturday souk and has an interesting **kasbah**, built by Moulay Ismail, used as a base by the bizarre pretender to the throne, Bou Hamra (see p.205), and now adapted as a storehouse.

South to Guercif

The road **south to Guercif** (N15, formerly S333), heading off 8km west of Mont Araoui, is narrow and sealed. It crosses the fertile Plaine de Gareb and makes an interesting alternative to Taza or Oujda, with its vistas of palms and scrub, and the occasional wandering camel.

Al Hoceima to Zeghangane (Segangane)

Begun in 2003, and recently completed, the 230-kilometre Mediterranean Rif Highway is part of King Mohammed VI's plan to revive the Rif and Mediterranean region, by opening up this section of the coast to tourist development. For the moment, however, the highway is a lonely stretch of tarmac only occasionally disturbed by the odd rural village, hilltop mosque or roadworkers' camp. At the time of writing there was no public transport taking this route, and no facilities to speak of other than a few cafés in the town of **Tazaghine**, 175km from Al Hoceima. Nevertheless, should you have your own transport, it's a breathtakingly scenic drive, and with time, the odd café-restaurant, hotel or petrol station should start popping up along the route. The highway terminates at the junction with the P39 as it heads into Nador, at the village of **Zeghangane** (sometimes spelt Segangane) just 2km north of Selouane.

Nador and the coast

Entering or leaving Morocco at the Spanish enclave of Melilla you will have to pass through **NADOR**. If you're a bird-watcher, the marshes and dunes of Kariat Arkmane and Ras el Ma, 30–40km east of the town, may well entice a stay of several days (see Box, p.190). If not, you will probably want to move

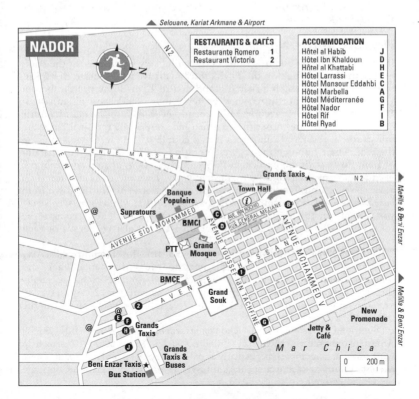

NADOR

Selouane, Kariat Arkmane & Airport

RESTAURANTS & CAFÉS	
Restaurante Romero	1
Restaurant Victoria	2

ACCOMMODATION	
Hôtel al Habib	J
Hôtel Ibn Khaldoun	D
Hôtel al Khattabi	H
Hôtel Larrassi	E
Hôtel Mansour Eddahbi	C
Hôtel Marbella	A
Hôtel Méditerranée	G
Hôtel Nador	F
Hôtel Rif	I
Hôtel Ryad	B

AVENUE MASSIRA

Grands Taxis

Town Hall

Banque Populaire

Supratours

AVE. IBN ROCHD

RUE GÉNÉRAL MEZIANE

BMCI

AVENUE SIDI MOHAMMED

AVENUE DES F.A.R.

PTT

Grand Mosque

AVENUE YOUSSEF IBN TACHFINE

BMCE

AVENUE HASSAN II

AVENUE MOHAMMED V

Grand Souk

Grands Taxis

New Promenade

Jetty & Café

Beni Enzar Taxis

Grands Taxis & Buses

Bus Station

Mar Chica

0   200 m

▶ Melilla & Beni Enzar

▶ Melilla & Beni Enzar

straight out and on. Nador itself, the bulk of which lies between the Selouane–Melilla road to the west, and the lagoon of Sebgha Bou Areq (or Mar Chica – "small sea") to the east, is earmarked as a centre for economic development and on first appearance has little to offer conventional tourists. However, it's worth breaking your journey here, if only to walk on the seaside promenade by the lagoon, and unwind at the relaxing café on the jetty at the far end of Boulevard Mohammed V.

When the Spanish left in 1957, Nador was just an ordinary Riffian village, given work and some impetus by the port of Melilla. Its later choice as a provincial capital was perhaps unfortunate. There was little to do for the local university students, while the iron foundry proposed to fuel the Rif's mining industry never materialized: two reasons that explain why the 1984 riots started in this town. The past decade has seen some attempt to address these problems, along with much new building, but the effective closure, in 1994, of the Algerian border was such a major blow to local business and tourism that only recently has the tide started to turn, thanks largely to increased passenger ferry traffic from both Melilla and the recently upgraded Beni Enzar port. Driving in from Selouane, turn right at the first sign to "Centre Ville" and you'll find yourself at the **Municipalité** and the landmark *Hôtel Ryad*. From there, **Avenue Mohammed V**, with its palms and orange trees, runs down to a little jetty on the lagoon corniche. Parallel, and to the south, **Avenue Youssef Ibn Tachfine** runs past the **Grand Mosque** with its tall, thin minaret down to the *Hôtel Rif* on the corniche. Halfway down, it is bisected by **Avenue Hassan II**, where you will find the two-storey **Grand Souk**.

Practicalities

If you're arriving by **bus** or **grand taxi**, you'll likely be dropped at the ranks nearby the Grand Souk on the town's third main avenue, **Avenue des FAR**; from here you can catch a shared grand taxi to Beni Enzar and the border with Melilla, 8km north. Arriving by ferry into Nador, you disembark at **Beni Enzar**. The ferry terminal has recently been re-furbished but has little in the way of facilities other than a café. Once out of the terminal, there are offices for all the ferry companies plus a couple of new restaurant-cafés on the road. Three hundred metres west along this road is the main roundabout of Beni Enzar with the border post only another 100m or so away. From the roundabout, shared grands taxis constantly ply the route to Nador for 10dh a seat. Some grands taxis drop you off on the western edge of the town from where it is about a ten-minute walk into the centre, whilst others will take you downtown to the busy bus and grand taxi station. There seems to be no system as to why this occurs other than by popular consensus of each taxi's occupants.

Nador's ONMT **tourist office** is at 88 Bd Ibn Rochid (Mon–Fri 8.30am–4.30pm; ☎036 33 03 48), next to the Rif cinema. There are numerous **banks** in town, all with ATMs and foreign exchange facilities, and **Internet** access is available at Club Internet at 126 Av des FAR (9.30am–4pm & 7pm–midnight) or from various Internet cafés near the bus and grand taxi station.

The friendly staff of the Al Khouzama **travel agency** at 9 Bd Général Amezian, opposite the town hall (☎036 60 71 55, ℱ036 60 77 10), can help with travel arrangements, particularly ferry journeys to mainland Spain. There are also a number of travel agencies on Avenue Youssef Ibn Tachfine, opposite the Grand Mosque.

Accommodation

There is a wide choice of **hotels**, many of them built in the more optimistic climate of the late 1980s/early 1990s, with most of the cheapies grouped around the two bus stations.

Cheap

Hôtel Ibn Khaldoun 91 Av Ibn Rochid ℡036 60 70 42. A reasonable *pension*, with some en-suite rooms, and hot water in the evenings. Breakfast included. ❶

Hôtel al Khattabi Rue Hay el Khattabi, opposite the *Hôtel Nador* ℡036 33 03 90. Clean and functional budget hotel with en-suite hot-water showers in most rooms. ❶

Hôtel Larrassi 16 Rue Hay el Khattabi ℡036 60 28 28. Friendly place with simple but adequate en-suite rooms. ❷

Hôtel Nador 49 Rue Hay el Khattabi ℡036 60 70 71. The best cheap hotel in town by far, with low prices, clean en-suite rooms and hot water round the clock. ❶

Moderate to expensive

Hôtel al Habib 11 Rue Hay el Khattabi ℡036 33 29 24. Newly built hotel, modern and clean. A grand marble staircase leads to upper floors, each with a small lounge/reading area and airy, light en-suite rooms. ❸

Hôtel Mansour Eddahbi 105 Rue de Marrakesh ℡036 60 31 73, ℱ036 60 65 83. A modern hotel, with a restaurant, café and bar. ❹

Hôtel Marbella 75–77 Av Youssef Ibn Tachfine ℡036 60 39 00, ℱ036 60 42 18. A two-star hotel, possibly the best mid-range choice in town. Most of the spacious rooms have balconies and all have en-suite bathrooms – with bathtubs. ❹

Hôtel Méditerranée 42–44 Av Youssef Ibn Tachfine ℡036 60 64 95, ℱ056 60 66 11. A good-value alternative to the above, opposite the prominent *Hôtel Rif*. Friendly, with comfortable rooms, the best of which have a balcony. ❹

Hôtel Rif Av Youssef Ibn Tachfine ℡036 60 65 35, ℱ036 33 33 84. An outpost of the Maroc-Tourist chain, overlooking the lagoon. Equipped with a swimming pool, restaurant and bar, but with a rather sad, empty air about it. ❸

Hôtel Ryad Av Mohammed V ℡036 60 77 17, ℱ036 60 77 19. A modern and spectacular wedding cake of a hotel, with a/c, restaurant, two bars, and use of a car park over the road. ❺

Eating and drinking

For **meals**, besides the hotel-restaurants, the *Restaurante Romero* at 48–50 Av Youssef Ibn Tachfine, overlooking the Grand Souk (noon–10pm; cheap), is highly recommended for fish dishes, as is *Restaurant Victoria* at 392 Bd Hassan II, near the corner with Avenue des FAR (daily 11am–midnight; moderate). Here you can treat yourself to a luscious fish paella or a *parrillada*, a fry-up of small portions of almost every fish/seafood locally available. Next door is the popular **patisserie** *Marjan*. Alternatively, if you have your own transport, you should definitely try *Restaurant Brabo* at Selouane (see p.188). Finally, for an early evening drink and a slice of cake, head to the *café* on the jetty over the Mar Chica. This former lighthouse is the most relaxing and scenic spot in town to cool down after a hot summer's day and watch the locals stroll up and down the seaside promenade.

Moving on

As Nador is a duty-free port, buses between here and Fes are invariably used for smuggling duty-free goods and therefore subject to numerous police and even customs checks and subsequent delays. Therefore, if you are heading for Fes, Taza or Oujda, the best course is to take the Supratours bus to **Taourirt**, on the Fes–Oujda train line, and continue your journey by rail. The bus currently leaves at 7.45pm from the ONCF/Supratours office at 28 Av Sidi Mohammed (daily 7am–noon & 3–8pm; ℡036 60 72 62).

CTM and some private **buses** to Casablanca, Fes, Meknes, Al Hoceima and Oujda leave from a terminal on Rue General Meziane, across the avenue from the *Hôtel Ryad*. Other buses leave from the main bus station opposite the grand

Birds and dunes: east of Nador

The coast east of Nador offers compelling sites for bird-watching – and plant wildlife – with a series of highly frequented freshwater and saline sites.

At **KARIET ARKMANE** a path leads out, opposite the village mosque, past salt pans and a pumping station (right-hand side) to an **extensive area of salt marsh**. This is covered by the fleshy-stemmed **marsh glasswort** or *salicornia*: a characteristic "salt plant" or *halophyte*, it can survive the saline conditions through the use of glands which excrete the salt. The **insect life** of the salt marsh is abundant, including damselflies, brightly coloured grasshoppers and various ants and sand spiders. The **birds** are even more impressive, with black-winged stilt, greater flamingo, coot, great-crested grebe, and various gulls and terns wheeling overhead.

Further along the coast, a walk east of the resort of **RAS EL MA** demonstrates the means by which plants invade **sand dunes**: a sequential colonization is known as **"succession"**, where one plant community gradually cedes to the next as a result of its own alteration of the environment. Typical early colonizers are marram grass and sea couch, which are eventually ousted by sea holly and sea spurge and finally by large, "woodier" species such as pistacihu, juniper and cistus species. Whole sequences can be seen occurring over time along the beach. The area attracts a variety of interesting **sea birds** as well, including the internationally rare **Audouin's gull** (thought to breed on the adjacent offshore Chafarinas Islands; see below). Other more familiar birds include dunlin, Kentish plover and oystercatcher.

Even further along the coast is the freshwater lagoon system which marks the mouth of the **OUED MOULOUYA**. The lagoons here are separated from the sea by a remarkable series of sand spits, no more than fifty metres across, and the **birdlife** is outstanding. Secluded among the reedbeds, it is possible to locate grey heron, white stork and little egret while the water's surface is constantly patrolled by the ever-alert black terns and kingfishers. Other varieties which you should manage to spot, wading in the shallows, are redshank, spotted redshank (in summer) and black-tailed godwit. The mouth and adjacent wetlands are under serious threat from government-encouraged and European-financed tourism developments a couple of kilometres to the east. In response to local and international pressure, a small parcel of wetland encompassing the mouth has been declared a protected area funded by, amongst others, the Global Environmental Fund and UNDP. Bird hides and information signboards have been erected along a marked walking path.

The Spanish-owned **Islas Chafarinas**, incidentally, are another important wildlife site, which Spanish ecologists are attempting to have declared a nature park. The three small islets support the Mediterranean's largest sea-bird colonies, and are home to the only known pair of **monk seals** surviving anywhere in Spanish waters. These are strictly protected as only about five hundred pairs exist in the world.

taxi stand, with half-hourly services to Oujda, four daily to Al Hoceima and three daily to Chefchaouen.

The Moroccan-Spanish border towns of Beni Enzar and Melilla are 8km to the north of Nador. At the time of writing there were no local buses running between Nador and the border but there is a constant stream of grands taxis plying the route, most of them departing from Nador's bus and grand taxi station located at the lagoon end of Avenue des FAR. A seat in a shared taxi will cost 10dh or you can charter one for around 150dh. They will drop you off at Beni Enzar's main roundabout from where it is a 100m walk north to the border with Melilla or about 300m east to the Beni Enzar ferry terminal. Between the roundabout and the terminal entrance there are booking offices for the ferry companies plus a couple of café-restaurants. Details of the Nador–Almería and Nador–Sète (summer only) **ferries** appear on pp.32–33.

Nador's Taouima **airport** (☎036 36 10 75, ℉036 36 10 72) is located 10km south of the city and caters mainly for international flights, although RAM operates a direct flight to Casablanca twice a week. No regular bus or grand taxi routes go to the airport so you will have to charter a grand taxi to get you there for around 150dh. There are, however, usually grands taxis at the airport to meet scheduled flights and you should be able to pay for just a single seat in a shared taxi heading into Nador or further on to the border.

The coast

The closest **beach** to Nador is at Boukana, 10km out of town, on the road towards Melilla. A nicer beach is at **Kariet Arkmane** (also signposted Ariet Arekmane), 25km southeast of Nador, at the end of the lagoon (see below), which in summer becomes a popular campsite for Moroccan families.

Moroccans also set up camp at the beaches to the northwest of Nador, beyond Boughafar (30km northwest), and at the **Cap des Trois Forches**, the cape 35km north of Nador on the continuation of the Melilla road. There are no official campsites at either resort but you'd have no problem in joining the locals.

The coast to the east of Nador has some of the most interesting **wildlife** sites in Morocco (see box opposite), and good beaches as well. To get the most out of this area, a car would be a great help. However, you can make use of the grands taxis, or the daily bus from Nador (which runs along road 8101 to Kariet Arkmane and Ras el Ma, then turns round and heads back to town).

Kariet Arkmane (Ariet Arekmane)

The village of **KARIET ARKMANE**, 30km from Nador, gives access to a sand and shell-packed road along the spit of the lagoon. This is a desolate area but picturesque in its own way, with salt marshes that provide manifold attractions for bird-watchers. The road out follows the edge of the lagoon from Kariet, passing an old Spanish lookout post en route to a shell-beach – a popular weekend spot with Spaniards from Melilla – before giving out at a tiny fishing village. On the beach, 1km beyond Kariet, is a **campsite**, *Camping Karia Plage* (☎036 36 02 41 or 061 26 45 30; summer only), and a ribbon of easy and relaxed café-restaurants. Another option is to look into renting an **apartment** (500dh per day) in the massive concrete block opposite the campsite, behind the eucalyptus trees. Reportedly very busy with Moroccan families during the summer, it's almost empty off season. Ask at the restaurants or the campsite for the whereabouts of the *gardien*. The expensive villas east of the campsite are the holiday homes of wealthy Moroccans, and not generally available to the casual tourist.

Ras el Ma and the Oued Moulouya

The road **east of Kariet** is a pleasant drive, twisting into the hills, never far from the sea, and eventually bringing you to **RAS EL MA** (or Ras Kebdana, as it is also known), 70km from Nador – and closer to Saïdia and Berkane (see p.199). Facing another of Spain's offshore island possessions on this coast, the three tiny **Islas Chafarinas**, this charming fishing village has a good **beach**, a smattering of cafés and restaurants overlooking the small harbour, and a beachside **campsite**, *Camping Ras el Ma* (closed during winter). On the eastern edge of town on the road to Saïdia is the newly built *Auberge de Cap de L'eau* (☎036 64 02 64; ❸) with en-suite rooms sleeping up to four people and a large restaurant.

The Nador–Melilla border

On a good day you can cross the **Nador–Melilla border** in ten or fifteen minutes. At other times, you may need considerable time and patience. During the summer it's often extremely crowded, with Moroccans returning from (or going to) jobs in Europe, as well as travellers off the ferry. If you want to avoid the queues, it is a good idea to spend a couple of hours in Melilla after arriving off a ferry, to let the main traffic get through. Or travel on the next morning: Melilla is worth a stay.

It is also possible to **stay** in Beni Enzar, just over the border on the Moroccan side: the *Hôtel les Quatre Saisons* is conveniently located right by the border (☎036 34 99 54; ❷) and has basic rooms, some en suite. The *Hôtel de la Marine*, some 500m further on at 23 Av Hassan II (☎036 60 89 39; ❶), is basic but clean and pretty reasonable.

If you are **driving**, be aware that smuggling goes on at the border, with periodic police crackdowns; in recent years, trading has included both drugs and people, with Moroccans (and sub-Saharan Africans) attempting to cross illegally into mainland Spain. Driving at night, keep an eye out for road checks – not always well lit but usually accompanied by tyre-puncturing blockades. If driving to Nador, beware of the local police, eager to pounce and demand large "fines" from newly arrived foreigners for the slightest infraction.

The two hundred metres that separate the Moroccan and the Spanish sides of the border are much more than just a geopolitical anomaly. They are a no-man's land isolating a prosperous European town from an unemployment-ridden Moroccan one. After spending a day in Melilla and returning in the evening to Nador, you begin to understand why so many Moroccans risk – and lose – their lives trying to reach the Spanish coast on makeshift rafts in search of better prospects. If you have already spent some time in Morocco before visiting Melilla, be prepared for an inverse culture-shock.

If you have your own transport, you could complete a loop back towards Nador from Ras el Ma, trailing the **Oued Moulouya** on road 8100 to the small town of Zaïo on the N2 – or take the road across the river (once the border between the French and Spanish Protectorates) to the beaches around Saïdia (see p.199). Along this road the dunes used to run virtually undisturbed to the Algerian border but are now being levelled, some would say desecrated, for two massive European-funded residential golf resorts developed as part of the king's strategy to attract tourism to the region.

Melilla (Mlilya)

Spanish-occupied **MELILLA** is a friendly little place, much more so than Ceuta (see p.145), with a new-found pride in its **mix of cultures** – Christian, Muslim, Jewish and Hindu – and an interesting selection of early twentieth-century **modernist architecture**. More conventional tourist pleasures are to be found, too, in an exploration of the walled old town, **Medina Sidonia**, with its stunning views out across the Mediterranean. And if you're here in August, there's the marvellous, if misleadingly titled **Semana Naútica**, when the port fills with sailing boats from mainland Spain and further afield for a fortnight of maritime extravaganzas and regattas.

Together with Ceuta, Melilla is the last of Spain's Moroccan enclaves on Moroccan soil – a former penal colony that saw its most prosperous days under

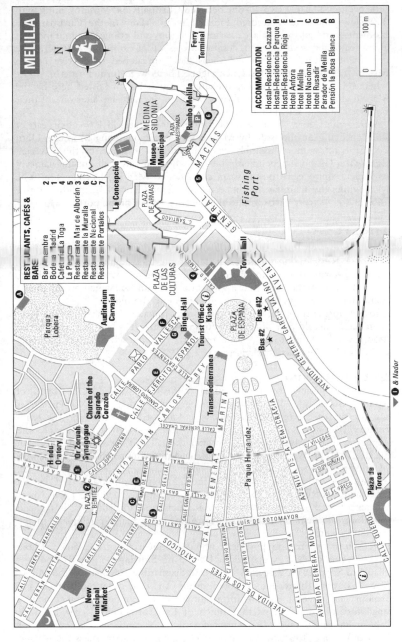

MELILLA

N

RESTAURANTS, CAFÉS & BARS

Bar Alhambra	2
Bodega Madrid	1
Cafetería La Toga	4
La Pepa	5
Restaurante Mar de Alborán	3
Restaurante la Muralla	6
Restaurante Nacional	C
Restaurante Portalos	7

ACCOMMODATION

Hostal-Residencia Cazaza	D
Hostal-Residencia Parque	H
Hostal-Residencia Rioja	F
Hotel Anfora	I
Hotel Melilla	C
Hotel Nacional	G
Hotel Rusadir	A
Parador de Melilla	A
Pensión la Rosa Blanca	B

0   100 m

Ferry Terminal

MEDINA SIDONIA

Rumbo Melilla

Museo Municipal

PLAZA MAESTRANZA

La Concepción

MACIAS

PLAZA DE ARMAS

C. SANTIAGO

GENERAL

Fishing Port

Parque Lobera

Auditorium Carvajal

PLAZA DE LAS CULTURAS

Town Hall

CALLE ALFONSO

Bingo Hall

Tourist Office Kiosk

PLAZA DE ESPAÑA

Bus #42

Bus #2

AVENIDA GENERAL GARCÍA VALIÑO

Church of the Sagrado Corazón

Hindu Oratory

Or Zoruah Synagogue

CALLE LÓPEZ MORENO

CALLE PABLO VALLESCA

CALLE EJÉRCITO ESPAÑOL

CALLE CERVANTES

REY

CALLE CANDIDO LOBERA

CALLE JUAN CARLOS I

Transmediterránea

MARINA

AVENIDA DE CASTELAR

PLAZA C. BENÍTEZ

CALLE GENERAL PAREJA

CALLE PRIM

CALLE GENERAL CHACEL

Parque Hernández

CALLE GENERAL

MARINA

CALLE GENERAL MARGALLO

CALLE GENERAL CAPITÁN

CALLE GRAN CAPITÁN

CALLE LÓPEZ DE VEGA

CALLE SOR ALEGRÍA

New Municipal Market

CALLE PRIMO DE RIVERA

CALLE GAS

CALLE GENERAL O'DONNELL

CALLE GENERAL PINTOS

CALLE CASTILLEJOS

CALLE LUIS DE SOTOMAYOR

CALLE DE LA DEMOCRACIA

C. VILLEGAS

C. GONZALO

C/ GRECO

CALLE CATÓLICOS

CALLE DE LOS REYES

C/ ALONSO MARTÍN

C/ ANTONIO FALCÓN

AVENIDA GENERAL MOLA

CALLE M. ZAZA

CALLE QUEROL

Plaza de Toros

& Nador

the Protectorate, when it was the main port for the Riffian mining industry. Since Moroccan independence in 1956, the city's population has halved to a little over 65,000, split two-to-one between Christians and Muslims, along with 3000 Jews and a few hundred Indian Hindus. Many of the Christians are Romanies, and all the enclave's various religious and ethnic communities get along reasonably well together, despite an episode of rioting in 1986, after the enactment of Spain's first real "Aliens Law" threatened to deprive certain Muslim families of their residence rights. There were further riots in 1996, when 400 Spanish Foreign Legionnaires, a tough bunch posted here by the Madrid authorities out of harm's way, went on the rampage after one of their number had been killed in a bar brawl.

Along with Ceuta, Melilla achieved autonomous status in 1995 after years of shilly-shallying on the issue by Madrid for fear of offending Morocco. Until 2003, the autonomous assembly was dominated as in Ceuta by the maverick right-wing Grupo Independiente Liberal, whose initials spell out the name of its leader, controversial businessman and Atlético Madrid chairman Jesús Gil. Meanwhile, the mainstay of the economy, as at Ceuta, remains the double anomaly of an army garrison plus the duty-free status of the port.

The Town

Melilla centres on **Plaza de España**, overlooking the port, and **Avenida Juan Carlos I Rey**, leading inland off it. This is the most animated part of town, especially during the evening *paseo*, when everyone promenades up and down, or strolls through the neighbouring **Parque Hernandez**, which on the town's numerous festival days hosts a fairground late into the night.

To the northeast, occupying a walled promontory, and adjacent to the ferry terminal, is the old part of town, **Medina Sidonia**. It is here that you should head, if you have time to fill waiting for a ferry – or you want to avoid queueing at the border after disembarking (see box, p.192).

Medina Sidonia

Until the beginning of the twentieth century, the walled "Old Town" of **Medina Sidonia**, wedged in above the port, was all there was of Melilla. This was the site of the original Phoenician colony of Rusadir around the tenth century BC, which the Spanish took in 1497, a kind of epilogue to the expulsion of the Moors from Spain after the fall of Granada in 1492. As an enclave, its security was always vulnerable, and at various periods of expansionist Moroccan rule – it was blockaded throughout the reign of Moulay Ismail – the Spanish population was limited to their fortress promontory and its sea approaches. The quarter's streets suggest the Andalusian Medinas of Tetouan or Chefchaouen, though inside the design is much more formal; it was in fact laid out along the lines of a Castilian fort, following a major earthquake in the sixteenth century.

Steps near the fishing port lead up to the quarter's main square, **Plaza Maestranza**, entered by the Gothic **Puerta de Santiago**, a gate flanked by a chapel to St James the Apostle – known to Spaniards as *Matamoros*, "the Moor-Slayer". Beyond the recently restored square you come to an old barracks and armoury, and, if you follow the fortifications round from here, you'll come to a small fort, below which is the church of **La Concepción**, crowded with baroque decoration, including a revered statue of *Nuestra Señora de Victoria* (Our Lady of Victory), the city's patroness. Back on Plaza Maestranza is the **Museo de la Ciudad Autonoma de la Melille** (Tues–Sat 10am–2pm & 4–8.30pm,

Sun 10am–2pm; free), which houses a miscellany of historical documents, coins and ceramics. Also interesting is the nearby **Rumbo Melilla** museum (Tues–Sat 10am–2pm & 4–8.30pm; Sun 10am–2pm; free), which shows a fifteen-minute audiovisual projection on the history of the various peoples to have occupied and influenced the town. These and other places of interest are all signposted and numbered as part of a short tourist walk within the Medina.

The new town: Art Nouveau

In the new town, many of the buildings around **Plaza de España** were designed by **Enrique Nieto**, a *modernista* (Art Nouveau) disciple of the renowned Catalan architect, Gaudí. Nieto arrived in 1909 at the age of 23 and proceeded, over the next four decades, to transform Melilla's architecture. The tile and stucco facades left by Nieto and his imitators – in a style more flowery than Gaudí's – are a quiet delight of the New Town if you cast your eyes above the shops.

A short, circular **walk** taking in these delights starts in Plaza de España with Melilla's most famous Art Deco building, the town hall, a Nieto building of 1947. Avenida Juan Carlos I Rey, leading away from the Plaza de España, begins with the 1917 Trasmediterranea building on the left, followed by another fine piece of Art Nouveau at no. 9, built in 1915. From here head for Calle Ejército Español to have a look at no.16 and continue up Calle Lopez Moreno, checking out the *modernista* buildings on the right-hand side, among them Nieto's **Or Zoruah (Holy Light) Synagogue**, built in 1924, and, opposite, the Polygon Mosque, also by Nieto, and dating to 1945. Back on Avenida Juan Carlos I Rey, you have quite a selection around Plaza Comandante Benitez and, just down Calle Reyes Catolicos, have a look at those on Calle Sor Alegría, before heading along Avenida General Prim for a look at the building on the corner of Castelar. The last building, the bingo hall, has another fine stucco facade, in Art Deco style this time, on the corner of Comandante Emperador and Ejército Español, just off Plaza de España, and bringing you back to the start.

Practicalities

Bus #19 and **grands taxis** from Nador (from the eastern end of Avenue des FAR, or from the main road, just north of the town hall) drop you at the border post of **Beni Enzar**, and from there, once the often time-consuming process of crossing the border is out of the way, buses on the Melilla side will take you to Plaza de España (#42 or #70; every 15min; takes 15min, €0.60 or the equivalent in dirhams). **Rented cars** are not allowed across the border, so if you want to take a day-trip to Melilla from Morocco, you'll have to use public transport. Melilla's **ferry terminal** is at the far end of Avenida General Macias and is only a short walk from the main square, Plaza de España. Within the terminal is an office for Acciona Trasmediterranea and there are a couple of travel agencies just outside. Arriving at the **airport** (☎952 69 80 12), 3km southwest of the town, means a €6.50 taxi ride into the centre.

The **tourist office** (Mon–Fri 10am–2pm & 5–8.30pm; ☎952 67 54 44, ⓦwww.melillaturismo.com) is in the Palacio de Exposiciones y Congresos, c/Fortuny 21, near the Plaza de Toros, and in the more conveniently located kiosk by the town hall (Mon–Sat 9am–2pm & 4–8.30pm, Sun 10am–2pm). When **phoning Melilla** from Morocco (or anywhere else outside Spain), you must prefix phone numbers with the international code (☎00 34). Dialling numbers within Melilla you must include the old local code 952 as part of the new nine-digit number. To **phone Morocco from Melilla**, you need to dial ☎00 212, followed by the local code (minus the initial zero) and number. Note that Melilla works to Spanish time, which is one hour (in winter) and two hours (in summer) ahead of Morocco.

There are a number of **banks** on or near Avenida Juan Carlos I Rey which will change cheques, sterling, dollars or dirhams. Banco Central is at c/Ejército Español 1 and Banco de España is on Plaza de España itself. Note that some banks in Melilla (Mon–Fri 9am–2pm) charge outrageous rates of commission for changing small amounts of cash, while others charge none at all, so ask first. There are black-market moneychangers who hang out on the stretch of Avenida de Juan Carlos I Rey nearest to Plaza de España, especially in the evenings, though the usual rules of caution about changing money on the street apply.

In case of medical emergency, head to the **Hospital Comarcal** at c/Remonta 2 (☎952 67 00 00) or the **Hospital Militar** at c/General Polavieja s/n (☎952 67 47 43).

Accommodation

Accommodation in Melilla is not easy to find; rooms tend to be in short supply – and are expensive by Moroccan standards. If you have problems, the tourist office (see p.195) might be able to help. If you plan to stay during the Semana Náutica make a reservation well in advance as most hotels will be fully booked for the two weeks of the event.

Hostal-Residencia Cazaza c/Primo de Rivera 6 ☎952 68 46 48. The rooms are a little sombre, but it's a friendly, well-maintained place, with TV and large bathroom in all rooms, and there's a small café on the ground floor for breakfast. €40
Hostal-Residencia Parque c/Generál Marina 15 ☎952 68 21 43. The location – opposite the park – is the best thing about this hotel, as its rooms are very average. Nonetheless, it's a popular choice, invariably full. €42
Hostal-Residencia Rioja c/Ejército Español 10 ☎952 68 27 09. Simple and clean with shared bathrooms but hot water round the clock. €28
Hotel Anfora c/Pablo Vallesca 16 ☎952 68 33 40, ☏952 68 33 44. A two-star hotel, with a/c rooms. Has a bar and café and a top-floor restaurant with great views. €60
Hotel Melilla Puerto Esplanada de San Lorenzo s/n, 100m from town centre ☎952 69 55 25, ⓦwww.hotelmelillapuerto.com. Upmarket hotel, geared towards the business traveller. €122

Hotel Nacional c/Primo de Rivera 10 ☎952 68 45 40, ☏952 68 44 81. Small but comfortable rooms with TV, a/c and newly refurbished bathrooms. It also has the only kosher restaurant in town, open to nonresidents, which is certainly a must if you are after quality homemade cuisine. Guests can arrange car rental here for day-trips to Morocco. €56
Hotel Rusadir c/Pablo Vallesca 5 ☎952 68 12 40, ⓔhotelrusadir@wanadoo.es. An upmarket hotel that's comfortable enough but lacks character or indeed anything much to justify its price – there's not even a pool. €75
Parador de Melilla Avda de Candido Lobera – overlooking the Parque Lobera ☎952 68 49 40, ⓦwww.parador.es. The best upmarket choice with fine views over the town, and a swimming pool. €115
Pensión la Rosa Blanca c/Gran Capitan 7 ☎952 68 27 38. A charming, quiet little *pension* worth booking ahead as it is often full in summer. Some rooms have balconies. €33

Eating and drinking

Melilla has some great tapas bars, but not much in the way of restaurants. Coming from Morocco, the easy availability of alcohol and open drinking culture are refreshing in more ways than one. The main concentration of **restaurants** and **tapas bars** lies in the area east of Avenida Juan Carlos I Rey, between the Plaza de España and the Municipal Market.

Bar Alhambra c/Castelar 3. A fairly large bar, popular with locals, serving cold beers, tapas and *bocadillos*. Daily except Sun 10am–3pm & 6–11pm. Cheap.

🦐 **Bodega Madrid** c/Castelar 6. An excellent beer and tapas bar with huge rations of freshly cooked fish and seafood (you may want to go for a half-portion) eaten standing at wine-barrel tables; one of Melilla's livelier evening hangouts. Daily 11.15am–3pm & 7–10.45pm. Cheap to moderate.

Cafetería La Toga Plaza de las Culturas. A friendly café-bar, good for a breakfast of hot chocolate and *churros* (long dough fritters), or a *carajillo* (coffee with a slug of brandy) at any time of day. Daily except Sun 6.30am–10pm.

La Pergola Avda Generál Macias, alongside the fishing port. Open-air coffee, beer and cocktails served Mon–Fri 3pm–2.30am (3am in summer), Sat & Sun 11.30am–3am. Meals available 8–11.30pm in winter, all day in summer. Moderate.

Restaurante Mar de Alborán c/Generál Prim 24. *The* place in town to eat paella. Daily noon–3.30pm & 7–11.30pm. Moderate.

Restaurante la Muralla c/Mirador de Florentina s/n, near the southeast corner of Medina Sidonia ☏952 68 10 35. Fantastic views over the port from a restaurant that also serves as a chef school. Moderate.

Restaurante Nacional *Hotel Nacional*, c/Primo de Rivera 10. This small family-run kosher restaurant offers a selection of traditional recipes, with a menu including generous portions of lamb in caramelized onion sauce, boneless *corvina* fish, delicious home-made *imozonot* bread (with orange juice in the dough) and Jewish sweets. An €18 menu allows you to sample small portions across the range. Daily 11am–3pm & 7–11pm. Moderate.

Restaurante Portalos Avda Generál Macias 9. Popular eatery across from the fishing port with a pizzeria, seafood dishes and €8–11 *platos combinados*. Open for breakfast, lunch and dinner. Cheap to moderate.

Moving on

Ferries from Melilla (see p.217) run almost daily to **Malaga** and **Almería**, twice daily to Almería in summer. Making advance bookings is essential in August – with waits of up to three days possible if you just turn up for a boat – and the period at the end of Semana Santa (Easter week) is also best avoided.

Alternatively, there are Iberia **flights** to **Malaga**, **Barcelona**, **Almería**, **Granada** and **Madrid**. Again, reserve ahead of time if possible, and be warned that flights don't leave in bad weather. The Iberia/Air Nostrum office is at the airport (☏952 67 38 00) and there is an Iberia Airlines agency in town at 20 c/Generál Marina. You can find more detailed information on flights from and to Melilla on Ⓦwww.iberia.es or Ⓦwww.aena.es (official site of the Spanish airport authority), both of them available in English. A helpful **travel agency** for information and reservations is Viajes Mariaire, Avda Juan Carlos I Rey 30 (Mon–Fri 9am–1pm & 4.30–8pm; ☏952 68 10 17, Ⓕ952 69 00 23).

Travelling into Morocco you can usually pick up collective grands taxis for **Nador** just over the border, but if there are none, or if they try to make you charter a whole taxi and you don't want to, then walk 100m to the roundabout and pick one up there. There are also city buses (#19) to Nador.

The Zegzel Gorge, Berkane and Saïdia

The **route east from Nador to Oujda** is fast, efficient and well served by buses and grands taxis. It holds little of interest along the way, but if you've got the time (and ideally a car), there's an attractive detour around Berkane into the **Zegzel Gorge**, a dark limestone fault in the Beni Snassen mountains – the last outcrops of the Rif. And on the coast there is the considerable attraction of **Saïdia**, one of the country's most pleasant and relaxed seaside resorts.

The gorge route

The **Oued Zegzel** is a tributary of the Moulouya, which as it runs south of Berkane has carved out a fertile shaft of mountain valleys. For centuries these marked the limits of the Shereefian empire.

The route through these valleys is easily accessible today but still forbiddingly steep: virtually all traffic goes anticlockwise (down) from Berkane to Taforalt, taking the N2 (formerly P27) out of town and, after 10km, turning south onto the S403, climbing up to Taforalt, 10km from the turn-off. If you've got a car, this is the route to follow. If you're using public transport, stay on the bus to Berkane, where you can get a seat in a grand taxi to Taforalt and there negotiate another one back, this time via the gorge road. Neither is an expensive operation because the routes are used by local residents as well as tourists.

Taforalt, the Grotte du Chameau and the gorge

TAFORALT (Tafoughalt) is a quiet mountain village, active (or as active as it ever gets) only for the **Wednesday souk**. It does, though, have a reliable supply of grands taxis (though it's not served by any buses), and you should be able to move on rapidly towards the Zegzel Gorge; before settling on a price, get the driver to agree to stop en route at the Chameau cave.

This – the **Grotte du Chameau** – is 10km from Taforalt, a cavern of vast stalactites, one of which is remarkably camel-like in shape (hence the name). The cave, with various tunnels leading off, is completely uncommercialized and it is not always open (you will need to locate the *gardien* to unlock the entrance); a torch is also essential. Near the entrance to the cave is a hot stream, which locals use for bathing. Local boys stationed by the main road, just before the site, will charge 5dh per vehicle for the use of the car park. Even if the cave is closed you can still enjoy the soothing picnic area next to it, underneath towering limestone buttresses and shaded by dense cedar trees. There is a grocery stall selling soft drinks, tea and biscuits and a few garden tables where you can soak up the tranquillity of the place, particularly off season, when there might only be a couple of Moroccan families having a barbecue. If you feel energetic you can go for a **walk** along the footpath that leads from the picnic site into the gorge, although the usual precautions about flash-floods apply.

The Zegzel Gorge, or rather **gorges**, begins about a kilometre beyond the cave. A rough track branches off the main road, only suitable for 4x4 vehicle and perennially subject to rock avalanches and flash-floods. The gorges are terraced and cultivated with all kinds of citrus and fruit trees. As the track crisscrosses the riverbed, they progressively narrow, drawing your eye to the cedars and dwarf oaks at the summit, until you eventually emerge (22km from Taforalt) onto the Berkane plain.

Berkane

BERKANE is a strategic little market town, French-built and prosperous, set amid an extensive region of orchards and vineyards. If you stay, you're likely to be the only Westerner in the town – so there aren't any hustlers.

The town's main square is at the top end of town on the N2 road. Buses and Oujda grands taxis hang out in the street running south from here. There are good eating places on the long, unpaved street running uphill from Boulevard Hassan II, along with lots of very dark, tented souks. Best of the cheap **hotels** is the *Majestic* (no phone; ❶), on Boulevard Hassan II, 50m west of the main square. There is also *Hôtel Zaki* (☎036 61 37 43; ❺), 500m east of the main square on the road towards Oujda, slick and comfortable, and mainly catering to businesspeople, with air-conditioning, heating and satellite TV in all rooms, an in-house pizzeria, and a fitness room.

There isn't much to see in Berkane, but one thing worth a glance if you're in town is the now disused **church**, just north of the main road, 50m east of the

A note on Algeria

Throughout the 1990s and into the early 2000s Algeria was effectively off limits to all foreign visitors. During the civil war between 1992 and 1998 over 100,000 people were killed in attacks and reprisals by Islamic fundamentalists and the army; foreigners, as well as Algerian intellectuals, journalists and musicians, were particular targets. Since the 1999 elections, and the Islamic Salvation Army (the armed wing of the Islamic Salvation Front or FIS) disbanded in early 2000, the situation has improved. However, occasional ambushes on government forces and attacks on villages still persist, with problems including an ongoing, sometimes violent, campaign for autonomy by the ethnic Berber minority and continuing skirmishes with militant Islamic extremists.

Algeria recognizes the Saharawi Arab Democratic Republic and supports the Polisario guerillas against Morocco's occupation of the Western Sahara (see p.685) – over 100,000 Saharawi refugees from the Western Sahara are living in camps on the Algerian side of the border and it is this dispute that led to the 1994 closing of the land border – and this remains the stumbling block to better relations with Morocco. In mid-2004, in an attempt to improve those relations, Morocco lifted all visa entry requirements for Algerians. Despite this, although it is still possible for non-Moroccans to obtain entry visas for Algeria, and there is a consulate at Oujda (see p.213), the land border between the two countries remains closed.

main square, painted in red ochre, with a row of strange grimacing faces picked out in yellow along the top of its facade.

Moving on from Berkane is straightforward, with frequent buses and grands taxis to Nador, Oujda and Saïdia; there's a CTM service to Casablanca (via Fes, Meknes and Rabat) currently departing at 7pm. Buses leave from just off the main square, as do grands taxis for Oujda. Grands taxis for Nador are to be found 200m west along the main road, while those for Saïdia leave from just north of the roundabout 300m east of the main square.

Saïdia

Sited almost on the Algerian border, **SAÏDIA** is a good choice for staying put for a few days. A very low-key resort, rambling back from the sea in the shadow of a still-occupied nineteenth-century kasbah, it is fronted by one of the best beaches on the Mediterranean – an immense, sandy strand, stretching west to face the tiny Chafarinas islands at Ras el Ma (see box, p.190), and east, across the Oued Kiss, towards Algeria. Although the border is still closed and the political situation in Algeria is still far from rosy, in recent years the obvious tension in the town has subsided. This is most visible at the **Sunday souk**, held under giant fig trees between the market and kasbah, whereby Moroccans and Algerians – the border may officially be closed but every (Algerian) man and his dog seems free to wander across the usually trickling Oued Kiss – mingle freely between the random stalls selling used TVs, clothing and kitchen wares. This relative tranquility may rapidly change, however, on the completion of two massive, linked tourist developments frantically taking shape just west of the town. The resort will eventually boast a 740-berth marina, three 18-hole golf courses, at least six luxury hotels and numerous shopping complexes.

For the time being at least, you're likely to be a rare foreign visitor, though you might find the occasional bird-watcher in residence, and a small number of European tourists in the know spending their summer holidays here. Saïdia has rewarding bird sites in the marshes and woodland stretching behind the beach

△ Oued Moulouya, near Saïdia

towards the Oued Moulouya (see box, p.190). The town really only comes into its own in July and August, when many Moroccan families camp by the beach, and several hotels that are closed for the rest of the year open their doors – reservation is advisable at this time, wherever you intend to stay. The main square becomes pretty animated in summer when the town hosts the August **Festival du Raï et des Arts Populaires**, centred in the Palais du Festival building, at the far northern end of the beachside Boulevard Mohammed V, as well as on Place 20 Août and the beach. The two-week festival is an opportunity to listen to some indigenous *chaâbi*, *raï* and *amazigh* music, and see *raggada* and *laäoui* folk-dancing ensembles.

Practicalities

Buses and **grands taxis** will drop you by the northwest corner of the kasbah, from which the beach is a couple of blocks to the north. Down by the beach are two main thoroughfares running parrallel to each other: the beachfront Boulevard Mohammed V and Boulevard Hassan II. The town's small square, Place 20 Août, connects the two towards the eastern end. On Boulevard Hassan II, close to Place 20 Août, are branches of the **banks** Banque Populaire and Wafa, both with ATMs, as well as the **post office** (Mon–Fri 8am–6pm, Sat 8am–noon), two blocks west of *Hôtel Atlal.*

Accommodation

For a town of its size, Saïdia has a fair number of mid-range and upmarket hotels. Most are located on Boulevard Mohammed V with some dotted around nearby Place 20 Août; ask for discounts out of season. The views from the sea-facing rooms in any of the hotels on Mohammed V are simply fantastic.

There are three **campsites** in town, all offering large sites and full facilities but closed during winter. *Camping Chemse* (no phone) and *L'Amazone Camping International* (T 036 62 46 46), are situated next door to each other at the eastern end of Boulevard Hassan II, one block back from the beach. On the road heading west out of town is *Camping Mansour*, with self-catering bungalows and tents to rent. Should the campsites be full, campervans are usually allowed to stay overnight in the flood-lit car park opposite the beachfront *Samy Playa Pizzeria*, about halfway along Boulevard Mohammed V.

Hôtel Atlal 44 Bd Hassan II T 036 62 50 21, E atlalben@menara.ma. Award-wining hotel with spacious and light family rooms, some with balconies and others with a small private patio ideal for those with small children. Solar-heated hot water. Downstairs there's a fully fledged restaurant with fish specialities and a reasonable selection of Moroccan wines and a cosy bar. Breakfast included. **⑥**

Hôtel Hannour Place 20 Août T 036 62 51 15, F 036 62 43 43. A lively three-star establishment with smart rooms and a good restaurant. **④**

Hôtel Manhattan Bd Mohammed V T 036 62 42 40. One of a trio of seafront hotels, located above its own popular café-restaurant. All rooms are en-suite with TV and are tiled throughout. Slightly overpriced during season. **⑤**

Hôtel Paco Bd Hassan II opposite the *Atlal* T 036 62 51 10. A rather spartan hotel with good value en-suite rooms and hot showers. **③**

Hôtel Rimal Bd Mohammed V T 036 62 41 41, F 036 62 41 42. Very similar in both style and price to the neighbouring *Manhattan*, including the ground-floor café-restaurant. Also has some larger suites. **⑤**

Hôtel Titanic Bd Mohammed V T & F 036 62 40 71. A large poster of the blockbuster movie presides over the reception hall of this blue and cream hotel, the best of the three neighbouring seafront choices. The modern, airy rooms are glazed all round and lead onto good-sized balconies offering unbeatable sea views. Closed during winter. **⑤**

Eating and Drinking

There are a few lively **café-restaurants** by the market and kasbah and, during the holiday season, on the beach. The best restaurants, however, are around Place 20 Août and are open all year round. Both *Hôtel Atlal* and *Hôtel Paco* have **bars**, whilst next door to *Hôtel Hannour* is the relaxed *Mediterrania Club* with pool tables, café and *shisha*-pipes.

Chez Said Bd Hassan II, opposite Hôtel Hannour T 036 62 54 11. Small, friendly restaurant serving seafood specialities like royal paella. Lunch & Dinner daily. Moderate.

Hôtel Atlal 44 Bd Hassan II T 036 62 50 21. The best restaurant in town, with a nice, warm atmosphere renowned for its fish

specialities. It also has a reasonable selection of Moroccan wines. Daily lunch and dinner. Moderate.

Le Nimois Place 20 Août. American diner-type café-restaurant with an extensive menu of Moroccan and Italian dishes. Open daily until late. Moderate.

The Route de L'Unité: Ketama to Fes

At the end of the Spanish Protectorate in 1957, there was no north–south route across the Rif, a marked symbol both of its isolation and of the separateness of the old French and Spanish zones. It was in order to counteract these aspects – and to provide working contact between the Riffian tribes and the French-colonized Moroccans – that the **Route de l'Unité** was planned, cutting right across the range from Ketama south to Fes.

The Route (more prosaically known as the R509, formerly S203), completed in 1963, was built with volunteer labour from all over the country – Hassan II himself worked on it at the outset. It was the brainchild of Mehdi Ben Barka, first president of the National Assembly and the most outstanding figure of the nationalist Left before his exile and subsequent "disappearance" in Paris in 1965. Ben Barka's volunteers, 15,000-strong for much of the project, formed a kind of labour university, working through the mornings and attending lectures in the afternoons.

Today the Route de l'Unité sees little traffic – travelling from Fes to Al Hoceima, it's quicker to go via Taza; from Fes to Tetouan, via Ouezzane. Nevertheless, it's an impressive and very beautiful road, certainly as dramatic an approach to Fes as you could hope for. However, see the **warning** about driving through here on pp.174–175.

Taounate, Aïn-Aïcha and Tissa

Going by bus, the village which most tempts a halt is **TAOUNATE**. The largest community along the Route, it stands on a hill above the valley of the Oued Ouerrha. If you can make it for the huge **Friday market** here, you should be able to get a lift out to any number of villages in the region. There's quite a pleasant little hotel, the *Entente* (☎035 68 82 91; ❶), halfway down the hill on the left-hand side, with panoramic views. There are also a couple of cafés in the village.

On the R509 to Fes, shortly after Taounate, is **AÏN-AÏCHA**, a mostly modern town with a picturesque old quarter across the Oued Ouerrha, comprising a cluster of whitewashed houses built up a little hillock and overlooked by a rocky outcrop.

Continuing south along the Route, there is a turning, 33km from Taounate, to **TISSA**, announced by a sign at the entrance to the village as the "Berceau des Chevaux". The region around Tissa is known for its thoroughbred Hayani horses. Here, in late September/early October, horses and riders from the region gather to compete at the annual **horsefair**. The climax is the competitive **fantasias** judged on speed, discipline and dress. Elsewhere, *fantasias* – traditional cavalry charges culminating in firing of muskets in the air – are put on largely for tourists, but these are the real thing, for aficionados.

West of Taounate

To the west of Taounate lies **RAFSAÏ**, the last village of the Rif to be overrun by the Spanish, and the site of a December **Olive Festival**. In recent years over 600,000 olive trees have been planted in the region as part of a local campaign to find an economically viable alternative to cannabis. Rafsaï is reached by taking the S304, which used to continue further west to the village of Fes el Bali until the construction of the Barrage al Wahda, and then turning northwards on the S305. If you are into scenic roads and have transport, you might consider taking a forty-kilometre dirt road out from Rafsaï to the **Djebel Lalla Outka**, the peak reputed to offer the best view of the whole Rif range. The road is reasonable as far as the village of Tamesnite, but thereafter is very rough *piste* – accessible only in summer.

Fes el Bali is, since 1997, to be found only on the maps. The Oued Ouerrha has been dammed – the **Barrage al Wahda** – at Mjara, 20km downstream of the old village of Fes el Bali. After Aswan in Egypt, al Wahda is the second largest dam in Africa, with a total height of 90m. The lake formed by the dam is 34km long, designed to irrigate 2000 square kilometres of the **Gharb** coastal plain and protect them from floodwaters. It also contributes ten percent to the national electricity grid.

East: Aknoul

Going **east from Taounate**, an attractive though less spectacular route heads through cork and holm oak forests towards the scattered and rather grim village of **AKNOUL**. From here you can pick up a daily bus or grand taxi down to Taza, or the one bus a day over to Nador or Al Hoceima.

Taza and the Djebel Tazzeka

TAZA was once a place of great importance: the capital of Morocco for periods of the Almohad, Merenid and Alaouite dynasties, and controlling the Taza Gap, the only practicable pass from the east. It forms a wide passage between the Rif and Middle Atlas and was the route to central power taken by Moulay Idriss and the first Moroccan Arabs, as well as the Almohads and Merenids, both of whom successfully invaded Fes from Taza. Each of these dynasties fortified and endowed the city but as a defensive position it was never very effective: the local Zenatta tribe were always willing to join an attack by outsiders and, in the nineteenth century, they managed to overrun Taza completely, with centralized control returning only with the French occupation of 1914.

Modern Taza seems little haunted by this past, its monuments sparse and mostly inaccessible to non-Muslims. It is, however, a pleasant market town – an easy place to get acclimatized if you have arrived in Morocco at Melilla – and its Medina is saved from anonymity by a magnificent hilltop terrace site, flanked by crumbling Almohad walls. In addition, there is a considerable attraction in the surrounding countryside – the national park of **Djebel Tazzeka**, with its circuit of waterfalls, caves and schist gorges.

Taza splits into two parts, the **Medina** and the French-built **Ville Nouvelle**, distinct quarters separated by 2km of road. The Ville Nouvelle was an important military garrison in the Riffian war and retains much of the barrack-grid character. Its focal point, **Place de l'Indépendance**, actually serves a population of 70,000, but it's so quiet you'd hardly know it.

The Medina

Buses from Place de l'Indépendance run up to **Place Ahrrache**, a busy little square overlooking the Ville Nouvelle, or you can climb up to it on the steps from the main road junction opposite the gendarmerie. Lab Photo Touzani in the southwest corner of the square sells some interesting panoramic prints of Taza, including one displaying the town covered in snow. The **Medina**, to the west of the square, is a compact, modernized quarter – easy enough to navigate, though you may need to ask directions for the few scattered sites. The quarter spreads out from a long main street, called the **Mechouar** on its initial stretch and changing name to Rue Koubet and Rue Cherkiyne as it approaches the **Grand Mosque**.

The Andalous Mosque and Palais Bou Hamra

From between Place Ahrrache and its southern extension, **Place Moulay Hassan**, Zenqat el Andalous, which starts roughly opposite the post office, runs west to the twelfth century **Andalous Mosque**. The mosque is the largest building in the southern section of the Medina – though its courtyards are characteristically well concealed from outside view. The minaret is best viewed

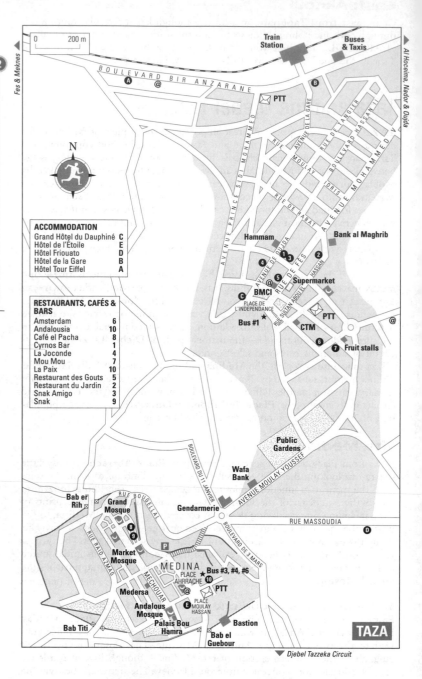

Al Hoceima, Nador & Oujda

0   200 m

Train
Station

Buses
& Taxis

BOULEVARD BIR ANZARANE

Ⓐ @

PTT

Ⓑ

RUE DE LA GARE
RUE DE TANGIER
AVENUE MOULAY DRIS
BOULEVARD HASSAN II
AVENUE MOHAMMED V

RUE MOULAY

RUE DE RABAT

N

ACCOMMODATION
Grand Hôtel du Dauphiné   **C**
Hôtel de l'Étoile   **E**
Hôtel Friouato   **D**
Hôtel de la Gare   **B**
Hôtel Tour Eiffel   **A**

**RESTAURANTS, CAFÉS &
BARS**
Amsterdam   **6**
Andalousia   **10**
Café el Pacha   **8**
Cyrnos Bar   **1**
La Joconde   **4**
Mou Mou   **7**
La Paix   **10**
Restaurant des Gouts   **5**
Restaurant du Jardin   **2**
Snak Amigo   **3**
Snak   **9**

Hammam

Bank al Maghrib

AVENUE PRINCE SIDI MOHAMMED

AVENUE DE OUJDA

Ⓒ BMCI
@

RUE DE FES

RUE SULTAN ABOU EL HASSAN

❶ ❸ ❷
❹
❺
Supermarket

PLACE DE
L'INDEPENDANCE

Bus #1

PTT

CTM

❻
❼ Fruit stalls

@

Public
Gardens

Wafa
Bank

AVENUE MOULAY YOUSSEF

BOULEVARD DU 11 JANVIER

Gendarmerie

RUE MASSOUDIA

Ⓓ

Bab er
Rih

RUE BOUGELLAI

Grand
Mosque

BOULEVARD DE 3 MARS

RUE RAID ATMAG

❽
❾

Market
Mosque

MECHOUAR

MEDINA

P

Bus #3, #4, #6
PLACE
AHRRACHE ★ ❿
@

PTT

Medersa

Ⓔ PLACE
MOULAY
HASSAN

Andalous
Mosque

Bab Titi

Palais Bou
Hamra

Bab el
Guebour

Bastion

TAZA

Djebel Tazzeka Circuit

from the Mechouar. Close by the mosque, just west of the Mechouar, is the Merenid-era **Bou Abul Hassan Medersa**. An inconspicuous building, it is usually kept locked; if you can locate the *gardien*, there are rewards to be had in a classic court and beautiful mihrab.

To the rear of the Andalous Mosque is the **Palais Bou Hamra**, the largely ruined residence of Bou Hamra, the *Rogui* or pretender to the throne, in the early years of the twentieth century. There is little to see today, but for a decade or so this was a power base controlling much of eastern Morocco. Like most protagonists of the immediate pre-colonial period, Bou Hamra was an extraordinary figure: a former forger, conjurer and saint, who claimed to be the legitimate Shereefian heir and had himself proclaimed Sultan at Taza in 1902.

The name Bou Hamra – "man on the she-donkey" – recalled his means of travel round the countryside, where he won his followers by performing "miracles". One of these involved talking to the dead, which he perfected by the timely burying of a disciple, who would then communicate through a concealed straw; the pronouncements over, Bou Hamra flattened the straw with his foot (presumably not part of the original deal) and allowed the amazed villagers to dig up the by-then-dead witness.

Bou Hamra's own death – after his capture by Sultan Moulay Hafid – was no less melodramatic. He was brought to Fes in a small cage on the back of a camel fed to the court lions (who refused to eat him), and was eventually shot and burned. Both Gavin Maxwell and Walter Harris give graphic accounts (see "Books" in Contexts, p.769 & p.772).

The souks and Grand Mosque

Taza's **souks** branch off to either side of the main street (by now Rue Koubet), midway between the Andalous and Grand Mosque. Since there are few and sporadic tourists, these are very much working markets, free of the artificial "craft" goods so often found. In fact, one of the most memorable is a souk for used European clothing – a frequent feature of country and provincial markets, the more fortunate dealers having gained access to the supplies of international charities. The **granary** and the covered stalls of the **kissaria** are also worth a look, in the shadow of the **Market Mosque** (Djemaa es Souk).

Taza's **Grand Mosque** is historically one of the most interesting buildings in the country, though, like that of the Andalous, it is so discreetly screened that it's difficult for non-Muslims to gain any glimpse of the interior. Founded in the twelfth century by the Almohad sultan Abd el Moumen, it is probably the oldest Almohad structure in existence, predating even the partially ruined mosque at Tin Mal (see p.511), with which it shares most stylistic features. If you are Muslim, you will be able to pop in for a look at the sumptuous stuccowork on the mihrab and on the domed ceiling in front of it. Like the ivory-inlaid *minbar* and the magnificent pagoda-like brass lamp overhanging the main aisle, these date from the end of the thirteenth century when the mosque was enlarged and endowed by the Merenids. For non-Muslims, on the other hand, even the outside of the mosque is elusive, shielded by a net of buildings; you have to walk up towards Bab er Rih for a reasonable impression of its ground plan.

Bab er Rih and the bastions

Above the Medina, at **Bab er Rih** (Gate of the Winds), it is possible to get some feeling for Taza's historic and strategic significance. You can see up the valley towards the Taza Gap: the Djebel Tazzeka and the Middle Atlas on one side, and the reddish earth of the Rif behind on the other. The only drawback to this vantage point is the smell of rubbish thrown down the hillside below.

The actual gate now leads nowhere and looks somewhat lost below the road, but it is Almohad in origin and design. So, too, is most of the circuit of walls, which you can follow round by way of a **bastion** (added by Moulay Ismail, in Spanish style) back to Place Moulay Hassan.

Practicalities

City bus #1 runs between **Place de l'Indépendance** and **Place Ahrrache**, in the Medina. The **train station** and adjacent **bus stand** and **grands taxis** terminals are at the north end of the Ville Nouvelle, 2km from Place de l'Indépendance (bus #3, #4 or #6 from Place Ahrrache; 3dh), which is where CTM services will drop you. Petits taxis are available for rides between the stations, Ville Nouvelle and Medina.

Internet access is available east of Place de l'Indépendance at Cyber fNet (10am–6am next day).

Accommodation

Taza doesn't have a great choice of accommodation – and there's no campsite – but you should find a room any time of year. If you're not too fussy about comfort, Place de l'Indépendance is the best location, with a scattering of cafés and restaurants nearby.

There are **hammams** off Place de l'Indépendance at 34 Av d'Oujda (two blocks north of the *Grand Hôtel du Dauphiné*), where men and women can go at the same time, though not together, with separate entrances (left for men, right for women) and sections (open 6am–9pm; 10dh).

In the Medina, the main hammam also has separate entrances, but also separate times. Men enter through the tiled doorway at 13 Zenkat Khtitl (first right up Zenqat el Andalous, the street off Place Ahrrache opposite the post office) and bathe from 8pm through to noon the next day; women enter via a similarly tiled doorway at 10 Zenqat Hadj Mimoune (second right up Zenqat el Andalous), and bathe from noon to 7pm.

Grand Hôtel du Dauphiné Pl de l'Indépendance ☎035 67 35 67. An old Art Deco hotel with decent-sized rooms, some of which are en suite. There is hot water mornings and evenings, and you'll find a cross-sectional plan of the Friouato cave (see p.208) in the lobby, along with some photos of French explorers visiting the cave back in 1951. ❸

Hôtel de l'Étoile Place Moulay Hassan, the southern extension of Place Ahrrache ☎035 27 01 79. This is a bargain cheapie – a friendly, family-run place with twelve decent rooms off a tiled courtyard. The nearby hammam compensates for the absence of showers, but there's not much in the way of places to eat round here. ❶

Hôtel Friouato Rue Massoudia ☎035 67 25 93, ℉035 67 22 44. A rather charmless concrete outpost, set in its own grounds amid the scrubland between the Ville Nouvelle and Medina. Still, there's a functional swimming pool, a bar

and a reasonable restaurant, and the rooms are pleasant, comfortable and heated in winter. ❺

Hôtel de la Gare Corner of Bd bir Anzarane & Av de la Gare, opposite the train station ☎035 67 24 48, ℉035 67 08 44. Handy for transport though a long haul from the Medina. Rooms are off a small courtyard with a banana tree, and many have showers and toilets, and hot water mornings and evenings. There's a *téléboutique*, and a café for breakfast attached. ❷

Hôtel Tour Eiffel Bd bir Anzarane ☎035 67 15 62, ℉035 67 15 63. A slightly overrated three-star hotel, with a scale model of the Parisian icon above the front door, located a petit taxi ride from Place de l'Indépendance. The rooms boast all mod cons but lack character, and it doesn't offer the same value for money as the *Dauphiné*. However, the restaurant, open to nonresidents and with a good selection of fish specialities, like *friture de poisson*, is worth a try. It can also arrange taxi circuits of Djebel Tazzeka starting at 250dh. ❺

Eating and drinking

Most of the **cafés and restaurants** are around **Place de l'Indépendance**. The *Restaurant des Gouts*, a block north of the square on Rue de Fes (daily 6am–11pm), is a good, cheap choice for brochettes, chicken or tajine, while the *Restaurant du Jardin*, a block northeast at 46 Rue Sultan Abou el Hassan, opposite the Bank al Maghrib (daily noon–midnight) offers pizzas as well as tasty tajines. Offering similar menus are *Snak Amigo*, next door to the *Cyrnos Bar*, and *Mou Mou*, which also serves panini and schwarma, on Boulevard Moulay Youssef. There are two good **patisseries** near the centre, *La Joconde* and *Amsterdam*; both have a fantastic selection of freshly made pastries and cakes. There is a small **supermarket** on Rue de Fes, opposite *Restaurant des Gouts*.

In the **Medina**, you won't find any restaurants as such, though shops around Place Ahrrache will sort you a sandwich. A good place for a mint tea or a coffee-and-croissant breakfast is the ✕ *Andalousia* café, above *Laiterie Ahrrache* on the south side of Place Ahrrache, overlooking the square and next door to *La Paix* **patisserie**. Nearer the Grand Mosque, you will find the simply named *Snak* sandwich shop and the nearby *Café el Pacha*, which has fantastic views overlooking the town and beyond.

Down below the Medina, there's a **bar** – and a passable restaurant – at the rather forlorn *Hôtel Friouato* or you could try *Cyrnos Bar*, across from *La Joconde*.

Moving on

Taza is quite a transport junction, with good connections west to Fes, east to Oujda and north to Nador and Al Hoceima. Grands taxis and all buses other than CTM services leave from right by the train station. There's no actual bus station building in Taza: ask someone to direct you to the ticket sellers for buses to your destination.

For **Fes** there's a wide choice of options. Grands taxis run throughout the day (just ask and wait for a place), arriving in Fes at Bab Ftouh (where you'll need to pick up a city taxi or bus to get to the hotels at Bab Boujeloud or the Ville Nouvelle). Fes is also served by four daily trains, plus a number of buses, but note that buses that originate from Nador will be subject to numerous police and customs checks en route, making the journey time rather longer. **Oujda** is easiest reached by train – a quick route across the eastern steppes, through Guercif and Taourirt (see p.210), though there are buses too.

For the **Rif**, most buses leave very early in the morning. There are plenty to **Nador** (most leaving in the morning), but only one going via **Aknoul** (currently at 3pm), the others over a more direct road via Taourirt (on the N6). There are also one or two buses each morning to **Al Hoceima**, via Aknoul. From Aknoul you can catch sporadic grands taxis across the southern slopes of the Rif to Taounate on the Route de l'Unité – the local bus that used to cover the route was not operating at the time of writing. Travelling to Al Hoceima by grand taxi, you may have to change vehicles at Kassita.

CTM buses leave from Place de l'Indépendance with daily services to Al Hoceima and Oujda (currently at 3pm); Tangier (10pm); plus two to Rabat and Casablanca and five to Fes.

The Djebel Tazzeka and beyond

A loop of some 123km around Taza, the **Cirque du Djebel Tazzeka** is really a car-driver's route, with its succession of mountain views, marking a transition between the Rif and Middle Atlas. However, it has a specific "sight" in the

Wildlife in the Djebel Tazzeka

The **Djebel Tazzeka National Park** is one of northern Morocco's most rewarding wildlife sites, positioned, as it is, at the point where the Rif merges with the Middle Atlas. The range's lower slopes are covered in cork oak, the prime commercial crop of this area, and interspersed with areas of mixed woodland containing holm oak, the pink-flowered cistus and the more familiar bracken.

These woodland glades are frequented by a myriad of **butterflies** from late May onwards; common varieties include knapweed, ark green fritillaries and Barbary skippers. The forest floor also provides an ideal habitat for **birds** such as the multi-coloured hoopoe, with its identifying crest, and the trees abound with the calls of wood pigeon, nuthatch, short-toed treecreeper and various titmice. The roadside telegraph lines also provide attractive hunting perches for such brightly coloured inhabitants as rollers and shrikes, both woodchat and great grey, who swoop on passing insects and lizards with almost gluttonous frequency.

immense **Friouato Cave** (Gouffre du Friouato), 22km from Taza, and the whole route is fertile ground for bird-watching and other wildlife (see box above). If you don't have transport, you could negotiate a grand taxi in Taza (at the rank by the train station) to take you to the cave and back, either waiting while you visit or picking you up later in the day; obviously, you'll want to pay at the end of the trip.

The cirque – and the Friouato cave

The **Cirque du Djebel Tazzeka road** starts out curling around below Taza's Medina before climbing to a narrow valley of almond and cherry orchards. About 10km out of Taza you reach the **Cascades de Ras el Oued**, a series of small waterfalls reduced to a trickle in the dry summer months. Two kilometres past the waterfalls is the village of **Ras el Ma** and the source of the ravine that feeds the oued. Unfortunately the spring here is partially built up with concrete pipes and looks like it is used as a makeshift toilet by locals and visitors alike. The *Café Ras el Ma*, an inconspicuous roadside building at the entrance to the village, is worth a a pit-stop not so much for its workaday menu of Moroccan staples and sandwiches as for the aerial views of the village afforded by its shaded terrace. Beyond here the road, prone to rock avalanches but generally in good condition, loops towards the first pass (at 1198m), passing some great picnic spots and eventually emerging onto the Chiker Plateau. Here, in exceptional years, the **Dayat Chiker** appears as a broad, shallow lake. More often than not, though, it is just a fertile saucer, planted with cereals; geographers will recognize its formation as a classic limestone polje.

At this point, the road divides; to reach the Friouato cave, take the right fork – the left leads to Meghraoua and Midelt, see opposite for details. After 4km, midway along the polje, you'll pass a sign to the **Gouffre du Friouato**, 500m to the right of the road. The cave complex, explored down to 180m, is said to be the deepest in North Africa – and it feels it – entered by descending into a huge "pot", over 30m wide, with five hundred wall-clinging steps down to a scree-filled base. The sense of descending into the entrails of the earth is exhilarating, but from the foot of the steps, it's a tight, slippery and strenuous squeeze back up to the top, through an entrance tunnel to a maze of passages which go deeper and deeper. Warm clothing is essential, as are sturdy shoes (it can be muddy), and more than one torch if exploring alone. If you are unused to potholing, it would be wise to employ the services of Mustapha Lachhab

(☎067 64 06 26), who has been the *gardien* here since 1980; if he's not at the cave, try his house by the junction with the main Taza road. He charges 200dh for an exploratory trip 2km into the cave, for a maximum of ten people. Alternatively you can go as far as the base of the steps for 5dh and come back. The complex has hardly been developed but there is a small café, and a map of the system is on sale; it is open to visitors 6am–10.30pm and kept locked at other times.

Grands taxis between Taza and the cave are available on a one-way fare basis until 2pm during the high season. After 2pm or throughout the day in the low season you will have to pay a return fare from Taza to get to Friouato, (around 150dh).

There's a *gîte d'étape* near the cave at **Aïn Bechar** on Dayat Chiker, offering very basic but decent rural **accommodation** in a flat-roofed adobe house as part of a local ecotourism initiative. A serene place with wonderful views across the plains, it sleeps up to six people in two rooms (☎067 25 44 21, ⓦwww.geocities.com/ainbecharass; 80dh per person, full board 180dh per person), with a communal shower and toilet. It is signposted on the main road (S311), 500m before the junction to the cave, a mile along a very rough *piste* across the plateau. Although most of the *piste* can be done – just! – in a normal car, the small creek crossing 200m before the house is only suitable for a 4x4. You can, however, leave your car before the stream, since the locals will keep an eye on it.

Beyond Friouato, the road runs up through the dark schist gorges of the Oued Zireg. At **Bab Bou Idir**, a low-key *éstivage* site 8.5km from Friouato, there is an office (sporadically open) for the **Tazzeka National Park** (see box opposite); more or less alongside, a small café and campsite operate in summer.

The most dramatic and scenic stretch of the cirque is undoubtedly the **ascent of Djebel Tazzeka** itself. It can be climbed by walking up the *piste* that turns off some 15km beyond Bab Bou Idir and serves a communication mast at the summit. The view from the top, encased in forests of cedars, stretches to the Rif, to the mountains around Fes and to much of the eastern Middle Atlas. Slightly further on from the turn off is a picnic site, *Vallèe des Cerfs* (Valley of the Stags), set in amongst the cork trees. The road wends on pleasantly, through cork oak forests where cork production is much in evidence, to rejoin the Fes–Taza road at Sidi Abdallah Des Rhiata.

A route to Midelt

For anyone with sturdy transport, there is an adventurous route **through the Middle Atlas to Midelt**. The start of this is the left fork (route 4822) at the beginning of the Chiker Plateau described above; it is paved road as far as Merhaoua, where a dirt road (very rough) takes over to Talzemt, where you join the 4656. This road eventually hits the R503 (formerly P20), a few kilometres south of Boulemane; from here you follow the road all the way south to Midelt (see p.313).

Taza to Oujda

The route from **Taza to Oujda** is as bare as it looks on the map: a semi-desert plain, broken by little more than the odd roadside town. Nonetheless, if you've got time to spare, and transport, there are a trio of recommendable detours.

Msoun

MSOUN, 29km east of Taza, and 3km north of the main road, is the first point of interest. The village, inhabited by a hundred or so members of the semi-nomadic Haoura tribe, is built within a **kasbah**, dating to the reign of Moulay Ismail (1672–1727) which is still turreted and complete on three sides. You can view its original rainwater cistern and grain silos, alongside the settlement's shop, post office and mosque.

Back on the main road, just opposite the track to Msoun, is the *Motel La Kasbah* (☎035 67 46 51; ❶), a friendly place for a meal or overnight stop.

Guercif, Gouttitir and the Cascades

At the agricultural centre of **GUERCIF**, at 37km from Taza, is another small **hotel**, the *Hôtel Howary* (☎035 62 50 62; ❷); it's a modest, friendly place with a reasonable restaurant at street level. There are also a number of grill café-restaurants surrounding the main roundabout. Midway between here and Taourirt, you might consider a brief detour from the main road, off to the left, to the hamlet of **GOUTTITIR**. Signposted "Thermal Spring", this comprises a few buildings set around a **hot spring**, in a rocky, steep-sided gully, whose waters are pumped up to supply a hammam (used by men during the day; women after dusk). There are very basic **rooms** (no beds) and **meals** to be had nearby at the *Café Sidi Chaffi*.

There's another possible detour: north of the road, 12km on from the Gouttitir turning, are the **Bou Mazouz Cascades**. These are reached by turning left (north) for 9km along the road to the Melga el Ouidane barrage. In contrast to the barren landscape either side of the main Taza road, this takes you past orange and olive orchards watered by the Oued Za. Look for a small mosque, with prominent loudspeaker, on the right; leave the road at this point and follow a rough track to the waterfalls – you can swim in a natural pool here, and camp beside it if you want.

Taourirt

TAOURIRT, the largest town along the route, was the crossroads between the old north–south caravan route linking Melilla and the ancient kingdom of Sijilmassa (see p.588), and the Taza corridor between Morocco and Algeria. The presence of the army (who occupy the old kasbah) and of prominent radio aerials confirms its continuing strategic importance, and for travellers it is a useful train and road junction, with buses north to Nador connecting reasonably well with train arrivals from Oujda or Fes. If you need to break your journey here, try the *Hôtel Mansour* (☎036 69 40 03; ❷), just off the roundabout in the centre of town and next door to a branch of the Wafa bank. Taourirt itself is of little interest, save for its large **Sunday souk**, but two spots nearby are well worth exploring. The first is the **Zâa Waterfalls**, on the Oued Zâa, reached by following the road to Taza westwards for 6km and turning right onto the N19 (signposted); the waterfalls are 9km further on. The second is the **Zâa Gorges**, about the same distance southeast from Taourirt, but not accessible by car; after driving 5km or so from town to the end of the S349, you must continue on foot into the narrow canyon.

Oujda and around

Open and easy-going, with a large and active university, **OUJDA** has that rare quality in Moroccan cities – nobody makes demands on your instinct

OUJDA

▲ Nador & Melilla

▲ Grands Taxis

▲ Chefchaouni

▲ Taza

▲ Figuig

▶ Sidi Yahia

0   200 m

0   50 m

RESTAURANTS & CAFÉS
Bar Restaurant du Palais	5
Brasserie Restaurant de France	2
Café Edahab	9
Le Palace	7
Ramses Restaurant	8
Restaurant el Hana	4
Restaurant National	6
Restaurant Oslo	1
Restaurant Wassila	3

ACCOMMODATION
Chic Hôtel	C	Hôtel Oujda	N
Hôtel Afrah	D	Hôtel Raiss	H
Hôtel Angad	F	Hôtel Ryad	O
Hôtel Concorde	G	Hôtel Simon	E
Hôtel Hanna	A	Hôtel 16 Août	I
Hôtel des Lilas	K	Hôtel Victoria	B
Hôtel Lutetia	M	Ibis Hôtel	J
Hôtel al Manar	L	Orient Oujda	P

Bab el Ouahab

Kissaria

SOUKS

Medersa

Kasbah

Grand Mosque

Cathédrale St Louis

MEDINA

MELLAH

Mosque Omar bin Abdullassiz

Bank al Maghrib

Hôtel de Ville

PTT

CTM

Bab el Gharbi

AL MOUTTAHIDA

Train Station

Market

Institut Français

Parque Lalla Aïsha

Bus Station

Grands Taxis

Oued Nachef

Cinema Theatre Royal

Bank al Maghrib

BMCI

Carlson Wagonlit

Hôtel de Ville

PTT

See inset map

RUE DE CASABLANCA
RUE DE RABAT
RUE DE FIGUIG
RUE DE FES
RUE DE MARRAKECH
AV DES MARCHES
PLACE DU MAROC
RUE DES MARCHES
PLACE SOUK EL MAI
PLACE EL ATTARIN
BD. RAMDANE EL GADI
BD MOHAMMED V
BD D'ASFER
RUE MARJANE
MOHADINE
RUE EL MAZOUZI
PLACE DU 16 AOÛT
RUE EL QUAHDA
BD. DE SIDI YAHIA
RUE SIDI ZIANE
BOULEVARD MAGHRIB
RIF IDRISS AL AKBAR
BEN ABDALLAH
ALLAL
RUE JAMAL
BMCI
RAI
Supermarket
BOULEVARD MOHAMMED ARDOU
RUE MOHAMMED DERFOUFI
RUE MOURABITINES
RUE AL MOURABITINES
BOULEVARD ZERKTOUNI
RUE IBN ABDOUN
BOULEVARD
RUE MOHAMMED
BD. ABDALLAH
BOULEVARD HASSAN LOUKILI
RUE MAMOUN
RUE HANSALI
BOULEVARD BIR ANZARANE
RUE IMAM CHAFI
YOUSSEF BEN TACHINE
Algerian Consulate
RUE DRISS BEN BOUCHAIB
R. TARIK IBN ZIAD
TA-NA
HAMDANE EL GADI
BOULEVARD MOHAMMED V
PLACE DU 16 AOÛT
RUE LIEUTENANT BEL HOUCINE

N

for self-preservation. After the Rif, it is a surprise, too, to see women in public again, and to re-enter a Gallic atmosphere – as you move out of what used to be Spanish Morocco into the old French Protectorate zone. Morocco's easternmost town, Oujda was the capital of French Maroc Orient and an important trading centre. It remains today a lively and relatively prosperous place, strikingly modern by Moroccan standards, and with a population approaching three quarters of a million.

With its strategic location at the crossroads of eastern and southern routes across Morocco and Algeria, Oujda, like Taza, was always vulnerable to invasion and has frequently been the focus of territorial claims. Founded in the tenth century by Berber chieftain Ziri Ben Attia, it was occupied for parts of the thirteenth and fourteenth centuries by the Ziyanids, whose capital at Tlemcen is today just across the Algerian border. From 1727 until the early nineteenth century Oujda was under Turkish rule – the only town in present-day Morocco to have been part of the Ottoman Empire. Following the French defeat of the Ottomans in Algeria, France twice occupied the town, prior to its incorporation within the Moroccan Protectorate in 1912: an early and prolonged association, which remains tangible in the streets and attitudes.

In more recent years, the town's proximity to the Algerian border and distance from the government in Rabat led to a reputation for dissidence and unrest. This was particularly evident during the Algerian border war in the early 1960s, and again, in the 1980s, in a series of student strikes. Just as important, however, was the restoration of Moroccan–Algerian relations in 1988, when for a time the city became truly pan-Maghrebi, with Algerians coming in to shop, and Moroccans sharing in some of the cultural dynamism of neighbouring Oran, the home of *raï* music. Alas, this is all in the past now, since the closure of the border.

The Town

Oujda consists of the usual **Medina** and **Ville Nouvelle**, the latter highly linear in its layout, having started out as a military camp.

The **Medina**, walled on three sides, lies right in the heart of town and is largely a French reconstruction – obvious by the ease with which you can find your way around. Unusually, though, it has retained much of the city's commercial functions and has an enjoyably active air with **Place du 16 Août**, the town's main square, at its northwest corner.

Entering from **Bab el Ouahab**, the principal gate, you'll be struck by the amazing variety of food – on both café and market stalls – and it's well worth a look for this alone. Olives are Oujda specialities, and especially wonderful if you're about after the September harvest. In the old days, more or less up until the French occupation, Bab el Ouahab was the gate where the heads of criminals were displayed.

Exploring the quarter, a good route to follow from the gate is straight down the main street towards **Place el Attarin**, flanked by a *kissaria* (covered market) and a grand *fondouk*. At the far end of the souks you come upon **Souk el Ma**, the irrigation souk, where the supply of water used to be regulated and sold by the hour. Walking on from here, you'll arrive back at Place du 16 Août.

Running along the outside of the Medina walls, the **Parc Lalla Aisha** is a pleasant area to seek midday shade. Following it round to the west takes you to the Bab el Gharbi – also called Bab Sidi Aisha – from which Rue el Ouahda runs north to the old French **Cathédrale Saint Louis**. Its present congregation (Mass Sat 6.30pm & Sun 9am) numbers about ten, the fonts are dry, and the statue niches empty, but there is a beautiful chapel; for admission, ring at the door of the presbytery at the back, on Rue d'Azila.

Practicalities

Arriving at the **train station** you are in easy walking distance of the centre. The new **bus station**, which handles most services, is more of a walk (or an inexpensive petit taxi ride), 500m southwest of the train station, across the Oued Nachef, but CTM services use their own terminal on Rue Sidi Brahim, by the Omar Bin Abdullah mosque. Oujda–Angad **airport** is 12km north of Oujda and inside the terminal you will find desks for Avis, Hertz and Europcar and a post office agency but no bureau de change. Grands taxis are usually waiting outside to meet all arrivals and should charge around 150dh to take up to six people into the city. For **car rental** there is a Hertz office at 3 Bd Mohammed V (☎036 68 38 02), or just around the corner is the efficient and privately run Benahmed Cars on Rue Anoual el Baraka (☎061 36 36 00). The **travel agency** Carlson Wagonlit, facing Place Mohammed V by the main boulevard (☎036 68 25 20, ⓔcwtoud1@menara .ma), acts as the agent for Europcar and Air France as well as dealing with general travel arrangements.

There is still an **Algerian consulate** at 11 Rue de Taza, about 300m west of Bab el Gharbi (Mon–Thurs 8am–3.30pm, Fri 8am–3pm, ☎036 71 04 52), though its staff may tell you to go to Rabat for a visa. For **car repairs**, mechanics are on Rue Ahfir, with a number of spares shops on Rue Madina el Mounaouara – the two streets meet at their junction with Boulevard Mohammed V. The Hôtel de Ville, the **post office**, several **banks** and the **tourist office** (Mon–Fri 8.30am–5.30pm; ☎036 68 20 36 or 68 56 31) are all grouped around Place du 16 Août. **Internet** access is available at Karamoss Cyber Lounge on Boulevard Mohammed V, opposite the Bank el Maghrib (daily 9am–10pm), and there is a *téléboutique* Internet at 13 Bd Mohammed Derfoufi (daily 8am–11pm). There is a **hammam** (Hammam du Jardin) 200m up the road into the Medina from Bab el Gharbi (men 4–8am & 6–11pm, women 8am–6pm; 7/8dh respectively; the entrance is the very conspicuous blue door on your right.

Accommodation

There are a number of **hotels** in the **Medina**; many are poor value, but the better choices are detailed below. Around the **Ville Nouvelle** is a range of much better hotels, many of them built in the early 1990s. Booking ahead is a good idea during holiday periods, when many Moroccan migrant workers return home to their families. The closest **campsite** is in Saïdia (see p.201).

Cheap

Chic Hôtel 34 Bd Ramdane el Gadi ☎036 69 05 66. The name's a bit optimistic but the hotel is clean, pleasant and well maintained. ❷

Hôtel Afrah 15 Rue Tafna ☎036 68 65 33. Located on a busy pedestrianized street, this modern hotel has comfortable en-suite rooms, heated in winter, and great views across the Medina from its rooftop café. ❷

Hôtel Hanna 132 Rue de Marrakech ☎ & ⓕ036 68 60 03. Neat and clean rooms, some of them with balconies but none en suite. The vast terrace

overlooks the minaret of the Omar Bin Abdullah mosque. ❶

Hôtel Lutetia 44 Bd Hassan Loukili ☎036 68 33 65. This old hotel has seen better days but is conveniently positioned right by the train station. Shared showers. ❷

Hôtel Simon corner of Rue Tariq Ibn Ziad and Idriss Ben Bouchaib (no phone). Located just inside the Medina, this was the first European-style hotel in Oujda – opened in 1910. It remains a nice, friendly place, with a restaurant and lively bar. All rooms have hot-water showers. ❶

Hôtel 16 Août 128 Rue de Marrakech ☎036 68 41 97. Best of the cheap hotels, with clean rooms and hot showers available (5dh). **①**

Hôtel Victoria 74 Bd Mohammed V ☎036 68 50 20. Rather uninspiring establishment better left as a fall-back if other hotels in town are fully booked. Communal toilets and cold showers. **①**

Moderate to expensive

Hôtel Angad Bd Ramdane el Gadi ☎036 69 14 51, ℱ036 69 14 52. Friendly and clean hotel with heated, en-suite rooms and breakfast café. **④**

Hôtel Concorde Bd Mohammed V ☎036 68 23 28, ℱ036 68 78 28. The freshly painted exterior belies a dark, gloomy interior and rather plain, en-suite heated rooms. Conveniently located for CTM departures. **④**

Hôtel des Lilas Rue Jamal Eddine el Afghani ☎036 68 08 40. A decent, modern hotel with small tiled en-suite rooms and secure parking next door. **③**

Hôtel al Manar 50 Bd Zerktouni ☎036 68 88 55, ℱ036 69 02 44. A smart, modest establishment, opened in 1992 and wearing well, with heating. Breakfast included. **⑤**

Hôtel Oujda Bd Mohammed V ☎036 68 44 82, ℱ036 68 50 64. A long-established landmark

hotel, undistinguished but with TVs, a/c, heating and a bath in each room, plus a popular bar and a small swimming pool. **⑤**

Hôtel Raiss Bd Mohammed V ☎036 70 30 58, ℱ036 68 80 08. A friendly, clean and comfortable new hotel with TVs and heating in all rooms – those at the back are quieter than those overlooking the street. Good breakfasts. **⑤**

Hôtel Ryad Av Idriss al Akbar ☎036 68 83 53. Good value, with clean, pleasant rooms, a restaurant, café and friendly bar; undergoing renovation at time of writing. **⑤**

Ibis Hôtel (*Moussafir*) Bd Abdellah Chefchaouini, near the train station ☎036 68 82 02, ⓦwww .ibishotel.com. One of the elegant "blue and white" chain of hotels located by major train stations. It has a restaurant, bar, swimming pool, a/c and TVs in all rooms, and all in all is pretty good value. **⑤**

Orient Oujda (formerly *Hôtel al Massira*) Bd Maghreb el Arabi ☎036 70 06 06, ⓦwww .hotelsatlas.com. Recently refurbished by the Atlas chain, with 98 a/c en-suite rooms, all with satellite TVs and balconies. Boasts three restaurants, two bars, a wellness centre and a large swimming pool. The adjoining *Alcazar* nightclub (daily 11pm–3am) is open to nonresidents. **⑦**

Eating, drinking and entertainment

Oujda has a strong cultural life and is one of the most enjoyable Moroccan cities in which to while away an evening. Hustlers don't really feature here and the bars and restaurants are sociable and open places. Most of the town's **bars** are in the hotels; good bets include the *Ibis*, the *Orient*, the *Ryad* and the *Simon*. A lively local place is *Bar Restaurant du Palais* on Boulevard Mohammed Derfoufi. For **cafés/patisseries** there's the gleaming *Café Edahab*, next to *Hôtel Ryad* on Avenue Idriss al Akbar; *Le Palace*, on Boulevard Mohammed V, serves possibly the best espresso in town – and fresh pastries to match. For groceries, there is an unnamed, but well-stocked, **supermarket** on Avenue Idriss al Akbar, opposite *Café Edahab*.

The Theatre Royal **cinema** on Rue Okba Ibn Nafia, opposite the Banque el Maghrib on the other side of Boulevard Mohammed V, has daily showings at 3pm and 9pm, with the usual choice of foreign and Moroccan films in French. The Institut Français at 3 Rue de Berkane (☎036 68 44 04, ⓦwww .ambafrance-ma.org/institut/oujda) organizes an eclectic selection of **cultural events** – from audiovisual talks to exhibitions, theatre and musical performances by local and visiting artists – listed in its quarterly brochure, available on the premises.

Restaurants

The focus of evening activity is **Bab el Ouahab**, around which you can get all kinds of grilled food from stalls. On the other side of the Medina, too, there are plenty of good eating places on, or just off, **Boulevard Zerktouni**.

In the **Ville Nouvelle**, in addition to those found in the hotels mentioned above, recommended restaurants include:

Brasserie Restaurant de France Bd Mohammed V. Despite the bubblegum furniture, this is one of the fancier places in town, offering a selection of well-prepared mostly French fish and meat dishes. It's located upstairs from a café-patisserie, and with a nightclub attached. Licensed. Daily 9am–11pm. Moderate.

Ramses Restaurant 2 Bd Mohammed V. Brand new and already popular with the university crowd. The downstairs restaurant (daily noon–11pm) serves mainly pizza and pannini whilst the upstairs café and patisserie (daily 5am–11pm) has a great breakfast menu and fresh juices. Cheap to moderate.

Restaurant el Hana 106 Bd Mohammed Derfoufi. A cheap-and-cheerful place with tasty spit-roast chicken plus soups, tajines, salads and various meats. Daily 7am–2am. Cheap.

Restaurant National Bd Zerktouni, corner of Bd Allal Ben Abdallah. A good place for tajines and meat dishes, which also offers a veg-only tajine, and *beldi* (country) chicken once a week, but avoid the salads, which are left out uncovered on the counter by the cash till. Seating upstairs. Daily 7am–11pm. Cheap.

Restaurant Oslo 130 Rue de Marrakech, next door to *Hôtel Hana*. Cheerful little place which serves kebabs, tajine and cous cous. Open daily 'til late. Cheap,

Restaurant Wassila 19 Rue Tafna. One of several small café-restaurants on the pedestrianized streets south of Place du 16 Août. A friendly place with a small menu of staples (meat, chips, tajines), all well prepared. Daily except Sun 7am–9pm. Cheap.

Moving on

Around fourteen independent transport companies operate from the main **bus station** across the Oued Nachef, between them running several daily departures to main towns around the country. You are unlikely to wait more than 45 minutes for a bus to the most immediate destinations, such as Saïdia, Berkane or Taza, regardless of the time of day. CTM services currently leave for Fes, Taza, and Al Hoceima via Nador. Oujda **train station** is at the easternmost end of the northern railway network, from where there is at least one daily direct service to Fes, Meknes, Tangier and Casablanca.

Grands taxis for Ahfir, Berkane and Al Hoceima leave from near the train station (you'll probably have to change taxis at Berkane for Saïdia or Nador, but you may strike lucky and get one direct), but those for Taourirt and Taza leave by the main bus station – you'll have to change at Taza for Fes, and there for most points beyond. The **airport**, Oujda–Angad, is 12km north, off the N2 (☎036 68 20 84, ℻036 68 44 62); there is no bureau de change at the airport. In town, RAM has an office alongside the *Hôtel Oujda* on Boulevard Mohammed V (☎036 68 39 09, ℻036 71 02 27), and operates daily flights to Casablanca. There are also less frequent direct services to various European destinations and connecting services to other Moroccan destinations via Casablanca.

Sidi Yahia

SIDI YAHIA, 6km south of Oujda, is a rather unimpressive little oasis for most of the year, with a "cascade" that is switched on at weekends. However, it's a place of some veneration, housing as it does the tomb of the *marabout* **Sidi Yahia**, a holy man identified by local tradition with John the Baptist. Nobody is quite sure where the saint is buried – several of the cafés stake an optimistic claim – but at the **moussems** held here in August and September almost every shrub and tree in the oasis is festooned with little pieces of cloth, a ritual as lavish and extraordinary as anything in the Mediterranean Church.

South to Figuig

In past years, before the eruption of civil war in Algeria, there was a well-established travel route from Oujda, south to the ancient **date palm oasis of**

Figuig, and across from there into the Algerian Sahara. This is no longer a possibility. However, those into isolated journeys might still want to consider the route from **Oujda** to **Figuig** – and on from there to the southern Moroccan oasis town of **Er Rachidia** (see p.580).

If you're on for the trip, be warned it's a long, hot haul: 369km from Oujda to Figuig, and a further 393km to Er Rachidia. You can travel by bus (there are three daily departures to Figuig; the 6am one continuing to Er Rachidia) or, if you have transport, you can drive: the road is sealed all the way. Whichever way you travel, expect to explain yourself at a number of military checkpoints: this is a sensitive border area.

The route

En route between Oujda and Figuig there are just a few roadside settlements and mining towns – for coal, copper, manganese and zinc. If you are driving, **AÏN BENIMATHAR**, 83km from Oujda, is a good point to break the journey: the village has a group of kasbahs, an important (and ancient) **Monday souk**, and some grill-cafés. About 4km to its west is a small oasis, **Ras el Aïn**, with a (highly seasonal) waterfall.

Another possible stop could be **TENDRARA**, 198km from Oujda, a larger settlement with an important **Thursday souk**; it has a traditional marketplace in the centre and sheep and goats corralled on the outskirts. Again, there are grill-cafés.

At 241km, you reach **BOUARFA**, the region's administrative centre and transport hub, with buses to Er Rachidia (as well as Figuig and Oujda), and a couple of hotels. For details of **Bouarfa, Figuig and the route to Er Rachidia**, see pp.598–600.

Travel details

Trains

Oujda to: Casablanca (2 direct & 1 connecting daily; 10hr); Fes (3 daily; 5hr 30min); Guercif (3 daily; 2hr 30min); Kenitra (2 direct & 1 connecting daily; 8hr 30min); Marrakesh (2 connecting daily; 14hr); Meknes (3 daily; 7hr); Rabat (2 direct & 1 connecting daily; 9hr); Tangier (1 direct & 1 connecting daily; 12hr); Taourirt (3 daily; 1hr 45min; connecting Supratours bus service to and from Nador); Taza (3 daily; 3hr 30min).

There are no longer any passenger services from Oujda to Bouarfa; nor currently across the border to Algeria.

Taza to: Casablanca (2 direct & 2 connecting daily; 7hr); Fes (4 daily; 2hr); Guercif (3 daily; 1hr); Kenitra (2 direct & 2 connecting daily; 5hr 15min); Marrakesh (3 connecting daily; 10hr); Meknes (3 direct & 1 connecting daily; 3hr 15min); Rabat (2 direct & 2 connecting daily; 6hr); Tangier (1 direct & 2 connecting daily; 8hr 20min).

Buses

Berkane to: Casablanca (1 CTM daily; 12hr 15min); Fes (1 CTM daily; 7hr 15min); Meknes (1 CTM daily; 8hr 15min); Nador (19 daily; 1hr 30min); Oujda (20 daily; 1hr 30min); Rabat (1 CTM daily; 10hr 45min); Saïdia (4 daily; 1hr).

Al Hoceima to: Aknoul (1 daily; 1hr 30min); Casablanca (1 CTM daily; 12hr) via Rabat (9hr); Fes (2 CTM & 6 others daily; 5hr); Meknes (2 CTM & 1 other daily; 6hr); Nador (2 CTM & 6 others daily; 3hr); Oujda (2 CTM & 1 other daily; 4hr 30min); Tangier (2 CTM & 5 others daily; 6hr); Tetouan (2 CTM & 8 others daily; 5hr 30min) via Issaguen (3 daily; 2hr 30min) and Chefchaouen (2 CTM & 5 others; Tangier line, only goes into Chefchaouen if requested, otherwise stops at Dardara; 4hr 30min).

Nador to: Aknoul (1 daily; 3hr 30min); Casablanca (2 CTM & 9 others daily; 12hr); Fes (2 CTM & 17 others daily; 5hr 30min); Figuig (1 daily; 9hr 30min); Guercif (at least one every hour; 3hr); Al Hoceima (3 CTM & 16 others daily; 3hr); Meknes

(2 CTM & 5 others daily; 6hr 30mins; Oujda (1 CTM & 16 others daily; 2hr 30min); Rabat (1 CTM & 16 others daily; 9hr); Er Rachidia (2 daily; 14hr); Rissani (1 daily; 16hr); Saïdia (1 daily; 2hr); Tangier (1 CTM & 7 others daily; 12hr) via Tetouan (9hr 30min); Taourirt (4 ONCF/Supratours daily; 1hr 30min; connecting with train service to Fes, Meknes, Kenitra, Rabat & Casablanca); Taza (at least one every hour; 4hr).

Oujda to: Bouarfa (2 daily; 5hr); Casablanca (2 CTM & at least 7 others daily; 11hr) via Rabat (9hr 30min); Al Hoceima (1 CTM & 1 other daily; 8hr); Fes (4 CTM & 18 others daily; 6hr 15min); Figuig (3 daily; 7hr); Meknes (4 CTM & 15 others daily; 7hr 15min); Nador (1 CTM & 12 others daily; 2hr 30min); Saïdia (2 daily; 1hr 30min); Taza (2 CTM & 15 others; 4hr).

Taza to: Aknoul (1 daily; 1hr 30min); Casablanca (2 CTM & 9 others daily; 7hr 30min) via Meknes (2hr 45min) and Rabat (6hr 15min); Fes (5 CTM daily & others roughly hourly; 2hr 30min); Al Hoceima (1 CTM & 1 other daily; 3hr 30min); Meknes (2 CTM & 3 others daily; 3hr 15min); ▮▮▮▮▮ (▮▮ ▮▮▮▮ ▮▮▮ ▮▮▮▮▮ ▮▮▮▮▮ ▮▮▮); Oujda (1 CTM daily & others roughly hourly; 3hr 30min); Tangier (1 CTM daily; 8hr).

Berkane to: Nador (1hr 30min); Saïdia (45min); Oujda (50min); Taforalt (45min).
Al Hoceima to: Issaguen (2hr); Kalah Iris (1hr); Kassita (1hr); Nador (3hr); Oujda (5hr 30min). Occasionally direct to Fes (4hr); Targuist (1hr 30min); Taza (4hr 30min).

Bab Berret to: Issaguen (45min); Chefchaouen (1hr).
Issaguen (Ketama) to: Bab Berret (45min); Al Hoceima (1hr 45min); Taounate (1hr 20min); Targuist (45min).
Nador to: Beni Enzar (15min); Berkane (1hr 30min); Al Hoceima (2hr 45min); occasionally direct to Oujda (2hr 30min).
Oujda to: Ahfir (45min); Berkane (50min); Al Hoceima (5hr 30min); Taza (3hr). Occasionally direct to Nador (2hr).
Saïdia to: Ahfir (30min); Berkane (30min).
Taounate to: Fes (1hr 30min); Issaguen (1hr 20min).
Targuist to: Al Hoceima (1hr 30min); Issaguen (45min); Kalah Iris (45min).
Taza to: Aknoul (1hr); Fes (1hr 30min); Guercif (45min); Kassita (2hr); Oujda (3hr). Occasionally direct to Al Hoceima (2hr 45min).

Ferries

Al Hoceima to: Almería (2 daily June–Sept; 5hr).
Nador (Beni Enzar) to: ▮▮▮▮▮ (10 ▮▮▮▮▮) in winter, 3–4 daily in summer; 6–7hr); Sète (every four days in summer only; 36hr).
Melilla to: Malaga (1–2 daily; 8–9hr); Almería (1 daily, 2 daily in summer, 6hr).
For further details on ferry services, see pp.32–33.

Flights

Nador to: Casablanca (2 weekly; 1hr 35min).
Oujda to: Casablanca (1–3 daily; 1hr 10min).

Meknes, Fes and the Middle Atlas

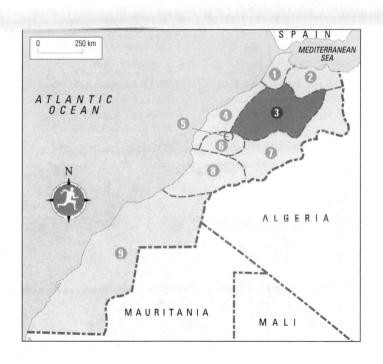

CHAPTER 3 # Highlights

✳ **The souks of Meknes**
Hassle-free and a pleasure to
browse – don't miss the spice
and sweet stalls. See p.236

✳ **Volubilis and Moulay Idriss**
Two remarkable Roman and
Islamic sites that can be
combined on an easy day-trip
from Meknes. See p.242

✳ **Borj Nord at sunset** Visit
for a fabled panorama of
Fes Medina; pure magic
accompanied by the call of
muezzins. See p.267

✳ **Bou Inania Medersa, Fes**
The finest Merenid Islamic
college in the country,
looking better than ever after
renovation. See p.269

✳ **The tanneries, Fes** A little
voyeuristic, but the view of
these leather-tanning vats
can have barely changed
since medieval days.
See p.280

✳ **Mibladene and El Ahouli** The
off-road drive to these derelict
mines is an adventure in itself.
See p.315

✳ **Cirque du Jaffar** The
classic Midelt driving route,
perfect for an excursion.
See p.317

✳ **The Cascades d'Ouzoud**
If you only visit one
waterfall in Morocco, make
it these spectacular falls.
See p.327

△ Bou Inania Medersa, Fes

Meknes, Fes and the Middle Atlas

he undoubted highlight of this chapter is **Fes**. The imperial capital for long periods under the Merenid Wattasid and Alaouite dynasties, the city has for the past ten centuries stood at the heart of Moroccan history – and for five of these it was one of the major intellectual and cultural centres of the West, rivalling the great university cities of Europe. Today, it is unique in the Arab world, preserving the appearance and much of the life of a medieval Islamic city. In terms of monuments, it boasts as many as the other Moroccan imperial capitals combined, while the souks, extending for over a mile, maintain the whole tradition of urban crafts.

In all of this – and equally in the everyday aspects of the city's life – there is enormous fascination and, for the outsider, a real feeling of privilege. But inevitably, it is at a cost. Declared a historical monument by its French colonizers, and subsequently deprived of its political and cultural significance, Fes today retains its beauty but is evidently in decline. Its university faculties have been dispersed around the country, with the most important departments in Rabat; the Fassi business elite have mostly left for Casablanca; and, for survival, the city depends increasingly on the tourist trade. Nonetheless, two or three days here is an absolute must for any visit to Morocco.

Meknes, like Fes (and Rabat and Marrakesh) an imperial city, sees comparatively few visitors, despite being an easy and convenient stopover en route by train from Tangier or Rabat, or by bus from Chefchaouen on the route south to the Middle Atlas or the Great Southern Oasis routes. The creation of megalomaniac Moulay Ismail, the most tyrannical of all Moroccan sultans, it is once again a city of lost ages, its enduring impression being that of an endless series of walls. But Meknes is also an important modern market centre and its souks, though smaller and less secretive than those of Fes, are almost as varied and generally more authentic. There are, too, the local attractions of **Volubilis**, the most impressive of the country's Roman sites, and the hilltop town of **Moulay Idriss**, home to the most important Islamic shrine in Morocco.

South of the two imperial cities stretch the cedar-covered slopes of the **Middle Atlas**, which in turn gradually give way to the High Atlas. Across and around this region, often beautiful and for the most part remote, there are two main routes. The most popular, a day's journey by bus, skirts the range beyond the market town of **Azrou** to emerge via **Beni Mellal** at Marrakesh. The

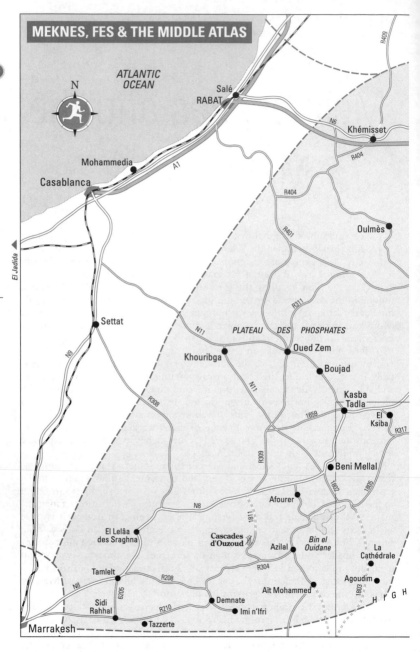

MEKNES, FES & THE MIDDLE ATLAS

El Jadida ▲

ATLANTIC
OCEAN

N

Salé
RABAT

Khémisset

R409

N6

R404

Mohammedia

A1

Casablanca

R404

R401

Oulmès

Settat

N11

PLATEAU DES PHOSPHATES

Oued Zem

R311

N9

Khouribga

N11

Boujad

R308

Kasba
Tadla

1659

El
Ksiba

R317

R309

Beni Mellal

1802

1805

Afourer

N8

1811

Cascades
d'Ouzoud

Azilal

*Bin el
Ouidane*

La
Cathédrale

El Lelâa
des Sraghna

R304

Agoudim

1803

H I G H

Tamlelt

6205

R208

Aït Mohammed

Sidi
Rahhal

R210

Demnate

Imi n'Ifri

Marrakesh

N8

Tazzerte

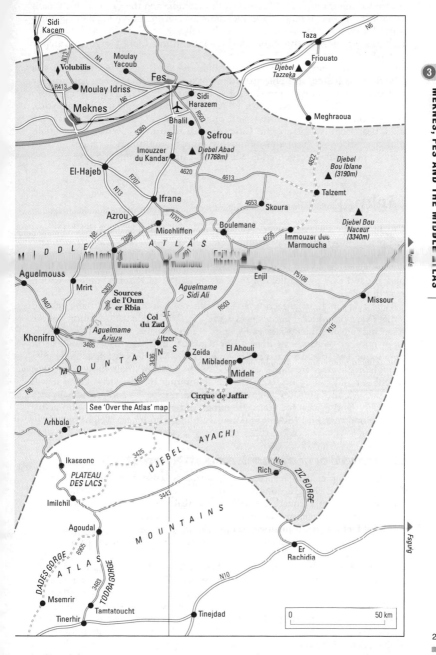

second climbs southeast from Azrou towards **Midelt**, an excellent carpet centre, before passing through great gorges to Er Rachidia and the vast date palm oasis of Tafilalt – the beginning of a tremendous southern circuit (see p.580). A third route leaves the main Azrou–Marrakesh highway at **El Ksiba** and makes its tortuous way **across the Atlas** via Imilchil and the Todra Gorge to Tinerhir (see p.574).

If you're travelling one of the main highways, and you've got the time, the Middle Atlas has considerable attractions of its own. Close to Fes, **Immouzer** and **Ifrane** are popular summer resorts, their air and waters a cool escape from the city. The Berber market town of **Azrou** is host to a great **Tuesday souk** and surrounded by cedar forests and mountain lakes. And off the Marrakesh road, near Beni Mellal, are the **Cascades d'Ouzoud** – spectacular waterfalls which crash down from the mountains, even in midsummer, plunging from pool to pool into a gorge beside which you can swim, camp and hike.

Meknes

Cut in two by the wide river valley of the Oued Boufekrane, **MEKNES** is a prosperous provincial city. Monuments from its past – notably the extraordinary creations of Moulay Ismail (see p.231) – justify a day's rambling exploration, as do the varied and busy souks of its Medina. In addition, the Ville Nouvelle is pleasant and easy to handle, and there is the appeal of Roman Volubilis within easy distance.

Almost as much an attraction as its architecture is the friendly and relaxed atmosphere on which Meknes prides itself. A large student population, whose male and female students mix easily, helps – and probably explains the relatively large number of bars – as does a population that is far smaller than that of neighbour Fes spread in a spacious town. True, Meknes's Medina and souks, though hassle-free, are tame compared with those of their more illustrious neighbour and can even seem rather disappointing by comparison. But if you visit first, Meknes prepares you a little for the drama of Fes and provides an idea of quality (and prices) for crafts shopping. And even those visitors who arrive here second may find Meknes's more easy-going atmosphere weighs heavily in its favour.

Orientation, arrival and information

Meknes is simpler than it looks on the map. Its **Ville Nouvelle** (*Hamriya* in Arabic) stretches along a slope above the east bank of the river, radiating from an impressive public square, the **Place Administrative** – a stretch of garden and a fountain, flanked by the main post office, a walloping Hôtel de Ville, and a helpful Délégué du Tourisme (see opposite). While you're here, the interior of the post office is worth a look for its vast Expressionist murals, painted by a Parisian professor in 1929.

The **Medina** and its neighbouring **Mellah** (the old Jewish quarters) occupy the west bank, with the walls of Moulay Ismail's **Ville Impériale** edging away, seemingly forever, to their south. The focal point of the Medina is **Place el Hedim**, remodelled in the 1990s into a pedestrian plaza with fountains, decorated arcades and shops. This is a good place to fix your bearings: downhill, petits taxis, grands taxis and buses run to local destinations, while uphill buses #5, #7 and #9 head towards the Ville Nouvelle. If you are **driving**, it's worth noting that traffic on Avenue Mohammed V and Avenue Allal Ben Abdallah is one-way, circulating anticlockwise. Parking near the Medina is available just west of Place el Hedim.

As an idea of distances, the walk between Place Administrative in the Ville Nouvelle and Place el Hedim in the Medina takes around twenty minutes, or costs about 12dh in a petit taxi.

The **tourist office** is at 27 Pl Administrative (Mon–Fri 8.30am–4.30pm; ☏035 51 60 22, ⓦwww.meknes-net.com), with unusually helpful staff and considerable, if sometimes dated, information on the noticeboard.

Arrival

Arriving by **bus** you will be dropped either at the main **bus station** on the north side of the New Mellah just outside the Bab el Khemis, or (if coming by CTM) at the **CTM bus station** on Avenue de Fes, east of the Ville Nouvelle.

Grands taxis from most destinations use a yard alongside the CTM bus station. Grands taxis from one or two local destinations use a yard across the road from the local bus stops below Place el Hedim in the Medina, and on Rue Omar el Moutahida in the Ville Nouvelle.

There are two **train stations**, both in the Ville Nouvelle on the east bank. The **main station** is a kilometre away from the central area; a smaller, more convenient one, the **Gare el Amir Abdelkader**, is a couple of blocks from the centre (behind the *Hôtel Majestic*). All trains stop at both.

Accommodation

Meknes' hotels are concentrated in the **Ville Nouvelle**, which is the best choice for comfort (unless you opt for one of the riads in the **Medina** or the **Ville Impériale**) and proximity to most bars and restaurants. It's only a twenty-minute walk from there to the Medina, monuments and souks.

Medina and Ville Impériale

As ever, all the cheapies have pretty basic facilities, although the trade off is their location just a few minutes from the sights.

Cheap

Hôtel Agadir 9 Rue Dar Smen ☏035 53 01 41. Clean and friendly, with small, basic rooms mostly tucked away in odd crannies of an eccentric rambling building. Free cold showers are available on the terrace and there's a hammam nearby (see p.241). ❶

Hôtel Meknes 35 Rue Dar Smen ☏060 83 86 80. Down-to-earth hotel with rooms on two floors arranged around an inner courtyard. It's between *Hôtel Nouveau* and *Hôtel Regina*, and best as a fall-back if both are full. Cold showers. ❶

Hôtel Nouveau 65 Rue Dar Smen ☏035 67 93 17. Opposite the Banque Populaire, this claims to be the first hotel in the Medina (despite the name) and is certainly the cheapest. Helpful, basic facilities and no external windows. Hot showers available at 5dh. ❶

Hôtel de Paris 58 Rue Rouamzine (no phone). Up from the *Maroc Hôtel* on the opposite side of the street, a tatty 1930s hotel that has seen better days. No showers but there's a hammam nearby (see p.241). ❶

Hôtel Regina 19 Rue Dar Smen ☏035 53 02 80. This old hotel is a mite more expensive than its neighbours and not necessarily better. Bar a few grubby corners, basic rooms with washbasins are clean enough and hot showers are available for 5dh. ❶

Maroc Hôtel 7 Rue Rouamzine ☏035 53 00 75. Cleanest and quietest of the Medina hotels; most rooms are pleasantly furnished and look onto a patio garden full of orange trees. Hot showers and a hammam nearby (see p.241). Rooftop sleeping in summer for 40–50dh. ❷

Moderate to expensive

Maison d'hôte Riad 79 Ksar Chaacha ☏035 53 05 42, ⓦwww.riadmeknes.com. Seven rooms in a modern but antique-filled complex attached to

225

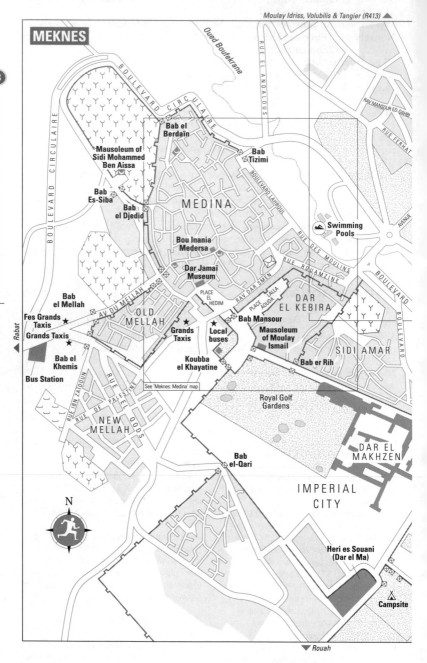

MEKNES

Moulay Idriss, Volubilis & Tangier (R413)

Oued Boufekrane

MEDINA

Bab el Berdaïn

Mausoleum of Sidi Mohammed Ben Aissa

Bab Tizimi

Bab Es-Siba

Bab el Djedid

Bou Inania Medersa

Dar Jamaï Museum

PLACE EL HEDIM

Bab el Mellah

AV DU MELLAH

OLD MELLAH

Fes Grands Taxis

Grands Taxis

Grands Taxis

Local buses

Bab Mansour

DAR EL KEBIRA

Mausoleum of Moulay Ismail

SIDI AMAR

Bab el Khemis

Koubba el Khayatine

Bab er Rih

Bus Station

See 'Meknes: Medina' map

NEW MELLAH

Royal Golf Gardens

DAR EL MAKHZEN

Bab el-Qari

IMPERIAL CITY

N

Heri es Souani (Dar el Ma)

Campsite

Rouah

3

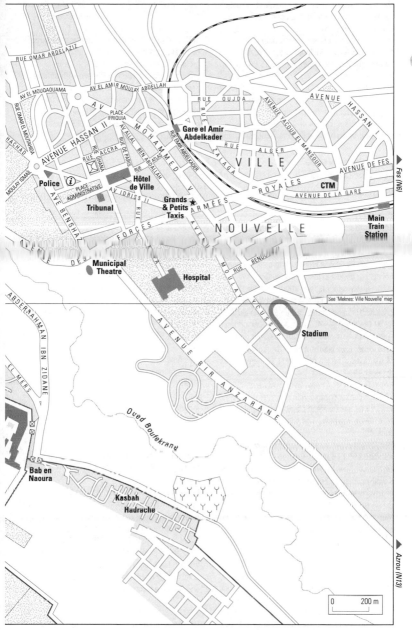

RUE OMAR ARDELAZIZ

AV EL MOUQAOUAMA

AV EL AMIR MOULAY ABDELLAH

RUE OMAR EL MOUTANABA

RUE OUJDA

AVENUE HASSAN I

AVENUE

PLACE
IFRIQUIA

Gare el Amir
Abdelkader

AVENUE ACOUB EL MANSOUR

VILLE

AVENUE DE FES

▶ Fes (N6)

AVENUE HASSAN II

RUE ACCRA

Police

RUE GHANA

ⓘ

PLACE
ADMINISTRATIVE

Hôtel
de Ville

ALGER

ROYALES

CTM

AVENUE DE LA GARE

MOULAY ISMAIL

Tribunal

AV IDRISS II

Grands
& Petits
Taxis

ARMÉES

NOUVELLE

Main
Train
Station

FORCES

Municipal
Theatre

Hospital

See 'Meknes: Ville Nouvelle' map

AVENUE BIR ANZARANE

Stadium

ABDERRAHMAN IBN ZIDANE

EL MERS

Oued Boufekrane

Bab en
Naoura

Kasbah
Hadrache

▶ Azrou (N13)

0   200 m

the *Restaurant Riad* (see p.239 for directions), individually decorated by theme – from sumptuous Arabic via a traditional tent to rustic Berber cottage. The style throughout is purest Moroccan, and created with traditional techniques and materials. Has a pool in the garden, too. A gem. Includes breakfast. **7**

Palais Didi 7 Dar el Kebira ☎035 55 85 90, ⊛www.palaisdidi.com. A seventeenth-century palace tucked away in the Ville Impériale through Bab er Rih (follow signs), now an upmarket courtyard hotel from the owner of the *Riad* (see p.239). Whiffs of chiffon on four-posters and zellij-tiled baths add romance to colourful rooms,

all with a/c. Also has small pool. Includes breakfast. **7**

🏃 **Riad Bahia** Tiberbarine, behind Dar Jamaï ☎035 55 45 41, ⓔoasis.ja@caramail.com. Not as glamorous as those in Fes, this Medina riad is charming nevertheless, restored by local artisans following strict aesthetic and architectural guidelines. All rooms are en suite and have a/c, many are furnished with antique painted woodwork, yet the vibe is one of laid-back luxury. A hammam is planned for 2007 and there's a small restaurant, open to non-residents on reservation (see p.239). Includes breakfast. **6**

Ville Nouvelle

Some of the prominent hotels in the Ville Nouvelle are fairly unsavoury; grubby or even used as brothels. Aim for those listed here to be on the safe side.

Cheap

Hôtel Bordeaux 64 Av de la Gare ☎035 52 25 63. Handy for early starts (or late arrivals) at the CTM station opposite. A small shuttered building and garden lend a bygone French air to a simple hotel. Rooms are basic and there's cold water only – hot public showers for men are 100m east, the nearest facilities for women are at a hammam by the *Café l'Abeille*, 100m up Marhaj Yacoub el Mansour. **2**

Hôtel Chellal 1 Rue Abou Hassan M'Rini, on the corner with Av Hassan II ☎035 52 08 87. This has seen better days but it's a better cheapie than most Medina places, with a handy petit taxi rank outside the door. **2**

Hôtel Touring 34 Av Allal Ben Abdallah ☎035 52 23 51. A central cheapie with pretty average facilities; a little threadbare in places, functional in others. Hot water evenings only. Some rooms en suite. **2**

Youth Hostel (Auberge de Jeunesse) Av Okba Ibn Nafi ☎035 52 46 98, ⓔauberge_meknes@yahoo.fr. Near the Hôtel Transatlantique, this is a well-maintained hostel around a garden courtyard, with single beds shoehorned into dorm rooms (45dh), plus functional doubles, triples and four-bed rooms and hot showers (5dh). It's open all year: 8am–10pm (till midnight in summer, closed 10am–6pm on Sundays). **2**

Moderate

Hôtel Akouas 27 Rue Amir Abdelkader ☎035 51 59 67, ⊛www.hotelakouas.com. All the mod cons – double-glazing, a/c, heating, satellite TV – in an international-standard business hotel near the CTM terminal and Meknes's lively nightlife; the *Akouas* also has its own nightclub. There's also a small indoor pool and a decent restaurant, *El Menzeh*

(see p.240), open to nonresidents. Includes breakfast. **5**

🏃 **Hôtel Majestic** 19 Av Mohammed V ☎035 52 20 35, ⓕ035 52 74 27. A 1930s hotel which marries vintage charm with comfortable, clean rooms (some en suite) with heating and balconies, and a terrace for al fresco breakfasts. Friendly management, too. Probably the best mid-priced choice in the Ville Nouvelle, and convenient for the El Amir Abdelkader train station. Includes breakfast. **4**

Hôtel de Nice corner Omar Ben Chemssi and Rue Antsirabé ☎035 52 03 18, ⓔnice_hotel@menara.ma. A friendly central place whose good-value refurbished rooms on the fourth or fifth floors provide bright modern en suites with three-star facilities, including a/c. Also has a bar and nightclub. Includes breakfast. **5**

Hôtel Ouislane 54 Av Allal Ben Abdallah ☎035 52 17 43. Use this as a standby if nothing else is available – a basic, old hotel, overpriced for the facilities on offer. Some rooms have a/c – at 90dh extra. **4**

Hôtel Palace 11 Rue Ghana ☎035 52 04 07, ⓕ035 40 14 31. A better choice than the *Hôtel Ouislane* and well priced, though spartan rooms (en suite with 24hr hot water) could do with a revamp. **4**

Hôtel Volubilis 45 Av des FAR ☎035 52 50 82. A bit of faded grandeur from the 1930s, complete with Art Deco lobby and facade. One of the oldest hotels in the quarter, and still decent with hot showers, but located at a noisy road junction. **4**

Expensive

Hôtel Bab Mansour 38 Rue Amir Abdelkader ☎035 52 52 39, ⓔhotel_bab_mansour@menara.ma. A modern hotel opposite the *Akouas* which

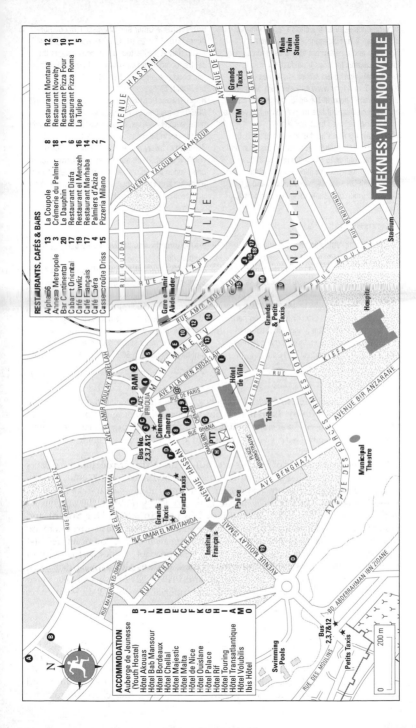

MEKNES: VILLE NOUVELLE

RESTAURANTS, CAFÉS & BARS

Apha26	6	La Coupole	13
Annex Metropole	3	Crémerie du Palmier	9
Bar Continental		Le Dauphin	20
Cabaret Oriental		Restaurant Diafa	17
Café Swilz		Restaurant el Menzeh	19
Café Français		Restaurant Marhaba	17
Café Oléra		Palmiers d'Aziza	4
Casse-croûte Driss		Pizzeria Milano	15
Restaurant Montana	12		
Restaurant Novelty	9		
Restaurant Pizza Four	10		
Restaurant Pizza Roma	11		
La Tulipe	5		
Restaurant el Menzeh	16		
Palmiers d'Aziza	2		
Pizzeria Milano	7		

ACCOMMODATION

Auberge de Jeunesse (Youth Hostel)	B
Hôtel Akouas	J
Hôtel Bab Mansour	L
Hôtel Bordeaux	N
Hôtel Chellal	D
Hôtel Majestic	E
Hôtel Malta	C
Hôtel de Nice	F
Hôtel Ouislane	K
Hôtel Palace	G
Hôtel Rif	H
Hôtel Touring	I
Hôtel Transatlantique	A
Hôtel Volubilis	M
Ibis Hôtel	O

229

recommends itself as the choice "pour hommes d'affaires". It has a garage, parking, a bar, a nightclub and a restaurant that is used to catering for vegetarians. Includes breakfast. ❺

Ibis Hôtel (also called *Moussafir*) Av des FAR ☎ 035 40 41 41, ⓦ www.ibishotel.com. Modern and upmarket hotel of the Accor-owned Ibis chain, on the main thoroughfare from the Ville Nouvelle to the Medina. Includes breakfast. ❺

Hôtel Malta 3 Rue Charif el Idnssi ☎ 035 51 50 20, ⓦ www.hotelmaltamaroc.com. A spacious and friendly newcomer to Meknes's upmarket hotel scene, with four-star facilities in its en-suite rooms, each with ISDN sockets, plus two bars and a nightclub (midnight–3am). Includes breakfast. ❻

Hôtel Rif Rue Omar Ben Chemssi, formerly Rue Accra ☎ 035 52 25 91, ⓔ hotel_rig@menara.ma. An upmarket 1950s tour group hotel bang in the centre, comfy in an old-fashioned way and with a bar, good restaurant and small pool. Includes breakfast. ❻

Hôtel Transatlantique Rue el Marinyen ☎ 035 52 50 50, ⓔ transat01@menara.ma. Meknes's luxury hotel, with two wings: a characterful older arm, with tiled floors in Moroccan-styled rooms and patio doors on to lovely gardens, and a modern wing, comfy if bland. There are tennis courts, two outdoor pools (open to non residents from 50dh) and a new nightclub and terrace bar with astounding views to the Medina. Includes breakfast. ❼

Camping

Camping Belle-Vue also called *Camping Zerhouane* on the road to Moulay Idriss, 14km from Meknes ☎ 035 54 41 68. A shaded site with a small café and a few rooms to let. Not as good as *Camping Aguedal* and inconvenient unless you have a car, though buses to and from Moulay Idriss (9km away) will drop or pick you up here. Can also be found 11km along the direct road from Volubilis to Meknes, though roads here are poorly marked – it's easiest located by

asking directions to the nearby *Refuge Zerhouane*.

Camping Caravaning International also called *Camping Aguedal* ☎ 035 55 53 96. A half-hour walk from Place el Hedim (or a 13dh petit taxi ride), the city campsite is sited opposite the Heri es Souani. Although a little pricey, it's a pleasant, shaded site (*aguedal*, or *agdal*, means "garden"), with good facilities (hot water showers available). The restaurant has menus from 60dh – reservations required.

The Imperial City

More than any other town in Morocco, Meknes is associated with a single figure, **Sultan Moulay Ismail** (see box opposite). During his 55-year reign (1672–1727), the city was tranformed from a forgettable provincial centre into a spectacular capital with twenty gates and over fifty palaces enclosed within 45km of exterior walls.

The principal remains of Ismail's creation – the **Ville Impériale** of palaces and gardens, barracks, granaries and stables – sprawl below the Medina amid a confusing array of walled enclosures. It's a long morning's walk to take in everything. Starting from the Ville Nouvelle, make your way down to the main street at the southern edge of the Medina (**Rue Rouamzine/Rue Dar Smen**), and along to **Place el Hedim** and its immense gateway, **Bab Mansour**. There are usually **guides** hanging around here if you want to use one; you don't need to, but if you can find someone entertaining, he'll probably elaborate the story of the walls with some superbly convoluted local legend. Alternatively, drivers of horse-drawn carriages in Place el Hedim and Place Lalla Aouda will take up to six passengers on an hour-long tour of the imperial city for 120dh – easier on the legs if rather rushed.

Bab Mansour and around

Place el Hedim ("square of demolition and renewal") immediately recalls the reign of Moulay Ismail. Seeking a grand approach to his palace quarter, the *Dar Kebira*, the sultan demolished the houses that formed the western corner of the Medina to create the square. He also used it as a depot for marble columns and construction material he had gathered from sites and cities throughout

The Sultan Moulay Ismail (1672–1727)

"The Sultan Moulay Ismail," wrote his chronicler, Ezziani, "loved Mequinez, and he would have liked never to leave it." But leave it he did, ceaselessly campaigning against the rebel Berber chiefs of the south, and the Europeans entrenched in Tangier, Asilah and Larache, until the entire country lay completely under government control for the first time in five centuries. His reign saw the creation of Morocco's strongest ever – and most coherent – army, which included a crack Negro guard, the Abid regiment, and, it is reckoned, a garrison force of one in twenty of the male population. The period was Morocco's last golden age, though the ruthless centralization of all decisions and the fear with which the sultan reigned, led to a slide into anarchy and weak, inward-looking rule.

Ismail's achievements were matched by his tyrannies, which were judged extreme even by the standards of the time – and contemporary Europeans were burning their enemies and torturing them on the rack. His reign began with the display of 400 heads at Fes, most of them of captured chiefs, and over the next five decades it is estimated that he was responsible for over 30,000 deaths, not including those killed in battle. Many of these deaths were quite arbitrary. Mounting a horse, Ismail might slash the head off the eunuch holding his stirrup; inspecting the work on his buildings, he would carry a weighted lance, with which to batter skulls in order to "encourage" the others. "My subjects are like rats in a basket," he used to say, "and if I do not keep shaking the basket they will gnaw their way through."

Yet the sultan was a tireless builder throughout Morocco, constructing towns and ports, and a multitude of defensive kasbahs, palaces and bridges. By far his greatest efforts were focused on Meknes, where he sustained an obsessive building programme, often acting as architect and sometimes even working alongside the slaves and labourers. Ironically, time has not been kind to his constructions in Meknes. Built mainly of *tabia*, a mixture of earth and lime, they were severely damaged by a hurricane even in his lifetime, and were left to decay thereafter, as subsequent Alaouite sultans shifted their capitals back to Fes and Marrakesh. Walter Harris, writing only 150 years after Ismail's death, found Meknes "a city of the dead. . . strewn with marble columns and surrounded by great masses of ruin". Thankfully, more recent city authorities have tackled the restoration of the main monuments with more energy.

Morocco, including Roman Volubilis. From late afternoon it takes on a festive air as storytellers and astrologers, acrobats and traditional doctors, gather until mid-evening, like Marrakesh's Djemaa el Fna in miniature.

The centrepiece of the city's ensemble of walls and gateways is the great **Bab Mansour**, startlingly rich in its ceremonial decoration and almost perfectly preserved. Its name comes from its architect, one of a number of Christian renegades who converted to Islam and rose to high position at Ismail's court. A local tale relates that the sultan inspected the completed gate, then asked El Mansour whether he could do any better, a Catch 22 for the hapless architect, whose response ("yes") led to his immediate execution. That said, the story may be apocryphal because the gate was completed under Ismail's son, Moulay Abdallah.

Whatever the truth, the gate is the finest in Meknes and an interesting adaptation of the classic Almohad design, flanked by unusual inset and fairly squat bastions which are purely decorative and whose marble columns were brought from Volubilis. Indeed, they are more impressive than any that remain at the site itself. The decorative patterns on both gate and bastions are basically elaborations of the Almohad *darj w ktarf* motif (see *Moroccan Architecture* colour section), the space between each motif filled out with a brilliant array of zellij created by a layer of cutaway black tiles, just like the ornamental inscription above, which extols the triumph of Ismail and, even more, that of Abdallah, bragging that no gate in Damascus or Alexandria is its equal. Alongside Bab Mansour is a smaller gateway in the same style, **Bab Djemaa en Nouar**.

Nowadays, traffic passes through neither gate – indeed, the inside of Bab Mansour is used as an arts and crafts market, sometimes displaying work from the Ensemble Artisanal (see p.236). Passing through the gateway to the left of Bab Mansour as you face it, you reach Place Lalla Aouda. Leave at the far right corner and you enter an open square, in the far right corner of which is the green-tiled **Koubba el Khayatine** (daily 9am–noon & 3–6pm; 10dh), an anonymous zellij-covered reception hall for ambassadors to the imperial court. More intriguing is a vast series of subterranean vaults that are reached via a stairway behind and which are, by popular tradition, the **Prison of Christian Slaves** (same ticket). Whatever the name, this was probably a storehouse or granary, although there were certainly several thousand Christian captives at Ismail's court. Most were seized by the Sallee Rovers (see p.346) and brought to Meknes as slave labour for the interminable construction projects. The story goes that any who died were simply buried in the walls they were building, although no human remains have come to light even though most of the walls have crumbled away. Nevertheless, the damp vaults are impressively atmospheric and a true architectural feat: seven hectares of subterranean chambers and passages lit only by the skyholes that stud the lawn above, and three tunnels which lead towards Fes, Volubilis and the Middle Atlas according to local legend.

Ahead of the *koubba*, set within the long wall and at right angles to it, are three modest **gates**. The one in the centre is generally closed and is at all times flanked by soldiers from the royal guard; within, landscaped across a lake and the sunken garden of Ismail's last and finest palace, are the **Royal Golf Gardens** – private and strictly *interdit* unless you play a round on one dedicated section (p.241). The gate on the left opens onto an apparently endless corridor of walls and, a few metres down is the entrance to the **Mausoleum of Moulay Ismail**.

The Mausoleum

Together with the tomb of Mohammed V in Rabat, and the Medersa Bou Inania in Fes, **Moulay Ismail's Mausoleum** (daily 9am–12.30pm & 3–6pm, except Friday mornings, tomb open to Muslims only; free) is the only active Moroccan shrine that non-Muslims may visit. Modest dress, for both women and men, is required.

The mausoleum has been a point of reverence since Ismail's death (it was constructed in his own lifetime) and remains held in high esteem. Given tales of the ruler's excesses, this seems puzzling to Westerners, but in Morocco Ismail is remembered for his achievements: bringing peace and prosperity after a period of anarchy, and driving out the Spanish from Larache and the British from Tangier. His extreme observance of orthodox Islamic form and ritual also conferred a kind of magic on him, as, of course, does his part in founding the ruling Alaouite dynasty. Although, technically, the dynasty began with his brother, Moulay Rachid, Ismail is generally honoured as the founder.

Entering the mausoleum, you are allowed to approach the **sanctuary** in which the sultan is buried, though cannot go beyond this annexe. More interesting than the bright zellij and spiralling stuccowork in the series of courts and chambers – fine, if unspectacular – is the reverance with which the shrine is treated. It was thoroughly renovated in the 1950s at the expense of Mohammed V, and the sarcophagus is still the object of veneration. You will almost invariably see villagers here, especially women seeking *baraka* (charismatic blessing) and intercession from the saintly sultan's remains.

The Dar el Makhzen and Heri es Souani

Beyond the mausoleum, a gate on your left leads into the dilapidated quarter of **Dar el Kebira**, Ismail's great palace complex. The imperial structures – there were originally twelve pavilions within the complex – can still be seen between and above the houses here: ogre-like creations of massive scale compared with the modest dwellings. They were completed in 1677 and dedicated at a midnight celebration, when the sultan personally slaughtered a wolf so its head could be displayed at the centre of the gateway.

Some later commentators saw a conscious echo of Versailles – its contemporary rival – in the grandeur of Ismail's plan, though it would be another decade until the first reports of Louis XIV's palace reached the imperial court. When they did, however, Ismail's interest was pricked. In 1699, he sent an ambassador to Paris to negotiate the addition of Louis' daughter, Princess Conti, to his harem. The ambasssador returned without the girl, but bearing some magnificent clocks, offered as a conciliatory gesture by the Sun King and now on display in the mausoleum.

On the opposite side of the long-walled corridor, beyond the Royal Golf Gardens, more immense buildings are spread out, making up Ismail's last great palace, the **Dar el Makhzen**. Unlike the Kebira, which was destroyed by the great earthquake of 1755 (the same one that levelled Lisbon), this is still a minor royal residence, though Mohammed VI rarely visits Meknes. The most you can get are a few brief glimpses over the heads of the guards posted by occasional gates in the crumbling, 20ft walls.

The corridor itself, which eventually turns a corner to bring you out by the campsite and the Heri es Souani, may be the **"strangee"** recorded by eighteenth-century travellers. A mile-long terrace wall, shaded with vines, it was a favourite drive of the sultan – according to several sources, he was driven around in a bizarre chariot drawn by his women or eunuchs.

At the corridor's end, a thirty-minute walk from Bab Mansour, is the chief sight of the Imperial City, the **Heri es Souani** (or Dar el Ma), which is often introduced by local guides as "Ismail's stables" (daily 9am–noon & 3–6pm; 10dh). In fact, the stables are further south, and the startling series of high vaulted chambers here were storerooms and granaries, filled with provisions for siege or drought. They give a powerful impression of the complexity of seventeenth-century Moroccan engineering. Each of Ismail's palaces had underground plumbing (well in advance of Europe), and here you can find a remarkable system of chain-bucket wells built between each of the storerooms. One on the right, near the back, has been restored; you can switch on lights for a better look.

Just as worthwhile is the view from the **roof** of the Heri es Souani, which is accessed through the second entrance on the right, although frequently closed to visitors. From its garden, you can gaze out over the Dar el Makhzen and the still **Agdal Basin**, built as an irrigation reservoir and pleasure lake, beside which people sometimes picnic and wash their cars.

Over to the southwest, in the distance, you can make out another seventeenth-century royal palace, the **Dar el Baida** (the "White House"), now a military academy, and beyond it, the **Rouah**, or stables.

Horses and mules

The Haras de Meknes

The **Haras de Meknes** (☎035 53 07 53, ☏035 55 79 34; Mon–Fri 9–11am & 3–4pm; free) is the largest national stud farm in Morocco. It is located in the Zitoun quarter on the southwest edge of town, near the military academy and the Rouah – the old imperial stables (see below). Take the road to Azrou or bus #14 or #16 from the Ville Nouvelle and get off near the science and arts faculties of the university.

It's well worth an informal visit for anyone with even a passing equestrian interest, if only to check out the *Première Ecurie*, the first stable to the left of the entrance. Here you will see glossy stallions of Arab (horse name on red signs at the stable), Berber (green signs) or mixed (red/green) stock, all highly valuable. The cousins of such horses can be seen at riding stables around the world, and at *fantasias* throughout Morocco.

SPANA

The British charity **SPANA** (Society for the Protection of Animals Abroad) has a small centre in Meknes on Rue de Laine, which runs from Bab el Qari (☎035 53 32 94, ⊛www.spana.org.ma); you will recognize the street by the wool traders (*laine* is wool). SPANA is at no. 72 on the left. Visitors are welcome by arrangement, morning or afternoon.

In the morning, staff visit local markets and treat donkeys and mules on the spot; in the afternoon, the centre is open to treat all manner of animals brought by their owners. Mohamed Fafaite at the centre is particularly keen on improving the footwear of the beasts of burden. Makeshift "shoes" made of old car tyres are not good for the animals and he encourages blacksmiths through the Meknes Association of Blacksmiths, which works nationally.

The Rouah

The ramshackle ruins of Moulay Ismail's stables, the **Rouah,** are officially closed to visitors and not really worth the thirty-minute walk from the Heri es Souani unless you have a serious interest in archaeology. If you are committed, turn up and ask around for a *gardien* who will usually let you have a quick look. To find the site, follow the road diagonally behind *Camping Aguedal* and the Heri es Souani for half a kilometre, then turn right at the next junction to reach the **Djemaa Rouah** (Stable Mosque), a large, heavily restored building preceded by a well-kept gravel courtyard. Behind it off to your right are the **stables** – a massive complex, perhaps twice as large as the Heri es Souani.

In contemporary accounts, the Rouah is often singled out as the greatest feature of all Ismail's building projects: some three miles in length, traversed by a long canal, with flooring built over vaults used for storing grain, and space for over 12,000 horses. Today, they've been replaced by a few scrambling goats in a conclusive ruin – piles of rubble and zellij tiles line the walls and high-arched aisles of crumbling *pisé* extend out in each direction. More than anything else in Meknes, it recalls the scale and madness of Moulay Ismail's vision.

The Medina

Although taking much of its present form and size under Moulay Ismail, the Medina bears far less of his stamp. Its main sights, in addition to the extensive **souks**, are a Merenid *medersa* (an Islamic college, see box, p.270) – the **Bou Inania** – and a nineteenth-century palace museum, the **Dar Jamaï**, both rewarding and easy to find.

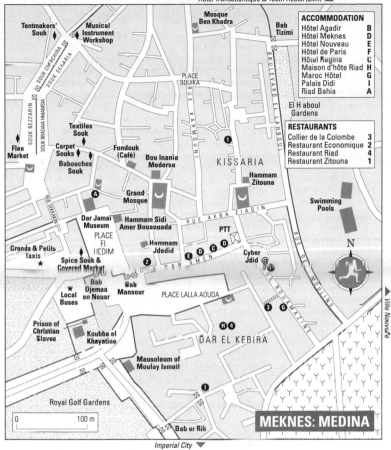

ACCOMMODATION

Hôtel Agadir	B
Hôtel Meknes	D
Hôtel Nouveau	E
Hôtel de Paris	F
Hôtel Regina	C
Maison d'hôte Riad	H
Maroc Hôtel	G
Palais Didi	I
Riad Bahia	A

RESTAURANTS

Collier de la Colombe	3
Restaurant Economique	2
Restaurant Riad	4
Restaurant Zitouna	1

MEKNES, FES AND THE MIDDLE ATLAS | Meknes

MEKNES: MEDINA

Imperial City ▼

The Dar Jamaï

The **Dar Jamaï** (daily 9am–5pm; closed Tues; 10dh) stands discretely down a stairway at the back of Place el Hedim. One of the finest examples of a late nineteenth-century Moroccan palace, it was built in 1882 by the same family of viziers (high government officials) who erected the Palais Jamaï in Fes. After 1912, it was used as a military hospital, becoming the Museum of Moroccan Art in 1920.

Today, it houses one of the best museums in Morocco. Its exhibits, some organised to recreate the gloriously cluttered reception rooms of nobility in the late-1800s, are predominantly of the same age as the palace, though some pieces of **Fes** and **Meknes pottery** date back to around Ismail's reign. These ceramics – elaborate polychrome designs from Meknes and strong blue and white patterns from Fes – make an interesting comparison, with Fes's strong handicrafts tradition coming out as superior. A display of Berber jewellery also catches the eye, though the best is that of **Middle Atlas carpets**, in particular the bold geometric designs of the Beni Mguild tribe.

Arts and crafts

The **Ensemble Artisanal** on Avenue Zine el Abidine Riad (Mon–Thurs 8.30am–noon & 2.30–6.30pm, Fri 8.30–11am & 3–6.30pm; ☎035 53 09 29) is housed in a prominent, reddish building above the local bus station, near the *grands taxi* park west of Place el Hedim. It is large and trains apprentices but there is little to buy. However, there is a lot to be seen, including the work of young craftsmen making **zellij** tiles. The building also houses several active cooperatives, including **La Cooperative Féminine de Céramique**.

In the Medina, **Espace Berbère** at 32 Rue Tiberbarine has an interesting and eclectic collection of craft items; the knowledgeable owner Abdel can instruct you in the art of sorting worthwhile carpets from mere souvenirs. For a genuine Meknesi product, head for **Kissaria Lahrir** (see opposite), where you can buy traditional **silver damascene** tableware and other items.

The **Village des Potiers** is in the valley of the Oued Boufekrane, which divides the Ville Nouvelle from the Medina. It's to the north, between Bab el Berdaïn and the *Hôtel Transatlantique*; if in doubt or taking a petit taxi, ask for Farharine. It's just about worth a visit, but you can give it a miss if Safi is on your itinerary.

The **Music Conservatoire** of Meknes is the impressive French-style building near Place Ifriquia, between avenues Mohammed V and Allal Ben Abdallah. Students study classical Arab-Andalous music, together with *milhûn* and, less so, *gharnati*, and the conservatoire gives occasional concerts. The **Institut Français**, Place Farhat Hachad (☎035 52 40 71, ⓦwww.ambafrance-ma.org/institut/fes-meknes), has a programme of music, theatre, cinema and literature events, plus a popular student café. Its cultural activities are more comprehensive than those in Fes, and well priced at 30dh per adult, or 15dh for the cinema.

Artefacts and antiques aside, the museum is worth a visit as much for the building, boasting a gorgeous upper-floor reception room with intricate wood carvings on the ceiling. The viziers' Andalusian Garden has also been preserved, a lush courtyard with palm, banana, lemon and orange trees, as well as papyrus, roses and cypresses, usually twittering with birds.

The souks

The most accessible souk from Place el Hedim is **Souk Atriya**, or **covered market** (closed Fri), which runs all along the west side of the square. This is the produce market where locals do their shopping; row upon row of multicoloured vegetable and spice stalls, olives piled into pyramids, butchers (not for the squeamish), and sweet stalls so loaded with cakes you can hardly reach the stall-holder to pay.

A lane immediately behind the Dar Jamaï (Rue Tiberbarine) from Place el Hedim leads into other souks. Follow it and you emerge in the middle of the Medina's major market street; on your right, leading to the Grand Mosque and Bou Inania Medersa, is **Souk es Sebbat**; on your left is **Souk en Nejjarin**.

Turning first to the left, you enter an area of textile stalls, which give way to the carpenters' (*nejjarin*) workshops after which the souk is named. Shortly after this, you pass a mosque on your left, beyond which is an entrance to a parallel arcade. The **carpet market**, or **Souk Joutiya es Zerabi**, is just off here to the left. Quality can be very high, as can prices, though because Meknes lacks the constant stream of tourists of Fes or Marrakesh, dealers are more willing to bargain. Don't be afraid to start low.

At the end of Souk en Nejjarin you come to another souk, the **Bezzarin**, which runs up at right angles to the Nejjarin, on either side of the city wall.

This looks an unpromising, run-down neighbourhood, but things get more interesting if you follow the outer side of the wall to an assortment of crafts-workers, grouped in trade guilds and often fronted by an old *fondouk* or warehouse. There are **basketmakers**, **ironsmiths** and **saddlers**, and at the top near **Bab el Djedid** you'll find **tent-makers** – although they rarely sew any traditional tents these days – and a couple of **musical instrument workshops** in the gate itself. Just through this on the right, is a rough-and-ready area of **metal workers** who fashion intricate iron grilles.

Going the other way beyond the Dar Jamaï, on **Souk es Sebbat**, you reach a classier section of the market – starting off with *babouche* vendors and moving on to the fancier goods aimed at tourists near the medersa, before finally exiting into a covered **kissaria** dominated by kaftan sellers. From here it's easy to find your way to the Bou Inania Medersa, whose imposing portal is on the left-hand side of the street. If you want a tea break, a nineteenth-century **fondouk**, a short way back, doubles as a café and carpet/crafts emporium – look for its open courtyard. Incidentally, Meknes mint is reputed to be the best in Morocco.

An idiosyncratic local souk is the **auction market**, or **Souk Dlala** (daily except Fri after the third call to prayer, for about 2hr), held in a covered area 100m north of the Dar Jamaï, where you can find the occasional antique (although these are likely to have been spotted – and already bought – by local dealers) amid interesting junk.

Not far from Souk Dlala and near the Bou Inania Medersa (see p.238) is the **Kissaria Lahrir**, where you can see traditional **silver damascene** being made, the hair-thin silver thread slowly engraved in steel and used to decorate plates, jugs and other items. The family of Essaidi M'barek has passed on the skills for such delicate work from one generation to the next; his English-speaking son, Saidi, will explain the process if you're interested. To find this kissaria turn right

△ A souk in Meknes

as you face the entrance of Bou Inania, then take the lane first on the right; after 30m you will see the entrance of the souk on your left.

Bou Inania Medersa

The **Bou Inania Medersa** (daily 9am–noon & 2–6pm; 10dh) was built around 1340–50, so is more or less contemporary with the great medersas of Fes. It takes its name from the notorious Sultan Abou Inan (see p.269), though it was founded by his predecessor, Abou el Hassan, the great Merenid builder behind the Chellah *zaouia* in Rabat and Salé medersa.

A modest and functional building, the medersa follows the plan of Hassan's other principal works in that it has a single **courtyard** opening onto a narrow **prayer hall**, and is encircled on each floor by the students' **cells**, with exquisitely carved cedar screens. It has a much lighter feel to it than the Salé medersa, and in its balance of wood, stucco and zellij achieves a remarkable combination of intricacy – no area is left uncovered – and restraint. Architecturally, the most unusual feature is a ribbed dome over the **entrance hall**, an impressive piece of craftsmanship that extends right out into the souk.

From **the roof**, generally open to visitors, you can look out – and feel as if you could climb across – to the tiled pyramids of the **Grand Mosque**; you can just catch a glimpse of the interior. The souk is mainly obscured from view, but you can get a good, general panorama of the town and the mosques of each quarter. Inlaid with bands of green tiles, the minarets of these distinctive mosques are unique to Meknes; those of Fes or Marrakesh tend to be more elaborate and multicoloured.

North from Bou Inania

North of the medersa and Grand Mosque, the Medina is largely residential, dotted with the occasional fruit and vegetable market, the **Ben Khadra Mosque**, which has beautiful polychrome doors and some exquisite coloured stucco, and a carpenters' souk. If you continue this way, you'll eventually come out in a long, open square, which culminates in the monumental **Bab el Berdaïn** (The Gate of the Saddlers). This was another of Ismail's creations, a rugged, genuinely defensive structure, which looks like a more muscular version of the central section of Bab Mansour.

Outside, the city walls extend along the main road to Rabat. Follow it and you will catch occasional glimpses on your left of an enormous **cemetery** – almost half the size of the Medina in extent. Non-Muslims are not permitted to enter the enclosure near the centre, home to the *zaouia* and shrine of one of the country's most famous and curious saints, **Sidi Ben Aissa**.

Reputedly a contemporary of Moulay Ismail, Ben Aissa conferred on his followers the power to eat anything, even poison or broken glass, without suffering any ill effects. His cult, the Aissaoua, became one of the most important in Morocco, and certainly the most violent and fanatical. Until prohibited by the French, some 50,000 devotees regularly attended the saint's annual moussem on the eve of Mouloud. Entering into a trance, they were known to pierce their tongues and cheeks with daggers, eat serpents and scorpions – a scene vividly described in Joseph Thomson's book (see p.770) – or devour live sheep and goats. The only other confraternity to approach such frenzy was the Hamadcha of Moulay Idriss, whose devotees were known to cut each other's heads with hatchets or, during more extreme rites, toss heavy stones or cannonballs into the air, so they landed on their heads. Both cults continue to hold moussems, though successive Moroccan governments have effectively outlawed the more outrageous activities.

A road wraps all around the cemetery, then around the western side of the Medina and the Old Mellah, the former Jewish quarter, until it arrives after 1.5km or so at the **Bab el Khemis** (or Bab Lakhmis) near the bus station west of Place el Hedim. Another fine gate, only second in stature to Bab Mansour, it is decorated with a monumental inscription etched in black tiles as a frieze across the brickwork.

Restaurants, bars and nightlife

Meknes is a small town compared with Fes or even Tangier. In the Ville Nouvelle, most of the action is within a few blocks of the central Place Administrative.

Restaurants

In the **Ville Nouvelle** you'll find a dozen or so good restaurants, most serving a daily three-course menu. Eating in the **Medina** is largely at basic café-grills – as well as those listed here, cheap hole-in-the-wall joints with fried fish and brochettes line Rue Rouamazine, near the *Maroc Hôtel*. However, there are also palatial restaurants – the *Collier de la Colombe*, the *Riad/Palais Didi* and the *Riad Bahia*– where you can tuck into excellent food at a fraction of the price you'd pay in the touristy equivalents in Fes. All smarter options – and a few of the moderates – are licensed to serve alcohol.

Medina

Collier de la Colombe 67 Rue Driba ☏035 55 50 41. A smart but far from costly restaurant in the ornate mansion of "Sultan" Lakhal, a non-Alaouite pretender to the throne on the death of Moulay Youssef in 1927. Night and day, the views across the valley to the Ville Nouvelle are stunning, especially from the roof terrace. Atlas trout stars alongside tajines with fruit and olives on an à la carte menu or reasonable set menus (from 110dh). Daily 11am–4pm & 7–11pm. Moderate to expensive.

Restaurant Economique 123 Rue Dar Smen, opposite Bab Mansour and alongside *Restaurant Bab Mansour*, both are good café-restaurants, the *Economique* being marginally better. Daily 11am–9pm. Cheap.

🏃 **Restaurant Riad** 79 Ksar Chaacha, Dar el Kebira ☏035 53 05 42. A lovely little place snug in the last of Moulay Ismail's original twelve pavilions, the only one to have survived the 1755 earthquake. It's tricky to find (follow green arrows from the entry to Dar el Kebira by Bab er Rih), but well worth the effort to sample refined traditional cuisine – the best in town, say some locals – in beautifully restored salons or in the patio garden that's magic in the evening. As well as very reasonable à la carte eating (*mechoui* needs to be ordered up to 3hr in advance), set menus start at 150dh. Daily 11am–3pm & 6.30–11pm. Moderate to expensive.

Restaurant Riad Bahia Rue Tiberbarine, just behind the Dar Jamaï museum ☏035 55 45 41.

Heavenly pastilla and tanjia, the beef stew cooked in an old clay pot in the low heat of a hammam's embers (see p.470 for more). Rachid, the chef and owner's brother, personally takes the pots to the nearby hammam, where they simmer for over five hours. Daily noon–3pm & 7–10pm; reservations required. Moderate to expensive.

Restaurant Zitouna 44 Jamaâ Zitouna. All the usual Moroccan dishes, served in the courtyard and rooms of a renovated late-19th century palace; often swamped by tour groups during lunch, so best left to evenings. Not licensed. Daily 11am–3pm & 7–11pm. Moderate.

Ville Nouvelle

Annexo Metropole 11 Rue Charif Idrissi. A modest-looking little place which serves excellent cooking beneath a carved roof. There are three set menus from 120dh, plus unusual dishes like fish brochettes. Daily 10am–3pm & 5.30–11pm. Moderate.

Casse-croûte Driss 34 Rue Amir Abdelkader, next to the Regent cinema. One of the few cheapies in the area, this friendly and unpretentious little café-restaurant prepares the usual snacks plus fresh fried fish and chips. Daily noon–2am. Cheap.

La Coupole Corner of Av Hassan II and Rue du Ghana. Popular with locals for an extensive range of reasonably priced Moroccan and European dishes and a set menu (110dh); grilled meats are the house special. There's also a bar and a noisy nightclub. Daily noon–3pm & 6–11pm. Moderate.

Le Dauphin 5 Av Mohammed V, entrance at side. Managed by the *Hôtel Bab Mansour*, this is a smart, old-fashioned French place, with reliable cooking and a reputation for excellent seafood; the fish is guaranteed fresh each day. Decent winelist too. Daily noon–3pm & 7–11pm. Expensive.

Pizzeria Milano 14 Av Hassan II. Good selection of pizzas and fish dishes from 35dh. Daily 10am–11pm. Cheap to moderate.

Restaurant Diafa 12 Rue Badr el Kobra. What looks like a private house has extremely good and reasonably priced cooking, with two set menus though not a vast choice of dishes. Daily noon–3pm & 7pm–midnight. Moderate.

Restaurant el Menzeh *Hôtel Akouas* Rue Amir Abdelkader. A good selection of menus from 95dh and attentive service in a clean, if fairly unremarkable environment. Daily 10am–10pm. Moderate.

Restaurant Marhaba 23 Av Mohammed V, not to be confused with the café *Glacier Marhaba* which fronts Av Mohammed V. A no-nonsense eating house, popular with locals for a cheap bite of thick *harira* soup from 4dh, brochettes and tajines. Daily noon–9pm. Cheap.

Restaurant Novelty 12 Rue de Paris. A café-restaurant above an all-day bar. Good-value *plat du jour* 50dh are listed on a board and set menu starts at 60dh. Daily noon–3pm & 7–9pm. Cheap.

Restaurant Pizza Four 1 Rue Atlas, near *Hôtel Majestic*, off Av Mohammed V. Omelettes, pizzas and tenuously Italian food in a bizarre – and rather gloomy – mock Italian-Tudor interior. Daily 11am–3pm & 6.30pm–midnight. Moderate.

Restaurant Pizza Roma 8 Rue Accra, alongside the *Hôtel de Nice*. Limited menu, beyond the pizzas, but good value, and handy for out-of-hours snacks. Open 24hr. Cheap.

Cafés and patisseries

Meknes's finest patisseries are in the Ville Nouvelle, the classiest located near Place Ifriquia.

Alpha 56 16 bis Av Mohammed V. A heavenly *tarte tatin* and a few profiteroles could make this patisserie a favourite haunt in Meknes. Scrumptious, although at prices to match. Daily 6am–9pm.

Café Dawliz Av Moulay Ismail, behind the *McDonald's*. A smart new café with panoramic views over the Medina to the west – especially atmospheric at sunset. Daily 8am–11pm.

Café Opéra 7 Av Mohammed V. A blend of café and patisserie which attracts a young crowd and stays open daytime during Ramadan. Daily 6am–11pm.

Crémerie du Palmier 53 Av des FAR, next to the *Hôtel Excelsior*. Another excellent patisserie, with

good *rayeb* (set yoghurt in a glass) and fresh fruit juices. Daily 3am–10pm.

Palmiers d'Aziza 9 Rue de Tarfaya, near Place Ifriquia. The chicest option of Meknes's café scene, the palm tree on its terrace is to honour the owner's origins in Figuig, south Morocco. There's a choice of terraces, all ruled by waiters in black and whites and frequented by a trendy clientele. Daily 6.30am–10pm.

La Tulipe Pl Maarakat Lahri. A semi-smart place to indulge yourself in ice cream, which you can eat in a fondant-hued interior, a quiet terrace or take away. Daily 6am–9.30pm.

Bars

Many of the Ville Nouvelle hotels have bars and nightclubs, often quite lively in the evenings. The stylish new bar of the *Hôtel Transatlantique* is your best bet for a mellow drink, especially recommended for Medina views at sunset, or the nightclub of the *Hôtel Rif* is a mite more lively, and kicks off with a Scheherezade-style floor show. The bars below are more boisterous and although some have female staff, women may find the raucous, all-male clientele intimidating.

Bar Continental By the *Hôtel Continental*, on the opposite side of Av des FAR. Outside tables are blighted by traffic, so go inside, a rather seedy dive, but fun if you're in the mood for a no-nonsense boozey vibe. Daily 6am–10.30pm.

Cabaret Oriental Av des FAR (next to *Café Français*). Occasionally hosts bands into the small hours. 9pm–3am.

Café Français (also called *Club de Nuit*) By the *Hôtel Excelsior*, on Av des FAR. A rather bunker-like bar behind a brick facade, pepped up with funky 1970s mirrors. Bar open daily 6am–11pm, club nightly 9pm–2am.

Volubilis Nightclub part of the *Hôtel Volubilis* (entrance down an alley under the arch to the right of the hotel). Pop sounds plus the occasional Western hit. Nightly 9pm–3am.

Listings

Airlines Royal Air Maroc has an office at 7 Av Mohammed V ☎035 52 09 63 (Mon–Fri 8.30am–12.15pm & 2.30–7pm, Sat 8.30am–noon & 3–6pm); the nearest airport is at Saïs, south of Fes.

Banks are concentrated around Pl Administrative, and along Av Mohammed V (the Crédit du Maroc is at no. 28, Banque Populaire at no. 17, BMCE at no. 9) and Av des FAR (Crédit du Maroc; BMCE is at no. 98). In the Medina, the Banque Populaire on Rue Dar Smen, near Bab Mansour, has exchange facilities and a cashpoint, as does BMCE in Rue Rouamazine. BMCI by Dar Jamaï in Place el Hedim has a bureau de change open Sun 10am–noon & 3–5pm. The *Hôtel Rif* (see p.230) will exchange cash round the clock.

Bookshop The best in town, with a vast selection of literature in French, is Dar el Kitab at 10 Av Allal Ben Abdellah (Mon–Fri 8.30am–1pm & 3–8pm), 50m southeast of the Camera cinema.

Car rental None of the major companies has offices in Meknes. Try Bab Mansour Car, 3 rue Iuriss II (on Av Hassan II at its western end; ☎ & ℗035 52 66 31) or Meknes Car, on the corner of Av Hassan II and Rue Safi (☎035 51 20 74), both with small three-doors from 250dh per day.

Car repairs Car mechanics and car spare parts shops are concentrated around Bd el Kods in the New Mellah, and the beginning of Zenkat Zalaka and Zenkat Nador at their junction with Av des FAR. Renault garages are to be found on Rue Charif Idrissi (at the corner of Av Mohammed V, just north of Place Ifriquia) and out on the Route de Fes.

Cinemas Central ones include the Camera on Place Ifriquia and the Regent, next door to the *Hôtel Bab Mansour*, both of which show a varied programme of Bollywood, American and French movies, including recent blockbusters; and the Rif on Bd el Kods by the New Mellah. The Camera has two daily screenings at 2.45pm and 8.45pm, each offering a double-bill for the price of a single ticket. Cinema Dawliz on Av Moulay Ismail is handy for the Medina and shows Bollywood and western films.

Festivals The city's Ben Aïssa Moussem (aka Moussem Cheikh el Kamal) is one of the country's most impressive. Also worth planning for are the Beni Rached Moussem (seven days after Mouloud; at the village of Beni Rached, out of town on the Moulay Idriss road) and the Moulay Idriss Moussem (at Moulay Idriss, second week of August).

Golf The Meknes Royal Golf Club at Bab Belkari Jnane Lbahraouia (☎035 53 07 53, ℗035 55 79 34), has a nine-hole, par 36 course within the confines of the Royal Palace gardens.

Hammams In the Medina, the Hammam Sidi Amer Bouaouada (women 1–9pm; men 9pm–1am & 6am–1pm) is one of a very few where you can see the basement heating system; the hammam is 20m on the right on the lane off the northeast corner of Pl el Hedim. Harder to find is the Hammam Zitouna (women 1–9.30pm; men 9.30pm–1pm next day); at the northern tip of Rue Rouamazine, head through an archway on your left and continue 50m to a small square by a mosque, at the far right of which another passageway contains the hammam, on the left. A third hammam in the Medina is near the *Hôtel Nouveau*; from the hotel take the second road to the right as you head for Pl el Hedim, then take the first lane to the left and continue for 30m. In the Ville Nouvelle, ask for Hammam al Hadika, off the western end of Av Hassan II, at 4 Rue Patrice Lumumba, with separate sections for women and men (both 7am–9pm).

Internet access is available at Cyber Express on Rue de Paris, near the Camera cinema (9am–9pm), and Quicknet at 28 Rue Amir Abdelkader (9am–11.30pm); the latter has a/c and a café counter. In the Medina, Cyber Jdid (9am–4pm daily) in a mall near the *Hôtel Paris* has fast connections.

Laundry Atlas Pressing, 26 Av Allal Ben Abdallah, opposite Collège Allal Ben Abdallah; Pressing Marhaba, by the steps leading from Rue Rouamazine up to the *Collier de la Colombe* restaurant; Pressing Koala on Rue de la Voûte, near *Hôtel Majestic* (left as you leave the hotel, then first left and first right).

Medical services English-speaking doctors include Dr Mohammed Dbab at 4 Rue Accra (☎035 52 10 87).

Pharmacies The emergency night pharmacy in the *Hôtel de Ville* on Pl Administrative (☎035 52 33 75) is open 8.30pm–8.30am, and there's another night pharmacy and dispensary behind the local bus stands just south of Pl el Hedim.

Police The local HQ is at Pl Ferhat Hached, at the western end of Av Hassan II (☎19). There's a smaller station next to Bab Djemaa en Nouar in the southwest corner of Pl el Hedim.

Post office The PTT is just off Pl de France (Oct to mid-July Mon–Fri 8am–6.30pm & Sat 8–11.30am; mid-July to Sept 8am–3.30pm; Ramadan 9am–3.30pm); the telephone section is open daily 8am–8.30pm and sells stamps, while there are public callboxes by the entrance and many téléboutiques on Av Mohammed V and elsewhere. Branch post offices include one in the

Medina at the corner of Rue Dar Smen and Rue Rouamazine (Mon–Fri 8.30am–4.15pm & Sat 8.30am–noon). Both have a Western Union bureau de change.

Swimming pools There are two public pools down by the Oued Boufekrane, reached along a lane from Bd el Haboul or from the intersection of avenues Hassan II and Moulay Ismail, both open June–Sept only. The first is very cheap at 5dh; just to its north is CODM Natation – classier, less crowded, and six times the price.

Moving on

CTM has several daily departures for **Fes**, **Casablanca** and **Rabat**. Other destinations covered at least once daily by CTM and private companies include Tangier, Nador, Oujda, Marrakesh, Agadir and Rissani; it's a good idea to buy your ticket in advance. The same destinations are covered even more frequently from the main bus station west of the Old Mellah – Fes and Moulay Idriss at least hourly for most of the day.

The most convenient **train station** is Gare el Amir Abdelkader, near the *Hôtel Majestic* in the Ville Nouvelle, which has direct trains to Casablanca, Fes, Marrakesh, Oujda, Rabat, Tangier and Taza.

Grands taxis use a yard alongside the bus station, and destinations regularly include Moulay Idriss, Sidi Slimane, Ouezzane, Kenitra, Casablanca, Ifrane, Midelt, Er Rachidia and Khenifra (those for Fes leave just across the street). Some grands taxis for Fes and Oujda also leave from next to the CTM bus station (most grands taxis for Fes will set you down at the train station there, rather than the *gare routière*). Grands taxis for one or two local destinations use a yard across the road from the local bus stops below Place el Hedim in the Medina, and on Rue Omar el Moutahida in the Ville Nouvelle, though it is unlikely that you will need to use these. There's also a **taxi** rank (grands and petits taxis – but the former again for local destinations only, unless you charter one) at the junction of Avenue des FAR and Avenue Mohammed V.

Volubilis and Moulay Idriss

An easy excursion from Meknes, **Volubilis** and **Moulay Idriss** embody much of Morocco's early history: Volubilis as its Roman provincial capital, Moulay Idriss in the creation of the country's first Arab dynasty. Their sites stand 4km apart, at either side of a deep and very fertile valley, about 30km north of Meknes.

Practicalities

You can take in both sites on a leisurely day-trip from Meknes. **Grands taxis** make regular runs to **Moulay Idriss** (10dh a place) from near the new bus station by Bab el Khemis in the Medina and from near the French Cultural Centre just off Avenue Hassan II in the Ville Nouvelle. For **Volubilis**, you can take a Ouezzane **bus** and ask to be set down by the site (which is a 500m walk downhill from the N13 – formerly P28 – road), or you could charter a grand taxi. The whole taxi (*une course*) should cost 60dh (six times the price of a *place* to Moulay Idriss a little further on), which can be split between up to six passengers; if you pay more, the driver will wait at Volubilis and take you on to Moulay Idriss, where you can look round at leisure and then get a regular place in a grand taxi back to Meknes. To charter a private taxi for a half-day tour, expect to pay 380dh.

You could also **walk** between Volubilis and Moulay Idriss, which are only around 4km apart – ask the grand taxi driver to drop you at the junction of the

N13 and the Moulay Idriss road, which will save you about 1km. The walk from the junction (known to taxi drivers as "*le carrefour*") to Volubilis is a scenic and safe fifty-minute stroll, particularly enjoyable in the early morning when locals join you on their way to the olive groves. If you **drive** to Volubilis from the north, turning east after Sidi Kacem, note that the route might be signposted only to Oualili, the Arabic for Volubilis (which is a corruption of *oualili*, meaning oleander).

Accommodation and eating

Until recently, non-Muslims were not permitted to stay overnight in Moulay Idriss, the last place in Morocco to keep this religious prohibition. But after King Mohammed VI decreed this unfair following a visit in 2005, several family-run *maison d'hôtes* have appeared. The best are: *Dar Al Andalousia* (Derb Zouak 169, ☏035 54 47 49, ✉andalous@maisondhote-volubilis.com); *Dar Diafa Lhaj Dhbi-Senhaji* (Ou Bab Kasbah 32, ☏035 54 43 54, ✉senhab @hotmail.com); or *La Colombe Blanche* (21 Derb Zouak Tazga, ☏035 54 45 96, 🖷060 04 02 83). All are clean and are priced around 200dh for a double room (including breakfast).

The only **hotel** hereabouts is 3km from Moulay Idriss, the *Volubilis Inn* (☏035 54 44 05, 🖷035 54 42 80; ❼) 1km north of the site. Reopened in 2006 after renovation into a smart four-star, it is geared towards tour groups and justifies its high prices with a pool and astounding views over the ruins from every room, presumably what attracted the Prince of Wales to its previous incarnation in 1996. A cheaper option in the village near the site is *A L'Ombre des Oliviers* (☏074 57 53 57), or there is a campsite, *Camping Belle-Vue*, 11km from Volubilis and 9km from Moulay Idriss (see p.230). A café at the site entrance serves basic food and drink.

Volubilis

A striking sight, visible for miles on the bends of the approach roads, **VOLUBILIS** occupies the ledge of a long, high plateau. Below its walls, towards Moulay Idriss, stretches a rich river valley; beyond lie dark, outlying ridges of the Zerhoun mountains. The drama of this scene – and the scope of the ruins – are undeniably impressive, so much so the site was a key location for Martin Scorsese's film *The Last Temptation of Christ*.

Some history

Except for a small trading post on the island off Essaouira, Volubilis was the Roman Empire's most remote and far-flung base. It represented – and was, literally – the end of the imperial road, having reached across France and Spain, then down from Tangier, and despite successive emperors' dreams of "penetrating the Atlas", the southern Berber tribes were never effectively subdued.

In fact, direct Roman rule here lasted little over two centuries – the garrison withdrew early, in 285 AD, to ease pressure elsewhere. But the town must have taken much of its present form well before the official annexation of North African Mauretania by Emperor Claudius in 45 AD. Tablets found on the site, inscribed in Punic, show a significant Carthaginian trading presence in the third century BC, and prior to colonization it was the western capital of a heavily Romanized, but semi-autonomous, Berber kingdom that reached into northern Algeria and Tunisia. After the Romans left, Volubilis experienced very gradual change. Latin was still spoken in the seventh century by the local population of Berbers, Greeks, Syrians and Jews; Christian churches survived until the coming

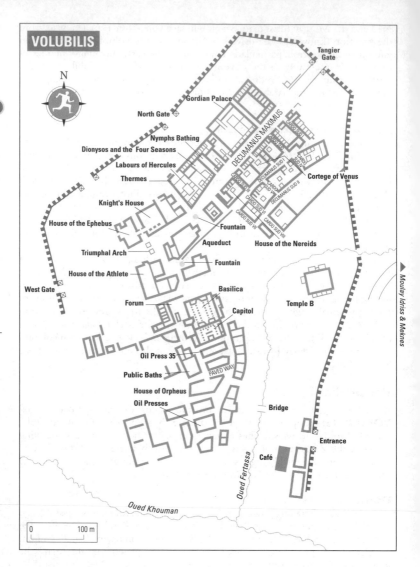

of Islam; and the city itself remained alive and active well into the eighteenth century, when its marble was carried away by slaves for the building of Moulay Ismail's Meknes.

What you see today, well excavated and maintained, are largely the ruins of second- and third-century AD buildings – impressive and affluent creations from its period as a colonial provincial capital. The land around here is some of the most fertile in North Africa, and the city exported wheat and olives in considerable quantities to Rome, as it did wild animals from the surrounding hills. Roman games, memorable for the sheer scale of their slaughter (9000 beasts were killed for the dedication of Rome's Colosseum alone), could not have happened without the African provinces, and Volubilis was a chief source of their lions. Within just two hundred years, along with Barbary bears and elephants, they became extinct.

The site

The entrance to the site (daily 8am–sunset in theory, in practice around 5.30pm; 20dh) is through a minor gate in the city wall, built along with a number of outer camps in 168 AD, following a prolonged series of Berber insurrections. Just inside are the **ticket office** and *Café Oualili* on a hillside spur. A new administrative office is slowly being built below and will house a small **museum**. From time to time, funds permitting, there are further excavations and discoveries – and attempts at the restoration of the fallen structures.

The best of the finds – which include a superb collection of bronzes – have been taken to the Rabat museum, which is worth a visit for that reason alone. Volubilis, however, has retained *in situ* the great majority of its **mosaics**, some thirty or so, which are starting to show the effects of being exposed to the elements. Bar those subject to heavy-handed restoration, the once-brightly coloured tiles have faded to a subtle palette of ochres and greys, sometimes overlaid with a skin of grime built up over the centuries. Similarly, the site requires a bit of imagination to reconstruct a town from the jumble of low walls and stumpy columns. Nevertheless, you leave with a real sense of Roman city life and its provincial prosperity while it is not hard to recognize the essentials of a medieval Arab town in the layout.

Guides hang around by the ticket office and café (120dh per hour) or you can explore at leisure on the following **itinerary**; most showpiece buildings are demarcated with a plaque. Until the new administrative centre is finished, turn left off beyond the café on a path that leads across a bridge over the Fertassa stream, and you climb up a hillside to a mixed area of housing and industry, each of its buildings containing the remains of at least one **olive press**. The extent and number of these presses, built into even the grandest mansions, reflect the olive's central importance to the city and indicate perhaps why Volubilis remained unchanged for so long after the Romans' departure. A significant proportion of its 20,000 population must have been involved in some capacity in the oil's production and export.

Somewhat isolated in this suburban quarter is the **House of Orpheus**, an enormous complex of rooms just beside the start of a paved way. Although substantially in ruins, it offers a strong impression of its former luxury – an opulent mansion, perhaps for one of the town's richest merchants. Its two main sections – public and private – each have their own separate entrance and interior court. The private rooms, which you come to first, are grouped around a small patio, which is decorated with a more or less intact **dolphin mosaic**. You can also make out the furnace and heating system (just by the entrance), the kitchen with its niche for the household gods, and the **baths**, an extensive system of hot, cold and steam rooms.

A little further inside, the house's public apartments are dominated by a large **atrium**, half reception hall, half central court, and again preserving a very fine mosaic, **The Chariot of Amphitrite Drawn by a Seahorse**. The best mosaic here, however, from which the house takes its name, is that of the **Orpheus Myth**, located to the south in a room which was probably the *tablinium*, or archives.

Just north of the House of Orpheus, you pass first through the remains of the city's main **Public Baths**. Restored by the Emperor Gallienus in the second century AD, these are clearly monumental in their intent, though sadly the

△ Volubilis mosaic

mosaics are only fragmentary. Immediately after the baths is the **Oil Press 35**, restored in 1990 and featuring a reconstruction of the grinding mechanism, including both grinding stones.

Above the Orpheus House, a broad, paved street leads up towards the main group of public buildings – the Capitol and Basilica, whose sand-coloured ruins dominate the site. The arrangement of the **Forum** is typical of a major Roman town: built on the highest rise of the city and flanked by a triumphal arch, market, capitol and basilica.

Inscriptions date the **Capitol**, the smaller and lower of the two main buildings, to 217 AD, when this public nucleus seems to have been rebuilt by the African-born Severian emperors. Adjoined by small forum **baths**, it is a simple building with a porticoed court that leads on to a small temple and altar dedicated to the official state cult of Capitoline Jove, Juno and Minerva. The large five-aisled **Basilica** to its side served as the courthouse, while immediately across the **forum** were the small court and stalls of the central market. Storks have colonized some columns of the Capitol and Basilica; on a quiet day you will hear their clacking noises and will almost certainly see a few circling above or gliding on and off their nests.

The **Triumphal Arch**, right in the middle of the town, had no purpose other than to create a ceremonial proscenium for the principal street, the Decumanus Maximus. It was erected to honour the Severian emperor Caracalla and once topped with a bronze chariot, according to a weathered inscription. This and the nymphs that once shot water into basins below are gone, though the arch remains an impressive monument, thanks to tall Corinthian columns of imported marble and its sheer bulk. The heavy eroded medallions on either side presumably depict Caracalla and his mother, Julia Donna, who is also named in the inscription.

Mansions and mosaics

The finest of Volubilis's mansions – and its mosaics – line the **Decumanus Maximus**, fronted in traditional Roman and Italian fashion by the shops built in tiny cubicles. Before you reach this point, however, take a look at the remains of an **aqueduct** and **fountains** across from the triumphal arch; these once supplied yet another complex of public baths. Opposite them is the **House of the Athlete** (also called House of the Acrobat), which retains an impressive **Mosaic of an Athlete** or "chariot jumper" – depicted receiving the winner's cup for a *desultor* race, a display of great skill which entailed leaping on and off a horse in full gallop.

First of the Decumanus Maximus mansions, the **House of the Ephebus** takes its name from the bronze of a youth found in its ruins (and today displayed in Rabat). In general plan it is very similar to the House of Orpheus, once again containing an olive press in its rear section, though this building is on a far grander scale – almost twice the size of the other – with pictorial mosaics in most of its public rooms and an ornamental pool in its central court. Finest of the mosaics is a representation of **Bacchus Being Drawn in a Chariot by Panthers** – a suitable scene for the *cenacula*, or banqueting hall, in which it is placed.

Separated from the Ephebus House by a narrow lane is a mosaic-less mansion, known after its facade as the **House of Columns**, and adjoining this, the **Knight's House** with an incomplete mosaic of **Dionysos Discovering Ariadne** asleep on the beach at Naxos; both houses are largely ruins. More illuminating is the large mansion which begins the next block, similar in plan, but with a very complete mosaic of the **Labours of Hercules**. Almost comic caricatures, these give a good idea of typical provincial Roman mosaics. The next house along, the **House of Dionysos**, holds the site's best preserved mosaic, **Dionysos and the Four Seasons**, which still hints at the exuberant original colours. In the neighbouring house is a mosaic of the **Nymphs Bathing**, severely deteriorated around its central area.

Beyond this area, approaching the partially reconstructed **Tangier Gate**, stands the **Palace of the Gordians**, former residence of the procurators who administered the city and the province. Despite its size, however, and even with evidence of a huge **bath house** and pooled courtyards, it is unmemorable, stripped of its columns and lacking any mosaics. Its grandeur may have made it a target for Ismail's building mania. Indeed, how much of Volubilis remained standing before his reign is an open question; Walter Harris, writing at the turn of the twentieth century, found the road between here and Meknes littered with ancient marbles, left as they fell following the announcement of the sultan's death.

Back on the Decumanus, cross to the other side of the road and walk down a block to a smaller lane below the street, heading for the isolated cypress tree opposite the Palace of the Gordians. In the house by the tree is the most exceptional ensemble of mosaics in Volubilis – the **Cortege of Venus**. You cannot enter the house but most of the fine mosaics can be seen by walking round the outside of the ruins. If you imagine walking into the main section of the house, a central court is preceded by a paved vestibule and opens onto another, smaller patio, around which are grouped the main reception halls (and mosaics). From the entrance, the **baths** are off to the left, flanked by the private quarters, while immediately around the central court is a small group of mosaics, including an odd, very worn representation of a **Chariot Race** – with birds instead of horses. The villa's most outstanding mosaics lie beyond, in the "public" sections. On the left, in the corner, is a geometrical design, with medallions of **Bacchus Surrounded by the Four Seasons**; off to the right are **Diana Bathing** (and surprised by the huntsman Acteon) and the **Abduction of Hylas by Nymphs**. Each of these scenes – especially the last two – is superbly handled in stylized, fluid animation. They date, like that of the **Nereids** (two houses further down), from the late second or early third century AD, and were a serious commission. It is not known who commissioned the house, but its owner must have been among the city's most successful patrons; bronze busts of Cato and Juba II were also found here and now form the centrepiece of Rabat's museum.

Leaving the site by a path below the forum, you pass close by the ruins of a **temple** on the opposite side of the stream. The Romans dedicated it to Saturn, but it seems to have previously been used for the worship of a Carthaginian god; several hundred votive offerings were discovered during its excavation.

Moulay Idriss

MOULAY IDRISS takes its name from its founder, Morocco's most venerated saint and the creator of its first Arab dynasty. His tomb and *zaouia* lie right at the heart of the town, the reason for its sacred status and the object of constant pilgrimage – a trip here is worth a fifth of the *hajj* to Mecca – not to mention an important summer **moussem** in the third week of August. For most Western tourists, there is little specific to see and certainly nothing that may be visited – non-Muslims are barred from the shrines. But you could lose a happy day exploring the tangled lanes which shimmy between the sugar-cube houses that are scattered over two hills, enjoying delightful window-views, or just absorbing the easy-going holiday atmosphere. Few tourists bother to stay overnight – another reason to linger.

The Town

Grands taxis and buses for Moulay Idriss drop you at a square at the very base of the town. From here, walk up the steep road to another square – almost directly ahead are the green-tiled pyramids of the shrine and *zaouia*, flanked on either side by the hillside residential quarters of Khiber and Tasga. Locals say the town looks like a Bactrian camel, with the shrine and *zaouia* as the saddle between the two humps.

The souks, such as they are, line the streets of the Khiber (the taller hill) above the *zaouia*. They offer a variety of religious artefacts for Muslim visitors,

Moulay Idriss and the foundation of Morocco

Moulay Idriss el Akhbar (The Elder) was a great-grandson of the Prophet Muhammad; his grandparents were Muhammad's daughter Fatima, and cousin and first follower, Ali. Heir to the Caliphate in Damascus, he fled to Morocco around 787, following the Ommayad victory in the great civil war which split the Muslim world into Shia and Sunni sects.

In Volubilis, then still the main centre of the north, Idriss seems to have been welcomed as an *imam* (a spiritual and political leader), and within five years had succeeded in carving out a considerable kingdom. At this new town site, more easily defended than Volubilis, he built his capital, and he also began the construction of Fes, continued and considerably extended by his son Idriss II, that city's patron saint. News of his growing power filtered back to the East, however, and in 792 the Ommayads had Idriss poisoned, doubtless assuming that his kingdom would crumble.

They were mistaken. Alongside the faith of Islam, Idriss had instilled a sense of unity among the region's previously pagan (and sometimes Christian or Jewish) Berber tribes, which had been joined in this prototypical Moroccan state by increasing numbers of Arab Shiites loyal to the succession of his *Alid* line. After his assassination, Rashid, the servant who had travelled to Morocco with Idriss, took over as regent until 807, when the founder's son, Idriss II, was old enough to assume the throne.

especially plain white candles for the shrines, together with excellent local nougat and, in autumn, *arbutus* (strawberry tree) berries.

Rebuilt by Moulay Ismail, **Moulay Idriss's shrine and zaouia** are cordoned off from the street by a low, wooden bar to keep out Christians and beasts of burden. To get a true sense of its scale, you have to climb up towards one of the vantage points near the pinnacle of each quarter – ideally, the **Terrasse Sidi Abdallah el Hajjam** right above the Khiber, now a panoramic restaurant (see below). It's not easy to find your way up through the winding streets (most end in abrupt blind alleys), and, unless you enjoy the challenge of it all, you'd do better to enlist the help of a guide in the *place*. Should you decide to venture on your own, from the entrance of the shrine (as you face its courtyard) take the left passageway and climb the steps towards a fountain, 50m beyond, where the lane splits in two; take the right fork for another 30m or so and then turn left up another flight of steps; continue up the steps (150 of them), negotiating some switchbacks on the way, until you (hopefully) get to the café-restaurant.

On your way up, aim for the unusual modern minaret of the **Idriss Medersa**, now a Koranic school. The Medersa was built with materials taken from Volubilis and the cylindrical minaret was built in 1939 by a *hadji* who had been inspired by those he had seen in Mecca. A *surah* (chapter) from the Koran is inscribed in Kufic script in green mosaics.

There are several grill **cafés** on the square by the shrine and *zaouia*. For more substantial fare, try the *Restaurant Dar Diaf* (moderate) near the shrine, and the cheaper *Restaurant Baraka* (open lunchtime only; moderate), a small white building, near the *fantasia* ground on the way into the town. Better if only for its views is the *Restaurant Trois Boules d'Or*, up though the labyrinthine streets on the Terrasse Sidi Abdallah el Hajjam (daily summer 10am–midnight, winter 10am–6pm). Considering its premium position and glorious views, it is reasonably priced, with a few à la carte mains and menus both from 70dh.

On the way back you could reward yourself for the steep climb at the local **hammam**; coming down the steps, you'll find it on the right, 30m before the *zaouia*. Bathing hours for men are 6am to 1pm and for women 1pm to 8pm, after which time the hammam's steamy rooms are available for private hire for 100dh to 200dh.

Around Meknes

Heading **north** from Meknes, towards Larache, Tangier or Chefchaouen, Volubilis (see p.243) provides by far the most interesting excursion; there is little to delay you on the hour-long journey east to Fes. Covered below are the routes **west to Rabat** and **south to Azrou**, both of which offer a few points of interest along the way. For details on the trains, buses and grands taxis from Meknes, see pp.332–333.

West to Rabat: Khémisset and Lake Roumi

The road **west of Meknes** (N6, formerly P1) is a pleasant drive, running at first through a rich, cultivated landscape, then cutting across low, forested hills, with lavender (planted for perfume) on the lower slopes.

KHÉMISSET, 46km from Meknes, is a small market town, created by the French to encourage settlement of the scattered Zemmour Berbers of the region. It hosts a Tuesday souk, known for its carpets and wood carvings, and has a pleasant **hotel**, the *Diouri* (℡ & ℻037 55 26 45; ❸) on Boulevard

MohammedV, on the eastern outskirts of town. Driving from Meknes to Rabat, the hotel is about midway and its restaurant makes a good stop for lunch. If you want just a quick snack, try the *Café Yasmina* next door.

If you're in no hurry, a diversion to the **Dayet er Roumi** – a lake – is highly recommended. This lies 15km southwest of Khémisset, just off the R404 (formerly S106), and it's a gorgeous place whose shimmering water, birdsong and wood smoke from the fires of shepherds are every inch the pastoral idyll. From April to October, a **campsite** (℡037 55 29 77) and **café** operate by the water's edge and rent out pedalos to while away the afternoon. Swimming here is also good, and you can fish if you already have a permit.

To reach the café and campsite, you need to turn left off the R404, onto a rough road by a cactus field with five trees; the signposted road to the lake, 1500m beyond, leads only to a group of lakeside houses. If you don't have a car, it's possible to charter a grand taxi at Khémisset.

South to Azrou: Agouraï, El Hajeb and the Paysage d'Ito

South of Meknes is one of Morocco's best known **wine-growing areas**. Under French rule, Morocco and Algeria produced up to a third of the table wine consumed in France and had some respectable vintages. After decades of slow decay, new plantings and investment is seeing a marked upgrade in Moroccan wines. Some decent reds – marketed as *Toulal* – are produced at **AÏT-SOUALA**, on the minor S3065 road, west of the main Azrou road, and if you're curious, the vineyards can be visited. Continuing along the 3065 brings you out at the **kasbah** of **AGOURAÏ**, built by Moulay Ismail and now enclosing a small Berber village. It's an interesting spot, with water sluicing down the main street, and a buzzing Thursday **souk**. There is a **café** but no rooms or meals to be had, just drinks and cakes.

Back on the main road to Azrou, the N13 (formerly P21), the cultivation changes to wheat, planted in the *poljes* or depressions of this classic karst countryside. The small town of **EL HAJEB** ("eyebrow" in Arabic) occupies a high, cliffside site, alongside a ruined nineteenth-century fort. It has a Monday **souk**, a bank and several cafés.

Just south of the town, the road divides, with a minor route, the S309, leading through cedar forests to Ifrane (see p.304). The N13 to Azrou, though, is the better road to take because after 18km (17km north of Azrou) you reach the remarkable **Paysage d'Ito** – a natural roadside balcony on the edge of a volcanic plateau, with an astounding panorama, stretching for some seventy kilometres. The landscape is wonderfully bizarre, with outcrops of extinct volcanoes, and was used as the backdrop for many of the science fiction films of the 1950s and 1960s.

Nearby is the *Auberge d'Ito*. You can no longer sleep here, nor eat, unless you order in advance, but you can **drink** – and you won't be the only one. Be warned, it's a little rough.

Fes (Fez)

The history of Fes is composed of wars and murders, triumphs of arts and sciences, and a good deal of imagination.

Walter Harris: *Land of an African Sultan*

The most ancient of the Imperial capitals and the most complete medieval city of the Arab world, **FES** stimulates all the senses: a barrage of haunting and beautiful sounds, infinite visual details and unfiltered odours. It has the French-built Ville Nouvelle of other Moroccan cities – familiar and modern in looks and urban life – but a quarter or so of Fes's 800,000 inhabitants continue to live in the extraordinary Medina-city of **Fes el Bali**, which owes little to the West besides electricity and tourists. More than any other city in Morocco, the old town seems suspended in time somewhere between the Middle Ages and the modern world.

As a spectacle this is unmissable, and it's difficult to imagine a city whose external forms (all you can really hope to penetrate) could be such a source of constant interest. But stay in Fes a few days and it's equally hard to avoid the paradox of the place. Like much of "traditional" Morocco, the city was "saved" then re-created by the French, under the auspices of General Lyautey, the Protectorate's first Resident-General. Lyautey took the philanthropic and startling move of declaring the city a historical monument; philanthropic because he certainly saved Fes el Bali from destruction (albeit from less benevolent Frenchmen), and startling because until then Moroccans were under the impression that Fes was still a living city – the Imperial Capital of the Moroccan empire rather than a preservable part of the nation's heritage. More conveniently for the French, this paternalistic protection helped to disguise the dismantling of the old culture. By building a new European city nearby – the Ville Nouvelle – then transferring Fes's economic and political functions to Rabat and the west coast, Lyautey ensured the city's eclipse along with its preservation.

To appreciate the significance of this demise, you only have to look at the Arab chronicles or old histories of Morocco – in every one, Fes takes centre stage. The city had dominated Moroccan trade, culture and religious life – and usually its politics, too – since the end of the tenth century. It was closely and symbolically linked with the birth of an "Arabic" Moroccan state due to their mutual foundation by Moulay Idriss I, and was regarded as one of the holiest cities of the Islamic world after Mecca and Medina. Medieval European travellers describe it with a mixture of awe and respect, as a "citadel of fanaticism" yet the most advanced seat of learning in mathematics, philosophy and medicine. Tourism posters still boast of Fes as the country's *capitale spirituelle*.

The decline of the city notwithstanding, **Fassis** – the people of Fes – have a reputation throughout Morocco as successful and sophisticated. Just as the city is situated at the centre of the country, so its inhabitants are at the heart of government and most government ministries are headed by Fassis. What is undeniable is that they have the most developed Moroccan city culture, with an intellectual tradition and their own cuisine, dress and way of life.

The development of Fes

When the city's founder, Moulay Idriss I, died in 792, Fes was little more than a village on the east bank of the river. It was his son, **Idriss II**, who really began the city's development, at the beginning of the ninth century, by making it his capital and allowing in refugees from Andalusian Cordoba and from Kairouan in Tunisia – at the time, the two most important cities of western Islam. The impact on Fes of these refugees was immediate and lasting: they established separate, walled towns (still distinct quarters today) on either riverbank, and provided the superior craftsmanship and mercantile experience for Fes's industrial and commercial growth. It was at this time, too, that the city gained its intellectual reputation. The tenth-century Pope Silvester II studied here at the Kairaouine University, where he is said to have learned the Arabic mathematics that he introduced to Europe.

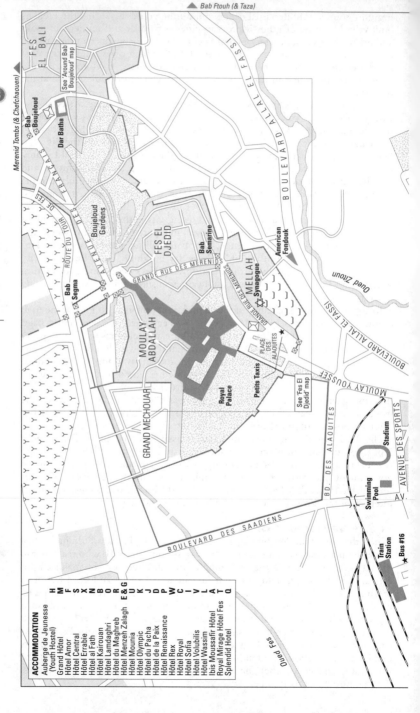

▲ Bab Ftouh (& Taza)

FES EL BALI

See 'Around Bab Boujeloud' map

◀ Merenid Tombs (& Chefchaouen)

Bab Boujeloud

Dar Batha

Boujeloud Gardens

FES EL DJEDID

Bab Semarine

American Fondouk

Oued Zitoun

GRANDE RUE DES MERENIDS

Bab Segma

ROUTE DU TOUR DE FES

AVENUE DES FRANÇAIS

BOULEVARD ALLAL EL FASSI

ISS

MELLAH

Synagogue

GRANDE RUE DES MERENIDS

MOULAY ABDALLAH

PLACE DES ALAOUITES

See 'Fes El Djedid' map

Royal Palace

Petits Taxis

GRAND MECHOUAR

BOULEVARD ALLAL EL FASSI

MOULAY YOUSSEF

BD. DES ALAOUITES

Stadium

Swimming Pool

AVENUE DES SPORTS

AV.

BOULEVARD DES SAADIENS

Train Station

★ Bus #16

Oued Fes

ACCOMMODATION

Auberge de Jeunesse (Youth Hostel)	H
Grand Hôtel	M
Hôtel Amor	F
Hôtel Central	S
Hôtel Errabie	X
Hôtel al Fath	N
Hôtel Kairouan	B
Hôtel Lamdaghri	O
Hôtel du Maghreb	R
Hôtel Menzeh Zalagh	E & G
Hôtel Mounia	U
Hôtel Olympic	K
Hôtel du Pacha	J
Hôtel de la Paix	D
Hôtel Renaissance	P
Hôtel Rex	W
Hôtel Royal	C
Hôtel Sofia	I
Hôtel Volubilis	V
Hôtel Wassim	L
Ibis Moussafir Hôtel	A
Royal Mirage Hôtel Fes	T
Splendid Hotel	Q

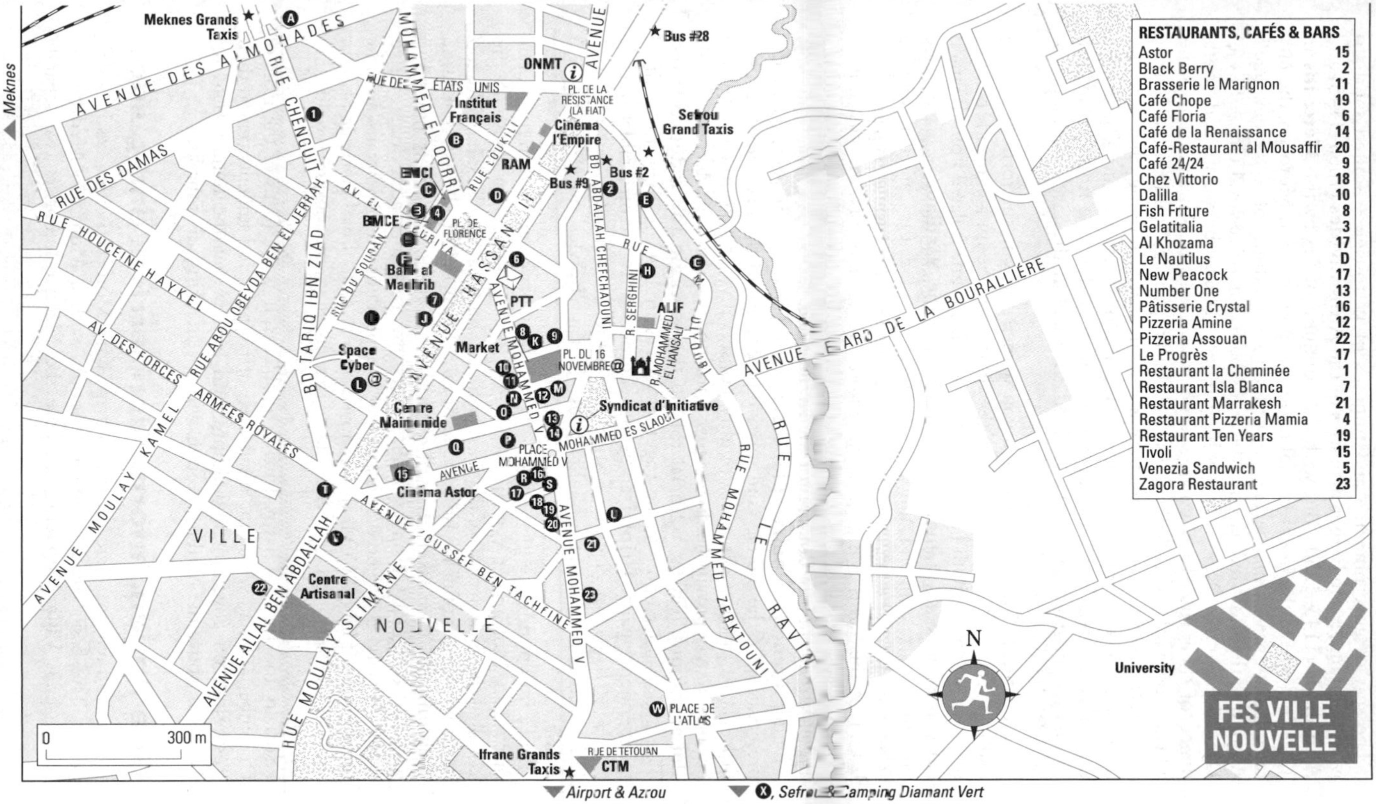

FES VILLE NOUVELLE
RESTAURANTS, CAFÉS & BARS
Astor 15
Black Berry 2
Brasserie le Marignon 11
Café Chope 19
Café Floria 6
Café de la Renaissance 14
Café-Restaurant al Mousaffir 20
Café 24/24 9
Chez Vittorio 18
Dalilla 10
Fish Friture 8
Gelatitalia 3
Al Khozama 17
Le Nautilus D
New Peacock 17
Number One 13
Pâtisserie Crystal 16
Pizzeria Amine 12
Pizzeria Assouan 22
Le Progrès 17
Restaurant la Cheminée 1
Restaurant Isla Blanca 7
Restaurant Marrakesh 21
Restaurant Pizzeria Mamia 4
Restaurant Ten Years 19
Tivoli 15
Venezia Sandwich 5
Zagora Restaurant 23
Meknes
Meknes Grands Taxis
AVENUE DES ALMOHADES
RUE CHENGUIT
RUE DES DAMAS
RUE HOUCEINE HAYKEL
AV. DES FORCES ARMÉES ROYALES
RUE AROU OBEYDA BEN EL JERRAH
BD. TARIQ IBN ZIAD
AVENUE MOULAY KAMEL
AVENUE ALLAL BEN ABDALLAH
RUE MOULAY SLIMANE
VILLE
NOUVELLE
Centre Artisanal
Space Cyber
Centre Maimonide
Cinéma Astor
Market
PTT
BMCI
BMCE
Bank al Maghrib
RUE DU SOUDAN
PL. DE FLORENCE
Institut Français
RUE DES ÉTATS UNIS
MOHAMMED EL QORRI
RUE LOUKILI
RAM
ONMT
PL. DE LA RESISTANCE (LA FIAT)
Cinéma l'Empire
Bus #9
Bus #2
Bus #28
Sefrou Grand Taxis
BD. ABDALLAH CHEFCHAOUNI
R. SERGHINI
R. MOHAMMED EL HANSALI
ALIF
AVENUE HASSAN II
AVENUE MOHAMMED V
PL. DU 16 NOVEMBRE
Syndicat d'Initiative
MOHAMMED ES SLAOUI
PLACE MOHAMMED V
AVENUE YOUSSEF BEN TACHFINE
RUE MOHAMMED ZERKTOUNI
RUE LE RAVIN
AVENUE DE LA BOURALLIÉRE
PLACE DE L'ATLAS
RUE DE TETOUAN
CTM
Ifrane Grands Taxis
University
N
0 300 m
Airport & Azrou
Camping Diamant Vert

The seat of government – and impetus of patronage – shifted south to Marrakesh under the Berber dynasties of the **Almoravides** (1068–1145) and **Almohads** (1145–1250). But with the conquest of Fes by the **Merenids** in 1248, and their subsequent consolidation of power across Morocco, the city regained its pre-eminence and moved into something of a "golden age". Alongside the old Medina, the Merenids built a massive royal city – **Fes el Djedid**, meaning "New Fes" – which reflected both the wealth and confidence of their rule. They enlarged and decorated the Kairaouine mosque, added a network of *fondouks* (inns) for the burgeoning commercial activity and greatly developed the Kairaouine University, building the series of magnificent **medersas**, or colleges, to accommodate its students. Once again this expansion was based on an influx of refugees, this time from the Spanish reconquest of Andalusia, and it helped to establish the city's reputation as "the Baghdad of the West".

It is essentially Merenid Fes which you witness today in the form of the city and its monuments. From the fall of the dynasty in the mid-sixteenth century, there was decline as both Fes and Morocco itself became isolated from the main currents of Western culture. The new rulers – the **Saadians** – in any case preferred Marrakesh, and although Fes re-emerged as the capital under the **Alaouites**, it had begun to lose its international stature. Moulay Ismail, whose hatred of the Fassis was legendary, almost managed to tax the city out of existence, and the principal building concerns of his successors lay in restoring and enlarging the vast domains of the royal palace.

Under **French colonial rule**, there were positive achievements in the preservation of the old city and relative prosperity of the Ville Nouvelle, but little actual progress. As a thoroughly conservative and bourgeois city, Fes became merely provincial. Even so, it remained a symbol of Moroccan pride and aspirations, playing a crucial role in the **struggle for independence**. The nationalist factions came together in Fes in 1943 to form the unified independence party: **Istiqlal**; an event recorded in Arabic on a tablet outside the *Hôtel Batha*, on Place de l'Istiqlal. And the subsequent events in Fes in 1955 were marvellously brought to life in Paul Bowles' novel *The Spider's House*.

Since **independence** in 1956, the city's position has been less than happy. The first sultan, Mohammed V, retained the French capital of Rabat, and with this signalled the final decline of the Fassi political and financial elites. In 1956, too, the city lost most of its Jewish community to France and Israel. First-generation rural migrants have taken their place in the Medina, often poorly housed in mansions designed for single families but now accommodating four or five, while the city as a whole is increasingly dependent on handicrafts and the tourist trade. If UNESCO had not moved in with its Cultural Heritage plan for the city's preservation, it seems likely that its physical collapse would have become even more widespread.

Socially, too, the city has had major problems. It was a focus of the riots of December 1990, in which the disaffected urban poor and students vented their frustrations on government buildings, and burned out the luxury *Hôtel des Merenides*, above the Medina, though without attacking any tourists.

Orientation, information, arrival and guides

Even if you felt you were getting to grips with Moroccan cities, Fes is bewildering. The basic layout is simple enough, with a Moroccan **Medina** and French-built **Ville Nouvelle**, but here the Medina comprises two separate

Petits taxis and city buses

Petits taxis in Fes use their meters, so offer good value. Useful petit taxi ranks include:

Pl Mohammed V (Ville Nouvelle). Main PTT on Ave Hassan II (Ville Nouvelle).

Pl des Alaouites (Fes el Djedid).

Pl Baghdadi (north of Bab Boujeloud, Fes el Bali).

Dar Batha (south of Bab Boujeloud, Fes el Bali).

Bab Guissa (north gate, by Palais Jamaï, Fes el Bali).

Bab er R'cif (central gate, south of the Kairaouine Mosque, Fes el Bali).

Bab Ftouh (southeast gate, Fes el Bali).

City buses Useful city bus routes are detailed, where relevant, in the text. As a general guide these are the ones you're most likely to want to use:

#2	Av Mohammed V to Bab Semarine (by Av Hassan II and Pl des Alaouites).	#20	Pl de Florence to the Arms Museum.
#3	Pl de la Résistance (La Fiat) via Bd Allal el Fassi to Bab Ftouh.	#27	Dar Batha to Pl er R'cif, south of the Kairaouine Mosque.
#9	Pl Mohammed V to Route de Sefrou via Bab Boujeloud.	#28	Pl de la Résistance (La Fiat) via Bab Ftouh to Sidi Harazem.
#10	Train station via *gare routière* to Bab Ftouh.	#29	Pl de l'Atlas to Pl er R'cif, south of the Kaira-ouine Mosque.
#12	Bab Boujeloud to Bab Ftouh.		
#16	Train station to the airport.	#38	From Pl de l'Atlas to Ain Bedia via the *Camping International* (see p.263) on the Sefrou road.
#17	Pl de Florence, opposite Banque al Maghrib to Aïn Chkeff for the *Diamant Vert* campsite (see p.263).	#45	Hay Adarissa to Pl R'cif via Pl l'Istiqlal
#18	Dar Batha to Sidi Boujida via Bab Ftouh.	**Note.** These numbers **are marked on the sides** of the buses; those on the back are completely different.	
#19	Train station to Pl er R'cif, south of the Kairaouine Mosque.		

cities: **Fes el Bali** (Old Fes), in the pear-shaped bowl of the Sebou valley, and **Fes el Djedid** (New Fes), established on the edge of the valley during the thirteenth century.

Fes el Djedid, dominated by a vast enclosure of royal palaces and gardens, is relatively straightforward. But **Fes el Bali**, where you'll want to spend most of your time, is an incredibly intricate web of lanes, blind alleys and souks. It takes two or three days before you even start to feel confident of where you're going and on an initial visit you may well want to pay for a guide (see p.257) to show you the main sights and layout. The learning process is not helped by the fact that most of the street signs are in Arabic only.

Fes's **tourist office**, the ONMT's reluctant *Délégation de Tourisme,* is in Immeuble Bennani at the corner of Avenue Moulay Youssef at Place de la Résistance, also called La Fiat (Mon–Fri 8.30am–2.30pm; ☏035 62 34 60). Don't expect much help, however. Better is a *Syndicat d'Initiative* on the east side of Place Mohammed V, which opens Mon–Fri 8.30–noon & 2.30–6.30pm plus Sat 9am–noon during summer.

Arrival

By train

The train station (☎035 93 03 33) is in the Ville Nouvelle, ten minutes' walk from the concentration of hotels around Place Mohammed V. If you prefer to stay in Fes el Bali, either take a petit taxi or bus #10 or #47 to Bab Boujeloud, where most of the old city's hotels are to be found; if you walk to Avenue Hassan II, you can pick up the #9 bus to nearby Dar Batha (pronounced *dar baat-ha*). From the train station, the #10 bus passes the main bus station and the #16 bus runs to the airport. Other buses from the train station run to outlying suburbs.

Beware of **unofficial taxi drivers**, who wait at the station and charge very unofficial rates for the trip into town; in a petit taxi during daytime (prices increase after dark), the fare to Bab Boujeloud is around 10dh (supplements for more than one person will increase this by a few dirhams), and will be about this per person in standard taxis. Be prepared for a certain amount of hustling, though the authorities have largely stopped this in obvious places.

By bus

Coming in by bus can be confusing, since there are terminals in the Ville Nouvelle and by the various gates to the Medina. Coming from most destinations, however, you will arrive at the main **bus station** or *gare routière* just north of Bab Mahrouk, between Kasbah Cherada and Borj Nord (see map, p.264). CTM has its own principal station on the corner of Rue Tetouan and Avenue Mohammed V in the Ville Nouvelle (☎035 73 29 84 – see Ville Nouvelle map, p.253); buses call here before, in theory, continuing on to the main bus station. The other exception is if you're coming from **Taza and the east**: buses stop at the Medina's southeast gate, **Bab Ftouh**, before continuing to the main bus station.

By grands taxis

Like buses, grands taxis mostly operate from the *gare routière* outside Bab Mahrouk. Exceptions are those from **Immouzer**, **Ifrane** and **Azrou** (and sometimes Marrakesh), which use a rank opposite the CTM office, 100m west of Place de l'Atlas (see Ville Nouvelle map p.253) and those from/to **Sefrou** (and sometimes Immouzer), which use a rank 100m down southeast of Place de la Résistance (La Fiat). **Meknes** grands taxis arrive outside the train station. Grands taxis from **Sidi Harazem**, **Taza**, and **Taounate** arrive at **Bab Ftouh**.

By air

Fes's Saïs **airport** is 15km south of the city, off the N8 (formerly P24) to Immouzer. From here you can reach town by grand taxi – ranks are just outside the terminal building on the left – or on bus #16 to the train station, which leaves the airport at least every hour.

By car

Be prepared for "motorbike guides" – Morocco's most annoying hustlers – who haunt the approach roads to Fes, attach themselves to tourist cars and insist on escorting you to a hotel. While efforts have been made to stamp the practice out, they are impossibly persistent and can be deeply unpleasant and not best countered by aggression; if they follow you, make it clear to the hotel receptionist that they have not guided you there and to the hustlers that you do not want a guided tour of the city.

Central options for **parking** in the Ville Nouvelle include: Place de Florence; the square backed by *Hôtel Sofia* one block south; and Place du 16 Novembre. If you intend to stay in Fes el Bali (or just drive there for the day), you can leave your car in car parks around Bab Boujeloud; west on the wasteground opposite the Lycée or south by the Batha Museum, from where it is only a short walk to the Medina and its hotels. Other useful car parks are off Route du Tour de Fes, near the centre of Talâa Kebira (just south of *Maison Blue 'Le Riad'* hotel on the map p.265) and by Bab el Guissa. Expect to pay the *gardien* at each around 10dh per day, 20dh overnight.

Maps

The **maps** in this guide are as functional as any available. On pp.252–253 is a plan of the Ville Nouvelle, showing the outline of Fes el Djedid and edge of Fes el Bali; on pp.264–265 is a general plan of Fes el Bali (with enlargements of the Bab Boujeloud area on p.259 and the Kairaouine Mosque area on p.275). An additional map of Fes el Djedid is on p.284. Inevitably, all maps of Fes el Bali are hugely simplified: more than any other Medina in Morocco, the old city is composed of an impenetrable maze of lanes and blind alleys whose precise orientation and localized names do not exactly lend themselves to cartography. **Topographical maps** (1:5000, 1:100000, 1:250000) are available from the *division cartographique* on Avenue Chefchaouini (☎035 94 03 17).

Guides

A half-day tour from an **official guide** is a useful introduction to Fes el Bali; no matter how many people are in your group, the fee is 150dh for a half-day and 250dh for a whole day, although it is always a good idea to clarify in advance exactly what is meant by a "full" day. Official guides identify themselves by laminated identity cards around their necks and can be engaged at the Syndicat d'Initiative on the east side of Place Mohammed V, outside the more upmarket hotels or at the youth hostel.

Guides who tout their services are likely to be **unofficial** and technically illegal. This doesn't necessarily mean they're to be avoided – some who are genuine students (as most claim to be) can be excellent. But you have to choose carefully, ideally drinking a tea together before settling a rate or declaring interest. One of the downsides of taking an unofficial guide is that in order not to be spotted by their offical counterparts, they sometimes follow convoluted and ill-frequented routes around the Medina, or call out directions from a few metres in front of or behind you, so they don't look like they are at your service – not a good way to gain information about the places you are walking by. More disreputable guides play an unpleasant trick of leading you into Fes el Bali and, once you're disorientated, maybe with dusk descending, demand more than the agreed fee to take you back to your hotel. Don't be intimidated – appeal to passers-by, who will be happy to direct you back to your hotel.

Whether you get an official or unofficial guide, it's essential to work out in advance the **main points you want to see**: a useful exercise would be to mark them on our map of Fes el Bali and show this to your guide. At all events, make it absolutely clear if you are not interested in **shopping**. If you enter a shop with a guide, official or otherwise, they will take a commission from the shopkeeper on anything you buy, which will be added to the price you pay, except for new carpets whose price is fixed by the state, in which case it is deducted from the shopkeeper's profit. Official guides are worse in this respect because they can command a much higher commission, often as much as forty percent. For some hints on shopping on your own, see "Shopping for Crafts" on p.293.

Despite what some *faux guides* may say, the Medina is not a dangerous place. However, some female visitors report experiencing unwanted attention from teenage touts. If a stern word does not work, appeal to older Fassis nearby, who will be as shocked as you at their lack of respect. In the Ville Nouvelle, locals warn that robbery is a problem at night on the isolated main road between Dar Batha and Place de La Résistance in the Ville Nouvelle; if you must walk it, do so only in groups of at least three people. Also, avoid the overgrown hillside east of Place de la Résistance, between the McDonald's restaurant and the train track, where muggings have occurred even during daytime.

Accommodation

Staying in Fes used to mean either comfort (and a reliable water supply) in modern **Ville Nouvelle** hotels or roughing it in the Medina hotels of **Fes el Bali** and **Fes el Djedid**. No longer. Not only has plumbing in the Medina improved somewhat, the rise and rise of Fes's riad scene, means there is class and character in renovated palaces – if you are prepared to pay for it. Either way, hotel space is at a premium in all categories, so be prepared for higher prices than usual and reserve in advance if possible.

If you are not overly concerned about the size and cleanliness of your room or can afford one of the growing number of upmarket options, **Fes el Bali** is undoubtedly the place to be. You will be at the heart of the city's souks and traditional life, well placed to explore the monuments and witness to the amazing sound of muezzins from hundreds of mosques simultaneously striking up the early morning call.

Visitors who prefer their hotel to come with the full complement of mod cons (not always on offer even in the riads) may prefer the **Ville Nouvelle**, whose wide choice of hotels is adequate if unexciting and where there is a youth hostel. A few of the better hotels here have swimming pools, so can be worth a splurge in midsummer, when the heat of the plateau can be overwhelming. The Ville Nouvelle hotels also offer advantages in their proximity to restaurants and bars and the train station.

Fes el Bali

With the notable exceptions of the *Hôtel Batha, Palais Jamaï* and a fast-growing number of pricey riads (60 at the last count), all hotels in Fes el Bali are basic *pensions*, most of which could do with a makeover and better plumbing. Some are also overpriced, charging the equivalent of one-star prices when they can get away with it in peak season. So long as your expectations are modest, most are adequate and the group around Bab Boujeloud are an ideal launchpad from which to explore the old city's sights and souks. The problem of water – or rather lack of it in summer – in many of the bargain-basement hotels can be overcome by taking a steam bath in the nearby hammam.

Bab Boujeloud

Bab Boujeloud is the western gateway to Fes el Bali and offers pedestrian access to Fes el Djedid. Bus and petit taxi ranks for getting to and from the Ville Nouvelle are in nearby **Place de l'Istiqlal**. The hotels listed below are keyed on the map of the Bab Boujeloud area, opposite. There is also a hammam nearby (see p.295).

Dar Bouânania 21 Derb ben Salem (off Talâa Kebira) ☎ & ℻ 035 63 72 82 (map p.264). Not as | classy as the riads yet a cut above other Bab Boujeloud cheapies. Simple characterful rooms

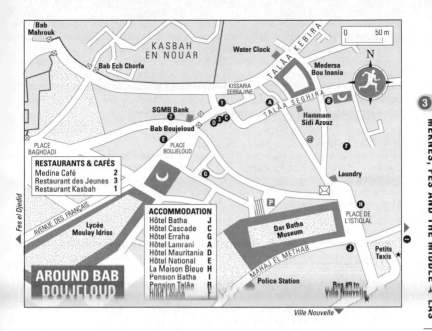

(two en suite) are arranged around an intimate courtyard of painted woodwork and zellij that hints at riad charm at a fraction of the price. ❹

Hôtel Batha Pl de l'Istiqlal ☎035 74 10 77, @hotelbatha@menara.ma. A tour group favourite next to the Dar Batha museum, this three-star is comfy if a little bland, its character concealed in the bar of the older block behind, formerly the British consulate. Also has a small swimming pool. Worrying reports of individual reservations not honoured suggest
you should reconfirm all bookings. Breakfast included. ❺

Hôtel Cascade 26 Rue Serajine ☎035 63 84 42. Smallish but clean rooms, most with windows, hot showers around the clock, plus the best terrace of the Boujeloud hotels, where you can sleep for 30–50dh (depending on demand). Popularity has added a hint of hustle, but always busy with a young international crowd. ❷

Hôtel Erraha Signposted by Boujeloud Mosque ☎035 63 32 26. Rooms in the "*Relax*" are basic and a little tatty, although hot showers are available. Good top terrace too. ❷

Hôtel Lamrani Talâa Seghira, opposite the Hammam Sidi Azouz ☎035 63 44 11. A friendly place with small but clean rooms, most with double beds. Hot showers (10dh) available. ❷

Hôtel Mauritania 20 Rue Serajine ☎035 63 35 18. A fall back to – and overpriced compared with – the *Hôtel Cascade* next door. Washbasins in cell-like rooms, hot showers on the corridor. ❷

Hôtel National Pl Boujeloud, no tel. Basic but clean(ish), best seen as a fall back – traffic noise can be a problem in front rooms. Cold showers. ❷

Pension Batha 8 Sidi Lkhayat Batha ☎035 74 11 50, ☏035 74 88 27. Close to place de l'Istiqlal and away from the hustle around the gateway, this has pleasant old fashioned decor in the rooms – rooms 4 and 5 feature nice stuccowork on the ceiling – and some en-suite hot showers. Price includes breakfast. ❹

Pension Talâa Talâa Seghira (opposite Medersa Bou Inania) ☎035 63 33 59. A warm welcome in a well-maintained and well-located pension, with pleasant doubles, though singles are rather hutch-like. A more mellow alternative to the *Cascade*. Shared hot showers. ❸

Bab Ftouh

An alternative group of cheap hotels, all pretty basic, is by **Bab Ftouh**, a gate at the southeast corner of the Fes el Bali (see map, pp.264–265), an untouristed area whose hotels are used almost exclusively by Moroccans. It's also a rather underworld sort of area where even Moroccans watch their step. Grands taxis to Sidi Harazem, Taounate and other points east and north of Fes leave from Bab Ftouh, and buses to and from Taza and Al Hoceima should call here after/before the main bus station; double-check with the driver if arriving. Although three of these hotels only have cold showers and one has no shower at all, hammam Douche Andalous has hot showers and a traditional steam bath. From Bab Ftouh take a left immediately after *Hôtel el Andalous* and it's on the left; open for women 1–6pm, for men 6am–noon and 6.30–10pm.

Hôtel el Andalous 31 Rue Kaid Khammer ℡ 035 64 82 62. The best of the four hotels in the quarter, the same price as the others but cleaner and quieter with a roof terrace and rooms around a central patio. **❶**

Hôtel el Hamra Rue Bab el Hamra (no phone). A last choice if you're desperate; just as basic as the others in the area, but costing slightly more. **❶**

Hôtel Bahia Rue Sidi Ali Boughaleb ℡ 035 64 92 01. A bed in cell-like rooms and no showers. **❶**

Hôtel Moulay Idriss 2 Bab Ftouh ℡ 035 64 91 86. Unused to tourists, with only Arabic spoken. **❶**

Riads and upmarket hotels in Fes el Bali

Staying in style in Fes el Bali means the best of both worlds, but it doesn't come cheap. Fes's riad scene is fast catching up with that in Marrakesh as owners cotton on that period atmosphere means high prices – some are overpriced, so it pays to be choosy. That said, their charm is unquestionable and a few houses now restored as luxurious *maisons d'hôtes* offer one small room at prices to tempt even those on tighter budgets into a splurge. Reservation is recommended and breakfast is included in all prices.

Dar el Ghalia 13/15 Ross Rhi ℡ 035 63 41 67, ⓦ www.maisondhotes.co.ma (see map, pp.264–265). First-floor suites are the pick in Hadj Omar Lebbar's riad, created from an 18th-century palace and with heavier, more traditional furnishings. **❽**

Dar Seffarine 14 Derb Shoa Lougote (alley 20m north of Pl Seffarine) ℡ 035 63 52 05, ⓦ www.darseffarine.com (see map, p.275). In the old heart of Fes el Bali, with some of the oldest zellij and stucco of Fes's riads and rooms styled in a sort of Moroccan minimalism by its designer-architect owners; the palatial Koba suite is a knock-out. Add in a community spirit that sees guests breakfast together and you have one of the most appealing – and well-priced – options. **❻**

La Maison Bleue 2 Pl de l'Istiqlal ℡ & ℡ 035 74 18 43, ⓦ www.maisonbleue.com (see map, p.259). The first riad in Fes and still one of the best, an intimate world of luxury opposite the Batha Museum where rooms, some with a private terrace, are named after female members of the family who built and still own it. Style is a mix of Moroccan and classy European pieces and there's excellent traditional dining in its restaurant (expensive; open to non-guests). More romantic still is the sister house 🏃 *La Maison Bleue* "*Le Riad*", across a car park north of Talâa Kebira at 33 Derb el Miter (℡ 035 74 18 73, ℡ 035 74 06 86, ⓦ www.maisonbleue.com; see map, pp.264–265). This has the added appeal of a garden and a swimming pool in the courtyard, plus a hammam hidden away among its many levels. Both **❾**

Riad Arabesque 20 Derb el Mitter ℡ 035 63 53 21, ⓦ www.arabesquehotel.com (see map, pp.264–265). Located near the *Hôtel Palais Jamaï* – ask here for directions – this riad aheres to the sumptuous style favoured by the Edwardian Fassi elite; rich and gloriously cluttered with an eclectic mix of antiques and objets d'art and with generous use of expensive *tadelakt* wall finish, fireplaces and four-posters in rooms. A fountain and pool in the garden courtyard add to the exotic atmosphere, particularly in the evening. **❼**

Riad al Bartal 21 Rue Sournas ℡ 035 63 70 53, ⓦ www.riadalbartal.com (see map, pp.264–265). The light touch of French owners Mireille and Christian Laroche abounds in this *maison d'hôte*, from the arty, pared-down decor in a plant-filled courtyard to individually styled rooms with painted ceilings and *tadelakt* walls. Suites are worth the extra 150dh. **❼**

Riad Fes Derb Ben Slimane ℡ 035 94 76 10, ⓦ www.riadfes.com (see map, pp.264–265). Less a *maison d'hôte* than a boutique hotel, architecturally the grandest in Fes and whose carving and zellij in the courtyard score high on the wow factor. There's a stylish bar in the extension, a plunge pool in the garden and immaculate service everywhere. **❽**

Riad Louna 21 Derb Serraj off Talâa Seghira ℡ & ℡ 035 74 19 85, ⓦ www.riadlouna.com

(see map, p.259). One of the best value riads, traditionally restored by its Belgian owner with six rooms and three suites set around a lovely garden of palms, orange trees and a fountain. It is easiest located from Place de l'Istiqlal: leaving the PTT on your left, take the first right down steps then right down a narrow alley. A window-less room priced ⑤ is just about worth it for the charm outside, others from ⑥.

Riad Norma 16 Derb Sornas ☎035 63 47 81, ⓦwww.riadnorma.com (see map, pp.264–265). We get consistently good reports of this charming riad, simpler than others and elegantly furnished with antiques, with more modern style in six suites and a plunge pool in the garden. ⑦

Ryad Mabrouka 25 Derb el Miter ☎035 65 63 45, ⓦwww.ryadmabrouka.com (see map, pp.264–265). Through a door in an unassuming dead-end alley, Moroccan style is paired with French antiques and

modern art, a reflection of the eclectic tastes of French owner Michel Trezzy. There's also a plunge pool in an idyllic garden and great views of the Medina from the terrace to boot. ⑦

Sofitel Palais Jamaï Bab Guissa (north gate) ☎035 63 43 31, ⓦwww.sofitel.com (see map, pp.264–265). Along with Marrakesh's *Mamounia*, the most famous and historic hotel in Morocco, a five-star number founded on a nineteenth-century vizier's palace (see p.281). It also served as a principal setting for Paul Bowles' novel *The Spider's House*. That said, unless you pay upwards of 6000dh for a palace suite, you're in the modern block behind, whose smallish rooms are rather pricey for the bland international style; the best offer excellent views to the Medina. There are also three restaurants, including the excellent Al Fassia, two spas and a large pool in beautiful gardens. ⑧

Fes el Djedid

An alternative to the backpacker hostels around Bab Boujeloud, these are within a ten- to fifteen-minute walk of Fes el Djdid and less frequented by tourists (and hustlers). See map on p.284 for locations.

Hôtel Glacier Near Pl des Alaouites ☎035 62 62 61. Located at the bottom of an alleyway off Rue des Merenides, this brightly painted hotel has clean and basic rooms arranged around an interior courtyard. Run by two friendly women, who speak only Arabic. Best budget choice in this part of town; shared cold-water showers. ①

Hôtel du Parc Off Grand Rue des Merenides ☎035 94 16 98. Overlook squalid toilets, grubby rooms and cold-water showers and this friendly place has a certain shabby appeal, plus a terrace with views of the ramparts. It's also by far the cheapest bed in the Bab Boujeloud area. ①

The Ville Nouvelle

As cheap rooms can be tricky to obtain in Fes, we have listed most of the Ville Nouvelle hotels – the good and not so good. All are marked on the map on pp.252–253.

Cheap

Auberge de Jeunesse (Youth Hostel) 18 Rue Abdeslam Seghrini ☎035 62 40 85, ⓦwww .fesyouth-hostel.com. One of the best Moroccan youth hostels; easy-going, friendly and refur-bished to provide spotless dorms from 55dh and doubles from 130dh; free hot showers 8.15–10am. It's set in a small garden in a quiet backwater near the *Hôtel Zalagh*, which usually allows hostel guests to swim in its pool for a reduced fee. Its enthusiastic Fassi manager is also a mine of local information. Doors close 11.30pm summer, 10pm winter. ②

Hôtel Amor 31 Rue Arabie Saoudite, previously Rue du Pakistan ☎035 62 27 24. One block from Av Hassan II, behind the Bank al Maghrib. Attractive tiled frontage; restaurant and reasonably-priced accommodation. ③

Hôtel Central 50 Rue Brahim Roudani, also called Rue du Nador ☎035 62 23 33. Good value, popular one-star that's often full. Rooms are clean and bright, heated in winter, some with small en-suite shower cubicles. ③

Hôtel Errabie 1 Rue de Tangier ☎055 64 01 00, ⓕ035 65 9 163. Just off the bottom, southern edge of the map – on the Route de Sefrou. A modern, well-built complex on the corner of a major junction, with three petrol stations. Café, patisserie, boulangerie and small swimming pool – simply but well finished, all rooms en suite, some with a/c. Easy parking. ③

Hôtel al Fath formerly the *Excelsior*, at the corner of Av Mohammed V and Rue Larbi el Kaghat ☎035 94 46 50. New managemenet but still rather spartan. Friendly, though, and hot showers mornings and evenings. ③

Hôtel Kairouan 84 Rue de Soudan ☏ 035 62 35 90. A simple, well-kept hotel with large rooms (all with hot showers) but sited somewhat in no-man's-land site between the train station and town centre. ❷

Hôtel Lamdaghri Rue Abbas Msaadi ☏ 035 62 03 10. Big rooms with cupboard-size en-suite bathrooms; restaurant on first floor and lively bar next door. Reasonable value, bright and well placed at the centre of the Ville Nouvelle. ❸

Hôtel du Maghreb 25 Av Mohammed es Slaoui ☏ 035 62 15 67. One of the cheaper hotels in the Ville Nouvelle, fairly tatty and sometimes not terribly clean, although high-ceilinged rooms are spacious. ❷

Hôtel du Pacha 32 Av Hassan II ☏ 035 65 22 90. An old-style downmarket hotel, catering mainly to Moroccans. The big minus is that not all rooms have (cold) showers, and there are no shared ones. ❷

Hôtel Renaissance 29 Rue Abdelkrim el Kattabi ☏ 035 62 21 93. Despite a rather gloomy entrance and only functional rooms, a friendly and clean billet in a central position with shared hot showers. ❷

Hôtel Rex 32 Pl de l'Atlas ☏ 035 64 21 33. A basic place, with shared facilities throughout and a café on the ground floor. Handy for CTM departures (or late arrivals). ❷

Hôtel Royal 36 Rue de Soudan ☏ 035 62 46 56. Convenient for the train station and near the *Hôtel Kairouan*. Its simple rooms vary somewhat; those on the first floor with shared facilities are cheaper, but better en suites are worth the extra. ❷

Moderate

Grand Hôtel Bd Abdallah Chefchaouni ☏ 035 62 32 45, ✉ granotel@hotmail.ma. An old colonial hotel with an Art Deco facade and similarly impressive proportions in refurbished rooms, somewhat spartan though all with a/c, heating and en suite; many have a bath. Facilities include a bar, restaurant, nightclub and garage. ❻

Hôtel Mounia 60 Bd Zerktouny ☏ 035 62 48 38, ⊕ www.hotelmouniafes.ma. A friendly modern hotel that has been recently refurbished to provide smart rooms, all with central heating, a/c and satellite TV. One of the best mid-range choices in the Ville Nouvelle. ❻

Hôtel Olympic Rue Houman el Fatouaki, off Av Mohammed V, facing one side of the covered market ☏ 035 93 26 82, ⓕ 035 93 26 65. A keenly priced option, clean and reliable with a reasonable restaurant. Recently refurbished throughout – all rooms now have bathroom, TV, and heating in winter. ❹

Hôtel de la Paix 44 Av Hassan II ☏ 055 62 50 72, ✉ hoteldelapaix@iam.net.ma. An old-established tour group hotel, well worth a call. Red-carpeted corridors lead to modern(ish) spotless rooms with full bathroom suite, TV, a/c and heating. The hotel's good seafood restaurant, *Le Nautilus*, is open to nonresidents. ❹

Hôtel Wassim Rue du Liban – off Av Hassan II ☏ 035 65 49 39, ⊕ hotelwassim.ifrance.com. Classy in an understated kind of way, this four-star has scheduled for a makeover of its three restaurants and bar in 2007, while fully equipped rooms, though on the small side, are tasteful and spotless. Also has a nightclub (free for residents but open to all). ❻

Ibis Moussafir Hôtel Pl de la Gare/Av des Almohades ☏ 035 65 19 02, ⊕ www.ibishotel.com. An always-busy member of Accor's international Ibis chain, modern and bright if rather impersonal in its smallish pleasant rooms. Also has a so-so restaurant, a bar and small swimming pool. ❺

Splendid Hôtel 9 Rue Abdelkrim el Khattabi ☏ 035 62 21 48, ✉ splendid@menara.ma. An efficient modern hotel in the heart of the Ville Nouvelle with newly refurbished and very pleasant en-suite rooms, a good restaurant, bar and small swimming pool. One of the best-value options in the Ville Nouvelle when not booked out by tour groups. ❺

Expensive

Hôtel Menzeh Zalagh 10 Rue Mohammed Diouri ☏ 035 62 55 31, ⊕ www.menzeh-zalagh.ma. A formerly state-owned hotel, now privatized, with quite a chic clientele (even the tour groups are select), and a new annexe on Rue Diyouri at the corner of Rue de Ravin, the Hôtel Menzeh Fes. Facilities include the hotel's own hammam. The swimming pool is open to nonresidents, but expensive at 70dh. On the other hand, the fine views across to Fes el Djedid are anyone's for the cost of an orange juice. ❼

Hôtel Sofia 3 Rue Arabie Saoudite, formerly Rue du Pakistan ☏ 035 62 42 65, ⊕ www.hotelsofia.ma. Four-star standards in a central modern chain hotel with a pool and all the works, frequented almost exclusively by tour groups; bar and nightclub open to nonresidents. Reasonably priced for a quality hotel. ❻

Hôtel Volubilis Av Allal Ben Abdallah next to the Centre Artisanal ☏ 035 62 30 98, ⓕ 035 62 11 25. Another four-star, whose main attraction is a central garden with two pools. The rooms are rather functional but most enjoy views over the garden. Nightclub from midnight, daily except Sunday, free to residents and 100dh for nonresidents. ❻

Royal Mirage Hôtel Fes Av des FAR ☎ 035 93 09 09, ℮ reservations.fes@royalmiragehotels. com. A former member of the *Sheraton* chain, now independent, though still a large and not particularly distinguished tour group hotel on the fringe of the Ville Nouvelle, rather pricey for the bland decor of its rooms. Useful features include a large swimming pool, car rental firm, First Car, with a desk in the lobby (no fixed working hours, so contact the main branch first, see p.293) and an office of postal chain DHL. ❽

Camping

Camping International Route de Sefrou ☎ 035 61 80 61, ℗ 055 61 81 73. A relatively new site next to the new football stadium 4km from the city centre, accessible by bus #38 from Pl de l'Atlas. Well kept, with plenty of greenery, shade and constant hot water, it is pricey as campsites go, although for your money you get a pool, a bar, tennis courts and horse riding. The pool is also open to nonresidents (daily 9am–5pm; 15dh). **Camping Diamant Vert** Fôret d'Aïn Chkeff 6km south of the city ☎ 035 60 83 67, ℮ diamantfes@yahoo.fr. Although well out of town, this is a pleasant and shady site, with its own swimming pool, restaurant, café, playground and Barbary apes. More welcoming and generally quieter than *Camping International*, it is a good choice for tourers, motorbikers and cyclists. Staying here also gives easy access to the neighbouring **Reda leisure complex**, which includes a swimming pool, sports facilities, restaurants and a disco/nightclub often with a live band. Bus #17 from Pl Florence – opposite Banque al Maghrib – in Fes Ville Nouvelle runs past the campsite.

Fes el Bali

With its mosques, medersas and *fondouks*, combined with a mile-long labyrinth of souks, there are enough sights in **Fes el Bali** to fill three or four days just trying to locate them. Even then, you're unlikely to stumble across some except by chance or the whim of a guide. In this the apparently wilful secretiveness – lies part of Fes's fascination and there is much to be said for Paul Bowles' somewhat lofty advice to "lose oneself in the crowd – to be pulled along by it – not knowing where to and for how long . . . to see beauty where it is least likely to appear". Do the same and you must be prepared to get really lost. However, the Medina is not a dangerous place despite what some hustlers say, and there's always someone around to ask for directions or to lead you towards a landmark: Bab Boujeloud, Talâa Kebira, the Kairaouine Mosque, Bab er R'cif or Bab Ftouh, for example. The flow of life eases considerably on Friday, when much of the Medina takes a day off and crowds thin.

To help visitors, tourism masterminds have scattered star-shaped signs throughout Fes el Bali, directional markers for colour co-ordinated routes that

---

Getting in and out of Fes el Bali

There are four principal entrances and exits to Fes el Bali: **Bab Boujeloud**. The western gate, easily identified by its bright polychrome decoration and the hotels and cafés grouped on either side. **Bab er R'cif**. A central gate by the square (and car park) beside the Mosque er R'cif, this is a convenient entrance, just a few blocks below the Kairaouine Mosque. Bus #19 and bus #29 run between the square and Avenue Mohammed V in the Ville Nouvelle, #19 continuing to the train station, #29 to Place de l'Atlas. Bus #27 runs between the square and Dar Batha. **Bab Ftouh**. The southeast gate at the bottom of the Andalous quarter, with cemeteries extending to the south. Bus #18 runs between here and Place de l'Istiqlal (near Bab Boujeloud) and there is also a petit taxi rank. **Bab Guissa**. The north gate, up at the top of the city by the *Hôtel Palais Jamaï*: a convenient point to enter (or leave) the city from (or heading to) the Merenid tombs. Petits taxis are available by the gate.

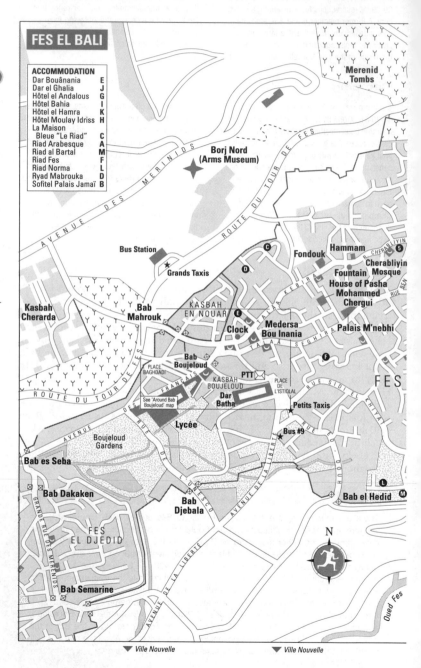

FES EL BALI

ACCOMMODATION

Dar Bouânania	E
Dar el Ghalia	J
Hôtel el Andalous	G
Hôtel Bahia	I
Hôtel el Hamra	K
Hôtel Moulay Idriss	H
La Maison Bleue "Le Riad"	C
Riad Arabesque	A
Riad al Bartal	M
Riad Fes	F
Riad Norma	L
Ryad Mabrouka	D
Sofitel Palais Jamaï	B

Borj Nord (Arms Museum)

Merenid Tombs

Bus Station

Grands Taxis

Kasbah Cherarda

Bab Mahrouk

KASBAH EN NOUAR

Clock

Medersa Bou Inania

Fondouk

Hammam

Cherabliyin Mosque

Fountain

House of Pasha Mohammed Chergui

Palais M'nebhi

FES

Bab Boujeloud

PLACE BAGHDADI

PTT

PLACE DE L'ISTIQLAL

KASBAH BOUJELOUD

Dar Batha

See 'Around Bab Boujeloud' map

Lycée

Petits Taxis

Bus #9

Boujeloud Gardens

Bab es Seba

Bab Dakaken

Bab Djebala

Bab el Hedid

FES EL DJEDID

Bab Semarine

N

ROUTE DU TOUR DE FES

AVENUE DES MERINIDS

AVENUE DE LA LIBERTE

AVENUE DES FRANÇAIS

RUE DE L'UNESCO

GRANDE RUE DES MERINIDS

RUE ED DOUH

RUE SIDI EL KHITAT

TALAA KEBIR

TALAA SEGHIRA

R. CHERABLIYIN

Oued Fes

Ville Nouvelle   *Ville Nouvelle*

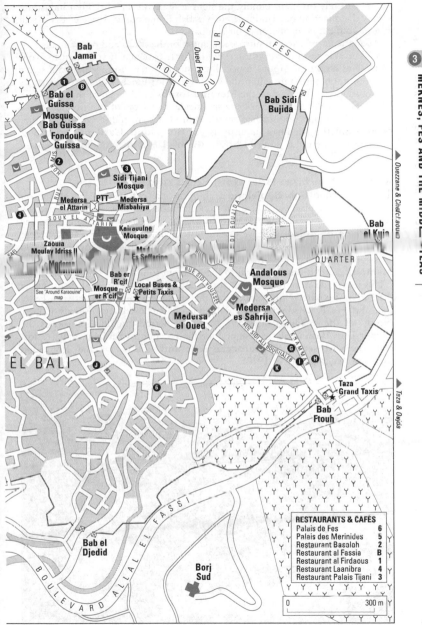

▶ Ouezzane & Chefchaouen

▶ Taza & Oujda

Bab Jamaï

Bab el Guissa

Mosque Bab Guissa

Fondouk Guissa

Sidi Tijani Mosque

Medersa el Attarin PTT **Medersa Misbahiya**

SOUK EL ATTARIN

Kairaouine Mosque

Zaouia Moulay Idriss II

Medersa

Medersa Es Seffarine

Bab er R'cif

Mosque er R'cif

Local Buses & Petits Taxis

See 'Around Karaouine' map

Medersa el Oued

EL BALI

Bab Sidi Bujida

RTE DU EQUIDA

Bab el Kuin

QUARTER

Andalous Mosque

RUE SIDI YOUSSEF

RUE LAIB KTAMAR

Medersa es Sahrija

RUE SIDI ALI BOURHALEB

Taza Grand Taxis

Bab Ftouh

Bab el Djedid

BOULEVARD ALLAL EL FASSI

Borj Sud

RESTAURANTS & CAFÉS
Palais de Fes	6
Palais des Merinides	5
Restaurant Basalah	2
Restaurant al Fassia	B
Restaurant al Firdaous	1
Restaurant Laanibra	4
Restaurant Palais Tijani	3

0   300 m

are depicted on public street maps; there's one at the tourist office near Place de la Résistance, another adjacent to the mosque on Place Boujeloud. Although it's best not to rely on them blindly, the signs at door-top height, often indicating simply the direction of a landmark such as Bab Boujeloud or Place er R'cif, will at least confirm your own in-built compass.

Making your own way in purposeful quest for the souks and monuments, you should be able to find everything – with a little patience. If you want to avoid coinciding with tour groups, especially in summer, try visiting the main sights between noon and 2pm, when the groups stop for lunch. Before you start, it's not a bad idea to head up to the **Merenid tombs** on the rim of the valley (see box opposite), where you can get a spectacular overview of the city and try to make out its shape undisturbed by the rush of human traffic within. Another escape from the Medina's intensity is the **Boujeloud Gardens** (Jnane Sbil; open 8am–6.30pm), a peaceful haven west of Bab Boujeloud with a pleasant open-air café.

Into the Medina: Bab Boujeloud and Dar Batha

The area around **Bab Boujeloud** is the principal entrance to Fes el Bali for most visitors; a place with a great concentration of cafés, stalls and activity where people come to talk and stare. Provincial buses leave throughout the day from **Place Baghdadi** (just west of the gate), while in the early evening there are occasional entertainments and a flea market spreading out towards the old Mechouar (the former assembly point and government square) and to **Bab el Mahrouk**, an exit onto the road to the Merenid tombs.

This focus and importance is all comparatively recent because it was only at the end of the nineteenth century that the walls were joined up between Fes el Bali and Fes el Djedid and the subsequently enclosed area was developed. Nearly all the buildings here date from this period, including those of the elegant **Dar Batha** palace, designed for the reception of foreign ambassadors and now a **Museum of Moroccan Arts and Crafts**, and Bab Boujeloud itself, constructed only in 1913.

△ View of Fes from the Merenid tombs

A crumbling and fairly obscure group of ruins, the **Merenid tombs** are not of great interest in themselves. People no longer know which of the dynasty's sultans had them erected and there is not a trace remaining of the "beautiful white marbles' vividly coloured epitaphs" which so struck Leo Africanus in his sixteenth-century description of Fes. Poised at the city's skyline, however, they are a picturesque focus and a superb vantage point. All round you are spread the Muslim cemeteries which ring the hills on each side of the city, while looking down you can delineate the more prominent of Fes's reputed 365 mosque minarets.

Getting up to the tombs is no problem. You can walk it in about twenty minutes from Bab Boujeloud, or take a taxi (around 10dh from the Ville Nouvelle). From the Boujeloud area, leave by **Bab el Mahrouk**, below the new bus station, and once outside the walls, turn immediately to the right. After a while you come to a network of paths worn into the hillside, which you can scramble up if sufficiently able-bodied to reach the stolid fortress of **Borj Nord** (a longer but more sedate route is to follow the road round from Bab el Mahrouk). Despite its French garrison-like appearance, this and its southern counterpart across the valley were actually built in the late sixteenth century by the Saadians. The dynasty's only endowment to the city, they were used to control the Fassis rather than to defend them. Carefully maintained, the Borj now houses the country's **arms museum** (in theory, daily except Tues 8.30am–noon & 2.30–6pm; 10dh) – daggers encrusted with stones and an interminable display of row upon row of muskets, most of them confiscated from the Riffians in the 1920s rebellion. Pride of place is given to a cannon 5m long and weighing twelve tonnes, said to be used during the Battle of the Three Kings (see p.709).

Clambering across the hillside from Borj Nord – or following (by road) Route du Tour du Fes past *Hôtel des Merenides* – you soon emerge at **the tombs** and an expectant cluster of guides. Wandering round here, you will probably be standing on the city's original foundations, before its rapid expansion under Moulay Idriss II. But it is **the view** across the deep pear-shaped bowl of the valley below which holds everyone's attention – Fes el Bali neatly wedged within it, white and diamond-shaped, and buzzing with activity.

Immediately below is Adourat el Kairaouine, or the Kairaouine quarter: the main stretch of the Medina, where Idriss settled the first Tunisian refugees. At its heart, towards the river, stands the green-tiled courtyard of the **Kairaouine Mosque**, the country's most important religious building, preceded and partially screened by its two minarets. The main one has a dome on top and is whitewashed, which is an unusual Moroccan (though characteristically Tunisian) design, the slightly lower one to its right (square, with a narrower upper floor) is Borj en Naffara (The Trumpeter's Tower), from which the beginning and end of Ramadan are proclaimed. Over to the right of this, and very easily recognized, are the tall pyramid-shaped roof and slender, decoratively faced minaret of the city's second great religious building, the **Zaouia of Moulay Idriss II**.

The **Andalous quarter**, the other area settled by ninth century refugees, lies some way over to the left of this trio of minarets – divided from the Kairaouine by the appropriately named **Bou Khareb** (The River Carrying Garbage), whose path is marked out by a series of minarets. **Djemma el Andalous**, the principal mosque of this quarter, is distinguished by a massive, tile-porched, monumental gateway, behind which you can make out the roofs enclosing its great courtyard.

Orientation aside, there is a definite magic if you're up here in the early evening or, best of all, at dawn. The sounds of the city, the stillness and the contained disorder below all seem to make manifest the mystical significance which Islam places on urban life as the most perfect expression of culture and society.

From the tombs you can enter Fes el Bali either through **Bab Guissa** (which leads to the Souk el Attarin), or by returning to **Bab Boujeloud**. There is a petit taxi stand by Bab Guissa.

Bus #18 from the Ville Nouvelle has a stop more or less outside Dar Batha in Place de l'Istiqlal, two minutes' walk below Bab Boujeloud. Here, and around the gate, you'll be pestered with offers of a **guide**. If you don't want one, be firm and explain that you're only going down to Bou Inania – which will probably be your first move anyway. Most hustlers give up after about fifty metres or so. To get a **petit taxi** in the Bab Boujeloud area, return to Place de l'Istiqlal or walk up to Place Baghdadi by the Boujeloud bus terminal.

Dar Batha

The **Dar Batha** (Mon, Wed–Sun 8.30am–4.30pm; closed Tues; 10dh) is worth a visit just for its courtyards and gardens, which provide a respite from the exhausting pace of the Medina. The entrance is 60m up the lane separating it from the *Hôtel Batha*.

The art and crafts collections concentrate on local artisan traditions. There are displays of **carved wood**, much of it rescued from the Misbahiya and other medersas; another room of **Middle Atlas carpets**; and examples of **zellij-work**, **calligraphy** and **embroidery**. Above all, it is the **pottery** rooms which stand out. The pieces, dating from the sixteenth century to the 1930s, are beautiful and stress the preservation of age-old techniques rather than innovation. This timeless quality is constantly asserted as you wander around Fes. There is no concept here of the "antique" – something is either new or it is old, and if the latter, its age could be anything from thirty years to three centuries. This same quality is occasionally reinforced at the museum itself when the work of local cooperatives is displayed for sale.

Into the Medina: Talâa Seghira and Talâa Kebira

Until you get to grips with Fes el Bali, it's useful to stick with **Bab Boujeloud** as a point of entry and reference. With its polychrome tiled facades – blue (the traditional colour of Fes) on the outside, facing the ramparts, and green (the colour of Islam) on the interior, facing into the Medina – it is a pretty unmistakeable landmark and once inside, things are initially straightforward. To the right of Bab Boujeloud, as you face it, is the ancient **water collectors** building, closed to visitors. This ingenious hydraulic complex is where water from the Oued Fes was collected and distributed, via a dense network of vaulted underground canals, to the houses, medersas and mosques of Fes el Bali.

Once through the gate you will find yourself in a small square (see map on p.259), flanked by the *Hôtel Cascade* on your right, the *Restaurant Kasbah* on your left and a couple of minarets almost directly ahead. Just beyond the *Hôtel Cascade*, an entrance straight ahead leads into the Kissaria Sejjarin, a small yard of craft shops. The road chicanes around sharply to the right, then the left, past a handful of small foodstalls where you can buy chunks of pastilla, the great Fassi delicacy of pigeon pie, then leads under an arch to begin its descent into the Medina.

This is **Talâa Seghira** (also known, in its French translation, as Rue du Petit Talâa), the lower of two lanes which run into the Medina in parallel for much of their length, traversed by dozens of alleys. Further down, the lane (renamed Rue Ben Safi) has little of specific interest bar the occasional craftshop until it loops up to rejoin the upper lane at the Souk el Attarin. One point of interest en route is the **Palais M'nebhi**, where the agreement for the France-Morocco protectorate was signed in 1912. The palace now operates as a venue for private functions, though you can usually look into its impressive hall or hunt in lanes behind to locate a courtyard with an impressive zellij fountain.

Backtrack and turn right fifty metres before the palais down Derb el Horra – look for a sign pointing to a craft shop of Fabrication de Percussion et de

Poterie – and after 150m you will find the **Dar Ba Mohammed Chergui** (in theory daily 8.30am–9pm; 10dh), the former house of the eighteenth-century pasha Mohammed Chergui. Sadly, the palace is suffering from neglect, semi-derelict on our last visit, with only a couple of rooms and the labyrinthine garden of star-shaped planters with delicate zellij tilework maintained. The lane continues to link up midway along Talâa Kebira (see p.272).

The upper lane, **Talâa Kebira** (Rue du Grand Talâa) is the major artery of the Medina, a route lined with craft shops and stalls which runs right through to the Kairaouine Mosque (albeit under different names). From Bab Boujeloud it is reached through the Kissaria Sejjarin or from an entrance opposite the *Hôtel Cascade*. The latter leads into one of the most atmospheric parts of the Medina, thick with the smoke of char-grilled kebabs, dappled by slats of light that slip through its thatched cover.

The Bou Inania medersa and clock

About a hundred metres further down the Talâa Kebira is one of the most brilliant of all the city's monuments, the **Medersa Bou Inania** (Mon–Thurs, Sat & Sun 8.30am–noon & 2–5pm, Fri 8–11am & 2–5pm, daily 9am–4pm during Ramadan, 10dh). If there is just one building you seek out in Fes – or, not to put too fine a point on it, in Morocco – this should be it. The most elaborate, extravagant and beautiful of all Merenid monuments, immaculate after renovation, it comes close to perfection In every aspect of its ornamentation, its dark cedar is faultlessly carved, the zellij tilework classic, and the stucco a revelation.

In addition, the medersa is the city's only building still in religious use that non-Muslims are permitted to enter. Of course, non-believers cannot enter the prayer hall, which is divided from the main body of the medersa by a small canal, but they can gaze across to it from the exquisite marble courtyard. Set somewhat apart from the other medersas of Fes, the Bou Inania was the last and grandest built by a Merenid sultan. It shares its name with the one in Meknes, which was completed (though not initiated) by the same patron, **Sultan Abou Inan** (1351–58). But the Fes version is infinitely more splendid. Its cost alone was legendary – Abou Inan is said to have thrown the accounts into the river on its completion because "a thing of beauty is beyond reckoning".

At first, Abou Inan doesn't seem the kind of sultan to have wanted a medersa – his mania for building aside, he was more noted for having 325 sons in ten years, deposing his father, and committing unusually atrocious murders. The *Ulema*, the religious leaders of the Kairaouine Mosque, certainly thought him an unlikely candidate and advised him to build his medersa on the city's garbage dump, on the basis that piety and good works can cure anything. Whether it was this or merely the desire for a lasting monument that inspired him, he set up the medersa as a rival to the Kairaouine itself and for a while it was the most important religious building in the city. A long campaign to have the announcement of the time of prayer transferred here failed in the face of the Kairaouine's powerful opposition, but the medersa was granted the status of a Grand Mosque – unique in Morocco – and retains the right to say the Friday *khotbeh* prayer.

The medersa

The basic **layout** of the medersa is quite simple – a single large courtyard flanked by two sizeable halls and opening onto an oratory – and is essentially the same design as that of the wealthier Fassi mansions. For its effect it relies on the mass of decoration and the light and space held within. You enter the

③

The function of Medersas

Medersas – student colleges and residence halls – were by no means unique to Fes. Indeed they originated in Khorassan in eastern Iran and gradually spread west through Baghdad and Cairo, where the Al Azhar Medersa was founded in 972 and became the most important teaching institution in the Muslim world. They seem to have reached Morocco under the Almohads, although the earliest ones still surviving in Fes are Merenid, dating from the early fourteenth century.

The word medersa means "place of study" and there may have been lectures delivered in some of the prayer halls. However, most medersas served as little more than dormitories, providing room and board to poor (male) students from the country-side, so that they could attend lessons at the mosques. In Fes, where students might attend the Kairaouine University for ten years or more, rooms were always in great demand and "key money" was often paid by the new occupant. Although medersas had largely disappeared from most of the Islamic world by the late Middle Ages, the majority of those in Fes remained in use right up into the 1950s. Since then, restoration work, partly funded by UNESCO, has made them more accessible, although several restored medersas are accommodating students again. This means visitors are sometimes welcome only at certain times; as restoration continues, accessibility is impossible to predict.

courtyard – the medersa's outstanding feature – through a stalactite-domed entrance chamber, a feature adapted from Andalusian architecture.

Off to each side of the courtyard are stairs to the upper storey, lined with student cells, and to the roof. This may still be closed but if you can go up, head straight for the roof to get an excellent (not to mention useful) overview of this part of the city. The cells, as is usual in medersas, are bare and monkish except for their windows and decorated ceilings.

In the courtyard, the **decoration**, startlingly well preserved, covers every possible surface. Perhaps most striking in terms of craftsmanship are the wood carving and joinery, an unrivalled example of the Moorish art of *laceria*, "the carpentry of knots". Cedar beams ring three sides of the courtyard and a sash of elegant black Kufic script wraps around four sides, dividing the zellij (ceramic tilework) from the stucco, thus adding a further dimension; unusually, it is largely a list of the properties whose incomes were given as an endowment, rather than the standard Koranic inscriptions. Abou Inan is bountifully praised amid the inscriptions and is credited with the title caliph on the foundation stone, a vainglorious claim to leadership of the Islamic world pursued by none of his successors.

The water clock, latrines and ablutions

More or less opposite the medersa entrance, just across Talâa Kebira, Bou Inania's property continued with an extraordinary **water clock**, built above the stalls in the road. This was removed over a decade ago for research and possible restoration; the woodwork has now been restored, but the metal parts have yet to be replaced. An enduring curiosity, it consisted of a row of thirteen windows and platforms, seven of which retained their original brass bowls. Nobody has yet been able to discover exactly how it functioned, though a contemporary account detailed how at every hour one of its windows would open, dropping a weight down into the respective bowl.

Clocks had great religious significance during the Middle Ages in establishing the time of prayer, and it seems probable that this one was bought by Abou Inan as part of his campaign to assert the medersa's pre-eminence; there are accounts of similar constructions in Tlemcen, just across the border in Algeria. Fassi conspiracy theories are told to account for its destruction – most of them revolve round the miscarriage of a Jewish woman passing below at the time of its striking and a Jewish sorcerer casting the evil eye on the whole device. The building to which the clock is fixed, once owned by a rabbi, is popularly known as "The House of the Magician".

Completing the medersa complex, opposite the main entrance and immediately adjacent to the clock, are the original **latrines and ablutions** (*wudu*) built for Friday worshippers. These have recently been restored but remain closed to the public at the time of writing. Predating their counterparts in the West by around four centuries, these "Turkish-style" toilets were very functional, flushed by impressive volumes of running water.

Further down Talâa Kebira

Making your way down the **Talâa Kebira**, you eventually emerge at the labyrinth of lanes round the Kairaouine Mosque and Zaouia Moulay Idriss II. It's a straightforward route to follow that is interesting less for specific sights than the accumulation of stimuli which barrage the senses. Diarist Anaïs Nin reacted in terms of odours: ". . . of excrement, saffron, leather being cured, sandalwood, olive oil being fried, nut oil so strong at first that you cannot swallow". To which should be added sound – the shouts of muleteers (*balak!*, meaning "look out!"), beggars' mantric aria, the bells of water vendors, the clang of metalsmiths' hammers and, above all, the sight of the people, seen in shafts of light filtered through the rush roofings which cover much of the Talâa's length.

Along the first stretch, heading down from the Bou Inania Medersa, you pass a number of old **fondouks**. Before the advent of French-style cafés in Morocco at the beginning of the twentieth century, the *fondouks* – or caravanserais as they were called in the East – formed the heart of social life outside the home. They provided rooms for traders and richer students, and frequently became centres of vice, intrigue and entertainment. There were once around two hundred in Fes el Bali and many of those that survive now serve as small factories or warehouses, often graced with beautiful fourteenth- and fifteenth-century decorations.

The first *fondouk* you pass, on your left at no. 49 Talâa Kebira, has become a workshop making drums, while one just past it at no. 59 is now private residences. More interesting is the large *fondouk* 100m beyond at no. 89, the *Qa'at Sman*, which was originally a **Merenid prison**, fitted out with solid colonnades and arches. Further down and across the street, no. 54 has also been turned into private homes, while another *fondouk*, on the left after another 100m, is used for curing animal skins (and smells awful).

An interesting feature of Talâa Kebira, which can also be found on a few other lanes of the Medina, like Derb el Keddane, is the **mzara**. Looking like inoperative fountains, these little fenced-off alcoves in the walls are points of reverence to Moulay Idriss for those who can't spare the time to go to his mausoleum further down the road.

Rue ech Cherabliyin

A little way beyond the last-mentioned *fondouk*, the street twists round to the right, past a small mosaic fountain, and changes name to become **Rue ech Cherabliyin**. Continuing past the **hammam** Bourous, the oldest hammam still in use in Fes (men only), you find yourself in a district of **leather stalls and shoemakers**. Fassis claim their local-made *babouches* (leather slippers) are the best in the country – naturally, this is hotly disputed in Tafraoute in the south. Unusually, Fes also produces sophisticated-looking grey and black pairs in addition to the classic yellow and white. If you want to buy a good pair, spend some time examining the different qualities and be prepared to bargain hard; prices will vary from 60dh to 600dh depending on quality – the very best are lightweight, made with *ziouani* leather (top-quality goatskin) and *metfoul* (with no stitching visible).

Passing through a gateway here, you will see ahead of you the green minaret of the **Cherabliyin** (Slippermakers) **mosque**, in the midst of the quarter. The mosque was endowed by the Merenid sultan Abou el Hassan, builder of the Chellah complex in Rabat. It has been substantially restored, though the minaret is original. If you've seen the Koutoubia in Marrakesh or the great Almohad monuments of Rabat, you'll recognize the familiar *darj w ktaf* motifs (see *Moroccan Architecture* colour section) of its decoration.

Souk el Attarin

Beyond the Cherabliyin Mosque, the street again changes name again to Rue de Tarafin then Souk Tiyalin, lined by more leather-workers and then a forgettable sequence of handicraft shops. Just past the *Palais des Merinides* restaurant (see p.292), lower arterial street Talâa Seghira links up at last (see pp.268–269), while further along Rue de Tarafin an arched gateway leads to **Souk el Attarin**, the "Souk of the Spice Vendors". This was the formal heart of the old city and its richest and most sophisticated shopping district. It was traditionally around the grand mosque of a city that the most expensive commodities were sold and kept, a pattern more or less maintained as you approach the Kairaouine. Spices are still sold here (closed evenings and Fri), alongside modern beauty products and perfumes, while in the web of little squares off to the left, you'll find all kinds of manufactured goods.

There are a few small cafés inside the spice souk and on the main street on the left is **Dar Saada**, a nineteenth-century mansion now housing an expensive restaurant (see p.291), opposite which is one entrance to Souk el Henna (see p.274). Just beyond the restaurant, this time on the right of the street, is the principal **kissaria**, or covered market, again dominated by textiles and modern goods and nothing very special – most of its character went up in smoke during a fire in the 1950s.

Reaching the end of Souk el Attarin you come to a **crossroads of lanes** lying slightly askew from the direction of the street. On your right (and ahead) are the walls of the **Kairaouine Mosque**; to your left, and entered a few yards up the lane, is the magnificent **Attarin medersa** (see p.276). Beforehand, however, take a look at the area below the Souk el Attarin, dominated as it has been for five centuries by the **shrine and zaouia of Moulay Idriss II**, the city's patron saint.

The Zaouia of Moulay Idriss II and around

The principal landmark south of the Souk el Attarin is the **Zaouia Moulay Idriss II**, one of the holiest buildings in the city. Although enclosed by a confusing web of lanes, it is not difficult to find: take the first lane on the right – Rue Mjadliyin – as soon as you have passed through the arch into the Attarin and you will find yourself in front of a wooden bar which marks the beginning of its *horm*, or sanctuary precinct. Until the French occupation of the city in 1911, this was as far as Christians, Jews or mules could go, and any Muslim who went beyond it had the right to claim asylum from prosecution or arrest. These days, non-Muslims are allowed to walk around the outside of the *zaouia*, and although they are not permitted to enter, it is possible to glimpse discreetly inside the shrine and even see the saint's tomb.

Passing to the right of the bar, and making your way around a narrow alley, you emerge on the far side of the *zaouia* at the **women's entrance**. Looking in from the doorway, the **tomb** of Moulay Idriss II is on the left amid a scene of intense and apparently high-baroque devotion all around. Women – Idriss's principal devotees – burn candles and incense here, then proceed around the corner of the precinct to touch or make offerings at a round brass grille that opens directly onto the tomb. A curious feature, common to many *zaouias* but rarely visible from outside, are the numerous European clocks – prestigious gifts and very popular in the nineteenth century, when they were shipped from Manchester by Fassi merchant families (their main export base for the cotton trade). Muslim visitors can enter to check out the mosaics on the walls and the stucco-work on the ceilings, as well as the original, beautifully carved wooden *minbar*. The zellij (tilework) motif repeated throughout the interior of the *zaouia* is based on a sixteen-pointed star, often doubled up to make 32 points.

There is no particular evidence that Moulay Idriss II was a very saintly *marabout*, but as the effective founder of Fes and the son of the founder of the Moroccan state, he has considerable *baraka*, the magical blessing that Moroccans invoke. Originally it was assumed that Idriss had been buried near Volubilis, like his father, but in 1308 an uncorrupted body was found on this spot and the cult was launched. Presumably, it was an immediate success, since in addition to his role as the city's patron saint, Idriss has an impressive roster of supplicants. This is the place to visit for poor strangers arriving in the city, for boys before being circumcized and for women wanting to facilitate childbirth. For some long-forgotten reason, Idriss is also the protector of Morocco's sweetmeat vendors. The shrine itself was rebuilt in the eighteenth century by Sultan Moulay Ismail – his only act of pious endowment in this city.

Round the other side of the *zaouia* is a tight network of lanes called the Kissaria, full of clothes shops. There is nothing especially exciting about it, but if you want a **fez** hat, this is the place to come – the best shop is a small, plain-looking stall next to the kissaria entrance by the southeast corner of Moulay Idriss's *zaouia*. The red cylindrical hat with its black tassel, more correctly known as a Fassi tarbouche, is not only worn and manufactured in Fes, but as far afield as Egypt and Syria. In the eighteenth and nineteenth centuries the fez became associated with the Ottoman Empire and in some places it was donned as a mark of support for the empire, a gesture which led to it being banned by Kemal Atatürk when he took power in Turkey and abolished the empire. The fez is also going out of fashion in its home town, and tends to be worn only by older men – most young men now prefer the Tunisian *chechia* or baseball caps.

Place en Nejjarin

Standing at the women's entrance to the *zaouia*, you'll see a lane off to the left – **Rue du Bab Moulay Ismail** – full of stalls selling candles and silverware for devotional offerings. Follow this around to the wooden bar, go under it (turning to the right), and then, keeping to your left, you should come out in the picturesque square of **Place en Nejjarin** (Carpenters' Square).

Here, a beautiful canopied fountain, the **Nejjarin Fountain**, best known of several mosaic fountains in the Medina, stands next to the imposing **Nejjarin Fondouk**, built at the same time in the early eighteenth century. The *fondouk* was in pretty bad shape but still used until a few years ago as a hostel for students at the nearby Kairaouine university. It has now been restored and opened to the public as a woodwork museum (daily 10am–5pm; 20dh). The museum's exhibits are not of great interest to a nonprofessional, bar perhaps the fourteenth- to eighteenth-century cedarwood friezes exhibited on the middle floor, and, on the top floor, a *rabab* (string instrument – see p.748) beautifully inlaid with mother-of-pearl. However, the interior of the building itself is worth the entrance fee, wonderfully restored after six years of work – a small exhibit on the roof terrace covers the renovation, where there's also a café and fine views over the city.

In the alleys that lead off the square, you'll find the **Nejjarin souk**, best located by the sound and smell (one of Morocco's finest) of its carpenters chiselling away at sweet-smelling cedarwood. They produce mainly stools and tables – three-legged so they don't wobble on uneven ground – along with implements for winding yarn, wooden storage boxes and coffins. You may also see them working on special ornamented tables for weddings, created with edges and used for parading the bride and groom at shoulder level – a Fassi custom.

A short distance from Place en Nejjarin are the nearby **tanneries of Sidi Moussa**, less well known than the famous ones near Place Seffarine (see p.280), but arguably just as interesting and certainly less visited. The best way to get a sense of the complex of vats and dye baths is to head to the inevitable craft-shop-cum-vantage-point (signposted by the Nejjarin *Fondouk* entrance) on 19 Derb Mina. Its terrace offers rewarding and relatively close-up views of the dyers' workshop below, and there's only moderate pressure to buy what are reasonably priced items.

South of Place en Nejjarin is the **Belghazi Museum**, tucked away in a maze of narrow lanes at 19 Rue Guerniz Derb el Ghorba (daily 10am–6.30pm; 40dh); to find it, trust the signs either around Place en Nejjarin, near the Karaouine Mosque or after the Banque Populaire on Talâa Seghira – keep your eyes peeled because, depending on where you start from, you will be following them for more than 300m. Housed in a traditonal riad house built in the seventeenth century, the museum explains the basic layout and features of this type of architecture.

At the end of the Nejjarin souk, a passage leads off to the right; at the end of that, turn left to get back to Souk el Attarin.

Souk el Henna

Just off Souk el Attarin via an arch opposite the *Dar Saada* restaurant – and also accessible from the passage that leads to the Place en Nejjarin (first left off it) 50m further down – is the **Souk el Henna**, a quiet, tree-shaded square adjoining what was once the largest madhouse in the Merenid empire, an imposing building now in use as a storehouse. Stalls here continue to sell henna and other traditional cosmetics such as *kohl* eyeliner (traditionally antimony but usually now lead sulphide, which is cheaper but also toxic), and lip reddener made from crushed poppy petals; on one side of the square there is a huge pair of scales used for weighing the larger deliveries. In addition several outlets here offer the more esoteric ingredients required for medical cures, aphrodisiacs and the odd magical spell. Get talking to the stallkeepers and you'll be shown an amazing collection of plant and animal (often insect) derivatives.

That said, they are in a minority because **pottery stalls** are gradually encroaching on this traditional pharmacological business. Cheap but often striking in design, the pieces include Fassi pots, which are usually blue and white or simple black on earthenware; those from Safi, the pottery most commonly exported from Morocco, distinguished by heavy green or blue glazes; and from Salé, often elaborate modern designs on a white glaze.

The Kairaouine Mosque

The **Djemaa el Kairaouine** – the Kairaouine Mosque – was the largest mosque in Morocco until the construction of the new Hassan II Mosque in Casablanca – and vies with Cairo's Al-Azhar for the title of world's oldest university. It remains today the fountainhead of the country's religious life, governing, for example, the timings of Ramadan and the other Islamic festivals. An old Fassi saying goes that all roads in Fes lead to the Kairaouine, a claim which retains some truth.

The mosque was founded in 857 by the daughter of a wealthy refugee from the city of Kairouan in Tunisia, but its present dimensions, with sixteen aisles and room for 20,000 worshippers, are essentially the product of tenth- and twelfth-century reconstructions: first by the great Caliph of Cordoba, Abd Er Rahman III, and later under the Almoravids.

For non-Muslims, who cannot enter the mosque's courts and prayer halls, the Kairaouine is a rather elusive sight. Even before current piecemeal restoration began, the building is so thoroughly enmeshed into the surrounding houses and shops that it is impossible to get any clear sense of its shape, and at most you can get only partial views of it from the adjoining rooftops or through the four great entrances to its main courtyard. Nobody seems to object to tourists gaping through the gates, though inevitably the centrepieces that would give order to all the separate parts – the main aisle and the main mihrab – remain hidden from the view of non-Muslims. The overall layout was inspired by the Great Mosque of Cordoba in Spain. The courtyard is open to the sky, with a large fountain at its centre and two smaller ones under porticoes at each side, added in the seventeenth century and based on originals in the Alhambra at Granada. In summer, this area serves as the main prayer area, with its own mihrab directly opposite the main entrance, from which it is easily visible. It is backed by a

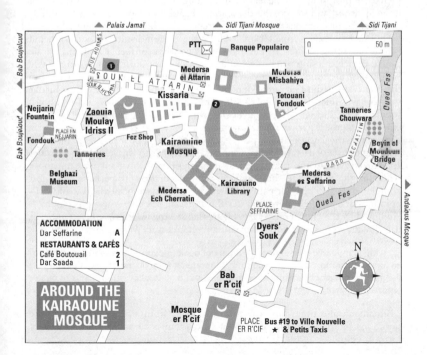

AROUND THE KAIRAOUINE MOSQUE

ACCOMMODATION
Dar Seffarine   A
RESTAURANTS & CAFÉS
Café Boutouail   2
Dar Saada   1

cedarwood screen decorated with kufic inscriptions and the hexagrams and six-pointed stars that are the Kairaouine's dominant zellij motif.

Beyond the cedarwood screen (and invisible to non-Muslims), is the main aisle of the inner prayer area, above which are a series of five domes decorated under the Almoravids with stucco stalactites and kufic calligraphy, each more elaborate than the last, leading to another and even more richly decorated mihrab. The main aisle is also hung with the mosque's most venerable brass lamps, the largest of which was added by the Almohads in the early thirteenth century. The beautiful wooden *minbar* is Almoravid, dating from 1144. The rest of the inner prayer area is covered by row upon row of round arches, built when the mosque was enlarged in 956, again inspired by those in the Great Mosque of Cordoba. Here, however, the arches are painted plain white, the ceiling is similarly plain and unadorned, and simple rush matting covers the floor.

The best way to avoid getting lost in the vicinity of the mosque is to try to keep it on one side as you circumnavigate; for example, on your right if you go clockwise. The best **point of reference** around the Kairaouine – and the building most worth visiting if the renovation under way at the time of writing is complete – is the Medersa el Attarin, whose entrance is at the far end of the Souk el Attarin, at the northwest corner of the Kairaouine Mosque. From here you can make your way around the mosque to a succession of other medersas and *fondouks*, picking up glimpses of the Kairaouine's interior as you go through some of its sixteen gates.

The Medersa el Attarin

After the Bou Inania, the **Medersa el Attarin** (before renovation daily 8.30am–5pm; 10dh) is the finest of the city's medieval colleges, graced by an incredible profusion and variety of patterning. For all the startling richness of its zellij, wood and stucco, the decoration retains an air of ease, and the building's elegant proportions are never threatened with being overwhelmed.

The medersa was completed in 1325 by the Merenid sultan, Abou Said, and is thus one of the earliest in Fes. Its general lightness of feel is achieved by the simple device of using pairs of symmetrical arches to join the pillars to a single weight-bearing lintel – a design repeated in the upper storeys and mirrored in the courtyard basin. The later Merenid design, as employed in the Bou Inania, was to have much heavier lintels (the timbers above the doors and windows) supported by shorter projecting beams; this produces a more solid, step-like effect, losing the Attarin's fluid movement.

However, the basic ground plan is more or less standard: an entrance hall opening onto a courtyard with a fountain, off which to the left are the latrines and directly ahead the prayer hall. If it has reopened, on your way in, stop a while in the **entrance hall**, whose zellij decoration is perhaps the most complex in Fes. Its circular pattern, based on an interlace of pentagons and five-pointed stars, perfectly demonstrates the intricate science – and philosophy – employed by the craftsmen. As Titus Burckhardt explains in *Moorish Art in Spain*, it is directly opposed to the pictorial representation in Western arts:

> . . . with its rhythmic repetitions, [it] does not seek to capture the eye to lead it into an imagined world, but, on the contrary, liberates it from all the pre-occupations of the mind. It does not transmit specific ideas, but a state of being, which is at once repose and inner rhythm.

Burckhardt also notes how the patterns radiate from a single point as a pure simile for the belief in the oneness of God, manifested as the centre of every form or being.

In the **courtyard** you'll notice a change in the zellij base to a combination of eight- and ten-pointed stars. This probably signifies the hand of a different *maallem* (master craftsman), most of whom had a single mathematical base which they worked and reworked with infinite variation on all commissions. In comparison with these outer rooms, the **prayer hall** itself is very bare and meditative, focusing on its mihrab (or prayer niche) flanked by marble pillars and lit by a series of small zellij-glass windows.

Around the second floor, usually out of bounds to visitors, are **cells** for over sixty students, and these operated as an annexe to the Kairaouine University until the 1950s. Budgett Meakin (in 1899) estimated that there were some 1500 students in the city's various medersas, something of an overestimate, perhaps, since it was based not on a count of the students, but on how many loaves of bread were prepared for them each day. Non-Muslims were not allowed into the medersas until the French undertook their repair at the beginning of the Protectorate, and were banned again (this time by the colonial authorities) when the Kairaouine students became active in the struggle for independence.

Views of the Kairaouine

If you can get onto it, one of the most complete possible **views of the Kairaouine Mosque** is available from the roof of the Medersa el Attarin. Unfortunately, it rarely seemed to be open to the public even before the renovation began, although you could try your luck with the *gardien* to let you on to it.

Looking out across the mosque's green roof tiles three **minarets** are visible. The square one on the left belongs to the Zaouia Moulay Idriss. To its right are the Kairaouine's Burj an-Naffara (Trumpeter's Tower) and original minaret. The latter, slightly thinner in its silhouette than usual – most minarets are built to an exact 5:1 (height:width) ratio – is the oldest Islamic monument in the city, built in the year 956. Below it, you can also make out a considerable section of the central courtyard of the mosque, the **sahn**.

For a closer glimpse of the *sahn* at ground level, the best vantage point is the Bab Wouroud near the entrance to the Medersa el Attarin: turn left as you step out of the medersa, then immediately left again and down the lane for a few yards. At the end of the courtyard, a pair of magnificent pavilions are visible – the last additions to the structure of the mosque, added by the Saadians in the sixteenth century. They are modelled on the Court of the Lions in Granada's Alhambra Palace, and may have been constructed by Spanish Muslim craftsmen.

Around the Kairaouine and Place Seffarine

A further angle onto the *sahn* of the Kairaouine is from the **Bab Khessa**, a gate near the end of this first stretch of the mosque wall. Opposite is another college, the semi-derelict **Misbahiya Medersa**, closed for renovation for several years and with precious little signs of progress. Peer through the boarding and it has some fine details, although much of its best wood carving is now displayed at the Dar Batha museum. The elegant central basin was brought over by the Saadians from Almería in Spain; the marble floor in which it is set level came from Italy. Surprisingly large, with courtyards (and two latrines/ablutions) at each corner, it was built a couple of years before Bou Inania, again by the Merenid sultan, Abou el Hassan.

Moving around the corner of the Kairaouine, you pass the **Tetouani fondouk** (aka the *Tastawniyine*), a well-preserved Merenid building where traders from Tetouan once stayed, now largely occupied by a carpet store. You can look inside without any obligation and you'll probably be shown the huge, ancient door lock which draws across its gateway.

A few doors down, past a much smaller *fondouk,* is the original **Palais de Fes**, a grand nineteenth-century mansion. Another entrance to the Kairaouine, essentially of Almoravid construction, is bang opposite the Palais de Fes; it is one of the ten which are opened only for Friday prayers. Notice the cedar panelling along the walls which guided the blind towards the mosque.

Place Seffarine, the Kairaouine Library and the Medersa es Seffarine

Further along, the alley pinches tighter before you emerge into a wedge-shaped square. This is **Place Seffarine**, almost wilfully picturesque with its metal-workers hammering away surrounded by immense iron and copper cauldrons for weddings and festivals, and a gnarled tree at its centre.

The tall, simple entrance in the whitewashed walls on your right leads into the **Kairaouine Library**. Established by the Kairouan refugees in the ninth century, then stocked by virtually the entire contents of Cordoba's medieval library, it once held the greatest collection of Islamic, mathematical and scholarly books outside Baghdad. That much of the library was lost or dissipated in the seventeenth century is a pointed marker of Fes's decline. Restored and in use again by scholars hunched over texts in the large study hall, it is one of the most important in the Arab world.

Despite the studious atmosphere of the library, the **university** here has been largely usurped by modern departments around Fes el Djedid and the Ville Nouvelle, and dispersed throughout Morocco. However, until recent decades it was the only source of Moroccan higher education. Entirely traditional in character, studies comprised courses on Koranic law, astrology, mathematics, logic, rhetoric and poetry – very much as the medieval universities of Europe. Teaching was informal; professors gave lectures in a corner of the mosque to a group of students who contrived to absorb the body of the professors' knowledge. Of course, study was an entirely male preserve.

△ Souks, Place Seffarine, Fes

Opposite the library is the **Medersa es Seffarine**, the earliest of these Fes colleges and the only medersa still used as a hostel for students studying at the Kairaouine, which means you can pop in for a look at any reasonable time with no charge. Built around 1285 – twenty years before the Attarin, 42 before the Bou Inania – the Seffarine is unlike all the other medersas in that it takes the exact form of a traditional Fassi house, with an arched balcony above its courtyard and still with suggestions of former grandeur in the lofty prayer hall. Elsewhere, the wandering vine and delicate ablutions pool give it a domestic air; in the far left-hand corner are washbasins and latrines.

Next door are two newer medersas housing students from the Lycée.

Onward from Place Seffarine

A chance for a breather after the intensity of the Medina, Place Seffarine is a good place to get your bearings before taking one of a number of onward routes. You can continue around the mosque by taking the first lane to the right as you leave the square to the south – **Sma't el Adoul** (The Street of the Notaries). The notaries, professional scribes, have gone out of business, but the route lets you peek through a number of gates into the Kairaouine's rush-matted and round-arched interior as you loop back to the Attarin medersa. Continue straight ahead instead of taking this turning and you enter souks specializing in **gold and silver jewellery** and used metal goods, especially ornate **pewter teapots**. As this route veers left downhill a right turn leads up to the **Medersa ech Cherratin** then eventually back to Zaouia Moulay Idriss.

The Medersa Ech Cherratin

Very different from the Seffarine (and indeed all the previous medersas), the **Medersa ech Cherratin** dates from 1670 and the reign of Moulay Rachid, founder of the Alaouite dynasty. The design represents a shift in scope and wealth to an essentially functional style, whereby the student cells are grouped around three corner courtyards and latrines/ablutions around the fourth.

The craftsmanship here represents a significant decline, although there is some impressive woodwork around the individual courtyards. Instead, the interest is as a rare surviving building from this period. That said, the medersa is being restored like the Karouine mosque it adjoins – before renovation became serious it was open to the public (daily 6am–8pm; 10dh).

Continuing down the lane beyond the entrance to the Medersa es Seffarine, swinging down the hill to the right, you reach **Rue des Teinturiers** (The Dyers' Souk: see the following section) and a bridge over the Oued Fes, below which you can leave the Medina by the square beside the **Mosque er R'cif**.

South and east of the Kairaouine: the dyers' souk and tanneries

The antidote to the medieval prettiness of the central souks and medersas is the region just below the Kairaouine – the dyers' and tanners' souks on which the city's commercial wealth from the tenth to the nineteenth century was founded and the prosaic often smelly underside of everything you've seen until now.

The dyers' souk

The **dyers' street** – **Souk Sabbighin** (or Rue des Teinturiers, in French) – is directly below the Seffarine Medersa. Continue past the medersa to your left, then turn right immediately before the bridge ahead. Short but bizarre, the souk is draped with fantastically coloured yarns and cloth drying in the heat.

Below, workers in grey overalls toil over ancient cauldrons of multicoloured dyes in an atmosphere that is thick and mysterious, and not a little disconcerting so close to one of the city's main entrances.

At the end of the dyers' souk you come to a second bridge, the humpbacked **Qantrat Sidi el Aouad**, almost disguised by the shops built on and around it. On the other side is the **Andalous quarter** (see p.282), and if you follow the main lane up to the left, Rue Sidi Youssef, you'll come out at the Andalous Mosque. Staying on the Kairaouine side of the river and taking the lane down to your right at the end of the souk you emerge at the open square by the R'cif Mosque; take buses #19, #29 or #45 – or a petit taxi – if you want to return to the Ville Nouvelle.

The tanneries Chouwara

For the main tanneries quarter – the **Souk Dabbaghin** – return to Place Seffarine and take the right-hand lane at the top of the square (the second lane on your left if you're coming from the Palais de Fes). This lane is known as **Derb Mechattin** (Combmakers' Lane), and runs more or less parallel to the river for 150m or so until it reaches a T-junction. The right-hand branch leads down to the river and **Beyin el Moudoun Bridge** – another approach to the Andalous Mosque. The left winds up at **Derb Chouwara** amid a maze of eighteenth-century streets for another 150 to 200m until you see the tanneries on your right. It sounds a convoluted route but is actually one that's plied constantly by tourists to visit the **tanneries Chouwara**, the biggest tanneries in Fes and the most striking sight in the Medina. The best time to visit is in the morning, when the tanneries are at their most active. You will be asked to pay a small fee – 10dh is usual – to one of the *gardiens*. Shops overlooking the tanneries will often invite you for a look in return for the opportunity to show you what they have for sale (generally at high prices) – the Terrasse de la Tannerie, just past the entrance to the main tanneries at 10 Hay Lablida Choura, sells leather goods and goes lighter on the heavy sales pressure. Remember that if you are enticed in by a promise that there's no obligation to buy, you are perfectly within your rights to hold the shop owner to that.

There is a compulsive fascination about the tanneries. Cascades of water pour through holes that were once the windows of houses, hundreds of skins lie spread out on the rooftops to dry, while amid the vats of dye and pigeon dung (used to treat the leather), an unbelievably gothic fantasy is enacted as tanners treat the skins. The rotation of colours in the honeycombed vats follows a traditional sequence – yellow (supposedly "saffron", in fact turmeric), red (poppy), blue (indigo), green (mint) and black (antimony) – although vegetable dyes have largely been replaced by chemicals, to the detriment of workers' health.

This innovation and the occasional rinsing machine aside, there can have been little change here since the sixteenth century, when Fes replaced Cordoba as the pre-eminent city of leather production. As befits such an ancient system, the ownership is also intricately feudal: the foremen run a hereditary guild and the workers pass down their specific jobs from generation to generation.

For all the stench and voyeurism involved, there is a kind of sensuous beauty about the tanneries. However, it is a guilty pleasure. Look across at the gallery of camera-touting foreigners snapping away and there are few more pointed exercises in the nature of comparative wealth. Like it or not, this is tourism at its most extreme.

North to Bab Guissa and the Palais Jamaï

This region – **north from Souk el Attarin** towards Bab Guissa and the *Palais Jamaï Hôtel* – is something of a tailpiece to the Kairaouine quarter of Fes el Bali. Few tourists bother to see what are more curiosities than monuments, but that is part of the area's appeal. The only monument as such hereabouts is the **Mosque of Sidi Tijani** north of the Attarin Medersa, the *zaouia* of an eighteenth-century *marabout* that is the traditional stopover for West African pilgrims en route to Mecca to do *hajj*. The interior is closed to all but Muslims, but you can look in when the doors are open for prayer. At other times, look on the exterior for a hole to the right of the eastern doorway, included for donations and above which there's a mirror with good bronzework. Past the mosque, the route loops around to reach the Chouwara tanneries from the north.

Alternatively you can cut west, then north through the alleys of the Sagha district towards Bab Guissa, then walk to the **Merenid Tombs**, an astounding spot to watch dusk descend over the Medina.

A route to Bab Guissa – and the jewellers' souk

Off **Souk el Attarin**, dozens of lanes climb north in the general direction of Bab Guissa, many of them blind alleys which send you scuttling back to retrace your steps. One of the more straightforward and interesting approaches is the first lane on your left inside the souk's entrance, about 15m before the Dar Saada restaurant. Initially it follows a marvellous produce market, crowded and intense and one of the most atmospheric spots of the Medina, then emerges at the small square of **Joutia**, the ancient fish and salt market.

Head for the top-right lane to leave the square and follow it for about 80m, then take the right fork and you reach **Place Sagha**, the **jewellers' quarter** which is flanked by the eighteenth-century **Fondouk Sagha** and a small inoperative fountain. The *fondouk* serves as a warehouse for neighbouring shops and if it's open you may be allowed to take a look at the elegant cedar woodwork and (heavily restored) stucco.

Backtracking to the main lane up from Joutia, you turn right and continue to **Place Achabin**, a herbalists' square where remedies are still sold. The **café-restaurants** in the area provide some of the best-value feeds in Fes el Bali, serving simple solid dishes or mint tea and fresh orange – good for a break while you ramble around the Attarin/Kairaouine area. Most are located in Rue Hormis.

A lane to the near-left off Place Achabin heads uphill through an area filled with carpenters' workshops and a *kissaria*, or covered market. Continue up the right fork beyond the kissaria towards Bab Guissa and you pass the **Fondouk Guissa** – or Fondouk el Ihoudi (the Jews' Fondouk) – on the left-hand side. This dates to the thirteenth century and was at the centre of the Jewish community until it was removed to the Mellah in Fes el Djedid. Today is is a warehouse for skins brought up from the tanneries.

Bab Guissa and the Hôtel Palais Jamaï

Bab Guissa and **Mosque Bab Guissa** at the top of the hill were rebuilt in the nineteenth century to replace a string of predecessors and are of little interest. The fountain adjoining the mosque, on the other hand, is one of the city's most spectacular pieces of mosaic work, albeit one that is neglected and used as an unofficial public toilet.

A quick right just before the gate threads to the **Sofitel Palais Jamaï**, a hotel whose luxury comes as quite a shock after the Medina below. The original palace – dwarfed by a 1970s hulk behind – was built towards the end of the 1800s by the Jamaï brothers, viziers to Sultan Moulay Hassan and effectively the most powerful men in Morocco. Fabulously rapacious, the brothers fell from power at the accession of Abdul Aziz in 1894 in a giddy whirl of intrigue. In *Morocco That Was*, Walter Harris records the brothers' ignominious fate – "perhaps the blackest page of Moulay Abdul Aziz's reign".

They were sent in fetters to Tetouan, and confined, chained and fettered, in a dungeon. In the course of time – and how long those ten years must have been – Hadj Amaati (The Elder) died. The governor of Tetouan was afraid to bury the body, lest he should be accused of having allowed his prisoner to escape. He wrote to the court for instructions. It was summer, and even the dungeon was hot. The answer did not come for eleven days, and all that time Si Mohammed remained chained to his brother's corpse! The brother survived. In 1908 he was released after fourteen years of incarceration, a hopeless, broken, ruined man. Everything he had possessed had been confiscated, his wives and children had died; the result of want and persecution. He emerged from his dark dungeon nearly blind, and lame from the cruel fetters he had worn. In his days of power he had been cruel, it is said – but what a price he paid!

A hint of former glory can be sensed in the palace gardens, a tranquil oasis of palms, and orange trees, box-hedge courtyards and fountains. A drink on the terrace of the *Al Mandar* bar merits the prices and if you can afford a splurge, the Moroccan cuisine of the *Al Fassia* restaurant in a palatial old salon is so exquisite that King Mohammed VI visits whenever he's in town. The palace quarters themselves function as suites and conference rooms, but if they're unoccupied by any passing president or state dignitary, you may be permitted a look – ask at reception if a porter can show you the "Royal Suites"; a tip will be expected.

From **Bab Guissa** you can take a short cut through the cemetery to the Merenid tombs or follow the road up and around. At **Bab Ferdaous**, just outside the *Palais Jamaï*, there's a petit taxi stand, and a stop for **bus #10** which runs to the train station in the Ville Nouvelle.

The Andalous Quarter

The eastern side of Fes el Bali across the **Bou Khareb** river is known as the Andalous Quarter. Crossing the river from the Kairaouine – now by the Tarrafine Bridge south of Place Seffarine or the Bein el Moudoun Bridge ("The Bridge Between the Cities") near the main tanneries – to the **Andalous bank** is hardly the adventure it once was. For the first three centuries of their existence, the two quarters were separate walled cities and the intense rivalry between them often erupted as factional strife. It still lingers enough to give each area a distinct identity, although since the thirteenth century this has been a somewhat one-sided affair: according to Fassis, the Andalousis had more beautiful women and braver soldiers, but the Kairaouinis have always had the money.

Whatever the truth of the tale, nearly all of the most famous Andalusian scholars and craftsmen lived and worked on the other side of the river and as a result the atmosphere in the quarter has a somewhat provincial character. Monuments are few and comparatively modest, and the streets are quieter and predominantly residential. As such, it can be a pleasant quarter to spend the early evening and get caught up in the rhythms of daily life in Fes el Bali. Most street trading here (and in the southern quarters of the Kairaouine side, too) revolves around daily necessities, providing a link between the "medieval" town and continuing urban life. And your relationship with the city changes accordingly as you cease to be a consuming tourist – there is a near-total absence of "guides" and hustlers.

As well as from the Kairaouine area, you can reach the Andalous Mosque from Place er R'cif (**bus**: #19, #29 or #45 from the Ville Nouvelle; #27 from Dar Batha) or more directly from Bab Ftouh (**bus**: #3 from Place de la Résistance (La Fiat), #12 from Bab Boujeloud or #18 from Place l'Istiqlal, by the Dar Batha).

The Medersa es Sahrija and Andalous Mosque

A goal for your wanderings in the Andalous Quarter, the **Medersa es Sahrija** (daily 8am–6pm; 10dh), is the quarter's most interesting monument and is generally rated the third finest medersa in the city after the Attarin and Bou Inania. Anywhere else but Fes it would be a major sight. But such is the brilliance of the more accessible monuments, it rarely receives the attention it deserves.

What makes it worth the visit is the considerable range and variety of the original decoration, looking better than ever after restoration. The zellij is among the oldest in the country, and the palmettes and pine cones of the cedarwood carving hark back to Almohad and Almoravid motifs. Built around 1321 by Sultan Abou el Hassan, it is slightly earlier than the Attarin and a more or less exact contemporary of the medersa in Meknes, which it resembles in many ways. Interestingly, the perspective of the central pool is such that the far end always appears to be shallowest regardless of which end you look into the water.

There is little to be seen of the nearby **Andalous Mosque** other than the monumental entrance gates because it is built at the highest point of the valley. Like the Kairaouine, it was founded in the late-ninth century and saw considerable enlargements under the Almoravids and Merenids. The Sahrija Medersa originally served as a dormitory annexe for those studying at the mosque's library and under its individual professors.

A last medersa, the **Medersa el Oued**, is across the street just west of the Sahrija. It also functions as a working mosque (Lranja Mosque), so only Muslims are allowed in.

Towards Bab Ftouh and the potters' quarter

Going south from the Andalous Mosque – out towards **Bab Ftouh** – you emerge into a kind of flea market: clothes sellers at first, then household and general goods and odds and ends. At the top of the hill, on the edge of a cemetery area, entertainers – storytellers and the occasional musician – sometimes perform to large audiences.

This region of the city, a strange no-man's-land of **cemeteries** and run-down houses, was once a leper colony, and is traditionally known as a quarter of necromancers, thieves, madmen and saints. At its heart, close by Bab Ftouh, is the whitewashed **koubba of Sidi Ali Ben Harazem**, a twelfth-century mystic who has been adopted as the patron saint of students and the mentally ill. The saint's moussem, held in the spring, is one of the city's most colourful; in past centuries it was often the cue for riots and popular insurrections. This also used to be the **potters' quarter**, although they have been moved east to Aïn Nokbi, some 2km along the Taza road and pinpointed for miles around by the columns of black smoke. If you're interested in the techniques – the moulding, drying and decorating of the pots and tiles – it's possible to look around the workshops of the Complexe Céramique du Maroc on the left of the road, where the designs and workmanship remain traditional despite the new premises.

At **Bab Ftouh** you can pick up a petit taxi to any part of town (the route up to the Merenid tombs has good views) or you can catch bus #18 back to the Ville Nouvelle, also with good views from Boulevard Allal el Fassi.

Fes el Djedid

Unlike Fes el Bali, whose development and growth seems to have been almost organic, **Fes el Djedid** – "Fes the New" – was a planned city, built by the Merenids at the beginning of their rule as a practical and symbolic seat of government. Work began around 1273 under the dynasty's second ruling sultan, Abou Youssef and finished after a feat of manic building within three years. The capital for much of its construction came from taxes levied on the Meknes olive presses, though the Jews were also taxed to build a new grand mosque, and the labour, at least in part, was supplied by Spanish Christian slaves.

The chronicles present the Merenids' decision to site their city some distance from Fes el Bali as a defence strategy, although it is hard to escape the conclusion that this was less against marauders than to safeguard the new dynasty against the Fassis themselves. It was not an extension for the people in any real sense, being occupied largely by the vast royal palace of **Dar el Makhzen** and a series of garrisons. This process continued with the addition of the **Mellah** – the Jewish

▲ Merenid Tombs (Route du Tour de Fes)   ▲ Merenid Tombs

Kasbah Cherarda

Bab Boujeloud

PTT

Bab Segma

VIEUX MECHOUAR

Dar Batha

Bab Dekkakine

AVENUE DES FRANÇAIS

Jardins de Boujeloud

Lycée

Jardins Beïda

RUE DE L'UNESCO

Makina

❶
Ⓐ

PETIT MECHOUAR

Grand Mosque

Bab Djeba

Moulay Abdallah Mosque

Bab Bou Jat

MOULAY ABDALLAH

GRANDE RUE DE FES DJEDID

FES EL DJEDID

ACCOMMODATION
Hôtel Glacier   **B**
Hôtel du Parc   **A**

Bab Semarine

RESTAURANT
Café-Restaurant la Noria   **1**

Royal Palace

RUE BOU KHESSISSAT

GRANDE RUE DES MERINIDES

MELLAH

N

AVENUE DE LA LIBERTÉ

PLACE DES ALAOUITES

Ⓑ Ibn Danan Synagogue

Habanim Synagogue

AVENUE DE LA

EL FASS

0   200 m

BOULEVARD ALLAL

FES EL DJEDID

▼ Ville Nouvelle

ghetto – at the beginning of the fourteenth century. Forced out of Fes el Bali after one of the periodic pogroms, the Jews provided an extra barrier (and scapegoat) between the sultan and his Muslim faithful, not to mention a source of ready income conveniently located by the palace gate.

Fes el Djedid's fortunes generally tracked those of the city. It was hugely prosperous under the Merenids and Wattasids, fell into decline under the Saadians, lapsed into virtual ruin during Moulay Ismail's long reign in Meknes, but revived with the commercial expansion of the nineteenth century – at which point the walls between the old and new cities were finally joined.

Yet the greatest change has come during the last century. As a "government city" under the French Protectorate, Fes el Djedid had no obvious role after the transfer of power to Rabat – a vacuum which the French filled by establishing a huge *quartier reservé* (red-light district) around the Grand Mosque. If that move was a blow for the city's identity, the immediate aftermath of independence in 1956 was a disaster. Concerned about their future status, their position made untenable by the Arab-Israeli war, the Mellah's 17,000 **Jewish population** emigrated to Israel, Paris or Casablanca virtually en masse. Today the future of the Jewish community in Fes is more fragile than ever. At the time of writing, there were just a handful of Jewish families in the Ville Nouvelle and virtually no young people: most had followed the custom of emigrating to study abroad and very few had returned. The Jewish Community Centre, Centre Maimonide, is at 21 Rue el Housslie el Khaddar (☎035 62 05 03; open Mon–Fri 8.30am–noon, 2.30–6pm), opposite the copse that faces the *Splendid Hôtel*. Rabbi Abraham Sabbagh (☎035 62 32 03), who officially accompanies predominantly Jewish visiting parties around the Mellah and other Jewish sites, is a mine of information about Jewish history in Fes; with his help or that of others at the centre, you could learn more about the community or old synagogues in Fes el Djedid (see pp.287–289).

You can reach Fes el Djedid in a ten-minute walk from **Bab Boujeloud** (the route outlined below) or from the Ville Nouvelle by walking – be aware that locals advise against taking the isolated route at night unless in large groups – or by taking a **bus** (#2 from Place de la Résistance, also called La Fiat) to **Place des Alaouites** and **Bab Semarine** beside the Mellah.

West from Boujeloud

The scale shifts as you walk to Fes el Djedid from Bab Boujeloud. Gone are the labyrinthine alleyways and souks of the Medina, to be replaced by a stretch of massive walls. Within them, on your left, are a series of gardens. the private **Jardins Beida**, behind the Lycée, then the public **Jardins de Boujeloud**, Jnane Sbil (daily 8am–6.30pm), their pools diverted from the Oued Fes. The latter have an entrance in the middle of Avenue des Français (or at the far end if that's closed) and are a vital lung for the old city. If everything gets too much, wander in, lounge on the grass and spend an hour or two at the tranquil **café-restaurant** (see p.291) by an old waterwheel, at their west corner.

The Petit Mechouar

Continuing west along Avenue des Français, you pass through a twin-arched gate to reach an enclosed square, the **Petit Mechouar**, once the focus of city life and a stage for the sort of snake charmers, jugglers and storytellers that are still found in Marrakesh's Djemaa el Fna. They were cleared out when the Mechouar was closed for repairs in the mid-1970s and have not been allowed back.

The Petit Mechouar has five exits. One of the two on its eastern side leads onto Avenue des Français and just south of that another double archway, **Bab**

Baghdadi, through which Fes el Djedid proper begins as main street the **Grande Rue** (see opposite). On the west flank of the Petit Mechouar, Bab Moulay Abdallah leads to the eponymous Moulay Abdallah quarter (see below), while to the south **Bab Mechouar** opens onto the grounds of the Royal Palace. From here, ordinary citizens would approach the palace to petition the king – the mechouar was where they would wait for admission.

To the right is the monumental **Bab Dekkakine** (Gate of the Benches), more correctly known as **Bab es Seba**, a Merenid structure which was the main approach to the Royal Palace and Fes el Bali until King Hassan realigned the site in 1967–71. It also served as a gallows for the Infante Ferdinand of Portugal, who was hanged here, head down, for four days in 1443. He had been captured during an unsuccessful raid on Tangier and was doomed after his country failed to raise the ransom. As a further, salutary warning, his corpse was cut down, stuffed and displayed beside the gate, where it remained for the next three decades.

The Vieux Mechouar

Once through the three great arches on the north side of the Petit Mechouar, you enter a much larger courtyard, the **Vieux Mechouar**. Laid out in the eighteenth century, this is flanked along the whole of one side by the **Makina**, an arms factory built by Italians in 1886 and today partially occupied by a rug factory and local clubs.

A smaller gate, the nineteenth-century **Bab Segma**, stands at the far end of the court, forcing you into an immediate turn as you leave the city through the Merenid outer gateway, whose twin octagonal towers slightly resemble the contemporary Chellah in Rabat.

If you are walking to the **Merenid tombs** from here, you can either turn sharp right and scramble up the hillside after the Borj Nord, or go straight ahead along the longer Route du Tour de Fes. The latter takes you past the huge **Kasbah Cherada**, a fort built by Sultan Moulay Rashid in 1670 to house – and keep at a distance – the Berber tribes of his garrison. The partially walled compound is now the site of a hospital, a school and an annexe of the Kairaouine University.

Quartier Moulay Abdallah and the souks

Back at the Petit Mechouar – and before turning through the double arch onto the Grande Rue de Fes el Djedid – a smaller gateway leads off to the right at the bottom of the square. This enters the old *quartier reservé* of **Moulay Abdallah**, home to the French cafés, dance halls and brothels. The prostitutes

---

The evening roost in Fes

For bird-watchers, the evening roost at Fes can make a spectacular sight. The performance begins with the frenzied activities of the resident starlings (including spotless starlings), but these are soon eclipsed by the overhead passage of dozens of little egrets, gracefully returning to their roost sites in the Middle Atlas and environs. The skies soon appear to swarm with literally thousands of alpine swifts, wheeling on crescent-shaped wings in search of insects for their young in nests in the city walls. To complete the spectacle, it is worth casting an eye along the rooftop silhouette as the light begins to fade. With a little perseverance it is possible to locate the characteristic body profiles of white storks on their rooftop nests along the perimeter walls which line Fes el Djedid.

were mostly young Berber girls, lured by the chance of a quick buck; most returned to their villages after they had earned enough to marry or keep their families. The quarter today has a slightly forlorn feel about it on a main street that twists to Fes el Djedid's 1276 **Grand Mosque**. West of this, on the way to Bab Bou Jat, is the **Moulay Abdallah Mausoleum**, a mosque and medersa complex which also contains the tombs of four sultans of the current Alaouite dynasty, from the eighteenth and twentieth centuries. To get here from the Grand Mosque follow the street to the west for 50m onto a small square with fountains; cross the square and take the right fork at the far end. You will see the minaret of the mausoleum shortly after, from which you can reach Bab Bou Jat by heading northwest. Bab Bou Jat leads on to the **Grand Mechouar**, a large open space that can also be entered from the main road to its north.

East of the Moulay Abdallah quarter and through the main gateway, the **Grand Rue** zigzags slightly before leading down to the Mellah. There are **souks**, mainly for textiles and produce, along the way but nothing much to detain you long. Just by the entrance, though, immediately to the left after you go through the arch, a narrow **lane** curves off into an attractive little area on the periphery of the Boujeloud gardens. There's an old **waterwheel** here which used to supply the gardens, and adjacent, the *Café-Restaurant la Noria* (see p.291).

The Mellah and Royal Palace

Once home to Jewish families, few of which remain, the **Mellah** has been largely resettled by poor Muslim emigrants from the countryside. Although the quarter's name came to be used for Jewish ghettos throughout Morocco, it originally applied only to this one in Fes, christened from the Arabic word for "salt" (*mellah*) perhaps in reference to the Fassi Jews' job of salting the heads of criminals before they were hung on the gates.

The enclosed and partly protected position of the Mellah fairly accurately represents the historically ambivalent position of Moroccan Jews. Arriving for the most part with compatriot Muslim refugees from Spain and Portugal, they were never fully accepted into the nation's life. Yet nor were they quite rejected as in other Arab countries. Inside the Mellah, they were under the direct protection of the sultan (or the local *caid*) and maintained their own laws and governors.

Whether the creation of a ghetto ensured the actual need for one is debatable. Certainly, it greatly benefited the reigning sultan, who could depend on Jewish loyalties and also manipulate the international trade and finance that they came to dominate in the nineteenth century. But despite their value to the sultan, even the richest Jews led extremely circumscribed lives. In Fes before the French Protectorate, no Jew was allowed to ride or even to wear shoes outside the Mellah, and they were severely restricted in their travels elsewhere.

Houses, synagogues and cemeteries

Since the Protectorate ended, whereupon many of Fes's poorer Jews left to take up an equally ambivalent place at the bottom of Israeli society (although this time above the Arabs), memories of their presence have faded rapidly. What remains are their eighteenth- and nineteenth-century **houses**, conspicuously un-Arabic, with their tiny windows and elaborate ironwork. Cramped even closer together than the houses in Fes el Bali, they are interestingly designed if you are offered a look inside.

The **Hebrew Cemetery** (Mon–Fri & Sun 7.30am–sunset, closing slightly earlier on Fri for Jewish Sabbath) lies east of the Place des Alaouites on the edge

△ The Hebrew Cemetery, Fes el Djedid

of the Mellah, its iron gate just up from a car park, between the Garage Sahar and the start of the flea market on the side street.

Inside, white, rounded gravestones extend to the edge of the valley of the Oued Zitoun (see Fes el Djedid map, p.284); 12,000 have names, around 600 are anonymous, mostly victims of a typhus epidemic in 1924, and none are more pitiful than the tiny tombs of children. Visitors leave a pebble on the gravestone to mark their visit or burn a candle in the recess provided. The most visited tombs are those of former chief rabbis, notably that of eighteenth-century Rabbi Yehuda ben Attar, which is covered in green and black mosaic tiles, and that of Lalla Solika Hatchouel, topped by three vase-like turrets. She caught the eye of Prince Moulay Abderrahman, who asked her to convert to Islam, so he could marry her. She refused and was promptly imprisoned and executed for the affront, and has since been venerated as a martyr.

At the northeast corner of the cemetery is the **Em Habanim Synagogue** (same hours as the cemetery), built in 1928 and until fairly recently in regular use for services and as a religious school. It has been restored by the Jewish-Moroccan Heritage Foundation and the Moroccan Ministry of Culture, and opened as a museum, containing a massive clutter of bric-a-brac, much of it only tangentially related to Fes's Jewish community. The centrepiece is a *huppa* (wedding canopy) and two bridal costumes, and the ark in the eastern wall, which marks the direction of prayer and contains a 300-year-old Torah scroll, is surmounted with beautiful stuccowork. There's also a room full of photographs, the most interesting of which are a series of postcards of Fes, including the Mellah, dating back to 1912.

During opening hours, there is always someone to show you round the cemetery and museum. There is no charge but a donation is expected. The *gardien* of the cemetery can also direct you to other synagogues on, or just off, the Grande Rue des Merenides. At one time there were 38, of which most are now shops or private residences. The oldest is the seventeenth-century **Ibn Danan Synagogue** down the side street off Grande Rue des Merenides by no. 86, reopened following restoration in 1999. The most striking feature of an otherwise unremarkable interior is its collection of brass and glass lamps and, just as many mosques are adjoined by a hammam, so this synagogue has a *mikve* (ritual bath) in its basement. Other synagogues in the quarter – nearly as old, but smaller – include the **El Fassayine Synagogue**, now a martial arts club, and the **Synagogue Mansano**, now a private residence. The only actively **working synagogues** are in the Ville Nouvelle; the Sadoun Synagogue is on Rue de Serbie (Rabbi Abraham Sabbagh), the Beth-El Synagogue on Rue Mohammed Kghat (Rabbi Jacob Pinto) and the Talmud Synagogue on Rue Zerktouni (Rabbi Ishoua Kesselassy).

The Royal Palace

At the far end of the Mellah's main street – Grand Rue des Merenides (or Grand Rue de Mellah) – you come into **Place des Alaouites**, fronted by the new ceremonial gateway to the **Royal Palace**. The palace, which has been constantly rebuilt and expanded over the centuries, is one of the most sumptuous complexes in Morocco, set amid vast gardens, with numerous pavilions and guest wings.

Even in the 1970s, it was possible to gain a permit to visit part of the palace grounds, which were described in Christopher Kininmonth's *Travellers' Guide* as "the finest single sight Morocco has to offer . . . many acres in size and of a beauty to take the breath away". Today, the palace complex is strictly off limits to all except official guests, though it was reputedly little used by Hassan II, the previous king, who divided most of his time between his palaces in Ifrane, Rabat and Marrakesh.

Eating and drinking

By day, there's little to keep you in the **Ville Nouvelle**, the new city established by Lyautey at the beginning of the Protectorate. Unlike Casa or Rabat, where the French adapted Moroccan forms to create their own showplaces, this is a pretty lacklustre European grid. However, the Ville Nouvelle is home to most of the faculties of the city's university, and is the city's business and commercial centre. If you want to talk with Fassis on any basis other than guide or tout to tourist, your best chance will be in the cafés here, and it's more likely that the students you meet are exactly that. The quarter is also the centre for most of the city's restaurants, cafés, bars, bookshops and other facilities.

Fes el Bali and **Fes el Djedid** are quieter at night, except during Ramadan (when shops and stalls stay open till two or three in the morning). As with Medina quarters throughout Morocco, they are bereft of bars, and with the exception of the smarter palace-restaurants, some of which only open for lunch, or those in hotels, their eating places are on the basic side.

Ville Nouvelle

The Ville Nouvelle has a decent selection of restaurants, though few justify the city's reputation as the home of Morocco's finest cuisine. Cafés, at least, are plentiful – and there are a few bars. The following are all on the map on pp.252–253.

Restaurants

Café-Restaurant al Mousaffir 47 Bd Mohammed V ☎035 62 00 19. This delicately tiled establishment, which prides itself on not depending on tour groups and agencies for its survival, offers a wide selection of meat and fish dishes, and local wines from 60dh to 180dh; menu 100dh. Daily 10am–3pm & 6pm–midnight. Moderate.

Café 24/24 Pl 16 Novembre at the corner of Rue Hamoun el Fetouaki (by *Hôtel Olympique*). A café-restaurant worthy of note for its claim to supply a meal (burgers, steak, brochettes) at any time of the day or night, so handy if you get the munchies in the wee hours. Open 24hr. Cheap.

Chez Vittorio 21 Rue du Nador, (Brahim Roudani), almost opposite the *Hôtel Central*.

Reliable place whose decor makes a decent stab at a trattoria and whose chef prepares a small menu of pizzas and pasta dishes. Daily noon–3pm & 6.30–11.30pm. Moderate.

Fish Friture 138 Bd Mohammed V, at the far end of a short passageway off the main street ☎035 94 06 99. Tasty fish dishes are the mainstay, though the paella must be one of the best you'll get this side of the Straits of Gibraltar. Service is courteous and quick, and there are meat dishes and omelettes as well as fish, with menus starting at 60dh. Daily 7am–11pm. Cheap to moderate.

Al Khozama 23 Av Mohammed es Slaoui. A small place adjacent to the *Hôtel du Maghreb*, good for a cheap eat of savoury crepes, brochettes and grills, fish and pizzas from 30dh. Daily 7am–11pm. Cheap.

Le Nautilus First floor of the *Hôtel de la Paix*, 44 Av Hassan II. A rather classy restaurant renowned for its fish and seafood. Mon–Sat noon–3pm & 7pm–midnight. Moderate to expensive.

Pizzeria Amine A couple of doors before the *Grand Hôtel*, near Pl Mohammed V. An excellent pizzeria with quick and friendly service. As well as pizzas to eat in or take away, it serves panini, sandwiches and hamburgers. Cheap.

Pizzeria Assouan 4 Av Allal Ben Abdallah. A pizzeria that also serves pasta and tajines, not to mention Chinese and Vietnamese if you fancy a change from European and North African food. An adjoining upmarket café and patisserie, also called *Assouan*, provides tea and gateaux after a visit to the Centre Artisanal. Daily 11am–3pm & 5pm–midnight. Moderate.

Restaurant la Cheminée 6 Av Lalla Asma (Rue Chenguit) on way to the train station ☎035 62 49

02. Small and friendly licensed restaurant specializing in meat grills. Daily 7pm–midnight. Moderate.

Restaurant Isla Blanca 32 Av Hassan II. "Atlas trout" and seafood specialities plus Italian dishes, a Moroccan menu at 130dh and à la carte from 200dh. Good wine list too. Daily noon–3pm & 6pm–1am. Moderate to expensive.

Restaurant Marrakesh 11 Rue Omar Amkhtar (between Av Mohammed V and *Hôtel Mounia*). Small, with a limited menu, but the food is well cooked and tasty. Daily 10am–midnight. Cheap.

Restaurant Pizzeria Mamia Between BMCI and BMCE on Pl de Florence ☎035 62 31 64. Comprehensive selection of Moroccan and international dishes, as well as omelettes and hamburgers for quicker snacks and takeaway pizzas. Central and popular with locals. Daily 11am–11pm. Moderate.

Restaurant Ten Years (formerly *Roi de la Bière*) 61 Av Mohammed V. A reasonable but not tremendously exciting restaurant whose set menu (70dh) includes options for couscous, lamb tajine with prunes or chicken tajine with lemon and olives. Also prepares so-so Italian dishes. Daily 10am–3pm & 6–11pm. Cheap.

Venezia Sandwich 7 Av el Houria, formerly Av de France, round the corner from the *Hôtel Amor*. A superior fast-food joint with grilled sausages, fish and *kefta*, plus a range of salads. Daily 11am–midnight. Cheap.

Zagora Restaurant 5 Bd Mohammed V ☎035 94 06 86. In a shopping mall off the main street, this classy place serves French dishes à la carte or a set menu (130dh) of Moroccan cuisine; service is immaculate and helpful. Daily noon–3pm & 6.30–11pm. Moderate.

Cafés and bars

Cafés and **patisseries** are scattered throughout the Ville Nouvelle, with some of the most popular around Place Mohammed V. The *Café de la Renaissance* was an old Foreign Legion hangout, now a popular gathering point for weekend football matches on TV; the *Patisserie Crystal*, opposite the tourist office, has a vintage 1960s vibe in a split-level interior ruled by uniformed waiters and is a good place for a quiet drink. Just up the road, the *Brasserie le Marignon*, screened by fig trees opposite the market, is a mite more stylish and suffers less traffic fumes. Another cluster of decent cafés can be found along Avenue Mohammed es Slaoui, Avenue Hassan II and Boulevard Mohammed V. Two of the most popular of these, are the *Café Floria*, a block north of the PTT on Avenue Hassan II, boasting excellent croissants (and very clean toilets), and the *Number One* in Avenue Lalla Asma, with mirror-tile decor dating from the disco era. The *New Peacock*, a few metres down the road at no. 29, is a rather elegant café which also serves savoury pastries. Good **ice creams** are to be had at *Black Berry*, 59 Bd Abdallah Chefchaouni, or *Gelatitalia* on Rue Libya, just off Rue el Houria near Place de Florence.

For **bars**, you have to look a little harder. Some might enjoy the seedy but cheap *Dalilla* at 17 Bd Mohammed V, decorated with futuristic metal panels and whose upstairs bar is a place for serious drinking. The *Astor*, by the cinema of the same name at 18 Av Mohammed es Slaoui, has a cellar bar that doubles up as the city's only **kosher restaurant**, while at the *Tivoli* just 50m to its east at no. 46, the back bar is more relaxed than the loud front bar. Around the corner, on Boulevard Mohammed V, the *Café Chope*, with its neon-illuminated interior, does decent bar snacks. *Le Progrès* at 21 Av Mohammed es Slaoui, with a pool table and a crowd of regulars, is a dark, boozy place which seems permanently stuck at 2am. Beyond these options (none likely to feel very comfortable for women, though the downstairs bar at the *Astor* should be all right because it's also a restaurant), you're left with the handful of **hotel bars**: in the *Ibis*, *de la Paix*, *Mounia*, *Lamdaghri*, *Splendid* and *Grand*, and the upmarket and rather dull *Royal Mirage Hôtel* and *Sofia*. Alternatively, an off-licence opposite *Hôtel Olympic* by the market sells a large selection of wine, beer plus some spirits.

Fes el Bali

Fes el Bali has possibilities for budget meals and, at greater cost, for sampling (relatively) traditional cuisine in some splendid old palaces. **Fes el Djedid** also has a few basic café-restaurants, although none worth specially recommending, save for *Café Restaurant la Noria* in the Jardins de Boujeloud (see p.292), a relaxing and usually quiet spot for a meal.

Café-restaurants and snacks

There are two main areas for **budget eating** in Fes el Bali: just inside Bab Boujeloud; and along Rue Hormis, which runs up from Souk el Attarin towards Bab Guissa in the north and has good hole-in-the-wall places. Other cheap café-restaurants are to be found near Bab Ftouh. If your money doesn't allow a full meal, you can get a range of **snacks** around Bab Boujeloud, including delicious chunks of pastilla from the stalls near the beginning of Talâa Seghira, *kefta* or brochettes around the corner on Talâa Kebira, and freshly made crisps (potato chips) from the corner opposite the Hammam Mernisi. The following are all marked on the map on p.259, unless otherwise stated.

Restaurant Basalah Rue Hormis almost opposite the Cine Hillal (Mon–Thurs & Sat–Sun noon–7pm, see map, pp.264–265). Simple but tasty Moroccan staples in a very popular but unsignposted joint. Cheap.

Restaurant des Jeunes Bab Boujeloud, below the *Hôtel Mauritania* (daily 8am–9pm). Basic brochettes and tajines, couscous and salads in an old-timer on the square, still there despite increasing competition. Menus at 40dh help, although double-check your bill for occasional service charges. Cheap.

Restaurant Kasbah Bab Boujeloud, opposite

Hôtel Cascade. The most appealing option in Bab Boujeloud due to two terraces with views and zellij-covered walls. The 70dh menu is acceptable if uninspiring, à la carte brochettes, *kefta* and pastilla are better. Daily 11.30am–midnight. Cheap.

Medina Café Bab Boujeloud, just up from SGMB bank. A more laid-back option in Bab Boujeloud, with the obligatory pastilla, veggie couscous and tajines, though a little more expensive too and not all dishes merit the extra few dirhams. Daily 11am–midnight. Cheap–moderate.

Restaurants

For a Fassi banquet in an appropriate palace setting, most restaurants charge around 150–200dh a head. Some places, particularly those in the heart of Fes el Bali, serve lunch only because they are tricky to find even in daylight. The following are all marked on the map on pp.264–265, unless otherwise stated.

Dar Saada 21 Rue el Attarin ⊕035 63 73 70. Tasty pastilla or (ordered a day in advance) *mechoui*, all in vast portions – two people could order one main dish and a plate of vegetables – in

another century-old palace whose fine carving was renewed after a fire in 1972. It is located in the Souk el Attarin and labelled on our map on p.275. Lunches only. Daily 8am–5.45pm. Expensive.

Palais de Fes 15 Makhfia er R'cif, off Pl er R'cif behind the Cinéma el Amal ☎035 76 15 90. A delicious pastilla and Medina views are the specialities of this highly regarded restaurant and carpet shop behind the cinema, both served on the best terrace in town. The menu features a choice of set menus and reservation is recommended if only to request a free car to pick you up from your hotel. Daily 10am–midnight. Expensive.

Palais des Merinides ☎035 63 40 28, 100m east of the Cherabliyin Mosque. Beautifully restored palatial decor inside and good views from the terrace out. There's a choice of themed set menus from 195dh – the Fassi menu features chicken pastilla (pigeon if ordered 24hr in advance) – or à la carte eating from around 230dh. Daily noon–11.30pm or the last customer. Expensive.

Restaurant al Fassia Sofitel Palais Jamaï Hôtel, Bab Guissa ☎035 63 43 31. A distinguished Moroccan cuisine restaurant, with a terrace overlooking the Medina, open evenings only, with a belly-dancing floorshow and musicians. There are few more stylish ways to spend an evening, but count on at least 400dh each, more if you order (24hr in advance) one of the specials such as mechoui or stuffed sea bass. Daily 8–11pm. Expensive. The hotel also has a fine French restaurant, Al Jounaina, and Mediterranean cuisine poolside at l'Oliveraie.

Restaurant al Firdaous 10 Rue Zenjifour, Bab Guissa – just down from the Hôtel Palais Jamaï ☎035 63 43 43. A rich merchant's house of the 1920s. Meals, with music and a floorshow (featuring mock weddings, fire dancing and belly-dancing) in the evenings. There's a choice here of several set menus costing from 290dh. Daily 8.30am–11.30pm. Expensive.

Restaurant Laanibra 61 Aïn Lkhail ☎035 74 10 09. A wonderful seventeenth-century palace that's home to a friendly restaurant, one that's more intimate than the grander Palais des Merinides nearby (see last column). Only open for lunch, it serves à la carte dishes and a choice of menus from 200dh. Find it west of the Palais de Merinides, signposted down a lane on the left. The entrance is under a little archway on the right – look for a heavy wooden door. Daily noon–4pm. Expensive.

Restaurant Palais Tijani 51–53 Derb Ben Chekroune, east of Sidi Ahmed Tijani Mosque ☎035 74 11 28. Less grandiose than the other palace-style eateries and without the floorshow, but better value for money. The emphasis here is on the food ("Fes seen through its cuisine", it advertises) and the atmosphere is more intimate than the other palais, the diners as likely to be Moroccan as foreign. Menus start at 120dh. Daily 11am–midnight. Moderate.

Cafés

There are plenty of small **cafés** all over the Medina, but few worthy of special mention. At the very heart of the Old City, at the northwest corner of the Kairaouine Mosque and opposite the Attarin Medersa, the Café Boutouail (Mon–Thurs & Sat–Sun 6am–10pm, Fri 6am–12.30pm & 7–9.30pm) does a good line in coffee and pastries – extra seating is hidden away upstairs – but its speciality is panachi, a mixture of milk, almond milk, and raisins, with a blob of ice cream on top for good measure. The Café Restaurant la Noria, by the water-wheel off the Boujeloud Gardens and accessible from Avenue des Français and Grande Rue des Merenides, is a good spot to have breakfast or stop for a coffee (daily 6.30am–10.30pm; ☎055 62 54 22; moderate to expensive).

Listings

Airlines Royal Air Maroc has an office at 54 Av Hassan II in the Ville Nouvelle (☎035 62 55 16; Mon–Thurs 8.30am–12.15pm & 2.30–7pm, Sat 8.30am–noon & 3–6pm).

Arabic Language Institute in Fes (ALIF) is at 2 Rue Ahmed Hiba (☎035 62 48 50, ⓦ www.alif-fes .com) near the youth hostel and the Hôtel Menzeh Zalagh. This American initiative offers a range of courses plus private/specialized lessons. There are three-week (60hr) and six-week (120hr) courses in Colloquial Moroccan Arabic or Modern Standard

Arabic at all levels. ALIF also has its own residence for students, or the option of a homestay with a Moroccan family. Since ALIF doubles as an English school, the American Language Center, it is also a good place to meet up with young Moroccans.

Banks Most banks are grouped along Bd Mohammed V. As always, the BMCE (branches at Pl Mohammed V, Pl Florence and Pl de l'Atlas) is best for exchange and handles Visa/Mastercard transactions, as well as traveller's cheques. There is a BMCI office a few metres beyond BMCE in

Shopping for crafts

Fes has a rightful reputation as the centre of Moroccan traditional crafts but if you're buying rather than looking, bear in mind that it also sees more tourists than almost anywhere except Marrakesh. However much you bargain, rugs and carpets will probably be cheaper in Meknes, Midelt or Azrou, and although the brass, leather and cloth here are the best you'll find, you will need plenty of energy, a good sense of humour and a lot of patience to get them at a reasonable price. Fassi dealers are expert hagglers – making you feel like an idiot for suggesting a ludicrously low price, jumping up out of their seats as if to push you out of the shop or lulling you with mint tea and elaborate displays.

This can be all good fun, but it requires confidence and some idea of what you're buying and how much you should be paying for it. For some guidelines on **quality**, look at the historic pieces in the **Dar Batha** museum – keeping in mind, of course, that exhibits here are the best available. If you want to check on the prices of more modest and modern artefacts, browse the shops along Avenue Mohammed V in the **Ville Nouvelle**, which have fairly fixed prices (and are easy to leave). Alternatively, visit the government-run and strictly fixed-price Centre Artisanal, out past the *Royal Mirage Hôtel Fes* on the left-hand side of Avenue Allal Ben Abdallah (☎035 62 10 07; daily 9am–12.30pm & 2.30–6.30pm). It's not the best in the country – the one in Marrakesh leaves it standing – but it's worth a visit, time permitting.

Two shops that deserve a quick look are Tissage Berbère (☎035 63 56 45) and Chez Hamidou (☎062 34 77 82), both on the way to the main tanneries on Derb Chouwara. Contrary to what you might expect in a street so frequently plied by tourists, these carpet and cushion shops, respectively, are generally overlooked by tour groups in the rush to visit the tanneries and continue with their itinerary. **Carpet** prices at Tissage Berbère are reasonable, and bartering with the informative owner enjoyable; to find it, follow the signs on Derb Chouwara near the main entrance to the tanneries. Chez Hamidou is a few metres before Tissage Berbère and consists of no more than a hole in the wall stacked with **cushion covers**, the speciality of the shop and reputedly the best in the Medina.

Pl Florence. Others include: Banque Populaire (Av Mohammed V), with quick service for currency and travellers' cheques and opposite the Royal Palace on Rue Bou Khessiscat, Fes el Djedid, with change facilities and cashpoint; Crédit du Maroc (Av Mohammed V) and SGMB (at the intersection of Rue el Houria and Rue Soudan). Banque Populaire also has three branches in Fes el Bali: halfway down Talâa Seghira, north of the Medersa el Attarin by Sidi Tijani, and on Rue Kaid Khammar by Bab Ftouh. SGMB by Bab Boujeloud is closed Friday afternoon but open Saturday morning. Banque Commercial du Maroc has branches at the far east end of Talâa Seghira and by Bab Semarine in Fes el Djedid (open Mon–Fri only). The SGMB just outside Bab Boujeloud opens Sat 10.15am–12.30pm, otherwise outside banking hours you can change money at Karima Voyages at 106 Bd Mohammed V (☎035 65 02 47; Mon–Sat 8.30am–12.30pm & 2.30–8pm, Sun 8.30am–12.30pm only). Most of the four- or five-star hotels also change money and cheques.

Bookshops The Librairie du Centre, 134 Bd Mohammed V (near the post office), has a good selection of books in French, including some poetry, and a small shelf of books in English, mostly classic novels.

Car rental Fes has quite a number of rental companies, though none are as cheap as the best deals in Casa. Call around the following, which all allow return delivery to a different centre: First Car, Av des FAR, (☎035 93 09 09), also at the *Royal Mirage Hôtel*; Avis, 50 Bd Abdallah Chefchaoueni (☎035 62 69 69, ✆avis.fes@iam.net.ma); Budget, 6 Rue Chenguit also called Av Lalla Asmae (☎035 94 00 92, ✆055 94 00 91); Europcar, 45 Av Hassan II (☎035 62 65 45, ✆022 31 03 60); Hertz, Bd Lalla Maryem, 1 Kissariat de la Foire (☎035 62 28 12); Tourvilles, 13 Bis Rue Mokhtar Soussi, off Bd Mohammed V (☎035 62 66 35, ✆reservation @tourvilles.net). First Car, Avis, Europcar, Budget and Hertz have desks at the airport.

Car repairs Mechanics can be found in the vicinity of the train station. The garage on Rue

Soudan (☏ 035 62 22 32) is good for Renault repairs.

Cinemas Several in the Ville Nouvelle show foreign films – mainly dubbed into French; the Empire, on Av Hassan II near Place de la Résistance, has showings at 3.20pm & 9pm.

Festivals and cultural events Since 1995, Fes has hosted a **Festival of World Sacred Music** (held in June), which has developed into the country's most interesting and inspiring cultural festival. Recent years have seen Sufi chanters from Azerbaijan, Tibetan dancers, dervishes from Kurdistan, a Javanese gamelan, and a Byzantine choir from Greece. Concerts take place at Pl Moulay Hassan north of the Mechouar by Bab Makina, at the Batha Museum, and sometimes further afield, such as amid the ruins of Volubilis. Details are available from the secretariat (☏ 035 74 05 35, ✉ info@fesfestival.com), or on the festival's website at ⊕ www.fesfestival.com. Major local festivals are the students' moussem of Sidi Harazem (held outside the city in Sidi Harazem at the end of April) and the Moulay Idriss II moussem (held in the city, in September). There are other moussems held locally – ask at the tourist office for details – and some good events a little further out, like the Fête des Cerises at Sefrou (see p.297) in June, and the Fête du Cheval at Tissa (see p.202) in September.

Two nearby spas: Moulay Yacoub and Sidi Harazem

The spa villages of **Moulay Yacoub** and **Sidi Harazem**, respectively 20km northwest and 15km southeast of Fes, are largely medicinal centres, offering cures for the afflicted as they have for centuries. They are local rather than tourist attractions, loved by Moroccan families, but Moulay Yacoub, in particular, makes a pleasant day-trip for a swim and hot bath. Either site can be reached by grand taxi from the *gare routière* to Moulay Yacoub (10dh) and from Bab Ftouh to Sidi Harazem (5dh). Buses to Moulay Yacoub run hourly from the main bus station and bus #28 runs to Sidi Harazem at least every hour from the stand 400m northeast of Place de la Résistance, on Boulevard Allal el Fassi.

Moulay Yacoub

The trip to **MOULAY YACOUB** takes you across pleasant, rolling countryside, with wonderful views south across the plain of Saïss to the Middle Atlas beyond. Legend relates that the village was named either after Sultan Moulay Yacoub Ben Masour – cured after his first bath, they say – or from the corruption of Aquae Juba, the spring of a local berber king, Juba, who was envious of Roman hot baths. Either way, the hillside village's fame is founded on its 36–40°C sulphur-rich spa waters. Cars and taxis park at the top of the village, leaving you to descend flights of steps past stalls whose bathing goods add a chirpy resort atmosphere. The swimming pool (6am–10pm; separate areas for men and women; 7dh), as well as most of the hotels, is near a square halfway down the hill. The old thermal baths (or *baignoires or anciennes thermes*; 6am–10pm) are a short walk from the pool, and have a more medicinal purpose – albeit fairly basic to western eyes – and are usually busy, but you can enjoy a hot bath on your own (*baignoire individuelle*; 15dh for 30min) or with a friend (25dh for 30 min). Massage and Jacuzzi are also available for 35dh each or masseurs in the thermal baths charge around 15–20dh for a hammam-style scrub. Beware that both facilities – baths and pool – are only cleaned once a week on Tuesday, when they close at 6pm, so you're probably best not swimming that afternoon.

Continue down the steps to the foot of the hill and you reach the newer and more upmarket baths of the Thermes de Moulay Yacoub (☏ 35 69 40 64, ✉ accueil @sothermy.ma), a spa for serious medical treatment – mostly rheumatism and respiratory problems – and serious self-indulgence that is as exclusive as it gets in Morocco. Not surprisingly, prices rise accordingly: a 30-minute dip in the pool starts at 90dh, albeit including a bathrobe, towel and cloakroom. The main reason to come, however, is that the main pool is mixed – a rare chance for male/female couples to bathe together. Prices for the various massages, manicures, pedicures and facials average 150dh.

Among the selection of generally good hotels in town – most located just above or along the steps that go downhill – are the following:

Cultural events in the city are relatively frequent, both Moroccan- and French-sponsored. Again, ask for details at the tourist office, where you can buy tickets, or at the Institut Français (℡035 62 39 21) on Rue Loukili. A *Son et Lumière* show is presented from March to October; daily except Sun, 7.15pm (9.30pm May–Sept); the show lasts 45min and costs 100dh. The show is in Arabic, English, French or Spanish – check that it will be in a language you understand on the night you intend to go. The audience views the show from the Borj Sud, which is south of Bd Allal el Fassi, the broad avenue which links the Ville Nouvelle with Bab el Djedid and Bab Ftouh, between which a track leads uphill alongside the Bab Ftouh cemetery (see Fes el Bali map, pp.264–265).

Golf The Fes Royal Golf Club, 15km from Fes on the Route d'Ifrane (℡035 66 52 10), was designed by Cabell B Robinson and has an 18-hole, par 72 course.

Hammams Hammam Sidi Azouz is on Talâa Seghira opposite *Hôtel Lamrani*; hours are women 1–10pm, men 10pm–noon, with Fri–Sun the busiest days. If you are unfamiliar with the routine, and since the staff may well speak Arabic and Berber only, it is best, especially for women, to ask someone at your hotel to escort you. The oldest hammam in Fes (Hammam Kantarte Bourous – for

Hôtel Aleonard ℡035 69 40 98. At the top of steps, with all the mod cons of a newly built hotel. Friendly too. **⑤**

Hôtel Fadoua ℡035 69 40 50. Bright, sunny rooms are on the small side, but a location opposite the public baths is excellent. **①**

Hôtel Hanae ℡055 69 41 91. Not quite as modern as the nearby Aleonard, but clean and comfy rooms, all with a/c. **④**

Grand Hôtel ℡035 69 41 60. A cheapie just past the public baths, with basic but clean en suites. Arabic only spoken. **③**

Hôtel Moulay Yacoub ℡035 69 40 35, ⓦ www.sogatour.com. The smartest place in town, by the turn off to the village, has bright, spacious rooms that face the hills and marble floors in its en-suite bathrooms. Bungalows for four to six people are also available. **⑥**

For coffee and cake, try the *Pâtisserie Glacier* below the *Hôtel Aleonard*; it also serves luscious fruit cocktails and smoothies.

Sidi Harazem

The eucalyptus-covered shrine of **SIDI HARAZEM** was established by Sultan Moulay er Rachid in the seventeenth century, though the centre owes its current fame to its bestselling mineral water, said to treat kidney conditions and high cholesterol as well as arthritis. At the weekend Fassi families come to stock up on the sodium- and calcium-rich water. Around the central fountain, the hub of activity of the spa, you give a few dirhams to any of the attendants who are authorized to dispense the venerated liquid – the fountain is chained all-round and you are not allowed to step inside. Innumerable stalls around the square sell plastic containers for those who have left their own behind.

The other focal point of a visit is the Piscine du Palmier (daily 8am–5pm; 17dh). There are two pools, one for men and women (although in practice only men use it) and another smaller one for women only, cleverly out of sight but still in the open air. Both pools are clean and well maintained, particularly the latter, and there's a café by the pool, often animated in the evening by local bands.

For anyone not seeking a cure or a swim, the reason to visit is for one of the biggest moussems in the Fes region, held in March/April.

The refurbished four-star *Sidi Harazem* **hotel** (℡035 69 01 35, ℻035 69 01 36, ⓦ www.sogatour.com **⑥**) of the Sogatour group offers bright, tastefully decorated rooms, plus a private pool and garden. Just below it, apartment blocks (℡035 69 00 47; **④**) also run by Sogatour – known locally as the *pension* – are fairly spartan, with squat toilets and cold showers, offer very good value; they sleep up to six people and are fitted with cooker, fridge and a private lawned area.

For a meal, there's the pricey hotel restaurant or you could walk 600m to the grill complex beyond the hotel; follow the charcoal smoke and smell of brochettes.

men only) is on Rue ech Cherabliyin. Don't forget to take your towel, soap, shampoo and swimsuit (or change of underwear).

Internet access In the Ville Nouvelle there is Space-Cyber at 12 Av Hassan II (second floor), next to Café Riad (daily 8.30am–midnight), and Cybercafé Oumnia (daily 9am–9pm) above the café behind the market. CyberNet, at 68 Rue Bou Khessissat, is a handy place for Internet access in Fes el Djedid – halfway down the road from Bab Semarine to the Royal Palace, on the left (daily 8am–9pm). Bathanet on Derb Douh, between Cinéma Boujeloud and Pl de l'Istiqlal, is conveniently located near the budget hotels in Fes el Bali (daily 10am–midnight).

Laundry In the Ville Nouvelle, try Pressing Dallas, 44 Rue Asilah near *Hôtel Mounia*; near Bab Boujeloud, there's a laundry, Blanchisserie Batha, at the northern end of Place de l'Istiqlal facing the local post office (daily 7.30am–10pm).

Left luggage/baggage A deposit is available at the bus and train stations.

Newspapers Some British dailies are usually on sale at newsagents stalls on Av Mohammed V (for example on the corner of Rue Abdelkrim el Khattabi), otherwise try the newsagent at 16 Pl 16 Novembre for the *USA Today* and the British *Guardian Weekly*, as well as *Time*, *Newsweek* and *The Economist*; the *International Herald Tribune* is sometimes sold at 34 Av Hassan II.

Petrol stations Several are to be found around Pl de l'Atlas, near the beginning of the road to Sefrou and Midelt, and off Bd Abdallah Chefchaoueni.

Pharmacies There are numerous pharmacies throughout the Ville Nouvelle, one just outside Bab Boujeloud, another at the northern end of Pl de l'Istiqlal, and another on Grande Rue des Merenides in the Mellah. Any of these will display the rota of night services for the week. The Pharmacie du Municipalité, just up from Place de la Résistance, on Av Moulay Youssef, stays open all night.

Police There are *commissariats* by the post office on Av Mohammed V and off Pl de l'Istiqlal on the road to the right of the post office that leads to Cinéma Boujeloud. The police emergency number is ☎19.

Post office The main PTT is on the corner of Bd Mohammed V/Av Hassan II in the Ville Nouvelle (Mon–Fri 8.30am–6.30pm, Sat 8–11am); the **poste restante** section is inside the main building; the **phones section** (daily 8.30am–9pm) has a separate side entrance when the rest is closed. Just outside Fes el Bali there is a PTT at Pl de l'Istiqlal; there are also branch post offices on Pl des Alouites on the edge of the Mellah, and in the Medina just north of Medersa el Attarin.

Swimming pools There is a municipal pool (open mid-June to mid-Sept) on Av des Sports, just west of the train station. The upmarket *Hôtel Menzeh Zalagh* (see p.262) has an open-air pool, although at 80dh for nonresidents, this is a little pricey.

Moving on

Buses for most destinations leave from the main **bus station** or *gare routière* just north of Bab Mahrouk, between Kasbah Cherada and Borj Nord. Most CTM services now leave from here too before calling at the CTM station in the Ville Nouvelle, on the corner of Rue Tetouan and Avenue Mohammed V. For buses for Nador/Melilla, ONCF/Supratours run connecting buses from Taorirt on the Oujda line; you can buy tickets straight through.

Like buses, **grands taxis** mostly operate from the *gare routière*. Exceptions are those for **Immouzer**, **Ifrane** and **Azrou** (and sometimes Marrakesh), which use a terminal across from the *Hôtel Mounia*, on Boulevard Mohammed V, and those to **Sefrou** (and sometimes Immouzer), which use a rank 100m southeast of Place de la Résistance (also called La Fiat). **Meknes** grands taxis depart from outside the train station. Grands taxis based at Bab Ftouh run to **Sidi Harazem**, **Taza**, **Taounate** and other points east and north of Fes. Leaving Fes by bus for the south, note that convenient **night buses** cover most routes – to Marrakesh and Rissani, for example.

Fes's tiny **airport** is 15km south of the city, at Saïs, off the N8 to Immouzer (☎035 62 47 12, ☏035 65 21 61), and is most easily reached by chartering a grand taxi from the *gare routière*, though you can also get to it on bus #16 from the train station.

The Middle Atlas

Most people heading south from Fes take a bus straight to either **Marrakesh** or to **Er Rachidia**, the start of the great desert and *ksour* routes. However, both journeys involve at least ten to twelve hours of continuous travel, which in summer is reason enough to stop off along the way.

A second, better reason if you have the time (or, better still, a car), is to get off the well-trodden tourist routes and into the mountains. Covered in forests of oak, cork and giant cedar, the **Middle Atlas** is a beautiful and relatively little-visited region. The brown-black tents of nomadic Berber encampments immediately establish a cultural shift away from the European north, the plateaux are pockmarked by dark volcanic lakes, and, at **Ouzoud** and **Oum er Rbia**, there are some magnificent waterfalls. If you just want a day-trip from Fes, the Middle Atlas is most easily accessible at **Sefrou**, a relaxed market town, 28km southeast of Fes.

On the practical front, **bus** travellers may find a few problems stopping en route between Fes and Marrakesh, as many of the buses arrive and depart full. The solution is flexibility. Take the occasional grand taxi or stop for a night to catch an early bus and you will never be stuck for long. This is especially true of the Fes–Azrou–Midelt–Er Rachidia route, where buses are plentiful. This is the old *Trek es Sultan*, or Royal Road, an ancient trading route that once carried salt, slaves and other commodities with caravans of camels across the desert from West Africa.

Sefrou and around

The fate of **SEFROU** is to be just 28km south of Fes. Anywhere else in Morocco, this ancient walled town at the foothills of the Middle Atlas would receive a steady flow of visitors, just as it did when it served as the first stop on the caravan routes to the Tafilalet; until the Protectorate, it marked the mountain limits of the Bled el Makhzen – the governed lands. Instead, the pull of the larger city leaves Sefrou, once known as the Jardin du Maroc, virtually ignored by most tourists, a source of some local resentment and the reason, perhaps, for the extreme persistence of the few hustlers here.

To add insult to injury, Sefrou actually predates Fes as a city and might well have grown into a regional or imperial capital if Moulay Idriss I and II had not acted differently. Into the 1950s, at least a third of the then 18,000 population were Jews. There seems to have been a Jewish-Berber population here long before the coming of Islam and, although most converted, a large number of Jews from the south settled again in the town under the Merenids. Today, only a handful remain, most having left for Israel, Paris or Casa.

From Fes, the town can be reached in less than an hour by **bus** or **grand taxi**; the former leave from Bab Ftouh in Fes el Bali (9dh) and the latter from just below Place de la Résistance (or "La Fiat") in the Ville Nouvelle. Situated some 880m above sea level, it makes a cool day-trip in summer, and in winter is at times covered in snow, and there are decent walks in the area, which you'll usually have to yourself.

The town draws sizeable crowds during the annual **Fête des Cerises**, a cherry festival in June, usually over the last weekend, with music, folklore and

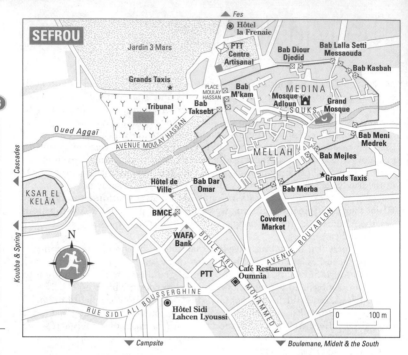

sports events and whose climax is the crowning of the Cherry Queen on Saturday evening; and during the August **Moussem of Sidi Lahcen Lyoussi**, a seventeenth-century saint from neighbouring Azzaba, 13km to the east of Sefrou – his *zaouia* and tomb in the Medina on the north bank of the Oued Aggaï.

The Town

Although Sefrou is not a large place – the population today is only 40,000 – its layout is a little confusing. If you are coming in by bus or grand taxi, you are usually dropped in the landscaped **Place Moulay Hassan**, off which is **Bab M'kam**, the main entrance to the Medina. On the other side of Place Moulay Hassan, the old cemetery has been transformed into the **Jardin 3 Mars**, a rather scruffy park whose southernmost section contains the massive modern Tribunal (High Court) building.

Beyond the square, the road and some of the buses continue round a loop above the town and valley, crossing the **Oued Aggaï** and straightening out onto **Boulevard Mohammed V**, the principal street of the modest Ville Nouvelle.

The Medina

In comparison with Fes, the Medina of Sefrou inevitably feels rather low-key. However, it is equally well preserved on its modest scale – a pocket-size version of Fes el Bali that is far less intimidating for many visitors – and the untouristy atmosphere makes it a pleasant place to explore by instinct. The **Thursday souk**, for example, remains a largely local affair, drawing Berbers from neighbouring villages to sell garden produce and buy basic goods. Western products and clothing are gradually replacing local ones in the stalls of the Medina, but you'll still see traditional trades such as ironmongery and carpentry being plied in a couple of lanes beyond the Grand Mosque (see below).

Enclosed by its nineteenth-century ramparts and split in two by the river, the Medina isn't difficult to find your way around, not least because the river provides a handy reference if you get lost. Coming from the P11 on Boulevard Mohammed V, you can take a short cut down on the right of the road by way of **Bab Merba**, straight into the Mellah; if you were then to turn left, you would eventually wind to Place Moulay Hassan by way of the small **Mosque Adloun** and the nearby **Hammam Adloun**, notable by its unique chimney. You would arrive on the *place* through a new, small gate, **Bab Taksebt**.

The most straightforward approach, though, is through **Bab M'Kam**, the old main gate on the *place*. Beyond Bab M'Kam, the main street of the old Arab town winds clockwise down to the river, passing through a region of **souks**. When you reach the first bridge across the river you will find the Mosque Adloun on your left. Following the north bank of the river east from here, you soon emerge at the **Grand Mosque,** with its domed minaret. A second bridge here lets you cross the river and head right (southwest) for Bab el Merba, or left (southeast) to come out of the Medina via Bab Mejles. Or you could explore the more traditional souks behind the Grand Mosque – walk clockwise around the mosque, negotiating some convoluted alleys, to end up on the other side. Here, a third bridge offers a good view of the Grand Mosque's southern wall. Heading east after crossing this bridge eventually takes you out of the Medina via Bab Meni Medrek. Alternatively, if you stay on the north bank of the river and continue straight on, you will pass a lively fresh produce market, where locals do their shopping. The market stretches all the way to the northern gate of Bab Lalla Setti Messaouda.

The Mellah

A dark, cramped conglomeration of tall, shuttered houses and tunnel-like streets, the **Mellah** lies across the river from the Grand Mosque. Even though many of the Jews only left for Israel after the June 1967 Six-Day War and the population is now largely Muslim, the district still seems distinct.

The Sefrou Jewish community had become quite well-off during the French Protectorate thanks to the good agricultural land they owned in the environs. But living conditions must have been pretty miserable when most of their houses were built in the mid-nineteenth century. Edith Wharton, visiting in 1917, found "ragged figures . . . in black gabardines and skull-caps" living one family to a room in most of the mansions, and the alleys were lit even at midday by oil lamps. "No wonder," she concluded sanctimoniously, "[that] the babies of the Moroccan ghettos are nursed on date-brandy, and their elders doze away to death under its consoling spell."

From the Mellah, you can return, still clockwise, to the *place* by way of the Mosque Adloun (see above).

Into the hills

High enough into the Middle Atlas to avoid the suffocating dry heat of summer, Sefrou is a good base for some modest walking. Dozens of **springs** emerge in the hills above the town and a few waterfalls are active for part of the year.

For a relatively easy target, take the road up behind the Ville Nouvelle post office on Boulevard Mohammed V, which will divide into a fork after about a kilometre. The right branch goes up past the campsite; the left leads to a small, deserted, French military post, known as the **Prioux**, and to the **koubba** of one

Sidi Bou Ali Serghin. The views from around here are exciting: in winter, the snow-capped Mischliffen; in summer, the cedars and holm oaks cresting the ridges to infinity.

You can also reach the *koubba* and French fort on a road that forks left in front of the fortified *kelâa* (settlement), quite interesting in itself and reached on **Rue de la Kelâa** west of the sharp bend in the main road across the **Oued Aggaï**. However, go right in front of the *kelâa* and you'll get to a junction signposted "Cascades". From here a single-lane tarmac road continues up beside the river, flanked by some expensive holiday homes. After a short distance you will pass a small hydroelectric power station on your right, then 250m beyond, below imposing rocky outcrops, are the waterfalls, at their best in spring. Flash floods regularly wash away the path here, so repair work may bar your access to a pool beneath for a paddle.

Practicalities

One reason for Sefrou's lack of visitors may be its lack of **hotels** – just two at the last count. First choice is *Hôtel Sidi Lahcen Lyoussi* (☎035 68 34 28; ❸), which has an alpine chalet feel in en-suite rooms with balconies (grubby bathrooms and often no hot water, though), an erratic restaurant, a popular cellar bar and a swimming pool – sometimes even full of water in summer (20dh non residents). Its rival, *Hôtel la Frenaie* (no phone; ❷) is on the left as you enter Sefrou, with seven functional rooms and shared facilities above a bar which prepares snacks. Alternatively, a couple of kilometres to the west of town, there is a well-maintained **municipal campsite** (☎035 66 00 01), with plenty of shade, hot showers and friendly staff.

For **food and drink**, in addition to the hotels, hole-in-the-wall grills flank either side of the covered marked by Bab Merba. Otherwise, you are limited to *Café-Restaurant Oumnia* on Boulevard Mohammed V (daily 8.30am–11.30pm; cheap), whose dining room is beyond a smokey cafe.

Internet access is available at a cyber-café (daily 8.30am–midnight) adjacent to *Hôtel la Frenaie*. The town's two **banks** are on Boulevard Mohammed V, neither very wised up to cashing cheques, though they have no problems with cash exchange and have ATMs.

Just up from Bab M'kam on Place Moulay Hassan, the tiny **Centre Artisanal** (Mon–Fri 8am–noon & 2–7pm), though small beer compared with those in Fes or Marrakesh, with just a handful of shops which open in rotation, is worth a visit, and you can usually see woodcarvings, brassware and carpets being created by hand.

Around Sefrou

Signposted off the Fes road, 7km northwest of Sefrou, **Bhalil** claims pre-Islamic Christian origins. Locals say it was founded by emigrants from Roman Volubilis (see p.243), who introduced red hair and blue eyes into the village's gene pool, apparently. More visibly, Bhalil retains a number of troglodyte dwellings. The **cave houses** are to the rear of the village, reached by a dirt road; ask directions from Mohammed Chraibi (BP 42, Bhalil), the official guide, who will show you his own cave home.

The village itself – or at least the old part of it – is charming, its whitewashed houses tumbling down a hillside connected by innumerable bridges. Coming from Fes by car, it is signposted off on the right 5km before Sefrou. Without your own transport, grands taxis for Bhalil (3dh) depart from just off Place Moulay Hassan in Sefrou.

South and east of Sefrou are some of the most attractive swathes of the Middle Atlas: dense, wooded mountains, with great scope for hiking or *piste* driving, and not a hint of tourism. Immediately south of the town is the Massif du Kandar, which loops round to Imouzzer du Kandar. To the east, further afield, are the Bou Iblane mountains – an exploration of which could be combined by drivers with the Djebel Tazzeka circuit, near Taza (see p.207).

If you are heading south, there is a daily bus to **Midelt**, via the quiet roadside town of **Boulemane**, but none to Ifrane or Azrou on the Fes–Marrakesh road. Short of returning to Fes, the only way to cross onto this route is by grand taxi to Immouzer du Kandar (11dh). Boulemane itself can be worth a stop for its Sunday souk which serves a wide and diverse area.

The Massif du Kandar

The 4620 route over the Massif du Kandar leaves the R503 Sefrou–Midelt road 14km south of Sefrou. It has some rough stretches of track but is passable in summer with a standard car; in winter, you need to check conditions locally. For those without transport, it would be possible to charter a grand taxi in Sefrou (or, travelling west–east, in Immouzer du Kandar) for the 36km route.

Shortly after the *piste* turns off from the Sefrou–Midelt road, it begins to climb up into the hills around the **Djebel Abad** (1768m). If you reckon your car can make it – or you feel like walking – you can follow a rocky 4km track almost to the summit of the mountain; this leads off, to the right of the road, 10km down the 4620, coming from the Sefrou direction.

The Djebel Bou Iblane

East of Sefrou – and southeast of Fes – is a huge area of high country, culminating in the two mountains of **Djebel Bou Iblane** (3190m) and **Djebel Bou Naceur** (3340m). It is an extraordinarily varied landscape: the northern aspects rise from the cedar forests, while the south is stark and waterless, although demarcated by the great Oued Moulouya. The whole area is sparsely populated and trekkers are almost unknown, yet it's a rewarding area and has relatively easy access. From either Sefrou or Fes, you could arrange a grand taxi to take you to the centre of the range, dropping you either at the forestry hut of **Tafferte** or at the largely abandoned ski resort under Djebel Bou Iblane, where the local *caid* has an office; he is responsible for this great empty quarter.

From here, a web of *pistes* radiate throughout the area, and a circular trek with a mule would be memorable.

Grands taxis run to **Skoura** (on route 4653) and **Immouzer des Marmoucha** (on route 4656) giving access from the east. As with so many lesser-known ranges, the best sources of information are the Peyron Guides (see p.290) and AMIS (see p.36).

Imouzzer du Kandar, Ifrane and Mischliffen

The first hills you see of the Middle Atlas, heading directly south from the plains around Fes, seem distinctly un-Moroccan thanks to their lush forests. The towns en route feel different, too, their flat gabled European-style houses lending an Alpine resort feel. The French colonial chiefs retreated from the heat at the "hill station" resort of **Ifrane**, where the king now has a summer palace, and there's modest skiing at **Mischliffen**. En route is another small French-built hill station, **Immouzer du Kandar**, easy-going but rather mundane, and, in the wet season, a gorgeous freshwater lake, the **Dayet Aaoua**.

Imouzzer du Kandar

IMOUZZER DU KANDAR, 36km south of Fes at 1345m high, is a one-road, one-square kind of place. There's nothing specific to see, but it's an easy-going, friendly resort where Fassis come to swim, picnic and spend a few days when the summer heat becomes over bearing. There's a large number of hotels if you feel like doing the same and some good restaurants, too.

A small Monday **souk** is held just off the central square within the ruined kasbah, location for music and dance events during a Fête des Pommes **festival** in August. The kasbah itself is reduced to crumbling walls, although it conceals a couple of the troglodyte dwellings that were once common in the area – most were filled in by local French governors, who were appalled at the idea of people living in caves. You'll find them, both private, on the lane on the immediate right as you enter the kasbah gate.

Three kilometres west of town is the **Aïn Soltane** spring, a tranquil spot among grassy hillocks and old pine trees; it's a pleasant stroll from town, particularly in the late afternoon or early evening when locals do likewise. To get here from town, head through the park (southeast) by the *Hôtel Royal* and across the canals beyond, then turn right on the tarmac lane and continue for about 500m, past some villas and holiday homes. Alternatively just take a petit taxi from town for 5dh.

Birdlife in the Dayet Aaoua and Middle Atlas lakes

Like other freshwater lakes in the Middle Atlas, when it's full **Dayet Aaoua** has a good mosaic of habitat types and supports a wide variety of animals. Green frogs take refuge from the summer drought within the lake's protective shallows, and a multitude of dragonflies and damselflies of shimmering reds, blues and greens patrol the water's surface.

The **birdlife** is similarly diverse, attracting all kinds of waders and wildfowl. Waders include black-winged stilt, green sandpiper, redshank and **avocet** (one of Morocco's most elegant birds), and the deeper waters provide food for flocks of grebes (great-crested, black-necked and little varieties), and in the spring the magnificent **crested coot** (which has spectacular bright red knobs on either side of its white facial shield, when in breeding condition). The reedbeds provide cover for **grey heron** and **cattle egret** and ring with the songs of hidden **reed-** and **fan-tailed warbler**.

The water's edge is traced by passage grey and yellow wagtails and in summer the skies are filled with migrating swallows and martins – the sand martin especially. This abundance of life proves an irresistible draw for resident and migrant birds of prey – there are regular sightings of the acrobatic **red kite** at Aaoua, usually circling overhead. You may also see flocks of collared pratincole, whose darting flight is spectacular, and, quartering overhead, the **Montagu's harrier**, ever alert for any unsuspecting duck on the lake below.

If the lake is dry, you will find, in the words of John Keats, that "the sedge has withered from the lake and no birds sing". But there are still birds to be seen alongside – or close to – the 17km stretch of the N8 between Ifrane and Azrou. Here you will find the endemic Levaillant's green **woodpecker**, **firecrest**, **nuthatch**, short-toed **tree creeper** and local variants of the **jay** and **blue tit**.

White storks, **ravens** and a colony of **lesser kestrels** have been recorded in the low hills behind the *Hôtel Panorama* in Azrou (see p.309).

Grands taxis for Azrou and Ifrane leave by the market; those for Fes and Sefrou leave from a parking area 100m north on the main road. **Buses** pass regularly en route between Fes and Azrou.

Around the town centre, there are several decent **restaurants**, the best of which is *Le Rose des Vents* (☎035 66 37 66, 11am–3pm & 7–10pm; moderate), which serves up heavenly lamb chops in tomato and rosemary sauce and some elaborate fish dishes. A rather ritzy **patisserie** downstairs serves delicious cakes and French pastries.

Immouzer has one **bank**, a Banque Populaire with an ATM, located behind *Hôtel la Chambotte*.

Hotels

Immouzer has a good choice of **hotels**, except at the very bottom of the scale, where options are limited. At the time of writing, one of the two smart hotels, the three-star *Hôtel Royal* (☎035 66 31 86; ❹), opposite *Hôtel la Chambotte* and with a nightclub (11pm–3am), was closed due to management problems.

Hôtel Bellevue, behind *Hôtel Chaharazed* (see below) ☎079 42 37 83. A very spartan option above a bar; communal facilities, cold showers and not even a belle vue. Best seen as a fall-back if everywhere else is fully booked. ❷

Hôtel Chaharazed 2 Pl du Marché ☎035 66 30 12, ℱ035 66 34 45. On the main road, opposite the square, and currently the smartest hotel in town – reservations advisable in summer. Comfortable rooms with heating, a/c, TV and a balcony, plus a reasonable restaurant, two bars, and friendly, efficient staff. Includes breakfast. ❹

Hôtel la Chambotte Bd Mohammed V ☎ & ℱ 035 66 33 74. A French-style auberge with a good restaurant and smallish characterful rooms; rooms 6 and 7 are en suite. Showers are

Gouraud's Cedar

Eight kilometres from Azrou, and marked on the Michelin map, is the legendary **Cèdre Gouraud**. This is well signposted from the main road and the Gouraud cedar itself is singled out among others of much the same stature by a sign nailed to the tree. The 130ft giant, with a girth of around 25ft, is reputed to be at least 800 years old. The history of its name is a mystery. Colonel Gouraud was Lyautey's second in command from 1912 to 1914 and some locals say Lyautey's cedar is nearby. Why two soldiers should lend their names to trees is not clear, the confusion confounded by a recent authority which claims that Gouraud's cedar was actually felled at the turn of the century, when it was at least 980 years old. Maybe the sign is moved from tree to tree, possibly by the **Barbary apes** you will see hereabouts (see box p.310). They are no friend of the cedar; they gnaw the trees' buds and tear off strips of bark.

Another enemy is the **processionary caterpillar** which eats the foliage. In spring, they form a colony cocooned within a white shroud-like "tent" to protect themselves from feathered predators, then venture out under the cover of darkness to eat the surrounding foliage. When that is gone, one caterpillar is dispatched to scout out more foliage, returning to lead the colony in procession, head-to-tail to the new feeding ground. Here a secure new tent is spun and the process begins again. Naturally, the caterpillars are a favourite of TV documentaries, notably featured in David Attenborough's BBC series *The Private Life of Plants* in 1995.

Details of two local guides who could help with the trip to the Gouraud Cedar – one offical the other not, but both well-informed about the Azrou region – are provided on p.308.

hot (on demand) and there's central heating when called for. Also has six duplex apartments in an annexe. Rooms ❸ , apartments ❹

Hôtel du Rif 500m south of main square on the Ifrane road ☎035 66 33 92. Sombre and basic ensuites, although cheapest in town and a quiet location. Cold showers. ❶

Hôtel Smara on the main square, opposite the *Chaharazed* ☎035 66 34 64. Basic but clean and friendly, with a lively café-restaurant attached. Few double rooms – most are singles. Shared hot-water showers. ❷

🏃 **Hôtel des Truites** 200m north of the main square on the Fes road ☎ & ⓕ035 66 30 02. A delightful old-fashioned place with a quirky rustic French-style bar and (unpredictable) restaurant, and great views north towards Fes. Rooms in the annexe are en suite. Charming owners, too. ❸

Dayet Aaoua

A good excursion from Immouzer, or an alternative place to break the journey south, is the lake of **Dayet Aaoua**; it is sited just to the east of the N8, 9km south of Immouzer. You can camp around the lakeside, but, like other lakes in the Ifrane area, Aaoua is often dry due to the prevalence of limestone and sometimes to climatic changes. On the other hand, when it is full of water, it has a rewarding **birdlife habitat** – see box p.302.

The N8 continues past the lake to Ifrane, climbing through ever-more dense shafts of forest. If you are driving, it's possible to reach Ifrane by a longer and more scenic route, following a *piste* (4627) up behind the Dayet Aaoua, then looping to the right, past another (often dry) lake, **Dayet Hachlef**, on *piste* 3325, before joining the S309 back to Ifrane.

Since the *Restaurant Chalet du Lac* (☎035 66 31 97; moderate) on the north bank of the lake stopped providing rooms, the only accommodation is in *Le Gîte du Lac* (☎035 60 48 80, ✉aouagite@yahoo.com; includes breakfast; ❹), an inviting chalet-style house with wood-panelled rooms and a rustic alpine feel. It can also arrange treks and horse-riding excursions in the area, and rents mountain bikes from 100dh per day.

Ifrane

With its globe lights in manicured parks, its fountains in ornamental lakes, or its pseudo-Alpine villas on broad leafy streets, **IFRANE** is something of an anomaly among Moroccan towns; a little prim, even perhaps a little smug. Although the name reveals the site has long been inhabited – "*yfran*" are the "caves" in which local Berbers once lived – the modern town was created by the Protectorate in 1929 as a self-conscious "poche de France" (pocket of France), *then* adopted enthusiastically after independence by Moroccan government ministries and the wealthier bourgeoisie, who own the gleaming top-of-the-range marques parked throughout town from June to September. In recent times, the town won extra prestige with the addition of a **Royal Palace**, whose characteristic green tiles (a royal prerogative) can be seen through the trees on the descent into a valley.

Ifrane is also the site of another royal initiative. On January 16, 1995, King Hassan II inaugurated the **Al Akhawayn University**, on the northern edge of town, beyond the *Hôtel Mischliffen*. Its chalet-style buildings, cream walls and russet-tiled roofs, mirroring those in Ifrane, were designed by Michel Pinseau, the architect who designed the king's showpiece Mosquée Hassan II in Casablanca. The name Al Akhawayn ("brothers" in Arabic) denotes it as the brainchild (and beneficiary) of the Moroccan king and his "brother" King Fahd of Saudi Arabia; it has also been funded by the United States and, to a lesser extent, by the British Council. The undergraduate and postgraduate curricula are modelled on the American system of higher education and English is used for lectures.

King Hassan was keen to underpin his creation with the religious and cultural values of Christianity and Judaism as well as of Islam. The university is dedicated to "practical tolerance between faiths" and a mosque, church and synagogue are on campus to provide, as the king put it, "a meeting place for the sons of Abraham", a concept endorsed by the Prince of Wales when he visited Ifrane on February 28, 1996.

Inevitably, there have been criticisms of the new university, not least that it is an elite initiative restricted to those who can pay. There is also something of an anti-French feel, too; Moroccan academics are trying to escape the French educational straitjacket and have begun to "arabize" science teaching in the established universities. Should you want to visit the campus, try to go on a weekday afternoon when the students are about.

As befits a royal resort and aspiring academia, **Ifrane town** is no average Moroccan settlement – its Alpine resort-style centre is squeaky clean and spacious, and there's a steady growth of costly new houses. Unsurprisingly, it is also expensive – even provisions in the shops are pricier than elsewhere – and being a relatively new resort, it rather lacks the human touch. In summer, a policeman is even posted to stop anyone clambering onto the resort's landmark **stone lion** – located in a copse by the central *Hôtel Chamonix*, it was carved by an Italian prisoner of war, apparently – and when the court is in residence in summer, security is very tight.

Usually, however, Ifrane retains an easy-going, affluent air. A walk by the river below the royal palace is pleasant, as is the easy mountain air, and there's an excellent municipal swimming pool (summer only) signposted off the main road 250m north of the turning for the *Hôtel Mischliffen*.

Practicalities

Ifrane has a *Syndicat d'Initiative* **tourist office** in Place du Syndicat, on the corner of avenues Mohammed V and Prince Moulay Abdallah (☎035 56 68 21, ☎035 56 68 22; Mon–Fri 8.30am–4.30pm). The **bus station** is behind the municipal market off the Meknes road, 400m from the town centre, with frequent services to Fes and Azrou, but fewer to Meknes, Rabat, Casablanca and Marrakesh. CTM destinations include Casa via Meknes and Rabat (9am); Marrakesh via Khenifra and Beni Mellal (7.30am); and Agadir via Marrakesh (9pm). **Grands taxis** gather just beside the bus station, and ply routes to Fes, Azrou and Immouzer on a regular basis, and, less frequently, Meknes.

Accommodation

To help maintain its air of exclusivity, Ifrane doesn't do cheap **accommodation**, nor is it always easy to obtain in summer, when reservations are recommended. Those on a budget should consider rooms in Immouzer du Kander. However, there is a municipal **campsite** (☎035 56 61 56) on Boulevard Mohammed V (the Meknes road), near the market, open all year, with a little shop open in summer.

Grand Hôtel Av de la Marche Verte ☎035 56 75 31, ✉grandhotelspaifrane@menara.ma. Recent restoration has buffed up this 1941-vintage hotel into the best and most stylish in the region – stone walls, recycled 1930s cedarwood beams and fireplaces sit comfortably with modern hardwood floors and furnishings to create a stylish take on the Alpine lodge. Also has a gym, Jacuzzi and hammam and a nightclub (midnight–3am). **7**

Hôtel Chamonix Av de la Marche Verte ☎035 56 60 28, ☎035 56 68 26. A good-value hotel in the centre of town, with light, spotless rooms done out in pastel green, and heating, a/c and TV in each. There's also a nightclub open Fri and Sat nights (11pm to 3am), open to nonresidents. **5**

Hôtel Mischliffen Route de Fes ☎035 56 66 07, ☎035 56 66 22. When doors reopen in Jan 2008 after renovation, this hotel should offer modern

luxury facilities and two pools. Views from its hilltop 800m north of the centre will be just as superb. Formerly ⑥
Hôtel Perce-Neige Rue des Asphodelles ☎035 56 63 50, ⓦwww.hotelperceneige.com. An upmarket place, friendly and efficiently run, its small but comfortable carpeted rooms refurbished in early 2007, some with a terrace, and all

with satellite TV, heating and a/c. There's also a good restaurant, a cosy bar, and daycare facilities for children. ⑤
Hôtel les Tilleuls Rue du Tilleul ☎035 56 66 58, ⓕ035 56 60 79. A rather tired town-centre hotel, whose simple, old-fashioned rooms, though en-suite, are poor value compared with the similarly priced *Hôtel Chamonix* nearby. ⑤

Restaurants

Café Restaurant La Rose Rue de la Cascade, behind *Hôtel Chamonix*. A cosy wood-panelled place – a mite too snug on the first floor – with various forms of Atlas trout and 60dh menus. Daily 9am–11pm. Cheap.
Cookie-Craque Av des Tilleuls. Everything from pastas and grills to crepes and gâteaux in a retro Alpine place from the team behind the *Grand Hôtel*. Log fires in winter too. Daily 8am–10.30pm. Cheap.
Grand Hôtel Av de la Marche Verte. International cuisine and upmarket Moroccan dishes served in a rustic-chic dining room decorated with Alpine antiques. Menus 170dh. Daily 11am–3pm & 6.30–11pm. Expensive.

Hôtel Chamonix Av de la Marche Verte. A decent if unspectacular option, with reasonably priced menus at 80dh and 110dh. Daily noon–3pm & 7pm–11pm. Moderate.
Rendezvous des Skieurs Av de la Marche Verte. Pizzas cooked in a wood-fired oven, plus well-priced dishes such as rabbit tajine or menus in a decent café-style option. Daily 6am–11pm. Cheap.
Restaurant Pizzeria la Paix Av de la Marche Verte, next to *Hôtel Chamonix*. An upmarket modern place, where à la carte meals start at 150dh. An attached café-cum-patisserie provides cheaper sandwiches and pizzas (cheap). Daily 9am–11pm. Expensive.

The Mischliffen

The Mischliffen is simply a shallow bowl in the mountains – the crater of an extinct volcano – enclosed on all sides by cedar forests. There's no village here and few buildings, and, it's only of interest mainly for the minor skiing area.

In season (Jan–March, but snow cover is often patchy) there are taxis from Ifrane up to the resort's **refuge-club** (restaurant and bar, but no accommodation) and to the rather ancient **ski lifts**. You can **rent ski equipment** in Ifrane from the manager of the *Hôtel Chamonix* for about 100dh per day.

Azrou

The first real town of the Middle Atlas, **AZROU** grew at the crossroads of two major routes – north to Meknes and Fes, south to Khenifra and Midelt. As might be expected, it's an important market centre (the main souk is on Tuesday) and it has long held a strategic role in controlling the mountain Berbers. Moulay Ismail built a kasbah here, the remains of which survive, while more recently the French established the prestigious **Collège Berbère** – one plank in their policy to split the country's Berbers from the urban Arabs.

The college, now the Lycée Tarik Ibn Ziad and still a dominant building in the town, provided many of the Protectorate's interpreters, local administrators and military officers. But in spite of its ban on using Arabic and any manifestation of Islam, the policy was a failure. Azrou graduates played a significant role in the nationalist movement – and were uniquely placed to do so, as a new French-created elite. However, since independence their influence has been minor outside of the army, in part because many Berber student activists of the

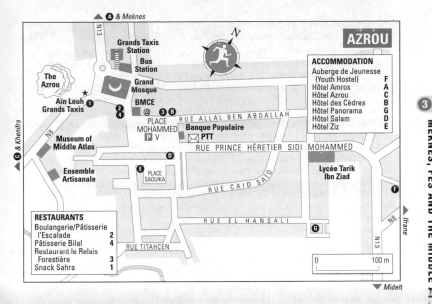

1950s and 1960s pledged allegiance to Mehdi Ben Barka's ill-fated socialist UNFP party (see p.718).

The town's relaxed atmosphere (bar one or two over-persistent touts) and the possibilities for walks and treks nearby make Azrou a pleasant spot to break your journey or even spend a few days.

The town and its souk

Once the defining feature on arrival in Azrou was the massive knobble of rock on its western edges – the *azrou* ("rock" in Berber) after which it is named. Now, your view is somewhat impeded by the impressive new Grand Mosque which adjoins the main square, **Place Mohammed V**.

Bar a public swimming pool behind the rock – signposted 300m along the Khenifra road and almost reason enough to stop in summer – or until the opening of a large Museum of the Middle Atlas in mid-2007, the most compelling reason to visit Azrou is its **Tuesday souk**, which draws Berbers from surrounding mountain villages. It is held a little above the main part of town – just follow the crowds up to the quarter across the valley. At first it appears to offer little more than fruit and vegetable stalls, but keep going and you'll see a stretch of wasteland – often with a few musicians and storytellers performing – beyond which is a smaller section for carpets, textiles and general goods.

On other days, the **craft stalls** in the old quarter of town around Place Saouika (Place Moulay Hachem Ben Salah) and Place Mohammed V can turn up some beautiful items, fairly priced if not exactly bargains, although the lack of a regular supply of tourists means that touts can be persistent. There's less hard sell at a **carpet shop** by the *Hôtel des Cèdres*, which has a comprehensive selection of carpets and rugs from the various Beni M'Guild tribes in the Middle Atlas, most with bright, geometric designs based on traditional tribal patterns, plus wood carving and fossils. Affable owner Amraoui Saïd is a knowledgeable *chasseur des tapis* (carpet hunter), as he calls himself, who will explain

The Benedictines of Tioumliline

The functional monastery of Tioumliline was built in 1926 by French Benedictines, and until the mid-1990s played an important role in the life of the local Berber community. The focus of the monastery's life was its *dispensaire* or clinic, outside the walls of the complex and by the road to Aïn Leuh. The clinic offered free medical treatment and medicines to any passer-by; Berber families in isolated mountain villages used to bring their sick relatives to be treated and looked after by the monks. As well as free medical care, the monastery supplied the poorest Berber families – and generally anyone whose harvests failed – with basic foodstuffs.

The end of the monastery came in the mid-1990s as a result of increasing animosity against Christians in the area. Most of the monks of Tioumliline were relocated to the Abbey of Calcat in France, while their superior, Father Gilbert, went to the Abbey of Saint Benoît de Koubiri, near Ouagadougou in Burkina Faso. The Benedictines of Tioumliline are affectionately remembered by many of the locals, including Monsieur Boudaoud, who lives with his family in the former dispensary. He can tell you stories about the monastery and show you around the ruins.

the difference between good Berber carpets and mere souvenirs if you show enough interest. Another source of rugs and carpets is the **Ensemble Artisanale** (Mon–Fri 8.30am–noon & 2.30–6.30pm), on the Khenifra road; this has seen better days – it's a bit sleepy compared with other cooperatives – but some decent modern rugs, plus stone and cedar carvings, are still produced.

There's little else to keep you in the town itself, but good walks are to be had in the surrounding hills – lush when watered by seasonal springs and home to Barbary apes – or down to the river, which is reputedly well stocked with trout. A pleasant afternoon stroll goes to the derelict twentieth-century **Benedictine Monastery of Tioumliline** (see box above), 3km away in the hills above Azrou, reached along the road to Aïn Leuh, which branches off the N13 to Midelt. On your way back to town you can cut across the hills south of the monastery on any of the footpaths that crisscross the area. Further afield are extensive cedar forests; see box, p.310. For guides to the area contact: Moulay Abdellah Lahrizi (☎062 19 08 89 or 063 77 26 87, ℮lahrizi37@ yahoo.co.uk), president of the Ifrane and Azrou branch of the Association of Mountain Guides; or Boujemâa Boudaoud (☎063 76 08 25, ℮boujemaa_ boudaoud@yahoo.com), an unofficial but knowlegable guide whose family live in the monastery dispensary. Both speak good English and charge around 200dh per day.

Practicalities

The **bus station** is just north of the central Grand Mosque, the **grand taxi** station just behind and downstairs from it. **Petit taxis** wait on streets north and east of the mosque.

Two **banks** (BMCE and Banque Populaire) are in Place Mohammed V; both have change facilities for travellers' cheques and cashpoints. The **PTT** is just east of the square, behind the Banque Populaire. **Internet** access is available at Internet Abrid (daily 9am–midnight) and Cyber Canadien (same hours), both on the first floor of a mall to the left of the BMCE, or Cyber Kawtar (daily 9am–midnight) at the bus station is a convenient place to email while you wait for a bus. There is a handy **laundry** 50m south of Place Saouika, by the army garrison – ask for directions at the *Hôtel des Cèdres*.

Accommodation

Azrou's position at a major road junction means that there are plenty of **hotels** in town; bear in mind that the nights are cold, particularly in winter, and central heating is only provided in dearer (and more distant) places.

Auberge de Jeunesse (Youth Hostel) Route de Midelt-Ifrane ☏ 035 56 37 33. On the outskirts of town, about 1km from the centre and before the road forks to Midelt/Er Rachidia (N13) and to Ifrane/Fes (N8). Friendly and well run, with good views too. A pack of bad-tempered dogs hangs around the dirt track to the hostel, so you might want to take a petit taxi all the way to reception.

Hôtel Amros 6km out on the Meknes road ☏ 035 56 36 63, ℱ 035 56 36 80. An upmarket hotel for which you will need a petit taxi. According to season, there is a nightclub, a swimming pool and tennis courts, as well as a restaurant – which gets mixed reports – and bar. ⑤

Hôtel Azrou Route du Khenifra, 300m downhill to the southwest of Place Mohammed V ☏ 035 56 21 16, ℱ 035 56 42 73. A good-value place, with pleasant rooms, some en suite, a good restaurant and bar, and English spoken. ③

Hôtel des Cèdres Pl Mohammed V ☏ & ℱ 035 56 23 26. The best value in central Azrou. Spacious comfortable rooms are enjoyably old-fashioned, all with high ceilings and washbasins, and a shared balcony overlooks the square. Heating in winter and shared hot showers (10dh). ②

Hôtel Panorama Rue el Hansali ☏ 035 56 20 10, ℱ 035 56 18 04. There's a solid old-fashioned hotel feel to this minor pile 10min walk north of the centre. Rooms are spacious but somewhat spartan, but the entrance hall, with a working fireplace, is bright and relaxing. Some rooms en suite; hot water, central heating, a good restaurant and a bar. ⑤

Hôtel Salam Off Pl Saouika ☏ 035 56 25 62, ℮ hotel.salam@gmail.com. Boxy small rooms in a central clean hotel, with shared facilities and free hot showers. A good fallback if the Cèdres is full. *Café Salam* next door is good. ②

Hôtel Ziz 83 Pl Saouika ☏ 035 56 23 62. Not too impressive – and cold showers. Best as a reserve if other cheaples are full and just better than the nearby *Hôtel Atlas*. ①

Eating

The best place to **eat** in town – though it tends to be colonized by drinkers in the evening – is the restaurant of the *Hôtel Azrou* (daily 11.30am–3pm & 6–11pm; cheap to moderate), where the trout in particular is recommended. After that, the best choice is the restaurant of the *Hôtel Panorama* (daily noon–3pm & 7–11pm; expensive) with a gourmet menu from 130dh. Another reasonable restaurant is at the adjoining *Hôtel des Cèdres* (daily noon–3pm & 7–10pm; cheap to moderate), which is warmed by a log fire in winter. Bizarrely, it is sometimes cheaper to eat à la carte than to order the set menu at both. The down-to-earth *Restaurant le Relais Forestière* (daily noon–3pm & 5–9pm; cheap), next to the *Hôtel des Cèdres*, has main dishes from about 40dh.

For even cheaper eating, basic grills line the roads around the Grand Mosque and prepare the usual brochettes, tajines and spit-roast chicken; as ever, doublecheck that the birds were not left on the spit overnight if you choose the latter for lunch. The stalls towards the *azrou* rock tend to be better than those towards the bus station – *Snack Sahra* serves a generous portion of *kefta*, fries and salad for 25dh.

The town has two classy **patisseries** near Place Mohammed V: *Patisserie Bilal* (winter 5am–midnight, summer 24hr) has a sitting area inside and a small terrace by the road, while *Boulangerie/Patisserie l'Escalade*, just round the corner, sells a variety of French bread as well as cakes and pastries, some of them savoury.

Moving on

There are several daily **bus** services to Fes, Meknes, Khenifra, Beni Mellal, Midelt and Er Rachidia, fewer to destinations like Marrakesh, Casablanca and Rabat, and only one to Aïn Leuh. CTM also has several daily services, the most frequent being to Fes, Meknes and Midelt. If you don't want to get the only night-time bus to Er Rachidia and Rissani, take the Midelt bus and change there. Similarly, to reach Marrakesh, you may have to change at Beni Mellal. Because most bus services are just passing through, tickets sometimes only go on sale when the bus arrives and the conductor tells the people in the ticket office how many places are available – cue a mad scramble for tickets if seats are scarce. Arrive early and set up a place by the ticket window, and you will be at the front of the queue if that happens.

Grands taxis run regularly to Midelt, Meknes, Ifrane and Fes, and occasionally to Khenifra and sporadically Beni Mellal. Grands taxis for Aïn Leuh have their own station at the beginning of the Khenifra road opposite the Grand Mosque and the *azrou*.

Aïn Leuh and the waterfalls of Oum er Rbia

South of Azrou lies some of the most remote and beautiful country of the Middle Atlas: a region of cedar forests, limestone plateaus and polje lakes that is home to some superb wildlife (see box below), including Barbary apes.

It is rewarding countryside for a few days' exploration, either by car or on foot. At the heart of the region – an obvious focus for a trip – are the **waterfalls of Oum er Rbia**, the source of Morocco's largest river. If you don't have transport, you can get a daily **bus** from Azrou to **Aïn Leuh**, 30km along the route (and with some minor falls of its own), or, if you have the money or can round up a group, you could charter a **grand taxi** from Azrou.

Aïn Leuh

AÏN LEUH (17km from Azrou along the main Khenifra road, then 13km up the S303) is a large Berber village, typical of the Middle Atlas, with its flat-roofed houses tiered above the valley. As at Azrou, there are ruins of a kasbah built by Moulay Ismail and in the hills behind the town there are **springs** and a more or less year-round waterfall.

Barbary apes and other cedar forest wildlife

The **cedar forests** which lie to the **south of Azrou** are a unique habitat in Morocco, their verdant atmosphere contrasting starkly with the surrounding aridity and barrenness of the Middle Atlas range. They shelter several troupes of **Barbary apes**, a glimpse of which is one of the wildlife highlights of a visit to Morocco. They can be found feeding along the forest margins – sometimes on the outskirts of Azrou itself – but they are shy animals and any excessive intrusion is likely to be met with a retreat to the sanctuary of the treetops.

Almost as interesting is the forest **birdlife**, which includes Morocco's two species of woodpecker, the pied and red great spotted and green and yellow Levaillant's varieties. Other avian highlights include the splendid **booted eagle**, often seen soaring on outstretched wings in an attempt to avoid the attention of resident ravens. Kestrels nest in the Oum er Rbia gorge, near the falls (see above) in spring.

The cedars also provide shelter for a vibrant carpet of flowers – pink peonies, scarlet dianthus, blue germander, golden compositae and a variety of orchids – which makes an ideal haven for a host of **butterflies** (from April onwards), among them the brilliant sulphur cleopatra, large tortoiseshell and cardinal.

△ Barbary ape on the road near Azrou

Aïn Leuh's **souk** is held on Wednesday (a good day to hitch), though it can extend a day in either direction. It serves as the weekly gathering of the **Beni M'Guild** tribes, still semi-nomadic in this region – you may see them camping out with their flocks in heavy, dark tents. As a colonial *zone d'insécurité*, this part of the Atlas was relatively undisturbed by French settlers, and the traditional balance between pasture and forest has remained largely intact.

The Oum er Rbia sources and Aguelmane Azigza

The road to the **Oum er Rbia cascades** continues just south of Aïn Leuh, signposted "Aguelmane Azigza/Khenifra". Though paved along its entire course, with several new bridges over the Rbia, it can still become waterlogged and impassable in winter, when you should ask about conditions in Azrou or Khenifra before you set out. For the most part it runs through mountain forest, where you're almost certain to come across apes.

About 20km south of Aïn Leuh, to the left of the road, there's a small lake, **Lac Ouiouane**, and beside it a couple of farms and a large *maison forestière*. A stretch of more open country, dotted with grazing sheep and odd pitched-roof farmsteads, leads to the descent to the Oum er Rbia valley. Here, the road twists down, bends through a side valley and round to a concrete bridge over the Rbia, with a small parking area by the river. (Coming from the south, the descent to the Oum er Rbia – around 45km from Khenifra – is unmistakeable.)

Guides may offer to lead you to the **walk to the falls** but they are unnecessary because a clear path leads up to the gorge – a ten- to fifteen-minute walk. Along the river's edge, the water comes out in forty or more springs (*sources*), many of them marked with café-shelters. Beyond, where the gorge is barred, a small waterfall flows down the rocks, with a fish hatchery below. Swimming is not advisable as the currents are extremely strong.

Aguelmane Azigza

On past the bridges, the main road heads off to the west, crossed by a confusing array of *pistes*. After 18km, a turnoff on the left leads to the **Aguelmane Azigza**, a dark and deep lake, secluded among the cedar trees. You can camp and swim here, as many Moroccans do. Azigza has terrific **wildlife**. The wooded slopes of the lake throng with insect life, including the brilliant red and black grasshopper and the small Amanda's blue butterfly, while the forest provides nesting and feeding areas for woodland finches and titmice, including the elusive hawfinch, identified by a heavy bill. There's more birdlife in the waters, too, notably diving duck (mainly grebes and coot) and marbled teal in autumn and winter.

Improved *pistes* and often surfaced roads wend through this huge area of cedar forest, offering tours unlike anything else in Morocco. The Atlas cedar (*Cedrus atlantica*) can soar to over 40m, often flat-topped, the trees are carefully nurtured and rejuvenating successfully. The best west–east routes are as follows: from just south of Aïn Leuh across the R13 to the Mischliffen; from just south of the Azigza turnoff on to Itzer from where either the R13 or R503 can be reached; and, almost 20km south of Khenifra an excellent road by El Kbab (Monsouk) up the O.Serou to Kerrouchen and the Tizi Rechou to the R503. A web of *pistes* link these and are popular with bikers and 4x4s.

South to Midelt and Er Rachidia

If you're travelling the southern circuits of the ksour and kasbahs of the south, you're almost certain to take this route in one direction or the other. It's 125km from **Azrou to Midelt** and a further 154km to **Er Rachidia** – feasible distances to cover in a single bus trip or a day's driving, but more satisfying when made in a couple of stages. You cross passes over both Middle and High Atlas ranges, catch a first glimpse of the south's fabulous *pisé* architecture and end up in the desert.

Azrou to Midelt

Climbing up from Azrou, the Midelt road (R13, which becomes the N13) follows a magnificent stretch of the Middle Atlas, winding through the forests to emerge at the **valley of the Oued Gigou**, the view ahead taking in some of the range's highest peaks. By bus you have little alternative but to head

Moroccan architecture

Many features of Moroccan architecture – such as the familiar pointed horseshoe arches of doorways and city gates – come from the Middle East and arrived with the Arabs. Though the style has been refined, and decorative details added over the centuries, the country's architectural traditions have changed little since then. The colonial period did, however, make its mark, and there are some particularly fine examples of Art Deco and Art Nouveau styles to be found, though they are confined to the French-built Villes Nouvelles, leaving the traditional Medinas often remarkably untouched.

◄ Balcony of the Radiology Clinic, Casablanca

Some history

As far as we can tell from their only surviving building of note – the Koubba Ba'adiyn in Marrakesh – it was the **Almoravids** who first used many of the decorative elements that have become so typical of the country's architecture, including *merlons* (battlement-like castellations), a ribbed dome, and stylized plant-inspired designs resembling pine cones and palm fronds. The **Almohads** introduced the classic Moroccan square minaret, as seen in the Koutoubia at Marrakesh, the Hassan Tower in Rabat, and the Giralda at Seville in Spain. Architectural styles were refined but not radically altered under the **Merenids** and the **Saadians**, who brought in techniques of zellij tilework and carved stucco and cedarwood.

The next big change came with the **colonial period**, when European styles – and the Europeanized North African style known as Mauresque – began to appear in the Villes Nouvelles of larger cities, most notably in Casablanca. **Art Nouveau** made a major impact on the Spanish enclave of Melilla, and **Art Deco** similarly dominates the former Spanish enclave of Sidi Ifni.

Concrete-and-glass modern architecture has not made many inroads in Morocco, though you'll see it on the outskirts of Casablanca if you're coming in from the south. Nor has post-World War II European architecture especially impressed Moroccans – one of Le Corbusier's brutalist blocks was demolished in the centre of Meknes in 2004 without much comment. Morocco's most impressive modern building, the Mosquée Hassan II in Casablanca, was built using completely traditional styles and techniques.

Mosques

Mosques follow the same basic plan regardless of their age or size. All mosques face Mecca, the birthplace of Islam and the direction in which all Muslims pray. This direction is indicated by an alcove called the *mihrab*, set in the Mecca-facing *qibla* wall. Next to the *mihrab* in larger mosques is a pulpit, usually wooden, called the **minbar**. Larger mosques will also have a courtyard, often with a fountain for ablutions, but the *qibla* end is taken up by a covered **prayer hall**. The **minaret** is a tower from which, back in the day, the *muezzin* would climb to call the faithful to prayer. Moroccan mosques invariably have only one minaret, and since the days of the Almohads in the twelfth century, almost all Moroccan minarets have been square in shape, with a ratio of 5:1 height to width.

A **zaouia** is a mosque built around the tomb of a *marabout*, or Islamic saint; typically the saint's tomb will be located next to the prayer hall, and surmounted by a dome or **koubba**.

Morocco's most important mosque architecture includes the Koutoubia in Marrakesh, the Kairaouine Mosque and the Zaouia of Moulay Idriss in Fes, the Hassan Tower in Rabat, and the Mosquée Hassan II in Casablanca. Non-Muslims, unfortunately, are not allowed inside most mosques.

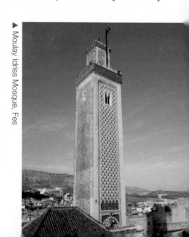

▶ Moulay Idriss Mosque, Fes

Medersas

A **medersa** (or *madrasa*) is a religious school where students come to study Islam, and unlike mosques, *medersas* are open to non-Muslims. Typically they consist of a large courtyard, with rooms around it for teaching, and rooms upstairs where the students sleep. The *medersas* of Fes in particular, such as Bou Inania and the Attarin, are richly decorated with carved stucco and cedarwood, and zellij mosaic tilework. Because Islam is suspicious of representational art (lest it lead to idol worship), religious buildings such as *medersas* are decorated with geometric designs and calligraphy, the latter almost always consisting of quotations from the Koran. Other architecturally interesting *medersas* include the Abou el Hassan in Salé, and the Ben Youssef in Marrakesh.

Traditional homes

People's houses in Morocco do not look outward, like a Western home, but rather inward, to an enclosed **patio**, an arrangement that guards privacy, particularly for women, who traditionally observed purdah and did not allow men outside the family to see them. Rooms are arranged around the patio, usually on two floors with a roof terrace. At one time, most homes would have had a well in the middle of the patio to supply drinking water. A grand house or mansion might have a whole garden in the patio, typically with orange trees, and sometimes a second patio too. The **ceilings** would be wooden and often beautifully painted.

The very best way to take in Moroccan domestic architecture is to stay in an old riad, particularly in a city such as Marrakesh or Fes. Second best is to visit one of the palatial restaurants in those two cities. In Marrakesh, the Bahia Palace and Dar el Glaoui are also worth a visit.

Kasbahs

A **kasbah** can be a walled residential district (as in Fes), or the citadel of a walled city (as in Tangier and Marrakesh), but in southern Morocco, most impressively in Telouet, Tamdaght and the Skoura Oasis, a kasbah is a fortified citadel, something like a castle, where everyone in a village could take refuge in times of trouble (see box p.538). Built of mud bricks, these kasbahs are rectangular structures with turrets at each corner, usually decorated with Berber motifs.

Architectural motifs

Darj w ktarf This fleur de lys-like pattern, used on Marrakesh's Koutoubia and the Moulay Idriss mosque, has been a favourite in Moroccan architecture since the time of the Almohads.

Stucco Intricate decorative designs are carved into plaster on lintels, cornices and walls.

Zellij A mosaic of specially shaped pieces of tile put together to form a geometric pattern, usually based on a star with a specific number of points.

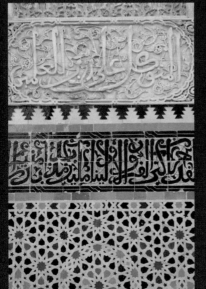

Carved cedarwood Especially in the form of panels and lintels, cedarwood with inscriptions and stylistic designs carved into it surmounts walls, doorways and recessed fountains.

Painted wooden ceilings The cedarwood ceilings of mansions and palaces in cities such as Fes and Marrakesh are adorned with beautiful hand-painted traditional designs.

Merlons The battlement-like castellations seen atop so many city gates and palaces are decorative as much as defensive.

◄ Zellij tiles and calligraphy decoration in Bou Inania Medersa, Fes

> ## Birdlife around Zeïda
>
> Thirty kilometres north of Midelt and within 15km of Zeïda is a stony desert area renowned for the elusive **Dupont's lark**. Other species to be found on the vast, open scrubby plain are the **red-rumped wheatear**, **thick-billed lark**, **lesser short-toed lark** and **trumpeter finch**. The area east and west of the N13 between kilometre posts 27 and 28 is recommended for bird-watching.
>
> North of Zeïda, the aqueduct, parallel with the road, has **rock sparrows** and **spotless starlings**.

straight to Midelt, reached in around two hours, via the market village of Timadhite (large **Thursday souk**). With a car, there are two very brief and worthwhile detours.

The first of these comes 52km from Azrou, as the road levels out on a strange volcanic plateau littered with dark pumice rock. A turnoff to the left directs you to **Aguelmane Sidi Ali**, the largest of the region's many mountain lakes that pooled in extinct craters; long, still and eerily beautiful yet only a kilometre from the road. Besides an occasional shepherd's tent and flock, there is unlikely to be anything or anyone in sight, and the lake itself is reputed to be teeming with trout, pike and perch.

The other paths where you might want to leave the road is taken further down, past the Col du Ziad, a 2178m pass across the Middle Atlas. Superb trekking country lies west of the col, leading to the Oued Sefrou. South of the col, a road leads for 6km to the small village of **ITZER**, whose **market** (Mon & Thurs) is one of the most important in the region, and can be a good source of Berger rugs and carpets.

Back on the main road, you pass road junctions near Boulôjul (the R503 – formerly P20 – from Boulemane) and Zeïda (with the R503 from Khenifra). A few kilometres south of Zeïda is a small, but good, tourist complex, the *Centre Timnay* (see p.316), including a shop, café restaurant, swimming pool (in summer) and a clean **campsite**, with shared accommodation available for those without tents. The centre has been developed by its owner, Aït Lemkaden Driss, as a base for **Land Rover**, **mountain bike** and **walking** expeditions in the region.

Midelt

At **MIDELT**, approached through a bleak plain of scrub and desert, you have left behind the Middle Atlas. As you approach from the north, the greater peaks of the High Atlas appear suddenly through the haze, rising behind the town to a massive range, the **Djebel Ayachi**, at over 3700m. The sheer drama of the site – tremendous in the clear, cool evenings – is one of the most compelling reasons to stop over. Certainly, the town itself does nothing to entice as you approach – a drab carpet of ochre and rusty cubes spread over a dusty plain when seen from afar – and even up close it seems little more than a street with a few cafés and hotels and a small souk. But it's a pleasant place to break a journey, partly because so few people do, partly because of the easy-going (and predominantly Berber) atmosphere of the town. Indeed, there is a hint of the frontier town about Midlet, a sense reinforced by the **derelict mines** at Mibladene and El Ahouli, northeast of Midelt, in the nearby gorge of Oued Moulouya (see box, p.315), which are well worth a visit.

Midelt is so far inland that it has a microclimate of extremes: bitterly cold in winter and oppressively hot in summer. Consequently, one of the best times to visit is autumn, particularly at the start of October, when the town hosts a

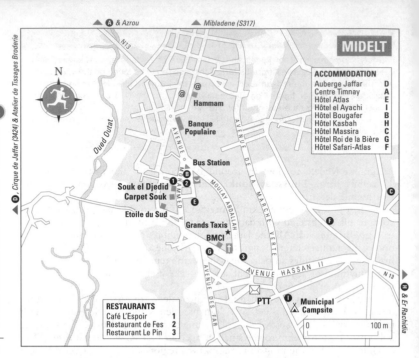

▲ ⓐ & Azrou   ▲ Mibladene (S317)

MIDELT

ACCOMMODATION
Auberge Jaffar   D
Centre Timnay   A
Hôtel Atlas   E
Hôtel el Ayachi   I
Hôtel Bougafer   B
Hôtel Kasbah   H
Hôtel Massira   C
Hôtel Roi de la Bière   G
Hôtel Safari-Atlas   F

◀ ⓓ Cirque de Jaffar (3424) & Atelier de Tissages Broderie

Hammam

Banque
Populaire

Bus Station

Souk el Djedid
Carpet Souk

Etoile du Sud

Grands Taxis
BMCI

AVENUE HASSAN II

RESTAURANTS
Café L'Espoir   1
Restaurant de Fes   2
Restaurant Le Pin   3

PTT   Municipal
             Campsite

0   100 m

▶ ⓗ & Er Rachidia

modest apple festival; fields south of the town are planted with orchards. And year-round, if you get the chance, try to arrive for the huge **Sunday souk**, which spreads back along the road towards Azrou.

The Town

The most interesting section of town, meriting at least a stop between buses, is the area around the old souk – **Souk Djedid**, behind the stalls facing the bus station. Just to the south of the main souk, a daily fruit and vegetable market, is an arcaded **carpet souk**, whose stalls rotate their wares in the sunlight (for natural bleaching) and pile up rugs in bewildering layers of pattern and colour. This is a relaxed place for shopping and the rugs are superb – mostly local, geometric designs from tribes of the Middle Atlas. Ask to see the "antique" ones, few of which are actually more than ten or twenty years old, but which are usually the most idiosyncratic and inventive. Good examples can also be seen at the Etoile du Sud carpet shop, behind the *Hôtel Occidental* just south of the souk and which has a large stock in three showrooms, or at the smaller Maison Berbère a few doors up from the *Hôtel Atlas*. Be prepared to bargain hard to secure a decent price – it goes without saying, don't turn up with a guide.

A more worthy place to buy carpets – plus blankets and beautiful traditional embroidery – is the **Atelier de Tissages et Broderie** (Mon–Thurs & Sat 8am–noon & 2–5.30pm), also known as Kasbah Myriem (☎035 58 24 43) in a former convent building; the entrance is just beyond that to the convent itself (see opposite). The atelier is run by six Franciscan nuns, who welcome visitors to see carpets and textiles being made from start to finish by local women. Girls learn techniques from as young as five years old, and women who choose to continue after marriage, rather than focus on domestic duties, are paid for their work. Consequently, the women practise and pass on traditional skills and designs, and also contribute to their own domestic economies.

The nuns operate this programme in conjunction with literacy courses; up to twelve local women spend two years labouring in the workshop for part of the day, then attending Arabic lessons. Admittedly, this is not the cheapest place to buy a carpet, but your money contributes directly to the local economy – next to no intermediaries are involved – and the pieces are of high quality; all *"fait avec amour"*, as the nuns put it. The atelier is located on the western outskirts of Midelt, to the left past a new mosque on the road to **Tattiouine,** where a Coopérative de Tissages is run by semi-nomadic families, also assisted by the Franciscan community.

The convent building itself, Nôtre Dame de l'Atlas, is home not to the nuns – who live in a house opposite – but to five elderly Trappist monks, among them Frère Jean-Pierre, one of only two survivors of the massacre of seven Jesuit monks in Tibhirine, Algeria, in 1996. He had been visiting when the Islamic extremists swooped. Mass is held at the convent (times are posted on the metal gate at the entrance) and visitors are welcome to join in.

If you follow the Tattiouine road a few kilometres further, you enter very different countryside from that around Midelt, where eagles soar above the hills

Mibladene and El Ahouli: Moroccan klondike

Less than an hour's drive from Midelt, on the banks of the **Oued Moulouya** where it emerges from its spectacular gorge, is the deserted mining settlement of **El Ahouli**. You can reach it by car from Midelt, first along the S317, past **Mibladene** (11km from Midelt) and then, by the 3419, to El Ahouli (another 14km). At the outset, the route from Midelt is not easy to find because it is not signposted. Leave by Avenue Moulay Idriss. Alternatively, 4x4 and fossicking excursions run by *Hôtel Safari-Atlas* (see p.316) cost from 300dh per person per day.

Once past Mibladene (appropriately, "our mother earth" in Berber) where modest excavations are still being worked, the road deteriorates and the tarmac virtually disappears as you approach El Ahouli. In some respects the barren and tortuous route from Mibladene, and the desolate landscape around it, are reason enough to do the trip. The bleak plateau where Mibladene is located leads to a narrow and picturesque gorge, which you negotiate with frequent crossings of the river on rattling wooden bridges. On a clear day the reddish landscape provides a dramatic contrast with the blue sky.

Soon, you reach the mining ruins on both sides of the river. From the turn of the twentieth century, and long before on a more modest scale, the locals mined **lead**, which contained **silver**. In 1979, around three thousand people still worked here but all had gone by the mid-1980s. You don't have to be an industrial archeologist to be impressed by the tunnels, aqueducts, aerial ropeways, barrack-like living quarters and, above all, the mine buildings, pressed high against the cliff face like a Tibetan monastery. Tracks cut across the sides of the gorge – first used by mules, then a mineral-line railway passing through the tunnels – and everywhere there is rusting ironmongery.

Beyond El Ahouli, a rough track continues downstream to **Ksabi** from where you can complete the circuit to Midelt by the N15 and N13. Realistically, most of the route beyond Mibladene needs a 4x4 because the track is regularly subjected to flash floods. If you find a grand taxi whose driver agrees to do the trip – not everyone will, because of the poor condition of the track – expect to pay between 200dh and 300dh for a return trip to the mines, including a two-hour stopover at the site.

and mule tracks lead down to valleys dotted with an occasional kasbah. For more on this area – and the Cirque Jaffar beyond – see opposite.

Practicalities

Midelt's **bus station**, in the centre of town, has regular departures to Azrou, Meknes, Fes, Er Rachidia and Rissani, with fewer services to Casablanca and Rabat. The **grand taxi** stand, behind it on Avenue Moulay Abdallah, has regular runs to Azrou, Fes, Meknes, Zeida, Khenifra and Er Rachidia. There is a small men-only **hammam** on Avenue Tarik Souk Jamâa (daily 7am–9pm; 6dh). For **Internet** access, Cyber Panorama opposite the bus stop (daily 9.30am–1pm & 2.30–10.30pm) is handy to knock off an email while waiting for a bus, otherwise Cybre Melouya at 3 Av Moulay Idriss and Cyber el Ayachi, at 43 Av Tarik Souk Jamâa, are both open daily from 9am–midnight.

The hotel *Safari-Atlas* arranges **4x4 excursions** to the El Ahouli mines, the Djebel Ayachi and Cirque Jaffar; a Land Rover for up to six people costs from 1200dh per day, including driver service and food.

Accommodation

Midelt has a reasonable spread of accommodation, but **hotels** are often full by mid-afternoon in peak season, so arrive early or make a reservation the day before. There is a **municipal campsite** (☎070 18 07 04) behind the *Hôtel el Ayachi*, rather bare and stony, but with a pool in summer (5dh nonresidents) and hot showers. The *Centre Timnay*, 30km northwest of Midelt on the N13 to Azrou (see below), is a better place to camp if you have your own transport.

Auberge Jaffar 5km west of town on the Cirque du Jaffar road ☎035 58 34 15. Fantastic views over the Djebel Ayachi, friendly management and the bonus of a pool. ❹

Centre Timnay signposted on the N13 30km northwest of Midelt ☎035 57 69 53, ✉timnay@iam.net.ma. A very popular spot with excellent facilities and friendly management. As well as tent spaces it offers basic, clean rooms with communal facilities, or for 30dh you can sleep under a Berber tent. Treks and 4x4 excursions can also be arranged. ❷

Hôtel Atlas 3 Rue Mohammed Amraoui (☎035 58 29 38). A lovely small *pension* run by a charming Berber family, their ten cosy rooms spotless and sweet. It's popular, so arrive early or book in advance. You can sleep on the terrace for 30dh. Hot showers 10dh. ❶

Hôtel el Ayachi Rue Agadir: follow the signs ☎035 58 21 61, ☏035 58 33 07. Midelt's main upmarket hotel, once chockablock with tour groups, now rather frayed at the edges. The best rooms are comfy but dated – those at the rear look over the garden to High Atlas peaks. A 1990 *International Gastronomy Award* remains on display in the restaurant (menu 100dh) – still the best in town when it pulls out the stops. ❺

Hôtel Bougafer 7 Av Mohammed V ☎ & ☏035 58 30 99, ⊕www.bougaferweb.com. A friendly, modern place above a café with rooms distributed over two

floors: en-suites on the first floor are the newest and most expensive; those above are cheaper with shared facilities (hot showers 10dh). There are great views from the roof terrace, where you can sleep out for 25dh or in a Berber tent for 50dh, and a restaurant. Locks its doors at 11pm. ❶

Hôtel Kasbah 2km south on the Er Rachidia road ☎035 58 04 05, ☏035 58 39 45. An impressive pile that is styled after a traditional kasbah but has three-star facilities: a/c in rooms, a flamboyantly decorated restaurant and a pool. Some readers have reported surly management. ❺

Hôtel Massira 11 Av des Anciens Combattents ☎035 36 10 10, ☏035 36 10 10. A fallback if the other cheapies are full, its 20 rooms functional rather than pleasant, though most have washbasins and hot showers are free. ❶

Hôtel Roi de la Bière corner of Av Hassan II and Av des FAR ☎ & ☏035 58 26 75. A pleasant and comfortable place founded in 1938, clean and well kept – some rooms have en-suite (hot) showers. No beer in the bar anymore, mind. ❹

Hôtel Safari-Atlas 118 Bd Palestine ☎ & ☏035 58 00 69, ✉safariatlas_hotel@yahoo.com. One of the better mid-range hotels in town, this has spacious and comfortable en-suite rooms, all fairly modern and with a/c. It has a restaurant – usually open to residents only – with menus from 60dh; just below the hotel there is also a patisserie. Includes breakfast. ❹

Eating

A clutch of café-restaurants south of the bus station on Avenue Mohammed V prepare simple **meals**; try the *Café L'Espoir* (no tel; daily 10am–9pm; cheap), or opposite on Rue Lalla Aïcha, the *Restaurant de Fes* (*Chez Fatima et Fils*) (☎062 05 77 54; daily noon–3pm & 6–9pm; moderate), which offers a generous *menu du jour* for 80dh, with vegetarian tajines and quince stewed in sugar and cinnamon for afters. Outside the hotels, other options include the *Restaurant Le Pin*, part of a tourist complex on Avenue Moulay Abdallah (daily 10am–3pm & 7–10pm; moderate), whose offerings include tajines, brochettes and omelettes. More relaxing than its hall-like dining room are the bar and tent-syled café in the gardens – a pleasant spot for breakfast.

The Cirque Jaffar, Djebel Ayachi and beyond

The classic route around Midelt is the **Cirque Jaffar**, a good *piste* which leaves the Midelt–Tattiouine road to edge its way through a hollow in the foothills of the **Djebel Ayachi** (see box, p.318). This runs round the *cirque*, then loops back to the Midelt–Azrou road after 34km (turn right, onto the 3426, near the *Maison Forestière de Mitkane*); it is only 79km in all back to Midelt, but takes a good half-day to complete.

Across the Atlas

Standard cars make it over the Atlas from Midelt to Tinerhir in summer, though it's a lot easier with four-wheel-drive vehicles; everyone needs a pick and spade for the occasional very rough detour (beware of scorpions when shifting rocks, by the way), some warm clothes and a tent for sleeping out at night – Atlas nights are chilly even in summer. If you don't have a vehicle, you can use Berber lorries over the various stages, which provide a kind of bus service most days. Travelling this way, you should reckon on up to three days for the journey to Imilchil (though you might make it in one), and a similar number from there down to the Todra Gorge and Tinerhir (see p.566). Note that you can also reach Imilchil on daily mini-buses from Rich (see p.318).

South towards Er Rachidia

There's less adventure in continuing **south from Midelt to Er Rachidia**, though the route is a striking one, marking the transition to the south and the desert. The area was long notorious for raids upon caravans and travellers carried out by the Aït Haddidou, a nomadic Berber tribe, fear of whom led the main spring along this route to be known as *Aïn Khrob ou Hrob* – "Drink and Flee". The tribe were pacified with great difficulty by the French, with skirmishes only fizzling out as late as the 1930s, and as a result traditional *ksour* (fortified villages) are often shadowed by old Foreign Legion posts.

The Tizi n'Talrhmeht and Rich

Around 30km south of Midelt, you heave up across one of the lower passes of the High Atlas, the **Tizi n'Talrhmeht** (Pass of the She-Camel), before descending onto a sparse desert plain. At Aït Messaoud, just beyond the pass, there's a distinctly *Beau Geste*-like Foreign Legion fort, and a few kilometres further down, you come across the first southern *ksar*, Aït Kherrou, a river oasis at the entrance to a small gorge. After this, the *ksour* begin to dot the landscape as the road follows the meanders of the great Ziz River.

Djebel Ayachi and Tounfite

Djebel Ayachi can be climbed from Midelt, either returning to the town, or as part of a through-trek to Tounfite. From Midelt, a taxi or pick-up can be arranged to the springs 2km beyond Tattiouine, and the long **Ikkis valley** followed, with a bivouac at its head (the col at the end leads to the Cirque du Jaffar). An easy ascent leads to the many summits of this huge range, which was long thought to be the highest in Morocco (it is 3700m – compared to Toubkal at 4167m). A descent south to the Oued Taarart valley brings you to several villages and a Wednesday truck out to Tounfite.

At **Tounfite**, rooms are available and buses and taxis link it with **Boumia** (with a Thurs souk), Zeïda and Midelt. The village also gives access to the Djebel Masker (3265m) – a long day's climb, rising from cedar forests. Ayachi and Masker are long wave-crests; seen from a distance they appear to curve over the horizon such is the scale.

Serious expeditions

From Tounfite, an interesting *piste* runs west, between the Toujjet and Oujoud peaks to the head of the Melwiya plains and Arghbala, beyond which lies the main *piste* across the Central Atlas via Imilchil. South of Djebel Masker lies a chaos of spectacular peaks, little visited. The only information in English at present is in Michael Peyron's *Grand Atlas Traverse* guide, which details the whole zone between Midelt and the Toubkal massif.

The main settlement in these parts is **RICH**, a dusty, red-washed market town and administrative centre, spread on a plain between mountains. Enclosed by palms that are watered by a *seguia* or *khettera* (irrigation channel) from the Oued Ziz, the town developed around a *ksar* and was an important fort during the Protectorate. It still has shades of *Beau Geste* about it, as well as a lively Monday **souk**. Several **hotels** lie just off the main square, the best of which is *Hôtel Isli* (☎035 36 81 91; ❶), which has clean rooms and free hot showers above a café-restaurant. In the unlikely event that it's full, on the same street are the basic *Hôtel Salama* (☎035 58 93 43; ❶) and the *El Massira* (☎035 58 93 40; ❶), marginally preferable and which has hot showers and a restaurant.

Over the Atlas from Rich

West of Rich, the Atlas mountains stretch into the distance, skirted by a road up behind the town which trails the last section of the Oued Ziz. The R317 (formerly 3443) road west from Rich begins as the R706 (formerly 3442) and is surfaced all the way to Imilchil. Minibus taxis ply this impressive route daily, a wonderful three-hour trip through great gorges and ever-more barren valleys. They depart in the morning from a *place* one block east of the bus station, by the road sign to Imilchil, then head to the bridge across the Ziz; you can pick them up at either place, usually from around 7am.

The route can also be travelled in stages by **Berber lorries** (*camions*), which head for the Imilchil souk on Fridays. Land Rover taxis also cover the route and, if there are enough customers, you will be able to pay for a *place* rather than chartering the whole vehicle. The most promising day to set out from Rich by *camion* or Land Rover is Friday (or early Saturday morning), when you might get a shared vehicle all the way to Imilchil for its Saturday souk; make enquiries at the Rich hotels.

The Ziz Gorges

The scenic highlight of the regular Midelt–Er Rachidia route is the dramatic **Ziz Gorges**, tremendous erosions of rock which carve a passage through the Atlas. The route follows the Ziz valley from **AÏT KROJMANE** (7km from Rich) onwards, just past the Ziz ("gazelle" in Berber) filling station. About 20km from Rich, you will see a cluster of modern buildings on the right between the road and the river, signposted **Hammat Moulay Ali Cherif**. This is a small, but well-known spa, whose outdoor hot springs (over 36°C), rich in magnesium and sulphates, are said to cure rheumatic disorders and kidney problems. You will see the afflicted hopefuls in steamy thickets nearby. Men and women bathe on alternate days and there is a café and some primitive rooms to rent.

A further 5km on, you enter the gorges proper, around 25km from Rich, shortly after the **Tunnel du Légionnaire**, built by the French in 1930 to open up the route to the south and still guarded by drowsy soldiers. The gorges are truly majestic, especially in late-afternoon, when they are lit by great slashes of sunlight and the mountain landscape reveals sudden vistas of brilliant green oasis and red-brown *ksour*.

You emerge from the gorges near the vast **Barrage Hassan Addakhil**, built in 1971 to irrigate the valley of the Tafilalt beyond, and to supply electricity for El Rachidia. The dam also regulates the flow of the Oued Ziz, preventing the serious flooding which occurred frequently before it was built, as witnessed by the deserted *ksour* in the gorges above and below the lake.

Azrou to Kasba Tadla

The **main route from Azrou to Marrakesh** – the N8 – skirts well clear of the Atlas ranges. The towns along the way are dusty, functional market centres, unlikely to tempt you to linger, and the interest is all in the subtle changes of land, cultivation and architecture as you move into the south. In addition, the Middle Atlas is close at hand if you leave the main road and take to the *pistes*. A great network of them spreads out behind the small town of **El Ksiba**, itself 4km off the N8, but easily hitched to from the turn-off or reached by bus from Kasba Tadla.

Khenifra

With long-distance buses regularly passing through the provincial centre of **KHENIFRA**, you are unlikely to get stranded here. Nor are you likely to want to: the once fast-flowing **Oued Oumer Rbia** is sluggish and grubby, and the modern quarters, bisected by the Fes-Marrakesh road (N8), are not much more enticing. Perhaps, the only reasons to stop are to head to the Cascades of Oum er Rbia (see p.311) if you are travelling up from Marrakesh, or to browse a Sunday souk or a Berber rug auction on Saturday afternoons, held just across the bridge near the bus station.

Indeed, Khenifra now seems far too mundane to have been a focus of resistance under Moha ou Hammou. Yet in the early years of the Protectorate, the French suffered a costly victory here, losing six hundred men when they took the town in 1914. There used to be an impressive **monument** recording the event, 7km south on the road to Marrakesh, but this seems to have disappeared, for understandable reasons. The town also played an important part in the struggle for independence which climaxed on August 20, 1955. In his book *Lords of the Atlas* (see p.772), Gavin Maxwell records that Gilbert Grandval, the Resident General, returned from Paris to Rabat:

> **at 2am on the 20th, and at 7am the Director of the Interior, General Leblanc, telephoned to him with the opening words, 'It is war.' Massive rioting had broken out at Khenifra, and the General asked authorization to use aircraft. The Medina was surrounded by troops, but mounted tribesmen were visible on all the ridges that could be seen from the town. Grandval gave his authorization, but on the condition that use of aircraft should be limited to low flying dispersal of tribal cavalry, and that no shot be fired or bomb dropped. This was only the beginning; during the next few hours, the situation was repeated at Boujad, Safi, Ouezzane, Petit Jean, Casablanca and Rabat.**

The revolution proved unstoppable – Morocco was independent within a year.

Practicalities

Arriving from the north on the N8 Fes–Marrakesh road, named Avenue Zerktouni, the **bus station** is on your right, served by frequent daily services to Marrakesh, Meknes, Fes, Kasbah Tadla, Beni Mellal and Azrou, plus destinations as far as Tetouan or Rissani. Less frequent services go to Midelt and even Er Rachidia – if the wait is long you could always take a bus to "Trente Trois", the junction of the N8 Fes–Marrakesh road with the R503 road towards Midelt, and pick up a connection there. Southbound **grands taxis** – including those for El Ksiba – leave behind the bus station, those for Fes and Meknes leave from a station in the Medina.

Turning left 200m north of the bus station, at the junction with main thoroughfare Avenue Mohammed V, you cross the river. On the far side of the bridge on your right, the small **Souk Central des Tapis** has a few Berber carpet stalls, beyond which on opposite sides of the street are the **PTT** and BMCE **bank**. Just past the PTT, the **municipal market** marks the beginning of the **Medina**, with lively narrow streets, but nothing of special interest. **Internet** facilities are available at cyber-cafés every 50m or so north of the bus station on Avenue Zerktouni, or Cyber Zahranet opposite *Hôtel Melilla* (see opposite) is open 10am–midnight.

Accommodation and eating

The best place to **eat** is the restaurant of the *Hôtel de France* (noon–3.30pm & 7pm–midnight; moderate), offering all the usual dishes plus good steaks and 80dh menus, though it's a long walk unless you take a petit taxi (see directions below). Otherwise, there are a number of cafés and restaurants around the junction of Avenue Zerktouni and Avenue Mohammed V; the *Hôtel Najah* (12.30–5pm & 7–9pm; moderate) prepares well-cooked menus for 90dh, although the dining room is rather impersonal, and *La Coupole* (11am–9pm; cheap) just north offers charcoal-oven pizza to eat in or take away from 30dh.

Hôtel Arego Av Zerktouni, just south of main junction ☎035 58 64 87. Simple but clean and friendly, with shared bathrooms. It's on the main road, so you either have noisy, bright rooms at the front, or dingy, quiet rooms at the rear. ❷

Hôtel de France Quartier des FAR ☎035 58 61 14, ℻035 38 45 20. Clean old-fashioned

en-suites and service with a smile. The restaurant is excellent – far better than the hotel in fact. Cross the river then go past the Medina on a palm-fringed road for another 800m. The hotel is behind the Mobil petrol station. A petit taxi will cost around 8dh from the bus station. ❸

Hôtel Jaouharat al Atlas (formerly *Hôtel Rif*), Av Zerktouni, just north of the bus station ☎ 035 58 80 30. Modest but comfortable and clean place, usually with hot water. ❷

Hôtel Melilla Off Av Zerktouni, next to the bus station ☎ 035 38 46 09. Opened in 1995, standards seem to be gradually falling, with hutch-sized basic rooms. The bus station is noisy even at night, so avoid the rooms facing it. ❷

Hôtel Najah Av Zerktouni, just north of the junction with Av Mohammed V ☎ 035 58 83 31, ☎ 035 58 78 74. A central business hotel, with comfortable and heated rooms – all en-suite,

all spotless and with satellite TV. Has a good restaurant too. ❺

Hôtel Sahara 3 Av Bir Anzarane, just behind the municipal market ☎ 035 38 53 18. No frills (literally) in functional rooms – the cheapest option in town. ❶

Riad Zayani (formerly *Hôtel Hammou Zayane*), Cité el Amal, 500m uphill east from the junction of avenues Zerktouni and Mohammed V ☎ 035 58 60 20, ☎ 035 58 65 3. No riad, whatever the name change. Rather, the same dated establishment poshed up by a health and beauty spa. Friendly, though, and dated decor in good en-suite rooms has a retro appeal. Also has tennis courts and swimming pool. ❹

Northwest of Khenifra: Oulmès

The R407 (formerly 2516) from Khenifra leads northwest through the Djebel Mouchchene, a forested outcrop of the Middle Atlas, towards Rabat. Although little known to tourists, the hill country here is attractive: rolling hills, often forested, are topped with volcanic peaks and riven by the deep gorges of northwesterly flowing rivers, most entering the sea as the Oum er Rbia between Rabat and Sale. Wild boar roam the hills and there is good birdlife and a rich flora in spring. There is a major **souk** at the crossroads settlement of Aguelmouss each Saturday.

Midway along the route is the small town of **OULMÈS** and, some 4km off along a side road, the spa-hamlet of **OULMÈS LES THERMES (TARMILATE)**, home of the Moroccan mineral waters Oulmès (fizzy) and Sidi Ali (still). Standards are exacting – bottle tops bear not only the date but the time of production – and you can witness the whole process, from the bottles being made, to being loaded full onto lorries ready for the off, on tours organized by the spa's **hotel**, *Hôtel des Thermes* (closed July & Aug; ☎ 037 52 31 56; ❸), still owned by the company. Staff are welcoming, meals huge and rooms good – altogether excellent value. The walk down to the gorge and hot springs is recommended for the fit.

El Ksiba, Aghbala and across the Atlas

EL KSIBA is a busy Berber village lying 4km south of the N8 Fes–Marrakesh road, enclosed by apricot, olive and orange groves and with a **Sunday souk**. Two buses arrive daily from Kasba Tadla, as do **grands taxis** from Khenifra and Kasba Tadla. The village, dusty and not terribly inspiring, has a **bank** and

---

Olive oil

On the main road (N8) near El Ksiba, and particularly either side of Tirhboula (45km from Beni Mellal), you will see plastic bottles hanging from roadside trees to advertise the availability of olive oil crushed from local olives in the adjacent domestic presses. Regardless of whether you have a passion for cooking or drizzling your salads with olive oil, it's well worth a stop in early autumn to see the presses at work. You'll be welcome to visit – and to buy.

When ripe, the black olives contain up to sixty percent oil. Some of them are harvested unripe or green and then pickled in salt. Both ripe and unripe olives are normally bitter; this can be corrected by soaking them first in an alkaline solution.

a passable small **hotel**, the *Henri IV* (☎ & ℱ023 41 50 02; ❸), in the Quartier Administrative; from the centre of the village, head uphill from opposite the petrol station and bear left after about 300m – if coming by car from the N8, take the left before you enter the village. The hotel is in attractive surroundings, with plenty of scope for day walks or overnight treks. The **PTT** is next door. A little beyond here, the road divides, the left fork following a rough track for 800m to reach the *Auberge des Artistes* (☎023 41 54 90 or 062 11 94 05; ❹). Managed by French couple Patricia and François, the *auberge* is a charming spot in the middle of the countryside, with double rooms, dorm beds (150dh) and **camping** facilities, and a restaurant which is open all hours in theory (menu 120dh). The campsite, favoured by overland expeditions and bikers en route to Imilchil, is a better choice than another 2km further on, the *Camping Taghbalout*, notoriously rowdy and with an erratic water supply.

South of El Ksiba, the road crosses the Atlas by way of Imilchil and the Todra gorge to Tinerhir (see map, p.575). Once a challenging *piste*, this is now mostly tarmac and measures are being taken to avoid past wash-out danger spots.

From El Ksiba, the R317 road twists through forest to a panoramic col, then descends to a river and a junction with the R306 to Ouaouizaght and Azilal via the Bin el Ouidane reservoir (see p.327), a fine scenic drive. **Ouaouizaght** has a busy Wednesday souk, and one hotel, the *Hôtel Atlas* (☎023 44 20 42; ❶) at the top end of town.

The R317 meanwhile turns upwards by a gorge and continues through varied forest to cross the **Tizi n'Isli** pass (a village of the same name is just off the road). From here, it snakes down to a junction, at which an unnamed road branches off eastward to **Arhbala**, a busy market town with a Wednesday souk, and cafés that have rooms to rent (see p.578). This road continues to meet the R503 Beni Mellal–Midelt road, an attractive circuit, surfaced but in a poor state.

Heading south from the junction, route R317 (also known here as the trans-Atlas road) crosses a girder bridge and continues on a rough road to **Ikassene**, something of a staging post on this route, with several cafés, and rooms available. Beyond Ikassane, a new line leads on to Tassent, then hauls upwards on many bends (periodic landslides may block it) to a high valley and a col, giving a view to the Tislit lake, beyond which lies Imilchil (see p.578).

Kasba Tadla

KASBA TADLA takes its name from a fortress Moulay Ismail built here, strategically positioned beside the Oum er Rbia river. It remains a military town, not that you'd know it in a surprisingly sleepy, leafy town centre. The only site – such as it is – is a walled **kasbah** at the southern end of the main street, Avenue Mohammed V. This features an impressive derelict Grand Mosque with a crumbling brick minaret, and an interesting smaller mosque,

---

The R503

The road linking the Kasba Tadla–Khenifra N8 and the Azrou–Midelt–Er Rachidia N13 has some attractive scenery in its western end and a visit to the lively souk at Ek Kbab is recommended, with a scenic drive continuing up the Oued Serrou to Kerrouchen (on the edge of the cedar country) and the Tizi n' Rechou which leads to Zeïda. The R503 gives views over the huge Moulaya plain with Ibel Ayachi and Ibel Masker dipping beyond horizons east and west.

whose minaret has the same protruding perches as that of the Great Mosque in Tiznit (see p.649). The rest of the area inside the walls is taken up with the poor makeshift homes typical of Morocco's *bidonvilles*.

As you enter town, keep an eye open for four tall, square pillars near the turn-off on the N8 Fes–Marrakesh road (about 1km from the town centre). This is a **memorial** to the French soldiers killed hereabouts from 1912 to 1933, and affords a fine view of the *bidonville* by the river and the town beyond. The town's other main feature is a sizeable **souk** held on Mondays.

For anyone stranded, there are two cheap and very basic **hotels** off Avenue Mohammed V, a few blocks north of the kasbah. The better of the two is the ramshackle *Hôtel des Alliés* at 38 Av Mohammed V (☎023 41 85 87; cold showers; ❶), with iron bedsteads in rooms and a barn-like bar that could have been transported from 1930s pastoral France; no alcohol, though. The only other option is the cheaper and even more basic *Hôtel Atlas*, round the block at 46 Rue Majjati Obad (no phone; ❶).

Your best bet in town for **eating** is the *Restaurant Kordouba* (daily 8am–10pm; cheap) a couple of blocks south of the *Alliés* at the corner of Avenue Mohammed V and Rue Tarik Ibn Ziad, serving chicken, brochettes and steak. The *Café St Clair* (daily 8am–11pm; cheap) opposite the *Hôtel des Alliés* has decent snacks. For out-of-hours meals, there's the aptly named *Restaurant Jour et Nuit* (daily 24hr) at the bus station. The **banks** there are on Rue Majjati Obad near the *Hôtel Atlas* – Banque Populaire and BCMP have machines, WAFA offers Western Union transfer facilities – and the **PTT** is on Avenue des FAR (parallel with Avenue Mohammed V, two blocks east) heading out of town towards the N8 Fes–Marrakesh road.

On the same road in the other direction, 500m north of the town centre, the **bus** station has frequent departures for Beni Mellal and Khenifra, two a day to El Ksiba, and more long-distance services to Marrakesh, Fes, Meknes, Midelt and Casablanca, with even one daily departure each for Tangier and Agadir. The **grand taxi** yard opposite offers regular runs to Beni Mellal, El Ksiba, Khenifra and Marrakesh.

Beni Mellal

Ideally sited between Marrakesh and Fes, and on the main routes to Casa and Rabat, **BENI MELLAL** is one of Morocco's fastest-growing towns, whose haphazardly planned new suburbs nibble deeper into the surrounding olive groves with every year. A largely modern town, it has few specific sights – and even fewer tourists – but makes a break en route to Marrakesh or a good transit point for other destinations; it is well connected by bus services. It also serves as a market centre for the broad, prosperous flatlands to the north, hosting a large **Tuesday souk** which is good for woollen blankets that feature unusual Berber designs. Olives are grown on the lower slopes of the Djebel Tassemit and the plain is well known for its oranges.

Moulay Ismail's **kasbah** in the old Medina has been restored to the point of no interest. Your time is better spent walking to the smaller **Kasbah de Ras el Aïn** – local wags joke you can see the sea on a clear day – and the nearby spring of **Aïn Asserdoun**, both south of town. The latter (signposted on a Circuit Touristique from town, which peters out thereafter, presumably for a lack of sights) is a pleasant spot, feeding a series of artificial falls amid well-tended gardens (Moroccans love waterfalls). A petit taxi (8dh) or bus #3 from the

El Ksiba

Kasba Tadla & Fes

Ain
Asserdoun

Kasbah
Ras el Aïn

N

N8a

AVENUE MOHAMMED V

AVENUE IBN SINA

RUE IBN HASSAN

NEW
MEDINA

Ensemble
Artesanal

CTM

RUE TARIK
IBN ZIAD

RUE TARIK IBN HASSAN

RUE TARIK EL HASSAN

PLACE DE LA
LIBERTÉ

Banque
Populaire
& BMCE

Souk

Grands Taxis

AVENUE DES F.A.R.

Bus
Station

Grand
Taxi
Stand

RUE CHOUKI

AVENUE MOHAMMED V

PTT

Crédit
du Maroc

Stadium

Banque Populaire

AVENUE HASSAN II

AVENUE HASSAN II

Grands Taxis

1 km

0

AVENUE MOHAMMED V

N8a

Marrakesh

Casablanca

BENI MELLAL

RESTAURANTS

Café Restaurant Tawada	4
Restaurant Noumidia	2
Safa-Glace	3
Snack Bensouda	1

ACCOMMODATION

Hôtel Aïn Asserdoun	D
Hôtel al Bassatine	E
Hôtel Chems	J
Hôtel Gharnata	I
Hôtel Kamal	C
Hôtel Ouzoud	K
Hôtel de Paris	F
Hôtel es Saada	G
Hôtel Tassamet	H
Hôtel Venisia	A
Hôtel Zidania/	
Hôtel Charaf	B

Medina (summer only) will take you to the *source*, from where you can walk to the kasbah, fifteen minutes up the footpath behind the car park – start from the steps at the far left.

If you're in Beni Mellal on a Saturday, it's worth a trip to what is traditionally the Middle Atlas's largest weekly **market**, held 35km southwest of the town at **Souk Sebt des Oulad Nemâa**, and linked by regular buses.

Practicalities

The main road from Fes to Marrakesh (the N8) cuts into the northern suburbs of Beni Mellal as the N8a and leads to the **bus station**; if you can't face the 20min walk to the centre, a petit taxi will cost around 7dh. The old Fes–Marrakesh road carves through the town centre as **Avenue Mohammed V**, offering a glimpse of the plain to the north midway along. The focus of the old **Medina** is the cream-and-white arcaded **Place de la Liberté**.

There are plenty of **banks** around the **PTT**, all with ATMs, or out of banking hours; you can change money at Imilchil Voyages, 333 Av Mohammed V (Mon–Sat 8.30am–9pm; also open Sunday in summer; ☏023 48 72 59, ℱ023 48 54 90), and at the helpful Torin Voyages, across the road at 412 Av Mohammed V (☏023 48 01 91, ℱ023 48 02 60); the latter is also an agent for RAM, Air France and British Airways. The **tourist office** is on Avenue Hassan II, just south of the junction with Boulevard Mohammed V (☏023 10 86 63, Mon–Fri July & Aug 7.30am–3.30pm, Sept–June 8.30am–noon & 2–6.30pm). For details of local guides – and adventure tours – into the Atlas from Beni Mellal, see box, p.326.

Accommodation

If the Medina **hotels** listed here are full – unlikely, admittedly – try more basic options on Place de la Liberté.

Hôtel Aïn Asserdoun Av des FAR ☏ & ℱ023 48 34 93). A friendly place, with a small restaurant (menu 80dh), comfortable accommodation and en-suite bathrooms; popular with Moroccans passing through. ❸

Hôtel al Bassatine Ouled Hamdane, Route de Fkih Ben Salah ☏023 48 22 47, ✉al_bassatine@yahoo .fr. A tour group favourite on the outskirts, set in its own gardens and whose good rooms all have balconies. Has a large swimming pool too. The food is disappointing, though. Includes breakfast. ❺

Hôtel Chems ☏023 48 34 60, ℱ 023 48 85 30. One of two garden hotels on the original Marrakesh road, this is less flash than the nearby *Hôtel Ouzoud* (see below), but also more friendly. Accommodation is modern, facilities include a pool, tennis courts and a nightclub. Includes breakfast. ❻

Hôtel Gharnata Corner of Rue Chouki and Av Mohammed V ☏023 48 34 82, ☏023 42 24 27. Nothing special and two-star rooms are on the small side, but well-placed in the town centre. ❸

Hôtel Ouzoud ☏023 48 37 52, ⊕www.sogatour .ma. This looks indistinguishable from the nearby *Hôtel Chems*, but is a swish, international-standard place favoured by visiting executives; good restaurant, bar, tennis courts and swimming pool. Includes breakfast. ❼

Hôtel de Paris Hay Ibn Sina, New Medina ☏023 48 22 45, ℱ023 48 42 27. A 1950s-style hotel, fifteen minutes from the town centre. Pleasant rooms, all with a/c, have a country vibe thanks to pine furniture. Good restaurant too. ❹

Hôtel es Saada 129 Rue Tarik Ibn Ziad ☏023 48 29 91. A cheap but clean place with helpful management; hot showers for 7dh next door. ❶

Hôtel Tassamet 186 Rue Ahmed el Hansali, just off the street ☏023 42 13 13. A cut above the usual Medina cheapie, clean and welcoming, with constant hot water and en-suite rooms (❸), and good views from front-facing rooms – ask for a balcony – and the roof terrace. ❶

Hôtel Venisia Round the corner from *Hôtel Zidania* on Bd 20 Août ☏023 48 23 48. Newest and best of the trio of similarly priced hotels facing the bus station, with well-kept and comfortable en-suite rooms. If it's full, the *Hôtel Kamal* (☏023 48 69 41) on the main road is a better bet than the twinned *Hôtel Zidania/Hôtel Charaf* (☏023 48 18 98) nearby. ❸

Eating

Beni Mellal is not blessed with choices for eating out, and many options are choked by exhaust fumes on Avenue Mohammed V. For upmarket **meals**, try *Hôtel Ouzoud* (daily 11.30am–3pm & 6.30–11pm; moderate to expensive), whose smart restaurant serves international and Moroccan dishes, or *Hôtel de Paris* (daily 10.30am–3pm & 6.30–11.30pm; moderate), which offers a self-service buffet and à la carte. In the town centre, tasty fare at lower prices is rustled up at the *Café Restaurant Tawada* (11.30am–3pm & 7–11pm; cheap)

South of Beni Mellal: Atlas hikes and pistes

The mountains south and southeast of Beni Mellal and the Bin el Ouidane reservoir are ideal trekking and Land Rover country. In the foothills, **Djebel Tassemit** (2248m) – which towers like a high wall behind Beni Mellal – offers a challenge and fine views; reached by Aïn Asserdoun and the Kasbah de Ras el Aïn. **Djebel R'Nim** (2411m) can be climbed from the pass to **Ouaouizaght**. The road from Marrakesh to Aghbala via Azilal, Bin el Ouidane and Ouaouizaght is surfaced all the way and offers grand scenery, far more interesting than the N8 across the plain through Beni Mellal.

The real mountains lie to the south. A road crosses the east end of the reservoir to wend its way through to Tillouguïte (which has a Saturday souk), becoming a Jeepable *piste* at the col. It continues spectacularly to reach the Oued Ahansal (bridge washed out in 1999), from where one branch goes up the Oued Mellal to Anergui (*gîte*), access for **Mouriq** (3223m), Laqroun (3117m) and the **Mellal Gorges**. The other branch goes to Tamga, facing the soaring limestone walls of the peak nicknamed *"La Cathédrale"* (a spectacular goat path actually leads to the summit dome). The *piste* then makes a high and tortuous ascent to **Zaouia Ahancal**, a *marabout's* shrine at the village of **Agoudim** in what are known as "the Dolomites of Morocco" (70km from Tillouguite).

Zaouia Ahancal is also reached by a *piste* from Aït Mohammed and Azilal, descending under Aroudane's massive cliffs. Agoudim's tower architecture is unique north of the Atlas, and it has long been a religious centre, besides being strong enough to stop the Glaoui chieftains (see p.516) from expanding their fiefdom further east. The Taghia gorges upstream from the village, and the plateau country beyond, offer some of the best trekking in the Atlas, and can be combined with a start/finish in the more popular Bou Guemez.

Practicalities

It would be possible to cover this route in stages, using irregular local Berber lorries or jeeps. Abderrahman Tissoukla (Rue 26, 4 Biad Somâa, ☎023 42 08 99 or 068 96 28 83), the president of the local Guides Association, is one of several local **guides** who know the area well, and can organize means of transport such as mules or Land Rovers – if you need a guide elsewhere in the Middle Atlas he can help too. For maps, contact Atlas Maps, the same firm as AMIS (see p.36), which also regularly treks this area. Land Rover expeditions are also arranged by **Imilchil Voyages** in Beni Mellal (see p.325). Across and down the road from Imilchil Voyages is another helpful travel agency, Torin Voyages at 412 Bd Mohammed V (☎023 48 01 91, ☎023 48 02 60), which is also a bureau de change and agent for RAM, Air France, BA and Alitalia.

For **accommodation**, Agoudim has several *gîtes*, and there is another at Amezraï, by the perched *agadir* a kilometre to Agoudim's north. A **topographical guide**, *Randonnées Pédestres dans le Massif du Mgoun*, is published in Morocco (and unobtainable anywhere else). While useful, the gorge explorations mentioned in it are highly dangerous scrambles rather than sedate walks, and the text should be treated with caution.

adjacent to the Total garage on Avenue Mohammed V – the rabbit tajine with raisins and cinnamon takes some beating.

As ever, the cheapest eats are in the Old Medina, where *Restaurant Noumidia* at 141 Rue Ahmed el Hansali (daily 10am–midnight; cheap) is the best of a trio of popular eateries doing roast chicken, brochettes and *kefta* kebabs. Another popular unpretentious place, offering exotic fare such as liver and brain kebabs alongside the usuals, is *Snack Bensouda* at 136 Av Mohammed V (daily noon–midnight; cheap), though outside tables are blighted by traffic. *Safa-Glace* at 40 Rue Chouki (11.30am–4pm & 6–11.30pm; cheap) has a more pleasant location, plus tasty pizzas and ice cream; frequented by a young crowd, it is particularly lively in late-evenings. A clutch of smart **cafés**, popular with businessmen and flashy young bravos, lines Avenue Mohammed V, just east of the junction with Avenue Hassan II.

Moving on

Beni Mellal is at a strategic crossroads of the Middle Atlas foothills, so is served by a wealth of **buses**. There are several daily services to Rabat, Meknes, Midelt, Marrakesh, Agadir, Casablanca and Er Rachidia. CTM has daily services to Fes, Casablanca and Marrakesh from the main bus station, where there's an erratic CTM counter – another is at the north corner of the Medina.

Grands taxis to Fes and Azrou leave from the esplanade opposite the CTM office; those to Marrakesh, Azilal, Ouaouizerhte, Fquih Ben Salah and Rabat as well as Kasba Tadla and El Ksiba, leave from a parking area behind the bus station.

The Cascades d'Ouzoud

The **Cascades d'Ouzoud** are the most spectacular in Morocco, their amphitheatre of waterfalls falling into pools in a lush valley that remains invisible till the last moment. The wide spread of cataracts at the top isn't entirely natural – water from the *oued* is channelled through a variety of irrigation channels towards the rim of the falls – but the result is an image that is not too far removed from the Muslim idea of Paradise depicted on gaudy prints throughout the nation. Nor has the site been overcommercialized – despite the cascades appearing in every national tourism brochure, the atmosphere remains laid-back and relaxing. Camping spots and cafés abound, and the good paths, high summer apart, are never too busy; the site is at its best from March until mid June, hot in summer. That there are pleasant walks in the locale is just another reason to stay overnight – to swim in pools below the cascades by moonlight (technically forbidden) is something special, and in late afternoon, arching rainbows appear in the mist around the falls.

Ouzoud lies 18km down a surfaced road off the R304 Marrakesh–Azilal road, 21km before Azilal. You could try your chances hitching from the turn-off, but it's safer to go into Azilal, where there are regular grands taxis to the falls (17dh a place or 100dh for the whole taxi). Getting back to Azilal is generally no problem, with grands taxis regularly shuttling from the falls. From Beni Mellal, a grand taxi to the falls should cost around 360dh (60dh per person if you can fill it). From Marrakesh, tourist agencies offer day-long tours.

Bin el Ouidane and Azilal

The quickest road from Beni Mellal to Azilal heads off 20km along the N8 through Afourer and hauls uphill, providing a vast panorama of the huge plain that sweeps east into the distance, then crests a pass to descend zigzagging through the hills to the **Bin el Ouidane reservoir**. This was one of the earliest (1948–55) and most ambitious of the country's irrigation schemes and has changed much of the land around Beni Mellal – formerly as dry and barren as the phosphate plains to the northwest. It also supplies much of central Morocco's electricity.

There's a small **hotel** beside the barrage, the *Auberge du Lac* (T023 44 24 65, F023 44 24 30; ❹), which offers decent rooms and camping by the river downstream of the dam. It also has a bar, a restaurant, boats for rent, and fishing; swimming is prohibited. Be warned, it is cold up here in winter – ask for extra blankets because there is no heating in the rooms.

AZILAL, 27km further on, **feels** more oversized village than provincial capital, yet its loose affiliation of streets have a garrison, banks and hotels, and a Thursday souk, and there are good transport links. There is also a **tourist office** on the main road (Rue Tarik Ibn Ziad), a few metres up from *Hôtel Assounfou*, but rarely open.

Buses drop you on a patch of wasteground behind the main square (backed by a large mosque) near the budget **hotels** on Avenue Hassan II. The best of these is the friendly *Hôtel Dades* (T023 45 82 45, Wwww.members.lycos.fr/hoteldades; ❶) 300m east (left) of the bus station and with colourful rooms around a plant-filled courtyard. On the way, you'll pass the *Tissa* (T023 45 85 89; ❶), the *Ouzoud* (T023 45 84 82; ❶) and the *Souss* (T023 45 89 17; ❶). The smartest option in town – still rather shabby – is the *Hôtel Assounfou*, 200m west of the town square on Avenue Hassan II (T023 45 92 20, F023 45 84 42; ❸). The only places to **eat** are simple café-restaurants, among them the down-to-earth *Ibnou Ziad Restaurant* (daily 7.30am–9.30pm; cheap) 50m west of the town square on Avenue Hassan II. Be aware that menus are limited in the evening. The Banque Populaire opposite the main square has an **ATM**, and there's a Crédit Agricole 200m east of it, beyond which, about 800m out of town, are the **PTT** and Complexe Artesanal. **Internet** access is widely available on the main drag; try Cyber Adrar beside *Hôtel Assounfou* (daily 8am–midnight).

Buses from Azilal serve Marrakesh four times daily, two continuing to Agadir. There are also five direct buses to Beni Mellal, three morning buses to Casablanca and two departures to Demnate, although most Marrakesh and Agadir buses also call here. **Grands taxis** from a rank beside the bus yard mostly serve Beni Mellal, plus some to the Cascades d'Ouzoud. You may also be able to get one 45km west to Tanant, and one from there to Demnate. The Bou Guemez valley is reached by a surfaced road, with a daily bus service from Azilal. Should you need a guide, seek advice at the *Hôtel Dades*.

The Cascades

The **Cascades d'Ouzoud** are a popular destination in summer, with both Moroccan and foreign tourists attracted by the falls and an easy-going ambience that is refreshingly uncommercialized – for now. The falls face northwest, so are shrouded in darkness for much of the morning and early afternoon; for the best photos, visit from mid- to late-afternoon and bring a wide-angle lens if you have one. The largest rainbows are best seen from the first of the outlook spots, halfway down the path to the bottom of the falls.

Before you descend, however, have a look at the lip of the falls just past the *Riad Cascades d'Ouzoud* (see opposite) at the top of the village. The over-sized hutches here shelter small **watermills**, some still grinding wheat into flour as the river is diverted through the wheels before it plunges over the edge. Worn grindstones are sold in some of the stalls that line the path down the valley. It starts from the top of the village, to the left of the *Dar Essalam* hotel (see below), then zigzags past **cafés and souvenir stalls to** the great basins below the **cascades**, where boatmen in rickety rafts offer to row visitors to the main pool. Although strictly speaking it's not permitted, you can swim in one of the lower natural pools – currents are dangerous in the main pool beneath the falls – and you might spot the occasional Barbary ape under the oak and pomegranate trees. Your best chance is at daybreak or an hour or so before dusk, when they come to drink in the river.

For a memorable short **hike**, go beyond the lower pools to the so-called "Mexican village" (officially named Tanaghmelt, though some guides prefer "Berber village"), a fascinating place connected by semi-underground passages. To get there, follow the path past the lower pools and you will see a path climbing up on the left, past a farmhouse and up to the top of the plain. Follow this west and the village is sited on the slopes of the wooded hills, about 1km along the path, which drops to a stream before climbing up to the houses. Allow four hours for a circuit. Another path follows the river valley beyond the falls at its narrowest and most impressive after 7km at the Gorges de l'Ouzoud-el-Abid. With your own transport, you could see this on the road north towards the N8 or unofficial guides tout their services for dayhikes; ask in hotels or at the café at the top of the village, by the turn-off towards *Hôtel Restaurant de France*.

Accommodation options start 100m beyond the taxi stand with the friendly *Dar Essalam* (☎067 51 85 07, **❶**), built around a courtyard; you can rent bare rooms or sleep on the roof (20dh). More comfortable is *Hôtel Chellal d'Ouzoud* (☎023 45 96 60, ℻023 45 95 32; **❸**) at the start of the path downhill, redecorated, clean and cool, and with its own terrace to sleep on (25dh). The restaurant offers a menu of Moroccan staples for about 60dh. For something more tranquil, the *Hôtel Restaurant de France* (☎023 45 90 17; **❸**) is among olive groves 500m from the top of the village, and has bright rooms, some en suite, and a pleasant garden. The only upmarket choice is the ⚜ *Riad Cascades d'Ouzoud* (☎023 42 91 73, ⓦ www.ouzoud.com; includes breakfast; **❻**), at the top of the village, a beautifully restored house whose rustic chic sits comfortably alongside traditional features and which has open fires in rooms in winter. Several **campsites** lie at the top of the village, all fairly basic but offering shady spots for tents and motorhomes; the first you come to is *Camping Amalou* (☎070 25 43 76). Closer to the waterfalls, cafés on the path downhill have space for camping for a few tents, either for a small fee, or free if you eat at them during your stay. All tend to attract a young backpacking clientele.

On from Ouzoud

Continuing to Marrakesh from Ouzoud on local transport, it's easiest to backtrack to Azilal, picking up a bus there to Beni Mellal or (if you time it right) direct to Marrakesh. However, if you are driving you could head down to **Khemis des Oulad** on the Beni Mellal–Marrakesh road (N8) – 51km of tarred road.

Bou Guemez valley and Ighil Mgoun

The **Bou Guemez valley** ("La Vallée Heureux") is second only to Djebel Toubkal in popularity among mountain-lovers, not only for its own unique

Ighil Mgoun, at 4068m, is Morocco's only summit above four thousand metres outside the Toubkal massif, and a popular target for hill-goers, giving an easy but long ascent from a base on the Tessaout Sources/Tarkeddid plateau, itself most easily reached from the Bou Guemez valley. This remote spot is the start of the Oued Tessaout, which descends the spectacular Wandras gorge (climbing involved) and also the Arouss gorge (climbing) to the Bou Guemez and, eastwards then south, drains out to Imi n'Wakka and Kelaal de Mgouna; three to four days including many hours of wading gorges (flash flood risk), easy but dramatic. Tarkeddid (3565m) gives excellent climbing on its traverse. West of Mgoun, two rarely visited peaks of 3883m and 3877m, are the highest between Mgoun and the Toubkal area. Other peaks too make this a deservedly popular area. Several *gîtes* make walking in the Bou Guemez itself worthwhile, while east, between Azourki (3677m) and Ouaougoulzat (3763m), both skiers' objectives in winter, is the seasonal Lac Izoughar (Izourar), beyond which lies the vast nomad plateau and gorges between Zaouia Ahancal and the Dadès (see p.326).

The Tessaout Valley

Demnate is the gateway into the Tessaout valley, and to Imi n'Wakka and Tarbat n'Tirsal, below vast Djebel Rhat and near Tizi n'Tirghyst, with the finest area of rock carvings in Morocco (and the continuation of the Bou Willi/Bou Guemez valleys). From the Tuesday souk at Aït Tamlil, the Oued Tessaout gives high-class trekking to its source under Mgoun. Djebel Rhat (3781m) and Djebel Tignousti (3825m) to the north, and a whole crest of peaks to the south, are all worth climbing. Passes south from Toufghine/Aït Tamlil (surfaced), Magdaz (the most beautiful village in the Atlas, now also accessible by *piste*) and Amezri (reached by *piste* from the south) allow exits by *piste*, *piste* routes covered by a daily truck except from Magdaz (mule pass only). From Aït Tamlil, trekking links can also be made to Telouet (see p.515), either north or south of Djebel Anghomar (3610m).

beauty, but also as a base for **Ighil Mgoun** (4068m), the highest summit in Morocco outside the Toubkal massif (see box above). There are also some astonishing gorges and passes on the southward trek through the mountains to exit at Kelaal de Mgouna.

A road, turning off near Aït Mhammed and highly spectacular, gives access to the lower end of the Bou Guemez and Bou Willi valleys. Most visitors arrive by Land Rover from Marrakesh, but a daily minibus service operates from Azilal (see p.328), and more infrequently from Aït Mhammed via the old *piste*, which enters over an eastern pass that is often blocked in winter. Trekkers are recommended to tackle the two-day walk in to the Bou Guemez from Aït Mhammed via the pretty hamlet of **SREMPT** (with a *gîte*, run by Sabre Brahim), and the **Tizi n'Aït Ouriat** (2606m), which has great views of the mountain ranges. Another possible approach is via Demnate (see opposite) from where trucks go on to the road end at **Imi n'Wakka** (Tarbat n'Tirsal) under the bulk of Djebel Rhat. A spectacular trek of several days heads down the Bou Willi valley to connect with the Bou Guemez. On the **Tizi n'Tirghyst** (2390m) are prehistoric rock-carved pictures of battles and symbols from 4000 years ago.

A longer circuit goes round the west flank of **Djebel Rhat** (3797m) and **Djebel Tignousti** (3825m) to reach the **Oued Tessaout** which is followed to its head under Ighil Mgoun to rejoin the Bou Guemez. East from the Bou Guemez, the seasonal lake of **Izoughar** is dominated by Djebel Azourki and other big hills. A *tizi* leads to Arouadane and the Zaouia Ahancal area of spectacular gorges. **Agoudim**, a village of remarkable architecture, has several *gîtes* (1km south of Zaouia Ahancal), as has **Taghia**, which faces the finest gorge and cliff scenery in the country, a rock-climbers' playground of Dolomitic scope. There are many other ticks, peaks, climbs and gorges of note, well covered in Peyron (see p.89), and making use of local experts is highly recommended.

Several of the Bou Guemez valley villages have *gîte* accommodation, meals and mule hire (see lists in the ONMT Atlas guide). The *Auberge Dar Itrane* (☎023 45 93 12; ❸) in **IMELGHAS** is a more expensive option but worth considering if you plan to make a stopover in the village. Mohammed Achari (Donar Iskattefen, Aït Bou Guemez, Bureau Tabant, par Azilal ☎023 45 93 27) is an experienced mountain guide who has helped many British parties, and offers a full range of services, including Land Rover rental.

Azilal to Marrakesh: Demnate

Having come as far as Azilal and the cascades, it is easier to continue along the R304 road to Marrakesh rather than the descent to the N8 main road from Beni Mellal, in any case the more interesting route.

Demnate

You may have to change buses along the way at **DEMNATE**, a walled market town with a Glaoui-era kasbah, an old Mellah (half the population were Jews until the 1950s) and a **Sunday souk,** held 2km out of town on the Sidi Rahal road. The souk is by far the largest in the region, an interesting and unaffected event and worth rejigging your travel plans to see. There is also a small daily souk just outside the ramparts and along the nearby streets, as well as a central market with butchers, bakers and fruit and vegetable stalls.

The surrounding area is renowned for **olives** and attractive glazed **pottery**, which is made at out-of-town Bougrhat – signposted and also worth a visit. Another trip, possible by grand taxi (3dh per *place*) from a square 300m beyond the town gate, is to an impressive natural bridge **Imi n'Ifri** (around 6.5km from Demnate). The arch spans a yawning gorge, the result of the partial collapse of an underground cave system, and guaranteed to unnerve anyone of a vertiginous disposition. It's a quiet untouristed spot, with a seasonal restaurant to sit in and little to do but watch the aerobatic displays of choughs and swifts, with their white rumps and square tails, or the *sibsib* (ground squirrels) on roadside walls. Close by is a series of springs, the cause of the Demnate valley's intense cultivation and the site of a large moussem held two weeks after the Aïd el Kebir.

Demnate sees few tourists and makes for a relaxed stopover. **Buses** drop you at a stop 400m to the right of the old town gate Bab el 'Arabi (the Gate of the Arabs), **grands taxis** to and from Azilal, Marrakesh and Beni Mellal stop and leave from the gate. The **PTT** just inside the gate has an ATM, unlike a nearby Banque Populaire. **Accommodation** is one of two basic but extremely cheap establishments: the *Hôtel Imi-Nifri*, just inside the gate (☎023 50 60 03; ❶) and the friendly and slightly better *Hôtel Ouzoud* (☎061 24 10 99; ❶), 150m or so back down the street outside the gate. Both can be grubby in places, so ask to see several rooms. Superior to anything in the town is a delightful **gîte** (☎ & ⨍023 50 64 73, mobile 062 10 51 68; ❷) run by a mountain guide, Ezzaari Thami, situated 500m beyond Imi n'Ifri. The *gîte* enjoys a beautiful garden setting and offers delicious Berber dishes; you can also camp here.

The land between Demnate and Marrakesh is poor and rocky, distinguished only by sporadic clusters of farmhouses or shepherds' huts. If you take the bus, it might follow either of the routes to Marrakesh – the R208 (formerly S508) via Tamlelt (where you rejoin the N8) or the well-paved R210 (formerly 6206) road via Tazzerte and Sidi Rahal. Given the choice, go for the latter. En route is an old Glaoui village, **TAZZERTE**, which has four crumbling kasbahs off the road, from which the clan (see p.516) used to control the region and the caravan routes to the north. There is a small Monday market held here, and a larger one on Fridays at **SIDI RAHAL**, 7km further on and named after a fifteenth-century *marabout*. It is also a point of local pilgrimage, especially for a small, but important moussem during Aïd el Kebir. The saint in whose honour the festivities take place has an unusual Judeo-Muslim tradition, and is the subject of a multitude of stories of magic and legend. The most popular yarns recount his power to conduct himself and other creatures through the air, a "talent" which apparently led to one of his followers accidently knocking down the upper storey of the Koutoubia minaret in Marrakesh with his knee. His favours are sought by the mentally ill and their families.

Coming into Marrakesh from either Demnate or Beni Mellal, you skirt part of the huge **palmery** which encloses the northern walls of the city. Buses go to the main **bus station** by Bab Doukkala – a ten-minute walk from the centre of Gueliz (the Ville Nouvelle), or twenty minutes (or a 10dh taxi ride) from Place Djemaa el Fna and the Medina.

Travel details

Trains

Fes to: Casablanca (9 daily; 4hr 15min); Kenitra (9 daily; 2hr 45min); Marrakesh (7 daily; 7hr 40min); Meknes (10 daily; 45min); Oujda (3 daily; 5hr 25min); Rabat (9 daily; 3hr 20min); Tangier (6 daily; 5hr 30min); Taza (4 daily; 2hr).

Meknes to: Casablanca (9 daily; 3hr 30min); Fes (11 daily; 55min); Kenitra (9 daily; 2hr); Marrakesh (7 daily; 7hr); Oujda (3 daily; 7hr 15min); Rabat (9 daily; 2hr 20min); Tangier (6 daily; 4hr 40min); Taza (4 daily; 3hr 20min).

Buses

Azilal to: Afourer (3 daily; 40min); Agadir (2 daily; 7hr); Beni Mellal (5 daily; 1hr 30min); Casablanca (3 daily; 5hr); Demnate (2 daily; 1hr); Marrakesh (4 daily; 3hr).

Azrou to: Agadir (1 CTM & 1 other daily; 13hr); Aïn Leuh (1 daily; 40min); Beni Mellal (2 CTM & 9 others daily; 5hr); Casablanca (2 CTM & 2 others daily; 5hr 30min); Fes (2 CTM & 17 others daily; 1hr 30min) via Ifrane (20min) and Immouzer (45min); Khenifra (2 CTM & over 18 others daily; 1hr 40min); Marrakesh (2 CTM & 6 others daily; 9hr); Meknes (4 CTM & 18 others daily; 1hr); Midelt

(3 CTM & 18 others daily; 3hr); Rabat (2 CTM & 7 others daily; 4hr); Er Rachidia (2 CTM & 14 others daily; 6hr); Rissani (1 CTM & 4 others daily; 9hr); Tangier (1 daily; 8hr); Tetouan (2 daily; 7hr).

Beni Mellal to: Agadir (1 CTM & 6 others daily; 8hr); Azilal (3 daily; 1hr 30min); Azrou (2 CTM & 9 others daily; 5hr); Casablanca (1 CTM & over 2 others daily; 3hr 30min); Demnate (6 daily; 3hr); Essaouira (1 daily; 6hr); Fes (1 CTM & 9 others daily; 6hr); El Jadida (2 daily; 5hr 30min); Midelt (2 daily; 4hr 30min); Meknes (6 daily; 5hr); Rabat (4 daily; 2hr 30min); Er Rachidia (1 daily; 6hr); Safi (2 daily; 6hr).

Demnate to: Azilal (2 daily; 1hr); Marrakesh (9 daily; 1hr 30min).

Fes to: Agadir (1 CTM & 4 others daily; 12hr); Azrou (2 CTM & 16 others daily; 1hr 30min); Beni Mellal (2 CTM & 9 others daily; 6hr); Casablanca (9 CTM & 24 others daily; 5hr 30min) via Rabat (4hr); Chefchaouen (4 CTM & 8 others daily; 5hr); Al Hoceima (1 CTM & 6 others daily; 5hr); Ifrane (1 CTM & 16 others daily; 1hr 30min); Immouzer (hourly; 45min); Khenifra (2 CTM & 12 others daily; 4hr); Marrakesh (1 CTM & 12 others daily; 10hr) via Beni Mellal (7hr); Meknes (3 CTM daily & others hourly 7am–7pm; 50min); Midelt (2 CTM, 7 others daily; 5hr 30min); Moulay Yacoub (roughly hourly; 30min); Nador (2 CTM & 17 others daily; 5hr 30min); Oujda (3 CTM & 18 others daily; 5hr 30min); Er Rachidia (7 daily; 8hr 30min); Rissani (2 CTM & 5 others daily; 10hr 30min); Sefrou (17 daily; 30min); Tangier (3 CTM & 7 others daily; 5hr 45min); Taza (3 CTM daily & others roughly hourly; 2hr 30min); Tetouan (3 CTM & 12 others daily; 5hr 20min).

Meknes to: Agadir (2 CTM & 2 others daily; 12hr); Azrou (1 CTM & 16 others daily; 1hr 30min); Beni Mellal (6 daily; 6hr); Casablanca (1 CTM & 7 others daily; 4hr 30min); Chefchaouen (5 daily; 5hr 30min); Fes (7 CTM daily & others hourly 7am–7pm; 50min); Al Hoceima (2 CTM & 1 other daily; 6hr); Larache (3 CTM & 8 others daily; 5hr 30min); Marrakesh (1 CTM & 8 others daily; 9hr); Midelt (2 CTM & 12 others daily; 5hr 30min); Nador (2 CTM & 5 others daily; 6hr 30min); Ouezzane (7 daily; 4hr); Oujda (2 CTM & 15 others daily; 6hr 30min); Rabat (7 CTM & 15 others daily; 3hr); Er Rachidia (1 CTM & 4 others daily; 8hr 00min); Rissani (1 CTM & 1 other daily; 10hr 30min); Tangier (3 CTM & 6 others daily; 7hr); Taza (4 CTM & 9 others daily; 3hr 15min); Tetouan (2 CTM & 7 others daily; 7hr).

Midelt to: Azrou (2 CTM & 18 others daily; 3hr); Beni Mellal (3 daily; 4hr 30min); Casablanca (1 CTM & 2 others daily; 8hr); Khenifra (5 daily; 3hr); Marrakesh (2 CTM & 5 others daily; 8hr 30min); Meknes (1 CTM and 9 others daily; 5hr); Nador (2 daily; 6hr); Ouarzazate (2 daily; 9hr 30min); Rabat (1 CTM & 8 daily; 7hr); Er Rachidia (2 CTM & 8 others daily; 3hr); Rissani (2 CTM & 8 others daily; 6hr); Tangier (3 daily; 12hr).

Grands taxis

Azilal to: Beni Mellal (1hr); the Cascades d'Ouzoud (40min).

Azrou to: Aïn Leuh (20min); Fes (1hr 30min); Meknes (45min); Midelt (2hr 30min); Ifrane (20min); occasionally Beni Mellal (3hr 30min) and Khenifra (1hr 30min).

Beni Mellal to: Azilal (1hr); Azrou (3hr 30min); Kasba Tadla (40min); Khenifra (2hr); Marrakesh (3hr).

Fes to: Azrou (1hr 30min); Casablanca (3hr 30min); Ifrane (1hr); Immouzer (40min); Meknes (40min); Moulay Yacoub (30min); Rabat (2hr 30min); Sefrou (30min); Sidi Harazem (30min); Taounate (1hr); Taza (1hr 15min).

Ifrane to: Azrou (20min); Fes (1hr); Immouzer (30min); Meknes (1hr).

Imouzzer du Kandar to: Azrou (45min); Fes (40min); Sefrou (40min); Ifrane (30min).

Khenifra to: Beni Mellal (2hr); Zaouiet ech Cheikh (40min); "Trente Trois" (15min); Midelt (2hr 30min); occasionally Er Rachidia (4hr 30min).

Meknes to: Azrou (45min); Fes (40min); Kenitra (1hr 30min); Khenifra (1hr 30min); Moulay Idriss (35min); Ouezzane (2hr 30min); Sidi Slimane (1hr).

Midelt to: El Ahouli mines (1hr); Azrou (2hr 30min); Fes (4hr); Meknes (4hr); Zeida (20min); "Trente Trois" (2hr 15min); Khenifra (2hr 30min); Er Rachidia (2hr).

Zaouiet ech Cheikh to: Kasba Tadla (40min); Khonifra (40min); El Ksiba (20min).

Flights

Fes to: Casablanca (1–3 daily; 45min).

The West Coast: from Rabat to Essaouira

CHAPTER 4 # Highlights

✳ **Hassan Mosque, Rabat**
Never completed, the minaret
of this Almohad mosque
is a masterpiece of Islamic
architecture. See p.354

✳ **Chellah, Rabat** As beautiful
a ruin as you could imagine,
with Roman remains and royal
tombs from the Merenids.
See p.356

✳ **Salé** Once the capital of a
pirate republic, now a sleepy
little town, a ferry ride across
the river from Rabat. See p.364

✳ **Colonial architecture,
Casablanca** Casa's city centre
is a monument to French
1930s Art Deco styles.
See p.381

✳ **Mosquée Hassan II,
Casablanca** Second in size
only to Mecca, Hassan II's
great mosque can (unusually)
be visited by non-Muslims.
See p.385

✳ **Cité Portugaise, El Jadida**
Walk round the ramparts or
check out the cistern where
Orson Welles filmed *Othello*.
See p.399

✳ **Oualidia oysters** North
Africa's finest. See p.402

✳ **Essaouira** Morocco's most
relaxed seaside town, and
a top spot for kite- and
windsurfers. See p.409

△ Mosquée Hassan II, Casablanca

4

The West Coast: from Rabat to Essaouira

This chapter takes in almost five hundred kilometres of Atlantic coastline, from Kenitra in the north to the popular resort of Essaouira in the south and ranges through long stretches of scarcely developed lagoons and sands to Morocco's urban heartland. The cities of Rabat and Casablanca – the respective seats of government and of industry and commerce – together with the towns of Kenitra, Salé (near Rabat) and Mohammedia (near Casablanca) have a population of around five million, nearly a fifth of the country's total. It's an astonishingly recent growth along what was, until the French Protectorate, a neglected strip of coast. In Morocco now, the bulk of new investment is in the Casablanca and Kenitra areas – and around Settat, 68km from Casablanca, on the road to Marrakesh.

Inevitably, it is French and post-colonial influences that are dominant in these cities. Don't go to **Casa** – as Casablanca is popularly known – expecting some exotic movie location; it's a modern city that looks very much like Marseille. **Rabat**, too, which the French developed as a capital in place of the old imperial centres of Fes and Marrakesh, looks markedly European, with its cafés and boulevards, though it also has some of Morocco's finest and oldest monuments, dating from the Almohad and Merenid dynasties. If you're on a first trip to Morocco, Rabat is an ideal place to get to grips with the country. Its westernized streets make an easy cultural shift and it's an excellent transport hub, well connected by train with Tangier, Fes and Marrakesh. Casa is maybe more interesting after you've spent a while in the country, when you'll appreciate both its differences and its fundamentally Moroccan character.

South along the coast, populations and towns thin out, as the road skirts a series of beaches and dunes, with the odd detour inland when cliffs take hold. **El Jadida**, established as a beach resort by the French, now fulfils the same function for middle-class Casablanca. **Oualidia**, to its south, has a similar, though rather more relaxed and small-scale style. **Safi**, between Oualidia and Essaouira, is a predominantly industrial town, but a friendly place, with some excellent beaches nearby.

Finally, there is **Essaouira**, which is also easily accessible from Marrakesh, and is, to put it simply, Morocco's most enjoyable resort. A beautiful walled town, with an active fishing port, long sandy beaches and a very relaxed feel, its only

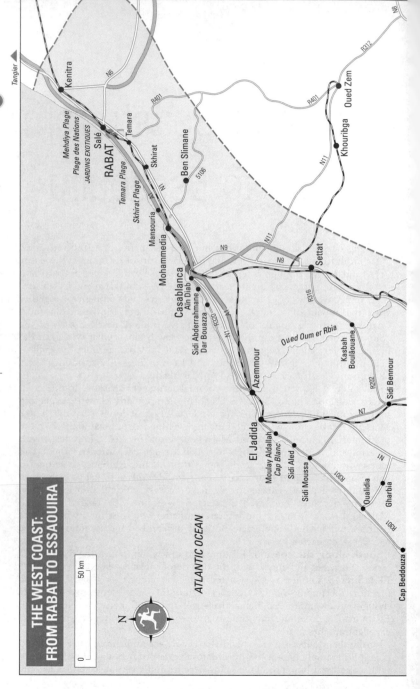

THE WEST COAST:
FROM RABAT TO ESSAOUIRA

0   50 km

N

ATLANTIC OCEAN

Tangier, Meknes & Fes

Tangier

Kenitra
N6

Mehdiya Plage
Plage des Nations
JARDINS EXOTIQUES
Salé
RABAT
Temara
Temara Plage
Skhirat Plage
Skhirat
Ben Slimane
N1
R401
S106
Mansouria
Mohammedia
Casablanca
Aïn Diab
Sidi Abderrahmane
Dar Bouazza
R320
N1
N9
N9
N11
N11
Settat
R316
Oued Oum er Rbia
Kasbah
Boulâouane
R202
Sidi Bennour
N7
Azemmour
El Jadida
Moulay Aïdallah
Cap Blanc
Sidi Aled
Sidi Moussa
R301
Oualidia
Gharbia
N1
R301
Cap Beddouza

Oued Zem
R312
N8
Khouribga
R401
N11

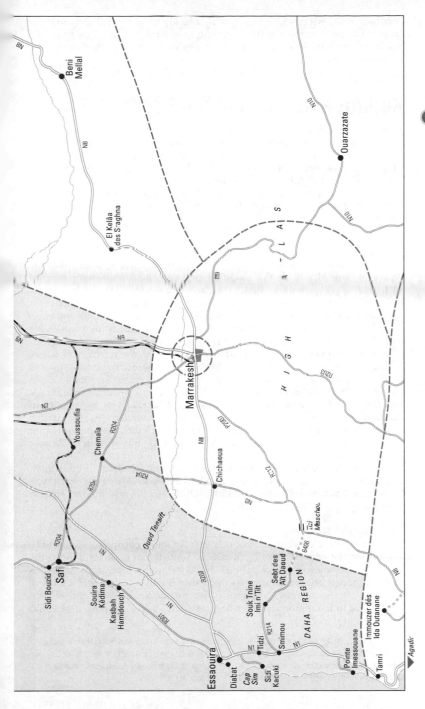

drawback is the wind, which can blow incessantly in spring and early summer (September to November is the best time to visit). However, even this wind has been used to help promote the town as Morocco's chief kite- and windsurfing resort.

Kenitra and the coast to Rabat

Travelling to Rabat from Tangier or Fes, you will bypass the stretch of coast around **Kenitra** – a friendly if not very exciting little town, with a scruffy beach nearby at **Mehdiya**. Further south there are pleasant detours to the **Plage des Nations** – Rabat's local beach resort – and to the botanical extravagance of the **Jardins Exotiques**; if you're dependent on buses, these can be visited as a day-trip from the capital. **Bird-watchers** may also want to explore the **Lac de Sidi Boughaba**, near Mehdiya, which has protected status due to its notable birds of prey.

Kenitra and Mehdiya

KENITRA was established by the French as Port Lyautey – named after the Resident General – with the intention of channelling trade from Fes and Meknes. It never quite took off, however, losing out in industry and port activities to Casablanca, despite the rich farming areas of its hinterland. It has a population today of around 300,000, employed mainly in paper mills and a fish cannery. It's livelier than most Moroccan towns of its size, with a noticeably friendly atmosphere that goes some way to make up for the paucity of sights.

There are two main streets: **Avenue Mohammed V**, the town's main artery, which runs east to west, and **Avenue Mohammed Diouri**, running north to south. The central square, dominated by the *baladiya* (town hall – *hôtel de ville* in French), is **Place Administrative**, two blocks north of Avenue Mohammed V and three blocks east of Avenue Mohammed Diouri. There are two **train stations**: Kenitra station, the most central, at the southern end of Avenue Mohammed Diouri; and Kenitra Medina (or Kenitra Ville), one stop north, off the eastern end of Avenue Mohammed V and near the **bus station** on Avenue John Kennedy.

The main **post office** is on Avenue Hassan II, just off Place Administrative, and **banks** can be found along Avenue Mohammed V. One of the best places for **Internet access** is Acces Pro at 12 Rue Amira Aïcha, next door to *Hôtel de Commerce*, which is open round the clock.

Accommodation

There's a reasonable selection of **hotels** in town and a **campsite**, *Camping La Chenaie* on the edge of town (approaching from Rabat look for signs to the left to the *Complexe Touristique*; ☎037 36 30 01), rather overgrown and run-down, although prices are pretty low and there's tennis, a pool and a football pitch. An alternative for campervans is the *Aire de Repose*, 8km out of town on the road to the motorway (see p.55), and there's also a campsite at Mehdiya (see opposite).

Hôtel Ambassy 20 Av Hassan II ☎037 37 99 78, ☎037 37 74 20. Comfortable and central, with nice stucco decoration; each room has a little laundry room as well as a bathroom, and there is a bar with a pool table. There's also a fish restaurant, *Le Turbot*, though it's not as good as the accommodation. Prices include breakfast. ⑤

Hôtel du Commerce 12 Rue Amira Aicha ☏ 037 37 15 03. A small hotel near the town hall. Simple, but adequate rooms with shared showers (5dh). Clean and well kept. ❷

Hôtel d'Europe 63 Av Mohammed Diouri ☏ 037 37 14 50. An older hotel, opposite the *Hôtel La Rotonde*. En-suite rooms are more expensive than those with separate facilities. Good value for money, and the *Sangria* restaurant on the ground floor is good too. Price includes breakfast. ❹

Hôtel Jacaranda (formerly Hôtel Farah) Pl Administrative ☏ 037 37 30 30, ©hoteljacaranda @menara.ma. This is the most upmarket place in town, with swimming pool, restaurant and nightclub. Ask for a room at the back, overlooking the pool. Price includes breakfast. ❺

Hôtel Mamora northern end of Av Hassan II, opposite the town hall ☏ 037 37 17 75, ℗ 037 37 14 46. Comfortable, with en-suite facilities, swimming pool and reasonable restaurant, albeit with a limited menu. Popular with businesspeople. Price includes breakfast. ❻

Hôtel de la Poste 307 Av Mohammed V ☏ 037 37 99 82. Basic, cheap and good value – double rooms have their own showers, singles don't. ❸

Hôtel La Rotonde 60 Av Mohammed Diouri ☏ & ℗ 037 37 14 01. Friendly place, with recently restored Art Deco exterior, though the interior is a little gloomy. Rooms are large and clean, if a bit basic. The downstairs bar and reception area is popular with locals, and it also has a good restaurant next door. Price includes breakfast. ❹

Eating, drinking and nightlife

There are a few good **restaurants** as well as the hotel ones mentioned: *Restaurant Chez Ouidad*, 52 Rue de la Maâmora, serves traditional dishes at cheap prices; *Champs Elysée*, 49 Rue Moulay Abdallah, roasts *shawarma*, brochettes, spaghetti and lasagne; and *Cafe Restaurant Ouazzani*, 8 Av Hassan II, near *Hôtel Ambassy*, offers tajine and other Moroccan standards.

For **bars** and **nightlife**, try the area around the triangular garden at the junction of Avenue Mohammed V, Avenue Mohammed Diouri and the pedestrianized Rue Reine Elizabeth, though don't expect too much. Look for *Mama's Club*, attached to *Les Arcades* bar at the corner of avenues Mohammed V and Mohammed Diouri; *Le Village* at the corner of Avenue Mohammed V and Rue de la Maâmora; and *007* at 93 Av Mohammed Diouri.

Mehdiya

MEHDIYA PLAGE, Kenitra's beach, 9km to the west, is a dull, greyish strip with a few houses and chalets, intermittent beach cafés and plenty of day visitors in summer. It's easily reached by grand taxi (from Avenue Mohammed Diouri in Kenitra), but if you're after a spot to break a journey and swim, you'd be better off at the more relaxed Plage des Nations, to the south.

The road from Kenitra to Mehdiya Plage runs along the left bank of the estuary of the Oued Sebou, passing first the large **fish cannery** and then continuing along below Mehdiya's ruined **kasbah**, overlooking the estuary. This was built by the Portuguese, extended by the Spanish, demolished and then restored by Moulay Ismail and, finally, knocked about in the course of US troop landings in World War II (see box, p.377); it shelters the remains of a seventeenth-century governor's palace. The kasbah is served from Kenitra by bus #9, the beach area by bus #15 (both from the northern end of Avenue Mohammed Diouri).

Accommodation is limited to a large **campsite**, *Camping & Caravanning Medhiya Plage* (summer only), and a **youth hostel** at Villa No. 6, Lotisement Amria (☏ 037 38 82 12; dorms 55dh with HI card, 60dh without, including breakfast, hot showers 5dh; July–Sept and at other times by prior arrangement). You may also get offers of a room with a family. For **eating** and **nightlife**, try the *Complexe Belle Vue* on the corniche road below the fort, which has a fish restaurant, bar and *Khaima* nightclub, or any of a number of restaurants down

Lac du Sidi Boughaba, just inland from Mehdiya, is a long, narrow freshwater lake, divided by a central causeway. The lake is the centrepiece of a larger wetland reserve which has been a RAMSAR site of International Importance since 1980. At the southern edge of the lake is the National Centre for Environmental Education (CNEE), a partnership between the government and the Moroccan arm of the British animal welfare NGO, SPANA (see p.67). The centre is focused mainly on environmental education for local schoolchildren but is open to visitors on weekends and public holidays (winter noon–4pm; summer noon–5pm).

The best viewing points for the lake's rich birdlife are either from the viewing deck at the education centre or on the causeway itself, where the ever-present damselflies and dragonflies provide a spectacular display of flight and colour. Marsh frogs and Berber toads also make their vocal contribution from the sanctuary of the northern reedbeds. Hiking trails begin from the education centre.

The **birdlife** of Sidi Boughaba is outstanding. The reedbeds throng with the calls of flitting reed and melodious warbler and the open stretches of water hold good numbers of crested coot (in spring) and marbled teal (in autumn and winter). It is, however, for its birds of prey that the site is best known. Circling almost constantly overhead are **marsh harriers**, with their characteristic low quartering flight, and these are joined on occasion by the smaller and whiter black-shouldered **kite** with its diagnostic black shoulders (and red eyes if you get close enough). In winter, look for the **European hobby**, **greater flamingo** and, at any time, **wading godwits**. At sunset you may also see the **African marsh owl**. In early spring, you will find wild crocuses, marigolds and white broom.

No camping is allowed on the reserve but there are great picnic spots, some with barbeque facilities, along the water's edge, accessible during the day only.

the other end of town opposite the beach. A couple of kilometres inland is the birdlife-rich **Lac du Sidi Boughaba** (see box above), flanked by a *koubba* that is the site of an August **moussem**.

The Plage des Nations and Jardins Exotiques

The Plage des Nations (22km south from Kenitra) and Jardins Exotiques (6km further) are easily visited if you are driving the coast road between Kenitra and Rabat or as a day-trip from Rabat. In summer, there are regular grands taxis to the beach from Rabat's satellite town of Salé, while throughout the year local bus #28 runs from Rabat's Avenue Moulay Hassan (via Boulevard Al Alaouiyne and Salé's Bab Khemis, almost opposite the train station), past the gardens and the turn-off to the beach. Alternatively, you could charter a grand taxi from Rabat, Salé or Kenitra to take you out to the gardens and/or beach, and back.

Plage des Nations

The **Plage des Nations**, or Sidi Bouknadel as it's sometimes known, was named after the foreign diplomats and their families who started swimming there – and continue to do so. Unlike the capital's Kasbah or Salé beaches, it has a very relaxed, friendly and cosmopolitan feel about it and is unusual in that young Moroccan women feel able to come out here for the day. The beach itself is excellent, with big, exciting waves – but dangerous currents, and is patrolled by lifeguards along the central strip. It's flanked by a couple of beach cafés and the *Hôtel Firdaous* (☏037 82 21 31, ℻037 82 21 43; ●), which has a swimming pool (nonresidents 70dh), plus a bar, restaurant and snack bar. It's a good place to stay, too – all rooms have a sea view, you can get a suite for not much more than the price of a room, and the 1970s decor manages to seem charmingly period rather than just outdated.

The beach lies 2km off the N1 coast road, reached along a surfaced track. On the main road, in an old villa directly opposite the turn-off, is the **Museé Dar Belghazi**, named after its enterprising Fassi owner (daily 8am–5pm; 40dh for a simple tour, 100dh for a complete tour including the reserve collection; ☏037 82 21 78, ✉museebelghazi@yahoo.com). The museum has a wealth of manuscripts, nineteenth-century carpets and textiles, eighteenth- and nineteenth-century ceramics, and examples of woodwork, armour and jewellery. The more tightly packed reserve collection holds further treasures including a reproduction eighteenth-century cedarwood carriage, and the 1812 *minbar*, which was removed from the Grand Mosque in Tangier a couple of years ago by the Ministry of Islamic Affairs (to the great outrage of many Tanjawis) and subsequently resurfaced here. Though it is undoubtedly a fine collection, no single piece is spectacularly compelling, there's not much by way of explanatory text other than a small booklet (in French and Arabic only), but if you do have a particular interest in Moroccan or Islamic art, then the trip out here is worthwhile.

Jardins Exotiques

The **Jardins Exotiques** (daily: winter 9am–5pm; summer 9am–7pm; 10dh) were laid out by one M. François in the early 1950s, in what contemporary French guidebooks called "une manière remarquable". They fell into decline in the 1980s but were rescued in 2003 by the king's "Fondation Pour la Protection de l'Environnement", and assiduously renovated before the grand reopening in November 2005. If you can visit the gardens in spring or early summer, they are a delight.

Entering the gardens, you find yourself directed across a series of precarious bamboo bridges and dot-directed routes through a sequence of regional creations. There is a **Brazilian rain forest**, dense with water and orchids; a formal **Japanese garden**; and then suddenly a great piece of **French Polynesia**, with rickety summerhouses set amid long pools, turtles paddling past, palm trees all round and flashes of bright red flowers. The last of the series, returning to a more local level, is an **Andalusian garden** with a fine collection of Moroccan plants. A map and information leaflet is available (free) at the entrance and the *Café Maure* is to your left as you enter the gardens.

Rabat

Capital of the nation since independence – and of the French Protectorate from 1912 to 1956 – **RABAT** is in many ways the city you'd expect: elegant in its spacious European grid, slightly self-conscious in its civilized modern ways, and, as an administrative centre, a little bit dull. If you arrive during Ramadan, you'll find the main avenues and boulevards an astonishing night-long promenade – at other times, it's hard to find a café open much past ten at night. Rabat, as they tell you in Casa, is provincial.

However, the city does have considerable historic and architectural interest – and across the estuary in **Salé** – which includes some of the finest and oldest

Airport & Meknes ▲ *Magic Park (Fair Ground),* **B** & **3**

Kenitra & Tangier ◀ ⊕ **Bab Mrisa**

Campsite ▲

SALÉ

Salé Beach

Oued Bou Regreg

ACCOMMODATION

Auberge de Jeunesse Youth Hostel	I
Le Dawiz Hôtel	R
Hilton Rabat Souissi	C
Hôtel Balima	T
Hôtel Berlin	K
Hôtel Bouregreg	S
Hôtel Chellah	G
Hôtel Central	W
Hôtel Dorhmi	A
Hôtel Gaulois	N
Hôtel al Maghrib al Jadid	O
Hôtel Majestic	F
Hôtel Majliss	B
Hôtel Marrakesh	X
Hôtel d'Orsay	Q
Hôtel la Paix	V
Hôtel Terminus	J
Hôtel des Voyageurs	E
Ibis Moussafir	P
Riad Kasbah	U
Royal Hôtel	H
Splendid Hôtel	M
Le Tour Hassan	D

RABAT

Beach

Kasbah des Oudaïas Ⓐ

Oudaïa Gate

MEDINA

Grand Mosque

Fountain

Market

Bab el Had

Bab el Alou

ALMOHAD WALL

AVENUE **HASSAN** *II*

AV MAGHREB EL ARABI

Bab el Djedid

MELLAH

Synagogue

Bab el Bahr

Bab el Mellah

Bab Chellah

Bab el Bouiba

BOULEVARD **ANDALUCIAN** *WALL*

Parc du Triangle du Vue

Théâtre National Mohammed V

BOULEVARD AL ALAOUIYNE

PLACE SIDI MAKLOUF

TARIK AL MARSA

BOULEVARD DU BOUREGREG

BOULEVARD ARRABATH

Hassan Tower

Mohammed V Mausoleum

British Embassy

PONT MOULAY HASSAN

Bab el Had

6 & Temara (coast road) ▼

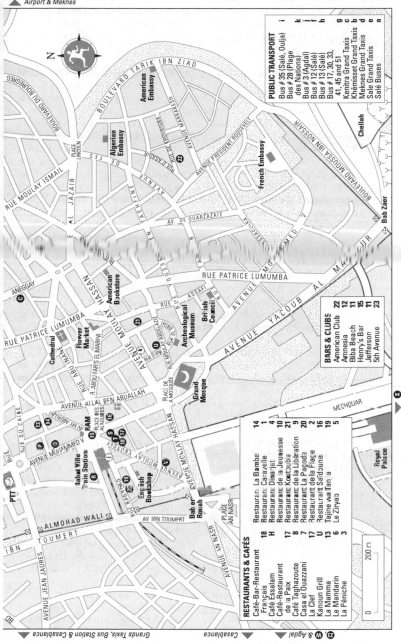

PUBLIC TRANSPORT
Bus # 35 (Salé, Oulja)	i
Bus # 28 (Plage des Nations)	k
Bus # 3 (Agdal)	j
Bus # 12 (Salé)	f
Bus # 13 (Salé)	h
Bus # 17, 30, 33, 41, 45 and 51	g
Kenitra Grand Taxis	c
Khémisset Grand Taxis	b
Meknes Grand Taxis	d
Salé Grand Taxis	e
Salé Buses	a

BARS & CLUBS
American Club	22
Amnesia	12
Biba Beach	15
Henry's Bar	11
Jefferson	23
5th Avenue	

RESTAURANTS & CAFÉS
Café-Bar-Restaurant Français	18
Café Essalam	H
Café-Restaurant de la Paix	17
Café Taghazoute	8
Casa el Ouazzani	7
La Clef	17
Kanoun Grill	U
La Mamma	13
Le Mandarin	6
La Péniche	3
Restaurant La Bamba	14
Restaurant Caravelle	4
Restaurant Dimarjet	10
Restaurant de la Jeunesse	21
Restaurant Koutoubia	9
Restaurant de la Libération	20
Restaurant La Pagode	2
Restaurant de la Plage	16
Restaurant Saïdouna	19
Tajine wa Tan'a	6
Le Ziryab	5

Arab monuments in the country, dating from the Almohad and Merenid dynasties. You can spend an enjoyable few days looking round these, and out on the local beaches, and there is a major plus in that, unlike Fes or Marrakesh, you can get round the place quite happily without a guide, and talk in cafés with people who do not depend on tourist money.

Some history

Rabat's **monuments** punctuate the span of Moroccan history. The plains inland, designated *Maroc Utile* by the French, have been occupied and cultivated since Paleolithic times, and there were Neolithic settlements on the coast south of Rabat, notably at present-day Temara and Skhirat.

Both Phoenicians and Carthaginians established trading posts on modern-day Rabat's estuary site. The earliest known settlement, Sala, occupied the citadel known today as **Chellah**. Here, after the demise of the Carthaginians, the **Romans** created their southernmost colony. It lasted well beyond the break-up of the empire in Africa and eventually formed the basis of an independent Berber state, which reached its peak of influence in the eighth century, developing a code of government inspired by the Koran but adapted to Berber customs and needs. It represented a challenge to the Islamic orthodoxy of the **Arab** rulers of the interior, however, and to stamp out the heresy, a *ribat* – the fortified monastery from which the city takes its name – was founded on the site of the present-day kasbah.

The *ribat's* activities led to Chellah's decline – a process hastened in the eleventh century by the founding of a new town, **Salé**, across the estuary. But with the arrival of the **Almohads** in the twelfth century, the Rabat kasbah was rebuilt and a city again took shape around it. The Almohad fort, renamed **Ribat el Fathi** (Stronghold of Victory), served as a launching point for the dynasty's campaigns in Spain, which by 1170 had returned virtually all of Andalusia to Muslim rule.

Under the Almohad Caliph **Yacoub el Mansour**, a new Imperial Capital was created. Its legacy includes the superb **Oudaïa Gate** of the kasbah, **Bab er Rouah** at the southwest edge of town, and the early stages of the **Hassan Mosque**. Until recent years, this was the largest ever undertaken in Morocco and its minaret, standing high above the river, is still the city's great landmark. Mansour also erected over 5km of fortifications – but neither his vision nor his success in maintaining a Spanish empire was to be lasting. He left the Hassan Mosque unfinished, and only in the last sixty years has the city expanded to fill his dark circuit of *pisé* walls.

After Mansour's death, Rabat's significance was dwarfed by the imperial cities of Fes, Meknes and Marrakesh, and the city fell into neglect. Sacked by the Portuguese, it was little more than a village when, as New Salé, it was resettled by seventeenth-century Andalusian refugees. In this revived form, however, it entered into an extraordinary period of international piracy and local autonomy. Its corsair fleets, the **Sallee Rovers**, specialized in the plunder of merchant ships returning to Europe from West Africa and the Spanish Americas, but on occasion raided as far afield as Plymouth and the Irish coast – Daniel Defoe's Robinson Crusoe began his captivity "carry'd prisoner into Sallee, a Moorish port".

The Andalusians, owing no loyalty to the Moorish sultans and practically impregnable within their kasbah perched high on a rocky bluff above the river, established their own pirate state, the **Republic of the Bou Regreg**. They rebuilt the Medina below the kasbah in a style reminiscent of their homes in the Spanish city of Badajoz, dealt in arms with the English and French, and even accepted European consuls, before the town finally reverted to government control under Moulay Rashid, and his successor, Moulay Ismail. Unofficial piracy continued until 1829 when Austria took revenge for the loss of a ship by shelling Rabat and other coastal towns. From then until the French creation of a capital, Rabat-Salé was very much a backwater.

Arrival

Rabat Ville train station is right in the middle of the Ville Nouvelle, a few minutes' walk from hotels there's a BMCE bureau de change and a Budget car rental desk (☎037 70 57 89) on the station concourse. There are three other stations in the Rabat–Salé area, which tourists are much less likely to use, though business visitors and diplomats may have cause to alight at **Rabat Agdal**, which serves the southern suburbs and the Royal Palace; the royal train is occasionally seen here in a siding. **Salé Ville** station serves Salé to the north of the estuary, with a relatively new station, **Salé Tabriquet**, serving the northern quarters of the town, but unlikely to attract many visitors.

The main **bus terminal** is located in Place Zerktouni – 3km west of the centre by the road junction for Casa and Beni Mellal. Local buses will take you from here to Bab el Had in town (bus #30 picks up right outside the terminal, buses #17 and #41 stop just behind it), or you can get a petit taxi (carrying up to three passengers; around 20dh into town on the meter). Easier, if you are coming by bus from the north, is to get off in **Salé** (see p.367) and take a grand taxi from there into Rabat.

Grands taxis from Fes and Casablanca will deposit you outside the bus station. Those from Meknes are likely to drop you on Boulevard Hassan II opposite Bab Chellah, while those from Kenitra will leave you further east along Boulevard Hassan II.

Rabat–Salé airport is 7km northeast of Rabat, and grands taxis are the only public transport into town from here. The current tariff for the ride is 150dh into the city centre (500dh to Casablanca), for up to six people. The airport has a post office agency, bureau de change and desks for all the main car rental companies. From **Mohammed V airport** near Casablanca, your best bet is to take a train (hourly 5.50am–9.50pm and then 11.50pm) and change at Aïn Sebaa for a connecting service to any of the four train stations mentioned above. The fare from the airport to Rabat is 55dh and the journey takes a little under two hours.

Useful local bus routes

#3 from just by Rabat Ville train station down Avenue Fal Ould Ouemir in Agdal to Avenue Atlas.

#12 and #13 from just off Place Melilla to Salé.

#17, #30 and #41 from just outside Bab el Had to the intercity bus station.

#28 from Avenue Moulay Hassan via Boulevard Al Alaouiyne to Salé, Jardins Exotiques, Bouknadel, Museé Dar Belghazi and the Plage des Nations turn-off.

#33 from just outside Bab el Had to Temara Plage.

#35 from Boulevard Al Alaouiyne to Salé, Magic Park and the Complexe des Potiers in Oulja.

Orientation, information and city transport

With its **Medina** and **Ville Nouvelle** bounded by the river and Almohad walls, central Rabat never feels like a big city, and indeed all the city's points of interest are within easy walking distance.

The ONMT **tourist office** is on the corner of Rue Oued el Makhazine and Rue Zellaka at the far end of the suburb of Agdal, about 3km southwest of the city centre (Mon–Fri 8.30am– 4.30pm; ☎037 67 39 18, ☏037 67 40 15). In the unlikely event that you decide to traipse off down there (by petit taxi is the best way), you can pick up a few free brochures, but don't expect too much.

Local bus services can be very useful in Rabat, and some bus stops are clearly marked, with the numbers of the buses that stop at them posted up, though there are still places where you're expected to know the location of the stop by osmosis. The most useful routes are listed in the box on p.347.

Petits and **grands taxis** can be found on Boulevard Hassan II and by the train station, but petits taxis are not allowed to run between Rabat and Salé.

Accommodation

Hotel space can be tight in midsummer, and especially in July, when budget-priced rooms in particular are at a premium, so it's a good idea to book in advance. A couple of cheapies aside, all of the better hotels are to be found in the Ville Nouvelle and there's little to gain from staying in the Medina, which is in any case only a stroll across the boulevard. The nearest **campsite** is across the river at Salé; see p.367.

Ville Nouvelle Hotels

Most of the Ville Nouvelle hotels are modest, French-built places. If your budget is limited, go for one of these, as the four- and five-star hotels are mostly standard chain efforts, and there are better splurges elsewhere.

Cheap

Auberge de Jeunesse (Youth Hostel) 43 Rue Marrassa ☎037 72 57 69. Conveniently sited just west of the Almohad walls of the Medina and to the north of Bd Hassan II. It's pleasant, clean and well furnished, with a courtyard, but no self-catering facilities. Closed 10am–noon & 3–6.30pm. Dorm beds with breakfast are 45dh per person with HI card, 50dh without.

Hôtel Berlin 261 Av Mohammed V ☎037 70 34 35. A small nine-room establishment, with shared bathrooms and sporadic hot water (shower 6dh); located above the Chinese *Restaurant Hong Kong*. Central, and reasonable value for money. ❷

Hôtel Central 2 Rue Al Basra ☎037 70 73 56, ☏037 70 73 56. Not to be confused with the *Hôtel du Centre* in the Medina (which is not recommended), this is one of the best cheapies in the city, located alongside the (prominent) *Hôtel Balima* on Av Mohammed V – and thus convenient for restaurants, banks, the train station, and a nightcap at the *Balima* bar. Some rooms with showers; hot water mornings and evenings. ❸

Moderate

Hôtel Gaulois corner of Rue Hims and Av Mohammed V ☎037 72 30 22, ☏037 73 88 48. Friendly old hotel with a spacious grand entrance and both shared-shower and en-suite rooms, the latter being pretty good value for money. ❹

Hôtel Majestic 121 Av Hassan II ☎037 72 29 97, ☏037 70 88 56. This is a friendly old hotel, refurbished with bright, spotless rooms, some overlooking the Medina; it's often full, though, and you'll be lucky to find a room much after midday. Sporadic hot water. ❹

Hôtel d'Orsay 11 Av Moulay Youssef, on Pl de la Gare ☎037 70 13 19, ☏037 70 82 08. Friendly, helpful, efficient and convenient for the train station and numerous café-restaurants. It's very popular with Moroccan (and overseas) businessmen, so book ahead. ❹

Hôtel la Paix 2 Rue Ghazza, on corner with Av Allal Ben Abdallah ☎037 72 29 26. Friendly staff and comfortable, if sombre, rooms with good en-suite bathrooms. ❹

Hôtel Terminus 384 Av Mohammed V ☎037 70 06 16, ☏037 70 19 26. Round the corner from the

Hôtel d'Orsay and a possible alternative if it's full. It's a large, featureless block, but the interior has been refurbished and rooms are comfortable, though some are a lot better than others, so it's worth looking at a few. ⑤

Splendid Hôtel 8 Rue Ghazza ☎037 72 32 83. The best rooms at this nice old hotel overlook a pleasant courtyard with flowers and banana trees, and some have their own showers. Opposite, the *Café-Restaurant Ghazza* is good for breakfast and snacks. ③

Expensive

Hilton Rabat Souissi ☎037 67 56 56, ✉rbahitw@meganet.net.ma. This deluxe five-star set among pleasant gardens has all the standard facilities and is wheelchair accessible, with a free shuttle service to the golf course, but it is rather inconveniently located in the suburb of Souissi, southwest of town, beyond the royal palace. ⑧

Hôtel Balima Corner of Rue Jakarta and Av Mohammed V ☎037 70 86 25, ✉hotelbalima @menara.ma. This was once Rabat's top hotel but has been long overtaken by the competition. It has been refurbished and still has quite reasonable prices, not least for its suites; T'hami el Glaoui, Pasha of Marrakesh (see p.456), stayed in one of these on his visits to the city in the early 1950s. The open-air café between the hotel and the avenue is shaded and popular. Price includes breakfast. ⑥

Hôtel Bélère 33 Av Moulay Youssef ☎037 20 33 01, ⓦwww.belerehotels.ma. Comfortable, a/c tour-group hotel, well positioned for the train station. Rooms are fine but somewhat overpriced. Price includes breakfast. ⑦

Hôtel Bouregreg corner of Rue Nador and Bd Hassan II ☎037 72 41 10, ✉hotel_bouregreg @menara.ma. This centrally placed hotel attracts tour groups and visitors with cars who appreciate the secure parking available. Pleasant courtyard restaurant and a bar. Price includes breakfast. ⑥

Hôtel Chellah, 2 Rue d'Ifni ☎037 66 83 00, ✉037 70 63 54. An upmarket tour-group hotel with comfortable rooms in a rather characterless block, handy for the archeological museum, with a good grill-restaurant, *Le Kanoun*. ⑧

Hôtel Majliss 6 Rue Zahla ☎037 73 37 26, ⓦwww.majlisshotel.ma. A modern deluxe hotel, overlooking the platforms of the Rabat Ville station. There's a choice of room styles, and standard rooms are equipped with orthopaedic beds. The more expensive ones at the back have views over the roof of the parliament building to the Atlantic Ocean. Price includes breakfast. ⑦

Ibis Moussafir 32–34 Rue Abderrahmane el Ghafki, Pl de la Gare Rabat Agdal ☎037 77 49 19, ⓦwww.ibishotel.com. Like all the Moussafir chain, this hotel is by a train station, which means that, being in Agdal, everything of interest is a taxi ride away. Still, it's comfortable and efficient with easy parking, and the price includes breakfast. ⑥

Royal Hôtel 1 Rue Amman, on corner with Av Allal Ben Abdallah ☎037 72 11 71, ⓦwww.mtds.com /royalhotel. A three-star hotel with comfortable and reasonable rooms – not huge, but refurbished, clean and well maintained. The best ones overlook the attractive Parc du Triangle de Vue. Price includes breakfast. ⑥

La Tour Hassan 26 Rue Chellah ☎037 23 90 00, ⓦwww.latourhassan.com. Rabat's plushest offering, with exquisite, palatial decor in the public areas and several grades of rooms and suites (mostly priced according to the views available from them) peaking at a whopping 12,500dh a night. The rooms, however, are not huge, and in fact the *Majliss* has the edge on it comfort-wise. ⑧

Medina hotels

Hôtel Dorhmi 313 Av Mohammed V ☎037 72 38 98. Refurbished to a decent standard, and nicely positioned, just inside Bab el Djedid and above the pleasant *Café Essalam*. Competitive prices, though hot showers are extra (10dh). ②

Hôtel al Maghrib al Jadid 2 Rue Sebbahi ☎037 73 22 07. Basic and clean, though the decor is a garish combination of candy pink and bright blue. Hot showers are available at 7.50dh a go. ②

Hôtel Marrakesh 10 Rue Sebbahi ☎037 72 77 03. Run by the same people as the *Maghrib al Jadid* down the street, and similar in just about every respect, including the colour scheme. ②

Hôtel des Voyageurs 8 Souk Semarino, by Bab Djedid ☎037 72 37 20. Inexpensive, popular and often full. Clean, airy rooms but no showers, though there are public ones for men nearby, and for women not too far away. The same stretch of street has several similar places. ①

🏃 **Riad Kasbah** In the kasbah at 39 Rue Zirara, on your left as you enter through Bab Oudaïas ☎037 70 23 92, ⓦwww.riadoudaya.com. This small riad oozes simplicity and authenticity. It's nicely furnished and the staff are overwhelmingly attentive. There's 24hr hot water and breakfast is included. Minimum two-night stay and pre-booking is required. ⑦

The Medina and souks

Rabat's **Medina** – all that there was of the city until the French arrived in 1912 – is a compact quarter, wedged on two sides by the sea and the river, on the others by the twelfth-century Almohad and seventeenth-century Andalusian walls. It's not the most interesting Medina in the country – open and orderly in comparison to those of Fes or Marrakesh, for example – but coming here from the adjacent avenues of the modern capital it remains a surprise. In appearance, the quarter is still essentially the town created by Andalusian Muslim refugees from Badajoz in Spain, and with these external features intact, its way of life seems remarkably at odds with the government business and cosmopolitanism of the Ville Nouvelle.

That this is possible – here and throughout the old cities of Morocco – is largely due to **Marshal Lyautey**, the first, and certainly the most sympathetic to the indigenous culture, of France's Resident Generals. Colonizing Algeria over the previous century, the French had destroyed most of the Arab towns, replacing their traditional structures (evolved through the needs of Islamic customs) with completely European plans. In Rabat, Lyautey found this system already under way, the builders tearing down parts of the Medina for the construction of a new town and administrative quarters. Realizing the aesthetic loss – and the inappropriateness of wholesale Europeanization – he ordered work to be halted and the Ville Nouvelle built outside the walls.

It was a precedent accepted throughout the French and Spanish zones of the colony, a policy which inevitably created "native quarters", but one which also preserved continuity, maintained the nation's past and, at least so Lyautey believed, showed the special relationship of the Protectorate. Lyautey himself resigned and left Morocco in 1925 but when he died in 1934 he was returned to Morocco and buried in a Moorish monument in Rabat. Symbolism was reversed when, in 1961, his body was "repatriated" and entombed in Les Invalides, the soldiers' church, in Paris.

Into the Medina

The basic grid-like regularity of its Medina, cut by a number of long main streets, makes Rabat a good place to get to grips with the feel and lay-out of a Moroccan city. Its plan is typical, with a main market street – **Rue Souika** and its continuation **Souk es Sebbat** – running beside the Grand Mosque, and behind it a residential area scattered with smaller souks and "parish" mosques. The buildings, characteristically Andalusian, in the style of Tetouan or Chefchaouen, are part stone and part whitewash, with splashes of yellow and turquoise and great, dark-wood studded doors.

From **Boulevard Hassan II**, half a dozen gates and a series of streets give access to the Medina, all leading more or less directly through the quarter, to emerge near the kasbah and the hillside cemetery. On the west side, the two main streets – **Avenue Mohammed V** and **Rue Sidi Fatah** – are really continuations of Ville Nouvelle avenues, though, flanked by working-class café-restaurants and cell-like hotels, their character is immediately different. Entering along either street, past a lively, modern food market and a handful of stalls selling fruit, juice and snacks, you can turn very shortly to the right and come out at the cubicle shops on **Rue Souika**. Dominated by textiles and silverware along the initial stretch, these give way to a concentration of *babouche* and other shoe stalls as you approach the Grand Mosque. They are all fairly everyday – though quite high-quality – shops, not for the most part geared to tourists.

Stalls selling cheaper goods, and the *joutia* (flea market), are off towards the river, round the old Jewish quarter of the Mellah (see opposite). Along the way are few buildings of particular interest, as most of the medieval city – which predated that of the Andalusians on this site – was destroyed by Portuguese raids in the sixteenth century.

The **Grand Mosque**, founded by the Merenids in the fourteenth century, is a partial exception, though it has been considerably rebuilt – its minaret, for example, was only completed in 1939. Entry to the mosque is forbidden to non-Muslims. Opposite, there is a small example of Merenid decoration in the stone facade of a public **fountain**, which now forms the front of an Arabic bookshop.

The Mellah and Joutia

The most direct approach from Boulevard Hassan II to the Grand Mosque section of the Medina is through **Bab Chellah**, which gives way onto a broad, tree-lined, pedestrian way. Alternatively, continuing a couple of blocks past the *Hôtel Bouregreg*, you can go in by the **Bab el Mellah**, which gives onto Rue Oukassa.

To the east of this street is the **Mellah**, the old Jewish quarter, and still the poorest and most run-down area of the city. It was designated as a Jewish quarter only in 1808 – Jews previously owned several properties on Rue des Consuls, to the north – and no longer has a significant Jewish population. If you can find a local guide, you may be able to look into some of its seventeen former **synagogues**. None of these function; the only active synagogue in the city is a modern building, one block from here, at the bottom end of Rue Moulay Ismail.

With its meat and produce markets, the Mellah looks a somewhat uninviting and impenetrable area, but it is worth a wander through towards the river. A **joutia**, or **flea market**, spreads out along the streets below Souk es Sebbat, down to Bab el Bahr. There are clothes, pieces of machinery, and vendors touting wonderful old movie posters, garishly illustrating titles like *Police Militaire* and *La Fille du Désert*.

Towards the kasbah: Rue des Consuls

Beyond the Mellah, heading towards the kasbah, you can walk out by **Bab el Bahr** and follow an avenue near the riverside up to the Oudaïa Gate. At the time of writing there was major earthworks in progress on the river's shoreline (and also across on the Salé side). The end result is expected to be a beautiful grand promenade and corniche. Unfortunately the Ensemble Artisinal that was located here has been demolished in the process.

Rue des Consuls, a block inland, is not so busy and is a more interesting approach to the kasbah; like the Mellah, this, too, used to be a reserved quarter – the only street of the nineteenth-century city where European consuls were permitted to live. Many of the residency buildings survive, as do a number of impressive merchants' *fondouks* – most in the alleys off to the left. The main street, particularly at its upper end, is largely a centre for **rug and carpet shops** and on Monday and Thursday mornings becomes a **souk**, with locals bringing carpets – new and old – to sell.

Rabat carpets, woven with very bright dyes (which, if vegetable-based, will fade), are a traditional cottage industry in the Medina, though they're now often made in workshops, one of which you can see on the kasbah's *plateforme* (see p.353). Some of the traditional carpets on sale, particularly in the shops, will have come from further afield. They are officially graded at a special centre just off Rue des Consuls – to the right as you climb towards the kasbah.

The Kasbah des Oudaïas

The site of the original *ribat* and citadel of the Almohad, Merenid and Andalusian towns, the **Kasbah des Oudaïas** is a striking and evocative quarter. Its principal gateway, the **Bab Oudaïa**, is perhaps the most beautiful in the Moorish world, and within the kasbah walls is the **Musée National des Bijoux** (Museum of Moroccan Jewellery), housed in a seventeenth-century palace, and a perfect **Andalusian garden**.

The Bab Oudaïa

The **Bab Oudaïa**, like so many of the great external monuments of Morocco, is of Almohad foundation. Built around 1195, it was inserted by Yacoub el Mansour within a line of walls already built by his grandfather, Abd el Moumen. The walls in fact extended well to its west, leading down to the sea at the edge of the Medina, and the gate cannot have been designed for any real defensive purpose – its function and importance must have been purely ceremonial. It was to be the heart of the kasbah, its chambers acting as a courthouse and state-rooms, with everything of importance taking place nearby. The **Souk el Ghezel** – the main commercial centre of the medieval town, including its wool and slave markets – was located just outside the gate, while the original sultanate's palace stood immediately inside.

The gate itself doesn't impress so much by its size, which is not unusual for an Almohad structure, as by the visual strength and simplicity of its decoration. This is based on a typically Islamic rhythm, establishing a tension between the exuberant, outward expansion of the arches and the heavy, enclosing rectangle of the gate itself. Looking at the two for a few minutes, you begin to sense a kind of optical illusion – the shapes appear suspended by the great rush of movement from the centre of the arch. The basic feature is, of course, the arch, which here is a sequence of three, progressively more elaborate: first, the basic horseshoe; then, two "filled" or decorated ones, the latter with the distinctive Almohad *darj w ktarf* patterning, a cheek-and-shoulder design somewhat like a fleur-de-lys. At the top, framing the design, is a band of geometric ornamentation, cut off in what seems to be an arbitrary manner but which again creates the impression of movement and continuation outside the gate.

The dominant motifs – scallop-shell-looking palm fronds – are also characteristically Almohad, though without any symbolic importance.

Around the kasbah

You can enter the **kasbah** proper through the small gateway to the right of the Oudaïa Gate itself (which is sometimes used for exhibitions), or by a lower, horseshoe arch at the base of the ceremonial stairway. This latter approach leads through a door in the palace wall to Rue Bazo,

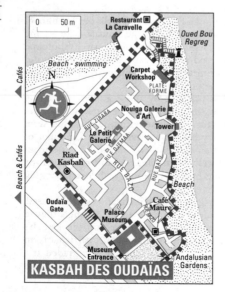

KASBAH DES OUDAÏAS

where a right turn will take you down to the **Café Maure**, beside the gardens, a fine place to retreat, high on a terrace overlooking the river, serving mint tea, brewed up on an ancient brazier, and trays of pastries. It's used as much by Moroccans as tourists, and is therefore reasonably priced.

An airy, village-like part of the city, the kasbah is a pleasant and very photogenic quarter in which to wander. Hardly more than 150m from one end to the other, it's not a place where you really need a guide; if you're approached, talk to the hustlers, be easygoing and explain you're only wandering down to *la plateforme*.

Once inside the Oudaïa Gate, it would actually be hard not to find the way down to the *plateforme* since the single main street, **Rue Djemaa** (Street of the Mosque), runs straight down to a broad terrace commanding views of the river and sea. Along the way, you pass by the **Kasbah Mosque**, the city's oldest, founded in 1050, though rebuilt in the eighteenth century by an English renegade known as Ahmed el Inglisi – one of a number of European pirates who joined up with the Sallee Rovers.

El Inglisi was also responsible for several of the forts built below and round the seventeenth-century **plateforme**, originally a semaphore station, on which was built an eighteenth-century warehouse, now housing a carpet cooperative workshop. The guns of the forts and the *plateforme* regularly echoed across the estuary in Salé. The Bou Regreg ("Father of Reflection") River is quite open at this point and it would appear to have left the corsair fleets vulnerable, harboured a little downstream, where the fishing boats today ferry people across to Salé. In fact, a long sandbank lies submerged across the mouth of the estuary – a feature much exploited by the shallow-keeled pirate ships, which would draw the merchant ships in pursuit, only to leave them stranded within the sights of the city's cannon. The sandbank proved a handicap in the early twentieth century and diverted commercial trade to the better-endowed Casablanca.

From the *plateforme*, it's possible to climb down towards the *Restaurant Caravelle* (see p.360) and the **beach**, crowded with locals throughout the summer, as is the Salé strip across the water, though neither is very inviting, and you'd be better off at the more relaxed (and less exclusively male) sands at the Plage des Nations or Temara Plage (see p.342 and p.368).

The Palace Museum and Gardens

South of the Oudaïa and horseshoe gates, a third gate leads to the Palace and the Andalusian Gardens, which are also accessible from within the kasbah via *Café Maure*.

The **palace** itself (daily 10am–6pm; 20dh) is seventeenth century, one of many built by Moulay Ismail, the first sultan since Almohad times to force a unified control over the country. Ismail, whose base was at Meknes, gave Rabat – or New Salé, as it was then known – a relatively high priority. Having subdued the pirates' republic, he took over the kasbah as a garrison for Saharan tribesmen who accepted military service in return for tax exemption, and who formed an important part of his mercenary army.

Formerly home to the Museum of Moroccan Arts and an interesting building in its own right, at the time of writing the palace was being transformed into the National Museum of Moroccan Jewellery. The design is classic: a series of reception rooms grouped round a central court, giving access to the private quarters. The rooms in the far left corner of the courtyard were once the hammam – a feature of all noble mansions – while the room through to the right of the courtyard was once the palace mosque.

The beautiful **Andalusian Gardens** occupy the old palace grounds. What you see today was constructed by the French in the twentieth century – though true to Andalusian tradition, with deep, sunken beds of shrubs and flowering annuals. If you're familiar with Granada, it's illuminating to compare the authentic Moorish concept here with the neat box hedges with which the Alhambra has been restored. But historical authenticity aside, it's a delightful place, full of the scent of tree daturas, bougainvillea and a multitude of herbs and flowers. It has a definite modern role too, as a meeting place for women, who gather here in dozens of small groups on a Friday or Sunday afternoon.

The Hassan Mosque and Mohammed V Mausoleum

The most ambitious of all Almohad buildings, the **Hassan Mosque** (daily 8.30am–6.30pm; free) and its vast minaret dominates almost every view of the capital – a majestic sight from the kasbah, from Salé, or glimpsed as you arrive across the river by train. If it had been completed, it would (in its time) have been the second largest mosque in the Islamic world, outflanked only by the one in Smarra, Iraq. Even today its size seems a novelty.

There is also the poignancy of its ruin. Designed by El Mansour as the centre-piece of the new capital and as a celebration of his great victory over the Spanish kings at Alarcos, the mosque's construction seems to have been more or less abandoned on his death in 1199. The tower was probably left much as it appears today; the mosque's hall, roofed in cedar, was used until the Great Earthquake of 1755 (which destroyed central Lisbon) brought down its central columns. Its extent, however, must always have seemed an elaborate folly. Morocco's most important mosque, the Kairaouine in Fes, is less than half the Hassan's size, but served a much greater population, with adequate space for 20,000 worshippers. Bearing in mind that it is only men who gather for the weekly Friday prayer – when a town traditionally comes together in its Grand Mosque – Rabat would have needed a population of well over 100,000 to make adequate use of the

△ Mosque and Mausoleum of Mohammed V, Rabat

Hassan's capacity. As it was, the city never really took off under the later Almohads and Merenids, and when Leo Africanus came here in 1600, he found no more than a hundred households, gathered for security within the kasbah.

The **tower**, or minaret, was begun by Yacoub el Mansour in 1195 – at the same time as the Koutoubia in Marrakesh and the Giralda in Seville – and it's one of the few Moroccan buildings to approach the European idea of monumentality. This is due in part to its site, on a level above the river and most of the city, but perhaps equally to its unfinished solidity.

The minaret is unusually positioned at the centre rather than the northern corner of the rear of the mosque. Some 50m tall in its present state, it would probably have been around 80m if finished to normal proportions – a third again the height of Marrakesh's Koutoubia. Despite its apparent simplicity, it is arguably the most complex of all Almohad structures. Each facade is different, with a distinct combination of patterning, yet the whole intricacy of blind arcades and interlacing curves is based on just two formal designs. On the south and west faces these are the *darj w ktarf* motifs of the Oudaïa Gate (see p.352); on the north and east is the *shabka* (net) motif, an extremely popular form adapted by the Almohads from the lobed arches of the Cordoba Grand Mosque – and still in contemporary use.

The Mohammed V Mausoleum

Facing the tower – in an assertion of Morocco's historical independence and continuity – are the **Mosque and Mausoleum of Mohammed V**, begun on the king's death in 1961 and inaugurated six years later. Hassan II and his brother, Moulay Abdellah, are buried here too, alongside their father. The **mosque**, extending between a stark pair of pavilions, gives a somewhat foreshortened idea of how the Hassan Mosque must once have appeared, roofed in its traditional green tiles.

The **mausoleum**, designed by a Vietnamese architect, Vo Toan, was one of the great prestige projects of modern Morocco. Its brilliantly surfaced marbles and spiralling designs, however, seem to pay homage to traditional Moroccan techniques, while failing to capture their rhythms and unity. It is, nevertheless, an important shrine for Moroccans – and one which, unusually, non-Muslims are permitted to visit. You file past fabulously costumed royal guards to an interior balcony; the tomb of Mohammed V, carved from white onyx, lies below, an old man squatting beside it, reading from the Koran. If possible, plan a morning or afternoon visit as the mausoleum usually closes for midday prayers in the adjoining mosque.

The Ville Nouvelle

French in construction, style and feel, the **Ville Nouvelle** provides the main focus of Rabat's life, above all in the cafés and promenades of the broad, tree-lined Avenue Mohammed V, and in the pleasant **Parc du Triangle de Vue** (daily 7am–6.30pm, Ramadan 7am–3.30pm), opposite the south wall of the Medina, with an open-air café that's a popular afternoon meeting place. Another attractive and colourful spot is the **Flower Market**, held in a sunken garden just to the north of Avenue Moulay Hassan.

There's a certain grandeur in some of the old, *Mauresque* public buildings around the main boulevards, too, which were built with as much desire to impress as any earlier epoch. However, it's the **Almohad walls and gates**, the excellent **Archeological Museum** and, just beyond, the **citadel of Chellah** (see p.356) that hold most of interest in the quarter.

More-or-less complete sections of the **Almohad walls** run right down from the kasbah to the Royal Palace and beyond – an extraordinary monument to Yacoub el Mansour's vision. Along their course four of the original **gates** survive. Three – **Bab el Alou**, **Bab el Had** and **Bab Zaer** – are very modest. The fourth, **Bab er Rouah** (Gate of the Wind), is on an entirely different scale, recalling and in many ways rivalling the Oudaïa.

Contained within a massive stone bastion, **Bab er Rouah** again achieves the tension of movement – with its sun-like arches contained within a square of Koranic inscription – and a similar balance between simplicity and ornament. The west side, approached from outside the walls, is the main facade, and must have been designed as a monumental approach to the city; the shallow-cut, floral relief between arch and square is arguably the finest anywhere in Morocco. Inside, you can appreciate the gate's archetypal defensive structure – the three domed chambers aligned to force a sharp double turn. They're used for exhibitions and are usually open.

From Bab er Rouah, it's a fifteen-minute walk down towards the last Almohad gate, the much-restored **Bab Zaer**, and the entrance to the **Chellah**. On the way, you pass a series of modern gates leading off to the vast enclosures of the **Royal Palace** – which is really more a collection of palaces, built mainly in the nineteenth century and decidedly off-limits to casual visitors – and, off to the left (opposite the *Hôtel Chellah*), the Archeological Museum.

The Archeological Museum

Rabat's **Archeological Museum** on Rue el Brihi (Mon & Wed–Fri 8.45am–4.30pm; 10dh; ☎037 70 19 19) is the most important in Morocco. Although small – surprisingly so in a country which saw substantial Phoenician and Carthaginian settlement and three centuries of Roman rule – it houses an exceptional collection of Roman-era bronzes.

The bronzes are displayed in a special annexe with a separate entrance; although included in the entry fee, it's sometimes closed. If so, ask one of the attendants at the museum's entrance to open it up for you. They date from the first and second centuries AD and were found mainly at the provincial capital of Volubilis (near Meknes), together with a few pieces from Chellah and the colonies of Banasa and Thamusida. Highlights include superb figures of a guard dog and a rider, and two magnificent portrait heads, reputedly those of Cato the Younger (Caton d'Utique) and Juba II – the last significant ruler of the Romanized Berber kingdoms of Mauretania and Numidia before the assertion of direct imperial rule. Both of these busts were found in the House of Venus at Volubilis.

Back in the main building, there are showcases on two floors; each contains finds from different digs, of little interest unless you have already visited the area – or plan to do so. Captions are in French and, if you ask, you may be provided with a guide to the museum – also in French.

Citadel of Chellah

The most beautiful of Moroccan ruins, **Chellah** (daily 9am–5.30pm, last ticket sold 5pm; 10dh) is a startling sight as you emerge from the long avenues of the Ville Nouvelle. Walled and towered, it seems a much larger enclosure than the map suggests, and it feels for a moment as if you've come upon a second Medina. The site is, in fact, long uninhabited – since 1154, when it was abandoned in favour of Salé across the Bou Regreg. But for almost a thousand years prior to that, Chellah (or *Sala Colonia*, as it was known) had been a

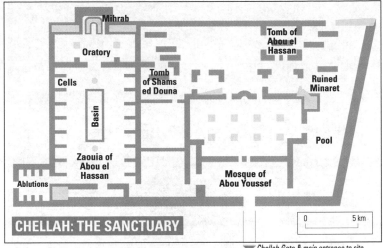

CHELLAH: THE SANCTUARY

0   5 km

▼ Chellah Gate & main entrance to site

thriving city and port, one of the last to sever links with the Roman Empire and the first to proclaim Moulay Idriss founder of Morocco's original Arab dynasty. An apocryphal local tradition maintains that the Prophet himself also prayed at a shrine here.

Under the Almohads, the site was already a royal burial ground, but most of what you see today, including the gates and enclosing wall, is the legacy of the Merenid sultan, **Abou el Hassan** (1331–51). The greatest of Merenid rulers, conquering and controlling the Maghreb as far east as Tunis, Abou el Hassan, "The Black Sultan", was also their most prolific builder. In addition to Chellah, he was responsible for important mosques in Fes and Tlemcen, as well as the beautiful medersas of Salé and Meknes.

The **main gate** here is the most surprising of Merenid monuments, its turreted bastions creating an almost Gothic appearance. Its base is recognizably Almohad, but each element has become inflated, and the combination of simplicity and solidity has gone. In its original state, with bright-coloured marble and tile decoration, the effect must have been incredibly gaudy – a bit like the nineteenth-century palaces you see today in Fes and Marrakesh. An interesting technical innovation, however, is the stalactite (or "honeycomb") corbels which form the transition from the bastion's semi-octagonal towers to their square platforms; these were to become a feature of Merenid building. The Kufic inscription above the gate is from the Koran and begins with the invocation: "I take refuge in Allah, against Satan."

To your left, as you enter, and signposted "Site Antique", are the main **Roman ruins** (same times and admission as Chellah). They are of a small trading post dating from 200 BC onwards, are well signposted and include a forum, a temple and a craftsmen's quarter.

The Sanctuary

From the main gate, the **Islamic ruins** are down to the right, within a second inner sanctuary approached along a broad path through half-wild gardens of banana, orange and ancient fig trees, sunflowers, dahlias and poisonous datura plants.

△ Chellah, Rabat

Their most prominent and picturesque feature is a tall stone-and-tile **minaret**, a ludicrously oversized stork's nest perched invariably – and photogenically – on its summit. Storks, along with swallows and house buntings, have a certain sanctity in Morocco, and storks nesting on minarets is a sign of good fortune.

The sanctuary itself appears as a confusing cluster of tombs and ruins, but it's essentially just two buildings: a mosque, built by the second Merenid sultan, Abou Youssef (1258–86), and a *zaouia*, or mosque-monastery, added along with the enclosure walls by Abou el Hassan. You enter directly into the *sahn*, or courtyard, of **Abou Youssef's Mosque**, a small and presumably private structure built as a funerary dedication. It is now in ruins, though you can make out the colonnades of the inner prayer hall with its mihrab to indicate the direction of prayer. To the right is its minaret, now reduced to the level of the mosque's roof.

Behind, both in and outside the sanctuary enclosure, are scattered **royal tombs** – each aligned so that the dead, dressed in white and lying on their right sides, may face Mecca to await the Call of Judgement. Abou Youssef's tomb has not been identified, but you can find those of both **Abou el Hassan** and his wife **Shams ed Douna**. Hassan's is contained within a kind of pavilion whose external wall retains its decoration, the *darj w ktarf* motif set above three small arches in a design very similar to that of the Hassan Tower. Shams ed Douna (Morning Sun) has only a tombstone – a long, pointed rectangle covered in a mass of verses from the Koran. A convert from Christianity, Shams was the mother of Abou el Hassan's rebel son, Abou Inan, whose uprising led to the sultan's death as a fugitive in the High Atlas during the winter of 1352.

The **Zaouia** is in a much better state of preservation, its structure, like Abou el Hassan's medersas, that of a long, central court enclosed by cells, with a smaller oratory or prayer hall at the end. Each of these features is quite recognizable, along with those of the ablutions, preceding the main court, for the worshippers' purification. There are fragments of zellij tilework on some of the colonnades and on the minaret, which again give an idea of its original brightness, and there are traces, too, of the mihrab's elaborate stucco decoration. Five-sided, the **mihrab** has a narrow passageway (now blocked with brambles) leading to the rear – built so that pilgrims might make seven circuits round it. This was once believed to give the equivalent merit of the *hadj*, the trip to Mecca a tradition, with that of Muhammad's visit, probably invented and propagated by the *zaouia's* keepers to increase their revenue.

Off to the right and above the sanctuary enclosure are a group of **koubbas** – the domed tombs of local saints or *marabouts* – and beyond them a **spring pool**, enclosed by low, vaulted buildings. This is held sacred, along with the eels which swim in its waters, and women bring hard-boiled eggs for the fish to invoke assistance in fertility and childbirth. If you're here in spring, you'll get additional wildlife, with the storks nesting and the egrets roosting.

At the far end of the sanctuary, you can look down a side-valley to the Bou Regreg estuary. From here, you can appreciate that this site was destined, from early times, to be settled and fortified. The site was easy to defend and the springs provided water in times of siege.

Nowadays, you can also appreciate from here the steady expansion inland of Salé – with its sprawling suburb, Betana. Salé is also expanding, ribbon-like, either side of the main road north towards Kenitra.

Eating, drinking and nightlife

For a capital city, Rabat is pretty quiet, but it does have the country's best collections of restaurants – many of them moderately priced or inexpensive – plus loads of good cafés, some reasonable bars and, as Moroccan nightlife goes, some not-too-terrible clubs.

Medina and beach area restaurants

As ever, the cheapest places to eat are to be found in the **Medina**, with a group of good, everyday **café-restaurants** just inside Bab Djedid – clean enough and serving regular Moroccan fare. They are excellent value, especially at lunchtime, when many have fixed-price meals for the office and shop workers. There are also a couple of good upmarket restaurants to the north of the Medina towards, or on, the beach.

Café Essalam Beside the Bab Djedid, set in the walls. Popular with locals downstairs and a plusher restaurant upstairs. Cheap.

Café Taghazoute 7 Rue Sebbahi. This café serves simple dishes, including tasty fried fish, and also omelettes, which makes it a good option for breakfast. It tends to be busy with office workers at lunchtime. Cheap.

Casa el Ouazzani 155 Av Mohammed V. A hole-in-the-wall pizzeria which also serves pannini and has what must be the world's smallest al-fresco dining area at the front. Cheap.

La Péniche Av du Bou Regreg, on the Salé side of the Bou Regreg river between the Royal Nautical Club and the Magic Park ⊤ 037 78 56 61. This floating restaurant in a canal boat serves excellent seafood, and is licensed. Moderate to expensive.

Restaurant Caravelle in the bastion to the north of the kasbah ⊤ 068 28 66 49. A scenic spot for tajine, brochettes, pastilla or even paella, with a terrace overlooking Salé and the beach. Moderate.

Restaurant Dinarjat 6 Rue Belgnaoui, off Bd el Alou ⊤ 037 70 42 39. This palatial eatery with fine Moroccan dishes and musical entertainment, in a seventeenth-century mansion at the northern end of the Medina, makes a good choice if you wish to spoil yourself. Expensive.

Restaurant de la Jeunesse 305 Av Mohammed V. One of the city's better budget eateries, with generous portions of couscous, and decent tajines. Cheap.

Restaurant de la Libération 256 Av Mohammed V. Another spot serving tajines and other Moroccan staples, including couscous on Fri. Cheap.

Restaurant de la Plage On the beach below the Kasbah des Oudaïas ⊤ 037 20 29 28. A fine fish restaurant overlooking the beach, offering the latest catch, well cooked. Expensive.

Le Ziryab 10 Impasse Ennajar, off Rue des Consuls ⊤ 037 73 36 36, ⊛ www.restaurantleziryab.com. Opened in 2004, this is a popular eatery on the business and embassy circuit, with good reason: the 500dh set menu is first-class Moroccan fare. Dinner only, closed Sun. Expensive.

Ville Nouvelle restaurants

In the **Ville Nouvelle** you can pick from a fine selection of Moroccan and French restaurants, plus a few Oriental places for a change of cuisine.

Café-Bar-Restaurant Français 3 Av Moulay Youssef, just off Pl de la Gare and alongside the *Hôtel d'Orsay*. Another downstairs bar with upstairs restaurant, like *La Clef* nearby, and arguably the best and most consistent place around the train station. Moderate.

Café-Restaurant de la Paix 1 Av Moulay Youssef, just off Pl de la Gare. As with the nearby *La Clef* and *Français*, there's some heavy drinking in the ground-floor bar, but you can eat well in the upstairs restaurant. Moderate.

La Clef Rue Hatim, a narrow side street just off Av Moulay Youssef, and near the *Hôtel d'Orsay*. There's serious drinking in the bar downstairs, but the restaurant upstairs is quiet and serves good French and Moroccan dishes. Try the tajines, brochettes and excellent pastilla. Moderate.

Hôtel Balima Av Mohammed V ⊤ 037 70 86 25, Ⓕ 037 70 74 50. Mainly Moroccan dishes in the snack bar, European ones in the main restaurant, but they're nothing special – the indoor bar and outdoor café under the trees are more the thing here. Moderate.

Kanoun Grill 6th floor, *Chellah Hôtel*, 2 Rue Ifni, ⊤ 037 70 10 51. The best place in town to sink your teeth into a good steak, or any other meat grilled over charcoal. Open daily for dinner, reservation recommended. Expensive.

La Mamma 6 Rue Tanta ⊤ 037 70 73 29. Opposite *La Bamba* and its Italian-style rival, with a range of good pizzas and pasta dishes. *La Dolce Vita*, next door to *La Mamma*, is owned by the same patron and provides luscious Italian-style ice cream. Moderate.

Le Mandarin 100 Av Abdel Krim Al Kattabi ⊤ 037 72 46 99. Popular Chinese restaurant in L'Océan quarter, not far from Bab el Alou. Closed Wed. Moderate to expensive.

Restaurant La Bamba 3 Rue Tanta, a small side street behind the *Hôtel Balima* ⊤ 037 70 98 39. European and Moroccan dishes, with good-value set menus for 80–120dh. Licensed. Moderate.

Restaurant Koutoubia 10 Rue Pierre Parent, off Rue Moulay Abdelaziz, and near the *Hôtel Chellah* ⊤ 037 72 01 25. There's an upmarket bar and, with a separate entrance through a quaint wood and glass extension, an old-style restaurant, serving excellent food. It claims the late King Hassan among past clientele, and an elderly patron who knew his father, Mohammed V. Expensive.

Restaurant La Pagode 13 Rue Baghdad, parallel to (and south of) the train station ⊤ 037 70 93 81. Has been around for a while now and is still one of the more popular Asian food –

mainly Chinese and Vietnamese – restaurants in town. Recently refurbished, they also have a take-out and home delivery service. Moderate. **Restaurant Saïdoune** In the mall at 467 Av Mohammed V, opposite the *Hôtel Terminus*. A good Lebanese restaurant run by an Iraqi, which also has a bar. Closed Fri. Moderate.

Tajine wa Tanjia 9 Rue Baghdad ☎037 72 97 97. Great little restaurant with a nice atmosphere accompanied most nights by live *oud* playing. The menu is mainly Moroccan fare, well presented, with a range of tajines, tanjia (jugged beef or lamb), and, on Fridays, couscous. Closed Sun. Licensed. Moderate.

Agdal restaurants

The suburb of **Agdal**, about 3km southwest of the city centre and favoured by Rabat's expat residents, has some fine restaurants and a reasonable variety of cuisines, though it's a bit of a haul if you're not already based there.

Fuji Restaurant 2 Av Michliffen, at the western end of Av Atlas ☎037 67 35 83. An upmarket Japanese restaurant favoured by Rabat's Japanese community (such as it is), and widely considered to have the best Oriental food in Rabat: sushi, sashimi, tempura and bento lunch boxes. Closed Tues and lunchtime Wed. Expensive. **Mijana** Av Atlas between Rue Oum Errabia and Rue Melouiya ☎037 77 00 97. Lebanese snacks and meze, with good falafel and koubba, hummus,

tabouleh, a choice of chicken or beef shawarma, and Lebanese (Turkish) coffee to round it off. Home delivery available. Cheap. **Pousse-Pousse** 41 Av Atlas ☎037 68 34 35. Reasonable Vietnamese- and Chinese-style food to eat in, take out or have delivered. Moderate. **Restaurant Entrecôte** 74 Av Fal Ould Oumeir ☎037 67 11 08. A well established restaurant with a good French menu and excellent fish dishes. WiFi connected. Expensive.

Cafés, bars and nightlife

Avenues Mohammed V and Allal Ben Abdallah have some excellent **cafés**, for coffee, soft drinks and pastries. Particularly pleasant spots include the *Hôtel Balima* outdoor café, which is very popular with locals and something of a male cruising spot, the *Café Maure* in the kasbah (see p.353), and the café in the shady Parc du Triangle de Vue, just south of Boulevard Hassan II, which is usually full of students working or arguing over a mint tea, but only opens in the daytime.

Bars – outside the main hotels – are few and far between. The bar and adjoining courtyard inside the *Hôtel Bouregreg* is pleasant enough though it's a little out of the way if you're not staying there. The one inside the *Hôtel Balima* is a trifle seedy but it does tend to stay open as late as there are customers and attracts an interesting crowd of Moroccan drinkers.

The restaurants *La Clef*, café-restaurant *de la Paix* and *Restaurant Koutoubia* all have bars. *Henry's Bar* on Place des Alaouites, pretty much opposite the train station, is a decent enough place as Moroccan city bars go, though it closes at 8pm. Americans can drink at the *American Club*, 15 Rue de Khouribga (☎037 76 22 65), there are imported beers, and decent club sandwiches, but it closes at 9pm.

Most of Rabat's **discos**, notably those around Place de Melilla, are little more than pick-up joints, though they expect you to dress up in order to get in. *Jefferson* and *Biba Beach*, both just off Place de Melilla, are open until the early hours by which time, frankly, you don't want to be there. One reasonable place for a dance is *Amnesia* at 16 Rue de Monastir, which attracts quite a mixed crowd. Another popular dance-club is *5th Avenue*, near the Moulay Youssef Sport complex, in the Agdal quarter, south of the centre, easiest reached by petit taxi. If you go early, you could eat first at the *Pizza Reggio* in the complex; the prices are reasonable and there's a good atmosphere.

In addition to the listings below, you may want to consult *Telecontact*, an annual directory with Yellow Pages-style listings for businesses and services in the Rabat/Casablanca/Kenitra region. It comes out around the New Year and is available from newsstands.

Airlines Royal Air Maroc is just across from the train station on Av Mohammed V (℡ 037 70 97 10) and Air France (℡ 037 70 75 80 or 037 70 77 28) is on the same avenue just north of the *Hôtel Balima* at no. 281. The nearest British Airways and Iberia offices are in Casablanca (℡ 022 22 94 64 & ℡ 022 43 95 42 respectively).

Banks Most are along avenues Allal Ben Abdallah and Mohammed V. BMCE's main branch at 340 Av Mohammed V has a bureau de change (daily 8.15am–noon & 2–7.30pm), and there's also one at Gare de Ville train station open similar hours.

Bookshops The English Bookshop, 7 Rue Al Yamama (Mon–Sat 9am–12.30pm & 3–6pm; ℡ 037 70 65 93), stocks new titles plus a wide selection of secondhand paperbacks. The American Bookstore, at the corner of Rue Moulay Abdelhafid and Rue Boujaad (Tues–Fri 10am–12.30pm; ℡ 037 76 12 69), has a good range of novels and non-fiction, as well as a small selection of books about Morocco and Islamic culture. Both these shops are marked on the map on p.345. You can get coffee-table books on Morocco and phrasebooks from several of the bookshops along Av Mohammed V – Kalila Wa Dimna, no. 344, and Éditions La Porte, just north of *Hôtel Balima*, both have a good selection.

Car rental Cheaper deals are available in Casablanca, but there are twenty or so rental agencies in Rabat. Main companies include: Avis, 7 Zankat Abou Faris Al Mairini ℡ 037 72 18 18, (F) 037 76 75 03; Budget, Rabat Ville train station ℡ 037 70 57 89, (F) 037 70 14 77; Europcar, 25 bis Rue Patrice Lumumba ℡ 037 72 41 41, (F) 037 20 02 41; Hertz, 467 Av Mohammed V ℡ 037 70 73 66 or 037 70 92 27, (F) 037 70 92 27; National, corner of Rue de Caire and Rue Ghandi ℡ 037 72 27 31, (F) 037 72 25 26; Visa Car, 9 Rue Bait Lahm ℡ 037 70 13 58, (F) 037 70 14 53. Avis, Budget, Europcar, Hertz and National have desks at Rabat–Salé airport.

Cinemas There are several cinemas on or near Av Mohammed V: Cinéma Renaissance at 360 Av Mohammed V, just north of the post office, has the latest US and French films; Cinéma Royal on Rue Amman, diagonally opposite *Royal Hôtel*, is more given to Kung Fu and Bollywood double bills. More of an arts cinema is the smaller Salle de 7ème Art on Av Allal Ben Abdallah, also near the *Royal Hôtel*; advance booking advisable. The Théâtre National

Mohammed V on Rue du Caire (℡ 037 20 83 16) puts on a range of concerts (Arabic and Western classical music) and films.

Cultural centres British Council, 36 Rue de Tanger (℡ 037 76 08 36) has a library with English-language books and British newspapers (Mon–Fri 8.30am–7.30pm, Sat 8.30am–5.30pm), and puts on various films and events in English. It's also a possible source of information if you want to stay on in Morocco and teach English. The German Goethe Institute, 7 Rue Sanaa (℡ 037 73 65 44) and the French Institut Français, 1 Rue Abdou Inane (℡ 037 68 96 50, ⊛ www.ambafrance-ma.org) also put on exhibitions and cultural events.

Dentist Dr Karim Yahyaouti, 5 Rue Tabaria ℡ 037 70 25 82

Embassies Algeria, 46 Bd Tariq Ibn Ziad ℡ 037 76 55 91 (but note that the land border with Morocco is still closed at present); Canada, 13 bis Rue Jaâfar as Sadiq, Agdal ℡ 037 68 74 00; France, embassy 3 Rue Sahnoun, Agdal ℡ 037 68 97 00, consulate 49 Rue Allal Ben Abdallah ℡ 037 26 81 81; Italy, 2 Zankat Driss el Azhar ℡ 037 70 68 82; Mauritania, 6 Rue Thami Lamdouar, Quartier OLM, Souissi ℡ 037 65 66 78, Mon–Thurs 9am–3pm, Fri 9am–noon but note that visas are only issued by their consulate in Casablanca (see p.391); Netherlands, 40 Rue de Tunis ℡ 037 73 35 12; Norway, 9 Rue de Khénifra, Agdal ℡ 037 76 40 84 or 85; South Africa, 34 Rue des Saadiens ℡ 037 70 67 60; Spain, 3 Rue Madnine ℡ 037 26 80 00; Sweden, 159 Av John Kennedy, Souissi ℡ 037 63 32 10; UK, 28 Av SAR Sidi Mohammed, Souissi ℡ 037 63 33 33, Mon–Thurs 8am–4.30pm, Fri 8am–1pm; USA, 2 Av Mohammed el Fassi (Av Marrakesh) ℡ 037 76 22 65, Mon-Fri 8am–noon & 1–5pm. Australia is represented by the Canadian embassy and New Zealanders by their embassy in Madrid (℡ 00-34/91 523 0226), but they may get help from the Brits in cases of dire emergency. The nearest Irish and Danish representation are their consulate in Casablanca (see p.391).

Fairgrounds If you have some children in tow, they may appreciate a visit to the riverside Magic Park on Av du Bou Regreg, on the Salé side of the river, served by bus #35 from Bd Al Alaouiyne in Rabat via Salé's Bab Mrisa. There are carousels and other gentle fairground rides, as well as bumper cars, and the park is open Wed, Sat & Sun in winter, daily in summer 11am–9pm (Ramadan Mon–Fri 8pm–1am, Sat & Sun 1pm–1am); entry is 5dh for children, 10dh for accompanying adults, 25dh for adults with no children, and a 40dh ticket gives access to all rides.

Galleries Unusually for Morocco, Rabat has a number of worthwhile art galleries, showing works by contemporary artists. The Bab Oudaïa often opens its mammoth doors for exhibitions, and there's also a gallery inside the gate at Bab er Rouah (just south of the gap used by traffic – entrance on the western side; ☎037 70 05 30), with regular exhibitions by local artists. In the kasbah, along Rue Djemaa, is Le Petit Galerie and the larger Nouiga Galerie d'Art, the latter regularly showcasing local photographers.

Golf The Dar es Salaam Royal Golf Club, 7km out of Rabat on Zaers Rd (☎037 75 58 64, ℗037 75 75 71) is one of the country's finest, with two eighteen hole and one nine hole course designed by Robert Trent-Jones.

Hiking maps Division de la Cartographie, Av Hassan II, ☎⋯⋯⋯⋯⋯⋯⋯⋯⋯⋯⋯⋯⋯ ask for *Residence Oum Kaltoum* If you're lost ☎037 29 50 34. You may be able to get hiking maps to the Toubkal area over the counter, but other topographic maps of the main hiking areas in the High and Middle Atlas, which can be selected from the official index, have to be ordered and collected 48hr later, discounting Sat and Sun, but only if officially sanctioned (there's no postal service). These are good maps, at up to 1:50,000, but the policy and the service make buying them a major bureaucratic exercise, and even if you go down to the office, apply, and wait the statutory 48hr, it is very likely that you will be refused the maps.

Internet access Student Cyber, 83 Av Hassan II (daily 8.30am–11.30pm); ETSI Net, 12 Av Prince Moulay Abdellah (daily 9am–11pm); Phobos, 113 Bd Hassan II by *Hôtel Majestic* (daily 8am–10pm). If you're in Salé, there's a good and cheap Internet station, Perfect Computer, just inside Bab Djedid (daily 8am–8pm).

Medical aid Dr Youssef Alaoui Belghiti, 6 Pl des Alaouites ☎037 70 80 29; Dr Mohammed el Kabbaj, 8 Rue Oued Zem ☎037 76 43 11. For emergencies call the Service Médical d'Urgence on ☎037 20 21 21. The US embassy maintains a list of useful medical contacts online at ⋯⋯⋯⋯⋯⋯⋯⋯⋯⋯⋯⋯⋯⋯⋯ /list_of_physicians.html.

Police The main station is on Av Tripoli, near the cathedral (☎037 72 02 31), with a police post at Bab Djedid. For emergencies call ☎19.

Oulja: the Complexe des Potiers

On the Salé side of the estuary, 3km out from the town, the suburb of **Oulja** houses one of Morocco's finest **potteries**. It has been open since 1980, established around a rich vein of clay, so its techniques and kilns are relatively modern. For instance, while just three out of the 180 kilns at Safi (Morocco's largest potting town; see p.407) are fired by gas or electricity, here the ratio is almost exactly the reverse, with just a few specialist kilns using tamarisk wood fuel. Nevertheless, despite different techniques, lovely and wonderfully imaginative objects are produced at both Oulja and Safi.

The complex also has a craft shopping centre, an area specializing in basketwork, and a clean and modern restaurant. Visitors are made welcome, with a minimum of sales hassle, at the twenty-odd potteries on the complex and you could pick interesting potteries at random. Good ones, however, include:

#12 **Poterie Demnate** ☎ & ℗037 81 36 29, ⊕www.poteriedemnate.fr.st. The patron, Bennami Abdelaziz came here after working in Demnate. Wares include ashtrays, butter dishes, plates and miniature tajines.

#10 **Poterie Hariky** ☎037 81 13 19, ℗037 80 98 90. Superb Islamic designs, by family-named business. Tajines, cups and saucers, and vases are among the objects for sale, the bigger ones decorated with calligraphy and geometric designs.

#9 **Poterie el Attar** ☎064 92 93 64. Light, modern designs, with many tea sets and mugs – some of their work can be seen in the Hassan II Mosque in Casablanca.

Oulja can be reached by bus #35 from Rabat (Boulevard Al Alaouiyne) or Salé (Bab Mrisa). If you want to walk back to Rabat, head east to cross the first bridge; you can then cut up to the high ground towards the Tour Hassan.

Post office The central PTT is at the junction of
avenues Mohammed V and Jean Jaurès, opposite
the Bank Al Maghrib (Mon–Fri 8am–6pm, Sat
8am–noon).
Supermarkets Label Vie, 4 Av Maghreb el Arabi,
about 100m west of Bab el Had, and at the junction
of Av Fal Ould Oumeir & Bd Ibn Sina (500m west of
Agdal train station) are open daily 8.30am–9pm.
There is also the Marjane hypermarket between
Rabat and Salé.

Moving on

Leaving town by **train** is easy, with Rabat Ville station slap-bang in the city
centre. Services to Casa are extremely frequent, and most run to the more
convenient Port station rather than the less central Voyageurs. There are also
fairly frequent services to Meknes and Fes, and six a day to Tangier.

The main **bus terminal** is at Place Zerktouni, 3km out from the centre by
the road junction for Casa and Beni Mellal (around 20dh by petit taxi, or 3dh
by #17 or #30 bus from just outside Bab el Had). CTM services from here
serve Casa, Fes, Meknes, Marrakesh, Agadir, Tangier and Tetouan. To Casa in
particular, though private firms have departures every few minutes, it's worth
taking the CTM, which drops you right in town rather than at Casa's *gare
routière* out in the back of beyond. Private services to Fes on the other hand
(which leave every half-hour, via Meknes) drop you at the *gare routière* near Bab
Boujeloud, which most tourists will find far more convenient than the CTM
station in the Ville Nouvelle. Private companies also have departures pretty
much hourly for Marrakesh, Agadir and Tangier.

Grands taxis for Fes and Casa leave from outside the bus terminal. For
Meknes, they leave from Boulevard Hassan II at the corner of Avenue Chellah,
while those for Kenitra and Khémisset also leave from just off Boulevard
Hassan II, a few blocks to the east.

Rabat–Salé Airport (☎037 81 02 21 or 29) is 7km northeast of Rabat,
served by no public transport other than privately hired grands taxis (150dh
for up to six people). Flights from here serve various domestic and UK
destinations and Paris. At the airport is a post office agency, bureau de
change, car rental desks and a small café. **Mohammed V Airport**, out
beyond Casablanca (☎022 53 90 40), is served by hourly trains from
Casablanca's Aïn Sebaa station, reached by connecting services from Rabat
with a total journey time of just under two hours, although it is best to give
yourself extra time.

Salé

Although it's now essentially a suburb of Rabat, **SALÉ** was the pre-eminent of
the two right through the Middle Ages, from the decline of the Almohads to
the uneasy alliance in the pirate republic of Bou Regreg (see p.346). Under the
Merenids, in particular, it was a port of some stature, and endowed as such, the
most notable monument being its superb **Medersa Bou Inan**.

In the last century, following the French creation of a capital in Rabat, and the
emergence of Casablanca as Morocco's great port, Salé became a bit of a
backwater. The original Ville Nouvelle was restricted to a small area around the
bus station and the northern gates. More recently, however, Salé has spread
inland and along the main road north towards Kenitra. The increased Salé-
Rabat traffic has called for an additional road bridge over the Bou Regreg and
new train station (see p.364). Nevertheless, Salé still looks and feels very distinct
from Rabat, particularly within its medieval walls where the souks and life
remain surprisingly traditional.

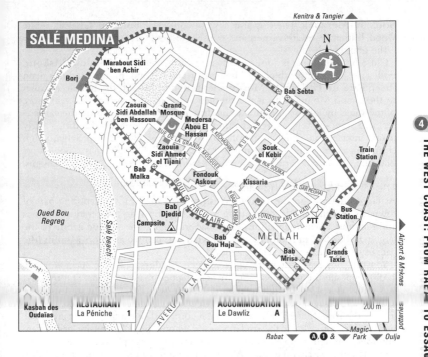

The Medina

The most interesting point to enter Salé's Medina is through **Bab Mrisa**, near the grand taxi terminal. Its name – "of the small harbour" – recalls the marine arsenal that used to be sited within the walls, and explains the gate's unusual height. A channel running here from the Bou Regreg has long silted up, but in medieval times it allowed merchant ships to sail right into town. Robinson Crusoe was brought into captivity through this gate in Daniel Defoe's novel. The gate itself is a very early Merenid structure of the 1270s, its design and motifs (palmettes enclosed by floral decoration, bands of Kufic inscription and *darj w ktarf*) still inherently Almohad in tone.

The souks

Inside Bab Mrisa you'll find yourself in a small square, at the bottom of the old **Mellah** (Jewish) quarter. Turning to the left and continuing close to the walls for around 350m, you come to another gate, **Bab Bou Haja**, beside a small park. If you want to explore the souks – the route outlined below – veer right and take the road – Rue Bab el Khebaz – which runs along the left-hand side of the park. If not, continue on just inside the walls to a long open area; as this starts to narrow into a lane (about 40m further down) veer to your right into the town. This should bring you out more or less at the **Grand Mosque**, opposite which is the **Medersa of Abou el Hassan.**

The park-side street from Bab Bou Haja is **Rue Bab el Khebaz** (Street of the Bakers' Gate), a busy little lane that emerges at the heart of the **souks** by a small **kissaria** (covered market) devoted mainly to textiles. Most of the alleys here are grouped round specific crafts, a particular speciality being the pattern-weave mats produced for the sides and floors of mosques – to be found in the

Souk el Merzouk. There is also a wool souk, the **Souk el Ghezel**, while wood, leather, ironware, carpets and household items are in the **Souk el Kebir** – the grand souk.

Close by the *kissaria* is a fourteenth-century hospice, the **Fondouk Askour**, with a notable gateway (built by Abou Inan), and beyond this the Medina's main street, **Rue de la Grande Mosque**, leads uphill through the middle of town to the Grand Mosque. This is the simplest approach, but you can take in more of the souks by following **Rue Kechachin**, parallel. Along here are the carpenters and stone-carvers, as well as other craftsmen. In **Rue Haddadin**, a fairly major intersection which leads off to its right up towards Bab Sebta, you'll come upon gold- and coppersmiths. At 72 Rue al Eskandaria is Coopérative Nakasha, a women's carpet cooperative producing interesting, modern designs.

The Grand Mosque and Medersa

As far as buildings go, the **Grand Mosque** marks the most interesting part of town, its surrounding lanes fronting a concentration of aristocratic mansions and religious *zaouia* foundations. Almohad in origin, the mosque is one of the largest and earliest in Morocco, though what you can see as a non-Muslim (the gateway and minaret) are recent additions.

You can, however, visit its recently restored **Medersa** (daily 8.30am–4.30pm; 10dh), opposite the mosque's monumental, stepped main entrance. The medersa was founded in 1341 by Sultan Abou el Hassan (see p.357), and is thus more or less contemporary with the Bou Inania medersas in Meknes and Fes. Like them, it follows the basic Merenid plan of a central courtyard opening onto a prayer hall, with a series of cells for the students – for whom these "university halls" were endowed – round its upper floors. If this is the first example you've seen, it will come as a surprise after the sparse Almohad economy of the monuments in Rabat. The great Merenid medersas are all intensely decorated – in carved wood, stucco and zellij – and this is no exception. Within the entrance gate, there is hardly an inch of space which doesn't draw the eye away into a web of intricacy.

The patterns, for the most part, derive from Almohad models, with their stylized geometric and floral motifs, but in the latter there is a much more naturalistic, less abstracted approach. There is also a new stress on calligraphy, with monumental inscriptions carved in great bands on the dark cedarwood and incorporated within the stucco and zellij. Almost invariably these are in the elaborate cursive script, and they are generally passages from the Koran. There are occasional poems, however, such as the beautiful foundation inscription, set in marble against a green background, on the rear wall of the court, which begins:

Look at my admirable portal!
Rejoice in my chosen company,
In the remarkable style of my construction
And my marvellous interior!
The workers here have accomplished an artful
Creation with the beauty of youth . . .

Translation from Richard B. Parker, *Islamic Monuments in Morocco*

The medersa is only sporadically visited and you'll probably have it to yourself (except for the sparrows and the caretaker) – a quiet, meditative place. Close to its entrance there is a stairway up to the former cells of the students (now partially renovated to look almost livable) and to the **roof**, where, looking out across the river to Rabat, you sense the enormity of the Hassan Tower.

Round the Grand Mosque, and over to the northwest, you can view (but not enter, unless you are Muslim) a trio of interesting buildings.

The first of these is the **Zaouia Sidi Ahmed el Tijani**, whose elaborate portal faces the Grand Mosque and Medersa. *Zaouias* are a mix of shrine and charitable establishment, maintained by their followers, who once or more each year hold a moussem, a pilgrimage festival, in the saint-founder's honour.

The most important of Salé's moussems is that of its patron saint, **Sidi Abdallah Ben Hassoun**, whose **zaouia** stands at the end of the Rue de la Grande Mosquée, a few steps before the cemetery. The saint, who for Muslim travellers plays a role similar to St Christopher, lived in Salé during the sixteenth century, though the origins and significance of his moussem are unclear. Taking place each year on the eve of Mouloud – the Prophet's birthday – it involves a spectacular procession through the streets of the town with local boatmen, dressed in corsair costumes, carrying huge and elaborate wax lanterns mounted on giant poles. Much of it can be witnessed away from the forbidden precincts.

At the far end of a cemetery (again forbidden to non-Muslims), which spreads down to the river, is a third revered site, the white *koubba* and associated buildings of the **Marabout of Sidi Ben Achir**. Sometimes known as "Al Tabib" (The Doctor), Ben Achir was a fourteenth century ascetic from Andalusia. His shrine, said to have the ability to attract shipwrecks and quell storms – good pirate virtues – reputedly effects cures for blindness, paralysis and madness. Enclosed by nineteenth-century pilgrim lodgings, it, too, has a considerable annual moussem on the eve of Mouloud.

Practicalities

From Rabat you used to be able to cross the river to Salé by rowing boat ferry but whether this will still be possible once the riverside promenade development is complete is not known. The only public transport option at the moment is to take one of the many **buses** (#12, #13, #14, #16, #34, #38 & #42) that pick up from the eastern end of Boulevard Hassan II; some can be picked up further west – #12 and #13 for example, which start just off Place Melilla. The buses drop you at an open terminal just outside the town's principal gate, **Bab Mrisa**. **Grands taxis** from various points on Boulevard Hassan II and Rue An Nador serve specific places in Salé; those for Bab Mrisa leave from the corner of Rue An Nador with Zenkat Deldou.

Salé has a basic **campsite**: *Camping de la Plage* (☎063 59 36 63; open all year), near the beach, but unless you want to use the campsite as a base for Rabat, there seems little reason to stay. To the east of the Medina and overlooking the river is the top end *Le Dawliz Hôtel* (☎037 88 32 77, ⓦwww.ledawliz.com; ❼ including breakfast) which boasts 45 large rooms with all mod cons plus a complex of bars, restaurants and a nightclub.

In the evenings, you can eat reasonably at one of the many **cafés** along Rue Kechachin, but the streets empty even earlier than those in Rabat.

The coast from Rabat to Casa

It's a little over an hour by grand taxi from Rabat to Casa (under an hour by express train) and, if you're making a quick tour of Morocco, there's little to

THE WEST COAST: FROM RABAT TO ESSAOUIRA | The coast from Rabat to Casa delay your progress. The landscape, wooded in parts, is a low, flat plain, punctuated inland by a series of scruffy light-industrial towns.

On the coast, things are slightly more promising: **Mohammedia** has a fine beach and good restaurants, and is, with the smaller resorts of **Temara** and **Skhirat**, a popular seaside escape for the affluent of Rabat and Casablanca. For visitors, however, there's a lot more to get excited about on the coast south from Casa towards Agadir.

Rabat to Mohammedia

Temara Plage, some 14km to the south of Rabat, is (along with Plage des Nations, see p.342), the capital's closest beach resort. If you are planning a day-trip from Rabat, you can take local bus #33 from just outside Bab el Had or, in summer, a grand taxi from Boulevard Hassan II (around 20min).

If you're driving, the **coast road** (R322) is more scenic than the inland N1, though both routes are built up almost the whole way. Leaving Rabat, follow Tarik al Marsa past the Kasbah des Oudaïas for the coast road, or take Boulevard Misr alongside the Medina wall, then bear left onto Avenue Al Moukaouma and its continuation Avenue Sidi Mohammed Ben Abdallah for the N1. The latter route passes by the vast **Complexe Olympique**, built for the 1983 Mediterranean games.

Temara Ville and Plage

TEMARA VILLE (served by bus #17 from outside Bab el Had in Rabat, and by some trains between Casa and Rabat) has an old **kasbah**, dating from Moulay Ismail's reign. Other than that, there's little to delay you, unless you want to stock up for picnics on the beach or the campsites further south. To get from here to Temara Plage (about 4km), you'll need to take the road that leads west off the N1 about 500m north of the train station.

TEMARA PLAGE (served by bus #33 from outside Bab el Had in Rabat) consists of several sandy strips, plus a cluster of discos that provide a summer alternative to the lack of action in Rabat. Few people stay here overnight, other than the well-heeled of Rabat, who maintain summer villas. However, there are a number of **hotels**, the newest and most deluxe being the *Yasmina Club Hotel* (☎037 64 14 03, ⓕ037 64 13 54; ❻ including breakfast), just north of the road from Temara Ville, which boasts a restaurant, bar, nightclub, fitness club and swimming pool. A kilometre or so south of here sits the now-closed *Hôtel St Germain en Laye* and a small guesthouse nearby, the *Hôtel Studio Temara Plage* (☎037 74 45 39 or 067 71 07 46; ❹), run by a very friendly local family who also operate a foreign- (including English) language school in nearby Tamara Ville. Two kilometres south, by the beach known as Plage Les Sables d'Or, the *Hôtel La Felouque* (☎037 74 43 88; ❺ including breakfast) has a swimming pool, tennis courts and a well-regarded **restaurant**, *Les Sables d'Or*. Nearby, on the main road, at the very end of the #33 bus route, the *Hôtel Panorama* (☎037 74 42 89, ⓕ037 74 48 19; ❺ including breakfast) is better value, with friendly staff, a terrace overlooking the beach, and reasonably well-maintained lawns and gardens. There's a campsite, *Camping les Sablettes*, off the main road a little way south of *Hôtel St Germain en Laye*, open summer only (though campervans can park up for the night outside when it's closed).

Back on the coastal road, there is a good **restaurant**, the *San Francisco*, built by a Moroccan returned from thirty years in California, and decorated with a full-size Ford Mustang bursting through the bar mirror.

Ech Chiana

ECH CHIANA, also known as Rose Marie Plage, is 9km south from Temara and a slightly plusher resort, with a luxury beachside **hotel**, *La Kasbah* (☎037 74 91 16, ⓦwww.hotelkasbahclub.com; ❻), popular with French package tourists. A little back from the beach, on the inland side of the road, there is also the cheaper *Hôtel Les Gambusias* (☎037 74 95 25, Ⓕ037 74 91 88; ❹), which does good meals, especially fish dishes, and has a swimming pool and a seasonal campsite. A second campsite (July–Sept) is attached to the highly regarded beachside **restaurant-bar** *Rose-Marie* (☎037 74 92 51).

Skhirat Plage

The **Royal Palace** at **SKHIRAT PLAGE** was the site of a notorious coup attempt by senior Moroccan generals during King Hassan's birthday celebrations in July 1971. The coup was mounted using a force of Berber cadets, who took over the palace, imprisoned the king and massacred a number of his guests. It came within hours of being successful, being thwarted by the apparently accidental shooting of the cadets' leader, General Mohammed Medbuh, and by the strength of personality of Hassan, who reasserted control over his captors. Among the guests who survived was Malcolm Forbes (see p.119).

The palace still stands, though it has understandably fallen from royal favour, and there are a good many holiday French-style villas in the vicinity – some old, some new, many unfinished. Right next to the palace, the gleaming white and spanking new *L'Amphitrite Palace* (☎037 62 10 00, Ⓕ037 62 10 10; ❽) ranks as one of Morocco's most de luxe beach hotels.

Getting to the resort by public transport, take any of the slow **trains** (there are about six a day, departing early morning or mid- to late-afternoon) on the Rabat–Casa line to Skhirat Ville, a small (and uninteresting) farming town, on the hillside, a couple of kilometres up from the beach.

Bouznika and Mansouria

Before Mohammedia, the coastal plain is increasingly barren and the beaches are less developed, indeed isolated, and in places reached only by sandy tracks from the main road. At **BOUZNIKA PLAGE** and **DAHOMEY PLAGE**, around 20km before Mohammedia, there are primitive summer **campsites**. Further south, 6km before Mohammedia, **MANSOURIA** has two more campsites, the *Oubaha* (☎023 32 33 36; June–Sept) and the rather better *Mimosa* (☎ 023 32 33 25; open all year).

The last place of note before Mohammedia is **PORT BLONDIN**, at the mouth of the Oued Nefifikh and the beginning of the Mohammedia sands. There is a fairly consistent surf break here, especially during winter with a north-westerly swell. It's flanked by a couple of seasonal campsites and the *Hôtel La Madrague* (☎ & Ⓕ023 32 20 20; ❺), a rambling building, but well maintained by friendly staff.

From here, it's a straight run into Mohammedia, its approach heralded by bright new villas either side of the road.

Mohammedia

Formerly known as Fedala, but renamed following the death of Mohammed V in 1961, the port of **MOHAMMEDIA** has a dual identity. As the site of Morocco's main oil refineries, and the base of its petrochemical industry, it's an important industrial and commercial city, with a population of some 170,000. Yet it's also a big-name resort – a holiday playground for Casablanca – with one

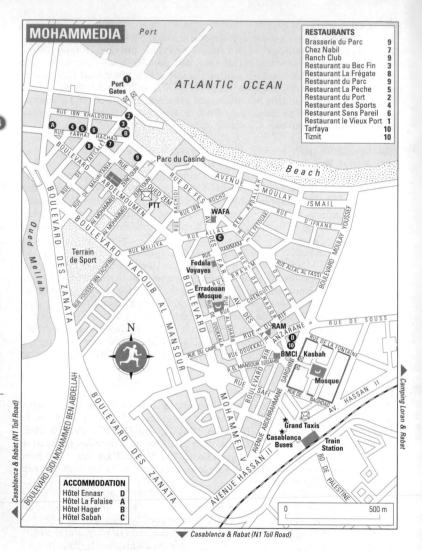

MOHAMMEDIA

Port

ATLANTIC OCEAN

RESTAURANTS
Brasserie du Parc   9
Chez Nabil   7
Ranch Club   9
Restaurant au Bec Fin   3
Restaurant La Frégate   8
Restaurant du Parc   9
Restaurant La Peche   5
Restaurant du Port   2
Restaurant des Sports   4
Restaurant Sans Pareil   6
Restaurant le Vieux Port   1
Tarfaya   10
Tiznit   10

Port Gates

RUE IBN KHALDOUN

RUE FARHAT HACHAD

BOULEVARD DE TATFILALET

BOULEVARD DE MAURITANIA

Parc du Casino

Beach

AVENUE MOULAY ISMAIL

PTT

WAFA

Terrain de Sport

Oued Mellah

Fedala Voyayes

Erradouan Mosque

RAM

BMCI Kasbah

Mosque

RUE DE SOUSS

Grand Taxis

Casablanca Buses

Train Station

N

BOULEVARD DES ZANATA

BOULEVARD SIDI MOHAMMED BEN ABDELLAH

Casablanca & Rabat (N1 Toll Road)

AVENUE HASSAN II

BD DE PALESTINE

0   500 m

ACCOMMODATION
Hôtel Ennasr   D
Hôtel La Falaise A
Hôtel Hager   B
Hôtel Sabah   C

Camping Loran & Rabat

▼ *Casablanca & Rabat (N1 Toll Road)*

of the best beaches on the Atlantic, a racecourse, the Ibn Batouta yacht marina and the Mohammedia Royal Golf Club (☎023 31 48 02, ℉023 32 11 22) where the game was originally played in the sand in the 1920s, before a Frenchman, Pierre Uruguayen, shaped the present eighteen holes.

These two faces of the city – tourism and industry – are kept quite distinct, with the latter contained in a zone to the southwest of the city centre and beach. In summer, the city's population is given a huge boost by Moroccan tourists, mainly from Casa, who camp by the beach in what is called *Moham-media-Est*: a sequence of tented villages that stretch northeast towards Port Blondin and Mansouria. For foreign visitors, there is perhaps less to tempt a stay. Despite a longish history as a trading port, this was still a small village at the turn of the twentieth century and the city has little in the way of monuments of "old Morocco". The only sight to speak of is a modern building, the **Erradouane Mosque**, which, with its elegant minaret, has become a landmark of Mohammedia since it was inaugurated in March 1991.

Still, Mohammedia makes a very pleasant stopover, with its friendly, easy-going atmosphere, and a fine selection of restaurants. If you are flying in or out of Casablanca, you could do a lot worse than spend a first or last night here; it's only twenty minutes by train from Casa and there are a dozen or so trains a day each way. In July, it may be worth a special trip, too, for the week-long **Mohammedia Festival**, which encompasses all kinds of cultural activities, craft and floral exhibitions, a *fantasia*, cycling races and a marathon.

Practicalities

Orientation is not difficult as "downtown" Mohammedia covers quite a small area. Between the **train station** and the **Ville Nouvelle**, there is a small square **kasbah**, built during a period of Portuguese occupation and still preserving its original gateway. To the west of the kasbah, a sequence of boulevards leads down to the beach. **Buses** and **grands taxis** operate from Avenue Hassan II, just in front of the train station. Travelling to Casablanca, the best bus to take is #900, which drops you in the city centre.

There is a branch of the BMCI bank at the top end of Avenue des FAR, facing the small roundabout in front of the main entrance to the kasbah, and a branch of the BMCE on Rue Rachidi, one block to the west of Rue de Fes. The **post office** is on Avenue Mohammed Zerktouni, also one block to the west of Rue de Fes – and facing the Parc du Casino. The **travel agency** Fedala Voyages at 35 Avenue des FAR (☎023 32 73 90) is helpful for confirming flights and arranging car rental. Royal Air Maroc has an office on the corner of Avenue des FAR and Rue du Rif. Rue Baghdad near the station is the place for car repairs, with a slew of mechanics and spares shops. There is a Marjane **supermarket** on the way out to the N1 toll road from the port end of town.

Accommodation

There are four **hotels** in Mohammedia, and a campsite, *Camping Loran*, 2km north of town on the Rabat road (☎023 32 49 46), which is closed in winter, and sometimes even in summer, so sites up the coast are better options (see p.340, p.341, p.367, p.368 & p.369).

Hôtel Ennasr Rd Moulay Youssef (no phone). This basic hotel with cubicles (no outside windows) off a first floor corridor has shared showers and a ground-floor café that is lively or noisy, depending on your point of view. Make sure you are clear from the outset how much you have agreed to pay for the room. ❶

Hôtel La Falaise Rue Farhat Hachad ☎023 32 48 28. A lovely little place run by an energetic Frenchwoman, with eight spotless rooms, but only one en suite, a tree-shaded central courtyard and a bar. It's often full so it's worth booking ahead. ❹

Hôtel Hager Rue Farhat Hachad ☎023 32 59 21, ✉hotelhager@menara.ma. This is a modest but modern hotel, with bright, sparkling rooms, two excellent restaurants (one on the roof), and a patisserie next door. Price includes breakfast. ❺

Hôtel Sabah 42 Av des FAR ☎023 32 14 54, ✆023 32 14 56. A modern, expensive hotel, halfway between the kasbah and the port, it caters more for businesspeople than tourists. Price includes breakfast. ❻

Eating and drinking

For its size, Mohammedia's choice of **restaurants** is impressive, especially for fish. As well as the options listed below, the *Hôtel Hager's* two eateries are both worth trying (the downstairs one is even open daytime during Ramadan, when it is something of an oasis). **Breakfast and snacks** are available from several pavement cafés facing the main entrance to the kasbah: the *Tiznit* and *Tarfaya* both serve grills and brochettes. Just inside the main gate of the kasbah, on the right, there are a number of similar café–restaurants worth a try.

Mohammedia has a few **bars** apart from those at the restaurants and hotels, including the *Ranch Club* (☎023 32 22 11), on Rue de Fes facing the Parc du Casino, and *Brasserie du Parc* just around the corner. The bar at the *Hôtel la Falaise* is also not a bad place. For nightlife, however, it's better to stay in Casa and explore the Aïn Diab corniche (see p.386 & p.390).

Chez Nabil Rue de Tafilalet. A café-restaurant with fried fish and paella to eat in or take away. Cheap.

Restaurant au Bec Fin Rue Cheikh Chouaib Doukali, near the port gates ☎023 32 44 29. A small, but highly recommended restaurant with a truly Spanish flavour. Moderate.

Restaurant La Frégate Rue Oued Zem, near the *Hôtel Hager* ☎023 32 44 47. Lobster, prawns, shrimps and all manner of seafood served in generous helpings, particularly of shellfish paella. There's a take-away and delivery service too. Moderate to expensive.

Restaurant du Parc Rue de Fes, facing the Parc du Casino and next to the *Ranch Club* ☎023 32 22 11. Excellent place, with fish specialities. Moderate.

🏃 **Restaurant La Peche** Rue Farhat Hachad. Unpretentious though popular seafood restaurant serving some of the best calamari, fish, oysters and paella in town. Can get very busy on Sundays with well-to-do Casablancans enjoying their weekly seafood feast. Lunch and dinner. Cheap to moderate.

Restaurant du Port 1 Rue du Port, opposite the port gates ☎023 32 58 95. This is the town's best-known restaurant, renowned for its charcoal grills, served in a flower-strewn garden. Indoors, the decor is strongly nautical. Same patron as Casablanca's *La Brasserie Bavaroise* (see p.388). Moderate to expensive.

Restaurant des Sports Rue Farhat Hachad ☎023 32 35 32. Large and classy, with excellent seafood and "folkloric spectacles" at weekends in the season. Dinner only. Moderate to expensive.

Restaurant le Vieux Port In the fishing port. Oysters, paella, fish and seafood, fresh as can be, well cooked and not outrageously priced (many items, including lobster, are priced by weight). Moderate.

Casablanca (Casa, Dar el Baida)

The principal city of Morocco, and capital in all but administration, **CASABLANCA** (Dar el Baida in its literal Arabic form) is now the largest port of the Maghreb – and busier even than Marseilles, the city on which it was modelled by the French. Its development, from a town of 20,000 in 1906, has been astonishing but it was ruthlessly deliberate. When the French landed their forces here in 1907, and established their Protectorate five years later, Fes was Morocco's commercial centre and Tangier its main port. Had Tangier not been in international hands, this probably would have remained the case. However, the demands of an independent colonial administration forced the French to seek an entirely new base. Casa, at the heart of *Maroc Utile*, the country's most fertile zone and centre of its mineral deposits, was a natural choice.

Superficially, with a population of over three million, Casa today is not unlike a large southern European city: a familiarity that makes it fairly easy to get your bearings and a revelation as you begin to understand something of its life. Arriving here from the south, or even from Fes or Tangier, most of the preconceptions you've been travelling round with will be happily shattered by the city's cosmopolitan beach clubs or by the almost total absence of the veil. But these "European" images shield what is substantially a first-generation city – and one still attracting considerable immigration from the countryside – and perhaps inevitably some of Morocco's most intense social problems.

Alongside its show of wealth and its prestige developments – most notably the vast Mosquée Hassan II, on a promontory looking out to the Atlantic – Casablanca has had a reputation for extreme poverty, prostitution, crime, social unrest and the *bidonvilles* (shanty towns) which you will see both sides of the train track as you approach the city. In fact, the word – literally "tin-can town" in French – was coined in Casablanca in the 1920s, when construction workers on a building project in the Roches Noires district, east of the port area, knocked up some temporary accommodation next to their main quarry. Over the decades, other migrant workers followed suit, and the *bidonville* problem escalated, partly from the sheer extent of population increases – which exceeded one million in the 1960s – and partly because few of the earlier migrants intended to stay permanently. Most of them sent back their earnings to their families in the country, meaning to rejoin them as soon as they had raised sufficient funds for a business at home.

The pattern is now much more towards permanent settlement, and this, together with a strict control of migration and a limited number of self-help programmes, has eased and cleared many of the worst slums. Also, *bidonville* dwellers have been accorded increasing respect during recent years. They cannot be evicted if they have lived in a property over two years, and after ten years they acquire title to the land and building, which can be used as collateral at the bank for loans. The dread of every *bidonville* family is to be evicted and put in a high-rise block, which is regarded as the lowest of the low on the housing ladder.

The problem of a concentrated urban poor, however, is more enduring and represents, as it did for the French, an intermittent threat to government stability. Through the 1940s and 1950s Casa was the main centre of anti-French rioting, and post-independence it was the city's working class that formed the base of Ben Barka's Socialist Party. There have been strikes here sporadically in subsequent decades, and on several occasions, most violently in the food strikes of 1982, they have precipitated rioting. Whether Casa's development can be sustained, and the lot of its new migrants improved, must decide much of Morocco's future.

Arrival

The best way to arrive in Casa is by **CTM bus**, which will drop you at the CTM terminal on Rue Léon l'Africain, right in the centre of town. Second best is on a **local train** from Kenitra or Rabat, most of which run into the relatively central **Casa Port** station (Gare du Port), at the end of Boulevard Houphouet Boigny, 150m from Place des Nations Unies. **Intercity trains** arriving from Marrakesh, Fes, Meknes and Tangier stop at the less convenient station of **Casa Voyageurs** (Gare des Voyageurs), 2km from the centre at the far end of Boulevard Mohammed V. Few trains run from Voyageurs to Port station, so if there isn't one in the offing, you'll have to either take a taxi into town (about 10dh), or walk (a good 20 minutes – straight ahead down Boulevard Mohammed V, curving slightly to the left as you come to the next main square, Place el Yassir), or take bus #2 from outside the station. Alternatively, change trains at Rabat on the way.

Private **buses** (except CTM) and most grands taxis (exceptions detailed below) arrive at the **Ouled Ziane Gare Routière**, 4km southeast of the city centre. The easiest way to get into town from here is by petit taxi (about 20dh on the meter). Buses #10 and #36 go into town (Boulevard Mohammed V by Marché Central) from a bus stop over the main road, next to the pharmacy. The *gare routière* has a 24hr left-luggage office (*consigne*), which costs 10dh per item per day.

4

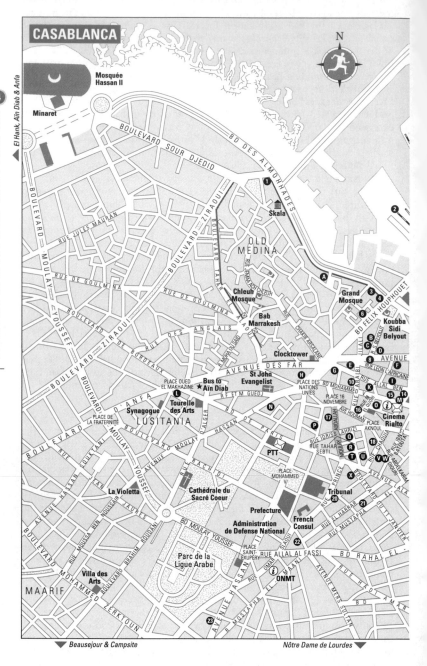

CASABLANCA

N

◄ El Hank, Aïn Diab & Anfa

Mosquée
Hassan II

Minaret

BOULEVARD SOUR DJEDID

BD DES ALMOHADES

BOULEVARD JULES MAURAN

RUE JULES MAURAN

BOULEVARD MOULAY YOUSSEF

RUE DE GOULMINA

RUE DE GOULMINA

BOULEVARD ZIRAOUI

BOULEVARD ZIRAOUI

BOULEVARD ZIRAOUI

BOULEVARD TAHAR

RUE DES ANGLAIS

RUE DE BORDEAUX

J

Skala

OLD
MEDINA

RUE IBNOU BOT CHLEUH

Chleuh
Mosque

RUE TAHAR SEBTI

Bab
Marrakesh

Clocktower

AVENUE DES FAR

A

Grand
Mosque

BD FELIX HOUPHOUET

3
4
6

Koubba
Sidi
Belyout

B
C
D

E

AVENUE

RUE LEON L'AFRICAINE

F

2

RUE ALLAL BEN

St John
Evangelist

PLACE OUED
EL MAKHAZINE

Bus to
Aïn Diab

PLACE DES
NATIONS
UNIES

PLACE 16
NOVEMBRE

H

G

BD MOHAMMED

RUE EL M'GUEDJ

L

Tourelle
des Arts

Synagogue

LUSITANIA

D'ANFA

BOULEVARD D'ALGER

HASSAN

RUE DE PARIS

AVE HOUMAN

10
K

8

I

15 14
M

16
i

Q

Cinema
Rialto

PLACE
AKNOUL

N

17

P

RUE IDRISS LAHRIZI

RUE TAHAR
SEBTI

Q
R

18

T U

V W

PLACE DE
LA FRATERNITÉ

BOULEVARD

RUE

BOULEVARD MOULAY

AVENUE MOULAY

RUE RACHDI

La Violetta

AVENUE HASSAN

RUE MOUSSA BEN NOUSSAIR

RUE JAURÈS

Cathédrale du
Sacré Coeur

BD MOULAY YOUSSEF

PTT

PLACE
MOHAMMED
V

Prefecture

Administration
de Defense National

PLACE
SAINT-
EXUPERY

RUE ALLAL AL FASSI

Parc de la
Ligue Arabe

Villa des
Arts

MAARIF

BOULEVARD MOHAMMED ZERKTOUN

BOULEVARD BRAHIM ROUDANI

X

Tribunal

20

21

French
Consul

RUE EL HARRAB

RUE MUSTAPHA

BD RAHAL EL

AVENUE LALLA

BD

22

RUE OMAR SLAOUI

RUE MAANI

i

ONMT

23

R. MOSTAPHA

R. MUSTAPHA

AVENUE MERS SULTAN

AVENUE NUE

BD

▼ Beausejour & Campsite

Nôtre Dame de Lourdes ▼

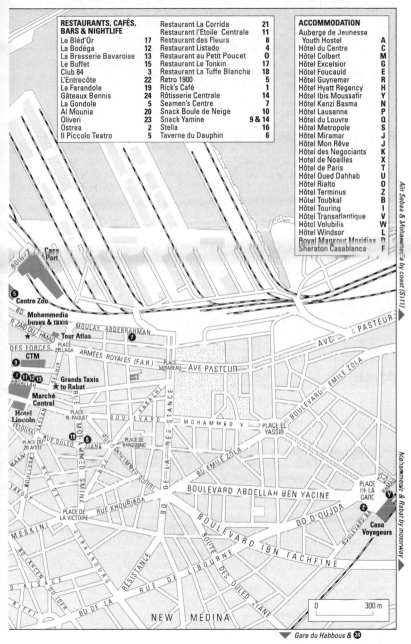

Most **grands taxis** arrive in front of the Ouled Ziane Gare Routière. The main exceptions include those from Rabat, which deposit passengers in town on Boulevard Hassan Seghir, very near the CTM terminal, and those from Mohammedia, which go to Rue Zaid ou Hmad, close to Casa Port train station. Grands taxis from El Jadida, Safi and Essaouira leave you on Boulevard Brahim Roudani, by the junction with Boulevard Bir Anzarane, 2km from the city centre. From here it's a twenty-minute walk into town, or take a petit taxi (about 10dh), or hop on bus #7 to Place des Nations Unies.

Coming from the **Aéroport Mohammed V**, used by all international and most domestic flights, there is an hourly train service (6.50am–9.50pm then 11.50pm) to Casa Voyageurs (35 min; 30dh; see p.373).

The CTM airport shuttle bus is no longer operating, so if you don't want to take the train you will need to organize a transfer with your hotel or take a grand taxi, located outside the entrance of the terminal. The official rate is 230dh per person but it often seems to depend on how many passengers and the time of day. There are numerous bank ATMs and bureaux de change in the arrivals terminal. You could also rent a car on arrival (see p.390), though driving in Casablanca is pretty nightmarish, and you'd be better off waiting until you leave town.

Orientation and information

Casa is a large city by any standards and it can be a bewildering place in which to arrive, but once you're in the city centre, orientation is relatively straightforward. It's focused on a large public square, **Place Mohammed V** (but note box below), and most of the places to stay, eat, or (in a rather limited way) see, are located in and around the avenues that radiate from it. A few blocks to the north, still partially walled, is the **Old Medina**, which was all there was of Casablanca until around 1907. Much further out to the south is the **Habous** quarter – the **New Medina**, created by the French, while to the west, along the Corniche past the Mosquée Hassan II, lies the beach suburb of **Aïn Diab**.

Casablanca has two **tourist offices**, both unusually helpful. The more convenient of the two is the **Syndicat d'Initiative** at 98 Bd Mohammed V (Mon–Fri 8.30am–4.30pm, Sat 8.30am– 12.30pm; ☏022 22 15 24). Among other things, they have a map of the city on their desk which goes out a lot further than our map, including the areas of Beauséjour, Habbous or Aïn Diab. Alternatively, there's the ONMT **Délégation du Tourisme**, in the southern reaches of the

---

New names and new avenues

The names of Casa's chief squares –-**Place Mohammed V** and **Place des Nations Unies** - are a source of enduring confusion. In 1991, Hassan II declared that the old Place des Nations Unies (around which are grouped the city's main public buildings) be known as Place Mohammed V, while the old Place Mohammed V (the square beside the Medina) became renamed Place des Nations Unies.

Note also that, as elsewhere in Morocco, many of the old French street names have been revised to bear Moroccan names; older people and many petit taxi drivers still use the old names – as do some street maps still on sale. Significant conversions include:

Rue Branly – Rue Sharif Amziane
Rue Claude – Rue Mohammed el Qorri
Rue Colbert – Rue Chaouia
Rue Foucauld –-Rue Araibi Jilali
Rue de l'Horloge – Rue Allal Ben Abdallah

city centre at 55 Rue Omar Slaoui (Mon–Fri 8.30am–4.30pm; ☎022 27 11 77), with friendly staff who are happy enough to answer questions.

Good but pricey street **maps** of greater Casablanca are available at most bookshops.

City transport

Petits taxis are easy to find along the main avenues and are invariably metered – as long as the meter is switched on you will rarely pay more than 8dh per taxi

You must remember this . . .

Probably the best-known fact about Casablanca is that it wasn't the location for the movie – all of which was shot in Hollywood. In fact, Warner Bros, upset by the Marx Brothers filming *A Night in Casablanca*, attempted to copyright the very name Casablanca – which could have been inconvenient for the city.

The film, of course, owes its enduring success to the romantic tension between Humphrey Bogart and Ingrid Bergman, but at the time of its release it received a major publicity boost by the appearance of Casablanca and Morocco in the news. As the film was being completed, in November 1942, the Allies launched **Operation Torch**, landing 25,000 troops on the coast north and south of Casablanca, at Kénitra, Mohammedia and Safi. The troops were commanded by General Eisenhower and consisted principally of Americans, whom Roosevelt believed were less likely than the British to be fired on by the Vichy French government in Morocco. An even more fortunate coincidence, however, took place in the week of the film's première in Los Angeles in January 1943. Churchill and Roosevelt had arranged an Allied leaders' summit, and the newsreels revealed its location: the **Casablanca Conference**, held in a hotel (long since gone) in the affluent suburb of Anfa, out beyond Aïn Diab. Such events – and the movie – are not, it has to be said, evoked by modern-day Casa.

Attempting to reverse this is ﹠ **Rick's Café**, located on the edge of the Medina at 248 Bd Sour Jdid, on the corner with Bd des Almohades (daily noon–3pm & 6.30pm–12.30am; ☎022 27 42 07, ⊛www.rickscafe.ma). *Rick's* was opened in 2004 by American woman Kathy Kriger, who has lived in Morocco since 1998 and who greets each customer every night. The restored interior of the multi-levelled former Medina residence is dominated by the central courtyard with its authentic 1930s *Pleyel* piano. Local pianist Issam Chabaa creates a Forties and Fifties musical ambience every night except Monday – apparently, he never tires of playing the inevitable "As Time Goes By", which, let's face it, is the main reason most visitors will come here. On Sunday nights he "gets the place jumpin'" with the weekly jazz jam session that has become a staple of the Casa social scene and regularly sees international musicians drop by. The movie is screened nightly in an upstairs viewing room. It's not a cheap place to drink (beers start at 50dh and the Dom Perignon is a decidedly chilled 2500dh) nor eat (rib steak for 150dh), and it depends upon your own expectations and theatrical sense as to whether a visit is worthwhile or not. If you are suitably impressed, there is a range of souvenirs – including a delightfully tacky *Rick's* coffee mug – for sale.

The movie is also commemorated by the **Bar Casablanca** in the *Hôtel Hyatt Regency* on Place des Nations Unies (see p.379), decorated with stills from the movie and selling drinks and souvenirs almost as expensive as *Rick's*. For a glimpse of True Brit expat life, as it used to be lived, there is always the **Churchill Club** at 1 Rue de la Mediterranée (Rue Pessac) in Aïn Diab (☎022 79 72 80). Established in 1922, as the "British Bank Club", its one condition of membership is that "the English language only should be spoken on the premises". One of the social highlights of the week is still the post-church and pre-Sunday lunch drinks, while the Tuesday night suppers are also popular. The bar is open until 11pm (even during Ramadan), and English-speaking visitors are always welcome.

for a trip round town. For Aïn Diab the fare is currently 20dh (5dh extra if you get the driver to detour en route round the Mosquée Hassan II). There is a fifty-percent surcharge at night.

You may want to make use of **city bus** services if you arrive at or leave from Casa Voyageurs (#2), Ouled Ziane *Gare Routière* (#10 or #36), or the Essaouira/El Jadida taxi stand in the suburb of Maarif (#7), or if you're staying at *Camping Oasis* (#31). The other useful services are #15 from Boulevard Félix Houphouët Boigny and Place Oued el Makhzine to Mosquée Hassan II, and #9 from the same stops to Aïn Diab. Be warned that buses can get very crowded at rush hours.

Traffic is a nightmare in Casa, and roads are frequently gridlocked: if you can avoid **driving**, try to do so. If you have a car, the larger hotels at Aïn Diab offer more security than those in the city centre. Alternatively, stay in Rabat or Mohammedia and commute in by train.

Accommodation

Although there are a large number of hotels in Casa, they operate at near capacity for much of the year and can fill up at short notice for conferences. If possible, phone ahead for a room, or at least arrive fairly early in the day. Even if you have a reservation, it's wise to phone ahead the day before to confirm. If there is a royal-patronage event on, your hotel may well be commandeered.

City centre

The recommendations listed below are in the main, central area of the city. No hotels in the Old Medina have been included, as most overcharge for miserable rooms; in the "new city", by contrast, many of the cheaper places are quite stylish Art Deco buildings. Most of the more expensive places offer discounts off-season.

Cheap

Auberge de Jeunesse (Youth Hostel) 6 Pl Ahmed el Biolaoui, previously Amiral Philibert ℡022 22 05 51, ℻022 22 76 77. A friendly, airy place, nicely sited just inside the Medina, and well maintained. Neither IYHF nor national YHA cards are required, it's good value for money (45dh in dormitory, 120dh double room, including breakfast. hot shower 6dh), and popular – reservations are advisable June–Sept. Open 8–10am & noon–midnight. There's a good café, small PTT, Internet and a hammam on the leafy square.

Hôtel Colbert 38 Rue Chaouia (Rue Colbert) ℡022 31 42 41. Conveniently located – one block from the CTM – and surprisingly large, though the hotel sign is difficult to see; it's across the street from the daily flower stalls against the outer wall of the Marché Central. A bit gloomy, but clean and friendly. Rooms with showers cost more. There are several grill-cafés alongside for a quick snack or meal. ❸

Hôtel Foucauld 52 Rue Araibi Jilali ℡022 22 26 66. A good-value hotel with a gaily painted facade, nice stuccowork in the lobby, and clean, if bare, salmon-pink rooms, some en suite. ❸

Hôtel du Louvre 36 Rue Nationale ℡022 27 37 47. Central and pleasant, but rooms are a bit

glum, and some are better than others, so check before deciding. All rooms have a shower (some right at the end of the bed), but there's only hot water in the mornings. ❸

Hôtel Miramar 22 Rue León l'Africain ℡022 31 03 08. Only 50m from the CTM, this is currently the cheapest of the little hotels in the city centre. It has an old-fashioned feel, and bathroom facilities are shared (shower 10dh), but the rooms are fine for the price. ❷

Hôtel Mon Rêve 7 Rue Chaouia (Rue Colbert) ℡022 31 14 39. A friendly little place, and one that has long been a favourite with budget travellers, though some of the rooms are way up the steep spiral staircase. Showers on the corridor. ❸

Hôtel des Negociants 116 Rue Allal Ben Abdallah ℡022 31 40 23. Opposite *Hôtel Touring* (see opposite), and very similar, though currently priced slightly higher. It has recently been refurbished, with clean, comfortable rooms (some en suite), and is a popular choice with Moroccan families. ❹

Hôtel Oued Dahhab 17 Rue Mohammed Belloul (Rue Pegoud) ℡022 22 38 66, ✉hotelguynemer @yahoo.com. Owned by the same family as the nearby *Hôtel Guynemer*, this is a rare budget option in this area of the city centre with basic but large, airy rooms, some en suite. Airport (and sometimes bus) pick-ups if prearranged. ❹

Hôtel Rialto 9 Rue Salah Ben Bouchaib ☎022 27 51 22. Opposite the Cinema Rialto and just off Bd Mohammed V. All rooms have a shower, some have toilets too, and there's hot water mornings and evenings. ❸

Hôtel Terminus 184 Bd Ba Hamad ☎022 24 00 25. Close to Casa Voyageurs, so quite convenient: clean, decent rooms with hot showers on the corridor. It's not in the same league as the nearby *Hôtel Ibis* (see next column) but then it's less than one third of the cost. ❸

🏃 **Hôtel Touring** 87 Rue Allal Ben Abdallah ☎022 31 02 16. A friendly old French hotel that's been refurbished and is excellent value, with clean, comfortable rooms, some with their own shower, and hot water all day (bar a couple of hours around noon). It's even got its own little mosque. Definitely the first choice on this street. ❸

Moderate

Hôtel du Centre 1 Rue Sidi Belyout, corner of Av Mohammed V ☎022 44 61 78. Old-fashioned hotel with a creaky antique lift, but some nice Art Deco ironwork on the staircase, and rooms cheered up by a lick of paint and sparkling en-suite bathrooms. ❹

Hôtel Excelsior 2 Rue el Amraoui Brahim, off Pl des Nations Unies ☎022 20 02 63, ℱ022 26 22 81. A once-grand hotel, opened in 1915 and thus Casa's oldest surviving hotel. Though outclassed these days by the big chain hotels on Av des FAR, it retains an elegance and has a central and very convenient location, near Casa Port. ❹

Hôtel Guynemer 2 Rue Mohammed Belloul (Rue Pegoud) ☎022 27 57 64, ✉hotelguynemer@yahoo.com. A fairly well-appointed, family-run hotel just off Rue Prince Moulay Abdellah and Av Idriss Lahrizi in the most architecturally interesting part of town. Great Art Deco touches on the exterior and a recently refurbished interior – ask for one of the newer, larger rooms. It has a licensed restaurant and the staff are very friendly, helpful and speak good English. Free Internet and WiFi. Airport (and sometimes bus) pick-ups if pre-arranged. ❻

Hôtel Lausanne 24 Rue Tata (Rue Poincaré), off Av Idriss Lahrizi, opposite the Cinéma Lusitania ☎022 26 86 90, ℱ022 26 80 83. The owner has lived in Switzerland where, according to Bernard Shaw, they know all about hotels. The *Hôtel Lausanne* illustrates his point: it's efficient and well managed, with a *salon de thé* next door, but the lift is not safe for children. ❺

Hôtel Metropole 89 Rue Mohammed Smiha ☎022 30 12 13, ℱ022 30 58 01. Off Bd Mohammed V, this is quite a comfortable hotel, though the decor is a bit gaudy. ❺

Hotel de Noailles 22 Bd du 11 Janvier, just off Av Lalla Yacout ☎022 20 25 54, ℱ022 22 05 89. Though starting to show its age, this is a pleasant and tasteful hotel with a *salon de thé* and a touch of class. ❻

Hôtel de Paris 2 Rue Sharif Amzian, on the corner with the pedestrianized length of Rue Prince Moulay Abdallah ☎022 27 38 71, ℱ022 29 80 69. In the centre of town and highly recommended, though rooms at the front can be noisy; it's often full, so book or arrive early. ❺

Hôtel Volubilis 20/22 Rue Abdelkrim Diouri ☎022 27 27 72, ℱ022 29 47 92. Built in 1919, the *Volubilis* re-opened in 2006 after a complete refurbishment, with a suitably Roman-themed reception area. There are 45 (mostly small) rooms, some with balcony and adjoining doors, good for families, and there's a small lift. Breakfast in the ground floor restaurant included. ❺

Hôtel Windsor 93 Pl Oued el Makhazine ☎022 20 03 50, ℱ022 88 08 05. A comfortable hotel with large rooms with either a large bathroom or (cheaper) just a shower. There's also a decent bar. ❺

Expensive

Hôtel Hyatt Regency Pl des Nations Unies ☎022 43 12 34, ⊛www.casablanca.hyatt.com. Casablanca's most prominent deluxe hotel, with all the facilities you could want – pool (summer only), gym, sauna, basketball court, squash courts, private hammam, guarded parking, three restaurants, the *Casablanca* bar (themed on the movie) and a nightclub, plus of course extremely plush rooms and suites. Nor is the price too outrageous compared with the competition. ❽

Hôtel Ibis Moussafir Bd Ba Hamad, Pl de la Gare ☎022 40 19 84, ⊛www.ibishotels.com. As with all hotels in this popular chain, the site is by the train station; in this case Casa Voyageurs, so it's hardly central, though convenient for a late arrival (book in advance) or early departure. Restaurant, (sometimes noisy) bar, and car park. Breakfast is included in the price. ❻

Hôtel Kenzi Basma 35 Av Moulay Hassan I, just off Pl des Nations Unies ☎022 22 33 23, ℱ022 26 89 36. Efficient and comfortable, this newish four-star business hotel is in a horrible-looking building, but some of its rooms have great views over the Medina and towards the Mosquée Hassan II. ❼

Hôtel Toubkal 9 Rue Sidi Belyout, off Av des FAR ☎022 31 14 14, ⊛www.bestwestern.com/ma /hoteltoubkal. One of the Best Western chain, centrally located with a/c rooms, restaurant, bar, cabaret and safe parking, but nothing very special for the price. ❼

🏃 **Hôtel Transatlantique** 79 Rue Chaouia (Rue Colbert) ☎022 29 45 51, ⓦwww .transatcasa.com. Founded in 1922 in a Lyautey colonial building, and recently refurbished with a great mix of colonial decor (including two big brass lions in the foyer) and traditional stucco, tilework and stained glass, the *Transatlantique* boasts very comfortable rooms, a bar, restaurant and nightly cabaret. Past guests include Edith Piaf. ❼

Royal Mansour Meridien 27 Av des FAR ☎022 31 30 11, ⓦwww.starwoodhotels.com/lemeridien. This centrally located, modern deluxe hotel has a fitness centre, a gym, two restaurants, a piano bar and a hammam, but no swimming pool and very high prices. ❽

Sheraton Casablanca 100 Av des FAR ☎022 43 94 94, ⓦwww.sheraton.com/casablanca. A very modern top-end hotel right in the centre of the Ville Nouvelle, with every conceivable facility – pool, business centre, three restaurants, nightclub, sauna, gym, Jacuzzi, hammam, beauty parlour – plus state-of-the-art rooms (including some disabled-adapted). If you've still got money to spare, you could splash out on a "Tower" room, with personal Internet access, workdesk and ergonomic chair plus a host of minor perks, or suites up to 31,800dh. ❾

Aïn Diab

The seaside suburb of Aïn Diab (about 15dh from the centre by petit taxi, 3dh on bus #9) provides an alternative base if you can afford any of the hotels below; all are comfortable business/tourist places, close to the beach. The few cheaper hotels in the area cater exclusively for Moroccan guests, and tourists are unlikely to find rooms on offer.

Azur Hôtel 41 Bd de la Corniche ☎022 79 74 93, ⓦwww.azurhotel.ma. Across the road from the beach, but equipped with a decent-size swimming pool, a bar and a restaurant, its rooms are quite elegantly furnished, with satellite TV, a/c and heating, and a slightly maritime feel. Breakfast is included in the price. ❼

Hôtel Bellerive 38 Bd de la Corniche ☎022 79 75 04, ☎022 79 76 39. A modern hotel overlooking the beach, with a good pool, safe parking and a restaurant serving burgers, club sandwiches and kebabs. The rooms are a bit small, but comfortable. Breakfast is included in the price. ❻

Hôtel de la Corniche Bd de la Corniche ☎022 79 81 81, ⓦwww.hoteldelacorniche.com. Stylish hotel with light, airy rooms with a/c and satellite TV, a small pool and safe parking, but no direct beach access. The price may be negotiable in winter, but not in summer when you'll need to book ahead. ❻

Hôtel de la Côte Bd de la Corniche ☎022 79 70 35, ☎022 79 70 43. Getting a little weather-worn but still comfortable enough, with a bar, restaurant and pool. ❻

Church of St John the Evangelist

The **Church of St John the Evangelist**, on Rue Félix and Max Guedj near the Hôtel Hyatt Regency, stood in open fields when it was built in 1906. It now stands, partially hidden by a high wall and the tall trees surrounding it, in the centre of modern Casablanca – testimony to the phenomenal growth of the city.

Within twelve months of its consecration, the church was involved in events which led to the **first French landings** here. Some Europeans working on the port were murdered as Shaweea tribesmen from the interior invaded the town. They sacked the church, destroying the organ and ripping up the lectern Bible. Peace of a sort was restored by a French bombardment and subsequent occupation of the town.

In 1942, during **World War II**, the church was filled with troops involved in Operation Torch, when American troops landed at Casablanca and elsewhere on the Atlantic coast. An early member of the congregation at this time was General George Patton, who had led his troops ashore at Safi. He presented the oak pulpit, which still stands in the church, "in memory of the men of all nations who fell in the fighting around Casablanca".

Details of services are displayed on the door in the high wall.

Camping

For details of other campsites in the area, see the Rabat to Mohammedia coast
p.367, p.368 & p.369, or the coast southwest to El Jadida p.394 & p.398.

Camping Oasis Av Jean Mermoz, Beauséjour
☎022 23 42 57. This is the nearest site, 4km out
past Maarif in the suburb of Beauséjour (bus #31
from Place Oued el Makhzine). If driving, head
out on Bd Brahim Roudani, which becomes Av
Omar el Khayyam – the campsite is on the left,
just past Beauséjour market.

The City

Guidebooks used to declare, with some amazement, that Casa had not a single
"real" monument. Given the scale and success of the colonial landmarks of the
city centre – including the ensemble of public buildings on **Place Mohammed
V** designed by the French architect d'Henri Prost – this was never quite true.
However, the city did undoubtedly lack any one single, great building: a
situation that, in part, prompted King Hassan II's decision to construct the
Mosquée Hassan II on a truly epic scale. The mosque is literally unmissable,
standing beside the sea on the road to Aïn Diab. Casablanca also has the only
Jewish museum in the Muslim world, but the city's true delight remains the
Mauresque and Art Deco architecture built during the colonial period, in
particular the 1920s and 1930s, and the best way to take it all in is simply to go
for a stroll through the centre of town. One possible route – following roughly
an arc, from Boulevard Mohammed V down to Place Mohammed V and the
cathedral, and then round to Place Oued el Makhazine – covers the most
outstanding colonial buildings in the city centre and is outlined below.

Casablanca's colonial architecture

The French-built city centre and its formal, colonial buildings already seem to
belong to a different and distant age. The style of the administrative buildings in
particular is known as **Mauresque**, or sometimes as "Neo-Moorish", essentially

△ Hôtel Lincoln, Casablanca

a French idealization and "improvement" on traditional Moroccan styles, with lots of horseshoe arches, and even the odd touch of *darj w ktarf*, originally an Almohad motif (see *Moroccan Architecture* colour section). Many private buildings of the early colonial period (from 1912 until the early 1920s) were heavily influenced by the flowery **Art Nouveau** of late nineteenth- and early twentieth-century Europe, but following the 1925 Exposition des Arts Decoratifs in Paris, a new and bolder style, named **Art Deco** after the Exposition, began to take hold. Art Deco took its inspiration from many sources, including traditional Moroccan design, and it in turn had a major influence on later Mauresque private architecture, with trademarks such as wrought-iron windows, staircases and balconies, and floral, animal and geometric designs on stuccoed pediments and friezes. The authorities are now taking steps to preserve these buildings as part of Casablanca's architectural heritage, and the following route will take you past some of the most outstanding examples. Be sure to look upwards, though, since most of the finer features stop short of ground-floor level.

Boulevard Mohammed V and around

Most guidebooks mention the **Hôtel Lincoln** on Boulevard Mohammed V, opposite the Marché Central, an early example of colonial Mauresque, dating from 1916. Once a lovely building, it is now sadly derelict although there is word that the city council is planning to restore it to its former glory by way of a museum or boutique hotel. No matter, it makes as good a starting point as any. Heading west from here along the south side of **Boulevard Mohammed V**, there's a whole row of splendid facades dating from the same period, starting with the post office at no. 116, which incorporates a Europeanized version of the Almohad *darj w ktarf* motif (see *Moroccan architecture* colour section). The most striking facade on this strip, however, is the *Maroc Soir/Le Matin du Sahara* newspaper office, one block west, which boasts a wonderful frontage based on a hexagram motif, topped with a lovely green-tiled roof, although the resident pigeons are doing their best to camouflage it. There are more fine buildings on both sides of the boulevard for a couple of blocks past here, but if you take the next left up Rue Mohammed el Qorri, you'll see the **Rialto Cinema**, a gorgeous 1930 Art Deco picture palace which was receiving a major facelift at the time of writing.

Continuing up Rue Mohammed el Qorri, you emerge at Place Aknoul, and now you really are in the thick of some of Casa's finest colonial-era buildings. The road straight ahead, **Rue Tahar Sebti**, is full of them and **Rue Abdelkarim Diouri**, over to your left, has a nice little bunch of buildings at its junction with Rue Ibn Batouta (two blocks up), especially the *Bar Lyonnais*. Opposite is the 1919 **Hôtel Volubilis** and behind that, the 1922 **Hôtel Translantique**, both of which have recently been lovingly restored (see p.379 & p.380).

Heading west from Place Aknoul, down Rue Idriss Lahrizi towards the post office, there are more great facades along both sides of the street. It's worth making a detour to take the first street on the right, Rue Pergoud, where the **Hôtel Guynemer** (see p.379), at the first corner on the left, has some smashing Art Deco panels up on its cornerpiece. A right here brings you to the pedestrianized stretch of **Rue Prince Moulay Abdallah**, where there's a whole row of Mauresque and Art Deco facades on both sides, and some lovely little touches too: the Art Deco doorway at no. 48, for example, has a bird of paradise incorporated into the ironwork (as does 25 Rue Mouftakir Abdelkader, in the same block, just round the corner), while no. 72 is topped with some pretty Art Nouveau ironwork reminiscent more of Brussels or Barcelona than of Marseille, the city with which Casablanca is most often compared. At the northern end of the pedestrianized street is **Place 16**

Novembre, where no. 19 is the most handsome of a trio of charming Art Deco buildings, while at the southern end Boulevard de Paris leads west to Place Mohammed V. On the way, check out the fine group of buildings around the junction with Rue Tata (Rue Poincaré).

Place Mohammed V and around

Place Mohammed V (the former Place des Nations Unies) is truly grand in scale, as are the public buildings that surround it. They served as models for administrative architecture throughout Morocco, and to an extent still do. The square stood at the centre of a network of boulevards drawn up by Resident General Lyautey's chief architect, **d'Henri Prost**, who made his plan based on a projected population of 150,000, considered far too high by many when he proposed it in 1914, but already exceeded by the time he left in 1923. Prost was keen to combine traditional Moroccan forms with current European town planning ideas, and he more than anyone else was responsible for Casablanca's shape, and much of its architectural style.

The effect of the central ensemble in Place Mohammed V is very impressive indeed, the only feature out of place being a clocktower in the old **Préfecture**, on the south side of the square —an irresistible French colonial addition. The **law courts** on the east side of the square, and the **Bank al Maghrib** on the north are both solidly imposing too, and unlike much of the city's architecture, barely seem to have aged at all, probably because the many more modern buildings are modelled on them. On the west side of the square, the **post office**, which opened in 1919, incorporates lots of surprisingly traditional features, in the tilework around the door for example, as well as the ceiling and brass chandelier within.

To the south of the square, at the junction of Avenue Hassan II with Rue d'Agadir and Rue Allal el Fassi, check out the building at 2 Place Saint-Exupéry, an imposing edifice with an impressive semicircular facade. Opposite, across Avenue Hassan II, the Administration de Défense Nationale building, dating from 1916, represents an earlier and much simpler style of Mauresque, reminiscent of buildings in the Spanish zone of northern Morocco. Off Avenue Hassan II, you'll find some fine 1920s buildings along **Avenue Mers Sultan**, especially around *L'Entrecôte* restaurant and the next main junction, Place Mers Sultan.

The cathedral and around

From Avenue Hassan II, Boulevard Moulay Youssef heads west towards Casablanca's most classic piece of Christmas-cake colonial architecture, the **Cathedral of Sacré Cœur**, at the far end of the **Parc de la Ligue Arabe**. More European in style, though again adopting traditional Moroccan forms, the cathedral was built to a wonderfully balanced and airy design, paying genuine homage to its Moroccan setting. After independence it was used as a school and then as a theatre and cultural centre; after a long period of neglect it is now being given some, not a lot, attention and is again playing host to the odd cultural soirée. Most days you should be able to have a look around inside and if you're lucky, the *gardien* may escort you to the top of the tower for a brilliant view of the city and port.

Some 500m south of the cathedral at 30 Bd Brahim Roudani, an Art Deco villa has been lovingly restored and now houses the **Villa des Arts** (Tues–Sat 9am–7pm, except Ramadan 10am–3pm & 8.30pm–10.30pm; free; ☎022 29 50 87 or 94), an exhibition centre concentrating on contemporary art and a peaceful haven away from the noisy traffic. Alongside the cathedral and heading north, there are more fine colonial-era buildings along **Rue d'Alger**, especially nos. 54 and 78, which despite their numbering are pretty much next to each other. On the corner of Boulevard Rachidi, the **Tourelle des Arts** is another restored Art Deco villa which opened briefly as an exhibition centre much like Villa des Arts; it closed when its owner died in 2002 and although a lovely café has moved in onto the terrace, its future is still uncertain. Further up Rue d'Alger towards Place Oued el Makhazine, the balconies on the Radiology Clinic at no. 12 are classic Art Deco. Finally, to round off your tour of Casa's colonial architecture, there's another slew of handsome 1920s buildings along the south side of **Avenue Moulay Hassan I**, from Rue d'Alger to Place des Nations Unies, excluding the hideous *Hôtel Kenzi Basma*, which may be comfortable within (see p.379), but is something of an eyesore without.

The Old Medina

The **Old Medina**, lapsing into dilapidation above the port, is largely the product of the late nineteenth century, when Casa began its modest growth as a commercial centre. Before that, it was little more than a group of village huts, half-heartedly settled by local tribes after the site was abandoned by the Portuguese in 1755. Casa Branca, the town the Portuguese founded here in the fifteenth century after the expulsion of the pirates, had been virtually levelled by the great earthquake of that year. Only its name ("White House": *Casablanca* in Spanish; *Dar el Baida* in Arabic) survives.

Now relatively underpopulated, the Medina has a slightly disreputable, if also fairly affluent, air. It is said to be the place to go to look for any stolen goods you might want to buy back – a character well in keeping with many of the stalls. There's nothing sinister though, and it can be a good source for cheap snacks and general goods. A single main street, which starts from the top end of Boulevard Félix Houphouëy Boigny by a restored clocktower as **Rue Chakib Arsalane**, becomes **Rue Jemaa Ach Chleuh** halfway along. This street edges its way right through the quarter, past most of the market stalls and the principal mosque from which it takes its second name. At the far end, a small eighteenth-century bastion, the **Skala**, has been restored, with some old cannons. The walls on the west side of the Medina, starting with the restored Ottoman-style clock tower, have also been renovated.

The one other building of interest hereabouts is the **Koubba of Sidi Belyout**, on the left as you walk up Boulevard Félix Houphouët Boigny from the Gare du Port. There's a high wall round a small enclosure (which is forbidden to non-Muslims) but through the open door you can see the white domed tomb. Sidi Belyout is the patron saint of Casablanca and he has lent his name to the district southeast of the port. Legend has it that he despaired of mankind, blinded himself and went to live with animals who took care of him.

Quartier Habous – the New Medina

About a kilometre to the southeast of the city centre, at the end of Avenue Mers Sultan, is the **New Medina** – or **Quartier Habous** – which displays a somewhat bizarre extension of Mauresque. Built in the 1930s as a response to the first *bidonville* crisis, it was intended as a model quarter, and it still has a kind of Legoland look, with its neat little rows of streets. What's most unreal, perhaps, is the neighbourhood mosque, flanked by a tidy stretch of green just as if it were a provincial French church.

South again from the New Medina, at the junction of avenues Mers Sultan and 2 Mars, alongside the Rond-point de l'Europe, is one final sight – the **Church of Notre-Dame de Lourdes**. Completed in the 1950s, it's smaller than the cathedral and still in use. Its beautiful stained-glass windows, the work of Gabriel Loire, a master craftsman from Chartres, are its pride and joy.

The Mosquée Hassan II

Once upon a time, Casablanca had no "sights" as such. Then, in a speech given on July 9, 1980 (his birthday and Youth Day), King Hassan II said:

I wish Casablanca to be endowed with a large, fine building of which it can be proud until the end of time . . . I want to build this mosque on the water, because God's throne was on the water. Therefore, the faithful who go there to pray, to praise the creator on firm soil, can contemplate God's sky and ocean.

Work on the **Mosquée Hassan II** was launched the same year, and the mosque was inaugurated on August 30, 1993. The whole complex, however, and the proposed remodelling of the avenues leading towards it from Place des Nations Unies, is unlikely to be completed in the next decade. Raised on a rocky platform reclaimed from the ocean, it represents the late monarch's most ambitious building project, and his legacy to Moroccan architecture. Unusually, the mosque is open to all, on accompanied one-hour visits which also visit the mosque's huge and elaborate basement hammam (tours daily except Fri 9am, 10am, 11am & 2pm in winter, 2.30pm in summer; 120dh, students 60dh, children under 12yrs 30dh).

Designed by the French architect, Michel Pinseau, the mosque is a phenomenal undertaking. Looking out towards it from the city centre, its huge size tricks you into thinking it's far nearer than it is. Its minaret is actually two hundred metres high, making it by far the tallest structure in the country – as well as the tallest minaret in the world; a laser on its summit projects a beam towards Mecca – to "point out the way to Allah". The mosque itself provides space for 25,000 worshippers within, and a further 80,000 in its courtyard. A glass floor in the mosque reveals the ocean below, a reminder of the Koran's statement (11:7), reiterated by Hassan II, that God's throne is upon the water. In order that the faithful can "contemplate God's sky", the enormous roof of the Mosque rolls open on occasions. The Mosque is second only to Mecca's in size, and St Peter's in Rome could fit comfortably inside it. Eventually, the complex will include a medersa, museum and library. The medersa has been completed; the other two were started in 1987, and due for completion in August 1993, but are still not yet finished. Only Muslims can visit the medersa, but it's assumed that, when completed, all visitors will be welcome in the museum, if not the library.

The facts of the mosque's construction are almost as startling as its size. During the early 1990s, when it was being readied for opening, 1400 men worked by day and a further 1100 by night. Most were master-craftsmen, working marble from Agadir, cedar from the Middle Atlas, granite from Tafraoute, and (the only import) glass from Murano near Venice. Equally extraordinary was its cost – which is reckoned to have exceeded £500m/US$750m, raised by not entirely voluntary public subscription. Despite resentment in some quarters at this, there is also a genuine pride in the project, and pictures of the mosque are displayed in homes and cafés throughout the land (though cynics may point out that any business not displaying one was asking for trouble). The mosque had a knock-on effect on the economy, too; at one stage the level of donations was so high that it temporarily reduced Morocco's money supply and brought down inflation.

The fact that the mosque bears the late king's name inspired rumours that it was designed in part as his mausoleum, along the lines of that of his father,

Mohammed V, in Rabat. However, as we now know, he wished in fact to rest alongside his father, and that is where his tomb is to be found. It's important to add that in addition to his secular position, Hassan was also "Commander of the Faithful", the spiritual leader of Moroccan Muslims, and the building's site, in addition to reflecting his wish to give the city a heart and a memorable symbol, is designed to represent God's creation of earth, sea and sky.

A brisk twenty-minute walk from the city centre along Boulevard Moulay Youssef, the mosque can also be reached by petit taxi (less than 10dh on the meter), or by bus #15 (see p.378).

Aïn Diab: the beach

You can get out to the beach suburb of **Aïn Diab** by bus #9 (see p.378), by petit taxi (about 20dh on the meter from Place des Nations Unies) or – if you fancy a long walk (30–45min) – on foot. The beach starts around 3km out from the port and Old Medina, past the Mosquée Hassan II, and continues for about the same distance.

A beach right within Casa may not sound alluring – and it's certainly not the cleanest and clearest stretch of the country's waters – but Aïn Diab's big attraction is not so much the sea, in whose shallow waters Moroccans gather in phalanx formations, as the **beach clubs** along its front. Each of these has one or more pools, usually filled with filtered seawater, a restaurant and a couple of snack bars; in the fancier ones there'll also be additional sports facilities like tennis or volleyball and perhaps even a disco. The novelty of coming upon this in a Moroccan city is quite amazing, and it's a strange sight to see women veiled from head to toe looking down onto the cosmopolitan intensity unfolding beneath them.

The prices and quality of the **beach clubs** vary enormously and it's worth wandering round a while to check out what's available. Most locals have annual membership and for outsiders a day or weekend ticket can work out surprisingly expensive (80–160dh), but there's quite often one place which has thrown its doors open for free in an attempt to boost its café business. If you are taking a petit taxi from the Mosquée Hassan II or the city centre, ask to be set down at any one of *Tahiti*, *Tropicana* or *Miami*, then reconnoitre and make your choice.

Out beyond Aïn Diab, along the Corniche and inland from it, is the suburb of **Anfa**, where the city's wealthy have their villas, and companies their corporate headquarters –including the striking **OCP** (Office Chérifien des Phosphates) shiny black block alongside the Old Casablanca airport, now known as Aéroport Casa Anfa and used for private and business internal flights. Here, too, are the villas of rich Saudis, and overlooking the Corniche, the wealthy **Ibn Saud Foundation** and its beautiful mosque.

The Jewish Museum

Five kilometres south of town, in the suburb of Oasis, the **Jewish Museum of Casablanca** at 81 Rue Chasseur Jules Gros (Mon–Fri 10am–6pm; 30dh; wheelchair accessible; ☎022 99 49 40, Ⓦwww.casajewishmuseum.com) is Casablanca's one museum, and the only Jewish museum in any Muslim country. It is also an important resource of information on Morocco's massive Jewish heritage, one that rather dwarfs the country's 5000-strong Jewish population, of whom more than sixty percent live in Casablanca.

The museum, set up and run jointly by the Jewish-Moroccan Cultural Heritage Foundation and the Ministry of Culture, is housed in a bright, modern building. It exhibits photographs of synagogues, ancient cemeteries and Jewish holy sites nationwide, many of which are covered in this book, as well as reconstructed synagogue interiors, books and scrolls, traditional costumes, both full- and doll-size, and sacramental items, mostly made of silver and some hailing from Manchester, England. In fact, since silverwork was once the preserve of Morocco's Jews – even today, you'll find the jewellery souk in the Mellah (Jewish quarter) of many Moroccan towns – there are exhibits of Jewish-made silver jewellery, and a reconstructed jeweller's workshop. There are also photos of ancient synagogues such as the Ibn Danan in Fes (see p.288) and others in Ifrane de l'Anti-Atlas (see p.646) and elsewhere, which the Foundation and Ministry have restored or are in the process of restoring.

Morocco's Jews, and Casablanca's in particular, have once again found their niche in Moroccan society, after the mass emigration and bad feeling sparked by the creation of the State of Israel and its long war against the Palestinians, with whom of course nearly all Moroccans strongly sympathize. The position of Casablanca's Jewish community looked rather less secure in May 2003 when sectarian fundamentalist bombers attacked six targets in Casablanca, most of them Jewish-owned or related. The twelve bombers killed 45 people including themselves, eight foreigners and 25 passers-by, all Moroccan Muslims. If they expected to stir up hatred against the Jewish community, however, they miscalculated: hundreds of people came out onto Casablanca's streets the next day in spontaneous protests against sectarian hatred. The following week saw tens of thousands (organizers claimed over a million, but that is almost certainly an exaggeration) march in the biggest demonstration Morocco had ever seen, a march led by members of the city's Jewish community bearing a banner reading "Jews and Muslims: we are all citizens; we are all Moroccans." As the museum's director says, "This is the only country in the Arab world where Jews and Muslims have reached an understanding." One of the museum's aims is to increase that understanding.

You can get to the museum by petit taxi from the city centre (about 20dh), or by train from Casa Voyageurs. From Oasis station, turn left and head towards a motorway bridge across the road. Take the last street on the right before the bridge (Rue Abu Dhabi, though it isn't signposted), turning left after about 300m by no. 53, and the museum is just ahead on your left.

Eating, drinking and nightlife

Casa has the reputation of being the best place to eat in Morocco, and if you can afford the fancier restaurant prices, this is certainly true. There are fine seafood restaurants along the Corniche at Aïn Diab and the bays beyond, and some stylish old French colonial ones round the central boulevards. On a budget, your choice is somewhat more limited, but there are plenty of chicken rôtisseries and snack joints, so you won't starve.

The city is equally well known for its **patisseries**, of which the most famous by far is *Gâteaux Bennis*, 2 Rue Fkih el Gabbas in the Quartier Habous (T022 30 30 25). In town, one of the more renowned is *Le Blé d'Or* at 38 Rue Prince Moulay Abdallah. **Ice-cream parlours** are also popular: one of the best is *Oliveri*, 132 Av Hassan II, which is also quite a refined café. More central, though it's take-away only, is *Stella*, at the corner of Rue Mohammed el Quorri and Avenue Houman Fetouki, boasting over eighty flavours (though only about thirty or so are available at any one time), and waffle cones freshly made on the premises.

Restaurants

In addition to the places listed here, there are inexpensive hole-in-the-wall eateries in the **Old Medina**, and if you're putting together a picnic, the

Marché Central (daily 6am–2pm) on Rue Chaouia groans under the weight of the freshest and best produce in Morocco.

Downtown

La Bodéga 127 Rue Allal Ben Abdallah ☏022 54 18 42, ⊛www.bodega.ma. Spanish cuisine, including various seafood tapas, fajitas, burritos and grilled steaks in a lively taverna-style setting. It can get very busy, and there's a downstairs bar and dancefloor. You come here for the vibe and alcohol more than the food on its own. Dinner only, closed Sun. Moderate to expensive.

La Brasserie Bavaroise 129–131 Rue Allal Ben Abdallah ☏022 31 17 60, ⊛www.labavaroise .com. A fine selection of fish and meat dishes at this French-style brasserie. Closed Sat dinner & Sun. Expensive.

Le Buffet 99 Bd Mohammed V. Quick, bright and popular, with a reasonable 65dh *menu du jour* and 12dh breakfast. Unlicensed. Cheap to moderate.

L'Entrecôte 78 Av Mers Sultan, next to a RAM office. French cuisine in a relaxed setting. Moderate to expensive.

La Farandole 74 Rue Mohammed Smiha. Small café and restaurant with a surprisingly varied menu of French, Italian and Moroccan dishes. Not licensed. Moderate.

La Gondole Centre 2000, by Casa Port station ☏022 27 74 88. Restaurant and piano bar serving good pizza and basic Moroccan food. Cheap to moderate.

Al Mounia 95 Rue du Prince Moulay Abdallah ☏022 22 26 69. Traditional Moroccan cuisine served in a salon or out in the garden. You can eat well for 250dh. Closed Sun. Moderate to expensive.

Ostrea Port de Pêche de Casablanca ☏022 44 13 90, ⊛www.ilove-casablanca.com/ostrea. This place, tucked away in the port area, deserves to be better known, especially for its Oualidia oysters. Other fabulous fresh fish dishes include lobster or crayfish sold by weight. Moderate to expensive.

Il Piccolo Teatro Centre 2000, by Casa Port station ☏022 27 65 36. Franco-Italian dishes, such as four-cheese ravioli al pesto, and various options involving duck, in a relaxed setting, albeit in a down-at-heel shopping centre. Expensive.

Restaurant La Corrida 35 Rue el Avaar (Rue Guy Lussac), parallel to Rue Mustata Al Maani ☏022 27 81 55. Informal tapas-style Spanish restaurant run by a Spanish-French couple. In summer, you can eat in the garden. Closed Sun and the whole of August. Moderate.

Restaurant l'Etoile Centrale 107 Rue Allal Ben Abdallah ☏061 63 75 24. The most "local" of the

three resturants on this street, with a spartan interior but good atmosphere and specialities like pastilla and *mechoui*. Daily for dinner only. Cheap to moderate.

Restaurant des Fleurs 42 Av des FAR ☏022 31 27 35. The snack bar downstairs is good for breakfast; upstairs, there is a more formal restaurant serving French and Moroccan dishes. Moderate to expensive.

Restaurant Listado 133 Bd Félix Houphouët Boigny. A fish restaurant with an imaginative menu. Open for lunch and dinner. Moderate.

Restaurant au Petit Poucet 86 Bd Mohammed V. A slice of old Casablanca style, this French restaurant is dressed up like a 1920s Parisian salon (which is what it was). It was here that the French aviator and writer Saint-Exupéry used to recuperate between his mail flights south to the Sahara; a couple of framed sketches by him grace the walls. You come for the decor rather than the food, which is fine but nothing special, though the *soupe à l'oignon* is pretty good. Prices are moderate and there is a (much cheaper) snack bar next door.

Restaurant Le Tonkin 34 Rue Prince Moulay Abdallah ☏022 22 19 13. First-floor restaurant on the pedestrianized length of the street, serving Chinese and Vietnamese dishes in an "exotic setting". Moderate, with a 90dh set menu.

Restaurant La Tuffe Blanche 57 Tahar Sebti. One of the few remaining Jewish eating places, it serves kosher dishes and alcohol. Convenient for the *Hôtel Guynemer* and *Hôtel de Paris*. Cheap to moderate.

Retro 1900 Centre 2000, by Casa Port station. The most upmarket choice in this rather gone-to-seed shopping centre, serving French cuisine with flair, supervised by chef Jacky Rolling. Popular with businessmen for lunch and *bon viveurs* for dinner. Closed Sun. Expensive.

Rick's Café 248 Bd Sour Jdid, off Bd des Almohades ☏022 27 42 07, ⊛www .rickscafe.ma. A varied menu consisting of a fusion of five-star Moroccan, French and Californian cuisine, including chicken pie and fish and chips. The American breakfast (confusingly on the lunch menu) is a splurge at 80dh. Sat Is oyster night. See box, p.377. Expensive.

Rôtisserie Centrale 36 Rue Chaouia. The best of a bunch of cheap chicken-on-a-spit joints on this little stretch of road opposite the Marché Central. Chicken, chips and salad here won't set you back much more than 30dh.

Snack **Boule de Neige** 72 Rue Araibi Jilali. Open all hours (except daytime during Ramadan), serving tasty, cheap snacks.

Snack **Yamine** 5 & 32 Rue Chaouia. Café-restaurant with two locations, both premises specializing in seafood dishes like paella, grilled calamari and marlin steaks or you are just as welcome to sit and have a coffee. Lunch and dinner. Cheap to moderate.

Taverne du Dauphin 115 Bd Félix Houphouët Boigny ✆022 22 12 00. Long-established and very popular fish restaurant. You may need to queue, or you could make a reservation. Moderate to expensive.

On the coast

During the summer holiday season, Casa's corniche restaurants can be very busy but if you stroll along and have a browse at the restaurants on offer, you should find a free table soon enough. The listings below are from east to west along the corniche to Aïn Diab and beyond.

Mystic Garden 33 Bd de la Corniche, Aïn Diab ✆022 79 88 77. Minimalist, stylish restaurant-bar serving fine French cuisine. A ground floor bar leads out to a pleasant garden setting whilst the split-level restaurant looks out over the sea. Expensive.

La Tangage 51 Bd de la Corniche, Aïn Diab ✆061 38 26 76. Simple restaurant with a choice of seafood, grills, pizza and burgers. Cheap to moderate.

La Criée 1st floor, 51 Bd de la Corniche, Aïn Diab (No phone). Specialist seafood restaurant, albeit in an over-the-top maritime setting. Great sea views from both the restaurant and terrace. Licensed. Open for lunch & dinner. Expensive.

Notre Alsace 59 Bd de la Corniche, Aïn Diab ✆022 36 71 91. A very pleasant bar-restaurant-brasserie with a good choice of fish and meat dishes. Moderate.

A Ma Bretagne Sidi Abderrahmane, 2km west of Aïn Diab ✆022 39 79 79. French gastronomes visit Casablanca purely to eat at this restaurant, which is run by André Halbert, one of just three Maîtres Cuisiniers de France working in Africa and recipient of an award for the best French cooking in the continent. Specialities include *huîtres au Champagne* and *salade de l'océan au foie gras*; the site is delightful, close to the little island *marabout* of Sidi Abderrahmane (see p.394). Naturally, it's not cheap and you should anticipate upwards of 350dh a head. Closed Sun and throughout Aug.

Bars and nightclubs

Casa has a surprisingly elusive nightlife, at least in the centre, where the clubs tend to be rather tacky cabaret joints. **Bars** are plentiful, but as usual they tend to be all-male preserves, and women wanting a hassle-free drink are going to be hard-put. Two notable exceptions offering a place to socialize and drink no matter what your gender are the recently opened ⅃ *La Bodéga* (Mon–Sat 7pm–1am), a lively Spanish-styled taverna with a great atmosphere serving, among other things, draught beer, sangria and seafood tapas, and a salsa night on Tuesdays in the downstairs dance club, and the rather more refined *Rick's Café*. You could also try the *Churchill Club* in Aïn Diab, where the bar is open till 11pm, or the admittedly pricey *Casablanca Bar* in the *Hôtel Hyatt Regency*, decorated with stills from the movie (see box, p.377 for the last three). The *Seamen's Centre* on Boulevard Moulay Abderrahman (✆022 30 99 50) is really only for members and mariners, but they'll usually admit and serve foreigners, and as bars go, it's a good one, with a pool table and space to relax. Hotel bars worth a try include the *Transatlantique*, the *Windsor* and the *Noailles*. Of ordinary bars around town, *Au Petit Poucet*, 86 Bd Mohammed V, attached to the restaurant of the same name is quite relaxed and there are also a few around the Rialto Cinema. If you want to check out some typical all-male hard-drinking dens, you'll find a row of them next to *La Bodega*, along Rue Allal Ben Abdallah behind the Marché Central.

Nightclubs generally open around 11pm, close about 3am, and charge around 100dh to get in. The term in general use for a dance-floor nightclub is "disco", while "nightclub" usually means a place with tables and a cabaret floorshow. Some discos also have performers, among them *La Cage* in Centre 2000, the shopping centre next to Casa Port station, and *La Arizona* on Rue el Amraoui Brahim, next to the *Hôtel Excelsior*. Of the dance clubs, *Club 84* on Bd el Mouahadine, very near Casa Port station, is worth a try, while the clubs attached to five-star hotels, such as the *Black House* at the *Hyatt Regency* and *Caesar* at the *Sheraton*, are slightly pricier and attract a more upmarket crowd. In summer especially more happens out at Aïn Diab on the coast, where the top clubs include *Le Tube* at 1 Bd de la Corniche, *Velvet Chic* and *Pulp Club* next door at no. 3, *Le Village* at no. 11 (which has quite a large gay contingent), the quite upmarket *La Notte* at no. 31, and *Metropolis* in the *Hôtel Suisse* at the junction of Bd de la Corniche with Boulevard Biarritz. *Calypso* at 61 Bd de la Corniche is more relaxed, a bar with a dance floor rather than a disco as such.

Listings

In addition to the listings here, you may want to consult *Telecontact*, an annual directory with Yellow Pages-style listings for businesses and services in the Rabat/Casablanca/Kenitra region. It comes out around the New Year and is available from newsstands.

Airlines Air France, 15 Av des FAR ℡022 43 18 18; Alitalia, Tour Habous, Av des FAR near the *Sheraton* hotel ℡022 31 41 81; British Airways, Centre Allal Ben Abdallah, 47 Rue Allal Ben Abdallah ℡022 43 33 00; Emirates, Sania Building, 140 Bd Zerktouni, fourth floor ℡022 43 99 00; Gulf Air, Centre Allal Ben Abdallah, 47 Rue Allal Ben Abdallah ℡022 49 12 12; Iberia, 17 Av des FAR ℡022 43 95 42; KLM, 6 Bd Félix Houphouët Boigny ℡022 20 32 22; Lufthansa, Tour Habous, Av des FAR near the *Sheraton* hotel ℡022 31 24 02; Regional Air Lines, 19 Av des FAR ℡022 53 80 80; Royal Air Maroc, 44 Av des FAR ℡022 32 11 22 and 44 Pl Mohammed V ℡022 20 32 70.
All, except Gulf Air and KLM, have desks at the airport.

American Express Represented by Voyages Schwartz, 112 Av Prince Moulay Abdellah ℡022 37 63 30; and S'Tours, 4 Rue Turgot, Quarties Racine ℡022 36 13 04.

Banks Most banks have main branches with ATMs along Av des FAR between Pl des Nations Unies and Pl Zellaqa, and other branches with ATMs on Bd de Paris east of Pl Mohammed V. Most of the larger hotels (*Hyatt Regency, Sheraton, Mansour Meridien*) will change money outside banking hours.

Books and newspapers For English-language books try the American Language Center Bookstore, 1 Pl de la Fraternité just off Bd Moulay Youssef (℡022 27 77 65), with a reasonable selection of classics, contemporary fiction and books on Moroccan and Islamic issues. British newspapers and the *International Herald Tribune* are available from stands around Pl des Nations

Unies (and in the *Hyatt Regency* on the square) and at the Gare du Port.

Car rental *Telecontact* lists over a hundred car rental firms in Casa. Competition is stiff and deals are generally the best in the country, if you spend a while phoning around, or call in at the offices grouped along the Av des FAR. The big international franchises are: Avis, 19 Av des FAR ℡022 31 24 24, ℻022 31 11 35; Budget, Tour des Habous, Av des FAR near the *Sheraton* hotel ℡022 31 31 24, ℻022 31 30 76; Europcar, Tour des Habous, Av des FAR. near the *Sheraton* hotel ℡022 31 37 37, ℻022 31 03 60; Hertz, 25 Rue Araibi Jilali ℡022 48 47 10, ℻022 29 44 03; National, 12 Rue Araibi Jilali ℡022 27 71 41. Cheaper deals may be had from local firms. One of the best is Afric Cars, 33 Rue Mohammed Radi Slaoui ℡022 24 21 87. Others include: Ennass Car, 18 Bd Anfa ℡022 22 08 13 or 31, ℻022 22 07 78; First Car, 30 Rue Sidi Belyout ℡022 31 87 88; Goldcar, 5 Av des FAR ℡022 20 09 50; Weekend Cars, second floor, 39 Rue Omar Slaoui ℡022 47 25 58. Hertz, Avis, Budget, Europcar and National all have car rental desks at the airport, as do several smaller firms.

Car repairs Garages include Fiat and Alfa Romeo: Ital Car, 261 Bd Brahim Roudani ℡022 99 11 45; Ford: AutoHall, 44 Av Lalla Yacout ℡022 31 90 56; Leyland and Fiat: Afric Auto, 147 Rue Mustapha el Maoui ℡022 27 92 85; Peugeot: Siara, 193 Av des FAR ℡022 30 17 62; Renault, Rue de Karachi ℡022 30 05 91. There's a mechanic and repair shop next door to Ital Car at 263 Bd Brahim Roudani, and a Mobil service centre along the road at no. 462. There are tyre replacement shops on Bd

Brahim Roudani at nos. 106, 136 and 246, and at 4 Bd Bir Anzarane.

Cinemas Casa is well served by cinemas. The Dawliz chain has two: Dawliz Habous (two screens), 48 Av des FAR ☎022 31 48 22; and Dawliz Corniche (three screens) near *McDonald's* on the Corniche in Aïn Diab ☎022 39 69 43. Others include Cinéma Rif on the corner of Av des FAR with Rue Araibi Jilali (Rue Foucault), the Lusitania opposite the *Hôtel Lausanne* on Rue Tata, the Art Deco Rialto on the corner of Rue Mohammed el Quorri with Rue Salah Ben Bouchaib (see p.382), and the Lynx at 55 Av Mers Sultan.

Consulates Algeria, 159 Bd Moulay Idriss I ☎022 80 41 75 (but the land border with Morocco is still closed); Denmark, 50 Av Pasteur ☎022 43 76 20; Ireland, Copragñ Building, Bd Moulay Ismail, km 6-3, Route de Rabat, Aïn Sebaa ☎022 66 03 66; Mauritania, 382 Rue d'el Jadida, Beauséjour ☎022 25 78 78 (Rahabus – not RATC – #7 from Pl des Nations Unies) – visas (apply 9–11am, collect 2–3pm the next day) cost 200dh plus two passport photos and a photocopy of the ID page from your passport; Netherlands, 26 Rue Nationale, first floor ☎022 22 18 20; Norway, c/o Scandinavian Shiphandlers SA, Villas Paquet, 44 Rue Mohammed Smiha ☎022 30 59 61; Spain, 29 Rue d'Alger ☎022 22 07 52; Sweden, 29–30 Lotissement Attaoufiq, Rue 1, Sidi Maârouf ☎022 43 71 71; UK, 36 Rue de la Loire, Polo ☎022 85 74 00; USA, 8 Bd Moulay Youssef ☎022 43 05 78.

Cultural centres The Complex Cultural Sidi Belyout, 28 Rue Léon Africain (☎022 30 37 60), behind the CTM bus station, has a programme of music, drama and dance. The Institut Français, 121–123 Bd Mohammed Zerktouni (☎022 77 98 70) has an extensive programme, particularly in winter: films, concerts, recitals, exhibitions, and library. Details of these and other events are to be found in the local press, or online at @www .ambafrance-ma.org/institut/casablanca/index.cfm. The German Goethe Institute, 11 Pl du 16 Novembre (☎022 20 04 45) also puts on exhibitions and cultural events.

Dentists Dr Hassan Belkady, 305 Bd Bir Anzarane ☎022 36 10 39; Dr Hicham Benhayoun, 3 Bd Mohammed Abdou ☎022 27 33 14.

Fairgrounds Children may appreciate a visit to Parc des Jeux Yasmina, an amusement park with children's fairground rides on Bd Moulay Youssef in Parc de la Ligue Arabe (daily 11am–8pm, Ramadan 11am–4pm; entry 1.50dh). Out in Aïn Diab, beyond the hotels on the Corniche, there is the Sindibad amusement park, with a huge cut-out of Sinbad the Sailor, plus pedalos, dodgems, roundabouts and slides.

Ferry agent Comanav Voyages, 30 Av des FAR (☎022 31 20 50, ☎022 48 48 44), will give details and sell tickets for most ferry departures from Morocco.

Hammams Every neighbourhood has several – ask at your hotel; better ones include the pricey Hammam Zaki at 25 Rue Abou Assalt el Andaloussi, just off Bd Brahim Roudani in Maarif. For men, there's also the Turkish hammam at 131 Rue Oussama Ibnou Ziad (Rue Jura), also off Bd Brahim Roudani in Maarif.

Internet access Internet stations are surprisingly sparse in downtown Casablanca, and they open and shut all the time. Current options include: Cybernet, 38 Rue Mouftaker Abdelkader (daily 8.30am–11pm); G@NET, 29 Rue Mouftaker Abdelkader (daily 9am–10pm); LG Net, 81 Bd Mohammed V, first floor (Mon–Sat 9am–midnight, Sun 10am–midnight).

Laundry Lavomatic International, 24 Rue Salah Ben Bouchaib, near Rialto Cinema.

Medical aid Dial ☎15 for emergency services or call SOS Médecin (☎022 20 20 20 or 022 44 44 44) or SOS Médecins Maroc (☎000 98 98 98 or 022 98 98 98) for a doctor, or SAMU (☎022 25 25 25) for an ambulance. Clinics open round the clock for emergency treatment include: Clinique Badr, 35 Rue el Alloussi Bourgogne (☎022 49 23 80 84) and Clinique Yasmine, Bd Sidi Abderrahman Hay el Hana (☎022 39 69 60). English-speaking doctors include: Dr Mohammed Bennani, 45 Rue Atlas Maarif ☎022 98 02 28–9; Dr Alain Guidon, 6 Rue Jean Jaurès ☎022 26 71 53. Large hotels should also have addresses for doctors. There's an all-night pharmacy (9pm–8am) in the Préfecture in Pl Mohammed V (☎022 26 94 91; details of other pharmacies open out of hours appear in the local press, or on lists displayed by all pharmacies. The US Consulate maintains a list of useful medical contacts online at @http://casablanca.usconsulate .gov/list_of_physicians.html.

Photographic supplies and developing Chez Faugra, 36 Av Mers Sultan; Studio Restinga, 27 Rue Tahar Sebti.

Police Main station is on Bd Brahim Roudani (☎022 98 98 65). For emergencies call ☎19.

Post office The main PTT is on Pl Mohammed V (Mon–Fri 8am–6pm & Sat 8am–noon). The most useful branch office is at 116 Bd Mohammed V, on the corner of Rue Chaouia (Rue Colbert) (Mon–Fri 8am–4.15pm).

Shopping If you need a department store, try Alpha 55 at 55 Av Mers Sultan, with a good seventh-floor restaurant, or the Twin Centre mall at 191 Bd Mohammed Zerktouni. For shoes and general clothing, have a browse along the pedestrianized section of Rue Prince Moulay Abdallah. Casablanca is not the place to buy Moroccan crafts, fossils or similar souvenirs but, if you need a last-minute purchase before you fly home, there are shops on both sides of Bd Félix Houphouët Boigny – beware of *trafika* (phoney fossils for example), and expect to pay higher prices for lower quality than elsewhere in Morocco. More reliable but at least as expensive (though prices are fixed) is the Exposition Nationale d'Artisanat at the junction of Av Hassan II with Rue Maarakat Ohoud (across from the Hyatt Regency), which has crafts from around the country. Moorish antiques can be found at Amazonite, 15 Rue Prince Moulay Abdallah. For music, the Comptoir Marocain de Distribution de Disques at 26 Av Lalla Yacout has an excellent selection of Moroccan, Algerian and Middle Eastern sounds on CD and vinyl. Supermarkets are mainly out of the city centre, save for two branches of Acima: 21 Rue Pierre Parent at Pl Nicolas Paquet (Place Georges Mercie) by the junction of Bd Mohammed V with Rue Mohammed Smiha; and on Bd Rahal el Meskini at the corner of Bd Lahcen Ouider.

Sports Casa is the best place in Morocco to see football; the city's rivals, Raja and Wydad (also known as WAC) both play at the Complexe Mohammed V on Rue Socrate in Maarif; check the local press for fixtures. The complex also houses an Olympic-size indoor swimming pool, and has facilities open to the public (☎022 36 23 72 or 36 21 35). The city also boasts a racecourse, the Hippodrome, at Anfa (active some Sundays, mainly in winter) and, beside it, a nine-hole Royal golf course (closed Mon; ☎022 36 53 55, ℻022 39 33 74); there are eighteen-hole courses along the coast at Mohammedia (see p.370) and El Jadida (see p.396). As well as the beach clubs on the Corniche, and the Complexe Mohammed V, you can swim in the open-air Piscine Océanique in Aïn Sebaa. The pool at the *Hyatt Regency* hotel costs 200dh for nonresidents.

Tours KTI Voyages, based in Casa, is a very reliable operator, used by British companies like Hayes & Jarvis and Kuoni; its head office is at 122 Av Hassan II (☎022 27 62 44).

Moving on

CTM buses run from their city-centre terminal (☎022 26 80 61) to just about everywhere, including Safi, Essaouira, Agadir, Tiznit and various European destinations; tickets and times are available from the terminal on Rue Léon Africain. The 9am departure to Fes is direct and nonstop.

All **private bus** firms operate out of the Ouled Ziane *gare routière*, 4km southeast of the city centre. To get there, you can take a petit taxi, or a #10 or #36 bus from Boulevard Mohammed V opposite the Marché Central. For Mohammedia, you alternatively take local bus #900, which leaves from Rue Zaid ou Hmad, as do Mohammedia grands taxis.

Grands taxis for Fes, Meknes and Tangier operate from outside the Ouled Ziane *gare routière*. Those for Rabat leave from the Boulevard Hassan Seghir, very near the CTM terminal, while the grand taxi station for El Jadida, Safi and Essaouira is on Boulevard Brahim Roudani in Maarif, some 2km from the city centre, and served by #7 bus from Place des Nations Unies.

Trains for El Jadida, Mohammedia, Rabat and Kenitra are best caught at Casa Port station (☎022 27 18 37), but for Marrakesh, Tangier, Meknes, Fes and Oujda, you'll need to get to Casa Voyageurs station (☎022 24 38 18), a long walk, a short taxi ride, or a hop on a #2 or #30 bus from Place des Nations Unies or Boulevard Mohammed V. Casablanca's Mohammed V **Airport** (☎022 53 90 40) is around 25 km and 230dh from town by grand taxi (taking up to six people) or 55dh by train from Casa Voyageurs (hourly 6.05am–9.05pm and then 11.05pm; 35min). Getting there by train from Casa Port is possible but involves changing at Aïn Sebaa – about an hour's journey time in total. All flights depart from terminal 1 other than Royal Air Maroc flights to Canada, Germany, the Netherlands, Italy and USA, which depart from terminal 3. There is a free shuttle service between the two terminals. All airport bureaux de change claim they will exchange your unused Moroccan dirhams back into Euros or US dollars (though not Pounds Sterling). Both a pharmacy and post/fax bureau operate on the upper level between the departure and arrival areas.

For details of destinations, frequencies and journey times for buses, trains, grands taxis and internal flights out of Casablanca, see pp.425–426.

Settat and around

The road and train line run side by side, south across the plains from **Casa** to **Marrakesh**. To the east lies the desolate and dusty phosphate-mining region, the Plateau des Phosphates. To the west, the land is more fertile and watered by Morocco's greatest river, the Oum er Rbia, and its tributaries, inevitably dammed wherever convenient for irrigation and hydroelectricity.

SETTAT, 60km south of Casablanca, is the major city on the way to Marrakesh – a sizeable town and still growing. Though the bulk of new investment is in the Casablanca area, Kenitra and Settat are joint second, with the Rabat-Salé area representing only a small percentage of new investment. Already, Settat is the centre of the Moroccan **cotton industry**: spinning, weaving and ready-made clothes. In 1990, the Spanish company Tavex, a leading European producer of denim cloth, built a factory here and it now produces half the denim needed for Morocco's clothing industry.

The wealth of Settat is to be seen in its civic architecture and commercial edifices, mostly banks. The entry to the town follows a well-watered valley with green lawns and trees on both sides and then the university and the nine-hole Settat University Golf Club (☎023 40 07 55, ℻023 40 20 99). There's also the luxurious *Hôtel du Parc* (☎023 40 39 51, ℻023 40 42 08; ❼). In the town itself there are two adequate hotels, both on Place Mohammed V: *Hôtel de la Place* (☎023 40 30 62; ❶) and *Hôtel Al Massira* (☎023 40 20 72, ℻023 40 10 92; ❸).

Boulaoune (Boulaouane): kasbah and wine

Fifty kilometres west of Settat, and halfway to El Jadida on the coast, is the impressive **Kasbah de Boulaoune** and the revitalized vineyards famous for **Gris de Boulaoune**, Morocco's best-known rosé. Despite these attractions, the area is rarely visited, mostly due to a lack of public transport and the necessity of a car, but, if it's possible, a detour en route from Settat to El Jadida can be most rewarding. If you fancy a visit and don't have your own transport, it's best to arrange a taxi for a half or full day-trip from Settat.

The **kasbah** stands high on a rocky outcrop above a great loop of the Oum er Rbia, a natural site for a stronghold. It was built by Moulay Ismail in 1710 as a control post on the inland route from the Sahara to the Mediterranean, and to stand astride the rival regions of Doukkala, the hinterland of Safi and El Jadida, and Chaouia, the hinterland of what is now Casablanca.

Though strategically important, the kasbah rarely saw any action, and it appears today very much as it did in the eighteenth century. It has a well-preserved gateway, bearing the details of its construction. The high crenellated walls are complete with seven bastions, and the square minaret still stands; the mosque below, however, is not in such good shape. Alongside is the Koubba of Sidi Mansana. A *gardien* will no doubt greet you at the gateway and gladly show you round.

The future of the kasbah is uncertain. The French made it a historic monument in 1924 but took no steps to restore it. There have been discussions about restoration, but lack of finance and a quarrel between present-day Doukkala and Chaouia seem to have indefinitely postponed a start.

The **Gris de Boulaoune** has a history too, but it's only in the last few years that it's come into its own. Nowadays, as you drive through the area, the impressive rolling countryside is dotted with copses of eucalyptus and conifers, between which are the large vineyards producing the wine. The efforts of this Moroccan–French enterprise over the last ten or so years, including the construction of new irrigation channels, has resulted in a wine that is, according to one Moroccan monthly magazine, "*le plus célèbre du Maroc*". Unfortunately an onsite visit and tastings are, as yet, unavailable.

Casablanca to El Jadida

Buses and trains cover the ninety-odd kilometres from **Casablanca to El Jadida** on swift inland routes, of no great interest save for the town of **Azemmour**, an old Portuguese fortress-town at the estuary of the Oum er Rbia. Using public transport, Azemmour is easiest visited as an excursion from El Jadida, which is only 16km further southwest.

If you have transport of your own, the old **R320 road** is an enjoyable alternative, trailing the coast the whole way from **Casa to Azemmour**. As you clear the urban area, the beaches are increasingly enticing and, as yet, virtually undeveloped.

Sidi Abderrahmane and around

En route to Azemmour, the most attractive spot is the beach facing the picturesque little island **Marabout of Sidi Abderrahmane**, 10km from central Casa, in the first bay that you come to after passing through Aïn Diab. The island itself is a tiny outcrop of rock, under fifty metres from the rock shore, from which it's possible to walk across at low tide. Non-Muslims, however, may not enter the shrine, which is entirely occupied by the *marabout* – or pilgrim centre – laid out around the shrine of Sidi Abderrahmane, a Muslim Sufi from Baghdad. The pilgrims are, for the most part, the mentally ill, for whom the saint has supposedly curative powers, and their families.

Nearby, overlooking the beach, is *A Ma Bretagne* (see p.389), the finest – and most expensive – **restaurant** in the Casablanca area. If you can afford it, and read this in time to make an advance booking, it will most likely be the best meal you have in Morocco.

Further along towards Azemmour, there's little beyond a slew of **campsites**, fronting onto stretches of beach. First of these, 16km from Casa, is *Camping Desserte des Plages* (☏022 29 03 42), reached by turning right off the R320, 5km before Dar Bouazza. It's a modest family affair, with a summer-only café. The other established site, *Camping des Tamaris* (☏022 33 00 60), is at Hajra Khala; 19km from Casablanca turn right and it's then a further 5km to the coast and campsite. This takes its name from the surrounding tamarisk bushes whose combustible branches fuel the pottery kilns of Safi. Just inland of the *Tamaris* is *Camping International*, with full facilities including bungalows and two swimming pools.

Azemmour

AZEMMOUR has an oddly remote feel – and history, considering its strategic site on the great Oum er Rbia river. It has long been outside the mainstream of events. When the Portuguese controlled El Jadida, Safi and Essaouira, they stayed here for under thirty years; later, when the European traders moved in on this coast, the town remained a "closed" port. Little bothered by the French, it remains today very much a backwater and sees possibly fewer tourists than any other Moroccan coastal town which, it could be said, is a good thing and makes a visit, especially of the largely residential medina, worthwhile.

The Medina

The Portuguese remained in Azemmour long enough to build a circuit of walls, which are stacked directly above the banks of the river and dramatically extended by the white, cubist line of the **Medina**. The best view of all this – and it is impressive – is from across the river, on the way out of town towards Casablanca.

To look round the Medina, make your way to Place du Souk, on the landward side of the ramparts, where you will see a sixteenth-century **gate** with an unusual, European-style, semicircular arch. Through it extends the old **kasbah** – largely in ruins but safe enough to visit. If you wait around, the local *gardien* will probably arrive, open things up and show you round; if he doesn't turn up, you might find him by asking at the cafés. Once inside the ruins, you can follow the parapet wall round the ramparts, with views of the river and the gardens, including henna orchards, along its edge. You'll also be shown **Dar el Baroud** (The House of Powder), a large tower built over the ruins of an old gunpowder store; note also the ruined Gothic window.

The old **Mellah** – Azemmour had a substantial Jewish population until the 1960s – lies beyond the kasbah at the northern end of the Medina. Here, beside ramparts overlooking the Oum er Rbia, you will be shown the old town synagogue which is still well maintained and visited occasionally by practising Jews from Casablanca and El Jadida. It's cared for by a local family and you can – for an additional tip – see inside, where rests the tomb of Rabbi Abrahim Moul Niss – still a shrine for Jewish pilgrims and the focus of an August moussem.

These sights might not sound like much on paper, and you'll have to negotiate the final tip with the *gardien*, but all in all it's an interesting and enjoyable break from El Jadida, or a stop en route to the town, and easily combined with a swim.

Practicalities

The town is easily reached from El Jadida by **bus** (#101 from the roundabout 200m south of the bus station) or **grand taxi** (from Rue Abdelmoumen el Mouahidi by the bus station). It's also served by four **trains** daily from Casa Voyageurs and El Jadida, though the station is inconveniently located 2km out of town, on the far side of the N1.

Once in town, getting your bearings is pretty straightforward. The main thoroughfare of the new town is **Avenue Mohammed V**, which leads to the main square, **Place du Souk**, with the **Medina** straight ahead.

There are two magical little **riads** that have recently opened within the medina. *L'Oum Errebia* at 25 Derb Chtouka (T023 34 70 71, Wwww .azemmour-hotel.com; ●, mid-week discounts), once the kitchen and servant quarters for the town's *caid*, has been renovated with a distinctly modern touch, accentuated by the many bright, abstract paintings adorning almost every spare bit of wall space. The river view from the terrace is unequalled. There are six rooms, two of which share a bathroom. *Riad Azama*, 17 Derb Ben Tahar (T023 34 75 16, Wwww.riadazama.com; ●), has six rooms of varying sizes that have all been restored with a traditional feel. Meals can be taken on the terrace overlooking the medina or in the intricately decorated dining, or *douiria*, room. Outside the Medina is the basic *Hôtel de la Poste* at

78 Av Mohammed V, on Place du Souk (☎023 35 77 02; ❶). The town also has several **café-restaurants**, best of which is the *Café el Manzeh* on Place du Souk, with an active card school upstairs (look for the Coca-Cola awnings). There are also two café-restaurants down at the beach (see below). You'll be able to find **Internet** around Place du Souk.

Haouzia beach – and birds

The river currents at Azemmour are notoriously dangerous, but there's a nice stretch of **beach** half an hour's walk through the eucalyptus trees beyond the town. If you go by road, it's signposted to the "Balnéaire du Haouzia", a small complex of cabins and camping occupying part of the sands. There are two **restaurants** here: *La Perle* (☎023 34 79 05), which is fairly expensive but good (around 150dh per person), serving paella and other fish dishes; and the newer *Cap Blanc*, serving similar fare to its neighbour. In summer, you can camp in the private complex; in winter, you can safely camp alongside the restaurants.

For **bird-watchers**, the scrub dunes around the mouth of the river should prove rewarding territory.

The golf club

The coast between Azemmour and El Jadida is showing signs of development, the most ambitious complex being the **El Jadida Royal Golf Club** (☎023 35 22 51, ☞023 35 41 50), beside the sea, 10km from Azemmour and 7km from El Jadida. The eighteen-hole golf course was designed by the American Cabell B. Robinson and is one of the most attractive in Morocco, with mimosa, sand dunes, a large lake and, across the bay, the skyline of El Jadida. Alongside is the four-star *Sofitel Royal Golf Hôtel* (☎023 37 91 00, ⓦwww.sofitel.com; ❽) set among beautiful gardens and with all mod cons including two restaurants, a swimming pool and tennis court.

El Jadida (Mazagan)

EL JADIDA is a stylish and beautiful town, retaining the lanes and ramparts of an old Portuguese Medina. It was known as Mazagan under the Portuguese, who held it from 1506 until 1769, and it is under this name that the medina was granted World Heritage status in 2004 as "an outstanding example of the interchange of influences between European and Moroccan cultures". The city was taken from the Portuguese by Sultan Sidi Mohammed Ben Abdallah and then in the nineteenth century Moroccan Mazagan was renamed El Jadida – "The New" – after being resettled, partly with Jews from Azemmour, by Sultan Abd er Rahman. Under the French, it grew into a quite sizeable administrative centre and a popular beach resort.

Today it's the beach that is undeniably the focal point, for the locals at least. Moroccans from Casablanca and Marrakesh, even Tangier or Fes, come here in droves in summer, and, alongside this mix, there's an unusual feeling of openness. The bars are crowded (a rare feature in itself), there's an almost frenetic evening promenade and – as in Casa – Moroccan women are visible and active participants.

Arrival, orientation and information

The **bus station** is at the southern end of town, from where it's a fifteen-minute walk to the Medina or to most hotels. Coming by **train** (there are four

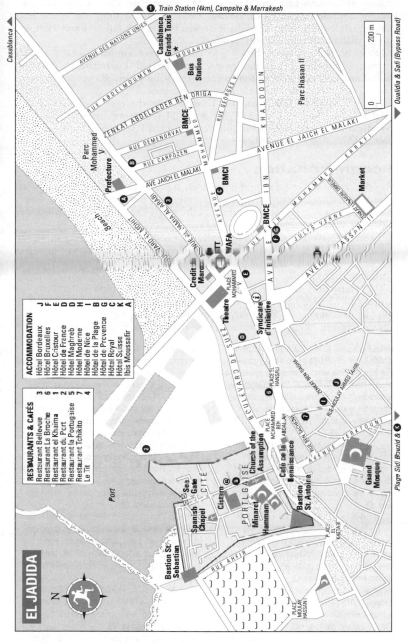

▲ ❶, Train Station (4km), Campsite & Marrakesh

◀ Casablanca

▶ Oualidia & Safi (Bypass Road)

EL JADIDA

AVENUE DES NATIONS UNIES

Casablanca
Grands Taxis ★

EL MOUAHIDI

Bus
Station

RUE ABDELMOUMEN

ZENKAT ABDELKADER BEN ORIGA

RUE GEORGES V

Parc Hassan II

BMCE

RUE DEMENORVAL

MOHAMMED

KHALDOUN

Parc
Mohammed
V

RUE CARPOZEN

RUE DEMORVAL

AVENUE EL JAICH EL MALAKI

Prefecture

AVE JAICH EL MALAKI

BMCI

IBN

ERRAFI

Beach

AVENUE

AFA

BMCE

Market

ZENKAT TAHOBE OBBOL

DE JUIFS VERNE

Credit
Maroc

Theatre

Syndicate
d'Initiative

HASSAN

RESTAURANTS & CAFÉS
Restaurant Bellevue   3
Restaurant Le Broche   6
Restaurant el Khaima   1
Restaurant du Port   2
Restaurant la Portugaise   5
Restaurant Tchikito   7
Le Tit   4

ACCOMMODATION
Hôtel Bordeaux   J
Hôtel Bruxelles   F
Hôtel C'ristour   E
Hôtel de France   D
Hôtel Maghreb   D
Hôtel Moderne   H
Hôtel de Nice   I
Hôtel de la Plage   B
Hôtel de Provence   G
Hôtel Royal   C
Hôtel Suisse   K
Ibis Moussafir   A

PLACE
MOHAMMED V

BOULEVARD DE SUEZ

PLACE EL
HANSALI

ZENKAT BEN BASHA

RUE BEN TACHFINE

PLACE
MOHAMMED
BEN
ABDALLAH

Café de la
Renaissance

RUE ABDULLAH AHMED TAURI

AVENUE ZERKTOUNI

Port

Sea
Gate

Cistern

PORTUGAISE
CITÉ

Spanish
Chapel

Church of the
Assumption

Minaret
Hammam

Bastion
St Antoine

Grand
Mosque

Bastion St
Sebastian

RUE AHFIR

PLACE
EL
KATIB 3

PLACE
MOULAY
HASSAN

▶ Plage Sidi Bouzid & ❸

N

0   200 m

daily services to and from either Casa Port or Casa Voyageurs) you arrive at a station 4km south of town along the Marrakesh road (N1); petits taxis are usually available (about 15dh). **Grands taxis** from Casa drop you by the bus station, while those from Oualidia leave you by the lighthouse, about 1km up the Oualidia road from the city centre.

Once you realize that the beach faces northeast, not southwest as you would expect, orientation is straightforward, with the old **Portuguese Medina**, walled and looking out over the port, and the **Ville Nouvelle** spreading to its south along the seafront towards Plage Sidi Bouzid.

There's a helpful **Délégation de Tourisme** on the corner of Avenue des FAR and Rue Nador (℡023 34 47 88, ℱ023 34 47 89) and the more accessible **Syndicat d'Initiative** at 33 Pl Mohammed V (℡023 37 06 56), who might be able to help with accommodation.

Accommodation

Rooms can be very hard to find in summer, so prices are higher and it's a good idea to book in advance. In fact, at all times you may prefer to make some phone calls before pacing the streets, as the town extends for some distance along the seafront.

If you are staying for a week or more, there are flats and villas for rent: ask for information at the Syndicat, or check out the Locations Saisonnières website, with both English- and French-language versions, at ⓦwww .jadidalocations.com.

The **campsite**, *Camping Caravaning International*, on Avenue des Nations Unies (℡023 34 27 55), offers moderate facilities with lots of shade and is a popular site due to its proximity to the beach; the only disadvantage is its distance: fifteen minutes to the bus station and another fifteen to town.

Hôtel Bordeaux 47 Rue Moulay Ahmed Tahiri ℡023 37 39 21, ℱ023 34 06 91, signposted from Rue Ben Tachfine, down a small side street. An old hotel – the oldest in town, so the patron claims – it is attractively refurbished and immaculately clean, though the showers (5dh) are on the corridor. Good-value but slightly pricier than some of the other cheapies. ❷

Hôtel Bruxelles 40 Av Ibn Khaldoun ℡023 34 20 72, next to *Hôtel de Provence*. Bright and cheerful, with pleasant, clean rooms, and balconies at the front. For drivers, the guarded parking (10dh) here is a big plus. ❶

Hôtel Cristour 7 Av Mohammed V ℡023 34 26 43. Opposite the theatre and behind the prominent *Café Français*, with small cabin-like rooms off a courtyard. Adequate, but noisy and a little overpriced, it is a useful fall-back at the bottom end of the market. ❶

Hôtel de France/Hôtel Maghreb 12/16 Rue Lescoul ℡023 34 21 81. This is in reality one hotel – though with two entrances, stairways and names. Great value and creaking with character, it's old and roomy, with fabulous views of the sea and hot showers on the landing (5dh). ❶

Hôtel Moderne 21 Av Hassan II ℡023 34 31 33. Very much a family hotel, with a small garden. Hot showers on the corridor (5dh). ❶

Hôtel de Nice 15 Rue Mohammed Smiha ℡023 35 22 72. Off Rue Ben Tachfine and on the same street as the *Restaurant Tchikito*, which is well signposted. Cheaper than the nearby *Bordeaux*, though not as bright and modern. ❸

Hôtel de la Plage 3 Av al Jamia al Arabi ℡023 34 26 48. Despite the rather grim bar on the ground floor, this is friendly, with clean, perfectly adequate rooms and separate facilities on the corridor. Convenient for the bus station and the *patron* also owns the campsite. ❶

Hôtel de Provence 42 Av Fqih Mohammed Errafi ℡023 34 23 47, ℱ023 35 21 15. This grand old dame is still the best mid-range choice, with a good restaurant, a garden for breakfast, and large rooms. Be sure to reserve ahead, particularly in the high season. ❹

Hôtel Royal 108 Av Mohammed V ℡023 34 28 39, ℱ023 34 00 60. Large, airy rooms with erratic plumbing, a garden and lively bar. Convenient for the bus station. ❹

Hôtel Suisse 175 Av Zerktouni ℡023 34 28 16. Small, friendly, with a garden and patio; en-suite facilities and pleasant café next door (same owner) for breakfast. Good value. **②**

Ibis Moussafir Place Nour el Kamar ☏ 023 37 95 00, ⓦ www.ibishotel.com. Unlike most hotels in this chain, this one has a prime location right on the beach. Rooms have a/c and heating, and two are wheelchair-friendly. There is a restaurant, bar, swimming pool and secure parking. **⑥**

The town and beaches

El Jadida's **Medina** is the most European-looking in Morocco: a quiet, walled and bastioned seaside village, with a handful of churches scattered on its lanes. It was founded by the Portuguese in 1513 – and retained by them until 1769 – and it is still popularly known as the **Cité Portugaise**. As they withdrew, the Portuguese blew up several of the churches and other important buildings. The Moors who settled here after the Portuguese withdrawal tended to live outside the walls. Budgett Meakin, writing in the 1890s (see p.770), found an "extensive native settlement of beehive huts, or *nouallahs*" spreading back from the harbour, while European merchants had re-established themselves in the "clean, prosperous and well-lighted streets" of the Medina. As in all the open ports on this coast, there was also an important Jewish community handling the trade with Marrakesh; uniquely, old Mazagan had no separate Jewish *mellah*.

The Cité Portugaise

The **Cité Portugaise** is steadily being restored, thanks largely to its recently gained status as a World Heritage site, and it round its newly spruced-up ramparts is not to be missed. Nor, above all, is a visit to the beautiful old **Portuguese Cistern** (daily 9am–1pm & 3–6.30pm; 10dh), a subterranean vault that mirrors its roof and pillars in a shallow film of water covering the floor. It's entered midway along the Medina's main street, Rua Carreira (now renamed Rue Mohammed Ali Bahbai), on the left walking down past some souvenir shops.

The cistern was used to startling effect in Orson Welles's great film of *Othello*; he staged a riot here, provoked by Iago to discredit Cassio, and filmed it from within and above. It also featured in a Moroccan TV ad for Samar coffee and

△ Inside the Portuguese Cistern, El Jadida

locals associate it with that, rather than Orson Welles. If the idea of competing with either appeals, you'll need a fast film for the refracted light.

At the entrance to the cistern there is a useful model of the Cité Portugaise, and if you continue up Rua Carreira you'll come to its most prominent feature – the **Sea Gate** (Bab el Bahr), the original gate onto the port. From here you can climb onto the ramparts (daily 9am–6.30pm; free), and walk all the way round and onto all the bastions, should you so desire. By Bastion St Sebastian, the restored former synagogue has an interesting crescent and Star of David on its back wall. The Christian churches and chapels of the Portuguese City, long converted to secular use, are generally closed; but, if you have time, you can look for the small Spanish chapel, now closed and bricked up bar a small part section used as a shop. More impressive is the seventeenth-century Portuguese Church of the Assumption by the entrance to the Cité Portugaise, now sitting dormant after initially being restored and used as a cultural centre. The minaret of the **Grand Mosque** here was once a five-sided watchtower or lighthouse, and is said to be the only pentagonal minaret in Islam.

The beaches

El Jadida's town **beach** spreads northeast from the *cité* and port, well beyond the length of the town. It's a popular strip, though from time to time polluted by the ships in port. If it doesn't look too good, or you feel like a change, take a petit taxi 3km further north along the coastal road, past the **Phare Sidi Ouafi** (lighthouse), to a broader strip of sand where dozens of Moroccan families set up tents for the summer. Good swimming is to be had and there are makeshift beach cafés in the summer.

Plage Sidi Bouzid, 2km southwest, is more developed, flanked by some fancy villas and with a few restaurants well-known for their seafood, *Le Requin Bleu* (☏023 34 80 67) and *l'Alligator*. The beach can be reached on bus #2 from alongside Place Mohammed Ben Abdallah, or by grand taxi.

Eating and drinking

For its size, El Jadida is well served by **restaurants**, and has most other facilities you might want to make use of. **Bars** are to be found mainly in the hotels – try the lively one at *Hôtel de la Plage*, *de Provence*'s pleasant bar or the more upmarket *Palais Andalous*. There's also the bar *Le Tit*, 2 Av Al Jamia el Arabi, which, if you don't mind being the only one, is female traveller friendly.

In high season, there are many more eateries: stroll through Place el Hansali and Place Mohammed Ben Abdallah or along Boulevard el Mohit towards Parc Mohammed V until somewhere catches your eye.

Restaurants

Hôtel-Restaurant de Provence 42 Av Fqih Mohammed Errafi ☏023 34 23 47. Well-prepared, French-inspired meals, open to nonresidents, and licensed. Worth making a reservation. Moderate to expensive.

Restaurant Bellevue 46 Av Al Jamia Al Arabi. French cuisine in a stylish setting a short walk from Place Mohammed V. Expensive.

Restaurant La Broche 46 Pl el Hansali. Offers an inexpensive menu of the day plus the usual meat or chicken dishes and omelettes. Daily for lunch & dinner. Cheap.

Restaurant el Khaima Av des Nations Unies, between the beach and the campsite ☏023 37 21 74. Good-value Moroccan and Italian dishes make it well worth the walk or taxi ride. Moderate.

Restaurant du Port at the northern end of the port ☏023 34 25 79. This first-floor restaurant in an unprepossessing building has a great view of the sea and serves good and plentiful seafood. Closed Sun evening. Moderate to expensive.

Restaurant la Portugaise Rua Carreira (Rue Mohammed Ali Bahbai), Cité Portugaise. A very pleasant little restaurant serving French rather than

Portuguese dishes. The food is good but the portions are not huge. Set menus at 56dh (chicken or tajine) and 66dh (fish). Open for lunch and dinner. Moderate.

Restaurant Tchikito Rue Mohammed Smiha. A memorable fish restaurant, with generous helpings and Koranic decorations. Unlicensed but the atmosphere is intoxicating. Moderate.

Listings

Banks with ATM include: Crédit du Maroc on Av Al Jamia Al Arabi behind the post office; BMCE at the corner of avenues Ibn Khaldoun and Fqih Mohammed Errafi, and the corner of Av Mohammed V and Rue Demenorval; and BMCI at the corner of avenues Mohammed V and Jaich El Malaki; WAFA at the corner of Av Mohammed V and Rue Mohammed Errafi.

Car rental No major agencies, but there are a couple of recommended local ones: Azama Cars, 100 Av Mohammed VI ☎061 06 55 94. Narjiss, shop 2, Central Market, Zenkat Lenaigre Dubreuil (Aristide Briand) ☎023 35 14 82;

Car spares and repairs Mechanics' workshops are grouped behind the bus station, on and around Rue Abdelmoumen el Mouahidi, with tyre changers and spare parts shops to its north and south on Av Mohammed V.

Hammam There's one in the Cité Portugaise at 1 Rue No. 45 (enter the double gate, turn left along Rua do Arco and it's on the third corner on your right). It's usually open mornings for women and evenings for men.

Internet access The best place is Mellah Net, with relatively fast connnections, in a little side street by 40 Rua Carreira in the Cité Portugaise, almost opposite the entrance to the cistern (daily 9am–2pm & 3pm–midnight). @Kiltec, 62 Pl el Hansali, is open daily from 11am - midnight.

Post office The main PTT is on Pl Mohammed V (Mon–Fri 8am-6pm, Sat 8am–noon).

Souk A Wednesday souk takes place by the lighthouse northwest of town.

Travel agency Fedala Voyages, 4 Av Ibn Khaldoun ☎023 34 21 99. Royal Air Maroc has an office at the corner of Av Mohammed VI & Av Des FAR ☎023 37 93 00, ☎023 37 93 04.

El Jadida to Safi

Once again, the main road (and express buses) south, from **El Jadida to Safi**, take an inland road, across the plains. The coast road, however, is almost as direct, and a very pleasant drive, with little development, lovely stretches of beach, a minor ancient ruin at **Moulay Abdallah** and major **bird habitats** around the low-key resort of **Oualidia**. It's not much frequented by tourists, who seem to visit either El Jadida from Casa or Essaouira from Marrakesh – rarely both.

Moulay Abdallah and the ruins of Tit

MOULAY ABDALLAH, 11km from El Jadida, is a tiny fishing village, dominated by a large *zaouia* complex and partially enclosed by a circuit of walls in ruins. At the *zaouia* an important **moussem** is held towards the end of August, attracting tens of thousands of devotees – and almost as many horses in the parades and *fantasias*.

The village walls span the site of a twelfth-century **ribat**, or fortified monastery, known as 'Tit ("eyes" or "spring" in the local Berber dialect) and built, so it's thought, in preparation for a Norman invasion: a real threat at the time – the Normans having launched attacks on Tunisia – but one which never materialized. Today, there is little to see, though the minaret of the modern **zaouia** (prominent and whitewashed) is Almohad in origin; behind it, up through the graveyard, you can walk to a second, isolated minaret, which is thought to be even older. If it is, then it is perhaps the only one surviving from the Almoravid era – a claim considerably more impressive than its simple, block-like appearance might suggest.

Sidi Abed and Sidi Moussa

The first good beach beyond Cap Blanc is at **SIDI ABED**, a small village with a café-restaurant and a scattering of villas, 27km from El Jadida. A couple of kilometres before the village, and on the right travelling towards it, is *Le Relais* (☏023 34 54 98; ❺), with showers in the rooms and toilets on the corridor; it's also a restaurant (year-round, except for Ramadan), and is worth a stopover if only to enjoy a mint tea and the view from the terrace overlooking the small bay.

The coast hereabouts is an alternation of sandy beach and rocky outcrops, and past **SIDI MOUSSA**, 36km from El Jadida, it's backed by huge dunes, then, towards Oualidia, cut off by a long expanse of salt marshland. From here on south, for the next 70km or so, bird-watchers are in for a treat (see box below) but Sidi Moussa is attractive to non-twitchers, too, with its estuary-like lagoon, a beach and a very pleasant **hotel**, the *Villa la Brise* (☏023 34 69 17; ❹), with French cooking, a bar and a swimming pool that's full in summer. It's a popular base for fishing parties.

South of Sidi Moussa, the roadside is flanked by saltpans and by extensive plastic hothouses, for intensive cultivation of tomatoes and other vegetables; 63km from El Jadida, there's a Friday souk at **Souk el Djemaa**, as the name suggests.

Oualidia

OUALIDIA, 78km from El Jadida, is a stunningly picturesque little resort – a fishing port and lagoon beach, flanked by a kasbah and a royal villa. The **kasbah** is seventeenth century, built by the Saadian Sultan el Oualid (after whom the village is named) as a counterweight and alternative to El Jadida, then held by the Portuguese. Until Sultan Sidi Mohammed took El Jadida, the extensive lagoon made an excellent harbour and, as late as 1875, a French geographer thought that "by a little dredging the place would again become the safest shipping station on the whole Moroccan seaboard". The **royal villa**, which now stands empty, was built by Mohammed V, who celebrated many birthdays and other family events here.

Today, most Moroccans know Oualidia for its **Japanese oysters**; Morocco's first oyster farm was launched here in 1957 and nowadays it harvests some 200 tonnes a year, most of which are sold locally. But the town really deserves to be better known as a resort: its beach is excellent for surfing and windsurfing and swimming is safe and easy thanks to the shielded lagoon. The atmosphere for most of the year is very relaxed, aside from August when the place is absolutely jam-packed with Moroccan holidaymakers. A recent spate of

---

Bird habitats around Oualidia

The 70km of coast between Sidi Moussa (36km south of El Jadida) and Cap Beddouza (34km south of Oualidia) is one of the richest **birdlife habitats** in Morocco. The coastal wetlands, sands and saltpans, the jagged reefs, and the lagoons of Sidi Moussa and Oualidia shelter a huge range of species – flamingos, avocets, stilts, godwits, storks, terns, egrets, warblers and many small waders. Numerous country-side species come in, too; golden oriole and hoopoe have been recorded, and flocks of shearwaters are often to be seen not far offshore.

The best watching locations are the two **lagoons** and the rocky headland at **Cap Beddouza**.

residential development overlooking the lagoon also suggests that Oualidia is to become more than just a summer holiday village and it remains to be seen whether this will add to or detract from its coastal village vibe.

Practicalities

Oualidia is served by local **buses** from Safi, one CTM bus each way between Casa and Safi (two in summer), one bus from Marrakesh, Agadir and Tiznit, and several from Casa and El Jadida. Buses stop on the main road near the petrol station. Oualidia is also served by collective **grands taxis** from El Jadida and Safi, which stop across the street near the road that leads down to the beach. There's one **bank** in town, the Banque Populaire, with an ATM, and there's a **post office**, a **pharmacy**, and a **doctor's surgery** next door. The lagoon and beach are both a ten-minute downhill walk from the main road.

The **campsite**, *Camping Sables d'Or* (℡023 36 65 56; open all year but overflowing with Moroccan holidaymakers during August) is off the beach, opposite *Motel-Restaurant à l'Araignée Gourmande*. The hotels down by the lagoon are mostly very good too, and offer excellent seafood meals to residents and nonresidents alike. There are a number of other restaurants up on the main road; two to look out for are *Restaurant Thalassa*, which has set menus for 50dh, and, north of town, *Le Parc à Huîtres No. 007* (also called *Ostrea II*, and run by the same people as *Ostrea* in Casablanca; see p 388), which serves and sells oysters.

Complexe Touristique Chems ℡023 36 69 40. Next to *l'Araignée Gourmande*, with cabins of various sizes, from singles to fully equipped bungalows for up to five people, all with hot showers, but getting a bit shabby. The restaurant is still reasonable, though. ❻

Hôtel Hippocampe ℡023 36 61 08, ℻023 36 64 61. A delightful place, halfway up the slope from the lagoon to the village at the top. Immaculate rooms off a flower-filled garden and steps down to a "private" beach; also has a pool and a good restaurant, but guests have to take half-board. ❼

L'Initiale Hôtel Restaurant Oualidia Plage ℡023 36 62 46, ℻023 36 62 46. A family-run place that's the last along the beach road, with a mixture of food on offer in the restaurant, including vegetarian options. Most of the six rooms have a sea view. Booking advisable, breakfast included, and half-board compulsory at weekends. ❺

Motel-Restaurant à l'Araignée Gourmande ℡023 36 64 47, ℻023 36 61 44. This stands alongside the lagoon beach, and offers good-value, well-kept rooms and an excellent fish restaurant with set menus starting at 100dh, or a lobster set menu for 230dh. Price includes breakfast. ❻

Kasbah Gharbia

The Doukkala plains, inland from the El Jadida–Safi coast have long been a fertile and fought-over region, and there are scattered forts and kasbahs at several villages. One of the most interesting and accessible is at **GHARBIA**, 20km from Oualidia on a road that takes you across an undulating limestone plateau. The **kasbah** here is a vast enclosure, four kilometres long on each side, bastioned at intervals, and with a gate at each point of the compass, giving onto roads to Oualidia, Safi, El Jadida and Marrakesh: a strategic site. Within, a few houses remain in use and there's a large white house in the centre, occupied by the *caid* in the days of the Protectorate. If you visit – the trip is only really feasible if you have transport – you will be shown round by a charming bunch of locals, intent on pointing out the various features.

Cap Beddouza and Lalla Fatna

Continuing south from Oualidia, the road climbs a little inland and above the sea, which is hidden from view by sand dunes. It's a pretty stretch and the more so as you approach **Cap Beddouza**, where the rocky headland gives way intermittently to sandy beaches, sheltered by cliffs. At the cape there is a lighthouse and the *Auberge Cap Beddouza* (☏024 62 58 43; ❹), with a restaurant, bar and basic, rather overpriced cabins on the cliff top.

The best of the cliff-sheltered beaches is known as **Lalla Fatna**, 51km from Oualidia and just 15km short of Safi (with which it's connected by local bus #10 or #15). It's totally undeveloped, with nothing more than a **koubba** and in summer a few Moroccan tents, sometimes a café. If you stay here, you'll need your own transport and to take provisions. The beach is a steep two-kilometre descent from the road; camping on the beach, make sure you've pitched your tent far enough back from the tides. There is a **moussem** at the *koubba* on the thirteenth day of Shaban (the month before Ramadan).

Finally, beyond Cap Safi, you pass the *marabout* of Sidi Bouzid, overlooking Safi with its Medina, port and industry. Down below is **Sidi Bouzid beach** – Safi's local strand – where on November 8, 1942, American troops under General Patton landed as the southernmost thrust of *Operation Torch* (see box, p.377), the Vichy French position offering little resistance.

If you'd prefer a **hotel** here rather than in Safi itself, try the sprawling *Hôtel Atlantique Panorama* (☏024 66 84 90, ⓦwww.hotel-atlantique-panorama .com; ❻) which has a restaurant, three bars, two hammams, a nightclub and, perhaps its redeeming feature, a huge swimming pool overlooking the sea. There are also a couple of nice **restaurants** nearby: *La Corniche* (☏024 46 35 84) and *Le Refuge* (☏024 66 80 86).

Safi and around

Flanked by a strip of fertilizer factories, a vast grain silo and sardine-canning plants, **SAFI** is not the prettiest of Moroccan towns. It does, however, provide a glimpse of an active, modern and working community and the old **Medina** in its centre, walled and turreted by the Portuguese, holds a certain interest. The city – it merits the name with a population of over 300,000 – also has a strong industrial-artisan tradition, with a whole quarter devoted to **pottery workshops**. These have a virtual monopoly on the green, heavily glazed

---

Thor Heyerdahl and Safi

Thor Heyerdahl, of Kon Tiki fame, had a theory that ancient Mediterranean people could have crossed the Atlantic to Central America long before Columbus made the same voyage in 1492. To test his theory he built *Ra*, a reed ship, in 1969 in Safi, and prepared to sail across the Atlantic from the town. When asked why he had chosen Safi, Heyerdahl replied:

Safi is one of the oldest African ports beyond Gibraltar. Casablanca is a modern port, but Safi has been known from ancient times. Safi lies just where a coastal sailor coming from the Mediterranean world would be most likely to be swept out to sea by the elements. Just beyond Safi, the Canary current and the trade wind seize anything that floats, and sends it to America.

His first attempt in *Ra* failed, but a year later, in 1970, *Ra II* successfully crossed the Atlantic and reached Barbados, proving Heyerdahl's theory correct.

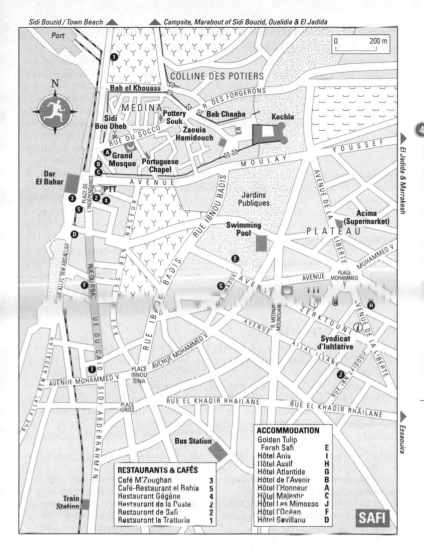

COLLINE DES POTIERS

Port

N

Bab el Khouass

MEDINA

Sidi Bou Dheb

Pottery Souk

R. DES FORGERONS

Bab Chaaba

Kechla

Zaouia Hamidouch

RUE DU SOCCO

Grand Mosque

Portuguese Chapel

Dar El Bahar

AVENUE

MOULAY

YOUSSEF

PLACE DE L'INDEPENDANCE

PTT

RUE BEN NACEUR

RUE IBNOU BADIS

Jardins Publiques

AVENUE DE LA LIBERTE

Acima (Supermarket)

RUE ALLAL BEN ABDALLAH

RUE DU RBAT

RUE IBNOU BADIS

Swimming Pool

PLATEAU

AVENUE

AVENUE MOHAMMED V

PLACE MOHAMMED V

MOHAMMED V

R. MEDINA MOUNOUARE

AVENUE

ZERKTOUN

AVENUE DE LA LIBERTE

Syndicat d'Initiative

ALLAL ISLANE

AVENUE MOHAMMED V

PLACE IBNOU SINA

RUE DU CAID SIDI ABDERRAHMN

RUE IB

RUE EL KHADIR RHAILANE

RUE IBN ZAIDOUF

RUE EL KHADIR RHAILANE

PLACE IDRISS

Train Station

RUE ALLAL BEN ABDALLAH

Bus Station

RESTAURANTS & CAFÉS

Café M'Zoughan	3
Café-Restaurant el Bahia	5
Restaurant Gégéne	4
Restaurant de la Poste	2
Restaurant de Safi	2
Restaurant la Trattoria	1

ACCOMMODATION

Golden Tulip Farah Safi	E
Hôtel Anis	I
Hôtel Assif	H
Hôtel Atlantide	G
Hôtel de l'Avenir	B
Hôtel l'Honneur	A
Hôtel Majestic	C
Hôtel Les Mimosas	J
Hôtel l'Océan	F
Hôtel Sevillana	D

SAFI

roof tiles used on palaces and mosques, as well as providing Morocco's main pottery exports, in the form of bowls, plates and garden pots.

The main interest in Safi is in its **Medina**, the adjoining **Dar el Bahar** fort, and the **Colline des Potiers**, the potters' quarter on the hill northeast of the Medina. Further out, on the Oualidia road, is the main industrial quarter and the new port.

South of Safi, the **coast** is heavily polluted and industrialized, and for a beach escape you'll want to head north. Local buses #10 and #15 run to **Lalla Fatna** and **Cap Beddouza** (see opposite) from the Place de l'Indépendance. In summer there are also local buses to **Souira Kedima** (see p.408).

Arrival, orientation and information

Arriving by **bus** – or **grand taxi** from Essaouira, Marrakesh, El Jadida and Casa – you should find yourself at the bus station, around 1.5km south of the Medina. The **train station** – Safi has two trains a day to and from Benguerir, where they connect for Settat, Marrakesh, Casa, Rabat, Meknes and Fes – is a similar distance. From either terminal, if you don't want to walk into town, you can take a petit taxi or city bus into one of the main squares, **Place de l'Indépendance**, just south of the Medina, or **Place Mohammed V** on the higher ground (known by the French as the *Plateau*); recently it's been spruced up with gardens, and is flanked by most of the city's major public buildings, including the PTT and the Municipalité. Most of the **banks** are around Place de l'Indépendance, while **Internet access** is cheaper here than elsewhere in Morocco: offices include Catric Cybercafé on Avenue Ibn Khaldoun near the bus station (daily 9am–11pm); Club Internet at 29 Rue du R'bat (daily 9am–midnight); and Lascala opposite the post office on Avenue Sidi Mohammed Abdallah (daily 10am–midnight). This last is also a pool hall and café. An Acima **supermarket** with a liquor outlet is on Avenue de la Liberté.

Safi boasts two **tourist offices**: the ONMT Délégation de Tourisme, south of the bus station at 26 Rue Imam Malik (Mon–Fri 8.30am–noon & 2.30–6.30pm; ☎024 62 24 96, ⊛www.safi-ville.com/tourisme.asp); and the more conveniently located Syndicat d'Initiative, on Avenue de la Liberté near the *Hôtel Assif* (no phone, same hours).

Accommodation

Safi has a reasonable range of **hotels**, catering more for Moroccan business travellers than tourists. Nonetheless, you should find a room without great difficulty.

The **campsite**, *Camping International Safi*, is 2km north of town, signposted to the right of the road to Oualidia (☎044 46 38 16; summer only). Spacious and well shaded, with a shop, pool and usual facilities, it has some great views over the town and towards the sea and is 1km from the beach at Sidi Bouzid.

Golden Tulip Farah Safi (formerly Hôtel CMKD) Av Zerktouni ☎024 46 42 99, ⊛www.goldentulipfarahsafi.com. Taken over and totally refurbished in 2003 by this worldwide chain. Rooms are spacious, modern and have all mod cons and the hotel boasts three restaurants, two bars, a nightclub, secure parking and has commanding views over the city. **❼**

Hôtel Anis Corner of Rue du R'bat and Rue de la Falaise ☎024 36 40 78. Rooms with en-suite facilities and a few "apartment" suites, good for families and/or long stays with a 25 percent reduction after the first night. Also has car parking. **❸**

Hôtel Assif Av de la Liberté ☎024 62 29 40, ⊛www.hotel-assif.ma. The best mid-range hotel, with small but homely rooms, each with TV and balcony, and there's an underground car park and a good restaurant. **❺**

Hôtel Atlantide Rue Chaouki ☎024 46 21 60, ℗024 46 45 95. A pleasant old hotel, with views over the town from the balconies, a swimming pool and good restaurant. **❺**

Hôtel de l'Avenir 1 Impasse de la Mer (no phone). The best of a trio of cheap hotels tucked just inside the Medina (the *Essaouira* and *Paris* are tolerable fall-backs). Hot showers (5dh) on the corridor, grand views of the sea and a busy café downstairs. **❶**

Hôtel l'Honneur (Foundouq esh Shraf) 56 Pl Douane (no phone). At the beginning of Rue du Socco, a homely little place with plain but clean rooms around a central patio (most windows only opening inward). Shared showers, and hot water if you're lucky. **❶**

Hôtel Majestic Place de l'Indépendance ☎024 46 40 11, ℗024 46 24 90. Fine views of the Dar el Behar and the sea, from fairly spacious, clean and pleasant rooms; hot showers (5dh). Marginally the best of the cheapies. **❷**

Hôtel Les Mimosas Rue Ibn Zaidoun ☎024 62 32 08, ℗024 62 59 55. An old hotel, now moved into a new wing, with good-size rooms, the *Golden Fish* disco/nightclub (10pm–1am) and a bar across the street. It is good value for money, but not central. **⑤**

Hôtel l'Océan Rue du R'bat on the corner of Derb Merchiche (no phone). A cheap hotel with plain,

bare rooms and shared showers (5dh); a decent fall-back, but not first choice. **①**

Hôtel Sevillana 1 Rue Ben Hassan ℡ 024 46 23 91. The blue-painted rooms are clean but a bit cramped, with shared hot showers, and a terrace with views over the Medina. **②**

Dar el Bahar, Kechla and the Medina

The **Dar el Bahar**, or Château de la Mer (Mon–Fri 9am–noon & 2.30–6.30pm; 10dh), is the main remnant of Safi's brief Portuguese occupation (1508–41). Sited on the waterfront, above the old port, it was built – in the Manueline style of the day – as the governor's residence, and saw subsequent use as a fortress and prison. Within, you can see the old prison cells at the foot of a spiral staircase to the ramparts, where a line of Dutch and Spanish cannon is ranged pointing out to sea.

The old Medina walls climb north, enclosing the Medina, to link with another and larger fortress known as the **Kechla** – again, Portuguese in origin, and housing the town's modern prison until 1990. It's now the National Ceramics Museum (daily except Tues 8.30am–noon & 2–6pm; 10dh; ℡024 46 38 95) with a not too exciting collection of local ceramics, marginally better than that in the Dar Batha Museum in Fez. Of rather more interest are further cannon (British this time), garden ornamentation and Portuguese coats-of-arms.

In the **Medina** proper, there is one further relic of the Portuguese, the **Cathédrale Portugaise** (daily 9am–noon & 2.30–6.30pm; 10dh), actually just the choir gallery of what was to be the cathedral – left uncompleted when the Portuguese withdrew – and again adorned with Manueline motifs. It's most easily found by heading up the Rue du Socco – the Medina's main street – for about 100m, until it opens out a little; there on your right, by the entrance to the Grand Mosque, a sign painted on the wall points the way through a small doorway. Beyond here, Rue du Socco leads uphill past a series of **souks**, food and domestic-goods markets, to the old city gate of **Bab Chaaba** and, through it, to the Colline des Potiers. En route, and just before the city gate, you pass through the **Souk de Poterie**. If you are looking to buy goods, you are likely to find better pieces here than in the showrooms at the foot of the Colline des Potiers itself.

If you are Muslim, you can enter two important Sufi shrines in the Medina: the **Marabout Sidi Bou Dheb** (at the bottom end of Rue du Socco) and the **Zaouia of Hamidouch** (near the Kechla). Sidi Bou Dheb is perhaps the best-known Sufi saint in Morocco and both his *marabout* and the Hamdouchia *zaouia* host **moussems** (held in May in recent years) attended by their respective brotherhoods; these feature music, dervish type dancing and, often, trance-induced self-mutilation with hatchets and knives. Heady stuff.

A more recent religious building is the **Jewish meeting place** and **synagogue** on Avenue Zerktouni. Built on the site of an ancient holy spot, it was opened in July 1993 under the patronage of the governor of Safi.

Colline des Potiers

The **Colline des Potiers** (potters' quarter) sprawls above the Medina and is impossible to miss, with its dozens of whitewashed beehive-kilns and chimneys, merging into the cemeteries beyond. The processes here remain traditional – electricity and gas have made scarcely an inroad on the tamarisk-fired kilns – and the quarter is worth at least the time it takes to wander up the new concrete steps and pathways. At the foot of the hillside is a street of showrooms. The products on display are of interest, but the colour dyes and garish designs are hardly comparable to the beautiful old pieces that can be seen around the country's crafts museums. Indeed, you are as likely to see U-bends for toilets being fired as anything else. There is every likelihood that a faux guide will introduce himself to you at the potters' quarter. Whilst the kilns are easily located without assistance, some of the guides are pretty good and can take you to a few of the more remote kilns and also make it a bit easier to take photographs and ask a few questions about the process. If you do accept an offer of a guided "tour" make sure you agree a price beforehand (perhaps 10dh per person) and don't be intimidated into purchasing anything.

And the sardines?

Safi's famed sardines are caught in the deeper waters of the Atlantic from Boujdour in the south to Safi in the north. There are around five hundred 18–20m wooden trawlers in the town fleet and you can still see them being made in the boatyards at Safi, Essaouira and Agadir. The fleet lands 350,000 tonnes of sardines annually and most of them are canned in Safi. Increasingly, those caught further south are landed at the nearest port and brought to Safi in refrigerated trucks. Most of the tins get sold abroad – Morocco being the world's largest exporter of sardines.

Eating

Safi is no gastronomic paradise with most of the town's restaurants offering the usual Moroccan fare along with a few seafood dishes. For anything above the average try the restaurants within the hotels *Atlantide* and *Golden Tulip Farah* or alternatively head up to the clifftop restaurants overlooking the city's beach, Plage Sidi Bouzid (see p.404).

Café M'Zoughan Pl de l'Indépendance. Café-patisserie which is good for breakfast.
Café-Restaurant El Bahia Pl de l'Indépendance. Café downstairs and restaurant above, with fancy Moroccan dishes. Moderate.
Restaurant Gégéne 8 Rue de la Marine, just off Pl de l'Indépendance ☏ 024 46 33 69. A lively restaurant with separate bar and a limited but satisfying menu. Moderate.
Restaurant de la Poste 40 Pl de l'Indépendance. The upstairs restaurant is

good: French cuisine and seafood. Licensed. Moderate.
Restaurant de Safi 3 Rue de la Marine, next to *Gégéne*. Friendly little restaurant serving up tajine and brochettes. Cheap to moderate.
Restaurant La Trattoria 2 Route de l'Aouinate ☏ 024 46 31 76 or 024 62 09 59. Near the Délégation des Pêches Maritime de Safi, follow the signs to *La Trattoria*. Upmarket and very pleasant Italian restaurant. Live music Thurs–Sat evenings. Moderate to expensive.

Safi to Essaouira: Kasbah Hamidouch

Travelling by bus, you usually have no option but to take the inland N1, if heading southwest from **Safi to Essaouira**. With your own transport, or in a grand taxi, you could follow the R301 coast road, which runs past the canning plants towards **Souira Kedima**, around 30km south of Safi. This is a fine beach fronted by a rather bleak holiday-bungalow complex, used by people from Safi and Marrakesh on their summer holidays; nearby, on a windswept headland, there is an old Portuguese fortress known as **Agouz**.

A little beyond Souria Kedima, a new bridge allows you to cross the Oued Tensift to reach, along a stretch of good but sandy *piste*, the large and isolated fortress of **Kasbah Hamidouch**. This was built by the ever-industrious Moulay Ismail to control the mouth of the Tensift – one of the most active Moroccan rivers, which here finishes its course from Marrakesh. You can reach its ramparts across the fields.

South of the kasbah, a new and quite **scenic road** (R301) heads off along the coast towards Essaouira via **Cap Hadid**; it joins the Marrakesh-Essaouira road (R207) 4km outside Essaouira.

Djebel Hadid was once mined for iron ore and, indeed, in the nineteenth century, this coast was known as the Iron Coast.

Essaouira (Mogador)

ESSAOUIRA is by popular acclaim Morocco's most likeable resort: an eighteenth-century town, enclosed by medieval-looking battlements, facing a cluster of rocky offshore islands, and trailed by a vast expanse of empty sands and dunes. Its whitewashed and blue-shuttered houses and colonnades, wood workshops and art galleries, boat-builders and sardine fishermen and feathery Norfolk Island pines, which only thrive in a pollution-free atmosphere, all provide a colourful and very pleasant backdrop to the beach. Many of the foreign tourists making their own way to Essaouira are drawn by the wind, known locally as the *alizee*, which in spring and summer can be a bit remorseless for sunbathing but creates much-sought-after waves for **windsurfing** and, increasingly, **kitesurfing**. In recent years, the town has gained quite a reputation in this respect, promoting itself as "Wind City,

Essaouira art galleries

Essaouira has become quite a centre for painting and sculpture, and many of its artists have made a name for themselves in both Morocco and Europe. Artists with their own distinctive styles tend to have an entourage of second-rate imitators, so it's worth checking that the artist whose works you're looking at really is the one whose work you were interested in, as it should be in any of the galleries listed here.

Association Tilal 4 Rue du Caire ☎024 47 54 24. A gallery exhibiting the work of half a dozen or so local painters with quite distinctive styles. Many of the pieces exhibited here have been knocked up quickly to sell at low prices: to buy some of the artists' better work, you'll have to speak to them personally and perhaps commission something. The association should be able to put you in touch.

Atelier Hassan el Kass (see shopfront sign Travail sur Peau) 58 Rue Sidi Mohammed Ben Abdallah. A small shop run by a local artist whose work consists mainly of calligraphy and pseudo-calligraphy on parchment.

Espace Othello 9 Rue Mohammed Layachi, behind the *Hôtel Sahara* (daily 9am–1pm & 3–8pm). This gallery was opened in 1993 by the *patron* of the nearby *Restaurant el Minzah* to display paintings and sculptures by local artists.

Galerie d'Art Frederic Damgaard on Av Oqba Ibn Nafia (daily 9am–1pm & 3–7pm) ☎024 78 44 46, ℻024 47 58 57. Paintings and sculptures by twenty or so locally based artists, in a gallery run by a Danish furniture designer, who uses the traditional thuya techniques in a highly imaginative, modern context. There's also an atelier at 2 Rue el Hijalli, just off Pl Chefchaouni.

La Petite Galerie Just off the north end of Pl Prince Moulay el Hassan in the passage through to Rue Ibn Rochd . A small but well-chosen selection of works by local painters.

Afrika" and hosting national and international windsurfing contests. The same winds make Essaouira pretty terrible for **surfing** – those in the know head down the coast to Taghazout (see p.622).

The life of the resort, too, is easy and uncomplicated, and very much in the image of the youthful Europeans and Marrakshis who come here on holiday. Not that Essaouira is exclusively a backpackers' resort – these days it attracts all kinds of independent travellers, and increasing numbers of packages, with new chain hotels and villas springing up along the Corniche. But, as yet, it's very far from spoilt, and remains a thoroughly enjoyable base to rest up after being in the cities, the Atlas or the desert.

Some history

Fronted by dramatic sea bastions and fortifications, Essaouira seems a lot older than it is. Although a series of forts were built here from the fifteenth century on, it was only in the 1760s that the town was established and the present circuit of walls constructed. It was known to European sailors and then traders as **Mogador**, said to be a reference to the prominent *koubba* of Sidi Mgdoul, used for navigating entry to the bay. Less likely is the legend that the town's patron saint was a Scotsman named McDougal who was shipwrecked here in the fourteenth century. To the Moroccans it was known as Seurah, from the Berber "little picture".

The work on the town's walls, which was completed in 1770, was ordered by the sultan **Sidi Mohammed Ben Abdallah**, and carried out by a French military architect, Theodore Cornut, which explains the town's unique blend of Moroccan Medina and French grid layout. The sultan's original intention was to provide a military port, as Agadir was in revolt at the time and Sultan Mohammed Ben Abdallah needed a local base. It lent itself superbly to the purpose, as its series of forts ensured complete protection for the bay. Soon,

Orson Welles's Othello

Orson Welles filmed much of his **Othello** in Essaouira, returning the Moor (played by Welles himself) to his homeland. The film opens with a tremendous panning shot of the Essaouira ramparts, where Welles placed a scene-setting "punishment" of Iago, suspended above the sea and rocks in a metal cage. Later locations included a local hammam for the murder of Rodrigo – the costumes Welles had ordered from Jewish tailors in the Mellah were not ready, so he had to shoot a scene with minimal clothing – and the Portuguese cistern in El Jadida (see p.399).

The film was something of a personal crusade for Welles, who financed it himself, leaving the cast at intervals to try and borrow money off friends in Italy and France. During the course of the filming, he got through at least four – and perhaps six – Desdemonas, beginning with his fiancée Lea Padovani, until she soured relations by beginning an affair with one of the crew. In the end they were all dubbed, as indeed were many other of the characters – Welles performing most himself.

On its release in 1952, *Othello* was panned by the critics, and at Welles' death it was the only one of his dozen films to which he owned the rights. Forty years on, however, it was restored by his daughter for its anniversary, and shown at film festivals worldwide, and to huge acclaim. Even Essaouira had an open-air showing, in the presence of King Mohammed VI (Prince Héritier at the time); this event was accompanied by the official naming of a park area on the front, **Orson Welles' Square**, complete with a thuya wood memorial made by Samir Mustapha, one of the town's most talented young craftsmen.

however, commercial concerns gained pre-eminence. During the nineteenth century, Mogador was the only Moroccan port south of Tangier that was open to European trade, and it prospered greatly from the privilege. Drawn by protected trade status, and a harbour free from customs duties, British merchants settled in the kasbah quarter, and a large Jewish community in the Mellah, within the northeast ramparts.

Decline set in during the French Protectorate, with Marshal Lyautey's promotion of Casablanca. Anecdote has it that he arrived in Essaouira on a Saturday when the Jewish community was at prayer; he cast a single glance at the deserted streets and decided to shift to the port of Casablanca further up the coast. The decline was accelerated after independence, by the exodus of the Jewish community. These days, however, the town is very much back on its feet, as a fishing port, market town and ever more popular resort.

Arrival

Buses (both CTM and private lines) arrive at a bus station, inconveniently sited on the outskirts of the town, about 500m north of Bab Doukkala and the site of much building and roadworks. Especially at night, it's worth taking a petit taxi (about 5dh) or horse-drawn calèche (about 10dh) into town. Taxis cannot enter the Medina city walls, but you can hire one of the barrow boys who are usually on hand to meet arriving buses and wheel your luggage to a hotel for you – bargain for the price. **Supratours** buses from Agadir and Marrakesh arrive and depart from their office at the end of a short cul de sac by the south bastion (off Av Lalla Aicha).

Grands taxis operate from the bus station, though they will often drop arrivals at Bab Doukkala or even by Place Prince Moulay el Hassan. There is a **petit taxi rank** by the car park at the southern end of Avenue Oqba Ibn Nafia, and taxis serving the Medina also run to and from Bab es Sebaa and Bab Doukkala.

If you are driving, it's worth making use of the **car parking** space, manned round the clock (20dh for 24hr) in front of the harbour offices, south of Place Prince Moulay el Hassan.

The best way into town from the **airport**, 15km south of town, is by grand taxi (about 50dh for up to six passengers). If you really want to scrimp, you can take local bus #2 for 7dh (9 daily; 1hr).

Orientation and information

Though having long outgrown its ramparts, Essaouira is a simple place to get to grips with. At the northeast end of town is the **Bab Doukkala**; at the southwest is the town's pedestrianized main square, **Place Prince Moulay el Hassan**, and the fishing **harbour**. Between them run two main parallel streets, **Avenue de l'Istiqlal/Avenue Mohammed Zerktouni** and **Rue Sidi Mohammed Ben Abdallah**.

The **tourist office** is on Avenue du Caire opposite the police station (due to re-open after renovations in early 2007; June to mid-Sept Mon–Sat 9am–1pm & 3–7pm; mid-Sept to May Mon–Fri 9am–noon & 3–6.30pm; ☎024 78 35 32). Alternatively there's **Jack's Kiosk**, 1 Pl Prince Moulay el Hassan (daily 10am–10pm; ☎024 47 55 38, ⓕ024 47 69 01), a newsagent and bookshop that has long served informally as an information booth and accommodation agency. It still lets apartments, has an international phone and fax centre, and sells English-language newspapers.

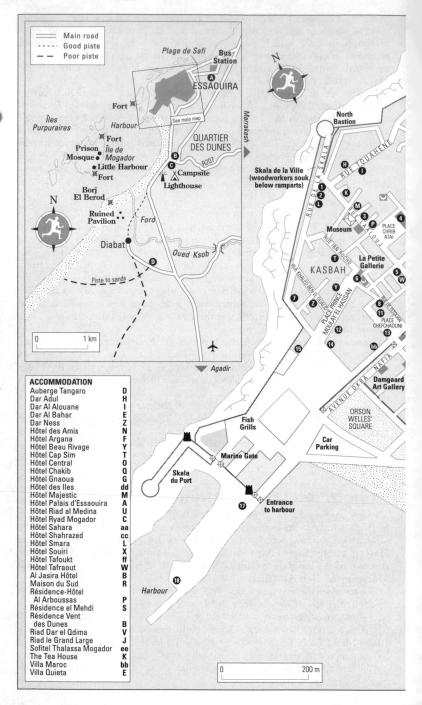

ACCOMMODATION

Auberge Tangaro	D
Dar Adul	H
Dar Al Alouane	I
Dar Al Bahar	E
Dar Ness	Z
Hôtel des Amis	N
Hôtel Argana	F
Hôtel Beau Rivage	Y
Hôtel Cap Sim	T
Hôtel Central	O
Hôtel Chakib	Q
Hôtel Gnaoua	G
Hôtel des Iles	dd
Hôtel Majestic	M
Hôtel Palais d'Essaouira	A
Hôtel Riad al Medina	U
Hôtel Ryad Mogador	C
Hôtel Sahara	aa
Hôtel Shahrazed	cc
Hôtel Smara	L
Hôtel Souiri	X
Hôtel Tafoukt	ff
Hôtel Tafraout	W
Al Jasira Hôtel	B
Maison du Sud	R
Résidence-Hôtel	
Al Arboussas	P
Résidence el Mehdi	S
Résidence Vent	
des Dunes	B
Riad Dar el Qdima	V
Riad le Grand Large	J
Sofitel Thalassa Mogador	ee
The Tea House	K
Villa Maroc	bb
Villa Quieta	E

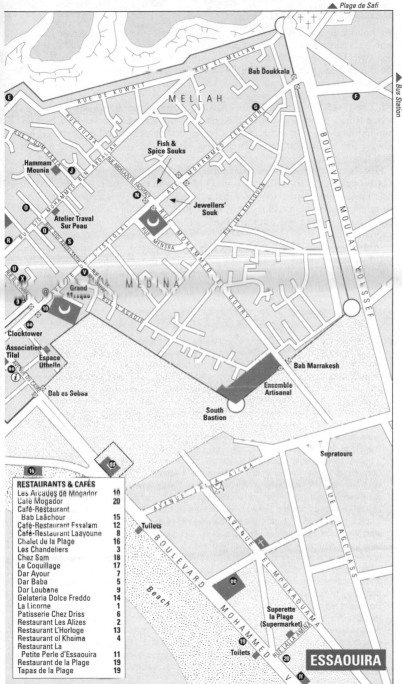

▲ Plage de Safi

▲ Bus Station

4

MELLAH

Bab Doukkala

RUE EL MELLAH

RUE DE KUWAIT

RUE OUJDA

RUE D'UM RABIA

Hammam
Mounia

Fish &
Spice Souks

Jewellers'
Souk

Atelier Traval
Sur Peau

MEDINA

Grand
Mosque

Clocktower

Association
Tilal

Espace
Othello

Bab es Sebaa

Bab Marrakesh

Ensemble
Artisanal

South
Bastion

Supratours

BOULEVARD MOHAMMED

Beach

Toilets

Superette
la Plage
(Supermarket)

Toilets

ESSAOUIRA

413

RESTAURANTS & CAFÉS

Les Arcades de Mogador	10
Café Mogador	20
Café-Restaurant	
Bab Laâchour	15
Café-Restaurant Essalam	12
Café-Restaurant Laayoune	8
Chalet de la Plage	16
Les Chandeliers	3
Chez Sam	18
Le Coquillage	17
Dar Ayour	7
Dar Baba	5
Dar Loubane	9
Gelateria Dolce Freddo	14
La Licorne	1
Patisserie Chez Driss	6
Restaurant Les Alizes	2
Restaurant L'Horloge	13
Restaurant ol Khaima	4
Restaurant La	
Petite Perle d'Essaouira	11
Restaurant de la Plage	19
Tapas de la Plage	19

Quartier des Dunes, Campsite, ▼Agadir & Marrakesh

Accommodation

At holiday times (summer, Christmas/New Year), you need to arrive early or book ahead to ensure the accommodation of your choice; if you plan to stay for a week or more, it can be worth renting an **apartment** or a villa. You can do this through Jack's Kiosk (see p.411, or check its website at ⓦwww.essaouira .com/apartments), through Karimo, whose office is just off the north end of Place Prince Moulay el Hassan in the passage through to Rue Ibn Rochd (ⓣ024 47 45 00, ⓦwww.karimo.net), or through the *Restaurant Essalam* on Place Prince Moulay el Hassan (see p.421). You may also be accosted by key-waving local residents at the bus station as you arrive with offers of rooms, but always check out what's on offer carefully, and be sure of the price and services you have agreed on before accepting.

Hotels and apartments are proliferating as Essaouira's popularity grows, as are **riads** (*maisons d'hôte*), within Essaouira's Medina to meet the rise in demand for accommodation. A riad may offer that warm, homely feel associated with B&Bs in other parts of the world but this comes at a price, whereas the hotels perhaps won't be as atmospheric, but the rooms can be considerably cheaper with much the same facilities.

Although some of the **beach hotels** are very near town, others are 2km south in the **Quartier des Dunes** district. This removes you somewhat from the life of the town, though it's an easy enough walk along the beach by day, or a short taxi hop at night.

The Île de Mogador and Eleonora's falcon

Out across the bay from Essaouira lie the **Îles Purpuraires**, named from the dyes for purple imperial cloth that the Romans once produced on the islands from murex shellfish. Here also, Sir Francis Drake ate his Christmas lunch in 1577, commenting on the "verie ugly fish". The largest of the islands, known as the **Île de Mogador**, is flanked on each side by a fort which, together with the fort on the islet just off the town harbour and the Bord el Berod on the beach, covers all possible approaches to the bay. It also has a small harbour, a mosque, a few rusting cannons and a nineteenth-century prison used for political exiles but long closed. Recent excavations have revealed that there was a Phoenician settlement on the landward side of the island dating back to the late seventh century BC.

It is of most interest these days, however, as a nature reserve, for this is the only non-Mediterranean breeding site of **Eleonora's falcon** – Morocco's most dramatic bird. They are not hard to see, with binoculars, from the beach. The best time is the early evening half-light, when you might spot as many as two or three dozen of these magnificent birds, gliding in low over the sea to hawk for insects. The falcons are summer visitors to Morocco, staying between May and October before making the long return journey south to Madagascar for the winter. They are often seen hunting over the dunes south of Oued Ksob. The nearby river course also has many **waders** and **egrets** and occasional rarities such as gull-billed tern and Mediterranean gull.

The island has no inhabitants, save for a *gardien* who keeps an eye on the falcons. If you want to visit —and this is strongly discouraged when the birds are resident – you'll first have to get a *permit d'autorisation* from the *Province*, signposted inland from Boulevard Mohammed V after the *Hôtel Tafkout*, and then the approval of the harbour-master in his office before the Marine Gate; the latter's say-so depends on the state of the tide and the weather forecast. Then, and only then, can you negotiate for a boat ride. Don't pay for the ride until you've been collected and returned to the town.

A visit such as this is problematic, time-consuming and calls for perseverance – but it is possible. Allow a couple of days at least for due processes.

The **campsite**, *Camping Sidi Magdoul*, is 3km out of town on the Agadir road and near the lighthouse (☎ 024 47 21 96). It's clean, friendly and well-managed, with hot showers and bungalows, though the ground is rather hard and shade is sparse.

In town

Cheap

Hôtel des Amis 24 Rue Abdelaziz el Fachtaly (no phone). A basic but very cheap travellers' hotel in the middle of the Medina with shared hot showers (8dh); there's an inexpensive restaurant next door offering various set menus, one of them vegetarian. ❶

Hôtel Argana Pl Bab Doukkala ☎024 47 59 75. Not the cheapest cheapie, and certainly not the best located, but the rooms are clean and it's handy for the bus station. Shared showers (5dh). ❷

Hôtel Cap Sim 11 Rue Ibn Rochd ☎ & ℱ024 78 58 34, ✉hotelcapsim@menara.ma. Central, clean and popular with a fourth-floor terrace. The price includes breakfast, but en-suite rooms cost considerably more than those with shared shower facilities. ❸

Hôtel Central 5 Rue Bal Dheb, off Av Mohammed Ben Abdallah ☎024 78 36 23. Cheap and cheerful basic rooms and friendly staff in a nice old house around a patio with a fig tree and shared hot showers (5dh). ❷

Hôtel Chakib 2 Rue Sidi Abdelsmih ☎024 47 52 91. Not great value as Essaouira's budget hotels go but a useful fall-back if the others are full, with basic but decent rooms, shared hot showers (7dh) and negotiable prices off-season. ❷

Hôtel Majestic 40 Rue Laâlouj ☎024 47 49 09. The former French colonial courthouse (opened in 1914, according to the plaque on the side of the building), and not bad value with decent-sized rooms and hot showers, though only two rooms are en suite. ❸

Hôtel Sahara Av Okba Ibn Nafia ①024 47 52 92, ℱ 024 47 61 98. Big rooms around a central well, and hot water mornings and evenings. Some rooms are en suite. ❹

Hôtel Smara 26 Rue Skala ☎ 024 47 56 55, ℱ024 47 51 75. A small hotel with small rooms, but the sea view from the terrace and the front rooms is a bonus. Price includes breakfast. ❸

Hôtel Souiri 37 Rue Attarine ☎& ℱ024 47 53 39. Very central and very popular, with a range of rooms, the cheaper ones having shared bathroom facilities. Rooms at the front are considered the best, though those at the back are quieter. Price includes breakfast. ❹

Hôtel Tafraout 7 Rue de Marrakesh ☎024 47 62 76. Recently renovated with friendly staff and comfortable rooms, some en suite, but not much

character, and not all rooms have outside windows. Hot water evenings only, but there are public showers for both sexes right next door. ❸

Moderate to expensive

Hôtel Beau Rivage 4 Pl Prince Moulay el Hassan ☎024 47 59 25, ⓦwww.beaurivage -essaouira.com. This travellers' favourite with its prime location on the square offers clean, modern en-suite rooms each with its own balcony. Those overlooking the square, however, can be a bit noisy. There is a popular restaurant down below and a terrace up top with fantastic Medina and sea views. ❺

Hôtel Gnaoua 89 Av Zerktouni ☎ & ℱ024 47 52 34. A newish place towards Bab Doukkala and away from the more touristy parts of the Medina, spick and span but a little overpriced. All rooms are en suite but not all have outside windows. ❺

Hôtel Palais d'Essaouira 5 Av 2 Mars ① 024 47 23 87, ⓦwww.essaouiranet.com/palais. A nicely done-out place with comfortable en-suite rooms, not brilliantly located but convenient for the bus station, which is just across the road. Discount of 25 percent after the first night. ❹

Hôtel Riad al Medina 9 Rue Attarine ☎024 47 59 07, ⓦwww.riadalmadina.com. A former palatial mansion built in 1871, which had by the 1960s fallen on hard times and become a budget hotel for hippies – guests supposedly included Jimi Hendrix, Frank Zappa, Jefferson Airplane and Cat Stevens. Now refurbished with 49 rooms and suites, it gets mixed reports: some people love it, and it's certainly friendly with bags of character; others hate it, largely because it's quite basic by package-tour standards, and expensive for what you get, though the price includes breakfast. ❼

Hôtel Shahrazed 1 Rue Youssef el Fassi, entrance on Rue de Caire ☎024 47 29 77. Opposite the police station. Well equipped, with spacious, almost spartan rooms, most en suite. ❹

Résidence-Hôtel Al Arboussas 24 Rue Laâlouj, in a small alley opposite the museum ☎024 47 26 10, ℱ024 47 26 13. A large house, nicely converted. The rooms are small, but impeccably clean, en suite and comfortable. Price includes breakfast. ❺

Résidence el Mehdi 15 Rue Sidi Abdelsmih ☎ & ℱ024 47 59 43, ⓦwww.el-mehdi.net. A modernized old house with nice, airy rooms, two patios (one covered, one open), two terraces and a reliable kitchen, plus a couple of apartments and a suite. Price includes breakfast. ⑤

Riads

Dar Adul 63 Rue Touahene (near the Skala) ☎ & ℱ024 47 39 10. Lashings of whitewash give this place a bright, airy feel, and help to keep it cool in summer. It's French-run, with a selection of different-sized rooms, some split-level, and the largest with a fireplace to make it cosy in winter. Breakfast included. ⑦

🏃 **Dar Al Alouane** (also called La Maison des Couleurs) 66 Rue Touahene ☎024 47 61 72, ℮dar_al_alouane@yahoo.fr. Simple and stylish newcomer with a choice of brightly painted rooms for up to four people sharing. Shared bathroom but still good value for this standard. ⑤

Dar Al Bahar 1 Rue Touahene ☎024 47 68 31, ⓦwww.daralbahar.com. Wild sea views, especially from the terrace, cool whitewashed rooms and paintings and window blinds by some of the best local artists make this an excellent choice, though it's a bit tucked away. Price includes breakfast. ⑥

Dar Ness 1 Rue Khalid ben Oualid ☎ & ℱ024 47 68 04, ⓦwww.darness-essaouira.com. A nineteenth-century house turned into an attractive riad by its French owner, simply but tastefully furnished. Price includes breakfast. ⑦

Maison du Sud 29 Rue Sidi Mohammed Ben Abdallah ☎024 47 41 41, ⓦwww.essaouiranet .com/maison-du-sud. An eighteenth-century house built around a covered patio with fountain. Most rooms are split-level with a sitting area and bathroom below the sleeping area. Prices include breakfast. ⑥

Riad Dar el Qdima 4 Rue Malek Ben Rahai ☎024 47 38 58, ⓦwww.darqdima.com. A small riad in an eighteenth-century house with a variety of rooms around a covered patio, or adjoining the roof terrace. Prices include breakfast. ⑤

Riad le Grand Large 2 Rue Oum Rabii ☎024 47 28 66, ⓦwww.riadlegrandlarge.com. Despite its name, a small, cosy place with ten smallish rooms, lovely staff, a restaurant and a roof terrace café. Good value, with reductions off-season. Prices include breakfast. ⑤

🏃 **The Tea House** 74 Rue Laâlouj, in an alley off the street ☎024 78 35 43, ⓦwww .theteahouse.net. Two self-contained and well-equipped apartments, each sleeping four adults, comprising two bedrooms each with own shower, a sitting room, kitchen and bathroom, in an old house run by a British woman and her Marrakshi husband. There is also a new upper terrace with sea views. Among services offered are help with souvenir shopping, and a neighbour who'll come in and cook a Moroccan meal. Prices include breakfast. ⑦

Villa Maroc 10 Rue Abdallah Ben Yassin, just inside the Medina wall near the clocktower ☎ 024 47 61 47, ⓦwww.villa-maroc.com. Established long before riads became trendy, from two old houses converted into a score of rooms and suites, heated in winter and decorated with the finest Moroccan materials. It even has its own hammam. Most of the year you will need to book several months ahead, though it's always worth a call on the off-chance. Nonresidents can dine here if they reserve before 4pm. Though accessible only on foot, they have porters on hand to carry your luggage from the car park. Prices include breakfast. ⑦

Near the beach

Hôtel des Iles Bd Mohammed V ☎024 78 36 36, ⓦwww.hotel-des-iles.com. Outside, but close to, the Medina. Comfortable, but a bit dull with rooms in a main block and chalet rooms round the swimming pool. Nonresidents can use the pool for 75dh a day. Overpriced, but discounts out of season. ⑦

Hôtel Ryad Mogador where Bd Mohammed V leaves the seafront and turns inland to become the R207 ☎024 78 35 55, ⓦwww.ryadmogador.com. A four-star beach hotel (though some 200m off the beach) with a good-sized pool, quite spacious rooms and nice decor. Better value for money than the Sofitel.. ⑦

Hôtel Tafoukt 58 Bd Mohammed V ☎024 78 45 04, ℮h.tafoukt.essa@wanadoo.net.ma. One

kilometre south of the old town, facing the beach, this comfortable block is showing signs of wear on the outside but the decent-sized rooms are nicely done out in sky blue or sunny yellow. There's a good restaurant, La Petite Algue, and a bar, both open to nonresidents. Book early for peak periods. Price includes breakfast. ⑥

Al Jasira Hôtel 18 Rue Moulay Ali Cherif, Quartier des Dunes ☎024 78 44 03, ⓦwww.aljasirahotel -mogador.com. Some 200m off the beach, behind Villa Quieta, with spacious rooms but a very small pool. Rooms without a sea view are much cheaper than those with. Price includes breakfast. ⑥

Résidence Vent des Dunes Villa 20, 26 Quartier des Dunes ☎ & ℱ024 47 53 91,

Essaouira and its nearby beaches are Morocco's prime wind- and kitesurfing centre, drawing enthusiasts almost year-round. The trade wind at Essaouira is northwesterly and blows year-round; it's stronger in summer – if you're a novice try to get out early in the morning – but the swell is bigger in winter. The winds can be quite strong (sails required are 5.03.5) but the curved shape of Essaouira's bay, along with a gently sloping sandy bottom that creates a wide shallow area along the shoreline, makes it ideal for novices. Even during summer the water temperature rises only to 20 degrees maximum, so a wetsuit is required all year. There are numerous surf shops and schools in Essaouira, as well as one or two in Sidi Kaouiki and Point Imessouane (see p.423 & p.424) further south. Surfers should be warned that for most of the year Essouaria's non-stop winds, though great for windsurfing, can be a disappointment for board surfing and you might be better off down at Point Imessouane with its easterly facing bay.

Surfing supplies

Club Mistral The closest beachside operator to the Medina, opposite the *Sofitel* hotel ☏024 78 39 34, ⓦwww.club-mistral.com. Rents out mainly wind- and kitesurfing gear and offers lessons in both as well. It is also heavily involved in local initiatives that are putting more and more school – and street – children on the water.

Gipsy Surfer 14 Rue de Tetouan ☏061 01 79 98. Rents surfing and windsurfing equipment and posts weather reports.

Hotel Ocean Vagabond ☏024 47 92 22, ⓦwww.oceanvagabond.com. Has a surf school at the far southern end of the beach where it also offers kitesurfing lessons and posts the weather forecast.

Magic Fun Afrika Av Mohammed V, 100m south of *Hôtel Tafoukt* ☏ 024 47 38 56, ⓦwww.magicfunafrika.com. Rents out kayaks, kitesurfing, surfboards and windsurfing equipment, offers surf lessons and posts the weather forecast daily.

No Work Team 2 Rue Skala & 7 Rue Houmam el Fatouki ☏024 47 52 72, The British-owned place sells surfwear and surfing equipment from its two shops.

The Royal Windsurfing Club (*Royal Club de Planche à Voile*), next to Magic Fun. Offers windsurfing lessons.

ⓦwww.essaouiranet.com/ventdesdunes. Behind the *Al Jasira*, a good-value place with cheerful rooms, satellite TV, friendly staff, a terrace and tent on the roof for breakfast, and a nearby annexe with apartments, but no pool. Includes breakfast. ⑤
Sofitel Thalassa Mogador Rd Mohammed V ☏024 47 90 00, ⓦwww.sofitel.com. The most expensive hotel in Essaouira by a very long chalk, and possibly the best, though certainly not by the same kind of margin. It has a pool, two bars, two restaurants, a thalassotherapy centre (if a swim in

the sea isn't sufficient), and – which might make it worth the price if you need it – a room adapted for wheelchair users. ❻
Villa Quieta 86 Rd Mohammed V, Quartier des Dunes ☏024 78 50 04, ⓦwww.villa-quieta.com. A luxurious mansion built in semi-traditional style by the current owner's father in the 1950s, some 2km south of town. The rooms are tasteful and comfortable, and the place retains the feel of an upscale guesthouse rather than a hotel. There's no pool, though it's only 150m to the beach. ❼

The Town

There are few formal "sights" in Essaouira, but it's a great place just to walk around, exploring the **ramparts**, the **harbour** and the **souks** – above all the **thuya wood workshops** – or wandering along the immense windswept **beach**.

The Skala de la Ville, thuya wood workshops and galleries

The ramparts are the obvious place to start a tour of Essaouira. If you head north along the lane at the end of Place Prince Moulay el Hassan, you can gain access to the **Skala de la Ville**, the great sea bastion that runs along the northern cliffs. Along the top of it are a collection of European cannon, presented to Sultan Sidi Mohammed Ben Abdallah by ambitious nineteenth-century merchants, and at its end is the circular **North Bastion**, with panoramic views across the Medina, kasbah and Mellah quarters, and out to sea (closes at sunset).

Along the Rue de Skala, built into the ramparts, are a number of **marquetry and wood-carving workshops**, long established in Essaouira. Here – and in workshops around town – artisans produce amazingly painstaking and beautiful marquetry work from **thuya** (also spelt *thuja*; *arar* in Arabic), an aromatic mahogany-like hardwood from a local coniferous tree, from which they adapt both the trunk and the roots (or *loupe*). With total justice, they claim that their produce is the best in the country. If you see good examples elsewhere they've probably come from Essaouira, and if you're thinking of buying – boxes and chess sets are for sale, as well as traditional furniture, and some striking modern carvings – this is the best place to do it. To gauge quality and prices before you come to make a purchase, visit Afalkay Art at 9 Pl Prince Moulay el Hassan (opposite the *Hôtel Beau Rivage*), a vast and somewhat impersonal emporium where you can browse with no commitment to buy.

The **Musée Sidi Mohammed Ben Abdallah**, on Rue Laâlouj next to the post office (Mon, Wed–Sun 8.30am–6.30pm; 10dh), is in a nineteenth-century mansion that served as the town hall during the Protectorate. Recently re-opened after a lengthy renovation, the collection of traditional jewellery, coins, carpets, costumes and Gnaoua musical instruments decorated with marquetry along with a gallery of pictures of old Essaouira, is well worth a look.

△ Skala de la Ville at dusk, Essaouira

Spice and jewellery souks and the Mellah

The town's **other souks** spread around and to the south of two arcades, on either side of Rue Mohammed Zerktouni, and up towards the Mellah. Worth particular attention are the **Marché d'Epices** (spice market) and **Souk des Bijoutiers** (jewellers' market). Stallholders in the spice souk will extol the virtues of their wares, including exotic remedies for baldness, infertility and so on.

The jewellery business was one of the traditional trades of Essaouira's Jewish community, who have long since deserted the **Mellah**, in the northwest corner of the ramparts. A gloomy-looking part of the town, it was locked at night up until the end of the nineteenth century.

There have been various estimates as to the size of the **Jewish community** in the last quarter of the nineteenth century, ranging from four thousand to nine thousand – the likelihood being at the top end of the scale. It is also probable that they comprised around half of the total population. Trade was carried out mainly with Marseille and London, but there were never more than three hundred Europeans living in the Mellah, engaged primarily in trade. The principal exports were almonds, goatskins, olive oil and ostrich feathers; and the principal imports were cotton goods (half the total value) and tea. **Sir Moses Montefiore**, the nineteenth-century leader of Britain's Jewish community, was born here.

Today, the old Jewish quarter is noticeably in decline, with many of its houses deserted and in a dangerous condition. A dozen or so Jewish families currently live in Essaouira, but not in the Mellah.

At the northeast corner of the Medina, **Bab Doukkala** leads to a small Christian cemetery dating from colonial times (100m on the left). The area just outside the gate was until 2002 one of the last places in Morocco – apart from Marrakesh's Djemaa el Fna (see p.442) – where storytellers and other performers still gathered to entertain; alas it has now become a commercial and residential development. Some 400m beyond Bab Doukkala there is further evidence of the former Jewish community in the extensive Jewish cemetery – two vast grey lanes of tombstones, carefully tended and well ordered, in a site on both sides of the road. The principal entrance is on the right.

The port

At some point, it's worth making your way down to the **harbour** via the Marine Gate. Essaouira is the country's third fishing port after Agadir and Safi, and the port area bustles with life for most of the day, with the local wooden fishing boats being built or repaired, and the fishing fleet bringing in the day's catch. The sea bastion by the harbour, the **Skala du Port**, is open to the public (daily 8.30am–noon & 2.30–6pm; 10dh), and worth popping in to climb on the ramparts and enjoy the views.

Just outside the port area, is a line of **fish grill-cafés**, with wooden tables and benches laid out overlooking the main square. These are an absolute must for a stay in Essaouira (and some would say a must for every day of a stay), with a feast of sardines and other fish, freshly caught and grilled in front of you. Despite the initial hustle for custom, the atmosphere is relaxed and standards high.

The beach

Essaouira has beaches to the north and south. The main town beach, to the **south**, extends for miles from the town, often backed by dunes, out towards Cap Sim. On its early reaches, the main activity, as ever in Morocco, is football. There's virtually always a game in progress and at weekends a full-scale local league, with a dozen matches side by side and kick-offs timed by the tides. If you're a player, you'll be encouraged to join in, but the weekend games are fun just to watch, and on occasions half the town seems to turn out.

The southern beach also has a dozen or so **camel** men, offering rides up and down the sands, or out to the dunes. Most of them operate in pairs and they can be fiercely competitive for custom (they're not beyond galloping off as soon as they've enticed you to ride). So, if you have young kids, watch the scene for a while and be sure to pick someone you feel confident about – it's a long way to fall. You'll need to bargain for rates.

The beach to the north of town, known as the **Plage de Safi**, is good in hot weather and with a calm sea, but the water can be dangerous if the wind is up. It's reached from the north end of town by skirting left through a malodorous area, the reward being miles of often delightfully empty sand.

Bordj el Berod and Diabat

Walking further along the beach to the south, past the football and the crowds, you pass the riverbed of the Oued Ksob (note that you can't cross this at high tide) and come upon the ruins of an old fort, the **Bordj el Berod**. According to local mythology, this was the original Castle Made of Sand that inspired the track of that name on Jimi Hendrix's *Axis Bold As Love* album, and it is said that Hendrix played impromptu concerts here for his fellow hippies back in the old days. Nice though it would be to believe this, Hendrix stories in Essaouira want taking with a pinch or two of salt – *Axis Bold as Love*, for example, was released in January 1968, but Hendrix didn't visit Morocco until July 1969; he spent a week touring the country, of which a few days at most were in Essaouira. The fort is nonetheless an excellent viewing spot for the Iles Purpuraires, offshore, and their birdlife (see box, p.414). Inland you can see the ruins of a royal summer pavillion.

A little further south, inland through the scrub, is the small Berber village of **Diabat**. This was once a legendary hippy hangout, and local mythology has it that both Jimi Hendrix and Cat Stevens (a favourite in Morocco for having converted to Islam) spent time in the colony. These days, it has reverted to an ordinary Berber farming village but is about to be overwhelmed by a residential golf development.

Few venture beyond the Oued Ksob, from which an aqueduct once carried water to Essaouira, but a walk to Cap Sim and back is an all-day challenge. The majority of the walk is quite isolated and two tourists were attacked here in 2005. This may be an isolated and opportunistic incident but it's worth bearing in mind. Take plenty of water, take care with the tides and visit the *Auberge Tangaro* on the way back (see p.423).

Eating and drinking

With its fishing fleet and market, Essaouira offers a good range of cafés and restaurants – and a few of the upmarket ones are licensed to sell alcohol. However, for an informal lunch, or early evening meal, you can do no better than eat at the line of **grills** down at the port, an Essaouira institution, and cooking fish as fresh as it is possible to be. Finish off with a scoop of excellent Italian-style **ice cream** from *Gelateria Dolce Freddo*, on the corner of Place Prince Moulay el Hassan, at a mere 5dh a pop. The Superette la Plage, on Rue Lalla Amina, stocks a wide range of **groceries** and food items.

Essaouira doesn't have much by way of **nightlife** – it's a café more than a bar scene – but there are a few places where you can have a drink, namely the restaurants *Les Chandeliers* and *Chalet de la Plage*, (though the latter prefers customers to eat as well), *Le Mechouar* (next to *Hôtel Sahara*) and the seafront *Restaurant de la Plage* and *Café Mogador*, along with the hotels *Tafoukt* and *des Iles*; at the last of these, Moroccans gather to drink beer and play chess and draughts.

Dar Ayour, at 16 Rue de la Skala, is a relaxed café and *salon de thé* where young locals gather to play **billiards and pool**.

Les Arcades de Mogador 2 Av de l'Istiqlal. Small, busy restaurant serving delicious Moroccan fare always accompanied with a stereo playing funky Gnaoua, Arabic and French jazz music. There are some interesting pictures of old Essaouira on the wall. Open early 'til late. Cheap to moderate.

Café-Restaurant Bab Laâchour Bab Laâchour, by Pl Prince Moulay el Hassan ☎ 024 47 35 72. A café favoured by locals downstairs, with a more tourist-oriented restaurant on the floor above. The menu includes fish and tajines. Moderate.

Café-Restaurant Essalam 23 Pl Prince Moulay el Hassan ☎ 024 47 55 48. The cheapest set menus in town (28–40dh), and certainly value for money, though the choice is a little bit limited. The bare walls you will see small watercolours by Charles Kérival who often visits and paints in Essaouira. Born in Brittany, he discovered Morocco when the oil-tanker on which he was working visited Casablanca in 1956. Cheap.

Café-Restaurant Laayoune 4 bis Rue Hajjali ☎ 024 47 46 43. Recently refurbished and still a good place for tajines and other Moroccan staples in a relaxed setting with friendly service. Moderate, with tajine- and couscous-based menus at 58–78dh.

Chalet de la Plage Bd Mohammed V, on the seafront, just above the high tide mark ☎ 024 47 59 72. Built entirely of wood by the Ferraud family in 1893, the building is now a little gloomy and barnacled with marine mementos, but the seafood and sea views are truly memorable. Avoid lunchtime when day-trippers overwhelm the place. Licensed. Moderate to expensive, with 150dh and 180dh set menus.

Les Chandeliers 14 Rue Laâlouj ☎ 024 47 58 27. A well-established restaurant and wine bar run by a French family and offering both continental and Moroccan options. Licensed; dinner only. Moderate to expensive.

Chez Sam in the harbour ☎ 024 47 65 13. An Essaouira institution – a wooden shack, built like a boat, set seductively right by the waterfront in the harbour. Service can be a bit hit-and-miss but the portions are generous, the fish is usually cooked pretty well, there's beer and wine available, and fishing boats to watch through the portholes. Moderate to expensive, with set menus at 85dh, or 220dh with lobster.

Le Coquillage (Restaurant du Port) in the harbour ☎ 024 47 66 55. A seashell-bedecked competitor to the older *Chez Sam*, and offering a similar menu in slightly more refined surroundings. Moderate to expensive, with a three-course set menu at 90dh, four-course at 150dh, and four-course with lobster for 250dh.

Dar Baba 2 Rue de Marrakech, on the corner with Rue Sidi Mohammed Ben Abdallah (same street as *Hôtel Tafraout*, on 1st floor). Italian dishes: spaghetti, pasta, pizza. Cheap.

Dar Loubane 24 Rue du Rif, a stone's throw from Pl Chefchaouni ☎ 024 47 62 96. Upmarket restaurant on the ground-floor patio of an attractive eighteenth-century mansion. Moroccan and French cuisine, friendly service, interesting semi-kitsch decor and exhibits which are of interest. Live Gnaoua music takes place on Saturday evenings when it's advisable to make a booking. Closed mid Nov to mid-Dec. Moderate to expensive.

La Licorne 26 Rue Skala ☎ 024 47 36 26. An upmarket Moroccan restaurant serving some of the best traditional French and Moroccan food in town. The chocolate mousse is particularly recommended, but doesn't feature on the 135dh set menu. Expensive.

🏃 **Patisserie Chez Driss** 10 Rue Hajjali, just off Pl Prince Moulay el Hassan. Long established and one of the town's most popular meeting places. Delicious fresh pastries and coffee in a quiet leafy courtyard. Ideal for a leisurely breakfast. Cheap.

🏃 **Restaurant Les Alizes** 26 Rue Skala ☎ 024 47 68 19. Next to the *Hôtel Smara* and away from the mainstream, this restaurant has built up a good reputation for Moroccan dishes – choice is limited to an 85dh set menu, but everything is delicious. Wine is available; booking advised. Closed Nov.

Restaurant L'Horloge Pl Chefchaouni. Moderately priced Moroccan meals, standard and lacking imagination, but good value for money. Housed in a one-time synagogue.

Restaurant el Khaima Pl Chrib Atai, off Rue Laâlouj. Rather pricey meals in an upstairs room done out as a traditional tent (hence *Khaima*), set far back from the street, almost opposite the museum and on a square that it shares with

lock-up workshops. It's licensed, takes cards and stays open late. Moderate to expensive.
Restaurant La Petite Perle d'Essaouira 2 Rue el Hajjalli ☎024 47 50 50. A small place with low divan seating and generous servings of good traditional Moroccan cooking. Moderate, with set menus for 55–95dh.

Listings

Banks BCM, Banque Populaire and Crédit du Maroc are in the big open area just south of Pl Prince Moulay el Hassan; BMCE is just off the square to the north; Société Générale is on Av Okba Ibn Nafia; and WAFA is at 60 Av de l'Istiqlal, all with ATMs.

Bookshops Galerie Aide bookshop, 2 Rue Skala, run by a former New Yorker, has a small but good selection of English-language books and some nice antiques and bric-a-brac. There's a secondhand book store on Rue Sidi Mohammed Ben Abdallah by the turning for the *Hôtel Central* with a selection of used books in English, mostly pulps.

Car rental Of the big international firms, only Avis has an office here, at 28 bis Av Oued el Makhazine (☎024 47 52 70), and at the airport (☎024 47 49 26). Smaller, local firms include Dzira Location, 50 Bd Mohammed V (☎ & ☏024 47 37 16), and Isfaoun Rent-a-Car, 62 Bd Mohammed V (☎024 47 49 06, ⊛www.essaouiracar.com).

Festivals A dozen or so local moussems, fairs and festivals are held between March and October. The main event is the Festival d'Essaouira in late June, the main focus of which is Gnaoua music; see *Festivals and music* colour section. For further information, check the festival website at ⊛www.festival-gnaoua.co.ma. In October, the air rally commemorating the Aéropostale Service of the 1920s passes through Essaouira. An annual music festival is held each spring.

Hammam Hammam Mounia on Rue d'Oum Rabia near *Riad le Grand Large* is clean and tourist-friendly: women daily 12.30–6.30pm, men 6.30–10.30pm.

Internet access There are numerous Internet cafés on Av de L'Istiqlal, some open all day, every day. There is also Internet Club on Av du Claire, next to *Hotel Shahrazed*.

Post office The PTT is outside the ramparts on Av Lalla Aicha (Mon–Fri 8am–6pm; Sat 8am–noon), with branch offices in Rue Laâlouj and by the bus station (similar hours but closed for lunch at noon).

Shopping Despite its size, Essaouira rivals Marrakesh and Fes as a centre for attractive items, and it's relatively hassle-free. As usual, however, beware of tourist emporiums selling *trafika* (simulated antiques and fossils) – tiles with Hebrew lettering, supposedly old tiles from the Mellah, are a favourite scam here, and any shop selling them is probably worth avoiding. Hippy-style clothing is a good buy in Essaouira – a couple of shops on Rue el Hajjali are good for tunics and drawstring trousers. Thuya wood crafts are also good value (see p.418), and paintings by local artists are worth a look if you feel like spending a bit more (see box p.409). Argan oil and its associated beauty products are widely sold but relatively pricey: Argad'or, at 3 Rue Ibn Rochd (close to *Hôtel Cap Sim*) and shops on Rue Sidi Mohammed Ben Abdallah by the turning for the *Hôtel Central* are the best places to look for it.

Moving on

Leaving Essaouira for **Marrakesh**, there is a nonstop Supratours bus which leaves from a lane off Avenue Lalla Aicha three times daily (roughly at 6am, noon & 4pm; ☎024 47 53 17) and arrives at Marrakesh train station to connect with trains for Casa, Rabat, Meknes, Fes and Tangier; tickets should be bought from the nearby kiosk the day before, and you can get through tickets for the train too.

The best direct bus to **Casablanca** is the overnight CTM, which leaves Essaouira daily at 1am, arriving Casa at 6am. There's also a daytime CTM and a SATAS service; CTM is preferable, though it costs about 10dh more, as it takes you into the city centre. **Grands taxis** to Marrakesh, Casa, Safi and Agadir operate from a yard by the bus station, and are best caught early in the morning.

Royal Air Maroc run two **flights** a week to both Casablanca and Paris-Orly from Essaouira's airport, which is 15km south of town on the Agadir road

(☎024 47 67 04/05). A new terminal building is being built but at this stage there is no ATM or bureau de change, or much else for that matter. You can get there by grand taxi from the bus station (about 50dh for up to six passengers), or by bus #2 from Bab Doukkala (10dh). RAM does not have an office in town – for enquiries, call them in Casablanca on ☎022 32 11 22.

South of Essaouira

The main road south from Essaouira to Agadir (N1) runs inland for the first 100km or so, with just the occasional *piste* leading down to a beach or fishing hamlet scattered along the rugged, cliff-lined coast. Along this stretch there is just one resort, **Sidi Kaouki**, which has the reputation of being Morocco's best windsurfing beach, as well as providing a good wave for the stand-up surfers.

The region **inland** is known as the **Haha**, populated by Tashelhaït-speaking Berbers, and actually the westernmost range of the High Atlas. Its slopes are covered in **argan trees** (see p.621), which might have a goat halfway up, nibbling away at the fruit. Several tarred roads and *pistes* head into the hills from the coast road to come out on the Tizi Maachou road from Marrakesh to Agadir (see p.519).

Diabat, Sidi Kaouki and Cap Sim

The main road south from Essaouira crosses the river Oued Ksob upstream before joining the N1 (formerly P8) to Agadir. A turning to the right just before this junction takes you to Diabat by a metalled side road (see inset map on p.412.)

En route to **Diabat** and signposted from the main road is the *Auberge Tangaro* (☎024 78 57 35; ❼), an Italian-owned place that provides an alternative to staying in Essaouira if you have transport. Half-board is compulsory though it serves excellent meals, and the place is little used except at weekends, when groups of French and German windsurfers arrive from Casablanca and Marrakesh. Prices are steep however, especially considering that there isn't any electricity and the chic, rustic allure is starting to show signs of tiredness. Next door is a small **campsite**. The beach is a half-hour hike.

Back on the N1, a further 7km brings you to a side road signposted to **SIDI KAOUKI**. The beach here attracts **windsurfers** virtually year-round, and this small village looks set for mainstream development. Presumably in expectation of this, the government designated Sidi Kaouki as a showcase for its alternative energy strategies in rural areas and has installed wind generators – giant modern-day windmills – to supply up to 95 percent of the village's electricity.

For a village of only 120 or so inhabitants, Sidi Kaouki has an astonishing seven **accommodation** establishments, all of them set back 100m or so from the beach and signposted. Among them are *Résidence La Kaouki* (☎024 78 32 06, ⓦ www.sidikaouki.com; ❻ including breakfast) and its neighbour *La Pergola* (☎024 78 58 31; ❹ including breakfast), which both offer a range of comfortable en-suite rooms with hot showers. In a similar vein are the solar-powered *Hotel Villa Soleil* (☎024 47 20 92, ⓦ www.hotelvillasoleil.com; ❺ including breakfast) and the newer *Auberge de la Plage* (☎024 47 66 00, ⓦ www.kaouki.com; ❻ including breakfast). All of these hotels have restaurants serving lunch and dinner, though nonresidents are advised to pre-book.

Directly opposite the beach, at the southern edge of the village, are two **campsites**. *VHM Camping* is run by Essaouira-based surf company Magic Fun

Afrika (see p.417) and has hot showers and a restaurant but is only open during summer. The other site, *Camping Atlantic,* offers no more than a bit of shade and very basic ablutions, albeit with a million dollar view.

There are a number of **cafés** at the northern end of the beach. Light meals are also available at the Sidi Kaouki Surfclub (Ⓦ www.sidi-kaouki.com) – a two-storey "skyscraper" plonked right in front of the beach. They also rent out gear for both windsurfers and surfers. Near the beach is the original **Marabout of Sidi Kaouki**, which has a reputation for curing female sterility, and beyond that is **Cap Sim**, backed by long expanses of dunes.

Sidi Kaouki makes a good base for **camel trekking** along the coast south from Essaouira, which has a succession of fine sands and headlands. It's not a cheap option, but the vast, empty sands, blue-painted fishing boats, bird migrations, flowers and local hospitality all make for memorable walking, the heat is tempered by strong sea breezes, and the camels do the carrying. One guide who can organize this is Aït Idir Mohammed, BP 26, Asni (Ⓣ & Ⓕ 024 48 56 16). April to June and September to October are the best months for trekking, and you should allow about a week in total. Food and a mess tent are provided.

Twenty-six kilometres south of Essaouira, and accessible by local bus #8 from Bab Doukkala in Essaouira, at **Tidzi**, the Commune Rurale de Tidzi is a women's agricultural cooperative making high-quality argan oil for the food and cosmetics markets and *amalou,* a mixture of honey, almonds and argan oil. Grouped into an association – called Targanine – with another in the nearby village of Tamanar, these were Morocco's first argan oil producing cooperatives, bringing employment, business skills and literacy to more than 450 rural women. Riding on this success and subsequent world-wide publicity, a number of "displays" have popped up on the road into Essaouira from Marrakesh.

On towards Agadir

For off-road vehicles, the *pistes* south along the coast from Sidi Kaouki offer a mix of long strands, dunes and scenic headlands, with occasional blue-painted fishing boats. Eventually the main road (N1) is rejoined north of **SMIMOU**, a one-street town with a petrol station and a couple of café-restaurants. A few kilometres before Smimou, a metalled road which soon turns to *piste* leads west to **IFRANE**, one of the finest beaches.

Just south of Smimou, inland, lies the forested whaleback of **Djebel Amsittene** (905m). A challenging *piste* climbs to traverse the crest of this grand viewpoint, and descends not far from **Imi n'Tilt**, a busy Monday souk, and a recommended venture if you have 4WD. A little further south of Smimou, another scenic *piste* leads westward to **Cap Tafelney**, below which lies a curious village and a bay full of fishing boats.

The coast is rockier if approached from **TAMANAR**, a larger town with a few restaurants. Fifteen kilometres south, a surfaced road leads to **POINTE IMESSOUANE**, which used to be a picturesque little harbour with a few fishermen's cottages, but it has now changed beyond recognition.

Thanks to aid from the Japanese government, it is now a grand complex of apartments and (mostly empty) shops around a large square and modern fish market. Besides (or despite) this well-meaning development the village is still relatively unspoilt and worth a visit, especially if you windsurf or surf. No matter what swell, tide or wind condition prevails, the point's two bays should offer something for all. Two **surf schools**, Kahina and Planet Surf Morocco, and the unimaginatively named Surf Shop, which rents out secondhand surf gear, are all within fifty metres of each other down near the market. There are a

number of **cafés** offering, among other things, excellent grilled sardines.
Accommodation is presently limited to ⚲ *Kahina l'Auberge* (☏028 82 60 32,
Ⓦ www.kahinasurfschool.com; ❸), which has a prime site overlooking **Imoucha,**
the east bay, and a restaurant with good seafood, open to nonresidents. Three
kilometres to the north is the *Auberge Tasra* (☏028 82 05 97; ❸) and opposite is
a track leading to a large, open campsite overlooking the west bay. There are also
many **caves** in this limestone region.

A few kilometres beyond the roadside settlement of **TAMRI** (117km; see
p.623), the Agadir road rejoins the coast, passing a lagoon, which might detain
bird-watchers, and the fishing village of Taghazoute (see p.622) before the final
run to Agadir. Honey and bananas are on sale by the roadside, the latter to boost
your sense of arrival in the south.

Travel details

Trains

Note that Supratours buses connect at Marrakesh
for Essaouira, Agadir, Laayoune and Dakhla, at
Taïne Sidi Lyamani (on the Tangier line) for Tétouan,
and at Taourirt (on the Oujda line) for Nador, with
through tickets available from any train station.

Casablanca Port to: El Jadida (4 daily;
1hr 40min); Kenitra (25 daily, 1hr 30min) via
Mohammedia (20min) and Rabat (1hr); Rabat
(30 direct daily; 1hr).

Casablanca Voyageurs to: Mohammed V airport
(hourly 5am–10pm; 35min); Asilah (3 direct & 3
connecting daily; 5hr); Fes (9 daily; 4hr 30min);
Kenitra (12 direct daily; 1hr 30min); Marrakesh
(9 daily; 3hr 25min); Meknes (9 daily; 3hr 30min);
Oujda (2 direct & 1 connecting daily; 10hr); Rabat
(13 direct daily; 1hr); Settat (9 daily; 1hr); Tangier
(3 direct & 3 connecting daily; 5hr 40min).

El Jadida to: Casa Port (4 daily; 1hr 40min) via
Casa Voyageurs (1hr 30min). One service connects
at Casa Voyageurs for Marrakesh, 3 for Meknes and
Fes, 1 for Tangier (changing again at Sidi Kacem).

Kenitra to: Asilah (3 direct & 3 connecting daily;
3hr 25min); Casa Port (25 daily, 1hr 30min); Casa
Voyageurs (13 direct daily; 1hr 30min); Casablanca
Mohammed V airport (13 daily 5.30am–8.30pm,
changing at Aïn Sebaa; 2hr 10min); Fes (9 daily;
3hr); Marrakesh (8 direct & 1 connecting daily;
5hr); Meknes (9 daily; 2hr); Oujda (2 direct & 1
connecting daily; 8hr 40min); Rabat (38 daily;
30min); Tangier (3 direct & 3 connecting daily;
4hr 10min).

Rabat Ville to: Asilah (3 direct & 3 connecting
daily; 4hr); Casa Port (half-hourly 6.30am–8pm,
last at 9pm; 1hr); Casa Voyageurs (13 direct daily;
1hr); Casablanca Mohammed V airport (hourly
6am–9pm, changing at Aïn Sebaa; 1hr 40min);

Fes (9 daily; 3hr 30min); Kenitra (38 daily; 30min);
Marrakesh (8 direct & 1 connecting daily;
4hr 35min); Meknes (9 daily; 2hr 30min); Oujda
(2 direct & 1 connecting daily; 9hr); Settat (9 direct
& 1 connecting daily; 2hr); Tangier (3 direct & 3
connecting daily; 4hr 40min).

Safi to: Benguerir (2 daily; 1hr 50min) via Yous-
soufia (1hr 5min), connecting at Benguerir for
Casablanca (2hr 20min); Fes (6hr 50min);
Marrakesh (50min) and Rabat (2hr 25min).

Buses

Casablanca to: Agadir (9 CTM and 34 others
daily; 9hr), Beni Mellal (1 CTM daily & others
roughly every half-hour; 3hr 30min); Essaouira (2
CTM & 46 others daily; 7hr); Fes (10 CTM & 15
others daily; 5hr 30min); El Jadida (5 CTM daily &
others every 15min; 2hr 30min); Kenitra (3 CTM &
14 others daily; 2hr), Laayoune (2 CTM & 1 other
daily; 19hr); Marrakesh (9 CTM daily & others half-
hourly 4.30am–9pm; 4hr); Meknes (10 CTM & 5
others daily; 4hr 30min); Nador (1 CTM & 10
others daily; 12hr); Ouarzazate (1 CTM daily; 8hr
20min); Oujda (1 CTM & 15 others daily; 11hr);
Rabat (5 CTM daily & others half-hourly 6am–
8.30pm; 1hr 20min); Er Rachidia (1 CTM & 11
others daily; 10hr 15min); Safi (4 CTM & 30 others
daily; 4hr 45min); Settat (half-hourly 9am–6.45pm;
2hr); Tangier (4 CTM & 35 others daily; 6hr
30min); Tetouan (2 CTM & 23 others daily; 6hr);
Tiznit (4 CTM & 7 others daily; 11hr).

Essaouira to: Agadir (1 CTM & 43 others daily; 3hr
30min); Casablanca (2 CTM & 46 others daily; 7hr);
Marrakesh (2 Supratours & 15 others daily; 3hr
30min); Rabat (12 daily; 8hr 30min); Safi (2 CTM &
9 others daily; 3hr 30min); Tangier (1 daily; 14hr);
Taroudannt (3 daily; 10hr).

El Jadida to: Casablanca (5 CTM daily & others every 15min; 2hr 30min); Marrakesh (9 daily; 4hr); Oualidia (3 daily; 1hr 30min); Rabat (9 daily; 4hr); Safi (3 CTM & 9 others daily; 2hr 30min); Settat (4 daily; 2hr 30min).

Rabat to: Agadir (2 CTM daily & others hourly 8.30am–11.30pm; 11hr); Casablanca (5 CTM daily & very frequent private services; 1hr 20min); Essaouira (12 daily; 8hr 30min); Fes (4 CTM daily & others half-hourly 5am–7pm; 4hr); El Jadida (every 15min 6.30am–7pm; 2hr 30min); Marrakesh (3 CTM daily & others hourly 8.30am–11.30pm; 5hr 30min); Meknes (4 CTM daily & others half-hourly 5am–7pm; 3hr); Nador (1 CTM & 4 others daily; 9hr 30min); Ouarzazate (5 daily; 9hr 30min); Safi (16 daily; 6hr); Salé (frequent; 15min); Tangier (4 CTM daily & 35 others; 5hr); Tetouan (2 CTM & 18 others daily; 5hr).

Safi to: Agadir (1 CTM & 16 others daily; 5hr); Casablanca (4 CTM & 30 others daily; 4hr 45min); Essaouira (2 CTM & 9 others daily; 3hr 30min); El Jadida (3 CTM & 9 others daily; 2hr 30min); Marrakesh (17 daily; 2hr); Oualidia (1 CTM & 8 others daily; 1hr 25min); Rabat (16 daily; 6hr); Tangier (1 daily; 11hr).

Grands Taxis

Casablanca to: Fes (3hr 30min); El Jadida (2hr); Mohammedia (30min); Rabat (1hr 20min); Safi (3hr 30min); Tangier (5hr).

Essaouira to: Agadir (2hr 30min); Casablanca (5hr); Marrakesh (2hr 30min); Safi (2hr 30min).

El Jadida to: Casablanca (2hr); Oualidia (1hr); Safi (2hr).

Rabat to: Casablanca (1hr 20min); Fes (2hr 30min); Kenitra (1hr); Meknes (1hr 50min); Salé (15min).

Safi to: Casablanca (3hr 30min); Essaouira (2hr 30min); El Jadida (2hr); Marrakesh (2hr 30min).

Flights

Note that some flights within Morocco are a code share between Royal Air Maroc (RAM) and Regional Air Lines.

Essaouira to: Casablanca (2 weekly with Regional Air Lines; 50min).

Casablanca Mohammed V to: Agadir (3–4 daily with RAM, 1–2 daily with Regional Air Lines; 1hr); Dakhla (3 weekly with RAM, 2 weekly with Regional Air Lines; 3hr 15min); Essaouira (2 weekly with Regional Air Lines; 50min); Fes (3 daily with Regional Air Lines, 1 daily with RAM; 40min); Laayoune (3 weekly with RAM, 10 weekly with Regional Air Lines; 1hr 30min); Marrakesh (6–8 daily with RAM, 2 daily with Regional Air Lines; 40min); Nador (2 weekly with Regional Air Lines; 1hr 20min); Ouarzazate (1 daily with RAM, 4 weekly with Regional Air Lines; 1hr 10min); Oujda (1 daily with RAM, 2 weekly with Regional Air Lines; 1hr 30min); Tangier (3–5 daily with RAM; 1hr).

Marrakesh

CHAPTER 5 # Highlights

✳ **Djemaa el Fna** The most wonderful city square in the world, an open-air circus of snake charmers, acrobats, musicians and storytellers. See p.442

✳ **Koutoubia Mosque** The most perfect minaret in North Africa, simple but beautifully proportioned, and a classic piece of Almohad architecture. See p.444

✳ **Almoravid koubba** This tiny ablutions kiosk is the last remnant of the original city, and the only intact Almoravid building in Morocco. See p.452

✳ **Ben Youssef Medersa** Stucco, zellij tilework, and carved cedarwood mark this beautiful medersa. See p.453

✳ **El Badi Palace** The "Incomparable Palace", now an incomparable ruin. See p.459

✳ **Bahia Palace** The ideal of Arabic domestic architecture expressed in a nineteenth-century politician's mansion. See p.463

✳ **Majorelle Garden** A sublime garden, with cacti, lily ponds, and an Islamic Arts museum housed in a stunning pavilion. See p.466

✳ **Tanjia** Jugged beef or lamb, left to cook slowly in the embers, is the great speciality of Marrakshi cuisine. See p.471

△ Ben Youssef Medersa

5

Marrakesh

Marrakesh – "Morocco City", as early foreign travellers called it – has always been something of a pleasure city, a marketplace where the southern tribesmen and Berber villagers bring in their goods, spend their money and find entertainment. For visitors it's an enduring fantasy – a city of immense beauty, low, red and tent-like before a great shaft of mountains – and immediately exciting. It's known as the **Red City** from the natural red-ochre pigment that bedecks its walls and buildings, but there's certainly no shortage of other colours.

At the heart of it all is a square, **Djemaa el Fna**, really no more than an open space in the centre of the city, but the stage for a long-established ritual in which shifting circles of onlookers gather round groups of acrobats, drummers, pipe musicians, dancers, storytellers, comedians and fairground acts. However many times you return there, it remains compelling. So, too, do the city's architectural attractions: the immense, still basins of the Agdal and Menara gardens, the delicate Granada-style carving of the Saadian Tombs and, above all, the Koutoubia Minaret, the most perfect Islamic monument in North Africa.

Like all Moroccan cities, Marrakesh is a town of two halves: the ancient walled **Medina**, founded by Sultan Youssef Ben Tachfine in the Middle Ages, and the colonial **Ville Nouvelle**, built by the French in the mid-twentieth century. Each has its own delights – the Medina with its ancient palaces and mansions, labyrinthine souks and deeply traditional way of life, and the Ville Nouvelle with its pavement cafés, trendy boutiques, gardens and boulevards.

Unlike Fes, for so long its rival as the nation's capital, Marrakesh seems much more rooted in the present than the past. After Casablanca, it's Morocco's second largest city and its population continues to rise. It has a thriving industrial area and is the most important market and administrative centre of southern Morocco. This is not to suggest an easy prosperity – there is heavy unemployment and poverty here, as throughout the country – but a stay in Marrakesh leaves you with a vivid impression of life and activity. And for once this doesn't apply exclusively to the new city; the Medina, substantially in ruins at the beginning of the twentieth century, was rebuilt and expanded during the years of French rule and retains no less significant a role in the modern city.

The last few years have seen Marrakesh established as Morocco's **capital of chic**, attracting the rich and famous from Europe and beyond. Though the vast majority of its residents are poor by any European standard, an increasing number of wealthy visitors are taking up residence and their influence on the tourist experience is evident.

Marrakesh has **Berber** rather than Arab origins, having developed as the metropolis of Atlas tribes – Maghrebis from the plains, Saharan nomads and former slaves from beyond the desert. Once upon a time, Marrakesh was the entrepôt for goods – slaves, gold, ivory and even "Morocco" leather – brought by caravan from the ancient empires of Mali and Songhay via their great desert port of Timbuktu. All of these strands of commerce and population shaped the city's souks and its way of life, and even today, in the crowds and performers of the Djemaa el Fna, the nomadic and West African influence can still seem quite distinct.

Some history

Marrakesh was founded near the onset of **Almoravid** rule – around 1062–70 – and must have taken the initial form of a camp and market with a *ksour*, or fortified town, gradually developing round it. Though founded by the first Almoravid dynasty ruler, **Youssef Ben Tachfine**, who maintained both Fes and Marrakesh as bases for his empire, it was his son, **Ali Ben Youssef**, who made Marrakesh the dominant centre. The first seven-kilometre **circuit of walls** was raised in 1126–27, replacing an earlier stockade of thorn bushes. These, many times rebuilt, are essentially the city's present walls – made of *tabia*, the red mud of the plains, mixed and strengthened with lime.

Of the rest of the Almoravids' building works, hardly a trace remains. The dynasty that replaced them – the **Almohads** – sacked the city for three days after taking possession of it in 1147, but they kept it as their empire's capital.

With the 1184 accession to the throne of the third Almohad sultan, **Yacoub el Mansour**, the city entered its greatest period. *Kissarias* were constructed for the sale and storage of Italian and Oriental cloth, a new kasbah was begun, and a succession of poets and scholars arrived at the court – among them Ibn Rochd, also known as *Averroes*, the most distinguished of Arabic medieval philosophers, who was born in Cordoba (1126) and died in Marrakesh (1198). Mansour's reign also saw the construction of the great **Koutoubia Mosque** and minaret.

By the 1220s, the empire was beginning to fragment amid a series of factional civil wars, and Marrakesh fell into the familiar pattern of pillage, ruination and rebuilding. In 1269, it lost its status as capital when the Fes-based **Merenids** took power, though in 1374–86 it did form the basis of a breakaway state under the Merenid pretender Abderrahman ibn Taflusin.

Taking Marrakesh, then devastated by famine, in 1521, the **Saadians** provided a last burst of imperial splendour. Their dynasty's greatest figure, **Ahmed el Mansour**, having invaded Mali and seized control of the most lucrative caravan routes in Africa, had the **El Badi Palace** – Marrakesh's largest and greatest building project – constructed from the proceeds of this new wealth, and the dynasty also of course bequeathed to Marrakesh their wonderful mausoleum, the **Saadian Tombs**.

Under the **Alaouites** Marrakesh lost its status as capital to Meknes, but remained an important imperial city, and the need to maintain a southern base against the tribes ensured the regular presence of its sultans. But from the seventeenth to the nineteenth century, it shrank back from its medieval walls and lost much of its former trade.

During the last decades prior to the Protectorate, the city's fortunes revived somewhat as it enjoyed a return to favour with the Shereefian court. **Moulay Hassan** (1873–94) and **Moulay Abd el Aziz** (1894–1908) both ran their governments from here in a bizarre closing epoch of the old ways, accompanied by a final bout of frantic palace building. On the arrival of **the French**, Marrakesh gave rise to a short-lived pretender, the religious leader El Hiba, and for most of the colonial period it was run as a virtual fiefdom of its pasha,

T'hami el Glaoui – the most powerful, autocratic and extraordinary character of his age (see p.456).

Since **independence**, the city has undergone considerable change, with rural emigration from the Atlas and beyond, new methods of cultivation on the Haouz plain and the development of a sizeable tourist industry. The impressive **Palais des Congrès**, opened in 1989, has given Marrakesh international prestige, hosting national and international events. All of these factors combine to make Marrakesh Morocco's best-known city and, after Casablanca, the country's largest trading base and population centre, with around 850,000 inhabitants.

Arrival

Arriving at the **train station**, on the edge of the new town Guéliz, a petit taxi is a good idea, unless you fancy a fifteen-minute walk to the Guéliz hotels, or a longer walk or bus ride to the Medina; the taxi fare should be no more than 15dh to the Medina, less to hotels in Guéliz. Buses #3, #8, #10 and #14 run from the bus stop opposite the station to the Place de Foucauld, alongside Place Djemaa el Fna. The youth hostel is very close to the station – just five minutes on foot.

The **gare routière** (for long-distance bus services other than CTM or Supratours) is just outside the walls of the Medina by Bab Doukkala. Most long-distance collective **grands taxis** arriving in Marrakesh terminate immediately behind this bus station, though they may drop you off in front of it on Place Mourabiton. You can walk into the centre of Guéliz from the *gare routière* in around ten minutes by following Avenue des Nations Unies (to the right as you exit the bus station, then straight on bearing right). To the Place Djemaa el Fna it's around 25 minutes: follow the Medina walls (to your left as you exit the bus station) down to Avenue Mohammed V, then turn left. A petit taxi is about 10dh to the Djemaa el Fna, less to Guéliz. Alternatively, catch bus #16, from outside the station, which runs through the heart of Guéliz, or buses #3, #8, #10, #14 or #16, which stop directly opposite Bab Doukkala (though the bus stop is not obvious), and head south to the Koutoubia.

Supratours services from Essaouira, Agadir, and the Western Sahara arrive next to the train station, **CTM** services at their office in Guéliz. Grands taxis from the **High Atlas villages** of Asni, Imlil, Setti Fatma and Oukaïmeden arrive at their own *gare routière*, 2km southwest of Bab er Robb – a 15dh taxi ride from the Djemaa el Fna, 20dh to Guéliz.

The city's **airport** is 4km to the southwest. Bus #19 (20dh) leaves on the hour every hour from 7am to midnight bound for Place de Foucauld (by the Koutoubia) and Avenue Mohammed V (Guéliz). Petits taxis or grands taxis are a more comfortable option, though you will have to haggle for a reasonable fare – petits taxis in particular will try to overcharge you, but you should be able to get one into town for 50dh (the price on the meter, if they used it, would be under 20dh). Grands taxis currently charge a fixed rate of 60dh for up to six passengers for the trip from the airport to the Djemaa el Fna, double at night.

Arriving at the airport late at night, you won't always find the BMCE or Banque Populaire kiosk open to change money or travellers' cheques, but there are ATMs in the arrivals hall; taxis will in any case usually accept euros, and sometimes even dollars or sterling, at more or less the equivalent dirham rate, or you can have them call at an ATM en route (see p.478).

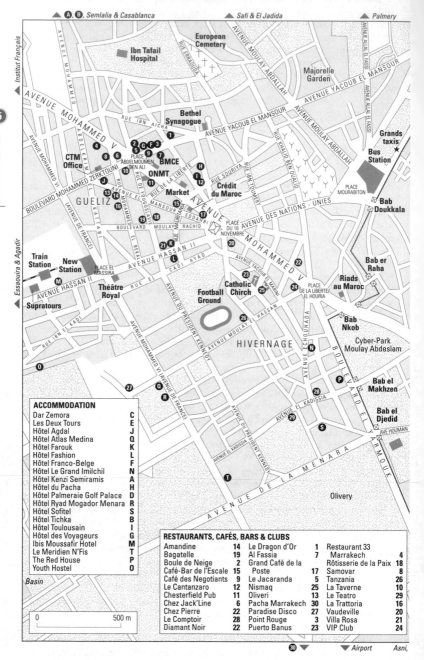

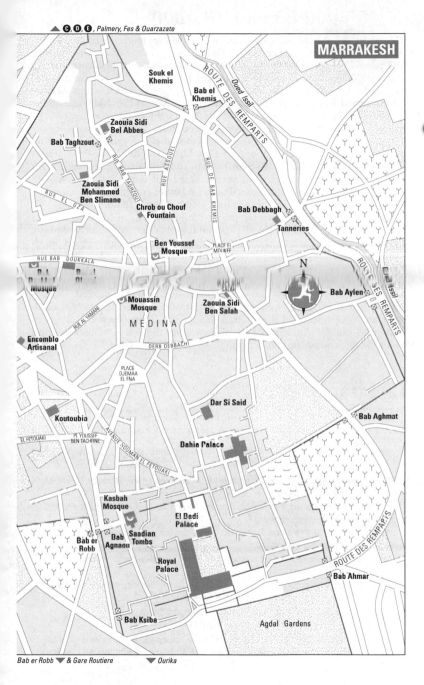

MARRAKESH

Souk el Khemis

Bab el Khemis

Zaouia Sidi Bel Abbes

Bab Taghzout

Zaouia Sidi Mohammed Ben Slimane

Chrob ou Chouf Fountain

Bab Debbagh

Tanneries

Ben Youssef Mosque

PLACE EL MOUKEF

RUE BAB DOUKKALA

Mosque

N

Bab Aylen

Mouassin Mosque

Zaouia Sidi Ben Salah

MEDINA

Encomblo Artisanal

DERB DEBBACHI

RUE AL YAMANI

PLACE DJEMAA EL FNA

Dar Si Said

Koutoubia

Bab Aghmat

EL FETOUAKI

PL. YOUSSEF BEN TACHFINE

Dahia Palace

Kasbah Mosque

El Badi Palace

Bab er Robb

Bab Agnaou

Saadian Tombs

Royal Palace

Bab Ahmar

Bab Ksiba

Agdal Gardens

Orientation and information

Despite its size and the maze of its souks, Marrakesh is not too hard to navigate. The broad, open space of **Djemaa el Fna** lies right at the heart of the **Medina**, and almost everything of interest is concentrated in the web of alleyways north and south of the square. Just to the west of the Djemaa el Fna is the unmistakeable landmark of the **Koutoubia** minaret – in the shadow of which begins **Avenue Mohammed V**, leading out through the Medina walls at Bab Nkob and up the length of the French-built new city, **Guéliz**. You might want to consider hiring a guide to explore the Medina, but given a decent map, it really isn't necessary.

The ONMT office in Marrakesh, also called the Délégation Régional du Tourisme, is on Place Abdelmoumen Ben Ali in Guéliz (Mon–Fri 8.30am–4.30pm; ℡024 43 62 39). It seems now to function mainly as a gallery for selling paintings, but the staff do keep a dossier of useful information with listings of hotels, campsites, car-rental firms and other contacts, and they may be prepared to answer questions if they have nothing better to do.

The best **website** for Marrakesh information is the I Love Marrakech site at ⓦ www.ilovemarrakech.com, with pages on the city's history, golf in Marrakesh, the latest weather forecast and Marrakesh news. The similarly named, much more commercially oriented ⓦ www.ilove-marrakesh.com has listings of upmarket hotels, riads and restaurants, plus write-ups and some photos of the main tourist sights.

Frankly, our own Rough Guide **city map** of Marrakesh, printed on tear-proof paper, is by far the best you'll get. It's not usually on sale in Marrakesh itself, and is best obtained abroad, though Librairie Chatr (see p.478) has been known to stock it. Among maps available locally, the best is Marocity's "Plan Guide Map", costing around 17.50dh.

City transport

It is a fairly long walk between Guéliz and the Medina, but there are plenty of **petits taxis**, which will take you between the two for around 10–15dh. There

---

Local bus routes

The following buses leave from Avenue el Mouahidine alongside Place de Foucauld, opposite *Hôtel de Foucauld*:

#1 along Av Mohammed V to Guéliz, then up Av Mohammed Abdelkrim el Khattabi (Route de Casablanca) to Semlalia.

#3, #8, #10, #13 & #14 all go to Bab Doukkala (for the bus station), then on down Av Hassan II past the train station.

#4 to Bab Doukkala (for the bus station), then swings by the Jardin Majorelle and on to Daoudiate swimming pool.

#5 to Bab Doukkala (for the bus station), then round the city walls past Bab el Khemis, Bab Debbagh and Bab Aylen to Bab Ahmar.

#6 and **#20** to Bab Ighli and the entrance to the Agdal gardens.

#17 and #26 to the Route de Fes for the palmery.

#19 circular route from the airport to Place de Foucauld, then north up Avenue Mohammed V, south down Avenue Mohammed Abdelkrim el Khattabi and back to the airport.

Sightseeing bus tours

If you don't have much time and you want to scoot around Marrakesh's major sights in a day or two, the **hop-on hop-off Marrakech Tour bus** (☎025 06 00 06, ⓦwww .marrakech-tour.com, though the website is currently only in French and Spanish) could be for you. Using open-top double-deckers, with a commentary in several languages including English, the tour follows two circular routes: the first tours the Medina and Guéliz, calling at Place de Foucauld (for the Djemaa and Koutoubia), Place des Ferblantiers (for the Bahia and El Badi Palaces, plus the Mellah), and the Menara Gardens; the second tours the palmery, following the Circuit de la Palmeraie. The Medina/Guéliz bus departs from outside *Boule de Neige* café in Place Abdelmoumen Ben Ali every 30min from 9am till 5pm; the palmery bus leaves from the same place every 80min from 9.50am till 3.50pm. You can get on and off where you like, and tickets (130dh) can be bought on board, or at Place Abdelmoumen Ben Ali or Place de Foucauld. They are valid for 24hr, so even if you start your tour after lunch, you can finish it the following morning.

are taxi ranks at most major intersections in Guéliz, and in the Medina in the northwest corner of Place Djemaa el Fna, outside the *Grand Hôtel Tazi*, and at the Place des Ferblantiers end of Avenue Houman el Fetouaki. **Bus** #1 and #16 also run along Avenue Mohammed V between Guéliz and the Koutoubia in the Medina (for other bus routes, see box opposite).

Petits taxis have meters, which they should use; most trips should cost around 10–15dh during the day, or 15–20dh at night, when there is a surcharge on the meter price. If a taxi driver doesn't want to use the meter, it is because they intend to overcharge you. If you get a petit taxi out to somewhere on the periphery, such as the palmery or one of the golf courses, and especially if the driver doesn't try to pull any stunts over the fare, it's worth getting a phone number to call them for the return journey.

In addition to taxis, there are **calèches**, horse-drawn cabs which line up on Place Foucault near the Koutoubia, and at some of the fancier hotels. These can take up to five people and are not much more expensive than petits taxis – though be sure to fix the price in advance, particularly if you want a tour of the town.

An alternative for exploring the more scattered city sights, such as the Agdal and Menara gardens or the palmery, is renting a **bicycle** or **moped** (see p.478); bicycles will cost around 100dh a day, mopeds more like 300dh. **Grands taxis** can also be chartered by the day for around 200dh – very reasonable if split between four people (the taxis take up to six passengers, but four is comfortable). Negotiate at the ranks in Djemaa el Fna or by the post office in Guéliz. By law grands taxis have to display prices for specified trips; these prices are per trip and not per person, as drivers sometimes claim.

Accommodation

The **Medina** has the main concentration of small, budget hotels, especially in the area around the Djemaa el Fna. It is also where you'll find most of Marrakesh's **riads**, usually hidden away deep in its backstreets. **Guéliz**, whose hotels tend to be concentrated in the mid range, is handier for transport, especially for the train station. Hotels in **Hivernage** and **Semlalia** are upmarket, in modern buildings with swimming pools, but they're pretty soulless.

Advance bookings are a wise idea, especially for the more popular places in the Medina. The worst times are the **Easter** and **Christmas/New Year** holiday periods, when virtually every decent place can be full to capacity.

Medina hotels and riads

Most of the hotel accommodation in the Medina is concentrated in the small area south of the Djemaa el Fna. The riads are more widely scattered, and can be found in just about every quarter of the walled city.

Budget hotels

The small hotels listed below are the pick of those available, but there are many others in the same small area, which may be worth a try if those we've recommended are full. All these are shown on the map on p.443.

Hôtel Aday 111 Derb Sidi Bouloukat ☎024 44 19 20. Friendly budget hotel, well kept, clean and pleasantly decorated. The rooms, grouped around a central patio, are small and most have only inward-facing windows. Shower facilities are shared (5dh), with hot water round the clock. Single rooms are half the price of doubles, making them a very good deal for lone travellers, and you can sleep on the roof for 30dh. ➊

Hôtel Arsete el Bilk Rue Bani Marine ☎024 44 31 13. An attractive alternative to the nearby *Gazelle* and *Ichbilia*, with well-kept little rooms, all en suite. Rates include breakfast and dinner. ➍

Hôtel CTM Pl Djemaa el Fna ☎024 44 23 25. Rooms are a decent size and clean but drab, and there's no hot water in the shared bathrooms, though en-suite rooms have hot showers. The hotel is above the old bus station (hence its name), now used as a car park, and handy if you're driving. Breakfast (included in the room rate) is served on the roof terrace, which overlooks the square, as do rooms 28–32, though that does of course make them noisy. ➋

Hôtel Challah 14 Rue de la Recette ☎ & ☎024 44 29 77. A good-value budget hotel with nice, fresh rooms around a large formal patio with orange trees and a fountain, though the bathroom facilities are shared (hot showers 10dh), and the roof terrace is nothing to write home about. ➌

Hôtel Essaouira 3 Derb Sidi Bouloukat ☎024 44 38 05. One of the most popular cheapies in Marrakesh – and with good reason. It's a well-run, safe place, with thirty rooms, hot showers for 5dh, a laundry service, baggage deposit and rooftop café. ➋

Hôtel la Gazelle 12 Rue Bani Marine ☎024 44 11 12, ✉hotel_lagazelle@hotmail.com. Well-kept hotel on a street with foodstalls and small grill cafés, with rooms around a covered patio – windows of downstairs rooms open onto the patio, those upstairs open to the outside. Some rooms have bathrooms, and there's a discount on the room price after three nights. ➌

Hôtel Ichbilia 1 Rue Bani Marine ☎024 38 15 30. Near the Mabrouk cinema, and well placed for shops, banks and cafés, with comfortable rooms off a covered gallery, some with private bathroom. Sometimes referred to as *Hotel Sevilla* (*Ichbilia* is the Arabic for Seville). ➌

Hôtel Medina 1 Derb Sidi Bouloukat ☎024 44 29 97. Clean, friendly and pretty good value, with an English-speaking proprietor and hot shared showers (5dh). In summer there's also the option of a cheaper (30dh) bed on the roof. ➋

Hôtel Nissam 76 Derb Sidi Bouloukat ☎024 38 60 81. A cheerful little place, with bright rooms around a pretty courtyard, ample enough to allow light into the rooms even though the windows all face inward. Bathroom facilities are shared but there's hot water 24/7. ➋

Moderate and expensive hotels

All these hotels are shown on the map on pp.450–451, unless otherwise stated.

Dar les Cigognes 108 Rue de Berrima, Medina ☎024 38 27 40, ⊛www.lescigognes.com. A luxury boutique hotel run by a Swiss–American couple in two converted Medina houses. It's done up in traditional fashion around the patio, but with modern decor in the rooms and suites. There's a library, a hammam, a Jacuzzi, a salon and a terrace where you can see storks nesting on the walls of the royal palace opposite (hence the name, which means "house of the storks"). Prices include breakfast. ➑

Dar Salam 162 Derb Ben Fayda off Rue el Gza near Bab Doukkala, Medina ☎024 38 31 10, ⊛www.dar-salam.com. A Moroccan family home which takes in guests, this is a true *maison d'hôte* as opposed to a riad, a place to relax and put your feet up rather than admire the decor. The food is similarly unpretentious – tasty home-style Moroccan cooking, like your mum would make if she were Marrakshi. ⑤

Hôtel Ali Rue Moulay Ismail; see map p.443 ☏024 44 49 79, ✉hotelali@hotmail.com. A popular hotel with en-suite rooms (heated in winter, a/c in summer), and dorm beds (60dh). Breakfast is included in the price, and there's a restaurant with all-you-can-eat buffet suppers, served on the rooftop terrace in summer. The hotel is used by groups heading to the High Atlas, so it's a good source of trekking (and other) information; it also changes money, and can arrange car, minibus or 4x4 rental. Consequently, at times it has the air of a transport terminal. Booking ahead is advisable, but so is checking your room before taking it (some are a bit whiffy). Prices include breakfast. ④

Hôtel de Foucauld Av el Mouahidine, facing Pl de Foucauld; see map p.443 ☏024 44 08 06, ℱ024 44 13 44. Rooms are a little sombre and some are a bit on the small side, but they're decent enough, with a/c, heating and constant hot water (with a choice of tub or shower). There's a roof terrace with views of the Koutoubia, and a restaurant with buffet suppers. The friendly staff can arrange tours, help with local information, and put you onto guides for High Atlas trekking. Prices include breakfast, and supper too in high season, when half-board is compulsory. ⑥

Hotel Gallia 30 Rue de la Recette; see map p.443 ☏024 44 59 13, ⊛www.ilove-marrakesh.com /hotelgallia. Beautifully kept hotel in a restored Medina mansion with immaculate en-suite rooms off two tiled courtyards, one with fountain, palm tree and caged birds. There's central heating in winter and a/c in summer. A long-term favourite and highly recommended. Book online, at least a month ahead if possible. Breakfast included. ⑥

Hôtel Islane 279 Av Mohammed V. ☏024 44 00 81 or 83, ℱ024 44 00 85. A very central location,

only a short walk from the Djemaa el Fna, facing the Koutoubia. The rooms are quite airy (though they have horrible laminated floors), and the views compensate for the traffic noise from rooms at the front. There is also a rooftop restaurant with great Koutoubia views. Breakfast included. ⑤

Hôtel La Mamounia Av Bab Jdid ☏024 44 44 09, ⊛www.mamounia.com. Marrakesh's most famous hotel, in palatial grounds, with full facilities, including a hammam and sauna, a pool (of course), several bars and restaurants, and a casino, plus 1920s Art Deco touches by Jacques Majorelle (of Majorelle Garden fame). Despite the history, the fame and all the trimmings, standards of service do not always match the price. At last check it was closed for a major refit, due to reopen in 2008. For a description of the gardens and some history of the hotel, see p.445. ⑧

Hôtel Sherazade 3 Derb Djama, Rue Riad Zitoun el Kedim; see map p.443 ☏024 42 93 05, ⊛www .hotelsherazade.com. Before riads took off big time, this place was already on the scene, an old merchant's house, prettily done up, that gets rave reviews from our readers. Besides a lovely roof terrace, the hotel offers a wide variety of well-maintained rooms at different prices, not all en suite. Run very professionally by a German-Moroccan couple, it's extremely popular, so book well ahead. ④

Les Jardins de la Medina 21 Derb Chtouka, Kasbah ☏024 38 18 51, ⊛www .lesjardinsdelamedina.com. A beautiful old palace transformed into a luxury hotel, its rooms set around an extensive patio garden with hammocks slung between the trees and a decent-sized pool. What the hotel really plugs, however, is its hammam-cum-beauty-salon where you can get manicured, pedicured, scrubbed and massaged till you glow. ⑧

🏃 **Jnane Mogador Hôtel** Derb Sidi Bouloukat by 116 Rue Riad Zitoun el Kedim; see map p.443 ☏024 42 63 23, ⊛www.jnanemogador .com. Set in a beautifully restored old house, with

Riad-booking agencies

Marrakesh Medina 102 Rue Dar el Bacha, Northern Medina ☏024 44 24 48, ⊛www .marrakech-medina.com. A firm that's actually in the business of doing up riads as well as renting them out, with a reasonable selection in all price ranges.

Marrakech Riads Dar Cherifa, 8 Derb Charfa Lakbir, Mouassine, Northern Medina ☏024 42 64 63, ⊛www.marrakech-riads.net. A small agency with only five riads; committed to keep it chic and authentic.

Riads au Maroc 1 Rue Mahjoub Rmiza, Guéliz ☏024 43 19 00, ⊛www.riadsomaroc .org. One of the first and biggest riad agencies with lots of choice in all price categories.

charming rooms around a lovely fountain patio, its own hammam, and a roof terrace where you can have breakfast, or tea and cake. It's run by the same management as the *Essaouira*, rather more upmarket, but still great value. ❺

La Maison Arabe 1 Derb Assebbe Bab Doukkala, behind the Doukkala mosque ☎024 38 70 10, ⓦ www.lamaisonarabe.com. Though not as famous as the *Mamounia*, this is Marrakesh's classiest hotel, boasting high standards of service in a gorgeous nineteenth-century mansion restored with fine traditional workmanship. The furnishings are sumptuous, as is the food (this was a restaurant before it was a hotel, and it even offers cookery classes –1600dh 1–2 people, 500–600dh per person for small groups). There are two

beautifully kept patios and a selection of rooms and suites, all with TV, minibar, a/c and heating, some with private terrace and Jacuzzi. There is no pool on the premises, but a free shuttle bus can take you to the hotel's private pool nearby. ❽

Villa des Orangers 6 Rue Sidi Mimoun, off Pl Youssef Ben Tachfine ☎024 38 46 38, ⓦ www .villadesorangers.com. Owned by the French firm Relais et Châteaux, this luxury establishment is officially a hotel, and not family-run, but it's a riad in the true sense of the word: an old house around a garden patio – two in fact – with orange trees and lots of lovely carved stucco. There's a range of rooms and suites, many with their own private terrace. The 3200dh price includes breakfast and light lunch. ❽

Riads

Marrakesh is where the **riad** craze started, and the number is growing all the time. Some are seriously overpriced, so it pays to shop around; those at the top end of the market tend to offer best value for money. Prices quoted for riads include breakfast. Unless otherwise stated, they are shown on the Medina map on pp.450–451. Though not officially classified as riads, the *Dar les Cigognes, Gallia, Jnane Mogador, Sherazade* and *Villa des Orangers* (see p.436, p.437 and above) are all worth considering too.

Bordj Dar Lamane 11 Derb el Koudia (Derb Kabbadj), off Pl Ben Salah ☎024 37 85 41. Easy to find from Pl Ben Salah (the arch leading to it has a sign painted over it), this is a Moroccan-owned riad in an interesting part of the Medina, far enough from the Djemaa el Fna to avoid the tourist throng, but near enough to be there in ten minutes when you want to be. The decor is based on traditional features such as painted woodwork, and there's a lovely flower-filled roof terrace. English is spoken. ❼

Dar el Assafir 24 bis Arset el Hamed ☎024 38 73 77, ⓦ www.riadelassafir.com. Located in a rather atypical part of the Medina, behind the town hall, this is a late nineteenth-century colonial mansion done out in colonial rather than traditional way. It's quite spacious, with two patios and a nice pool, singing birds in a little aviary and Belle Époque-style rooms with orientalist ornaments. ❻

Dar Mouassine 148 Derb Essnane, off Rue Sidi el Yumani ☎024 44 52 87, ⓦ www.darmouassine .com. The rooms are done out in classic Moroccan decor, the salon and the patio less so, though the latter has a fountain and banana trees. There are well-chosen and interesting prints on the walls, all rooms have CD players, and the better ones have painted wooden ceilings. ❼

Riad Bayti 35 Derb Saka, Bab el Mellah ☎024 38 01 80, ⓦ www.riad-bayti.com. A great old house, formerly owned by a family of

Jewish wine merchants in the Mellah, with that quarter's distinctive high ceilings and wide verandah giving a spacious feel. Run by a dynamic young French couple with warm modern decor that perfectly complements the classic architecture and the smell of spices wafting in from the market below. Their mint tea gets high ratings too; their lukewarm showers don't. They also offer safe childcare facilities. ❼

Riad Blanc 25 Riad Zitoun el Djedid ☎024 38 27 60, ⓦ www.riadblanc.com. An old Medina house located between Maison Tiskiwin and Dar Si Said, and restored with just enough stucco, carved cedar and zellij to be classic without going over the top. The rooms similarly manage to be stylish without looking over-designed. There's a plunge pool in the patio, a Jacuzzi on the roof, and an in-house hammam. ❼

Riad el Ouarda 5 Derb Taht Sour Lakbir, near the Zaouia of Sidi Bel Abbes ☎024 38 57 14, ⓦ www.riadelouarda.com. A stylish riad in a seventeenth-century house with lots of original features, including oodles of stucco, painted wooden doors and ceilings, zellij floors and lots of kellims. The rooms are warm but uncluttered, and the terrace has great views over Sidi Bel Abbes and the Medina. ❼

Riad Jonan 35 Derb Bzou, off Rue de la Kasbah ☎024 38 64 48, ⓦ www.riadjonan.com. Cosy British-run riad in the Kasbah with understated decor, lots of brick and terracotta tiles, Thai food and a very relaxed atmosphere. Due to expand into the house next door with a pool (covered and heated in winter) and rooftop Jacuzzi. ●

Riad Kaïss 65 Derb Jedid, off Rue Riad Zitoun el Kedim ☎024 44 01 41, ⊛www.riadkaiss.com. A luxury riad in a nineteenth-century house done out in quite an interesting contemporary Moroccan style – the light, modern decor seamlessly incorporates traditional features such as windows with stained glass in vivid primary colours. Rooms mostly surround a large open courtyard with orange trees, a fountain and recesses with divans to lounge on. There's also a large, cool salon, an in-house hammam, and a multi-level roof terrace with pavilions and a pool. ●

Riad Malika 29–36 Derb Arset Aouzal ☎024 38 54 51, ⊛www.riadmalika.com. Sumptuous decor – modern but with colonial and 1930s touches – bedecks this very stylish riad owned by architect and interior designer Jean-Luc Lemée. There's loads of checkered tiling, a lovely pool, a warm salon and plush bedroom furnishings. It's very popular and needs booking well ahead, if it's full, Jean-Luc runs another, almost equally good riad – *Dar Doukkala* – very nearby at 83 Rue Bab Doukkala. ●

Riad Omar 22 Rue Bab Agnaou; see map p.443 ☎024 44 56 60, ⊛www.riadomar.com. Reasonably priced riad located just off the Djemaa el Fna. It used to be a hotel rather than a private home, but it's been well done out and the room decor is light but attractive. Nonetheless, the real appeal of this riad is price and location rather than chic-ness or luxury. It is also child-friendly, with family rooms and babysitting services available. ●

Riad Sahara Nour 118 Derb Dekkak ☎024 37 65 70, ⊛www.riadsaharanour-marrakech.com. More than just a riad, this is a centre for art, self-development and relaxation. Art workshops in music, dance, painting and calligraphy are held here, with the emphasis on a cross-fertilization of European, African and Middle Eastern ideas; self development

programmes are available including those in meditation and relaxation techniques. Guests who wish to hold artistic happenings are encouraged. However, you don't need to take part in these activities in order to stay here; you can enjoy the calm atmosphere on the patio, shaded by orange, loquat and pomegranate trees. ●

Riad 72 72 Derb Arset Aouzal ☎024 38 76 29, ⊛www.riad72.com. A very sleek and stylish riad, with just four rooms, sparse but extremely tasteful modern decor, palms and banana trees in the courtyard and its own hammam (but no pool). The catering is Moroccan. Rates include breakfast and afternoon tea. ●

Riad Sindibad 413 Arset Ben Brahim, just inside Bab Yacout ☎024 38 13 10, ⊛www.riad-sindibad .com. Thoughtfully done up by its French owners, with Moroccan touches, the feel here remains predominantly European. The rooms, set around an intimate patio with a small pool, are comfortable and en suite, and there's a Jacuzzi and hammam on the roof terrace. The location is a bit of a way from the main Medina sights however. ●

Riad Zitoun 31 Derb Ben Amrane, off Rue Riad Zitoun el Kedim; see map p.443 ☎024 42 67 93, ⊛www.riadzinoun.com. A friendly little riad, run by a French–Moroccan couple. Not the most chic of its kind in the Medina, but very pleasant and set around a patio (covered in winter, open in summer) in a nicely refurbished old house. ●

🐾 **Riyad al Moussika** 17 Derb Cherkaoui, off Rue Douar Graoua ☎024 38 90 67, ⊛www.riyad-al-moussika.com. A gem of a riad, formerly owned by Thami el Glaoui, with absolutely gorgeous decor, all designed to exact specifications in traditional Moroccan style by its Italian owner. The resulting combination of Moroccan tradition and Italian flair is harmonious and beautiful – like a traditional Marrakshi mansion, but better. The walls are decked with contemporary paintings by local artists, and the owner's son, a cordon bleu chef, takes care of the catering – in fact, the riad claims to have the finest cuisine in town. ●

Guéliz

Hotels listed here are shown on the map on p.432.

Hôtel Agdal 1 Bd Mohammed Zerktouni ☎024 43 36 70, ⊛www.hotelagdal.com. One of the better Guéliz hotels, with a pool, bar and restaurant; well situated for the restaurants and cafés around Pl Abdelmoumen Ben Ali. Rooms are smallish but have a/c, satellite TV and balcony. ●

Hôtel Farouk 66 Av Hassan II ☎024 43 19 89, ⓔhotelfarouk@hotmail.com. Owned by the same

family as the *Ali* in the Medina, and housed in a rather eccentric building, with all sorts of branches and extensions, it offers a variety of rooms – have a look at a few before choosing – all with hot showers. Staff are friendly and welcoming, and there's an excellent restaurant. Breakfast included. ●

Hôtel Fashion 45 Av Hassan II ☎024 42 37 07, ⓔfashionhotel@menara.ma. Terracotta-tiled rooms and bathrooms, nicely carved black-painted wooden furnishings, reliable hot showers with a strong jet (a rarity in Marrakesh), and large windows grace the rooms at this promising new three-star. Breakfast is included but not exactly copious. ⑥

Hôtel Franco-Belge 62 Bd Mohammed Zerktouni ☎024 44 84 72. Decent but rather drab ground-floor rooms, some with shower, around a courtyard in what claims to be the oldest hotel in Guéliz, with hot water mornings only. ②

Hôtel du Pacha 33 Rue de la Liberté ☎024 43 13 27, ℱ024 43 13 26. A 1930s-built hotel with large if rather drab rooms, most around a central courtyard, with a/c and satellite TV. There's a good restaurant, but no pool. Breakfast included. ⑤

Hôtel Toulousain 44 Rue Tariq Ben Ziad ☎024 43 00 33, ⓦwww.geocities.com/hotel_toulousain. This

excellent budget hotel was originally owned by a Frenchman from Toulouse (hence the name), and has a secure car park and a variety of rooms, some with shower, some with shower and toilet, some with shared facilities. ③

Hôtel des Voyageurs 40 Bd Mohammed Zerktouni ☎024 44 72 18. This long-established budget hotel has rather an old-fashioned feel, but it's well kept, with spacious if rather sombre rooms and a pleasant little garden. ②

Ibis Moussafir Hotel Av Hassan II/Pl de la Gare ☎024 43 59 29 to 32, ⓦwww.ibishotel.com. Tasteful chain hotel located right by the train station, not the most exciting accommodation in town, but good value, with efficient service, a swimming pool, a restaurant, a bar in the lobby and good buffet breakfasts included in the rate, though you're better off taking lunch and supper elsewhere. ⑥

Hivernage

Hivernage is an area devoid of any interest but with a concentration of upmarket hotels, mostly used by package tours. The chain four- and five-stars have frankly rather amateurish standards of service in comparison with their equivalents abroad, and few people travelling independently bother with them nowadays as there are so many excellent deluxe riads in the Medina which are far more attractive. What some upmarket Hivernage hotels do offer, however, that riads do not, is wheelchair access; they're also more child-friendly, and have large pools. The hotels listed here are shown on the map on p.432.

Hôtel Atlas Medina Av Moulay el Hassan ☎024 33 99 99, ⓦwww.hotelsatlas.com. The Atlas chain's top offering in Marrakesh set in five hectares of gardens and plugged mostly for its spa facilities, which incorporate traditional Moroccan treatments. The lobby is very stylish, with Art Deco-style touches and Berber motifs; the rooms are quite plush, with a warmer feel, though still incorporating the same styles. Three rooms are adapted for wheelchair users. ⑧

Hôtel Le Grand Imilchil Av Echouhada ☎024 44 76 53, ℮hotel_imilchil@maroc.zzn.com. This well-run three-star is an oasis of tranquillity in a location near Place de la Liberté that's handy for both the Medina and the Ville Nouvelle. The swimming pool may be small but service is punctilious and the hotel is good value for the price. ⑥

Hôtel Ryad Mogador Menara Av Mohammed VI (Av de France) ☎024 33 93 30, ⓦwww .ryadmogador.com. Five-star (though really more like a four-star) whose facilities include a health club and three restaurants but, alcohol is banned from the premises. The lobby is done out in classic style, with painted ceilings, chandeliers

and a very Moroccan feel, and the receptionists wear traditional garb. Rooms, on the other hand, are modern, light and airy. There's a babysitting service, and four rooms are adapted for wheel-chair users. ⑧

Hôtel Sofitel Marrakech Rue Harroun Errachid ☎024 42 56 00, ⓦwww.sofitel.com. Quite a classy five-star incorporating classical elements into the design of both its exterior and its grand rooms, all done out in royal red. It also has 61 suites, and four rooms adapted for wheelchair users, plus two restaurants, two bars and a fitness centre with a sauna, Jacuzzi and hammam. ⑧

Le Meridien N'Fis Av Mohammed VI (Av de France) ☎024 33 94 00, ⓦwww.lemeridien.com. The rooms here are nothing special, but are equipped with satellite TV, a/c and heating. The public areas are quite tastefully decorated however, and the hotel boasts its own pool, hammam, sauna, fitness centre and crêche, plus five restaurants. Two rooms are adapted for wheelchair users. ⑧

The Red House Bd el Yarmouk opposite the city wall ☎024 43 70 40 or 41, ⓦwww.theredhouse -marrakech.com. A beautiful nineteenth-century mansion (also called *Dar el Ahmar*) full of fine stucco and zellij work downstairs, where the restaurant offers gourmet Moroccan cuisine.

Accommodation consists of eight luxurious suites – extremely chic and palatial – though European imperial rather than classic Moroccan in style. ⑧

Semlalia and the palmery

Semlalia might suit you if you have a car, or if you want to spend a good part of your time in Marrakesh lazing by the pool, with trips into the Medina by taxi (15–20dh). The two Semlalia hotels listed here are next to each other, about 3km out of town up Avenue Mohammed Abdelkrim el Khattabi (the Route de Casablanca), served by bus #1 from the Koutoubia. Further out, the **palmery** is peaceful and quite rural, though rather inconveniently located, and taxi drivers are very loth to use the meter when driving you there or back.

Dar Zemora 72 Rue el Aandalib, palmery ☎024 32 82 00, ⓦwww.darzemora.com. A luxury villa stylishly done out with a mix of traditional and modern features, a nice garden with a heated pool, a masseur on call, and a view of the Atlas from the roof terrace. All rooms have CD players, but not TV (except by special request). To find it take the next left (Rue Qortoba) off the Route de Fes after the Circuit de la Palmeraie, then the first right (Rue el Yassamin), fork left after 300m and it's 300m round the bend on the right. ⑧

Les Deux Tours Douar Abiad, Circuit de la Palmeraie, Palmery ☎024 32 95 25 to 27, ⓦwww.les-deuxtours.com. The *deux tours* (two towers) of the name flank the gateway to this cluster of luxury villas, designed by locally renowned architect Charles Boccara and located in rather a raggedy patch of the palmery, not signposted (take a turn-off to the east about halfway along the Route de la Palmeraie, signposted "Villa des Trois Golfs", then continue for about 400m, ignoring any further signs to the Trois Golfs). It's a beautiful, tranquil spot, with four rooms to each villa, all built in traditional Moroccan brick and done out in restful earth colours, each villa with its own little garden. There's a hammam, swimming pool, restaurant and bar as well as extensive shared gardens to wander or relax in. ⑧

Hôtel Kenzi Semiramis Triangle d'Or, off Av Mohammed Abdelkrim el Khattabi (Route de Casablanca), BP 595, Semlalia ☎024 43 13 77, ⓦwww.kenzi-hotels.com. A five-star hotel, part of the Kenzi chain which specializes in sports holidays – this hotel specializes in golf, running a shuttle service to the Amelkis golf course (see p.479). Expensive, but there are sometimes promotional rates. ⑧

Hôtel Palmeraie Golf Palace Circuit de la Palmeraie, off the Route de Casablanca, Palmery ☎024 30 10 10, ⓦwww.pgp.co.ma. Large five-star, some way out of town, set among wooded countryside with five swimming pools, plus squash and tennis courts, riding stables and, most importantly, its own eighteen-hole golf course. A favourite with Morocco's last king, Hassan II, though most tourists find it rather corporate and impersonal. ⑧

Hôtel Tichka Triangle d'Or, off Av Mohammed Abdelkrim el Khattabi (Route de Casablanca), BP 894, Semlalia ☎024 44 87 10, ⓔtichkasalam ⓐmenara.ma. State-of-the-art four-star hotel, with fine architecture and internal decor by American designer Bill Willis, including columns in the form of palm trees and, most notably, the use of a super-smooth, beautifully coloured plaster glaze called *tadelakt*, which was traditionally used in hammams to waterproof the walls, and whose use here by Willis made it massively trendy in Moroccan interior design. ⑦

Camping and youth hostel

There is no **campsite** in town, but there are two campsites to the north, and a **youth hostel** not far from the station.

Camping Caravanning Ferdaous 13km from the city centre on the Casablanca road (N9, formerly P7) ☎024 30 40 90, ⓕ024 30 23 11. Good facilities and fine for an overnight stay if using a car or campervan, but not really convenient as a base for exploring Marrakesh on foot.

Relais de Marrakech 10km from the city centre on the Casablanca road, opposite Grand Stade football ground ☎064 71 73 28, ⓦwww.lerelaisdemarrakech.com. Upmarket campsite, with a pool, and also permanent "nomadic" tents – choice of standard, superior or deluxe

doubles – as well as the option of pitching your own, or parking a campervan. ❹
Youth Hostel Rue el Jahid, Guéliz; see map p.432 ☎024 44 77 13. Friendly, quiet and sparkling clean, with a small garden. Useful first-night standby if you arrive late by train, just five minutes' walk from the station (8–9am & 2–10pm: HI cardholders given priority), with dorm beds (60dh) and double rooms, prices including breakfast. ❸

The Djemaa el Fna

There's nowhere in Morocco like the **Djemaa el Fna** – no place that so effortlessly involves you and keeps you coming back for more. By day it's little more than a market, with a few snake charmers, storytellers and an occasional troupe of acrobats. In the evening it becomes a whole carnival of musicians, clowns and street entertainers. When you arrive in Marrakesh, and after you've found a room, come out here and you'll soon be immersed in the ritual: wandering round, squatting amid the circles of onlookers, giving a dirham or two as your contribution. If you want a respite, you can move over to the rooftop terraces of the *Café de France* or the *Restaurant Argana* to gaze over the square and admire the frame of the Koutoubia.

As a foreigner in the Djemaa el Fna, you can feel something of an interloper. Sometimes the storyteller or musician will pick on you to take part or contribute generously to the end-of-show collection and, entering into the spectacle, it's best to go denuded of the usual tourist trappings – watches, belt-wallets, etc; **pickpockets** do operate. One scam popular in the past (though we haven't heard of it lately) involved women selling "silver" jewellery, and then giving a "present" to tourists who declined to make a purchase; the victim would then be surrounded by large male accomplices, accused of stealing the trinket, and forced to pay for it. The crowds around performers are also sometimes used as an opportunity to grope female foreigners, and by male Moroccans and gay male tourists for cruising.

Some say that tourists are now vital to the Djemaa's survival, though apart from the snake charmers, monkey handlers and water vendors (all of whom live

The development of the Djemaa el Fna

Nobody is entirely sure when or how Djemaa el Fna came into being – nor even what its name means. The usual translation is "assembly of the dead", a suitably epic title that seems to refer to the public display here of the heads of rebels and criminals. This is certainly possible, since the Djemaa was a place of execution well into the nineteenth century; the phrase, though, might only mean "the mosque of nothing" (djemaa means both "mosque" and "assembly" – interchangeable terms in Islamic society), recalling an abandoned Saadian plan to build a new grand mosque on this site.

Whichever is the case, as an open area between the original kasbah and the souks, the square has probably played its present role since the city's earliest days. It has often been the focal point for rioting and every few years there are plans to close it down and to move its activities outside the city walls. This, in fact, happened briefly after independence in 1956, when the new "modernist" government built a corn market on part of the square and tried to turn the rest into a car park. The plan, however, lasted for only a year. Tourism was falling off and it was clearly an unpopular move – taking away an important social focal point as well as eliminating a perhaps necessary expression of the past. As novelist Paul Bowles said, without the Djemaa el Fna, Marrakesh would become just another Moroccan city.

by posing for photographs), there's little that has compromised itself for outsiders. In many ways it actually seems the opposite. Most of the people gathered into circles round the performers are Moroccans – Berbers from the villages and lots of kids. There is no way that any tourist is going to have a tooth pulled by one of the dentists here, no matter how neat the piles of molars displayed. Nor are you likely to use the scribes or street barbers or, above all, understand the convoluted tales of the storytellers, round whom are gathered perhaps the most animated, all-male crowds in the square.

Nothing of this, though, matters very much, and should certainly not deter you from visiting. There is a fascination in the remedies of the herb doctors, with their bizarre concoctions spread out before them. There are **performers**,

Henna tattoos

Henna is a shrub (*Lawsonia inermis*) native to the Mediterranean region, whose leaves have been used as a hair conditioner and hair dye since at least the seventh millennium BC. The dried leaves are ground and made into a paste with lemon juice and sometimes other ingredients such as sugar. This can be applied to hair or skin and, after a few hours, will leave a rust-brown stain that can last for anything from two weeks to three months. In Morocco, Berber women in many regions stain their hands in different ways with henna, and a bride traditionally has her hands and feet decorated with a very fine henna design prior to her wedding. Henna "tattoos" of this sort are offered in many tourist areas, notably in Marrakesh's Djemaa el Fna. The colour of the design will vary according to your complexion, and will be less prominent if your skin is very dark (in which case, you might want a bolder design with heavier lines rather than something too filigree), but you should beware of preparations containing black henna, a toxic synthetic additive correctly called para-phenylenediamine or PPD, which is carcinogenic and can hypersensitize the skin, causing a nasty allergic reaction. If you do go for a henna "tattoo", especially in the Djemaa, agree the price beforehand.

too, whose appeal is universal. The square's acrobats, itinerants from Tazeroualt (the region around Tighmi; see p.652), have for years supplied the European circuses – though they are perhaps never so spectacular as here, thrust forward into multiple somersaults and contortions in the late afternoon heat. By day too, you'll see sad-looking trained monkeys, snake charmers and, dressed in their magnificent red regalia, the water sellers.

In the evening, these give way to storytellers and above all – the Djemaa's enduring sound – dozens of **musicians** playing all kinds of instruments. Late at night, when only a few people are left in the square, you encounter individual players, plucking away at their *ginbris,* the skin-covered two- or three-string guitars. Earlier in the evening, there are full groups: the *Aissaoua*, playing oboe-like *ghaitahs* next to the snake charmers; Andalous groups, with their *ouds* and violins; and the Gnaoua trance-healers who beat out hour-long hypnotic rhythms with iron clanging castanets, and pound tall drums with long curved sticks.

For refreshment, stalls offer orange and grapefruit juice (but have it squeezed in front of you if you don't want it adulterated), while neighbouring handcarts are piled high with dates, dried figs, almonds and walnuts, especially delicious in winter when they are freshly picked in the surrounding countryside. As dusk falls, the square becomes a huge open-air dining area, packed with stalls lit by gas lanterns, and the air is filled with wonderful smells and plumes of cooking smoke spiralling up into the night (see box, p.470).

The Koutoubia

The absence of architectural features on the Djemaa el Fna serves to emphasize the drama of the **Koutoubia Minaret**. Nearly seventy metres high and visible for miles on a clear morning, this is the oldest of the three great Almohad towers (the others are the Hassan Tower in Rabat and the Giralda in Seville) and the most complete. Its pleasing proportions – a 1:5 ratio of width to height – established the classic Moroccan design.

Completed under Sultan Yacoub el Mansour (1184–99), work on the minaret probably began shortly after the Almohad conquest of the city, around 1150. It displays many of the features that were to become widespread in Moroccan architecture – the wide band of ceramic inlay near the top, the pyramid-shaped, castellated *merlons* (battlements) rising above it, the use of *darj w ktarf* ("cheek and shoulder"; see *Moroccan architecture* colour section) and other motifs – and it also established the alternation of patterning on different faces. Here, the top floor is similar on each of the sides but the lower two are almost eccentric in their variety. The semicircle of small lobed arches on the middle niche of the southeast face was to become the dominant decorative feature of Almohad gates. At the summit are three great balls made of copper – the subject of numerous legends, mostly of supernatural interventions to keep away thieves. They are thought to have originally been made of gold, the gift of the wife of Yacoub el Mansour, presented as penance for breaking her fast for three hours during Ramadan.

Close to the arches, the stones of the main body of the tower become slightly smaller, which seems odd today, but not originally, when the whole minaret was covered with plaster and painted, as on the Kasbah Mosque (see p.459). There was talk about restoring this on the Koutoubia back in 2000, but the authorities settled for a straight clean-up – to stunning effect, especially when it's floodlit at night. At the same time, archeologists excavated the original mosque, which predates the tower, confirming that it had had to be rebuilt to correct its alignment with Mecca.

Alongside the mosque, and close to Avenue Mohammed V, is the **tomb of Fatima Zohra** in a white *koubba*. She was the daughter of a seventeenth-century religious leader and tradition has it that she was a woman by day and a white dove by night; women still dedicate their children to her in the belief that her blessing will protect them.

To the south and west of the Koutoubia are the **Koutoubia Gardens**, attractively laid out with pools and fountains, roses, orange trees and palms, very handy for an afternoon stroll, and giving excellent views of the Koutoubia, especially when it is floodlit at night.

Hôtel La Mamounia

West of the Koutoubia, it's worth having a look round the gardens of the luxurious **Hôtel La Mamounia**, though it was closed at the time of writing for renovations (expected to reopen in 2008). Walled from the outside world, yet only ten minutes' walk from the Djemaa el Fna, these were once royal grounds, laid out by the Saadians with a succession of pavilions. Today they're slightly Europeanized in style but have retained the traditional elements of shrubs and walkways.

For the cost of a drink or some tea on the terrace – the latter not cripplingly exorbitant – you can sit and admire the surroundings. Visitors are not supposed to enter wearing shorts or jeans, and the swimming pool is reserved strictly for residents.

Usually open only to hotel residents, the **Winston Churchill suite** is preserved as visited by its namesake. There are editions of Churchill's books on the shelves, a truly sultan-like bed (and smaller sleeping quarters for his manservant) and photographs of him painting in the gardens. Churchill was a frequent visitor to Marrakesh from the 1930s to the 1950s, and he thought the *Mamounia* gardens were, as he remarked when he was there with Franklin D. Roosevelt in 1943, the loveliest spot in the whole world. Significantly, it was here that Churchill painted his only picture during World War II.

Even though the hotel has been rebuilt and enlarged since Churchill's day, it's not hard to understand the lasting appeal. Decoratively, it is of most interest for the 1920s Art Deco touches of **Jacques Majorelle** (see p.466), and their enhancements, in 1986, by King Hassan II's then-favourite designer, **André Paccard**.

The souks and northern Medina

It is spicy in the souks, and cool and colourful. The smell, always pleasant, changes gradually with the nature of the merchandise. There are no names or signs; there is no glass . . . You find everything – but you always find it many times over.

Elias Canetti: The Voices of Marrakesh

The **souks** of Marrakesh sprawl immediately north of Djemaa el Fna. They seem vast the first time you venture in, and almost impossible to navigate, though in fact the area that they cover is pretty compact. A long, covered street, **Rue Souk Smarine**, runs for half their length and then splits into two lanes – **Souk el Attarin** and **Souk el Kebir**. Off these are virtually all the individual souks: alleys and small squares devoted to specific crafts, where you can often watch part of the production process. At the top of the main area of souks, too, you can visit the Saadian **Ben Youssef Medersa** – the most important monument in the northern half of the Medina and arguably the finest building in the city after the Koutoubia Minaret.

If you are staying for some days, you'll probably return often to the souks – and this is a good way of taking them in, singling out a couple of specific crafts or products to see, rather than being swamped by the whole. To get to grips with the general layout, though, you might find it useful to walk round the whole area once with a **guide** (see box below), but it's certainly not essential: with a reasonable map, you can quite easily navigate the souks on your own, and besides, getting a little bit lost is all part of the fun.

The most interesting **times** to visit are in the early morning (6.30–8am) and late afternoon, at around 4 to 5pm, when some of the souks auction off goods to local traders. Later in the evening, most of the stalls are closed, but you can wander unharassed to take a look at the elaborate decoration of their doorways and arches; those stalls that stay open, until 7 or 8pm, are often more amenable to bargaining at the end of the day.

The main souks

On the corner of Djemaa el Fna itself there is a small potters' souk, but the main market area begins a little further beyond this. Its **entrance** is initially confusing. Standing in front of the *Café de France*, look across the street and you'll see the *Terraces de l'Alhambra* (see p.469). The lane straight ahead of you leads to the Souk Ableuh, dominated by stalls selling olives. Continue through

Guides

Official guides (150dh for half a day) can be arranged at the ONMT or large hotels; unofficial ones are rare now following police clampdowns, but may still occasionally offer their services around the Djemaa el Fna, and in general are best avoided. Some guides are fine, but others escort you into shop after shop that you don't want to visit. Since entering with a guide will always raise the price of anything you buy, it's always best to leave any shopping until you are guide-free, and it's worth specifying in advance that you don't want to visit any shops, though your guide may not like this. Sometimes hustlers may offer to take you to a "Berber market", supposedly open "only today"; in fact, all the main souks are open every day, though they're quiet on Friday mornings and some shops close on Friday afternoons. Even the big Souk el Khemis (the Thursday Market, held outside Bab Debbagh) now operates most days of the week.

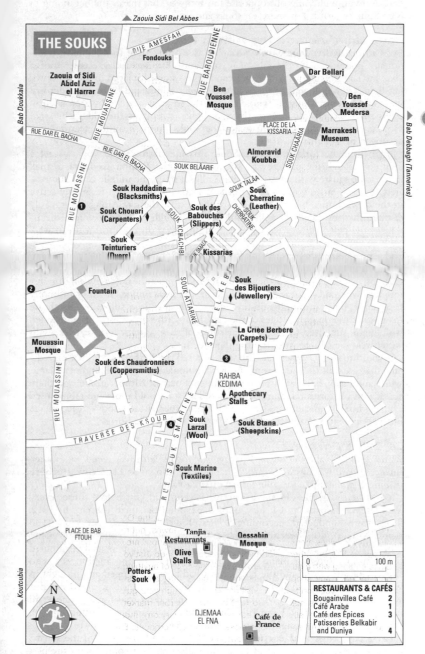

THE SOUKS

Zaouia Sidi Bel Abbes

RUE AMESFAH

RUE BAROUDIENNE

Fondouks

Bab Doukkala

Zaouia of Sidi
Abdel Aziz
el Harrar

Ben
Youssef
Mosque

Dar Bellarj

Ben
Youssef
Medersa

RUE MOUASSINE

RUE DAR EL BACHA

RUE DAR EL BACHA

PLACE DE LA
KISSARIA

SOUK CHAARIA

Marrakesh
Museum

Bab Debbagh (Tanneries)

SOUK BELÁARIF

Almoravid
Koubba

RUE MOUASSINE

SOUK TALÁA

❶

Souk Haddadine
(Blacksmiths)

Souk Chouari
(Carpenters)

SOUK KCHACHBI

Souk des
Babouches
(Slippers)

Souk
Cherratine
(Leather)

SOUK
CHERRATINE

Souk
Teinturiers
(Dyers)

KSMARA

Kissarias

❷

Fountain

SOUK EL KEBIR

Souk
des Bijoutiers
(Jewellery)

SOUK ATTARINE

Mouassin
Mosque

La Criée Berbère
(Carpets)

❸

Souk des Chaudronniers
(Coppersmiths)

RUE MOUASSINE

RAHBA
KEDIMA

Apothecary
Stalls

RUE SOUK SMARINE

TRAVERSE DES KSOUR

❹

Souk
Larzal
(Wool)

Souk Btana
(Sheepskins)

Souk Marine
(Textiles)

PLACE DE BAB
FTOUH

Tanjia
Restaurants

Qessabin
Mosque

Olive
Stalls

Potters'
Souk

N

Koutoubia

DJEMAA
EL FNA

Café de
France

0   100 m

RESTAURANTS & CAFÉS

Bougainvillea Café	2
Café Arabe	1
Café des Épices	3
Patisseries Belkabir and Duniya	4

here and you will come out opposite the archway that marks the beginning of Rue Souk Smarine. For more on souks and shopping see p.476.

Souk Smarine and the Rahba Kedima

Busy and crowded, **Rue Souk Smarine** is an important thoroughfare, traditionally dominated by the sale of textiles and clothing. Today, classier tourist "bazaars" are moving in, with American Express signs displayed in the windows, but there are still dozens of shops in the arcades selling and tailoring traditional shirts and kaftans. Along its whole course, the street is covered by a broad, iron trellis that restricts the sun to shafts of light; it replaces the old rush (*smar*) roofing, which along with many of the souks' more beautiful features was destroyed by a fire in the 1960s.

Just before the fork at its end, Souk Smarine narrows and you can get a glimpse through the passageways to its right of the **Rahba Kedima**, a small ramshackle square with a few vegetable stalls set up in the middle of it. Immediately to the right, as you go in, is **Souk Larzal**, a wool market feverishly active in the dawn hours, but closed most of the rest of the day. Alongside it, easily distinguished by smell alone, is **Souk Btana**, which deals with whole sheepskins – the pelts laid out to dry and then displayed on the roof. You can walk up here and take a look at how the skins are treated.

The most interesting aspect of Rahba Kedima, however, is the **apothecary stalls** grouped round the near corner of the square. These sell all the standard traditional cosmetics – earthenware saucers of cochineal (*kashiniah*) for liprouge, powdered *kohl* (traditionally made of stibnite, a mineral form of antimony trisulphide, but commonly substituted with cheaper lead sulphide – both are toxic) for darkening the edges of the eyes, henna (the only cosmetic unmarried women are supposed to use) and the sticks of *suak* (walnut root or bark) with which you see Moroccans cleaning their teeth.

In addition to such essentials, the stalls also sell the herbal and animal ingredients that are still in widespread use for manipulation, or spellbinding. Magic, white and black, has always been very much a part of Moroccan life, and there are dozens of stories relating to its effects. The stalls hold roots and tablets used as aphrodisiacs, and there are stranger and more specialized goods – dried pieces of lizard and stork, fragments of beaks, talons and gazelle horns.

La Criée Berbère

At the end of Rahba Kedima, a passageway to the left gives access to another, smaller square – a bustling, carpet-draped area known as **La Criée Berbère** (the Berber auction), also called the **Souk Zrabia**.

It was here that the old **slave auctions** were held, just before sunset every Wednesday, Thursday and Friday, until the French occupied the city in 1912. They were conducted, according to travel writer Budgett Meakin's 1900 account (see p.770), "precisely as those of cows and mules, often on the same spot by the same men . . . with the human chattels being personally examined in the most disgusting manner, and paraded in lots by the auctioneers, who shout their attractions and the bids". Most had been kidnapped and brought in with the caravans from Mali, travelling on foot – those too weak to make it were left to die en route. Meakin saw two small boys sold for £5 apiece, an eight-year-old girl for £3 and 10 shillings and a "stalwart negro" went for £14; a beauty, he was told, might fetch £130 to £150.

These days, **rugs and carpets** are about the only things sold in the square, and if you have a good deal of time and willpower you could spend the best part of a day here while endless (and often identical) stacks are unfolded and displayed before you. Some of the most interesting are the Berber rugs from the High Atlas – bright, geometric designs that look very different after being laid out on the roof and bleached by the sun. The dark, often black, backgrounds usually signify rugs from the Glaoui country, up towards Telouet; the reddish-backed carpets are from Chichaoua, a small village nearly halfway to Essaouira, and are also pretty common.

Around the kissarias

Cutting back to **Souk el Kebir**, which by now has taken over from the Smarine, you emerge at the **kissarias**, the covered market at the heart of the souks. The goods here, apart from the many and sometimes imaginative *couvertures* (blankets), aren't that interesting; the *kissarias* traditionally sell the more expensive products, which today means a sad predominance of Western designs and imports. Off to their right, at the southern end of the *kissarias*, is **Souk des Bijoutiers**, a modest jewellers' lane, which is much less varied than the one established in the Mellah (see p.461) by Jewish craftsmen. At the northern end is a convoluted web of alleys that comprise the **Souk Cherratin**, essentially a leather workers' souk (with dozens of purse-makers and sandal cobblers), though it's interspersed with smaller alleys and souks of carpenters, sieve-makers and even a few tourist shops. If you bear left through this area and then turn right (or vice versa), you should arrive at Place de la Kissaria, an open space surrounded by the Almoravid Koubba (see p.452), the Marrakesh Museum (see p.452), and the mighty Ben Youssef Mosque; the medersa (see p.453) is off to its east.

The Dyers' Souk and around

Taking the earlier left fork along **Souk el Attarin** – the spice and perfume souk – brings you out on the other side of the **kissarias** and the long lane of the **Souk des Babouches** (slipper-makers) or **Souk Smata**.

The main attraction in this area is the little **Souk des Teinturiers** – the dyers' souk. To reach it, turn left along the first alley you come to after the Souk des Babouches. Working your way down this lane (which comes out in a square by the Mouassin Mosque), look to your right and you'll see the entrance to the souk about halfway down – its lanes rhythmically flash with bright skeins of wool, hung from above. If you have trouble finding it, just follow the first tour group you see.

North of here sprawls the main section of **carpenters'** workshops, **Souk Chouari** – with their beautiful smell of cedar – and beyond them the **Souk Haddadine** of blacksmiths – whose sounds you'll hear long before arriving.

West of the dyers' souk, the street widens out into a square opposite an elaborate triple-bayed **fountain** adjoining the Mouassin Mosque. Built in the mid-sixteenth century under the prolific Saadian builder, Abdallah el Ghalib, it is one of many such fountains in Marrakesh with a basin for humans set next to two larger troughs for animals; its installation was a pious act, directly sanctioned by the Koran in its charitable provision of water for men and beasts. To get back to the Djemaa el Fna from here, continue on past the Mouassin Mosque and take a left down Rue Mouassine. The coppermakes' souk, **Souk des Chaudronniers**, is just to the east of this road as you descend.

Around Place de la Kissaria

At the northern end of the souks area, is **Place de la Kissaria**, an open space surrounded by important public buildings. Its north side is dominated by the **Ben Youssef Mosque**, successor to an original put up by the city's Almoravid

Palmery ▶

Palmery ▶

Guéliz ▼

Guéliz ▼

RESTAURANTS

Café-Restaurant el Badi	10
Café Restaurant Maryland	8
Dar Marjana	2
Dar Mima	5
Palais Gharnata	6
Le Pavillon	3
Pizzeria Portofino	K
Pizzeria Venezia	7
Restaurant el Bahia	K
Restaurant Yacout	1
Riad des Mers	B
La Rotunda	11
Le Tanjia	9
Le Tobsil	4

ACCOMMODATION

Bordj Dar Lamane	J
Dar el Assafir	G
Dar les Cigognes	R
Dar Mouassine	I
Dar Salam	K
Hôtel Islane	M
Hôtel La Mamounia	F
La Maison Arabe	T
Les Jardins de la Medina	H
Riad 72	Q
Riad Bayti	N
Riad Blanc	S
Riad Jonan	P
Riad Kaïss	A
Riad el Ouarda	B
Riad Sahara Nour	D
Riad Sindibad	L
Riyad al Moussika	O
Villa des Orangers	

ROUTE DES REMPARTS

Bab Kechich

Bab el Khemis

RUE BAB EL KHEMIS

RUE ASSOUEL

Thursday Market

Bouiba al Layadi

KAA EL MECHRA

RUE DE SIDI GHALEM

Zaouia of Sidi Bel Abbès

RUE EL ABBES

Moulay Rachid Fountain

Bab Inane Bel Abbès

Bab Arset Ben Brahim

Taghzout

RUE DE BAB TAGHZOU

Zaouia of Sidi Mohammed Ben Slimane

RUE SIDI BEN SLIMANE

Chrob ou Chouf Fountain

Tomb of Sidi Abdel Aziz

Ben Youssef Mosque

Ben Youssef Medersa

Marrakesh Museum

PLACE BEN YOUSSEF

RUE SIDI BOU HABBA

RUE BAB DEBBAGH

Bab Debbagh

TANNERIES

RUE ESSEBTIYNE

Zaouia of Sidi Ben Salah

SOUKS

SOUK EL KEBIR

SOUK SEMMARINE

RAHBA KEDIMA

RUE MOUASSINE

Mouassin Mosque

Dar el Glaoui

RUE BAB DOUKKALA

RUE DE BAB DOUKKALA

RUE DE BAB EL ABOUS

Bab Yacout

Grands Taxis

Bab Moussoufia

Bab Boutouil

RUE FIGA

RUE FATIMA ZOHRA

RUE JEBEL LAKHDAR

Doukkala Mosque

Ensemble Artesanal

Town Hall

RUE EL ADALA

AVENUE ALLAL EL FASSI

AVENUE DES NATIONS UNIES

Gare Routière

RUE BOUTOUIL

Bab Doukkala

Place Mourabiton

Bab er Raha

Bab Nkob

Cyber-Park Moulay Abdeslam

Majorelle Garden

Buses to Koutoubia

AV MOULAY ABDALLAH

AVENUE DES NATIONS UNIES

PLACE DE LA LIBERTÉ

RUE MOHAMMED EL MELLAKH

AVENUE MOHAMMED V

AVENUE AHMED OUAGALLAH

Bab Aylem

MARRAKESH MEDINA

N

ROUTE DES REMPARTS

ROUTE DES REMPARTS

Caid Ayad Mosque

Bab Aylen

RUE EL KADI AYAD

Tomb of Sidi Youssef Ben Ali

Bab Aghmat

RUE BA HMAD

RUE RIAD ZITOUN EL DJEDID

RUE SIDI BOULBAD

BEN CHEGRA

RUE IMAM EL EZZALI

Miâara Jewish Cemetery

Bahia Palace

Bab Hmar

RUE DE BAB HMAR

RUE DABBACHI

Dar Si Said

Maison Tiskiwin

Lazama Synagogue

MELLA

Berrima Mosque

Jardin Agdal

See Souks map

RUE RIAD ZITOUN EL DJEDID

RUE RIAD ZITOUN EL KEDIM

BRIANTES

RUE BAB BERRIMA

Bab er Rih

El Badi Palace

Royal Palace

Jardin Agdal entrance ▶

DJEMAA EL FNA

PLACE BAB FTEUH

See Around Djemaa el Fna map

AVENUE HOUMAN EL FETOUAKI

AVENUE HOUMAN EL FETOUAKI

RUE DE BAB AGNAOU

RUE ARSE EL MAACH

RUE IBN RACHID

Kasbah Mosque

Saadian Tombs

RUE DE LA KASBAH

KASBAH

GRAND MECHOUAR

Bab el Aghdar

RUE OUMECHOUAR

Caléches

Place Foucauld

Buses

Tourist Police

RUE DE BAB AGNAOU

RUE OUBA BEN NAFIA

Bab Agnaou

Bab Ighli

Bab Ksiba

RUE DE BAL RHAL

Tomb of Sidi Moulay el Ksour

RUE SIDI MIMOUN

AVENUE MOHAMMED V

Koutoubia Gardens

Tomb of Sidi Ali Belkacem

Bab Sidi Ghrib

Bab Makhzen

Bab Djedid

Hôtel La Mamounia

AVENUE HOUMAN EL FETOUAKI

Hôtel Mamounia Gardens

Youssef Ben Tachfine

Bab er Robb

Tomb of Sidi es Soheili

Bab er Robb Gare Routière (500m) ▶

BOULEVARD EL YARMOUK

AVENUE DE LA MENARA

Bab Djedid Olive grove

◀ Jardin Menara

500 m

0

founders. The mosque was completely rebuilt under the Almohads, and several times since, so that the building you see today dates largely from the nineteenth century. The only surviving remnant from the original mosque, the **Almoravid Koubba**, stands below ground level in an excavated area directly across the square, though to enter it you'll have to buy a ticket to the **Marrakesh Museum** at the square's western end, right next to the mosque's impressively decorated Merenid **medersa**.

The Marrakesh Museum

On the west side of Place de la Kissaria is the **Marrakesh Museum** (daily: April–Sept 9am–7pm; Oct–March 9am–6pm; 40dh ticket includes entry to Almoravid Koubba, combined ticket with Ben Youssef Medersa 60dh), housed in a magnificent late-nineteenth-century palace, **Dar Mnebbi**. The palace was built for Mehdi Mnebbi, defence minister of Moulay Abdelziz (1894–1908), who later became Moroccan ambassador in London, before returning to live in Tangier, and selling his palace to T'hami el Glaoui, pasha of Marrakesh. With independence in 1956, the palace was taken over by the state but left in an increasing condition of neglect for many years.

In 1995, Omar Benjoullan, a patron of the arts, bought and restored the derelict building, and in March 1997 it opened as the Marrakesh Museum. It houses exhibitions of Moroccan art and sculpture, both traditional (in the main hall and surrounding rooms), and contemporary (in what were the palace kitchens). It is the restoration itself, however, that is most remarkable, especially in what was the hammam, and in the now-covered inner courtyard with its huge brass lamp hung above a central fountain. There's also a small café and bookshop in the entrance courtyard.

The Almoravid Koubba

On the southern side of Place de la Kissaria, opposite the Ben Youssef Mosque, the **Almoravid Koubba** (Koubba Ba'adiyn; daily: April–Sept 9am–7pm; Oct–March 9am–6pm; buy ticket at Marrakesh Museum) is a small, two-storey kiosk, recently restored, which at first seems little more than a grey dome and

△ Tomb of Sidi Abdel Aziz, near Place Kissaria

a handful of variously shaped doors and windows. Look closer, though, and you may begin to understand its significance and even fascination. For this is the only Almoravid building to survive intact in Morocco (excepting possibly a minaret in Tit near El Jadida; see p.401), and its style is at the root of all Moroccan architecture. The motifs used in later buildings such as the nearby Ben Youssef Medersa (see below) – the pine cones, palms and acanthus leaves – were all carved here first. The windows on each of the different sides became the classic shapes of Almohad and Merenid design – as did the merlons, the Christmas tree-like battlements; the complex "ribs" on the outside of the dome; and the dome's interior support, a sophisticated device of a square and star-shaped octagon, which is itself repeated at each of its corners. Once you see all this, you're only a step away from the eulogies of Islamic art historians who sense in this building, which was probably a small ablutions annexe to the original Ben Youssef Mosque, a powerful and novel expression of form.

Excavated only in 1952, the *koubba* had previously been covered over amid the many rebuildings of the Ben Youssef Mosque. It was built well below today's ground level, which is well above its upper floor. You have to go down two flights of stairs to get to the level it was built at, now uncovered once again thanks to recent excavations. Once down there, you can also look around the attendant facilities, including a large water cistern, and remains of latrines and fountains for performing ablutions, much like those you will still find adjacent to many Moroccan mosques.

The Ben Youssef Medersa

Just thirty metres north of the museum is the entrance to the **Ben Youssef Medersa** (daily: April–Sept 9am–7pm; Oct–March 9am–6pm; 40dh, combined ticket with Marrakesh Museum and Almoravid Koubba 60dh), a koranic school attached to the Ben Youssef Mosque, where students learned the Koran by rote.

Like most of its counterparts up in Fes (see p.270 for a description of their development and function), the Ben Youssef was a Merenid foundation, established by one of Morocco's most illustrious rulers, the "Black Sultan" Abou el Hassan (1331–49). In the 1560s, under the Saadians, it was almost completely rebuilt and their intricate, Andalusian-influenced art dominates it. As with the slightly later Saadian Tombs, no surface is left undecorated, and the overall quality of its craftsmanship, whether in carved wood, stuccowork or zellij tilework, is startling. That this was possible in sixteenth-century Marrakesh, after a period in which the city was reduced to near ruin and the country to tribal anarchy, is remarkable. Revealingly, parts have exact parallels in the Alhambra Palace in Granada, and it seems likely that architects from Muslim Spain were employed in its construction.

The **central courtyard**, its carved cedarwood lintels weathered almost flat on the most exposed side, is unusually large. Along two sides run wide, sturdy, columned arcades, which were probably used to supplement the space for teaching in the neighbouring mosque. Above them are some of the windows of the **dormitory quarters**, which are reached by stairs from the entry vestibule, and from which you can get an interesting perspective – and attempt to fathom how over eight hundred students were once housed in the building. One room is furnished as it would have been when in use.

At its far end, the court opens onto a **prayer hall**, where the decoration, mellowed on the outside with the city's familiar pink tone, is at its best preserved and most elaborate. Notable here, as in the court's cedar carving, is a predominance of pine cone and palm motifs; around the mihrab (the horseshoe-arched prayer niche) they've been applied so as to give the frieze a highly three-dimensional appearance. This is rare in Moorish stuccowork, though the inscriptions themselves, picked out in the curling, vegetative arabesques, are quotations from the Koran, the most common being its opening invocation: "In the name of God, the Compassionate, the Merciful".

The tanneries and northern gates

The main souks – and the tourist route – stop abruptly at Place de la Kissaria. Beyond them, in all directions, you'll find yourself in the ordinary **residential quarters** of the Medina. There are few particular "sights" to be found here, but if you've got the time, there's an interest of its own in following the crowds, and a relief in getting away from the central shopping district of Marrakesh, where you are expected to come in, look round and buy.

North of the entrance to the Ben Youssef Medersa, you quickly reach a fork in the side street. Bear right and keep going as straight as possible, and after about fifteen minutes, you'll reach the tanneries and the ramparts by Bab Debbagh. Before the tanneries you'll cross a small square and intersection, **Place el Moukef**, where a busy street to the left leads to Bab el Khemis. Turning right instead, you arrive within ten minutes at Place Ben Salah and the **Zaouia of Sidi Ben Salah** with a very fine prominent minaret, commissioned by a fourteenth-century Merenid sultan.

Bab Debbagh and the tanneries

Bab Debbagh is supposedly Almoravid in design, though over the years it must have been almost totally rebuilt. Passing through the gate, you become aware of its very real defensive purpose: three internal chicanes are placed in such a manner as to force anyone attempting to storm it to make several turns. Just before the gate, several shops on the left give good views over the quarter from their roofs, and shopkeepers will let you up (for a small fee – agree it first or you'll be mercilessly overcharged).

Looking out, you get partial views over the **tanneries**, more scattered and thus less interesting to look at than those at Fes. They were built here at the edge of the city not only because of the smell, but also for access to water: a stream, the Oued Issil, runs just outside the walls. If you want to take a closer look at the tanning process, come in the morning, when the cooperatives are at work. The smell comes largely from the first stage, where the hides are soaked in a vat of pigeon droppings. The natural dyes traditionally used to colour the leather have largely been replaced by chemicals, many of them carcinogenic – a fact to remember when you see people standing waist-deep in them. One tannery that's easy to find is on the north side of the street about 200m before Bab Debbagh, opposite the blue-tiled stand-up fountain, with another one about 200m further west. Ignore hustlers trying to persuade you that you have to pay them for entry. From outside the gate, bus #5 runs back to the Koutoubia.

Bab el Khemis

The road north from Bab Debbagh, outside the ramparts, takes you up to **Bab el Khemis**, another reconstructed Almoravid gate. Built at an angle in the walls, it is surrounded by concentric rings of decoration and topped with Christmas-tree-like castellations. Its name, means "Thursday Gate", a reference to the market held outside, 400m to the north, past a *marabout's* tomb and a former cemetery, now landscaped as a little park. Although the main market is held on a Thursday morning, there are stalls out most days. It is really a local produce market, though odd handicraft items do occasionally surface. Bab el Khemis, like Bab Debbagh, is served from the Koutoubia by bus #5.

North of the Ben Youssef Mosque

The area immediately **north of the Ben Youssef Mosque** is cut by two main streets: Rue Assouel (which leads up to Bab el Khemis) and Rue Bab Taghzout, which runs up to the gate of the same name and to the Zaouia of Sidi Bel Abbes. These were, with Bab Doukkala, the principal approaches to the city until the twentieth century and along them you find many of the old **fondouks** used for storage and lodging by merchants visiting the souks.

One of these *fondouks* is sited just south of the mosque and a whole series can be found along **Rue Amesfah**, which, if you bear left under the archway north

The seven saints of Marrakesh

Some two hundred holy men and women have their tombs in Marrakesh, but the most important are the **Sabatou Rijal**, literally "seven men" though usually translated in English as **"seven saints"**. Other than being holy men who are buried in Marrakesh, the seven don't have a lot in common: they lived at different times, came from different places, and didn't even all die in Marrakesh. The circuit of their tombs was established in the seventeenth century under the Alaouite ruler Moulay Ismail, to give the city some religious significance and to attract pilgrims (tourists, in other words). The tombs get their most visitors during a rather low-key week-long annual moussem held in their honour in late March, and they are visited in a specific order, travelling anticlockwise round the Medina. In that order, these are the seven:

(1) **Sidi Youssef Ben Ali**, whose tomb is located just outside Bab Aghmat, at the Medina's southeastern corner, was a Marrakshi leper who spent most of his life in a leper colony just outside the walls here, where he died in 1196 or 1197, and if you've got a touch of leprosy, this is the saint to visit for *baraka*.

(2) **Caïd Ayad** was born in Ceuta in 1083 and studied theology in Muslim Spain under Andalusia's greatest teachers before moving to Marrakesh. He was employed in turn by both the Almoravids and the Almohads, and died in 1149. His *zaouia* is just inside Bab Aylen,

(3) **Sidi Bel Abbes** (see p.456) was known for the strictness of his religious observance (he knew the Koran by heart at the age of sixteen), and for his acts of charity, especially towards blind people. It is said that in his day, a blind person never went hungry in Marrakesh, and the visually impaired still come to him for *baraka*.

(4) **Sidi Mohammed Ben Slimane el Jazouli**, a descendant of the Prophet, was expelled from Safi around 1560 because the governor feared his shereefian status and reputation as a holy man made him a potential political rival. He neither lived nor died in Marrakesh, but his body was moved to a series of locations after his death before finally being laid to rest in 1524 in a mausoleum about 200m southwest of Sidi Bel Abbes, and 200m north of Rue Riad el Arous.

(5) **Sidi Abdel Aziz el Harrar** was born in Marrakesh, but made his name in Fes, where he was based in the Medersa el Attarine (see p.276). He died in 1508 and was buried in a mausoleum on Rue Mouassine, near the junction of Rue Amesfah with Rue Baroudienne.

(6) **Sidi Moulay el Ksour** was a Berber from the mountains who studied in Fes and Grenada before coming to Marrakesh to become a disciple of Sidi Abdel Aziz el Harrar. When Portuguese forces attacked the city in 1514, he led the popular resistance movement that kept them out, and died in 1528, to be buried only 300m northwest of the Djemaa el Fna, not far from Bab Fteuh.

(7) **Sidi es Souheili** was a great Islamic jurist from Malaga who came to Marrakesh around 1182 at the call of the Almohad sultan Yacoub el Mansour. He died here three years later, and his *zaouia*, in a cemetery just outside Bab er Robb (inaccessible to non-Muslims), hides a former gate in the wall called Bab ech Charia.

of the entrance to the Ben Youssef Medersa and continue to the junction with **Rue Baroudienne**, is the street more or less directly ahead of you. Most of the *fondouks* are still used in some commercial capacity, as workshops or warehouses, and the doors to their courtyards often stand open. Some date from Saadian times and have fine details of woodcarving or stuccowork. If you are interested, nobody seems to mind if you wander in.

The Zaouia of Sidi Bel Abbes

If you follow Rue Baroudienne north from its junction with Rue Amesfah, and turn right at the end, you pass another *fondouk*, opposite a small sixteenth-century recessed fountain known as **Chrob ou Chouf** ("drink and look"), which is worth a second glance for its carved cedarwood lintel. Take the next left, and around 500m further north is the old city gate of **Bab Taghzout**. This marked the limits of the original Almoravid Medina, and continued to do so into the eighteenth century, when Sultan Mohammed Abdallah extended the walls to enclose the quarter and the **Zaouia of Sidi Bel Abbes**.

Sidi Bel Abbes was born in Ceuta in 1130. As a *marabout* and a prolific performer of miracles, particularly giving sight to the blind, he is the most important of Marrakesh's seven saints (see box, p.455), and his **zaouia**, a kind of monastic cult centre, has traditionally wielded very great influence and power, often at odds with that of the sultan and providing a refuge for political dissidents.

The present buildings date largely from a reconstruction by Moulay Ismail, an act that was probably inspired more by political motivation than piety. Non-Muslims are not allowed to enter, but may see something of the complex and its activities from outside the official boundary, though they should not try to pass through the long central corridor. The *zaouia* has always prospered and still owns much of the quarter to the north and continues its educational and charitable work, distributing food each evening to the blind.

West to Bab Doukkala: Dar el Glaoui

West from Ben Youssef **towards Bab Doukkala**, the route, once you've found your way down through Souk Haddadine to **Rue Bab Doukkala**, is a sizeable

---

El Glaoui: the Pasha of Marrakesh

T'hami el Glaoui, the famous pasha of Marrakesh during the French Protectorate, was the last of the great southern tribal leaders, an active and shrewd supporter of colonial rule (see p.516) and a personal friend of Winston Churchill. Cruel and magnificent in equal measure, he was also one of the most spectacular party-givers around – in an age where rivals were not lacking. At the extraordinary *difas* or banquets held at the Dar el Glaoui, his Marrakesh palace, "nothing", as Gavin Maxwell wrote, "was impossible" – hashish and opium were freely available for the Europeans and Americans to experiment with, and "to his guests T'hami gave whatever they wanted, whether it might be a diamond ring, a present of money in gold, or a Berber girl or boy from the High Atlas".

Not surprisingly, there was little enthusiasm for showing off the palace since El Glaoui's death in 1956, an event that led to a mob looting the palace, destroying its fittings and even the cars in the garages, and then lynching any of Glaoui's henchmen to be found.

However, passions have burnt out over the years, and the family has been rehabilitated, and one of T'hami's sons, Glaoui Abdelssadak, rose to high rank in the Moroccan civil service and became vice president of Gulf Oil.

Crafts and souvenirs

Handicrafts are big in Morocco, and pretty much every part of the country has its speciality. In cities like Fes and Marrakesh, different parts of the Medina produce different goods, from furniture to ironwork to sandals to musical instruments. Jewellery and carpets tend to come in from the countryside, where each region – each village even – has its own style and its own techniques. The advantage of shopping in a big city is that you'll have a huge range to choose from, but there's a very special pleasure in tracking the souvenir you want down to the place where it's made, and even seeing the artisans at work making it.

Carpets, rugs and blankets

Morocco produces some lovely carpets, in wonderful warm colours – saffron yellow, cochineal red, antimony black – that look great flung across the floor in any living space. Nowadays most carpets are coloured with synthetic dyes, but their inspiration remains the natural dyes with which they were traditionally made. The most expensive carpets are hand-knotted, but there are also woven rugs called kellims.

Knotted carpets are not cheap – you can pay €1500 and more for the finer Arab designs in Fes or Rabat – but **rugs and kellims** come in at more reasonable prices, with a range of strong, well-designed weaves from €50–70. Most of these kellims will be of Berber origin and the most interesting ones usually come from the High and Middle Atlas. You'll find a big selection in Marrakesh, but if you're looking seriously, try to get to the town souk in Midelt or the weekly markets in Azrou and other villages in the region. The chain of Maison Berbère shops in Ouarzazate, Tinerhir and Rissani are good hunting grounds too, but one of the best ways to find carpets is to wander around villages or parts of town where they are made, listen for the tell-tale sound of the loom in use, and ask at the weavers' homes if they have any carpets for sale.

On a simpler and cheaper level, the **Berber blankets** (*foutahs*, or *couvertures*) are imaginative, and often very striking with bands of reds and blacks; for these, Tetouan and Chefchaouen, on the edge of the Rif, are promising.

▲ Tajines being made in Safi

Ceramics

Pottery is colourful if fairly crudely made on the whole, though the blue-and-white designs of Fes and the multicoloured pots of Chefchaouen (both produced largely for the tourist trade) are highly attractive. The essentially domestic pottery of Safi – Morocco's major pottery centre – is worth a look, too, with its colourful plates, **tajines** and **garden pots**. Safi tajines are nice to look at, but for practical use, the best are those produced by the Oulja pottery at Salé, near Rabat, in plain red-brown earthenware.

Jewellery

Arabic-style **gold** jewellery tends to be a bit fussy for Western tastes, but **silver** is another story. In the south particularly, you can pick up some fabulous Berber necklaces and bracelets, always very chunky, and characterized by bold combinations of semiprecious (and sometimes plastic) stones and beads. Women in the Atlas and the Souss Valley regions in particular often wear chunky silver bracelets, belts embellished with old silver coins, or heavy necklaces with big beads of **amber**, **coral** and **carnelian**. Silver brooches are used to fasten garments, and many of the symbols

▲ Berber jewellery

found in Moroccan jewellery, such as the "hand of Fatima" and the five-pointed star, are there to guard against the evil eye. Essaouira, Marrakesh and Tiznit have particularly good jewellery souks.

Minerals and fossils

You'll see a variety of semiprecious stones on sale throughout Morocco, and in the High Atlas they are often aggressively hawked on the roadsides. If you're lucky enough to be offered genuine amethyst or quartz, prices can be bargained to very tempting levels. Be warned, however, that all that glitters is not necessarily the real thing. Too often, if you wet the stone and rub, you'll find traces of dye on your fingers.

Fossils too are widely sold in Morocco, and can be as beautiful as they are fascinating. The fossil-rich black marble of the Erfoud region, for example, is sold in the form of anything from ashtrays to table tops. But again, things aren't always what they seem, and a lot of fossils are in fact fakes, made out of cement. This is particularly true of trilobites, or any black fossil on a grey background. For more on fossils and minerals, see the box on p.591.

Wood

Marquetry is one of the few crafts where you'll see genuinely old pieces – inlaid **tables** and shelves – though the most easily exportable objects are boxes. The big centre for marquetry is Essaouira, where cedar or thuya wood is beautifully inlaid with orange-tree wood and other light-coloured woods to make trays, chess and backgammon sets, even plates and bowls, and you can visit the workshops where they are made.

Fes, Meknes, Tetouan and Marrakesh also have souks specializing in carpentry, which produce not only furniture, but also chests, sculptures, and kitchen utensils such as the little ladles made from citrus wood that are used to eat *harira* soup.

◀ Essaouira marquetry

Clothes

Moroccan clothes are easy to purchase, and though Westerners – men at least – who try to imitate Moroccan styles by wearing the cotton or wool **djellaba** (a kind of outer garment) tend to look a little silly in the street, they do make good nightgowns. Some of the cloth on sale is exquisite in itself, and walking through the dyers' souks is an inspiration. Women will find some sumptuous gowns if they look in the right places – Marrakesh in particular has shops selling beautiful dresses, kaftans, **gandoras** (sleeveless kaftans) and tunics. Brightly coloured **knitted caps** are more likely to appeal to men, and there are plenty of inexpensive multicoloured **silk scarves** on offer too. Even ordinary jackets and trousers are often on sale in the souks at bargain prices.

▲ Tanneries, Fes

Leatherware

Morocco leather is famously soft and luxurious. In towns like Fes, Marrakesh and Taroudannt you can even visit the tanneries to see it being cured. It comes in a myriad of forms from belts, bags and clothing to pouffes and even book covers, but Morocco's best-known leather item is the *babouche*, or slipper. Classic Moroccan babouches, open at the heel, are immensely comfortable, and produced in yellow (the usual colour), white, red (for women) and occasionally grey or (for the truly fetishistic) black; a good pair – and quality varies enormously – can cost between €9 and €22. Marrakesh and Tafraoute are especially good for *babouches*.

thoroughfare and very straightforward to follow. Midway, you pass the **Dar el Glaoui**, the old palace of the pasha who ruled Marrakesh on behalf of the French during the colonial period, when he was feted by Europeans, and hated by Marrakshis (see box opposite). His palace was a place of legendary exoticism throughout the first half of the twentieth century, and after years of neglect it is now being restored and is expected to be open to the public as a museum at the end of 2007.

The Lower Medina: the Royal Palace, Saadian Tombs and Mellah

Staying in Marrakesh even for a few days, you begin to sense the different appearance and life of its various Medina quarters, and nowhere more so than in the shift from the area to the north of Djemaa el Fna and that to the south of it. At the southern extremity (a kind of stem to the mushroom shape of the city walls) is **Dar el Makhzen**, the royal palace. To its west stretches the old inner citadel of the **Kasbah**; to the east the **Mellah**, once the largest Jewish ghetto in Morocco, while rambling to the north of it is a series of mansions and palaces built for the nineteenth-century elite.

All in all, it's an interesting area to wander round, though you inevitably spend time trying to figure out the sudden and apparently arbitrary appearance of ramparts and enclosures. And there are two obvious focal points, not to be missed: the **Saadian Tombs**, preserved in the shadow of the Kasbah Mosque, and **El Badi**, the ruined palace of Ahmed el Mansour.

The Saadian Tombs

The **Saadian Tombs** (daily 8.30–11.45am & 2.30–5.45pm; 10dh), belonging to the dynasty which ruled Morocco from 1554 to 1669, escaped plundering by the rapacious Alaouite sultan Moulay Ismail, probably because he feared bad luck if he desecrated them. Instead, he blocked all access bar an obscure entrance from the Kasbah Mosque. The tombs lay half-ruined and half-forgotten until they were rediscovered by a French aerial survey in 1917, and a passageway was built to give access from the side of the Kasbah Mosque. Restored, they are today the kasbah's main "sight" – over lavish, maybe, in their exhaustive decoration, but dazzling nonetheless. They are housed in a quiet, high-walled enclosure, shaded with shrubs and palms, which seems as much a pleasure garden as a cemetery. The best time to go is first thing in the morning, before the crowds arrive, or late in the afternoon when they, and the heat, have largely gone.

Some form of burial ground behind the royal palace probably predated the Saadian period, though the earliest of the tombs here dates from 1557, and all the principal structures were built by Sultan Ahmed el Mansour. This makes them virtual contemporaries of the Ben Youssef Medersa – with which there are obvious parallels – and allows a revealing insight into just how rich and extravagant the El Badi must once have been. A few prominent Marrakshis continued to be buried in the mausoleums: the last, in 1792, was the "mad sultan", Moulay Yazid, whose 22-month reign was one of the most violent and sadistic in the nation's history. Named as the successor to Sidi Mohammed, Moulay Yazid threw himself into a series of revolts against his father, waged an inconclusive war with Spain, and brutally suppressed a Marrakesh-based rebellion in support of his brother. A massacre followed his capture of the city, though he had little time to celebrate his victory – a bullet in the head during a rebel counterattack killed him soon after.

The mausoleums

There are two main **mausoleums** in the enclosure. The finest is on the left as you come in – a beautiful group of three rooms, built to house Ahmed el Mansour's own tomb and completed within his lifetime. Continuing round from the courtyard entrance, the first hall is a **prayer oratory**, a room probably not intended for burial, though now almost littered with the thin marble stones of Saadian princes. It is here that Moulay Yazid was laid out, perhaps in purposeful obscurity, certainly in ironic contrast to the cursive inscription round the band of black and white zellij: "And the works of peace they have accomplished", it reads amid the interlocking circles, "will make them enter the holy gardens."

Architecturally, the most important feature of this mausoleum is the mihrab, its pointed horseshoe arch supported by an incredibly delicate arrangement of columns. Opposite this is another elaborate arch, leading to the domed **central chamber** and **Ahmed el Mansour's tomb**, which you can glimpse through the next door in the court. The tomb, slightly larger than those surrounding it, lies right in the middle, flanked on either side by those of the sultan's sons and successors. The room itself is spectacular, faint light filtering onto the tombs from an interior lantern in a tremendous vaulted roof, the zellij full of colour and motion and the undefined richness of a third chamber almost hidden from view. Throughout, there are echoes of the Alhambra in Granada, built two centuries previously, and from which its style is clearly derived.

The **other mausoleum**, older and less impressive, was built by Ahmed in place of an existing pavilion above the tombs of his mother, Lalla Messaouda, and of Mohammed ech Sheikh, the founder of the Saadian dynasty. It is again a series of three rooms, though two are hardly more than *loggias*. Messaouda's tomb is the niche below the dome in the outer chamber. Mohammed ech Sheikh is buried in the inner one – or at least his torso is, since he was murdered in the Atlas by Turkish mercenaries, who salted his head and took it back for public display on the walls of Istanbul.

Outside, **round the garden and courtyard**, are scattered the tombs of over a hundred more Saadian princes and members of the royal household. Like the privileged 66 given space within the mausoleums, their gravestones are brilliantly tiled and often elaborately inscribed. The most usual inscription reads quite simply:

There is no God but Allah.
Muhammad is God's messenger.
Praise Be to God.
The occupant of this tomb died on . . .

But there are others – epitaphs and extracts from the Koran – that seem to express the turbulence of the age to a greater degree, which, with Ahmed's death in 1603, was to disintegrate into nearly seventy years of constant civil war. "Every soul shall know death", reads one tombstone; "Death will find you wherever you are, even in fortified towers", reads another. And, carved in gypsum on the walls, there is a poem:

O mausoleum, built out of mercy, thou whose
walls are the shadow of heaven.
The breath of asceticism is wafted from thy tombs
like a fragrance.
Through thy death
the light of faith has been dimmed,
the seven spheres are fraught with darkness
and the columns of glory
broken with pain.

Getting to the Saadian Tombs, the simplest route from the Djemaa el Fna is to follow **Rue Bab Agnaou** outside the ramparts. At its end you come to a small square flanked by two gates. Directly ahead is **Bab er Robb**, leading out of the Medina towards the High Atlas mountains. To its left, somewhat battered and eroded, is **Bab Agnaou**, one of the two original entrances to the kasbah, though the magnificent blue granite gateway which stands here today was built in 1885. The name actually means "black people's gate", a reference to its use by swarthy commoners, while the fair-complexioned aristocracy had their own entrance into the kasbah (now long gone). The gate is surrounded by concentric arches of decoration and topped with an inscription in decorative script, which reads: "Enter with blessing, serene people." Notice how the semicircular frieze above the arch creates a three-dimensional effect without any actual depth of carving.

Passing through the gate, the **Kasbah Mosque** is in front of you: its minaret looks gaudy and modern but is, in fact, contemporary with both the Koutoubia and Hassan towers – it was restored to its exact original state in the 1960s. The narrow passageway to the Saadian Tombs is well signposted, at the right-hand corner of the mosque.

El Badi Palace

The ruins of the **El Badi Palace** (daily 8.30–11.45am & 2.30–5.45pm; 10dh) are off Place des Ferblantiers (see p.462), 700m south of the Djemaa el Fna along Rue Riad Zitoun el Kedim. On the south side of Place des Ferblantiers,

△ El Badi Palace

a gate known as **Bab Berrima** opens onto a long rectangular enclosure, flanked on either side by walls; go through it, and on your right you'll come to the Badi's entrance.

Though substantially in ruins, and reduced throughout to its red *pisé* walls, enough remains of **El Badi** to suggest that its name – "The Incomparable" – was not entirely immodest. It took the sultan Moulay Ismail over ten years of systematic work to strip the palace of everything moveable or of value, but even so, there's a lingering sense of luxury and grandeur. The scale, with its sunken gardens and vast, ninety-metre-long pool, is certainly unrivalled, and the odd traces of zellij and plaster still left evoke a decor that was probably as rich as that of the Saadian Tombs.

What you see today is essentially the ceremonial part of the **palace complex**, planned on a grand scale for the reception of ambassadors, and not meant for everyday living. It seems likely that El Mansour and the multiple members of his court each had private palaces – smaller, though built to a similar ground plan – to the west and south, covering much of the area occupied by the Dar el Makhzen, the present Royal Palace.

The palace's **entrance** was originally in the southeast corner of the complex, but today you enter from the north, through the Green Pavilion – its walls, like everything else in this complex, of enormous height. From here you emerge into a vast **central court**, over 130m long and nearly as wide. In its northeast corner, you can climb up to get an overview from the ramparts, and a closer view of the **storks** that nest atop them.

Within the central court are four **sunken gardens**, two on the northern side and two on the southern side. **Pools** separate the two gardens on each side, and there are four smaller pools in the four corners of the court, which is constructed on a substructure of vaults in order to allow the circulation of water through the pools and gardens. When the pools are filled – as during the June folklore festival which takes place here – they are an incredibly majestic sight, especially the main two, joined by an island that was originally surmounted by an elaborate double fountain.

On each side of the courtyard were summer pavilions. Of the Crystal Pavilion, to the east, only the foundations survive. On the opposite side, a monumental hall that was used by the sultan on occasions of state was known as the **Koubba el Hamsiniya** (The Fifty Pavilion), after the number of its columns. Though part of the floor remains intact, none of the columns still stand today, but strangely enough, their size and splendour were documented by an observer

---

The Marrakesh Festival

Marrakesh utilizes the Badi Palace – and other venues in the city – for an annual two-week **Festival National des Art Populaires** (ⓦwww.maghrebarts.ma/festivals/fnap.html). This is the country's biggest and best folklore and music festival, held in June or July each year. If you are interested in Moroccan music, it would be worth planning your trip around it.

The festival comprises a series of totally authentic and unusual performances, with groups of musicians and dancers coming in from all regions of Morocco and beyond. A typical programme will span the range of Moroccan music – from the Gnaoua drummers and the panpipers of Jajouka, to Berber *ahouaches* from the Atlas and southern oases, to classical Andalous music, originally from Muslim Spain.

The shows are held each evening from around 9pm to midnight; before they start, towards sunset, there is a **fantasia** at Bab el Djedid – a spectacle by any standard, with dozens of Berber horsemen firing their guns in the air at full gallop.

Ahmed el Mansour

The El Badi Palace was begun shortly after Ahmed el Mansour's accession, its initial finance coming from the enormous ransom paid out by the Portuguese after the Battle of the Three Kings at Ksar el Kebir. Fought in the summer of 1578, this was one of the most disastrous battles in Christian medieval history; ostensibly in support of a rival Saadian claimant, but to all intents a Portuguese crusade, it was led by the young king, Dom Sebastião, and supported by almost his entire nobility. Few escaped death or Moorish capture. Sebastião himself was killed, as were both the Saadian claimant and the ruling sultan.

As a result, Ahmed – dubbed *El Mansour* (The Victorious) – came to the throne, undisputed and commanding immediate wealth from the ransoms paid for the captured Portuguese nobles. He reigned for 25 years, trading in sugar and slaves with Britain, Spain and Italy; seized the gold route across the Sahara with the resultant capture of Timbuktu, which earned him the additional epithet *Ed Dahbi* (The Golden); and maintained peace in Morocco through a loose confederation of tribes. It was the most prosperous period in the country's history since the time of the Almohads – a cultural and political renaissance reflected in the coining of a new title, the Shereefian Empire, the country's official name until independence in 1956.

who never came to Morocco: the French philosopher Montaigne, while travelling through Italy, saw craftsmen preparing the columns – "each of an extreme height for the king of Fes and Barbary".

You can pay another 10dh (at the main gate) to see the original **minbar** (pulpit) from the Koutoubia mosque (see p.444), housed in a pavilion in the southwest corner of the main courtyard. It may not sound like anything much, but this *minbar* was in its day one of the most celebrated works of art in the Muslim world. Commissioned from the Andalusian capital Cordoba in 1137 by the last Almoravid sultan, Ali Ben Youssef, it took eight years to complete, and the whole structure was covered with the most exquisite inlay work, of which, sadly, only patches remain. When the Almohads took power shortly afterwards, they installed the *minbar* in their newly built Koutoubia mosque. There it remained until 1962, when it was removed for restoration and eventually brought here. Unfortunately, members of the public are not usually allowed to walk around it and inspect the surviving inlay work, but the *gardien* may relent if you show a particular interest. Photography is not usually allowed.

South of the courtyard, accessed just to the right of the building housing the *minbar*, are ruins of the palace **stables**, and beyond them, leading towards the intriguing walls of the present royal palace, a series of **dungeons**, used into the last century as a state prison. You can explore part of these and could easily spend a whole afternoon wandering round the various inner courts above, with their fragments of marble and zellij and their water conduits for the fountains and hammams. The most enduring account of the palace concerns its state opening, a fabulous occasion attended by ambassadors from several European powers and by all the sheikhs and *caids* of the kingdom. Surveying the effect, Ahmed turned to his court jester for an opinion on the new palace. "Sidi," the man replied, "this will make a magnificent ruin."

The Mellah

It was in 1558 – five years before Ahmed's accession – that the Marrakesh **Mellah**, the separate Jewish quarter in Morocco, was created. There is no exact record of why this was done at this particular time. Possibly it was the result of a pogrom, with the sultan moving the Jews to his protected kasbah – and they, in turn, forming a useful buffer zone (and scapegoat) between his palace and the populace in times of social unrest. But, as likely as not, it was simply brought about to make taxation easier. The Jews of Marrakesh were an important financial resource – they controlled most of the Saadian sugar trade, and comprised practically all of the city's bankers, metalworkers, jewellers and tailors. In the sixteenth century, at least, their quarter was almost a town in itself, supervised by rabbis, and with its own souks, gardens, fountains and synagogues.

The present Mellah, which is now known officially as the **Hay Essalam** quarter and is much smaller in extent, is now almost entirely Muslim – most of the Marrakshi Jews left long ago for Casablanca (where some 6000 still live) or emigrated to France or Israel. The few who remain, outwardly distinguishable only by the men's small black skullcaps, are mostly poor or old or both. Their quarter, however, is immediately distinct: its houses are taller than elsewhere, the streets are more enclosed, and even the shop cubicles are smaller. Until the Protectorate, Jews were not permitted to own land or property – nor even to ride or walk, except barefoot – outside the Mellah; a situation that was greatly exploited by their landlords, who resisted all attempts to expand the walls. Today, although this is not a prized neighbourhood in which to live, its air of neglect and poverty is probably less than at any time during the past three centuries.

Around the quarter

The easiest approach to the Mellah is from **Place des Ferblantiers** – the tinsmiths' square. Formerly called Place du Mellah, this was itself part of the old Jewish souk, now prettied up into quite a pleasant little square, surrounded by the workshops of lantern makers. North of here, off the street leading up to Rue Riad Zitoun el Djedid, is a **jewellers' souk**, one of the traditional Jewish trades now more or less taken over by Muslim craftsmen.

East from here, leading along the southern side of the Bahia Palace, is the main road into the Mellah. The first left (under a low arch) takes you to **Place Souweka**, a small square at the centre of the Mellah, very much like the goal in a maze. If you ignore that turning, the main road does a twist, and the next left (Derb Ragraga) takes you after 100m to the unmarked **Lazama Synagogue**, the last door on the left before the street widens out (no. 36; no sign, just knock on the door; Sun–Thurs 9am–6pm, Fri 9am–1pm, closed Sat and Jewish hols; free, but a tip is expected). The synagogue is still in use but the interior is modern and not tremendously interesting. Like all the Mellah's synagogues, it forms part of a private house, which you'll notice is decorated with Star of David zellij tiling. Would-be guides may offer (for a tip, of course) to show you this, and some of the Mellah's other, smaller synagogues (*s'noga*), now disused. Even when in active use, these were as much private houses as temples – "... serving also as places in which to eat, sleep and to kill chickens", according to Budgett Meakin (see p.770).

Some 200m to the east is the **Jewish cemetery**, the **Miâara** (Sun–Thurs 7am–6pm, Fri 7am–3pm; closed Sat and Jewish holidays; no charge but tip expected), reckoned to date from the early seventeenth century. More sprawling than the cemetery in Fes (see p.287), it is well tended and boasts eleven Jewish *marabout* (*tsadikim* in Hebrew) shrines.

Just outside the Mellah, on Rue Arset el Mâach (Rue de l'Electricité), the first-floor **Bitoun Synagogue** is out of use and closed to the public, but it's worth checking out the unusual exterior, up above a herb shop, in mustard yellow with, naturally, a Star of David motif.

North of the Mellah

Heading north from the Mellah, back towards Djemaa el Fna, there are three direct and fairly simple routes. To the left of Place des Ferblantiers, **Avenue Houman el Fetouaki** will bring you to the Koutoubia. North of the square, two parallel streets, **Rue Riad Zitoun el Kedim** and **Rue Riad Zitoun el Djedid** lead up to the Djemaa el Fna.

Riad Zitoun el Kedim is a shopping street lined with grocers, barbershops and a couple of hammams. Riad Zitoun el Djedid is more residential, and it is here that you find the concentration of **palaces and mansions** built in those strange, closing decades of the nineteenth and the first few years of the twentieth century, when the sultans Moulay Hassan and Moulay Abd el Aziz held court in the city.

The Bahia

By far the most ambitious and costly of these mansions was the **Bahia Palace** (Sat–Thurs 8.45–11.45am & 2.45–5.45pm, Fri 8.45–11.30am & 3–5.45pm; 10dh), at the southern end of Rue Riad Zitoun el Djedid, originally built in 1866–7 for **Si Moussa**, a former slave who had risen to become Moulay Hassan's chamberlain, and then grand vizier. His son, **Bou Ahmed**, who himself held the post of chamberlain under Moulay Hassan, became kingmaker in 1894 when Hassan died while returning home from a *harka*. In something of a coup, Ahmed managed to conceal news of the sultan's death until he was able to declare Hassan's fourteen-year-old son Moulay Abd el Aziz sultan in his place, with himself as grand vizier and regent (see p.717). The wily Bou Ahmed thus attained virtually complete control over the state, which he exercised until his death in 1900.

Ahmed began enlarging the Bahia (meaning "brilliance") in the same year as his coup, and added a mosque, a hammam and even a vegetable garden; much of the palace has been restored to its original glory. Visitors enter the palace from the west, through an arcaded courtyard which leads to a **small riad** (enclosed garden), part of Bou Ahmed's extension. The riad is decorated with beautiful carved stucco and cedarwood, and salons lead off it on three sides. The eastern salon leads through to the **council room**, and thence through a vestibule – where it's worth pausing to look up at the lovely painted ceiling – to the **great courtyard** of Si Moussa's original palace. The rooms surrounding the courtyard are also all worth checking out for their painted wooden ceilings.

South of the great courtyard is the **large riad**, the heart of Si Moussa's palace, fragrant with fruit trees and melodious with birdsong, approaching the very ideal of beauty in Arabic domestic architecture. To its east and west are halls decorated with fine zellij fireplaces and painted wooden ceilings. From here, you leave the palace via the **private apartment** built in 1898 for Ahmed's wife, Lalla Zinab, where again you should look up to check out the painted ceiling, carved stucco, and stained-glass windows.

There is a certain pathos to the empty, echoing chambers of the palace, and the inevitable passing of Bou Ahmed's influence and glory. London *Times* correspondent Walter Harris (see p.769), who knew the vizier, described his demise and the clearing of his palace in *Morocco That Was*, published just twenty years after the events, by which time Bou Ahmed's name had already become "only a memory of the past":

For several days as the Vizier lay expiring, guards were stationed outside his palace waiting in silence for the end. And then one morning the wail of the women within the house told that death had come. Every gateway of the great building was seized, and no one was allowed to enter or come out, while within there was pandemonium. His slaves pillaged wherever they could lay their hands. His women fought and stole to get possession of the jewels. Safes were broken open, documents and title-deeds were extracted, precious stones were torn from their settings, the more easily to be concealed, and even murder took place . . . A few days later nothing remained but the great building – all the rest had disappeared into space. His family were driven out to starvation and ruin, and his vast properties passed into the possession of the State. It was the custom of the country.

For some years during the Protectorate, the palace was used to house the Resident General, and it is still called into use when the royal family is in the city, usually during the winter months, at which times there is no public admission.

Maison Tiskiwin

The **Maison Tiskiwin** (daily, in principle 9.30am–12.30pm & 3.30–5.30pm; 15dh), at 8 Rue de la Bahia, is a beautiful townhouse, built at the beginning of the twentieth century in Spanish-Moroccan style. The house is easy to find: 200m north of the Bahia Palace on Rue Riad Zitouan el Djedid, where the street opens out to the left, take a right turn (under an arch), and it's 100m ahead on the right (look for the yellow sign).

△ Maison Tiskiwin

Within lies a unique collection of Moroccan and Saharan artefacts, billed as "a journey from Marrakesh to Timbuktu and back". The items on display are furnished from the collection of a Dutch anthropologist, Bert Flint, a Moroccan resident since 1957. Each of the rooms features carpets, fabrics, clothes and jewellery from a different region of the Sahara, and explanatory notes in French describe the exhibits room by room. The exhibition illustrates the longstanding cultural links across the desert, a result of the centuries of caravan trade between Morocco and Mali.

Dar Si Said

The next left after the Maison Tiskiwin brings you to **Dar Si Said** (daily except Tues 9am–12.15pm & 3–6.15pm; 20dh), a smaller version of the Bahia Palace, built for a brother of Bou Ahmed, who, though something of a simpleton, nonetheless gained the post of royal chamberlain. It's a pleasurable building, with beautiful pooled courtyards, scented with lemons, palms and flowers, and it houses an impressive **Museum of Moroccan Arts**.

The museum is particularly strong on its collection of eighteenth- and nineteenth-century artwork, some of it from the Glaoui kasbahs and most of it in cedar wood. Besides the furniture, there are Berber doors, window frames and wonderful painted ceilings. There are also (upstairs) a number of traditional **wedding palanquins** – once widely used for carrying the bride, veiled and hidden, to her new home. Today, such chairs are still made in the souks and used, albeit symbolically, to carry the bride from her womenfolk in one room to the groom's menfolk in the next room.

One of the museum's most important exhibits, originally from the Ben Youssef Medersa, and not always on display, is a marble **basin**, rectangular in shape and decorated along one side with what seem to be heraldic eagles and griffins. An inscription amid the floral decorations records its origin in tenth-century Cordoba, then the centre of the western Muslim world. Although most Islamic artwork eschews images of plants and animals in favour of abstract patterns, the Ummayad caliphs for whom it was constructed had few reservations about representational art. What is more surprising is that it was brought over to Morocco by the highly puritan Almoravid sultan Ali Ben Youssef and, placed in his mosque, was left untouched by the dynasty's equally iconoclastic successors, the Almohads.

On the way out of the museum, don't miss the **fairground ride seats**, part of a contraption like a small wooden Ferris wheel, in which children commonly rode at moussems until the early 1960s. Photographs illustrate the apparatus as it was in use.

The Ville Nouvelle, gardens and palmery

Marrakesh's **Ville Nouvelle** radiates out from **Guéliz**, its commercial centre. Though it's hardly chock-a-block with attractions, it does have one must-see: the **Majorelle Garden**, east of Guéliz and just northwest of the Medina. South of Guéliz, the **Hivernage** district, built as a garden suburb, is where most of the city's newer tourist hotels are located, but it's devoid of any interest.

With summer temperatures of 34 to 38°C – and peaks well above that – one way to escape the heat is in one of the city's gardens. There are two large ones – the **Agdal** and **Menara** – designed for just this purpose. Each rambles through acres of orchards and olive groves and has, near its centre, an immense, lake-size pool of water. This is all – they are not flower gardens, but, cool and completely still, they are a luxurious contrast to the close city streets. Further out, Marrakesh's **palmery** will not impress those who have seen the great southern oases that we cover in Chapter Seven, but it's a cool and peaceful break, and a taster of the southern oases for those unable to reach them.

To get to the Agdal or Menara gardens, or to the palmery, you will want **transport** – either a petit taxi or calèche. If you are considering a calèche trip at any stage, the Agdal, Menara and palmery are perfect destinations. Alternatively, to take in both gardens and tour the ramparts and palmery, you could rent a **bike** or charter a grand taxi for the day.

Guéliz

The heart of modern Marrakesh, Guéliz has a certain buzz that the sleepy old Medina rather lacks. Its main thoroughfare, **Avenue Mohammed V**, runs all the way down to the Koutoubia, and it's on and around this boulevard that you'll find the city's main concentration of upmarket shops, restaurants and smart pavement cafés. Its junctions form the Ville Nouvelle's main centres of activity: Place de la Liberté, with its modern fountain; Place 16 Novembre, by the main post office; and Place Abdelmoumen Ben Ali, epicentre of Marrakesh's modern shopping zone. Looking back along Avenue Mohammed V from Guéliz to the Medina, on a clear day at least, you should see the Koutoubia rising in the distance, with the Atlas mountains behind.

One sight of minor interest is Marrakesh's **Catholic church**, on Rue de l'Imam. Built in 1930, it could easily be mistaken for a little church in rural France, but for its distinctly Marrakshi red-ochre hue. The church is dedicated to six Franciscan friars ("les saints martyrs") who insisted on preaching Christianity on the city's streets in the year 1220. When the sultan ordered them to either desist or leave, they refused, and were promptly beheaded. For their rather foolhardy bravery, they were later canonized.

Another remnant of the colonial era is the **European Cemetery** on Rue Erraouda (daily: April–Sept 7am–7pm; Oct–March 8am–6pm; free). Opened in 1925, it's a peaceful plot with lots of wild flowers, and some quite Poe-esque French family mausoleums. The first thing you'll notice on entry is the large white obelisk dedicated to the soldiers who fell fighting in Africa for Free France and democracy during World War II; 333 of these men have their last resting places in the cemetery's section H. Section B is devoted to children who died in infancy, and the oldest part, to the left of the obelisk as you come in, contains the tombs of colonists from the 1920s and 1930s, most of whom seem to have been less than forty years old when they died. The cemetery is nowadays also home to a colony of cats.

The Majorelle Garden

The **Majorelle Garden**, or Jardin Bou Saf (daily 8am–5.30pm; 30dh; no dogs, no unaccompanied children, no picnics, no smoking), is a meticulously planned twelve-acre botanical garden, created in the 1920s and 1930s by French painter Jacques Majorelle (1886–1962), and now owned by fashion designer Yves Saint Laurent. The entrance is on a small side street off the jacaranda-lined Avenue Yacoub el Mansour. Refreshments are not available in the garden, so it may be worth bringing your own, though picnicking is banned.

The feeling of tranquillity here is enhanced by verdant groves of bamboo, dwarf palm and agave, the cactus garden and the various lily-covered pools.

The Art Deco pavilion at the heart of the garden is painted in a striking cobalt blue – the colour of French workmen's overalls, so Majorelle claimed, though it seems to have improved in the Moroccan light. This brilliantly offsets both the plants – multicoloured bougainvillea, rows of bright orange nasturtiums and pink geraniums – and also the strong colours of the pergolas and concrete paths – pinks, lemon yellows and apple greens. The enduring sound is the chatter of the common bulbuls, flitting among the leaves of the date palms, and the pools also attract bird residents such as turtle doves and house buntings. The garden became better known abroad when it was featured by Yves Saint Laurent in a brilliant reproduction at the 1997 Chelsea Flower Show in London.

In Majorelle's former studio, housed within the pavilion, a **Museum of Islamic Arts** (15dh) exhibits Saint Laurent's fine personal collection of North African carpets, pottery, furniture and doors; Saint Laurent was himself born in Algeria. It also has many of Jacques Majorelle's engravings and paintings – mainly of Atlas scenes fifty years ago, including the fortified village of Anemiter and the Kasbah of Aït Benhaddou, near Ouarzazate.

When leaving, ignore the taxi drivers waiting outside, who run a cartel and will run a taxi you unless you pay well over the odds. The answer is simply to walk down to the main road and hail a passing taxi there.

Menara Gardens

Southwest of Hivernage, the **Menara Gardens** (daily 8am–6pm; free) are a popular picnic spot for Marrakshi families, as well as tourists, centred on a rectangular pool providing a classic postcard image beneath a backdrop of the High Atlas mountains. Aside from the pool, the garden is largely filled with olive trees. It couldn't be simpler to find: just follow Avenue de la Menara from Bab Djedid, by the *Hôtel La Mamounia*. In summer, it has several drinks stalls.

The Menara, originally dating from the twelfth century, was restored and its pavilions rebuilt in the mid-nineteenth century. The poolside *minzah* (daily 8am–12.30pm & 3–6pm; 15dh) is said to have replaced an original Saadian structure. At night, except in January and February, the pool becomes the scene for a Marvels and Reflections show (Mon–Sat 10pm, daily in April, May & Aug; 250dh or 400dh), featuring fireworks, dancers and acrobats. There's a ticket office at the park entrance, but it only seems to open very sporadically; for further information, call ☎024 43 95 78. Should you want to get up on a camel for a little jaunt, there's usually someone by the park entrance offering rides.

Agdal gardens

Open on Fridays and Sundays only, the **Agdal** (8am–5.30pm; free) is a confusingly large expanse – some 3km in extent and with half a dozen smaller irrigation pools in addition to its *grand bassin*. It's a long (4km) walk from town, south along Rue de la Kasbah from the Saadian Tombs and left at the end into Rue du Mechouar, or along the road outside the ramparts south from Bab Agnaou/Bab er Robb, and then left as you are about to leave the city at Bab Ighli; either route will bring you into the Grand Mechouar (a kind of parade ground) by the Royal Palace, across which (on the western side) another gateway leads to the Interior Mechouar, where a sharp right takes you into the garden. Alternatively, just take a petit taxi, or hop on bus #6.

The garden is watered by an incredible system of wells and underground channels, known as *khettara,* that go as far as the base of the Atlas in the Ourika

Valley and date, in part, from the earliest founding of the city. Over the centuries, the channels have at times fallen into disrepair and the gardens been abandoned, but the present nineteenth-century layout probably differs little from any of its predecessors. It is surrounded by walls, with gates at each of the near corners, while inside, the orange, fig, lemon, apricot and pomegranate orchards are divided into square, irrigated plots by endless raised walkways and broad avenues of olive trees.

At the heart of the park are a series of pools, the largest of which is the **Sahraj el Hana** (Tank of Health – now a green, algae-clogged rectangle of water), which was probably dug by the Almohads and is flanked by a ramshackle old *minzah*, or summer pavilion, where the last few precolonial sultans held picnics and boating parties.

The palmery

Marrakesh's **palmery**, or oasis, is northeast of town between the Route de Fes (N8) and the Route de Casablanca (N9). As oases go, it's far from being the most spectacular in the country, but it does make a change from the urban landscape if you're spending time in town. Dotted with the villas of prosperous Marrakshis who can afford to live out in the leafy suburbs, the palmery also boasts a golf course and a couple of luxury hotels. The clumps of date palms look rather windswept, but the palmery does have a certain tranquillity, and it's 5° cooler than the Medina, which could make it a particular attraction in summer. The most popular route through the oasis is the **Circuit de la Palmeraie**, which meanders through the trees and villas from the Route de Fes to the Route de Casablanca. The classic way to see it is by calèche, but you'll need to bargain hard to get a good price. You could also do the Circuit de la Palmeraie on foot, taking bus #17 or #26 to the Route de Fes turn-off, and bus #1 back from the Route de Casablanca (or vice versa). It's also possible to ride around the palmery on a camel – men by the main road offer rides.

Eating, drinking and nightlife

Marrakesh **eating and entertainment options** break down less rigidly than usual between the Ville Nouvelle and the Medina. **Guéliz**, naturally enough, is where you'll find most of the city's French-style cafés, bistros and restaurants, and virtually all the bars. In the **Medina**, however, there's plenty of choice for meals, including the spectacle of the Djemaa el Fna food stalls, many inexpensive café-restaurants, and a number of upmarket palace-restaurants.

Medina cafés and restaurants

Recommendations for the Medina span the range: from 50dh to 550dh a head; from a bench in the Djemaa el Fna to the most sumptuous palace decor. Only places listed under "Moderate" or "Expensive" are licensed to sell alcohol.

Note that many of the **palace-restaurants** are well hidden in the Medina and often difficult to find, especially at night; if in doubt, phone in advance and ask for directions – sometimes the restaurant will send someone to meet you. Be wary of palace-restaurants that aren't listed below; they tend to be geared towards tour groups, with kitsch belly-dancing entertainment, and uninteresting food.

△ Evening stroll, Rue Bab Agnaou

Overlooking the Djemaa

All these places appear on the map on p.443.

Argana The closest vantage point over the Djemaa, right on top of the action, and not at all a bad place to eat. Menus are 90–150dh, and dishes include lamb tajine with prunes, and seafood pastilla, a new-fangled variation on the traditional Fassi dish.

Café du Grand Balcon Next door to the *Hôtel CTM*, this place has the fullest view over the Djemaa, taking it all in from a perfect vantage point, but it isn't as close up as the *Argana*, and it serves only drinks (tea, coffee and sodas) – no food at all.

Chez Chegrouni Come at a quiet time if you want to bag one of the seats on the upstairs terrace that actually do overlook the square. Popular with tourists (you won't see a Moroccan in here), this place does decent couscous and tajines at moderate prices (mostly 50dh a throw), though the portions are on the small side.

Hôtel du Café de France The hotel itself is wretched but the restaurant and café are reliable

and reasonably priced – with a view over the eastern side of the Djemaa.

Hôtel CTM The rooftop café here does a very good-value continental breakfast, but otherwise serves only drinks, and gives a view onto most of the square.

Les Prémices Good Moroccan and European food including tasty gazpacho, well-prepared tajines, steaks, fish, pizzas and even crème brulée. It's on the very southeastern corner of the square, but close enough for a view of the action, and very moderately priced (you can eat pretty well for 100dh, very well for 150dh).

Terrasses de l'Alhambra Rather a tourist trap, and the food is overpriced and not consistently good, but it does have a great location overlooking the northeastern arm of the Djemaa, with two covered terraces, menus at 115dh and 130dh and lots of pizzas, pasta and salad.

Cheap cafés and restaurants

Apart from the Djemaa itself (see box, p.470), there's a a concentration of cheap and basic eateries on Rue Bani Marine, a narrow street that runs south from the post office and Bank al Maghrib on Djemaa el Fna, between and parallel to Rue Bab Agnaou and Rue Moulay Ismail. Another street of cheap eats, with grills on one side and fried fish on the other, is the small street that runs from Arset el Maach alongside Place des Ferblantiers to the entrance of the El Badi

Palace (see map p.469). There's also a row of places just outside the walls at Bab Doukkala, between the bus station and the grand taxi stand. All the following are on the map on p.443, unless stated.

El Bahja 24 Rue Bani Marine. This place (whose patron has appeared on a British TV food programme) is popular with locals and knowing tourists alike. Don't miss the *viande hachée* and house yoghurt. Set menus 52–65dh.

Café des Épices Place Rahba Kedima, north side; see map p.447. A small café offering refuge from the hubbub, with orange juice, mint tea, coffee in various permutations, including spiced with cinnamon, and views over the Rahba Kedima from the upper floor and the roof terrace.

Café-Restaurant el Badi by Bab Berrima; see map pp.450–451. On a rooftop looking out over Pl des Ferblantiers and towards the Mellah, this is one place to get close to the storks nesting on the walls of the El Badi Palace. It serves a limited range of hot and soft drinks, and a modest 80dh set menu of soup, salad and couscous, with a Moroccan sweetmeat for afters.

Café Restaurant Maryland Rue Ibn Rachid; see map pp.450–451. Reasonably priced and very tasty Moroccan dishes, including wonderful tajines (the rabbit is especially delicious, with lemon and raisins, but watch out – it may include the head), with tables indoors or out front. Expect to pay around 50–80dh for a three-course meal.

Chez Bahia Rue Riad Zitoun el Kedim, 50m from Djemaa el Fna. A café-diner offering pastilla, wonderful tajines and low-priced snacks, plus breakfasts of *bisara* and *harsha*. You can eat well here for 50dh.

Grillade Chez Sbai 91 Rue Kassabine. The tables are upstairs but you order downstairs at this tiny hole-in-the-wall eatery. It isn't much to look at, but the food is good, the portions are ample and the prices are low. Most customers go for the spit-roast chicken, but the best deal is a big plate of chicken *shwarma* with chips and salad, a snip at 22dh.

Patisserie Belkabir and Patisserie Duniya 63–65 Souk Smarine, by the corner of Traverse el Ksour; see map p.447. Two shops, side by side, specializing in traditional Moroccan sweetmeats, stuffed with nuts and drenched in syrup, and particularly popular during the holy month of Ramadan, when of course they are eaten by night. A kilo of assorted sticky delights costs 100dh.

Pâtisserie des Princes 32 Rue Bab Agnaou. A sparkling patisserie with mouth-watering pastries at prices that are a little high by local standards but worth the extra. They also have treats like almond milk and ice cream. The *salon de thé* at the back is a very civilized place to take breakfast, morning coffee or afternoon tea.

Djemaa el Fna foodstalls

Even if you don't eat at one of them, at some stage you should at least wander down the makeshift lane of food stalls on the Djemaa el Fna. They look great in the evening, lit by lanterns, and have boundless variety. As well as couscous and pastilla, there are spicy merguez sausages, *harira* soup, salads, fried fish, or, for the more adventurous, stewed snails (over towards the eastern side of the square), and sheep's heads complete with eyes. To partake, just take a seat on one of the benches, ask the price of a plate of food and order all you like. It's probably worth avoiding places that try to hustle you, and it's always wise to check the price of a dish before you order. Stalls patronized by Moroccans are invariably better than those whose only customers are tourists. If you want a soft drink or mineral water with your meal, the stallholders will send a boy to get it for you. Guides often suggest that the stalls aren't very healthy, but, as the cooking is so visible, standards of cleanliness are doubtless higher than in many hidden kitchens. On the southern edge of the food stalls, a row of vendors sell a hot, spicy ginseng drink (*khoudenjal*), said to be an aphrodisiac, and taken with a portion of nutty cake. Orange and grapefruit juice stalls line both sides of the foodstall area at all hours of the day, but check the price first and insist on having the juice pressed in front of you – if they pull out a bottle of ready-pressed juice, it'll most likely be watered down and quite possibly mixed with squash.

The dish for which Marrakesh is known in the rest of Morocco is tanjia. As with tajine, paella or casserole, the word tanjia correctly refers to the vessel rather than the food, in this case a kind of urn. The contents are beef or sometimes lamb, cooked very slowly to be extremely tender. Some say that the best meat to use is the tongue, cheek and penis, but don't worry – you won't get those unless you ask for them. Most good restaurants offer tanjia, but there are also cheap tanjia joints which serve nothing else. Almost every district in the Medina has such a place – recognized by the tanjia urns standing at the front – but the most convenient are a trio located opposite the olive stalls in Souk Ableuh, a small square just off the Djemaa el Fna. Here you can order your tanjia in advance, and pay for it by the kilo. They will then put the meat in the urn for you, with the right seasonings, and take it to the man who stokes the furnace at the local hammam. He'll bury it in the embers for a few hours, and when it emerges, the meat will be tender and ready to eat. In fact, local butchers rent out tanjia urns to customers, so you could even pack one with cuts of your choice and take it to the hammam furnace stoker yourself. On the whole, though, it's easier to get your tanjia ready-cooked.

Restaurant Oscar Progrès 20 Rue Bani Marine. One of the best budget restaurants in town, with friendly service, excellent-value set menus, and lovely, fragrant couscous. You can fill up here for around 50dh, or be a real pig and go for the 80dh set menu.

Onaak Café Toubkal in the far corner of the Djemaa el Fna, beyond *Hôtel CTM* and best recognized by its backdrop of a dozen colourful carpets for sale. As well as fruit juices, home-made yoghurts, and patisseries, there are salads, tajines and couscous, and good-value breakfasts too.

Moderate cafés and restaurants

Bougainvillea Café 33 Rue Mouassine; see map p.447. An upmarket café and quiet retreat in the middle of the Medina, handy for a break after a hard morning's shopping in the souks. There are salads, sandwiches, cakes, juices, coffee and tea – including tea flavoured with mountain herbs from the Atlas – but most of all it's a pleasant space to relax in, doubling as an art gallery, with exhibits by a different local painter each month, and live music Saturday evenings from 8pm.

Café Arabe 184 Rue Mouassine; see map p.447 ⓦ www.cafearabe.com. A sophisticated bar and eatery in the heart of the Medina, very handy for the souks. As well as excellent Moroccan and European cooking, not to mention snappy service, there's a fine selection of alcoholic drinks including wines, plus juices, teas, cocktails and mocktails, served on the terrace, in the patio or in the salon. Expect to pay around 200dh plus drinks.

Café Restaurant Iceberg Av el Mouahidine; see map p.443. Formerly an ice-cream parlour, hence its name, this place is central and popular with Marrakshis. Downstairs, it serves the best coffee in the Medina, and it also serves beer; upstairs there's a comfortable restaurant serving French and Moroccan food, with a 60dh set menu.

Dar Mima 9 Derb Zaouia el Khadiria, off Rue Riad Zitoun el Djedid; see map pp.450–451. ☎024 38 52 52, ⓦ www.ifrance.com/darmima. A modest nineteenth-century townhouse converted into a simple but comfortable restaurant, open evenings only, from 8pm. The fine à la carte menu represents what guests might be served in the home of a well-to-do Marrakchi family. Expect to pay around 250dh per person plus wine, and be sure to book in advance (they may even arrange for somebody to meet you and show you the way).

Hôtel Ali Rue Moulay Ismail; see map p.443. Justifiably popular restaurant with à la carte lunches, and a great-value buffet every evening, featuring, *harira*, salads, couscous and ten or more tajine-style dishes – eat as much as you like for 70dh (residents 60dh).

Pizzeria Portofino 279 Av Mohammed V; see map pp.450–451 ⓦ www.portofinomarrakech.com. Quite a posh ambience, tablecloths and all, and wood-oven pizzas that are well cooked, but slightly bland, though this is easily remedied with a splash of the garlic-and-chilli olive oil they thoughtfully provide.

Pizzeria Venezia 279 Av Mohammed V; see map pp.450–451. Rooftop restaurant whose main attraction is its unparalleled view of the Koutoubia rather than its so-so pizzas, but it isn't a bad place for breakfast.

Expensive restaurants

All the following are marked on the map on pp.450–451.

Dar Marjana 15 Derb Sidi Ali Tair, off Rue Bab Doukkala ☎024 38 51 10. This restaurant is housed in an early nineteenth-century palace, said by some to be the most beautiful in the Medina. Look for the sign above the entrance to a passageway diagonally across the street from the corner of the Dar el Glaoui; take the passage and look for the green door facing you before a right turn. The set menu costs 660dh. Advance booking only; daily except Tues from 8pm.

Palais Gharnata 5–6 Derb el Arsa, off Rue Riad Zitoun el Djedid ☎024 38 96 15, ⊛www.gharnata .com. From the car park of the Dar Si Said Museum, take the gate to the right of the Préfecture de Marrakesh Medina and, after passing the Maison Tiskiwin on your right, look for signs to the restaurant. The sixteenth-century decor is magnificent, the central alabaster fountain is also sixteenth century and from Italy. The food, however, is rather mediocre, and individual diners play second fiddle to groups. Past diners (who presumably didn't get that sort of treatment) have included Jacqueline Kennedy and the Aga Khan, and scenes from *The Return of the Pink Panther* were shot here. Open evenings only, from 8pm (book before 5pm). Cost 500dh per head.

Le Pavillon 47 Derb Zaouia ☎024 38 70 40. Best approached from Rue Bab Doukkala, round the back of the Bab Doukkala mosque – look for the sign over the first archway on the right, head down the passage and it's the last door on the right. The restaurant is in a beautifully restored middle-class residence, with a tree-shaded patio and Berber wall hangings. Among the specialities whipped up by Michelin-starred French chef Laurent Tarridec are lobster ravioli and a Grand Marnier soufflé. At around 300–400dh à la carte, it's more than worth the price.

Restaurant el Bahia 1 Rue Riad Zitoun el Djedid, by the Bahia Palace ☎024 37 86 79. A beautifully restored palace, all finely carved stucco and painted wooden ceilings, with bargain-priced menus off-season (lunch 80dh, supper 120dh), or, in summer, a choice of pricier set menus based on the specialities of Marrakesh (350dh, with beef and prune tajine, seven-vegetable couscous and *chakchouka*), or of Fes (380dh, featuring pastilla, and chicken tajine with olive and lemon). Music and dancing in the evening if they have enough customers to make it worthwhile.

Restaurant Yacout 79 Sidi Ahmed Soussi ☎024 38 29 00 or 29. In a gorgeous old palace, with columns and fireplaces in super-smooth orange- and blue-striped *tadelakt* plaster, courtesy of American interior designer and Marrakesh resident Bill Willis. After a drink on the roof terrace, you move down into one of the intimate salons surrounding the courtyard for a selection of salads, followed by a tajine, then lamb couscous and (if you have room) dessert. The classic Moroccan tajine of chicken with preserved lemon and olive is a favourite here, but the fish tajine is also rated very highly. The cuisine has received Michelin plaudits in the past, though standards are beginning to slip as the tour groups move in. The menu costs 700dh per person.

Riad des Mers 411 Derb Sidi Messaoud ☎024 37 53 04. They bring their own supplies in from the coast for this French fish and seafood restaurant in a patio garden (covered in winter), run by the proprietors of the neighbouring *Riad Sindibad* (see p.439). You can start with oysters or razor shells, continue with sea bass, king prawns or monkfish brochettes, and finish with chocolate pudding. Evenings from 8pm only; closed Mon.

La Rotunda 39 Derb Lamnabha, Kasbah ☎024 38 15 85. Two menus and two chefs, one Italian, one Moroccan, at this bi-national restaurant that's made a name for itself very quickly serving fine food from both countries amidst beautifully ornate decor from the owner's collection of fine Moroccan and Venetian antiques, or with a view of the Atlas should you care to eat on the roof terrace.

Le Tanjia 14 Derb Djedid, Hay Essalam/Mellah, near Pl des Ferblantiers ☎024 38 38 36, ⊛www.ilove-marrakesh.com/letanjia. Very stylish bar restaurant billed as an "oriental brasserie" serving well-cooked Moroccan dishes, including vegetarian options, in an old mansion done out in modern decor, and not outrageously expensive by any means (count on around 300dh per head plus wine). On Sun they do a 190dh buffet brunch.

Le Tobsil 22 Derb Abdellah Ben Hessaien, near Bab Ksour ☎024 44 40 52. Sumptuous Moroccan cuisine in an intimate riad, now considered by many to be the finest restaurant in town, though the wine (included in the price) doesn't match the quality of the food. Open evenings only (7–11pm) and closed Tues; worth booking ahead; set menu 600dh.

Guéliz restaurants

Although Guéliz is not so picturesque a setting for a meal, it would be a mistake to dismiss it as Frenchified and un-Moroccan: it is, after all, the city's main centre. In fact, its restaurants are generally good value, and the pricier ones are licensed to serve wine (about 90dh a bottle). If you want to menu-browse, the main concentration of places is around Place Abdelmoumen Ben Ali. All Guéliz restaurants are shown on the map on p.432.

Cafés, patisseries and cheap restaurants

Amandine 177 Rue Mohammed el Bekal. If you're on a diet, look away now, because this is a double whammy: a café-patisserie, stuffed full of scrumptious almond-filled Moroccan pastries and French-style cream cakes, and right next-door, a plush ice-cream parlour where you can sit and eat in comfort. You can have a coffee with your choice of sweetmeat in both halves, but the ice-cream section is more spacious.

Boule de Neige 20 Rue de Youqoslavie, close to Pl Abdelmoumen Ben Ali. This lively patisserie serves continental and American breakfasts and all-day snacks, as well as good ice cream and coffee, and toast with amalou. On Sat and Sun evenings, there's live Moroccan pop music too.

Café des Negotiants Pl Abdelmoumen Ben Ali. Slap bang on the busiest corner in Guéliz, this grand café is the place to sit out on the pavement and really feel that you're in the heart of modern Marrakesh. It's also an excellent venue in which to spend the morning over a coffee, with a choice of different croissants (plain, chocolate, almond), or even crêpes and fruit juice, to accompany your caffeine fix.

Nismaq Rue de l'Imam Ali, opposite the church. It can be hard to find an honest to-goodness cheap Moroccan eatery in the Ville Nouvelle, but this place serves tasty tajines at 15–25dh a shot, great value and very popular with workers on their lunch break.

Oliveri Av el Mansour Eddahbi, behind Hôtel Agdal. Marrakesh branch of the long-established Casablanca firm (see p.387). You can eat your scoop from a proper ice-cream goblet among elegant surroundings, accompanied, should you so desire, by coffee; or else you can take it away in a waffle cone.

Moderate restaurants

Bagatelle 101 Rue de Yougoslavie ☏ 024 43 02 74. Photos of Marrakesh in the 1950s deck the walls, and there's a lovely vine-shaded garden to eat in at this French-style restaurant which first opened its doors in 1949. You can start with an entrée such as pork and guinea fowl terrine, or pan-fried lamb's brain with capers, take in some Portuguese-style veal tongue, or duck confit with baked apple for your main course, and finish off with tart of the day or lemon and vodka sorbet. Throw in a coffee or a mint tea, and you'll pay around 200–250dh per head. Closed Wed.

Le Cantanzaro 50 Rue Tarik Ibn Ziad ☏ 024 43 37 31. One of the city's most popular Italian restaurants, crowded at lunchtime with Marrakshis, expats and tourists. Specialities include saltimbocca alla romana and rabbit in mustard sauce, and there's crème brûlée or tiramisú to round it off with. You're strongly advised to book, but you can also just turn up and queue for a table. Mon–Sat noon–2.30pm & 7.15–11pm.

Chez Jack'Line 63 Av Mohammed V, near Pl Abdelmoumen Ben Ali ☏ 024 44 75 47. French, Italian and Moroccan dishes are all served here under the skilful direction of the indefatigable Jack'Line Pinguet and the beady eye (upstairs) of Ulysses, her parrot. You can eat splendidly for 150dh à la carte, plus wine — top choices are the steaks and pasta dishes, including superb cannelloni — or go for the 80dh set menu based on couscous or tajine. Daily noon–2.30pm & 7–11pm

Chez Pierre Rue Oum Rabia, next to the Diamant Noir nightclub. Sandwiches, omelettes, crêpes and pizzas, all served round the clock – very handy if you emerge from a night's clubbing with a ravenous hunger. The walls are decorated with 1960s black-and-white stills featuring personalities of the era from Brigitte Bardot to Jimi Hendrix, but it's the hours rather than the decor which most appeal. Daily 24hr.

Le Dragon d'Or 82 Bd Mohammed Zerktouni ☏ 024 43 06 17. Vietnamese and Chinese cuisine, with bright and cheerful decor; it's popular with local families and there's a takeaway service. Prices are reasonable if a group of several people pick and mix. Open lunchtime and evenings.

Hôtel Farouk 66 Av Hassan II. From noon the hotel restaurant offers an excellent-value 60dh set menu with soup, salad, couscous, tajine or brochettes, followed by fruit, ice cream or home-made yoghurt. Alternatively, tuck in to one of their excellent wood-oven pizzas (30–50dh).

Restaurant 33 Marrakech 33 Av Mohammed V. Quite smart for a mid-range place, with royal blue table cloths, and the usual favourites – tajine, couscous and tanjia – on the menu, along with a big choice of brochettes – lamb, veal, chicken, turkey, fish, *kefta* (minced lamb) and spicy merguez sausage. Wine is served, and there's a good-value 80dh menu. Daily noon–3pm & 7pm–midnight.

Rôtisserie de la Paix 68 Rue de Yougoslavie, alongside the former cinema Lux-Palace ☎024

43 31 18, ⓦ www.restaurant-diaffa.ma/rotisserie. An open-air grill, established in 1949, specializing in mixed grills barbecued over wood, usually with a fish option for non-meat-eaters. It's all served either in a salon with a roaring fire in winter, or in the shaded garden in summer. Couscous served on Fridays only. Daily noon–3pm & 7–11pm.

La Taverne 22 Bd Mohammed Zerktouni ☎024 44 61 26. As well as a drinking tavern, this is a pretty decent restaurant – in fact, it claims to be the oldest in town – where you can dine on French and Moroccan fare indoors or in a lovely tree-shaded garden. The 110dh four-course set menu is great value. Daily 12.30–3pm & 7–10.30pm.

Expensive restaurants

Le Comptoir Av Echouada, Hivernage ☎024 43 77 02, ⓦ www.comptoirdarna.com. Downstairs it's a restaurant serving reliably good Moroccan and international cuisine (with a specific choice of Moroccan or foreign dishes for each course). Upstairs it's a chic lounge bar, very popular with Marrakesh's young and rich, with cabaret entertainment.

🏃 **Al Fassia** 232 Av Mohammed V ☎024 43 40 60. Truly Moroccan – both in decor and cuisine –specializing in dishes from the country's culinary capital, Fes. Start with that great classic, pigeon pastilla, followed by a choice of four different lamb tajines, among other fine Fassi offerings. There's a lunchtime set menu for around 150dh, but dinner will cost twice that. The ambience and service are superb. Note that Al Fassia has had to change location in the recent past, and word is that it may have to again, so keep your ear to the ground.

Grand Café de la Poste Rue el Imam Malik, just off Av Mohammed V behind the post office ☎024 43 30 38. More grand than café, this is in fact quite a posh restaurant serving international cuisine (roast chicken with thyme and olives, for example, or even English-style roast beef). Main courses go for 100–150dh. Wash it down with a cup of Earl Grey, or a choice of rums, tequilas and fine brandies if you prefer something harder. Daily 8am–1am.

Le Jacaranda 32 Bd Mohammed Zerktouni, on Pl Abdelmoumen Ben Ali ☎024 44 72 15, ⓦ www.lejacaranda.ma. Reliable French and Moroccan cuisine, starting with the likes of locally renowned oysters from Oualidia on the coast, beef carpaccio, or snails in garlic butter, followed by duck confit with baked apples and

wild mushrooms, or perhaps a fish trilogy tajine. À la carte eating will set you back around 300dh a head plus wine, or there are lunchtime set menus for 80–105dh. The restaurant doubles as an art gallery, with different exhibits on its walls each month.

Puerto Banus Rue Ibn Hanbal, opposite the police headquarters in the Royal Tennis Club ☎024 44 65 34. A Spanish fish restaurant – though French-managed – with specialities such as gazpacho, paella and Oualidia oysters. There's also a good selection of French and Moroccan dishes, including seafood pastilla. Count on 200dh per head without wine eating à la carte, though at lunchtimes there's a good-value 95dh buffet including a serve-yourself salad bar.

The Red House Bd el Yarmouk, opposite the Medina wall, Hivernage ☎024 43 70 40, ⓦ www .theredhouse-marrakech.com. You'll need to reserve ahead to eat at this palatial riad, beautifully decorated in stucco and zellij. There's a Moroccan set menu (450dh), featuring pigeon pastilla and lamb tajine with prunes and sesame, or you can dine à la carte on the likes of prawn and *langouste* ravioli or sashimi of trout and John Dory.

La Trattoria 179 Rue Mohammed el Bekal ☎024 43 26 41, ⓦ www.latrattoriamarrakech.com. This place serves the best Italian food in town, with impeccable, friendly service and excellent cooking. The restaurant is located in a 1920s house decorated by the acclaimed American designer Bill Willis (as in the *Hôtel Tichka*; see p.441). As well as freshly made pasta, steaks and escalopes, there are specialities like *tagliata de boeuf* – made with beef, capers and herbs from the Atlas mountains – plus a wonderful tiramisú to squeeze in for afters. Daily 7–11.30pm.

Vaudeville Rue de la Makhazine at Pl 16 Novembre ℡ 024 49 59 55, 🌐 www .ilove-marrakesh.com/levaudeville. French brasserie serving what passes in France for plain home-style cooking, with lots of meat dishes and red wine to accompany it. There's a lunchtime set menu for 150dh, and one in the evening for 250dh. Closed Mon.

Villa Rosa 64 Av Hassan II, next to the *Hôtel Farouk* ℡ 024 43 08 32. French-owned restaurant with light wood, pastel shades, silk drapes, a French menu and faultless dishes. There's also a jazz bar and a courtyard of citrus trees. You can eat well for 450dh a head plus wine.

Bars and nightlife

Entertainment and nightlife in the **Medina** revolve around Djemaa el Fna and its cafés, though sometimes there might be a music group playing in an enclosure behind the Koutoubia on Avenue Mohammed V. For a drink in the Medina, choices are limited; apart from the *Tazi* (listed below), you can get a beer in the *Café Restaurant Iceberg* (see p.471), or, more sophisticated, is the *Café Arabe* (see p.471). In **Guéliz**, there's more variety, with a sprinkling of decent bars and nightclubs. In particular, you'll find several **bars** that bear no resemblance to the usual Moroccan drinking dens full of stupefied inebriates. **Nightclubs in Marrakesh can be fun too; most play a mix of Western and Arabic** music, but it's the latter that really fills the dance floor. None of them really gets going until around midnight (in fact, some don't open until then), and they usually stay open until 3 or 4am.

Unless otherwise stated, all the places listed below are in Guéliz, and shown on the map on p.432.

Bars

Café-Bar de l'Escale Rue Mauretania, just off Av Mohammed V. This place has been going since 1947 and specializes in good bar snacks, such as fried fish or spicy merguez sausages – you could even come here for lunch or dinner (there's a dining area at the back), but it isn't recommended for unaccompanied women. Open 11am 10.30pm.

Chesterfield Pub 119 Av Mohammed V. Next to the *Nassim Hôtel*, this supposedly English pub – it's nothing of the sort – is one of Marrakesh's more sophisticated watering holes, with a comfortable if rather smoky bar area, all soft seats and muted lighting. There's also a more relaxed, open-air poolside terrace to lounge about on with your draught beer or cocktail of a summer evening. Daily 10am–midnight.

Grand Hôtel Tazi Corner of Rue Bab Agnaou and Rue el Mouahidine, Medina; see map p.443. Once, this was the only bar in the Medina where you could get a drink, and it's still the cheapest (beers from 25dh). There's nothing fancy about the bar area – squeezed in-between the restaurant and the lobby, and frequently spilling over into the latter – but it manages to be neither rough nor pretentious (a rare feat among Marrakesh drinking dens) and women should have no worries about drinking here.

Hôtel Agdal 1 Bd Mohammed Zerktouni. Pretty cosy as Moroccan bars go, and one where women should feel reasonably comfortable. Open till 12.30am.

Samovar 145 Rue Mohammed el Bekal, next to the *Hôtel Oudaya*. An old-school, low-life drinking den, a male hangout with bar girls in attendance. The customers get increasingly wasted as the evening progresses – if you want to see the underbelly of Morocco's drinking culture, this is where to come. Definitely not recommended for women visitors, however. Daily 10am–11pm.

Nightclubs

Diamant Noir Rue Oum er Bia, behind *Hôtel Marrakesh*. Look for the signpost on Av Mohammed V to find this lively dance club where Western pop and disco alternate with Algerian and Moroccan raï music. There are two bars, quite a sophisticated range of drinks (the 100dh entry ticket includes one), and a mainly young crowd, with a gay contingent.

🏃 **Pacha Marrakech** Av Mohammed VI (southern extension), Nouvelle Zone Hôtelière de l'Aguedal ℡ 024 38 84 00, 🌐 www .pachamarrakech.com. The Marrakesh branch of the famous Ibiza club claims to have the biggest and best sound system in Africa, and it's certainly the place to come if DJing skills, acoustics and visuals are important for your clubbing experience. Big-name DJs from abroad regularly play here – check the website for current line-ups. There's even a free shuttle service to and from town (call to arrange). Sun–Thurs 100–150dh; Fri & Sat: 200–250dh; occasionally as much as 350dh for a big event; entry includes one drink.

Paradise *Hôtel Kempinski*, Bd el Mansour Eddahbi, Hivernage. A plush and trendy club that tries to be reasonably exclusive (so dress smartly). The clientele of well-heeled Moroccans, with a sprinkling of expats, plus a few tourists staying at the attached five-star hotel, dance to some well-mixed sounds, mostly at the commercial – or at least, the more tuneful – end of house and techno. The drinks list is impressively long, and impressively expensive. Entry is 150dh weekdays, 200dh weekends.

Point Rouge 68 Bd Mohammed Zerktouni. Not the poshest joint in town (in fact, truth be told, rather a dive), but it's got to be the most good-natured and the least pretentious of Marrakesh's nightspots. Drunken bonhomie reigns as a mixed crowd of all ages do their thing to the sound of a four-piece Arabic folk band with female vocalist, interspersed with disco, pop and hip-hop records. No one stands on ceremony and a good time is generally had by all. The 50dh entry ticket includes your first drink.

Tanzania Moulay Hassan I Kawab Center, Avenue Moulay el Hassan, Hivernage ☏024 42 44 49. Sophisticated open-air club-restaurant offering food, drink, music and dancing. Entry is usually free.

Le Teatro Hotel Es Saadi, Av el Kaissia (Qadassia) ☏024 44 88 11. Currently Marrakesh's most happening nightclub, located in, as its name suggests, an old theatre.

VIP Club Pl de la Liberté. The gullet-like entrance leads down to the first level, where there's an "oriental cabaret" (meaning a belly-dancing floor-show), and then further down to the deepest level, where there's what the French call a *boîte*, meaning a sweaty little nightclub. It's got a circular dancefloor and a small bar area, but despite its diminutive size, the place rarely seems to be full. Entry is 100dh during the week, 150dh weekends.

Casino

Grand Casino in the *Hôtel La Mamounia*, Av Bab Djedid Ⓦwww.grandcasinomamounia.com. Walking in from the Medina, you'll find this grand high-class casino pretty unreal. Under huge chandeliers and Art Deco glass panels, you can – so long as you are not Muslim – gamble away your life savings on roulette, craps or blackjack (daily 9pm–4am), or feed your change to the slot machines (from 5pm weekdays, 3pm weekends). Entrance is free, but scruffy clothes are not permitted, and men need a jacket and tie. The casino remains open while the rest of the hotel undergoes renovation.

Shopping

There are a massive number of shops in Marrakesh selling all kinds of crafts, but there's nothing you won't get cheaper elsewhere. Marrakesh's attraction is that you don't have to go elsewhere to get it, and if you're flying home out of Marrakesh, then buying your souvenirs here means you won't have to lug them round the country with you.

Before setting off into the souks in search of rugs, blankets, or whatever, it's worth taking a look at the **Ensemble Artisanal** (Mon–Sat 8.30am–7pm, Sun 8.30am–1pm), on Avenue Mohammed V, midway between the Koutoubia and the ramparts at Bab Nkob. This government-run complex of small arts and crafts shops holds a reasonable range of goods, notably leather, textiles and carpets. Shopping here is hassle-free, and the prices, which are supposedly fixed (though actually you can haggle here too), are a good gauge of the going rate if you intend to bargain elsewhere. At the back are a dozen or so workshops where you can watch young people learning a range of crafts including carpet-weaving. Another place with supposedly fixed prices is **Entreprise Bouchaib Complexe d'Artisanat** at 7 Derb Baissi Kasbah, on Rue de la Kasbah near the Saadian Tombs (daily 8.30am–8pm; Ⓦwww.bouchaib.net). The "fixed" prices here are only slightly higher than what you might pay in the souks, and, though you won't be allowed to browse freely, the sales assistants who follow you round are generally quite charming and informative. In particular it's a good place to check out carpets and get an idea of the absolute maximum prices you should be paying.

Otherwise, the best place to buy **carpets** is, naturally enough, in the carpet souk (Souk des Tapis), just off Rahba Kedima by the Criée Berbère, with old rugs and carpets on sale at Bazar du Sud (nos.14 & 117), and new ones at Bazar Jouti (nos.16 & 119). The carpets here come from all over the south of Morocco, and most are coloured with natural dyes such as saffron (yellow), cochineal (red) and indigo (blue). A large carpet might cost 2000dh, but you might be able to find a small rug for around 500dh.

For **jewellery**, there's a souk for the kind of gaudy gold variety favoured by Moroccan women just off Souk el Kebir, but tourists tend to favour chunkier silver pieces. Boutique Bel Hadj, at 22 & 33 Souk Fondouk Louarzazi, off the north side of Place Bab Fteuh, is a good place to look for those. Abdellatif Bellawi, 56 & 103 Kissariat Lossta (one of the passages in the *Kissaria* between Souk el Kebir and Souk Attarine) also has big silver Berber bangles, as well as lots of beads from West Africa, the Sahara and Yemen as well as Morocco. For something smarter, not to mention a lot pricier, you need to head to Guéliz, where shops like Amazonite (94 Bd El Mansour Eddahbi) and Bazar Atlas (129 Av Mohammed V) have some lovely pieces.

tourists. For ordinary Moroccan kaftans, gandoras (sleeveless kaftans) and such like, try the covered souk just to your left as you come into Souk Smarine from the Djemaa el Fna. For something smarter, Maison du Kaftan Marocain at 65 Rue Sidi el Yumani has some beautiful but pricey robes, tunics and kaftans in shimmering silks and velvets, and sells to celeb customers like Jean-Paul Gautier and Samuel L. Jackson, whose photos are displayed on the wall. Not far away, Kulchi, at 1 Rue des Ksour, is a chic little boutique selling Moroccan clothes aimed at Western women, while in the heart of the souks, Femmes de Marrakech, at 67 Souk el Kchachbia, is a fair-trade co-op selling excellent hand-made cotton and linen dresses and kaftans.

Other good buys include **babouches** (Moroccan slippers), for which there's a whole souk (Souk Smata; see p.449) dedicated to nothing else, or there are tin, brass and iron **lanterns**, made and sold in several places, but especially in Place des Ferblantiers. At the southern end of Rue Riad Zitoun el Kedim, shops that originally sold buckets and flip-flops for hammam use now sell all sorts of goods made from **recycled rubber tyres**, including tuffets and picture frames. For **musical instruments**, the place to look is Rue Riad Zitoun el Djedid. **Wooden kitchen implements** (including wooden scissors for cutting home-made pasta) can be found around the junction where Souk Smarine forks to become Souk el Kebir and Souk el Attarine, while the main shop in town for **tajines** – practical rather than decorative ones – is Herman at 3 Rue Moulay Ismail, just off Place Foucault. In the way of **foodstuffs**, the shops in the olive souk, just off Djemaa el Fna by *Terraces de l'Alhambra,* has not only lots and lots of olives, but also lemons preserved in brine – very handy if you want to try your hand at a chicken tajine at home.

Listings

Airlines Atlas Blue, Menara Airport ☏ 024 42 42 00; British Airways, Menara Airport ☏ 024 22 94 64; Royal Air Maroc, 197 Av Mohammed V ☏ 024 42 55 00 or 01. Regional Air Lines do not currently have an office in Marrakesh, but can be contacted via their Casablanca call centre (☏ 022 53 80 80).

5

American Express Represented by Voyages Schwartz, Immeuble Moutaouakil, 1 Rue Mauritanie, Guéliz ☎024 43 74 69, ✉schwartz@wanadoo.net.ma; also by S'Tours, Immeuble F, 61 Rue de Yougoslavie, Guéliz ☎024 43 67 46, ✉dmc@stours.co.ma.

Banks The main area for banks in the Medina is off the south side of the Djemaa el Fna on Rue Moulay Ismail. In Guéliz, the main area is along Av Mohammed V between Pl Abdelmoumen Ben Ali and the market. Most major branches have ATMs. BMCE's branches in Guéliz (144 Av Mohammed V), the Medina (Rue Moulay Ismail on Place Foucault) and Hivernage (Av de France, opposite *Hôtel Atlas*) also have bureaux de change which open Mon–Fri 8am–7pm, Sat 9am–1pm & 2–6pm, Sun 9am–4pm. The post office on Pl 16 Novembre will change cash during opening hours, while in the Djemaa el Fna, the post office's bureau de change is round the back, by the telephones, and opens Mon–Sat 8am–6pm. Even outside these hours, the *Hôtel Ali* (see p.437) and most upmarket hotels will change travellers' cheques and major hard currencies, though the posh hotels are likely to give bad rates.

Bicycles, mopeds and motorbikes You can rent bicycles on Pl de la Liberté and a number of roadside locations in Hivernage, most notably at the junction of Av el Kaissia (also spelt Qadassia) with Av du Président Kennedy. Mopeds and scooters can be rented at Loc2Roues on the upper floor of Galerie Élite, 212 Av Mohammed V (☎024 43 02 94, ⦿www.loc2roues.com) and Marrakesh Motos, also called Chez Jamal Boucetta, 31 bis Av Mohammed Abdelkrim el Khattabi (☎073 01 84 48). Expect to pay around 100dh a day for a bicycle, 300dh for a moped or scooter.

Bookshops The best bookshop in town is Librairie Chatr 19 Av Mohammed V, Guéliz, with lots of books on Morocco in French, including books on trekking and off-roading, plus a small selection of titles in English. Librairie d'Art in *Résidence Taïb*, 55 Bd Mohammed Zerktouni, Guéliz, has lots of art and coffee-table books on Marrakesh and Morocco. In the Medina, there's a small bookshop which sells French books and a range of stationery, Librairie Ghazali, 51 Rue Bab Agnaou.

Car rental Marrakesh rates are generally the most competitive after Casablanca. The best-value deals are usually from local agencies, of which there are many, and with whom you can bargain for discounts (but those hustling tourists on the street are of course best avoided). Try: Concorde Cars, 154 Av Mohammed V ☎024 43 11 16; Fathi Cars, 183 Av Mohammed V ☎024 43 17 63; Najm Car, shop 9, Galerie Jakar, 61 Av Mohammed V

☎024 43 78 91, ⦿www.najmcar.com; or Nomade Car, 112 Av Mohammed V ☎079 56 36 11. National/international agencies include: Avis, 137 Av Mohammed V ☎024 43 25 25, ℗024 43 12 65; Budget, 66 Bd Mohammed Zerktouni ☎024 43 11 80, ℗024 43 74 83; First Car, 234 Av Mohammed V ☎024 43 87 64, ℗024 43 87 49; Hertz, 154 Av Mohammed V ☎024 43 99 84, ℗024 43 99 83; National, 1 Rue de la Liberté ☎024 43 06 83; most have desks at the airport, or will meet arrivals by arrangement. Many hotels can also arrange car rental, often at competitive rates. For minibus or 4x4 rental, try Sahara Expeditions on the corner of Rue el Mouahdine with Rue Bani Marine (☎024 42 79 77, ⦿www.saharaexpe.ma).

Car spares and repairs A good place to start is Bd Moulay Rachid between Av Mohammed Abdelkrim el Khattabi and Rue Mohammed el Bekal, where you'll find mechanics' workshops on one side of the street, and spare parts shops on the other. Another place is Rue Mohammed el Mellakh, opposite the city wall west of Bab Doukkala, where there's a garage, a spares shop and a service station. More spares dealers are on Av el Mansour Eddahbi, by the junction of Rue de la Liberté, while grand taxi drivers mostly seem to use the mechanics between Rue Oqba Ben Nafi and Rue Ibn Rochd in Arset el Maach just south of Av Houmann el Fetaouki. Recent recommendations include (for Mercedes, Chrysler and Jeep in particular) Auto Star in the industrial estate out on the Agadir road. For tyres, if you don't trust good old Moroccan mechanics, try the Goodyear Garage (Guéliz Pneus), 60 Av Mohammed Abdelkrim el Khattabi, Route de Casablanca (☎024 44 75 26).

Cinemas In Guéliz, the Colisée, alongside the *Café Le Siroua* on Bd Mohammed Zerktouni, is one of the best, showing general releases. In the Medina, there's the Cinéma Mabrouka on Rue Bab Agnaou. The Cinéma Eden, off Rue Riad Zitoun el Jedid, is more downmarket, but watching a film at the Eden is a real Moroccan experience, especially when it puts on the traditional Bollywood/kung fu double bill, known locally as "*l'histoire et la géographie*".

Consulates France, 1 Rue Ibn Khaldoun ☎024 38 82 00; UK Honorary Consul, *Résidence Taib* (entrance A, mezzanine floor), 55 Bd Mohammed Zerktouni, ☎024 43 50 95.

Cookery courses The *Maison Arabe* (see p.438) offers workshops in Moroccan cooking for groups of up to eight people, at 1600dh a day for one or two people and 500–600dh per person for groups of three to eight. It's also possible to learn Moroccan cooking with the Rhode School of Cuisine (see p.37), who offer week-long courses from \$2395 per person, including villa accommodation in the palmery and meals on site.

Courier delivery services FedEx (℡ 024 44 82 57) and DHL (℡ 024 43 76 47 or 48) have offices next to each other at 113 Av Abdelkrim el Khattabi, just northwest of the junction with Bd Mohammed Zerktouni.

Dentist Dr Bennani, 112 Av Mohammed V (first floor), opposite the ONMT office, Guéliz (℡ 024 44 91 36), is recommended and speaks some English.

Doctors Dr Abdelmajid Ben Tbib, 171 Av Mohammed V, Guéliz (℡ 024 43 10 30), is recommended and speaks English. Dr Frédéric Reitzer, Immeuble Moulay Youssef (4th floor), Rue de la Liberté, Guéliz ℡ 024 43 95 62 also speaks some English. There's also an emergency call-out service, SOS Médecins (℡ 024 40 40 40), which charges 400dh per consultation. See also "Hospitals" next column.

Festivals and events As well as the two week Festival National des Arts Populaires held in June (see p.460), Marrakesh has an annual Marathon, run on the third or fourth Sunday in January (see ⓦ www.marathon-marrakech.com for details), and the Marrakesh Film Festival in November (ⓦ www .festivalmarrakech.com), in which the featured movies are shown at cinemas across town, and on large screens in the El Badi Palace and the Djemaa el Fna. Held for the first time in 2000, the festival has royal patronage, and has helped to encourage the use of Marrakesh and its hinterland as a location in Hollywood productions.

Food shopping The municipal market on Rue Ibn Toumert, in Guéliz, is convenient for food supplies, as is the covered market between Av Houmane el Fetouaki and Arset el Maach in the Medina. There are a couple of hypermarkets on the outskirts, but the best supermarket actually in town is Aswak on Av 11 Janvier at the junction with Av Prince Moulay Abdallah, across the street from the bus station.

Gay Marrakesh For gay men, a certain amount of cruising goes on in the crowds of the Djemaa el Fna in the evening, and there's a gay presence at the Diamant Noir nightclub (see p.475). The gay tourist scene in Marrakesh is growing, and a number of riads are run by gay couples, but there is no easily perceptible lesbian scene in Marrakesh as yet.

Golf There are three eighteen-hole golf courses in Marrakesh: the Marrakesh Royal Golf Club (℡ 024 40 47 05), 10km out of town on the old Ouarzazate road, once played on by Churchill and Eisenhower; the Palmeraie Golf Club (℡ 024 30 10 10), built, as the name suggests, in the palmery, off the Route de Casablanca, northeast of town; and the Amelkis Golf Club, 12km out on the Route de Ouarzazate

(℡ 024 40 44 14). All courses are open to non-members, with green fees at 400–600dh per day.

Hammams There are plenty of hammams in the Medina. The three closest to the Djemaa el Fna are Hammam Polo on Rue de la Recette, one on the same street as *Hôtel Afriquia*, and one at the northern end of Rue Riad Zitoun el Kedim. All are marked on our map on p.443, and open simultaneously for men and women with separate entrances for each. A growing trend in Marrakesh is expensive hammams that are exclusively for tourists; one such is Hammam Ziani, 14 Rue Riad Zitoun el Djedid (℡ 062 71 55 71, ⓦ www .hammamziani.ma), open for both sexes (separate areas) daily 8am–10pm, costing 50dh for a simple steam bath, or 270dh for an all-in package with massage; even dearer is Les Bains de Marrakesh, 2 Derb Sedra, by Bab Agnaou in the kasbah (℡ 024 38 14 28, ⓦ www.lesbainsdemarrakech .com), where prices start at 150dh; despite this you won't (unless you've sent by able to share a steam bath experience with your partner – if you want to do that, you'll have to stay at one of the many riads with their own in-house hammam.

Hospitals Private clinics that have high standards and are accustomed to settling bills with insurance companies include: Clinique Yasmine, 12 Rue Ibn Toumert, Guéliz ℡ 024 43 96 94; and Polyclinique du Sud, at the corner of Rue de Yougoslavie and Rue Ibn Aïcha, Guéliz ℡ 024 44 79 99.

Internet access One of the best places to get online is at the Moulay Abdeslam Cyber-Park, on Av Mohammed V opposite the Ensemble Artisanal (daily 10am–7pm); there's a super-modern Internet office, with fast connections and low rates (5dh/hr) though, annoyingly, you have to guess how much time you're going to use and pay for it in advance. Also, almost the entire park, especially the area near the Internet office, is a free Wi-Fi zone. Internet cafés around the Djemaa el Fna include Cyber de la Place in an arcade off Rue Bani Marine by the *Hôtel Ichbilia* (daily 10am–10pm; 7dh/hr), Hanan Internet at the southern end of Rue Bab Agnaou (daily 9am–midnight; 7dh/hr), but you get a cheaper deal at Cyber Internet Riad, 62 Rue Riad Zitoun el Kedim (daily 9am–10pm; 4dh/hr). In Guéliz, Internet cafés are surprisingly thin on the ground; try Jawal, in a yard behind the CTM office on Bd Mohammed Zerktouni (daily 9am–10pm; 6dh/hr), the Café Siraoua a block to the east (daily 9am–midnight; 8dh/hr), or Espace Internet, in the basement at 185 Av Mohammed V (Mon–Sat 8.30am–9.30pm, Sun 11am–10pm; 10dh/hr).

Laundry In Guéliz, Pressing Oasis, 44 Rue Tarik Ibn Zaid, two doors from *Hôtel Toulousain*; in the Medina, Pressing du Sud, 10 Rue Bab Agnaou, near the Djemaa el Fna (entrance on Rue de la Recette).

Newspapers The most reliable newsagent for American and British newspapers is outside the ONMT office on Av Mohammed V, though you'll find *USA Today*, the *International Herald Tribune*, and various British dailies on sale at stalls elsewhere, especially around the south side of Place Djemaa el Fna.

Pharmacies There are several along Av Mohammed V, including a good one, the Pharmacie de la Liberté, just off Pl de la Liberté, which will call a doctor for you if necessary. In the Medina, try Pharmacie de la Place and Pharmacie du Progrès on Rue Bab Agnaou just by Pl Djemaa el Fna. There's an all-night pharmacy by the Commissariat de Police on Djemaa el Fna and another on Rue Khalid Ben Oualid near the fire station in Guéliz. Other all-night and weekend outlets are listed in pharmacy windows.

Photography Photographic equipment, film and batteries can be obtained from Wrédé, 142 Av Mohammed V (☎024 43 57 39).

Police The tourist police (*brigade touristique*) are based at the northern end of Rue Sidi Mimoun (☎024 38 46 01). There's also a police station on the west side of the Djemaa el Fna.

Post office The main post office, which receives all *poste restante* mail, is on Pl 16 Novembre, midway down Av Mohammed V in Guéliz (Mon–Fri 8am–4.30pm for full services; Mon–Fri 8am–6.30pm & Sat 8–11.45am for stamps, Western Union and money changing). There is a separate office, round the side, for sending parcels. The Medina post office on Pl Djemaa el Fna is open similar hours, but has a separate bureau de change (see p.478).

Swimming pools Many hotels (but, alas, not the *Mamounia*) allow nonresidents to use their pools if you have a meal, or for a fee. Useful if you're staying in the Medina is the *Grand Hôtel Tazi* (50dh). In the palmery, there's *Nikki Beach* (formerly the *Sunset Club*), Route de la Palmeraie by the *Golf Palace* hotel (daily 9am–7pm; 200dh; ☎024 36 87 27). Handy if you're with kids who hate sight-seeing is Oasiria, at km4, Route du Barrage, on the Asni/Oumnass road (daily 10am–6pm; weekdays 160dh full day, 130dh half-day, children under 1.5m 80dh/70dh, weekends adults 180dh/140dh, children 100dh/80dh; ☎024 38 04 38, ⊛www.oasiria.com); it even runs free shuttle buses from town in July–Oct, and offers a 10 percent discount to readers presenting a copy of this book at reception.

Travel agents Local tour operators include: Travel Link, 19 Rue Mauritania, Apartment 8, Guéliz ☎024 44 87 97, ⊛www.travellink.ma; Sahara Expeditions, corner of Rue el Mouahadine with Rue Bani Marine ☎024 42 79 77, ⊛www.saharaexpe.ma.

Moving on

Trains are the most comfortable way of getting to Casablanca and Rabat. The station is on Avenue Hassan II, a fifteen-minute walk west of Guéliz (served by buses #3, #8, #10, #13 and #14 from Place Foucault). If you're heading to **Tangier** it's possible to do the trip in one go, most easily by booking a couchette on the night train (350dh), preferably on the morning of the day of travel.

Buses to most **long-distance destinations** leave from the main terminal at **Bab Doukkala**, a ten-minute walk from Guéliz, twenty minutes from the Djemaa el Fna (☎024 43 39 33; served by the same buses that go to the train station). Buy tickets a day in advance – or turn up early – for the more popular destinations such as Fes, El Jadida, Taroudannt or Zagora; **CTM** and all the private companies have their own individual ticket windows – choices can be more extensive than at first appears. CTM also has an office on Boulevard Mohammed Zerktouni in Guéliz (☎024 44 83 28), where you can buy tickets, and where CTM buses all stop.

Supratours express buses for Essaouira, Agadir, Ouarzazate and the Western Sahara leave from outside the train station in Guéliz, though they only sell tickets if there is space after the allocation for train passengers from Casablanca/Rabat. Grands taxis are generally on hand to pick up the overflow at these times and are good value, a place to Agadir costing around 84dh.

Collective grands taxis can also be useful for other destinations and run from behind Bab Doukkala bus station, or (for High Atlas destinations) from the Bab er Robb *gare routière*, which is actually 2km beyond Bab er Robb. To Oukaïmeden, shared taxis operate during the skiing season only, heading up in the morning and back in the evening, and you will have to pay for the round trip, even if staying the night, which may also leave you without any sure transport back.

Marrakesh's **airport** (☎024 44 78 55 or 024 44 79 10) is 4km southwest of town, past the Menara Garden. It's not advisable to walk it (muggings are not unheard of), but you can take a petit taxi (they won't use the meter; expect to pay around 50–60dh) or an hourly bus leaving from Place Foucault every hour from 6.15am to 11.15pm, before heading north up Avenue Mohammed V, where you can pick it up between a quarter and half past the hour; it should reach the airport at a quarter to.

Travel details

Trains

Marrakesh to: Casablanca Voyageurs (9 daily; 3hr 10min); Fes (7 daily; 7hr 40min); Kenitra (9 daily; 4hr 50min); Meknes (7 daily; 6hr 45min); Oujda (2 daily changing at Casa or Fes; 13hr 40min); Rabat (9 daily; 4hr 15min); Safi (2 daily changing at Benguerir; 2hr 55min); Settat (9 daily; 2hr 5min); Tangier (1 direct & 4 connecting daily; 9hr 40min).

Buses

Marrakesh to: Agadir (4 CTM, 3 Supratours & 20 others daily; 4hr); Aoulouz via Tizi n'Test (3 daily; 9hr); Asni (10 daily; 1hr 30min); Azilal (2 daily; 3hr); Beni Mellal (2 CTM & some 30 others daily; 4hr); Casablanca (4 CTM daily and others roughly half-hourly 4am–9pm; 4hr); Dakhla (1 CTM, 1 Supratours and 3 others daily; 24hr); Demnate (9 daily; 1hr 30min); El Jadida (11 daily; 4hr); Essaouira (1 CTM, 2 Supratours & 12 others daily; 3hr 30min); Fes (2 CTM & 16 others daily; 10hr); Goulimine (3 CTM, 4 Supratours & 7 others daily; 9hr 30min); Laayoune (2 CTM, 2 Supratours & 2

others daily; 15hr); Meknes (11 daily; 9hr); Ouarzazate (3 CTM, 1 Supratours & 14 others daily; 5hr); Rabat (1 CTM & 31 others daily; 5hr); Safi (7 daily; 2hr); Smara (1 CTM, 1 Supratours & 1 other daily; 13hr 15min); Taliouine (3 daily; 9hr); Tafraoute (4 daily; 10hr); Taroudannt (1 CTM & 7 others daily; 6hr 30min); Tangier (3 daily; 10hr); Tetouan (3 daily; 10hr); Tata (2 daily; 10hr); Tiznit (3 CTM, 4 Supratours & 7 others daily; 7hr); Zagora (1 CTM & 6 others daily; 9hr 30min).

Grands taxis

Bab Doukkala to: Agadir (3hr); Azilal (2hr 30min); Casablanca (2hr 30min); Essaouira (2hr 30min); Ouarzazate (3hr); Taroudannt (4hr).

Bab er Robb station to: Asni (1hr); Moulay Brahim (1hr); Oukaïmeden (winter only; 2hr); Setti Fatma (2hr).

Flights

Marrakesh to: Agadir (RAL 6 weekly; 40min); Casablanca (RAM 4–6 daily, RAL 6 weekly; 40min).

6

The High Atlas

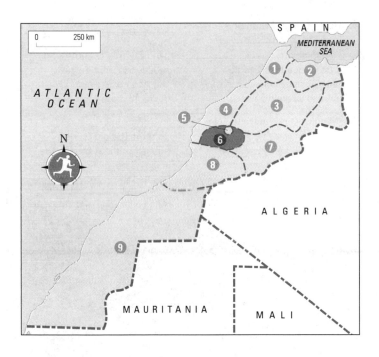

Highlights

* **Atlas Berbers** The High Atlas is a beautiful mountain area, populated mainly by Berbers who have a unique culture, dress and traditions.
See p.487

* **Ourika Valley** An easy day-trip from Marrakesh, the valley is a delight, with its waterfalls and riverside cafés.
See p.488

* **Atlas flora and fauna** Birds include flocks of bee-eaters, falcons, and other birds unique to the region. Early summer sees acres of orchids. See p.490

* **Skiing at Oukaïmeden** Want to say you've skied in Morocco? Ouka is easy to reach and inexpensive.
See p.491

* **Imlil and Aroumd** These Toubkal trailhead villages are remote enough to get a taste of Berber mountain life, even if you go no further.
See p.495 and p.500

* **Djebel Toubkal** North Africa's highest peak is the goal for most Atlas trekkers. It is a walk, rather than a climb, accessible in summer for anyone reasonably fit.
See p.501

* **Tin Mal** This twelfth-century mosque in the heart of the Atlas can, uniquely, be visited by non-Muslims.
See p.511

* **Telouet** The old feudal kasbah of the "Lords of the Atlas" is hugely evocative.
See p.515

△ Ourika Valley, High Atlas

The High Atlas

T he **High Atlas**, North Africa's greatest mountain range, contains some of the most intriguing and most beautiful regions of Morocco. A historical and physical barrier between the northern plains and the pre-Sahara, its Berber-populated valleys feel – and indeed are – very remote from the country's mainstream, or urban life. For visitors, it is, above all, trekking country, with walks to suit all levels of difficulty and commitment, from casual day-hikes to weeks of serious expedition routes combining a series of peaks (*djebels*) and passes (*tizis* or, in French, cols). One of the joys of Atlas trekking is that you can walk unencumbered: mules are available to hire, along with muleteers and mountain guides, who are invaluable if you are doing anything off the main routes. Rock-climbing and ski mountaineering are other options, and mountain biking, too, is increasingly popular on the dirt tracks (*pistes*) and mule paths. There are horses for hire at Ouirgane for organized local treks, while the adventurous might consider buying (and reselling) a mule at one of the local souks, and taking off into the wilds.

Despite the forbidding appearance of its peaks, these are surprisingly populated mountains; their slopes drop away to valleys and streams, with Berber villages terraced into their sides. At many of the **villages** – particularly in the two main hiking centres around Morocco's highest peak **Djebel Toubkal** (4167m) and the **Bou Guemez Valley** (see p.329) – *gîte*-style accommodation is offered in local houses, and there is an established infrastructure of guides and mules for trekking. It must be stressed, though, that part of the attraction of Atlas trekking is that it remains so undeveloped in comparison with, say, the Pyrenees or Alps. The network of *pistes* and paths was once vital for trade and travel. Today more vehicle access is possible, changing the old ways.

This chapter – although entitled "The High Atlas" – actually covers only the **Western part of the range**; for more on **easterly peaks and routes**, which offer four-wheel drive or travel on local Berber trucks, as well as trekking, see Chapter Seven.

Routes and passes

The **Djebel Toubkal** massif provides the focus for most trekking expeditions and can be reached easily from Marrakesh by driving, or taking a bus or taxi, to **Asni** – just over an hour's journey – and then up to the trailhead at **Imlil**. The region can also be approached from **Ouirgane** or **Ijoukak**, a little further west, or, the **Ourika Valley** from the east – a summer playground for Marrakesh – or the ski resort of **Oukaïmeden**. Some trekkers, with time to spend, also approach from the south, through the Tifnoute valley and Lac d'Ifni.

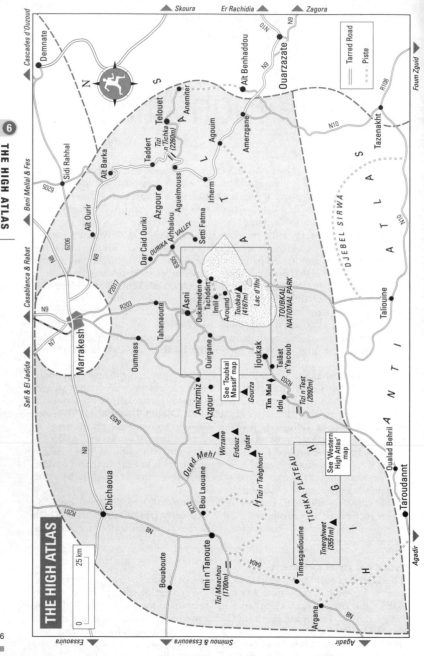

THE HIGH ATLAS

Asni, Ouirgane and Ijoukak all lie on the dramatic **Tizi n'Test road**, which runs over an Atlas pass to connect Marrakesh with Taroudannt: a switchback of hairpin curves to be driven with care. As well as its scenic appeal and trekking possibilities, the route has an easily accessible historic attraction in the ruins of the twelfth-century mosque of **Tin Mal**, the base from which the Almohads swept down to conquer Morocco and much of Spain.

Southeast of Marrakesh is the **Tizi n'Tichka**, a more substantial road pass, and for much of its length a spectacular piece of engineering. It was built to replace the old caravan route to the Drâa and the South, which was controlled during the nineteenth century and for much of the twentieth by the legendary **Glaoui family**, "the Lords of the Atlas" (see p.516). Their kasbah, a bizarre cluster of crumbling towers and kitschy-looking 1930s reception halls, still stands at **Telouet**, just an hour from the main road.

To the west, the **Tizi Maachou** has less drama, unless you leave the main road behind to get into the hills for some trekking in the Western Atlas – a beautiful area that is beginning to attract walkers. For most travellers the pass simply offers a fast route between Marrakesh and Agadir; it is cluttered with lorries, and can

High Atlas Berbers

Until recent decades, the High Atlas region – and its **Berber inhabitants** – was almost completely isolated. When the French began their "pacification" in the 1920s, the way of life here was essentially feudal, based upon the control of the three main passes (*tizis*) by a trio of "clan" families, "the Lords of the Atlas". Even after the French negotiated the cooperation of these warrior chiefs, it was not until the spring of 1933 – 21 years after the establishment of the Protectorate – that they were able to subdue them and control their tribal land, and only then with the cooperation of the main feudal chief, **T'hami el Glaoui**, who continued to control the region as pasha of Marrakesh (see p.516).

These days, the region is under official government control through a system of local *caids*, but in many villages the role of the state remains largely irrelevant, and if you go trekking you soon become aware of the mountains' highly distinctive culture and traditions. The longest established inhabitants of Morocco, the Atlas Berbers, never adopted a totally orthodox version of Islam (see Contexts, p.728) and the Arabic language has, even today, made little impression on their indigenous **Tachelhaït dialects**. Their music and ahouache dances (in which women and men both take part) are unique, as is the village **architecture**, with stone or clay houses tiered on the rocky slopes, craggy fortified **agadirs** (collective granaries), and **kasbahs**, which continued to serve as feudal castles for the community's defence right into the twentieth century.

Berber women in the Atlas go about unveiled and have a much higher profile than their rural counterparts in the plains and the north. They perform much of the heavy labour – working in the fields, herding and grazing cattle and goats and carrying vast loads of brushwood and provisions. Whether they have any greater status or power within the family and village, however, is questionable. The men retain the "important" tasks of buying and selling goods and the evening/night-time irrigation of the crops, ploughing and doing all the building and craftwork.

As an outsider, you'll be constantly surprised by the friendliness and openness of the Berbers, and by their amazing capacity for languages – there's scarcely a village where you won't find someone who speaks French or English, or both. The only areas where you may feel exploited – and pestered by kids – are the main trekking circuits around Djebel Toubkal, where tourism has become an all-important source of income. Given the harshness of life up here, its presence is hardly surprising.

be dangerous though ongoing work is upgrading it. The older, good *piste* road runs parallel, slightly east–west, and offers an attractive alternative.

Seasons and dangers – snow and floods

The High Atlas are subject to **snow** from **November to April**, and even the major Tizi n'Tichka and Tizi n'Test passes can be closed for periods of a day or more. If you are driving across the Atlas, and get caught by the snow, the easiest route from Marrakesh to the south is the Tizi Maachou pass (the N8 – formerly P10 – Agadir road) then the N10 (formerly P32) through Taroudannt and Taliouine, but the passes are seldom blocked for long and notices outside Marrakesh on the roads inform if they are open or closed.

The **thaw** can present problems, too, when the snows melt in spring causing swollen rivers, dangerous to cross. And the possibility of spring/summer **flash floods** must be taken seriously, as they can erupt suddenly and violently and are extremely dangerous. In August 1995, summer storms caused devastating flooding in the Atlas; dozens of buildings and bridges were washed away and more than a thousand lives lost. It's wise, at almost any time of year, to camp on high ground, avoiding any spot where water can lie or that might become a course for the torrents when they descend. This includes (although it's hard to believe in summer) dried up and apparently terminally inactive riverbeds.

For more on **trekking seasons** – and be aware that winter activities above the snow line are a serious endeavour here – see box, pp.498–499.

The Ourika Valley and Oukaïmeden

The **Ourika Valley** is an enjoyable and popular escape from the summer heat of Marrakesh, with the village of **Setti Fatma** a big weekend resort for young Marrakshis, who ride out on their mopeds or BMWs to lie around beside the streams and waterfalls. The village lies at the end of the road, but a *piste* (to Timichi) and then a mule track continues up the valley to passes to Tachddirt and **Oukaïmeden**, which has the best skiing in Morocco and interesting prehistoric rock carvings, and through to Imlil and Toubkal, making it a useful starting/finishing point for trekkers. A high pass also leads to the **Oued Zat Valley**, dominated by Taska n'Zat, a peak and valley offering demanding treks that are best left to the experienced. Setti Fatma itself has many pleasant spots, including waterfalls to visit and streamside cafés, and one of the country's biggest **moussems** takes place here in mid-August.

Getting to the Ourika Valley

Setti Fatma is an easy drive from Marrakesh (67km), and there is a regular service of **buses**, **minibuses** and **grands taxis** leaving from the city's main terminus out on the Asni road (see pp.480–481); the buses take a little under two hours. If taking public transport, make sure you will be dropped either at Setti Fatma or its adjoining village of **Asgaour** (63km from Marrakesh), and not at the near end of the valley at **Dar Caid Ouriki** (33km) or **Arhbalou** (50km). Returning to Marrakesh, you might have to walk to Asgaour to pick up a bus or taxi.

Into the valley

The Ourika Valley proper begins at **SOUK TNINE DE L'OURIKA** (30km from Marrakesh), a small roadside village, which, as its name proclaims, hosts a Monday **souk** – an excursion offered by many of the tour hotels in Marrakesh.

Just beyond it, across the river, is **DAR CAID OURIKI**, with a picturesque *zaouia* set back in the rocks, near the ruins of an old *caidal* **kasbah**.

Beyond here, scattered at intervals over the next forty kilometres, are a series of tiny hamlets, interspersed with a few summer homes and the occasional hotel or café-restaurant. The one sizeable settlement is **ARHBALOU** (50km from Marrakesh), where most of the local people on the buses get off. The village has a "palace-restaurant", *Le Lion d'Ourika* (℡024 44 53 22), and basic rooms to let in the village. A road west into the mountains leads to the trekking trailhead and ski resort of Oukaïmeden.

Moving on through the valley **towards Setti Fatma**, those with transport might want to stop at the **antiques/crafts shop**, Le Musée d'Arhbalou, 4km south of Arhbalou, which often has interesting stock. A further 2km on, there are pleasant **rooms** at the *Hôtel Amnougar* (℡024 44 53 28; ◐), and there are a number of tempting riverside cafés, too.

From the village of **TAZZIDFOUNT** a track leads up east to the Adrar Yagour − a good trekking area, where you can see prehistoric rock carvings; see "Treks from Setti Fatma" (below) for more on this.

Setti Fatma

SETTI FATMA is the most compelling Ourika destination, at least for a day-trip. It is a straggly riverside village, substantially rebuilt, expanded and made safer, after its 1995 devastation by floods. The setting, with grassy terraces and High Atlas peaks rising on three sides to over 3600m, feels like a real oasis after the dry plains around Marrakesh, and in the rocky foothills above the village are a series of six (at times, seven) **waterfalls**.

To **reach the falls** you first have to cross the stream by whatever bridge has been thrown up after the last floods; at certain times of year they can be completely inaccessible. Near the beginning of the climb are several cafés, where you can order a tajine for your return. The first waterfall is a fairly straightforward clamber over the rocks, and it is flanked by another café, the *Immouzer*. The higher ones are a lot more strenuous, and quite tricky when descending, requiring a head for heights and solid footwear. Returning, from the first of the falls you can loop back to Setti Fatma via the village's twin, **Zaouia Mohammed**, a few hundred metres further down the valley.

Setti Fatma Moussem

The **Setti Fatma Moussem** − one of the three most important festivals in the country − takes place for four days around the middle of August, centred on the **Koubba of Setti Fatma**, some way upstream from the *Café des Cascades*. Entry to the *koubba* is forbidden to non-Muslims, but the festival itself is as much a fair and market as religious festival and well worth trying to coincide with on your travels.

Treks from Setti Fatma

Ourika cuts right into the **High Atlas**, whose peaks begin to dominate as soon as you leave Marrakesh. At Setti Fatma these mountains provide a startling backdrop that, to the southwest, include the main **trekking/climbing zone of Toubkal**. The usual approach to this is from Asni (see p.493) but it is possible to set out from Setti Fatma, or from Oukaïmeden (see p.491).

Approaching Toubkal from Setti Fatma, one route is to trek via **Timichi** and **Oukaïmeden** and take the trail from there to Tachddirt. It is around five hours' walk along the *piste* from Setti Fatma to Timichi (which has several *gîtes*; see

The High Atlas has unique flora and fauna, which are accessible even to the most reluctant rambler if you base yourself at **Oukaïmeden, Imlil** or **Ouirgane**.

The spring bloom on the lower slopes comprises aromatic thyme and thorny caper, mingling with golden spreads of broom. Higher slopes are covered by more resilient species, such as the blue tussocks of hedgehog broom. The passes ring to the chorus of the painted frog and the North African race of the green toad during their spring breeding seasons, while some species of reptile, such as the **Moorish gecko,** have adapted to the stony walls of the area's towns and villages. **Butterflies** which brave these heights include the Moroccan copper and desert orange tip, and painted ladies heading from West Africa to western England. Other inhabitants include the almost-invisible praying mantis, the scampering ground squirrel and the rare elephant shrew.

Birds to be found among the sparse vegetation include Moussier's redstart and the crimson-winged finch, which prefers the grassy slopes where it feeds in flocks; both birds are unique to North African mountains. The rocky outcrops provide shelter for both chough and alpine chough and the mountain rivers are frequented by dippers who swim underwater in their search for food. Overhead, darting Lanner falcon or flocks of brilliantly coloured bee-eaters add to the feeling of abundance which permeates the slopes of the High Atlas. In the cultivated valleys look out for the magpie which, uniquely, has a sky-blue eye mark; there are also storks galore. Other High Atlas birds, as the snow melts, include shore larks, rock bunting, alpine accentor, redstarts and many species of wheatear.

Flora is impressive, too. The wet meadows produce a fantastic spread of hooped-petticoat daffodils, *romulea* and other bulbs, and Oukaïmeden in May/June has acres of orchids.

p.504). From Timichi, it is about 5–6 hours on a mule track to Oukaïmeden, including a steep ascent to the Tizi n'ou Attar. The ridge connecting this *tizi* with the Tizi n'Itbir, under Argour, gives pleasant rock scrambling (3100m).

The two-day trek direct from **Timichi to Tachddirt** is ideally done in the opposite direction, so is thus described on p.504.

Other **adventurous treks** from Setti Fatma – all of them requiring proper equipment, supplies and planning – include the **Djebel Yagour**, with its many prehistoric rock carvings; **Adrar Meltzen**, via **Tourcht**; and the secluded **Oued Zat** region reached by the demanding Tizi n'Tilst. The **Taska n'Zat–Arjoût peaks** require scrambling (up gorges and on the crests) while the way down the Oued Zat offers some days of splashing through gorges to reach the *piste* out. An ancient route climbs to the **Tizi Tazarzit** and reaches the N9 (formerly P31) at **Agouim** south of the range. These are some of the hardest options in the Atlas and it is a good idea to enlist one of the guides from Imlil (such as Aït Idir Mohammed; see p.500), or Hosain Izahan (who can be contacted through the *Café Azapza* in Setti Fatma).

Practicalities

Setti Fatma has an ever-growing number of **places to stay** and outside of weekends, or at festival time (when there'll be nothing going – but a huge impromptu campsite), you should have little problem finding a room. For **meals**, the *Asgaour* and *Restaurant Le Noyer* are the best bets.

Café Atlas At the north end of the village, the *Atlas* has roof space.

Café des Cascades The first café on the route to the falls, it has decent if basic rooms. ❷

Café-Restaurant Asgaour. This is in Setti Fatma village proper, and though the rooms are a bit basic, they are spotless, and overlook the river. The patron, Chebob Lahcen, also cooks excellent meals. **❷**
Hôtel Gare. One of a row of little hotel-restaurants that line the concrete road by the taxi turning area – and marginally more appealing than its neighbours. **❷**
Hôtel Tafoukt and La Perle d'Ourika These two modest and modern hotels are in Asgaour –-once a separate village (and labelled as such on most maps) but now basically the beginning of Setti Fatma. They both have en-suite rooms. **❸**

Oukaïmeden

The village and ski centre of **OUKAÏMEDEN** is a much easier trekking base than Setti Fatma from which to set out towards Toubkal – and a good target in its own right, even if you don't have anything that ambitious in mind. In summer, there are some attractive day-hikes, and the chance to see prehistoric rock carvings (see box below), while in winter, of course, there is the chance to **ski** – and it's hard to resist adding Africa to a list of places you have skied.

"Ouka", as it's known, is reached via a good modern road which veers off from Ourika just before Arhbalou. **Grands taxis** sometimes go up from Marrakesh in the winter for the skiing or you can charter a whole taxi for yourself. The road has a toll charge too in winter. A snowplough keeps the road open during the ski season.

Skiing

The slopes of **Djebel Oukaïmeden** offer the best **skiing** in Morocco, and up until the war the resort could boast the highest ski lift in the world – which, at 3273m, still remains impressive today (it was re-strung in 2003). It gives access to good *piste* and off-*piste* skiing, while on the lower slopes a few basic drag lifts serve nursery and intermediate runs. For **cross-country skiers**, several crests and cols are accessible, and ski mountaineers often head across to Tachddirt.

Snowfall and snow cover can be erratic but the **season** is regarded as February to April; the lifts close at the end of April (even if there are perfect skiing conditions). **Equipment** can be rented from several shops around the resort, at fairly modest rates; prices and, more particularly, quality of equipment fluctuate from one place to another, so ask around. Ski passes are

---

Prehistoric rock carvings in the Atlas

Details of the fascinating **prehistoric rock carvings of the Atlas**, showing animals, weapons, battle scenes and various unknown symbols, can be found in an indispensable guidebook (on sale in the Oukaïmeden CAF chalet and in Marrakesh bookshops), *Gravures Rupestres du Haut Atlas*. Several sites are located near Oukaïmeden and (in summer) a local will guide you to the better sites for a small tip.

A puzzling related feature of prehistoric rock sites in the Atlas are **cupmarks** – groups of small circular hollows (Peter Ustinov suggested they were egg-cups) with no apparent pattern carved into exposed rock surfaces at ground level. They had been noted down the western side of Scotland and Europe, but were unknown in Africa until recently, when Atlas explorer and *Rough Guide to Morocco* co-author Hamish Brown discovered them. Since then, he has come across them several times in his wanderings. Unlike the usual rock art, they appear in granite (in the western Atlas) and conglomerate (at Tinerhir) as well as sandstone (in the Middle Atlas). If anyone discovers further sites in Morocco, we would be grateful to hear from them so that the information can be passed on.

very cheap (around US$5), and there are also very modest charges if you want to hire a **ski guide**, or instructor.

Trekking: Oukaïmeden to Tachddirt

The **walking trails** from Oukaïmeden are strictly summer only: routes can be heavily snow-covered even late into spring. However, weather conditions allowing, the **trail to Tachddirt** (3hr) is pretty clear and easy-going, being a *piste* as far as the pass, the **Tizi n'Eddi** (2928m), reached in about two hours. On the descent, the trail divides in two, with both branches leading down into Tachddirt. For more details of this route, described in reverse, and routes on from Tachddirt, see p.504.

Practicalities

There are several **hotels** in the resort, as well as a rather basic **campsite**. The hotels cater mainly for the ski season, but most stay open year-round.

Chalet-Hôtel de l'Anglour (also called *Chez Juju*) ☎024 31 90 05. An excellent little *auberge*, owned by a Canadian couple, with decent French cooking and a bar. Open all year. ❹

Club Alpine Chalet ☎024 31 90 36 (26dh per night for members, 52dh non-members). Well equipped, with a bar and restaurant, which does substantial meals. The warden usually has Atlas trekking guidebooks for sale. ❷

Kenzi Louka ☎024 31 90 80 or 86; ⓦwww .kenzi-hotels.com/hotels/ouka/ouka.html. This 100-room, four-star hotel has terrific views from its pyramid-tiered rooms. Facilities include two restaurants, a bar, an indoor swimming pool, a hammam, a gym and even conference rooms. ❻

The Djebel Toubkal Massif

The **Toubkal Massif**, enclosing the High Atlas's highest peaks, is the goal of almost everyone who goes trekking in Morocco. You can reach its trailhead villages in just two to three hours from Marrakesh, and its main routes are well charted. Walking even fairly short distances, however, you feel transported to a very different world. The Berber mountain villages look amazing, their houses stacked one on top of another in apparently organic growth from the rocks, and the people are immediately distinct from their city compatriots, with the women dressed in brilliantly coloured costumes even when working in the fields.

From late spring to late autumn (see note on seasons on p.498), the region's trails are accessible for anyone reasonably fit. Mule tracks round the mountain valleys are well contoured and kept in excellent condition, and there's a network of village *gîtes*, houses and CAF refuge huts for accommodation, that makes camping unnecessary unless you're going well away from the villages (or if you are climbing Toubkal in peak season and the refuges are full).

In summer, **Djebel Toubkal**, at 4167m the highest peak in North Africa, is walkable right up to the summit; if you're pushed for time, you could trek it, and be back in Marrakesh, in three days – though at the risk of altitude sickness. Alternatively, if you are really short on time, or feel unable to tackle an ascent of Toubkal, it's possible to get a genuine taste of the mountains by spending a couple of days exploring the beautiful valleys around Imlil or Aroumd.

More committed trekkers will probably want to head further afield, away from the busy Toubkal trail. A tempting target is **Lac d'Ifni**, over a demanding pass, but there are infinite variations on **longer treks**, from local circuits to the two-to-three-week trek to Ighil Mgoun (see p.330).

Moulay Brahim

MOULAY BRAHIM is a picturesque village, just off the main Marrakesh Asni road and dominating the gorges leading up from the plains. The **Kik Plateau** and its escarpment, which runs above the main road towards Ouirgane, is botanically rich and offers perhaps the best panorama of the Atlas mountains. It can be reached from the top end of the town, on a *piste* past marble quarries (see p.494). A *piste* (being upgraded) crosses the plateau to descend to the Oued Nfis and Amizmiz.

The village is a popular weekend spot for Marrakshis and an alternative base for a first night in the Atlas, with several **hotels** – mostly cheapies such as the central *Alfouki* and the *Talfoukt* at the entrance to the town (both ❷) plus the better equipped and larger *Star's Hôtel* and the uninspiring *Haut Rocher* (both ❸) above the town. There are plenty of good eating places, and regular **buses** and **taxis** to and from Asni and Marrakesh. It hosts a large **moussem** two weeks after Mouloud.

Asni

The end of the line for most buses and grands taxis, **ASNI** is little more than a roadside village and marketplace, from where you can head straight on to Imlil, though a night here is quite pleasant – at least once the touts have left off. You may find it pays to make some small purchase, and take a mint tea with one of the sellers; after all, they have little else to do, and you may as well stay easy-going.

The most interesting time to be here before heading on to Toubkal is for the **Saturday souk**, when the enclosure behind the row of shop cubicles is filled with local produce (this is a big fruit-growing region) and livestock stalls, plus the odd storyteller or entertainer. An advantage of arriving on Saturday morning (or Friday night) is that you can stock up with cheap supplies before heading into the mountains.

Accommodation and eating

Accommodation is limited. The *Grand Hotel du Toubkal*, which was indeed a rather grand old hotel, has been closed for a decade and shows no sign of re-opening, which leaves you a choice between one guesthouse, a youth hostel and a few touted rooms. Or moving straight on to Imlil or Ouirgane. For **meals**, most of the café-stalls by the souk will fix you a tajine or *harira*.

Auberge de Jeunesse At the south end of the village. Asni's youth hostel is open all year and to all-comers, with slightly higher charges for non-IYHF members. There are cold showers and you'll need your own sleeping bag, though blankets can be rented; the location by the river can be very cold in winter. Nonetheless, it is a friendly place and good meeting point. They will store luggage if you want to go off trekking unencumbered. ❶

Villa de l'Atlas near the top end of the long straight road heading for Imlil ℡ & ☏ 024 48 4855 or ☏ 061 66 77 36. A pleasant new guesthouse, some way out of town, so worth taking a taxi if you have much luggage. ❸

Moving on

Transport from Asni on **to Imlil** is pretty straightforward, with minibuses and taxis shuttling back and forth along the 17km of road, along with larger lorries on Saturdays for the souk. All normally wait until they fill their passenger quota, though they can be chartered.

Buses from Asni run to Marrakesh, Moulay Brahim or Ijoukak and – at around 6am – over the Tizi n'Test for Taliouine (change at Ouled Berhil for

Taroudannt; see p.634), but check in advance as the service changes occasionally. From Asni a place in a **grand taxi** can be negotiated to Marrakesh, Moulay Brahim or Ouirgane, and (in stages) over the Tizi n'Test.

Buses and taxis leave from the souk entrance area (main destinations); from the roadside up from the petrol station (for up-valley destinations); and from the smaller souk entrance (on Saturdays).

Walks around Asni and Moulay Brahim

There's no need to rush up to Toubkal. There are many local walks in the fruit-growing areas around Asni and Moulay Brahim, which will get you acclimatized for the higher peaks. They are not much explored and so have a charm of their own.

The Kik Plateau

The forested slopes above Asni and Moulay Brahim are dominated by a rocky scarp which is the edge of the hidden limestone **Kik Plateau**. In spring a walk up here is a delight, with a marvellous spread of alpine flowers and incomparable views. To get the best from it, set off early in the day and carry water; six to eight hours' walking will bring you over the plateau if you take a bus or taxi up to the start.

If you are walking from Asni, follow the Tizi n'Test road to where it swings out of sight (past the red conical hill). Just past a souvenir stall a large track breaks off and can be seen rising up the hillside. Take this to reach the pass. Turn right again, through fields, and you eventually join the plateau edge, which you can follow to **Moulay Brahim**; leave the crest to join a *piste* down to the left, which passes big marble quarries just before the village. You can also cut down to Asni by a path leaving the route midway along.

An alternative day's trek on the plateau is to make for **Ouirgane**, further along the Tizi n'Test road (see p.507). On the rise to the plateau keep on, forking left, to the pass/village of Tizi Ouadou and then follow the dip to where it's crossed by a rough *piste*. Take this down to the road at Tizi Ouzla and follow the road down, with salt mines apparent below. Turn off right to work through paths to join the Nfis River and follow this to Ouirgane. (Dam construction work may force you to take a detour at some stage of this walk.)

There's also a spectacular road across the Kik Plateau, surfaced except for below the scarp, which should be completed in 2007. Crossing from Asni, you descend towards the reservoir of Lalla Takerkoust, and you will eventually emerge on the Amizmiz–Marrakesh road.

Valley approaches

The valleys of Asni, Imlil (Mizane), Tachddirt (Imenane) and Tizi Oussem/Ouirgane (Azzadene) offer fine walks, which you might do to acclimatize yourself before tackling Toubkal or other high mountains. They are all much easier if you walk them downhill – back to Asni/Ouirgane, from which it is easy enough to return to Imlil by taxi. The directions below are accurate at the time of writing, but there are a number of new *piste* roads being driven up these valleys.

Imlil to Asni. This is a pleasant half-day walk. From Imlil, walk back down the road, then, after about an hour, swap over to the old mule track on the east side of the valley. Follow this for about two hours, then at an area of purple, yellow and red soils, climb up to a pass and end by the lower Imenane; or go out to the last bump of the crest for a grand view.

Tachddirt to Asni. There is a long but straightforward *piste*/trail from Tachddirt down-valley to Asni, taking seven to nine hours. It's an enjoyable route through a fine valley – a good (and neglected) exit from the mountains. You could also do this route from Imlil, heading off down from the Tizi n'Tamatert (1hr from Imlil) to the bottom of the valley at Tinhourine. If you want to camp out at night, en route, there are possible places to pitch a tent below Ikiss or Arg. There are also **gîtes** at Ikiss and Amsakrou. A fine pass rises opposite Ikiss to cross a *tizi* to Aguersioual and so back to Imlil, an excellent round trip.

Imlil

The trip from Asni to **IMLIL** is a startling transition. Almost as soon as it leaves Asni, the road begins to climb; below it the valley of the Oued Rhirhaia unfolds, while above, small villages crowd onto the rocky slopes. As you emerge at Imlil the air feels quite different – silent and rarefied at 1740m. Paths and streams head off in all directions.

If you want to make an early start for the Toubkal (Neltner) hut and the ascent of Toubkal, Imlil village is a better trailhead than Asni, as is Around (the small village on towards Toubkal ??? ??? ??? ??? ??? ??? ??? ??? ??? ??? ??? ??? ??? ??? ??? ??? of Marrakesh in one day; the altitude can kick in and spoil your chances of climbing the peak.

Accommodation

Imlil has many provisions shops and a fair choice of accommodation including a CAF refuge and a fast-growing cluster of **hotel-cafés** and *gîtes*... and a kasbah treat.

Atlas Tichka ℡024 48 52 23, ℻024 48 56 28. One of the best of the new village-run hotels, with charming atmosphere and service. ❸

CAF refuge This old-established French Alpine Club refuge provides bunk beds, camping mattresses and blankets, as well as kitchen and washing facilities and luggage storage; rates vary according to membership of Alpine Club, YHA, and so on, but are around 50dh a head. The *gardien* can provide meals. ❶

Chez Lahcen Askary ℡ & ℻024 48 56 17. A fine *gîte*, set above the village, managed by Lahcen Askary (who runs the "Shopping Centre" facing the Imlil refuge). ❹

Chez Mohammed ℡ & ℻024 48 56 18. This *gîte* (200m beyond the school) is run by the guide Aït Idir Mohammed, who can also arrange other pleasant *gîtes*. Contact him here, or at the shop behind the concrete route indicator. Baggage can be stored while trekking. ❷

Hôtel El Aïne ℡024 48 56 25. Lower down the main street, this has reasonable rooms around an attractive courtyard. ❸

Hôtel-Café Aksoual ℡024 48 56 12. Facing the CAF refuge and with clean, comfortable rooms. ❸

Hôtel-Café Soleil ℡024 48 56 22, ℻024 48 56 22. On the square by the river, this place offers decent rooms and does superb tajines. It also offers camping, self-catering, and rooms at the *Auberge La Vallée* (℡024 48 52 16), at the top of the village. ❸

Hôtel Etoile de Toubkal ℡024 48 56 18. Decent enough, but without much care or character. ❹

Kasbah du Toubkal ℡024 48 56 11, ℻024 48 56 36; or through Discover Ltd in the UK (℡01883 744392, ⊛www.kasbahdutoubkal .com). This caïd's kasbah above Imlil was restored by the British company Discover using local crafts and workers, and offers a treat unlike any other in the area. Accommodation ranges from shared Berber-style hostel rooms (which cater for school trips) to luxury private rooms. The setting is tremendous, as is the decor, and the cooking. Martin Scorsese filmed much of *Kundun* here, the kasbah standing in for the home of the Dalai Lama. The kasbah can organize treks and guides, and has a small reception office by the car park in Imlil. ❻

Trekking resources and guides

Good sources of **information** include the CAF refuge and its *gardiens* (wardens), the *Kasbah du Toubkal*, and the long-established "Shopping Centre"

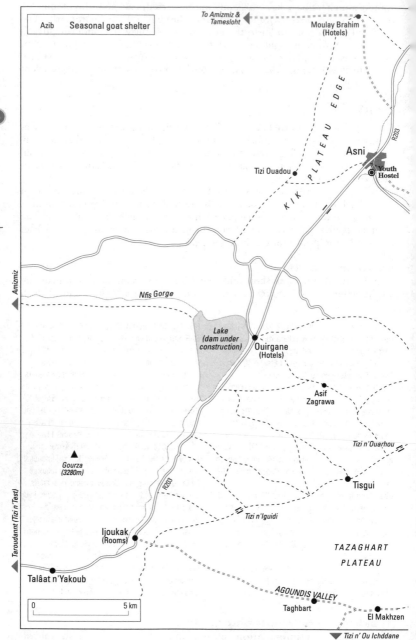

Azib   Seasonal goat shelter

To Amizmiz & Tamesloht

Moulay Brahim (Hotels)

K I K   P L A T E A U   E D G E

R203

Asni
Youth Hostel

Tizi Ouadou

Amizmiz

Nfis Gorge

Lake (dam under construction)

Ouirgane (Hotels)

Asif Zagrawa

Tizi n'Ouarhou

Gourza (3280m)

R203

Tisgui

Tizi n'Iguidi

Taroudannt (Tizi n'Test)

TAZAGHART PLATEAU

Ijoukak (Rooms)

Talâat n'Yakoub

AGOUNDIS VALLEY

Taghbart

El Makhzen

0   5 km

Tizi n' Ou Ichddane

TOUBKAL MASSIF

N

Oukaïmeden
(Hotels/refuge)

Ski Lift

Timguist

Timichi
(Rooms)

Agouns

Oukaïmeden
(3273m)

Tizi n'Eddi

Angour
(3616m)

Adrar
n'Ineghmar
(3892m)

Tamadout

AÏT MIZANE VALLEY

INEMANE VALLEY

Tizi n'Tachddirt

Amoqkrou

Ikiss

Tachddirt
(Rooms)

Oumskra
(Rooms)

Bou
Iguenouane
(3882m)

Aguersioual

Aït Souka

Tizi n'Tamatert

Tizi n'Likemt

Matat

Mzic

Imlil
(Refuge/rooms)

Aksoual
(3842m)

Azib Likemt

Id Aissa

Aroumd
(Rooms)

Azib Tifni

Tizi
Oussem
(Rooms)

Tizi Mzic

Sidi
Chamarouch
(Rooms)

Tizi n'Tagharat

Tizi n'Terhalino
(3247m)

Tizi n'Ouraï
(3109m)

Aguelzim

Azib
Tamsoult

Afekoï

Tazaghart
Refuge

Tadat

Tissaldaï

Tazaghart
(3845m)

Tizi Melloul

Toubkal
(4167m)

Toubkal
Refuges

Tizi n'Ouanoums
(3664m)

Timzakane

Ras
n'Ouanoukrim

Tizi n'Ouagane

Lac d'Ifni
(2312m)

Amsouzart
(Rooms)

Aït Youb

Imhilene

Imlil

Equipment and experience

Unless you're undertaking a particularly long or ambitious trek – or are here in winter conditions – there are no technical problems to hold anyone back from trekking in the Toubkal area, or climbing the peak itself. However, the mountain needs to be taken seriously. You must have decent **footwear and clothing** – it's possible to be caught out by summer storms as well as bad winter conditions – and you should be prepared to camp out if you are going on longer treks (or find the Toubkal refuge is full). It's important to keep to a gentle pace until you are properly acclimatized: there are high altitudes (3000–4000m) throughout the Toubkal region, which can be quite demanding, combined with the midday heat and walking over long sections of rough boulders or loose scree.

Seasons

Toubkal is usually under **snow** from November until mid-June. If you have some experience of winter trekking and conditions, it is feasible to climb the peak, and trek the low-level routes, year round, though for Toubkal itself you may need to wait around a couple of days for clear weather, and carry and know how to use an ice axe and crampons (which can usually be rented in Imlil).

For beginners, spring or early summer trekking is better limited to below the snow line. And only those with winter climbing experience should try going much beyond hut level, from November to May; ice axe, crampons, appropriate clothing and winter competence are required, as several fatalities have recently shown. Full rivers and flash floods in spring and high summer can pose additional problems.

Altitude

Toubkal is 4167m above sea level and much of the surrounding region is above 3000m, so it's possible that you might get **acute mountain sickness (AMS)**, also called altitude sickness. Aspirins can help, but just sucking on a sweet or swallowing often is as good as anything. Most people experience some symptoms of AMS but serious cases are rare. Hurrying is a major cause of altitude sickness so pace your ascent, allowing your body time to acclimatize. If you do develop more than slight breathlessness and really feel like vomiting, going down straight away is the best, and almost immediate, cure.

Accommodation

At most Atlas villages, it is usually possible to arrange a room in a local house; just turn up and ask. At some of the villages on more established routes, there are official *gîtes*, often the homes of mountain guides, who can provide mules and assistance – as well as food, showers, toilets and sometimes hammams. All *gîtes* are graded by the tourist authorities, who sometimes have lists of them available. Most charge 50–100dh per person for a night and for a further 60–75dhs will provide meals.

There are also three refuge **huts**, Toubkal (formerly known as *Neltner*), Tazaghart (formerly known as *Lépiney*) and Tachddirt, run by the *Club Alpin*; they charge about 50dh for a bed (less for members of Alpine Clubs). Toubkal, the best appointed, is often heavily booked and is always crowded in March/April (when ski-touring is popular) and July–September (the main trekking season). However, an independent hostel has been built alongside it, to a similar standard, which has relieved the pressure.

If you are planning to **camp**, there are designated areas. You will need a tent and warm sleeping bag – nights can be cold, even in summer, and you must use the inside toilets.

Guides and mules

Guides can be engaged at Imlil and at a number of the larger villages in the Toubkal region; **mules**, too, can be hired, usually in association with a guide or porter. Rates are around 250dh a day for a guide, 100dh for a mule. One mule can usually be shared among several people – and if you're setting out from Imlil, say, for Lac d'Ifni, or the Toubkal or Tazaghart refuges, it can be a worthwhile investment. Two extras are to be added to the price – a small fee to the car park supervisor in Imlil and a tip to the muleteer at the end. (Payment to all parties, incidentally, is best made at the end of a trip.)

Note that guides are more reluctant – and reasonably so – to work during the month of **Ramadan** (see p.61).

Water

Bottled **water** (Sidi Ali and Sidi Harazem are both spring sourced) is readily available at Atlas villages. If you are heading off main routes, a litre bottle of water is enough because you can refill it regularly. However, Giardiasis **bacteria** is present in many of the streams and rivers downriver from human habitation (including the Toubkal huts), so purification tablets are highly advisable, as, of course, is boiling the water to make it safe.

Clothes

Even in the summer months you'll need a warm sweater or jacket and a wind-breaker. Hiking boots are ideal though you can get by with a decent pair of trainers or jogging shoes. Some kind of hat is essential and sunblock and sunglasses are helpful.

Other things to bring

You can buy **food** in Asni, Imlil and some of the other villages – or negotiate meals – though it gets increasingly expensive the higher and the more remote you get. Taking along a variety of canned food, plus tea or coffee, is a good idea. Water purification tablets are worthwhile on longer trips, as are stomach pills, insect repellent and wet wipes (which should be used before meals).

Children constantly ask you for cigarettes, bonbons and *cadeaux* – but it's perhaps better for everyone if you don't give in, and limit **gifts** to those who offer genuine assistance. A worthwhile contribution trekkers can make to the local economy is to trade or give away some of your gear – always welcomed by the guides, who need it.

Guidebooks and maps

There are almost limitless Atlas trekking routes, only a selection of which are detailed in these pages. For other ideas, either engage a guide at Imlil, or invest in the Atlas Mountain trekking guidebooks by **Michael Peyron** (West Col), **Richard Knight** (Trail blazer), **Robin Collomb** (West Col), or **Karl Smith** (Cicerone Press).

Large-scale survey **maps** are available for the region; most are 1:100,000, though Toubkal is also mapped at 1:50,000. These, like the guidebooks above, are best obtained in advance from specialist map/travel shops, though occasionally guides or shops at Imlil or Oukaïmeden (or the *Hôtel Ali* in Marrakesh, see p.437) may have some stock to sell.

Ski-touring

The Toubkal Massif is popular with **ski-mountaineering** groups from February to April. Most of the *tizis* (cols), and Djebel Toubkal and other peaks, can be ascended, and a *Haute Route* linking the huts is possible. The route from the Toubkal summit to Sidi Chamarouch must rank as fine a mountain ski descent as you'll ever find.

The Toubkal refuge can get pretty crowded at these times, and the Tachddirt refuge (or, for a serious approach in winter, Tazaghart refuge) can make better bases.

facing the refuge, run by Lahcen Askary, an experienced, English-speaking guide. Also helpful is the *Hôtel-Café Soleil*'s owner, Aziam Brahim, who works for part of the year for a French trekking company, and his brother, Ibelaid Brahim.

Lahcen and the Brahim brothers and Aït Idir Mohammed (who runs *Chez Mohammed*) are among Imlil's **qualified guides** listed in the guides' office in the corner of the car park near the CAF Refuge. They can all arrange treks, ascents, mules, camping, guides, *gardiens* for your baggage and food.

Imlil to Djebel Toubkal

Most trekkers leaving Imlil are en route for the **ascent of Djebel Toubkal** – a walk rather than a climb, after the snows have cleared, but a serious business nonetheless (see box, pp.498–499). The route to the ascent trailhead, however, is fairly straightforward, and is enjoyable in its own right, following the Mizane Valley to the village of **Aroumd** (4km from Imlil; 1hr–1hr 30min) and from there through the pilgrim hamlet of **Sidi Chamarouch** to the **Toubkal (Neltner) Refuge** (3200m; 12km from Imlil; 5–6hr in all), at the foot of Toubkal's final slopes.

If you start out late in the day, Aroumd can be a useful first base, though most trekkers set out early to mid-morning from Imlil to stay the night at the Toubkal refuge, starting out at first light the next morning for Toubkal in order to get the clearest possible panorama from its heights. Afternoons can be cloudy.

Arriving at the Toubkal refuge early-ish in the day is advisable as it can be full, which would mean either camping or backtracking. This also gives you time to acclimatize and rest: many people find the hardest bit of the experience is the last hour's trek up to the hut. Take it easy.

Imlil to Aroumd

To **walk from Imlil to Aroumd,** you basically follow the course of the Mizane river. On the west side there's a well-defined mule track that zigzags above the river for about 2km before dropping to the floor of the valley, just before a crossing point to Aroumd; there is also a more circuitous *piste*, driveable in a reasonably hardy vehicle. On the east bank, there's a rough path – much the same distance but slightly harder to follow.

AROUMD (also called AROUND, AREMD) is the largest village of the Mizane Valley, an extraordinary looking place, built on a huge moraine spur above the valley at 1840m. Steep-tiered fields of potatoes, onions, barley and various kinds of fruit line the valley sides, their terraces edged with purple iris. The village is used as a base or overnight stop by a number of trekking companies, and several houses have been converted to well-equipped **gîtes**; among them are *Restaurant Résidence Aremd* (❸), overlooking the school, and the *Atlas Toubkal/Chez Omar le Rouge* (☎024 48 57 50; ❸), by the west bank of the river, which has a tented restaurant and also offers camping. If you're cooking for yourself, supplies are best brought along; there is only one small shop.

Aroumd to Sidi Chamarouch and Toubkal Refuge

From Aroumd, the **Toubkal trail** goes up the flood plain, with unavoidable river crossings, only problematic sometimes (hitch a mule over them). At the end of flood plain the track zig zags up to make its way along, high above the gorge. If you have been following the main mule trail on the west side of the valley from Imlil to Aroumd, you can join the Toubkal trail without going round into Aroumd.

The river is crossed once more by a bridge just before you arrive at the hamlet of **SIDI CHAMAROUCH** (1hr 30min–2hr from Aroumd). Set beside a small waterfall, this is an anarchic row of houses, all built one into another. Its seasonal population of ten or twelve run soft drinks/grocery shops for tourist trekkers and for Moroccan pilgrims, who come to the village's *marabout* shrine – sited across the river from the village and reached by a concrete bridge which non-Muslims are strictly forbidden to cross. The shrine is probably a survival of a very ancient nature cult – in these parts often thinly veiled by the trappings of Islam; on the approach to the village you may notice a tree, sacred to local tradition, where the Berbers hang strips of cloth and make piles of stones. Basic **rooms** (❶) are available and **camping** is possible – below the hamlet down by the stream. (Do not drink untreated water here, or around the Toubkal hut.)

Beyond **Sidi Chamarouch**, the Toubkal trail climbs steeply in zigzags and then traverses the flank of the valley well above the Mizane. The trail is clear the whole way to the **Toubkal Refuge**, which, at 3207m, marks the spring snow line. In winter the snow line can drop to Sidi Chamarouch and mules have to be replaced by porters if you want assistance to the Toubkal Refuge.

The Toubkal Refuge

Even in mid-August it feels pretty cold up at the **Toubkal Refuge** (formerly *Refuge Neltner*, ❷) once the sun has disappeared behind the ridge. You will probably, therefore, want to take advantage of its shelter. The refuge is open all year and has hot showers, sitting rooms and a self-catering kitchen; meals can also be ordered from the *gardien*. A separate building houses local guides, and mules. The hut is pricier than others in the Atlas, at 80dh a head (less with Alpine Club membership), but pretty reasonable, nonetheless. A new, privately-run **hostel** (❷) has been built alongside, which has helped with peak season crowds (when the main refuge is often full). There is also a designated area for **camping**. If you camp, you can (indeed must) use the refuge toilets; the authorities are trying to get the area a bit more hygienic.

If you are camping, you can do so near the hut, or head off on your own up-valley; either way, take care to protect the local water supply. Things can get distinctly unhygienic here in summer, and it is important to use the hut's toilets.

Climbing Toubkal

At the Toubkal Refuge you're almost bound to meet people who have just come down from **Djebel Toubkal** – and you should certainly take advantage of talking to them and the refuge *gardien* for an up-to-the-minute description of the routes and the state of the South Cirque (Ikhibi Sud) trail to the summit. If you don't feel too confident about going it alone, take a guide – they are usually available at the refuge – but don't let them try and rush you up the mountain (see box, p.498 for further details).

As you toil up the scree, you might reflect that – while the African explorer Joseph Thomson identified Toubkal as the highest peak in the Atlas in 1888 – Toubkal was first climbed only in 1923, a dozen years after Amundsen's expedition had reached the South Pole!

The South Cirque

The **South Cirque** (Ikhibi Sud) is the most popular and straightforward ascent of Toubkal and, depending on your fitness, should take between 2hr 30min and 3hr 30min (2–2hr 30min coming down). There is a well-worn path and with reasonable instructions on the spot it is easy enough to follow without a guide. More of a problem – and something you should be careful about at any time of the year – is finding the right track down though the slopes of loose scree.

The **trail** begins above the Toubkal Refuge, dropping down to cross the stream and then climbing over a short stretch of grass and rock to reach the first of Toubkal's innumerable fields of boulders and scree. These – often needing three steps to gain one – are the most tiring (and memorable) feature of the trek up, and gruelling for inexperienced walkers. The summit, a sloping plateau of stones marked by a tripod, is eventually reached after a lot of zigzagging up out of the cirque.

It should be stressed that **in winter even this ascent is a snow climb** and not for walkers. Slips can and have had fatal consequences. If you are properly equipped, check out the start the night before, and set off early. Ice axes and crampons are essential.

The North Cirque

An alternative – though longer (4hr 30min) and more ambitious – ascent is the **North Cirque** (Ikhibi Nord). En route you will pass the remains of an aircraft (it crashed while flying arms to Biafra) and the small peak of Tibherine has its engine as a cairn. The final ridge to the summit area calls for some scrambling and in general the route calls for experience. You should descend by the South Cirque.

Toubkal Refuge to Lac d'Ifni and beyond

Lac d'Ifni is one of the largest mountain lakes in the Atlas – and the only one of any size in the Toubkal region. From the refuge it's about a 4–5hr trek, again involving long, tedious stretches over loose rock and scree, and with odd stretches of snow remaining into July. On the way back, the scree demands are even more pronounced. To make the trip worthwhile, take along enough food for a couple of days' camping; there are no facilities of any kind en route.

Toubkal to Lac d'Ifni

The **Lac d'Ifni trail** begins at the Toubkal Refuge, climbing up a rough, stony slope and then winding round to the head of the Mizane Valley towards the imposing **Tizi n'Ouanoums**. The pass is reached in about an hour and the path is reasonably easy to follow. The trail up the pass itself is a good, gravel path, zigzagging continually until you reach the summit (3664m), a narrow gap in the rocky wall.

The views from the *tizi* are superb, taking in the whole route that you've covered and, in the distance to the south, the hazy green outline of the lake (which disappears from view as you descend). At this point the hard work seems over – but this is a false impression. The path down the valley to Lac d'Ifni is steep, the scree slopes apparently endless, and the lake doesn't come back into sight until you are almost there. It is, in fact, virtually enclosed by the mountains, and by what look like demolished hills – great heaps of rubble and boulders. All of which makes **Lac d'Ifni** a memorable sight, its only human habitations a few shepherds' huts, and the only sound that of water idly lapping on the shore; it is unusually deep – up to 50m over much of its area.

Sadly, the lakeside is a poor place to camp, with its scrubby terraces, somewhat fly-ridden by day, and no drinking water source (the lake waters are polluted). You can camp much more enjoyably by carrying on for another hour until you reach the first patches of irrigated valley, high above the village of Imhilene.

From all the villages south of Toubkal taxis/minibuses operate down the Tifnoute valley to **Aoulouz** (see p.636), passing a big reservoir.

On from Lac d'Ifni: a loop to Tachddirt or Sidi Chamarouch

Most people return from Lac d'Ifni to the Toubkal refuge by the same route but it's quite feasible to make a longer, anticlockwise, loop towards **Tachddirt** or **Sidi Chamarouch**.

Lac d'Ifni to Sidi Chamarouch

From the lake, you can strike east to the valley above Imhilene, and beyond it to the kasbah-like village of **Amsouzart**, reached in around three hours. There is a café/campsite here and *gîte* accommodation (❷) and meals at Omar's house; ask for him at the café or shop, which is your last chance of supplies on this route.

From Amsouzart, follow the up-valley path to reach the village of **Tissaldaï** in about four hours; camping is possible in the valley above. From here, it's at least four hours of strenuous trekking to get up the **Tizi n'Terhaline** (3247m). It's worth all the effort as you descend into a beautiful valley. After about two hours' walking from the pass, you will reach **Azib Tifni**, a collection of shepherds' huts, few more than a metre or two high.

You can then follow the valley west over another high pass, Tizi n'Tagharat for the long, steep, hard descent to **Sidi Chamarouch**. Or you can loop to Tachddirt.

The loop to Tachddirt

From Azib Tifni you can follow either a small but impressive gorge, or a pass to avoid it, down the **Tifni valley** to reach Azib Likemt – a region of intense cultivation and magnificent spring flowers. Another pass from the Lac d'Ifni, Tizi n'Ouraï, descends here. About 2km further down the Tifni, climb up to the village of **Azib Likemt**, from which a mule track climbs steeply to the **Tizi Likemt** (3555m), the spot from which Joseph Thomson noted Toubkal as the highest Atlas peak in 1888. From here there's a reasonably clear path down across some of the worst screes of the region. A big spring at the foot of the descent makes a good campsite, or you can cross over to the **CAF refuge** at **Tachddirt**, or, if that's full, there are rooms available in Tachddirt village.

The country east of Azib Likemt, the **Kissaria Gorges**, is wild in the extreme, and too hard even for mules. However, there is a magnificent, if very demanding (on people or mules) route over to the Ourika Valley by the splendid Tizi n'Oumchichka that sidesteps the Kissaria.

Tachddirt and beyond

TACHDDIRT (2000m), 8km east of Imlil, is an alternative and in many ways more attractive base for trekking expeditions. As at Imlil, there is a CAF refuge, and a fine range of local treks and onward routes. But despite its comparatively easy access – a pleasant mule track up the valley to the Tizi n'Tamatert (more direct than the tortuously winding *piste*) – the village sees only a handful of the trekkers who make it up to Toubkal.

You can walk **from Imlil** in three to four hours, or there is a daily Berber **lorry** along the *piste*. There is only one small shop in Tachddirt, so you may want to bring provisions. The **CAF refuge** (❶) has soft drinks and cooking facilities, and its *gardien* will provide meals on request; it is sited at the down-valley edge of the village and is kept locked, though the *gardien* should soon appear. He can arrange a guide and mules. **Rooms** (❶) are also available in the village.

The next village down, **Oumskra**, has a couple of **gîtes** (❷), and following the valley from here to Imlil is an enjoyable option.

Tachddirt to Setti Fatma

This is one of the best routes for anyone contemplating more than a simple day-trip into the hills. Taken at a reasonable pace, the route takes two days. There is a well-defined mule track all the way, so no particular skills are needed beyond general fitness and a head for heights. Several sections of the trail are quite exposed and steep.

You'll probably want to carry some food supplies with you. However, meals are offered at the village of Timichi, so cooking gear and provisions are not essential, but if you are carrying gear, you might want to hire mules at Tachddirt.

Tachddirt to Timichi

Tachddirt to Timichi is a superb day's walk. The first three hours or so are spent climbing up to the Tizi n'Tachddirt (3616m), a route with ever more spectacular views. The character of the valley changes abruptly after the pass, green terraced fields giving way to rough and craggy mountain slopes. The path down is one of the more barren sections of the route. As you approach Timichi the valley again becomes more green and cultivated.

TIMICHI has several *gîtes* (❷) and makes a good overnight stop. A hard but impressive pass, **Tizi n'ou Attar** (3050m), leads to Oukaïmeden and it is possible to follow the valley up and out under the peak of Angour. The normal three-day recommended route is Oukaïmeden–Tachddirt–Timichi–Oukaïmeden.

Timichi to Setti Fatma

Timichi to Setti Fatma is another beautiful trek, taking half a day. At first you follow the river fairly closely, passing several villages before you get to a *piste* which climbs up to avoid a gorge, with a great view from the last spur before it zigzags down to the flood plain of the Ourika Valley about 2km north of Setti Fatma. Following the gorge offers a bit more fun.

Tachddirt to Oukaïmeden

This is a fairly straightforward route – a three- to four-hour walk on a steep mule track by way of the 2960m **Tizi n'Eddi/Tizi nou Addi**.

The Angour Traverse

The ridge of Angour is pretty demanding, taking a full day from Tachddirt and requiring basic climbing skills; a guide is useful for this.

From the **Tizi n'Tachddirt** (3hr 30min from Tachddirt), head north up a rough, grassy slope, to break through crags onto the sloping **plateau**, which can be followed to the **summit of Angour** (3616m). This plateau is an unusual feature on a peak with such dramatic cliffs. It is split by a valley. With care, you can scramble along an exposed ridge down from here to **Tizi n'Eddi** (to pick up the Oukaïmeden trail), or cut down to Tachddirt once you are onto easy but still very steep ground.

Tachddirt to Imlil via Tizi n'Aguersioual

An alternative route back from **Tachddirt to Imlil** is by way of **Tizi n'Aguersioual**. This takes you down-valley to the hamlets of Tinerhourhine (1hr) and Ikiss (15min further down; soft drinks/rooms). From Ikiss a good path on the other side of the valley (ask someone to point it out) leads up to the Aguersioual pass and then zigzags down to the village of **Aguersioual**, from where you can follow the Asni road back up to Imlil. Aguersioual has a **gîte**, *Le Mont Blanc* (☎024 8 56 47; ❸).

West of Imlil: Tizi Oussem and the Tazaghart Refuge

The area west of Imlil and the Djebel Toubkal trail offers a good acclimatization trek to **Tizi Oussem** village, harder treks to the south to the **Tazaghart Refuge** (❶), accessible also from the Toubkal Refuge and Aroumd, and the possibility of one- or two-day treks out to **Ouirgane** or **Ijoukak** on the Tizi n'Test road, or back to the Asni–Imlil road at **Tamadout**.

Tizi Oussem and on to Ouirgane

The village of **TIZI OUSSEM** is in the next valley west of Imlil and is reached in about four hours over the **Tizi Mzic**; the track is not that easy to find, so ask for directions. The most interesting section is the path down from the pass to Tizi Oussem. If you are heading for the **Tazaghart Refuge**, another path from the pass follows round the hillside to Azib Tamsoult, and then to the gorge for the ascent to the refuge.

Once at Tizi Oussem, you could follow its **valley** in a long day's trek down to Ouirgane on the Tizi n'Test road. This route is quite tricky, however, as the 1995 flood devastated the valley bed. From the village you need to keep initially to the east bank and then drop onto the flood plain to gain the west bank at a narrowing. The path keeps high then zigzags down to cross the river to gain height on the east side, passing the walled farm of Azerfsane. Beyond there, the path swings west and drops to the river where a mule track on the left bank helps you cross to pull up to a spur with a commanding view to the rich Ouirgane Valley. You can follow a stretch of *piste* from here, turning off where it heads to Marigha, and following cultivation paths on the left bank to reach Ouirgane, at the *Auberge Au Sanglier Qui Fume* (see p.507).

Tizi Oussem to Ijoukak

Experienced walkers could make a three-day expedition to reach **Ijoukak** (see p.510), with two camps en route, one just below the Tizi Ouarhou (2672m) and the second before the Tizi n'Iguidi.

The Tazaghart Refuge area

The **Tazaghart Refuge** (formerly known as the *Refuge Lépiney*; ❶) is essentially a rock-climbing base for the fine cliffs of **Tazaghart**. To get access, you (or a porter) may have to go down to the village of Tizi Oussem to get the hut *gardien*, Omar Abdallah, who is also a very good (and extremely pleasant) guide; he can arrange a room in the village, too. Details of a number of climbs from the refuge are given in the Collomb guide, but in winter they require crampons and ice axes – and climbing experience; there was a fatal accident here in 1989, involving an organized trekking party.

To **reach the refuge** from Imlil (6hr 30min–7hr 30min) follow the routes described above. Alternatively, you can follow a new mule path (summer only) which leads from Aroumd over the Tizi n'Tizikert, north of Aguelzim.

To the south of the Tazaghart Refuge, **Tizi Melloul** (3–4hr) allows access to **Tazaghart** (3843m), an extraordinary plateau and fine vantage point. From here, you could cross over the pass and, with a night's camping, walk **down the Agoundis Valley to Ijoukak**.

Tizi n'Test: Ouirgane, Ijoukak and Tin Mal

The **Tizi n'Test** (2092m), the road that extends beyond Asni to Taroudannt or Taliouine, is unbelievably impressive. Cutting right through the heart of the Atlas, it was blasted out of the mountains by the French from 1926 to 1932 – the first modern route to link Marrakesh with the Souss plain and the desert, and an extraordinary feat of pioneer-spirit engineering. Until then, it had been considered impracticable without local protection and knowledge: an important pass for trade and for the control and subjugation of the south, but one that few sultans were able to make their own.

Through much of the nineteenth century – and the beginning of the twentieth – the pass was the personal fief of the **Goundafi** clan, whose ruined kasbahs still dominate many of the crags and strategic turns along the way. Much earlier it had served as the refuge and power base of the Almohads, and it was from the holy city of **Tin Mal**, standing above the Oued Nfis, that they launched their attack on the Almoravid dynasty. As remote and evocative a mountain stronghold as could be imagined, Tin Mal is an excursion well worth making for the chance to see the carefully restored ruins of the twelfth-century mosque, a building close in spirit to the Koutoubia mosque in Marrakesh, and for once accessible to non-Muslims, except on Fridays.

Practicalities

The Tizi n'Test is not for the faint-hearted. If you are **driving**, some experience of mountain roads is advisable. The route is well contoured and paved, but between the pass and the intersection with the N10, the Taliouine–Taroudannt road, it is extremely narrow (one and half times a car's width) with almost continuous hairpin bends and blind corners. As you can see for some distance ahead, this isn't as dangerous as it sounds – but you still need a lot of confidence and have to watch out for local drivers bearing down on you without any intention of stopping or slowing down. Bus and lorry drivers are, fortunately, more considerate. Try to avoid driving the route at midday in the summer months when cars are liable to overheat.

Using public transport, a **shared taxi** is your best option, negotiated either at Marrakesh, Asni or (coming in the other direction) Taliouine or Taroudannt. **Buses** over the pass are erratic, though there is one service most days between Marrakesh and Taliouine, with a change at Oulad Berhil if you are heading for Taroudannt.

From November to the end of April, the pass is occasionally blocked with **snow**. When this occurs, a sign is put up on the roadside at the point where the Asni–Test road leaves Marrakesh and on the roadside past Tahanaoute.

The road to the pass

Leaving Marrakesh, the Tizi n'Test road runs over the Haouz plain to **Tahanaoute** (Tuesday souk) – a fairly monotonous landscape until you reach the gorges of the Moulay Brahim, near Asni. Twisting endlessly over a watershed, there is some impressive "Badlands" scenery, with salt leaking from the soil before the rich basin of Marigha is reached. Here a road right runs down past saltworks and over the hills to Amizmiz (see p.508). Continuing over a rise, the main road drops to the large green valley basin of Ouirgane, beside the Oued Nfis – whose gorges are currently in the process of being dammed.

△ Weekly market at Tahanaoute

Ouirgane

OUIRGANE is a tiny place, long touted by French guidebooks as an *étape gastronomique*. It is a wonderful place to rest up after a few days of trekking around Toubkal, and a very pleasant base in itself for day walks, mountain-bike forays or horse riding in its beautiful valley. The village hosts a small Thursday souk.

The main lure, though, is the village's very tempting cluster of **hotels**:

La Bergerie ☎024 48 57 16, ✉bergerie @rediscover.co.uk. Sited 2km outside the village, this place is French-run and has a nice garden setting, a (modest) pool and good French food. ⑥
Café Badaoui. This village café has a few simple rooms. ❶
Chez Momo ☎024 48 57 04, ⓦwww .aubergemomo.com. Another garden-set hotel – attractive, quiet, and with a small pool. Its restaurant does classic Berber dishes. ⑥
Le Moufflon ☎024 48 57 22. A small roadside inn. ❹
Résidence Ouirgane Adama ☎024 31 92 07, ⓕ024 43 20 95. A recent addition to the scene, this is a nice hotel, magnificently sited above the village and soon-to-be-created lake. ⑤

Résidence de la Roseraie ☎024 43 20 94, ⓕ024 43 20 95. Ouirgane's top hotel is one of the nicest in the country – a luxury retreat with 45 rooms scattered around a rose garden. It has a swimming pool, sauna, tennis, an equestrian centre (horse riding 350dh for a half-day – bring your own helmet), and a renowned restaurant. Most people are on half-board, which ranges from 220–300dh according to season. ❼–❽
🏃 **Au Sanglier Qui Fume** ☎024 48 57 07, ⓕ024 48 57 09. A very attractive, old-established French-run auberge, with excellent food and a delightful garden and pool. Prices are a lot lower than at the *Roseraie*, and in summer you usually need to book well in advance. ⑤

Treks around Ouirgane

A couple of hours' walking (or riding) in Ouirgane's valley will take you to a waterfall for an ice-cold plunge, or you could just wander around the area and see how the dam and lake are coming on. If you want to go further afield, a rewarding full-day trek is to head for **Tizi Ouadou** and the **Kik Plateau** – and then down to Asni and back by taxi (see p.494 for more on this).

Amizmiz

The small town of **AMIZMIZ** can be reached direct from Marrakesh – on a minor road with regular bus and grand taxi connections. A low-key, very pleasant Atlas base, it is the site of a long-established **Tuesday souk** – one of the largest Berber markets of the Atlas, and not on the tourist route. The town comprises several quite distinct quarters, including a *zaouia,* kasbah and former Mellah, separated by a small, usually dry, river. **Accommodation** is available at the *Rahha,* a simple hotel in the centre of town (**❷**), or at the classier, women-run *Restaurant Le Source Bleu* (☎024 45 45 95; **❸**), a nice *auberge* 4km out of town (ask for directions). There is also a **gîte** (☎062 29 69 10; **❷**) at **OUADAKER**, the next village to the west.

Amizmiz is a good base for some challenging **trekking** and also for **mountain biking** (see box below). You might also look at using the services of High Country, a **trekking/adventure company** run by Englishman Matthew Low

---

Mountain biking – and some routes from Amizmiz

Mountain biking in Morocco offers some of the best adventure riding in the world and there are routes suitable for all abilities. The High Atlas has an awesome number of jeep and mule tracks that cover the countryside and several **adventure companies** offer mountain biking as a pursuit in Morocco (for details see pp.35–37). Travelling independently it's important to be aware of local sensibilities; ride slowly through villages, giving way to people where necessary, especially those on donkeys and children tending livestock; pick your way carefully through cropped fields and palmeries, or take a detour if possible; and try not to pass through inhabited areas in large groups – be discreet and the rewards will be wonderful. If **renting a bike**, negotiate essential extras like a pump, puncture repair kit and/or spare inner tube. A helmet is recommended, as is carrying plenty of water. Filling up from village wells is possible, but always ask permission first. For general information on planning and problems see pp.48–50.

Of the **two routes** detailed below, the first can be done by a novice with a rented bike, whilst the second is best left to the proficient, preferably on their own bike. Both routes begin and end at *Restaurant Le Source Bleu* (see above) in Amizmiz; the first is possible as a day-trip from Marrakesh, the second, more taxing route, requires a stopover at *Le Source Bleu*. As few roads are signposted, the Amizmiz 1:100,000 **topographical map** is highly recommended, and best obtained from specialist map shops before you leave home. Times given for completing routes are rough guides only; allow yourself plenty of time to take photos, enjoy the hospitality offered en route, and fix the odd puncture.

Route 1 The Oued Amizmiz

This ride follows the **Oued Amizmiz** along an undulating jeep track, crossing the river at the natural point where track meets valley bottom, and passing by picturesque villages, crop terraces and bizarre rock formations. It is essentially flat, with only **two notable hills**, and ends with a **dramatic descent** back into Amizmiz. The track is good quality *piste* and **the route**, though easy enough for anyone to tackle, is still interesting enough for the serious biker to appreciate too. The 38km should take about three to four hours.

From *Le Source Bleu* take the jeep track down until it meets the *piste* road running from Amizmiz to Azegour and then head on uphill and past the *Maison Forestière* (ranger's station). About 1.5km beyond the station a narrow jeep track branches off left, taking you down the west side of the valley to pass through the village of Aït Ouskri, from where there are tremendous views up the valley, its arid slopes

(☎024 33 21 82, ⓦwww.highcountry.co.uk), who arrange trekking, climbing, skiing, kayaking and off-road 4WD expeditions.

En route to Amizmiz, and only half an hour's drive from Marrakesh, is a tempting small **hotel**, *Le Relais du Lac* (☎024 48 49 24, ⓦwww.hotel -relaisdulac-marrakech.com), overlooking the **Lalla Takerkoust lake** and dam. This has a French chef, a swimming pool, and canoes and other craft available for exploring the lake; it also has quad bikes and arranges luxurious camping trips.

Treks around Amizmiz

The mountains backing Amizmiz offer some of the best trekking in the Atlas, little known or described and entirely unspoilt save for the intrusion of a few *pistes*.

contrasting with the lush terraces below, to Djebel Gourza and Djebel Imlit. The *piste* continues, passing the villages of Tizqui, Touq al Kheyr and, after 10km, Imi n Tala and Imi-n-Tala (big spring), before crossing the Amizmiz river below **Addouz** and bringing you to the eastern side of the valley. Care should be taken if **crossing the river in spring**, when it can become swollen from melted snow. Following the *piste* through Imzayn, and sticking to the lower track, leads to Igourdan and, after about 12km, uphill, to **Aït Hmad**, with the earlier part of the route and the villages on the western edge of the valley clearly visible.

Leaving Aït Hmad behind, the road widens to become a full-width *piste* jeep track allowing a fast but safe downhill back into Amizmiz.

Route 2 Azegour and Toulkine

This ride is a great test of stamina, technical skills and route finding, taking in some of the best views and villages in the area; with strenuous uphills and a very technical final descent, it is really only for the fit and experienced. Good brakes and seven to eight hours are needed to cover the 42km.

The route starts as for Route 1 but at the junction beyond the *Maison Forestière* you keep going straight (instead of taking the track to the left), climbing up above the valley with increasingly stunning views. After about 10km the *piste* flattens and the going is easier as you head westwards to the next valley. You should pass mining ruins and, after crossing the Oued Wadaber ford, on the outskirts of **Azegour**, fork right. From there, you will reach the village of **Toulkine** in 2.5km.

Passing through Toulkine, the right-hand donkey track, lined with cairns, heads north, up and over the hill, to the hamlet of **Adghous**. From here the trail can be difficult to follow and you'll need to **ask locals** for directions to Amizmiz; common sense and your map are the best ways to keep on the right track. A path leads down through the houses of Adghous, the hamlet starting to spread out over another valley, where an improbable left turn, just past some beautiful stone and mud houses, takes you through a dip (you'll have to carry your bike) and picks up a donkey track on the far side. It's worth pausing for the **spectacular view** of Adghous, sitting on a spur overhanging the valley, before continuing on the upper (single) track – rutted, stony and eroded – until the pre-Atlas plains to the north become visible. There is an obvious single track leading down the valley towards these plains, and at the village of **Tiqlit**, this track widens to become a fast jeep track. Follow this until you leave the valley and are on the plains, where a jeep track to the right will lead you through the village of Wadaker and back to Amizmiz.

The **Amizmiz (Anougar) valley** up to the neighbouring peaks of **Imlit** (3245m) and **Gourza** (3280m) is beautiful and various passes can be crossed to the Nfis or Ougdemt valleys.

Southwest beyond Azgour, rolling country rises to the **Wirzane-Erdouz crest** (3579m), so prominent from Marrakesh rooftop views, which is prime trekking country with several magnificent passes over to the Ougdemt valley. There is a fine descent above the Oued Wodaker, north of Azegour.

Ijoukak

IJOUKAK is an important shopping centre where the Agoundis Valley joins the Nfis. Buses stop at its many cafés, and there are **rooms** available at the *Café Ounaine* (*Chez Saïd*; ☏ 062 03 63 64; ❷), the last café at the Tizi n'Test end of the village, which is a nice place, with good tajine, and at *Café Badaoui* (☏ 068 16 45 91; ❷), at the lower end of the street.

Walking from Ijoukak, you can easily explore Tin Mal and Talâat n'Yacoub (see p.511 & p.513) or try some more prolonged **trekking in the Nfis and Agoundis valleys**. The Agoundis can also be enjoyable just as a day's wandering, if you have nothing more ambitious in mind, or you can take the winding forestry road up the hill dominating the village for its commanding view.

Treks around Ijoukak

Ijoukak gives access to some of the most enjoyable trekking in the High Atlas – all much less developed than the main Toubkal area. Starting from the village, you can trek east up the **Agoundis Valley towards Toubkal**, or west up the long **Ogdemt Valley**. The region to the **west of the Tizi n'Test road** is wilder still; for details – in reverse – of the trek to Afensou and Imi n'Tanoute (on the Marrakesh–Agadir road), see the "Tichka Plateau treks", p.519.

The **survey map** for the area (if you can get hold of it) is *Tizi n'Test* (1:100,000).

Agoundis Valley

East from Ijoukak winds the **Agoundis Valley**. It offers alternative access to Toubkal, but is seldom used. To reach the Toubkal Refuge takes two days of serious trekking. However, if "peak bagging" is not part of your plan, you could still enjoy a day's trek or an overnight trip up this way.

From Ijoukak head out on the Marrakesh road, cross the Agoundis Valley and turn right onto the up-valley *piste* passing several *gîtes*. The scenery grows ever grander yet fields will cling wherever possible and there are a surprising number of villages. After an hour's walking you reach the wreck of an old mineral processing plant, a gondola still high in the air on a cable stretched across the valley to mines that closed decades ago. After passing **Taghbart** there is a fork; the right branch crosses the river and makes an impressive ascent to the 2202m **Tizi-n-Ou-Ichddane** on the Atlas watershed. Past here branches lead to Aoulouz or to the R203 10km east of the Tizi n'Test turn-off, highly recommended 4x4 routes. Left at the fork, the up Agoundis *piste* soon passes **El Makhzen** and a prominent house in wedding-cake style before becoming progressively narrower, exposed and rough, passing perched villages and ending at Aït Youl. Enquire at *Chez Saïd* in Ijoukak (see above) about public transport up the valley, as **Aït Youl** is a long day's walk. From there strong walkers can reach the Toubkal refuge in a day, crossing the **Tizi n' Ougane**, where there's a risk of snow on the final slopes until May, passing through wild gorges and screes on the way. The descent to the Agoundis from Toubkal is easier.

Ougdemt Valley

West from Ijoukak and the Agoundis Valley lies the **Ougdemt**, a long, pleasant valley filled with Berber villages surrounded by walnut groves.

A dirt road ascends from **MZOUZITE** (3km beyond Tin Mal and 8km from Ijoukak) up to **ARG** at the head of the valley (6–7hr walking). From Arg you could aim for **Djebel Erdouz** (3579m) to the north of Tizi n'Tighfist (2895m), or the higher **Djebel Igdat** to the south (3616m), by way of Tizi n'Oumslama. Both are fairly straightforward when following the mule paths to the passes and can be reached in five to six hours from Arg. Be sure to take your own water in summer as the higher elevations can be dry. A two to three-day traverse of these peaks on to Djebel Gourza (3280m) and down to Tin Mal is a challenging adventure. The east ridge of Erdouz gives serious scrambling as does the east ridge of Igdat.

For the very adventurous, a further expedition could be undertaken **all the way to the Tichka plateau** – summer grazing pastures at the headwaters of the Nfis River – and across the other side to the Marrakesh–Agadir road. This would take at least six days from the Tizi n'Test road and require you to carry provisions for several days at a time. A brief summary of this trail, taken from the opposite direction, follows in the "Tichka Plateau" section on p.527.

Idni and the pass

At **IDNI**, well up on the pass, the small *Café Igdet* has very basic rooms with bed mats (●), hot meals and tea. From the hamlet, a path zigzags down to the Nfis which can then be followed out to the main road again.

The **Tizi n'Test** (2092m) itself is 18km beyond Idni. There's a small **café** on the col and another excellent one just down on the south side (with rooms); buses will stop on request. From the summit of the pass a *piste* rises up towards a platform mounted by a TV relay station, where the views down to the Souss Valley and back towards Toubkal can be stunning. Experienced climbers could backpack along the crest west from here to descend into the Nfis Valley later with the massive cliffs of Flillis dominating the view. There is also a *piste* (path direct from the *tizi* to join it) leading down to Souk Sebt Tanammert on the Nfis. Descending this and following the Nfis east is a good trek, with one bivouac.

Over the Tizi n'Test pass, the descent towards the **Taroudannt–Taliouine road** is dramatic: a drop of some 1600m in little over 30km. Throughout, there are stark, fabulous vistas of the peaks, and occasionally, hundreds of feet below, a mountain valley and cluster of villages. Taroudannt is reached in around 2hr 30min to 3hr by car or bus, Taliouine in a little more; coming up, needless to say, it all takes a good deal longer. For details on Taroudannt and Taliouine, see p.627 and p.636.

Tin Mal Mosque

The **Tin Mal Mosque**, quite apart from its historic and architectural importance, is a beautiful monument – isolated above a lush reach of river valley, with harsh mountains backing its buff-coloured walls. It has been partially restored and is a highly worthwhile stop if you're driving the Tizi n'Test. If you're staying at Ijoukak, it's an easy eight-kilometre walk, passing the riverside Goundafi kasbah near Talâat n'Yacoub (see p.513). You can return on the opposite side of the Nfis if a bridge (replaced seasonally) is in place – check first.

The mosque is set a little way above the modern village of Tin Mal (or Ifouriren) and reached by wandering uphill, across a road bridge. The site is kept locked but the *gardien* will soon spot you, open it up and let you look round undisturbed (10dh admission, and a tip is expected). The mosque is used for the Friday service, so closed to non-Muslims on that day.

The mosque

The **Tin Mal Mosque** was built by Abd el Moumen around 1153–54, partly as a memorial and cult centre for Ibn Toumert and partly as his own family mausoleum. Obviously fortified, it probably served also as a section of the town's defences, since in the early period of Almohad rule, Tin Mal was

Ibn Toumert and the Almohads

Tin Mal's site seems now so remote that it is difficult to imagine a town ever existing in this valley. In some form, though, it did. It was here that **Ibn Toumert** and his lieutenant, **Abd el Moumen**, preached to the Berber tribes and welded them into the **Almohad** ("unitarian") movement; here that they set out on the campaigns which culminated in the conquest of all Morocco and southern Spain; and here, too, a century and a half later, that they made their last stand against the incoming Merenid dynasty.

This history – so decisive in the development of the medieval Shereefian empire – is outlined in "The Historical Framework" in Contexts (pp.706–707). More particular to Tin Mal are the circumstances of Ibn Toumert's arrival and the appeal of his puritan, reforming teaching to the local tribes. Known to his followers as the *Mahdi* – "The Chosen One", whose coming is prophesied in the Hadith (Sayings of The Prophet) – Toumert was himself born in the High Atlas, a member of the Berber-speaking Masmouda tribe, who held the desert-born Almoravids, the ruling dynasty, in traditional contempt. He was an accomplished theologian and studied at the centres of eastern Islam, a period in which he formulated the strict Almohad doctrines, based on the assertion of the unity of God and on a verse of the Koran in which Muhammad set out the role of religious reform: "to reprove what is disapproved and enjoy what is good". For Toumert, Almoravid Morocco contained much to disapprove of and, returning from the East with a small group of disciples, he began to preach against all manifestations of luxury –above all, wine and performance of music – and against women mixing in male society.

In 1121, Ibn Toumert and his group arrived in Marrakesh, the Almoravid capital, where they began to provoke the sultan. Ironically, this was not an easy task – Ali Ben Youssef, one of the most pious rulers in Moroccan history, accepted many of Toumert's charges and forgave his insults. It was only in 1124, when the reformer struck Ali's sister from her horse for riding unveiled (as was desert tradition), that the Almohads were finally banished from the city and took refuge in the mountain stronghold of Tin Mal.

From the beginning in this exiled residence, Ibn Toumert and Abd el Moumen set out to mould the Atlas Berbers into a religious and military force. They taught prayers in Arabic by giving each follower as his name a word from the Koran and then lining them all up to recite it. They also stressed the significance of the "second coming" and Ibn Toumert's role as *Mahdi*. More significant, perhaps, was the savage military emphasis of the new order. Hesitant tribes were branded "hypocrites" and massacred – most notoriously in the Forty-Day Purge of the mountains – and within eight years none remained outside Almohad control. In the 1130s, after Ibn Toumert had died, Abd el Moumen began to attack and "convert" the plains. In 1145, he was able to take Fes and, in 1149, just 25 years after the march of exile, his armies entered and sacked Marrakesh.

entrusted with the state treasury. Today, it is the only part of the fortifications – indeed, of the entire Almohad city – that you can make out with any clarity. The rest was sacked and largely destroyed in the Merenid conquest of 1276 – a curiously late event, since all of the main Moroccan cities had already been in the new dynasty's hands for some thirty years.

That Tin Mal remained standing for that long, and that its mosque was maintained, says a lot about the power Ibn Toumert's teaching must have continued to exercise over the local Berbers. Even two centuries later the historian Ibn Khaldun found Koranic readers employed at the tombs, and when the French began restoration in the 1930s they found the site littered with the shrines of *marabouts*.

Architecturally, Tin Mal presents a unique opportunity for non-Muslims to take a look at the interior of a traditional Almohad mosque. It is roofless, for the most part, and two of the corner pavilion towers have disappeared, but the mihrab (or prayer niche) and the complex pattern of internal arches are substantially intact.

The arrangement is in a classic Almohad design – the T-shaped plan with a central aisle leading towards the mihrab – and is virtually identical to that of the Koutoubia in Marrakesh, more or less its contemporary. The only element of eccentricity is in the placing of the minaret (which you can climb for a view of the general layout) over the mihrab: a weakness of engineering design that meant it could never have been much taller than it is today.

In terms of decoration, the most striking feature is the variety and intricacy of the **arches** – above all those leading into the mihrab, which have been sculpted with a stalactite vaulting. In the **corner domes** and the **mihrab vault** this technique is extended with impressive effect. Elsewhere, and on the face of the mihrab, it is the slightly austere geometric patterns and familiar motifs (the palmette, rosette, scallop, etc), of Almohad decorative gates that are predominant.

On a less architectural note, don't miss the rooftop views – and the birds, with an owl family roosting up in the rafters and sky-blue rollers nesting in the walls.

The Goundafi kasbahs

The **Goundafi kasbahs** don't really compare historically, or as monuments, with Tin Mal – nor with the Glaoui kasbah in Telouet (off the Tizi n'Tichka; see p.515). But, as so often in Morocco, they provide an extraordinary assertion of just how recent is the country's feudal past. Despite their medieval appearance, the buildings are all nineteenth- or even twentieth-century creations.

Talâat n'Yacoub and other kasbahs

The more important of the kasbahs is the former Goundafi stronghold and headquarters near the village of **TALÂAT N'YACOUB** (which has an interesting mountain **souk** on Wed). Coming from Ijoukak, the kasbah is reached off to the right of the main road, down a very French-looking, tree-lined country lane; it is 6km from Ijoukak, 3km from Tin Mal, and clearly visible from the roadside at Talâat. Decaying, partially ruined and probably pretty unsafe, the **kasbah** stands at the far end of the village, by the river. Nobody seems to mind if you take a look inside, though beware its crumbling state – and the dogs near its entrance. The inner part of the palace-fortress, though blackened from a fire, is reasonably complete and retains traces of its decoration.

It is difficult to establish the exact facts with these old tribal kasbahs, but it seems that it was constructed late in the nineteenth century for the next-to-last Goundafi chieftain. A feudal warrior in the old tradition, he was constantly at war with the sultan during the 1860s and 1870s, and a bitter rival of the neighbouring Glaoui clan. His son, Tayeb el Goundafi, also spent most of his life in tribal campaigning, though he finally threw in his lot with Sultan Moulay Hassan, and later with the French. At the turn of the twentieth century, he could still raise some 5000 armed tribesmen with a day or two's notice, but his power and fief eventually collapsed in 1924. The writer, Cunninghame Graham, was detained here by the Goundafi in the 1890s, and describes the medieval scene well in his book, *Mogreb el-Acksa* (see Contexts, p.769).

Agadir n'Gouj and Tagoundaft

Another dramatic-looking Goundafi kasbah, **Agadir n'Gouj**, stands above the road overlooking the Kasbah Goundafi and is worth the climb up to its hilltop site. The interior has been cleared and some decorative details can still be seen. The structure is well preserved – as indeed it should be, having been built only in 1907, mainly to stable the Goundafi horses.

When the road begins to turn up and away from the river, another stark ruin looms up on the left. This is the **Tagoundaft**, the most imposing but seldom visited of the Goundafi kasbahs. It retains its vast cistern, though the aqueduct that once served this has gone. The walk up is worthwhile, if only to get a sense of its setting, like an eagle's eyrie.

Telouet and the Tizi n'Tichka

The **Tizi n'Tichka** – the direct route from Marrakesh to Ouarzazate – is not so remote or spectacular as the Tizi n'Test pass. As an important military (and tourist) approach to the south, the road is modern, well constructed and relatively fast. At **Telouet**, however, only a short distance off the modern highway, such mundane current roles are underpinned by an earlier political history, only five decades old yet seeming to belong more to medieval times. For this pass and the mountains to the east of it were the stamping ground of the extraordinary **Glaoui** brothers, the greatest and the most ambitious of all the Berber tribal leaders.

Their kasbah-headquarters, a vast complex of buildings abandoned only in 1956, are a rewarding detour (21km from the main road). And for trekkers, bikers or four-wheel-drivers, Telouet has an additional and powerful attraction, offering an alternative and superb *piste* to the south, following the old tribal **route to Aït Benhaddou**.

The Tizi n'Tichka

Telouet aside, it is the engineering of the Tichka road, and the views from its switchback of turns, that are the main attraction between **Marrakesh and the Tizi n'Tichka** – at 2260m. If you are driving south from Marrakesh, there's little to detain you before the pass. If you are driving north to Marrakesh, and want to stop for the night before reaching the city, the French-run **auberge**, *Le Coq Hardi* (☎024 48 00 56; ❸), set in gardens beside the **Zat river** bridge near Aït Ourir is a good bet. It has a bar, restaurant and pool (not always filled); it is often used by tour groups, so call ahead for a room.

The **road out from Marrakesh** runs through the **Haouz Plain**, but once across the Oued Zat it begins to contour forest slopes high about the Oued

Ghdat valley. From **ZERKTAN**, a Sunday souk, it is possible to drop down and head east over the Tizi n'Igli to Demnate: the road is part paved, part *piste*. Staying on the main road, constant twists and turns, passing small villages and fields in the river bends, leads to **TADDERT**, the last significant village before the Telouet turn-off and the Tichka pass. A popular transport break, it has wonderful views and a beautiful mountain stream, holm oaks and walnut trees. There are cafés and craft shops, and a pleasant half-hour walk to the village of Tamguememt, above the stream. It also has a rather gloomy and overpriced old **auberge**, *Les Noyers* (☎024 48 45 75; ❸).

After Taddert, the road climbs in an amazing array of hairpin bends to reach pastureland – "Tichka" means high pasture – before a final pull up to the **Tichka pass** (2260m), marked by cafés and tourist stalls. Not far down on the south side of the pass is the **turning to Telouet**.

If you keep on the main road south, you might want to stop at **IRHERM** (10km on), where there is a well-restored **agadir**. To find someone to unlock it, ask at the café or at the roadside **hotel**, *Chez Mimi* (☎024 88 00 56; ❷), which has basic garden rooms and a bar. Further on, at **AGOUIM** a road (part paved, part *piste*) heads west below the mountains to reach the Lac d'Ifni area (see p.502) and, 19km before Ouarzazate, a turning to the left leads to **Aït Benhaddou** and its kasbahs (see p.537).

Telouet: the Glaoui kasbah

The **Glaoui kasbah** at **TELOUET** is one of the most extraordinary sights of the Atlas – fast crumbling into the dark red earth, but visitable, and offering a peculiar glimpse of the style and melodrama of Moroccan political government and power well within living memory. There's little of aesthetic value – many of the rooms have fallen into complete ruin – but nevertheless, even after over a half-century of decay, there's still vast drama in this weird and remote site, and in the painted salon walls, often roofless and open to the wind.

△ Glaoui kasbah, Telouet

The Dar Glaoui

Driving through Telouet village you bear off to the right, on a signposted track, to the kasbah, or **Dar Glaoui** as it's known. The road twists round some ruins to a roughly paved courtyard facing massive double doors. Wait a while and you'll be joined by a caretaker-guide (tours 20dh per group), necessary in this case since the building is an unbelievable labyrinth of locked doors and connecting passages; it is said that no single person ever fully knew their way around the complex. Sadly, these days you're shown only the main halls and reception rooms. You can ask to see more – the harem, the kitchens, the cinema

The Glaoui

The extent and speed of **Madani** (1866–1918) and **T'hami** (1879–1956) **el Glaoui**'s rise to power is remarkable enough. In the mid-nineteenth century, their family were simply local clan leaders, controlling an important Atlas pass – a long-established trade route from Marrakesh to the Drâa and Dadès valleys – but lacking influence outside of it. Their entrance into national politics began dramatically in 1893. In that year's terrible winter, **Sultan Moulay Hassan**, on returning from a disastrous *harka* (subjugation/burning raid) of the Tafilalt region, found himself at the mercy of the brothers for food, shelter and safe passage. With shrewd political judgement, they rode out to meet the sultan, feting him with every detail of protocol and, miraculously, producing enough food to feed the entire 3000-strong force for the duration of their stay.

The extravagance was well rewarded. By the time Moulay Hassan began his return to Marrakesh, he had given *caid*-ship of all the lands between the High Atlas and the Sahara to the Glaouis and, most important of all, saw fit to abandon vast amounts of the royal armoury (including the first cannon to be seen in the Atlas) in Telouet. By 1901, the brothers had eliminated all opposition in the region, and when **the French** arrived in Morocco in 1912, the Glaouis were able to dictate the form of government for virtually all the south, putting down the attempted nationalist rebellion of El Hiba, pledging loyalty throughout World War I, and having themselves appointed **pashas of Marrakesh**, with their family becoming *caids* in all the main Atlas and desert cities. The French were content to concur, arming them, as Gavin Maxwell wrote, "to rule as despots, [and] perpetuating the corruption and oppression that the Europeans had nominally come to purge".

The strange events of this age and the legendary personal style of T'hami el Glaoui are beautifully evoked in Gavin Maxwell's *Lords of the Atlas*, the brooding romanticism of which almost compels a visit to Telouet:

At an altitude of more than 8000 feet in the High Atlas, [the castle] and its scattered predecessors occupy the corner of a desert plateau, circled by the giant peaks of the Central Massif . . . When in the spring the snows begin to thaw and the river below the castle, the Oued Mellah, becomes a torrent of ice-grey and white, the mountains reveal their fantastic colours, each distinct and contrasting with its neighbour. The hues are for the most part the range of colours to be found upon fan shells – reds, vivid pinks, violets, yellows, but among these are peaks of cold mineral green or of dull blue. Nearer at hand, where the Oued Mellah turns to flow though the Valley of Salt, a cluster of ghostly spires, hundreds of feet high and needle-pointed at their summits, cluster below the face of a precipice; vultures wheel and turn upon the air currents between them . . .

Even in this setting the castle does not seem insignificant. It is neither beautiful nor gracious, but its sheer size, as if in competition with the scale of the mountains, compels attention as much as the fact that its pretension somehow falls short of the ridiculous. The castle, or kasbah, of Telouet is a tower of tragedy that leaves no room for laughter.

– but the usual reply is "*dangereux*", and so it is: if you climb up to the roof (generally allowed) you can look down upon some of the courts and chambers, the bright zellij and stucco enclosing great gaping holes in the stone and plaster.

The **reception rooms** – "the outward and visible signs of ultimate physical ambition", in Maxwell's phrase – at least give a sense of the quantity and style of the decoration, still in progress when the Glaouis died and the old regime came to a sudden halt. They have delicate iron window grilles and fine carved ceilings, though the overall result is once again the late nineteenth- and early twentieth-century combination of sensitive imitation of the past and out-and-out vulgarity. There is a tremendous scale of affectation, too, perfectly demonstrated by the use of green Salé tiles for the roof – usually reserved for mosques and royal palaces.

The really enduring impression, though, is the wonder of how and why it ever came to be built at all.

Practicalities

Getting to Telouet is straightforward if you have transport: it is an easy 21km drive from the Tizi n'Tichka (N9) road, along the paved 6802. Using **public transport**, there is a daily bus from Marrakesh, departing from Bab el Khemis (daily at around 2–3pm), to Telouet and on to Anemiter (see p.518); it returns from Anemiter at 6.30am (7am from Telouet). Alternatively, there are shared **grands taxis** from Marrakesh to Anemiter, via Aït Ourir and Telouet.

Telouet itself is no more than a village; it has a Thursday **souk**, and makes a pleasant stopover at any time. Finding a **room** should be no problem. At the turn-off for the Dar Glaoui is the *Auberge Telouet* (☎024 89 07 17; ❸), with its nomad tent outside and new kasbah building across the road. It has good food and ambience, and the owner, Mohammed Boukhsas, can also arrange interesting accommodation in village houses. Alternatively, there is *Chez Bennouri* (❷), run by Mohammed Benouri (a trekking guide) and his father in part of an old *ksar*, and the simple *Auberge Le Pin* (☎024 89 07 09; ❷) at the west end of the village. There are several **cafés**, which serve meals.

Telouet to Aït Benhaddou

The **Tizi n'Tichka road** will bring you from the pass to Aït Benhaddou or Ouarzazate in a couple of hours (see p.515 for this route). However, if you have four-wheel drive (or a mountain bike), or want a good two-day walk, it is possible to reach Aït Benhaddou by the **Tizi n'Telouet** and the **Ounila Valley**. This is now a rather minor *piste* road but before the construction of the Tichka road it was the main route over the Atlas. Indeed, it was the presence in the Telouet kasbah of T'hami's xenophobic and intransigent cousin, Hammou ("The Vulture"), that caused the French to construct a road along the more difficult route to the west.

The route is surfaced as far as Anemiter but pretty rough beyond there, and requires fording streams at several points – most precariously just north of Aït Benhaddou.

The Ounila Valley

All in all, it is 35km from Telouet to Aït Benhaddou by the **Ounila Valley**. If you are walking or biking, the route offers tranquillity and unparalleled views of green valleys, a river that splashes down the whole course and remarkable coloured scree slopes amid the high, parched hillsides. Despite the absence of settlements on most of the maps, much of the **valley** has scattered communities, all making abundant use of the narrow but fertile valley. This unveils a wealth of dark red and crumbling **kasbahs** and **agadirs**, cliff dwellings, patchworks of wheatfields, terraced orchards, olive trees, date palms and figs – and everywhere children calling to each other from the fields, the river or the roadside.

If you are walking, you will need to take provisions for the trip but mules can be hired at Telouet or Anemiter.

Telouet to Anemiter

There are shared taxis (and the daily bus) between Telouet and **ANEMITER** (12km), one of the best-preserved fortified villages in Morocco. It is well worth a visit, even if you go no further along this route, and has some atmospheric **places to stay**. Mohammed Elyazid (☎024 89 07 80) offers simple nomad tent accommodation, camping, village house options, and meals, and can organize local treks.

Another possible stopover is at **TIGHZA**, 10km further on, up the Ounila Valley, where the brothers Bouchahoud, both mountain guides, have a fine **gîte** (☎024 44 54 99; ❷). They arrange local walks to the turquoise **Tamda lakes**, into the mountains, or to Anemiter and Telouet (by the crest of hills to the south). It is also possible to take mule tracks beyond the Tamda lakes to reach a new tarmac road over the Atlas from Demnate to Skoura, via the Oued Tessaout valley.

North of Anemiter lies a magnificent and almost unknown trekking area, surprising when it has such notable entry routes. The **Bou Guemez/Mgoun** area further east (see p.329) is second only to Toubkal in popularity, and trekking right through on long west–east links is highly recommended (routes are detailed in Peyron's guide).

Anemiter to Aït Benhaddou

There are occasional truck-taxis south of Anemiter, along the *piste*, but if you're setting out without transport it would be best to accept that you'll walk most of the way to Tamdaght, where the road resumes; it takes around ten hours.

Leaving Anemiter, the main track clings to the valley side, alternately climbing and descending, but with a general downhill trend as you make your way south. After three kilometres you cross a sturdy bridge. Beyond here the *piste* follows the left bank of the river to the hamlet of **ASSAKO** (2hr 30min walk from Anemiter), where it climbs to the left round some spectacular gorges and then drops steeply.

Walkers should aim to get beyond this exposed high ground before camping. At Tourhat, around six or seven hours from Anemiter, you might be able to find a room in a village home. Another three hours south of Tourhat, the trail brings you to **TAMDAGHT**, a scattered collection of buildings with a classic **kasbah**. This was used as a setting for an MGM epic, and retains some of its authentic Hollywood decor, along with ancient and rickety storks' nests on the battlements.

From **Tamdaght** the road is again paved to **Aït Benhaddou** (see p.537), where there are cafés and hotels, as well as taxis on to Ouarzazate.

Marrakesh to Agadir and Essaouira

The direct route from **Marrakesh to Agadir** – the **Imi n'Tanoute** or **Tizi Maachou** pass – is, in itself, the least spectacular of the Atlas roads, but if you are in a hurry to get south it is a reasonably fast trip (4hr drive to Agadir) and when the Test and Tichka passes are closed through snow, it normally remains open. Its hinterland also offers some exciting trekking, well off the beaten track, for more on which see "Tichka Plateau treks" below. And, not far off the main road, lies the old tribal **kasbah of the Mtouggi**, the third of the "Lords of the Atlas", with the Glaoui and Goundafi, and a ruin almost as impressive as Telouet.

Chichaoua, Imi n'Tanoute and the pass

Leaving Marrakesh, most Agadir traffic (including the majority of buses) follows the Essaouira road (N8) as far as **CHICHAOUA**, a small town and administrative centre set at a junction of routes, and famed in a small way for its **carpets**. Brightly coloured and often using stylized animal forms, they are sold at the local **Centre Coopératif** and also at the **Thursday market**. The village is a pleasant stop along the road to break your journey, though there's no reason to stay – and no great appeal in its basic souk hotels. Beyond Chichaoua, the **road to Essaouira** (R207) extends across the drab Chiadma plains. **Sidi Mokhtar**, 25km on from Chichaoua, has a **Wednesday souk** with an attractive array of carpets, a road from here (and another from Imi n'Tanoute) leads to Kasbah Mtouggi (see below).

Heading for Agadir, the N8 begins a slow climb from Chichaoua towards **IMI N'TANOUTE**, another administrative centre, with a **Monday souk**, and then cuts through the last outlying peaks of the High Atlas. Imi n'Tanoute is of little interest, though if you need to stay before setting out on a trek, there are **rooms** at a couple of the cafés, and provisions. A few kilometres further along the N8 from Imi n'Tanoute is the **Tizi Maachou**, at 1700m. The road south of the pass is often lined with locals selling bottles of golden argan oil (see p.621) and runs by the **dams of Tanizaourt** before descending to the fertile **Souss Valley**, with its intensive greenhouse cultivation.

There is also a minor tarred road, the **R212**, which breaks off the Essaouira road 23km west of Marrakesh, just after a bridge over the Nfis, and goes direct to Imi n'Tanoute. It's no faster but pleasantly unbusy. And if you have 4WD transport, you might alternatively want to consider the **old Tizi Maachou road**, a *piste* which runs east of the current N8; you can rejoin the main road at **Argana**, or head over the dramatic Tizi Iferd (Tizi Dahani) in the Souss Valley, nearer Taroudannt.

Kasbah Mtouggi

The Mtouggi dominated this western Atlas pass, just as the Goundafi and Glaoui did the eastern routes, and their **kasbah** near the village of **BOUABOUTE** looks, in its ruinous state, almost as large as Telouet. You can gain access to the ruins and see something of their one-time splendour, and the site is not hard to reach, either from Imi n'Tanoute on the Agadir road, or from Sidi Mohhtar on the Essaouira road. The road is paved.

Western High Atlas: Tichka Plateau treks

Exploring the **Tichka Plateau** and the **western fringes of the Atlas**, you move well away from the established tour-group routes, miles away from any organized refuge, and pass through Berber villages which see scarcely a foreigner

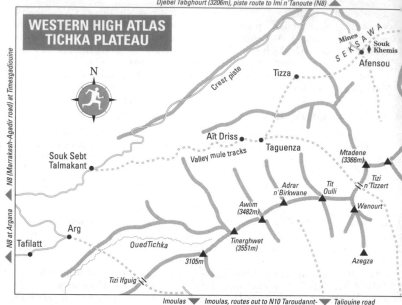

from one year to the next. You'll need to carry provisions, and be prepared to camp or possibly stay in a Berber village home if you get the invitation – as you almost certainly will. Sanitation is poor in the villages and it's not a bad idea to bring water purification tablets if you plan to take water from mountain streams – unless you're higher than all habitation (see also box, p.499). Eating and drinking in mountain village homes, though, is surprisingly safe, as the food (mainly tajines) is cooked slowly and the drink is invariably mint tea.

Getting into these mountains, there are approaches from both north and south: **Imi n'Tanoute**, **Timesgadiouine** and **Argana**, on the main Marrakesh–Agadir bus route (north and west), and **Taroudannt–Ouled Berhil** (south) or the Tizi n'Test road (east). From the north and west approaches, taxis, or rides on trucks bound for mines or markets at trailheads, have to be used; from the south, *camionettes* ply up daily to Imoulas, the Medlawa Valley and Tigouga. Up the Nfis from the Tizi n'Test road, a 4x4 can reach the valley from the pass. If you can afford it, hiring **Land Rover transport** to take you, and possibly a **guide**, to meet prearranged mules and a muleteer is the most efficient procedure. **El Ouad Ali** in Taroudannt (see p.630) is the recognized expert on the region and could make all arrangements. Or you could arrange a **small group trek** through the UK-based trekking company Walks Worldwide (see p.37); they organize, with El Ouad Ali, all levels of treks, from family walks through to an exceptional walk linking the Tichka Plateau to Djebel Toubkal.

The *IGN* 1:100,000 **maps** for the area are *Tizi n'Test* and *Igli*.

Imi n'Tanoute to the Tichka Plateau

A dirt road leads up into the mountains from Imi n'Tanoute to **Afensou**, nearby where a Thursday market (Al Khemis) is held, making your best chance of a lift up on Wednesday with one of the lorries. This trip takes several hours,

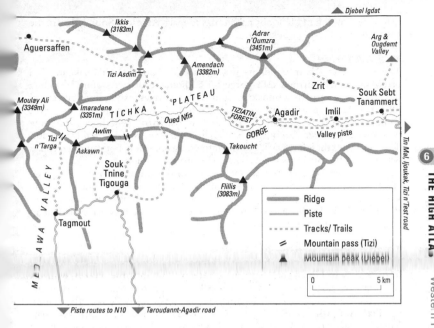

so don't arrive late in Imi n'Tanoute or you might get stranded. The road (not really suitable for ordinary passenger cars) crosses the **Tizi n'Tabghourt** at 2666m, from where you can ascend Djebel Tabghourt offering a magnificent panorama of the Western Atlas, often white with snow until early summer.

At Afensou you are in the **Haut Seksawa** with some of the highest mountain walks and climbs in the Atlas lying to the south and holding the romantic **Tichka Plateau** in their midst. **Moulay Ali** (3349m) dominates; the ridge from it to the main chain was climbed for the first time in 2001. The **Tizi Asdim** gives the easiest access to the Tichka Plateau, passing under **Djebel Ikkis** (3183m) and other climbing peaks. A few other *tizis* offer routes across the range and the traversing of the main ridge west of the plateau provides an exceptionally good multi-day trip with plenty of scrambling.

Timesgadiouine and the Aït Driss

The second access point to the mountains along the Marrakesh–Agadir road is **TIMESGADIOUINE**, about 50km south of Imi n'Tanoute. A signposted road leads off the N8 beside a café/petrol station. The actual village is 3–4km further on.

Souk Sebt Talmakant

SOUK SEBT TALMAKANT is most easily arrived at by using the lorries which drive up on Friday afternoons for the Saturday souks, or which go up during the week to the mines above Afensou, passing through Souk Sebt Talmakant on the way. Be prepared for a wait and a long dusty ride. If you ride up on Friday afternoon, you can camp overnight. Basic food items can be bought here. There are one or two cafés but no rooms, although the government workers posted to this nowhere place might offer you a room in their offices. A high level *piste* works along a crest with remarkable views, before descending in big loops past mines to reach Afensou/Souk Khemis, the easiest way to the high Seksawa.

The Aït Driss

The **Aït Driss River** winds its way just below Souk Sebt Talmakant. It's a pretty valley that narrows to a gorge for a kilometre or two before spreading out and filling up with walnut trees and Berber villages. As you trek up, several other tributaries come down on your right from the main ridge. The two most conspicuous peaks, **Tinerghwet** (3551m) and **Awlim** (3482m), are the same two you can see from Taroudannt, which lies in the Souss plain on their far side. Turn up any of these tributaries for an interesting day's trek. For camping, you're better off in the Aït Driss Valley, where the ground is flatter.

In September you'll see entire families out for the **walnut harvest**. The men climb high into the trees to beat the branches with long poles. Underneath, the women and children gather the nuts, staining their hands black for weeks from the outer shells. In this part of the Atlas, the women often wear their hair in coils that hang down the sides of their faces.

To the head of the Aït Driss

You can reach the **head of the Aït Driss** at Tamjlocht in a day's trekking from Souk Sebt Talmakent. From there a steep climb over the **Tizi n'Wannas** pass (2367m) takes you to Tizza, a small village at the head of the parallel valley, the Warguiwn. From Tizza trek east up a small valley 2–3km, then climb up **Tizi n'Timirout** (2280m) – which is not named on the survey map. There's a dramatic view of the main ridge from this pass, its rugged peaks stretching to the northeast. The most prominent one is Moulay Ali at 3349m. Afensou (see p.520) awaits you after a long descent, from where you can hitch back out to Souk Sebt Talmakent or Imi n'Tanoute or continue trekking to the Tizi n'Test road.

The Aït Driss Valley can be followed to its head (mule track) and the Tizi n'Tizzert crossed to southern villages (see below). This also gives access to Mtadene (3366m) and the main crest westwards.

Argana to Djebel Tichka

Argana, the third access point, lies off on a signposted road to the left some kilometres on down the Agadir road, a small town virtually abandoned since the new road bypassed it, and with something of the appearance of a frontier town in the Wild West. A French fort above points to its one-time importance.

Careful questioning and a long walk will lead you to **Tafilatt** and **Arg**, villages under the high wall of **Djebel Tichka**, gained by brutally steep tracks. A little below the crest on the other side lies the Oued Tichka, which breaks out to the south (a notable water channel leads its waters to the north side). Following this river up to reach the peaks of **Tinerghwet** and **Awlim** is one of the most rewarding ventures of its kind. Both peaks demand some scrambling and route-finding abilities and Awlim has acres of unclimbed cliffs. Passes southwards to Tasguint and Imoulas can round off a visit to this little-visited area.

Approaches to the Tichka Plateau

In the last few years the potential for mountain exploration in the Western High Atlas and "lost world" of the Tichka Plateau (and the beautiful valleys leading up to the heights) has been realized. Going it your own way, *camionettes* from Taroudannt and Ouled Berhil ply up to **Tasguint**, **Imoulas**, **Tagmout** and

Souk Tnine Tigouga, from where mule trails lead over the crests. From the east the Oued Nfis can be followed up to reach the Tichka Plateau in one or two days by dropping down to the valley from the Tizi n'Test and working upstream. The main routes from the south are outlined below.

Imoulas

IMOULAS is the most westerly market town of the foothills, with a Sunday souk. From here a *piste* extends for about 6km northwest to Tinighas, from where there is a dramatic route through a gorge to high *azibs* and a hard ascent to **Djebel Tinerghwet** (3551m), the highest peak in the area, and **Awlim** (3482m). East of Awlim extends the "**Ridge of a Hundred Peaks**", running on to the distant Tichka Plateau. Awlim's east face has climbing potential; a branch *piste* goes to Tasguint and the Tizi n'Ifguig which gives access to the Asif Tichka, Arg and the north of the range.

Tagmout

Houses may offer accommodation here or at the end of the *piste*, up the beautiful Medlawa Valley. A long zigzag mule track reaches the Tizi n'Targa, at the head of the Tichka Plateau. Tagmout/Tigouga *camionnettes* leave from east of Taroudannt so if you are approaching from Taroudannt, Imoulas is the easiest access point. A superb two-day trek (three if from Tasguint) leads to Alekjane and the Medlawa and can be arranged through El Ouad Ali in Taroudannt (see p.630).

Souk Tnine Tigouga

As the name suggests, **SOUK TNINE TIGOUGA** has a **Monday souk**, the easiest time to get a lift up, or out. Mule tracks west and east of Awlim give access to the Tichka Plateau and the only pass out north, the Tizi Asdim, to Aguersaffen, Afensou and Souk Khemis in the Seksawa. From Souk Tnine Tigouga a *piste* curls east to several villages and the Tizi n'Wadder mule track onto the lower Tichka Plateau. Djebel Flillis (3083m) in the ridges jutting to the south, is a worthy objective for experienced hill-goers, as is the granite Takoucht.

The Tichka Plateau

However you approach it, the **Tichka Plateau** is a delight. Grazing is controlled so the meadows are a mass of early daffodils and spring flowers. **Imaradene** (3351m) and **Amendach** (3382m) are the highest summits, west and east, and are superlative viewpoints. The plateau is drained by the Oued Nfis, first through the Tiziatin oak forest, using or bypassing gorges, then undergoing a series of villages, one, another Imlil, has a shrine to Ibn Toumert, the founder of the Tin Mal/Almohad dynasty.

A two-day trek from the plateau will take you to **SOUK SEBT TANAMMERT**. From this Saturday market, a lorry road climbs up to the Test road, not far from the pass itself. You can hitch out here or continue trekking for two more days to Mzouzite, near Tin Mal: one day north to Arg via Tizi n'Aghbar (2653m) and Tizi n'Tiddi (2744m), and the second day east along the long **Ougdemt Valley** to Mzouzite, as described under the Tizi n'Test section (see p.511). Passes from the Ougdemt Valley north over to Amizmiz are some of the hardest and finest in the Atlas. An excellent trail also descends the **Oued Nfis Valley** from Souk Sebt Tanammert, going through beautiful gorges and forested countryside.

Travel details

Buses

Marrakesh (Bab Doukkala terminal) to: Agadir (20 daily; 4hr); Ouarzazate (6 daily; 4–5hr); Taliouine (4 daily; 6hr).

Buses to Ourika, Asni (the trailhead for Djebel Toubkal; 1hr 30min), and Moulay Brahim, leave from the bus station out on the Asni road; some buses also run to Asni from the Bab Doukkala bus station.

Grands taxis

Marrakesh to: Ourika, Asni, Amizmiz and other Atlas trailhead towns – negotiate for these by the bus station out on the Asni road.

The great southern oasis routes

CHAPTER 7

Highlights

* **Kasbahs** Made with mud and straw *pisé*, some of these imposing traditional structures now house atmospheric hotels. See p.533, p.539 & p.545

* **Aït Benhaddou** The cream of the Deep South's desert architecture, used as a location for numerous movies. See p.537

* **Valley of Roses** Roses, used to make perfume, are the mainstay of this remote region – a superb trekking area. See p.555

* **Dadès Valley** Outlandish rock formations, ruined kasbahs and plentiful accommodation line this dramatic cleave in the High Atlas range. See p.562

* **Palmeries** Fed by ancient water courses, the great palmeries of Morocco's southern oases form an astounding contrast with the desert. See p.569

* **Todra Gorge** Simply one of the great natural spectacles of Morocco, at the head of a valley winding deep into the Atlas watershed. See p.571

* **Fossils** Stalls selling trilobites, ammonites, and other striking fossils litter southern roadsides, but the area around Alnif is a Mecca for serious collectors. See p.591

* **Erg Chebbi Dunes** Morocco's most impressive sand dunes, best explored on camel back. See p.596

△ Kasbahs at Aït Benhaddou

The great southern oasis routes

Immediately when you arrive in the Sahara, for this is the land that it is, you notice the stillness. An incredible, absolute silence prevails outside the towns; and within, even in busy places like the markets, there is a hushed quality in the air, as if the quiet were a constant force which, resenting the intrusion of sound, minimizes and disperses it straightaway. Then there is the sky, compared to which all other skies seem faint-hearted efforts. Solid and luminous, it is always the focal point of the landscape. At sunset, the precise, curved shadow of the earth rises into it swiftly from the horizon, cutting it into light section and dark section. When all daylight has gone, and the space is thick with stars, it is still of an intense and burning blue, darkest directly overhead and paling toward the earth, so that the night never really grows dark.

Paul Bowles: The Baptism of Solitude

The Moroccan pre-Sahara begins as soon as you cross the Atlas to the south. It is not sand for the most part – more a wasteland of rock and scrub which the Berbers call *hammada* – but it is powerfully impressive. The quote from Paul Bowles may sound over the top, but staying at M'hamid or Merzouga, or just stopping a car on a desert road between towns somehow has this effect.

There is, too, an irresistible sense of wonder as you catch a first glimpse of the great southern river valleys – the **Drâa**, **Dadès**, **Todra**, and **Ziz**. Long belts of date palm oases, scattered with the fabulous mud architecture of kasbahs and fortified *ksour* villages, these are the old caravan routes that reached back to Marrakesh and Fes and out across the Sahara to Timbuktu, Niger and old Sudan, carrying gold, slaves and salt well into the nineteenth century. They are beautiful routes, even today, tamed by modern roads and with the oases in decline, and if you're travelling in Morocco for any length of time, they are a must. The simplest circuits – **Marrakesh–Zagora–Marrakesh**, or **Marrakesh–Tinerhir–Midelt** – can be covered in around five days, though to do them any degree of justice you need a lot longer. With ten days or more to spare, the loop from Ouarzazate to Merzouga (via Boumalne and Tinerhir), and thence southwest to Zagora and M'hamid, becomes a possibility, stringing together the region's main highlights via good roads and dependable transport connections.

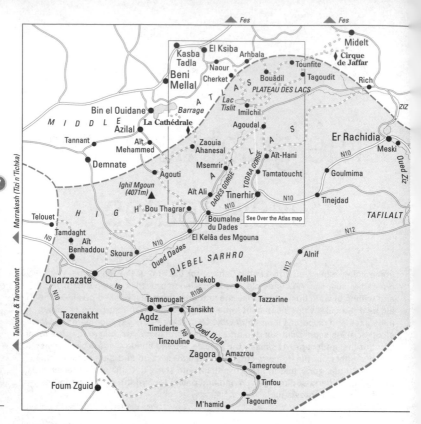

The **southern oases** were long a mainstay of the pre-colonial economy. Their wealth, and the arrival of tribes from the desert, provided the impetus for two of the great royal dynasties: the Saadians (1154–1669) from the Drâa Valley, and the current ruling family, the Alaouites (1669–present) from the Tafilalt. By the nineteenth century, however, the advance of the Sahara and the uncertain upkeep of the water channels had reduced life to bare subsistence even in the most fertile strips. Under the French, with the creation of modern industry in the north and the exploitation of phosphates and minerals, they became less and less significant, while the old caravan routes were dealt a final death blow by the closure of the Algerian border after independence.

Today, there are a few urban centres in the south; **Ouarzazate** and **Er Rachidia** are the largest and both were created by the French to "pacify" the south; they seem only to underline the end of an age. Although the date harvests in October, centred on **Erfoud**, can still give employment to the *ksour* communities, the rest of the year sees only the modest production of a handful of crops – henna, barley, citrus fruits and, uniquely, roses – the latter developed by the French around **El Kelâa des Mgouna** for the production of rose-water and perfume in May. To make matters worse, in recent years the seasonal rains have consistently failed, turning the palmeries pale yellow. Perhaps as much as half the male population of the region now seeks work in the north for at least part

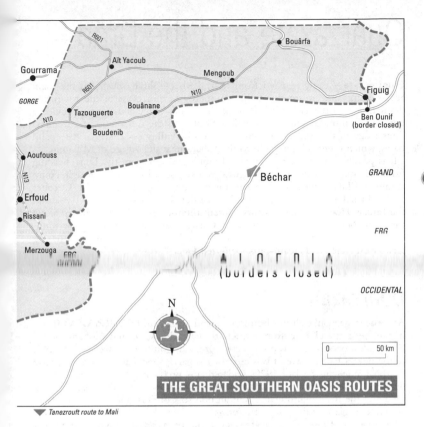

Tanezrouft route to Mali

of the year, while many of their women at home have been forced into poorly paid wage labour (there being insufficient fodder to feed the sheep and goats whose wool provided the basis of most families' income in the past).

Tourism brings in a little money, particularly to Ouarzazate and Zagora – once the Gate of the Desert (52 days to Timbuktu) – but has proved far from the economic miracle promised by developers in the early 1990s. That said you might be surprised by the number of visitors who make it this far south, even out of season, when the desert roads and *pistes* see a steady flow of camper vans and four-wheel-drives. Aside from the perennially dry weather (the area boasts an average of 300 cloudless days per year), most come to the pre-Sahara to see the **Dadès Valley**, whose picture-book *pisé* architecture sits at the foot of some extraordinary rock formations, and the still more spectacular **Todra Gorge**, further east, which remains one of the great spectacles of Morocco despite its relentless tourist traffic and attendant hassle. The region's undisputed scenic highlight, however, is the **Erg Chebbi dunes**, whose accessibility (they're the only large sand dunes in Morocco reachable by sealed road), not to mention their prominence on the Paris–Dakar Rally, have transformed the nearby village of **Merzouga** into a thriving tourist centre. Further southwest, the outpost of **M'hamid** is a more low-key alternative, with smaller dunes and correspondingly less pressure.

Ouarzazate and the Drâa

Ouarzazate – easily reached from Marrakesh (4–5hr by bus) – is the main access point and crossroads of the south. To the northeast of the town, the dramatic desert scenery and kasbah of the Dadès Valley and gorges, provide a compelling introduction to the region. South, on the other side of a tremendous ridge of the Anti-Atlas, begins the **Drâa Valley** – 125km of date palm oases, which eventually merge into the Sahara near the village of M'hamid.

It is possible to complete a circuit through and out from the Drâa, heading from the valley's main town, **Zagora**, across *piste* roads west through Foum Zguid and Tata to the Anti-Atlas, or north into the Djebel Sarhro (an October to April trekking area – see pp.558–562 for details), or east across to Rissani in the Tafilalt. However, most visitors content themselves with a return trip along the main **N9** (formerly P31) between Ouarzazate and Zagora: a great route, taking you well south of anywhere in the Tafilalt, and flanked by an amazing series of turreted and cream-pink-coloured *ksour*.

Ouarzazate

At some stage, you're almost bound to spend a night in **OUARZAZATE** and it can be a useful base from which to visit the *ksour* and kasbahs of Aït Benhaddou or Skoura. It is not exactly compelling in itself, however. Like most of the new Saharan towns, it was created as a garrison and administrative centre by the French in the late 1920s and remains pretty much the same today: a deliberate line of functional buildings, together with an array of modern hotels, set along the main highway and lent an odd sort of permanence by the use of concrete in place of the *pisé* of the *ksour*.

During the 1980s, Ouarzazate was a bit of a boom town. The tourist industry embarked on a wildly optimistic building programme of luxury hotels, based on Ouarzazate's marketability as a staging point for the "Saharan Adventure", and the town was given an additional boost from the attentions of movie-makers. The region first came to prominence in the film world forty-odd years ago, when David Lean shot *Lawrence of Arabia* (1962) at nearby Aït Benhaddou and in the Tafilalt, and since then numerous directors – most famously Bernardo Bertolucci, filming Paul Bowles's novel, *The Sheltering Sky* (1990), and Ridley Scott, who shot *Gladiator* here in 1999 – have been attracted to the Atlas Film Studios, 6km northwest on the main road (N9) towards Marrakesh.

Ouarzazate holds a mystic attraction for Moroccans, too – similar to the resonance of Timbuktu for Europeans. Indeed, many urban Moroccans respond to any mention of Ouarzazate with the odd rejoinder: "see Ouarzazate and die". Maybe this dates from the adventures of the Foreign Legion in the 1930s. If so, the only echo today is the early morning bugle sounding reveille behind the walls of the barracks.

Orientation, arrival and information

Orientation is simply a matter of getting your bearings along the old highway and main road, **Avenue Mohammed V**, at the east end of which

Southern practicalities

Transport

All the main road routes in this chapter are covered by regular buses, and often grands taxis. On many of the others, local Berber trucks (*camionettes*) or Land Rover and transit taxis (detailed in the text) run a bus-type service, charging standard fares for their trips, which are usually timed to coincide with the network of souks or markets in villages en route. The trucks cover a number of adventurous desert *pistes* – such as the direct routes from Zagora to Foum Zguid and Tata – and some very rough roads over the Atlas behind the Dadès or Todra gorges. If you plan to drive on these, you'll need to have a decent vehicle (4 x 4s are essential for some routes) and be able to do basic mechanical repairs.

Traveling by bus in the desert in summer, the main disadvantage is the sheer physical exhaustion involved: most trips tend to begin at dawn to avoid the worst of the heat and, for the rest of the day, it can be difficult to summon up the energy to do anything. If you can afford to rent a car – even for just two or three days –you'll be able to take in a lot more, with a lot less frustration, in a reasonably short period of time. There are numerous rental outlets in Ouarzazate, most of which allow you to return their vehicles to Agadir, Marrakesh, Fes, or even Casablanca.

Petrol stations can be found along all the main routes, but they're not exactly plentiful. Fill the tank whenever and wherever you have the opportunity. It's wise to carry water, too, in case of overheating, and, above all, be sure you've got a good spare tyre – punctures tend to be frequent on all southern roads. As throughout the country, however, local mechanics are excellent (Er Rachidia has an especially good reputation) and most minor – and routine – problems can be quickly dealt with (a puncture can be repaired for around 20dh).

Climate and seasons

Temperatures can climb well above 50°C in midsummer and you'll find the middle of the day is best spent being totally inactive. If you have the option, spring is by far the most enjoyable time to travel – particularly if you're heading for Zagora (reckoned to be the hottest town in the country), or Rissani-Merzouga. Autumn, with the date harvests, is also good. In winter, the days remain hot, though it can get fairly cool at night, and further south into the desert, it can actually freeze. Some kind of light hat or cap, and sunglasses, are pretty much essential.

Be aware, too, that the Drâa, in particular, is subject to flash floods in spring, as the snow melts in the Atlas and forges the river currents. Passes across the Atlas at this time, and even trips such as Ouarzazate to Aït Benhaddou or Skoura, can be difficult or impossible.

Health

Rivers in the south are reputed to contain **bilharzia**, a parasite that can enter your skin, including the soles of your feet, so, even when walking by streams in the oases, take care to avoid contact. Travellers are advised to drink only bottled mineral water in southern Morocco.

is the town's main sight, Kasbah Taorirt. The **CTM bus station** more or less marks the centre, with the **PTT** alongside. Private line long-distance **buses** now operate from the new Mahta bus station, 2km northwest on the bypass to the northwest of town. To reach the centre from here, you'll need to take a petit taxi (10–15dh). Most **grands taxis** also arrive outside the Mahta bus station, but some work from the CTM *gare routière* just off the main street. If you're unlucky, you may also be dropped 1km or so south of town across the Pont de Tabounte on the Zagora road (in which case you may prefer to head

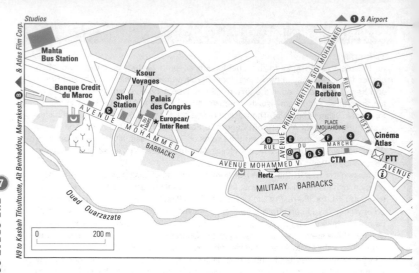

for one of the hotels in nearby Tabounte). Ouarzazate's **airport** is 2km north of town and served by local taxis (15–20dh). The helpful **tourist office** (Mon–Fri 8.30am–6.30pm; ☎024 88 24 85) is on Avenue Mohammed V, just across from the PTT.

Accommodation

Finding a hotel room should present few problems. Most of the cheaper and unclassified places are grouped in the centre of town; the more upmarket ones are mainly set back on the plateau to the north. Roughly 2km south across the river, the suburb of Tabounte holds most of the mid-range places; with your own vehicle, these are worth considering but otherwise lie inconveniently far from the centre. A more picturesque alternative would be to stay out at Aït Benhaddou (see p.537) or, if you've decided to skip the town altogether, press on to Skoura (see p.552).

The **campsite**, *Camping-Restaurant Ouarzazate* (☎024 88 46 36), is 2km east of the centre, signposted to the right just before the Kasbah Taorirt. It's a welcoming enough place, but has limited shade and the *blocs sanitaires* aren't always as clean as they might be. In the evenings noise from the adjacent tourist complex can also be a nuisance. Meals are available and you can swim at the municipal pool next door (now incorporated in the *Complexe Touristique Le Ouarzazate* – see p.536). For those with transport, a newer alternative is *Camping Tissa* (☎024 89 04 30), 20km west of town near the Aït Benhaddou junction. They have a small café-restaurant, a couple of rooms (still under construction when we passed through) and the staff speak English.

Cheap

Hôtel Amlal 24 Rue du Marché, near junction with Av Prince Héritier Sidi Mohammed ☎024 88 82 88, ⓕ024 88 46 00. A recently refurbished hotel with large en-suite rooms, dependable hot water supply and secure parking; demi-pensions are available and copious breakfasts are served in the salon for 25dh, a comfortable option although the back-street location is of little interest. ❹

Hôtel Atlas 13 Rue du Marché ☎024 88 77 45, ⓕ 024 88 64 85. Some rooms have showers, others use showers on the corridor; in both cases hot water in the evenings. A possible fall-back if the nearby *Hôtel Royal* is full. ❶

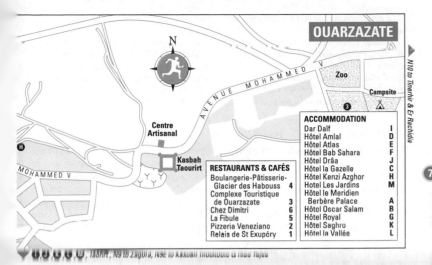

OUARZAZATE

ACCOMMODATION

Dar Daïf	I
Hôtel Amlal	D
Hôtel Atlas	E
Hôtel Bab Sahara	F
Hôtel Drâa	J
Hôtel la Gazelle	C
Hôtel Kenzi Azghor	H
Hotel Les Jardins	M
Hôtel le Meridien	
Berbère Palace	A
Hôtel Oscar Salam	B
Hôtel Royal	G
Hôtel Saghro	K
Hôtel la Vallée	L

RESTAURANTS & CAFÉS

Boulangerie-Pâtisserie-Glacier des Habouss	4
Complexe Touristique de Ouarzazate	3
Chez Dimitri	6
La Fibule	5
Pizzeria Veneziano	2
Relais de St Exupéry	1

Hôtel Bab Sahara Pl Mouahidine ☎024 88 47 22, ℻024 88 44 65. A 1990s-built hotel, convenient for the CTM bus station, grands taxis and shops. Rooms are available with showers and those that face the square have small balconies. Breakfast is available in the café. ➋

Hôtel Royal 24 Av Mohammed V ☎024 88 22 58. This is the best of the real cheapies: clean, well-maintained and with a variety of rooms, priced accordingly; it's central but can be noisy. ➊

Moderate

Hôtel Drâa 2km south in Tabounte ☎024 85 47 61, ℻024 85 47 62, 🌐www.ouarzazate.com/hoteldraa. Well-managed, modern place with fifty large rooms (most have balconies), small restaurant, large pool, and secure parking. ➌

Hôtel la Gazelle Av Mohammed V ☎024 88 21 51, ℻024 88 47 27. An old-established hotel, frayed around the edges but with a pleasant leafy garden courtyard. Handy for the bus station if you arrive late, but a bit of a plod from the centre. ➌

Hôtel Saghro 2.5km south in Tabounte ☎024 85 41 35, ℻024 85 47 09. A modern, friendly hotel offering impeccably clean rooms with, or without, attached bathrooms; a bargain, although again it's some distance from the centre. There's a small pool and restaurant, and a few shops nearby. Secure parking available. ➊–➍

Hôtel La Vallée 2km south in Tabounte ☎024 85 40 34, ℻024 85 40 43. Good value and well maintained; the only drawback is the distance from the town centre, compensated for by meals by the pool and dawn from the terrace. Used for

overnights by trekking groups, including Exodus and Explore. ➍

Riad Tajda 2km south in Tabounte Quartier Tarmigt ☎024 85 40 28, ℻024 85 41 09, ✉riadtajda.ifrance.com. This recently opened *maison d'hôte* in a converted town house provides one of the most unique accommodation options in the area. Each room is individually decorated and comfortably furnished. Price includes breakfast (self catering rooms available). ➍–➎

Expensive

Dar Daïf ☎ & ℻024 85 42 32, 🌐www.dardaif .ma. Beautifully restored *pisé* kasbah with romantic 1001 Nights decor and sublime views north from its terraces to the peaks of the High Atlas. Owned and run by a French mountain guide and his Moroccan wife, it's by far the most appealing place to stay in this category, although you'll need your own car to get here. Follow the Zagora road south across the river to Tabounte and look for the sign pointing left from the village centre. There is also a Hammam (100–120dh). ➎–➑

Hôtel Kenzi Azghor Av Prince Moulay Rachid ☎024 88 65 01, ℻044 88 63 53, ✉azgor @kenzi-hotels.com. This established hotel has fabulous views to the south and a good-sized swimming pool. For once, an upscale place that lives up to its prices. ➏–➐

Hôtel le Meridien Berbère Palace Quartier el Mansour Eddahbi ☎024 88 31 05, ℻024 88 30 71, ✉mberberpala@menara.ma. Ouarzazate's top hotel is a state-of-the-art five star incorporating traditional architectural motifs

533

and a magnificent pool, as well as a hammam and all the usual trimmings. ⑥

Hôtel Oscar Salam Atlas Film Corporation, 4.4km west along the Marrakesh road ☎ 024 88 21 66, ⓔ studio@iam.net.ma. Set up in the middle of the Atlas Studios to accommodate film crews and actors, but it usually has vacancies. Good-sized a/c rooms and a pool surrounded by pieces of old sets.

Recommended for movie buffs with their own transport. ⑤

Hotel Les Jardins 2km south in Tabounte ☎ 024 85 42 00, ⓕ 024 85 43 23, ⓔ hotellesjardins@ yahoo.fr, ⓦ www.lesjardinsdeouarzazate.com. This new faux-kasbah hotel offers comfortable rooms with hot showers available 24hrs, large garden area, swimming pool, and good food. ⑤

The town and kasbahs

Ouarzazate holds few sights of more than passing interest, but the local Glaoui Kasbah of **Taorirt**, and that of **Tifoultoutte**, 10km out on the old southern bypass, both deserve a visit. Movie fans may also enjoy a tour of the **Atlas Film Corporation Studios**, on the western outskirts of town, where you can see sets used in several international blockbusters. Other than that your best option is to get out for the day, either to Aït Benhaddou (see p.537) or a little along the Dadès to Skoura – a rambling oasis (see p.552), easily accessible as a day-trip using the Boumalne/Tinerhir buses.

Kasbah Taorirt

The **Kasbah Taorirt** (8am–6.30pm; 10dh) stands to the right of Avenue Mohammed V, at the east (Tinerhir direction) end of town. It's a dusty, twenty-minute walk from the centre of town.

Although built by the Glaoui, the kasbah was never an actual residence of its chiefs. However, located at this strategic junction of the southern trading routes, it was always controlled by a close relative. In the 1930s, when the Glaoui were the undisputed masters of the south, it was perhaps the largest of all Moroccan kasbahs – an enormous family domain housing numerous sons and cousins of the dynasty, along with several hundred of their servants and labourers, builders and craftsmen, even semi-itinerant Jewish tailors and moneylenders.

Since then, and especially since being taken over by the government after independence, the kasbah has fallen into drastic decline. The government has finally begun the task of "rehabilitating" the kasbah. Parts of the structure have disappeared, washed away by heavy rains, others are completely unsafe, and only a small section of the original – a kind of village within the kasbah – remains occupied today. That part is towards the rear of the rambling complex of rooms, courtyards and alleyways. What you are shown is just the main reception courtyard and a handful of principal rooms, lavishly decorated but not especially significant or representative of the old order of things. With an eye, perhaps, to tourism, they are known as "the harem".

Crafts

Opposite the Kasbah Taorirt is the **Centre Artisanal** (Mon–Fri 8.30am–6.30pm, Sat 8.30am–noon), a complex of half a dozen or so little shops with good-quality items at fixed (but not cheap) prices. Besides stone carvings and pottery, look for two local specialities: the geometrically patterned, silky woollen carpets of the region's Ouzguita Berbers, and the silver jewellery – necklaces and earrings incorporating *tazras* (chunky orange copal beads). There are also musical instruments used for the *ahouach*, a dance usually performed in the light of great fires until the first rays of daylight.

On the north side of town towards the airport, **Horizon Artisanat** (Mon–Fri 9am–6pm) has a shop selling attractive pottery, weaving and metalwork produced as part of a self-help scheme for less-able-bodied crafts workers. You can also visit workshops to watch them in action.

Avenue Mohammed V holds several small showrooms of traditional artefacts, old and new, and after studying the items at the Centre Artisanal, you may choose to try your bargaining skills there. Bazar du Sud is the most notable of the Mohammed V shops, located near the Super Market, which sells a variety of authentic tribal crafts and carpets at negotiable prices. Better still, but more difficult to find, is the **Maison Berbère** in the Tabounte district, the other side of the river on the road to Zagora; this is a branch of the Alaoui family chain selling high-quality carpets and rugs in towns south of Ouarzazate: Zagora, Tinerhir and Rissani.

Kasbah Tifoultoute

Around 10km from Ouarzazate is the **Kasbah of Tifoultoute** (8am–7pm; 10dh), originally owned by the Glaoui clan. It stands majestically on the banks of the Oued Tifoultoute, though it's rather more impressive from a distance than on entry. To reach it, cross the river to the Tabounte district and turn right at the petrol station where you see the sign for Tifoultoute.

In the 1960s, the kasbah was converted into a hotel for the cast of *Lawrence of Arabia*, since when it lapsed into a state of disrepair. Recent renovation, however, has transformed portions of the building, and it has started to feature on tour groups' itineraries again, hence the appearance of carpet and craft shops. Another part holds the *Restaurant Oued Tifoultoute*, which serves delicious mint and herb teas and menus ranging from 80–120dh on a pair of sunny terraces. It's also open for **visits**, which culminate with the panoramic views from the roof.

Atlas Film Corporation Studios

David Lean was the first to spot the potential of the Ouarzazate region as a source of exotic locations, filming *Lawrence of Arabia* here in the early 1960s. Since then a string of famous directors have followed in his wake to exploit the magnificent scenery, crisp light and plentiful supply of cheap, authentic-looking extras that have become the chief selling points of the **Atlas Film Corporation Studios**, 5km west of town on the Marrakesh road. International blockbusters shot here in recent years include Bertolucci's *The Sheltering Sky*, Scorsese's *Kundun*, Gillies MacKinnon's *Hideous Kinky*, Oliver Stone's *Alexander the Great* and Ridley Scott's *Gladiator*, *Black Hawk Down*, and most recently, *Kingdom of Heaven*.

As most of the filming takes place miles off the road in the desert, the studios are generally open to visitors (50dh for a 30min tour). Blue-Peter-badge-holder Youssef Ajama will show you around some of the sets surviving from projects past, among them a Tibetan monastery featured in Scorsese's *Kundun*, and a somewhat less authentic Egyptian temple used in a recent French version of *Cleopatra*.

Eating

There are pricey **restaurants** at all the large hotels and tourist complexes (see listings), and cheap **café-grills** grouped around the covered market at Place Mouahidine and along the nearby Rue du Marché. For breakfast, the sunnier north side of Boulevard Mohammed V is the area to head for, with a row of pleasant terrace cafés serving French baguettes and good coffee; the same places also serve tajines, grills and light salads at lunchtime for around 50–60dh, and are on the whole more hygiene than those in the market area.

Boulangerie-Patisserie-Glacier Des Habouss Pl Mouahidine. Ouarzazate's best bakery-cum-ice-cream parlour is a good spot for a coffee stop, serving several kinds of delicious Moroccan bread, in addition to crusty baguettes, croissants and pains au chocolat. They also do the full gamut of sticky local patisserie (sold by weight): try the *briouates* or *ouardas*, with crunchy almond fillings.

Chez Dimitri 22 Av Mohammed V (next to *Hôtel Royal*) ☎024 88 73 46. Founded in 1928 to serve the Foreign Legion, this bar-brasserie is licensed and has a wide-ranging menu of mostly Gallic standards (mains from around 80dh), served by uniformed waiters. Old photographs of the town and desert add to the colonial ambience, lapped up by French tour groups, but the food doesn't warrant the high prices. Reservations recommended. Expensive.

Complexe Touristique de Ouarzazate in the Sidi Daoud alongside the campsite ☎024 88 31 10. Upscale tourist restaurant seating 600 and pitched at groups, with displays of song, music and dance most evenings around the poolside. Served in Berber tents, the pricey *menus fixes* range from 130–150dh (for three courses) at lunchtime, to 230–300dh (four courses) for dinner. Specialities include lemon *harira* and pigeon tajine. Moderate to expensive.

La Fibule Bd Mohammed V. Currently the best of the lookalike budget café-restos lining the main street. The food – a predictable selection of tajines, omelettes, salads and *grillades* – is fairly priced (most mains around 50–65dh) and the service attentive. You can sit outside on the terrace or indoors. Cheap.

Pizzeria Veneziano Av Moulay Rachid ☎024 88 76 76. Unexpectedly smart little pizza joint serving a good range of inexpensive salads, European dishes and tajines, in addition to filling, tasty pizzas (from 30dh). They also offer plenty of veggie options and the staff are courteous. The most traveller-friendly budget restaurant in town. Cheap.

Relais de St Exupéry 13 Av Moulay-Abadallah, quartier Al-Gods ☎024 88 77 79. Just off the main Tinerhir road, near the airport (look for the signboards pointing left as you leave town, before the petrol station). Fine Moroccan cuisine, served in an attractive French-owned restaurant. Memorabilia from the *Aéropostale* days of *Little Prince* author Antoine de St Exupéry adorns the walls, but the food is the real attraction: try the wonderful pigeon pastilla, sea bass with orange or lamb in honey. Various fixed menus from 75–190dh. Moderate to expensive.

Listings

Airport The Aéroport Taorirt (☎024 88 23 83) is 2km north of town, and served by petits taxis (20dh). There are daily RAM flights to Casablanca and twice-weekly flights to Paris. RAM has an office at 1 Av Mohammed V (☎024 88 51 02, ℱ024 88 68 93).

Banks All the banks and ATMs are on the north side of Av Mohammed V. They include (moving west to east): Crédit du Maroc, Wafabank, BMCE, BCM and Banque Populaire.

Bikes – including mountain bikes – can be rented from Ksour Voyages, 11 Pl du 3 Mars (see "Tours", below).

Car rental Literally dozens of agencies operate in Ouarzazate, either from offices on Bd Mohammed V or out on Pl du 3 Mars. Shop around for the best deals; prices range from 200–350dh per day if you rent a vehicle for seven days, but it's always worth haggling – at least with local firms – and scrutinize the small print. As ever in Morocco, it's also advisable to opt for additional insurance to cover any damage excess (see our general advice in "Basics" on p.45); and check the car (front and back lights, petrol gauge and spare tyre) thoroughly before driving away. Standards here can be well below what you might be used to back home.

Amzrou Transport, Rue de l'Aviation, just off Bd Mohammed V ☎024 88 23 23; Avis, Pl du 3 Mars ☎024 88 78 70, ℱ024 88 43 10; Budget, Av Mohammed V, next to the Hôtel-Residence al Warda ☎024 88 28 92, ℱ024 88 42 12; Dune, Av Mohammed V ☎024 88 73 91, ℱ024 88 49 01; Europcar/InterRent, Pl du 3 Mars ☎024 88 20 35, ℱ024 88 40 27; Hertz, 33 Av Mohammed V ☎024 88 20 84, ℱ024 88 34 85.

Car repairs Garage Raquiq el Habib, Quartier Industriel No. 99 (☎024 88 49 33) is recommended.

Internet Access Satellite Net, near *Hôtel Amlal*, is the largest place in town and charges standard rates; otherwise, try Ouarzazate Web, on Bd Mohammed V.

Motorcycle rental and tours British-run Wilderness Wheels, at the far eastern end of Bd Mohammed V (☎024 88 81 28, ℗www.wildernesswheels.com), runs trips into the desert on Honda XR250R/ XR650R and KTM400 EXC trials bikes (from about €530 for a 2day/3night tour; which includes all equipment, including body armour, helmets, gloves, goggles and enduro jacket). This is a highly professional and experienced outfit, and the routes covered are superb. Motorbike licence essential.

Post office The PTT on Av Mohammed V has poste restante facilities, plus a direct-dialling international phone oootion; it's open Mon–Fri 8.30am–6pm, Sat 8.30am–noon.

Shopping The Super Marché, 73 Av Mohammed V, opposite Chez Dimitri, is well stocked, including beer and wine, and is open until 10pm.

Tours Swiss-run Iriqui Excursions, Pl du 3 Mars (☎024 88 57 99, ⊛www.iriqui.com) offers a range of well-organized tours, including a "Circuit St Exupéry", visits to places associated with the Paris–Dakar Rally and desert trips to a remote oasis 60km out of M'hamid. For day excursions in the area by minibus or Land Rover, try Ksour Voyages, also on Pl du 3 Mars (☎024 88 28 40, ☎024 88 48 99), or Amzrou Transport Touristique on Av Mohammed V (☎024 88 22 30). To arrange adventure trips into the High Atlas, including trekking and mountaineering, your best option is Désert et Montagne Maroc at the Hôtel Dar Daïf (⊛www.desert-montagne.ma; see p.533), run by French-qualified mountain guides Pierre and Zineb Datcharry.

Moving on

CTM bus services leave from their station near the PTT, to Agadir (via Taliouine, Taroudannt and Inezgane), Casablanca, Marrakesh, M'Hamid, Zagora, and Er Rachidia. SATAS and other privately run **long-distance buses** go from the new gare routière at Mahta, 2km from the centre (a 10–15dh taxi ride away); as ever, they're cheaper, but take longer. Between them they run as – or more – frequently than CTM, but timings often change. For a full rundown of destinations, see Travel details at the end of this chapter. If possible, book your ticket at least one day before departure.

Grands taxis leave from alongside the CTM bus station on regular runs along the Dadès to Boumalne (30dh a place; connections on towards Tinerhir and Er Rachidia), and for Marrakesh, Zagora and points westwards (including Tazenakht, Taliouine, Aloulouz, Ouled Berhil, Taroudannt and Agadir), with connections for the Tizi n'Test pass. The same range of destinations are served by grands taxis working from the less conveniently situated gare routière out at Mahta.

Aït Benhaddou

The first thing you hear from the guides on arrival at **AÏT BENHADDOU**, 32km from Ouarzazate, is a list of its movie credits. This is a feature of much of the Moroccan south (see p.535) but, even so, the Benhaddou kasbahs have a definite edge over the competition. Lawrence of Arabia was filmed here, of course; Orson Welles used it as a location for Sodom and Gomorrah; and for Jesus of Nazareth the whole lower part of the village was rebuilt. In recent years, more controlled restoration has been carried out under UNESCO auspices and, in 1994 the government announced plans to "rehabilitate" Aït Benhaddou in order to conserve the national and cultural heritage.

With its souvenir shops and constant stream of tour groups, Aït Benhaddou is not really the place to catch a glimpse of fading kasbah life but it is one of the most spectacular sights of the Atlas, piled upon a low hillock above a shallow, reed-strewn river. Its collection of kasbahs are among the most elaborately decorated and best preserved; they are less fortified than is usually the case along the Drâa or the Dadès, but, towered and crenellated, and with high, sheer walls of dark red pisé, they must have been near impregnable in this remote, hillside site.

As ever, it's impossible to determine exactly how old the kasbahs are, though there seem to have been buildings here since at least the sixteenth century. The importance of the site, which commands the area for miles around, was its position on the route from Marrakesh through Telouet to Ouarzazate and the south: the caravans passing through it carried salt across the Sahara and returned with gold, ivory and slaves. In time, this trade diminished, largely because the coast of West Africa was opened up: hence the colonial Ivory Coast and Gold Coast and the transatlantic slave trade.

In the twentieth century, the significance of this route disappeared with the creation of the new French road over the Tichka pass, which has led to severe depopulation over the last thirty years. There are now only half a dozen families living in the kasbahs, earning a sparse living from the valley's agriculture and rather more from the bus-loads of tourists who pass through.

Practicalities

Getting to Aït Benhaddou is simple enough by car. Leaving Ouarzazate on the N9 (Tizi n'Tichka) road, you turn right after 18km along a surfaced road. Without a car, the best solution is to get together with others and charter a grand taxi from Ouarzazate. Otherwise, you'll need to get a bus or grand taxi to the turn-off (8–10dh) and pick up another for the remaining leg to the village (5dh). At the "new village", on the west bank of the river, the road passes the *Hôtel-Restaurant Le Kasbah*, in front of which there's a parking area where guides hang around hoping to escort visitors across the river: in winter you sometimes have to wade across though the water is rarely more than knee-deep (when it is, donkeys will be on hand to help). Entry to the **kasbah** is free, although the gateways are "controlled" by people who may try to convince you

Ksour and kasbahs

Ksour (*ksar* in the singular), or **kasbahs**, are to be found throughout the southern valleys and, to an extent, in the Atlas. They are essentially fortified tribal villages, massive but transitory structures, built in the absence of other available materials out of the mud-clay *pisé* of the riverbanks and lasting only as long as the seasonal rains allow. A unique and probably indigenous development of the Berber populations, they are often monumental in design and fabulously decorated, with bold geometric patterns incised or painted on the exterior walls and slanted towers.

The kasbah, in its southern form, is similar to the *ksar*, though instead of sheltering a mixed village community, it is traditionally the domain of a single family and its dependants. *Agadirs* and *tighremts*, also variants of the *ksar* structure, used to serve as a combination of tribal fortress and communal granary or storehouse in the villages.

The Drâa kasbahs

Ksour line the route more or less continuously from Agdz to Zagora; most of the larger and older ones are grouped a little way from the road, up above the terraces of date palms. Few that are still in use can be more than a hundred years old, though you frequently see the ruins and walls of earlier *ksour* abandoned just a short distance from their modern counterparts. Most are populated by **Berbers**, but there are also Arab villages here, and even a few scattered communities of **Jews**, still living in their Mellahs. All of the southern valleys, too, have groups of **Haratin**, Blacks descended from the west Sudanese slaves brought into Morocco along these caravan routes. Inevitably, these populations have mixed to some extent – and the Jews here are almost certainly converted Berbers – though it is interesting to see just how distinct many of the *ksour* still appear, both in their architecture and customs. There is, for example, a great difference from one village to the next as regards women's costumes, above all in the wearing and extent of veils.

Visiting the region, bear in mind that all of the Drâa *ksour* and kasbahs tend to be further from the road than they look: it's possible to walk for several hours without reaching the edge of the oasis and the upper terraced levels.

otherwise (only pay the 10dh or so demanded if you want to see the inside of any houses). Follow the network of lanes uphill and you'll eventually arrive at the ruins of a vast and imposing **agadir**, or fortified granary, from where there are great views over the surrounding desert.

Leaving town by public transport at the end of the day can be tricky: local traffic tends to dry up by 4pm allowing taxis to charge what they think they can get away with. The only cheap alternative is to walk the 5km back to the highway and try to flag down one of the Marrakesh–Ouarzazate buses (which are likely to be full and not inclined to stop).

Accommodation and eating

Given how difficult it can sometimes be to find transport out of Aït Benhaddou, you may well end up deciding to spend the night here – in any case, it makes a more atmospheric stopover than Ouarzazate, and there's no shortage of accommodation options. Cafés and restaurants are somewhat thinner on the ground, with most people opting to eat at their hotel or guesthouse. For further suggestions, see also our reviews for Tamdaght on p.540.

Auberge el Bereke ⊕024 89 03 05, ℗024 88 62 11, 🌐baraka.hotel@hotmail.com. Twenty en suite rooms in the centre of the village, all with hot showers; there's also a roof terrace where you can bed down for 30dh and a good salon restaurant serving a four-course menu for 70dh (or 120dh half-board); there is also additional comfortable seating in two large Berber tents. *Taklia* – a kind of Berber tajine – is the house speciality, and the brothers lay on an informal "*tam tam*" show after supper. ❷

Auberge Étoile Filante ⊕024 89 03 22, ℗024 88 61 13. North of the village centre on the roadside, this has eleven rooms, all en suite and cool. It's clean and well managed, but a little characterless and not great value for money. Half board from 170dh per head. ❸

🏃 **Dar Mouna** ⊕048 84 30 54, ℗048 83 30 80, 🌐www.darmouna.com. Traditionally furnished rooms (all en suite) in a tastefully converted kasbah, on a bluff bang opposite the old village. The hotel is virtually self-sufficient with its own vegetable garden, bread ovens, natural well, and animals. Much the nicest place to stay, with arguably Aït Benhaddou's most romantic dining terrace and a cosy interior for the cool winter evenings. There is also a pool and traditional hammam. The restaurant offers a more adventurous menu than usual, too (100dh per head), with Egyptian *shorbah*, chicken crêpes and flambéed banana in addition to the Moroccan standards. ❻–❼

Defat Kasbah 3km north of Aït Benhaddou, on the riverside ⊕024 88 80 20, ℗024 88 64 85. Stylish budget hotel occupying a prime, tranquil spot with fine views up the valley. Owned by a young French-Moroccan couple, it's a friendly place with helpful staff and attractively furnished rooms (all en suite). Those on the upper floors have access to a nice terrace, and there's a pool and pleasant ground-floor salon restaurant. ❷–❸

Kasbah du Jardin ⊕024 88 80 19, ℗024 88 44 94. Rough and ready little *auberge* beyond the *Étoile Filante*, and the best budget fall-back if the *Ksar* is full. More peaceful than most of the competition, with traditional mud walls and wooden doors opening onto a plain concrete interior. Camping and secure parking available. ❷

Ksar ⊕066 60 60 84 (ask for Kamal). Newest and most appealing of the rock-bottom options, offering small but adequate rooms (all en suite and attractively decorated) at a roadside location just before Kasbah du Jardin. A bargain at 100dh per double and the meals are equally good value (60dh per head, or 100dh for half-board). ❶

Riad Maktoub ⊕024 88 86 94, ℗024 88 82 59, 🌐www.riadmaktoub.com. Located in the village centre on the main road, an attractive riad-style building with seven rooms and five suites surrounding a traditional long courtyard. Menus (60–75dh) are served in the salon or on either of the elegant terraces overlooking the kasbah. ❺

Tamdaght

Spread across a platform above a bend in the river, its fringes hemmed in by canyon walls, **TAMDAGHT**, 6km further up the valley from Aït Benhaddou, has a more authentic Berber feel than its neighbour. The village, which formerly flourished with the caravan route over the Tizi n'Tichka, is dominated by the

The shoreline of the El Mansour Eddahbi Barrage is an essential stop on the bird-watchers' itinerary. Throughout the year (especially late July–Nov & March–May) the area attracts a variety of migrants such as ruddy shellduck, other waterfowl and waders. There have also been sightings of a variety of desert-dwelling species such as mourning wheatear, trumpeter finch, blackbellied sandgrouse, thick-billed lark (and other larks) and raptors, including lanner falcon.

remnants of a crumbling Glaoui kasbah, its towers crowned by gigantic storks' nests. Few of the daytrippers that pass through Aït Benhaddou make it this far, but you can ford the river below the *Hôtel Dar Kasbah* (usually possible in a tourist vehicle) and either follow the road for another 4km or walk along the riverbank. Both lead through some spectacular desert scenery (featured by Ridley Scott in *Gladiator* and Oliver Stone in *Alexander the Great*), but on foot you've the added bonus of crossing the lush terraced gardens below the **kasbah**. Visits to the only section of the building still inhabited (one or two wings are on the verge of collapse) are possible; knock at the main door (facing the road) and expect to pay a donation of around 10dh.

From the end of the tarmac at Tamdaght, a *piste* leads 35km further northwest to Telouet and the Tizi n'Tichka pass. This has in recent years become a popular trekking and mountain bike itinerary, coverable in dry weather by 4 x4 but which should under no circumstances be attempted in a tourist vehicle; some sections are especially prone to landslides after rain. The route, however, penetrates increasingly magnificent landscape punctuated at regular intervals by villages, several of which have small *gîtes d'étapes*. At **Anemiter**, there's also a large Glaoui kasbah. Allow a half-day if following the *piste* by car, a full day by mountain bike and two to three days if on foot. (This route is covered in reverse from Telouet in the High Atlas chapter, see p.518.)

Practicalities

Tamdaght holds a couple of pleasant places to stay, both close to the kasbah on the edge of the village. The budget option is the eccentric *Auberge des Cigognes* (☎024 89 03 71; ❶), which offers four very basic rooms (with shared showers and toilets) in a rambling ancestral home for the bargain all-in price of 110dh full board. Its sole permanent occupant, owner Adelazize Taoufik, also has a cheap dorm frequented mostly by trekkers en route to or from Telouet.

At the opposite end of the scale, the neighbouring *Kasbah Ellouze* (☎067 96 54 83, Ⓦwww.kasbahellouze.com; ❺) is a much fancier French-run place recently established by a couple from Nîmes. Although modern, the building follows traditional lines, with *pisé* walls and cavernous rooms that combine stylish traditional Moroccan design with mod cons such as heaters and bathtubs. Copious, carefully prepared meals are also served on a lovely rear terrace (open to nonresidents for tea) overlooking the village orchards, river and valley. Full board here costs 640dh per person.

South to Zagora: the Drâa oases

The road from **Ouarzazate to Zagora** is well maintained and, for the most part, broad enough for two vehicles, though it does take its toll on tyres. As in the rest of the south, if you're driving make sure you have a good spare and the tools to change it with. If you're on the bus, get yourself a seat on the left-hand side for the most spectacular views.

Although Zagora is the ostensible goal and destination, the valley is the real attraction. Driving the route, try to resist the impulse to burn down to the desert, and take the opportunity to walk out to one or another of the *ksour* or kasbahs. Using local transport, you might consider hiring a grand taxi for the day – or half-day – from Ouarzazate, stopping to explore some of the kasbahs en route; if you intend to do this, however, be very clear to the driver about your plans.

Along certain stretches of the route you'll notice groups of kids brandishing boxes of **boufeggous dates**, highly prized in Morocco and worth stopping to taste – in some cases, the vendors may encourage you to do so by leaping in front of your car. Another hassle, prevalent throughout the south but refined along this road, are "**fake breakdowns**". People standing next to stationary cars will flag you down, ostensibly for help getting to a garage; but when you arrive at the next town they insist on returning the favour by offering you a "special price" on items from their handicraft shop.

The lake and over the Tizi n'Tinififft

The route begins unpromisingly. The course of the Drâa lies initially some way to the east and the road runs across bleak, stony *hammada*. After 15km, a side road, the P31F, leads 11km down to the **El Mansour Eddahbi Barrage and reservoir** (road closed to vehicles). In 1989 freak rains flooded the reservoir, and the Drâa, for the first time in recent memory, ran its course to the sea beyond Tan Tan.

On the main road, the first interest comes just beyond Aït Saoun, one of the few roadside villages along this stretch, where a dramatic change takes place. Leaving the plains behind, the road climbs, twists and turns its way up into the mountains, before breaking through the scarp at the pass of **Tizi n'Tinififft** (1660m). From the summit of the pass there are fine views north to the Atlas mountains that frame the horizon.

The pass is just 4km beyond Aït Saoun. Beyond it the road swings down through a landscape of layered strata, until finally, some 20km from the pass, you catch a first glimpse of the valley and the oases – a thick line of palms reaching out into the haze – and the first sign of the Drâa Kasbahs, rising as if from the land where the green gives way to desert.

Agdz

You descend into the Drâa Valley at **AGDZ** (pronounced Ag–a–dèz), 68km from Ouarzazate, a stopping point for many of the buses and a minor administrative centre for the region. The town consists of just one long street, blood-red coloured, save for the columns of its arcade of shops, picked out in flashes of white and blue. Many of these sell carpets and pottery – and in the few minutes before the bus leaves, prices can drop surprisingly. If you stop here – travelling in either direction – it is unlikely that you'll get a place back on the Zagora/ Ouarzazate bus; however, there are **grands taxis** (to either destination), which, like the buses, leave from the Grande Place, and it's possible to stay, too.

It's certainly worth a stop, for just to the north of the village begins a beautiful **palmery**. If the river here is low enough (take care to avoid the bilharzia-infested water) you can get across to view a few **kasbahs** on the far side, in the shadow of Djebel Kissane. Also worth a look is the Kasbah du Caïd Ali, reached by turning left off the main square (coming from Ouarzazate).

Accommodation and eating

The town has a handful of **hotels** that provide an attractive and low-key introduction to the valley. Of the budget options ranged around the Grande Place, the dirty, rundown *Hôtel Drâa* (☎024 84 31 53; ❶) is best avoided in favour of the more salubrious *Hôtel des Palmiers* (☎024 84 31 27; ❷) which has been recently renovated. By the ceremonial archway at the northern entry to the town is the pricier *Hôtel Kissane* (☎024 84 30 44, ⓕ024 84 32 58; ❹), a very pleasant place with obliging staff, a pool and a good salon **restaurant**. With your own transport you might want to venture further out of town to the *Maison d'Hôte Tansifte* (☎024 34 10 56; 400dh for 2 people full board), 4km from the centre (follow the main road towards Tazenakht and turn off where you see the signboard near the Total petrol station), which offers simple, attractively furnished rooms (with shared shower and toilet facilities) on a working farm. They've a large, well-tended garden to laze in and meals are prepared using home produce.

There are also a couple of better-than-average **campsites**. Alongside the Kasbah Asslim, the *Camping Kasbah de la Palmerie* (☎ & ⓕ024 84 36 40) is reached by turning left off the main street just after the Grande Place. The signpost says 2km, but it's possibly twice that. The site is run with great efficiency by a Frenchwoman, has plenty of shade, a swimming pool and clean toilet blocks, and there are a few rooms for rent in the kasbah (❶). Alternatively, try the cheaper *Camping Caravane Targui* ("Saïd's Bivouac"; no phone), which occupies a fabulous location beside the palmery. It's very basic, with no electricity or hot water, but offers good-value accommodation in nomad tents (❶) and decent meals, prepared by the owner, Saïd Youssifi (who also runs a nice little shop in the square selling antiques and curios from across North Africa).

West from Agdz to Tazenakht

Just north of Agdz, a junction marks the start of a little-travelled, but wonderfully remote route to **Tazenakht**, on the road to Taliouine (see p.636). The route has been paved and provides a much faster way to reach Tazenakht (as well as Agadir via Taroudannt) than the more roundabout route via Ouarzazate.

Settlements along the way include **Aït Smegane-n-el Grara** which has a café; **Bou Azzer**, which is just a mine and some workers' accommodation (east of Bou Azzer in Arhbar are extensive cobalt mines), and **TAZENAKHT**, a carpet weaving centre at the junction of the Agadir, Ouarzazate and Foum Zguid roads. The town is quite a transport hub, with regular buses and grands taxis to Ouarzazate, plus buses to Foum Zguid, Tissint and Tata. It also offers decent rooms and meals: the *Hôtel Zenaga* (☎024 84 10 32; ❷), on Avenue Moulay-Hassan, or the equally well-maintained *Hôtel Taghdoute* (☎024 84 13 93; ❷), also on Avenue Moulay-Hassan, whose owner organizes walking trips into the surrounding countryside. For cheap meals, you won't do better than the line of simple cafés opposite the *gare routière*, which knock up freshly grilled kebabs, spicy lentil stew (*ledus*) and fish steaks. There's also a Banque Populaire and petrol station. Alongside the *Café-Restaurant Étoile* is a large courtyard with a magnificent display of carpets, blankets and clothes, including many of the bold geometric designs of the Ouzguita tribe. If you have time on your hands, you could also visit the carpet cooperative. Souk days in Tazenakht are Friday and Saturday.

Tamnougalt, Timiderte and Tinzouline

Continuing south down the Drâa Valley, the *ksour* at **TAMNOUGALT** – off to the left of the road, about 6km past Agdz – are perhaps the most dramatic and extravagant of any in the region. A wild cluster of buildings, each is fabulously decorated with pockmarked walls and tapering towers. The village was once the capital of the region, and its assembly of families (the *djemaa*) administered what was virtually an independent republic. It's populated by a Berber tribe, the Mezguita. You can **stay** here at the welcoming *Jardin de Tamnougalt* (T024 84 36 14; ●), where proprietor Ismaïl Elalaoui has a handful of well-kept en-suite rooms in a family home, as well as limited camping space and a dining terrace shaded by olive and palm trees.

Another 13km south, on the opposite side of the river, is the more palace-like Glaoui kasbah of **TIMIDERTE**, built by Brahim, the eldest son of the one-time pasha of Marrakesh, T'hami el Glaoui. You'll have to ford the river again, this time on foot – ideally with some local assistance as the best crossing place isn't all that obvious – to reach another superb kasbah, the **Aït Hammou-Saïd**. Carpeted with palms producing the famous *boufeggous* dates (which you'll have seen sold from the roadside by kids along this stretch of the Drâa), the whole area is littered with wonderful old *ksour* dating from the era when the region was prone to attacks by nomads from the south.

The back country road from Rissani and Nekob meets the N9 just south of Timiderte (a route described on pp.590–593). Beyond the junction, another striking group of *ksour* dominated by a beautiful and imposing *caïd's kasbah*, stands back from the road at **TINZOULINE**, 57km beyond Timiderte (37km north of Zagora). There is a large and very worthwhile **Monday souk** held here and, if you're travelling by bus, the village is one of the better places to break the journey for a while. With some guidance, you can also follow a *piste* 7km west of the village to see a group of three-thousand-year-old rock carvings.

Zagora

ZAGORA seems unpromising at first sight: a one-street, modern market town with a big crop of hotels and government buildings. As the region's main staging post for trips to the fringes of the Sahara, it attracts far more tourist attention than it deserves in itself, not to mention hustlers in search of potential clients for camel treks. Two things, however, redeem it. The first is its location: this is the most productive stretch of the Drâa – indeed, of all the southern valleys – and you only have to walk a mile or so out of the town to find yourself amid the palms and oasis cultivation. The second is a distinct air of unreality. Directly behind the town rises a bizarre Hollywood-sunset mountain, and at the end of the main street is a mock-serious road sign to Timbuktu ("52 jours" – by camel – if the border were open).

Another draw for Zagora is its festivals. The Drâa's big event, the **Moussem of Moulay Abdelkader Jilali**, is celebrated here during the Mouloud, and like other national festivals here, such as the **Fête du Trône**, is always entertaining.

Orientation

Though it can seem a bit of a hassle on arrival, and in summer the oven-dry heat is staggering (as are the *frigidaire* nights in winter), Zagora is an easy place to get oriented. Almost everything of note is on the main street, **Boulevard Mohammed V**, or the lower – and lesser – **Avenue Hassan II**. Across the river, to the southeast, is the palmery and hamlet of **Amazrou**, a good alternative base, with a fast-growing group of hotels and two campsites.

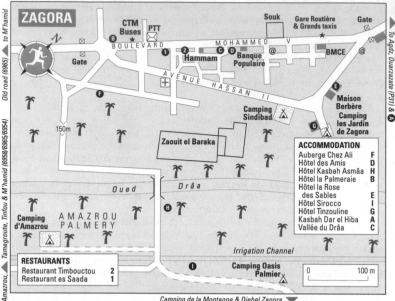

Camping de la Montagne & Djebel Zagora ▼

Accommodation

There is a good choice of **hotels** – in Zagora and Amazrou – and some nicely located **campsites**, especially for those with transport. Travellers on tight budgets should also note that many mid-scale hotels, including the *Sirocco* and *Kasbah Asmâa* (reviewed below) will let you bed down on roof terraces or in nomad tents for 50dh or less.

Hotels

Auberge Chez Ali Av Atlas Zaouit el Baraka ☎ 024 84 62 58, ✉ chez_ali@hotmail.com. A haven of greenery on the edge of town, offering clean, secure and relaxing accommodation in 12 comfortable rooms (8 en suite) or cosy Berber tents. The owner, Ali, is genuinely hospitable and has over two decades created a lovely garden filled with flowers and fruit trees, where you can dine and lounge around. Altogether the nicest address in Zagora, but far from a secret, so book ahead. ❷

Hôtel Des Amis Bd Mohammed V, ☎ 024 84 72 15. The cheapest rooms in town. Rooms overlooking the front have balconies. ❶

Hôtel Kasbah Asmâa 2km from the centre, over the Oued Drâa at Amazrou ☎ 024 84 72 41, ✉ ksbasmaa@iam.net.ma. A kasbah-style hotel, faced with traditional *pisé* and set in a beautiful garden overlooking the palmery, with a shaded swimming pool and top-notch restaurant. It's smaller, has better decor and a warmer welcome than its rival *Hôtel La Fibule du Drâa*. The best of the thirty or so

rooms are those in the new (and more expensive) block, some of which have great views. ❺

Hôtel la Palmeraie Bd Mohammed V ☎ 024 84 70 08, ☏ 024 84 78 78. At the far end of the main street, this popular hotel has close on sixty rooms, and caters for mainly budget groups. Non-a/c rooms start at 180dh per double; or 200dh per head for half-board (obligatory in Dec and April). They also provide no-frills space on outside terraces when asked and have an excellent pool and restaurant (80dh fixed menu). Occasionally a little frenzied, but a good choice. ❸

Hôtel la Rose des Sables Av Allal Ben Abdellah ☎ 024 84 72 74. Modest budget hotel lacking character, but offering clean and comfortable rooms, and far more welcoming than the competition. The ground-floor restaurant's good value, too, with a filling 60dh menu. ❶

Hôtel Sirocco On the outskirts of Zagora, 1km beyond the bridge on the left as you're leaving town, around 500m down a *piste* off the main road ☎ 024 84 61 25, ☏ 024 84 61 26. Smart

French-owned place with twenty a/c rooms that are well heated in winter, and a good-sized pool. You can also sleep on the terrace here for around 50dh, and the patron – a Paris-Dakar veteran – is a mine of information on the region's 4 x4 possibilities. ⑤

Hôtel Tinzouline Av Hassan II ☏024 84 72 52, ⓔtinsouli@menara.ma. Zagora's original "grand hotel" is showing its age, but still possesses lots of colonial-era charm. Housed in two huge wings, its rooms (some of which formerly served as a guest-house for the Moroccan royal family) are plush and most overlook splendid gardens. There's also a gourmet multi-cuisine restaurant, hammam and big pool. ⑥

Kasbah Dar el Hiba 8km north of town at Ksar Tissargat ☏024 84 78 05. Beautifully maintained hundred-year-old kasbah which, for once, has preserved its original layout and design – thus few windows and no en-suite bathrooms (water degenerates the *pisé*). The rooms are nevertheless attractively furnished, clean and comfortable, as are the showers and toilets (across the lane from the main building). The place feels a bit like a living museum, but has lots of atmosphere, especially in the evenings. ④

Vallée du Drâa Bd Mohammed V ☏024 84 72 10. Brighter of the two cheapies on the main drag. Handy for the bus station and they have a simple restaurant on the ground floor. ①

Camping

Camping d'Amazrou 1km south of town in the Amazrou palmery ☏024 84 74 19. Better suited to those with transport and more of a family site – with

its own camels available for rides over towards the mountain. Friendly staff, plenty of shade and hot showers, but the toilet blocks aren't always as clean as they might be.

Camping les Jardins de Zagora Rue Hassan II, next to the Hôtel Tinzouline ☏068 96 17 01. Immaculate, secluded little site within easy walking distance of the centre that's the first choice of most French RV drivers, with electric hook-ups and clean blocs sanitaires. They also have a couple of overpriced rooms and a little café serving simple, inexpensive meals to order.

Camping de la Montagne 4km from town ☏ & ⓕ024 84 75 58. This site is alongside the irrigation canal, and 2km from the main Zagora–Tameg-route road. It's older and cheaper than the other sites, but bleak and not too clean. Given the competition, it offers no advantages.

Camping Oasis Palmier – Chez Pixa Route Montagne, Amezrou ☏024 84 67 24, ⓔpixame-hareee@hotmail.com. On the far side of the river, reached via the piste turning left off the main M'hamid road after the bridge. Newest of the town's sites, and a pleasant mix of well-shaded pitches and Berber tents, set at the foot of the mountain, with clean toilet blocks, a relaxing café and friendly management.

Camping Sindibad next to the Hôtel Tinzouline ☏024 84 75 53. A small, pleasant site, with adequate shade and a tiny swimming pool (that's not always in use). Hot showers cost extra and they have a few rooms for rent (②). There's also a café with traditional meals for 50dh. Dedicated campers still report this as the best site in the centre.

Amazrou

Amazrou is a hamlet and palmery just to the southeast of Zagora, across the Drâa, and a great place to spend the afternoon, wandering (or biking – you can rent mountain bikes; see "Listings" overleaf) amid the shade of its gardens and *ksour*. The village is, inevitably, wise to the ways of tourism – children try to drag you into their houses for tea and will hassle you to adopt them as guides – but for all that, the oasis life and cultivation are still fairly unaffected.

The local sight, which any of the kids will lead you towards, is the old Jewish kasbah, **La Kasbah des Juifs**. The Jewish community here were active in the silver jewellery trade – a craft continued by Muslim Berbers after their exodus. It's possible to visit some of the workshops.

Djebel Zagora

Across the valley from Zagora are two **mountains**. Djebel Zagora is strictly speaking the bulky one, with a military post on top, but the name is also used for the smaller, sugarloaf hill above *Camping de la Montagne*.

Watching the sunset from the slopes of the mountain is something of a tradition. Take the road out to the *Hôtel La Fibule du Drâa/Hôtel Kasbah Asmâa*, then turn left almost at once at the river to follow the track/irrigation channel to *Camping de la Montagne*. Here, swing right on the rough track which leads to a pass between the two peaks, then bends back, rising across the hillside to make an elbow bend on a spur. This is the popular viewpoint, for the most part well-maintained and feasible in a Fiat Uno or, preferably, a 4 x4. The views are startling: you look out across the palmery to further *ksour*, to the Djebel Sarhro (see pp.558–562), and even to a stretch of sand dunes to the south. Just below the road are the remnants of a colossal eleventh-century Almoravid fort, built as an outpost against the powerful rulers of Tafilalt; later it was used to protect the caravans passing below, to and from Timbuktu. The road subsequently goes on to the military fort on the summit (entry forbidden) but the view gains little; from the spur a footpath runs across and down the hillside and can be followed back down to the road just opposite *La Fibule du Drâa*.

On foot you can climb the mountain more directly on an old zigzag footpath up from near the *Hôtel Kasbah Asmâa*.

Eating

All the hotels we've reviewed have dependable restaurants, and most offer competitive full-board deals. For a pleasant evening meal, you could do a lot worse than the little garden restaurant at *Auberge Chez Ali* on Avenue Atlas Zaouit el Baraka, which offers set menus from 60–80dh. The tables stand on lawns, surrounded by greenery and teeming birdlife, and most of the food comes straight from Ali's walled vegetable garden. For those on tighter budgets, the *Restaurant Timbouctou* and *Restaurant es Saada*, both on Avenue Mohammed V, do inexpensive Moroccan staples such as tajines (25–40dh), couscous (20–45dh) and salads (from 25dh), and are as popular with locals as tourists.

The **dates** of the Zagora oasis are some of the finest in Morocco and stall-holders at the market sell dozens of varieties: among them, the sweet *boufeggou*, which will last for up to four years if stored properly; the small, black *bousthami*; and the light, olive-coloured *bouzekri*.

Listings

Banks BMCE has a branch opposite the *gare routière*/grand taxi park and the Banque Populaire is on the same side, but midway down Bd Mohammed V. The latter has an ATM and will advance cash against Visa cards.

Bikes Good mountain bikes (VTTs) are available for rent at Azul Treck, Av Allal Ben Abdellah (☎024 84 82 78), situated in the road leading to *Camping Les Jardins de Zagora*; they are a good way to explore the palmery and kasbahs of Amazrou; rates are negotiable.

Camel trips Lots of the hotels and campsites have tie-ins with camel-riding outfits, and in some cases you might find yourself subjected to some pressure to book a ride. Trips range from half-day excursions around the hills and palmeries to the south, to full-blown three-week guided adventures. Rates, as ever, are negotiable; a good way to check out what's on offer is to ask a few of the agencies on Bd Mohammed V, such as Paradise Garden, Désert et Emotion and Les Amis du Sahara (*Auberge Chez Ali* arrange overnight trips to various desert locations for 350dh per night per person).

Internet access Boumessaoud Cyber/Cyber Sud on Av Hassan II; Cyber Centre, on Bd Mohammed V near the petrol station.

Petrol There is an Agip station by the Banque Populaire, and others by the exit from town on the Agdz/Ouarzazate road.

Post office The PTT on Bd Mohammed V offers poste restante and phones.

Shopping There's a branch of the Maison Berbère carpet/crafts shop on Av Hassan II. This is one of the best-quality outlets in the south, with other Alaoui family branches at Ouarzazate, Tinerhir and Rissani.

Souk Markets take place on Wed and Sun; with dates in autumn. There are daily stalls at the entrance for fresh vegetables and fruit.

Moving on

CTM **buses** for Ouarzazate, Marrakesh, Casablanca and, in the other direction, M'Hamid depart from the company's office on Boulevard Mohammed V;

private lines leave from the *gare routière*/grand taxi park further along the street. For a full rundown of destinations, see p.600.

Grands taxis have regular runs to Ouarzazate, from the rank by the *gare routière*. Grands taxis can also be negotiated for a trip south to Tamegroute and M'hamid (see below), and northeast to Nekob; most leave in the morning.

West from Zagora to Foum Zguid

West from Zagora, maps indicate a *piste* that heads west to **FOUM ZGUID**, where it joins up with the R111 road north to Tazenakht and the N12 to Tissint and Tata (see p.642). The *piste* was restricted to military use for many years but is now open to tourists, and can be covered in a 4x4, or a *camionette* (lorry) taxi. *Camionettes* run most days, but especially on Sunday and Wednesday (souk days in Zagora), and Monday (souk day in Foum Zguid, and also a good day for onward travel). The *piste* itself is rather monotonous, though the onward roads to Tazenakht and Tata are quite scenic in parts.

Foum Zguid is a tiny town with a Monday souk, a few small **hotels** (the best being the *Auberge Iriki*) and a few **cafés** opposite a welcome palmery and some *ksour*. It also has a campsite. There are three buses a day to Tazenakht and Ouarzazate, of which two continue to Marrakesh. In the other direction, all three run to Tissint and Tata, with one going on to reach Bou Izakarn, Goulimine and Tan Tan.

South to M'hamid

The **Zagora oasis** stretches for some 30km south of the town, where the Drâa dries up for a while, to resurface in a final fertile belt before the desert. You can follow this route all the way down: the road is now surfaced over the full 98km from **Zagora to M'hamid**, and with a car it's a fine trip with the option of a night's stop near the dunes at Tinfou, or beyond.

If you don't have transport, it's a bit of an effort; there are buses to Tamegroute and further south to M'hamid, but times are inconvenient: the CTM leaves Zagora at 7.30pm, and arrives at M'hamid at 10pm, and there are local minibuses which leave when full. It is possible to charter a grand taxi for an early morning departure, however, which would not be too expensive if you can find a group to share costs, and limit your sights to a day visit to **Tamegroute** and the **sand dunes** near Tinfou.

Tamegroute and Tinfou

Tamegroute (19km from Zagora) is reached by a good road (6958) down the left/east bank of the Drâa. Take care that you get onto this one; the old road to the south (6965 and still marked on some maps) to **Anagam**, on the right/west bank, is now out of use. **Tinfou** lies 10km on from Tamegroute at a point marked on the Michelin map as "Dunes".

Tamegroute

TAMEGROUTE is an interesting and unusual village. At first sight, it is basically a group of *ksour* and kasbahs, wedged tightly together and divided by low, covered passageways with an unremarkable Saturday souk and small potters' cooperative. Despite appearances, it was once the most important settlement in the Drâa valley; it appears on nineteenth-century maps – produced in Europe – as Tamgrat or Tamagrut, surrounded by lesser places whose names have little or no resonance today.

It owes its importance to its ancient and highly prestigious *zaouia*, which was a seat of learning from the eleventh century and, from the seventeenth century, the base of the Naciri Brotherhood. Founded by Abou Abdallah Mohammed Ben Naceur (an inveterate traveller and revered scholar), this exercised great influence over the Drâa tribes until recent decades. Its sheikhs (or holy leaders) were known as the "peacemakers of the desert" and it was they who settled disputes among the *ksour* and among the caravan traders converging on Zagora from the Sudan. They were missionaries, too, and as late as the 1750s sent envoys to preach to and convert the wilder, animist-minded Berber tribes of the Atlas and Rif.

Faux guides will try to show you the way to the **Zaouia Naciri** (daily 8am–12.30pm & 2–6pm; donations expected), at the back of the square, but it's easy enough to find un-aided: look for the tall white minaret. As for centuries past, the sanctuary is a refuge for the sick and mentally ill, whom you'll see sitting round in the courtyard; they come in the hope of miraculous cures and/or to be supported by the charity of the brotherhood and other benevolent visitors. The complex consists of a *marabout* (the tomb of Naceur, closed to non-Muslims), a medersa (theological college – still used by up to eighty students, preparing for university) and – most interesting of all – a small **library**, which welcomes non-Muslim visitors and where you can see illuminated Korans, some on animal hides, as well as twelfth-century works on mathematics, medicine and history. It was once the richest in Morocco, containing 40,000 volumes. Most have been dispersed to Koranic schools round the country, but Tamegroute preserves a number of very early editions of the Koran printed on gazelle hide, and some rare ancient books, including a thirteenth-century algebra primer featuring Western Arabic numerals, which, although subsequently dropped in the Arab world, formed the basis of the West's numbers, through the influence of the universities of Moorish Spain.

The **potters' cooperative** is on the left as you leave Tamegroute travelling towards Tinfou. Visitors are welcome (Mon–Fri 7am–7pm) and if you want to see the production of pottery in its simplest form, you'll find this an ideal opportunity. Don't be surprised to find the green glaze, on finished items, reminiscent of Fes pottery. This is no accident; the founders of the Naciri Brotherhood wanted to develop Tamegroute – to city status, they hoped. They invited merchants and craftsmen from Fes to settle in Tamegroute and two families, still working in the pottery, claim Fes forebears.

You can stay in Tamegroute at the homely *Jnane Dar* (☎024 86 85 22 or 061 34 81 49; ❸), opposite the *zaouia*. Run by a welcoming Moroccan-German couple, its seven rooms (showers and toilets in a separate block) and tents (❶) are set in a well-tended garden, and you can order copious traditional meals for 75dh.

Tinfou

The tiny hamlet of **TINFOU** stands at the edge of an impressive line of sand dunes – no substitute for Merzouga, but a worthwhile place to pause to sample real Moroccan sand desert.

Two hundred metres from Tinfou's large dune stands kasbah hotel *Sahara Sky* (☎024 84 85 62, ⊕024 84 70 02, ⓦwww.hotel-sahara.com, ⓦwww.saharasky .com, GPS location N 30° 14′ 10″ W 05° 36′ 28″; ❸). Both the name and clientele of this hotel has changed in recent years due to the addition of a small astro-observatory on the hotel's roof. Guests have the opportunity to gaze at the ░░░░░░░░░░░░░ through the hotel's telescope while astrophotographers and astronomers travel from all over the world to use the patron's second telescope, which at the time of writing happened to be the most powerful in Morocco (with the ability to view galaxies 2.2 billion light years away). The rooms are comfortable and the food good but expensive.

Besides the local dunes, the best **camel expeditions** will take you east to the Djebel Tadrant or south towards the Djebel Bani.

Tinfou to M'hamid

About 4km south of Tinfou, you cross the Oued Drâa, and shortly after that are joined by the old road from Zagora to M'hamid (6965). Ahead, apparently blocking the route, rises the great mass of the **Djebel Bani** (1095m), through which the road winds up and over a high-level pass. Once across, you enter a picturesque stretch of palmery. The next sizeable village, **TAGOUNITE** (74km from Zagora) has a **Thursday souk**, petrol station and a basic but serviceable **hotel**, *La Gazelle* (☎024 89 70 48; ❶), which can rustle up meals if the nearby *Café-Restaurant Saada* doesn't appeal. A *piste* to the west – suitable for 4x4 vehicles only – leads off to Foum Zguid (see p.547).

Continuing south, the road crosses another pass of the Djebel Bani, the **Tizi Beni Slimane**, to reach the last fertile belt of the Drâa, the **M'hamid el Gouzlane** – Plain of the Gazelles. A few kilometres on, at the palmery-village of **OULAD DRISS**, the Drâa turns sharply towards the west and the Atlantic; there are some well-preserved *ksour* to explore here, and a small, privately run **museum**, La Musée Big House (daily 8am–6pm; admission free, but donations welcome), in the village centre, whose modest collection of farming tools, textiles, pottery and weapons details the region's traditional life. Basic **accommodation** and camping facilities are available at the *Carrefour des Caravanes* (☎ & ⊕024 84 86 65; ❶), east of the main road, which offers rooms, Berber tents, meals and a small pool. Further out of the village in the same direction, the *Auberge Kasbah Touareg* (☎024 84 86 78; ❶), 800m down a *piste* off the main road, has more character, with six rooms inside an authentic *pisé* kasbah that's still inhabited by the family. The guest rooms are basic and gloomy (the showers and toilets are housed separately), but this is a hospitable place to stay, with a relaxing garden and plenty of atmosphere. Meals are available by request.

A signpost, echoing that of Zagora, tells you that it is "50 jours à Timbuktu"; the two days' camel ride thus far from Zagora takes around an hour and a half by car – though only a little further south of here, a camel would come into its own. On the final approach to M'hamid, sand has often drifted across the road, despite being lined with woven palm-leaf shields.

M'hamid

M'HAMID El DJEDID (new M'hamid), a small administrative centre centred on a café-lined square, is the climax of this trip. It was once an important market place for nomadic and trans-Saharan trade, but of this role only a rather mundane **Monday souk** remains. These days, you might, as a visitor, be forgiven for thinking the village's main *raison d'être* is as a platform for getting tourists onto camels. Although not on a par with the Erg Chebbi at Merzouga, the **dunes** in this area are worth braving the initial onslaught of *faux guides* to see. The most easily accessible are those at **Erg Lehoudi** ("Dunes of the Jews"), 8km north, which can be reached by tourist vehicle via a *piste* beginning 17km back along the main road towards Zagora. Roughly one hundred metres high, they see more than their share of daytrippers and hustlers. A more rewarding destination if your budget can stretch to it are the much larger, three-hundred-metre-high dunes at **Chigaga**, just under 60km away. A return trip there by camel takes around five days; by four-wheel drive you can get there in less than two hours.

Practicalities

There is no shortage of agencies in M'hamid to arrange a camel safari. **Prices** are pretty standard, at around 350dh per day per person, which should include the guide, camel to carry you and your gear, three meals and a tent to sleep in at the end of the day. Note that if you opt to extend the trip, the day rate quoted may rise dramatically. The explanation usually advanced for this is that a longer trip requires more provisions, extra camels to carry them, and thus extra camel men.

One outfit recommended by readers – for both camel excursions and 4x4 trips – is Sahara Services, opposite the *Hotel Sahara* (🄴saharacamel@hotmail .com), run by Abdelkhalek "Abdul" Benalila. Another is M'Hamid Travel located in the village to the left of *Hotel Sahara* (🅣024 88 57 77 or 068 16 79 18, 🅦www.mhamid-travel.com) which organizes camel trips to a large bivouac in the local dunes for 250dh per person per night as well as 4x4 excursions to the chigaga dunes (1,200dh for up to 6 people). As for **buses**, there's a daily CTM service from M'hamid to Casablanca, stopping at Zagora, Ouarzazate and Marrakesh; private services leave twice daily on the same route, the first at 6am and the second around early afternoon. Grands taxis also run to Zagora throughout the day, depending on demand.

Accommodation and eating

With most visitors heading off to the desert as quickly as possible, the choice of **places to stay and eat** in M'hamid is not as great as you'd imagine, though a growing number of new European-run hotels have opened along the road outside the village (which has angered the locals). In addition to the guesthouses listed, there are also a couple of **campsites**: *Camping Relais Hammada du Drâa* (🅣024 84 80 86) which also has a few basic rooms and a restaurant, 500m east of the village on the opposite side of the river, and *Paradise Garden* (🅣066 71 68 56), 4km north. Both have their own Berber tents where you can bed down for around 50dh per person. Meals can be arranged at all the places reviewed below, and at the friendly, *Restaurant Saharia Services* (near the main gate) which serves the usual range of couscous, omelettes, tajines, and salads, which can be served on the pleasant roof terrace upon request.

Al Khaima Across the river in the palmery ☎062 13 21 70. Ultra basic rooms in a traditional *pisé* house. Meals available. ❶

Hotel Iriqui Just off the main square ☎066 39 79 76. Marginally better maintained and organized than the competition, though still rudimentary, with shared showers and toilets; there's also a good-sized roof terrace with the regulation Berber tent. ❷

Hotel Kasbah Azalay Across the river ☎024 84 80 96, ℱ024 84 80 85, ⓦwww.azalay.com. This Spanish-run hotel represents the only upmarket

accommodation in the village and is by far the most comfortable choice with 22 tastefully decorated double rooms and two family suites arranged in a kasbah compound, with a restaurant (menus 150dh) and bar in the middle. ❻

Hotel Sahara On the village square ☎061 87 16 44, ℱ024 84 80 46, Ⓔsaharatrek@hotmail.com. M'hamid's original hotel has gone into decline since the death of its long-time patron, but has a certain character nonetheless. Basic rooms, common showers and bathrooms only. ❶

The Dadès and Todra

The **Dadès**, stretching northeast from Ouarzazate, is the harshest and most desolate of the southern valleys. Along much of its length, the river is barely visible above ground, and the road and plain are hemmed in between the parallel ranges of the High Atlas and Djebel Sarhro – broken, black-red volcanic rock and limestone pinnacles. This makes the oases, when they appear, all the more astonishing, and there are two here – **Skoura** and **Tinerhir** – among the most beautiful in the country. Each lies along the main bus route from Ouarzazate to Erfoud, offering an easy and excellent opportunity for a close look at a working oasis and, in Skoura, a startling range of kasbahs.

Impressive though these are, however, it is the two gorges that cut out from the valley into the High Atlas that steal the show. The **Dadès** itself forms the first gorge, carving up a fertile strip of land behind **Boumalne du Dadès**. To its east is the **Todra Gorge**, a classic, narrowing shaft of high rock walls, which you can trail by car or transit lorry from Tinerhir right into the heart of the Atlas. If you're happy with the isolation and uncertainties of the **pistes beyond**, it is possible, too, to continue across the mountains – a wonderful trip which emerges in the Middle Atlas, near Beni Mellal on the road from Marrakesh to Fes.

Trans Atlas To Demnate

This spectacular tarred road is an attractive alternative to the Tizi n' Tichka. About 15km east of Ouarzazate and before Skoura (marked as R307 on most road maps) it heads north across the plains to make a dramatic ascent through extremely barren country to reach the Tizi n'Fedrhate (2191m). The road loses this height in the descent to **Oued Tessaout** and the village of Toufrine where there is a small *gîte*. The area is popular with trekkers who use the Oued, which flows to the east, as a way to traverse the rugged terrain. After **Toufrine** there is a long ascent with some tremendous views all round before the road heads down to **Imi n'Ifri** and **Demante** (see p.331).

To the south of the Dadès, the **Djebel Sarhro** also offers exciting options from October to April, either trekking on foot, or exploring its network of rough *piste* roads in a 4x4 vehicle. Tours and treks can be arranged through British trekking companies (see "Basics", pp.35–37) or in the trailhead towns of El Kelâa des Mgouna, Boumalne du Dadès and Tinerhir; alternatively, you could approach the massif from the south via Nekob (see p.592).

The Skoura oasis

The **Skoura oasis** begins quite suddenly, around 30km east of Ouarzazate, along a tributary of the Drâa, the **Oued Amerhidl**. Although the recent drought has had a debilitating effect on the palms, it remains an extraordinary sight even from the road, which for the most part follows along its edge – a very extensive, very dense palmery, with an incredibly confusing network of tracks winding across fords and through the trees to scattered groups of *ksour* and kasbahs.

Skoura village

SKOURA village, which lies off the main road, at the east end of the oasis, consists of little more than a souk (Monday is market day) and a small group of administrative buildings, where buses stop. You'll probably want the services of a guide to explore some of the kasbahs, and possibly visit one or two that are still inhabited.

Accommodation in and around the area covers the full gamut, from a basic *gîte d'étape* to one of the world's most exclusive luxury hideaways. *Chez Slimani* (☎024 85 22 72 or 061 74 68 82; ❷), signposted off the main road before you enter the village down a *piste* track that meanders over a dry river bed and through the palmery (can be difficult to find especially at night, follow the terracotta painted rocks, you may want to seek assistance from the locals), is the best budget option, with a handful of basic rooms and shared washrooms on the ground floor of a grand old kasbah. The hot water supply is intermittent and the toilets aren't always as clean as they might be, but what this place lacks in comforts it more than makes up for with atmosphere. M. Slimani is a genial host, serving copious tajines in the traditional salon, or on a sunny roof terrace overlooking the palmery, and you've the run of a pleasant garden. If it's full, try the less appealing *Auberge La Palmerie* (☎062 15 30 49; ❷), 700m up a *piste* from the east end of the main street, on the opposite side of the village. Next door *Auberge Les Nomads* (☎061 89 63 29; ❷) is a slightly grander option with en-suite showers available and four rooms in turrets that overlook the palmery.

More upscale accommodation is available back on the main bypass road east of the village at *Aït Ben Moro* (☎ & ☎024 85 21 16, ✉hotelbenmoro@yahoo.fr; ❻). A thirteenth-century kasbah beautifully renovated by its Spanish expat owner, Juan Romero, from Cádiz, it comprises a dozen or so rooms, furnished and decorated in traditional style with an added western stone terrace from which to make the most of them. Moreover, the food is top-notch; count on 150dh per main meal, or 500dh per person half-board.

Recently opened, French-owned *Maison d'hotes Dar Lorkam* (☎024 85 22 40, ⓦwww.dar-lorkam.com; ❹–❺), located deep within the palmery and found by following green triangles painted on trees, is the most attractive mid-range accommodation in the area. Six pleasant double rooms and a couple of Berber tents are contained within a courtyard with a swimming pool at its centre. The restaurant serves a fusion of French and Moroccan dishes.

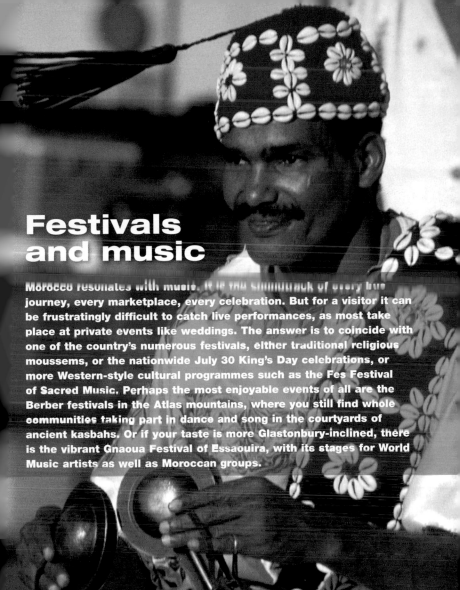

Festivals and music

Morocco resonates with music. It is the soundtrack of every bus journey, every marketplace, every celebration. But for a visitor it can be frustratingly difficult to catch live performances, as most take place at private events like weddings. The answer is to coincide with one of the country's numerous festivals, either traditional religious moussems, or the nationwide July 30 King's Day celebrations, or more Western-style cultural programmes such as the Fes Festival of Sacred Music. Perhaps the most enjoyable events of all are the Berber festivals in the Atlas mountains, where you still find whole communities taking part in dance and song in the courtyards of ancient kasbahs. Or if your taste is more Glastonbury-inclined, there is the vibrant Gnaoua Festival of Essaouira, with its stages for World Music artists as well as Moroccan groups.

Essaouira Gnaoua Festival

The **Essaouira Gnaoua Festival** is held every June in the charming seaside town of Essaouira. Established in 1998, it originally had the informal festive atmosphere of a *moussem* but in recent years the three-day festival has become more structured, with a programme of events and no less than nine stages to entertain up to 300,000 visitors. As the name suggests, the focus is Gnaoua (Gnawa) music – trance music hammered out to a backing of rhythmic metal castanets. Each year the organizers invite a number of prominent jazz and World Music artists (the French–Algerian star Rachid Taha was a recent visitor) alongside a half-dozen Gnaoua *ma'alem*s (band leaders who sing and play the *gimbri* – a form of lute) and popular Moroccan groups. The festival always ends with a monster jam session featuring as many *ma'alem*s as can be coaxed on to the stage. All of the main events are free but there are additional and more intimate Gnaoua performances, for which you'll need to buy tickets, held in the courtyards of traditional Moroccan riads in the Medina.

For details see ⓦwww.festival-gnaoua.co.ma.

◀ Musical instruments for sale in Marrakesh

Fes Festival of World Sacred Music

The **Festival of World Sacred Music** in Fes is a little more staid than the Essaouira Festival, but equally worth your time. Held over a week in early June, it features concerts of Moroccan music (usually *al-âla*, or explicitly religious music), alongside spiritual music from around the world. It is groundbreaking, in this respect, in the Islamic world, and part of its brief is to open barriers; alongside the concerts a valuable series of public discussions – *Fes Encounters* – are held on subjects such as cultural diversity and climate change.

As far as the music goes, you should find a few names familiar from the international festival circuit – past acts have included Ravi Shankar, Youssou N'Dour and Gilberto Gil – but new discoveries may be just as rewarding. And the venues in and around Fes el Bali are a treat in themselves.

For details see Ⓦwww.fesfestival.com.

Moussem madness

The place to hear the wildest Moroccan music is a **moussem** – a festival devoted to the memory of a holy man. Many are held during *mouloud*, the annual celebration of the Prophet's Birthday (the date of which changes according to the lunar calendar)

Like of the biggest moussems in the country is that of Sidi Ben Aissa (April 11–12) which sees thousands of **Aissaoua Sufis** flock to the shrine of the fifteenth-century saint in Meknes. Aissaoua is one of the main Sufi brotherhoods of Morocco, and its music is spectacular, with ceremonial trumpets, *ghaitas* (*shawms*, a type of oboe) and barrel drums.

The event is half-pilgrimage, half-festival, with screaming wooden oboes and the thunder of drums, smoking kebabs, freak shows and a fun fair, and thousands of hooded *jalabas* as far as the eye can see. Aissaoua groups from the whole country process to the shrine, led by ceremonial flags. As bands arrive, they bow their flags in veneration, and devotees and dancers form a ring around the musicians. From time to time a woman will enter the ring and be drawn by a female member of the troupe into a sort of trance. Eyes roll, heads shake and limbs flail. Members of the Moroccan Red Crescent are on hand with roll up stretchers to take several semi-conscious bodies away. The power of the music – and the obvious need for it – is overwhelming. This is popular spirituality and medicine at work, Moroccan style.

With additional text by Simon Broughton and Matthew Lavoie.

Ahouache nights

In Berber villages in the High and Middle Atlas whole communities take part in dance and song at festival times. Try, if you can, to coincide with an **ahouache** (High Atlas) or **ahidus** (Middle Atlas), which are usually performed at night in the courtyard of a kasbah. The dancers gather in circles – often a hundred or more strong – around the musicians, swaying in the night sky, chanting in multiple pitch, and clapping in complex, evolving rhythms. Singing poets take part as well, often performing a battle-like dialogue which elicits howls of laughter from the audience.

You can also take in Berber music and dance at one of a growing roster of popular arts festivals, held mainly in the south of the country. The **Timitar Festival** in **Agadir** (early July) features *ahouache* and *ahidus*, as well as *rwai* music from the Souss valley and Riffian music from the north. Or you could head for the **Ouarzazate Ahouache Festival** (September, currently), which takes place below the walls of the town's impressive kasbah. It was held for the first time in 2005 and draws up to 600 performers from various *ahouache* groups.

If money is no object, you might want to consider the ultra-chic *Dar Ahlam* (☎024 85 22 39, ⊛www.darahlam.com; ❸), hidden away in the depths of the palmery northeast of the village, amid an oasis that was once the local ruler's private falconry ground. Inside its red walls, a labyrinthine kasbah harbours eight luxurious rooms and three villas, designed by a team of Parisian architects around a heated T-shaped pool. The food is as *haute cuisine* as you'd expect, with desserts devised by the renowned French *pâtissier* Pierre Hermé. Doubles start at around US$820 which includes as many Moroccan clay scrubs and Thai massages as you can fit in. Extras such as balloon flights, camel trips and champagne picnics are priced separately.

For a quick, cheap bite to eat for those passing through, try one of the no-frills **restaurants** ranged around the junction where the main street peels off the bypass. *La Baraka, L'Atlas,* and *Restaurant La Kasbah* (also the bus stop for the CTM from Ouarzazate) all serve a standard range of omelettes, salads, tajines, brochettes and local goat's cheese, charging what they think they can get away with.

Kasbahs in the Skoura oasis

Navigating the tiny palmery roads by foot or by car can be quite confusing. If you wish to hire a guide there is no shortage of willing candidates to be found in the village (Mohammed from the Kasbah de Ben Moro would be a good choice or Skoura-born Mohammed Ouchiar who can be contacted by phone ☎068 88 53 87). In general guides expect around 50dh an hour.

The Skoura oasis comprises a thin line of irrigated palmery, with dry rocky slopes to either side. Animals are not permitted to graze in the precious, cultivated area and so are kept just on the dry side of the line; to feed them, women constantly struggle up from the valley with huge loads of greenery – a characteristic sight here and throughout the southern valleys. A swath of almond, olive and fig trees, vines and date palms, with alfalfa grass planted below for animal feed, the **palmery** itself used to be one of the lushest in Morocco. Recent drought, however, has left its mark; hundreds have yellowed and are dying – a melancholy spectacle indeed.

Following the paths behind the Kasbah de Ben Moro, you pass the half-hidden **Marabout of Sidi Aïssa** (Jesus in his Arabized form), and then the (usually dry) riverbed of the Oued Amerhidl. Straight across is the **Kasbah Amerhidl**, the grandest and most extravagantly decorated in the oasis, and again seventeenth century in origin. The owner's family lives there from time to time and so it is maintained properly. It may well look familiar; it's eminently photogenic and features in travel brochures and coffee-table books – and on the back of the current fifty dirham note.

Kasbah Amerhidl can also be reached by car, from a turning further along the Skoura road. If you come this way, you'll be surrounded by any number of boys as soon as you stop, and you really have no option but to pay one to watch your car or be your guide. The kasbah is open to small groups year round, with informal arrangements as to exact times – show up and someone will be around to let you in.

Beyond Kasbah Amerhidl, a track heads off southwest, past a couple of tumbledown buildings to another impressive-looking kasbah, the **Dar Aït Sidi el Mati**, and from here it's possible to complete a circuit on foot back to the N10 (formerly P32), emerging by the ruinous **Kasbah el Kabbaba**.

If you have transport – or a lot of energy – you could search out another kasbah, the isolated **Kasbah Ben Amar**. This is still lived in and well maintained. To find it, backtrack along the N10 towards Ouarzazate, and before the bridge

Kasbah maintenance and destruction

Several of the Skoura kasbahs date, at least in part, from the seventeenth and eighteenth centuries, though the majority here – and throughout the Dadès oases – are relatively modern. Most of the older fortifications were destroyed in a vicious tribal war in 1893, and many that survived were pulled down in the French pacification of the 1920s and 1930s. Once a kasbah has been left unmaintained, it declines very fast – twenty years is enough to produce a ruinous state, if the *pisé* walls are not renewed.

The kasbah walls in the Dadès – higher and flatter than in the Drâa – often seem unscalable, but in the course of a siege or war there were always other methods of conquest. A favourite means of attack in the 1890s, according to Walter Harris, who journeyed here in disguise, was to divert the water channels of the oasis round a kasbah and simply wait for its foundations to dissolve.

over the Oued Amerhidl, look for a track off to the left/southeast; follow the track for a couple of kilometres and you will see the kasbah ahead. It commands magnificent views of the course of the Oued Dadès.

North of Skoura

There are further impressive kasbahs to the north of Skoura village, but they are harder to find, and taking a guide along would be invaluable. To find them, drive through Skoura village and leave it just beyond the closed *Hôtel Nikhil*, crossing the dry riverbed which is quite wide at this point.

After about 4km, and still well within the palmery, you should come to a pair of kasbahs, **Dar Aït Sous** and **Dar Lahsoune**; the former, small but once very grand, is in a ruinous state, used only for animals; the latter, once a Glaoui residence, is state-owned, and private. A further 2km drive – and directions from locals – takes you to the magnificent **Kasbah Aït Ben Abou**, which is second in Skoura only to Kasbah Amerhidl. It lies on well-farmed land and is still inhabited.

Finally, on the edge of the palmery, you might follow the trail to the imposing **Marabout Sidi M'Barek ou Ali**. A high wall, broken only by a door, encloses the *marabout*, which doubles as a grain store – a powerful twofold protection on both spiritual and military levels.

Skoura to El Kelâa des Mgouna

From **Skoura**, eastwards towards **El Kelâa des Mgouna**, the road runs parallel to the Oued Drâa which flows, out of sight, across this semi-desert plateau. Seven kilometres before El Kelâa des Mgouna, is a small hamlet, **Amejgag**, with the riverside *Hôtel Rosadamaskina* (☎024 83 49 13, ⓕ024 83 69 69, ⓦwww.rosadamaskina.com; ❷), a small but brightly furnished place, with great charm and frequented by the artist Charles Kerival, whose watercolours successfully capture the feel of southern Morocco.

El Kelâa des Mgouna

Travelling through the Dadès in spring, you'll find Skoura's fields divided by the bloom of thousands of small, pink Persian roses – cultivated as hedgerows dividing the plots. At **EL KELÂA DES MGOUNA** (also spelt Qalat Mgouna),

50km east across another shaft of semidesert plateau, there are still more, along with an immense kasbah-style **rose-water factory** with two prominent chimneys. Here, the Capp et Florale company distil the *eau de rose*. In late May (sometimes early June), a **rose festival** is held in the village to celebrate the new year's crops: a good time to visit, with villagers coming down from the mountains for the market, music and dancing.

The rest of the year, El Kelâa's single, rambling street is less impressive. There's a **Wednesday souk**, worth breaking your journey for, but little else of interest beyond the locked and deserted ruins of a **Glaoui kasbah**, on a spur above the river. The local shops are always full of *eau de rose*, though, and the factory can be visited too, for a look at –and an overpowering smell of – the distillation process. A second factory, Aromag, alongside the Mobil petrol station, 13km out along the Tinerhir road, can also be visited; it is run by a French company, based – of course – at Grasse.

One of a hundred varieties, *Rosa Centifolio* has, as the name implies, hundreds of small leaves on each small bush. Folklore has it that they were brought from Persepolis by the Phoenicians. Aerial photographs testify to there being 4200km of low hedges; each metre yields up to one kilo of petals and it takes ten tonnes of petals to produce three litres of rose oil. The petals are picked by women who start very early in the morning before the heat dries the bloom.

Practicalities

Buses and grands taxis pull into the junction at the centre of town, close to the three **banks** (Banque Populaire – as usual in the south – Crédit Agricole and Wafabank), all with ATMs. Of the **hotels**, the cheapest option, on the main street, is the *Hôtel du Grand Atlas* (T024 83 68 38; ❶), a nondescript but service-able little place with a hammam out the back and a simple restaurant on the ground floor. It is run by Lahcen Aaddi and his son, Mustapha, who can put you in touch, if you wish, with guides for trekking in the Djebel Sarhro (see p.558) and Djebel Mgoun. The other hotel near the centre, on a hilltop overlooking town, is *La Rose M'gouna* (T024 83 63 36, F024 83 60 07; ❹), an old "Grand Hôtel du Sud", a decent mid-range option with a swimming pool and comfort-able rooms.

Much the nicest place to stay, though – and reason enough to break your journey in Kelâa – is the romantic ❧ *Kasbah Itran* (T024 83 71 03 or 063 78 10 06, W www.kasbahitran.com; ❹), 4km north up the *piste* to Bou Thrarar. Run by the hospitable Taghda brothers (all seven of them), it's a recent building in traditional style set high on an escarpment overlooking the mouth of the Imgoun river valley, with its spectacular ruined kasbah, *ksour* and irrigated gardens. The stylishly decorated rooms make the most of the views, which extend across the Dadès to the distant Djebel Sarhro and snow-covered Ighil M'Goun (4071m) in the background. Breakfasts are served on a magnificent terrace, and dinner indoors in a conventional Moroccan salon. From Kelâa, you can walk or jump in a grand taxi (bound for Hdida) and get down after 4km.

Vallée des Roses

North of El Kelâa des Mgouna begins one of the most scenic – but least explored – regions of the southern High Atlas. Tourist literature likes to refer to it as "**La Vallée des Roses**", but in fact the famous roses are grown not so much in a single valley as a tangle of different ones, drained by rivers that converge on the village of Bou Thaghrar. Served by regular minibuses, a spectacular 35-kilometre *piste* (just about passable in a Fiat) runs up the Hdida

Valley from Kelâa to Bou Thaghrar, traversing a plateau called Imi-n-Louh – where Berber nomads still pass the winter in little caves – to cross the Jbel Ta'Louit at a 2084-metre pass. From there, you can survey the full glory of the M'Goun massif to the north, before dropping steeply via some hair-raising switchbacks to the valley floor.

An agglomeration of three villages clustered around a broad river confluence, **BOU THRARAR** (pronounced "Boot-Ag-*ra*") holds some impressive ruined kasbahs and a few basic **gîtes d'étapes**, of which *Chez Fadil* (℡024 83 11 52; ❶), almost the first building you come to in the village on your right, is the best choice. Run by Atman Fadil, who was raised in France but returned to his parents' village to marry and settle down, it has a few simple rooms and shared washrooms and showers; half-board costs 130dh per person and meals tend to be rounded off with impromptu Berber singing and drumming. This is a good place to hook up with guides for treks into the valleys further north. If it's full, try *Chez el Hacine Houssein Azabi* (℡024 83 61 68; ❶) further down the hill in the village proper, which also offers rooms, meals and guided treks. A more comfortable option, this time on the edge of the village, is the *Hôtel Boutaghrar* (℡024 83 11 16, ℻024 83 60 54; ❸). With bright, modern en-suite rooms and a large terrace overlooking the valley, it's impeccably clean but a bit overpriced and soulless.

Trekking in the Vallée des Roses

Beyond Bou Thrarar, the *pistes* degenerate or disappear altogether, making this prime **trekking** territory, which for the most part remains blissfully beyond the reach of most 4 x4s. Fed by meltwater from the high peaks, a succession of *pisé* villages preside over carpets of terraced gardens and orchards, bordered by rose bushes and silver birch. April and May, while the roses are being harvested, are the best months to walk here, but the routes are practicable in all but the height of summer. Guides charge around 250dh per day and are essential, not just to show the way but also to help relate to local Berber people, few of whom see many trekkers. Your guide will also be able to help you pick the best of the *gîtes d'étapes* (standards differ greatly).

Depending on the amount of time you have, a typical route in the region could range from a day-hike through the satellite villages of Bou Thrarar, to a ten-day trek north through the magnificent **Gorges d'Imgoun** (a real adventure involving hours of wading waist-deep through meltwater). With only three days to spare, the varied (and mostly dry) walk to **Amskar**, via **Iasarm**, **Alemdoun** and **Amajgag** – the conventional approach route for mountaineers bound for the M'Goun summit – would be an ideal sampler, passing through a series of pretty villages and some superb gorges. At Amskar, you can stay in this area's best *gîte*, *Chez Brahim* (no phone; ❶), whose roof terrace looks west to the snow fields of the M'Goun massif. Committed trekkers press on from here to cross the watershed at the pass above Amskar, dropping down the far side to reach the Cascades d'Ouzoud in the Marrakesh region in around ten days – a route for which you should expect to have to pay your guide and mule driver a return fee.

Boumalne du Dadès

As main gateway to the Dadès Valley, **BOUMALNE DU DADÈS** is hard to avoid, although it holds little of interest in itself and presents a somewhat

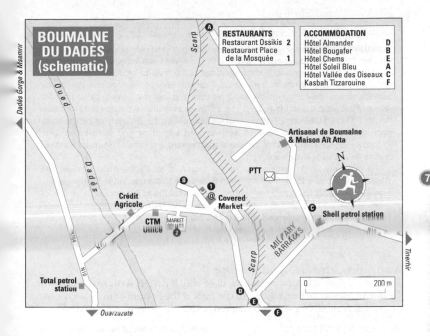

RESTAURANTS
Restaurant Ossikis **2**
Restaurant Place
de la Mosquée **1**

ACCOMMODATION
Hôtel Almander **D**
Hôtel Bougafer **B**
Hôtel Chems **E**
Hôtel Soleil Bleu **A**
Hôtel Vallée des Oiseaux **C**
Kasbah Tizzarouine **F**

bleak spectacle, its old town on the eastern bank of the Dadès climbing up to a plateau where a military barracks command the valley. On the plus side, the town has a better-than-average crop of hotels and is well poised for exploration of the Djebel Sarhro, as well as the bird-rich Vallée des Oiseaux.

Practicalities

After crossing the Oued Dadès the road the Ouarzazate road passes through a small square surrounded by a collection of shops and cafés which makes up the town centre. To the south of the centre is a large market square where the Wednesday souk takes place. Above the old *Hotel Adrar* at the north of the central square is a mosque and a covered market outside of which is, along with the market square, a departure point for **grands taxis** and pitstop for long distance buses. The CTM office is 150m back towards the river (services to Marrakesh and Er Rachidia daily). Past the square and up the hill are several hotels, a Shell petrol station, Banque Populaire, PTT, and two **shops**. Both of the shops – the Artisanale de Boumalne and Maison Aït Atta – are worth looking round for a range of carpets and carvings, on sale without great pressure.

Grands taxis make regular runs to Ouarzazate and Tinerhir. For Msemrir and the Dadès Valley, you can usually get a Land Rover taxi, transit or lorry; a transit/minibus leaves for Msemrir daily between noon and 2pm, returning at dawn the next morning.

Guides for trekking and bird-watching are contactable through the *Hôtel Soleil Bleu*, or you could hook up with mountain guide Hamou Ail Lhou at his office (℡067 59 32 92, ✉hamou57@voila.fr) above the *Café des Fleurs*, near the souk entrance in the middle of town.

Hammada birds and the Vallée des Oiseaux

Boumalne offers some exceptional bird-watching and wildlife possibilities – as can be seen from the logbook at the *Hôtel Soleil Bleu* (see hotel listings). To the south of the town are abundant and accessible areas of **hammada** or desert fringe, and a grassy valley. The hammada provides an austere environment, whose dry, sunny conditions are ideal for cold-blooded reptiles and are frequented by Montpelier snake, Atlas agama and fringe-toed lizard. The **grassy plains** provide food for small herds of Edmi gazelle and Addax antelope and shelter for a variety of bird species such as **cream-coloured courser, red-rumped wheatear** and **thick-billed lark**. Predatory **lanner falcon** patrol the skies and the rare and elusive **Houbara bustard** makes an occasional appearance.

The most rewarding birding trip in the region is to the so-called **Vallée des Oiseaux**, which heads off the 6907 from Boumalne to Iknioun in the Djebel Sarhro. This is the Tagdilt track and well known to bird-watchers; it's marked by a line of green shading on the Michelin map. Here, you'll find **Temmink's horned lark, bar-tailed desert lark, eagle owl** and several **sandgrouse**: pin-tailed, crowned and black-bellied. And, for extra measure, they make traditional pottery at Tagdilt.

Accommodation and eating

There is a decent selection of **hotels**, all of which have **restaurants**. In addition, for simple Moroccan fare, try one of the cafés at the bottom of town on the main street, which all serve a standard range of tajines, brochettes, grills and salads.

Hôtel Almander ☎ 024 83 01 72, ℮ aubergealmander@hotmail.com. A well-kept hotel on the main drag just below the *Chems* (see below) and sharing the same spectacular views. It has eleven rooms with tiny balconies overhanging the escarpment, and a small restaurant. ❷

Hôtel Bougafer ☎ & Ⓕ 024 83 07 68. Best of the cheapies: cosy little rooms with *pisé* walls, decent beds and clean toilets on the landings. There's also a popular café on the ground floor. ❶

Hôtel Chems ☎ 024 83 00 41, Ⓕ 024 83 13 08. A large, attractive hotel at the top of town, with a good restaurant and a spacious Moroccan salon. Built on the hillside, its 30 en-suite rooms overlook the valley and have great views (many rooms have private enclosed balconies). ❸

Hôtel Soleil Bleu ☎ 024 83 01 63, Ⓕ 024 83 03 94, ℮ le_soleilbleu@yahoo.fr. Reached along a *piste*, accessed by turning off the main road at *Hôtel Vallée Des Oiseaux* and continuing through a bland military area, this place is the most appealing in its category. It has sweeping views of the valley, psychedelic decor and two kinds of room: "standard" on the ground floor and more luxurious ones upstairs. There is space for camping outside with clean showers and toilets next to the site and budget travellers are welcome to sleep on the terrace or in the salon for 30–40dh. The food is delicious and inventive. The owners, the Najim brothers, specialize in tours and treks (particularly for bird-watchers); day visits to the Vallée des Oiseaux and other promising locations (see box above) are possible, and the hotel maintains an excellent birders' log. ❹

Hôtel Vallée des Oiseaux ☎ & Ⓕ 024 83 07 64. A dowdy, motel-style place with a pleasant garden but away from the edge of the plateau, so no views; some en-suite rooms. ❶–❷

Kasbah Tizzarouine ☎ 024 83 06 90, ℮ kasbah.tizzarouine@menara.ma. Impersonal, overpriced three-star, set in a huge compound half a kilometre beyond the *Hôtel Chems*, along a *piste*. Famous for having a few "chambres troglo-dytes" (which are nothing of the kind and were excavated by the hotel), most of its business is with large tour groups. ❺

The Djebel Sarhro

The **Djebel Sarhro** (or Saghro) lies south of the road from Ouarzazate to Tinerhir and east of that from Ouarzazate to Zagora. It's a starkly beautiful jumble of volcanic peaks, quite unlike the High Atlas or Anti-Atlas, and

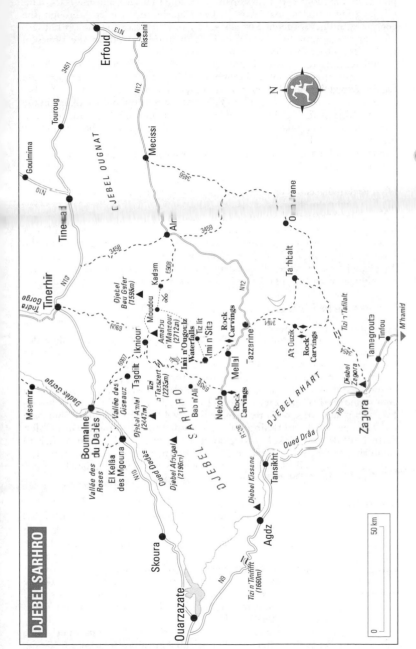

DJEBEL SARHRO

50 km

0

punctuated by gorges, ruined kasbahs, occasional villages, and the black tents of the semi-nomadic **Aït Atta** tribe. Fiercely independent through the centuries, and never subdued by any sultan, the Aït Atta were the last bulwark of resistance against the French, making their final stand on the slopes of Djebel Bou Gafer in 1933 (see box opposite).

Until recently, the Djebel Sarhro saw few visitors but it's becoming better known and more accessible through **trekking** operators like Explore and Sherpa Expeditions (see Basics, p.36 & p.37). They operate here from October to April, when the High Atlas is too cold and snow-covered for walking; in the summer, Sarhro itself is impracticable, being too hot and exposed, and with water, always scarce, quite impossible to find. In fact, Djebel Sarhro means "dry mountain" in Berber.

Independent exploration of the range is possible by **4x4** (many roads on our map are passable by Fiat Uno in reasonable weather, although bear in mind your insurance won't be valid driving on a *piste*). Road signs are rare and flash floods often lead to diversions or worse; navigation is not easy and taking along a local guide would be useful.

A **guide** is certainly recommended for trekking. They can be contacted through the *Hôtel Soleil Bleu* and the *Kasbah Tizzarouine* in Boumalne du Dadès and the *Hôtel Tomboctou* in Tinerhir. Alternatively, if you are approaching the Djebel Sarhro from the south, you could discuss your plans and hire a guide at Nekob, where there's a small *bureau des guides*; the one at El Kelâa des Mgouna is no longer a reliable option as it is rarely open.

Treks and routes

When planning a trek in the Sarhro, bear in mind the harshness of the terrain and the considerable distances involved. With the exception of the **Vallée des Oiseaux**, off the Boumalne–Iknioun road, which is a feasible destination for day trips (see box, p.558), this is not an area for short treks; nor does it have much infrastructure; you will need to be prepared to camp.

Given ten days, you could set out from El Kelâa des Mgouna, explore the area west of the **Tizi n'Tazazert** and loop back to El Kelâa or Boumalne. Alternatively, with about five days free, you could travel by local taxi from Boumalne du Dadès or Tinerhir to **Iknioun** and then walk south, by **Djebel Bou Gafer**, to **Imi n'Site** and **Nekob**, taking local transport from there either back to Boumalne or Tinerhir or across to Tansikht on the Ouarzazate–Zagora road.

You could also do the latter trip in the opposite direction from the Drâa Valley, arranging a guide at **Nekob**.

Iknioun to Nekob

The easiest access to the range for **trekkers** is a transit taxi from Boumalne to **IKNIOUN**; this runs most days, but Wednesday, after the Boumalne souk, is the most reliable. There are **rooms** in Iknioun, if you wish to stay. Alternatively, you can ask to be dropped at the junction of the *piste* 7km before Iknioun (there is a large sign here, so you shouldn't miss it), which you could follow in two or three days' **walk to Nekob** (35km). The people at the village 1km along the Nekob road will provide rooms for a first night's stop, though walkers should be prepared to camp beyond here. The Nekob souk is on a Sunday so you could plan to pick up a ride on the Saturday.

Following this route – which is also practicable with a four-wheel-drive vehicle – it takes about an hour's walk to reach a junction (at 2014m) to Tiouft: turn left here and climb steadily for an hour to a *faux* col, and then across an easy plateau for half an hour to the true col, **Tizi n'Tazazert** (2283m). From

The battle for Bou Gafer

For three centuries or more, the **Aït Atta** tribe were the great warriors of the south, dominating the Djebel Sarhro and its eastern extension, the Djebel Ougnat. At the beginning of the twentieth century, the British journalist Walter Harris reported seeing the young men at Touroug, one of their tribal strongholds (see map on p.559), practising running with galloping horses, holding onto their tails – a breakneck skill which enabled those on foot to travel as fast as the riders.

As guerrilla fighters, the Aït Atta resisted the French occupation from the outset. Led by **Hassou Ba Salem**, they finally retreated, at the beginning of 1933, to the rocky stronghold of the **Djebel Bou Gafer**, a chaos of gorges and pinnacles. Estimates vary, but the Aït Atta had at least a thousand fighting men, who, together with their families, totalled around 7000 people, accompanied by their flocks. They faced vastly superior French forces. Ali, the son of Hassou Ba Salem, says that, according to his father, these included 83,000 troops and four aircraft squadrons.

David Hart in the *Aït 'Atta of Southern Morocco* (1984) concluded that this was "the hardest single battle which the French had ever had to fight in the course of their 'pacification' of Morocco". The French first attacked the stronghold on February 21 and, after that, there were almost daily attacks on the ground and from the air. Many died on both sides but the Aït Atta did not surrender for over a month, by which time they were reduced to half their strength and had run short of ammunition. The victors, moving in on March 25, occupied, according to one of them, "an indescribable charnel house".

Hassou Ba Salem's conditions on surrender included a promise that the Aït Atta could maintain their tribal structures and customs, particularly insofar as law and order were concerned, and that they would not be "ruled" by the infamous T'Hami el Glaoui, the pasha of Marrakesh, whom they regarded as a traitor to their homeland. The French were content to accept, the battle meaning that their "pacification" was virtually complete, and giving them access to the valuable silver and copper mines at Moudou.

Hassou Ba Salem died in 1960 and was buried at Tagia, his birthplace, 5km from Tinerhir. Ali, his son, succeeded him as leader of the tribe, and took part in the 1975 Green March into the Western Sahara. He died in 1992 and is also buried at Tagia. As for the battlefield itself, local guides will show you the sites, including ruins of the fortress. It is still littered with spent bullets, which are covered in spring by colourful clumps of thyme, rockroses and broom.

here, it's downhill, through rocky scenery, with table-top mesas and volcanic cones visible to the west; there are traces of underground water, with palm trees in gullies, and camels grazing almost to the winter snow line. The *piste* zigzags down in two hours' walking (there are a lot of shortcuts for walkers), running due south down the main valley to **Nekob**. From **Nekob** – a full account of which appears on p.592 – transits run to the main road at **Tansikht**, on the Drâa, and eastwards to Tazzarine, Alnif and Rissani.

Other driving routes

In addition to the **north–south route over** the **Tizi n'Tazazert** to Tansikht, it is possible to drive over a much lower pass, the **Tizi n'Tafilalt**, to Zagora. There are also **east–west routes** between **Tansikht** and **Rissani** (in Tafilalt), which are much better established and are described at the end of the Ziz valley section (see pp.590–592).

From these roads, there are astonishing views of the surrounding mountains, of which the most notable are **Djebel Afougal** (2196m), **Djebel Amlal**

(2447m) and, the highest, **Amalou n'Mansour** (2712m). All of them are climbed by one or other of the trek operators. **Djebel Bou Gafer** (1598m) is lower and less remarkable but its history (see box, p.561) adds interest; it can be approached on foot from Moudou or Kadem, though either way a guide is again advisable and you may need to camp overnight to make the most of a visit to the battlefield.

Other less demanding attractions include the **Imi n'Ougoulz waterfalls** and **prehistoric rock carvings** near Nekob, Mellal and Tazzarine (local guides are essential for all of these).

The Dadès Valley

The **Dadès Valley**, with its high cliffs of limestone and weirdly shaped erosions, begins almost immediately north of Boumalne. Leaving the N10, you follow the R704 (formerly 6901) road, signposted "Mserhir" (Msemrir). Most travellers cover the first 25km or so by car or taxi, then turn back, which makes for a fine day's trip. If you have a 4 x 4, however, you could **loop over to the Todra Gorge** or continue **up and across the High Atlas** to the Beni Mellal–Marrakesh road. Alternatively, a couple of days' walking in and around the gorge from Boumalne will reward you with superb scenery, and plenty of kasbahs and *pisé* architecture to admire; there are rooms in several of the villages en route to Msemrir.

The Dadès gorge is accessible by local transport from Boumalne, with Peugeot taxis, transit vans and Berber pick-ups (*camionettes*) and lorries (*camions)* leaving regularly from the market square for Aït Ali (25km) and less often to Msemrir (63km). Pick-ups run occasionally to Atlas villages beyond but they do so more often on the Todra Gorge route (see p.571), which would make an easier access point if you plan to cross the Atlas on local transport. Returning to Boumalne, a transit/minibus leaves Msemrir daily at 4am. See **map** "Over the Atlas: beyond Todra and Dadès" on p.575 for routes.

Into the gorge: Boumalne to Msemrir

The road through the **Dadès Valley** is nowadays surfaced all the way to Msemrir (in fact, 15km beyond there to Aït Hani), and remains for the most part in good condition. The first section is badly potholed and slow going but usually passable by car nonetheless (beware of snowmelt flooding in winter). There are *ksour* and kasbahs clustered all along this stretch, many of them flanked by more modern houses, though even these usually retain some feature of the decorative traditional architecture.

In winter, temperatures in the gorge plummet at night and when choosing accommodation it's worth looking into what is on offer in terms of heating.

Boumalne to Aït Oufi

About eight kilometres along the road (R704) into the gorge from Boumalne, you pass the fine old **Glaoui kasbah** of Aït Youl, strategically sited as always to control all passage. Shortly after you climb over a little pass, flanked by the *Café-Restaurant Meguirne,* 18km from Boumalne. The views make this a fine place to stop for lunch (as tour groups do) and it also has seven basic, cheap en-suite **rooms** for rent (☏071 16 19 53; ❶–❷). Ali, the unfailingly cheerful owner, also prepares meals – in summer, his breakfast terrace is the first in the valley to catch the sun. Nearby is a hidden side-valley, entered by a narrow gorge, in which Ali

△ The Dadès Valley

takes a proprietary interest, organizing enjoyable half-day hikes and bivouacs. A kilometre north of the *Meguirne* on the roadside is another good-value place to stay, the *Hôtel-Restaurant Kasbah* (℡073 18 26 62; ❶–❷), with clean but garishly decorated rooms ranged around an attractive sheltered courtyard. Again, it caters for tour groups by day, laying on "Berber Weddings" and evening entertainment to order; there's also a flower-filled garden on the far side of the road, tumbling down to the riverbank.

The most impressive rock formations in this area lie another few kilometres down the road at **Tamnalt**, where an extraordinary cliff known by the locals as the "Hills of Human Bodies" rises from the far side of the valley. Geologically the rock is a weathered conglomerate of pebbles which probably lay where a great river entered a primordial sea. A superb group of **ksour** and **kasbahs** rise seamlessly from them, tinged with the colour of the earth, ranging from bleak lime-white to dark reds and greenish blacks.

A couple of simple restaurants-*auberges* have sprung up here, with small terraces that are perfectly placed for enjoying the spectacle over a mint tea. *Kasbah Aït Marghad* (℡024 83 03 11; ❶) is a tiny place with only a couple of en-suite rooms; next door, the *Kasbah Aït Arbi* (℡ & ℱ024 83 17 23; ❷) is slightly larger with a large terrace overlooking the valley. Both have hot water and offer good-value half-board rates. From the bridge below, an obvious path leads through a string of hamlets and high into the famous rocks, making one of the regions best **walks**. With the help of a guide, you can follow it for an hour or more to a narrow gorge that's barely a person's width in places. The views are memorable throughout.

Beyond Tamnalt, the valley floor is less fertile and the hills gentler. The road continues through the hamlet of Aït Ali to a spot known as **Aït Oudinar** (22km from Boumalne), where a bridge spans the river, and the gorge narrows quite dramatically. There is a little **hotel** here, the *Auberge des Gorges du Dadès – Chez Youssef* (℡024 83 01 53, ℱ024 83 02 21, ⓌMwww.aubergeaitoudinar.com; ❹), just after the bridge on the left, and an attractive place to stay, offering en-suite rooms with hot showers in slightly tacky nouveau Kasbah surroundings, bivouac tents on the terrace, or camping alongside the river where the few poplar trees provide some shade. The *auberge* serves meals (breakfast is included in the cost of most rooms) and arranges mule and 4 x4 trips into the gorge and Atlas. Its nearest neighbour – the *Auberge Chez Pierre* (℡024 83 02 67; ❺) – is an altogether more upmarket affair. Situated another 3km further along the road (on the right), it is owned and run by an expatriate Belgian chef who prides himself on providing one of the finest tables in Morocco, though you'll have to stay here (400dh per person for obligatory half-board) to enjoy it. Eight tastefully decorated rooms occupy a traditional-style *pisé* building, with its own pool and well-kept gardens.

The valley's largest concentration of hotels lies a further 5km up the road (27km from Boumalne), on the east bank of the river, hemmed in by slabs of cliff. They are, in order of appearance: the *Auberge du Peuplier* (℡024 83 17 48; ❶), the cheapest and most basic of the bunch with only seven rooms (doubles from 60dh); *Hôtel la Gazelle du Dadès* (℡024 83 17 53, ℱ024 83 17 53; ❷), which offers especially good-value half-board (130dh) and budget accommodation in Berber tents or on their terrace; ⚑ *Hôtel la Kasbah de la Vallée* (℡ & ℱ024 83 17 53/061 33 83 63; ❸), a long-established hotel run by its friendly English-speaking proprietor (Hammou) who offers comfortable rooms, balconies, hearty food, open fires in winter, and is the only place with a liquor license in the gorge; and finally, *Auberge Tissadrine* (℡024 83 17 45; ❶), located next to the river and a good budget option, recently refurbished in keeping with traditional style (you can bed on the terrace for 20dh). All of them have riverside camping.

At the 28km mark, another hotel cluster stands at a bend in the valley, next to the river. The *Auberge Atlas-Berbère* (☎024 83 17 42; ❷), is a mid-scale place offering cheaper mattress beds in its large salon, with a fine terrace overlooking the oued. Next up on the left side of the road, the much larger *Auberge le Vieux Château* (☎024 83 12 61, ℱ024 83 02 21; ❷) has a few rooms with balconies and in winter installs heaters on request. The salon restaurant is intimate and cozy; breakfast is included in the room price.

Just before the gorge narrows to a canyon, the welcoming ⟨ *Sourse Dadès* (☎024 83 12 58; ❸) ranks among the friendliest and best situated place to stay hereabouts. A traditional building that catches the sun in winter, it comprises only four rooms, all impeccably clean and well aired, priced at 130–200dh per person for obligatory half board; charm is derived from its striking location and hospitable service. The owners, Ahmed Oussidi and his brother, can point you in the direction of some good walks in the area, including one to the ridge above the guesthouse via an old spring.

On the far side of the canyon, 34km from Boumalne, the *Hôtel Berbère de la Montagne* (☎024 83 02 28/073 78 46 14; ❷) is one of the best value mid-scale places in the area – with six pleasantly furnished, immaculately clean rooms (some en suite), and carefully prepared meals served on a lovely streamside terrace. The hotel also has a campsite and makes a good base for short walks in and around the gorge; ask at reception for more details.

Aït Oufi to Msemrir

After passing the *Hôtel Berbère de la Montagne*, the road climbs by a coil of hairpin bends above the gorge, before squeezing through a tight, narrow gap to reach **Taghia n'Dadès** where there is the small and basic *Café-Hôtel Taghia* (no electricity, no phone and limited toilet facilities; ❶). Walking from here, you can scramble up the hill east to a cave with stalactites, or go north to a small but impressive gorge, with views down over the Dadès Valley.

Spring floods permitting, it is usually possible to drive on to Msemrir (63km in all from Boumalne). For a distance, the east side of the gorge is dominated by the **Isk n'Isladene** cliffs and then the road follows a canyon to **Tidrit** where it snakes up and crosses the face of one of the huge canyon loops before the final run to Msemrir. Two kilometres before Msemrir, the **Oussikis** valley, to the left, can be visited by an even rougher *piste*.

Msemrir and beyond

MSEMRIR, little more than a scattering of dusty government buildings and cafés, has a desultory, frontier feel to it. The lively Saturday souk provides the only real incentive to stop, but you might want to use the village as a staging post in a longer journey across the mountains. In this case you can find a room at the *El Warda* (☎024 83 16 09; ❶), a rundown little guesthouse on the main drag which is no more pleasant than nearby *Agdal* (no phone; ❶); a shabby café with a few rooms upstairs. The *Café-Restaurant Aït Atta* also has a basic *gîte d'étape* (☎024 83 04 47; ❶) in the village.

Beyond Msemrir, you've a choice of onward *piste* routes which are presented where the *piste* divides one kilometre outside Msemrir. One route heads east to join the Todra Gorge at Tamtatoucht (6–8hr by Land Rover), while the other heads north across the High Atlas. People drive tourist vehicles across both these routes in summer but they are not really suitable transport – and will break rental conditions. There are frequent wash-outs, bare slabs to cross and other hazards, and they are really best left for lorries or Land Rovers with four-wheel drive.

Over the Atlas

Heading over the High Atlas, the most direct route is to join the road from Todra at Agoudal: 60km or so of very rough driving, over the **Tizi n'Ouano**. Some details of the route beyond is included in the Todra Gorge section (see pp.576–578).

If you are looking for local transport, you may strike lucky with a lorry from Msemrir to Agoudal, but the route isn't driven nearly as regularly as that from Todra, so be prepared for a long wait at Msemrir – and winter often closes this road completely.

Across to Tamtatoucht

If you are intent on **crossing the Todra Gorge** to Tamtatoucht, there is virtually no chance of a local lorry, though you might just find a lift with fellow tourists. It's a long, uphill haul from the Dadès, and the seventy-odd kilometres of *piste*, often in a shocking state, can take a full day to travel. Most Atlas crossings are made from Tinerhir via the Todra Gorge as the route is considerably easier when driving from the opposite direction.

The Tamtatoucht track (not always worthy of the name) keeps on up the dry Oued Tiffaouine valley to reach **Tizi n'Uguent Zegsaoun** (2639m) followed by climbing up the ensuing gorge following the **Tizgui n'Ouaddou** valley which eventually arrives at a pass where the view opens out to the plains stretching to Aït Hani. The next section is defined by an extremely rugged descent over limestone which finally joins the plain and crosses it to hit the Tamtatoucht/Aït Hani *piste* (see p.576).

Tinerhir (Tinghir)

TINERHIR is largely a base for the trip up into the **Todra Gorge** – but it's also a much more interesting place than other administrative centres along this route. It's overlooked by a ruinous but ornamental Glaoui kasbah, and just east of the modern town is an extensive palmery, which feels a world apart, with its groups of *ksour* built at intervals into the rocky hills above. Don't be in too much of a hurry to catch the first lorry up to the Todra Gorge – the Tinerhir and, to the northeast, Todra **palmeries** are major attractions in themselves.

The palmeries seem all the more special after the **journey from Boumalne**: a bleak drive across desolate plains, interrupted by the sudden oases of **Imiter** (with several fine kasbahs) and Timadriouine. The **Djebel Sarhro** (see p.558) looms to the south for the latter part of the trip, dry barren outlines of mountains, like something from the Central Asia steppes; the drama of this part of the range was another memorable backdrop in David Lean's *Lawrence of Arabia*.

If you're interested in buying **crafts**, Tinerhir has a branch of the excellent **Maison Berbère** chain (run by the Alaoui family like those in Ouarzazate, Zagora and Rissani), which has high-quality rugs, carpets and especially silver. There are now two shops, both near the Place Principale: the first is simply called **Maison Berbère** and the second, **Maison De Cadeaux Berbère,** is found down an alley off Place Principale and is comprised of almost a dozen rooms filled with well-presented tribal treasure.

South of Imiter, in the foothills of the Djebel Sarhro, you will see – from the Boumalne-Tinerhir road (N10) – the spoil and silver mines of the Société

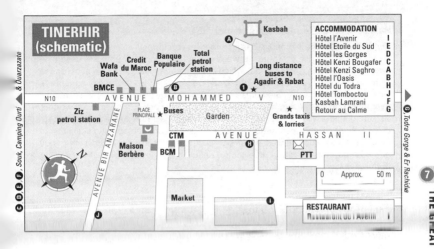

Métallurgique d'Imiter (SMI). Outside interest is not encouraged and rumours abound locally about other mining enterprises, possibly including gold mining; as you enter Tinerhir, you pass alongside the SMI company houses, signposted *Cité de Personnel.*

Practicalities

Orientation is straightforward. The centre of Tinerhir is a long **garden square**, flanked by hotels, café-restaurants and the **PTT**; here are to be found the **grands taxis** for standard runs to Boumalne, Er Rachidia and Erfoud and the **lorries** which go up the Todra Gorge to Tamtatoucht and Imilchil. In the **Place Principale** to the southwest of the garden square are the local **buses** and **CTM** office; long-distance buses, passing through Tinerhir en route for Agadir and Rabat, call here or stop on Avenue Mohammed V facing the central garden.

Four **banks** (Banque Populaire, Crédit du Maroc, Wafabank and BMCE) are on the northwest side of Avenue Mohammed V as it leaves the Place Principale towards Boumalne; all have ATMs. For counter service, the BMCE is most efficient.

There are now téléboutiques all over town; **Internet access** is available at Cyber Café Atlas, 72 Av Bir Inzaran, near the *Hôtel Tomboctou*. For **bicycle rental**, try *Hôtel l'Avenir* (see p.568), or Kamal's Bike, on Avenue Mohammed V, next to the pharmacy.

Accommodation

Most of the cheaper **hotels** line Avenue Hassan II, facing the central garden; the most expensive ones are a bit more scattered, but all are walkable from the set-down points of taxis and buses – with the possible exception of the *Hôtel Kenzi Bougafer* and *Kasbah Lamrani*, both of which are out on the Boumalne road opposite the souk.

There's a campsite, **Camping Ourti**, on Avenue Mohammed V (☎024 83 32 05, ℻024 83 45 99), the Boumalne road, beyond the souk. The site is enthusiastically managed by a young crowd, open year-round and has a good range of facilities – including hot showers and a swimming pool (April–Oct). There's a

The Carpets of the Nomad Women

For generations the Nomadic Berber tribes have stopped in Tinerhir during the winter months whilst en route between the Atlas mountains and the desert, in order to trade. During this period, which changes from year to year in accordance with the weather, many nomad women can be found in the *ksour* weaving carpets which are sold to support the nomadic families and buy provisions for the seasonal migration. If invited to see one of these workshops in action they are well worth a visit, and there will usually be someone nearby eager to explain the intricate cultural symbolisms woven into the carpet's pattern and the specific significance of different materials and weaves. Of course, there is the inevitable pressure to buy one yourself, though with a little tactful haggling the obvious benefits of buying from the source are clear.

restaurant (60dh) and a few bungalows, which sleep up to three people (40dh per head). The site can also arrange 4x4 transport, driver and guide for the gorge, or other expeditions.

Hôtel l'Avenir In the pedestrian zone near the central market ☎ & ⓕ 024 83 45 99, ⓔ mathieulavielle@yahoo.fr. An excellent little budget hotel above a cluster of shops, with good-value rooms, but in a noisy corner of town. ❶

Hôtel Etoile Du Sud Av Mohammed V, ☎ 066 01 48 63. A basic no-frills budget hotel, with a small café downstairs, rooms are simple but clean. ❶–❷

Hôtel les Gorges Av Mohammed V ☎ & ⓕ 024 83 48 00. A French-run place, 1km west of town on the Ouarzazate road. A bit bland from the outside, but the rooms (all en suite, on three storeys) are immaculate; and there's a terrace, a pool and mezzanine restaurant (80dh). The owner's a 4 x4 enthusiast and can help arrange jeep excursions in the area. ❷–❸

Hôtel Kenzi Bougafer Av Mohammed V ☎ 024 83 32 80, ⓕ 024 83 32 82, ⓦ www.kenzi-hotels.net. A modern, efficient hotel (opened 1993), located opposite the Monday souk. It's a luxurious place, already promoted from three to four stars, with very comfortable suites, rooms, a restaurant, bar and swimming pool. ❻

Hôtel Kenzi Saghro On a hill to the north of the town centre ☎ 024 83 41 81, ⓕ 024 83 43 52. Luxurious four-star on a hill overlooking the town, with a big swimming pool, restaurant, bar (residents only), and superb views of the palmeries. ❻

Hôtel l'Oasis Av Mohammed V ☎ & ⓕ 024 83 36 70. Another safe, central choice, including ten en-suite rooms, but is somewhat marred by noise from traffic and the busy downstairs café. ❶–❷

Hôtel du Todra Av Hassan II ☎ 024 83 42 49, ⓕ 024 83 45 65. Open since the 1980s, this place offers a range of differently priced rooms, ranging from basic to en-suite rooms with repro antique furniture. There's also a pleasant terrace and bar. ❶–❹

Hôtel Tomboctou Av Bir Anzarane ☎ 024 83 46 04, ⓕ 024 83 35 05, ⓦ www .hoteltomboctou.com. On a side road, opposite BMCE and to the left of Av Mohammed V (direction Boumalne). A kasbah built for Sheikh Bassou in 1944, tastefully converted by Moroccophile Spaniard Roger Mimó. Since his departure, standards (particularly in the kitchen) have dropped, but this remains one of the memorable small hotels of Morocco. The rooms, well-ventilated in summer and heated in winter, are tasteful and cozy. There's also a pool in the courtyard, a small bar, and a separate "riad" style area that houses a couple of attractive rooms. ❺–❻

Kasbah Lamrani Av Mohammed V, opposite the Monday souk ☎ 024 83 50 17, ⓕ 024 83 50 27, ⓔ elmrani.ali.alaoui@caramail.com. An upscale hotel owned by the Alaoui family, in ersatz kasbah style but with all mod cons including huge terraces with fountains, two restaurants, gardens, a big pool, and overpriced food. ❺

Retour au Calme On the outskirts of town, near the palmery (look for the signboard on the right of the main road, parking can be a problem) ☎ 024 83 49 24, ⓔ hote.calm@mageos.com. A modest, family guesthouse with simple rooms – as its name suggests, away from the bustle of the centre. Rooms with or without bath. Meals (45–65dh). ❷

Eating

Tinerhir is one of those towns where you're invariably better off eating in your hotel restaurant if it has one. If it doesn't, head out to *Chez Christophe* at the *Hôtel les Gorges*, which serves an 80dh *menu fixe*, and plenty of à la carte choices, in a pleasant mezzanine café. Of the places lining the square in the middle of town, only *Restaurant de l'Avenir* (no connection with the hotel of the same name nearby) stands out. It's staffed by a couple of eager young lads, who can turn out satisfactory grills, brochettes and salads; it's a good idea to order at least an hour before you want to eat, as they always seem to have to shop for the ingredients first. Most main courses cost 40–65dh, and the café itself is set back off the pavement, which ensures a degree of privacy.

Moving on

There are regular **buses** from Tinerhir to Ouarzazate (the 6am goes on to Marrakesh), to Fes and Meknes (leaving at 7pm), and to Rissani (6am; for Merzouga). **Grands taxis** in both directions (places available for Ouarzazate/ Boumalne/Er Rachidia/occasionally Fes and Rissani).

The **Berber lorries** (*camionettes*) make regular runs to villages in the **Todra Gorge and beyond**; on Mondays, from around noon (following the souk), numerous lorries set out for Atlas villages, including one that goes right over the mountains to Arhbala, driving through the night. Note that you can also arrange transport (and/or trips) for the **Todra Gorge** (or beyond) through the *Hôtel Tomboudou* or *Camping Ourti* (see p.567 & p.568).

The Tinerhir and Todra palmeries

Palmeries extend southeast and northeast of Tinerhir, lining both sides of the Todra River. For an overview, the *Hôtel Kenzi Saghro* has the town's best viewing point. To explore, you're best off renting a **bicycle** from the *Hôtel L'Avenir* or Kamal's Bike on Avenue Mohammed V – ride on the west side of the valley, where the road is higher and has better views (it's best late in the afternoon when the sun is low and the colours at their most vivid). Alternatively, catch a taxi or

△Palmeries

hitch out to the group of hotels and campsites at the entrance to the gorge (see opposite), and head south into the palmery on foot from there. Once in the palmery proper, the main paths are easy to follow, and you can peel right (west) at any stage to rejoin the main road, which runs above the houses.

The gardens follow the usual pattern in these valleys: date palms at the edge, terraces of olive, pomegranate, almond and fruit trees further in, with grain and vegetable crops planted beneath them. The **ksour** each originally controlled one section of the oasis, and there were frequent disputes over territory and, above all, over access to the mountain streams for each *ksour's* network of water channels. Even in the twentieth century, their fortifications were built in earnest, and, as Walter Harris wrote (melodramatically, but probably with little exaggeration): "The whole life was one of warfare and gloom. Every tribe had its enemies, every family had its blood feuds, and every man his would-be murderer."

Our map indicates several good viewing points, or **miradors**, and also names the most picturesque villages – many of which have **ksour and kasbahs** with extraordinarily complex patterns incised on the walls. Some include former Jewish quarters – Mellahs – though today the populations are almost entirely Berber and Muslim, mainly from the Aït Todra tribe north of Tinerhir and the Aït Atta tribe to the south. In the small village of **AFANOUR** (see map) an old earth mosque has been restored; it makes a pleasant destination for an afternoon ramble around the palmeries and provides a rare opportunity to see the interior of ancient mosque architecture (entry 20dh; ask at *Hotel Tomb, Boctou* for more information).

Southeast of Tinerhir there are potteries at **El Harat**, while at nearby **Tagia** are the tombs of the Aït Atta's chiefs, Hassou Ba Salam, and his son, Ali Ba

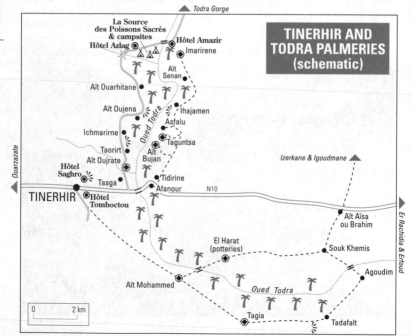

Salam (see box, p.561). There's a *marabout* near El Harat which is the focus of a June/July moussem; this area was originally settled by black slaves who were known as Haratin. For more on the **Todra palmery** – and the approach to the gorge – see below.

The Todra Gorge

Most tourist itineraries include a stop at the **Todra Gorge**, and with good reason. At its deepest and narrowest point, only 15km from Tinerhir, this trench through the High Atlas presents an arresting spectacle, its gigantic rock walls changing colour to magical effect as the day unfolds. In high season, the combination of its easy accessibility (a surfaced road now runs all the way through it), and the confined space makes it a prime hunting ground for southern Morocco's most persistent *faux guides* and touts, so choose wisely when hiring; recent positive feedback in guesthooks is in most cases the only available form of proof of a good international guide. The area has been increasingly recognized as a rock-climbing hot spot and now attracts a new clientele of independent climbers. Taxis up to the Todra Gorge are cheap and drop passengers off at a grouping of budget hotels just before the narrowing of the gorge.

Flash flooding has damaged what was a newly surfaced road up the Todra to the village of Tamtatouche, 32km from Tinerhir (or 17km from the main part of the gorge). The road is still easily passable by car (though hotel owners in the gorge may tell you otherwise in order to extend your stay) and there is pressure on the government to repair the damage as soon as possible. A further 15km from Tamtatouche the village of Aït Hani is accessible by paved road. Minibuses run regularly throughout the day to these villages from the eastern end of the municipal gardens in Tinerhir, although arranging a ride in one of them just as far as the gorge (10dh) can be difficult. Returning to Tinerhir, you stand a better chance of a taxi if you walk back to the *Zaouia* Sidi Abdelâli, 3km south of the gorge, or hitch a lift with day visitors or other tourists.

Beyond Aït Hani, *pistes* continue **over the Atlas** via the village of **Imilchil** (famed for its annual wedding market; see p.577), while another loops over to the Dadès Valley. You can arrange transport along the Imilchil route, either by chartering it at Tinerhir, or by paying for a place on a series of Berber lorries, which shuttle across for village souks. If you plan to drive the route, you will need a suitable (preferably 4x4) vehicle.

Tinerhir to the gorge

En route to the gorge proper, the road climbs along the west flank of the Todra palmery (see map opposite), a last, fertile shaft of land, narrowing at points to a ribbon of palms between the cliffs. There are more or less continuous villages, painted the pink-grey colour of the local rock, and the ruins of kasbahs and *ksour* up above or on the other side.

Around 9km from town, you cross a tributary of the Todra, and come to a string of well-established **campsites** and **hotels**, flanking a particularly luxuriant stretch of the palmery. The first of these, *Camping l'Auberge Atlas* (☎024 89 50 46; ❶), is the best equipped and situated, offering budget rooms (with shared toilets and showers) in addition to well-shaded camping (there is also a washing machine; 30dh). It's in better shape than the nearby *Camping du Lac – Jardin de l'Eden* (☎024 89 50 05; ❶) and *Auberge Camping de la Source des*

Poissons Sacrés (☎061 86 61 45; ➊–➋), both of which have basic rooms for around 100dh. The latter boasts a spring flowing into a pool where a shoal of sacred fish swim.

Just before the *Camping de la Source*, on the left side of the road, stands the most commendable **budget hotel** in this area, the *Hôtel Azlag* (☎024 89 52 17; ➊). Managed by a team of young lads, it has half a dozen simple en-suite rooms and a common veranda running the length of the building that overlooks the palmery. Breakfasts (20dh) and basic meals (from around 50dh) are available, and

△ Todra gorge

there is space to camp round the back. There are usually a couple of guides on hand who are able to lead walks in and around the gorge.

A short way further up the road on the right, the *Hôtel Amazir* (℡024 89 51 09, ℻024 89 50 50; ➎) is a more comfortable option, with a dozen newly fitted en-suite rooms, a lovely tiled salon where meals are served in the winter, and an airy *terrace panoramique* looking onto the river. Breakfast is included in the room price; half-board costs 600dh for two and there's a swimming pool on the terrace. This is the only quality hotel around the palmery and well worth shelling out a little extra for if it's normally beyond your budget. Beyond *Hôtel Amazir* on the left there is a sign for *Relax Appartment Meuble* (℡024 83 49 24; ➌), which provides a unique type of accommodation suited for families or groups of travellers/climbers in search of privacy (with the salon in use 6 adults could stay here comfortably). This apartment consists of two double bedrooms, a comfortable salon, self-catering kitchen (a cook can be provided on request) with fridge, gas cooker, and sink, a terrace, and garden, all of which can be had for 500dh a night.

Another mid-scale possibility a little way further up the valley is the new *Maison d'Hôte d'aïn* (℡024 83 43 10; ➌), 14km from Tinerhir, roughly halfway between the end of the palmery and the mouth of the gorge. It's on the roadside, but at a picturesque spot overlooking the river, surrounded by steep desert hillsides. The rooms are bright and clean, with tiled floors, good beds and immaculate en-suite bathrooms. Meals (80dh) are served in a ground-floor salon-café or, by request, on the rooftop.

The mouth of the gorge

The really enclosed section of **the gorge** extends for just a few hundred metres; it should certainly be walked, even if you're not going any further, for the drama of the scenery – although note the earlier warning about *faux guides* and stall holders, who can impede progress along the road.

It's possible to stay right at the foot of the 300-metre cliffs, where there's a cluster of small **hotels**. Given the traffic and crowds of tourists and hustlers who mill around them through the day, they're far from peaceful, and in winter can be very cold as the sun only reaches them at midday. However, things calm down considerably in the evening after the daytrippers have left, and their rooftops make ideal vantage points from which to admire the escarpments. Climbers congregate at the three budget places just before the entrance to the gorge, which all offer simple rooms with shared facilities from 60–100dh, in addition to dorm beds in salons from 30dh. They also keep log books with useful route descriptions for climbers. Pick of the crop, and generally cleaner than the competition, is the *Hôtel la Vallée* (℡024 89 51 26; ➊–➋). We've had some negative reports about the nearby *Hôtel el Mansour* (℡024 89 51 19; ➊), which may try to charge obligatory half-board rates, so make yourself clear if you just want a bed for the night. Next door the *Étoiles des Gorges* is much the same deal with basic rooms and a restaurant frequented by local touts (℡024 89 50 45; ➊).

Inside the most dramatic section of the gorge, beneath vast overhanging cliffs, are two mid-range places, *Les Roches* (℡024 89 51 34, ℻024 83 36 11, ⓦwww.les-roches.mezgarne.com; ➍) and *Yasmina* (℡024 89 51 18, ℻024 89 50 75, ⓦwww.todragorge.com; ➍). These each have restaurants, often under pressure from tour groups, but the food is good and the set lunches a bargain. Again, they offer a choice of accommodation, including en-suite rooms, or cheaper beds in the salon or tent dining rooms, or out on the terrace. Prices fluctuate according to season and thus demand.

Five kilometres from the mouth of the gorge, situated on a bank opposite the road, is ⚑ *Hotel Le Festival* (☎061 26 72 51, ✉aubergelefestival@yahoo .fr; ❷–❹), currently the only accommodation option between the mouth of the gorge and the village of **Tamtatoucht**. This intimate solar-powered hotel with its solitary location in the middle of the gorge has a true rustic mountain feel and provides an excellent base for climbers and trekkers. Apart from the simple comfortable rooms on the first floor of the hotel there are five inventive en-suite rooms built into the rock beside the hotel with natural cave-like interiors designed to be in keeping with the landscape; all and all a refreshingly different and atmospheric place to spend the night.

Climbing and walking

Having only recently been recognized for its climbing potential, the Hotels and excursion agencies of the Todra Gorge have yet to cash in on equipment rental and professional climbing excursions, which makes the area ideal for the experienced independent climber and underequipped for the novice. There are now more than 150 bolted routes, French Grade 5+ to 8, of between 25m and 300m, with new ones being added each year. The *Hôtel el Mansour* keeps an excellent French topo-guide for reference. Also worth consulting are hotel log books, which will alert you to any **problems** on the rock: over the past few years, kids have tampered with several access bolts, and even fixtures for top ropes. Whichever routes you follow, be warned that you'll need all your own gear as rental opportunities are extremely limited and unreliable. Hassan Mouhajir (☎010 13 42 94), who is best contacted through any of the budget hotels at the mouth of the gorge, has been working on the most comprehensive topo guide to the bolted routes in the area and can be hired as a climbing guide for 500dh (per person per day).

Most of the guides hanging around the gorge try to lead visitors on **walks**, but for the following route, which takes around one and a half to two hours to complete, you won't need help to find the way. It starts just beyond the narrowest section of the gorge. Once through the cliffs, look for a side valley leading quite steeply left (south) from the roadside to a pronounced saddle between two peaks – you'll be able to make out the path climbing on the left flank of the hillside. An easy ascent takes you to the pass in 45 minutes to one hour. From there you could potter up peaks for some great views over the gorge, or follow the path dropping downhill to your left, keeping to a line of silvery-grey rocks that fringe a dry riverbed. After around thirty minutes, the path then climbs briefly to a second saddle, from which it then descends to the edge of the Todra palmery, near the *Camping l'Auberge Atlas*.

Beyond Todra: over the Atlas

It's possible to continue via newly surfaced road (which has, as stated earlier, been damaged by recent flooding) beyond the Todra Gorge to **Tamtatoucht**, and from there across the High and Middle Atlas ranges, to emerge on either the N8 (Azrou–Beni Mellal; formerly P24), or the N13 (Midelt–Er Rachidia; formerly P21), via the beautiful village of **Imilchil**. In between, you are travelling on isolated and at times very rough tracks, for which four-wheel-drive vehicles (or mountain bikes) are essential: landslides are common after heavy rains and during the spring snow melt. With the uncertainty of road conditions in these areas it is important to enquire at Todra Gorge or

Tamtatoucht hotels about conditions before attempting the route beyond **Aït Hani**. If you don't have transport, you can travel on a succession of **Berber lorry–taxis** (*camionettes*), timed to coincide with local village souks. The attractions of this journey are considerable, offering a real experience of Berber mountain life – the villagers are generally very open and friendly – and some of the most exciting scenery in Morocco, in a succession of passes, mountains, rivers and gorges.

It's also possible to cross from the Todra Gorge to the **Dadès Valley** via a *piste* starting near Tamtatoucht (see p.576); cutting through sections of unstable limestone strata and shouldn't be attempted in anything other than a 4x4 vehicle or mountain bike.

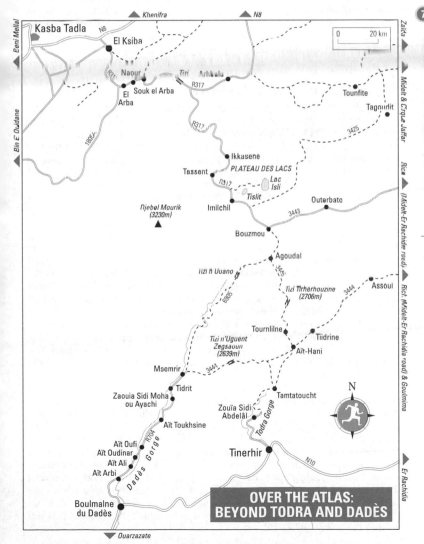

Practicalities

There are no **banks** between Tinerhir and Khenifra/Kasba Tadla/Rich, so you'll need to have enough cash for the journey. Don't underestimate the expense of buying **food** in the mountains (30–100 percent above normal rates), nor the prices charged for rides in the **Berber lorries**; as a very general guideline, reckon on about 20dh for every 50km. There are police stations at Aït Hani and Imilchil if you need serious help or advice on the state of the *pistes*.

Setting out on the lorries from Todra, the managers of the hotels at the mouth of the gorge usually have an idea of when the next *camionette* will pass through – and will help arrange your first ride. Promising days to start out are Wednesday (to coincide with Aït Hani's Thurs souk) and Friday (for Imilchil's Sat souk), but even at other times there's usually at least one lorry or taxi minibus heading in either direction. Eventually, everyone seems to get across to Arhbala (Aghbala) or Naour (where there are buses down to Kasba Tadla/Khenifra) or to Rich (on the Midelt–Er Rachidia road; see p.318), which is nowadays connected to Imilchil via a good surfaced road served by regular minibuses.

Tamtatoucht and beyond

The road up the Todra Gorge (from the hotels) grows gradually less spectacular as you progress uphill, but with your own vehicle it's worth pressing on to **TAMTATOUCHT**, 17km beyond the hotels *Yasmina* and *Les Roches*, for a taste of the high mountains. A sizeable sprawl with a growing number of attractive hotels and cafés (all of which have well-equipped camping areas), the village is situated beneath a ring of beautiful peaks, and with local guidance you can head off for rewarding day walks in the area. At the entrance a group of new hotels have sprung up; *Les Amis* (☎077 55 68 59; ❸), *Hotel Essalam* (☎024 83 58 43; ⓔhotel_essalam@yahoo.fr; ❷–❸), and *Kasbah Taymat* (☎024 83 40 71; ❷) all of which offer clean airy rooms, large camping areas, and demi-pensions.

Next is the friendly, brightly painted *Auberge Baddou* (☎024 83 40 71, ⓦwww.auberge-baddou.com; ❶), with clean rooms, hot showers, good food and *terrasse panoramique*. On the opposite side of the road, the *Boule de Neige* (no phone; ❶) and *Auberge Bougafer* (☎024 70 22 35; ❷–❸) are in a similar mould, offering cheap beds in Berber tents as well as basic rooms. Other options line the roadside on the opposite side of Tamtatoucht, 500m further along the road, including the *Amazigh* (no phone; ❶) and *Auberge Tafougt* (no phone; ❶); the latter crowns the top of a hillock and has exceptional views. When we last passed through, *Hotel Addoud* situated atop a hill overlooking Tamtatoucht (accessible via a good *piste* road just before *Amazigh*) was nearing completion and when finished will have 12 modern rooms and the best views in the village.

Across to the Dadès Valley

The turning for the *piste* that snakes **over to the Dadès Gorge** (see pp.562–566) lies north of Tamtatoucht, near Aït Hani. This is a particularly rough route; lifts are most unlikely, so it's basically an option for Land Rover-type vehicles. The ascent takes you over limestone pavements, after which the track goes over a small pass and then up the long **Tizgui n'Ouaddou** valley towards a huge scarp before the final sweeping bends to the **Tizi n'Uguent Zegsaoun** (2639m). The difficulties then increase; the road is in a bad state with wash-outs and diversions. Only when you edge the final plain and join the Msemrir-Agoudal *piste* does it improve – by which stage Msemrir is just around the corner.

The Imilchil Moussem

Held annually in the third or fourth week of September, the world-famous **Imilchil Moussem** – the "Fête des Fiancés" or "Marriage Market" – is the mother of all Moroccan mountain souks, a gathering of 30,000 or more Berbers from the Aït Haddidou, Aït Morghad, Aït Izdeg and Aït Yahia tribes. Over the three days of the fair (Fri to Sun), animals are traded, clothes, tools and provisions bought, and distant friends and family members reunited before the first snowfalls isolate their high villages. But what makes it especially highly charged is that it is here the region's youngsters come to decide who they're going to marry.

The tradition derives from colonial times, when the officials from the Bureau des Affaires Indigènes used to insist the Berbers assembled in Agdoul, site of a yearly transhumance fair, to register births, deaths and marriages. After Independence the custom was encouraged by the Moroccan tourist office, which the locals blame for propagating the myth that the marriages contracted here were entered into spontaneously. In fact, the matches are nearly all arranged in advance and merely formalized at the moussem. All the same, the fair provides the perfect opportunity for unmarried Berbers – particularly women trapped at altitude for most of the year – to survey their prospects. Dressed in traditional finery, with heavy jewellery and eyes rimmed with heavy black *kohl*, the girls parade around in groups, flirting outrageously with the boys as eagle-eyed elder relatives look on. Later, singing, dancing and drumming give both sexes further opportunities to mingle.

It all makes for a compelling spectacle, but one which in recent years has begun to feel less authentic thanks to the tourist circus surrounding it. Literally thousands of visitors pour in via the new road from Rich to attend the event, along with what seems like every *faux* Touareg and *faux guide* in the country. So if you travel hoping to sneak some good photos, come armed with plenty of cash. For the duration of the moussem weekend, **tents** sleeping a dozen or more people each are erected at the fairground, 24km from Imilchil at **Agdoul**. Rates for beds, food and water (which has to be brought in by lorry) tend to be greatly inflated, so fix prices in advance. It is also advisable to bring plenty of warm clothing as the nights at this altitude (over 2000m) can get bitterly cold by the end of September.

The precise **date** of the festival varies from year to year; contact the ONMT for more details.

Aït Hani and on to Imilchil

Continuing north from Tamtatoucht into the High Atlas, the tarmac ends at **AÏT HANI**, another large village almost the size of Tamtatoucht. It's just off the main route, and if you're driving you can keep going, turning after the town, rather than into it. On the outskirts, as you approach from the south, there is a police/military post, café and store, but no hotel or rooms. This region is generally high and barren landscape – the locals travel amazing distances each day to collect wood for fuel. A recently improved road leads east from Aït Hani towards Goulmima/Rich.

North of Aït Hani there is a stiff climb up to 2700m at **Tizi Tirherhouzine**, then down to **AGOUDAL**. This is a friendly village, and though again there is no official hotel, you'll probably be offered a room. It is in a less harsh setting, too, better irrigated, and the people seem more relaxed than at Aït Hani. You should be able to find a room at **BOUZMOU**, the next village on, and also pick up a *camionette* along the new surfaced road east to Rich on the Midelt–Er Rachidia road.

The road north improves greatly from Agoudal on, passing beyond Bouzmou through a fertile region to reach **IMILCHIL** (45km from Agoudal). This beautiful village, encircled by spectacular mountains and with a fine caidal kasbah, is for most people the highlight of the route. It's famed for its September moussem – the so-called **Marriage Market of Aït Haddidou** (see box, p.577) – which these days attracts streams of tourist traffic up the recently surfaced road from Rich, on the Er Rachidia–Midelt highway. The new artery has spurred development in the village, and there are a couple of simple **hotels** and café-restaurants here now, including *Hôtel Islane* (☏024 44 28 06; ❶) and *Hôtel Atlas* (☏024 44 28 28; ❶), both of which can arrange guides and mules for treks in the area. A handful of more basic places offering *gîte d'étape*-style accommodation in dorms have also sprung up. Among the resident trekking guides; Bassou Chabout is reliable and qualified.

Northeast of Imilchil spreads the **Plateau des Lacs** – flanked by the twin mountain lakes of **Isli** and **Tislit**, named after a couple from Berber folklore, whose love was thwarted and whose tears fell to form the two lakes. At Isli there's a rudimentary *gîte d'étape*; while at Tislit, the kasbah-style *Hôtel Tislit* (no phone; ❶) offers seven basic rooms, shared showers and indifferent meals – worth enduring for the sublime location, overlooked by 3000-metre peaks.

The main **route north** is now surfaced all the way to Arhbala, and provides a spectacular itinerary, with steep drops off the roadside and constant hairpin climbs and descents. This section has few settlements – and certainly nowhere the size of Imilchil, although that may well change with the completion of the new year-round Atlas crossing. **ARHBALA** itself (see p.322) has a very basic hotel near the marketplace (Wednesday souk), and a daily bus on to El Ksiba, where you can pick up connections to Khenifra and Beni Mellal. Another surfaced road heads off to join the Khenifra–Midelt road.

Tinerhir to Er Rachidia and Erfoud

East from Tinerhir, there is little to delay your progress to **Erfoud/Er Rachidia** and the Tafilalt. The more attractive route is the minor road (3451) from **Tinejdad to Erfoud**; the **Er Rachidia road** (N10) is a fast but dull highway through barren country that's broken only by the oases of Tinejdad and Goulmima.

Using local transport, you can get buses or grands taxis along the N10 to Er Rachidia; the taxis involve changes at **Tinejdad** (buses and taxis leave from the east end of the town) and **Goulmima**. Alternatively, a private-line bus leaves Tinejdad (from the square used by the grands taxis, on the main road) daily at 9.30am along the 3451 **to Erfoud and Rissani**, arriving at Rissani about four hours later; to make the connection, get a grand taxi from Tinerhir to Tinejdad.

Er Rachidia via Goulmima

GOULMIMA, a long, straggling palmery, is made up of some twenty or so scattered **ksour**. If you are interested in exploring, ask directions along the complex network of tracks to the *ksar* known as **Gheris de Charis**. Saïd Hansali, contactable through *Les Palmiers* (reviewed on the next page), is an excellent English-speaking guide who can show you around the labyrinthine *ksar* and adjacent palmery.

Modern Goulmima, beside the highway, is signalled by the usual "triumphal" entrance and exit arches of the south, and has little more within. There is, however, a Banque Populaire, and a small **hotel**, the *Gheris*, 2 Rue Saadian, off Boulevard Hassan II (℡035 78 31 67; ❷); despite the address it actually faces the main road. There is a small Internet café reserved for guests and an interesting display of herbs in the ground-floor café, whose terrace is much the best place in town for breakfasts. You can also stay over in the older end of town, where the ✤ *Maison d'Hôtes Les Palmiers* (℡035 78 40 04, Ⓔlespalmiers.odile@menara.ma; ❹) has five pleasantly furnished rooms in the suburban home of a welcoming French-Moroccan couple. The house opens out upon a large walled garden where you can camp. The owner organizes a variety of unique 4x4 excursions and treks, the highlights of which include camping in the **Gorges du Gheris** and fossil finding day trips in the nearby desert.

Erfoud – la Tinejdad

Covered by daily buses, this alternative route – **direct to Erfoud** – is, in parts, eerily impressive. It's well surfaced all the way, though sections are sometimes submerged with sand. The road branches off from the N10 to Er Rachidia at **TINEJDAD**; next to the junction itself stands the convenient and welcoming *Café Restaurant Oued Ed-Dahab*. Tinejdad is one long street, either side of which are the usual services: petrol station, post office, bank and cafés. An additional incentive to pull over here is the **Musée des Oasis** (daily 9am–6pm; admission 20dh), a collection of artefacts and photos showcasing local life. Guided visits (included in the ticket price) give you the chance to nose around an immaculate old *ksar*, recently restored by Spanish guidebook writer Roger Mimó. Roger's latest business venture is the adjacent *Maison d'Hôte el Khorbat* (℡035 88 03 55, ℻035 88 03 57, Ⓦwww .elkhorbat.com; ❻), where a handful of rooms have been stylishly converted, with en-suite bathrooms and Berber textiles; they're dark, but comfortable and cool. You can also eat here at a swish little **restaurant**, which offers a set menu of traditional oasis food, with some Continental as well as vegetarian options, priced at 120dh. There are tables indoors, or on a relaxing stone patio. Cheaper accommodation can be found on the western outskirts of the town on the Tinerhir road at *Hotel Reda* (℡070 67 58 49; ❷), a clean roadside café with half a dozen rooms upstairs.

From Tinejdad, the road follows a course of lush oases – populated by the Aït Atta tribe, traditional warriors of the south who used to control land and exact tribute as far afield as the Drâa, 175km to the southwest and on the far edge of the Djebel Sarhro (see p.561). There are some impressive kasbahs – ask directions to the **Kasbah Asrir**.

You leave the oasis at **MELLAB**, which has another fine **ksar**, and from then on it's more or less continuous desert *hammada* until the beginning of the vast palmery of **EL JORF** – the Tafilalt's largest *ksar* (population 6000) – on the approach to Erfoud. There are a few cafés in the modern village, a post office and a petrol station, but no hotel. Beside the road, over much of the distance from Mellab to Erfoud, the land is pockmarked by parallel lines of strange, volcanic-shaped humps – actually man-made entries to the old underground **irrigation channels** or *khettara*. Another curiosity, notable here and elsewhere along the oasis routes, is the Berber **cemeteries** walled off from the desert at the edge of the *ksour*. These consist of long fields of pointed stones thrust into the ground and the occasional cactus and thorn bush, but otherwise unidentified: a wholly practical measure to prevent jackals from unearthing bodies – and in so doing, frustrating their entry to paradise.

Er Rachidia, the Ziz Valley and the Tafilalt

The great date-palm oases of the **Oued Ziz** and **Tafilalt** come as near as anywhere in Morocco to fulfilling Western fantasies about the Sahara. They do so by occupying the last desert stretches of the **Ziz** Valley: a route shot through with lush and amazingly cinematic scenes, from its fertile beginnings at the *Source Bleue* (springwater pool) oasis meeting point of **Meski**, to a climax amid the rolling sand dunes of **Merzouga**. Along the way, once again, are an impressive succession of *ksour*, and an extraordinarily rich palmery – historically the most important territory this side of the Atlas.

Strictly speaking, the Tafilalt (or Tafilalet) comprises the oases south of **Erfoud**, its principal town and gateway. Nowadays, however, the provincial capital is the French-built garrison town and administrative centre of **Er Rachidia**. If you're making a circuit of the south, you will pass through here, from or en route to Midelt – a journey through the great canyon of the **Ziz Gorges** (see p.319). Er Rachidia is also a crossroads for the route east to Figuig –which used to be an important crossing point into Algeria when the frontier was open.

Er Rachidia

ER RACHIDIA was established by the French as a regional capital – when it was known as Ksar es Souk, after their Foreign Legion fort. Today, it represents more than anywhere else the new face of the Moroccan south: a shift away from the old desert markets and trading routes to a modern, urban centre. The town's role as a military outpost, originally against tribal dissidence, particularly from the Aït Atta (see p.561), was maintained after independence by the threat of territorial claims from Algeria, and there is still a significant garrison here.

The town is, nevertheless, a relaxed place to stay, with an air of relative prosperity, and a large student population, at the lycée and university.

Practicalities

Er Rachidia has a functional grid layout, with most facilities – banks, cafés and restaurants, a covered market and tourist office – strung along the highway/main street, **Avenue Moulay Ali Cherif**. This runs all the way

The Tafilalt was for centuries the Moroccan terminus of the **caravan routes** – the famous **Salt Road** to the south across the Sahara to West Africa, by way of Timbuktu. Merchants travelling south carried with them weapons, cloth and spices, part of which they traded en route at Taghaza (in modern-day Mali) for local **salt**, the most-sought after commodity in West Africa. They would continue south and then make the return trip from the old Kingdom of Ghana, to the west of Timbuktu, loaded with **gold** (one ounce of gold was exchanged for one pound of salt at the beginning of the nineteenth century) and, until European colonists brought an end to the trade, with **slaves**.

These were long journeys: Taghaza was twenty days by camel from Tafilalt, Timbuktu sixty, and merchants might be away for up to a year if they made a circuit via southern Libya (where slaves were still sold until the Italian occupation in 1911). They also, of course, brought an unusual degree of contact with other cultures, which ensured the Tafilalt a reputation as one of the most unstable parts of the Moroccan empire, frequently riven by religious dissent and separatism.

The separatism had a long history, dating back to the eighth century when the region prospered as the independent kingdom of **Sijilmassa** (see p.588); the dissent began when the *Filalis* – as Tafilalt's predominantly Berber population is known – adopted the **Kharijisite heresy**, a movement which used a Berber version of the Koran (orthodox Islam forbids any translation of God's direct Arabic revelation to Muhammad). Then in the fifteenth century it again emerged as a source of trouble, fostering the *Marabout* uprising that toppled the Saadian dynasty.

It is with the establishment of the **Alaouite** (or, after their birthplace, *Filali*) dynasty that the Tafilalt is most closely associated. Mounted from a *zaouia* in Rissani by Moulay Rachid, and secured by his successor Moulay Ismail, this is the dynasty which still holds power in Morocco, through Mohammed VI, the fifteenth sultan in the line. The Alaouites were also the source of the wealth of many of the old kasbahs and *ksour*; from the time of Moulay Ismail, through to the last century, the sultans exiled princes and unruly relatives out here to the edge of the desert.

The Tafilalt was a major centre of resistance to the French, who were limited to their garrison at Erfoud and an outpost of the Foreign Legion at Ouled Zohra until 1931.

The Tafilalt today – and Bayoud disease

The Tafilalt today, deprived of its contacts to the south, is something of a backwater, with a population estimated at around 80,000 and declining, as the effects of drought and Bayoud disease have taken hold on the palms. Most of the population are small-holding farmers, with thirty or so palms for each family, from which they could hope to produce around a thousand kilos of dates in a reasonable year. With the market price of dates around 6dh a kilo there are no fortunes to be made.

It is reckoned that two-thirds of Moroccan palmeries are infected with **Bayoud disease**. First detected in the Drâa at the beginning of the twentieth century, this is a kind of fungus, which is spread from root to root and possibly by transmission of spores. Palms die within a year of an attack, creating a secondary problem by leaving a gap in the wedge of trees, which allows the winds to blow through. The disease cannot be treated economically – the most that farmers can do is to isolate trees by digging a ditch round them – and the only real hope seems to lie in the development of resistant variety of palms. Moroccan and French scientists, in collaboration with the Total oil company, are at present working on new methods of propagation and cross-breeding. A variety species has already, in fact, been developed in France, but there's one problem: the dates, so far, taste awful.

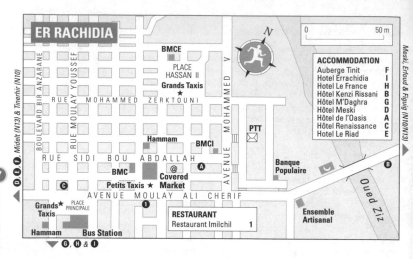

through town, between the familiar southern ceremonial roadside arches, turning into **Avenue El Massira** after crossing the bridge over the Oued Ziz.

All **buses** arrive at the main bus station, on the Place Principale, just south of Avenue Moulay Ali Cherif.

Accommodation, eating and drinking

Despite its size, Er Rachidia has a limited choice of decent **hotels** within the city centre and if you want to **camp**, the position is no better: the municipal site, still signposted just across the bridge, is closed and the *Source Bleue* at Meski, 21km south of Er Rachidia (see opposite), is the nearest possibility. Fortunately, the tourist complex at Meski has been improved and is a recommended alternative.

Several of the hotels listed below host decent restaurants, but the safest choice for an inexpensive tajine is the *Restaurant Imilchil*, in an attractive setting opposite the covered market.

Hotels

Auberge Tinit 3km west of the city centre on the Goulmima road, ☏ 035 79 17 59, ☏ 035 79 18 11, ✉ tinit_auberge2000@yahoo.fr. A new kasbah-style hotel with large pleasant rooms and a swimming pool in the courtyard. A convenient option for those wishing to stay outside the city centre. ⑤

Hôtel Errachidia 31 Iben Battouta ☏ 035 57 09 53. A simple two-star hotel with 21 rooms, the more expensive ones have a/c and balconies, breakfast is included in the room price. Next door to the bus station. ④

Hôtel Le France Rue Chekh El Islam ☏ 035 57 09 97. A pleasant café with mock-French décor, the rooms are simple and comfortable, but at 50dh the small tajines are slightly overpriced. ②

Hôtel Kenzi Rissani Av Al Massira ☏ 035/57 21 86, ☏ 035 57 25 85. Just across the bridge, on the right-hand side travelling towards Meski, this centrally a/c hotel is the smartest place to stay in town, with an upscale restaurant (meals from 180dh) and comfortable rooms from 700dh. ⑥

Hôtel M'Daghra 92 Rue Madaghra ☏ 035 57 40 47, ☏ 035 79 08 64. Much the best deal in this category, with 29 larger-than-average en-suite rooms (avoid the ones at the front of the building), a bar and a reasonable restaurant. ③

Hôtel Meski Av Moulay Ali Cherif ☏ 035 57 20 65, ☏ 035 57 12 37. 400m out of town, on the right as you come in from Midelt or Goulmima. Car parking is secure, but it's not convenient for public transport. Good-sized rooms (again, avoid those on the front side) with and without showers; the disorganized restaurant is alcohol-free. Best kept as a fall-back. **④**

Hôtel de l'Oasis 4 Rue Sidi Bou Abdallah ℡035 57 25 19, ℗035 57 01 26. A slightly shabby older hotel in the middle of town. The rooms are basic and clean and there's a small restaurant. **②**

Hôtel Renaissance 19 Rue Moulay Youssef ℡066 28 02 35. Cheap, simple rooms, some with

showers, and a decent restaurant, close to the bus station. A dependable budget choice. **①**

Hôtel Le Riad ℡035 79 10 06, ⓦwww .hotelleriad.com. An upscale affair on the Goulmima road 4km outside the city centre, the rooms face into a courtyard with a swimming pool and bar. Each of the en suite rooms has a small sitting area and is fitted with all the mod cons. **⑥**

Listings

Banks There are four banks – Banque Populaire, BMC, BMCE and BMCI – all shown on the map.

Car repairs The Renault agent on Pl Hassan II carries a large supply of parts and will order others efficiently from Fes.

Internet access Cyber Café Infoziz, 85 Rue Targa-Jdida, down the road just before the *Hôtel Meski* on the left, if you're approaching from Ouarzazate or – closer to the market – Cyber Challenge Internet.

Petrol stations There is a Ziz station on the Midelt road, and a Somepi station on the Erfoud road.

Petits taxis leave from outside the covered market on Av Moulay Ali Cherif.

Post office The PTT on Av Mohammed V has all the usual services.

Shopping The covered market is a reliable source of fresh food. There's a good craft shop, 6 Rue Sidi Ben Abdallah, by the *Hôtel de l'Oasis*; for once, the invitation to "just look" is sincere. The Ensemble Artisanal (8.30am–6.30pm) is on Av Moulay Ali Cherif, opposite the Banque Populaire, on the way out of town towards the *Hôtel Kenzi Rissani* it has a good display of local goods: pottery, brass, wood and, truly indigenous, basketware made of palm leaves.

Tourist office There's a helpful Délégation Provinciale du Tourisme at 44 Av Prince Moulay Abdallah (Mon–Fri: summer 7am–2pm; winter 8.30am–noon & 2.30–6.30pm; ℡035 57 09 44), found by leaving town on the Tinerhir road and turning right opposite the PTT.

Moving on

Buses leave at least six times a day for Erfoud/Rissani, and a similar number head north to Midelt and Fes or Meknes, via the dramatic Ziz Gorges. The CTM bus to Ouarzazate goes on to Marrakesh.

It's usually no problem to get a seat in a **grand taxi** to Erfoud or, paying the same price, to the Meski turning; these leave from opposite the bus station, as do grands taxis to Tinerhir. Grands taxis from Place Hassan II run to other destinations: check on your destination before setting out with baggage.

Meski and the Ziz valley

The small palm grove of **MESKI** is watered by a natural springwater pool – the famous **Source Bleue**, extended by the French Foreign Legion and long a postcard image and favourite campsite for travellers. It's set on the riverbank, below a huge ruined *ksar* on the opposite bank and, with several of the springs channelled into a **swimming pool**; it's as romantic a spot as any in the south. Outside midsummer, you might also consider walking part of the way downstream in the valley bottom, southeast of Meski. The superb four-hour **trek** along the Oued Ziz will bring you to **Oulad Aïssa**, a *ksar* with fabulous views over the upper Tafilalt.

Shaded by bamboo, palms and tamarisks, the **campsite** is well maintained by the local commune of M'Daghra, with a friendly little café-restaurant that serves meals given notice. The pool itself is safe to swim in, though be warned that the river may be infected with bilharzia.

Clearly signposted off the main road, the *source* lies 18km south of Er Rachidia. Coming by bus, ask to get out by the turn-off: from here it's only 400m down to the pool and campsite. **Going on** to Erfoud or back to Er Rachidia from Meski can be tricky, since most of the buses pass by full and don't stop. However, this is an easy place to hitch a lift from other tourists.

South from Meski: the Ziz palmery

Heading south from Er Rachidia and Meski, **towards Erfoud**, the N13 trails the final section of the **Oued Ziz**. Make sure you travel this in daylight, as it's one of the most pleasing of all the southern routes: a dry red belt of desert just beyond Meski, and then, suddenly, a drop into the valley and the great **Tizimi palmery** – a prelude of the Tafilalt, leading into Erfoud. Away from the road, **ksour** are almost continuous – glimpsed through the trees and high walls enclosing gardens and plots of farming land.

If you want to stop and take a closer look at the *ksour*, **AOUFOUSS**, midway to Erfoud, and the site of a **Thursday souk**, is perhaps the most accessible. There's also a pleasant little guesthouse here, the *Maison d'Hôtes Zouala* (no phone; ❷), in a traditional Berber house with en-suite rooms and hot showers. **MAADID**, too, off to the left of the road as you approach Erfoud, is interesting – a really massive **ksar**, which is considered to be the start of the Tafilalt proper.

Between Aoufouss and Maadid, 15km from Erfoud and to the west of the road near the one remaining tower of Borj Yerdi, you will see a couple of spectacular **chalybeate geysers** shooting aerated iron-bearing water up to five metres into the air: a photo-opportunity, if nothing else.

Erfoud

ERFOUD, like Er Rachidia, is largely a French-built administrative centre, and its desultory frontier-town atmosphere fulfils little of the promise of the Tafilalt. Arriving from Er Rachidia, however, you get a first, powerful sense of proximity to the desert, with frequent sandblasts ripping through the streets, and total darkness in the event of a (not uncommon) electrical blackout. Before the Rissani–Merzouga road was surfaced, Erfoud functioned as a launch pad for trips to the dunes at **Merzouga**. It has, however, been left high and dry since then and tends to be bypassed by travellers who arrive here early enough in the day to pick up onward transport. Its only point of minor interest, aside from the **date festival** (see box opposite), is the local **marble industry**, which produces a unique, high-quality black marble containing fossils. When polished, it's attractive and can be seen locally on every bar top and reception desk.

You can visit the marble works on the Tinerhir road; ask – or look for – the Usine de Marmar. A German sculptor, Fred Jansen, and his Arts Natura group, pioneered carving the marble so that the fossils are revealed in 3D and, at its best, this is most impressive.

Conventional sights are thin on the ground, but with time to kill you could walk to a popular viewpoint 1km south of town called **Le bordj**. It's reached by crossing the river and then turning left after 500m, where a *piste* scales the hillside to a small car park. At 937m, the hilltop hosts a military area, but in good weather the panorama over the palmery and surrounding desert is great. In addition, some well-preserved **ksour** and fine **palmeries** line the main road 3km north towards Er Rachidia.

The Festival of Dates

Erfoud's **Festival of Dates** is held over three days in October and you will be richly rewarded if you can visit at that time. As with all such events, it's a mixture of symbolism, sacred rites and entertainment. Traditionally, dates bring good luck: tied to a baby's arm they ensure a sweet nature, thrown at a bride they encourage fertility, and offered to strangers they signify friendship.

On the first morning of the festival, prayers are said at the mausoleum of Moulay Ali Shereef at Rissani and, the same evening, there is a fashion show of traditional costumes: a pride of embroidered silk, silver and gold headdresses, sequins and elaborate jewellery. Then there are processions, athletics and, on the last night, traditional music and spiritual songs.

Accommodation

Erfoud offers a good choice of **hotels**, at all price levels a legacy of the days when the town served as a staging host for dune trips which still offer dawn shuttles to Merzouga (at negotiable prices that start at around 100dh for one sharing with a group of six), but it's much cheaper to travel there by grand taxi or bus.

Hôtel el Farah Zouar Av Moulay Ismail ☏ & ⓕ 035 57 62 30. On the roundabout where roads to Rissani and to Tinerhir split. An elegant hotel, whose *terrasse panoramique* looks over the palmery towards Borj Est. It's a very friendly place and caters for individuals rather than groups. Restaurant, but no bar. ❹

Hôtel Kasbah Tizmi 2km west of town on the Tinerhir road ☏ 035 57 61 79, ⓕ 035 57 73 75, ⓔ katizimi@iam.net.ma. A modern *pisé* building on a down-to-earth scale, featuring traditional wood beams, ironwork and tiles. Ranged around patios and a flower-filled garden, the rooms are attractively decorated, and there's a large pool and spacious terrace with views. Count on 800dh half board for two. ❻

Hôtel Lahmada Av Moulay Ismail ☏ 035 57 69 97, ⓕ 035 57 60 80. A modern hotel offering excellent value for money at this price. The rooms are all en suite with quality furniture, and most have balconies. There's also a dependable, inexpensive restaurant. ❷

Hôtel Merzouga 114 Av Mohammed V ☏ 035 57 65 32. Reasonably clean en-suite rooms with hot showers; or you can sleep on the terrace for 25dh a head. Best of the rock-bottom options. ❶

Hôtel Sable d'Or 141 Av Mohammed V ☏ 035 57 63 48. Near the junction with Av Moulay Ismail and the Banque Populaire. Good on most counts: clean, comfortable, en-suite, hot showers, and views of the dunes from the third floor and terrace. ❸

Hôtel Salam Av Moulay Ismail ☏ 035 57 66 65, ⓕ 035 57 64 26. Swish four-star built in faux-kasbah style. The 156 rooms have a/c and there's

a large pool on the central patio, swathed in bougainvillea; also a sauna, restaurant and well-stocked bar. Good value in this category, but it does get swamped by groups. ❻

Hôtel Tafilalet Av Moulay Ismail ☏ 035 57 65 35, ⓕ 035 57 60 36. One of Erfoud's older hotels, slightly less expensive than the *Hôtel Salam* (see previous column) and in need of renovation though very friendly and comfortable nonetheless, with most mod cons (including a swimming pool). ❺

Kasbah Xaluca Maadid 6km North of town on the Er Rachidia road ☏ 035 57 67 93, ⓦ www .xalucamaadid.com. The most architecturally distinguished of the luxury *pisé* places in this area (though in many ways the abundance of decoration is slightly tacky). The rooms, opening onto small courtyards and a palm-fringed pool, are dominated by deep pastel colours, the furniture, decor and fittings make use of local arts and crafts. Unfortunately the size of the compound and its ability to cater for large groups tends to give the place an inauthentic resort-like feel. Half-board from 800dh for two. ❻

Riad Nour 6km north of town on the Er Rachidia road ☏ 035 57 77 48, ⓔ nriad01 @menara.ma. This tastefully decorated mock riad offers comfortable, cool rooms furnished with wrought iron that open onto a grassy hedge-rowed courtyard. There's a large swimming pool, fully licensed bar, and a pricey dinner menu (120dh). Breakfast is included in the room price. ❺

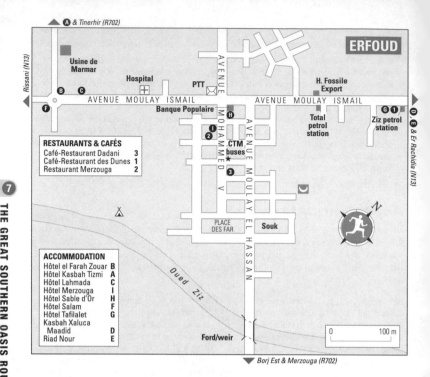

Borj Est & Merzouga (R702)

RESTAURANTS & CAFÉS
Café-Restaurant Dadani 3
Café-Restaurant des Dunes 1
Restaurant Merzouga 2

ACCOMMODATION
Hôtel el Farah Zouar B
Hôtel Kasbah Tizmi A
Hôtel Lahmada C
Hôtel Merzouga I
Hôtel Sable d'Or H
Hôtel Salam F
Hôtel Tafilalet G
Kasbah Xaluca
   Maadid D
Riad Nour E

THE GREAT SOUTHERN OASIS ROUTES | Erfoud

Eating

If you arrive in Erfoud too late to reach Rissani or Merzouga, you'll probably find yourself killing time in a café or restaurant. While you're here, try to sample the local speciality, *kalia* – a spicy stew of mutton or kid, flavoured with over forty spices and served in a tajine with vegetables, egg and parsley. Given a couple of hours' advance warning, most places – including those reviewed below – will also prepare southern Morocco's answer to pizza, *madfouna*: griddled-fried wheat-flour bases topped with onions, tomatoes, olives, minced lamb and cheese.

Café-Restaurant Dadani 103 Av Mohammed V ☏ 035 57 79 58. A congenial, hygienic budget restaurant with a large terrace, serving a range of Moroccan staples prepared with fresh ingredients, demonstrating good value for money. Mains from around 40dh.
Café-Restaurant des Dunes Av Moulay Ismaïl ☏ 035 57 67 93. *Kalia* is the house speciality of

this established little place, near the Zia petrol station. It's cheap and welcoming, with set menus from only 50dh.
Restaurant Merzouga 112 Av Mohammed V ☏ 035 57 65 32. On the ground floor of the popular budget hotel, and a good cheap option, with tasty vegetarian *harira*, couscous, omelettes and breakfasts. Menus from 40dh.

Moving on

CTM **buses** leave from the *gare routière* on Avenue Mohammed V; others from the Place des FAR. There are two daily private-line services to **Tinerhir** (one around 11.30am, the other around 3pm), via Tinejdad, avoiding the dogleg via Er Rachidia. A full rundown of destinations appears in "Travel Details" on p.600. **For Merzouga**, you can pick up local buses, taxis and minibuses from the Place des FAR, although you may have to change at Rissani; in any case, note that it's no longer necessary to pay for a 4 x4 to reach Merzouga as, contrary to what the hustlers may tell you, the road is surfaced all the way. There's also a morning CTM service, but it has a tie-in with one of the hotels on the dunes and may not drop you where you wish to stay. Other grands taxis – for Rissani, Er Rachidia and Tinerhir – leave from opposite the post office.

Rissani and around

RISSANI stands at the last visible point of the Ziz River; beyond it, steadily encroaching on the present town and its ancient *ksour* ruins, begins the desert. From the eighth to the fourteenth centuries, this was the site of the first independent kingdom of the south, Sijilmassa (see box, p.588). It was the first capital of the Tafilalt, and served as the last stop on the great caravan routes south. The British journalist Walter Harris reported thriving gold and slave auctions in Rissani as late as the 1890s.

Rissani has a special place in modern Moroccan lore. It was from the *zaouia* here – which is still an important national shrine – that the ruling Alaouite dynasty launched its bid for power, conquering first the oases of the south, then the vital Taza Gap, before triumphing finally in Fes and Marrakesh.

For visitors, its main interest lies in its proximity to the dunes at Merzouga, which can now be reached via a new paved road (previously, you had to catch a 4 x4 from Erfoud to cross the desert). This new springboard status means the town centre is swarming with *faux guides* trying to sign tourists up for camel rides and hotel packages; walk around with a rucksack and you'll be pestered from the moment you arrive. If you're driving, you'll probably be tempted to head straight through. This is unfortunate as Rissani has much to offer with many attractions of its own, including well-preserved medieval **ksour**, which the local tourist office have strung together on a waymarked 21km "**Circuit Touristique**" through the palmeries and a famous thrice-weekly **souk**. Rissani's proximity to the desert has established its souk as an important trading post for Nomadic Berber, Bedouin, and other Saharian tribes who travel from miles around to trade. In the early morning and afternoon the souk's main attraction is the animal market where goats, sheep, and cattle are bought and sold.

The Town

A quarter of Rissani's population still live in a large seventeenth-century **ksar**, in addition to which there is just the Place al Massira and one street, lined by the usual administrative buildings. It's a quiet place, which comes to life for the **souk** – held on Sunday, Tuesday and Thursday. This is more for locals than tourists but often turns up a good selection of Berber jewellery – including the crude, almost iconographic designs of the desert. Some of the basic products (dried fruits, farming implements and so on) are interestingly distinct from those of the richer north. Don't expect camels, as some guides promise: apart from the caravans, these were never very common in Tafilalt, the Berbers preferring more economical mules. They are still very much in evidence.

The souk aside, you might care to visit the modest **museum** (Mon–Fri 9am–6:30pm; free); most material has been moved to **Ksar al Fida** (see next page) though a library remains that contains a variety of information on the region. For example, there's a catalogue of rock carvings in southern Morocco. The staff are enthusiastic and will let you browse; as you would expect, the texts

Sijilmassa was founded in 757 by Berber dissidents, who had broken away from orthodox Islam, and for five centuries, until its collapse under civil unrest in 1393, it dominated southern Morocco. The early dominance and wealth of Sijilmassa was due to the fertility of the **oases** south of Erfoud. These are watered by parallel rivers, the Oued Rheris and Oued Ziz, which led to Sijilmassa's description as the "Mesopotamia of Morocco". Harvests were further improved by diverting the Ziz, just south of modern Erfoud, to the west of its natural channel, thus bringing it closer to the Rheris and raising the water table. Such natural wealth was reinforced by Sijilmassa's trading role on the **Salt Road** to West Africa (see box, p.581), which persisted until the west coast of Africa was opened up to sea trade, particularly by the Portuguese, in the fifteenth century. Coins from Sijilmassa in this period have been found as far as Aqaba in Jordan.

Historians disagree about the extent and pattern of Sijilmassa at its height. Some see it as a divided city, comprising several dispersed *ksour*, much as it was after the civil war at the end of the fourteenth century. Others view it as a single, elongated city, spread along the banks of the rivers: 14km from end to end, or half a day's walk.

There is still a gate to be seen on the east side of the Oued Ziz, at the ancient city's northern extremity, just south of El Mansouriya. This is known locally as the **Bab Errih** and may date from the Merenid period (1248–1465), although it has certainly undergone restoration since then. The Alaouites, who brought Sijilmassa to renewed prominence as the provincial capital of the Tafilalt in the seventeenth century, did a major restoration of the garrison. The southernmost point of the ancient city was near the *ksar* of Gaouz, on the "Circuit Touristique".

The (mainly Alaouite) central area is under excavation by a joint team from the Moroccan Institute of Archeology and the Middle Tennessee State University, under the direction of Dr Ronald Messier. The most accessible and visible remains are to be found a little to the west of Rissani, on the east bank of the Oued Ziz, and within the right angle formed by the north–south main road (N13) as it turns east into Rissani. Here can be traced the walls of a mosque with an early mihrab facing south, an adjoining medersa and the walls of the citadel with towers on the length by the river. In Rissani, there is a small museum and study centre where you may get help to explore the site.

With thanks to Dr Ron Messier.

---

are mainly in French. Two kilometres from the town centre in the direction of Merzouga there is a sign for **Ksar al Fida**, a nineteenth-century *ksar* that now houses the Alaouite museum (Mon–Sun 8am–7pm; 20dh) where you'll find interesting material about the Alaouite dynasty in what is quite a sparse exhibition.

Two permanent **craft shops** might also draw you into an hour or two's browsing: the **Maison Touareg** (☎035 57 54 93), on the left of the road out to Merzouga, and **Maison Berbère** (☎035 57 50 54), more difficult to find – across the open area alongside the *Centre de la Jeunesse* (not to be confused with the new youth hostel, see next page). The Maison Berbère is part of the Alaoui family chain that has a reputation for quality rugs – and no hassle.

Practicalities

Focused around a busy square and covered market area, the town centre is compact and easy to find your way around once you've got your bearings. Private buses pull into a new bus station 500m north, just outside a prominent triumphal arch; CTM services work from their offices in the square. If you're arriving by grand taxi, you'll probably be dropped near the post office, at the northern end of the medina walls outside the arch, or at a plot just west of the municipal compound. Rissani has a couple of **banks** (the Banque Populaire and Crédit du Maroc) both ranged around the square and with ATMs. The most convenient petrol station is the Ziz on the main square.

With the dunes now only down the road, few travellers choose to stay here, but you can do so at one or other of an uninspiring group of small **hotels** in the centre. The cheapest of them is the *Hôtel Panorama* (☎066 35 18 36; ❶), on the square, which has a little café; the owner also rents out decent **bicycles** for the "circuit touristique". The only mid-range option in the centre of town located behind *Hôtel Panorama* and next to **Maison Berbère**, *Dar Lamrani* (☎035 77 02 36, ⓦkasbahlamrani.com; ❹) is clean and accommodating, with tasteful rooms and two restaurant-salons downstairs with decent though overpriced food.

The best value option in town, further north close to the post office (turn left under the triumphal arch if you're arriving from the north), is the ✦ *Hôtel Sijilmassa* (☎035 57 50 42; ❷–❸), whose large rooftop terrace affords great views of the palmery, there is a pleasant café on the ground floor and if requested in advance, meals are freshly prepared for lunch or dinner. Otherwise, there's the friendly *Auberge de Jeunesse*, a couple of blocks south of the main square at 105 Hay Moulay Slimane Rissani (☎035 57 53 89, ⓕ035 77 40 71; ❶), which charges 25dh for dorm beds and 70dh for doubles, including breakfast. They also have a small kitchen where you can cook your own meals for no extra charge.

Kasbah Ennasra (☎035 77 44 03, ⓕ035 77 44 01, ⓦwww.kasbahennasra .com; ❻), two kilometres outside the town in the direction of Erfoud next to the petrol station, is Rissani's best luxury option, highlights include four-poster beds, an attractive patio, swimming pool, and a pricey first-class restaurant.

Eating options are limited in Rissani. The safest bet is the *Hôtel Sijilmassa's* restaurant (menus from 55dh), which features tasty *kalia* stew on its cheapest set menu. If the café terrace or cellar dining hall don't appeal, ask to be served on the airier rooftop terrace.

Moving on

Grands taxis and minivans (15dh) for the trip **onwards to Merzouga** leave from outside the *Hôtel Panorama*, in the central market, throughout the morning; in the afternoon, they're thinner on the ground and you may have to take a chance on one of the Berber lorries which run the route after the souk finishes; alternatively, walk out of town to the Merzouga road and hitch – there is always a fair bit of tourist traffic. From the centre, head through the town gates to the west (in the direction of the *Zaouia* of Moulay Ali Shereef and the "Circuit Touristique") and keep going straight on until you reach a junction. Bear left here, passing rows of shops to reach a second junction roughly 500m further on, where you should turn right; the new road swings decisively southeast at this point, crossing empty *hammada* desert with the dunes visible in the distance.

Heading **northwest** from Rissani, grands taxis and a couple of daily buses run direct to **Tinerhir** (45dh). An alternative route is the **road west to Zagora**, via Alnif, detailed on pp.590–593. Minivan taxis covering this back road usually leave from near the CTM office on Thursdays and Sundays, after the Rissani market, arriving in Zagora around ten hours later; arrange a place through your hotel.

Ksour around Rissani

Rissani's older monuments are well into the process of erosion – both through crumbling material and the slow progress of the sands. **Sijilmassa**, whose ruins were clearly visible at the beginning of the last century, has more or less vanished (though see the box on p.588). The various kasbahs and reminders of the Alaouite presence are also mostly in an advanced stage of decay, though there is just enough remaining to warrant a battle with the morning heat.

You can head towards a collection of *ksour* on the signposted "Circuit Touristique" (the circuit is especially beautiful in the golden light of sunset). Starting from the southern entrance to the circuit (found off the Merzouga road) the first *ksar* you encounter, about 2.5km to the southeast, houses the **Zaouia of Moulay Ali Shereef**, the original Alaouite stronghold and mausoleum of the dynasty's founder. Many times rebuilt – the last following floods in 1955 – the shrine is forbidden to non-Muslims.

Beside it, dominating this group of buildings, is the nineteenth-century **Ksar d'Akbar**, an awesomely grandiose ruin which was once a palace in exile, housing the unwanted members of the Alaouite family and the wives of the dead sultans. Most of the structure, which still bears considerable traces of its former decoration, dates from the beginning of the nineteenth century. A third royal *ksar*, the **Ksar Oualad Abdelhalim**, stands around 1.5km further down the road. Notable for its huge ramparts and the elaborate decorative effects of its blind arches and unplastered brick patterning, this is one of the few really impressive imperial buildings completed in the twentieth century. It was constructed around 1900 for Sultan Moulay Hassan's elder brother, whom he had appointed governor of the Tafilalt.

You can complete the circuit by passing a further group of *ksour* – **Asserehine**, **Zaouiet el Maati**, **Irara**, **Gaouz**, **Tabassant**, **Tinrheras** and **Ouirhlane** – and then looping back into town past a section of **Sijilmassa**. Tinrheras, a ruined *ksar* on a knoll, has fine views over Tafilalt.

West from Rissani to the Drâa

Around 3km north of Rissani, a recently surfaced road (N12) branches west off the main Erfoud highway towards Alnif, Tazzarine, and Nekob. The route sees little tourist traffic, but provides a dependable and scenic link between the Tafilalt and Drâa Valley, completing a circuit around the Djebel Sarhro and Djebel Ougnat massifs, whose escarpments and dark-brown peaks form a forbidding backdrop for most of the 240km journey. Aside from the landscape, **fossils** are this region's main attraction. The stretch between Alnif and Tazzarine, in particular, has become the centre of a low-scale mining industry whose principal export is large trilobites (see box opposite), sold from dozens of roadside stalls.

Daily **minibuses** and grands taxis run between Rissani and Nekob, but to reach Zagora in a single ride (10hr) you'll have to pick up the twice weekly CTM service (Thurs & Sun). Of the towns punctuating the route, Nekob is much the most appealing place to break the trip, with a good choice of accommodation; it also serves as a roadhead for hikes into the Djebel Sarhro.

Alnif and Tazzarine

Trilobites and potatoes are the stock in trade of **ALNIF**, 90km west of Rissani – the former scraped from ancient canyon walls around the town, the latter

Rocks, fossils and minerals

Along roadsides in the High and Anti-Atlas and down into the southeast, boys bound into the paths of oncoming cars to offer crystalline mementos of Morocco, and rocks, fossils and minerals are staples of most tourist shops in the south. Before purchasing, you might want to read these notes:

Geode Tennis-ball-sized specimens of crystals in a hollow geode cost around £12/$24 in Britain or the US; on the Moroccan hard-shoulder, they may cost more. Brilliant orange and red geodes and slices of rock crystal (quartz) look attractive but are unknown to natural science, as are the quartz geodes given an iridescent metal coating by vendors.

Ammonites Attractive spirals of ammonites (from Carboniferous to Jurassic) are common in the limestone areas of Britain but in Morocco they can be bought sliced and polished as well as "raw". Do not rely on the species name you are given by the shopkeeper – look at the centre of the spiral of the ammonite and at the ridge around its shell to check how far natural features have been "enhanced" by a chisel.

Trilobites Slightly older than ammonites, trilobites often appear in shops as identical beige-coloured fossils on grey slate. In nature, they are rarely so perfect – beware plaster casts. The early trilobite *paradoxides* is about the size of a hand, with long whisker-like spines. A deep-sea inhabitant, it is often found looking rather squashed sideways, where the silts on which it lived have been sheared by pressure. The *Calymene* and *Phacops* types of trilobites are about 200 million years younger than *Paradoxides*. They measure about two inches long, with a crab-like outer skeleton. The half-rounded shield-like skull, often found separated from the exo-skeleton, can appear in a shop with the rest of the skeleton carved around it as a tribute to modern Moroccan craftsmanship.

In the black limestone regions near Erfoud, the white crystalline shapes of **belemnites**, **ammonites** and **nautilus** are cross-sectioned and polished to emphasize the internal structure before being formed into ash-trays and even coffee tables, which can of course be transported for you at a cost. They may not look so good back home.

grown in the palmery winding northwards into the hills It's along the line of this old watercourse that a well-frequented *piste* cuts across a saddle dividing the Djebel Sarhro and Djebel Ougnat ranges to join the main Dadès highway, the N10, 21km southeast of Tinerhir. The route is generally in good condition and passable with a tourist vehicle, though as ever you'd do well to check on its state beforehand, and bear in mind that your insurance won't cover journeys on unsurfaced roads. Basic **accommodation** and meals are available here at the *Hôtel-Restaurant Bougafer* (T035 78 38 09, F035 88 42 89; ❷) in the town centre near the market, which has ten simple but clean rooms with showers, and cheaper beds in tents on the roof. Across the street *La Gazelle du Sud* (T035 78 38 13; ❷) is the only alternative, with a handful of simple rooms and a basic restaurant. The best place in the town centre for a quick meal for those passing through is *Restaurant Palmiers* (T072 02 30 25); a simple café with friendly staff and reasonably priced traditional food.

Continuing west, the scenery grows wilder as you approach **TAZZARINE**, set in a grassy oasis surrounded by bare mountains. The town hosts a weekly souk on Wednesdays, and there's a petrol station and a straggling row of shops, but little else you'd want to stop for, unless you find yourself having to overnight here. The town's budget option is *Bougafer* (T024 83 90 05; ❷), with 20 basic rooms that share showers, toilets and a hammam. Its owner has opened a new hotel and **campsite** on the edge of town, *Village Touristique Bougafer*

(☎024 83 90 05; ❺), just past the start of the bridge over the *oued*, a character-less concrete motel with 50 rooms, bar, swimming pool, two large restaurants, and a parking lot for campers. RV drivers, however, will prefer the *Camping Amasttou* (☎024 83 90 78, ℉024 83 96 35; ❷), which is found down a track to the left on the way out of town at the Nekob junction in a shady patch of palmery and has a couple of simple **rooms** as well as tents. At the entrance to the site is a **prehistoric rock carving** transported from elsewhere; you can see them *in situ* at Tiouririne (7km) and Aït Ouazik (26km) and one of the camp staff will gladly act as a guide to these or other local sights. Alternatively, *Auberge Ait Idir Isdaoune* (☎024 83 92 57; ❷), seven kilometres from Tazzarine in the direction of Tanoumrhit, has a large camping area and simple double rooms for 150dhs. The best accommodation in the area by far lies 10km from Tazzarine on the Nekob road in the small village of Tamsahalte, signposted off the main road. ⚘ *Kasbah Riad du Sud* (☎024 83 58 15, ℉024 83 22 23, ⓦwww.hotelriaddusud.com; ❻) is a genuine immaculate riad built around a courtyard; the rooms are attractive and traditional, the food is exceptional, and the staff friendly.

Nekob

NEKOB, 160km west of Rissani and only 38km from the junction with the Drâa Valley road, dominates the most spectacular stretch of this route, its kasbah-studded old quarter looking north from the rim of an escarpment across a large palmery to the peaks of the Djebel Sarhro. The number of grand houses in the town testify to its former prominence as a market hub for the region, but out-migration has taken its toll in recent years, compounded by the impact of a protracted drought that has yellowed the palms and dried up many of the old irrigation courses. For trekkers, Nekob serves as an important staging post for adventures in the mountains to the north (see next page): the Bureau des Guides (☎067 48 75 09) on the main street can hook you up with guides and ponymen, and advise on routes. In anticipation of the tourist traffic that is bound to accompany the completion of the tarmac link between the Drâa and Rissani, a handful of smart hotels have also opened here. For the time being, however, this remains a refreshingly off-track destination which you can explore free of hassle; other than a couple of **prehistoric rock carvings** (*gravures rupestres*) sites across the valley (which you'll need help from your hotel or guesthouse to find), there's nothing much to see, but the traditional *pisé* architecture and fine views from the roof terraces tempt many visitors into staying longer than they intended.

Nekob boasts a surprisingly good choice of **places to stay**. At the entrance to the town (as you approach from Tazzarine), the *Auberge-Restaurant Enakhil Saghro* (☎024 83 97 19, ℉024 83 97 89; ❷) is a pleasant, efficiently run roadside motel with a kasbah-style facade and glorious café-terrace overlooking the palmery. Its rooms are nothing special, but they're clean and light, and the common bathrooms are kept spick and span. On the right hand side as you enter town from the direction of Tazzarine there is a sign for *Auberge Ait Aata* (☎024 83 97 51; ❶) a converted town house that's the town's budget option; rooms are simple and there is limited running water, but the friendly staff, beautifully painted salon ceilings and character of the place make up for what are quite modest surroundings. Across town in the heart of the old quarter, the *Baha Baha* (☎024 83 97 63, ⓦwww.kasbahbahabaha.com; ❺) is a much grander place occupying a splendid renovated kasbah. Its nicest rooms are those in the square towers on the upper floors, decorated with plush Moroccan textiles and carpets. Outside, the garden features a couple of mock-Berber encampments flanking a pool (where you can stay for 80dh), and the whole site enjoys a great panorama over the valley. Nearby, *Kasbah Imdoukal* (℡024 83 97 98, Ⓦwww .kasbahimdoukal.com; ❻) is a new upscale kasbah hotel with tastefully decorated rooms and a beautiful roof terrace which affords some of the best views of the palmeries in the area.

Posher still, the *Ksar Jenna* (℡067 96 32 48, Ⓕ024 83 97 91, Ⓦwww .ksarjenna.com; 800dh for 2 people, obligatory half-board) stands just beyond the western outskirts of town as you head towards Ouarzazate/Zagora. Owned and run by an Italian-Moroccan couple, it's a self-consciously chic place whose rooms, high-ceilinged dining hall and salon are stylishly furnished with ceramics and expensive textiles. But the highlight here is a lush garden filled with flowers, fruit trees and a good-sized pool.

Just before *Ksar Jenna* (heading from town), *Camping Les Berbers* is the best **camping** option in the area.

Into the Djebel Sarhro

From Nekob, a spectacular *piste* – covered by daily minibuses – heads north to crest the Djebel Sarhro via the **Tazi n' Tazazart**, eventually dropping into the Dadès Valley at Iknioun, near Boumalne du Dadès (see p.556). Winding through dramatic rock formations and gorges, the route rivals the crossing of the main Atlas chain, with superb views from the pass. An added incentive to do it is the spectacular **pinnacles of Bab n' Ali**, which you can reach in a half-day's walk from a pleasant, conveniently situated *gîte d'étape* with camping space and dorm beds. You could also use the *gîte* as a base for ascents of several peaks, guided by the *gardien*.

Merzouga and Erg Chebbi

The **Erg Chebbi** dunes at **MERZOUGA** are indisputably one of the great sights of Morocco. Rising to 150m in places, these giant sand hills lining the Algerian border may not be as imposing nor as extensive as some in North Africa, but they come closer than anywhere else in the country (at least, anywhere else that's relatively accessible) to fulfilling most people's expectations of what a true desert should be. French travellers, in particular, are drawn here in droves, and there is no shortage of locals on hand eager to fuel their Saharan fantasies. The result is that Merzouga can sometimes feel less like the *désert profond* than a Saharan circus, with groups of luxuriously turbaned tourists posing for photographs with *hommes bleus* under the acacia trees, astride camels or rallying Paris–Dakar around the sand ridges. To stand any chance of experiencing the scenery in its essential state, therefore, you should aim to come here out of season (January and February are the quietest months) and choose your spot very carefully. At the height of summer, the few visitors who brave the fierce heat to reach Merzouga are mostly Moroccans, attracted by the reputed power of the sands to cure rheumatism. Sufferers are buried up to the neck for a minute or two – any longer than that can be fatal.

Arrival, accommodation and eating

Thanks to the new road from Rissani, **getting to Merzouga** is easy these days. The only obstacle you'll face are the gangs of *faux guides* lying in wait at Erfoud

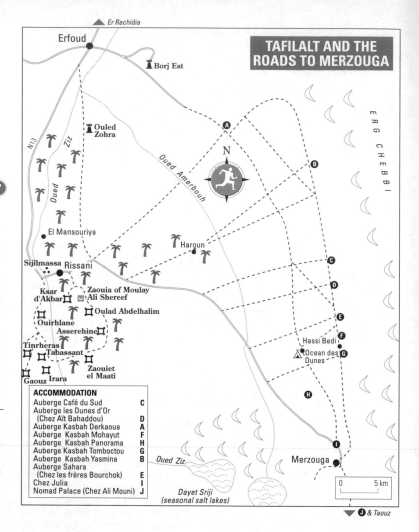

TAFILALT AND THE ROADS TO MERZOUGA

Er Rachidia

Erfoud

Borj Est

Ouled Zohra

N13

Ziz

Oued

El Mansouriya

Oued Amerbouh

Haroun

ERG CHEBBI

Sijilmassa Rissani

Ksar d'Akbar Zaouia of Moulay Ali Shereef

Oulad Abdelhalim

Ouirhlane Asserehine

Tinrheras Tabassant

Gaouz Irara Zaouiet el Maati

Hassi Bedi
Ocean des Dunes

Merzouga

Oued Ziz

Dayet Sriji (seasonal salt lakes)

0   5 km

J & Taouz

ACCOMMODATION

Auberge Café du Sud	C
Auberge les Dunes d'Or (Chez Aït Bahaddou)	D
Auberge Kasbah Derkaoua	A
Auberge Kasbah Mohayut	F
Auberge Kasbah Panorama	H
Auberge Kasbah Tomboctou	G
Auberge Kasbah Yasmina	B
Auberge Sahara (Chez les frères Bourchok)	E
Chez Julia	I
Nomad Palace (Chez Ali Mouni)	J

and Rissani, who'll try to convince you the road doesn't exist, that it's closed, or that you need a guide to find it, in an attempt to divert you to a hotel that will pay them commission. The welcoming posse is most vociferous at Merzouga village itself, where arrival by public transport can be as intimidating as almost anywhere in Morocco; the best tactic, as ever, is to **book your accommodation in advance** and try, if you don't have the luxury of your own vehicle, to get your hotel to meet you on arrival.

Before leaving Rissani, you'll also need to get a firm fix on where your chosen hotel actually is (see map above). **Places to stay** are strung across a wide area, nestled at the foot of the dunes in a straggling line. *Pistes* to them peel east off the main road at regular intervals (at junctions flagged by signboards), but this final leg across rough *hammada* can be a long one if you stay at the northern-most group of hotels, some of which lie more than 15km off the tarmac. The *pistes* are marked with coloured posts; if you're driving in a standard rental car, don't be tempted to improvise as there are many patches of soft sand where you might easily get stuck. Should this happen, rest assured that help will never be too far away, but expect to pay dearly for a 4 x4 rescue.

There is a **post office** and **internet café** in Merzouga as well as a few unremarkable **café-restaurants**; you'll get a much better deal if you eat at your hotel, paying an inclusive half- or full-board rate. The **auberges** reviewed below are listed from north to south. The majority of hotels offer a range of differently priced facilities, from comfy en-suite rooms with hot showers to basic beds in Berber tents. Outside high season, rates are surprisingly low, mainly because most places make their real money on camel trips as well as the fact that the steadily increasing number of *auberges* has led to a competition to reduce rates in order to attract custom.

Auberges

Auberge Café du Sud ☏061 21 61 66, ✉aubergedusud@gmail.com. Large *pisé* building whose rear terrace, dotted in oleanders, opens straight onto the sand. The welcoming owners, Ahmed and Mohamed Noghou, offer three categories of room: the more expensive ones (200dh) are larger, cleaner and tiled, with en-suite shower and toilet. ②–③

Auberge les Dunes d'Or (Chez Aït Bahaddou) ☏061 35 06 65, ⊛www.aubergedunesdor.com. A larger place built around a courtyard, 6km off the road (follow the pink and white posts). Once again, there are two types of room – dark standards and brighter, pricier tiled ones, as well as Berber tents. There's a deep swimming pool in the courtyard and great views extend from the sand hillock behind where there's a rusting fuselage of a plane used in a film of Antoine de Saint-Lxupéry's fable, *Le Petit Prince*. ②

🏃 **Auberge Kasbah Derkaoua** ☏035 57 71 40. Beautiful *pisé* complex in traditional style, set amid olive, almond and fruit orchards on the northern fringes of Erg Chebbi. The patron, Michel, was a *méhariste* in the French camel corps and enjoys a reputation as one of the best hosts in the country. His ten en suite rooms are comfortable enough, but you'll probably want to spend more time lazing in the lovely garden, which has two plunge pools and Berber tents. Recommended for animal lovers. Half-board (400dh per person) obligatory. Closed Jan, July & Aug. ⑥

🏃 **Auberge Kasbah Mohayut** Ksar Hassi Labiad ☏066 03 91 85, ✉mohamezan @yahoo.fr. Among the most appealing of the mid-range options. Very comfy, imaginatively furnished rooms in a modern *pisé* kasbah centred on an arcaded courtyard, bang opposite the highest dunes in Erg Chebbi. Count on around 200dh per head for (optional) half-board. ②–③

Auberge Kasbah Panorama ☏062 08 55 73, ✉aubergepanorama@yahoo.fr. Run by the hospitable Aït Bahaddou family (of *Les Dunes d'Or* fame) this budget *auberge* stands further from the sand than most, at the top of a hill outside Merzouga, but the views are stupendous: the sunset terrace enjoys arguably the best panorama this side of the Atlas. The rooms are well aired and pleasant, too, and the restaurant serves tasty tajines and *madfouna* ("pizza Berber"). ②–③

Auberge Kasbah Tombouctou ☏035 57 70 91, ⊛www.xalucamaadid.com. Part of the Xaluca chain of upscale hotels. Rooms are luxurious though a bit garish. There's a hammam, large pool, bar, and expensive restaurant. The overall glamour is somewhat out of place on the edge of the desert. ⑥

🏃 **Auberge-Kasbah Yasmina** ☏035 57 67 83, ✉yasminadesert@yahoo.fr. Old-established budget *auberge* right on the dunes, beside the seasonal lake where you might see flamingos if it's rained. The situation is spectacular and views from the sunny rear terrace superb. The rooms are pleasant and cool and most are now en suite. There is a large grouping of Berber tents at the edge of the dunes where you can stay for 50dh per person. Skis and snowboards are available for rent and they offer camel safaris at standard rates (325dh per person all in). ③–④

Auberge Sahara (Chez les frères Bourchok) Ksar Hassi Labiad ☏035 57 70 39, ⊛www .auberge-sahara-merzouga.com. Well-managed hotel with spacious, immaculately tiled rooms, relaxing Moroccan salon and fine views of the dunes from a rear terrace where you can chill out under huge palms. Rooms to fit any price range and better-than-average showers. Half-board 200dh per person. ①–⑤

🏃 **Chez Julia** ☏070 18 13 60. Situated within the village in a traditional desert house this small *auberge* is defined by an appealing combination of comfort and authenticity. Owned and run by Austrian painter and former church restorer, Julia Günther, the *auberge* has a handful of uniquely decorated colour-themed rooms. The à la carte menu features a combination of Moroccan and Austrian dishes all freshly prepared at reasonable prices. ❷–❸

Nomad Palace, Chez Ali Mouni 7km south of Merzouga, at Ksar Merzouga ☎ 061 56 36 11, ⓦ www.adventureswithali.com. The dunes aren't as high at this southern end of Erg Chebbi, but the area's much more peaceful as a result: you can expect to have the sand to yourself here for most of the year. The *auberge* itself boasts a huge Moroccan salon with open fire, and well-furnished rooms opening onto a quiet courtyard garden. Owner Ali Mouni also runs camel trips to a lesser frequented area on the far, east side of Erg Chebbi, via a more varied route than normal; and he takes guests out to hear wonderful Gnaoua music at a remote village nearby. Recommended for Land Rover enthusiasts. ❸

Camping

Ocean Des Dunes Ksar Hassi Labied ☎ 066 91 17 26. A cheap campsite overlooking the dunes with a small restaurant and four simple rooms. The best option for those with their own camping gear or RV. ❶

The dunes and camel trips

Tourist literature loves to give the impression the Merzouga **dunes** are the start of a vast sand sea, but compared with the *erg* of southern Algeria they're more of a pond – 28km from north to south and only 7km across at their widest point. The highest are those in the centre of the Erg Chebbi, near, or just north of, Merzouga village. Rising dramatically from a plain of blackened *hammada*, they're spectacular at any time of day, but early morning and late evening are the best times to view them. To find a relatively peaceful ridge free of footprints, however, you'll have to be prepared to walk for an hour or else arrange a **camel trip** through one of the *auberges* listed on p.595 and above. These can cost anywhere between 50dh and 100dh for a short amble of one to three hours, to 250–350dh for an overnight excursion taking you deep into the dunes to a camp of Berber tents, where you'll be well placed to enjoy the stars and a memorable sunrise the following day. A guide/cameleer, meals, tea and blankets are included in the price, but it's advisable to bring extra clothes and a sleeping bag – nights out on the sand can get excruciatingly cold.

Desert wildlife and the lake

Merzouga makes an excellent centre for the exploration of Morocco's sandy (or "true") desert, whose flora and fauna show ingenious adaptations to these least hospitable of living conditions. Bird-watchers will find most of interest. In early spring a lake, **Dayet Srji**, just to the west of Merzouga village, used to attract scores of pink flamingos, ruddy sheldrake and the rare Kittllitz's plover, but it hasn't formed for the past few years because of the drought. Water levels permitting, during the spring migration the bushes in the area may also harbour desert sparrow, Tristram's desert warbler, Egyptian nightjar and Arabian bustard.

The desert is also an ideal environment for **reptiles**, including the Algerian sand lizard and Berber skink, and typical **desert mammals** – more often located by their giveaway tracks in the morning sand than by nocturnal sightings – include the jerboa, desert hedgehog and fennec (desert fox).

Plant life is limited because of the extreme scarcity of water; the only survivors include the lichens and algae which can take up sufficient water from the condensation of dew which forms on the undersurfaces of rocks and stones, although even the desert has an all-too-brief **spring bloom** when the rains do come – dominated by pink asphodels and mauve statice.

△ Erg Chebbi Dunes

Each outfit works its own jealously guarded routes and camps, but it can be a matter of luck whether you hit a crowded section of the dunes or not. Basically, the further from the main agglomeration of *auberges* you go, the more chance you have of avoiding other camel trains and – even more importantly – 4x4 drivers whose antics can ruin the peace and quiet. Off-road traffic tends to peak around the time of the **Paris–Dakar Rally**, which hurtles straight through Merzouga sometime in January, bringing convoys of motor enthusiasts and sending hotel rates sky high.

East to Bouarfa and Figuig

The six- to eight-hour desert journey from **Er Rachidia to Figuig** (pronounced F'geeg) is spectacular in its isolation and scenically extraordinary: the real outlands of Morocco, dominated by huge empty landscapes and blank red mountains. It used to be quite a common route for travellers intent on entering Algeria, in the south, but the civil war there has ended such traffic and the border is closed. It is thus a somewhat perverse route to take – a lot of travelling in order to complete a loop via Bouarfa to northern Morocco at Oujda. You can, however, make the journey easily enough by car, the only diversion being the roadside *gendarmerie* who pass the time collecting car numbers and your mother's maiden name. Their concern makes more sense when you note the proximity of the "undefined boundary" with Algeria, shown on some maps and running parallel to the road.

It's 378km from **Er Rachidia** to **Figuig** via **Boudnib** and **Bouarfa**, and a further 386km from **Figuig** to **Oujda** via **Bouarfa** (see p.216), with few sights along the way.

Figuig

The southern oases are traditionally measured by the number of their palms, rather than in terms of area or population. **FIGUIG**, with something like 200,000 trees, has long been one of the largest – an importance enhanced by its strategic border position. The oasis has even less of an administrative town than usual, still basically consisting of its seven distinct villages which in the past feuded almost continuously over water and grazing rights.

At least twice Figuig has been lost by Morocco – in the seventeenth-century wars, and again at the end of Moulay Ismail's reign – and as recently as 1975 there was fighting in the streets here between Moroccan and Algerian troops. In recent decades the settlement reverted to a quiet existence, with a modest trade from its frontier position – including a trickle of tourists crossing into southern Algeria. Since the **Algerian civil war** erupted in the mid-1990s, however, the border has been effectively sealed and Figuig's economy has virtually collapsed.

Practicalities

Orientation is relatively simple, with almost everything on the road by which you enter the town. *Hôtel Figuig* (☎036 89 93 09; ❸), less than half a kilometre beyond the town centre, is the only current accommodation option. The rooms have hot showers and balconies, the restaurant is good, with menus from 70dh, and the view down the valley to the closed border, and Algeria beyond, is stunning. There is also a secure area for camping and a café that shares the hotel's famous views. There's a couple of **internet cafes** and a branch of the Banque Populaire, in town. Try the *Café de la Paix* for **snacks**, or the *Café Oasis* in the little park. Beyond that, there is nowhere else to eat.

Buses tend to arrive, and leave from the CTM office on the main street, with services to Oujda leaving early in the morning. Tickets are sold in advance but, as each bus is owned by a different company, you'll need to ask around to find out where to buy the ticket for the bus of your choice. Heading for **Er Rachidia,** there are just two buses a day from Bouarfa (at 8am and 2pm); you will need to catch the 5am bus from Figuig if you want to avoid a long wait at Bouarfa.

Exploring the ksour

Figuig's seven ksour are dispersed out of the oasis proper and in open ground at the base of the hill – each enclosing its own palmery within high turreted walls. Although sporadically organized into a loose confederation, they were until the last century fiercely independent – and their relations with each other were peppered with long and bitter blood feuds and, above all, disputes over the limited water supply. Their strange, archaic shape – with watchtowers rising above the snaking *feggaguir* (or irrigation channels) – evolved as much from this internal tension as from any need to protect themselves from the nomadic tribes of the desert. Likewise, within each of the *ksour*, the elaborate tunnel-like networks of alleys are deliberate (and successful) attempts to prevent any sudden or easy progress.

Your best chance of getting an overview of it all is to head for the *platforme*, a man-made lookout poised above the *ksar* of **Zenaga.** The view from here spans a large part of the palmery and its pink-tinged *ksour*, and you can gaze at the weird, multicoloured layers of the enclosing mountains. If you can find the energy – Figuig in summer feels a little like sitting inside a fan-heater – head down into Zenaga, the largest and richest of the seven villages. Going to your left, you should reach its centre, more developed than most in this area, with a couple of shops and a café in addition to a mosque. For a look at the other *ksour*, you would be well advised to hire someone local, preferably through your hotel, to guide you.

El Maiz is the prettiest village, with small vaulted lanes and houses with broad verandahs. In **El Hamam**, as the name suggests, there is a hot spring, used by the people for their ablutions. Anyone offering their services as a guide will take you to it. Back on the other side of the administrative road is the **Ksar el Oudarhir**, which also has some natural springs (one hot, one salty), and terraces similar to the ones in El Maiz.

All of the *ksour* have exclusively Berber populations, though up until the 1950s and 1960s there was also a considerable Jewish population. Until the beginning of the twentieth century, Figuig was also the final Moroccan staging point on the overland journey to Mecca.

Figuig to Oujda

Unless you have a strange fascination for very small town life, there is really nowhere else on this eastern plateau between Figuig and Oujda which offers much temptation. **TENDRARA** (Tuesday market) and **AÏT BENIMATHAR** both have basic café-hotels, if you need to stay overnight. Aït Benimathar is the better choice – a quiet little **hot water oasis**, full of tortoises and snakes. Even if you don't want to stay, it's not a bad place to spend the middle of an afternoon, which you can do by taking the early morning bus from Figuig, then catching a later one for the final 50km to Oujda.

Travel details

Buses

Erfoud to: Er Rachidia (4 daily; 1hr 30min); Fes (1 daily; 11hr); Rissani (4 daily; 1hr 30min); Tinerhir, via Tinejdad (2 daily; 8hr 30min).

Er Rachidia to: Casablanca (1 CTM daily; 10hr 15min); Erfoud/Rissani (12 daily; 1hr 30 min/3hr); Fes (10 daily; 8hr 30min); Figuig (1 daily via Bouarfa; 10hr); Marrakesh (1 CTM daily; 9hr 45min); Meknes (5 daily; 8hr); Midelt (5 daily; 3hr 30 min); Tinerhir (2 daily; 3hr).

Figuig to: Er Rachidia (via Bouarfa; 1 daily; 10hr); Oujda (4 daily; 7hr).

Ouarzazate to: Agadir (1 CTM daily; 8hr 30min); Casablanca (1 CTM daily; 8hr 20min); Er Rachidia (1 CTM, Tues, Thurs); Marrakesh (2 CTM & 6 others daily; 4–5hr); M'hamid (1 CTM daily; 7hr); Taliouine/Taroudannt (2 CTM daily; 3hr 30 min/5hr); Tinerhir (3 daily; 5hr); Zagora (1daily; 4hr).

Rissani to: Meknes (1 CTM daily; 8hr 30min); Tinejdad/Goulmima (1 daily; 3hr 30 min/4hr); Zagora (2 CTM weekly; 10hr).

Tazenakht to: Agadir (1 CTM & 4 others daily; 6hr) via Taliouine (1hr 30min) and Taroudannt (3hr 30min); Er Rachidia (1 daily; 6hr) via Tinerhir (3hr); Foum Zguid (3 daily; 1hr 30min); Goulimine (2 daily; 10hr 30min) via Tiznit (8hr); Marrakesh (1 CTM & 2 others daily; 6hr 30min); Ouarzazate (2 CTM & 8 others daily; 1hr 30min); Tan Tan (1 daily; 16hr 30min); Tata (3 daily; 4hr), Zagora (1 daily; 4hr 30min).

Tinerhir to: Er Rachidia (2 daily; 3hr); Ouarzazate (3 daily; 5hr); Rissani (2 daily; 4hr).

Zagora to: M'hamid (2 daily; 2hr); Marrakesh (2 daily; 9–11hr); Ouarzazate (4 daily; 4–5hr).

Grands Taxis

Boumalne to: Minivan taxis at least daily to Msemrir (3hr). Regular run to Tinerhir (50min).

Erfoud to: Fairly frequent runs to Rissani (1hr 30min) and Erfoud (2hr). Land Rover trips direct to Merzouga (1hr; relatively expensive).

Er Rachidia to: Fairly frequent runs to Erfoud (along the route you can negotiate a ticket to Meski) and to Tinejdad (2hr).

Ouarzazate to: Regularly to Zagora (3hr). Negotiable for Skoura (1hr) and Aït Benhaddou (1hr 45min, but expensive private trip).

Tinerhir to: Regular runs to Boumalne (50min) and Tinejdad (1hr; from there on to Er Rachidia).

Zagora to: Regularly to Ouarzazate (3hr); lorries to Rissani (10hr) and Foum Zguid (8hr).

Flights

Ouarzazate to: Casablanca (1 daily; 45min); Paris-Orly (Mon & Fri; 3hr 25min).

Agadir, the Souss and Anti-Atlas

CHAPTER 8

Highlights

* **Agadir beach** Golden sand, top-class hotels and sun pretty much all year round make this the country's number one seaside resort. **See p.614**

* **Surfing at Taghazout** Morocco's top surfing spot, a village beach resort with a whole series of excellent right breaks attracting tubehounds both local and foreign. **See p.623**

* **Taroudannt** Once the capital, this delightful walled town with two markets and bags of character is nowadays being dubbed "mini Marrakesh" by the tourist industry. **See p.627**

* **Ancient rock carvings** Across the whole region between Tafraoute and Tata, these prehistoric artworks attest to a time when elephants and giraffes roamed this neck of the woods. **See p.644**

* **Tafraoute** Tucked away in the Anti-Atlas mountains amid a landscape of strange rock formations, this friendly little town makes a great base to explore them from. **See p.651**

* **Sidi Ifni** A former Spanish enclave built from scratch in the 1930s with an Art Deco town hall, an Art Deco mosque, even an Art Deco lighthouse. **See p.662**

△ Agadir beach

Agadir, the Souss and Anti-Atlas

Southern Morocco's major tourist destination is **Agadir**, completely rebuilt after an earthquake flattened it in 1960, and now a popular beach resort with a fine sweep of sand, though very deliberately developed, and not a place to seek out "the real Morocco". To its north, **Taghazout**, still just a small fishing village, has become Morocco's number one surfing resort. Inland, **Paradise Valley** is a beautiful and exotic palm gorge, from which a mountain road trails up to the now-nearly-dry waterfalls of **Immouzer des Ida Outanane** – a superb one- or two-day trip. South of Agadir, the beaches are scarcely developed, ranging from solitary campsites at **Sidi Rbat** – one of Morocco's best locations for bird-watching – and **Sidi Moussa d'Aglou**, down to the old port of **Sidi Ifni** only relinquished by Spain in 1969 and full of splendid Art Deco colonial architecture.

Just over an hour away from Agadir, **Taroudannt**, capital of the wide and fertile Souss valley, has massive walls, animated souks and good hotels – a natural place to stay on your way to Marrakesh (which can be reached over the spectacular **Tizi n'Test** pass) or Ouarzazate. Further south, into the Anti-Atlas mountains, **Tafraoute** and its valley are even more compelling – the stone-built villages and villas set amid a stunning landscape of pink granite and vast rock formations.

For those with more time, a number of adventurous *piste* and desert trips can be made in the region. One of the best is the **Tata loop**, a surfaced but little-travelled road across the southern Anti-Atlas to the pre-Sahara. A more well-trodden route is down to **Tiznit**, quite a charming little walled town, though little more than a century old, and **Goulimine**, promoted by the tourist trade for its camel market, but most of interest as a stopping-off point for Sidi Ifni, local oases or the Western Sahara.

Agadir

AGADIR was, by all accounts, a characterful port, prior to the terrible earthquake of 1960 that completely destroyed it. Just four years into independence,

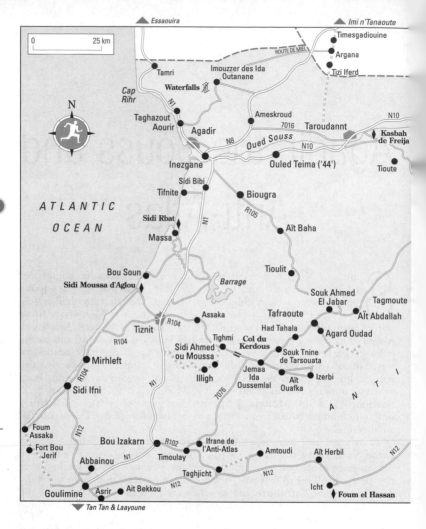

it was an especially traumatic event, which created a great will to re-create a city that showed Morocco in its best, modern face. Nearly half a century on, the result is quite impressive, with swathes of park and garden breaking up the hotel and residential zones. The beach, too, is magnificent and untrammelled by Spanish Costa-style high-rise building. However, it's hard to escape the feeling that the city lacks soul, and though the lack of bustle has novelty value coming from any other Moroccan town, it doesn't exactly merit a stay unless you just want to hang out on the beach.

Perhaps the city is best treated as a staging post – or a place to rest up – before moving on to Marrakesh, Essaouira, Taroudannt or Tafraoute. If you are booked on an Agadir package, you should certainly look at making a number of excursions, through your holiday company or going it alone. Renting a car for two or three days, the towns above are all in striking distance, while **Paradise Valley**

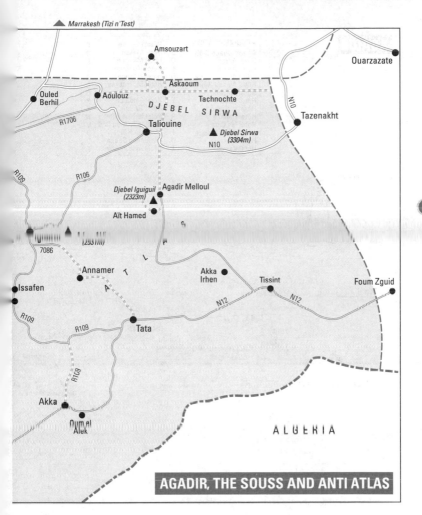

AGADIR, THE SOUSS AND ANTI ATLAS

and the waterfalls of **Immouzer des Ida Outanane** (see p.625), up in the mountains, are easy local trips.

Some history

Agadir's **history** closely parallels that of Morocco's other Atlantic ports. It was colonized first by the Portuguese in the fifteenth century, then, recaptured by the Saadians in the sixteenth, carried on its trading with intermittent prosperity, overshadowed, more often than not, by the activities of Mogador (Essaouira) and Mazagan (El Jadida).

Abroad, Agadir's name was known mainly for a crisis in colonial squabbling during the run-up to World War I (see box, p.606). The really big event in Agadir's history, however, was the devastating earthquake of February 29, 1960: a tremor that killed 15,000 and left most of the remaining 50,000 population

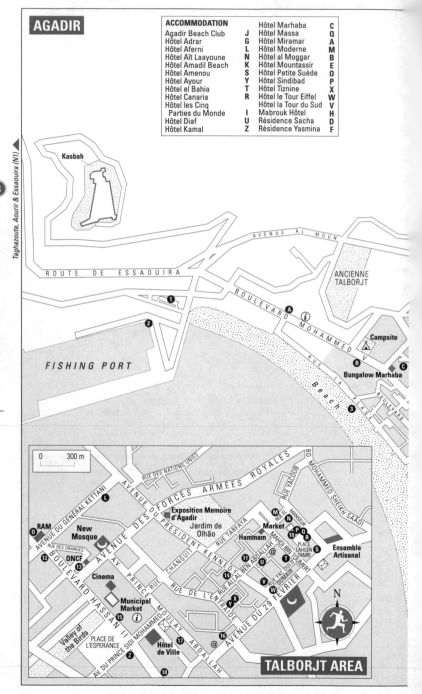

AGADIR

ACCOMMODATION

Agadir Beach Club	J	Hôtel Marhaba	C
Hôtel Adrar	G	Hôtel Massa	Q
Hôtel Aferni	L	Hôtel Miramar	A
Hôtel Aït Laayoune	N	Hôtel Moderne	M
Hôtel Amadil Beach	K	Hôtel al Moggar	B
Hôtel Amenou	S	Hôtel Mountassir	E
Hôtel Ayour	Y	Hôtel Petite Suède	O
Hôtel el Bahia	T	Hôtel Sindibad	P
Hôtel Canaria	R	Hôtel Tiznine	X
Hôtel les Cinq		Hôtel le Tour Eiffel	W
Parties du Monde	I	Hôtel la Tour du Sud	V
Hôtel Diaf	U	Mabrouk Hôtel	H
Hôtel Kamal	Z	Résidence Sacha	D
		Résidence Yasmina	F

Kasbah

AVENUE AL MOUN

ROUTE DE ESSAOUIRA

ANCIENNE
TALBORJT

BOULEVARD MOHAMMED

A ⓘ

Campsite

RUE LA PLAGE

B

Bungalow Marhaba

C

FISHING PORT

Beach

BOULEVARD

③

①

②

0   300 m

RUE DES NATIONS UNIES

AVENUE DES FORCES ARMÉES ROYALES

BD MOHAMMED SHEIKH SAADI

RUE YACOUB

AVENUE DU GÉNÉRAL KETTANI

L

**Exposition Memoire
d'Agadir**

Jardim de
Olhão

RUE MANSOUR

M RUE **N**

Market

P Q R

PLACE
LAHCEN
TAMRI

10

AVENUE DU PRÉSIDENT KENNEDY

RUE TARFAYA

Hammam

MAHDJ IBN TOUMERT

S

**Ensemble
Artisanal**

O RAM

**New
Mosque**

RUE DES ORANGES

12 BOULEVARD HASSAN II **13** ONCF

AV PRINCE RUE RUE

RUE CHANGUITT

RUE DE L'ENTRAIDE

RUE ALLAL BEN ABDALLAH

11

@

RUE FAL OULD OUMAIR

U

14

V W

AVENUE DU 29 FEVRIER

Cinema

**Municipal
Market**

ⓘ

15

**Valley
of
the Birds**

PLACE DE
L'ESPERANCE

RUE MOULAY MOHAMMED

Z

AV. DU PRINCE SIDI MOHAMMED

RUE MOULAY ABDALLAH

X
Y

16

17

**Hôtel
de Ville**

18

N

TALBORJT AREA

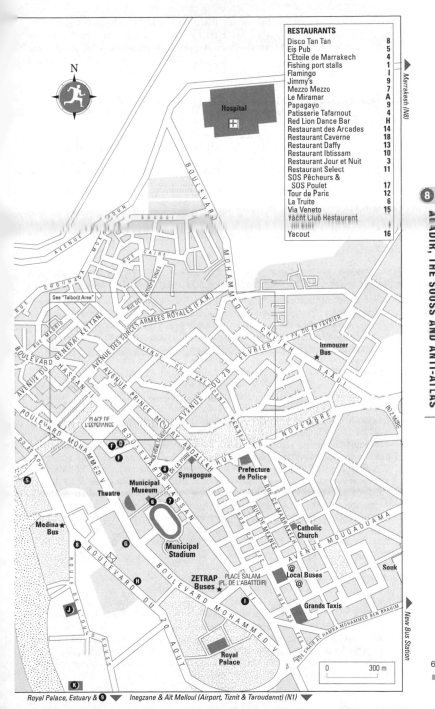

RESTAURANTS

Disco Tan Tan	8
Eis Pub	5
L'Étoile de Marrakech	4
Fishing port stalls	1
Flamingo	
Jimmy's	9
Mezzo Mezzo	7
Le Miramar	A
Papagayo	9
Patisserie Tafarnout	4
Red Lion Dance Bar	H
Restaurant des Arcades	14
Restaurant Caverne	18
Restaurant Daffy	13
Restaurant Ibtissam	10
Restaurant Jour et Nuit	3
Restaurant Select	11
SOS Pêcheurs &	
SOS Poulet	17
Tour de Paris	12
La Truite	6
Via Veneto	15
Yacht Club Restaurant	
Yacout	16

Hospital

Marrakesh (N8)

BOULEVARD MOULOUD

AVENUE

RUE CAIRE

RUE

CHOUHADA

RUE DES NATIONS UNIES

See "Talborjt Area"

RUE MAGRID

BOULEVARD DU GENERAL KETTANI

AVENUE DES FORCES ARMEES ROYALES (F.A.R.)

AVENUE

BOULEVARD HASSAN I

AVENUE DU HASSAN I

AVENUE DU PRESIDENT

AVENUE DU 29 FEVRIER

AV. DU 29 FEVRIER

CHEIKH SAADI

Immouzer Bus ★

AVENUE PRINCE MOULAY ABDALLAH

PLACE DE L'ESPERANCE

BOULEVARD MOHAMMED V

RUE DE LA FOIRE

AVENUE DU 18 NOVEMBRE

AV. 2 MARS

F D

F

⑤

Medina ★ Bus

⑧

Synagogue

④

Municipal Museum

Theatre

⑥ ⑦

Prefecture de Police

RUE DE MARRAKECH

RUE DE MEKNES

Catholic Church

AVENUE MOUQAOUAMA

G

Municipal Stadium

BOULEVARD HASSAN

Souk

H

BOULEVARD DU 20 AOUT

ZETRAP Buses ★

PLACE SALAM (PL. DE L'ABATTOIR)

Local Buses

@

@

J

I

Grands Taxis

ROUTE DE L'OUED SOUSS

BOULEVARD MOHAMMED V

RUE DE FES

RUE CHAIR AT HAMRA MOHAMMED BEN BRAHIM

K

Royal Palace

New Bus Station

N

0   300 m

607

homeless. In the aftermath, the whole place had to be rebuilt from scratch. Yet, though the events of 1960 still leave a traumatic scar in its memory, Agadir has recovered well. It is now Morocco's fifth-biggest city with a population of some 700,000. Its main industry, as will be immediately apparent to even a casual visitor, is tourism.

Orientation, information, arrival and city transport

"Downtown" Agadir is centred on the junction of **Boulevard Hassan II** and **Avenue Prince Moulay Abdallah** with **Avenue du Prince Sidi Mohammed**. Rebuilt in 1960s "modernist" style, it has all the trappings of a town centre, with office blocks, a tourist office, post office, Hôtel de Ville (town hall), municipal market and banks. Just to the northeast is an area known as **Talborjt**, where there is a concentration of budget hotels, local café-restaurants and, until the opening of the new bus station, most of the long-distance bus company offices. The fancier hotels are grouped along the avenues parallel to the beach: **Boulevard Mohammed V**, **Boulevard Hassan II** and **Boulevard du 20 Août**.

The Agadir Crisis

Morocco's strategic position at the mouth of the Mediterranean made it a big prize for the European colonial powers dividing up Africa at the beginning of the twentieth century. It was France that most had its beady eye on Morocco, as it lay next to Algeria, which the French already occupied. Germany, keen to limit France's influence, opposed the French claim on Morocco by strongly supporting Moroccan independence. France had just signed a new treaty with Britain, the Entente Cordiale, effectively an alliance against Germany, but the Germans believed they could use Britain and France's conflicting interests in Morocco to undermine the alliance. This policy failed spectacularly in 1905 however, when a visit by Kaiser Wilhelm to Tangier, apparently to reconfirm German recognition of Morocco's independence, only spurred Britain and Spain to cut a deal with France in order to keep the Germans out.

Franco-German rivalry blew up again in 1908 when French troops marched into the Kaiser's Casablanca embassy to seize three German deserters from the Foreign Legion. The dispute was eventually settled by international arbitration, but it was soon overshadowed by a much more serious incident, the **Agadir Crisis** of 1911.

Following a rebellion led by a pretender to the throne in northern Morocco, French troops occupied Fes, supposedly to protect the sultan and maintain order. The action riled both Britain and Spain, and the Germans saw a chance to hammer a wedge between their enemies. Claiming to be acting in defence of German subjects, Germany sent a warship, the *Panther*, to Agadir bay, and demanded that if France took control of Morocco, it should give Germany the Congo in exchange. To Germany's dismay, however, Britain backed France. In a speech at London's Mansion House, David Lloyd George – previously regarded as the British government's most pro-German and anti-war minister – threatened war on the side of France if Germany failed to withdraw. The Germans hastily recalled the *Panther* in exchange for a small strip of land in the Congo, leaving the French to split Morocco with Spain, while Britain got Cyprus and Egypt.

When war did come to Europe, three years later, the Entente Cordiale had been tried and tested. Britain and France, enemies for centuries, became allies against the Germans. Morocco meanwhile was left under European rule along with the rest of Africa, not to regain its independence for over forty years.

Agadir is for the most part a **walkable** city, though you may want to use petits taxis for transport between the Talborjt bus station and the beach hotels, or for getting to the grand taxi terminal at Place Salam. Alternatively, you can rent **mopeds** or **motor-bikes** (see p.618), which would also allow you to explore the beaches north and south of town.

There are also a few useful local bus routes: fares for most of these bus trips are 3.30dh on the municipal RATAG buses, which mainly operate out of Place Salam, or 4dh on the privately run ZETRAP services, which operate from the western end of Avenue Mouqaouama, just across Boulevard Hassan II from Place Salam.

RATAG #12 Place Salam – Av Mohammed V – Tamraght – Taghazout
ZETRAP #25, #28 Av Mohammed V – Place Salam – Inezgane
ZETRAP #60 Av Mouqaouama – Av Mohammed V – Tamraght – Taghazout
ZETRAP #61 Av Mouqaouama – Tamraght – Taghazout – Tamri
ZETRAP #50 Av Mouqaouama – Tamraght – Aourir – Imi Miki

To the southeast of Talborjt is a more working-class residential area and the **Place Salam local bus station**. To the northeast stands a hilly, grassed area known as **Ancienne Talborjt** – a memorial to the earthquake, under which lie the remains of the old Medina, which were bulldozed for fear of typhoid breaking out. Further north still, around the old **kasbah**, and beyond it, stands the new industrial port and suburb of **Anza**. Another industrial zone spreads south towards Inezgane.

The **ONMT** tourist office is in Immeuble Iguenwane, on Avenue Mohammed V west of town towards the port (Mon–Fri 8.30am–4.30pm; ☎028 84 63 77). Previously, there was also a locally-run tourist office called the *Syndicat d'Initiative* on Boulevard Mohammed V, opposite the end of Avenue Général Kettani (☎028 82 18 21), but this was closed at last check and it was not clear whether or not it would reopen.

Arrival

Agadir's **Al Massira airport** is 25km east of the city. It is well equipped and stays open all night, though the restaurants are closed from around 7pm (a small coffee bar stays open till 11pm), and car-rental offices open only during normal office hours and are closed on Sundays. At least one bank is generally open all the time, but taxis will usually accept foreign currency if you are unable to change it.

Holiday companies run their own buses to meet flights and shuttle passengers to their hotels, and if you've bought a flight-only deal it's worth tagging along with fellow passengers. If you don't get one of these, airport officials will direct you to the **grands taxis** outside, which charge a standard 150dh fare (200dh at night) to Agadir, or 100dh to Inezgane (13km southeast of Agadir; see p.620), which covers up to six passengers. If you plan to share a fare, arrange this inside the terminal. There is no bus to downtown Agadir, but if you don't want to shell out for a grand taxi, you can get to Inezgane on the blue and white GAB #22 bus from outside the airport building (every 40min; 6am–8pm; 4dh), and from there take a local ZETRAP bus or shared grand taxi (4dh) to Agadir. If you are planning to move straight on from Agadir, you would in any case be best off heading for Inezgane, from where there's a greater choice of onward transport, especially if you intend to travel by grand taxi. The #22 drops you off right next to the grand taxi stand in Inezgane; for the *gare routière* (bus station), just walk across to the other side of the grand taxi stand.

Renting a car at the airport on arrival should be no problem, as several agencies have branches there, including First Car (☎028 83 92 97), Budget (☎028 83 91 01), Europcar (☎028 83 90 66), Hertz (☎028 83 90 71), National (☎028 83 91 21) and Avis (☎028 83 92 44). Driving from the airport, you are well positioned for a first night at Agadir (30min drive), Taroudannt (45min), or even Marrakesh (about 4hr).

At present, most **long-distance buses** serving Agadir will drop you off at Rue Yacoub el Mansour, behind Place Lahcen Tamri (see map inset p.606), which is where the old *gare routière* stood. Exceptions are buses run by the train company ONCF, in conjunction with Supratours, which leave passengers outside their office in Rue des Oranges, off Boulevard Hassan II. This should change when Agadir's new bus station is completed, supposedly in mid-2007. The new terminus will be southeast of the centre on Rue Chair al Hamra Mohammed ben Brahim, just beyond the souk, and all long-distance buses should arrive at and leave from there, though there are fears that the new bus station will not have the capacity to handle all the buses that need to use it.

In any case, if you're coming in by bus from the south, you might find yourself dropped at Inezgane, 13km southeast (see p.620). Even buses continuing to Agadir may stop for an hour at Inezgane, so it's probably best to continue by local bus (ZETRAP #24, #25, #28, #40 or #45) or grand taxi (3dh a place), either of which will drop you by the local bus and grand taxi terminal at Place Salam (also called Place de l'Abattoir).

Accommodation

Agadir has a vast number of **hotels**, tourist apartments, "holiday villages" and self-catering *résidences* (in which the rooms are effectively suites with kitchenettes), but in high-season periods – Christmas/New Year, Easter, July and August – it is still worth booking ahead. Out of season, you can often get **discounts** at the large, four-star hotels, but budget hotels are much less likely to alter their rates. If you plan to move out of Agadir more or less immediately, you might be better off staying at **Inezgane** (see p.620), where budget hotels are cheaper, and where you have a greater number of long-distance buses and shared grands taxis for destinations in the south of Morocco.

Talborjt/city centre

Most of the budget hotels are in **Talborjt**, with more upmarket places in the city centre. Talborjt has the advantage of good shops, cafés and street life, whereas the centre is a bit bleak and lifeless.

Cheap

Hôtel Aït Laayoune Rue Yacoub el Mansour ☎028 82 43 75. Cheap and friendly, with shared shower facilities but constant hot water. The rooms are basic but clean. ❷

Hôtel Amenou 1 Rue Yacoub el Mansour ☎028 84 15 56. A plain and simple hotel with showers in some of the rooms, hot water round the clock, and a roof terrace in case you fancy a spot of sunbathing. On the downside, the bus stands are right outside, which can make it a bit noisy if you

get a room at the front, and some of the beds are soft and springy, so check yours before taking the room. ❶

Hôtel el Bahia Rue el Mahdi Ibn Toumert ☎028 82 27 24, ℉028 82 45 15. A fine little two-star hotel, beautifully modernized with three categories of room (with shower and toilet, with shower only, and with shared bathroom facilities), all with satellite TV, but not all with outside windows. ❸

Hôtel Canaria 2 Pl Lahcen Tamri ☎028 84 67 27. Best deal of the Talborjt cheapies. Rooms round a sunny central courtyard, so it doesn't matter that most have windows facing inwards only; some have en-suite showers, and there's guarded parking outside. **❶**

Hôtel Diaf Rue Allal Ben Abdallah ⊕028 82 58 52, ⓕ028 82 13 11. Reliable and comfortable with small but clean rooms. Some rooms have en-suite bathrooms, but hot water is available 7am–noon and 7–10pm only and reservations are only accepted if taken up before 2pm. The rooms on the roof are slightly cheaper but the ones on the first floor are a lot nicer. **❷**

Hôtel Massa Pl Lahcen Tamri ⊕028 82 24 09. Simple rooms but clean, around two upstairs court-yards, with shared bathroom facilities but 24-hour hot-water. **❶**

Hôtel Moderne Rue el Mahdi Ibn Toumert ⊕028 84 04 73. Tucked away in a quiet location, and quite prim and proper. Rooms are done out in salmon pink and sky blue, and have showers but not toilets en suite. **❸**

Hôtel Tiznine 3 Rue Drarga ⊕ & ⓕ028 84 39 25. A new hotel, all bright and gleaming, with pleasant if plain rooms, some en suite. Slightly pricier than the other Talborjt cheapies, but worth the differ-ence. **❷**

Hôtel le Tour Eiffel 25 Av du 29 Février ⊕028 82 37 12. A reasonable place with a café-restaurant downstairs which is handy for breakfast. The bathroom facilities are shared, and the hot water supply a bit iffy, but in theory it's on round the clock. **❶**

Moderate to expensive

Hôtel Aferni Av Général Kettani ⊕028 84 07 30, ⓦwww.aferni.com. It's worth asking for a room with a bathtub and balcony in this three-star hotel with a pool (heated in winter) and terrace, plus TVs and safes in each room. The only thing lacking is a bar, which you may consider a plus or a minus. **❺**

Hôtel Ayour 4 Rue de l'Entraide ⊕028 82 49 76, ⓔayour.hotel@gmail.com. Friendly, bright two-star, well-kept with nice modern rooms and satellite TV. **❹**

Hôtel Kamal Bd Hassan II ⊕028 84 28 17, ⓦwww.hotelkamal.ma. Centrally located three-star with quite large, cool, comfortable rooms set round a small swimming pool; of all the hotels in town, this one gets consistently good reports. **❺**

Hôtel Mountassir Rue de la Jeunesse ⊕028 84 32 28, ⓔh.almountassir@menara.ma. A city-centre concrete block that offers good value for money – the rooms are plain but decent enough, with balconies, and there's a small pool and garden as well as a café and restaurant. **❺**

Hôtel Petite Suède Bd Hassan II ⊕028 84 07 79, ⓔhotel.petite.suede@caramail.com. One of the first hotels built after the earthquake, and not too far from the beach. All rooms have en suite showers but shared toilets, and some have a balcony. There's also a sun terrace, and a ten percent discount for *Rough Guide* readers. **❹**

Hôtel Sindibad Pl Lahcen Tamri ⊕028 82 34 77, ⓕ028 84 24 74. Comfortable and popular hotel with a restaurant and bar, spotless a/c rooms, and a plunge pool on the roof. **❺**

Hôtel la Tour du Sud Av Kennedy ⊕028 82 26 94, ⓕ028 82 48 46. Small but immaculate, its en-suite rooms have smoked-glass windows and little balconies, built around two courtyards with large trees growing out of them. It's worth avoiding the ground-floor rooms, however, especially on the side facing the street. **❹**

Résidence Sacha Pl de la Jeunesse ⊕028 84 11 67, ⓦwww.agadir-maroc.com. Just off the town centre in a quiet square. French-managed, with a range of good-sized self-catering studios and apartments (some with private gardens), and a small swimming pool. **❾**

Résidence Yasmina Rue de la Jeunesse ⊕028 04 26 60, ⓦwww.residence.yasmina.com. Self catering apartments with small bedrooms but large sitting rooms and decent-sized kitchens, plus a lobby and salon done out in traditional zellij tilework, and a café, a swimming pool and a children's pool. **❺**

Main boulevards – towards the beach

The hotels along the **main boulevards**, and particularly towards the beach, are mostly rather fancy places.

Agadir Beach Club Route de l'Oued Souss ⊕028 84 43 43, ⓦwww.agadir-beach-club.com. A very grand hotel at the southern end of the beach, with no less than seven restaurants, four bars, a nightclub, a very large pool, and loads of sports facilities. Rooms are not huge but have a/c, satellite TV and a minibar, and there are ramps for wheelchairs, but no specifically adapted rooms. **❼**

Hôtel Adrar Bd Mohammed V ⊕028 84 04 17 or 37, ⓦwww.adrar-hotel.com. Not a very imposing building but it has charming staff and a good reputation for service, as well as a full range of facilities including pool and restaurant. The room decor is unconvincingly pseudo-Berber, but strangely pleasing nonetheless. All in all, great value. **❺**

Hôtel Amadil Beach Route de l'Oued Souss, south of the *Agadir Beach Club* ☎028 82 93 00, @amadil@iam.net.ma. A huge four-star package holiday complex on the beach, with a trio of pools and everything from sauna to pétanque; beach-trikes are rented nearby, too. ❼

Hôtel les Cinq Parties du Monde Bd Hassan II ☎028 84 54 81, ⓕ028 84 25 04. Handy for Place Salam bus and grand taxi station, with clean, pleasant rooms off a tiled courtyard, plus a decent restaurant. ❹

Hôtel Marhaba Bd Hassan II ☎028 84 06 70, ⓦwww.hotel-marhaba.com. An excellent-value three-star hotel with large, comfortable rooms, a nice pool and gardens, and promotional deals out of season. The beach isn't too far away, but it's across a busy main road. ❺

Hôtel Miramar Bd Mohammed V ☎028 84 07 70. This was the only hotel that survived the earthquake. It's a homely, twelve-room place, elegantly redesigned by André Paccard, doyen of the *Hôtel La Mamounia* in Marrakesh and several of King Hassan's palaces. It's value for money, with a good Italian restaurant (see p.617), but no pool. ❺

Hôtel al Moggar Bd Mohammed V ☎028 84 22 70 or 72 or 76, ⓦwww.hotelalmoggar.com. A large, well-equipped beach hotel complex, with a nightclub, a large pool, tennis courts, extensive gardens, and concrete bungalow-style rooms that are ugly without but spacious within and have balconies facing the beach. ❻

Mabrouk Hôtel Bd du 20 Août ☎028 82 87 01 or 02, ⓦwww.hmabrouk.ma. A small, friendly three-star hotel, with an attractive garden and large pool. Promotional prices often available off-season. Breakfast included. ❻

Between Agadir and Inezgane

There are a handful of good hotels off the road south of town towards **Inezgane** and the airport. The recommendations below are listed in order of appearance driving from **Agadir** on the Inezgane road, and detailed as being on the left or right of the road. All can be reached on any local bus or shared grand taxi travelling between Agadir and Inezgane.

Hôtel Jacaranda off Route de Inezgane, 5km from Agadir, right ☎028 28 03 16, ⓦwww.jacaranda -hotel-agadir.com. A new and very suave establishment, using ecologically sound thick walls, rather than a/c, to keep out the heat, but otherwise offering the usual four-star luxuries, with a solar-heated pool, original artworks in the rooms and some beautiful stucco-work in the lobby. ❼

Hôtel le Provençal Route de Inezgane, 9km from Agadir, on the edge of Inezgane, right ☎028 83 26 12, ⓕ028 83 34 31. A French-style *auberge*, with bungalow-style rooms arranged around a medium-sized swimming pool and a well-kept garden with flowers and banana trees. ❹

Hôtel-Restaurant la Pergola Route de Inezgane, 8km from Agadir, left ☎028 27 18 01 or 41, ⓦwww.lapergola.ma. Characterful French-run hotel, formerly a colonial villa, with parking facilities and a restaurant which, when on form, is memorable. ❹

Camping

Some old hands say that campers are better off staying away from Agadir. There are a lot of "no camping" signs, and one **official campsite**, which gets mixed but mainly negative reports: *Camping International Agadir*, Boulevard Mohammed V (☎028 84 66 83, ⓕ028 84 66 84). It is reasonably well located, within easy walking distance of the centre and beach, open all year and fairly secure, with a snack bar and other facilities but there's limited shade, campervans dominate, prices are relatively high and it's pretty crowded. Supposedly a new campsite is planned on Boulevard Mohammed V by the junction with Avenue du Prince Sidi Mohammed.

The town and beach

Agadir's life revolves round its beach. The town itself has few sights of any note. If you have kids to amuse, you might consider a ride on the "**tourist real train**", which does a thirty-minute run (10dh) around town every hour or two

△ Agadir town and beach

(listen for the whistle and bell), starting out from Boulevard 20 Août opposite the end of Rue de la Plage.

Along the beach

Agadir's **beach** is as good as they come: a wide expanse of fine sand which extends an impressive distance to the south of the town, is swept each morning and patrolled by mounted police. Along its course are a number of cafés which rent out sunbeds and umbrellas. The ocean – it should be stressed – has a **very strong Atlantic undertow** and is definitely not suitable for children unless closely supervised. Even adults are advised not to go out swimming alone.

At the south end of the beach, **wet-biking** (jet-skiing; 300dh for 20min) is available at the *Palm Beach Club* (20dh entry) and near the *Hôtel Amadil Beach*. Horse and camel rides are also available, and quad bikes and beach buggies can also be rented. You can ride on any of these along the sands, up on the dunes, and over to the estuary (see box opposite). This is reached past an area known as **Founty**, quite a pleasant place, where a hundred or so villas are scattered behind the sand dunes and eucalyptus forest.

The Valley of the Birds

As a break from the beach, you might wander into the **Valley of the Birds** (daily 9.30am–12.30pm & 2.30–6pm; 5dh), a small valley which runs down from Boulevard Hassan II, under Boulevard Mohammed V, to Boulevard du 20 Août. It's basically a narrow strip of parkland, with a little aviary of exotic birds, a small herd of Barbary sheep, a waterfall and a children's playground: all very pleasant, and the lush vegetation draws a rich variety of birds throughout the year.

A few blocks to the south is an outdoor theatre – built along Roman odeon lines – and a pedestrian precinct of tourist shops and restaurants where the small **Amazigh Heritage Museum** (Mon–Sat 9.30am–5.30pm; 20dh) has a collection of Berber cultural artefacts, including carpets and jewellery, but nothing wildly exciting.

The Jardim de Olhão

On Avenue Kennedy, just south of Avenue des FAR, a very pleasant outdoor space is the **Jardim de Olhão** (daily 8am–6.30pm; free), a landscaped garden with a café-restaurant and children's playground, opened in 2003 to celebrate the fourth anniversary of Agadir's twinning with the town of Olhão in Portugal. The walls and buildings in the garden are constructed in a traditional Berber style which some claim was inspired by Portuguese architecture, though the influence is hard to see, and could just as easily have been the other way round anyway. A small gallery by the entrance exhibits works by local artists.

Next to the Jardim de Olhão, at the junction of Avenue Kennedy with Avenue des FAR, the **Exposition Mémoire d'Agadir** (Tues–Sat 9.30am–12.30pm & 3–6pm; 20h) has some interesting photographs of Agadir as it was before the 1960 earthquake, and of the destruction wrought by that terrible event.

Markets

Agadir has two main markets, both containing stalls selling normal Moroccan goods, as well as tourist souvenirs. There's also a new "traditional" medina, where crafts are made and sold.

The **Municipal Market**, a two-storey concrete block, stands in the centre of town between Avenue des FAR and Avenue Prince Sidi Mohammed, with a display of wet fish downstairs cheek by jowl with fossils and handicrafts. Upstairs, it's almost all tourist shops selling goods from around the region, and indeed the country. Starting prices are very high, and you can certainly get some of the same things cheaper elsewhere, but there are some interesting goods here and it's worth a look around.

Much more Moroccan in style is the **souk**, in a massive walled enclosure on Rue Chair al Hamra Mohammed Ben Brahim, selling fruit, vegetables and household goods; here the tourist stalls are in a minority, albeit a significant one. **Talborjt** has a plain and simple Moroccan food market on Rue Mahdi Ibn Toumert just north-west of Place Lahcen Tamri.

Off the Inezgane road, 4km out of town, the new **"Medina d'Agadir"** (daily except Mon 8am–6pm; 40dh; ⓦwww.medinapolizzi.com) is a traditional-style artisans' village, where crafts are made and sold to tourists. The whole place was constructed using time-honoured techniques, as are the items sold within it. Nonetheless, no matter how carefully authentic they may have been, there really is very little authenticity about the atmosphere of the place, and obviously an enclosure selling handicrafts to tourists is nothing like a real living medina. It can be reached by minibus seven times daily (60dh round trip including entry to the Medina) from the kiosk at the junction of Boulevard du 20 Août and Chemin de Oued Souss, and from certain tourist hotels such as the *Agadir Beach Club*, and is signposted from the Agadir–Inezgane road.

Ancienne Talborjt and the old kasbah

The raised plateau of **Ancienne Talborjt**, which entombs the town demolished in the 1960 earthquake, stands to the west of the city centre. It is marked by a small mosque and unfinished memorial garden. Relatives of the 15,000 dead come to this park area to walk, remember and pray: a moving sight, even after so many years.

For visitors, a more tangible sight of old Agadir is the **kasbah**, on the hill to the north of the town. This is an eight-kilometre trip, worth making if you have transport, or by petit taxi, for a marvellous view of Agadir and the coast. You can see the kasbah quite clearly from central Agadir and more particularly a vast "Allah–King–Nation" slogan, picked out in Arabic, in white stones, illuminated at night, on the slopes below.

Athough it survived the quake, the kasbah is little more than a bare outline of walls and an entrance arch the latter with an inscription in Dutch and Arabic recording that the Netherlands began trading here in 1746 (capitalizing on the

---

The Souss estuary: birds and the palace

If the Oued Souss is flowing (it often dries out), the **estuary** is of interest to **bird-watchers**. The northern banks of the river have good views of a variety of waders and wildfowl including greater flamingo (most evident in Aug and Sept), spoonbill, ruddy shelduck, avocet, greenshank and curlew, while the surrounding scrubby banks also have large numbers of migrant warblers and Barbary partridge. An additional sight, of a rather different nature, is the **Royal Palace**, built in the 1980s in an imaginative blend of traditional and modern forms, which can be glimpsed from the riverbank. It cannot, of course, be visited.

To reach the estuary by road, take the Inezgane road out of town (green ZETRAP bus #24, #28 or #40 from Agadir) and turn right after 6km at the traffic lights and signpost for Golf des Dunes, but be warned that there have been reports of robberies, sometimes at knifepoint, so leave any valuables behind.

rich sugar plantations of the Souss plain). It's not much, but it is one of the few reminders that the city has any past at all, so complete was the destruction of the 1960 earthquake.

Eating, drinking and nightlife

For an international resort, Agadir is a bit staid, with little in the way of bars, clubs or discos, outside of the large hotels. However, there are plenty of **cafés** and **restaurants**, for all budgets, though most of those lining the beach and the boulevards are tourist traps, with waiters outside trying to hustle in any passing foreigner who shows an interest.

Restaurants

As with hotels, there's a concentration of inexpensive café-restaurants in **Talborjt**, where you can get regular Moroccan meals (including some bargain set menus) at pretty much regular Moroccan prices. There's also a scattering of cafés and mid-price restaurants on or near the **beach**, including two that stay open 24 hours, along with a fair range of more sophisticated places – a few of which almost justify a stopover in themselves. If your hotel doesn't provide **breakfast**, several places in Talborjt will do so (the *Ibtissam* and the *Select* for example), while many of the cafés around Place Salam bus station – notably the café belonging to the *Hôtel Massa* and its neighbour on Place Lahcen Tamri – have stalls outside selling *harsha* and *msimmen* (Moroccan breads) to eat with a coffee and croissant. The *Hôtel Sindibad* serves breakfast from around 6.30am, making it handy for early-morning bus travellers.

Talborjt/city centre

L'Étoile de Marrakech *Studiotel Afoud*, Rue de la Foire ☎028 84 39 99. Renowned for its traditional Moroccan dishes, the restaurant at the front of the hotel (serving the same food) is open daily 7.30–10.30am for breakfast, noon–3pm for lunch, 7.30–11pm for dinner, with snacks served in between times, while the *Étoile du Marrakech* itself, at the back of the hotel, gets going with live music at 11pm and continues until 2 or 3am. Moderate.

Restaurant des Arcades Rue Allal Ben Abdallah. The combination of a traditional-style painted stucco ceiling with glass chandeliers and seaside blue-and-white striped walls is a bit jarring, but the food isn't bad for the price and certainly fills a gap, with a good-value 40dh set menu, and snacks such as omelettes. Cheap.

Restaurant Caverne Bd Hassan II, near the *Atlantic Hotel*. Good food at reasonable prices, with a bargain set menu (60dh; changed daily), and Moroccan specialities for two – such as pastilla or rabbit tajine – if ordered a day in advance. Daily noon–3pm & 6–10pm. Moderate.

Restaurant Daffy Rue des Oranges. Pavement dining or couches around the inside tables, and reasonable set menus (55dh–60dh), or dishes like pastilla, mechoui or tanjia for two if ordered in advance. Daily noon–10.30pm. Cheap to moderate.

Restaurant Ibtissam Pl Lahcen Tamri. The best of a trio of cheapies all next to each other, handy for breakfast as well as for lunch and dinner. Serves Moroccan and international staples, with a bargain set menu (35dh), and vegetarian options if requested. Daily 8am–11pm. Cheap.

Restaurant Select 38 Rue Allal Ben Abdallah. Food varies from mediocre to delicious, but always good for the price. The set menu (40dh) is a great deal, or there are steaks, escalopes, and also juices. Daily 7.30am–10pm. Cheap.

SOS Pêcheurs and **SOS Poulet** Av Moulay Abdallah, near the post office. Two places next to each other, one doing fish (fried fish, fried cuttlefish, prawn tajine, paella), the other doing chicken meals (brochettes, sandwiches, or quarter, half or whole roast chickens with rice or chips), to eat in or take away. Daily noon–midnight. Cheap.

Tour de Paris 40 Bd Hassan II ☎028 84 09 01. Quite a high-quality place, with classic dishes like pastilla, couscous and several tasty tajines (meat with pears, for example, or beef noisettes with prawns and Roquefort cheese), along with live light music. Daily noon–2pm & 7–11pm. Moderate.

Via Veneto Bd Hassan II ☎028 84 14 67. This place used to serve the best Italian food in town, and still rustles up a decent wood-oven pizza, *osso bucco* or paella. Daily 11am–11pm. Moderate.

Main boulevards/towards the beach

Fishing port stalls outside Port d'Agadir. Not on a par with their equivalents in Essaouira (see p.420), but the gathering of stalls here will do you a freshly caught fish grilled over charcoal for not very much money – 34dh for shrimps, squid or whiting, 300dh for lobster, crawfish or king prawns. Daily winter noon–7pm, summer noon–11pm. Cheap.

Mezzo Mezzo Bd Mohammed V. Agadir's poshest pizzeria, with a wide selection of pizzas and dishes made with their own fresh pasta, all served in cosy modern surroundings. Daily 7pm–midnight. Moderate to expensive.

Le Miramar in the *Hôtel Miramar*, Bd Mohammed V ☎028 84 07 70. This is the city's most chic restaurant – a beautifully decorated place overlooking the fishing port. Fine international cuisine, particularly fish and seafood. Daily noon–2pm & 7–10.30pm. Moderate to expensive, but there's a 150dh set menu.

Restaurant Jour et Nuit on the beach off Rue de la Plage. International-style dishes such as lamb chops, steaks and roast chicken, and snacks including assorted sandwiches and a range of salads, plus a bar. Daily 24hr. Moderate.

La Truite between Bd Hassan II and Bd Mohammed V, opposite Amazigh Heritage Museum. Bacon and egg breakfasts, draught beer, and a sign that still says "Irish Pub", though the bar inside is decked out with cross of St George flags. It's pretty naff, of course, but it does show live English football, which makes it very handy if you need to catch a Premiership match (or if you're pining for a rasher of dead pig). Daily 8am–10pm. Moderate.

Yacht Club Restaurant du Port Port d'Agadir ☎028 84 37 08. An excellent place for fresh fish and seafood – as you'd expect from the location inside the fishing port, though the fish can be overcooked. Specialities include fillet of John Dory with orange sauce or fish brochette with saffron. Take your passport, as you have to go through customs. Daily noon–3pm & 7–11pm. Moderate.

Patisserie and ice cream

Eis Pub Centre Commercial Tafoukt, Bd du 20 Août. The best ice creams in Agadir – served up in waffle cones – and great cakes too. Daily 10am–10pm.

Patisserie Tafarnout Bd Hassan II at Rue de la Foire. Agadir's poshest patisserie, to indulge yourself with utterly sinful pastries including blackcurrant mousse on a chocolate cake base, or just a common-or-garden coffee and croissant. Daily 9am–8pm.

Yacout Av du 29 Février between Rue de l'Entraide and Rue Prince Moulay Abdallah. Patisserie selling Lebanese specialities such as *baklava* as well as excellent versions of almond-stuffed Moroccan favourites such as *corne de gazelle*. It also has a café and garden, great for a tea and pastry, or even a pastilla, but don't bother with the set menu (55dh). Daily 7am–10pm.

Bars and nightlife

The *Jour et Nuit* restaurant (see above) has a **bar** open 24 hours, while **clubs** and **hotel discos** tend to get going around 11pm or midnight. Nightclub entry tends to be 50dh Monday–Wednesday & Sunday, 100dh Thursday–Saturday (including the first drink). The club scene in Agadir can be quite sleazy – it's a good idea in the more popular clubs to pay for your drinks as you buy them rather than running up a tab to pay at the end of the evening, when you may be too drunk to notice the addition of extraneous items. Prostitution is rife (at the *Flamingo*, *Jimmy's* and the *Papagayo*, for example) but it's illegal, to the extent that girls and punters should travel in separate taxis to avoid police attention (if they travel together, the cab driver may flash police en route to alert them). A male **gay scene** also exists in Agadir – try *Jimmy's* in particular.

Disco Tan Tan in the *Hôtel Almohades*, Bd 20 Août ☎028 84 02 33. Long-established hotel disco, and generally a safe bet, not one of the "in" clubs in Agadir at present, but has the advantage of being nearer to town than most of the others.

Flamingo in the *Agadir Beach Club*, Bd 20 Août, ☎028 84 43 43. Lively if rather seedy nightclub attached to one of the bigger beach package hotels, but very popular with Moroccans as well as foreigners.

Jimmy's in the *Hôtel Al Madina Palace*, Bd 20 Août, ☎028 84 53 53. One of the better and trendier hotel nightclubs, popular with gay visitors as well as the usual mix of foreign and Moroccan clubbers.

Papagayo in the *Tikida Beach Hotel*, Bd 20 Août, ☎028 84 54 00. The most popular club at time of writing, very lively with the usual mix of Western with a few Arabic pop sounds. Tacky but fun. **Red Lion Dance Bar** in the *Mabrouk Hôtel* ☎028 82 87 01. Not a discothèque, but a bar with an Arabic band – it opens early, around 8pm, but you won't find anyone dancing much before midnight.

Listings

Airlines Royal Air Maroc, Av Général Kettani, opposite the junction with Bd Hassan II ☎028 82 91 20; Regional Air Lines, 16 Immeuble Hassania III, Bd Hassan II ☎028 82 03 30.

Banks The largest concentration of banks with ATMs is along Av Général Kettani between Bd Hassan II and Bd Mohammed V. In Talborjt, there's a BMCE and a Banque Populaire on Av Kennedy near the junction of Av du 29 Février (though the latter gets snooty about changing worn banknotes), and an SGMB on Rue Allal Ben Abdallah near Pl Lahcen Tamri. BMCE has a bureau de change on Bd du 20 Août, 300m south of *Hôtel Mabrouk* (Mon–Sat 9am–noon & 4.30–7pm). Just round the corner, on the road connecting Bd du 20 Août to Chemin de Oued Souss near the *Hôtel Amadil*, there's a bureau de change at Tarik Reisen travel agency, 20 Marché Cité Charaf (daily 8am–9pm), plus a couple more banks with ATMs. Most large hotels will also change money.

Bicycle and motorbike rental Various operators rent out motorbikes, scooters and bicycles along Bd du 20 Août south of Route de l'Oued Souss, but it pays to deal with a decent firm since a number of cowboy outfits operate. A reliable firm will rent for 24hr rather than just until nightfall, and will be able to show you full paperwork (rather than just a receipt) proving that the insurance, minimal though it might be, covers you (and passenger if necessary) and detailing help in the event of a breakdown. Bourida Motorent, outside *Hôtel Almohades*, Bd 20 Août (☎061 71 94 37) have motorbikes at 300dh per day, scooters at 200dh, bicycles at 100dh.

Books and newspapers A small selection of paperbacks and coffee-table books on Morocco are sold at Al Mouggar on Av Prince Moulay Abdallah opposite the end of Av du 29 Février. Atlas Bureau at 16–18 Av Prince Moulay Abdallah has some coffee-table and cookery books in English. British daily papers, as well as the *International Herald Tribune* can be found at Debit Pilote, 65 Bd Hassan II near the junction of Av des FAR, as well as at stands on Bd Hassan II between Av des FAR and Av Prince Sidi Mohammed, and at larger hotels.

Car rental If you're heading for the Anti-Atlas or southern oases, renting a car in Agadir makes a lot of sense. It's also very competitive, with a score or so companies vying for your custom. Shopping around, check that you are being offered an all-inclusive price (insurance, etc), and whether you can return the car to another city, or to Agadir airport. A good place to start looking is the Bungalow Marhaba on Bd Mohammed V (see map p.606), where you'll find Avis (☎028 84 17 55), Budget (☎028 84 82 22), Europcar (☎028 84 03 37), Hertz (☎028 84 09 39), and Tourist Cars (☎028 84 02 00), together with the local operators Youness Cars (☎028 84 07 50, of whom we've had good reports in the past), Weekend Cars (☎028 84 06 67) and Lotus Cars (☎028 84 05 88). The main agencies also have branches at the airport (see p.609). Other companies with offices in Agadir include First Car in Immeuble Oumlil, 17 Bd Hassan II, at the corner of Rue de l'Hôtel de Ville (☎028 82 67 96), National in Immeuble Sud Bahia on Bd Hassan II (☎028 84 00 26), and recommended local firm Amoudou Cars on Bd Hassan II, at the corner of Av Mouqaouama (☎028 82 50 10).

Car repairs Spare parts dealers are concentrated around the junction of Av Mouqaouama with Bd Hassan II, and there are a number of car mechanics with workshops on Bd 2 Mars between Rue 18 Novembre and Av Mouqaouama.

Cinemas The town has two: the Sahara on Pl Lahcen Tamri in Talborjt; and the Rialto, off Av des FAR behind the municipal market.

Consulates UK (honorary consul) Complet Tours, 26 Immeuble Oumlil, third floor, Bd Hassan II (☎028 82 34 01).

Courier services DHL, Immeuble Iguenwane, Bd Mohammed V, near *Hôtel Miramar* ☎028 84 07 03; FedEx, 9 Rue Changuit ☎028 84 44 06.

Craft shops Good first stops are Adrar, on Av Prince Moulay Abdallah, through the passageway behind the Crown English Bookshop, and the Uniprix shop at the corner of Bd Hassan II and Av Prince Sidi Mohammed, as they sell goods at fixed prices. So, too, does the chaotic Ensemble Artisanal (Mon–Fri 9am–7pm, though individual shops may open later, close for lunch or shut earlier) on Av du 29 Février, just north of Pl Lahcen Tamri. There is also the Medina d'Agadir off the Inezgane road (see p.615). If you buy anything elsewhere in Agadir – rugs, carpets, *babouches*, etc – you will have to do some very heavy bargaining indeed.

Food and drink shops The Uniprix shop (see above) also sells the cheapest spirits, beer and wine, along with general provisions, hidden away at the back behind the clothes and tourist tat.

Oawina Supermarket, 1 Rue Hôtel de Ville, just off Bd Hassan II near Rue de la Foire, has a good selection. The biggest supermarket is Marjane, just out of town on the Inezgane road. The honey shop at 129 Rue Marrakech, by the junction with Av Mouqaouama, sells various kinds of honey, and olive and argan oil. The souk on Rue Chair al Hamra Mohammed Ben Brahim and the market in Talborjt (see p.615) are good for fresh produce.

Festival In July 2004 Agadir hosted its first Timitar Festival, dedicated to nomadic music; it's not on a par with Essaouira (see p.422), but draws musicians from all over the south of Morocco, as well as from north and West Africa, France, Spain and even Latin America. For further details on this annual festival, check the festival website at Ⓦ www.festivaltimitar.com.

Golf Agadir has three golf clubs, all southeast of town: Agadir Royal Golf, 12km out on the Route d'Ait Melloul (Ⓣ028 84 85 51, Ⓔ royalgolfagadir @menara.ma), the smallest, with only nine holes and closed Mon, but the oldest-established, and generally considered the finest; Golf des Dunes (Ⓣ028 83 46 90, Ⓕ028 81 46 49), with three nine-hole courses; and Golf du Soleil (Ⓣ028 33 73 29, Ⓦ www.golfdusoleil.com), which is the newest and also has three nine-hole courses. Green fees are 400dh for nine holes, 550dh for eighteen, 1300dh for an unlimited seven-day pass, and include a free shuttle bus from the main beach hotels.

Hammam To sweat out the grime in Talborjt, the Bain Maure Essalama, on Rue Mahdi Ibn Toumert, is open daily for women 6am–6pm, and for men 6pm–midnight.

Internet access In Talborjt, there's Streamjet at 10

Rue Allal Ben Abdallah (Mon–Thurs 10.30am–10.30pm, Fri–Sun 2–10.30pm; 5dh/hr), and Copier Collier on Av du 29 Février near Yacout pâtisserie (daily 9am–midnight; 5dh/hr). There are also several places on Rue de Meknes by Place Salam bus station.

Medical care Most of the big hotels can provide addresses for English-speaking doctors. Current recommendations include a doctor – Dr Martinez Espinoza, Immeuble Oumlil, corner of Bd Hassan II and Rue Hôtel de Ville Ⓣ028 84 17 50 or 061 63 13 51 (surgery hours 9am–noon & 3–6pm); and a dentist – Dr Noureddine Touhami, Immeuble M2, Apt 4, second floor (behind *SOS Pêcheurs*), Av Prince Moulay Abdallah (Ⓣ028 84 63 20), by appointment only. For emergencies, get a taxi to the Clinique al Massira, on Av Prince Moulay Abdallah at the junction of Av du 29 Février (Ⓣ028 84 32 38). There's a night pharmacy at the town hall behind the main post office, and a list of *pharmacies de garde* (chemists open all night) posted in the windows of most town pharmacies.

Post offices The main post office is right in the middle of town at the top of Av Sidi Mohammed, Mon–Fri 8am–4.15pm for full services, and for sale of stamps, money changing and Western Union, Mon–Fri till 6.30pm and Sat 8am–noon. There's a branch post office on Av du 29 Février in Talborjt, opposite the Ensemble Artisanal, with similar hours, and a very small one on Bd du 20 Août near the junction of Chemin de Oued Souss.

Travel agents Menara Tours on the fourth floor of the blue-fronted building just south of the *Hôtel Miramar* on Bd Mohammed V (Ⓣ028 84 27 32) offers all the usual services, including car rental.

Moving on

Agadir is a reasonable **transport terminal**, with efficient buses to a range of destinations, and regular grands taxis run to Taroudannt and Tiznit. If you are going somewhere out of the way, you may need to connect with a bus or grand taxi at Inezgane. This can be reached most easily by grand taxi; they leave throughout the day from Place Salam, charging 4dh a place.

By air

The **airport** at Al Massira (Ⓣ028 83 91 02) is 25km east of town. The easiest way to get to it without your own transport is by grand taxi (150dh during the day or 200dh at night for up to six people), but there is a cheaper way if you're hard up: get a bus or shared grand taxi (4dh) to Inezgane, and from there take local GAB bus #22 (every 40min 6am–8pm; 4dh).

Driving to the airport from Agadir in your own vehicle, you have a choice of routes. The easiest is to leave Agadir by way of Aït Melloul and the Taroudannt (N10, formerly P32) road, turning right at the signposted junction. Alternatively, you can approach from the north, leaving Agadir on the Marrakesh (N8, formerly P40) road, then turning off (left) just after Tikiouine.

Airport Staff at Agadir have been known to tell passengers that valuables (such as cameras) are not allowed on as hand baggage and must be carried in in the hold. Note that such items are likely to go missing if not securely locked away.

By bus

Leaving Agadir by **bus**, the best services are operated by ONCF/Supratours (10 Rue des Oranges ☎028 84 12 07), CTM (Rue Yacoub el Mansour ☎028 82 20 77) and SATAS (Rue Yacoub el Mansour ☎028 84 24 70), though you may need to use other private lines for a few minor destinations, or travel via Inezgane. All services except Supratours and the daily Immouzer bus (see p.624) currently leave from their respective offices on Rue Yacoub el Mansour, but most are expected to move to a new *gare routière* on Rue Chair al Hamra Mohammed Ben Brahim just past the souk, as soon as it is completed. For journey times and frequencies see p.669.

By grand taxi

Agadir's **grands taxis** gather at a rank a block south of the local bus station at **Place Salam**. They run to Inezgane, as well as direct to Tiznit, Taroudannt and sometimes to other southern destinations, but it is often easier to take one to Inezgane and get a connection there, especially since the drivers at Agadir have started trying to charge tourists (but not Moroccans, of course) extra for their baggage. The fare in a shared taxi to Inezgane is 4dh, and grands taxis for points beyond will cost 4dh less from Inezgane than direct from Agadir, so you lose nothing by going there, and you could well get a faster connection, with no nonsense about extra charges for baggage. Taxis for Anza and Aourir run from right next to the local bus station itself, and also from outside the fishing port.

Inezgane

INEZGANE, on the north bank of the Oued Souss, is almost a suburb of Agadir, just 13km distant. The two could hardly be more different, though, for Inezgane is wholly Moroccan, and is a major transport hub for the region – much more so than Agadir – with buses and grands taxis going to most southern destinations.

It's connected with Agadir by local bus #25 and #28 (very frequent) and by frequent grands taxis (4dh a place, arriving/leaving Agadir at Place Salam). Each of these, along with intercity buses, have their own section of the *gare routière*, which is off Avenue Mokhtar Soussi, a wide street with arcades on both sides, running from the central Place al Massira to the main Agadir road. Across Avenue Mokhtar Soussi, through the arcades, is a wonderful city **market**, full of fruit, veg, spices, knick-knacks and traditional cosmetics, and a hundred times more authentic than anything you'll find in Agadir. From Place al Massira, the road makes a ninety-degree turn, and crosses Boulevard Mohammed V, Inezgane's main street, where you'll find the post office and most of the shops.

Useful **bus and grand taxi departures** from Inezgane include Taroudannt, Essaouira and Marrakesh (for a fuller list of destinations and journey times, see p.670).

Accommodation

If you arrive late at Agadir airport, and want to head straight on south, you could do a lot worse than stay here, rather than Agadir; you may be able to negotiate a slightly cheaper taxi from the airport, too (around 100dh). There are dozens of **hotels** near the bus station, all pretty basic, but prices are around half what they would be in equivalent Agadir hotels.

Hôtel Hagounia 9 Av Mokhtar Soussi ☎ 028 83 27 83. Right by the bus station on a busy intersection, with reasonable rooms, en-suite showers and 24-hour hot water. ❷

Hôtel al Qods 50 Pl al Massira ☎ 028 83 49 23. Friendly, reasonably clean, and much bigger than it looks from outside. Some rooms have an en-suite

shower, some have shower and toilet, the cheapest have shared bathroom facilities, and there's hot water round the clock. ❶

Hôtel de Paris 30 Bd Mohammed V ☎ 028 33 05 71. Extremely cheap, with an inexpensive restaurant too. Some rooms have en-suite shower, and there should be constant hot water. ❶

North of Agadir: the coast to Cap Rhir

Along the coast north of Agadir, tourist development rapidly begins to fade, and the beach at **Taghazout** (19km from Agadir) belongs to a different world, with entirely local accommodation and not a "proper" hotel in sight. This – and the coast further up here – is popular surfing territory. The route is also a good one for bird-watchers – as is the coastline south of Agadir.

Public transport is pretty straightforward. From Agadir, RATAG city bus #12, and ZETRAP buses #60 and #61 run regularly up the coast to Taghazout, #61 continuing to Tamri, while Essaouira buses take the route beyond, via Cap Rhir. The coast is a good target, too, if you rent mopeds or motorbikes in Agadir.

Agadir to Taghazout

The coast road north of Agadir begins unpromisingly, passing through the city's industrial sector, a strip known as **Cité Anza**. At 11km from Agadir, however, things improve, as you reach **AOURIR**, where a road heads inland to Paradise Valley and Immouzer des Ida Outanane (see p.624). Aourir and its sister village of **TAMRAGHT**, a kilometre beyond, are jointly known as "Banana Village" after the thriving banana groves that divide them, and the roadside stalls selling bananas in season. Both Aourir and Tamraght have **hotels**: Aourir's best offering is the *Hôtel Littoral* (☎028 31 47 26, ⓦwww.hotellittoral.com; ❹), just past the Immouzer turn-off, on your right if heading north, with spotless rooms, tiled floors, self-catering suites and a terrace, an amazing bargain compared to Agadir's hostelries, especially as breakfast is included in the room rate. Even more of a bargain is the lovely *Hôtel Riad Imourane*, 2km north of Tamraght on the landward side, beyond a popular surfing spot called Dynamic Beach (☎061 21 20 66; ❺), with immaculate rooms, beautiful tiled floors, carpets and tasteful traditional decor throughout.

You can **eat** extremely well at the roadside café-restaurants in Aourir, a weekend favourite among Agadiris 200m north of the Immouzer turn-off, opposite the Afriquia petrol station. The best is the *Baraka* (☎028 31 40 74; daily noon–midnight; moderate), which offers delicious chicken or lamb tajines, or *mechoui* (you pay by the kilo, around a quarter kilo is fine for one person), but no other options. Otherwise, the restaurant at the *Hôtel Littoral* (daily 7am–11pm; moderate) does a variety of fish and pasta dishes, including pesto or Napolitana for vegetarians, and has a 60dh set menu.

Aourir and Tamraght share "Banana Beach", a sandy strip, broken by the Oued Tamraght, the dividing line between the two villages. Banana Beach is used by surfers, and is especially good for the less experienced, with slower, fatter breaks than those at points to the north. A couple of doors north of the *Hôtel Littoral*, Mohammed le Cycliste rents out bicycles by the hour, the day or the week.

Around 2km north of Tamraght, a prominent rocky headland, **Les Roches du Diable**, is flanked by further good beaches. The southern one is used by fishermen who stay in bamboo huts here in the summer. Shortly beyond here (16km from Agadir but opposite a beach which calls itself "Km 17"), a signposted *piste* leads to Ranch R.E.H.A. (☎028 84 75 49, ⓔreha@wanadoo .net.ma), where you can go **horse trekking** into the mountains (book by phone, e-mail, or through larger Agadir hotels).

Taghazout

Eighteen kilometres from Agadir is the fishing village of **TAGHAZOUT** (Tarhazoute, or even Taghagant), flanked on either side – indeed, from way north of Cap Rhir down to Agadir – by a great swathe of **beach**, interrupted here and there by headlands and for the most part deserted. Many places in the village have no running water, and it inevitably attracts a rather different clientele from Agadir. At one time, it was Morocco's hippy resort *par excellence*, but the hippies have nowadays been replaced by surfers, many of them Moroccan. Several surf shops rent out, sell or repair boards, and sell surfing accoutrements (the oldest established is Free Surf on Rue Sidi Said Ouhmed, just opposite the main square).

The most obvious **accommodation** option in Taghazout is *Auberge Amouage Taghazout* overlooking the beach on Rue Taiought Atlas (☎028 20 02 72; ❸), with small but pleasant rooms, even a couple of suites, plus hot-water showers and a roof terrace with great views over the beach, perfect to relax on in the evening. Many visitors prefer to rent rooms from local families; rates are negotiable – try 400dh a week for two people. There's also a campsite south of the village, *Camping Taghazout*, favoured by campervan-driving retired Europeans (☎028 20 01 53) – it has sparse but growing shade in the form of argan trees. It's a popular site, and doesn't really have sufficient bathroom facilities, especially as it only permits hots showers 9–11am and 3–8pm and has nowhere for campervans to empty their toilets.

For right-footed surfers, the points just north of Taghazout are an absolute paradise, with a cluster of excellent right-hand breaks. Six kilometres north of the village, **Killers**, named after the killer whales which are often seen here, has one of the most consistent breaks, a powerful, perfectly peeling charger which breaks over a cliff shelf. **Source**, just south of Killers, is so called for the fresh water bubbling up underneath it. **Anchor Point**, 2km to the south of Killers, has long waves and big breaks, while at the north end of the village beach, **Hash Point** is supposedly used by those too stoned to make it to the others. A number of places in Taghazout, such as Almugar Surf Shop by the bus stop, rent and repair surfing equipment.

There are also good surf spots north and south of Taghazout, notably at **Banana Beach** between Aourir and Tamraght (see opposite), and **Dynamic Beach** just north of Tamraght, and at **Cap Rhir** near Tamri (see below). For further advice on surfing, see p.67. Further information about surf spots around Taghazout can be found on the Surf Maroc website at ⓦ www.surfmaroc.co.uk.

For instance, small restaurants in the village serve up grilled fresh fish at very reasonable prices. The *Panorama*, overlooking the beach at the south end of the village beach (daily 9am–midnight; cheap), does some excellent fish dishes, and there are several restaurants around the bus stop such as the *Café Restaurant Tenerife*, which dishes up steak, fish, brochettes or tajines at very reasonable prices.

Taghazout can be reached from Agadir by local bus #12, #60 or #61 (from Place Salam or Boulevard Mouqaouma via Boulevard Mohammed V). In theory the #12 and the #60 run every fifteen minutes, the #61 every half-hour. There are also frequent daily buses in each direction between Agadir and Essaouira, most of which will stop here.

On to Cap Rhir: beaches and bird-watching

North of Taghazout, a beach known as **25km Plage** (its distance from Agadir) is an attractive spot by a rocky headland, with good surfing. A further 5km brings you to – yes, **30km Plage**, flanked by smart summer villas, and the little village of Aghout. From here on to Cap Rhir, a stretch also known as **Paradis Plage**, are many little beaches, with caves on the rocky outcrops, including a really superb strand at Amesnaz, 33km from Agadir.

Cap Rhir (41km from Agadir) is distinguished by its lighthouse, one of the country's first, built by the French in 1926; the keepers welcome visits – and tips. There's a **surfing** spot here called **Boilers**, a powerful right break named after the relic of a shipwreck that's perched on an island: the paddle-out between the wreck and the shore demands good duckdiving or immaculate timing to avoid being washed up by sets. **Draculas**, a fast, shallow right named after its pin-cushion of sea urchins, breaks just inshore of Boilers. The whole area, together with **TAMRI** village and **lagoon**, 3km north (at the end of local bus route #61 from Agadir), is also particularly good for **bird-watching**, though we have heard of bird-watchers being menaced here by local youths, so it's best not to come alone. *Bird Watching* magazine has claimed some notable seabird sightings at the cape, among them Madeiran and Bulwer's petrels, "though you are more likely to see Cory's or Manx Shearwaters, Gannet and Common Scoter". At the lagoon, Audouin's gulls

The bald ibis

The scruffy-looking but highly distinctive **bald ibis** is one of the world's **rarest** birds. A large wader with shimmering dark green plumage, it is named after its white head, featherless on the crown, with a ducktail-like tuft behind. Once common across central and eastern Europe, the Mediterranean and the Middle Eastern Levant, the bald ibis had already disappeared from a lot of its traditional haunts by the beginning of the twentieth century and been hunted out of many Mediterranean habitats by the 1950s, when agricultural use of chemical pesticides killed it off in many more. Its last Middle Eastern colony, at Birecik in Turkey, disappeared in 1989. Now the colony at **Tamri** is just about the bald ibis's last hold-out. In 1993, Britain's Royal Society for the Protection of Birds began assisting the Moroccan government with a conservation programme for the bald ibis, and the planting in early 2000 of plastic dummy birds and artificial nests on cliff ledges (climbers from the British Mountaineering Council did this hazardous work) in an effort to attract the slaphead wader to new, safer sites. So far, the scheme has been highly successful, and the bald ibis population, which had fallen to less than fifty pairs in 1997, has now risen to over 85 pairs. Apart from three pairs recently discovered in Syria, these are the only bald ibises left in the wild anywhere in the world.

come in to bathe. This is the most reliable site to see the **bald ibis** (see box above) which roosts on the cliffs north of Tamri and feeds in the lagoon and on the surrounding hillsides. Passing motorists stop here to buy Tamri's excellent bananas from roadside stalls, and there are several **cafés** for other sorts of sustenance.

For the continuation of this route along the N1 (formerly P8), see pp.424–425, where it is covered in a north–south direction from Essaouira. For much of the distance the road runs some way inland, with just the occasional *piste* leading down to the sea.

Inland to Paradise Valley and Immouzer

The trip up to **Immouzer des Ida Outanane** – via **Paradise Valley**, a beautiful palm-lined gorge – is a superb excursion from Agadir. It is feasible in a day (Immouzer is 62km from Agadir) but much more enjoyable if you stay the night at one or other of the superb *auberges* or take time to explore and camp in the valley.

The 7002 road to Immouzer is surfaced the whole way; it leaves the N1 coast road at Aourir, 12km north of Agadir (make sure you take the right-hand fork in the village – the left-hand one is a dead-end, up a palmery). A daily bus leaves Agadir Thursdays at 7am, other days at 1pm (from a small parking area on Bd Mohammed Cheikh Saâdi, 200m southeast of its junction with Av du 29 Février), arriving in Immouzer four hours later; on Thursdays it goes back later in the day, otherwise it returns the following morning at 7am. Alternatively, take a grand taxi or city bus to Aourir, from where there are shared grands taxis to Immouzer, though mostly on Thursday for the weekly souk.

A surfaced road also connects Immouzer with the N8 Agadir–Marrakesh road, allowing easy access from Ameskroud, Taroudannt or Marrakesh, a highly scenic route.

Paradise Valley

Paradise Valley begins around 10km east of Aourir, as the road sweeps down into a deep, palm-lined gorge, with a river snaking along the base. The best stretch starts just after the turn-off for Immouzer. You can hire a mule to explore the valley's numerous Berber villages, and it's a glorious place to camp, though pitch your tent well away from the riverbed in case of flash floods.

There's an excellent place to stay 5km further along the "main road" (7002), at around the 35km mark from Aourir, in the form of a small **auberge**, the ♣ *Hôtel Tifrit* (☎028 82 60 44, ⓦhttp://tifrit.ifrance.com; ④). Set among palms and olives, with a river winding through, this is a rival for Immouzer's famous *Hôtel des Cascades* – and less than half the price. It is run by a charming family, has simple, cool rooms (with solar-powered electric lights) and a swimming pool, and provides fine Moroccan meals on its scenic terrace. A couple of kilometres further up, in the village of **Aqseri**, are two alternative places to stay, the *Auberge la Bonne Franquette*, which offers half-board accommodation (☎028 82 31 91, ⓦwww.bonnefranquette-agadir.com; ❷), and the ⌐⌐⌐⌐ ⌐⌐⌐⌐⌐⌐ ⌐⌐⌐⌐⌐ ⌐ ⌐ ⌐⌐ ⌐⌐⌐).

A further 20km of winding mountain road takes you up a steep ascent past a quiet corner with several pleasant café-restaurants before winding on to the village of **Immouzer des Ida Outanane**, tucked away in a westerly outcrop of the Atlas.

Immouzer des Ida Outanane and beyond

IMMOUZER DES IDA OUTANANE is a minor regional and market centre (of the Ida Outanane, as its full name suggests). The **waterfall**, for which the village was renowned, is nearby, and was best seen at its foot, 4km downhill to the northwest. Unfortunately the falls have been very adversely affected by drought over the last few years; tight control of irrigation now reduces the cascade on most occasions to a trickle, with the villagers "turning on" the falls for special events only. However, the petrified canopy of the falls is of interest in its own right, and there's a full **plunge pool**.

There's a hamlet just across the stream from the foot of the falls, and a **café** (*Café de Miel*) with basic food, near which you can camp out in the olive groves. The whole area is perfect for walkers. You can follow any of the paths with enjoyment – a good one, near the village, cuts up across the cliffs to the *Hôtel des Cascades* – or even trek off to the Marrakesh road (see p.626). The birdlife adds an exciting dimension, with birds of prey commonplace; Bonelli's eagle is a good bet, and you might well spot golden eagles or crag martins.

In Immouzer village, there's a **souk** every Thursday. The local speciality is honey, made by bees that browse on wild thyme, lavender and other mountain herbs. There's also a honey moussem every August for a week starting in the middle of the month.

Accommodation

♣ *Hôtel des Cascades* (☎028 82 60 16, ⓦwww.cascades-hotel.com; ⑥) in Immouzer is signposted from its main square. It's a really delightful place, set amid gardens of vines, apple and olive trees, roses and hollyhocks, with a panorama of the mountains rolling down to the coast (all rooms have a balcony and a share of the view), and a spectacular path down to the foot of the falls. The food, too, is memorable and there's a swimming pool (full in summer) and tennis court, and the hotel can organize trekking on foot or by donkey, and maintains a couple of *gîtes* to overnight in, as well as having arrangements with families further afield to put up guests.

Down beside the car park near the foot of the falls is the *Auberge Amalou* (☎061 59 09 35, Ⓦ www.aubergeamalou.com; ❸), with attractively tiled rooms (and even beds), currently undergoing an upgrade so that all rooms will have en-suite bathrooms.

East from Immouzer: treks and pistes

A road (gradually being surfaced) breaks off from the Immouzer–Agadir road, 5km south of Immouzer, and leads to the N8 Agadir–Marrakesh road, where you can catch a bus or taxi back to Agadir. The *Hôtel des Cascades* will run walkers to the end of the initial valley, from which the road winds up to cross a high limestone plateau. It then drops to circuit a huge hollow in the hills and descends to a (seasonal) river before climbing up to a pass through to the N8.

The route on from Immouzer to the N8, known as the Route de Miel ("Honey Road"), is also surfaced, and spectacular in places. The *Hôtel des Cascades* owns a few *gîtes*, and can organize **treks** in this attractive country. On the descent towards the N8 lies the eyrie-like *Hôtel-Restaurant Zolado* (☎061 38 04 40, Ⓕ028 82 06 36; ❹). The whole area between the N8 and the coast offers superb 4x4 exploring, and a lot of *pistes* are now being surfaced (and new ones created), allowing exploration in an ordinary vehicle too.

The coast south of Agadir

The stretch of coast south of Agadir and Inezgane is virtually undeveloped. It is accessible at a couple of points from the N1 Inezgane–Tiznit road, but there is little to go out of the way for until you reach the Massa lagoon.

On the main road, the hamlet of **Sidi Bibi**, (20km south of Agadir), has a wonderful open-air tajine restaurant, where those with their own transport might be tempted to take a break. A short way beyond Sidi Bibi, signposts point the way to **Tifnite**, a little collection of fishing huts that attracts a few campervan travellers; taxis wait at the turn-off to take local residents there from the main road. The turn-off can be reached from Inezgane on local bus #17.

The Massa lagoon

The **Massa lagoon**, on the coast around 40km south of Agadir, is part of the Souss–Massa National Park, and is possibly Morocco's most important **bird habitat** (see box opposite), attracting unusual desert visitors and often packed with flamingos, avocets and ducks. The immediate area of the lagoon is a protected zone, closed to visitors, but you can get in some rewarding bird-watching on a track overlooking the lagoon and on the long, wild beach and rolling sand dunes at Sidi Rbat. Various gazelles, oryx and even ostriches are now being reintroduced into the park. The best times to visit are March to April or October to November.

Transport of your own is a considerable advantage for exploring the lagoon area. The best approach from Agadir is to turn west off the N1 (formerly P30) Tiznit road at Aït Belfa; from the south you can turn west along the 7053 towards Tassila, shortly after reaching the Oued Massa. Either route will bring you to a T-junction in the centre of **Massa**, a long, straggling village. A left turn will lead you to the *Kasbah Tassila* (☎028 26 00 47), a restaurant that was originally a

The protected reserve of **Oued Massa** has perhaps the richest habitat mix in Morocco, drawing in a fabulous array of birds. The **sandbars** are visited in the early morning by flocks of sandgrouse (black-bellied and spotted species) and often shelter large numbers of cranes; the **ponds** and **reedbed** margins conceal various waders, such as black-tailed godwit, turnstone, dunlin, snipe, as well as the black-headed bush shrike (tschagra) and little crake; the deeper **open waters** provide feeding grounds for greater flamingo, spoonbill, white stork and black-winged stilt; and overhead the skies are patrolled by marsh harrier and osprey.

The surrounding **scrubby areas** also hold black-headed bush shrike and a variety of nocturnal mammals such as Egyptian mongoose, cape hare and jackal, while the Sidi Rbat complex offers its own wildlife highlights – a local population of Mauritanian toad in the shower block at night.

Enthusiasts with transport might also like to follow the Oued Massa inland, 20km to the east, to the **Barrage Youssef Ben Tachfine**, an enormous freshwater reservoir, edged by the Anti-Atlas. Possible sightings include black-shouldered and rock dove. By the lake is a car park where camping and sometimes overnight.

market compound built in 1851. It is popular with tour groups from Agadir who come down by the busload to eat here. The only hotel accommodation in Massa is the very upmarket *Ksar Massa* (T061 28 03 19; Wwww.ksarmassa.com; **7**), with de luxe comforts for those who can afford them.

In the opposite direction from the T-junction, 8km of sandy road lead alongside the coast and north of the lagoon to a *marabout's* tomb, **Sidi Rbat**. Pitching your tent where you can is still possible, however, and local fishermen sometimes let foreign visitors stay in their lock-up caves on the beach; one local resident, Chariki Omar, offers rooms or camping facilities in his courtyard (T078 86 99 68; **2**).

If you don't have transport, you could charter a taxi in Agadir or Inezgane for the day. Alternatively, take a local bus or grand taxi from Agadir to Inezgane, and local bus #17 (every 30min till 7pm) or a grand taxi from there to Massa. Bus #17 continues to Arbalo, halfway to Sidi Rbat, from where you can walk to the beach along the Oued, an area rich in birdlife. The beach itself is often misty and overcast – even when Agadir is basking in the sun – but on a clear day, it's as good as anywhere else and the walks are enjoyable.

Taroudannt and around

With its majestic, tawny-brown circuit of walls, **TAROUDANNT** is one of the most elegant towns in Morocco. It's a friendly, laid-back sort of place, with all the good-natured bustle of a Berber market town and it's a good base for trekking into the Western High Atlas or the Djebel Sirwa as well as for two superb road routes – north over the **Tizi n'Test** to Marrakesh (see pp.506–514), and south to **Tata** (see p.641), Foum el Hassan (see p.644) and beyond.

Taroudannt's position at the heart of the fertile Souss Valley has always given it a commercial and political importance but it never became an "imperial city". Even the Saadians, who made Taroudannt their capital in the sixteenth century (and built most of its circuit of walls), moved on to Marrakesh. The town's present status, as a major market centre with a population of around 60,000, is probably much as it always has been.

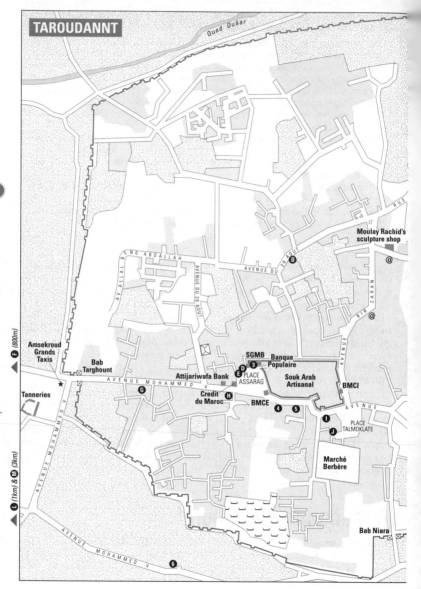

Arrival, orientation and accommodation

Despite its extensive ramparts and large tracts of open space Taroudannt is quite compact, and within the walled "inner city" there are just two main squares – **Place Assarag** (officially renamed Pl Alaouyine) and **Place Talmoklate** (officially Pl en Nasr) – with the main **souk** area between them to the north.

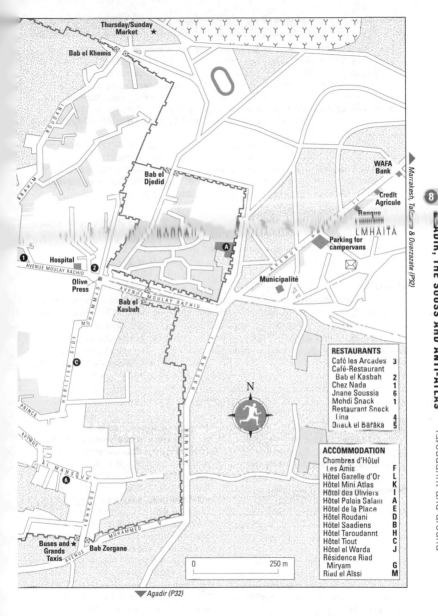

Thursday/Sunday
Market ★

Bab el Khemis

Bab el
Djedid

WAFA
Bank

Credit
Agricole

Banque

LMHAITA

Parking for
campervans

Hospital

Olive
Press

Bab el
Kasbah

Municipalité

N

RESTAURANTS

Café les Arcades	3
Café-Restaurant Bab el Kasbah	2
Chez Nada	1
Jnane Soussia	6
Mehdi Snack	1
Restaurant Snack Lina	4
Snack el Baraka	5

ACCOMMODATION

Chambres d'Hôtel Les Amis	F
Hôtel Gazelle d'Or	L
Hôtel Mini Atlas	K
Hôtel des Oliviers	I
Hôtel Palais Salam	A
Hôtel de la Place	E
Hôtel Roudani	D
Hôtel Saadiens	B
Hôtel Taroudannt	H
Hôtel Tiout	C
Hôtel el Warda	J
Résidence Riad Miryam	G
Riad el Aïssi	M

Buses and ★
Grands
Taxis

Bab Zorgane

0 —————— 250 m

Agadir (P32)

The pedestrianized area of Place Assarag, with its low arcaded front and many cafés, is very much the centre of activity. Over to the east is the old walled **kasbah**. **Private buses and grands taxis** will drop you at the **gare routière** outside the walls by Bab Zourgane, but the **CTM bus** leaves you just outside Bab Targhount.

From Taroudannt's rooftop terraces, the fang-like **peaks** of Awlim (3482m) and Tinerghwet (3551m) look temptingly close on the rugged northern skyline. The area is described on p.523, and is easily reached from Taroudannt, as is the Tichka Plateau (p.523). The Djebel Sirwa (pp.612–613) is also within practical reach of the town. You should really allow at least a week for a cursory visit, more if possible. One of the very best **trekking routes** in Morocco, nicknamed "The Wonder Walk", is a two-week trip up to the plateau and on to Djebel Toubkal (see p.501), Morocco's highest peak.

If you are interested in a **guided trek**, contact El Aouad Ali (BP127, Taroudannt 83000, Morocco ☎066 63 79 72, ⓦwww.trekmorocco.squarespace.com; or through the *Hôtel Roudani*. He is a highly knowledgeable, English-speaking mountain expert, and can organize treks at short notice if need be. It is best to avoid other agencies as there have been some unpleasant rip-offs by cowboy operators.

Getting round town, there are **petits taxis** (usually to be found in Pl Assarag) and, with similar tariffs, a few horse-drawn **calèches**, but in fact everything is within easy walking distance. You can also rent **bicycles** (see p.633).

Hotels

All the cheaper **hotels** are on or around Place Assarag or Place Talmoklate; not all have hot water, but public showers are close at hand (Douches Ramoq behind the *Hôtel Roudani*, for example). Fancier places are dotted round town, including the *Hôtel Gazelle d'Or*, the very poshest establishment in the whole south of Morocco. Less over-the-top upmarket options in the vicinity, for those with transport, include *Riad el Aïssi* (see opposite), *Dar Zitoun* (see next page) and *Riad Freija* (see p.634), and, further afield, the *Arganier d'Or* (see p.636). There's no **campsite** as such in Taroudannt, but campervans can park up in front of the *Palais Salam* hotel (tip the *gardien* 20dh a night).

Cheap

Chambres d'Hôte Les Amis 800m west of Bab Targhount ☎067 60 16 86, ⓦwww.maison -desamis.fr.fm. More like staying in a Moroccan family home than a hotel, with clean and pleasant rooms, constant hot water, a roof terrace, and use of the kitchen. Rates include breakfast. ❸

Hôtel Mini Atlas Av el Mansour Eddahbi ☎028 55 18 80, ⓕ028 85 17 39. Small but sparkling rooms with en-suite showers (hot water 6–10am & pm) and friendly staff. ❷

Hôtel des Oliviers Av du Prince Héritier Sidi Mohammed ☎028 85 20 21. Small, pretty basic rooms and shared bathrooms with no hot water, but cheap and friendly with a better "salon" for up to five people. ❶

Hôtel de la Place Pl Assarag ☎028 85 26 23. Slightly grubby and rather basic rooms, but okay for the price with friendly staff and a roof terrace, and hot water mornings and evenings. ❶

Hôtel Roudani overlooking Pl Assarag ☎028 85 22 19. Central and very popular with backpackers, though quite basic. Some rooms here have bathrooms but no hot water, and those with shared bathroom facilities are very cheap indeed. There's also a restaurant on the square, and a fine rooftop terrace for breakfast. ❶

Hôtel Taroudannt Pl Assarag ☎028 85 24 16, ⓕ028 85 15 53. A Taroudannt institution and the oldest hotel in town, this was run by a grand old French *patronne* up until her death in 1988, and retains her influence (and some of her old poster collection). Very good value, with a patio garden, a generally good restaurant, and a bar which is noisy but closes at 10pm. ❸

Hôtel el Warda 8 Pl Talmoklate ☎028 85 27 63. By far the best deal among the cheapies – clean, cosy rooms with en-suite toilets and shared hot showers that don't always work (depending on the water pressure), though there's always hot water in the bathroom taps, and a bucket. Rooms at the front have balconies overlooking the square; those at the back are quieter but get less light. ❶

Dar Zitoun 2km west of town, on the Agadir road ☎028 55 11 41 or 42, ⊛www.darzitoune.com. Twelve a/c bungalows set in a magnificent garden, with traditional-style decor and a big pool. A good upmarket choice. **❼**

Hôtel Gazelle d'Or 1km southwest of town, on the Ameskroud road ☎028 85 20 39, ⊛www .gazelledor.com. An extraordinary place: a hunting lodge created by a French baron in the 1920s, in a Morocco-meets-Provence style. It was converted to a hotel after World War II, and guests (mostly super-rich Brits) stay in bungalows in the lush gardens. Rates are astronomical, starting at 5510dh for a double – among the highest in North Africa – and one dresses for dinner. Facilities include horse riding and croquet. Advance reservation is compulsory, and you won't be allowed past the gate if you don't have it **❼**

Hôtel Palais Salam ☎028 85 25 01, ⓔsalamtaroudant@groupesalam.com. A package hotel located in a nineteenth-century palace, just inside the ramparts of the kasbah (entrance outside the walls). It's worth asking for a room or suite in the towers or garden pavilions, rather than on the new modern floor. Facilities include two swimming pools, a cocktail bar and tennis courts, and there are three restaurants. Breakfast included. **❼**

Hôtel Saadiens Bordj Oumansour ☎028 85 25 89, ⓔhotsaadi@iam.net.ma. A pleasant hotel, north of the two main squares, with a rooftop restaurant, a patisserie, hot showers (mornings and evenings) and a swimming pool. **❸**

Hôtel Tiout Av Prince Héritier Sidi Mohammed ☎028 85 03 41, ⊛www.hotiout.com. Spotless, airy and prettily decorated rooms, all with en-suite showers, some with baths, and most with a balcony, plus a restaurant, a car park, and a pleasant roof terrace with a fountain. Breakfast included. **❺**

🏃 **Résidence Riad Miryam** 40 Derb Maalem Mohammed, signposted off Av Mohammed V ☎066 12 72 85. Taroudannt's first riad, with four smallish rooms and a suite around a lovely patio garden. The decor isn't exactly tasteful, nor really even kitsch, but it has a certain charm, as do the couple who run the place. The food is as good that it has featured more than once in the French gourmet magazine Saveurs. Breakfast included. **❻**

Riad el Aïssi Nouayl el Homr, on the Ameskroud road ☎028 55 02 25, ⊛www.riadelaissi.com. A beautifully restful place in a little village 3km southeast of town (past the Gazelle d'Or), set amid nineteen hectares of orange, lemon and banana trees in a 1930 pasha's mansion. The rooms are enormous, though the decor is sparse, and there's a restaurant serving Moroccan and Italian food. Rates include breakfast. **❺**

The Town

Taroudannt's twin attractions are its **ramparts** – best toured by bicycle – and its **souks**. The latter are not large by Moroccan city standards, but are varied and authentic and much of the work you find here is of outstanding quality. On Thursdays and Sundays there is a **regional souk**, which brings in Tashelhait (Chleuh) Berbers from the villages to sell farm produce and a few odd pieces of craftwork; this takes place out by the northeast gate, **Bab el Khemis**.

The souks

There are two principal souks: the **Souk Arab Artisanal**, immediately east of Place Assarag (and north of Pl Talmoklate), and the **Marché Berbère**, south of Place Talmoklate.

The **"Arab" souk** – easiest approached along the lane by the BMCE bank (you will probably emerge in Pl Talmoklate – it's a tiny area) – is good for rugs, carpets, leather goods and other traditional crafts, but especially jewellery. This comes mainly from the Anti-Atlas villages nowadays (little of it is as "antique" as the sellers would have you believe), though until the 1960s there was an active artisan quarter here of predominantly Jewish craftsmen. For good-quality wares, the Antiquaire Haut Atlas, run by Licher el Houcine at 61 Souk el Kebir, is recommended (to find him, if entering the souk from Pl Assarag by the BMCE bank, continue roughly straight ahead, and his shop is on the right after 200m).

The **Marché Berbère** is a more everyday souk, with spices and vegetables, as well as clothing and pottery, and again jewellery and carpets. It is most easily

△ Taroudannt's ramparts

entered from Place Talmoklate. Interesting shops include the Cadeaux de Taroudannt, 35 Av Nasr (almost opposite the *Hôtel el Warda*).

For something a bit more offbeat, check out the distinctive sandstone sculptures sold by eccentric local artist Avolay Moulay Rachid from his shop at 52 Av Moulay Rachid.

The tanneries

The leather **tanneries** are outside the town walls on account of their smell – leather is cured in cattle urine and pigeon droppings – and for the proximity to a ready supply of water. In comparison to Marrakesh or Fes, the tanneries here are small, but tidy and quite an attraction. Sheep, cow and goat leather articles are all on sale, but sadly, various skins of rarer or endangered species may be on display and should not be bought, for legal as much as ethical reasons: their importation is banned in most Western countries, and obviously you encourage the illegal poaching of rare animals if you buy them (in fact, it is best not to patronize any shop which sells them at all). If you want to visit the tanneries, follow the continuation of the main street past the *Hôtel Taroudannt* to Bab Targhount, turn left outside, and after 100m take the signposted turning to the right.

The walls and kasbah

The town's various **walls and bastions** can hardly be ignored, and, outside the height of summer, they make an enjoyable circuit to explore. They total around five kilometres in extent and there are stairs up onto them in a couple of places, most notably at **Bab el Kasbah** (also called Bab Essalsla). Some people walk round the outside, but it's easier to rent a bicycle (see opposite) and cycle round instead, or to take a calèche from just inside Bab el Kasbah. The finest stretch runs south from there to Bab Zourgane.

Just to the north of Bab el Kasbah, check out the **kasbah**, now a kind of village within the town. Originally, it was a winter palace complex for the

Saadians and contains the ruins of a fortress built by Moulay Ismail. Outside the walls here are a couple of palm-shaded parks popular for an evening stroll.

Beyond the walls to the south, signs point to the *Hôtel Gazelle d'Or* (see below), a pleasant cycle ride. A mint tea on its terrace is just about afford-able and worthwhile for a look at the gardens, especially in spring, but call in advance as they do not allow admittance to nonresidents without a reservation.

Eating and drinking

There are a fair few **juice shops** around town, selling all kinds of concoctions including creamy avocado with almond milk, but for freshly pressed orange and grapefruit juice you can't beat the stalls on Place Talmoklate. The town's main **bar** is in the *Hôtel Taroudannt* (daily 5–10pm).

Café les Arcades Pl Assarag. A restaurant on the square serving reasonable tajines and sometimes couscous. Daily 8am–11pm. Cheap.

Café Restaurant Bab el Kasbah Av Moulay Rachid, opposite the oil press. A 24-hour café with a rather incongruous revolving door, serving meals noon–3pm & 7–11.30pm, tea, coffee and snacks round the clock. The impressive looking menu outside is just to pull in the punters – when you actually sit down, you are presented with a very much shorter list. The 50dh set menu isn't bad value, though the four salads advertised on it are all in fact exactly the same. Cheap.

Chez Nada Av Moulay Rachid. Excellent tajines, and also pastilla if ordered three hours in advance, upstairs and on the roof terrace. It's open daily noon–3pm & 7–10pm, while the café downstairs is open from 7am to 10pm. Moderate.

Hôtel Gazelle d'Or 1km out of town (☎028 85 20 39). The tented dining room here is quite a sight, especially at dinner (menu 650dh), when men are required to wear jackets and ties. Lunch by the pool is less costly (450dh). Reservations compulsory. Daily 1–3pm & 8–9.30pm.

Hôtel Roudani Pl Assarag. Tasty tajines and couscous, including vegetarian options. Daily 9am–10.30pm. Cheap.

Hôtel Saadiens Bordj Oumansour. Top-floor set-menu terrace restaurant, with a view of the High Atlas. You can eat à la carte, or there's an 80dh set menu. Daily 7–10pm. Moderate.

Hôtel Taroudannt Pl Assarag. Reasonable French and Moroccan meals, and alcohol is served. The cooking is variable, but good if you strike lucky, with 70dh and 90dh set menus. Daily noon–2.30pm & 7–9pm. Moderate.

Jnane Soussia outside the walls, south of town (☎028 85 49 80). A grandiose would-be tourist restaurant with a pool and promises of evening entertainment, except that there never seem to be enough customers. The food is good (the usual tajines and brochettes, plus dishes like *mechoui* or pastilla if ordered in advance), but it's all a bit soulless. Daily noon–3pm & 7–10pm. Moderate.

Mehdi Snack Directly behind *Chez Nada* (see previous column) and run by the same family, a low-priced fast-food joint, with salads, burgers, fried fish, and set menus (30–50dh) based around those. Daily 11am–11pm. Cheap.

Restaurant Snack Lina Av Sidi Mohammed, just east of Pl Assarag. Shiny tiles and fluorescent lighting make this diner rather stark. The *shawarma* and spit-roast chicken are all right, but make sure they're today's. The tajines are good though, and half the price of the ones on the square. Daily 11am–midnight. Cheap.

Snack el Baraka (Chez Moustapha) Av Sidi Mohammed – between the two squares. A small restaurant serving a variety of kebabs (lamb, chicken, liver, *kefta*), spit-roast chicken and sandwiches. Daily 9am–11pm. Cheap.

Listings

Banks Several banks on and around Pl Assarag have ATMs and exchange facilities, as do a trio east of Bab el Kasbah on Av Hassan II.

Bicycles can be rented by the hour, half- or full-day from a little shop on Av Mohammed V just off Pl Assarag between Crédit du Maroc and BCME (5–10dh an hour, 40–60dh a day).

Car repairs There are garages and spares shops just inside Bab Targhount.

Hammams Hammam Tunsi, 30 Av Mohammed V, 30m along from the *Hôtel Taroudannt* (green tiled entrance next to a butcher's, signposted in Arabic only) men 4–11am and 6pm–midnight, women 11am–4pm; 9dh admission (massage extra).

There's also a hammam with an entrance for men just next to the *Hôtel el Warda*, and an entrance for women round the block on the next side street (daily 6am–11pm; 9dh).

Internet access Internet surfing is cheap in Taroudannt – usually only 3dh or even 2dh an hour. Current locales include Club Roudana on Av Bir Zaran (daily 10am till last customer leaves), and the back of a *tabac* on Av Moulay Rachid, opposite Moulay Rachid's sculpture shop (daily 8am–9pm).

Moving on

The most reliable **bus services** are those operated by CTM (whose office is in the *Café les Arcades* in Place Assarag, and whose single daily bus departs from outside Bab Targhount) and SATAS (one daily through bus in each direction between Agadir and Ouarzazate). Note however that SATAS buses may already be full before they arrive, sometimes even bypassing the town completely as a result. For bus frequencies and journey times, see p.670.

Grands taxis, and all buses except the CTM, operate from the *gare routière* outside Bab Zourgane. There are shared grand taxi runs to Agadir or Inezgane. There are rarely direct shared grands taxis to Tata, and you risk getting stranded at Igherm if you take one that's only going that far.

There are no longer any bus services from Taroudannt to **Marrakesh via Tizi n'Test**, one of the most exciting mountain roads in Morocco: a series of hairpin bends cutting across the High Atlas, which is described, in the opposite direction, on pp.506–511. There are, however, three daily buses from Aoulouz via Ouled Berhil, two of them leaving Aoulouz at 10am, Ouled Berhil at 11am, the other starting in Taliouine at 4pm, and reaching Ouled Berhil at 6pm, which means that, unless you are travelling in summer, it will be too dark to catch the spectacular scenery. With your own transport, you can drive the route, but be aware that the road is pretty hairy going, and in winter it can occasionally get snowed up. An alternative is to charter a grand taxi to Ijoukak (see p.510), where there is basic accommodation and onward transport to Asni and Marrakesh.

Around Taroudannt: Freija and Tioute

East of Taroudannt, the oases and kasbahs of **Freija** and **Tioute** are close enough to explore in a half-day's trip by car (or an energetic day by rented bike). Freija lies 11km east of Taroudannt, on the south bank of the Oued Souss; Tioute is a further 26km.

Bird-watchers may find they don't actually reach either site, due to the attractions of the **Oued Souss** itself (see box, p.615).

Freija

The shortest **route to Freija** is to turn south from the Ouarzazate road (N10, formerly P32) at Aït Iazza, 8km out from Taroudannt. After a further kilometre, ford the riverbed (this may be impossible in spring if the river is in flood) and follow an abandoned causeway. Hourly local buses leave for Freija from Taroudannt's Bab el Kasbah.

Freija is an ancient, fortified village, standing on a low hill above (and safe from flooding by) the Souss, and affords sweeping views of the river, the fertile plains beyond, and the High Atlas. A little further to the south, alongside the road in from the R1706 (formerly 7027) the old kasbah, built of *pisé* (mud and gravel), has been reborn as the *Riad Freija* (℡028 85 10 03, Ⓦwww.riadfreija.com; ❺), which is owned by the same proprietor as the *Hôtel Tiout* in Taroudannt. The decor in the bedrooms isn't as posh as in some

The Oued Souss: bird-watching

The **Oued Souss** is another key Moroccan bird habitat, with a rich array of winter residents, and a huge range of migrants in the spring.

Using Taroudannt as your base, the bridge or causeway north of **Freija** (see opposite) would be good points to spend a day bird-watching. Hoopoe, woodchat shrike, orphean, sub-Alpine and Bonelli's warbler, bee-eater and nightingale are all likely sightings in the spring, while stone curlew, great grey shrike and serin are common in winter. Raptors are also likely to be evident: black and black-shouldered kite, griffon vulture and tawny eagle among them. In the evening, you might spot black-bellied sandgrouse and red-necked nightjar.

Another site, more scenic and likely to be even more rewarding for birds, is the **Aoulouz Gorge**, 90km east of Taroudannt (just off the N10 Taroudannt–Taliouine road – see p.636). Spring migrants include everything from booted eagle and black kite to white stork; Barbary falcon, Moussier's and black redstart, blue rock thrush and rock bunting all winter here.

Over **Taroudannt** itself, you can usually see little and pallid swift in the evenings and something hunting in as in egrets, while sorin and Spanish swallow are common in scrubby areas.

riads, but all are en suite with air-conditioning in summer, heating in winter, and the location is superb.

Tioute

TIOUTE can be reached directly from Freija by turning right off the R109 (former 7025) Igherm road 16km beyond Aït Iazza. Either way, you should arrive at one of the seven straggling villages which form Tioute palmery, with a hill before you, capped by a large, stone-built Glaoui kasbah.

A rough track leads up to the kasbah, which is one of the grandest in the south and still owned by the local caïd. Profiled against the first foothills of the Anti-Atlas, it is a highly romantic sight, and was used as a location in Jacques Becker's 1954 French movie of *Ali Baba and the Forty Thieves*, starring Fernandel. Equally impressive are its fabulous views over the luxuriant palmery, with the High Atlas peaks beyond. If you want to avoid sharing it with the tour groups (who arrive around lunchtime), be sure to get here early. It is possible to stay in Tioute, at the *Auberge Tigmi*, down by the main road (T028 85 05 55; ❺). Just by the *auberge*, at the Taitmatine all-women's argan oil producers' cooperative, you can see argan oil being made, and of course buy some if you wish. El Aouad Ali (see box, p.630) can organize day walks in the hills above Tioute.

Taliouine and the Djebel Sirwa

The roads east from **Taroudannt to Taliouine** lack the drama of Tizi n'Test – the great route from Taroudannt to Marrakesh – but they are efficient approaches to the southern oases. There are some scenic stretches, too, particularly the Taliouine–Ouarzazate section, which changes gradually to semi-desert and offers views of the weirdly shaped mountains of the Anti-Atlas.

For trekkers, the **Djebel Sirwa** (or Siroua), north of Taliouine, is one of the finest mountain sections of the Anti-Atlas. It is scarcely less impressive than the more established High Atlas trekking areas, and a great deal less frequented.

Taroudannt to Taliouine – and an approach to Toubkal

Direct grands taxis from Taroudannt to Taliouine take the R1706, which follows the **Oued Souss**, but it's a narrow tarmac strip with horrendous verges and drivers are better off sticking to the main road (N10, formerly P32), which the new road meets just south of the village of Aoulouz.

Buses run along the N10, with a major halt (and taxi stage) at **OULED BERHIL**, 43km east of Taroudannt. Grands taxis from here serve three destinations: Taroudannt, Aoulouz, and Tajingont (15km on the road to Tizi n'Test – but no onward connections). An old kasbah 800m south of the main road (signposted from the centre of the village) has been turned into a sumptuous **hotel-restaurant,** the ⅋ *Riad Hida* (restaurant open 7am–11pm, food must be ordered 1hr in advance; moderate, with a 100dh set menu), with rooms, suites and spacious grounds (☎028 53 10 44, ⓦwww.riadhida.com; ❻). The house formerly belonged to a Dane, who scrupulously restored its traditional and highly ornate ceilings and architecture. The garden is magnificent, and both the rooms and the meals are very good value indeed. The village's other hotel is the *Hôtel Café Restaurant Toudrt* (☎028 53 14 63, ⓔtoudrt146@hotmail.com; ❷), a simple place on the main road with hot water but shared bathroom facilities. For those with transport, there's an alternative place to stay, 20km east of Taroudannt and 23km west of Ouled Berhil on the N10, the *Complexe l'Arganier d'Or* at Zaouiat Ifergane (☎028 55 02 11, ⓦwww.larganierdor-hotel.com; ❻), with good food, a big pool, and breakfast included in the price.

AOULOUZ, 34km east of Ouled Berhil and the starting point for the morning bus to Marrakesh via Tizi n'Test (see p.634), gives onto a **gorge**, rich in bird-watching opportunities (see box, p.635). The best **accommodation** is the *Hôtel Sahara* on the main drag (☎028 53 95 54; ❷), with nice, fresh rooms and shared but clean bathroom facilities. There is another small hotel, the *Oued Souss* (☎066 31 12 60; ❶), also on the main road, with a restaurant but no showers, and the *Café Restaurant Sa'ada*, down the road from there, by the market (☎028 53 94 68; ❶), which has a few rooms, but is often full on Wednesdays and Sundays, which are souk days. Aoulouz is a regular **grand taxi** stage, with runs to Ouled Berhil (and sometimes direct to Taroudannt) and Taliouine.

Towards Toubkal; the Assif n'Tifnout

To the east of Aoulouz, a *piste* leads to **Taïssa**, at the southern end of the **Assif n'Tifnout** valley, which is trailed north by a rough *piste* to Amsouzart, just east of **Lac d'Ifni** and **Djebel Toubkal**. It is possible to drive this in a sturdy vehicle and you can make a two-day tour, returning to Taliouine (or doing it in the opposite direction – see below). Alternatively, you could walk it. From Aoulouz there are minibuses to Assarag, where you'll find rooms, and from where a few hours' walk north will take you to Amsouzart, which also has accommodation options; from there you can reach Lac d'Ifni and Djebel Toubkal.

Taliouine and around

TALIOUINE lies below a pass, its land gathered into a bowl, with a scattering of buildings on and above the roadside. More village than town, its dominant feature is a magnificent **kasbah** (east of the village) built by the Glaoui, though in a much-decayed state. It is nowadays used mainly to house farm animals, though the best-preserved section is still inhabited by a few families, who might offer to show you round. The kasbah's decoration is intricately patterned, its windows moulded with palm fronds (some still showing their original paint), and the towers (climb very much at your own risk) are built around squat, downward-tapering pillars.

With your own vehicle, you can set out from Taroudannt, visit the kasbah and move on easily enough to Ouarzazate the same day. Relying on public transport, you should reckon on staying, which is an attractive proposition, though it is also possible to take in Taliouine as a day-trip from Taroudannt and few tourists do stay, despite the presence of **hotels** in all price ranges. There are other kasbahs in the hills round the village, if you have time to explore them.

Taliouine is a centre for **saffron**, which is grown in the hill country around about and harvested in September and October. Morocco is a very small-scale producer of saffron and this is the only area that grows it, but it's among the world's best in quality. It can be bought in one-gram packets from the Cooperative Souktana de Safran at its office on the eastern edge of town, where they'll tell you all about it, and where they also have a small **museum** (daily 8am–8pm; free). You can buy saffron slightly more cheaply locally elsewhere (in the *Hôtel Ibn Toumert*, for example), but note that saffron is damaged by light, so it's best not to buy if it has been left out in glass jars for any length of time. If heading for Tazenakht, look out for the small *Café Tinfat*, some 25km out of Taliouine, whose proprietor weighs out handfuls on antique brass scales at bargain prices; you can sip saffron tea and see it growing.

Practicalities

Taliouine has several good **hotels**, **hammams** (your hotel can give you directions), and a Monday **souk**, held across the valley behind the kasbah.

Heading on by **bus** from Taliouine can occasionally be tricky as buses can arrive – and leave – full for Taroudannt or Ouarzazate; it might pay to go to the main bus stop in town – buses can pass the *Souktana* full and then leave half empty from the bus stop. **Grands taxis** from Taliouine make the run west to Aoulouz (change for Ouled Berhil and Taroudannt), and less frequently east to Tazenakht (see p.542). See p.670 for journey times and bus frequencies.

With 4x4 transport it is possible to head north from Taliouine (or east from Aoulouz) to **Barrage Chikoukane**, a dam containing an artificial lake (the *Auberge Souktana* offers two-day Land Rover trips), and from there to proceed up the Tifnoute Valley (the upper part of the Oued Souss) to Djebel Toubkal (see p.501) via the village of Amsouzart (see p.503).

Hotels

Auberge Askaoun just east of town ☏028 53 40 17, ℮aubergeaskaoun@yahoo.fr. Friendly with good food and simple but decent rooms, some with private bathrooms – a good alternative to the *Souktana*. ❶

Auberge Camping Toubkal 3.5km east of town ☏028 53 43 43, ⓦwww.maghrebtourism.com /Aubergetoubkal. Run by the same proprietor as the *Auberge Askaoun*, this is in principle a campsite and cheap restaurant, but it also has bungalow rooms, as well as a swimming pool. The campsite is ideal for campervans, but not so much for tents, as the ground is rather hard and there isn't much shade. ❸

Auberge Safran just east of town ☏028 53 40 46, ⓦwww.auberge-safran.fr.fm. A reasonable

fall-back if the *Souktana* is full, with bright, en-suite rooms, some with a/c and heating, solar-supplemented hot water and good food. ❷

Auberge Souktana opposite the kasbah 2km east of town ☏028 53 40 75, ℮souktana@menara.ma. A wonderful little place, run by Ahmed Jadid, his French wife, Michelle, and their son, Hassan (Ahmed and Hassan are excellent mountain guides – see pp.638–639), offering good meals and a choice of accommodation: en-suite rooms in the main building, bungalows, permanent carpeted tents with beds, and floor space in a big tent. You can camp here too, though they are about to open a separate campsite just up the Askaoun road (*Zagmouzen Bivouac Camping Restaurant*), to which they will direct campers in future, and where they will have tents available for those who don't have their own. ❷

Grand Hôtel Ibn Toumert right next to the kasbah ☎028 85 12 31. The most comfortable place in town, though rather impersonal, with a pool, a bar, and views of the kasbah from some rooms. ❺

Hôtel Atlass by the bus stop ☎028 53 45 13. Reasonable rooms with comfortable beds and hot water in shared bathrooms. ❶

Hôtel Camping Siroua town centre ☎028 53 43 04, ⓦwww.auberge-siroua.com. A good-value place with simple but attractively decorated en-suite rooms, a good restaurant, and a camping ground. It's central, but the surroundings aren't as pretty as in the places east of town. ❷

Hôtel Renaissance by the bus stop (no phone). A simple Moroccan hotel, very low in price and handy for onward transport, but with no showers, no hot water, and not top of the league for comfort. ❶

Djebel Iguiguil

South of Taliouine, **Djebel Iguiguil** is an isolated peak reaching 2323 metres in height and offering a good day's excursion. The road from the N10 (signposted to Agadir Melloul), once it has hauled up the first pass from Taliouine, is surfaced right through to the N12 Tata–Foum Zguid road just west of Tissint, a spectacular drive. From just below Agadir Melloul, a *piste* heads west to pass the village of **Aït Hamed**, whose old *agadir* is worth a visit, before curling up to the lower slopes of the highest peak between Djebel Aklim (the highest peak in the Anti-Atlas, reaching 2531m) and the Sarhro. Detailed information on this area can be obtained from AMIS in Scotland (see p.36).

The Djebel Sirwa (Siroua)

The **Djebel Sirwa** (or Siroua) is an isolated volcanic peak, rising from a high area (3000m-plus, so take it easy) to the south of the High Atlas. It offers trekking as good as you can find anywhere – rewarded by magnificent views, a cliff village and dramatic gorges. It is best in spring; winter is extremely cold. For those with 4x4, one of the great scenic *pistes* of Morocco circles north of Sirwa, a two- to three-day trip from Taliouine via **Askaoum** and **Tachnochte**, rejoining the N10 north of Tazenakht.

A week-long walking circuit taking in Djebel Sirwa is outlined on our map, the numbers being the overnight halts. Mules to carry gear, as well as tent rental, can be arranged by **Ahmed and Hassan Jadid** at the *Auberge Souktana* (see p.637) or by **El Aouad Ali** in Taroudannt (see box, p.630), though they don't

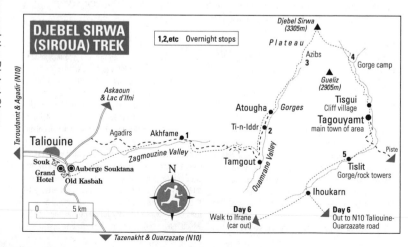

operate in the Sirwa in winter. Mules would be a worthwhile investment to ensure enjoyment – and accurate navigation. Having Ali or Ahmed along, however, is the best guarantee of success. Both are great characters – and cooks, and both speak fluent French and English.

If you are going it alone, the relevant survey maps are the 1:100,000 Taliwine and 1:50,000 Sirwa. Ahmed Jadid can show you these, and he dispenses advice whether or not you engage his guiding services.

The circuit

The initial day is a gentle valley ascent along a *piste* to **AKHFAME** where there are rooms and a kasbah. The *piste* actually reaches west of here as far as Atougha but, souk days apart, transport is non-existent and the walk is a pleasant introduction. Beyond Akhfame the *piste* climbs over a pass to another valley at **TAMGOUT** and up it to **ATOUGHA**, before contouring round into the upper valley, where you can stay at *azibs* (goat shelters) or bivouacs.

Djebel Sirwa (3304m) can be climbed from **Atougha** in five to six hours: a pull up from the southern cirque onto a plateau, crowned with rock towers: the nervous may want to be roped for one section of the final scramble. The sub-peak of **Guliz** is worth ascending, too, and a bivouac in the gorge below is recommended.

Beyond Guliz, you should keep to the lower paths to reach **TISGUI** – and don't fail to visit the unique **cliff village** just outside: its houses, ranked like swallows' nests on a 300m precipice, are now used as grain stores. Continuing the circuit, past fields of saffron, you reach **TAGOUYAMT**, the biggest village of the Sirwa area and connected by *piste* to the Taliouine road. Trails, however, leave it to pass through a couple of villages before reaching the river, which is followed to the extraordinary conglomerate features of the **Tislit gorges**. This natural sculpture park is amazing; you can camp or get rooms at the village.

On the last day, you can follow the valley to **IHOUKARN** and then to **IFRANE**, where it's possible to get a vehicle out; alternatively, a three-hour trek to the southeast leads to the Taliouine–Ouarzazate road, near its highest point, from where transport back to Taliouine is easier. Ahmed can arrange transport at either point to meet unaccompanied parties.

The Tata circuit

Heading **south** across the **Anti-Atlas** from Taroudannt, or east from Tiznit, you can drive, or travel by bus, or a combination of grands taxis and trucks, to the desert oases of **Tata**, **Akka** and **Foum el Hassan** to the west, or **Foum Zguid** to the east. This is one of the great Moroccan routes, increasingly popular since it was surfaced, though still very much a world apart, with its camel herds and lonely, weatherbeaten villages. As throughout southern Morocco, **bilharzia** is prevalent in the oases, so avoid contact with pool and river water.

The route can be covered in either direction, but transport can be sparse, which means you'll have to think ahead if you want to stop off at various places en route and be somewhere with a reasonable hotel by the time transport dries up. Grands taxis run from Tiznit to Bou Izakarn, and from there to Foum el Hassan, Tata and sometimes Akka. From Akka you should be able to get a grand taxi on to Tata so long as you don't leave it too late – the last shared grands taxis out of Akka and Tata often leave before 4pm, while buses between Tata and Bou Izakarn, especially westbound, can be booked up, and may refuse to take foreigners without a seat, so it's very easy to get stranded. The other problem is that smaller places like Oum el Alek and Aït Herbil have nowhere to stay and are not served by grands taxis – they'll drop you off, but are unlikely to be passing with a free space and picking you up. One way to solve these problems if you have the money is to rent a car. Hitching is possible but not advisable – we've heard of hitchhikers being robbed by motorists who've picked them up on the N12 road west of Tata.

Taroudannt to Tata

Leaving the N10 Taroudannt–Taliouine road after 8km at Aït Iazza, the R109 Tata road skirts through the edge of the oasis of **Freija**, and past the turning to **Tioute** (for both of which, see pp.634–635), before winding its way up into the stark Anti-Atlas mountains. Transport along the route is scarce – only three buses a day, two of which leave Taroudannt at 6am and 6.30am. Direct shared grands taxis are rare, as are shared taxis onward from Igherm, though you might find one if you are lucky early on Sunday or Thursday morning for the souk.

At **IGHERM** (also spelt Irherm, 93km from Taroudannt), where there's a **Wednesday souk**, buses will stop for a break, and most shared grands taxis from Taroudannt will terminate. The region was once known for its silver daggers and inlaid rifle butts, and Igherm itself, now an administrative centre and with some new buildings to prove it, was a copper town for centuries, carrying on trade with the Saharan caravans. The souk apart, it is a drab, sluggish town – not a place to get stranded, but if you do, basic rooms are available at the *Hôtel Restaurant Anzal* (☎028 85 93 12; ❶) and the *Hôtel Rendez-Vous* (☎070 08 89 67; ❶).

Not much **transport** is to be had out of Igherm, though there are grands taxis to Taroudannt, and three buses a day between Taroudannt and Tata (two early morning, one late afternoon). There's usually transport of some kind to Issafen, though you may have to wait around for it. If you want to enquire about trucks to Taliouine or Tafraoute, try asking around the main square (where there's a petrol station), or in the café-restaurant just off it, where the truck drivers hang out and play cards. Market day sees more transport between Tata and Igherm, but on other days, it's best to get a direct bus from Taroudannt to Tata, giving Igherm a miss.

Scenic tarmac roads link Igherm to **Taliouine** and **Tafraoute**, and there are plenty of adjoining *pistes* for exploration in a 4x4 if you have one. A rough *piste* heads south to Tata, though it has seen little traffic since the surfacing of the R109. Just down the old *piste* lies the oasis of **Anammer**, a blaze of almond blossom in March and dominated by one of the best-preserved *agadirs* in Morocco: a huge walled courtyard surrounded by layers of minute store-rooms, which are reached by tree-trunk ladders. If you want to see inside it, ask around for the *gardien*, who will of course expect a tip for his trouble.

The paved R109 road south from Igherm crosses the **Tizi Touzlimt** and then descends to **Issafen**, 32km down the road, also called Khemis Issafen for its Thursday souk. You may need to change vehicles here, and grands taxis to Tata should be more frequent from Issafen than from Igherm. Again, if stranded, there's very basic accommodation at the *Hôtel Restaurant Issafen* (no phone; ❶).

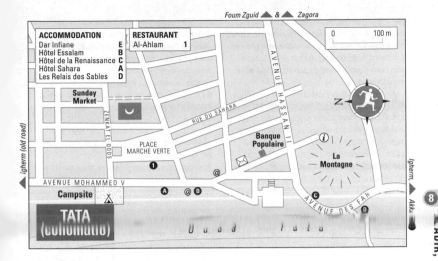

Tata

TATA is a small administrative and garrison town, flanking a large oasis. Its tiled and colonnaded streets are laid out in a rigid grid below a steep-sided hill – known as **La Montagne** (largely occupied by the military) – and flanked by the predictable duo of **Avenue des FAR** and **Avenue Mohammed V**. Just off the latter, in the centre of town, is the main square, **Place Marche Verte**, which **buses** run in and out of.

The town is a leisurely place with a friendly (if early-to-bed) air, and distinct desert influences in the darker complexion of the people, the black turbans of the men and the colourful sari-like coverings of the women (who wear black in the Anti-Atlas). It makes a good overnight stop along this circuit.

Practicalities

Tata has a Banque Populaire with an ATM, a post office, a few Internet offices (including Cyber de Luxe at 38 Av Mohammed V, open daily 8am–midnight, and Tatanet on the same street near the *Hôtel Essalam*, open daily 10am–10pm) and two petrol stations. There's a Sunday market in town and a very lively Thursday **souk** held at an enclosure – or, more accurately, a series of *pisé* courtyards known as El Khemis, 6km out on the Akka road (N12); the mainstay is dates. The Délégation de Tourisme is in the administrative enclosure at the bottom of the Montagne, which is at the southern end of Avenue Mohammed V (Mon–Fri 8.30am–4.30pm; ☎028 80 20 75).

Accommodation

Tata's **hotels** range from pretty comfortable to rock-bottom, but the cheaper rooms at the *Renaissance* should make it unnecessary to use the ultra-cheap options unless you really need to find the lowest possible price. Even then, you can take a mattress for less (20dh) in the hall at the **campsite**, *Camping Municipal* (☎028 80 33 56), which is on Avenue Mohammed V, overlooking the oued, with clean showers, and a certain amount of shade. The campsite also has a swimming pool, currently out of use but due to reopen in 2008 (insha'Allah).

Dar Infiane off the Akka road, in the palmery ☏028 80 24 08, ⊕www.darinfiane.com. Upmarket boutique hotel with six rooms and several terraces and patios, in a 500-year-old converted kasbah with palm-frond furnishings and traditional palm-wood ceilings. ❼

🏃 Hôtel de la Renaissance 9 Av des FAR ☏028 80 22 25, ✉stebelhotel@menara .ma. The best-value choice in town, welcoming you with large, gleaming, a/c suites or small, gleaming rooms, the latter at very reasonable prices. Hot water is solar-powered. The restaurant is good – and licensed, and there's a pool too. ❷

Hôtel Sahara 81 Av Mohammed V ☏072 50 82 29. The best of a trio of ultra-cheapies in town

(the others being the *Hôtel Essalam*, 41 Av Mohammed V (no phone), and the *Hôtel Marche Verte* by the bus station ☏062 46 47 88, both the same price as the *Sahara*). Rooms here are a bit better than those at the other two, and are grouped around a covered courtyard, but the hotel is still pretty basic, with no decent washing facilities for example. ❶

Les Relais des Sables Av des FAR ☏028 80 23 01, ☏028 80 23 00. A smart hotel with a swimming pool, bar and restaurant. The rooms are small but comfortable with en-suite showers and toilets, or there are mini-suites with a/c, sitting area and a complete bathroom. ❹

Eating and drinking

For **meals**, you'll find several grill-cafés under the colonnades on Avenue Mohammed V and on Place de la Marche Verte, the best of which is the *Café Restaurant Al-Ahlam* by the bus station on Place de la Marche Verte. For something more fancy (and/or a drink), your only choices are the restaurants in the *Relais des Sables* and *Renaissance* hotels – at the latter it's best to order meals a few hours in advance, if possible – they are reliably good. The *Renaissance* also has a **bar** (daily 10am–11pm).

Moving on

A number of **buses** start their journeys in Tata with destinations including Agadir, Bou Izakarn and Casablanca, via Igherm, Taroudannt and Marrakesh. For frequencies and journey times see, p.670. Waiting for **grands taxis** to get together enough passengers and set off can take quite a time, but there are occasional departures, especially in the morning, to Akka, Foum el Hassan, Bou Izakarn, Issafen, Tissint and Foum Zguid, as well as taxi-trucks to Foum Zguid (especially on Sunday night and Monday morning for Foum Zguid's Monday souk). Note however that transport dries up quickly in the afternoon, buses can easily be fully booked, and they may not let foreigners travel without a seat (it's illegal, and though Moroccan passengers can tip the *gendarmes* to do it, foreigners

East to Foum Zguid

The route from **Tata** to **Foum Zguid** and, for the intrepid, beyond to Zagora is a much more remote journey than the "Tata loop", and the second leg at least is strictly for the committed.

From **Tata**, there is a surfaced road, two daily buses, and regular grands taxis to Foum Zguid (see p.547), the buses continuing to Tazenakht (see p.542) and Ouarzazate (see p.530). The route runs through a wide valley, following the course of a seasonal river, amid some extremely bleak landscape, which is now and then punctuated by the occasional oasis and *ksar*, with the wave-like range of the Djebel Bani to the south. At **Tissint**, halfway to Foum Zguid, there's a gorge and waterfall, whose best vantage point is 2km before town on the road from Tata. There's also sometimes a police checkpoint, where you may be asked to show your passport. A surfaced road from Akka-Irhen (25km east of Tata, with a Thurs souk) heads north via Agadir Mellal (see p.638) to join the N10 Taliouine–Tazenakht road, an attractive motoring circuit, but without public transport.

are out of the *baksheesh* loop). Note if driving westward that the only fuel station before Bou Izakarn is the Ziz station at Aït Herbil, which is not necessarily reliable, so it's a good idea to fill your tank before heading west.

Akka and its oasis

Continuing along the circuit towards Tiznit, the N12 passes through **AKKA**, a roadside town with a large palmery extending to the north. It is said to have been one of the northern depots of the ancient caravan routes and still hosts an important weekly **souk**, on Thursdays, where the oasis dates (Akka means "dates" in the local Berber language) are much in evidence. There is also a smaller souk on Sundays, and the palmery rewards a visit, with its traditional oasis life.

At present, unfortunately, the town has just one **café-hotel**, the *Tamdoult* (☎028 80 80 30; ❶), an unwelcoming place with poor rooms, though decent food. If you ask, you may be able to pitch a tent in the municipal garden 200m along the Bou Izakarn road, under the shade of its date palms.

As well as five **buses** a day to Tata (one continuing to Ouarzazate, and one all the way to Meknes and Fes, via Taroudannt and Marrakesh), and four the other way to Bou Izakarn (two continuing to Goulimine and Tan Tan, the other two to Inezgane, Marrakesh and Casa), there are **grands taxis** to Tata and Bou Izakarn, though not usually to Foum el Hassan. Don't leave it too late however if you want onward transport – as at Tata, it dries up early, and given the dearth of accommodation, this is not a place you'll want to get stuck in.

Around the palmery

It's worth taking a morning to explore Akka's palmery. You will probably need to do so on foot, as most of the oasis *pistes* are impossible in a two-wheel drive vehicle. Its local sights include a **kasbah** and an **agadir**, southeast of the village of Aït Rahal, and **Les Cascades** – a series of shallow, dammed irrigation pools, enclosed by palms. Local people bathe in these pools, but they are reputed to harbour **bilharzia**, so avoid contact with the water – both here and in the irrigation canals. To reach them on foot, you leave Akka by crossing the dry riverbed by a concrete barrage and then follow a path through the almost continuous palmery villages of Aït Aäntar, Tagadiret and Taouriret.

A three-hour trek to the northwest of Aït Rahal is the **Targannt Gorge**, in which a cluster of oases are tucked between the cliffs. There are ruins of houses, though the place is deserted nowadays, save for the occasional nomadic camel herder. The route is across desert, passable to Land Rover-type vehicles, though the track is poorly defined. En route (and an aid to navigation) is a small hill on which the French built a barracks. There are **rock engravings** of oxen

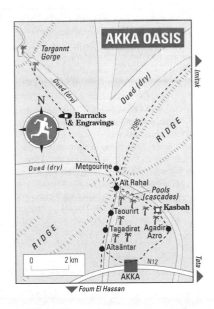

at the eastern end of the hill – some modern, others perhaps up to two thousand years old. Approaching the gorge, a lone palm tempts you to its mouth. A guide from the village would be helpful, while bringing food and a tent would reward you with a gorgeous camping spot.

Oum el Alek

There are more **rock carvings**, said to be prehistoric, near the village of **OUM EL ALEK** (or Oum el Aälague), 7km southeast of Akka, off the Tata road. Anyone with a particular interest is best advised to get in touch with the official *gardien*, Mouloud Taârabet who lives in Oum el Alek and can be contacted in the village, or through the *Café-Hôtel Tamdoult* in Akka. Mouloud knows all the rock carvings in the region, and should be able to take you to any of them you want to see, if you have a car or are prepared to charter a taxi. (See also Aït Herbil, below).

West to Foum el Hassan and Aït Herbil: rock carvings

The next major oasis beyond Akka is **FOUM EL HASSAN** (also spelt Fam el Hisn), 90km to the west – and 6km off the main road. This is basically a military post on the edge of an oasis. Some fighting with Polisario took place here in the early 1980s, but everything's quiet now. Buses between Tata and Bou Izakarn make the 6km detour to stop here, and you may find grands taxis to Bou Izakarn and Tata. There isn't much else in town aside from a few shops and a couple of cafés on the main square, of which the *Hôtel Café Sahara* (☎073 65 82 79; ❶) has basic rooms available.

Tircht

There are countless **prehistoric rock carvings** in this region, and engaging a guide you will probably be shown the local favourites. Those at **Tircht** can be reached by foot from Foum el Hassan by following the oued through the "V" in the mountains behind the town (bear right after 2km where it splits). Tircht is a peaked mountain to the left about 5km from town, but neither it nor the carvings are easy to find: you are best advised to employ someone from town as a guide. The best require a little climbing to get to, but they are among the finest in Morocco – elephants and rhinoceroses, 15–30cm high, dating roughly from 2000–500 BC, a time when the Sahara was full of lakes and swamps. Camping is possible here in the valley and preferable to staying in the town.

Aït Herbil

Less renowned are the rock carvings at the village of **AÏT HERBIL**, 2km off the N12, around 15km west of Foum el Hassan. The junction is easy to recognize, as it's right opposite a Ziz filling station. You can get there by grand taxi from Foum el Hassan, Akka, Tata or Bou Izakarn. For onward travel, however, you'll be lucky to find a passing grand taxi with places free, so short of hitching you'll have to depend on buses, of which there are only four a day in each direction. There are two series of rock carvings, marked as "A" and "B" on our map opposite, both easily accessible on foot. To get to them take the *piste* opposite the Ziz station (signposted to Tamanate and Tafraoute), bearing right towards Aït Herbil, a village worth seeing for its many patterned, colourful doors.

To reach **"A"**, when nearly through the village, turn right down a street that takes you across the dry riverbed. On the opposite bank is a steep rock fall, and to the right of a patch of distinctively lighter grey rocks (indicating several deep and dangerous wells) are perhaps as many as a hundred small carvings, depicting gazelles, bison, a giraffe and a bird or two. The rock fall looks recent but clearly, with the carvings all in the same place, it has not shifted for centuries, even millennia. The old ruined kasbah, which should be to your north (your left as you leave the village), is a useful landmark.

For **"B"** leave the village to the southeast, walking through the palmery and again across the dry riverbed, to find a concrete irrigation channel which at this point runs high above the level of the river. Before reaching the partly deserted village of Eghir, high on

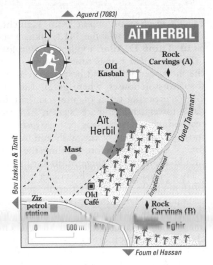

the left, look for carvings on the rocks to the left. Alternatively, follow the irrigation channel for 800m from the main road, where a signpost points the way. There are fewer examples here but they are larger.

Heading north from Aït Herbil, if you have your own transport, there's a *piste* up to the oases and gorges usually explored from Tafraoute (see p.660, and map p.656).

West to Bou Izakarn

Beyond Aït Herbil, the N12 continues across a barren patch of *hammada* to the oasis and roadside village of **TAGHJICHT** (or Tarhjijt), where a road heads off north to Amtoudi (see below). If you need to stay the night, en route, Taghjicht has a sizeable and friendly but underused **hotel**, the *Taghjijt* (☎028 78 87 80; ❸) with a bar and restaurant. The village also has regular grand taxi runs to Bou Izakarn; in the other direction you might be lucky and pick one up on its way to Foum el Hassan. At **TIMOULAY**, 26km further west, it is usually possible to get a grand taxi to Ifrane de l'Anti-Atlas (see p.646). You should also be able to get a taxi for the final 14km stretch to Bou Izakarn, on the main Tiznit–Goulimine road.

BOU IZAKARN is a larger village with a Friday **souk**, a post office, Banque Populaire, municipal swimming pool (summer only), and two basic **hotels**, the more convenient being the *Anti-Atlas* in the village centre (☎028 78 81 34; ❶). As a fall-back, there is also the *Aït Tamzkant* in the backstreets (☎061 10 95 27; ❷), for which you'll need to ask directions. There are regular buses and grands taxis. Taxi runs include Goulimine (these leave from a rank on the Goulimine road at the south end of the village), and Tiznit (for Tafraoute), Ifrane, Inezgane (for Agadir), and Foum el Hassan (all these leave from the main taxi rank in the town centre or, in the case of Ifrane, close by).

Amtoudi (Id Aïssa)

If you have transport, it's worth making an excursion from the Bou Izakarn/Tiznit road to visit **AMTOUDI** (or Id Aïssa, as it appears on most maps). This can be reached on a *piste* from Taghicht, or a surfaced road (signposted to Amtoudi) that leaves the N12 14km east of Taghicht. The two roads join at **Souk Tnine D'Adaï**, a village known for its decorative doors.

The sight that brings tour groups to Amtoudi is its **agadir**, which is one of the most spectacular and best preserved in North Africa. *Agadirs* are collective, fortified storehouses, where grain, dates, gunpowder and other valuables were kept safe during times of inter-clan conflict. Amtoudi's *agadir*, with its formidable towers and ramparts, sits on an eyrie-like setting atop the spur of a hill, reached up a steep zig-zag path. A *gardien* shows visitors round. There is a small museum, and parts of the walls and towers have been restored. Make sure the *gardien* is available before tackling the climb, as the *agadir* is kept locked. You should allow around three hours for the visit.

The approach road to the village ends at a parking lot by the *Hôtel Amtoudi* (☎028 78 93 94; ❹), a friendly *auberge* with simple rooms, hot water, a restaurant and a camping area. Alternatively, at the far end of the village, at the mouth of a gorge, *Ondiraitlesud* (☎028 78 94 14, ⓦondiraitlesud.ma .free.fr; ❹) offers half-board in a French-created *auberge* with a lot of character that promotes eco-tourism in the area. Both *auberges* can provide mules for the climb up to the *agadir*, or expeditions in the area's susbtantial gorges. A walk up the gorge at the end of the village leads to another *agadir*, with huge curtain walls, perched high above a cliff, and, 3km on, a spring and waterfall.

You can climb (or ride a mule) up a winding track and walk around the site, providing the *gardien* is there. If by chance you find the place overrun by visitors, you can escape the crowds with a walk down the palm-filled **gorge**; here another imposing but decaying *agadir* is perched on top of the cliff and, after about 3km, you'll come to a spring and waterfall.

Ifrane de l'Anti-Atlas

IFRANE DE L'ANTI-ATLAS is one of the most rewarding oasis detours on the Tata loop. A small Berber settlement in a long oasis, it comprises three surrounding *douar* (villages), each with its own kasbah and endless walls, together with **Souk Ifrane**, an administrative and market centre (Sat souk), with a pink, fort-like barracks. The place is particularly out of the way and visitors exploring the oasis can expect to be the object of attention, especially from children, but it's worth braving them: there are beautiful walks among the *douar*, springs, and ingenious water channels.

If you have a car, you may want to just stop a few hours, though there are very basic rooms available at the *Hôtel Karam* (☎076 71 79 79; ❶). This and a café opposite the mosque should be able to sort a meal out too, though it's best to ask in advance. There is a sealed road north to Tafraoute, but no public transport.

The oasis and Mellah

The Ifrane oasis is the centre of one of the oldest settled regions in Morocco – and was one of the last places in the south to convert to Islam. Across the dry riverbed stand the ruins of the old **Jewish kasbah**, or **Mellah**. Legend holds that Ifrane's Jews settled here in the sixth century BC, and certainly the Jewish community goes back to pre-Islamic days. It endured up until the 1950s, when, as elsewhere in the south, there was a mass exodus to Israel and, to an extent, Casablanca and Rabat. Thanks to a joint initiative by the Ministry of Culture and the Moroccan Jewish community's Heritage Foundation, the synagogue has

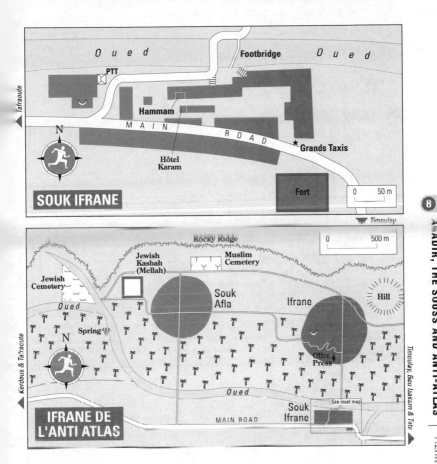

now been restored, and if you can find the *gardien*, you should be able to have a look inside.

Around the next bend in the stony riverbed, and up the hill on the right, lies the Jewish **cemetery**. Broken tombstones, inscribed in Hebrew, lie strewn about. Relatives still come here to visit the graves and burn candles in memory of the deceased. The Muslim past of Ifrane is evident as well, with white-domed tombs of saints and *marabouts* dotting the surrounding countryside.

Tiznit and around

Despite its solid circuit of walls, **TIZNIT** was founded as late as 1882, when Sultan Moulay Hassan (Hassan I) was undertaking a *harka* – a subjugation or (literally) "burning" raid – in the Souss and Anti-Atlas. In 1912 it was the base of **El Hiba**, known as the "Blue Sultan", who declared himself sultan after learning of Moulay Hafid's surrender to the French under the Treaty of Fes and led a Berber force on Marrakesh – which acknowledged his authority – before

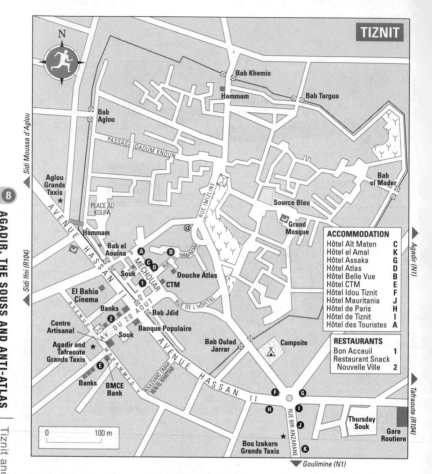

advancing on Fes in the spring of 1913. There they were defeated, though El Hiba's resistance continued, first in Taroudannt, later into the Anti-Atlas, until his death, near Tafraoute, in 1919, but the Tashelhaït (Chleuh) Berbers of the Anti-Atlas suffered their first true occupation only with the bitter French "pacification" of the early 1930s.

The town bears the stamp of its military history – huge *pisé* walls, neat administrative streets and a considerable garrison – but it's not a bad staging point en route to Tafraoute, Sidi Ifni or Tata. It is easily reached by bus from Agadir or grand taxi from Inezgane and has an exhilarating beach at **Sidi Moussa d'Aglou**, 17km distant, where the surf and the fierce Atlantic currents have warded off development.

The Town

Tiznit has five kilometres of walls and eight major gates, the most important of which are **Bab Ouled Jarrar** and **Bab Jedid**. The second of these was a French addition, as its name ("New Gate") indicates; it is also called Les Trois Portes ("the three gates"), though in fact it consists of four gateways. The walls, built little more than a century ago, encompassed a number of existing *ksour*, which are still clearly visible on the map as large angled enclosures.

Taking a brief loop through the town, start out at the **jewellery souk** (*Souk des Bijoutiers*), still an active crafts industry despite the loss to Israel of the town's large number of Jewish craftsmen. The jewellers occupy the northern part of the **main souk**, which can be entered from the Mechouar. Over to the south, across Avenue du 20 Août, is a larger **open-air market**, mainly selling food and produce, and there's a more workaday **municipal market** selling meat, fruit, veg and household goods, just off Avenue du 20 Août. The town's main weekly souk (Thurs) is held out on the Tafraoute road.

The walled town's main square, the **Mechouar**, was once a miltary parade ground, but now hosts a small gathering of traditional entertainers – storytellers, snake charmers, medicine men and the like – who appear in the evening, a faint echo of Marrakesh's Djemaa el Fna. North of the Mechouar, Rue de l'Hôpital winds round, past the hospital in John the main road from Bab Ouled Jarrar which then heads towards an arcade of shops and a mosque (at the top of Rue du Bain Maure). Taking a left just before the arcade of shops, bearing left at the T-junction and right at the next fork, brings you to the **Great Mosque**, which has an unusual minaret, punctuated by a series of perches. These are said to be an aid to the dead in climbing up to paradise, and are more commonly found south of the Sahara in Mali and Niger. Alongside the mosque is the **Source Bleue**, dedicated to the town's patroness, Lalla Tiznit, a saint and former prostitute martyred on this spot (whereupon water miraculously appeared). These days, more or less devoid of water, the spring is profoundly unflattering to her.

Following the street north of the *source*, you reach the north gate, **Bab Targua**, formerly an entry point for animals. The next gate round (clockwise) is **Bab el Mader**, beside a large Muslim cemetery with a picturesque white *marabout's* tomb, its corners picked out in green. To the north of the city wall is an area of rather mournful olive groves and an abandoned palmery.

Practicalities

Arriving by **bus** you'll find yourself set down either at the **Gare Routière** east of town (fifteen minutes from the centre on foot), or nearby at the main roundabout where the Tafraoute road meets the Goulimine road (Rue Bir Anzarane), with several hotels close by. Coming by **grand taxi** from Bou Izakarn, Goulimine or Tata you will probably be dropped on Rue Bir Anzarane within metres of the same roundabout, but from other destinations you'll be taken to a yard on Avenue Mohammed V opposite the post office.

Adjacent to the main **post office** is Avenue du 20 Août, where you'll find banks, a small municipal market and an Ensemble Artisanal. The avenue leads to Les Trois Portes, beyond which is the town's main square, the **Mechouar**, and most of the cheap hotels. **Internet access** is cheap, and is available at a number of places including Venmar on the corner of Rue el Hammam and Rue Imizline (daily 9am–midnight; 3dh/hr), or Anir, just off Rue el Hammam opposite the alley leading to Douche Atlas (daily 9am–11pm; 3dh/hr). There's a traditional **hammam** just inside the walls at Bab el Khemis, and the town's one **cinema**, the El Bahià, is just off Avenue Hassan II opposite Bab el Aouina.

Accommodation and eating

There are a dozen or more cheap **hotels** in the walled city, the best of which are listed below; not all can guarantee hot water, but in a cul-de-sac off Rue du

Bain Maure there is a public showerhouse, Douche Atlas (men and women 6am–8pm; 7dh). The **campsite**, *Camping Municipal* (☎028 60 13 54), just outside Bab Ouled Jarrar, is a secure but unshaded site.

There are numerous **café-restaurants** in and around the Mechouar, the best of which is the *Bon Accueil*, directly opposite the *Atlas* (meals served daily noon–3pm & 7–10pm; cheap). The *Hôtel el Amal*'s restaurant (daily noon–midnight; cheap) serves up excellent tajines, with soup and snacks available. On Avenue du 20 Août, *Restaurant Snack Ville Nouvelle* has a "panoramic terrace" (with huge TV screen but not much of a panorama) and non-smoking saloon on its top floor and offers spaghetti, steaks, brochettes and tajines as well as good-value breakfasts (daily 6am–9pm, meals served from noon; moderate). For a more upmarket meal, or a drink, your best bets are the restaurant of the *Hôtel de Paris* (meals served daily 10am–10pm; moderate), with a good selection of chicken, steak or brochette dishes, or the *restaurant gastronomique* at the *Hôtel Tiznit* (daily 7am–11pm; moderate).

Hotels

Hôtel Aït Maten 64 Mechouar ☎028 60 17 90. Spartan but clean and good value, with friendly staff and a terrace overlooking the square. Hot showers available (8dh). ❶

Hôtel el Amal Rue Bir Anzarane ☎028 86 24 62. A small hotel with spotless rooms, most with shower and toilet en suite, and friendly, efficient staff. Windows face inwards, however, so only those on the top floor get much natural light. ❶

🏃 **Hôtel Assaka** Rue Bir Anzarane, on main roundabout ☎028 60 22 86, @hotelassaka@hotmail.com. At the prices they were offering when we last checked, this is by far the best bargain in town, effectively a three-star hotel at backpacker prices. The rooms are nickel-clean, with a/c, heating, balcony, TV and good en-suite bathrooms. ❷

Hôtel Atlas 42 Mechouar ☎028 86 20 60. A popular hotel with quite a decent restaurant. Some rooms are slightly nicer (and dearer) than others, and there's access from the official roof terrace to a bit of the roof where you can sit undisturbed and watch the square. ❶

Hôtel Belle Vue Rue el Hammam ☎028 86 21 09. Best of the Rue el Hammam cheapies, though marginally dearer than the others – bright, clean and inviting, and quiet too. Hot showers available (8dh). ❶

Hôtel CTM opposite the grand taxi rank ☎028 86 22 11. A friendly place with clean rooms and showers, and a café-restaurant on the first floor, though no direct outside windows. ❶

Hôtel Idou Tiznit Av Hassan II ☎028 60 03 33, ⓦwww.idoutiznit.com. Tiznit's poshest option, a four-star that's part of a small nationwide chain, with spacious rooms, a/c, satellite TV, a pool, very professional staff, and usually some kind of promotional rate on offer, but it's a little bit soulless. ❼

Hôtel Mauritania Rue Bir Anzarane ☎028 86 36 32. Don't be fooled by the common-or-garden Moroccan eatery out front, this is a well-kept hotel with lovely little rooms, very cosy and beautifully turned out, on top of which there are parking facilities, and the staff are charming too. ❶

Hôtel de Paris Av Hassan II, by main roundabout ☎028 86 28 65, ⓕ028 60 13 95. A friendly and modestly priced hotel, with cosy rooms and a popular restaurant. ❷

Hôtel de Tiznit Rue Bir Anzarane, on main roundabout ☎028 86 24 11, ⓕ028 86 21 19. Formerly the poshest hotel in town, though looking a bit down-at-heel since the *Idou* opened opposite and upstaged it. Nonetheless, it's a decent enough three-star, with a bar and swimming pool, though the rooms are nothing special. ❺

Hôtel des Touristes 80 Mechouar ☎028 86 20 18. A deservedly popular backpacker hotel, with hot showers, friendly staff and old-fashioned iron bedsteads. The communal areas are decorated with pictures of Paris in the 1950s and an impressive collection of banknotes. ❶

Moving on

Buses that actually begin their journeys in Tiznit are supposed to leave from the *gare routière*, which is just off the Tafraoute road, a couple of hundred metres east of the Thursday souk, but in practice the *gare routière* is little used; some Tafraoute-bound buses use it, but otherwise most bus companies have their offices on the Mechouar, and departures tend to be from the roundabout where

Avenue Hassan II meets the Tafraoute and Goulimine roads. The most important departure is the evening CTM to Tangier via Agadir, Marrakesh, Casablanca and Rabat. Tickets on this, and on CTM buses southward to Laayoune and Dakhla can be booked at the CTM office in the Mechouar, but you cannot buy tickets for CTM services that pass through during the night, when the office is closed, nor can you board them, even if there are seats free.

Grands taxis operate from three different places. The main station is opposite the post office, and here you'll find vehicles serving Agadir, Inezgane, Tafraoute, Sidi Ifni and Mirhleft. For Bou Izakarn, Goulimine, Mirhleft, and, less frequently, Tan Tan and Laayoune, they start opposite the *Hôtel Mauritania* on Rue Bir Anzarane just south of the roundabout. Finally, those for Sidi Moussa d'Aglou leave from Avenue Hassan II near the southwestern corner of the Medina.

For further information on frequencies and journey times, see p.670.

Sidi Moussa d'Aglou

The beach at **SIDI MOUSSA D'AGLOU** is 17km from Tiznit along a barren, scrub-lined road. **Grands taxis** make routine runs from Tiznit (leaving from Avenue Hassan II by the southwestern corner of the Medina), though some only go to Aglou village, 3km short of the beach. What awaits you is an isolated expanse of sand, with a wild, body-breaking Atlantic surf. It has a dangerous undertow, and the beach is watched over in summer by military police coastguards, who only allow swimming if conditions are safe – if in doubt, ask them. **Surfing** can be good but you have to pick the right spots.

Quite a few Moroccans (many of them migrant workers from France) come down here in the middle of summer, and there's a trickle of Europeans in winter. Between times, however, the place is very quiet. If you want to stay, you'll find a municipal **campsite** (*Camping Plage Aglou*) about 500m before you get to the beach, on the right if coming from Tiznit. It's spacious though very basic, and bald ibises (see p.624) congregate on its walls in the late afternoon. A smaller site (*Camping Azrou Zougane*) with a few rooms can be found 2km south along the beach. Alternatively, by the beach, at the end of the road, is the *Hôtel Aglou Beach* (☎028 61 30 34, ✉agloubeach@hotmail.com; ⑤), which not only has comfortable rooms, but also a restaurant (daily 11am–3pm & 6.30–11pm; cheap) offering fish tajines and other tasty grub.

There are a couple of *marabout* tombs on the beach and, about 1.5km to the north, a tiny (and rather pretty) **troglodyte fishing village**, with a hundred or so primitive cave huts dug into the rocks. Southwards, a surfaced road follows the coast down to Mirhleft and Sidi Ifni.

Tafraoute

Approached by beautiful scenic roads through the Anti-Atlas from Tiznit or Agadir, or (with your own transport) Ifrane de l'Anti-Atlas, or Igherm and Tata, **Tafraoute** is worth all the effort and time it takes to reach. The town is the centre for villages built among a wind-eroded, jagged panorama of granite tors – "like the badlands of South Dakota", as Paul Bowles put it, "writ on a grand scale". To the northwest lies the **Ameln Valley**, with its many villages built below – or high among – the quartz range of the **Djebel el Kest**. A striking feature on it is the Lion's Face – a rock formation which really does look like the face of a lion in the afternoon light when seen from Tafraoute.

The best time for a visit to Tafraoute is early spring, when the almond trees are in full blossom, or in autumn, after the intense heat has subdued. In midsummer, it can be stunningly hot here, destroying almost all incentive to wander round the villages.

The routes from Tiznit and Agadir

Both the main approaches to Tafraoute are rewarding and, if you're driving, you may well want to take advantage of this by coming in from Tiznit and leaving for Agadir, or vice versa. If you're doing just one, the Tiznit approach has a distinct edge, winding through a succession of gorges and a grand mountain valley.

Buses and **grands taxis** cover the route from Tiznit several times daily, but there is only one bus a day along the road from Agadir via Aït Baha.

Tiznit to Tafraoute

The Tiznit–Tafraoute road (R104, previously numbered 7074) passes a succession of oasis-like villages, almost all of them named after the souk that they are host to (see p.794 for the Arabic day names). In winter and spring the road is sometimes crossed by streams but it is generally passable enough; the drive takes around two hours, but leave plenty of time to see (and navigate) the mountains before dusk.

At **ASSAKA** (20km from Tiznit), a substantial bridge has been built over the Oued Tazeroualt – the river that causes most difficulty in winter and spring. Around 19km further on, just before Tighmi, a road heads south into the **Anti-Atlas** to the **Zaouia of Sidi Ahmed ou Moussa** (10km), which for a while in the seventeenth century controlled its own local state, the Tazeroualt, whose capital was at nearby (and now deserted) **Illigh**. The *zaouia* remains active and hosts a **moussem** during the second or third week of August, which would be worth trying to attend. Sidi Ahmed is the patron saint of Morocco's acrobats, most of whom come from this region of Morocco – and return to perform.

Just beyond **TIGHMI** (Tirhmi; 42km from Tiznit), the road begins its ascent of the **Col du Kerdous** (1100m). At the top of the pass, the *Hôtel Kerdous* (☎028 86 20 63, ◍www.hotelkerdous.com; ◉), created from an old fortress, is worth at least a stop for a tea and breathtaking views. This area is also a hot spot for paragliding – Mohammed Ouhammou Sahnoun or Houssine Laroussi at the Coin des Nomades shop in Tafraoute (see p.655) have more details.

At the end of the descent is the village of **JEMAA IDA OUSSEMLAL** (64km from Tiznit), and the last petrol station before Tafraoute. The road

---

Ground squirrels

Along the road from Tiznit to Tafraoute, you may notice children holding little furry animals for sale – live, on a piece of string – by the roadside. These are **ground squirrels**, which are known locally as *anzid* or *sibsib*, and are destined for the **tajine** dish, in which they are considered quite a delicacy, their flesh being sweet since they subsist mainly on a diet of almonds and argan nuts. Recognizable by the prominent stripes down their backs, and by their long tails, ground squirrels are common in the tropics, and have long been ascribed medicinal properties in Morocco. You will not get *anzid* tajine in any restaurant however, unless perhaps you provide the squirrels yourself.

divides as you enter the village. The left fork, which runs downhill through the village (and past the hotel), is the direct road to Tafraoute, a picturesque route that drops into the Ameln Valley at Tahala (or Had Tahala), which was once a Jewish village. The right fork, a newer road, which skirts round Jemaa Ida Oussemlal, is a longer route but well surfaced, flatter and faster going, arriving in Tafraoute through a grand spectacle of mountains and the lunar landscape around Agard Oudad (see p. 000). Just after Aït Ouafka, it splits again – take the left-hand fork for **IZERBI**, where an ex-minister of housing has a Disney-style chateau.

Agadir/Inezgane to Tafraoute via Aït Baha
The R105 (formerly S509) road runs from Agadir to Tafraoute via Aït Baha. It is a bit drab between Agadir and Aït Baha, but the section from there on to Tafraoute is a highly scenic (and slow and winding) mountain ride past a series of fortified kasbah-villages. There's one daily bus along this route, plus another from Agadir to Aït Baha only.

AÏT BAHA is the largest village on the route, and becomes a lively shopping centre on souk day (Weds). It has one **hotel**, the *Al Adarissa* (⌂028 25 44 61, ℮h.eladarissa@menara.ma; ❸), two cafés and very little shade. More interesting accommodation lies 5km further down the road towards Tafraoute, in the thirteenth-century *Kasbah de Tizourgan* (⌂061 94 13 50, ℮tizourganekasbah @yahoo.fr; ❺), a popular place for a last night in Morocco among travellers with transport who are flying home from Agadir.

The most spectacular fortified village in the region, **TIOULIT**, is to the right of the road, around 35km from Aït Baha (the best views are looking back once you've passed it). Another 25km brings you to a junction of roads, with the left fork heading off to Igherm on the R109 Taroudannt–Tata road. Around 5km beyond this junction is the village of **SIDI ABDALLAH EL JABAR**, scene of a small, but lively moussem around its *zaouia*, celebrated annually (Oct 20–22).

Tafraoute

TAFRAOUTE is a small, pleasant place, created as an administrative centre by the French, and little expanded since. It is one of the most relaxed destinations in Morocco, though a few *faux guides* still make a nuisance of themselves, claiming to be the guides mentioned in this and other books, and spinning all sorts of yarns to coax the unwary into carpet shops where they can be subjected to the old hard-sell routine.

Tafraoute: village economics

Among Tafraoute villagers, **emigration** to work in the grocery and hotel trade – all over Morocco and France – is a determining aspect of life. The men return home to retire, however, building European-looking villas amid the rocks, and most of the younger ones manage to come back for a month's holiday each year – whether it be from Casablanca, Tangier, Paris or Marseille.

But for much of the year, it is the women who run things in the valley, and the only men to be found are the old, the family-supported or the affluent. It is a system that seems to work well enough: enormously industrious, and very community-minded, the Tafraoutis have managed to maintain their villages in spite of adverse economic conditions, importing all their foodstuffs except for a little barley, the famed Tafraoute almonds and the sweet oil of the argan tree.

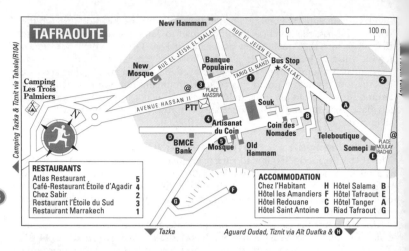

TAFRAOUTE

New Hammam

RUE EL JEISH EL MALAKI

RUE EL JEISH EL

0   100 m

Camping Tazka & Tiznit via Tahala(R104)

Camping
Les Trois
Palmiers

New
Mosque

RUE EL JEISH EL MALAKI

Banque
Populaire

TARIQ EL NAHZI

Bus Stop
MALAKI

②

AVENUE HASSAN II

@   ③ PLACE
    MASSIRA

PTT

④ Artisanat
du Coin

Souk

Coin des
Nomades

A

C

@

Teleboutique

PLACE
MOULAY
RACHID

N

D BMCE
Bank

Mosque

Old
Hammam

Somepi

E

RESTAURANTS

Atlas Restaurant   5
Café-Restaurant Étoile d'Agadir   4
Chez Sabir   2
Restaurant l'Étoile du Sud   3
Restaurant Marrakech   1

F

G

ACCOMMODATION

Chez l'Habitant   H   Hôtel Salama   B
Hôtel les Amandiers   F   Hôtel Tafraout   E
Hôtel Redouane   C   Hôtel Tanger   A
Hôtel Saint Antoine   D   Riad Tafraout   G

Tazka   Aguard Oudad, Tiznit via Aït Ouafka & H

Getting around the Ameln villages, you can use a combination of taxis and walking, or rent bicycles from Abid (who sets up shop between the Coin des Nomades and the *Hôtel Salama*) or from the Artisanat du Coin shop (60dh/day).

Accommodation

The **hotels** in Tafraoute are generally pretty good for their respective levels of the market. At the top level, the arrival of competition has made prices even more negotiable than usual, and it's worth shopping around between the *Amandiers*, the *Salama*, the *Saint Antoine* and the *Riad Tafraout* to see who'll offer you the best rates. Further accommodation options can be found just 4km to the north in the Ameln valley (see p.657). The most central **campsite**, *Camping les Trois Palmiers*, is ten minutes' walk from the centre (☎028 80 00 38). A small, secure enclosure with hot showers, it also has three rather musty rooms for rent (❶). It tends to overflow out of its enclosure and spread onto the surrounding land in winter and spring, when Tafraoute plays host to a swarm of campervans driven by sun-seeking retired Europeans, but there is a second campsite less than a kilometre, down the road, *Camping Tazka* (☎028 80 14 28, ⓦwww.campingtazka.com), whose prices are very slightly higher, though its facilities are cleaner and more adequate for the number of campers. Again, alternative sites, one with a pool, can be found just 4km away in the Ameln Valley (see p.657).

Chez l'Habitant 1km south of town, on the road to Napoleon's hat ☎062 02 93 05. Rustic accommodation in a Berber house with views of the Napoleon's hat and lion's face rock formations. You can take a basic room with a mattress or, in summer, camp out or sleep on the terrace (30dh). ❸

Hôtel les Amandiers on the hill above town ☎028 80 00 08, ⓦwww.hotel-lesamandiers.com. Formerly Tafraoute's top hotel, now getting a bit long in the tooth and upstaged by the new kids in town, it still has a certain old-fashioned charm, with a wood-panelled lobby, great views, and large,

rather grand rooms, which could do with a lick of paint. Breakfast included. ❺

Hôtel Redouane by the bridge ☎ & ⓕ028 80 00 66. A bit seedy with basic and not very clean rooms at erratic prices. Has a terrace restaurant on the first floor. ❶

Hôtel Saint Antoine Av Moktar Soussi ☎028 80 14 97 to 99, ⓦwww.hotelsaintantoine-tafraout .com. Slick, modern hotel, with efficient, English-speaking staff, cool, spacious rooms and a nice big swimming pool. ❹

Hôtel Salama across the river from the *Redouane* ☎028 80 00 26, ⓦwww.hotelsalama.com. A good-value hotel, recently refurbished, offering comfortable rooms, en-suite bathrooms, a roof terrace, a fire in winter, and a good restaurant. ❹

🏃 **Hôtel Tafraout** Pl Moulay Rachid, by the petrol station ☎028 80 00 60. By far the best of the budget hotels, with clean and pleasant rooms, a warm welcome, hot showers and very helpful staff. ❷

Hôtel Tanger across the road from the *Redouane* ☎028 80 01 90. Slightly better rooms than its competitor over the road, and cheaper for singles,

with friendly staff and quite a good restaurant where you can eat outside. ❶

Riad Tafraout Route de Tazka ☎028 80 00 31, ⓦwww.riad-tafraout.com. A very impressive hotel (not really a riad as such), tastefully done out (give or take the odd fox skin on the wall). The first-floor rooms are more attractive than those on the second floor, with straw-and-*pisé*-covered walls, and carved wooden doors from Mali. All rooms have a/c and satellite TV. Rates include breakfast, and discounts may be available. ❻

Eating

In addition to the hotels (of which the *Tanger* and the *Salama* both have reasonable restaurants, the *Tanger* offering a vegetarian tajine among other dishes), there are a few reasonable **restaurants** in town.

Atlas Restaurant Basic but well presented Moroccan nosh – chicken or lamb brochettes, liver, steak, sandwiches and breakfasts – in spotlessly bright café surroundings complete with blaring TV. Daily 6.30am–9pm. Cheap.

Café-Restaurant Etoile d'Agadir A great little place, serving classic tajines (lamb with prunes and almonds, chicken with lemon and olives) and other Moroccan dishes, all delicious and beautifully presented. Daily 8am–1pm. Cheap.

Chez Sabir 41 Route d'Amelne (100m from Pl Moulay Rachid, then left down a little alley, signposted). A small, intimate place with a good 65dh set menu, including vegetarian couscous, but

best ordered an hour ahead. It's also possible to eat on the roof terrace. On the downside, tables are at the same level as the seats, making eating rather uncomfortable. Daily 10.30am–10.30pm. Cheap.

Restaurant l'Etoile du Sud Av Hassan II. A set-menu restaurant (90dh) serving delicious Moroccan food, either indoors or outside in a Bedouin-style tent, with an occasional cabaret and floor show for tour groups. Daily 8.30am–10pm. Moderate.

🏃 **Restaurant Marrakech** An unpretentious family-run place with excellent-value meals (45dh set menu) and friendly service. The couscous here is particularly good. Daily 8am–10pm. Cheap.

Listings

Banks The Banque Populaire is open only on Wed and Thurs mornings for the town's souk, but there's an inconspicuous BMCE behind the post office, with standard opening hours and an ATM.

Car repairs You'll find a few mechanics north of the bus stop in the crook where the main road does a sharp bend.

Guides One guide highly recommended for trekking or four-wheel-driving around the region is Mohammed Ouhammou Sahnoun, who lives in the village of Tiouadou and can be contacted by phone or email (☎028 80 05 47, ⓔm_sahnoun @hotmail.com), or via either the *Hôtel Tafraout* or Houssine Laroussi, who runs the Coin des Nomades shop (☎061 62 79 21, ⓔtamayourt1 @caramail.com). Beware, however, of touts falsely claiming to know or to be these people – if someone who accosts you in the street claims to be Mohammed or Houssine, ask to see their state-issued ID cards. For excursions further afield, a recommended firm is Tafraout Adventure

on Pl Massira (☎028 80 13 66, ⓦwww .tafraout-adventure.com).

Hammam The old hammam is down a side street by the central mosque. There's another near the bend in the main street (behind the bakery, turn left and it's 100m further, under the arch), and a new one, off Pl Moulay Rachid (50m down the Ameln Valley road, then right and right again after another 50m). All the hammams have entrances for men and women, open from around 5am, but the women's side closes at around 5pm, the men's stays open till about 7.30pm.

Internet access Prices vary quite a bit, but better-value places include Cyber Leaga, just off Pl Moulay Rachid (daily 9am–10pm; 5dh/hr) and Aday.Net on Av Hassan II by Pl Massira (daily 9am–11pm; 4dh/hr till 4pm, 5dh/hr after).

Shopping There's a Wed souk, held in the centre of town. Worthwhile permanent crafts shops include the Coin des Nomades (also called Meeting Place of Nomads) and Artisanat du Coin, both unpressurized. Tafraoute is well known for its *babouches*, and a

narrow street of *cordonniers* sells quality slipper-wear just below the Coin des Nomades.
Post office The post office is open Mon–Fri 8.30am–4.15pm.

Sports Houssine Laroussi has information on rock-climbing sites, while Mohammed Ouhammou Sahnoun has information on paragliding sites. See "Guides", p.655, for contact details.

Moving on

Buses leave from the main street where the bus companies have their offices. Departure points and times change frequently, however, so always check them in advance. For frequencies and journey times see p.670. **Grands taxis** leave from the same street, opposite the CTM office. The only regular destination for collective taxis is Tiznit.

The Ameln Valley and around

You could spend days, if not weeks, wandering round the 26 villages of the **Ameln Valley north of** Tafraoute. Set against the backdrop of the rocks, they are all beautiful both from afar and close up – with springs, irrigation systems, brightly painted houses, and mosques. On no account, either, should you miss out on a walk to see the **painted rocks** in their albeit faded glory.

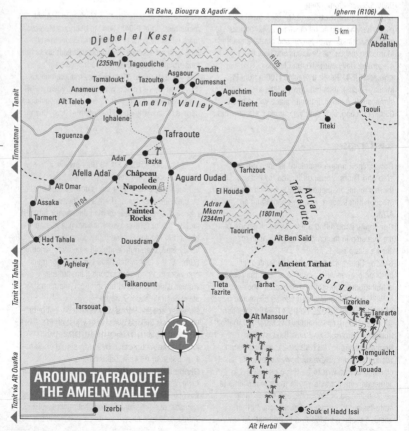

AROUND TAFRAOUTE: THE AMELN VALLEY

Starting out from Tafraoute, **Oumesnat**, 6km to the northeast, is a good first objective, as you can usually get a lift there, or charter a taxi at modest cost; taxis could also be arranged to pick you up from a village at the end of the day. From Oumesnat, you could walk the length of the valley from village to village: the walk to **Anemeur**, for example, is around 10–12km. More serious walkers might consider making the ascent of the **Djebel el Kest** (2359m) or, best of all, **Adrar Mkorn** (2344m), an isolated peak to the southeast with spectacular twin tops (this involves some hard scrambling). The area of the **lion's face** at Asgaour (and many other areas scattered on both the southern and northern slopes of the Djebel el Kest) offers excellent rock climbing on sound quartzite. If you intend doing any rock-climbing in the region, an invaluable source of information is *Climbing in the Moroccan Anti-Atlas* by Claude Davies (Cicerone, 2004), which details each site, showing the ascents on photographs of the rock face.

The **Ameln villages** are built on the lower slopes of the Djebel el Kest, between the "spring line" and the valley floor, allowing gravity to take the water through the village and on to the arable land below. Tracks link the villages, following the contour lines – and frequently the irrigation canals – and most are accessible from the road only by crossing an intricate network of these irrigation canals, orchards and allotments. Many of the villages have basic shops where you can buy drinks, if little else.

A number of **accommodation** options are clustered around the junction of the Ameln Valley road with the road from Tafraoute, which is 4km north of Tafraoute itself. By the junction itself, there's a small municipal **campsite** (☎070 46 79 65), surprisingly empty compared to the sites in town, and not yet colonized by the swarm of campervans that descends on Tafraoute each winter. In summer it even has a swimming pool (15dh). Right outside is a moderately-priced restaurant, the *Amnoggar*. Five hundred metres up the road, where the *piste* for Tamdilt and Asgaour branches off, there's the *Hôtel Camping L'Argannnien* (☎028 80 00 20, ✉argahotel@yahoo.fr; ❹), with small but sweet blue and white rooms and camping facilities. Directly opposite, the *Auberge la Tête du Lion* (☎028 80 11 65, ☻www.latetedulion.com; ❺) has large rooms, a bar and a panoramic roof terrace, but is not so well kept. Both have restaurants. Just 1km up the road to Tamdilt, the *Maison d'Hôte Yamina* (☎070 52 38 83, ☻www.2tafraout.com/yamina; ❹), run by a delightful French-Moroccan couple, is rather more charming and rather better value, in a traditional Berber house, upgraded with hot running water and en-suite bathrooms. All three of the places just mentioned have air-conditioning in summer, heating in winter, and offer deals for half- and full-board.

Oumesnat to Anameur – and a loop back to Tafraoute

OUMESNAT, like most Ameln settlements, emerges out of a startling green and purple rockscape, crouched against the steep rock walls of the valley – on which locals point out the face of a lion. From a distance, its houses, perched on the rocks, seem to have a solidity to them – sensible blocks of stone, often three storeys high, with parallel sets of windows. Close up, they reveal themselves as bizarre constructions, often built on top of older houses deserted when they had become too small or decrepit; a few of them, with rooms jutting out over the cliffs, are held up by enormous stilts and have raised doorways entered by short (and retractable) ladders.

One of the houses, known as **La Maison Traditionelle**, is owned by a blind Berber and his family, who will show visitors round (tip expected). They give an interesting tour, explaining the domestic equipment – grindstones, water-holders, cooking equipment – and the layout of the house with its guest room with separate entrance, animals' quarters, and summer terrace for sleeping out. To get the most from a visit, you may need to engage an interpreter, such as one of the guides recommended on p.655. The owners of the Maison Traditionelle also offer bed and breakfast (℡066 91 81 45, Ⓔmaisonhote@gmail.com; ❹) in two adjoining village houses, one with small, simple rooms, the other with more comfortable air-conditioned rooms (heated in winter).

From Oumesnat, you can walk through or above a series of villages to **ANAMEUR**, where there is a *source bleue*, or natural springwater pool, a meandering hike of around three hours. Along the way is **Tazoulte**, one of four local villages with Jewish cemeteries, remnants of a community now completely

△ Le Chapeau de Napoléon, near Tafraoute

departed, though Jewish symbols are still inscribed on the region's silverware, which was traditionally made by Jews.

The Ameln's highest village, **TAGOUDICHE** (Tagdichte on the road sign), where the trail up the **Djebel el Kest** (or Lekst) begins, is accessible by Land Rover along a rough *piste*. There is a shop, and a *gîte* (☎ c/o Hamid, 062 89 19 13; ❸) if you want to stay overnight for an early morning ascent. The Djebel el Kest is a rough and rocky scramble – there's no actual climbing involved – over a mountain of amethyst quartzite. There is a black igneous dyke below the summit pyramid, and the summit, being a pilgrimage site, has shelters on the top, as well as hooped petticoat daffodils blooming in spring. The easiest route is not obvious and a guide may be advisable.

Returning to Tafraoute from the Ameln Valley, you can walk over a pass back from the R104 road near Ighalenc in around three hours. The path isn't particularly easy to find but it's a lovely walk, taking you past flocks of sheep and goats tended by their child-shepherds. The route begins as a *piste* (east of the sky to Tagmoutil In). Then you follow a dry riverbed off to the right, up a side-valley, where the zigzags of an old track can be seen. Cross to go up here not straight on – and, once over the pass, keep circling left till you can see Tafraoute below.

Tirnmatmat

The road west along the Ameln Valley crosses an almost imperceptible watershed, beyond which, at Aït Omar (see map p.656), a *piste* heads north to **TIRNMATMAT**, a partly abandoned village. Around 200m further, on the north bank of the river, are numerous **carvings** in the rocks, depicting hunters and animals (some of these may be prehistoric), along with more modern graffiti (including a VW Beetle).

The **ridge walk** to the south of this village is taken by some trekking parties and is really special, with Bonelli's eagles circling below, goats climbing the argan trees, and wild boar snuffling round the bushes.

Agard Oudad and the painted rocks

A short but enjoyable walk from Tafraoute is to head south to **AGARD OUDAD** (3km from Tafraoute), a dramatic-looking village built under a particularly bizarre outcrop of granite. Like many of the rocks in this region, this has been given a name. Most of the others are named after animals – people will point out their shapes to you – but this one is known (in good French-colonial tradition) as **Le Chapeau de Napoléon** (Napoleon's hat).

A stranger sight, however, awaits you in the form of "Les Pierres Bleues" – the **Painted Rocks** – 1.5km to the southwest of the village. The painting was executed in 1984 by a Belgian artist, **Jean Verame**, together with a team of Moroccan firemen, who hosed some 18 tons of paint over a large area of rocks; Verame had previously executed a similar project in Sinai. The rocks have lost some of their sharpness of colour over the years but they remain weird and wonderful: blue and red hills, clusters of black and purple boulders, mesmerizing in effect. To reach them on foot, walk through the village and follow the flat *piste* round to the right, behind the Chapeau de Napoléon; you'll see the rocks on your left after a couple of kilometres. If you're in doubt about the route, you should be able to engage a young guide in the village to take you. For those coming by car, a smooth *piste* breaks off the Tiznit road 5km further on and wends its way up towards the rocks, leaving a ten-minute walk at the end. But unless you prefer this longer route, don't follow the road sign if you are on foot.

Tazka

Another easy walk from Tafraoute is to **TAZKA**, about 2km southwest, where there is a prehistoric carving of a gazelle. To get there, follow a path through the palmery, as shown on our Tafraoute map (p.654). When you emerge, past the remains of an old kasbah, you will see on your left the houses of Tazka at the foot of a high granite bluff. Take the lesser path to the right of the bluff and the carvings – a modern one on the rock face and an old one on the tilted surface of a fallen rock – are on your left after around 200m.

A southern circuit from Tafraoute

A beautiful day-trip from Tafraoute is to drive southeast towards Souk el Hadd Issi, a route that takes in some of the most beautiful country of the Anti-Atlas, including some fabulous gorges and palmeries. If you have a sturdy vehicle and a taste for bone-shaking *pistes*, you can make a loop of it, travelling down via Tizerkine, and returning via Aït Mansour. Minibuses (several, but all leaving at the same time) ply each of these routes once daily, leaving Tafraoute around noon, and returning from Souk el Had at 6am next morning. Local guide Mohammed Ouhammou Sahnoun (see Tafraoute "Listings", p.655) lives in **Tiouadou** and offers full-board **accommodation** at the *Auberge Sahnoun* (☎028 80 05 47, ⊜m_sahnoun@hotmail.com; ❺) for anyone interested in using it as a base to explore the local area. The accommodation is simple, but the setting is lovely, on the edge of Tiouadou's palmery, and hot showers are available; space is limited though, so it's best to call or email ahead. Mohammed can also arrange mule treks in the region, and help locate rock carvings.

Leaving Tafraoute, follow the road out past Agard Oudad, turning left around 3km south of the village. This road climbs over the hills, with superb panoramas back across Tafraoute and the Ameln Valley, to reach **TLETA TAZRITE** (15km from Tafraoute), which has a souk on Friday – not Tuesday as its name implies.

From here, a new surfaced road leads south to the massive palmery at **Aït Mansour**, and will eventually continue all the way to Akka. Heading east from Tleta, the road is also surfaced, but in a terrible condition. Following it past the modern village of **TARHAT** (Taghaout) you enter a canyon, which the *piste* follows for the next 46km, and just a little beyond here, high on your left, are the twelfth-century remains of **ancient Tarhat**, a fortified village and *agadir* perched on the lip of a sheer rock wall. A footpath leads up to it from the modern village.

At **TIZERKINE**, a lovely oasis snaking along the canyon, all semblance of paved road comes to an end. A passable *piste* continues (be sure to take the right fork, 5km from Tizerkine) to the village of **TEMGUILCHT**, dominated by the very large and impressive **Zaouia Sidi Ahmed ou Mohammed** (no entrance to non-Muslims), where there is a moussem in honour of the saint every August. The road continues past **Tiouada** and on to **SOUK EL HADD ISSI** (Souk el Had Arfallah Ihrir on the Michelin map), with a Sunday souk; then past a fine *agadir* (5km on); and finally north to meet the road from Aït Mansour.

Four kilometres west of Souk el Hadd Issi, a rougher *piste* heads southwards, and continues all the way to Aït Herbil (see p.644). Off this *piste* are a number of ancient **rock carvings**, though they are not easy to find and a guide would be advisable. The first and least difficult group of carvings to find are some 700m east of the *piste*, about 6.4km south of the junction. They feature long-horned cattle, and also elephants, which lived in this part of Africa when the carvings were made.

Tiznit to Goulimine – and Sidi Ifni

Heading **south from Tiznit to Goulimine**, you have a choice of routes: a fast inland road across scrubby desert via **Bou Izakarn**, where the road to Tata heads off east (see p.645); or a more circuitous journey along the coast, by way of the splendid former Spanish enclave of **Sidi Ifni**. A lot of people follow one route down and the other back.

Tiznit to Sidi Ifni: Mirhleft

The route down the coast from Tiznit to Sidi Ifni passes, around the midway point, the roadside village of **MIRHLEFT**, a friendly, bustling little place, set back a kilometre from a series of good beaches with crashing waves and strong currents, that attract surfers and campervans. A 1935 Spanish fort overlooks the village from the hill above, which you can climb to explore it; the fort itself is of no great interest, but beautiful views over the surrounding countryside make the climb worthwhile. The village also hosts a Monday souk, dealing mainly in secondhand items.

Mirhleft is served by grands taxis from Sidi Ifni, and buses plying between Ifni and Tiznit, most particularly the AGB #26 local bus, which passes in each direction at two-hourly intervals. There are no banks but the post office (Mon–Fri 8am–4pm, money changing till 3pm) will change cash from most major currencies. Internet facilities include Cyber Tzarzit (daily 9am–12.30pm & 2.30–10pm; 5dh/hr) and Tamohamat@Net (daily 9am–10pm; 5dh/hr), both reasonably easy to find in the middle of the village.

Accommodation

Hotels in Mirhleft are generally a little overpriced for what you get, especially as most people come here for the beach, and most of the hotels are at least a kilometre away in the village, but there are, nonetheless, some very agreeable places to stay, especially outside of the village itself.

Albergo de la Plage Plage Sidi Mohammed ben Abdallah, 2km south of town ☎028 71 90 56. A lovely little *auberge* standing all on its own at the end of a small beach dominated by an impressively large rock and overlooked by a mosque and a row of small shops. The rooms are nice and big, with pretty pictures and Berber rugs, and the beach is unspoiled and not suitable for surfing – which keeps most of the Mirhleft crowd away. ❺

Auberge des Trois Chameaux on the hill above town, just below the fort ☎028 71 91 87, ⓦwww.3chameaux.com. Classy maison d'hôte with a choice of "Berber rooms" (not all that special, nor particularly Berber, but very reasonably priced), suites (spacious and well-appointed, but pricey), and "royal suites" (spacious and well-appointed with private terraces and wonderful views). There's also a swimming pool, parking facilities, an in-house hammam, good food and great vistas over the countryside. Rates include breakfast. ❹

Hôtel Atlas opposite the souk ☎028 71 93 09, ⓦwww.atlas-mirhleft.com. Small, clean but simple rooms, some en-suite, with a roof terrace

giving views of the fort. Showers and toilets are impressively clean. Not a bad place, but overpriced, though rates include breakfast. ❹

Hôtel du Sud opposite the souk ☎028 71 91 07, ⓦwww.myspace.com/hotelsud. Fresh white rooms and hot-water showers, but it's still just a basic Moroccan hotel that's had a splash of paint and tripled its prices. ❸

Hôtel Restaurant Abertih on the corner of the main street with the Tiznit–Ifni road ☎028 71 93 04, ⓦwww.abertih.com. By common consent, the best hotel in the centre of the village, tastefully decorated with a good restaurant, well looked after by its French *patron*. ❹

Hôtel Tafoukt next to the souk ☎028 71 90 77. Of the simple hotels on the main street, this is the only one charging sensible rates, and in fact the cheaper rooms, with outside windows, are rather better than the slightly pricier ones, which have windows facing inwards. ❶

Maison d'Hôtes Aftas Beach Aftas beach ☎028 71 91 52, ⓦwww.aftasbeach.ifrance.com. A great location, on its own little beach, but not tremendously well kept, and you may well find, if you turn up unannounced, that there's nobody around. The rooms are also rather poky, and as almost the only building on the beach, it is a prime suspect for the litter and rubble that is unfortunately starting to accumulate there. ❹

Eating

On the main street, the *Restaurant à la Bonne Franquette* cooks up some tasty low-priced tajines, though you need to order them an hour ahead. *Hôtel Tafoukt* also serves good tajines at very reasonable prices, while *Hôtel Restaurant Albertih* offers posher **eating**, particularly fish. More geared up for the tourist trade is the *Sunset Pub Restaurant* on the Tiznit–Sidi Ifni road, which has pizzas, pasta, fish and even (if ordered half an hour in advance) paella, not to mention cold beer, and moderate prices.

Legzira Beach

This fine **beach**, with natural sea-worn rock archways, is just 10km north of Sidi Ifni, overlooked by an old Spanish fort from the hills above, whose marvellous thermal currents also attract hang-gliding enthusiasts from abroad. There's an informal campsite at the top of the cliff, just off the main road (pay the *gardien* 20dh a night per tent or campervan), and three *auberges* down on the beach itself, each with their own restaurant and generator (evenings only), and all offering half-board accommodation. The first and oldest of the three is *Auberge Legzira* (☏028 78 04 57, Ⓦwww.elgezira.free.fr; ❷), which is generally rated the best for meals. The other two – *Auberge Sables d'Or* (☏061 30 24 95; ❹), and *Auberge Beach Club* (☏028 87 50 13; ❹) – are newer, with brighter rooms, but they don't have the same degree of local knowledge and their food isn't as highly rated. You can get to Legzira on local bus #26 (every two hours) from Tiznit, Mirhleft or Sidi Ifni, but it's also possible to reach it on foot along the coast from Sidi Ifni, a pleasant two-and-a-half-hour walk along beach and cliffs, coming into Legzira under the rock archways.

Sidi Ifni

SIDI IFNI is uniquely interesting: a town that was relinquished by Spain only in 1969, after the Moroccan government closed off landward access to the colonial enclave. Built in the 1930s, on a clifftop site, it is surely the finest and most romantic Art Deco military town ever built. Many of its 1930s buildings have been the victims of neglect, but with a realization by the authorities that they attract tourists, steps are now being taken to conserve the town's heritage.

The town, or more accurately the site, then known as Santa Cruz del Mar Pequeño, "Holy Cross of the Small Sea", was held by the Spanish from 1476 to 1524, when the Saadians threw them out. In 1860, the Treaty of Tetouan – the culmination of Morocco's first military defeat by a European power in 200 years – gave it back to them, though they didn't reoccupy it until 1934, after they (or rather, the French) had "pacified" the interior.

Approaching Sidi Ifni from Tiznit, you pass through a modern and nondescript suburb called Colomina. Then the road swings down, across the Oued Ifni, and into Sidi Ifni proper. Once you've arrived in town, you should have no orientation problems: it's a straightforward grid, with steps leading down to the sea.

On Sundays a large **souk** takes place just east of the abandoned airfield, while on June 30 every year there's a **festival** to celebrate Ifni's 1969 reincorporation into Morocco. In recent years, Sidi Ifni has become something of a base for **surfing and paragliding**. Favourite spots for the former are on the main

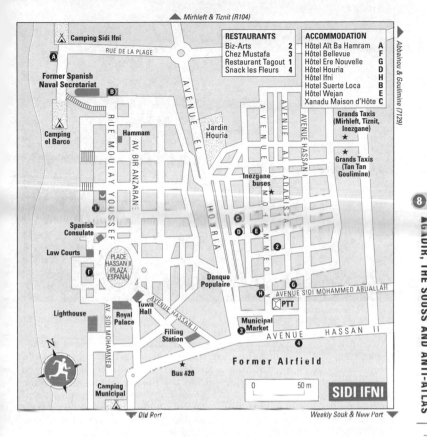

RESTAURANTS

Biz-Arts	2
Chez Mustafa	3
Restaurant Tagout	1
Snack les Fleurs	4

ACCOMMODATION

Hôtel Aït Ba Hamram	A
Hôtel Bellevue	F
Hôtel Ere Nouvelle	G
Hôtel Houria	D
Hôtel Ifni	H
Hotel Suerte Loca	B
Hôtel Wejan	E
Xanadu Maison d'Hôte	C

Camping Sidi Ifni

RUE DE LA PLAGE

Former Spanish
Naval Secretariat

Camping
el Barco

Hammam

AVENUE EL

Jardin
Houria

RUE MOULAY YOUSSEF

AV. BIR ANZARAN

AVENUE

AVENUE

AVENUE HASSAN I

AVENUE AL ADARISA

HOURIA

Grands Taxis
(Mirhleft, Tiznit,
Inezgane)
★

Grands Taxis
(Tan Tan
Goulimine)
★

Inezgane
buses ★

Spanish
Consulate

Law Courts

PLACE
HASSAN II
(PLAZA
ESPAÑA)

Danque
Populaire

AVENUE SIDI MOHAMMED ABDALLAH

PTT

Lighthouse

AV. SIDI MOHAMMED

Royal
Palace

Town
Hall

AVENUE HASSAN II

Filling
Station

Municipal
Market

AVENUE   HASSAN   II

Former Airfield

★
Bus #20

Camping
Municipal

0   50 m

SIDI IFNI

N

Old Port

Weekly Souk & New Port ▼

beach, just in front of the tennis courts, and another beach 100m south of the new port. Favourite paragliding spots are the hills behind Ifni, and at Legzira Beach, 10km to the north (see opposite).

The Town

It is the Spanish feel – and the **Art Deco architecture** – that is most attractive about Sidi Ifni. The town beach, with a *marabout* tomb at its northern end, is not that great (the beaches at Mirhleft, see p.661, are better) and is prone to long sea mists.

The obvious place to start out is the **Place Hassan II**, still commonly known by its original name, **Plaza de España**. It stands at the heart of the town and immediately sets a tone for the place, its centrepiece an Andalusian garden with Spanish tiled benches and a Moroccan tiled fountain, flanking a plinth which once bore the statue of General Capaz, who took Ifni for Spain in 1934. At one end of this square stands a **Spanish consulate** – a building straight out of García Márquez, now, it seems, terminally closed. Next to it, a **church** in Moorish-Art Deco style has now been adopted for use as the law courts. At the other end of the plaza, by a **town hall** complete with town clock, the former governor-general's residence is now the **royal palace**. Many of these buildings are in immaculate condition, with their stunning pastel shades picked out.

△ The Spanish Consulate, Sidi Ifni

More Art Deco splendour is to be seen off the square and along Avenue Hassan II, as well as around the **post office** which was also rather splendid before the top storey was demolished, and from where the town issued its own stamps under Spanish rule, featuring wildlife, traditional costumes and even the town's buildings. Next to the *Hôtel Suerte Loca* and alas sadly dilapidated nowadays, a building in the shape of a ship once housed the **naval secretariat** – its two forward portholes being windows of cells where miscreant sailors were held (it isn't the only ship-shaped building in town: the Banque Populaire, opposite the post office, is another). And there is a whole sequence of monumental **stairways**, rambling down towards the port and beach, and a magnificent Art Deco **lighthouse**. On Rue Moulay Youssef, there's even an Art Deco mosque.

To the south of the town is the **old port**, built by the Spanish, and out to sea is an odd little concrete island where ships used to dock. It was connected to the mainland by a unique cable car, which hauled goods as well as passengers. There's a **new port** further south, with big new sardine- and anchovy-processing factories. On the way to the latter is the former Spanish prison, now disused, and an airfield, also disused, whose last landing was an American locust-spraying plane, forced down here on one engine after being shot at by Polisario guerrillas in 1988. The airport building is now a meteorological station.

If you are interested in Ifni's past, you may care to call in on the barber's shop at 25 Av Mohammed V, where Hassan Aznag, the barber, will be glad to show you his collection of old photos of the town and to chat about its history.

Accommodation

Finding **accommodation** is easy enough, with seven hotels, all moderately priced. Of the three **campsites**, two are right by the beach at the end of Rue de la Plage: *Camping Sidi Ifni* (☏ 028 87 67 34), run by the proprietors of the

Hôtel Bellevue, which has a pool (15dh) and restaurant in summer, and high walls for security; and *Camping el Barco* (ⓣ028 78 07 07) which is longer established and more popular but more open to the elements – it has rooms (❹), though these are not good value compared with the hotels. *Camping Municipal* on Avenue Sidi Mohammed (ⓣ065 66 41 81) is the least attractive, rather spartan with little shade, and it can get rather crowded (in fact, it's often full).

Hotels

Hôtel Aït Ba Hamram Rue de la Plage – at the bottom of the steps ⓣ028 78 02 17. The town's best hotel, by the beach, with pristine en-suite rooms, a good restaurant and a bar. ❸

Hôtel Bellevue Pl Hassan II ⓣ028 87 50 72, ⓕ028 78 04 99. Three categories of room, all clean and well kept, though some are a bit on the small side, in an original Ifni Art Deco building on Pl de España with sweeping views over the beach, a noisy bar and a restaurant. Not the friendliest of places however. ❸

Hôtel Ere Nouvelle Av Sidi Mohammed Abdallah ⓣ028 87 52 98. The best of the four cheap hotels in the main part of town, with friendly staff and clean rooms, though not all have outside windows. ❶

Hôtel Houria (*Hôtel Liberté*) 9 Rue Mohammed el Kauzir, off Av Mohammed V; **Hôtel Ifni** Av Mohammed V ⓣ028 87 58 07; **Hôtel Wejan** 119 Rue Mohammed el Kauzir. A trio of small, basic hotels very close to each other, and all catering mainly for a Moroccan clientele. Prices are similar to those at the *Ere Nouvelle*, for which these can be considered as fall-back alternative options. ❶

Hotel Suerte Loca Rue Moulay Youssef ⓣ028 87 53 50, ⓕ028 78 00 03. A characterful place – the name ("Crazy Luck") and a building itself (and the name) reveal its small-town Spanish origins – which has been renovated and is run by a very welcoming English-speaking family. It has cheap rooms in the old Spanish wing, slightly pricier en-suite ones in a new wing, and is deservedly popular. It also has a good café-restaurant and a terrace overlooking the town and sea. ❷

Xanadu Maison d'Hôte 5 Rue el Jadida (look for the Ⲝ symbol on the door) ⓣ028 87 67 18, ⓦwww.maisonxanadu.com. Bright, cheerful *maison d'hôte* with lots of jolly pastel colours, breezy, modern, en-suite rooms and great views from the roof terrace. Rates include breakfast. ❺

Eating

There isn't a vast choice of places to eat in Sidi Ifni, but what there is should suffice. Of the hotels mentioned above, the *Aït Ba Hamram* has the best **restaurant**, though you can eat nearly as well and much more cheaply at the *Ere Nouvelle*. Other cheap options include a spit-roast chicken joint, *Snack Les Fleurs*, 13 Av Hassan II (daily 11am–1am), and a bunch of hole-in-the-wall eateries on the western side of the municipal market, with good fish tajines; of these, *Chez Mustafa*, the one nearest Avenue Hassan II (daily 9.30am–11pm), is the best. In addition there are a couple of restaurants in town that are worth trying: *Biz-Arts*, 15 Rue Casablanca, just off Avenue Mohammed V (Mon–Sat 9am–midnight; cheap), with a good-value 45dh set menu, though it needs to be ordered an hour or two in advance; and *Restaurant Tagout* off Rue Moulay Youssef (daily 8am–9pm; cheap), which has good tajines and fish dishes, though they probably won't have everything that's on the menu.

Moving on

Sidi Ifni has two early morning buses to Inezgane, one continuing to Marrakesh. Aside from those, the AGB bus #26 heads up to Tiznit via Legzira Beach and Mirhleft every two hours between 7am and 7pm. **Grands taxis** run to Mirhleft, Tiznit, Inezgane and Goulimine, leaving four blocks east of Avenue Mohammed V (see map). For further details see p.670.

There is little of note on the route south from Sidi Ifni to Goulimine, though the route itself is a pleasant one, especially in spring, when the slopes are green with a mass of euphorbia.

Goulimine and around

GOULIMINE (also spelt Guelmim or Gulimime) sounds pretty exciting in the brochures: "The Gateway to the Sahara", with its nomadic "blue men" and traditional **camel market**. The truth, sadly, is considerably more mundane. Goulimine is actually a fairly standard administrative town with a distinctly frontier feel to it, and a couple of small, fairly animated souks.

Though the scenery is indeed impressively bleak, you're still a long way short of seeing any Saharan dunes, and Goulimine's Saturday souk, known as the camel market, is a rather depressing sham, maintained largely for tour groups bussed in from Agadir. The market has all the usual Moroccan goods on sale: grain, vegetables, meat, clothes, silver, jewellery, sheep and goats. What it doesn't have in very great numbers is camels, as the beasts have steadily fallen from favour over the years in the wake of lorries and transit vehicles, and the caravan routes are more or less extinct. The few you do see here have been brought in either just for show or to be sold off for meat. If you are interested, the market is held a kilometre out of town on the road to Tan Tan; it starts around 6am, and a couple of hours later the first tour buses arrive. A couple of evening markets, one off the Route d'Agadir (now officially renamed Boulevard Mohammed VI) and one off Avenue des FAR, sell mainly food but are quite animated.

One or two local hustlers indulge in theatrical cons, usually involving invitations to see "genuine *hommes bleus*" in tents outside town; these are of course little more than an excuse to relieve tourists of some money. The nearest thing

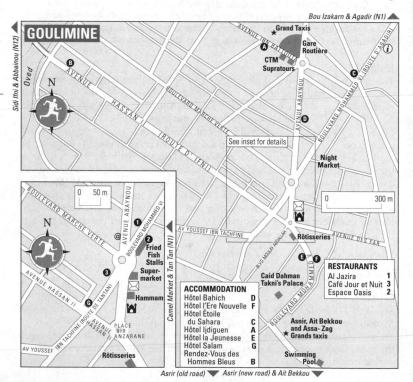

Goulimine has to a tourist sight is the remains of **Caid Dahman Takni's palace**, in the back streets behind the *Hôtel la Jeunesse*, ruined now but barely a hundred years old.

Practicalities

Arriving by bus or grand taxi, you'll probably be dropped at the *gare routière*, though night CTM services and some grands taxis may drop you elsewhere. At the heart of the town is the **Place Bir Anzarane**, with the main cluster of hotels and café-restaurants to its north.

There is a **tourist office** at 3 Résidence Sahara out on the Agadir road (Mon–Fri 8.30am–4.30pm; ☎028 87 29 11). There are plenty of **banks** with ATMs and also a small **supermarket**, Raji, in the centre of town, next to the **post office**. On the other side of *La Poste*, the town **hammam**, with showers as well as steam, is open for both sexes from 6am until 10pm. You can access the **Internet** at Horizons next to the Attijariwafa Bank on Avenue Abaynou (daily 8.30am–midnight; 4dh/hr).

Accommodation

There are quite a few very basic **hotels** in town, but not that many good ones. A trio of more interesting alternatives to a night in Goulimine are detailed in the "Around Goulimine" section on pp.668–669.

Hôtel Bahich 31 Av Abaynou ☎ & ☎028 77 21 78, ⓦwww.geocities.com/hotelbahich. An excellent deal, with comfortable rooms, some with en-suite showers, and 3-D paintings in the lobby by local artist, Hamid Kahlaoui. ❸

Hôtel Étoile du Sahara Bd Mohammed VI (Route d'Agadir) ☎028 87 10 95, ⓔhotel.residence.otoile .du.sahara@hotmail.com. A tall building topped by a panoramic terrace (though there isn't much to see), and offering a choice of ordinary rooms with shared bathroom facilities, or big rooms with a shower and a/c, all clean as a whistle, but only worth it if you need that a/c. ❹

Hôtel l'Ere Nouvelle 115 Bd Mohammed V ☎028 87 21 18. Best of the ultra-cheapies, basic but clean, with friendly staff and hot showers (7dh) on request. ❶

🏃 **Hôtel Ijdiguen** Av Ibn Battouta ☎ & ☎028 77 14 53. All new and shining, and right opposite the *gare routière*, with shared hot showers (7dh) and friendly staff; great if you've just arrived

on a late bus, or need to catch an early one, and a good halfway house between the most basic places and the better hotels ❷

Hôtel la Jeunesse 120 Bd Mohammed V ☎070 59 81 06. A reasonable fall-back if the *Ere Nouvelle* opposite is full. Located up a steep flight of steps. ❶

Hôtel Salam Av Youssef Ibn Tachfine (Route de Tan Tan) ☎028 87 20 57, ⓔhotel-salam@hotmail .com. Goulimine's top hotel (though not its most expensive), with large en-suite rooms round an open patio, a decent restaurant and the only bar in town. Like the *Bahich*, it has paintings by Hamid Kahlaoui in the lobby. ❸

Rendez-Vous des Hommes Bleus 447 Av Hassan II (Route d'Ifni) ☎028 77 28 21, ☎028 77 05 56. Located 600m up Av Hassan II, nearly at the oued, Goulimine's priciest hotel has satellite TV in all its cosy, clean, rather small rooms, but it isn't worth the price difference over the *Bahich* and the *Salam*. Despite the name, *hommes bleus* do not in fact tend to meet up here. ❺

Eating, drinking and entertainment

The *Hôtel Salam* has the best **meals** in town. For cheaper eating, there's a row of fried fish and tajine spots at the beginning of the Agadir road near the post office, and a bunch of *rôtisseries* (spit-roast chicken joints) on Avenue Mohammed V by Place Bir Anzarane. The *Hôtel Salam* has a **bar**, but nearly all its customers are male.

Al Jazira Bd Mohammed VI (Route d'Agadir). A popular joint selling spit-roast chicken, brochettes, sandwiches, salads and snacks. 10am–10pm. Cheap.

Café Jour et Nuit Av Youssef Ibn Tachfine (Route de Tan Tan). Cheap 24hr café (though it may close if there are no customers) slap-bang in the middle of town, which can rustle up a tajine at most times of the day or night should you need it, though it won't be the tastiest you'll have had in Morocco. **Espace Oasis** Bd Mohammed VI (Route d'Agadir). Pizzas, sandwiches (*panini*, no less) and coffee

served under a canopy or in a salon dominated by a pillar disguised as a palm tree and a couple of Hamid Kahlaoui paintings. Good for breakfast. 6am–11pm. Cheap.

Moving on

Daytime **bus departures** are from the *gare routière* on the Bou Izakarn road. **CTM** services leave from their office opposite the *gare routière* on Avenue Ibn Battouta (☎028 87 11 35), and **Supratours** buses leave from the Supratours office, a couple of doors from CTM (☎028 77 26 50).

Grands taxis leave from next to the *gare routière* for Ifni, Bou Izakarn, Tiznit, Inezgane, Agadir, Tan Tan, Laayoune and Smara, from a station on Avenue Hassan II, 100m north of the *Hôtel Salam* for Assaka (Land Rover taxis can also be found there), and from stations on the new Asrir road for Asrir, Aït Bekkou and Assa-Zag.

For frequencies and journey times see p.669 and p.670.

Around Goulimine: springs, oases and Plage Blanche

There are good little trips out from Goulimine to the hot springs of **Abbainou**, 15km northeast, and to the oasis of **Aït Bekkou**, 17km southeast; both offer pleasant alternative **accommodation** to a night in Goulimine. So, too, does the *auberge*-campsite at **Fort Bou-Jerif**, an old French Foreign Legion post, inland from **Plage Blanche** – the "White Beach" that stretches for sixty or so kilometres along the coast southwest of Goulimine.

A large **moussem** is held yearly in early June at **Asrir**, 10km southeast of Goulimine, with lots of camels and the chance to see **Guedra dancing**, a seductive women's dance of the desert, performed, from a kneeling position (developed for the low tents) to a slow, repetitive rhythm.

Abbainou

ABBAINOU (Abeïno) is a tiny oasis, located 15km northeast of Goulimine, and an easy excursion if you have transport (head up the Sidi Ifni road for a kilometre and it's signposted to the right). If you don't have a vehicle, you could negotiate a grand taxi (from the main rank by the souk). There are hot springs, which have been tapped, and on cool mornings the irrigation channels through the palmery can be seen steaming. There's a basic **campsite**, and a café and bakery in the village centre, but the main interest is the *station thérmale* at the immaculate *Hôtel Abainou* (☎028 87 28 92, ℱ028 77 04 24; ❹), where two indoor pools have been created, one for women at 28°C, the other for men, at a scalding 38°C! The village is certainly a more interesting place to stay than Goulimine.

Aït Bekkou

The largest and most spectacular oasis in the Goulimine area is **AÏT BEKKOU** (or Aït Boukka), 10km southeast along the road to Asrir, then a further 7km on *piste*. It can be reached by grand taxi from Goulimine (station on the Asrir road). Alongside the palmery is an impressive **hotel**, the *Tighmert* (☎028 77 08 06, ℱ028 77 20 11; ❺), built in mock-kasbah style and decorated, like the hotels *Bahich* and *Salam* in Goulimine, with paintings by Hamid Kahlaoui.

Aït Bekkou is a thriving agricultural community, with an especially lush strip of cultivation along a canal, irrigated from the old riverbed and emerging from a flat expanse of sand. You might even see the odd herd of camels being grazed out here. To reach the canal, head for the thicket of palms about 2km behind the oasis (or pick up a guide on the way).

Fort Bou-Jerif and Plage Blanche

Fort Bou-Jerif is a truly romantic spot, set beside the Oued Assaka, 13km from the sea, with a wonderful **auberge–campsite** (T072 13 00 17, Wwww .fortboujerif.com) in an old French Foreign Legion camp in the middle of nowhere, with excellent food (including camel tajine), and some superb four-wheel-drive excursions in the area, including, of course, trips to the Plage Blanche. Travellers heading for Mauritania and Senegal should also be able to pick up information here as a lot of overlanders stop over at the fort on their way down. They offer half-board accommodation in a "motel" (O), a "little hotel" (A) and a "hotel" (O) as well as camping (102dh for two people in a campervan), or a nomadic tent to sleep in if you don't have your own (40dh per person), plus power points for caravans, and rows of very clean showers (hot water) and toilets. If you book a room in advance, which you can do online, by mail (Fort Bou Jerif, BP 504, 81000 Goulimine) or by fax (F028 87 30 39), then you will have to take half-board, which is a good idea as the food is good and there is nowhere else to eat in any case.

The easiest route to the fort from Goulimine is via a paved road to Tisséguemane which branches left off the Sidi Ifni road a kilometre outside Goulimine, then 20km of *piste*, which you could probably persuade a grand taxi driver to take you along for a small fee, and which can be negotiated, with care, in a car or campervan. The fort can alternatively be approached on a paved road down the coast from Sidi Ifni to Foum Assaka, which leaves only 6km of *piste*. Failing that, you should be able to rent a Land Rover taxi from the station at the junction of Avenue Hassan II with Avenue el Moukaouama, about 300m north of the *Hôtel Salam*.

Travel details

Buses

Agadir to: Beni Mellal (1 CTM & 7 others daily; 8hr); Casablanca (5 CTM & 20 others daily; 9hr); Dakhla (2 CTM, 2 Supratours & 4 others daily; 19hr 30min); Essaouira (1 CTM & 25 others daily; 3hr 30min); Fes (9 daily; 12hr); Goulimine (4 CTM, 3 Supratours & 12 others daily; 4hr 30min); Immouzer (1 daily; 2hr 30min); Laayoune (4 CTM, 2 Supratours & 3 others daily; 11hr); Marrakesh (4 CTM, 3 Supratours & 20 others daily; 4hr); Meknes (1 CTM & 8 others daily; 12hr); Ouarzazate (3 daily; 7hr 30min); Rabat (3 CTM & 12 others daily; 11hr); Safi (1 CTM & 16 others daily; 5hr); Smara (1 CTM, 1 Supratours & 1 other daily; 9hr); Tafraoute (5 daily; 5hr); Tangier (1 daily; 16hr); Tan Tan (4 CTM, 3 Supratours & 8 others daily; 6hr); Taroudannt (5 daily; 1hr 30min); Tata

(5 daily; 9hr); Tiznit (4 CTM, 3 Supratours & 12 others daily; 2hr).

Goulimine to: Agadir (4 CTM, 3 Supratours & 12 others daily; 4hr 30min), via Tiznit (2hr 30min); Assa-Zag (2 daily; 3hr); Casablanca (3 CTM & 12 others daily; 14hr); Dakhla (2 CTM, 2 Supratours & 4 others daily; 15hr 30min); Laayoune (4 CTM, 2 Supratours & 3 others daily; 7hr); Marrakesh (3 CTM, 4 Supratours & 7 others daily; 9hr 30min); Ouarzazate (1 daily; 15hr) via Tata (9hr 30min), Foum el Hassan (6hr) & Akka (8hr); Rabat (1 CTM & 10 others daily; 16hr); Smara (1 CTM, 1 Supratours & 1 other daily; 6hr); Tan Tan (4 CTM, 2 Supratours & 19 others daily; 3hr).

Sidi Ifni to: Agadir (1 daily; 3hr 45min); Inezgane (2 daily; 3hr 30min); Marrakesh (1 daily; 8hr 30min); Tiznit (8 daily; 1hr 30min) via Mirhleft (40min).

Tafraoute to: Agadir (5 daily; 5hr); Aït Baha (1 daily; 2hr); Casablanca (5 daily; 14hr); Marrakesh (4 daily; 10hr); Rabat (1 daily; 16hr); Tiznit (5 daily; 3hr).

Taliouine to: Agadir (5 daily; 3hr 30min) via Taroudannt (2hr); Casablanca (2 daily; 13hr 30min); Er Rachidia (2 daily; 11hr); Goulimine (1 daily; 9hr) via Tiznit (6hr 30min); Marrakesh (3 daily; 9hr); Ouarzazate (3 daily; 3hr) via Tazenakht (1hr 30 min); Rabat (1 daily; 15hr 30min); Tinerhir (3 daily; 8hr); Zagora (1 daily; 6hr).

Taroudannt to: Agadir (5 daily; 1hr 30min); Casablanca (1 CTM & 5 others daily; 10hr); Marrakesh (1 CTM & 7 others daily; 6hr 30min); Ouarzazate (3 daily; 5hr) via Taliouine (2hr) & Tazenakht (3hr); Rabat (3 daily; 13hr); Tata (3 daily; 5hr) via Igherm (2hr 30min).

Tata to: Agadir (5 daily; 9hr); Bou Izakarn (3 daily; 6hr) via Akka (1hr 30min) and Foum el Hassan (3hr 30min); Casablanca (3 daily; 16hr); Marrakesh (2 daily; 10hr); Ouarzazate (2 daily; 5hr) via Foum Zguid (2hr 30min); Rabat (1 daily; 17hr); Tan Tan (1 daily; 12hr 30min) via Goulimine (9hr 30min); Taroudannt (3 daily; 5hr) via Igherm (2hr 30min); Tiznit (3 daily; 7hr).

Tiznit to: Agadir (4 CTM, 3 Supratours & 12 others daily; 2hr); Bou Izakarn (30 daily; 1hr); Casablanca (3 CTM & 9 others daily; 11hr); Dakhla (2 CTM, 2 Supratours & 4 others daily; 17hr 30min); Goulimine (4 CTM, 3 Supratours & 13 others daily; 2hr 30min); Laayoune (4 CTM, 2 Supratours & 3 others daily; 9hr); Marrakesh (3 CTM, 4 Supratours & 7 others daily; 7hr); Ouarzazate (1 daily; 9hr 30min); Rabat (2 daily; 13hr); Sidi Ifni (8 daily; 2hr) via Mirhleft (1hr); Smara (1 CTM, 1 Supratours & 1 other daily; 7hr); Tafraoute (5 daily; 3hr); Tata (3 daily; 7hr); Tan Tan (4 CTM, 3 Supratours & 13 others daily; 5hr 30min).

Grands taxis

Agadir to: Aourir (15min); Inezgane (15min); Taroudannt (1hr 15min); Tiznit (1hr 15min). Change at Inezgane for most southern destinations.

Aoulouz to: Ouled Berhil (30min); Taliouine (40min); Taroudannt (1hr).

Bou Izakarn to: Foum el Hassan (1hr 30min); Goulimine (1hr); Ifrane de l'Anti-Atlas (20min); Inezgane (3hr 30min); Tata (3hr 30min); Tiznit (1hr 30min).

Goulimine to: Agadir (4hr 45min); Aït Bekou (30min); Asrir (15min); Assaka (1hr); Assa-Zag (2hr); Bou Izakarn (1hr); Inezgane (4hr 30min); Laayoune (5hr); Sidi Ifni (1hr); Tiznit (2hr 30min); Tan Tan (2hr 30min).

Inezgane to: Agadir (15min); Essaouira (2hr 30min); Goulimine (4hr 30min); Laayoune (9hr); Marrakesh (3hr); Massa (45min); Ouled Teima (40min); Sidi Ifni (3hr 30min); Tan Tan (6hr 15min); Taroudannt (1hr 15min); Tiznit (2hr).

Ouled Berhil to: Aoulouz (30min); Taroudannt (40min).

Sidi Ifni to: Goulimine (1hr); Inezgane (3hr 30min); Mirhleft (45min); Tiznit (1hr 30min).

Taliouine to: Aoulouz (40min); Taroudannt (1hr 30min); Tazenakht (1hr).

Taroudannt to: Agadir (1hr 15min); Ameskroud (1hr); Aoulouz (1hr); Igherm (1hr 30min); Inezgane (1hr 15min); Marrakesh (4hr); Ouled Berhil (40min); Taliouine (1hr 30min).

Tata to: Akka (1hr); Bou Izakarn (3hr 30min); Foum el Hassan (2hr); Foum Zguid (2hr 30min); Issafen (2hr); Tissint (1hr).

Tiznit to: Agadir (1hr 15min); Bou Izakarn (1hr 30min); Goulimine (2hr 30min); Inezgane (1hr); Mirhleft (45min); Sidi Ifni (1hr 30min); Sidi Moussa d'Aglou (15min); Tafraoute (2hr).

Flights

Agadir to: Casablanca (RAM 4–5 daily, RAL 2 daily; 1hr–1hr 10min); Dakhla (RAM 1 weekly; 1hr 40min); Laayoune (RAL daily; 1hr 25min); Las Palmas (RAL 2 daily; 1hr 45min–2hr 45min); Marrakesh (RAL 6 weekly; 40min); Ouarzazate (RAL 3 weekly; 50min).

Goulimine to: Casablanca (RAL 3 weekly; 1hr 25min–2hr 25min); Tan Tan (RAL 1 weekly; 30min).

9

The Deep South and Western Sahara

CHAPTER 9

Highlights

✳ **Smara** A red ochre desert town, once the seat of local ruler the Blue Sultan, whose palace and great mosque constitute the town's main sights. See p.680

✳ **Tarfaya** A sleepy fishing village with an offshore fort, which you can walk over to at low tide. See p.683

✳ **Laayoune** A pioneering boom town built on subsidies and determination, with just a ghost, in its oldest quarters, of a Spanish colonial past. See p.687

✳ **Dakhla** The furthest south you can go by land from Europe without a visa – 22km from the tropics with sun all year round, and some lovely beaches within spitting distance of town. See p.693

△ Domed buildings, Laayoune

9

The Deep South and Western Sahara

F ew travellers venture south of Goulimine – and on the face of it there is little enough to commend the trip. The towns – **Tan Tan, Tarfaya**, **Laayoune** and **Dakhla** – are modern administrative centres, with no great intrinsic interest. The route, however, across vast tracts of *hammada* – bleak, stony desert – is another matter. The odd line of dunes unfolds on the horizon to the east, the ocean parallels much of the road to the west, and there is no mistaking that you have reached the **Sahara** proper. Returning, if you don't fancy a repeat of the journey, there are flights from Dakhla and Laayoune to Agadir, or from Laayoune to the **Canary Islands** (also accessible from Agadir).

An additional point of interest, now that the war with Polisario seems to be at an end, is the attention being lavished on the region by the Moroccan authorities. The **Saharan Provinces** (including – controversially – the former Spanish Sahara, claimed by Morocco with the 1975 Green March) begin just to the south of Tan Tan. **Laayoune**, never greatly regarded by the Spanish, has been transformed into a showcase capital for the new provinces; there are industrial plans for **Tarfaya**; and, with an eye to the traditional nomadic dwellers, the Moroccan authorities have also been assisting in building up the local camel herds.

The region's economic importance was long thought to centre on the phosphate mines at **Boukra**, southeast of Laayoune. However, these have not been very productive in recent years, and the deposits are not especially rich by the standards of the Plateau des Phosphates east of Casablanca. In the long term, the rich deep-water fishing grounds offshore are likely to prove a much better earner. This potential is gradually being realized with the development of fishing ports at Laayoune, Dakhla and Boujdour, together with industrial plants for fish storage and processing.

Throughout the Western Sahara and the Tarfaya strip (the southern part of the former Spanish protectorate), Spanish is fast being replaced by French as the dominant second language. Some older residents still speak Spanish, but officials, administrators, and other migrants into the Western Sahara from Morocco proper, as well as younger people in general, are much more likely to understand French.

THE DEEP SOUTH & WESTERN SAHARA

Canary Islands (Spain)

Lanzarote

Agadir

Sidi Ifni

Bou Izakarn

Goulimine

Foum El Hassan

Tenerife

Fuerteventura

Tan Tan Plage

Akhfenir

Tan Tan

Oued Drâa

ALGERIA

Gomera

Gran Canaria

Tarfaya

Tah

Abith

Border closed

27°40'

Al Haggaounia

ATLANTIC

Laayoune Plage

Foum El Oued

Lemsid

Laayoune

Lemseyed

Smara

Bir Lahlou

Boukra

Asli

Tifariti

26°

Boujdour

OCEAN

La Bouir

Oued Lakrâa

Galtat Zemmour

Dakhla

El Argoub

Bir Anzarane

23°30'

Imlili

Tropic of Cancer

Zouérat

MAURITANIA

Berm (desert wall)

Motel Dakmar

Bir Gandouz

Guerguarat

Nouadibhou

La Gouera

Choum

0   200 km

Nouakhott

Goulimine to Tan Tan

The approach from **Goulimine to Tan Tan** runs along 125km of straight desert road, across a bleak area of scrub and *hammada*. There are few features to speak of en route: a café and petrol station (55km from Goulimine); a small pass (85km); and finally a crossing of the **Oued Drâa** (109km), invariably dry at this point, where you will probably be asked to show your passport.

In colonial times, the Drâa was the border between the French and Spanish protectorates and a *piste* heads west to a last French **fort** at its mouth. Confusingly, the land immediately to the south of this point, the Tarfaya strip, was part of the Spanish Protectorate in Morocco, along with the area around Tetouan and Al Hoceima in the north. It was not considered part of Spain's two Saharan colonies (together known as the Spanish Sahara), of which the northernmost, Seguiat el Hamra, began at the 27°40′ N line just south of Tarfaya, while the southern one, Rio de Oro, began at the 26th parallel, just south of Boujdour. In 1958, two years after the rest of Morocco gained independence, the Spanish gave back the Tarfaya strip, but they kept the two Saharan colonies until November 1975 (see box, pp.684–685).

Tan Tan

Arriving at **TAN TAN**, between two sculptured camels, you might just find yourself wondering why you've bothered. A drab administrative centre, it survives in a low-key way through its status as a duty-free zone (the shops are full of radios and electric razors) and rather more so by its fishing port (25km distant), which is responsible for a large percentage of Morocco's sardine exports. Its one claim to fame is that it was a departure point for the famous **Green March** (La Marche Verte, or *el Massira el Khadra* – see p.684), an event commemorated on billboards and in street names throughout the south.

The town has around 50,000 inhabitants, many of them former nomads, who retain their distinctive pale blue robes. This clothing is much in evidence in the **souks** – the most animated part of a hot, sleepy town – as are a variety of *shesh*, strips of cotton that are wrapped round the head. The latter are a wise investment as sun protection if you're heading further south. In early June (or sometimes late May), Tan Tan livens up somewhat for the **Moussem of Sidi Mohammed Ma el Aïnin**, a tribal gathering featuring a camel fair and the sacrifice of a female camel.

Orientation and information

Tan Tan's main artery is the inevitable **Avenue Mohammed V**, and most of the town is spread out along it. Although the avenue is lined with buildings for

△ Camels being paraded at Tan Tan

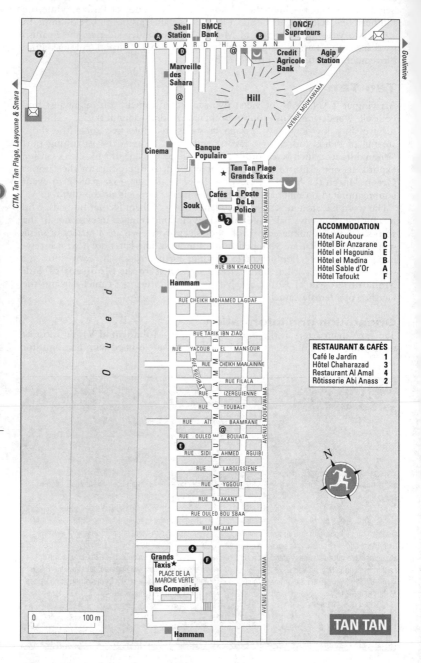

Goulimine

Shell Station
BMCE Bank
ONCF/ Supratours

Ⓐ Ⓑ

B O U L E V A R D   H A S S A N   I I

Ⓒ
Ⓓ
@

Credit Agricole Bank
Agip Station

Marveille des Sahara
@

AVENUE MOUKAWAMA

Hill

Cinema

Banque Populaire

★ **Tan Tan Plage Grands Taxis**

O u e d

Cafés
Souk
La Poste De La Police

AVENUE MOUKAWAMA

❶❷

❸ RUE IBN KHALDOUN

Hammam

RUE CHEIKH MOHAMED LAGDAF

RUE TARIK IBN ZIAD

RUE   YACOUB   EL   MANSOUR

RUE   CHEIKH MAALAININE

RUE RGUIBAT

AVENUE MOHAMED V

RUE FILALA

RUE   IZERGUIENNE

RUE   TOUBALT

RUE   AIT   BAAMRANE

@
RUE   OULED   BOUIATA

Ⓔ
RUE   SIDI   AHMED   RGUIBI

RUE   LAROUSSIENE

RUE   YGGOUT

RUE TAJAKANT

RUE OULED BOU SBAA

RUE MEJJAT

AVENUE MOUKAWAMA

❹

Grands Taxis★
Ⓕ
PLACE DE LA MARCHE VERTE

Bus Companies

Hammam

ACCOMMODATION	
Hôtel Aoubour	D
Hôtel Bir Anzarane	C
Hôtel el Hagounia	E
Hôtel el Madina	B
Hôtel Sable d'Or	A
Hôtel Tafoukt	F

RESTAURANT & CAFÉS	
Café le Jardin	1
Hôtel Chaharazad	3
Restaurant Al Amal	4
Rôtisserie Abi Anass	2

N

0   100 m

TAN TAN

the whole of its length, you can still catch glimpses down side streets of a parallel ridge, and to the west the riverbed of Oued Ben Khlil, overgrown in parts with castor oil plants and poisonous thorn apples, which "flows" north to join Oued Drâa.

Just off the bottom end of Avenue Mohammed V is the **Place de la Marche Verte**, with the **bus** and **grand taxi** rank, and several hotels. At the other end, a smaller square with several cafés and an arcade of shops down one side is referred to locally as **La Poste de la Police** because of the small police post that previously stood in the middle of it (now in the northeast corner – a snack bar has taken over its former location). **Petits taxis** can be found here, along with more cheap hotels, and **grands taxis** for Tan Tan Plage. Beyond the square, the street continues up to meet **Boulevard Hassan II**, the main road in and out of town, which enters from Goulimine between the sculptured camels and heads out, across the riverbed, towards Tan Tan Plage, the airport and Laayoune.

Most of the administrative buildings are at this (north) end of town. The main **post office** is on Boulevard Hassan II, with a branch office on the Laayoune road. There are a few **banks** on Boulevard Hassan II, as well as the Banque Populaire down near La Poste de la Police, all of which have ATMs. **Internet** access is available at numerous places including Mondial Net, 27 Bd Hassan II (daily 9am–midnight), Internet Club Yasser at the northern end of Avenue Mohammed V (daily 9am–11pm) and Cyber Abdou, 14 Rue Ouled Bouaita (daily 10am–3am); all charge 3dh/hr mornings, 5dh/hr evenings. Should you need a **hammam**, there's one for both sexes just behind the southern end of Place de la Marche Verte, and another at the far end of the street that leads north from the square. Tan Tan is not a place you may think of as good for **shopping**, but there are a couple of shops on Avenue Mohammed V that produce leather sandals and flip-flops: a nameless place at no. 338, and Merveille des Sahara at no. 72, which makes some quite attractive ones, mostly for women.

Accommodation

There are a number of unclassified hotels on and around Place de la Marche Verte and La Poste de la Police, most of them grotty if very cheap. Note that many of the cheaper places may balk at letting unmarried couples share a room. Better choices include:

Hôtel Aoubour junction of Av Mohammed V and Bd Hassan II ℡028 87 75 94. Handy for Supratours bus departures, with reasonably clean rooms (upstairs rooms are better than downstairs ones), but not great value compared to the *Bir Anzarane* down the road. ❶

Hôtel Bir Anzarane 154 Bd Hassan II ℡ & ℻028 87 78 34. The best deal in town, carpeted throughout, with shared but squeaky-clean bathrooms and very reasonable prices, though not all rooms have outside windows, and it's a bit of a haul from Pl de la Marche Verte. ❶

Hôtel el Hagounia 1 Rue Sidi Ahmed Rguibi ℡028 87 85 61. A cut above the other hotels in this part of town, with bare but large and generally clean rooms, and shared hot showers. ❶

Hôtel el Madina 68 Bd Hassan II ℡028 76 09 28, ℻028 76 56 83. En-suite rooms but no outside windows in this bright little unclassified hotel on the main road through town. ❷

Hôtel Sable d'Or Bd Hassan II ℡028 87 80 69. The best hotel in town, a two-star with large and immaculate en-suite rooms, some with balcony. ❸

Hôtel Tafoukt 98 Pl de la Marche Verte ℡028 87 70 31. The best value in Pl de la Marche Verte; reasonably clean, with shared hot showers (8dh a throw), though you're still better off popping up the street to the *Hagounia*. ❶

Eating and drinking

You are not spoilt for choice if you want a **meal** in Tan Tan. There are cafés around Place de la Marche Verte (the *Al Amal* on the north side of the square, for example) that claim to offer tajines, though you may well find that they don't actually have any on the go. The Poste de la Police square has a number of snack bars offering sandwiches and spit-roast chicken, newest and cleanest of which is the *Rôtisserie Abi Anass* on the north side (daily noon–midnight; cheap). The *Hôtel Chaharazad* on the south side of the square is your best bet for a meal, and should be able to rustle you up a decent tajine. The cafés to the south of the square are the best place to sip a mint tea and watch the world go by, in particular, the *Café le Jardin* (daily 7am–9pm) with a garden featuring a slide and swings, which younger travelling companions may appreciate. The two cafés at the northern end of the square, though nothing special, are also very popular and have a commanding view from their terraces over the comings and goings. The *Hôtel Sable d'Or* and the *Hôtel Bir Anzarane* should also be able to produce some food, especially if given notice.

There is no licensed bar in town, and entertainment is mainly limited to the Renaissance **cinema** between La Poste de la Police and the oued, which has a café, *Le Glacier*, attached, whose terrace overlooks the oued.

Moving on

All **buses** except Supratours and CTM leave from Place de la Marche Verte, the south side of which has a row of ticket offices. There are numerous daily services to Agadir, Marrakesh and Casablanca, a couple to Rabat and Laayoune, and one each to Tata and Ouarzazate.

ONCF/Supratours buses stop outside their offices on Boulevard Hassan II. There are two daily services to Laayoune, one of them continuing to Dakhla, one to Smara, and three daily to Agadir and Marrakesh. CTM buses stop at their office, 200m down the Laayoune road from the main post office, with services to Agadir, Marrakesh, Casablanca and even Rabat. Southbound services to Smara, Laayoune and Dakhla all pass through in the wee hours. **Grand taxi** runs include Goulimine, Inezgane, Agadir, Smara and Laayoune; if you strike lucky, you may also find direct taxis for Tarfaya and Tiznit (especially early mornings). They leave from Place de la Marche Verte except for taxis to Tan Tan Plage, which run from just north of La Poste de la Police.

Tan Tan Plage

TAN TAN PLAGE (also called El Ouatia), 28km from town on the coastal route to Laayoune, has been theoretically earmarked for development as a resort. The ambitious four-star *Hôtel Ayoub*, nearly twenty years under construction, will allegedly reopen some time, *insha'Allah*. In the meantime, there are three decent enough places to stay: the clean and cosy *Hôtel Belle Vue*, by the beach (T028 87 91 33; ❸), the older established *Hôtel Marin*, one block inland (T028 87 91 46; ❷), and the more functional *Hôtel Raja* on the main square (T028 87 94 11; ❷). The *Belle Vue* also has a decent restaurant, specializing in fried fish, and there's a Korean restaurant, *Korea House* (daily 11am–9pm; moderate) just round the corner. The **beach** is shadeless and often windswept, but it still gets quite crowded in summer.

A loop through Smara

It's possible to make a **loop** from Tan Tan along the new road, the R101 (formerly P44), to Smara, returning by way of the N1 (formerly P42) to Laayoune, and from there across to Tan Tan via Tarfaya – a circuit of some 800km. There are **buses** along each section (though not very frequent). If

Tourists can now travel freely in most Moroccan-controlled parts of what are called the **Saharan Provinces** (an administrative area created to include the **former Spanish Sahara**, while not coinciding with its boundaries), but do check first on the political situation. The government advisories listed on p.94 will have up-to-date information if any problems have arisen. Apart from this, the only obstacle would be for visitors who admit to being a writer or journalist: a profession not welcome in the region, unless under the aegis of an official press tour.

Otherwise, visiting Laayoune, Smara, Boujdour and Dakhla is now pretty routine, though it does involve answering a series of questions (name, age, profession, parents' names, passport number and date of issue, etc) at numerous **police checkpoints** along the way. This is all usually very amicable, but time-consuming (you'll be asked for these details four times, for example, between Laayoune and Dakhla, and taxi drivers may occasionally, as a result, be unwilling to carry foreigners. To save time it is a good idea to print out and/or photocopy several copies of a sheet with the following information listed, preferably in French (as given here in translation): family name (*nom*), given names (*prénoms*), date of birth (*date de naissance*), place of birth (*lieu de naissance*), marital status (*situation familiale*), father's name (*nom de père*), mother's name (*nom de mère*), nationality (*nationalité*), occupation (*profession*), address (*addresse* – which should be given in full), passport number (*numéro de passeport*), date of issue (*date de délivrance*), place of issue (*lieu de délivrance*), expiry date (*date d'expiration*), purpose of visit (*motif du voyage* – tourisme, for example), make of vehicle (*marque du véhicule* – you may of course have to leave this one blank), vehicle registration number (*matriculation* – ditto), date of entry into Morocco (*date d'entrée en Maroc*), place of entry (*ville d'entrée*) and police number (*numéro de police* – this is the number stamped in your passport alongside your first entry stamp into Morocco, typically six digits and two letters). For marital status, you could be single (*célibataire*), married (*marié* if male, *mariée* if female), divorced (*divorcé/divorcée*) or widowed (*veuf/veuve*). Armed with this, you can then give your details to police at every checkpoint, which will save them having to ask you for the information point by point.

Continuing south, the **border with Mauritania** is open (see p.697), a good surfaced road reaches the border with Mauritanian-held territory, and officials on both sides are now quite used to travellers passing through, so your only problem should be in finding transport (see p.696).

you're driving, you will find **petrol stations** in Tan Tan, Smara and Laayoune – petrol and diesel, incidentally, are subsidized throughout the Saharan provinces (including the former Spanish Sahara), and cost little more than half what you pay in Morocco proper – so if you embark on the trip be sure to fill up, and to carry good water supplies.

Tan Tan to Smara

The R101 between Tan Tan and Smara is almost devoid of habitation and features, though you will see some hills and valleys on either side of the road, starting around 20km out of Tan Tan. These peter out by the time you reach **ABITH** (or Abbatih), the route's single roadside hamlet, 75km from Tan Tan, where there are a couple of flyblown cafés and a flagpole. After another 36km, as you enter the Saharan Provinces, a couple of petrol stations allow you to take advantage of the lower fuel prices immediately. There is nothing else of interest before Smara, although the desert does get perceptibly darker in colour, due to the presence of black basalt.

Smara

SMARA (Es Semara) developed on an important caravan route across the Sahara, but today it is basically a military garrison town. The only link with its past is the remains of the Palace and Great Mosque of **Ma el Aïnin**, the "Blue Sultan", who controlled the region at the beginning of the twentieth century. If you do come to the town you should certainly see them.

The military presence in Smara includes both the Moroccan army and the UN, here to supervise the ceasefire and referendum. The difficulties of this are apparent even from a cursory look at the town, for there is a huge tented city outside of alleged former residents of Western Sahara brought in from Morocco proper; Polisario, inevitably, contest their origins and right to vote. Nonetheless, Smara manages quite an ambience, in spite of itself. The area around the souk in particular gets very lively of an evening, with grills in action along the street, traders selling their wares, and even the odd medicine man and snake charmer in attendance.

Information

The **post office** is by the local administration Province at the eastern end of Avenue Mohammed V. There are a couple of nameless **Internet** offices on Avenue Hassan II, one opposite the BMCE bank (daily 8.30am–11pm; 4dh/hr) and a block east (daily 9am–3am; 4dh/hr). The town also has a couple of **banks** (BMCE and Banque Populaire, both with ATMs), a **petrol station** and several garage-workshops for **car repairs**.

The town **hammam** is near the *Hôtel les Fleurs*. Coming up Boulevard de Stade from Avenue Hassan II, take the next right after the hotel and it's on the left. The first entrance is for women, the third for men, as illustrated above them (the second is for wood to heat the water). If you need a hot shower, the *Hôtel Amine* provides public showers round the back of the hotel.

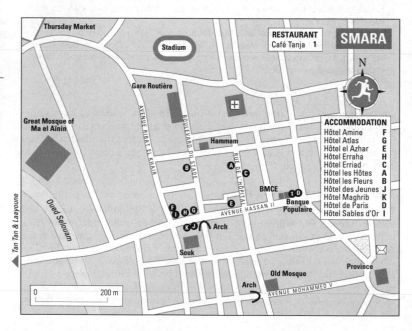

Accommodation

Smara has a dozen **hotels**, but most are extremely basic, with cold showers or none at all, and only one of the town's hotels has anything approaching comfort. You may have to check out the rock-bottom choices, however, if the more tolerable cheapies are full.

Hôtel Amine Av Ribat el Khair ☎ 028 88 73 68. The only really decent place to stay in town. The rooms are spotless, all with satellite TV, and there's a restaurant serving spit-roast chicken or tajines. The minus point, if you take a room that isn't en-suite, is that you'll have to leave the hotel and go round to the back of the building to take a shower. ❶

Hôtel les Fleurs 66 Bd du Stade ☎ 028 89 95 58. Very basic but friendly, with tolerably clean rooms and toilets. There should be hot showers ~~in the morning, and you are in any case near~~ the hammam. If this and the *Paris* are both full, and you need to stay somewhere very cheap, then you will have to try (in order of preference, and none of them recommended) the *Atlas* at 4

Bd du Stade, the *Erriad* at 49 Rue l'Hôpital, the *Erraha* at 16 Av Hassan II, the *Sables d'Or* at 1 Av Hassan II (next-door to the *Amine*), the *Hôtel des Jeunes* at 23 Av Hassan II, the *Les Hôtes* at 74 Rue l'Hôpital, or the *El Azhar* at 69 Rue de Figuig. ❶

Hôtel Maghrib el Arbi 15 Av Hassan II ☎ 028 89 91 51. Before the *Amine* opened this was Smara's top offering, which isn't saying much. No rooms are en suite, but they do have hot-water showers ~~and the rooms~~ ❶

Hôtel de Paris 156 Av Hassan II ☎ 010 78 09 88. Newer and generally better than Smara's other ultra-cheapies, with friendly staff, bright rooms, and hot showers in the evening. ❶

The Town

Ma el Aïnin's Palace is fairly well preserved. It stands near the oued and comprises the distinct residences of Ma el Aïnin's four main wives, one of which is now occupied by the *gardien* and his family. If you knock on the door, someone will open up and show you around, usually for a fee. Inside you can see the domed *zaouia*. Though plastered over, it is, like the rest of the palace, built of black basalt from the local hills. You can also see the palace's original armoured doors. What's left of the **Great Mosque** (daily 10am–noon & 3 6pm), a separate building further away from the river, is less well preserved, but you can still see the mihrab, and rows of basalt arches. To the south is a compound where Smara holds its **weekly market** every Thursday. A **festival** held in April 2007, sponsored by the Moroccan regional government and a number of businesses, featured a few musical entertainments and is expected to become an annual event.

The **old mosque** marked on our map is also made of local basalt, with a rather pretty stone minaret. This stands in the part of town built under Spanish rule, roughly bounded by the two arches and the *Hôtel Sables d'Or*. A distinctive aspect of the houses here (and elsewhere in the Western Sahara) is the eggshell-like domes which serve as roofs. The domes are said to keep the interior cooler by means of convection currents, but a more likely story is that the Spanish built them like this to prevent build-ups of wind-blown sand on the roofs of dwellings; the domes are certainly not traditional Saharawi structures, as the Saharawis were always nomads and their traditional homes were tents. Behind the mosque, you'll also find some of the strange tubular barracks put up by the Spanish to house their troops, now private homes. Like most buildings in Smara, they are painted a deep red ochre.

Eating

There isn't much in the way of **restaurants** in town, though there are open-air grills and fried fish stalls around the souk and on Boulevard de Stade. The best restaurant in town is at the *Hôtel Amine*. Avenue Hassan II has a lot of cafés, but few of them do food; one exception is the *Café Tanja*, next to the *Hôtel de Paris*, which has tajines.

Moving on

All **buses** and **grands taxis** leave from a yard on Boulevard de Stade near the stadium, where you'll find the offices of ONCF/Supratours, SATAS and CTM, the only firms that serve Smara, each with one daily departure to Marrakesh via Tan Tan, Goulimine, Tiznit and Agadir. ONCF/Supratours run the only daily service to Laayoune. All bus departures are currently in the morning. Grand taxi runs are to Laayoune, Tan Tan, Agadir and Marrakesh.

Note that the **road east from the town**, towards the Algerian town of Tindouf (where the Polisario have their main base), is firmly closed.

Smara to Laayoune

West from Smara, heading towards Laayoune, you pass through slightly more featured landscape than the route from Tan Tan to Smara. A new road has now been laid covering parts of the route. The old road cuts from time to time across the pre-existing *piste*, which is still marked by lines of cairns and poles. For the first 5km the desert remains black-ish from the basalt, before resuming its customary lighter hue for the rest of the route. There are prehistoric rock carvings to be found near **Asli**, 15km out of Smara, but you'd need local help and 4x4 transport to find these.

South of the new road, 30km from Smara stands a large brown flat-topped hill called **Gor el Bered** (Hill of the Wind). At the foot of its west side, just north of the old road is a small brown cupola-domed building resembling a *marabout* but it is in fact a structure built by the Spanish in the 1930s to extract chalk from the calcium-rich rock of the hill. A genuine *marabout* is to be found at **Sidi Khatari**, south of the new road some 90km from Smara. A couple of kilometres beyond, a water-processing plant desalinates the brackish water of the local well, before pumping it through recently laid pipes to Smara. Opposite is a **petrol station** and **café**.

There is little of any note to be seen for the next seventy-odd kilometres before the **turn-off to Boukra**, a mining town with a large garrison 25km to the southeast. Thereafter, however, you become aware of the **Boukra-Laayoune conveyor belt** snaking its way south of the road, bearing phosphates seaward for export. The vast region south of Boukra is a restricted military zone, and inaccessible to casual visitors.

As the road swings west for the last 50km before Laayoune its surface markedly improves and the canyon of the **Seguiat el Hamra** comes into view on the northern side. Seguiat el Hamra means "Red River" and, though there is no water in it for most of the year, the local clay turns it red when it does flow. The canyon is pretty impressive, but if you stop to take a snapshot be sure you are out of range of anything military. Meanwhile, signs along the road warn of animals crossing; the animal depicted, naturally, is a camel.

The oasis of **Lemseyed**, 12km before Laayoune, is a local beauty spot offering fine views over the canyon. Across the Oued, the **Fort of Dchira** was built by the Spanish in the very early days of their rule. It's currently occupied by the Moroccan army.

Tan Tan to Laayoune

The route between **Tan Tan Plage and Laayoune** cuts dramatically between desert and ocean. The coast, somewhat defying expectations, is mainly cliff – the desert dropping directly away to the sea, with only the occasional stretch of beach.

Tan Tan to Tarfaya

Between Tan Tan and Tarfaya there is little more than the roadside settlement of **AKHFENIR** (about 150km south of Tan Tan) with its 24-hour petrol station and several cafés, of which the *Café Paris* serves the best fresh fish in the area, while the *Café Puerto Cansado*, with its brightly painted cartoon characters and English-speaking owner, has the only pool table in town. The *Puerto Cansado* can also arrange accommodation, as well as trips to **Puerto Cansado**, 27km south (permit required) where you can see flamingos. Just beyond here is a rare stretch of accessible beach, with reputedly wonderful fishing. There are two places to stay: *Centre de Pêche et de Loisirs* (☎028 76 55 35 or 061 21 19 83, ⓔpechesicartakhfenir@menara.ma; half-board ❻); and *La Courbine d'Argent Centre de Pêche et Camping* (☎071 12 00 77, ⓦ www lacourbinedargent com ☎), which run strange fishing adventures and bird-watching excursions, and also has camping facilities.

Tarfaya

TARFAYA is a small town (population 6000) with a fishing port and a large monument to the Green March. It may be in line for greater things if an oil shale development, currently under consideration by Shell, goes ahead, but for the moment it's a quiet place, probably not far different from its years as a staging post for the Aéropostale Service – when aviators such as **Antoine de Saint-Exupéry** (author of *Night Flight* and *The Little Prince*) used to rest up here on their way down to West Africa.

The air service is commemorated annually in October by a "**Rallye Aérien**", with small planes flying south from Toulouse to Dakar in Senegal; Tarfaya is a night's stop. A monument to Saint-Exupéry in the form of a plane stands at the northern end of the beach. Very nearby, in the *Maison de l'Initiative* community centre, a **Musée Antoine de Saint-Exupéry** (Mon–Fri 8am–noon & 2–4pm; free) has a lot of quite interesting information about the air mail service that Saint-Exupéry pioneered, but even though this is the formerly Spanish zone of an Arabic-speaking country, the explanations are in French only.

Oddly enough, Tarfaya was actually founded, at the end of the nineteenth century, by a Scottish trader named Donald Mackenzie, and was originally called Port Victoria after Britain's queen. Mackenzie had a fort built, now known as **Casa Mar**, which is just offshore – a few metres' swim at low tide. During the Spanish occupation, the town was called Villa Bens and served as a very low-key capital for the "Southern Protectorate"; they abandoned it in 1958, leaving a church and a handful of villas.

These days Tarfaya has been overshadowed by Laayoune, but it's a beautifully lazy, do-nothing place to hang out for a day or two, and it has two basic **hotels**. The newer and better of them is the very welcoming *El Bahja* on a sandy street grandiosely named Boulevard Bir Anzarane (☎028 89 55 06; ❶). If that's full, you can fall back on the *El Massir*, close by off Rue Hassan II (☎071 58 13 85; ❶), which has slightly bigger but rather dingier rooms. Both can get quite busy during the fishing season (Dec–March). For **meals**, the *El Bahja* can whip up a tajine come lunchtime, but the cafés along the north side of the town's main street, Avenue Ahmed el Hayar, have excellent and very cheap fresh fried fish, or fish tajines – the best is the one nearest to the

The **Saharawi people** who live in the Western Sahara are largely descended from Arab tribes who moved into the area in the fifteenth century, and established themselves definitively with victory over the indigenous Sanhaja Berbers in the 1644–74 Char Bouba war. They speak an Arabic dialect called Hassania, which is much the same as that spoken in Mauritania, and somewhat different from the dialect spoken in most of Morocco. Their food and music are also more like those of Mauritania than of Morocco. However, Hassania-speaking Saharawis are not confined to the Western Sahara, and many live in southern Morocco too, as far north as Goulimine.

Spanish colonial rule

Spain held part of the Saharan coast in the early sixteenth century, but the **Saadians** drove them out in 1524, establishing **Moroccan control** over the coastline. In 1884, while European powers such as Britain, France and Portugal were carving up the rest of Africa, **Spain** got in on the act and declared the coast between Boujdour and the Nouadibhou peninsula to be a Spanish **"protectorate"**, gradually extending its boundaries inland and northward by agreement with other European powers. The Spanish didn't actually have much control over the area in practice, but built ports at La Gouera and Villa Cisneros (Dakhla), with occasional forays into the interior to "pacify" the Saharawi tribes. Full colonial rule was only introduced after the Spanish Civil War, when the territory was split into two colonies: **Rio de Oro**, with its capital at Villa Cisneros, and **Seguiat el Hamra**, with a new, purpose-built capital at Laayoune.

Following Moroccan independence and the 1958 return of the Tarfaya strip (see pp.674–675), Spain merged its two colonies to form the **Spanish Sahara**, which was considered a province of Spain itself, much like Ifni, Ceuta and Melilla. But it was only in the 1960s, after the discovery of **phosphates at Boukra,** that Spain actually started to develop the territory.

By that time colonialism was out of fashion. Britain and France had pulled out of most of Africa, and only the Fascist-ruled Iberian states of Spain and Portugal still held onto their African colonies, with international pressure mounting on them to quit. In 1966 for example, the **UN** passed a resolution calling on Spain to organize a referendum on independence in the Sahara. Meanwhile, as education became more widespread, the Spaniards were confronted with the same problem that they and the French had faced in Morocco thirty years earlier – the rise of nationalism. A **Movement for the Liberation of the Sahara** was formed in 1967, and in 1970 it organized a protest in Laayoune against Spanish rule. This was brutally put down, and the Movement was banned, but Spanish repression only succeeded in radicalizing opposition. In 1973, a group of militants formed the Frente para la Liberación de Seguiat el Hamra y Rio de Oro (**Polisario**), and began a guerrilla campaign for independence.

The Green March, and war

Under pressure from Polisario, and with its dictator General Franco on his last legs, Spain began to consider pulling out of the Sahara, but Morocco's King **Hassan II** now claimed sovereignty over the territory on the basis that it had been under Moroccan rule before Spanish colonization. The case went to the **International Court of Justice** in the Hague, which ruled that, though some Saharawi tribes had indeed paid allegiance to the Moroccan sultan, the territory had not been substantially Moroccan before colonization, and its people were entitled to self-determination. In accordance with this ruling, Spain reluctantly agreed to hold a referendum on independence. Under pressure at home over domestic issues, however (see p.718), Hassan saw advantages in waving the nationalist flag as a distraction, and the next month led a **"Green March"** (*Massira el Khadra*) of 350,000 Moroccan civilians (subsequently replaced by soldiers) across the border to claim the territory. At the same time a secret agreement was reached in Madrid to divide the territory between Morocco and Mauritania as soon as Spanish troops had withdrawn.

The Madrid signatories had however underestimated the Saharawis' determination to fight for their independence. In February 1976, when Spanish forces left, Polisario proclaimed the **Saharawi Arab Democratic Republic** (SADR), and fought back against Moroccan and Mauritanian occupation, backed by Algeria, and sometimes Libya, who saw the Sahara as a stick with which to beat their regional rivals. Thousands of refugees fled into Algeria, where they settled into increasingly unhygienic Polisario-run refugee camps rather than submit to Moroccan or Mauritanian rule. Algeria ceded the territory around the camps to the SADR; 200,000 people still live in them.

Polisario's early military successes were impressive, and Mauritania in particular did not have the resources to beat them. In 1978, the war's destabilization of the Mauritanian economy brought down the government. The new regime made peace with Polisario and pulled out of the Sahara (apart from La Güoüra and the western side of the Nouadibhou peninsula, which Mauritania still occupies). The Moroccans moved in to replace them, but by the early 1980s they had been pushed into a small area around Laayoune and Dakhla, and the phosphate mines lay idle. Polisario guerillas even managed to infiltrate into Morocco itself. But the Moroccans fought back and, beginning in 1981, built a series of heavily defended **desert walls** (*berm*) that excluded Polisario forces from successively larger areas. The sixth wall, built in 1987, established Moroccan control over two thirds of the territory, including all its economically important parts and the whole of the coastline. Polisario, now confined to areas behind the *berm*, particularly the region around Bir I ahlou and Tifariti, increasingly turned to diplomacy to gather support, with some success. In 1985, the OAU (now the African Union) admitted the SADR to full membership; Morocco left the organization in protest.

Ceasefire and future prospects

In 1988 a UN plan for a **referendum,** to choose between incorporation or independence, was accepted in principle by both sides, and 1991 saw a ceasefire, with the deployment of a UN peacekeeping force called MINURSO, but the years since have seen the UN aims frustrated, with arguments over the voting list leading to repeated postponement of the referendum; Morocco in particular has brought in large numbers of supporters to vote its way should the promised referendum ever be held. In theory, it will still take place, but observers are sceptical. Having invested so much in the territory – not only in military terms, as subsidies, tax concessions and infrastructure building have all been a heavy drain on the Moroccan economy – it seems inconceivable that Morocco will relinquish its claims. In 2002, Morocco's King Mohammed VI stated that he would never give up any part of the territory, and pro-independence protests in Laayoune and Dakhla are regularly put down by force, but the king has otherwise tried to be conciliatory, granting a royal pardon to hundreds of Saharawi political prisoners, and in 2007 he proposed a new settlement based on limited autonomy under Moroccan sovereignty, which Polisario inevitably rejected. Meanwhile Morocco has started building little villages all along the coast to establish "facts on the ground", and, as an important strategic ally of the West, is unlikely to face much international pressure on the issue. Truth is, prospects for independence are bleak, and limited autonomy is probably the best the Saharawis can hope for.

The case for and against Morocco's claim to the Western Sahara is, of course, keenly argued on the Internet. For the pro-independence side (though it may be sensible not to check these while in Morocco), see Ⓦwww.wsahara.net or Ⓦwww.arso.org. For the Moroccan case, see Ⓦwww.westernsaharaonline.net or (in French) Ⓦwww.saharamarocain.net.

post office by the Maison de la Pêche fishing supplies shop. Note that there is no bank in Tarfaya, so bring as many dirham with you as you'll need.

Transport is a little bit tricky; getting to and from Tarfaya, you may well have to wait a few hours before anything turns up. Grands taxis do make the run from both Tan Tan and Laayoune, provided they can find the passengers to fill them – as always, mornings are best. Local firm Najmat Sahara runs a daily bus from Tan Tan and one from Laayoune. Aside from

△ Fish market, Tarfaya

that, Supratours services between Tan Tan and Laayoune (two a day in each direction) call at Tarfaya, but SATAS and SAT services don't. CTM used to serve Tarfaya but have recently stopped, though it may be worth asking if they have resumed.

South to Laayoune

South of Tarfaya you cross into the Western Sahara just after **Tah**, where a red granite monument flanking the road commemorates the Green March, which set off from this windblown little hamlet in November 1975. From here on you begin to traverse real sand desert – the **Erg Lakhbayta**. The effect, however, is lighter than that implies, for along the way are a series of enormous **lagoons**, their water prevented from reaching the sea by long spits of sand, and **salt pans**, still being worked. These are important migratory sites, which should provide rewards for **bird-watchers**.

Laayoune

With a population of around 200,000, **LAAYOUNE** (AL AYOUN, sometimes spelt AAIUN in the Spanish colonial period) is the largest and the most interesting town in the Western Sahara, though it was only founded in 1940. Its development as a provincial capital is almost immediately obvious – and impressive, as you survey its building programmes such as the 30,000-seat stadium, with real grass, maintained for the area's handful of football teams. The city has the highest per capita government spending in Morocco and soldiers, billeted here for the conflict with Polisario, have been employed in many of the projects.

The population growth – from little more than a village when the Moroccans took over – has been aided by massive subsidies, which apply throughout the Western Sahara, and by an agreement that settlers should initially pay no taxes. They are a mix of Saharawis, many driven here by the drought of the last few years, and Moroccan immigrants induced to move down here in search of work. The fact that most of Laayoune's residents are here by choice – only a minority of current residents were actually born here – gives the place a dynamism and pioneering feel that contrasts quite sharply with the weight of tradition that hangs heavy on cities like Fes and Marrakesh. The result is that, although Laayoune has little in the way of obvious sights, its atmosphere is quite a change from that of towns in Morocco proper.

Orientation and information

The first sight of Laayoune, coming from Tarfaya, is across the steep-sided valley of the **Seguiat el Hamra**, which has been dammed to make another, shallow lagoon. The old **lower town**, built by the Spanish, lies on the southern slope of the valley, with the new **upper town**, developed since the Green March, on the high plateau beyond. Note that the main street uptown, Avenue Mecka al Mokarrama on street signs, is also called Avenue de la Mecque or Avenue Mekka.

There may be no tourists in town but there's a tourist delegation and **information** office on Avenue de l'Islam, hidden away in a compound opposite the *Hotel Parador* (Mon–Fri 8.30am–4.30pm; ☎028 89 16 94).

▲ Smara

◀ Tarfaya & Tan Tan

▼ Laayoune Plage, Boujdour & Dakhla

LAAYOUNE

0   200 m

N

Seguiat el Hamra

RESTAURANTS

Café Restaurant Yakout	4
La Comeda	3
Las Dunas	9
Haïti (Chez Aziz)	10
La Madone	8
Moyen Atlas	7
La Perla	6
Le Poissonnier	5
Restaurant el Bahja	1
Restaurant Marhaba	2

ACCOMMODATION

Hôtel Assahel	M
Hôtel Jodesa	H
Hôtel Lakouara	D
Hôtel Marhaba	C
Hôtel al Massira	G
Hôtel Mekka	I
Hôtel Naglir	E
Hôtel Parador	L
Hôtel Rif	B
Hôtel Sahara Line	J
Hôtel Sidi Ifni	A
Hôtel Smara	F
Hôtel Zemmour	N
Youth Hostel	K

Grands taxis

AVENUE ABOU BAKER ESSADIK

AVENUE DE LA MARINE

EJERCITO

AVENUE PRINCE MOULAY ABDALLAH

RUE ALLAL BEN ABDALLAH

SOUK EZ ZAJ

PLAZA DE LAS CANABIS

PLACE HASSAN II

BOULEVARD MOHAMMED V

BOULEVARD 28 FÉVRIER

Cathedral

AVENUE HASSAN II

RUE KADI EL GHALAOUI

Colline des Oiseaux

Water Towers

Paleis des Congrès

Place Mechouar

AVENUE DE L'ISLAM

Great Mosque

AVENUE MOULAY YOUSSEF

AVENUE MOULAY ISMAIL

Complexe Artisanal

COLOMINA

Supratours

Place Oum Saad

AVENUE MECKA AL MOKARRAMA

Atlas Garage

RUE AHMED EL MANSOUR

RUE BRAHMAN ENNACER

RUE KAIROUAN

Top Fly

Regional Air Lines

AVENUE 29 NOVEMBRE 1975

Binter

CTM. @

SATAS

PLACE BIR ANZARANE

AVENUE 24 NOVEMBRE

PLACE DOHRA

PLACE DOHRA

SAT ★

RAM

SATAS

AVENUE MOULAY IDRISSI

AVENUE MECKA AL MOKARRAMA

Nejmat Sahara ★

AVENUE OUM SAAD

RUE ATFILA

SOUK DJEMAL

Market

AVENUE SALEM BILA

Stadium

Airport ✈

Accommodation

Laayoune's **hotels** have done good business over the past few years with the UN, who block-book the best, though all now keep rooms aside for non-UN visitors. Unclassified hotels, of which there are maybe a score, are concentrated in the Souk ez Zaj and Souk Djemal districts (the former arguably the most interesting part of town to stay in), but they can be very basic indeed, and none too clean. There's a **youth hostel** behind the sports stadium (T028 89 34 02), but little reason to use it – it's inconveniently located, not especially salubrious, and a dorm bed (40dh) costs the same as a double room at a cheap hotel.

Cheap

Hôtel Assahel Av Moulay Idriss I T028 89 01 70. A good-value choice among the small group of cheapies off Pl Dchira, not very central but well placed for the Tan Tan and Dakhla grand taxi stations. The upstairs café, where you can smoke a sheesha pipe or drink a freshly squeezed orange juice, overlooks Pl Dchira. Hot showers are available (10dh). **①**

Hôtel Marhaba Av de la Marine, Souk ez Zaj T028 89 32 49. A good value, inexpensive hotel, a cut above most in this price range, but not the cleanest place you'll ever see (make sure your sheets are fresh, to start with). Hot showers available **①**

Hôtel Rif 99 Bd 28 Février, Souk ez Zaj, overlooking the Seguiat el Hamra T028 89 43 69. This was the best of Souk ez Zaj's cheapies, with clean rooms and less clean hot showers (10dh) but at last check they'd put the price up so high that it simply wasn't worth it, unless you can haggle them down to a sensible rate. **②**

Hôtel Sidi Ifni 12 Rue Sanhaja, Souk ez Zaj, off Av de la Marine (no phone). This place has, to its credit, the fact that it's at the heart the oldest part of town, and of Laayoune's original community, with rooms that are decent enough for the price, but it has no hot water (though installation is planned), and there's no hammam nearby. **①**

Hôtel Smara 130 Av Salem Bila, Souk Djemal (no phone). One of the better choices among the various cheap hotels in the Souk Djemal quarter; cleaner and more pleasant than most of the others, though still pretty basic, with no showers (Fl Fath hammam is 100m east, off Av Salem Bila by no.123), and it isn't as good value as the Souk ez Zaj options. **①**

🏃 **Hôtel Zemmour** 1 Av Oum Saad, just off Pl Dchira T028 89 23 23. Better, cleaner and brighter than any of the other budget options by a very long chalk; great value with pretty little apple-green rooms, some with a balcony. Bathroom facilities are shared but sparkling, and showers are hot. It costs slightly more than the rock-bottom options, but it's well worth the difference. **②**

Moderate to expensive

Hôtel Jodesa 223 Av Mecka al Mokarrama T028 99 20 64, F028 89 37 84. A very pleasant little place, with cosy carpeted rooms (some en suite), a roof terrace, a downstairs café, and a car rental service. **①**

Hôtel Lakouara Av Hassan II T028 89 33 78. A comfortable two-star with large rooms, en-suite bathrooms, satellite TV and 24hr hot water. Partly block-booked by the UN, but with rooms set aside for the general public. The upstairs café is used almost exclusively by hotel guests, so it's nice and quiet. **⑤**

Hôtel al Massira 12 Av Mecka al Mokarrama T028 09 42 25, F028 89 09 62. A smart and efficient modern hotel, conveniently located, though the rooms are quite small. It's partly block-booked by the UN, but keeps a number of rooms free. **⑦**

Hôtel Mekka 205 Av Mecka al Mokarrama T028 99 39 96. Clean and cosy with en-suite rooms, similar to the neighbouring *Jodesa* except that the rooms are smaller and have TVs (not satellite). **③**

Hôtel Nagjir 6 Pl Bir Anzarane T028 89 41 68, F028 89 39 11. Good-value four-star, recently refurbished, and with a good restaurant, and though most rooms are taken by the UN, they keep twenty-odd for casual visitors. **⑤**

Hotel Parador Av de l'Islam T028 89 20 14, F028 89 09 62. The old Spanish grand hotel, run by the same management as the *Al Massira*, but rather more traditional in style, with larger rooms and a pool. The corridors are decorated with photos of the 1975 Green March. **⑦**

🏃 **Hôtel Sahara Line** Av 24 Novembre at Rue Kairouan T028 99 54 54, ⊜tourismesahara@menara.ma. A four-star, though it doesn't have a bar or a pool. Charming management and lovely rooms, which aren't huge, but are equipped with satellite TV and a/c, and there are "suites" with a seating area, and even a presidential suite if you need something more spacious. They have a promotional discount of around 30 percent, which they offer on a permanent basis to anyone presenting this guidebook at reception. **⑥**

The Town

Most of the new building is in the upper town; the bulk of the old Spanish settlement, more dishevelled, lies down below, stretching eastwards from the old **cathedral**, which is open for Sunday morning mass. Failing that, the priest will normally let you have a look inside if you ring on his bell at a reasonable hour. Across the main square, on the east side, the **town hall** was formerly used by the Spanish administration, and is now largely occupied by the Moroccan military (so don't try to photograph it).

The district stretching east from here, **Souk ez Zaj** (Glass Market), is the oldest part of Laayoune, and many of its residents have been here since Spanish days. It's very run-down, as if forgotten amid the investment that's been pumped into the rest of town, but it's undoubtedly Laayoune's most atmospheric quarter. There's a smattering of cheap hotels, and many of the houses still have the eggshell-domed roofs typical of the Western Sahara (see p.681). One that doesn't, however, is **Laayoune's oldest house**, at 16 Bd 28 Février (on the corner of Rue No.18, and opposite the end of Bd Mohammed V). Though originally constructed in 1933 it was, like many one-storey houses of the period, extended upwards, losing the domed roof in the process. A few tiled Spanish street signs – or Arabic ones put up by the Spanish – are still in evidence around Souk ez Zaj, though most have been replaced by blue metal plaques painted in Arabic and French. The rather battered-looking **Plaza de las Canarias**, behind the *Hôtel Sidi Ifni*, and the tiled steps leading south from Rue de la Marine opposite Rue el Mouahidine, still have the ghost of a Spanish flavour.

East of Souk ez Zaj, the district of **Ejercito** (Spanish for army) houses Moroccan troops as it did their Spanish predecessors. South of Avenue de la Marine, some of the tubular barracks are now private houses, hemmed in by more modern, box-like, blocks of flats. The other district left from Spanish times is **Colomina**, to the south of Avenue Mecka al Mokarrama. It is nicknamed Colomina Tarduss (Kick) because, when the Spanish left, Moroccan settlers kicked in the doors to squat their houses. Nowadays, most of the quarter has been rebuilt. Apart from the areas just described, everything else in Laayoune was desert before 1975.

Of the Moroccan-built districts, **Souk Djemal**, west of the Goulimine grand taxi station is a workaday, working-class area, and the most animated part of town, especially around dusk. It is also where the **main market** is located, and it represents the first phase of Moroccan settlement here. The newer areas are more prosperous, stretching along **Avenue Mecka el Mokarrama**, and radiating outwards from **Place Dchira**.

Most striking of the modern developments is the **Place Mechouar**, which is flanked by the new **Great Mosque**. Lining one side of the square is a series of tent-like canopies for shade and at each corner are towers to floodlight the square at night. There is also an ambitious **Palais des Congrès**, designed by one of the late King Hassan's favourite architects, French-born André Paccard. Across the way is the new **stadium**, as fine as any in Morocco.

In addition to such public statements, there are a few pleasant corners, like the landscaped gardens of the **Colline des Oiseaux**, with their cages of exotic birds – with blinds to be drawn down over the cages in the event of sandstorms. It is now closed, and most of the birds gone, but if you go to the entrance on Avenue Ockba ben Nafaa, and ask the *gardien*, he may let you in for a tip. Of some interest, too, is the **Complexe Artisanal**, behind the Great Mosque, where twenty little workshops, capped with cupolas, provide space for metal, wood and jewellery craftsmen.

Eating

Plenty of restaurants in Laayoune serve Moroccan food, but none of them offer Saharawi food, which is typically meat or fish stew with rice – more like the food of Mauritania than that of Morocco. For an upmarket feed, the hotels *Al Massira*, *Nagjir* and *Parador* all have good **restaurants**. At the other end of the scale, the liveliest place to hang out in the evenings is **Souk Djemal**, where the cafés around the market serve cheap evening meals of tajine or fried fish, and also breakfasts, with *melaoui* and *harsha*, though coffee lovers should always check that the coffee they serve is real, since some of them have only instant (and don't warn you of this when you order). *Moyen Atlas* at 50 Av Mecka al Mokarrama, opposite the *Hôtel al Massira*, is a reasonably good patisserie where you can sit in or out and have your pastry with tea, coffee or orange juice.

Café Restaurant Yakout Av Talha Bnou Zubeir, behind Atlas garage. A Moroccan restaurant, prettily decorated with tourist souvenirs, with morning tajines and brochettes; it also offers apple-flavoured sheesha pipes and tea or coffee. Daily 8am–2am. Cheap.

La Comeda Av Hassan II. A diner serving spit-roast chicken, salads, burgers and snacks. Not gourmet eating by any means, but cheap and friendly, and plugs a gap. Daily 12.30pm–midnight. Cheap.

Las Dunas middle of Pl Dchira. You can get anything from a coffee and a croissant to a burger or a chicken tajine here, served in a pleasant a/c saloon or outside around a fountain in the square. Very civilized. Daily 7am–11pm. Moderate.

Haiti (Chez Aziz) 16 Rue No.1 ⊕028 99 44 42. A small but pleasant pizzeria-restaurant behind the *Hôtel Nagjir*, with pizza, pasta, fish kebabs, fried squid and roast chicken. The pizzas themselves aren't very good, but their fish dishes aren't bad and the prawn bisque is worth trying. Takeaways and home delivery available. Daily noon–3am. Moderate.

La Madone Av 24 Novembre ⊕028 99 32 52. A small pizzeria that's little more than a hole in the wall, but it does have a few tables both inside and out. The pasta dishes are pretty good (try the spaghetti aux fruits de mer), and they also do reasonable fish dishes and pizzas. Takeaways and home delivery available. Daily 11am–12.30am. Moderate.

La Perla 185 Av Mecka al Mokarrama. The menu looks great, with prawn bisque, gazpacho and a fine selection of fabulous-sounding fish dishes, but unfortunately it fails to live up to its promise, though it isn't bad for the price. Daily noon–3pm & 6.30–11pm. Moderate.

Le Poissonnier 183 Av Mecka al Mokarrama. It looks like *La Perla* next door, and the prices are similar, but the ambience is a bit slicker and the food is far superior, with excellent fish soup and wonderful grilled sea bass. Daily noon–3pm & 6.30–11pm. Moderate.

Restaurant el Bahja 8 Av Mohammed V, Souk ez Zaj. A popular but rather grubby Moroccan greasy spoon offering *kofta* (supposedly camel), lamb chops, and plenty of chips. The *Marhaba*, opposite, is much the same. Daily 10am–midnight. Cheap.

Listings

Airlines Binter 194 Av Mecka al Mokarrama ⊕028 98 05 17; RAM, Pl Bir Anzarane, next to *Hôtel Nagjir* ⊕028 99 58 10 to 12; Regional Air Lines, 176 Av Mecka al Mokarrama, opposite *La Perla* and *La Poissonnier* restaurants ⊕028 89 26 39; TopFly 149 Av Mecka al Mokarrama ⊕028 98 08 92.

Banks There are plenty of banks in town with ATMs and exchange facilities, with one group at the foot of Bd Mohammed V, near Pl Hassan II, and another in Pl Dchira.

Car rental No major firms are represented and there is a rapid turnover of small operators due to shortage of punters, but the biggest and

longest-established firm is Soubai, on Rue Afila just off Pl Dchira ⊕ & ⊕028 89 31 99.

Hammams There's one just off Av de la Marine (south side) between Pl Hassan II and *Hôtel Marhaba*, one in Souk Djemal off Av Salem Bila (north side) by no.123, and one in the backstreets behind the *Hôtel Nagjir*.

Internet access Loads of places around town, including: Cyber el Ihssane, 152 Av Mecka al Mokarrama (daily 9am–1.30pm & 3.30–11pm; 5dh/hr); and Dar el Khir, Av Moulay Ismail (daily 9am–11pm; 4dh/hr); W@dernet, on Av Mecka al Mokarrama, next to the water towers (daily 11am–midnight; 5dh/hr).

Post office The main office is on Pl Hassan II.
There's a branch office on Pl Dchira.

Supermarket Supermarket Dchira on Av 24
Novembre by Pl Dchira is small, but well stocked.

Moving on

Bus services mostly depart from Place Bir Anzarane or just off it. The exceptions are the **ONCF/Supratours** services, which leave from their office on Avenue Oum Saad at the southern end of Avenue Moulay Ismail (☎028 89 88 91), for Boujdour and Dakhla in the morning, and for Tarfaya, Tan Tan, Goulimine, Agadir and Marrakesh morning and evening. They also run the only bus to Smara.

CTM has two early morning departures down to Dakhla from outside its office at 198 Av Mecka al Mokarrama (☎028 99 07 63), and also runs services to Tarfaya, Tan Tan, Goulimine, Agadir, Marrakesh and Casablanca, (one continuing to Rabat). **SATAS**'s office is nearby on Place Bir Anzarane, from where its buses leave for Boujdour and Dakhla (the only evening departure southward), and for Agadir. Across the square, **SAT** has two daily buses in each direction between Dakhla and Marrakesh, and just opposite, sharing an office with Razma Car by *Café Ibiza*, **Najmat Sahara**'s one daily bus departs at noon for Tarfaya, connecting there for Tan Tan.

Grands taxis, which formerly departed from stations scattered all over town, now leave from a single stand located at the end of Avenue Abou Baker Essadik (roughly a continuation of Avenue Prince Moulay Aballah), about 2km east of the town centre.

The **airport** (☎028 89 33 46) is about a kilometre out of town, beyond Place Mechouar, with scheduled flights on RAM to Casablanca, Dakhla and Las Palmas in the Canary Islands, and by Regional Air Lines to Casablanca via Agadir. For details of frequencies and journey times on internal routes, see p.698.

Laayoune Plage

LAAYOUNE PLAGE is 20km distant: leave town on the N1 (formerly P41) towards Boujdour then, past the airport, turn right off the main road and quickly left at a sign to Camping Touristique. At the beach – which is very windy, year-round, with big Atlantic breakers – there is a sporadically open café-restaurant. Places to stay include the *Hôtel Josefina* (☎028 99 84 78; ⑤) at Laayoune Plage itself and, nearby at **Foum el Oued**, the *Hôtel Nagjir Plage*, a four-star hotel run by the same firm as the *Nagjir* in Laayoune (☎028 99 10 18, ℉028 99 52 70; ⑥).

South from Laayoune to Dakhla

Continuing **south of Laayoune** down to Dakhla is pretty routine now, and you no longer need special permission. There are six daily buses along this route from Agadir, as well as grand taxi runs; the buses are often full, so you may have to push your way on if you want to pick them up en route. The road is reasonably good, though drivers should beware of occasional sand-drifts, and camels grazing by or on the road. Foreigners will need to form-fill at checkpoints along the way (more easily avoided in a grand taxi, where the police or *gendarmes* may not notice there's a tourist aboard).

Laayoune to Dakhla

The first habitation along the road is **LEMSID**, 110km from Laayoune, where a small **café-shop** provides basic meals for the route's lorry drivers.

South of Lemsid, the sea is guarded by cliffs most of the way to the newly developed fishing port of **BOUJDOUR**, 188km southwest of Laayoune. The landscape here is a little more mellow, but the beach is dirty with dangerous rocks – the nearest beaches suitable for bathing (if you have the transport to reach them) are 20km south, below the cliffs, and 40km north, just beyond a military checkpoint and fishing settlement. Boujdour has a petrol station, various cafés and a handful of **hotels**, including the pleasant and friendly *Al Qods* (☏028 89 65 73; ❷). The street from the grand taxi stand down to the sea comes alive in the evening with restaurants frying up freshly caught fish, and stalls selling charcoal-grilled brochettes and sausages. There are also café-restaurants on the main road, especially around the SATAS and Supratours offices. The area behind these, which makes up most of Boujdour's residential area, is a large *bidonville*. The nearest thing to a sight in town is the lighthouse, though it's not open to the public. If you need a bank, the BMCE and Banque Populaire both have branches here with ATMs.

South again from Boujdour the road runs inland, rejoining the coast at a place called **La Bouir** – little more than a filling station and café-restaurant almost midway between Dakhla and Boujdour, where buses usually make a halt. There's a fishing settlement on the beach below the cliffs. The area behind the café at the top of the cliff, beyond the bit that's used as a public toilet, is full of fossilized snail shells. Five kilometres further south, at **Oued Lakrâa**, the Moroccans have built a small settlement, with Lego-like houses and a mosque, no doubt due to be occupied by people who will vote the right way should a referendum on Saharan independence ever be held.

Dakhla

Some 544km from Laayoune, you reach the town of **DAKHLA** (or Ad Dakhla) on a long spit of land, just 22km north of the Tropic of Cancer. Until 1975, this was a Spanish outpost, known as Villa Cisneros, and capital of the Rio de Oro colony. In those days, only the colonists and people working for them were allowed into town – the Saharawi nomads who lived in the desert were excluded. In 1975, the Spanish left and the Mauritanians moved in, to be replaced by the Moroccans four years later. Since then, Dakhla has grown somewhat, though it retains a lazy, sun-bleached atmosphere, with whitewashed, low-rise buildings and an easy-going feel. Increasing numbers of Europeans in camper vans are coming down this way in winter, drawn by the deserted beaches and year-round sunshine – even in January it's hot, and this is the furthest south you can get by land without needing a visa. The main industry is fishing, and there is also a strong military presence.

In March 2007, the Moroccan authorities and various businesses sponsored a three-day **festival**, similar to the one in Smara, not tremendously exciting and mostly designed to promote tourism, with a stage on Avenue Hassan II and a few bands. The festival looks set to be an annual fixture, and should at least be worth checking out if you happen to be in town at the time.

Arrival, orientation and information

Coming into town, you pass a **police checkpoint**, where you will have to show your passport and answer the full set of questions about your profession, parents' names and purpose of visit (see p.679). The town proper starts 3km

Campsite, Laayoune & Guerguerat ▲

New Terminal

Runway

Mosque

AVENUE MOHAMMED V

BOULEVARD EL WALAE

RESTAURANTS
Aya	3
Brochette restaurant	4
Casa Luis	2
La Real (Samarkand)	1

Airport Terminal

BMCE

AVENUE HASSAN I

BOULEVARD EL ACHARIATE

See Inset for details

BOULEVARD EL MASJID

AVENUE MOHAMMED V

Mosque

ACCOMMODATION
Hôtel Aigue	G
Hotel Bahia	E
Hôtel Doumss	A
Hôtel Erraha	D
Hôtel Mijik	B
Hôtel Riad	F
Hôtel Sahara	H
Hôtel Sahara Regency	C

Stadium
Municipal Market
New Mosque
SAT
Grands Taxis ★
AVENUE AHMED BELAFRIJ
★ Supratours

DAKHLA

0   200 m

AVENUE HASSAN II

0   100 m

RAM

BOULEVARD EL MOUKOUAMA

BOULEVARD EL WALAE

Centre Artesanal

Banque Populaire

BOULEVARD EL ACHARIATE

CTM

BOULEVARD 4 MARS

AVENUE MOHAMMED V

★ Supratours

AVENUE SIDI AHMED LAROUSSI

▼ Municipal Market

further down the road, which becomes **Boulevard el Walae**. The town centre starts when you cross **Avenue Hassan II**, which runs from east to west across the spit. A block further, the main road meets the eastern promenade, **Avenue Mohammed V**. A block to further south, Mohammed V meets **Boulevard el Moukouama**, and two blocks south of that, **Avenue Sidi Ahmed Laroussi** forms the heart of central Dakhla, with its largest concentration of cafés and street activity. At the western end of Sidi Ahmed Laroussi, **Boulevard el Achariate** heads down to meet **Bloulevard al Masjid**, which continues for a kilometre to the southern end of town, where you'll find the **municipal market**, the **new mosque**, the grand taxi stand and the main terminals for SAT and Supratours.

Should you need it, there is a **tourist office** on the second floor of Immeuble al Baraka, on the east side of Boulevard de Walae, 700m north of Avenue Hassan II (Mon–Fri 8.30am–4.30pm; ☎028 89 83 88 or 89). The main **post office** (Mon–Fri 8am–4.30pm, Sat 8am–noon) is on Boulevard el Moukouama. **Banks** with ATMs include the BMCE off Avenue Hassan II by the *Sahara Regency* hotel, and the Banque Populaire, a block south of the post office. There are also a couple opposite the new mosque at the southern end of town. For Moroccan crafts, there's an Ensemble Artisanal at the eastern end of Boulevard Moukouama.

Accommodation

Dakhla has quite a few hotels, and the cheap ones tend to be good value – mostly clean with hot water, and with a standard price per person (30dh at time of writing, in a room with shared bathroom facilities), though one person occupying a double room will have to pay for two places, and not many hotels have single rooms as such. Budget places often fill up early, so you may have to shop around. The main concentration is in the few blocks south of Avenue Hassan II and west of Avenue Mohammed V. There are in addition three mid-range hotels and one four-star, all listed below.

The **campsite**, *Camping Mousafir* (☎028 89 82 79; ❶) is 5km out of town, just north of the police checkpoint, in a pink-walled enclosure next to its own beach. It offers a small number of rather bare rooms (for which lone travellers pay single rates) as well as camping space, but is rather inconveniently located for town amenities – the only way into town without your own transport is either to walk, hitch, or wait for a petit taxi to turn up (which should charge 15dh to run you into town).

Hôtel Aigue Rue Laroussiyine, corner of Av Sidi Ahmed Laroussi ☎028 89 73 95. Bright, clean and friendly, with pleasant rooms and shared hot water showers, and not dissimilar to the neighbouring *Sahara*, for which it's a close second choice. Indeed, a couple of single rooms make it the first choice for budget minded lone travellers ❶

Hôtel Bahia 12 Av Mohammed V, corner of Rue Essaouira (no phone). Dakhla's oldest hotel, but not its best, with bare rooms, though clean, and no hot water but tepid showers. It does have some single rooms, but they tend to be booked up. ❶

Hôtel Doumss Bd el Walae, 500m north of Av Hassan II ☎028 89 80 46 or 47, ☏028 89 80 45. A comfortable two-star, not very central but handy for SATAS bus arrivals, and a good mid-market choice, with large en-suite rooms with balconies, and a bar. ❹

Hôtel Errana Av Ahmed Belafrij, at the southern end of town opposite the new mosque ☎028 89 88 11. A clean and bright hotel, all rooms en suite and sparkling, some way from the town centre but handy for SAT, Supratours and the grand taxi stand. ❸

Hôtel Mijik (or *Mijak*) on the seafront, behind the *Hôtel Doumss* ☎028 93 10 98, ✉hotelmijik @hotmail.com. Quieter and more seaside-like

than most of Dakhla's hotels, with small but well-kept rooms and a restaurant, overlooking a rocky and rather rubbish-strewn shore. En suite rooms with TV are available for twice the price of cheaper rooms (though that is still far from excessive). ❷

Hôtel Riad Rue Twarta ☎028 89 84 19. A nice, jolly little place on a pedestrianized street south of the CTM office, with Spanish tiles in the entrance and corridors, and shared showers with hot water. ❶

Hôtel Sahara Av Sidi Ahmed Laroussi ☎028 89 77 73. Dakhla's best budget hotel (though not to be confused with the *Sahara Regency*) is well-kept, friendly and central, with quite spacious, airy rooms and good hot showers. They can arrange transport to Mauritania at competitive prices. ❶

Hôtel Sahara Regency Bd de Walae, at the junction with Av Hassan II ☎028 89 80 71, ✇www.sahararegency.com. Dakhla's top offering, opened in 2002. Each room has separate en-suite bathroom and toilet, and a balcony. There are three bars, a rooftop restaurant and a pool (which non-residents can use for 50dh). They also organize jet skiing, kite surfing, 4x4 rental and visits to an oyster farm, but none of them cheaply. ❻

Eating

In addition to the **eating** places listed below, you'll find a handful of cheap places on and around Boulevard Ahmed Ben Chaqroun at the southern end of town. The *Hôtel Doumss* has a **bar**, but it closes early (daily 9.30am–7pm). The three bars in the *Hôtel Sahara Regency*, however, stay open until 10pm.

Aya Av Mohammed V near Av Sidi Ahmed Laroussi. Fast food (it even has a twin-arch "McAya" sign in the window, but it isn't that bad) including octopus and swordfish brochettes (in both cases frozen, not fresh), as well as burgers and *shawarma*. Daily noon–3pm & 8–11pm. Cheap

Brochette Restaurant Av Sidi Ahmed Laroussi, in front of *Hôtel Sahara*. Charcoal-grilled kebabs,

served with chips and salad, eaten out on the pavement. Daily noon–3pm & 7–10pm. Cheap.

Casa Luis 14 Av Mohammed V by *Hôtel Bahia*. Good Spanish fare including excellent omelettes and a very passable paella that makes up in flavour, fish and octopus what it lacks in shelled molluscs and crustaceans, though it's for a minimum of two and has to be ordered

40 minutes in advance. Serves beer and wine and has a 50dh set menu. Daily noon–3pm & 7–11pm. Moderate.

🏃 **Hotel Bahia** 12 Av Mohammed V, corner of Rue Essaouira. Excellent fish and seafood including paella (order 40 minutes in advance), *pulpo alla gallega* (octopus pan-fried with paprika),

swordfish steak or monkfish kebabs, but no alcohol. Daily 7am–11pm. Moderate.

La Real (Samarkand) Bd de la Achariate. A busy café restaurant serving pizzas, sandwiches, dishes such as beef stroganov or fish brochettes, and even banana split for dessert. Daily 7am–midnight. Moderate.

Moving on

If taking a **bus**, CTM's office is on Boulevard 4 Mars, three blocks south of Avenue Hassan II (☎028 89 81 66), with two daily departures to Agadir, one continuing to Marrakesh and Casablanca. ONCF/Supratours have their main office on Boulevard Ahmed Belafrij at the southern end of town, but their services also call at their old office, which is more conveniently located just around the corner from CTM, on Avenue Mohammed V (☎028 89 77 40). They also run two buses to Agadir, one of which continues to Marrakesh to connect with trains north. SATAS, 500m north of Avenue Hassan II on Boulevard de Walae, next to the *Hôtel Doumss* (☎028 93 04 60), has two departures to Agadir; SAT, near the new mosque at the southern end of town on Boulevard Ahmed Ben Chaqroun (☎028 93 05 11), has two daily buses to Marrakesh via Agadir. The **grand taxi** station, which is also at the southern end of town, southwest of the market and the stadium, has regular runs to Boujdour, Laayoune, Tan Tan and Agadir. Dakhla also has an **airport**, very centrally located, just off Boulevard de Walae almost opposite the *Sahara Regency* hotel (☎028 89 72 56), with flights to Agadir, Casablanca and Las Palmas. The airport is currently being extended with a new terminal due to open a kilometre or so to the north. RAM's office in town is directly behind the post office (☎028 89 70 49 or 50).

The road to Mauritania

If you are travelling south from **Dakhla to Mauritania**, you will need either to have your own transport, or to arrange some. The *Hôtel Sahara* is the best place to start – they can arrange a ride for just about the best rate in town (300dh/€30 to Nouadibhou, or 600dh/€60 to Nouakchott at time of writing). Otherwise, touts around town can put you in contact with Mauritanian drivers but you will need to bargain hard to get a fair price – try to find out the current rate in advance if possible. Alternatively, you could try asking around the campsite (or better still, stay there), as it is a favourite staging post for Europeans doing the run. Many of these will be bypassing Nouadibhou and heading straight for Nouakchott, which you may or may not see as an advantage (Nouakchott will get you to Senegal quicker, but Nouadibhou is where you need to go for the ore train to Choum). The number of European drivers heading in that direction has diminished somewhat since Senegal slapped a massive duty on the import of cars over five years old, thus putting the kibosh on an established trade in second-hand Peugeots from Europe, though these can still be sold in Mauritania, or beyond Senegal in Mali. It should be possible to obtain a **Mauritanian visa** at the border, for the same price as you would pay at the consulate in Casablanca (see p.391).

The road south is now surfaced all the way to the border, a distance of some 370km from Dakhla (including 38km from the town up the spit to the junction with the N1 road from Laayoune and Boujdour). The Mauritanian border post closes at 6pm, so it's best to set off early if you don't want to spend the night en route. The Moroccans are engaged in building settlements along the road, and little villages are springing up, each with identikit pretty new houses and a mosque. The first is 5km after the military post at **El Argoub**, opposite Dakhla across the lagoon enclosed by the spit; the next is at **Imlili**, some 50km further (124km from Dakhla). The **last fuel** and proper **accommodation** in Moroccan-held territory are at the *Café Restaurant Motel Dakmar* (formerly called *Barbas*), approximately 300km from Dakhla (T028 89 79 61; ❸), where you'll find clean rooms, comfortable beds, shared showers and good food. From there, it's 80km to the border post at **Guerguarat**, which is open daily 8am–7pm, but if you arrive after 5pm, you'll probably want to camp here for the night as the border post on the Mauritanian side closes at 6pm (these times may change however, so check in advance).

Five kilometres beyond Guerguarat, the tarmac ends and you enter Mauritanian-held territory. **Guides** are on hand just beyond the frontier to lead you to the **Mauritanian border post**, and it is wise to accept their assistance, as the area is heavily mined. The western side of the Nouadibhou peninsula is part of the Western Sahara, but occupied by Mauritania. Its main town, La Gouera (Lagwira), is used by the Mauritanian military and is off limits to foreigners. The Mauritanian border post is on the eastern side of the peninsula, in Mauritania proper, and once formalities have been completed, you can continue down to "**Quarante-Six**", where the road crosses the railway 46km out of Nouadibhou. If your lift is continuing across the desert to Nouakchott and you want to go to Nouadibhou, get off here to wait for a vehicle, but be warned that you may well be charged heavily for the journey, especially if it is getting late.

Coming from Mauritania, if you have a vehicle, you will need to get a permit from the Moroccan embassy in Nouakchott (see p.82). Note that you cannot obtain this from the consulate in Nouadibhou. If you do not have a vehicle, you will need to arrange transport. Ask around at the *auberges* (cheap lodges) and campsites used by travellers in Nouadibhou or even in Nouakchott. For further information on travelling in Mauritania and points beyond, see the *Rough Guide to West Africa*.

Travel details

Buses

Dakhla to: Agadir (7 daily; 19hr 30min) via Boujdour (5hr 30min), Laayoune (9hr), Tan Tan (13hr 30min) and Goulimine (16hr); Casablanca (2 daily; 28hr); Marrakesh (5 daily; 24hr); Rabat (1 daily; 30hr).
Laayoune to: Agadir (9 daily; 10hr 30min) via Tan Tan (4hr 30min), Goulimine (7hr) and Tiznit (8hr 30min); Dakhla (7 daily; 9hr) via Boujdour (3hr 30min); Casablanca (2 daily; 19hr); Marrakesh (6 daily; 15hr); Rabat (1 daily; 20hr); Smara (1 daily; 3hr); Tarfaya (3 daily; 1hr 30min).
Smara to: Agadir (3 daily; 9hr) via Tan Tan (3hr), Goulimine (5hr 30min) and Tiznit (7hr); Laayoune (1 daily; 3hr); Marrakesh (2 daily; 13hr 15min).

Tan Tan to: Agadir (15 daily; 6hr); Casablanca (12 daily; 16hr); Dakhla (7 daily; 13hr 30min); Goulimine (25 daily; 3hr); Laayoune (9 daily; 4hr 30min); Marrakesh (15 daily; 12hr); Ouarzazate (1 daily; 17hr 30min) via Tata (12hr 30 min); Rabat (3 daily; 17hr 30min); Smara (3 daily; 3hr); Tarfaya (3 daily; 3hr).

Grands taxis

Dakhla to: Boujdour (3hr 30min); Laayoune (9hr); Tan Tan (12hr).
Laayoune to: Inezgane (9hr); Dakhla (9hr); Goulimine (5hr); Laayoune Plage (20min); Smara (3hr); Tan Tan (3hr 30min); Tarfaya (1hr).

Smara to: Goulimine (4hr 30min); Laayoune (3hr); Marrakesh (12hr); Tan Tan (2hr).

Tan Tan to: Dakhla (12hr); Goulimine (2hr 30 min); Inezgane (6hr); Smara (3hr); Laayoune (3hr 30min); Tan Tan Plage (20min).

Flights

Dakhla to: Agadir (RAM 1 weekly; 1hr 40min); Casablanca (RAM 3 weekly; 2hr 10min); Las Palmas (TopFly 2 weekly; 1hr 10min).

Laayoune to: Agadir (RAL daily; 1hr 25min); Casablanca (RAM, RAL 1–3 daily; 1hr 30min–3hr 05min); Las Palmas (RAL, TopFly, Binter 2–3 daily; 50min).

Tan Tan to: Casablanca (RAM, RAL 1–3 daily; 1hr 55min–2hr 15min); Goulimine (RAL 2 weekly; 30min).

Contexts

Contexts

History

M orocco's emergence as a nation-state is astonishingly recent, dating from the occupation of the country by the French and Spanish at the turn of the twentieth century, and its independence in 1956. Prior to this, it is best seen as a patchwork of tribal groups, whose shifting alliances and sporadic bids for power defined the nature of government. With a handful of exceptions, the country's ruling sultans controlled only the plains, the coastal ports and the regions around the imperial capitals of Fes, Marrakesh, Rabat and Meknes. These were known as Bled el Makhzen – the governed lands, or, more literally, "Lands of the Storehouse". The rest of the Moroccan territories – the Rif, the three Atlas ranges and the outlying deserts – comprised Bled es Siba, "Lands of the Dissidents". Populated almost exclusively by Berbers, the region's original (pre-Arab) inhabitants, they were rarely recognized as being under anything more than local tribal authority.

The balance between government control and tribal independence is one of the two enduring themes of Moroccan history. The other is the emergence, expansion and eventual replacement of the various **sultanate dynasties**. These at first seem dauntingly complicated – a succession of short lived tribal movements and confusingly similar-named sultans – but there are actually just seven main groups. The first of them, the **Idrissids**, became the model by founding the city of Fes towards the end of the eighth century and bringing a coalition of Berber and Arab forces under a central *makhzen* (government) authority. The last, the **Alaouites**, emerged in the mid-seventeenth century from the great palm oasis of Tafilalt and, continuing with the current king, Mohammed VI, still hold constitutional power. It is around these groups – together with the medieval dynasties of the **Almoravids, Almohads, Merenids, Wattasids** and **Saadians** – that the bulk of the following sections are organized.

Prehistory

The first inhabitants of the **Maghreb** – the Arab term for the countries of North Africa – probably occupied the **Sahara**, for thousands of years a great savannah, fertile enough to support elephants, zebras and a whole range of other game and wildlife. Little is known about these ancestors of the human species, although it seems likely that there were groups of hunter-and-gatherer hominids here as early as 1,000,000 BC.

Around 15,000 BC there seem to have been **Paleolithic** settlements, and before the Sahara went into decline (from 3000 BC), primitive pastoral and agricultural systems had begun to develop. It is possible also to trace the arrival of two independent Stone-Age cultures in the Maghreb: the Neolithic **Capsian Man** (circa 10,000–5000 BC), probably emerging from Egypt, and, slightly later, **Mouillian Man**. From these people, fair-skinned and speaking a remote "Libyan" language, stem the cave and rock drawings of the pre-Sahara and High Atlas, the earliest archeological sites in Morocco.

Phoenicians and Carthaginians

The recorded history of the area begins around 1100 BC with the arrival of the **Phoenicians, a seafaring people from what is now Lebanon**. The Phoenicians eventually established a number of settlements along the coast, inlcuding Rusadir (Melilla), Tingis (Tangier), Zila (Asilah), Lixis (Larache) and Chellah (Rabat). Evidence of the Phoenician presence in these places dates back to the seventh century BC. The Phoenicians even had a settlement at Mogador (Essaouira) – of all their colonies, the furthest from their homeland – where they maintained a dye factory on the Îles Purpuraires (see p.414). The settlements were small, isolated colonies, most built on defensible headlands round the coast, and there was probably little initial contact between them and the inhabitants of the interior (known by their Greek name, *Barbaroi*, or **Berbers**). By the fifth century BC, one Phoenician colony, **Carthage** (modern Tunis), had become pre-eminent and gained dominance over the rest. Under Carthaginian leadership, some of the Moroccan colonies grew into considerable cities, exporting grain and grapes, and even minting their own coinage.

The Carthaginian Empire ended with its final defeat in the **Punic Wars** against Rome in 146 BC, but in these provincial outposts, life seems to have been little affected. If anything, the colonies grew in stature and prosperity, absorbing hundreds of refugees after the Roman destruction of Carthage. It was a first sign of Morocco's intrinsic historic and geographic isolation in what was to become known as Maghreb el Aska (Land of the Farthest West). Even after the Romans had annexed and then abandoned the country, Phoenician was still widely spoken along the coast.

Berber kingdoms and Roman rule

Prior to total Roman annexation, and the imposition of direct imperial rule in 24 AD, the "civilized" Moroccan territories for a while formed the **Berber kingdom of Mauretania**. This was probably little more than a confederation of local tribes, centred round **Volubilis** (near Meknes) and **Tangier**, but it gained a certain influence through alliance and occasional joint rule with the adjoining Berber state of **Numidia** (essentially modern Algeria).

The most important of the Berber rulers, and the only ones of which any substantial records survive, were **Juba II** (25 BC–23 AD) and his son **Ptolemy** (23–41 AD). Both were heavily Romanized: Juba, an Algerian Berber by birth, was brought up and educated in Rome, where he married the daughter of Antony and Cleopatra. His reign, if limited in its extent, seems to have been orderly and prosperous, and under his son the pattern might well have continued. In 41 AD, however, Emperor Caligula summoned Ptolemy to an audience in Lyons and had him assassinated – so the story goes, for appearing in a more brilliant cloak than his own. Whatever the truth, and Rome may just have been eager for more centralized rule, it was an inauspicious beginning.

Nevertheless, the following year, the new emperor Claudius divided Rome's North African domains into two provinces: Mauritania Caesarensis (the old

Numidia) and **Mauritania Tingitana** (essentially, Morocco). Tingis (Tangier) was the capital of Tingitana, while Volubilis became the seat of the provincial governor.

Roman rule

The early years of Rome's new imperial province were taken up with near-constant **rebellions** – the first one alone needing three years and over 20,000 troops to subdue.

Perhaps discouraged by this unexpected resistance, the **Romans** never attempted to colonize Morocco–Mauretania beyond its old limits, and the Rif and Atlas mountains were left unpenetrated. In this the Romans were establishing an enduring precedent: not just in their failure to subdue Bled es Siba, which also defied the later sultans, but also in their treatment of Morocco as a useful "corridor" to the greater agricultural wealth of Algeria, Tunisia and Spain. That said, Tingitana – although characterized as a backwater by Pliny – had a considerable Roman presence. The second century AD geographer Ptolemy listed more than thirty Roman cities in the province, and these provided exotic animals for Roman games, as well as grains, wines, fish sauce (garum), olive oil, copper and purple murex dye. **Volubilis**, the most extensive surviving Roman site in Morocco, was a significant city, at the heart of the north's fertile vineyards and grain fields.

However, as Roman power waned, and native Berber uprisings became more frequent, administration was moved from Volubilis to Tingis, and when the Roman legions were withdrawn in 253 AD, and the **Vandals** took power in southern Spain, the latter were interested only in taking Tingis and the neighbouring port of Ceuta for use as staging posts en route to northern Tunisia. Similarly, the **Byzantine General Belisarius**, who defeated the Vandals and laid claim to the Maghreb for Justinian's Eastern Empire, did little more than replace the Ceuta garrison.

It was understandable, of course. Any attempt to control Morocco would need manpower far in excess of these armies, and the only overland route through the country – across the Taza gap – was scarcely practicable even in peacetime. Not until the tenth century, and the great northward expansion of the desert nomads, was Morocco to become a land worthy of substantial exploitation in its own right, and even then only through the unifying and evangelizing impetus of Islam.

The coming of Islam

The irruption of **Islam** into the world began in 622 AD, when the Prophet Muhammad moved with his followers from Mecca to Medina. Within thirty years they had reached the borders of India, to the east, were threatening Byzantine Constantinople, to the north, and had established themselves in the Maghreb at Kairouan in present-day Tunisia.

After this initial thrust, however, sweeping across the old provinces of the Roman world, the progress of the new religion was temporarily slowed. The Berbers of Algeria – mainly pagans but including communities of Christians and Jews – put up a strong and unusually unified resistance to Arab control. It was only in 680 that the governor of Kairouan, **Oqba Ibn Nafi**, made an initial foray into Morocco, taking in the process the territory's last Byzantine stronghold at Ceuta.

What happened afterwards is unclear. There is a story, perhaps apocryphal, that Oqba embarked on a 5000-kilometre **march through Morocco**, raiding and subjugating all in his path, and preaching Islam all the way to the west – the Atlantic Ocean. But whether this expedition had any real Islamicizing influence on the Moroccan Berbers is questionable. Oqba left no garrison forces and was himself killed in Algeria on his way back to Kairouan.

Islam may, however, have taken root among some of the tribes. In the early part of the eighth century the new Arab governor of the west, **Moussa Ibn Nasr**, returned to Morocco and managed to establish Arab control (and carry out mass conversions to Islam) in both the northern plains and the pre-Sahara. However, like the Romans and Byzantines before him, his main thrust was towards **Spain**. In 711, the first Muslim forces crossed over from Tangier to Tarifa and defeated the Visigoths in a single battle; within a decade the Moors had taken control of all but the remote Spanish mountains in northern Asturias; and their advance into Europe was only halted at the Pyrenees by the victory of Charles Martel at Poitiers in 732.

The bulk of this invading and occupying force were almost certainly **Berber converts** to Islam, and the sheer scale of their military success must have had enormous influence in turning Morocco itself into a largely Muslim nation. It was not at this stage, however, in any way an Arab one. The extent of the Islamic Empire – from Persia to Morocco, and ancient Ghana to Spain – was simply too great for Arab numbers. Early attempts to impose taxes on the Moroccan Berbers led to a rebellion and, once again outside the political mainstream, the Maghreb fragmented into a series of small, independent **principalities**.

The Idrissids (eighth–eleventh century)

The Maghreb's fragmentation found an echo in the wider events of the Muslim world, which was undergoing its first – and most drastic – dissension, with the split into **Sunni** and **Shia** sects. In Damascus the Sunni Ummayad dynasty took power, the Shi'ites dispersing and seeking refuge to both the east and west.

One of them, arriving in Morocco around 787, was **Moulay Idriss**, an evidently charismatic leader and a direct descendant (great-grandson, in fact) of the Prophet Muhammad. He seems to have been adopted almost at once by the citizens of Volubilis – then still a vaguely Romanized city – and by the Aouraba Berber tribe. He was to survive for three more years, before being poisoned by order of the Sunni caliph, but in this time he managed to set up the infrastructure of an essentially Arab court and kingdom – the basis of what was to become the Moroccan nation. Its most important feature, enduring to the present with Mohammed VI, was his being recognized as *imam*. To the Moroccans this meant that he was both spiritual and political leader, "commander of the faithful" in every aspect of their lives.

Despite the brevity of Moulay Idriss's reign, and his sudden death in 791 or 792, his successors, the **Idrissids**, were to become the first recognizable Moroccan dynasty. Moulay Idriss himself left a son, born posthumously to a Berber woman, and in 807, after a period of an apparently orderly regency, **Moulay Idriss II** was declared sultan and *imam*. He ruled for a little over twenty years – something of a golden age for the emerging Moroccan state, with the extension of a central, Arabized authority throughout the north and even to the oases beyond the Atlas.

Idriss's most important achievement, however, was the establishment (if perhaps not the foundation) of the city of **Fes**. Here, he set up the apparatus of court government, and here he also welcomed large contingents of Shi'ite **refugees**. Most prominent among these were groups from Cordoba and Kairouan, then the two great cities of Western Islam. In incorporating them, Fes (and, by extension, Morocco) became increasingly Arabized, and was suddenly transformed into a major Arab centre in its own right. The **Kairaouine University** was established, becoming one of the three most important in Islam (and far ahead of those in Europe); a strong crafts tradition took root; and Fes became a vital link in the trade between Spain and the East, and between the Maghreb and Africa south of the Sahara.

Fes was to remain the major Moroccan city, and the country's Arab spiritual heart, right up until the twentieth century. The Idrissid state, however, split once more into **principalities**, most of which returned to their old isolation, until, at the turn of the tenth century, the context began to change. In Al-Andalus – the Muslim territories of Spain – the Western Caliphate collapsed and itself splintered into small rival states. Meanwhile in Tunisia, the well-established Fatimid dynasty moved their capital to Egypt, clashed with their nominated governors, the Zirids, and unleashed upon them the hostile nomadic tribe of the Banu Hilal.

It was a move that was to have devastating effects on the Maghreb's entire lifestyle and ecological balance, as the **Hilali** nomads swept westwards, destroying all in their path, laying to ruin the irrigation systems and devastating the agricultural lands with their goats and other flocks. The medieval Maghrebi historian, **Ibn Khaldun**, described their progress as being like a swarm of locusts: "the very earth seems to have changed its nature", he wrote, "all the lands that the Arabs have conquered in the last few centuries, civilization and population have departed from them".

The Almoravids (1062–1145)

Morocco was to some extent cushioned from the Hilali, and by the time they reached its southern oases (where they settled), the worst was probably over. But with the shattered social order of the Maghreb, and complex power struggles in Moorish Spain, came an obvious vacuum of authority.

It was this which created the opportunity for the two great Berber dynasties of the Middle Ages – the **Almoravids** and the **Almohads**. Both were to emerge from the south, and in each case their motivating force was religious: a purifying zeal to **reform** or destroy the decadent ways that had reached Morocco from the wealthy Andalusian Muslims of Spain. The two dynasties together lasted only a century and a half, but in this period Morocco was the pre-eminent power of western Islam, maintaining an **empire** that at its peak stretched right across the Maghreb to Libya, south to Senegal and ancient Ghana and north into Spain. Subsequent history and achievements never matched up to this imperial dream, though even today its memories are part of the Moroccan concept of nation. "**Greater Morocco**", the nationalist goal of the late 1950s, sketched out areas that took in Mauritania, Algeria, Tunisia and Libya, while even Morocco's current claim on the Western Sahara looks back to the reality of the medieval empires.

The **Almoravids** began as a reforming movement among the Sanhaja Berbers in Koumbi Saleh, capital of ancient Ghana, in what is now Mauritania. A nomadic desert tribe – similar to the Touaregs who occupy the area today – they had been converted to Islam in the ninth century, but perhaps only to nominal effect. The founders of the Almoravid movement, a local sheikh who had returned from the pilgrimage to Mecca and a *fakir* from the Souss plain, found widespread abuse of orthodox practice. In particular, they preached against drinking palm wine, playing licentious music and taking more than four wives. It held an appeal for this already ascetic, tent-dwelling people, and rapidly took hold.

Founding a *ribat* – a kind of warrior monastery similar to the Templar castles of Europe – the Almoravids soon became a considerable military force. In 1054, they set out from the *ribat* (from which the word Almoravids derives) to spread the message through a *jihad* (holy war), and within four years they had captured and destroyed the ancient empire of Ghana to the south. Turning towards Morocco, they established themselves in Marrakesh by 1062, and under the leadership of **Youssef Ben Tachfine** went on to extend their rule throughout the north of Morocco and, to the east, as far as Algiers.

At no time before had any one leader exercised such strong control over these territories; nor had the tribes before been united under a single religious doctrine – a simple, rigorous and puritanical form of Sunni orthodoxy. And so it remained, at least as long as the impetus of *jihad* was sustained. In 1085, Youssef undertook his first, and possibly reluctant, expedition to **Spain**, invited by the princes of **Al-Andalus** (as Muslim Spain was known) after the fall of Toledo to the Christians. He crossed over the Straits again in 1090, this time to take control of Spain himself. In this he was successful, and before his death in 1107, he had restored Muslim control to Valencia and other territories lost in the first wave of the Christian Reconquest.

The new Spanish territories had two decisive effects. The first was to reorient Moroccan culture towards the far more sophisticated and affluent Andalusian civilization; the second, to stretch the Almoravid forces too thin. Both were to contribute to the dynasty's decline. Youssef, disgusted by Andalusian decadence, had ruled largely from **Marrakesh**, leaving governors in Seville and other cities. After his death, the Andalusians proved disinclined to accept these foreign overlords, while the Moroccans themselves became vulnerable to charges of being corrupt and departing from their puritan ideals.

Youssef's son **Ali** was himself, in fact, extraordinarily pious, but he was unprepared for (nor interested in) ceaseless military activity; in Spain he turned to Christian mercenaries to maintain control. His reign, and that of the Almoravids, was effectively finished by the early 1140s, as a new movement, the Almohads, seized control of the main Moroccan cities one after another.

The Almohads (1145–1248)

Ironically, the **Almohads** shared much in common with their predecessors. Again, they were forged from the Berber tribes – this time in the High Atlas – and again, they based their bid for power on an intense puritanism. Their founder **Ibn Toumert,** attacked the Almoravids for allowing their women to ride horses (a tradition in the desert), for wearing extravagant clothes, and for being subject to what may have been Andalusian corruptions – the revived use of music and wine.

He also provoked a **theological crisis**, claiming that the Almoravids did not recognize the essential unitary and unknowable nature of God: the basis of Almohad belief, and the source of their name – the "unitarians". Banished from Marrakesh by Ali, Ibn Toumert set up a *ribat* in the Atlas at **Tin Mal**. Here he waged war on local tribes until they accepted his authority, and he eventually revealed himself to them as the Mahdi – "the chosen one" and the final prophet promised in the Koran.

Charismatic and brutal in his methods, Toumert was aided by a shrewd assistant and brilliant military leader, **Abd el Moumen**, who took over the movement after Toumert's death and extended the radius of their raids. In 1145, he was strong enough to displace the Almoravids from Fes, and two years later he drove them from their stronghold in Marrakesh. With the two cities subdued, he was now effectively sultan.

Resistance subsided and once again a Moroccan dynasty moved **towards Spain**, this time finally secured by the third Almohad sultan, **Yacoub el Mansur** (1184–1199), under his father's leadership. He also pushed the frontiers of the empire east to Tripoli, and for the first time, there was one single rule across the entire **Maghreb**, although it did not stretch as far south as under the Almoravids. With the ensuing wealth and prestige, Yacoub launched a great building programme – the first and most ambitious in Moroccan history – which included a new capital in **Rabat** and the magnificent (and in large part still surviving) gateways and minarets of Marrakesh and Seville.

Once more, though, imperial expansion precipitated disintegration. In 1212, Yacoub's successor, **Mohammed en Nasr**, attempted to drive the Spanish Christians as far back as the Pyrenees and met with decisive defeat at the battle of **Las Navas de Tolosa**. The balance of power in Spain was changing, and within four decades only the Kingdom of Granada remained in Muslim hands. In the Maghreb, meanwhile, the eastern provinces had declared independence from Almohad rule and Morocco itself was returning to the authority of local tribes. In 1248, one of these, the **Merenids** (or Beni Merin), took the northern capital of Fes and turned towards Marrakesh.

Merenids and Wattasids (1248–1554)

This last (300-year) period of Berber rule in Morocco is very much a tailpiece to the Almoravid and Almohad empires – marked by increasing domestic **instability** and economic stagnation, and signalling also the beginning of Morocco's **isolation** from both the European and Muslim worlds. Under the Merenids, the Spanish territories were not regained, and Granada, the last Moorish city, fell to Ferdinand and Isabella in 1492. Portuguese sea power saw to it that foreign seaports were established on the Atlantic and Mediterranean coasts. To the east, the rest of the Maghreb fell under Turkish domination, as part of the Ottoman Empire. The Portuguese ability to navigate beyond Mauritania also meant the eventual end of the trans-Sahara caravan route.

In Morocco itself, the main development was a centralized administrative system – the **Makhzen** – which was maintained without tribal support by standing armies of Arab and Christian mercenaries. It is to this age that the real distinction of Bled el Makhzen and Bled es Siba belongs – the latter coming to mean everything outside the immediate vicinities of the imperial cities.

The Merenids

Perhaps with this background it is not surprising that few of the 21 **Merenid sultans** – or their cousins and successors, the Wattasids – made any great impression. The early sultans were occupied mainly with Spain, at first in trying to regain a foothold on the coast, later with shoring up the Kingdom of Granada. There were minor successes in the fourteenth century under the "Black Sultan", **Abou el Hassan**, who for a time occupied Tunis, but he was to die before being able to launch a planned major invasion of Al-Andalus, and his son, **Abou Inan**, himself fell victim to the power struggles within the mercenary army.

The thirteenth and fourteenth centuries, however, did leave a considerable **legacy of building**, perhaps in defiance of the lack of political progress (and certainly a product of the move towards government by forced taxation). In 1279, the garrison town of **Fes el Djedid** was established, to be followed by a series of brilliantly endowed colleges, or **medersas**, which are among the finest surviving Moorish monuments. Culture, too, saw a final flourish. The historians **Ibn Khaldun** and **Leo Africanus**, and the travelling chronicler **Ibn Battuta**, all studied in Fes under Merenid patronage.

The Wattasids

The **Wattasids**, who usurped Merenid power in 1465, had ruled in effect for 45 years previously as a line of hereditary viziers. After their coup, they maintained a semblance of control for a little under a century, though the extent of the Makhzen lands was by now minimal.

The **Portuguese** had annexed and colonized the seaports of Ceuta, Tangier, Asilah, Agadir and Safi, while large tracts of the interior lay in the hands of religious warrior brotherhoods, or **marabouts**, on whose alliances the sultans had increasingly to depend.

The Saadians and civil war (1554–1669)

The rise and fall of the **Saadians** was in some respects a replay of all of the dynasties that had come before them. They were the most important of the *marabouts* to emerge in the early years of the sixteenth century, rising to power on the strength of their religious positions (they were Shereefs – descendants of the Prophet), climaxing in a single, particularly distinguished reign, and declining amid a chaos of political assassinations, bitter factional strife and, in the end, civil war.

As the first **Arab dynasty** since the Idrissids, they marked the end of Moroccan Berber rule, though this was probably less significant at the time than the fact that theirs was a government with no tribal basis. The Makhzen had to be even further extended than under the Merenids, and Turkish guards – a new point of intrigue – were added to the imperial armies.

Slower to establish themselves than the preceding dynasties, the Saadians began by setting up a small principality in the **Souss**, where they established their first capital in **Taroudannt**. Normally, this would have formed a regular part of Bled el Makhzen, but the absence of government in the south allowed them to extend their power to **Marrakesh** around 1520, with the Wattasids for a time retaining Fes and ruling the north.

In the following decades the Saadians made breakthroughs along the coast, capturing Agadir in 1540 and driving the Portuguese from Safi and Essaouira. When the Wattasids fell into bankruptcy and invited the Turks into Fes, the Saadians were ready to consolidate their power. This proved harder, and more confusing, than anyone might have expected. **Mohammed esh Sheikh**, the first Saadian sultan to control both the southern and northern kingdoms, was himself soon after Turkish troops, and was subsequently assassinated by a group of them in 1557. His death unleashed an incredibly convoluted sequence of factional murder and power politics, which was only resolved, somewhat fortuitously, by a battle with the Portuguese twenty years later.

The Battle of the Three Kings

This event, **The Battle of the Three Kings**, was essentially a Portuguese crusade, led by the youthful King Sebastião on the nominal behalf of a deposed Saadian king against his uncle and rival. At the end of the day all three were to perish on the battlefield, the Portuguese having suffered a crushing defeat, and a little-known Saadian prince emerged as the sole acknowledged ruler of Morocco.

His name was **Ahmed "El Mansour"** (The Victorious, following this momentous victory), and he was easily the most impressive sultan of the dynasty. Not only did he begin his reign clear of the intrigue and rivalry that had dogged his predecessors, but he was immensely wealthy as well. Portuguese ransoms paid for the remnants of their nobility after the battle had been enormous, causing Portugal to go bankrupt – the country, with its remaining Moroccan enclaves, then passed into the control of Habsburg Spain.

Breaking with tradition, Ahmed himself became actively involved in European politics, generally supporting the Protestant north against the Spanish and encouraging Dutch and British trade. Within Morocco he was able to maintain a reasonable level of order and peace, and diverted criticism of his use of Turkish troops (and his own Turkish-educated ways) by embarking on an **invasion of Timbuktu** and the south. This secured control of the Saharan salt mines and the gold and slave routes from Senegal, all sources of phenomenal wealth, which won him the additional epithet of *El Dhahabi* (The Golden One). It also reduced his need to tax Moroccans, which made him a popular man.

Civil war and piracy

Ahmed's death in 1603 caused abrupt and lasting chaos. He left three sons, none of whom could gain authority, and, split by **civil war**, the country once again broke into a number of principalities. A succession of **Saadian rulers** retained power in the Souss and in Marrakesh (where their tombs remain testimony to the opulence and turbulence of the age); another *marabout* force, the **Djila**, gained control of Fes; while around Salé and Rabat arose the bizarre **Republic of the Bou Regreg**.

The Bou Regreg depended almost entirely on **piracy**, a new development in Morocco, though well established along the Mediterranean coasts of Algeria and Tunisia. Its practitioners were the last Moors to be expelled from Spain – mainly from Granada and Badajoz – and they conducted a looting war primarily against Spanish ships. For a time they had astounding success, raiding as far away as the Irish coast, dealing in arms with the British and the French, and even accrediting foreign consuls. One writer, Giles Milton, has claimed that over a million Europeans were enslaved in North Africa during the seventeenth and eighteenth centuries, although most historians suggest the actual figures were far lower, and more likely in the tens of thousands.

Moulay Ismail and the early Alaouites (1665–1822)

Like the Saadians, the **Alaouites** were Shereefs, first establishing themselves as religious leaders – this time in Rissani in the **Tafilalt**. Their struggle to establish power also followed a similar pattern, spreading first to Taza and Fes and finally, under Sultan **Moulay Rashid**, reaching Marrakesh in 1669. Rashid, however, was unable to enjoy the fruits of his labour, since he was assassinated in a particularly bloody palace coup in 1672. It was only with Moulay Ismail, the ablest of his rival sons, that an Alaouite leader gained real control over the country.

Moulay Ismail

The reign of **Moulay Ismail**, perhaps the most notorious in all of Morocco's history, stretched over 55 years (1672–1727) and was to be the country's last stab at imperial glory. In Morocco, where his shrine in Meknes is still a place of pilgrimage, he is remembered as a great and just, if unusually ruthless, ruler; to contemporary Europeans – and in subsequent historical accounts – he is noted for extravagant cruelty. His rule certainly was tyrannical, with arbitrary killings and an appalling treatment of his slaves, but it was not much worse than that of the European nations of the day; the seventeenth century was the age of the witch trials in Protestant Europe, and of the Catholic Inquisition.

Nevertheless, Moulay Ismail stands out among the Alaouites because of the grandness of the scale on which he acted. At **Meknes**, which he made his new imperial capital, he garrisoned a permanent army of some 140,000 black troops, a legendary guard he had built up personally through slaving expeditions in Mauritania and the south, as well as by starting a human breeding programme. The army kept order throughout the kingdom – Morocco is today still littered with their kasbah garrisons – and were able to raise taxes as required. The Bou Regreg pirates, too (the so-called Sallee Rovers), were brought under the control of the state, along with their increasingly lucrative revenues.

With all this, Ismail was able to build a palace in Meknes that was the rival of its contemporary, Versailles, and he negotiated on equal terms with the **Europeans**. Indeed, it was probably the reputation he established for Morocco that allowed the country to remain free for another century and a half before the European colonial powers began carving it up.

Sidi Mohammed and Moulay Slimane

Like all the great, long-reigning Moroccan sultans, Moulay Ismail left innumerable sons and a terminal dispute for the throne, with the powerful standing army supporting and dropping heirs at will.

Remarkably, a capable ruler emerged fairly soon – Sultan **Sidi Mohammed** – and for a while it appeared that the Shereefian empire was moving back into the mainstream of European and world events. Mohammed recaptured the port of El Jadida from the Portuguese, founded the port of Essaouira, traded and conducted treaties with the Europeans, and even recognized the **United States of America** – the first ruler to do so.

At his death in 1790, however, the state collapsed once more into civil war, the two capitals of Fes and Marrakesh in turn promoting claimants to the throne. When this period drew to some kind of a close, with **Moulay Slimane** (1792–1822) asserting his authority in both cities, there was little left to govern. The army had dispersed; the Bled es Siba reasserted its old limits; and in Europe, with the ending of the Napoleonic wars, Britain, France, Spain and Germany were all looking to establish themselves in Africa.

Moulay Slimane's rule was increasingly isolated from the new realities outside Morocco. An intensely orthodox Muslim, he concentrated the efforts of government on eliminating the power and influence of the **Sufi brotherhoods** – a power he underestimated. In 1818 Berber tribes loyal to the Derakaoui brotherhood rebelled and, temporarily, captured the sultan. Subsequently, the sultans had no choice but to govern with the cooperation of local maraboutic and brotherhood leaders.

Even more serious, at least in its long-term effects, was Moulay Slimane's isolationist attitude towards **Europe**, and in particular to Napoleonic France. Exports were banned; European consuls banished to Tangier; and contacts that might have helped maintain Moroccan independence were lost.

European domination

Once started, the European domination of Moroccan affairs took an inevitable course – with an outdated, medieval form of government, virtual bankruptcy and armies press-ganged from the tribes to secure taxes, there was little that could be done to resist it.

The first pressures came from the **French**, who defeated the Ottomans in 1830 and occupied Algiers. Called to defend his fellow Muslims, Sultan **Abd Er Rahman** (1822–59) mustered a force but was severely defeated at Isly. In the following reign of **Mohammed III** (1859–73), **Spanish** aspirations were also realized with the occupation of Tetouan – regained by the Moroccans only after the offer to pay Spain massive indemnities and provide them with an Atlantic port (which the Spanish later claimed in Sidi Ifni).

Moulay Hassan

By the end of the nineteenth century outright occupation and colonization were proving more difficult to justify, but both the French and the Spanish had learned to use every opportunity to step in and "protect" their own nationals. Complaints by **Moulay Hassan**, the last pre-colonial sultan to have any real power, actually led to a debate on this issue at the 1880 **Madrid Conference**, but the effect was only to regularize the practice on a wider scale, beginning with the setting up of an "international administration" in Tangier.

Moulay Hassan could, in other circumstances, have proved an effective and possibly inspired sultan. Acceding to the throne in 1873, he embarked on an ambitious series of modernizing **reforms**, including attempts to stabilize the currency by minting the rial in Paris, to bring in more rational forms of taxation, and to retrain the army under the instruction of Turkish and Egyptian officers. The times, however, were against him. He found the social and monetary reforms obstructed by foreign merchants and local *caids*, while the European powers forced him to abandon plans for other Muslim states' involvement in the army.

Moulay Hassan played off the Europeans as best he could, employing a British military chief of staff, **Caid MacClean**, a French military mission and German arms manufacturers. On the frontiers, he built kasbahs to strengthen the defences at Tiznit, Saïdia and Selouane. But the government had few modern means of raising money to pay for these developments. Moulay Hassan was thrown back on the traditional means of taxation, the *harka*, setting out across the country to subdue the tribes and to collect tribute. In 1894, returning across the Atlas on just such a campaign, he died.

The last sultans

The last years of independence under Moulay Hassan's sons, Moulay Abd el Aziz and Moulay Hafid, were increasingly dominated by Europe.

The reign of **Abd el Aziz** (1894–1907), in particular, signalled an end to the possibilities of a modern, independent state raised by his reforming father. The sultan was a boy of fourteen at his accession, but for the first six years of his rule the country was kept in at least a semblance of order by his father's chamberlain, **Bou Ahmed**. In 1900, however, Bou Ahmed died, and Abd el Aziz was left to govern alone – surrounded by an assembly of Europeans, preying on the remaining wealth of the court.

The first years of the twentieth century in Morocco were marked by a return to the old ways. In the Atlas mountains, the tribal chiefs established ever-increasing powers, outside the government domain. In the Rif, a pretender to the throne, **Bou Hamra**, led a five-year revolt, coming close to taking control of Fes and the northern seat of government.

European manipulation during this period was remorselessly cynical. In 1904, the French negotiated agreements on "spheres of influence" with the British (who were to hold Egypt and Cyprus), and with the Italians (who got Tripolitania, or Libya). The following year saw the German kaiser Wilhelm visiting Tangier and swearing to protect Morocco's integrity, but he was later bought off with the chance to "develop" the Congo. France and Spain, meanwhile, had reached a secret arrangement on how they were going to divide Morocco and were simply waiting for the critical moment.

In 1907, the French moved troops into **Oujda**, on the Algerian border and, after a mob attack on French construction workers, into Casablanca. Abd el Aziz was eventually deposed by his brother, **Moulay Hafid** (1907–12), in a last attempt to resist the European advance. His reign began with a coalition with the principal Atlas chieftain, **Madani el Glaoui**, and intentions to take military action against the French. The new sultan, however, was at first preoccupied with putting down the revolt of Bou Hamra – whom he succeeded in capturing in 1909. By this time the moment for defence against European entrenchment, if indeed it had ever been possible, had passed. Claiming to protect their nationals – this time in the mineral mines of the Rif – the Spanish brought over 90,000 men to garrison their established port in Melilla. Colonial occupation, in effect, had begun.

The Treaty of Fes

Finally, in 1910, the two strands of Moroccan dissidence and European aggression came together. Moulay Hafid was driven into the hands of the French by the appearance of a new pretender in Meknes – one of a number during that period – and, with Berber tribesmen under the walls of his capital in Fes, was forced to accept their terms.

These were ratified and signed as the **Treaty of Fes** in 1912, and gave the French the right to defend Morocco, represent it abroad and conquer the Bled es Siba. A similar document was also signed with the Spanish, who were to take control of a strip of territory along the northern coast, with its capital in Tetouan and another thinner strip of land in the south, running eastwards from Tarfaya. In between, with the exception of a small Spanish enclave in Sidi Ifni, was to be French Morocco. A separate agreement gave Spain colonial rights to the Sahara, stretching south from Tarfaya to the borders of French Mauritania.

The arbitrary way in which these boundaries were drawn was to have a profound effect on modern Moroccan history. When Moroccan nationalists laid claim to the Sahara in the 1950s and to large stretches of Mauritania, Algeria and even Mali they based their case on the obsolete irrelevancy of colonial divisions.

C

The French and Spanish Protectorates (1912–56)

The fates of **Spanish and French Morocco** under colonial rule were to be very different. When **France** signed its Protectorate agreement with the sultan in 1912, its sense of **colonial mission** was running high. The colonial lobby in France argued that the colonies were vital not only as markets for French goods but because they fulfilled France's *mission civilisatrice* – to bring the benefits of French culture and language to all corners of the globe.

There may have been Spaniards who had similar conceptions of their role in North Africa, but reality was very different. **Spain** showed no interest in developing the Sahara until the 1960s; in the north the Spanish saw themselves more as conquerors than colonists. Its government there, described by one contemporary as a mixture of "battlefield, tavern and brothel", did much to provoke the Rif rebellions of the 1920s.

Lyautey and "Pacification"

France's first resident-general in Morocco was **General Hubert Lyautey**, often held up as the ideal of French colonialism with his stated policy: "Do not offend a single tradition, do not change a single habit." Lyautey recommended respect for the terms of the Protectorate agreement, which placed strict limits on French interference in Moroccan affairs. He recognized the existence of a functioning Moroccan bureaucracy based on the sultan's court with which the French could cooperate – a hierarchy of officials, with diplomatic representation abroad, and with its own social institutions.

But there were other forces at work: French soldiers were busy unifying the country, ending tribal rebellion; in their wake came a system of roads and railways that opened the country to further colonial exploitation. For the first time in Moroccan history, the central government exerted permanent control over the mountain regions. The **"pacification"** of the country brought a flood of French settlers and administrators.

In France these developments were presented as echoing the history of the opening up of the American Wild West. Innumerable articles celebrated "the transformation taking place, the stupendous development of Casablanca port, the birth of new towns, the construction of roads and dams . . . The image of the virgin lands in Morocco is contrasted often with metropolitan France, wrapped up in its history and its routines . . . ".

Naturally, the interests of the natives were submerged in this rapid economic development, and the restrictions of the Protectorate agreement were increasingly ignored.

Spain and revolt in the Rif

The early history of the **Spanish zone** was strikingly different. Before 1920 Spanish influence outside the main cities of Ceuta, Melilla and Tetouan was minimal. When the Spanish tried to extend their control into the Rif mountains of the interior, they ran into the fiercely independent Berber tribes of the region.

Normally, the various tribes remained divided, but faced with the Spanish troops they united under the leadership of **Abd el Krim**, later to become a hero of the Moroccan nationalists. In the summer of 1921, he inflicted a series of crushing defeats on the Spanish army, culminating in the massacre of at least 13,000 soldiers at **Annoual**. The scale of the defeat, at the hands of tribal fighters armed only with rifles, outraged the Spanish public and worried the French, who had Berber tribes of their own to deal with in the Atlas mountains. As the war began to spread into the French zone, the two colonial powers combined to crush the rebellion. It took a combined force of around 360,000 colonial troops to do so.

It was the last of the great tribal rebellions. Abd el Krim had fought for an independent **Rifian state**. An educated man, he had seen the potential wealth that could result from exploiting the mineral deposits of the Rif. After the rebellion was crushed, the route to Moroccan independence changed from armed revolt to the evolving middle-class resistance to the colonial rulers.

Nationalism and independence

The French had hoped that by educating a middle-class elite they would find native allies in the task of binding Morocco permanently to France. It had the opposite effect. The educated classes of Rabat and Fes were the first to demand reforms from the French that would give greater rights to the Moroccans. When the government failed to respond, the demand for reforms escalated into demands for total independence.

Religion also played an important part in the development of a nationalist movement. France's first inkling of the depth of nationalist feeling came in 1930, when the colonial government tried to bring in a **Berber dahir** – a law setting up a separate legal system for the Berber areas. This was an obvious breach of the Protectorate agreement, which prevented the French from changing the Islamic nature of government. Popular agitation forced the French to back down.

It was a classic attempt to "divide and rule", and as the nationalists gained strength, the French resorted more and more to threatening to "unleash" the Berber hill tribes against the Arab city dwellers. They hoped that by spreading

Christianity and setting up French schools in Berber areas, the tribes would become more "Europeanized" and, as such, useful allies against the Muslim Arabs.

Up until World War II, Morocco's **nationalists** were weak and their demands aimed at reforming the existing system, not independence. After riots in 1937, the government was able to round up the entire executive committee of the small nationalist party. But with French capitulation in the war, the climate changed. In 1943, the party took the name of **Istiqlal** (Independence); the call for complete separation from France grew more insistent.

The loyal performance of Moroccan troops during the war had raised hopes of a fairer treatment for nationalist demands, but postwar France continued to ignore Istiqlal, exiling its leaders and banning its publications. During the postwar period, it steadily developed into a mass party – growing from 10,000 members in 1947 to 100,000 by 1951.

To some extent, the developments of the 1950s, culminating in Moroccan independence in 1956, resemble events in Algeria and Tunisia. The French first underestimated the strength of local independence movements, then tried to resist them and finally had to concede defeat. In Algeria and Tunisia, the independence parties gained power and consolidated their positions once the French had left. But in Morocco, Istiqlal was never uncontested after 1956 and the party soon began to fragment – becoming by the 1970s a marginal force in politics.

The decline and fall of Istiqlal was due mainly to the astute way in which Sultan (later King) **Mohammed V** associated himself with the independence movement. Despite threats from the French government, Mohammed became more and more outspoken in his support for independence, paralysing government operations by refusing to sign legislation. Serious rioting in 1951 persuaded the French to act: after a period of house arrest, the sultan was sent into exile in 1953.

This only increased his popularity. After a brief attempt to rule in alliance with **T'hami el Glaoui**, the Berber pasha of Marrakesh who saw the sultan's absence as an opportunity to expand his power base in the south, the French capitulated in 1955, allowing the sultan to return. The government in Paris could see no way out of the spiralling violence of the nationalist guerrillas and the counterviolence of the French settlers. Perhaps equally significant, they could not sustain a simultaneous defence of three North African colonies – and economic interests dictated that they concentrate on holding Algeria. In 1956, Morocco was given full **independence** by France and Spain.

On independence, Sultan Mohammed V changed his title to that of king, foreshadowing a move towards a **constitutional monarchy**.

Mohammed V

Unlike his ancestor sultans, **Mohammed V** had inherited a united country with a well-developed industrial sector, an extensive system of irrigation and a network of roads and railways. But years of French administration had left little legacy of trained Moroccan administrators. Nor was there an obvious party base or bureaucracy for the king to operate within.

In 1956, Istiqlal party members held key posts in the first **government**. The regime instituted a series of reforms across the range of social issues. Schools and universities were created, a level of regional government was introduced and ambitious public works schemes launched. There were moves, also, against European "decadence", with a wholesale clean-up of Tangier, and against the unorthodox religious brotherhoods – both long-time targets of the Istiqlal.

Mohammed V, as **leader of the Muslim faith** in Morocco and the figurehead of independence, commanded huge support and influence in Morocco as a whole. In government, however, he did not perceive the Istiqlal as natural allies. The king bided his time, building links with the army – with the help of Crown Prince Hassan, whose period as commander-in-chief was a defining moment in his political development – and with the police.

Mohammed's influence on the army would prove a decisive factor in the Moroccan state withstanding a series of **rebellions** against its authority. The most serious of these were in the Rif, in 1958–59, but there were challenges, too, in the Middle Atlas and Sahara. The king's standing and the army's efficiency stood the test. Crown Prince Hassan, meanwhile, as the army commander, helped to translate internal pressures into renewed nationalism. The army began a quasi-siege in the south, exerting pressure on the Spanish to give up their claims to the port of **Sidi Ifni**.

In party politics, Mohammed's principal act was to lend his support to the **Mouvement Populaire** (MP), a moderate party set up to represent the Berbers, and for the king a useful counterweight to Istiqlal. In 1959, the strategy paid its first dividend. Istiqlal was seriously weakened by a split which hived off the more left-wing members into a separate party, the **Union Nationale des Forces Populaires** (UNFP) under Mehdi Ben Barka. There had always been a certain tension within Istiqlal between the moderates and those favouring a more radical policy, in association with the unions. A tendency towards parties dividing within and among themselves has been apparent in Moroccan politics ever since, helping to maintain the primal role of the Palace in the political arena.

Hassan II (1961–99)

The death of Mohammed V in 1961 led to the accession of **King Hassan II**, who was to dominate the kingdom for nearly four decades. For much of this reign Hassan ruled as an **autocrat**, albeit with a veneer of parliamentary party politics. But by the time that he died, in July 1999, the monarchy, although still by far the most powerful political institution in Morocco, was an institution that had begun to engage with other political and social forces – and had established the roots of a more open political culture.

The handover to Hassan's son **Sidi Mohammed Ben Hassan** – now reigning as **Mohammed VI** – was achieved peacefully after Hassan was buried with full national and international honours. Hassan's legacy included leaving a government led by a long-time opponent, Socialist leader **Abderrahmane el Youssoufi**, and a more rounded civil society than had seemed possible only a few years before. Thus, while the late king's legacy was widely glorified, the local media was by then sufficiently independent also to consider some of his failings as well in their analyses of Morocco's path **after Hassan**.

Hassan had presided over a period of **dramatic change**, forged upon a deeply **uneven** legacy of colonial rule. The French had built an administrative capital in Rabat and a relatively sophisticated infrastructure in Casablanca and other economically useful zones, but most other regions were left without adequate roads, health and education facilities or other trappings of a modernizing state.

In the kingdom's northern and southern extremities, Spanish colonial rule left even less on which the new state could base its policy of creating viable development. At independence, there was an almost total absence of doctors or graduates in the Spanish zones.

Despite the poverty still apparent in large areas of the country, much was done during Hassan's reign to bring the kingdom into the modern world. It was an achievement in the face of a huge **population explosion** in the 1970s and 1980s, which saw the population rise from eight million at Independence to more than thirty million today. It's a predominantly youthful population – more than forty percent are aged under fourteen – clamouring for the sort of education and jobs of which their parents and grandparents were routinely deprived.

Values and traditional roles

In many respects Hassan was a very modern monarch, regularly pictured playing golf, flying a jet fighter, or meeting fellow heads of state. As a power politician he had few peers. But he was also careful to maintain his status as a traditional ruler – one of the very few who remained in the Afro-Arab world. When in his flowing robes at a state occasion or religious festival, Hassan was very much the *Amir al-Muminin* (commander of the faithful), **Morocco's religious leader** as well as its temporal ruler.

This role is of great political significance to the monarchy, giving the ruler the sort of deep-rooted legitimacy so lacking in other developing countries – a fact not lost on young King Mohammed VI. Presiding over a complex system of traditional loyalties, ethnic and regional divisions, Hassan used traditions based in the days of the Sultanate to underpin his modern monarchy – maintaining the Palace at the centre of the Moroccan political universe. Indeed, according to his view of democracy, it would have been an abnegation of the king's religious role if he were not to play a central role in government.

Achieving the balance between continuity and change was not easy, as whatever formula the king chose would have to involve the genuine devolution of power. This only really happened right at the end of Hassan's reign, when multi party politics became a reality when the 1998 elections resulted in a coalition government led by former opposition parties. However, in the 1990s, the promotion of more responsive local authorities (*collectivités locales*) also set a form of **devolution** under way. Hassan even talked of dividing the country along federal lines, with the German *länder* as a model. A third pointer to the emergence of a new Morocco in this decade was the emergence of literally thousands of **non-governmental organizations** (NGOs) and other associations.

All of this was encouraging, especially given the continued postponement of general elections in the period 1989–97 – an impasse caused in large part by the political system's inability to develop a new configuration in which the Throne would remain dominant yet with genuine input from a wider **body of opinion**. Those pushing to be heard included a growing younger generation of professionals who felt alienated from the traditional political parties, which were mostly still run by men who had emerged during the independence struggle and Hassan's first years as monarch.

Dissatisfaction with Hassan's regime in the 1980s and 1990s surfaced in the form of protests by unemployed graduates (despite the dangers of political protest in Hassan's police state), and sometimes violent incidents in the kingdom's universities. In 1990, a general strike called by the CDT trade union federation led to riots in Fes and Tangier. On campus, the student movement linked to Morocco's biggest opposition party, the **Union Socialiste des Forces Populaires** (USFP) – in government since 1998 – went into retreat as a growing Islamist movement took control of student unions. This is one sign that the **rise of radical Islam** across the Arab world – and notably in neighbouring Algeria after civil conflict erupted in 1991–92 – has not left Morocco unaffected, for all that Hassan felt confident about his unique blend of religious authority and the efficiency of his security forces.

Constitution and elections

Domestic politics since independence has centred on a battle of wills between the dominant political forces in the kingdom: the Palace and its allies; a legalized opposition which has at times formed a part of the government; and underground movements such as the Marxist-Leninist Ilal Amam (which has all but disappeared) and, more recently, groups of Islamist radicals.

Even before independence, in a 1955 speech, Mohammed V had promised to set up "democratic institutions resulting from the holding of free elections". The country's first constitution was not ready until after his death, and it was only in 1962, under Hassan II, that it was put to, and approved by, a popular referendum. The constitution was drafted in such a way as to favour the pro-monarchy parties of the centre – setting the pattern that was to prevail up until the 1998 elections.

The 1960s were marked by the fragility of Morocco's political party structure and the authorities' greater enthusiasm for using the bullet and torture chamber rather than the ballot box to handle opposition. This mood was reflected in the **Ben Barka affair**, a notorious incident whose political ramifications endured for the next two decades, when Mehdi Ben Barka, leader of the opposition UNFP party, was assassinated in Paris, with apparent connivance between the governments of Morocco and France.

The opposition subsequently split, with the largest element of the UNFP going on to form the USFP, led by Abderrahim Bouabid until his death in 1992. These parties were largely ineffectual, especially after Hassan announced a new constitution in 1970, following a period of emergency rule. However, the events of 1971–72 showed the real nature of the threat to the monarchy.

In July 1971, a group of soldiers broke into the royal palace in Skhirat in an attempt to stage a **coup**; more than 100 people were killed, but in the confusion Hassan escaped. The following year another attempt was launched, as the king's private jet was attacked by fighters of the Moroccan Air Force. Again, Hassan had a very narrow escape – his pilot was able to convince the attacking aircraft by radio that the king had already died. The former interior minister, General Mohamed Oufkir disappeared (apparently murdered in custody) soon after and the armed forces were restructured. Typical of the younger Hassan's style, Oufkir's family remained imprisoned and incommunicado until 1991.

The Saharan conflict and the UMA

Hassan's great challenge was to give a sense of destiny to the country, a cause similar to the struggle for independence that had brought such prestige to his father. That cause was provided in 1975, when the Spanish finally decided to pull out of their colony in the **Western Sahara** (for more on which, see pp.684–685).

In the 1950s the nationalist Istiqlal party had laid claim to the Spanish Sahara, as well as to Mauritania and parts of Algeria and Mali, as part of its quest for a "Greater Morocco". By 1975, Hassan had patched up the border dispute with Algeria and recognized the independent government in

Mauritania, but he retained a more realistic design – Moroccan control of the Spanish Sahara.

Spanish withdrawal from the Western Sahara in 1975 coincided with General Franco's final illness and Hassan timed his move perfectly, sending some 350,000 Moroccan civilians southwards on **El Massira** – the **"Green March"** – to the Sahara. Spain could either go to war with Morocco by attacking the advancing Moroccans or withdraw without holding a referendum on independence, which they had agreed to call after pressure from the UN. Hassan's bluff worked, and the popular unrest of the 1960s and the coup attempts of 1971–72 were forgotten under a wave of patriotism. Without shedding any blood, Morocco had "recaptured" part of its former empire. But the Polisario guerillas who had led the fight against Spanish rule now began a campaign against Moroccan occupation. Despite early Polisario successes, the Moroccans managed to assert control over most of the territory, and all of its economically important areas, but in 1990 the two sides agreed a ceasefire under UN auspices, on the principle that a **referendum** would be held on the territory's future.

That promised referendum has yet to take place, but the dispute has damaged Morocco diplomatically; in particular it has left her isolated in African politics since the African Union recognized the Polisario-declared Saharawi Arab Democratic Republic, prompting Morocco to leave. A resolution is also essential if Morocco is to have normal relations with its neighbours, particularly Algeria, which has strongly backed Polisario throughout the Saharan conflict; the resulting friction between Morocco and Algeria has hampered efforts towards regional unity.

In February 1989 Algerian, Libyan, Mauritanian, Moroccan and Tunisian leaders, meeting in Marrakesh, had agreed to form the long-awaited regional grouping, the **Arab Maghreb Union,** known by its evocative acronym UMA (from the French Union du Maghreb Arabe but sounding like the Arabic word *'umma,* or community). However, the UMA has been stalled by disputes hinging on longstanding rivalries between the North African states. Chief among the UMA's problems has been Moroccan–Algerian hostility arising largely from the Saharan question. This led in 1994 to the closure of the Algerian–Moroccan border, which has not reopened since.

Economic and social problems

The Saharan war proved to be only a temporary distraction from discontent in Morocco itself. Moreover, the occupation of the Western Sahara and its demands on the economy added to the very problems it was designed to divert attention from. By 1981, an estimated sixty percent of the population were living below the poverty level, unemployment ran at approximately twenty percent (forty percent among the young) and perhaps twenty percent of the urban population lived in shantytowns, or *bidonvilles.*

Popular unrest erupted in the 1984 **"bread riots"** in cities across the country, most notably in Marrakesh, Oujda, Nador and Tetouan. The riots were triggered when the government raised the prices of staple foods following pressure from the International Monetary Fund (IMF) to repay its **burgeoning debt** while phosphate prices were depressed and the country was suffering one of its regular **droughts**. King Hassan had to intervene personally to reverse the decision and, in the opinion of many analysts, save his monarchy from a populist rising.

In the 1990s, Morocco embarked on one of Africa's biggest **privatization** drives as King Hassan firmly nailed his colours to the mast of economic liberalization. New efforts were made to encourage foreign investment in technologically advanced manufacturing industries, **textiles** and, an increasingly important earner, **tourism**. Modern management skills began to take hold with the emergence of a new managerial class independent of the old social loyalties. The decade ended with the Medi Telecom consortium bidding over US$1 billion for a licence to install a GSM mobile telephone system, and privately financed power plants helping to raise energy capacity.

Morocco's controversial application to join the **European Union**, made in the 1980s, was rejected. But Brussels has pushed European governments to develop closer relations with the kingdom and in 1996 Morocco's became only the second Arab government (after Tunisia) to join the European Union's **Euro-Mediterranean Partnership** agreement. This accord opens the way for the kingdom to join a free trade zone eventually planned for North Africa and the Mediterranean.

Change and elections

The opposition, which had been quiet through much of the 1980s, started to reassert itself in the 1990s, as traditional opposition parties showed revived enthusiasm for challenging the government – though not the king. They did this in the knowledge that if their opposition failed, younger Moroccans might be tempted to follow Islamist and other illegal political trends.

The mid-1990s saw Morocco cleaning up its previously appalling **human rights** record. In 1992, a leading dissident, Abraham Serfaty, was one of many well-known figures in a **release of political prisoners** that included many soldiers held, since the 1972 failed coup, in a dungeon prison at Tazmamart in the High Atlas. Indeed, several former student radicals who survived imprisonment and torture in the 1960s, '70s and '80s went on to hold positions of responsibility in the local press, universities and even government departments.

In 1996 Hassan judged there to be sufficient consensus on the direction of Moroccan politics to hold a referendum on constitutional reforms, opening the way for a new bicameral parliamentary system. Local and national elections were held in 1997 and for the first time there seemed the prospect of bringing the opposition into government, with genuine power.

Disappointingly, the elections produced a lacklustre campaign and much voter apathy, as a three-way split gave right-wing, centrist and left-wing/nationalist groupings a similar number of seats in the lower house of parliament. Hassan appointed as prime minister the USFP (Socialist) leader **Abderrahmane Youssoufi** at the head of a coalition government that included both USFP and Istiqlal ministers.

Islamist politics

While leftists dominated the opposition in the first three decades of independence, **radical Islam** posed the greatest challenge in the 1990s, and has continued to do so in the 2000s.

One notable factor in the 1997 general election was that Islamist deputies were voted into parliament for the first time, under the *Mouvement Populaire Constitutionnel et Démocratique* (**MPCD**) banner. This parliamentary debut for the Islamists came at a time when their calls for a change in views on public morality and private sector development were gaining appeal among those most alienated by increasing social tensions and allegations of corruption, but many have seen the administration's acceptance of the **MPCD**, who stand at the moderate end of the Islamist spectrum, as a classic piece of Moroccan divide-and-rule, aimed at splitting the Islamist movement.

Mohammed VI (1999–)

Even as he suffered his final illnesses, King Hassan II bestrode the Moroccan scene, and the possibility that he might depart leaving a political vacuum alarmed many Moroccans, as well as many of the king's allies abroad. This dread about the future was fuelled by concerns that the kingdom could be divided by ethnic and regional rivalries – a fear the Palace, ever schooled in Moroccan traditions of divide-and-rule, did nothing to play down.

However, the handover to **King Mohammed VI** went smoothly, and ushered in a **new style** of rule. Indeed, after years when the 35-year-old crown prince's ability to lead such a large and complex country had been widely questioned, Sidi Mohammed quickly emerged from his father's shadow as very much his own man, and has won widespread popular support. From the very start he made clear his more inclusive agenda by visiting the northern parts (long ignored by Hassan), restoring **civil rights** to those remaining political prisoners not covered by previous amnesties (with over 8,000 released in first year amnesties), and promising a more **relaxed and consensual** form of rule.

Also in the very first months of his rule, the new king quickly set a new tone and showed he could wield his own **authority** by sacking Hassan's powerful but unpopular right-hand man, Minister of State for the Interior **Driss Basri.** He also allowed a number of high-profile dissidents to return to Morocco, most notably leftist **Abraham Serfaty,** who he appointed as a personal adviser. In May 2000, he made headlines by freeing his father's most implacable critic, **Abdessalam Yassine,** leader of the banned **Al-Adl wal Ihsane** (Justice and Charity) movement. Dissent is not always tolerated however, and the king's forces have on occasion clamped down rather harshly on street protests, notably a protest by unemployed graduates in Rabat in June 2000, while newspapers still get prosecuted under laws against "undermining" the monarchy or Morocco's "territorial integrity". Nonetheless, the tenor of Mohammed's reign has been to extend democracy, human rights and free speech, albeit in a cautious fashion.

In March 2000, the king announced a **National Action Plan,** whose main feature was a Family Law that radically improved the **position of women** under Moroccan law, banning polygamy and introducing more equal family rights. The proposal sparked a backlash by Islamists, who mustered around a quarter of a million supporters at a march in Casablanca to protest the proposals, and the government responded by setting up a consultative commission to consider the question more carefully. After due consideration, parliament decided to go ahead with the proposals, which came into force in 2004, giving women greater legal rights in Morocco than anywhere else in the Muslim world, and more on a par with those of women in Europe.

The Moroccan government was swift to condemn the September 2001 **attacks by al-Qaida** on the Pentagon and the New York World Trade Center, but the apparent involvement of pro-Islamist Moroccans in those attacks and in the train bombs that killed over 200 people in Madrid in March 2004 severely embarrassed the Moroccan authorities. In Morocco itself, May 2003 saw attacks on Jewish and Western targets by suicide bombers in Casablanca, which resulted in the deaths of 33 people, aside from the bombers themselves. The attack severely dented fundamentalist appeal, but a hardcore of support for such actions does continue to exist in Morocco, a small minority though it may be. The authorities reacted to the bombings by rounding up over 1500 people

C

CONTEXTS | History

suspected of involvement with militant groups, of whom several hundred were given prison sentences of anything from three months to thirty years.

September 2002 saw **legislative elections** in which the moderate Islamist MPCD, now renamed the PJD (*Parti de la Justice et du Développement*), took thirteen percent of the vote and emerged as Morocco's third biggest political party after the USFP and Istiqlal, which formed an administration together with representatives of four other parties. All the government parties are essentially organizations for the distribution of patronage, and the ministries that they control are largely staffed by their own people. The PJD, which is the only ideologically based political party, is also the only serious opposition in parliament.

The birth of a son and heir, Prince Moulay Hassan, in 2003, gave the king an excuse to release some 9000 prisoners and remit the sentences of thousands more. The same year also saw a major extension of **rights for Berber speakers**, whose languages were taught for the first time in schools in the 2003–4 academic year. Programmes in Berber are also now broadcast on TV.

Despite his reforms, King Mohammed's Morocco is still very much dominated by the Palace – where a younger generation of advisers is settling in, many drawn from the **royal school** created by King Hassan to educate his sons with the brightest and best the kingdom could offer. These are an impressive body of men (and a few women now reaching top jobs), but while they talk the language of globalization, their political mandate remains essentially feudal. The government remains rooted in a political tradition in which they take orders from a king who is both monarch and *Al-Amir Al-Muminin* (commander of the faithful), but Mohammed is gradually edging towards a constitutional monarchy, and has at times berated his ministers for not acting on their own initiative.

To date, the king has proved surprisingly successful in rejuvenating the monarchical and political system. He has needed to do so, if he is now to address the **crucial issues** facing Morocco: unemployment, poverty, a huge young population, the need for a resolution in the Western Sahara, and the spectre of radical Islam. The hope is that the West, and in particular the European Union (where Morocco is seen by some as a buffer against African immigration) will provide support for both the king and system to prosper.

Chronology of Events and Monuments

10,000–5000 BC	**Capsian** and **Mouillian Man** spread across the Maghreb Neolithic cultures	**Rock carvings** in Oukaïmeden, Foum el Hassan and other less accessible sites
1100 BC	**Phoenician** settlements	Bronze Age. First trading port at **Lixis** (near Larache)
500 BC	**Carthaginians** take over Phoenician settlements and greatly expand them	Remains in Lixis, and in Rabat Archeological Museum
146 BC	Fall of Carthage at end of the Third Punic War; Roman influence spreads into **Berber kingdoms** of Mauretania-Numidia	Bust of Juba II (Rabat)
27 BC	Direct **Roman** rule under Emperor Caligula	**Volubilis** developed as provincial capital; other minor sites at Lixis and Tangier
253 AD	Roman legions withdrawn	Mosaics in Tetouan and Rabat museums
429	**Vandals** pass through	
535	**Byzantines** occupy Ceuta	

Islam

622	Muhammad and followers move from Mecca to Medina and start spread of Islam	
ca. 705	**Moussa Ibn Nasr** establishes Arab rule in north and pre-Sahara, and in 711 leads Berber invasion of Spain	

Idrissid Dynasty (788–923)

788	**Moulay Idriss** establishes first Moroccan Arab dynasty	Founding of Moulay Idriss and Fes
807	Moulay Idriss II (807–836)	**Fes** developed with Kairouan and Andalusian refugee quarters, and establishment of Kairaouine Mosque
10th–11th c.	Hilali tribes wreak havoc on Maghrebi infrastructure	

Almoravid dynasty (1062–1145)

| 1062 | **Youssef bin Tachfine** establishes capital in Marrakesh; first great Berber dynasty | **Koubba** in **Marrakesh** is only surviving monument, except for walls and possibly a minaret in **Tit** (near El Jadida) |
| 1090 | Almoravid invasion of **Spain** | |

Almohad dynasty (1145–1248)

1120s	**Ibn Toumert** sets up a *ribat* in Tin Mal in the High Atlas	Ruined mosque of **Tin Mal**
1145–1147	**Abd el Moumen** captures Fes and then Marrakesh	Extensive building of walls, gates and **minarets**, including the Koutoubia in **Marrakesh**
1195	**Yacoub el Mansour** (1184–99) extends rule to Spain, and east to Tripoli	New capital begun in **Rabat**: Hassan Tower, Oudaia Gate
1212	Defeat in Spain at Las Navas de Tolosa	

Merenid dynasty (1248–1465)

1250s	**Abou Youssef Yacoub** (1258–86) establishes effective power	*Zaouia* and mausoleum in **Chellah** (Rabat); new city (El Djedid) built in **Fes Medersas** in Fes (Bou Inania, Attarin, etc), Meknes and Salé
1330s–50s	**Abou el Hassan** (1331–51) and **Abou Inan** (1351–58), two of the most successful Merenids, extend rule briefly to Tunis	
1415	**Portuguese** begin attacks on Moroccan coast, taking Ceuta and later other cities	**Portuguese** cistern in El Jadida; walls and remains in Azzemour, Asilah and Safi

Wattasid dynasty (1465–1554)

1465	Wattasids – Merenid viziers – usurp power	**Chefchaouen** built and **Tetouan** founded again by refugees
	Fall of **Granada**, last Muslim kingdom in Spain; Jewish and Muslim refugees settle in Morocco over next 100 years or so	
15th–16th c.	*Marabouts* establish *zaouias*, controlling parts of the country	

Saadian dynasty (1554–1669)

1550s	**Mohammed esh Sheikh** (d. 1557) founds dynasty in Marrakesh	
1579	Battle of Three Kings leads to accession of **Ahmed el Mansour** (1578–1603), who goes on to conquer Timbuktu and the gold and slave routes to the south	**Saadian Tombs** and **Ben Youssef medersa** (Marrakesh); pavilion extensions to **Kairaouine** Mosque (Fes)
1627	Pirate **Republic of Bou Regreg** set up by Andalusian refugees	**Rabat** Medina built

Alaouite dynasty (1669–)

1670s–1720s	**Moulay Ismail** (1672–1727) founds the Alaouite dynasty on Morocco	New imperial capital in **Meknes** (Ismail's mausoleum, etc); **kasbahs** and **forts** built; **palaces** in Tangier and Rabat
18th–19th c.	**Sidi Mohammed** (1757–90) **Moulay Suleiman** (1792–1822)	Ismail and his successors rebuild **grand mosques**, especially in **Marrakesh**, capital for many Alaouites, and build many of the city's **pavilions** and **gardens** in the early 18th century
1894	Death of Moulay Hassan, last effective sultan of "Old Morocco"	Extensive **palace** building – El Badi (Marrakesh), Palais Jamai (Fes)
1912	**Treaty of Fes** brings into being **French and Spanish Protectorates**	European **Villes Nouvelles** built, **Mauresque** architecture developed for administrative buildings
	T'hami el Glaoui becomes pacha of Marrakesh and is used by French to conquer the southern tribes	**Glaoui palaces** in Telouet and Marrakesh; **kasbah** fortresses throughout the south
1921	Riffian revolt under Abd El Krim	
1943	Nationalist **Istiqlal** party formed in Fes	
1956	**Independence**	
1961	Accession of **Hassan II (1961–99)**	
1975	**Green March into Western Sahara**	New royal **palaces** in all major cities
1997	**Hassan II Mosque** in Casablanca	
1999	Accession of **Mohammed VI**	
2002	Legislative elections result in a four-party coalition administration, with a parliamentary Islamist opposition	
2003	Birth of heir to the throne **Prince Moulay Hassan**; bomb attacks in Casablanca; first Berber lessons in schools	
2004	**New Family Law** radically extends women's legal rights	
2007	King announces new peace initiative for **Western Sahara**	

Islam in Morocco

It's difficult to get any grasp of Morocco, and even more so of Moroccan history, without first knowing something of Islam. What follows is a very basic background: some theory, some history and an idea of Morocco's place in the modern Islamic world.

Beginnings: practice and belief

Islam was a new religion born of the wreckage of the Greco-Roman world beyond the Mediterranean. Its founder, a merchant named **Muhammad** (also spelt Mohammed) from the wealthy city of Mecca (now in Saudi Arabia), was chosen as God's Prophet: in about 609 AD, he began to receive divine messages which he transcribed directly into the **Koran** (*Qur'an*), Islam's Bible. This was the same God worshipped by Jews and Christians – Jesus (*Aïssa* in Arabic) is one of the major prophets in Islam – but Muslims claim that he had been misunderstood by both earlier religions.

The distinctive feature of this new faith was directness – a reaction to the increasing complexity of established religions and an obvious attraction. In Islam there is no intermediary between man and God in the form of an institutionalized priesthood or complicated liturgy, as in Christianity; and worship, in the form of prayer, is a direct and personal communication with God. Believers face five essential requirements, called **Pillars of faith:** prayer five times daily (*salat*); the pilgrimage (*hadj*) to Mecca; the Ramadan fast (*sanm*); almsgiving (*zakat*); and, most fundamental of all, the acceptance that "There is no God but God and Muhammad is His Prophet" (*shahada*).

The Pillars of Faith

The Pillars of Faith are still central to Muslim life, articulating and informing daily existence. Ritual **prayers** are the most visible. Bearing in mind that the Islamic day begins at sunset, the five daily times are sunset, after dark, dawn, noon and afternoon. Prayers can be performed anywhere, but preferably in a mosque (*djemaa* in Arabic). In the past, and even today in some places, a *muezzin* would climb his minaret each time and summon the faithful.

Nowadays, the call is likely to be less frequent, and prerecorded; even so, this most distinctive of Islamic sounds has a beauty all its own, especially when neighbouring *muezzins* are audible simultaneously. Their message is simplicity itself: "God is most great (*Allah Akhbar*). I testify that there is no God but Allah. I testify that Muhammad is His Prophet. Come to prayer, come to security. God is great." Another phrase is added in the morning: "Prayer is better than sleep".

Prayers are preceded by ritual washing and are recited with the feet bare. Facing Mecca (the direction indicated in a mosque by the *mihrab*), the worshipper recites the Fatina, the first chapter of the Koran: "Praise be to God, Lord of the worlds, the Compassionate, the Merciful, King of the Day of Judgement. We worship you and seek your aid. Guide us on the straight path, the path of those on whom you have bestowed your Grace, not the path of those who incur your anger nor of those who go astray." The same words are then repeated twice in the prostrate position, with some interjections of *Allah Akhbar*. It is a highly ritualized procedure, the prostrate position symbolic of the worshipper's role as servant (Islam literally means "obedience"), and the sight of thousands of people going through the same motions simultaneously in a mosque is a powerful one. On Islam's holy day, Friday, all believers are expected to attend prayers in their local grand mosque. Here the whole community comes together in worship led by an *imam*, who may also deliver the *khutba*, or sermon.

Ramadan is the name of the ninth month in the lunar Islamic calendar, the month in which the Koran was revealed to Muhammad. For the whole of the month, believers must obey a rigorous fast (the custom was originally modelled on Jewish and Christian practice), forsaking all forms of consumption between sunrise and sundown; this includes food, drink, cigarettes and any form of sexual contact. Only a few categories of people are exempted: travellers, children, pregnant women and warriors engaged in a *jihad*, or holy war. Given the climates in which many Muslims live, the fast is a formidable undertaking, but in practice it becomes a time of intense celebration.

The pilgrimage, or **hadj**, to Mecca is an annual event, with millions flocking to Muhammad's birthplace from all over the world. Here they go through several days of rituals, the central one being a sevenfold circumambulation of the Kaba, before kissing a black stone set in its wall. Islam requires that all believers go on a *hadj* as often as is practically possible, but for the poor it may well be a once-in-a-lifetime occasion, and is sometimes replaced by a series of visits to lesser, local shrines – in Morocco, for instance, to Fes and Moulay Idriss.

Based on these central articles, the new Islamic faith proved to be inspirational. Muhammad's own Arab nation was soon converted, and the Arabs then proceeded to carry their religion far and wide in an extraordinarily rapid territorial expansion. Many peoples of the Middle East and North Africa, who for centuries had only grudgingly accepted Roman paganism or Christianity, embraced Islam almost immediately.

Islam's development in Morocco

Islam made a particularly spectacular arrival in Morocco. **Oqba Ibn Nafi**, the crusading general who had already expelled the Byzantines from Tunisia, marked his subjugation of the "Far West" by riding fully armed into the waves of the Atlantic. "O God," he is said to have exclaimed, "I call you to witness that there is no ford here. If there was, I would cross it."

This compulsory appreciation of Morocco's remoteness was prophetic in a way, because over the succeeding centuries Moroccan Islam was to acquire and retain a highly distinctive character. Where mainstream Islamic history is concerned, its development has been relatively straightforward – it was virtually untouched, for instance, by the Sunni–Shia conflict that split the Muslim world – but the country's unusual geographical and social circumstances have conspired to tip the balance away from official orthodoxy.

Orthodoxy, by its very nature, has to be an urban-based tradition. Learned men – lawyers, Koranic scholars and others – could only congregate in the cities where, gathered together and known collectively as the *ulema*, they regulated the faith. In Islam, this included both law and education. Teaching was at first based entirely in the mosques; later, it was conducted through a system of colleges, or medersas, in which students would live while studying at the often adjoining mosque. In most parts of the Islamic world, this very learned and sophisticated urban hierarchy was dominant. But Morocco also developed a powerful tradition of **popular religion**, first manifested in the eighth-century Kharijite rebellion – which effectively divided the country into separate Berber kingdoms – and endures to this day in the mountains and countryside.

Marabouts

There are three main strands of this popular religion, all of them deriving from the worship of saints. Everywhere in Morocco, as well as elsewhere in North Africa, the countryside is dotted with small domed **marabouts**: the tombs of holy men, which became centres of worship and pilgrimage. This elevation of individuals goes against strict Islamic teaching, but probably derives from the Berbers' pre-Islamic tendency to focus worship round individual holy men. At its simplest local level, these saint cults attracted the loyalty of the Moroccan villages and the more remote regions.

More prosperous cults would also endow educational institutions attached to the *marabout*, known as **zaouias**, which provided an alternative to the official education given in urban medersas. These inevitably posed a threat to the authority of the urban hierarchy, and as rural cults extended their influence, some became so popular that they endowed their saints with genealogies traced back to the Prophet. The title accorded to these men and their descendants was Shereef, and many grew into strong political forces. The classic example in Morocco is the tomb of Moulay Idriss – in the eighth century just a local *marabout*, but eventually, the base of the Idrissid clan, a centre of enormous influence that reached far beyond its rural origins.

Loyalty to a particular family – religiously sanctified, but essentially political – was at the centre of the shereefian movements. In the third strand of popular devotion, the focus was more narrowly religious. Again, the origins lay in small, localized cults of individuals, but these were individuals worshipped for their

△ The Zaouia of Sidi Ben Salah in Marrakesh

magical and mystical powers. Taken up and developed by subsequent followers, their rituals became the focal point of **brotherhoods** of initiates.

The Aissaoua

Perhaps the most famous Moroccan brotherhood is that of **Sidi Mohammed Bin Aissa**. Born in Souss in the fifteenth century, he travelled in northern Morocco before settling down as a teacher in Meknes and founding a *zaouia*. His powers of mystical healing became famous there, and he provoked enough official suspicion to be exiled briefly to the desert – where he again revealed his exceptional powers by proving himself immune to scorpions, snakes, live flames and other hostile manifestations. His followers tried to achieve the same state of grace. Six hundred were said to have attained perfection – and during the saint's lifetime *zaouias* devoted to his teachings were founded in Figuig and elsewhere in the Maghreb.

Bound by its practice of a common source of ritual, the Aissaoua brotherhood made itself notorious with displays of eating scorpions, walking on hot coals and other ecstatic practices designed to bring union with God. It was perhaps the most flamboyant of these brotherhoods, but most at any rate used some kind of dancing or music. The more extreme and fanatical of these rites are now outlawed, though the attainment of trance is still an important part of the moussems, or festivals, of the various confraternities.

Towards crisis

With all its different forms, Islam permeated every aspect of the country's pre-twentieth-century life. Unlike Christianity, at least Protestant Christianity, which to some extent has accepted the separation of church and state, Islam sees no such distinction. **Civil law** was provided by the *sharia*, the religious law contained in the Koran, and **intellectual life** by the *msids* (Koranic primary schools where the 6200 verses were learned by heart) and by the great medieval mosque universities, of which the Karraouine in Fes (together with the Zitoura in Tunis and the Al Azhar in Cairo) was the most important in the Arab world.

The religious basis of Arab study and intellectual life did not prevent its scholars and scientists from producing work that was hundreds of years ahead of contemporary "Dark Age" Europe. The remains of a monumental water clock in Fes and the work of the historian Ibn Khaldun are just two Moroccan examples. Arab work in developing and transmitting multicultural influences (Greco-Roman, Persian, Indian and Chinese) was also vital to the whole development of the European Renaissance. By this time, however, the Islamic world – and isolated Morocco in particular – was beginning to move away from the West. The Crusades had been one enduring influence promoting division. Another was the Islamic authorities themselves, increasingly suspicious (like the Western Church) of any challenge and actively discouraging of innovation. At first it did not matter in political terms that Islamic culture became static. But by the end of the eighteenth century, Europe was ready to take advantage. Napoleon's expedition to Egypt in 1798 marked the beginning of a century in which virtually every Islamic country came under the control of a **European power**.

Islam cannot, of course, be held solely responsible for the Muslim world's material decline. But because it influences every part of its believers' lives, and because East–West rivalry had always been viewed in primarily religious terms, the nineteenth and twentieth centuries saw something of a **crisis in religious confidence**. Why had Islam's former power now passed to infidel foreigners?

Fundamentalism

Reactions and answers veered between two extremes. There were those who felt that Islam should try to incorporate some of the West's materialism; on the other side, there were movements holding that Islam should turn its back on the West, purify itself of all corrupt additions and thus rediscover its former power. While they were colonies of European powers, however, Muslim nations had little chance of putting any such ideas into effective practice. These could only emerge in the form of cooperation with, or rebellion against, the ruling power. But the postwar era of **decolonization**, and the simultaneous acquisition through oil of relative economic independence, brought the Islamic world suddenly face to face with the question of its own spiritual identity. How should it deal with Western values and influence, now that it could afford – both politically and economically – almost total rejection? A return to the totality of Islam – **fundamentalism** – is a conscious choice of one consistent spiritual identity, one that is deeply embedded in the consciousness of a culture already unusually aware of tradition. It is also a rejection of the West and its colonial and exploitative values. Traditional Islam, at least in some interpretations, offers a positivist brand of freedom that is clearly opposed to the negative freedoms of Western materialism. The most vehement Islamic fundamentalists, in Morocco as elsewhere, are not passive reactionaries dwelling in the past, but young radicals – often students – eager to assert their "anti-imperialist" religion.

Islam in Modern Morocco

There are two basic reasons why only a few Islamic countries have embraced a rigidly traditional or fundamentalist stance. The first is an ethical one: however undesirable Western materialism may appear, the rejection of all Western values involves rejecting also what the West sees as the "benefits" of development. Perhaps it is begging the question in strictly Islamic terms to say that the emancipation of women, for example, is a "benefit". But the leaders of many countries feel that such steps are both desirable and reconcilable with a more liberal brand of Islam, which will retain its place in the national identity. The other argument against militant Islam is a more pragmatic, economic one. Morocco is only one of many countries which would suffer severe economic hardship if they cut themselves off from the West: they have to tread a narrow line that allows them to maintain good relations both with the West and with the Islamic world.

Islam and the state

In Morocco today, Islam is the official state religion, and King Mohammed's secular status is interwoven with his role as "commander of the faithful". Internationally, too, he plays a leading role. Meetings of the Islamic Conference Organization are frequently held in Morocco and, in one of the most unlikely exchanges, students from Tashkent in Uzbekistan came to study at Fes University. For all these indications of Islamic solidarity, though, **state policy** remains distinctly moderate – sometimes in the face of extremist pressure. The 2004 law on the status of women is a good example of this: 100,000 people marched in Rabat to support the new law, and over 200,000 marched in Casablanca against it, a sign of increasing **polarization** on religious questions.

In the cities, there has long been tension between those for and against secularization, as well as a large body of urban poor, for whom Islamic fundamentalism can seem to offer solutions. In some circles, Islam is becoming very relaxed; in Casablanca, Rabat, El Jadida and Marrakesh, young people of both sexes can be seen socializing together, young women no longer wear the veil, and have exchanged their frumpy cover-alls for flattering, sexy clothes, while young couples visit nightclubs and even drink socially. But against this, the number of people going to pray at mosques is on the up, and among the poor especially, Islam is becoming a mark of pride and respectability. That this is reflected in politics is not surprising, and the moderate Islamist PJD is developing into a serious legal opposition with increasing support, one that could easily win an election and form a government in the future, but if that government's programme included the enforcement of religious strictures, it would be strongly resented by secular Moroccans.

Rural religion

Not surprisingly, all of this is more apparent in the cities than in the countryside – a difference accentuated by the gap between them that has always existed in Morocco. Away from the cities, religious attitudes have changed less over the past two generations. Religious brotherhoods such as the Aissaoua have declined since the beginning of the twentieth century, when they were still very powerful, and the influence of mystics generally has fallen. As the official histories put it, popular credulity in Morocco provided an ideal setting for charlatans as well as saviours, and much of this has now passed. All the same, the rhythms of **rural life** still revolve around local *marabouts*, and the annual moussems, or festivals-cum-pilgrimages, are still vital and impressive displays.

Wildlife

Few countries in the Mediterranean region can match the variety and quality of the wildlife habitats to be found in Morocco. Whether you are an expert botanist, a dedicated bird-watcher or simply a visitor with an interest in a totally different environment, the wildlife experience of your travels should be extremely rewarding.

Habitats

There are three main **vegetation zones** which can be distinguished as you travel through the country.

The most northerly and westerly zone – the **Mediterranean** and **northern Atlantic coastal strips** – is typical of the European Med region, encompassing semi-arid pastoral lands of olive groves and cultivated fields.

Further inland lie the barren **Rif mountains** (the home of *kif* or marijuana plants) and the more fertile **Middle Atlas range**, where the montane flora is dominated by cedar forest which, despite its reduction in more recent times, provides a unique mosaic of forest and grassland. The **High Atlas**, beyond, is more arid but has its own montane flora.

Finally, there is the most southerly zone of the desert fringe or **Sahel**, a harsh environment characterized by pebbly *hammada*, tussock grass, the occasional acacia tree and a number of sand dunes, or *ergs*.

These zones provide a wide variety of **habitat types**, from coastal cliffs, sand dunes and estuarine marshlands to subalpine forests and grasslands, to the semi-arid and true desert areas of the south. The **climate** is similarly diverse, being warm and humid along the coastal zones, relatively cooler at altitude within the Atlas ranges and distinctly hotter and drier south of the High Atlas, where midday temperatures will often climb higher than 40°C during the summer months. Not surprisingly, the plant and animal life in Morocco is accordingly parochial, species distributions being closely related to the habitat and climate types to which they are specifically adapted.

Many of these habitats are currently under threat from land reclamation, tourist development and the inevitable process of **desertification**, and the resulting habitat loss is endangering the existence of several of the more sensitive species of plants and animals to be found in Morocco. Human persecution of wildlife, however, is limited, as the tribes are largely disarmed and hunting is more the preserve of French tourists.

On the positive side, the *International Committee for Bird Preservation* (ICBP) and the *Administration des Eaux et Forêts* of the Moroccan Agriculture Ministry have been involved in the designation of protected status to several **wetland sites** along the Atlantic coast; at Merdja Zerga and Lac de Sidi Bourhaba, education centres have been set up with resident wardens and interpretative materials. The government has also done some good work on the problems of erosion and desertification and has implemented extensive and impressive schemes of **afforestation and reclamation**.

Birds

In addition to a unique range of **resident bird species**, distributed throughout the country on the basis of vegetation and climatic zonation, the periods of late March/April and September/October provide the additional sight of vast **bird migrations**.

Large numbers of birds which have overwintered south of the Sahara migrate northwards in the spring to breed in Europe, completing their return passage through Morocco in the autumn. Similarly, some of the more familiar north European species choose Morocco for their overwintering grounds to avoid the harshness of the northern winter. These movements can form a dramatic spectacle in the skies, dense flocks of birds moving in procession through bottleneck areas such as Tangier and Ceuta where sea crossings are at their shortest.

Resident species

The **resident species** can be subdivided on the basis of their preferred habitat type:

Coastal/marine species. These include the familiar moorhen and less familiar **crested coot**, an incongruous bird which, when breeding, resembles its northern European relation but with an additional pair of bright red knobs on either side of its white facial shield. Other species include the diminutive **little ringed plover** and **rock dove**.

South of the High Atlas. Among these are some of the true desert specialities, such as the **sandgrouse** (spotted, crowned, pin-tailed and black-bellied varieties), **stone curlew, cream-coloured courser** and **Houbara bustard** – the latter standing over two feet in height. Other well-represented groups include **wheatears** (4 varieties), **larks** (7 varieties) and **finches, buntings, warblers, corvids, jays, magpies, choughs** and **ravens** (crow family), **tits** (primarily blue, great and coal) and **owls** (barn, eagle, tawny and little). Although many of these species can be found in northern Europe, subtle variations in colour and pattern can be misleading and a closer look is often worthwhile.

Raptors (birds of prey) provide an enticing roll call of resident species, including **red-** and **black-shouldered kite, long-legged buzzard, Bonelli's, golden** and **tawny eagles, Barbary, lanner** and **peregrine falcons** and the more familiar **kestrel**.

Migrant species

Migrant species can be subdivided into three categories: summer visitors, winter visitors and passage migrants.

Summer visitors. The number of species visiting Morocco during the summer months may be low but includes some particularly interesting varieties. Among the **marine/coastal types** are the **manx shearwater, Eleonora's falcon** and the **bald ibis** – in one of its few remaining breeding colonies in the world (see p.624).

The **mountain species** include the small **Egyptian vulture** and several of the **hirundines** (swallows and martins) and their close relatives, the **swifts**, such as **little swift, red-rumped swallow** and the more familiar **house martin**.

A particularly colourful addition at this time of year in the **Sahel regions** is the **blue-cheeked bee-eater**, a vibrant blend of red, yellow, blue and green, unmistakeable if seen close up.

Winter visitors. The list of winter visitors is more extensive but composed primarily of the marine or coastal/estuarine varieties. The most common of the truly marine (*pelagic*) flocks include **Cory's shearwater, storm petrel, gannet, razorbill** and **puffin**. These are often found congregated on the sea surface, along with any combination of **skuas** (great, arctic and pomarine varieties), **terns** (predominantly sandwich) and **gulls** (including black-headed, Mediterranean, little, herring and the rarer Audouin's) flying overhead.

A variety of coastal/estuarine species also arrive during this period, forming large mixed flocks of **grebes** (great-crested, little and black-necked), **avocet, cattle egret, spoonbill, greater flamingo**, and wildfowl such as **shelduck, wigeon, teal, pintail, shoveler, tufted duck, pochard** and **coot**.

Migrant **birds of prey** during the winter months include the **common buzzard** (actually a rarity in Morocco), **dashing merlin** and both **marsh** and **hen harriers**.

Passage migrants. There are many birds that simply pass through Morocco en route to other areas, and are thus known as passage migrants. Well-represented groups include **petrels** (5 varieties) and **terns** (6 varieties) along coastal areas, and **herons** (4 varieties), **bitterns, cranes, white and black stork** and **crake** (spotted, little, Baillon's and corncrake) in the marshland/estuarine habitats.

Further inland, flocks of multicoloured **roller, bee-eater** and **hoopoe** mix with various **larks, wagtails** and **warblers** (13 varieties), forming large "windfall" flocks when climatic conditions worsen abruptly. Individual species of note include the aptly named **black-winged stilt**, an elegant black and white wader, with long, vibrant red legs, often found among the disused saltpans; and the nocturnal **nightjars** (both common and red-necked), which are most easily seen by the reflection of their eyes in the headlamps of passing cars.

Birds of prey can also form dense passage flocks, often mixed and including large numbers of **black kite, short-toed eagle** and **honey buzzard**. Over open water spaces, the majestic **osprey** may be seen demonstrating its mastery of the art of fishing.

"Vagrant" species. Finally, Morocco has its share of occasional or "vagrant" species, so classified on the unusual or rare nature of their appearances. These include such exotic varieties as **glossy ibis, pale-chanting goshawk, Arabian bustard** and **lappet-faced vulture**. Inevitably, they provide few, if any, opportunities for viewing.

Flora

In the light of its climatic harshness and unreliable rains, the flora of Morocco is remarkably diverse. Plant species have adapted strategies to cope with the Moroccan climate, becoming either specifically adapted to one particular part of the environment (a habitat type), or evolving multiple structural and/or biochemical means of surviving the more demanding seasons. Others have adopted the proverbial "ostrich" philosophy of burying their heads (or rather their seeds in this case) in the sand and waiting for climatic conditions to become favourable – often an extremely patient process.

The type of flowers that you see will obviously depend entirely on where and when you decide to visit. Some parts of the country have very short flowering seasons because of high temperatures or lack of available water, but generally the best times of year for flowering plants are either just before or just after the main temperature extremes of the North African summer.

The very best time to visit is **spring** (late March to mid–May), when most flowers are in bloom. Typical spring flowers include purple **barbary nut iris**, deep blue **germander** and the aromatic **claret thyme**, all of which frequent the slopes of the Atlas ranges. Among the **woodland flora** at this time of year are the red **pheasant's eye**, pink **viburnum**, violet **calamint** and purple **campanula**, which form a resplendent carpet beneath the cedar forests. By late spring, huge tracts of the High Atlas slopes are aglow with the golden hues of **broom** and, secluded among the lowland cereal crops, splashes of magenta reveal the presence of **wild gladioli**.

By **midsummer** the climate is at its most extreme and the main concern of plants is to avoid desiccation in the hot, arid conditions. Two areas of exception to these conditions are the **Atlantic coastal zones**, where sea mists produce a slightly more humid environment, and the upper reaches of the **Atlas ranges** which remain cool and moist at altitude throughout the year. Spring comes later in these loftier places and one can find many of the more familiar garden rock plants, such as the **saxifrages** and **anemones**, in flower well into late July and August.

Once the hottest part of the summer is past (September onwards), then a second, **autumn** bloom begins with later varieties such as **cyclamens** and **autumn crocus**.

Habitat varieties

The range of plants you are likely to encounter is similarly influenced by specific habitats:

Seashores. These include a variety of sand-tolerant species, with their adaptations for coping with water loss, such as **sea holly** and **sea stocks**. The dune areas contrast starkly with the Salicornia-dominated salt marshes – monotonous landscapes broken only by the occasional dead **tamarisk** tree.

Arable land. Often dominated by cereal crops – particularly in the more humid Atlantic and Mediterranean coastal belts – or **olive and eucalyptus groves**, which extend over large areas. On the coast around Essaouira and Agadir the indigenous **argan tree** – a relative of the olive – is common and is often seen with goats climbing its trunk. The general lack of use of herbicides allows the coexistence of many "**wild flowers**", especially in the fallow hay meadows which are ablaze with the colours of **wild poppy**, **ox-eye daisy**, **muscali** (borage) and various yellow composites.

Lowland hills. These form a fascinating mosaic of dense, shrubby species, known as *maquis*, lower-lying, more grazed areas, known as *garrigue*, and more open areas with abundant aromatic herbs and shrubs.

Maquis vegetation is dominated by **cistaceae** (**rockroses**) and the endemic **argan** tree. The lower-lying *garrigue* is more typically composed of aromatic herbs such as **rosemary**, **thyme** and **golden milfoil**. Among these shrubs, within the more open areas, you may find an abundance of other species such as **anemones, grape hyacinths** and **orchids**. The orchids are particularly outstanding, including several of the *Ophrys* group, which use the strategy of insect imitation to entice pollinators and as such have an intricate arrangement of flowers.

Mountain slopes. Flowering later in the year, the slopes of the **Atlas ranges** are dominated by the blue-mauve **pitch trefoil** and golden drifts of **broom**. As you travel south through the Middle Atlas, the verdant **ash**, **oak**, **atlantic cedar** and **juniper forest** dominates the landscape. Watered by the depressions

CONTEXTS | Wildlife

that sweep across from the Atlantic, these slopes form a luxurious spectacle, ablaze with colour in spring.

Among the glades beneath the **giant cedars** of the Middle Atlas, a unique flora may be found, dominated by the vibrant **pink peony**. Other plants which form this spectacular carpet include **geranium, anchusa, pink verburnum, saffron mulleins, mauve cupidanes, violet calamint, purple campanula**, the diminutive **scarlet dianthus** and a wealth of **golden composites** and **orchids**.

Further south, the **Toubkal National Park** boasts its own varieties and spring bloom; the thyme and thorny caper are interspersed with the blue-mauve **pit trefoil, pink convulvulus**, the silver-blue and pinks of everlasting flowers of **cupidane** and **phagnalon** and golden spreads of **broom**. At the highest altitudes, the limestone Atlas slopes form a bleak environment, either covered by winter snows or scorched by the summer sun. However, some species are capable of surviving even under these conditions, the most conspicuous of these being the widespread purple tussocks of the **hedgehog broom**.

Steppeland. South of the Atlas, temperatures rise sharply and the effect on flora is dramatic; the extensive cedar forests and their multicoloured carpets are replaced by sparse grass plains where the horizon is broken only by the occasional stunted **holm oak, juniper** or **acacia**. Commonly known as wattle trees, the acacia were introduced into North Africa from Australia and their large yellow flowers add a welcome splash of colour to this barren landscape. One of the few crop plants grown in this area is the **date palm**, which is particularly resistant to drought. The steppeland is characterized by the presence of **esparto grass**, which exudes toxins to prevent the growth of competing species. These halfa grass plains are only broken by the flowering of **broom** in May. Within rocky outcrops, this spring bloom can become a mini-explosion of colour, blending the hues of **cistus** and **chrysanthemum** with the pink of **rockrose**, yellow of **milfoil** and mauve of **rosemary**.

Desert fringe (*hammada*). Even the desert areas provide short-lived blooms of colour during the infrequent spring showers; dwarf varieties such as pink **asphodels**, yellow **daisies** and mauve **statice** thrive briefly while conditions are favourable. Under the flat stones of the *hammada*, colonies of lichens and microscopic algae eke out an existence; their shade tolerance and ability to obtain sufficient water from the occasional condensation which takes place under these stones allows them to survive in this harshest of environments. No matter how inhospitable the environment or extreme the climate, somewhere, somehow, there are plants surviving – if you take time to look for them.

Amphibians

There are very few remaining amphibians in Morocco – relics of a bygone, more fertile era, now restricted to scarce watery havens. They are more apparent by sound than sight, forming a resonant chorus during the night and early morning. One of the more common varieties is the **green frog**, typically immersed up to its eyes in water, releasing the odd giveaway croak. Another widespread individual, most abundant in the regions round Marrakesh, is the **western marsh frog**.

The toads are represented by the **Berber toad**, another nocturnal baritone, and the **Mauritanian toad** whose large size and characteristic yellow and brown-spotted coloration make it quite unmistakable.

Some Moroccan amphibians are capable of survival at surprisingly **high altitudes**. The **painted frog** is a common participant in the chorus that emanates from the *oueds* (riverbeds) of the High Atlas, while the wide-ranging whistle of the North African race of the **green toad**, famed for its ability to change its colour with the surrounding environment, can be heard at altitudes in excess of 2000m.

Reptiles

Reptiles are far more widespread in their distribution than their amphibious cousins. Their range extends from the Mediterranean coastal strip – where the few remaining **tortoises** (sadly depleted through "craft items" sold to the tourist trade) are to be seen – to the *hammada* itself.

The forested slopes of the Middle Atlas are frequented by the **blue and green-eyed lizard** and the **chameleon**; the former uses its size and agility to capture its prey, whereas the latter relies on the more subtle strategy of colour coordination, stealth and a quicksilver tongue.

Several species have adapted to the specific environment of the stony **walls** that form the towns and villages. The **Spanish wall lizard** is a common basker on domestic walls, as is the **Moorish gecko**.

Further south, the drier, scrub-covered slopes form an ideal habitat for two of Morocco's largest **snakes**. The **horseshoe snake** (which can exceed 2m in length) and **Montpelier snake** hunt by day, feeding on birds and rats. Also found in this harsh environment are the **Atlas agama** and **fringe-toed lizard**.

Finally, there are the **desert "specialists"**, such as the **Algerian sand lizard** and **Berber skink**. The skinks make a fascinating spectacle; commonly known as "sand fish", they inhabit the ergs and appear to "swim" through the sand, where their yellow-brown coloration provides the perfect camouflage. Of numerous species of lizard that live in the *hammada*, the more obvious include the many colours and varieties of the **spiny-tailed lizard** (*dhub* in Arabic), an omnivore feeding on a mixed diet of insects, fruit and young shoots. The one really poisonous species is the **horned viper**, only half a metre in length, which spends the days buried just below the surface of the sand and feeds by night on jerboas and lizards.

Mammals

Larger animal life in Morocco is dominated by the extensive nomadic herds of goats, sheep and camels which use the most inaccessible and barren patches of wilderness as seasonal grazing areas.

One of the most impressive of the wild mammals, however, is the **Barbary ape** – in fact not a true ape but a Macaque monkey. These frequent the cedar forests south of Azrou in the Middle Atlas and can be seen on the ground foraging for food in the glades. Other inhabitants of the cedar forest include **wild boar** and **red fox**.

A speciality of the Oued Souss, outside Agadir, is the **common otter**; this is now a rare species in Morocco and can only be seen with considerable patience and some fortune.

△ The elephant shrew

The majority of the smaller mammals in Morocco live south of the Atlas ranges in the *hammada*, where the ever-present problem of water conservation plays a major role in the lifestyle of its inhabitants. Larger herbivores include the **Edmi gazelle** and the smaller, and rarer, **Addax antelope,** which graze the thorn bushes and dried grasses to obtain their moisture.

Many of the desert varieties reduce the problems of body temperature regulation by adopting a nocturnal lifestyle. Typical exponents of this strategy are the **desert hedgehog** and numerous small rodents such as the **jerboa.** A common predator of the jerboa is the **fennec** (desert fox), whose characteristic large ears are used for both directional hearing (invaluable as a nocturnal hunter) and heat radiation to aid body cooling.

An oddity, found in the Djebel Toubkal area of the High Atlas, is the African **elephant shrew** – a fascinating creature, like a little mouse, with an elephantine trunk.

Insects

Insect life is widespread throughout Morocco, its variety of form occupying unique, overlapping roles.

Butterflies

Most colourful are the butterflies, of which over a hundred species have been recorded, predominantly in the Middle and High Atlas ranges. The most obvious, which can be seen from April onwards, are generally the largest and most colourful, such as the brilliant sulphur **Cleopatra, large tortoiseshell** and **cardinal**. Located on the grassy slopes within the ranges are less conspicuous varieties: the **hermit, Spanish marbled white, fritillaries, graylings, hairstreaks** and **blues** – such as the small **larquin's** and **false baton**.

Later in the year, from about June onwards, the glades and woodland edges of the Middle Atlas cedar forests provide the perfect habitat for **dark green fritillaries**, while in the higher flowery fields, at altitudes of up to 2000m, **knapweed fritillaries**, **large grizzled** and **Barbary skippers** abound. Particularly attractive is the **Amanda's blue**, found at altitudes in excess of 600m through till midsummer if nectar remains available.

On the rocky slopes of Toubkal National Park, south of Marrakesh, the **Moroccan copper butterfly** may be seen flitting through the thyme. In the higher Atlas gorges (1700m or more), the **desert orange tip** is more prevalent, being found on its larval food plant, the thorny caper. The Atlas also sees one of the world's most extraordinary butterfly migrations, when waves of painted ladies and Bath whites pass through, having crossed the Sahara from West Africa, en route across the Bay of Biscay to the west of England.

Other insects and arachnids

Other common groups include **grasshoppers**, **crickets** and **locusts**. In the High Atlas, **praying mantis** may be seen, such as **eremiaphila**, whose brown coloration provides excellent camouflage.

Beetles are another common group, though they tend to avoid the heat of the day, remaining in their burrows and emerging at night to feed. The **darkling beetles** are particularly abundant and voracious scavengers.

Finally there are **arachnids**, of which there are three major groups in Morocco – scorpions, camel spiders and spiders. **Scorpions** are nocturnal, hiding under suitable covered depressions during the day such as rocks and boulders (or rucksacks and shoes). Some of the six or so species which may be found in Morocco are poisonous but most are harmless and unlikely to sting

---

Field guides

There are few publications specifically about Moroccan wildlife, but some field guides to Mediterranean Europe extend coverage to North Africa, and most are in any case reasonably practicable for the area.

Birds
P. and F. Bergier *A Birdwatcher's Guide to Morocco* (Prion Press, UK). An excellent practical guidebook that includes site-maps and species lists.

M. Thevenot, R. Vernon, P. Bergier *The Birds of Morocco* (British Ornithologists' Union, UK). The definitive tome.

Heinzel, Fitter and Parslow *The Birds of Britain and Europe with North Africa and the Middle East* (Collins, UK; Stephen Green Press, US).

Flowers
Oleg Polunin and Anthony Huxley *Flowers of the Mediterranean* (Oxford UP, UK & US).

Mammals
Theodor Haltenorth and Helmut Diller *A Field Guide to the Mammals of Africa* (Collins, UK; Stephen Green Press, US).

Butterflies
Lionel Higgins and Norman Riley *A Field Guide to the Butterflies of Britain and Europe* (Collins, UK; Stephen Green Press, US).

unless provoked. The **camel spiders** (or wind-scorpions) are unique. They lack a poisonous tail but possess huge jaws with which they catch their main source of prey, scorpions.

Spiders are not common in Morocco, only being found in large numbers within the Atlas ranges. Here, it is possible to see several small species of **tarantula** (not the hairy South American variety) and the white **orb-web spider** *Argiope lobata*, whose coloration acts as a disruptive pattern against pale backgrounds.

Key wildlife sites

Features on key Moroccan wildlife, and especially bird habitats are to be found throughout the guide; the main entries are boxed. They include:

- **AGADIR/OUED SOUSS** Riverbank that attracts waders and wildfowl, migrant warblers and Barbary partridge. p.615 and p.635.

- **AGUELMAME AZIGZA** Middle Atlas occasional inland lake and forest: hawfinch, diving duck and marbled teal in autumn/winter. p.312.

- **BOUMALNE: DESERT HAMMADA** Atlas agama and fringe-toed lizard; specialist bird species such as cream-coloured courser, red-rumped wheatear and thick-billed lark. **Houbara bustard**. p.558.

- **CEDAR FORESTS SOUTH OF AZROU** Species include green-eyed lizard and chameleon; **butterflies** from April onwards; **Barbary apes**; Moroccan woodpecker and **booted eagle**. p.310.

- **DAYET AAOUA** Another Middle Atlas occasional lake: flocks of grebes, **crested coot**, grey heron and cattle egret; migrant birds of prey include **red kite**. p.302.

- **DJEBEL TAZZEKA NATIONAL PARK** Where the Rif merges with the Middle Atlas: slopes covered in cork oak and woodland; butterflies from late May/early June, and birds such as the hoopoe. p.208.

- **DJEBEL TOUBKAL NATIONAL PARK** High Atlas mountains: sights include Moorish gecko, rare butterflies; Moussier's redstart and crimson-winged finch, both unique to North African mountains; hooped-petticoat daffodils, *romulea* and various other bulbs in spring. p.490.

- **ESSAOUIRA** Coastal dunes, river and offshore islands attract **waders** and **egrets**; also **Eleanora's falcon** between May and October. p.414.

- **FES** Evening roost of egret and alpine swift; **white stork** on rooftop nests of walls. p.286.

- **LAC DU SIDI BOURHABA** Freshwater lake, with outstanding **birds of prey**. p. 000.

- **MARRAKESH: MAJORELLE GARDEN** Lush garden with turtle doves, house buntings and common bulbuls. p.466.

- **MERDJA ZERGA** Large wetland area guarantees good **bird** numbers at all times of year, especially **gulls and terns** (including the **Caspian tern**). p. 143.

- **MERZOUGA** Sandy (or "true") desert: all-too-brief **spring bloom** of pink asphodels and mauve statice; Algerian sand lizard and Berber skink; **birds** include fulvous babbler, blue-cheeked bee-eater, the rare desert sparrow and even Arabian bustard. p.596.

• **NADOR/KARIET ARKMANE/RAS EL MA** Salt marshes and coastal sand dunes, good for waders and gulls. p.190.

• **OUALIDIA** Mix of ragged, rocky coast, sands, lagoon, marshes and salt-pans. Good for small waders. p.402.

• **OUED MASSA** Important inland lagoon and reserve that is perhaps the country's number one bird habitat. p.627.

• **OUED MOULOUYA** Lagoons and sand spits, with outstanding birds. p.190.

• **TODRA GORGE** Marsh frog and green toad; ground squirrel; common bulbul, black wheatear, blue rock thrush and rock dove. **Bonelli's eagles** nest in the gorge. p.571.

C

CONTEXTS | Wildlfe

Moroccan music

Wherever you go in Morocco you are likely to hear music. It is the basic expression of the country's folk culture – indeed to many of the illiterate country people it is the sole expression. Traditional music remains very much a part of life, evident at every celebration, and most spectacularly so in the mountains, where long and ancient pieces are performed by the entire communities of Berber villages, while in the cities there is a strong Arabic classical tradition, of songs and instrumental music brought by the Arabs from the east and Andalusian Spain. And in recent decades Morocco has spawned a powerful indigenous strain of pop or *chaabi* music – sounds that you'll hear blaring out of buses and taxis and ghetto blasters.

Although the most ubiquitous musical phenomenon that you will hear is the **muezzin** calling the faithful to prayer, amplified from minarets, most Moroccan music is performed for the sake of entertainment rather than religion. At every weekly **souk**, or market, you will find musicians playing in a patch of shade, or a stall blasting out cassettes or CDs they have on sale. In the evenings many **cafés** feature musicians, particularly during the long nights of Ramadan. **Television** also plays its part, with two weekly programmes devoted to music, and the **radio stations** broadcast a variety of different styles. In fact, thanks to the huge penetration of satellite dishes and Internet cafés in recent years, Morocco has opened its ears to many of the same sounds that hold sway in Europe and North America – rap in particular.

Festivals are perhaps the most rewarding way of plunging into Moroccan's astoundingly rich traditional and folk music culture. Every popular or religious festival involves musicians, and the larger **moussems** (p.62 & p.64) are always rewarding. Keep an eye out for cultural festivals, too, in particular the summer **Asilah Festival** (p.125), the **Essaouira Gnaoua Festival** (see p.422), the **Marrakesh Festival of Popular Arts** (see p.460), and the **Festival of Sacred Music** held at the end of May in **Fes** (p.294). For more on these see the *Music and Festivals* colour section.

Berber music

Berber music is quite distinct from Arab-influenced forms in its rhythms, tunings, instruments and sounds. It is an extremely ancient tradition, long predating even the arrival of Arabs in Morocco, and has been passed on orally from generation to generation. There are three main categories: village music, ritual music and the music of professional musicians.

Village music is essentially a collective performance. Men and women of the entire village will assemble on festive occasions to dance and sing together. The best-known dances are the **ahouache**, in the western High Atlas, and the **ahidus**, performed by Chleuh Berbers in the eastern High Atlas. In each, drums (*bendirs*) and flute (*nai*) are the only instruments used. The dance begins with a chanted prayer, to which the dancers respond in chorus, the men and women gathered in a large ring in the open air, round the musicians. The *ahouache* is normally performed at night in the patio of the kasbah; the dance is so complicated that the musicians meet to prepare for it in a group called a *laamt* set up specially for the purpose. In the **bumzdi**, a variation on the *ahouache*, one or more soloists perform a series of poetic improvisations. Some of these soloists, such as **Raïs Ajmaa Lahcen** and **Raïs Ihya**, have a national reputation.

Ritual music is rarely absent from any rites connected with the agricultural calendar – such as moussems – or major events in the life of individuals, such as marriage. It may also be called upon to help deal with *djinn*, or evil spirits, or to encourage rainfall. Flutes and drums are usually the sole instruments, along with much rhythmic hand-clapping, although a community may have engaged professional musicians for certain events.

The **professional musicians**, or *imdyazn*, of the Atlas mountains are itinerant, travelling during the summer, usually in groups of four. The leader of the group is called the *amydaz* or poet. He presents his poems, which are usually improvised and give news of national or world affairs, in the village square. The poet may be accompanied by one or two members of the group on drums and *rabab*, a single-string fiddle, and by a fourth player, known as the *bou oughanim*. This latter is the reed player, throwing out melodies on a double clarinet, and also acting as the group's clown. *Imdyazn* are found in many weekly souks in the Atlas.

A group of women Berber musicians from the Houara region near Tarou-dannt have forged an international reputation over the last decade with their strident vocals and loping rhythms driven by the metal *naqqous* percussion. Originally called **Bnet Houriyat**, "The women of the Houara", they are now known as **Bnet Marrakech**. They are the "stage" incarnation of a musical culture that still exists at a grass roots level throughout Morocco.

Rwais

Groups of **Chleuh Berber** musicians, from the Souss Valley, are known as **rwais**; again they are professional musicians. A *rwai* worthy of the name will not only know all the music for any particular celebration, but have its own repertoire of songs – commenting on current events – and be able to improvise. A *rwai* ensemble can be made up of a single-string *rabab*, one or two *lotars* (lutes) and sometimes *nakous* (cymbals), together with a number of singers. The leader of the group, the **raïs**, is in charge of the poetry, music and choreography of the performance. Fine clothes, jewels and elaborate gestures also have an important part to play in this ancient rural form of musical theatre. Female *rwai* performers often lead their own ensembles of *raysat*, mainly comprising singers and *lotar* players.

A **rwai performance** will start with the *astara*, an instrumental prelude, played on *rabab*, giving the basic notes of the melodies that follow (this also makes it possible for the other instruments to tune to the *rabab*). The *astara* is not in any particular rhythm. Then comes the *amarg*, the sung poetry which forms the heart of the piece. This is followed by the *ammussu*, which is a sort of choreographed overture; the *tamssust*, a lively song; the *aberdag*, or dance; and finally the *tabbayt*, a finale characterized by an acceleration in rhythm and an abrupt end. Apart from the *astara* and *tabbayt*, the elements of a performance may appear in a different order. The arrangement and duration of the various parts are decided upon freely by the *rwais*.

The two current rwai favourites are **Aarab Aatigui** and the magnificent female star **Raysa Fatima Taabamrant**.

Andalous music

Morocco's classical music comes from the **Arab–Andalusian tradition**, and is to be found, with variations, throughout North Africa. It is thought to have evolved, around a thousand years ago, in Cordoba, Spain (then ruled by the Moors), and its invention is usually credited to an outstanding musician from Baghdad called **Zyriab**. One of his greatest innovations was the founding of the classical suite called **nuba**, which forms what is now known as **andalous music**, or **al-âla**. There are, in addition, two other classical traditions, **milhûn** and **gharnati**, each with a distinctive style and form.

Andalous music, far from being the scholastic relic you might expect, is very much alive, popular and greatly loved. Television, which plays an important part in the Moroccan music scene, broadcasts nightly programmes of andalous classics during Ramadan, and people who don't have their own TVs congregate at local cafés to watch the shows.

The nuba

Originally there were twenty-four **nuba** linked with the hours in the day, but only four full and seven fragmentary *nuba* have been preserved in the Moroccan tradition. Complete *nuba* last between six and seven hours and so are rarely performed in one sitting, and are usually chosen to fit the time of day or occasion. Each *nuba* is divided into five main parts, or *mizan*, of differing durations. These five parts correspond to the five different rhythms used within a suite. If a whole *nuba* were being performed then these five rhythms would be used in order: the *basît* rhythm (6/4); *qaum wa nusf* rhythm (8/4); *darj* rhythm (4/4); *btâyhi* rhythm (8/4); and *quddâm* rhythm (3/4 or 6/8).

Traditionally each *mizan* begins with instrumental preludes – *bughya*, *m'shaliya* and *tuashia* – followed by a number of songs, the *sana'a*. There can be as many as twenty *sana'a* within a given *mizan* although for shorter performances an orchestra may only play three or four before going on to the next rhythm.

The words to many *sana'a* deal, though often obliquely, with subjects generally considered taboo in Islamic society like alcohol and sex – perhaps signifying archaic, pre-Islamic and nomadic roots – although others are religious, glorifying the Prophet and divine laws. The fourteenth *sana'a* of the *basît mizan* in **Al-'Ushshâq** tells of the desire for clarity following an active night entirely given over to the pleasures of sex and wine:

Obscure night steals away
Chased by the light
that sweeps up shadows
The candle wax runs
as if weeping tears of farewell
And then, suddenly and behold,
the birds are singing
and the flowers smile at us.

When the Arabs were driven out of Spain, which they had known as Al-Andalus, the different musical schools were dispersed across Morocco. The school of Valencia was re-established in Fes, that of Granada in Toua and Chefchaouen. Today, the most famous **orchestras** are those of **Fes** (led by **Mohammed Briouel**), **Rabat** (led by **Haj Mohamed Toud**) and **Tetouan**. Many fans of andalous music mourn the passing of the "golden age" in the 1970s and 1980s, when a trio of much lamented masters – **Abdelkrim Rais**, **Abdesadak Chekara** and **Moulay Ahmed Loukili** – led the Fes, Tetouan and Rabat orchestras. But it seems that this venerable style, although ancient, is also very resilient, and it lives on in the new century.

A typical andalous orchestra uses the following instruments: *rabab* (fiddle), *oud* (lute), *kamenjah* (violin-style instrument played vertically on the knee), *kanun* (zither), *darabouka* (metal or pottery goblet drums), and *taarija* (tambourine). Each orchestra has featured unusual instruments from time to time. Clarinets, flutes, banjos and pianos have all been used with varying degrees of success.

Milhûn

Milhûn is a semiclassical form of sung poetry – a definition that sounds a lot drier than it is. Musically it has many links with andalous music, having adopted the same modes as *al-âla* orchestras, and, like them, it uses string instruments and percussion, though the result can be quite wild and danceable. Unlike andalous music, which has always been the province of an educated elite, *milhûn* was originally the poetic expression of artisans and traders. Indeed, many of the great *milhûn* singers of the twentieth century began their lives as cobblers, tanners bakers or doughnut sellers.

The *milhûn* suite comprises two parts: the *taqsim* (overture) and the *qassida* (sung poems). The *taqsim* is played on the *oud* or violin in free rhythm, and introduces the mode in which the piece is set. The *qassida* is divided into three parts: *al-aqsâm*, verses sung solo; *al-harba*, refrains sung by the chorus; and *al-drîdka*, a chorus where the rhythm gathers speed and eventually announces the end of the piece. The words of the *qassida* can be taken from anywhere – folk poetry, mystical poems or nonsense lines used for rhythm.

Al-Thami Lamdaghri, who died in 1856, was one of the greatest *milhûn* composers. He is credited with many well-known songs including *Al-'Arsa* (*The Garden of Delight*):

Open your eyes
Taste the delights and the generous nature
Of this heavenly garden
The branches of the wonderful
      trees intertwine
Like two lovers meeting again
And totter about, heady with happiness
The smile of flowers,
Mingled with the tears of the dew
Recall the melancholic exchange
Of a sad lover and his joyous beloved
Birds sing in the branches
Like as many lutes and rababs.

The **milhûn orchestra** generally consists of *oud*, *kamenjah*, *swisen* (a small, high-pitched folk lute related to the *gimbri*), the *hadjouj* (a bass version of the *swisen*), *taarija*, *darabouka* and *handqa* (small brass cymbals), plus a number of **singers**. The most renowned *milhûn* singer of recent times was **Hadj Lhocine Toulali**, who dominated the vibrant *milhûn* scene in the city of Meknes for many decades before his death in 1999. Contemporary singers of note include **Abdelkrim and Saïd Guennoun** of Fes, **Haj Husseïn** and **Abdallah Ramdani** of Meknes, **Muhammad Berrahal** and **Muhammad Bensaïd** of Salé, and the brothers **Mohammed and Ahmed Amenzou** from Marrakesh. In the past ten or so years, some female singers have become stars, including Touria Hadraoui (who is also a novelist) and Sanaa Marahati, whom many consider the future of *milhûn*.

Gharnati

Gharnati, the third music of Arab–Andalusian tradition, derives from the Arabic word for Granada, the great city of Arab Andalusia. It is mainly played in Algeria but there are two important centres in Morocco – the capital, Rabat, and Oujda, near the Algerian border. As with *al-âla*, it is arranged in suites or *nuba*, of which there are twelve complete and four unfinished suites.

The *gharnati* orchestra consists of plucked and bowed instruments together with percussion: the usual *ouds* and *kamenjahs* supplemented by the addition of banjo, mandolin and Algerian lute or *kwîtra*.

Brotherhoods and Trance music

Music in orthodox Islam is frowned upon unless it is singing God's praises. But in addition to the chants of the Koran, which are improvised on a uniform beat, the *adhan*, or call to prayer, and the songs about the life of the prophet Muhammad, there is another entire range of prayers and ceremonies belonging to the **Sufi brotherhoods**, or *tarikas*, in which music is seen as a means of getting closer to Allah. These include the music used in processions to the tombs of saints during moussems.

The aim is for those present to reach a state of mystical ecstasy, often through **trance**. In a private nocturnal ceremony called the *hadra*, the Sufi brothers attain a trance by chanting the name of Allah or dancing in a ring holding hands. The songs and music are irregular in rhythm, and quicken to an abrupt end. Some brotherhoods play for alms in households that want to gain the favour of their patron saint. Musically, the best known Moroccan brotherhood is the **Gnaoua**, or Gnawa.

Gnaoua

The **Gnaoua** is a religious confraternity – not sufi as such – whose members are descendants of slaves, servants and prisoners brought from across the Sahara by the Arabs. They have devotees all over Morocco, though the strongest concentrations are in the south, particularly in Essaouria, Marrakesh and Taroudannt.

The brotherhood claim spiritual descent from **Sidi Bilal**, an Ethiopian who was the Prophet's first *muezzin*. Most Gnaoua ceremonies, or *lilas*, so called because they usually last all night long (*lil* is the Arabic word for "night") are held to placate spirits, good and evil, who are inhabiting a person or place. They are often called in cases of mental disturbance or to help treat someone stung by a scorpion. These rites have their origins in sub-Saharan Africa, and an African influence is evident in the music itself. The principal instrument, the *ginbri* or *sentir*, is a long-necked lute almost identical to instruments found in West Africa. The other characteristic sound of Gnaoua music is the *garagab*, a pair of metal castanets, which beat out a trance-like rhythm.

Each Gnaoua troupe is lead by a *ma'alem*, or "master", who plays the *ginbri* and sings the lead vocal parts. The ceremonial part of the proceedings is usually led by a female *mogadema*, or "medium", who is mistress of the arcane spiritual knowledge and huge gallery of saints and spirits, both good and evil, that underpin and influence Gnaoui ritual.

During the late 1950s and early 1960s Tangier was as bohemian a city as any, attracting beats and, in their wake, rock stars. In 1968 the Rolling Stones paid the first of several visits and their then guitarist Brian Jones was introduced to the Berber Master Musicians of Jajouka in the foothills of the Rif Mountains. His recording of them, the *Pipes of Jajouka*, with its heavy sound treatments, was for many years the only record available of Moroccan music.

The Master Musicians are essentially trance musicians, producing an awesome sound through a multitude of double-headed drums and the dark drones and melodies of the *ghaita*, a double-reed pipe similar in sound to the oboe. They are a kind of brotherhood, and the leadership of the group is passed down from father to son. The present chief, Bachir Attar, inherited the post when his father died in the late 1980s.

Although the Rolling Stones returned to Morocco in the mid-1980s to use Jajouka on their Steel Wheels album, the Master Musicians were largely forgotten in the West until 1990 when American bassist and composer Bill Laswell travelled to Morocco. Using the latest digital technology, he produced an album of purity and power. Since then, the group (or, rather, two groups, under rival leaders) have experienced a revival of interest, spurred by the World Music scene, appearing at festivals around the world. They have recorded several further CDs, including a collaboration with British–Asian musician Talvin Singh.

Gnaoua music can be heard at festivals and in the entertainment squares of Marrakesh and elsewhere. And in recent decades, the music has been blended with many other forms of music including jazz, rock, funk, hip hop and drum and bass. Two of the most famous living *ma'alems* – **Mustapha Baqbou** and **Mahmoud Guinea**, both of whom belong to great Gnaoua dynasties – have recorded with American musicians Bill Laswell and Pharoah Saunders, as well as the Moroccan group, Jil Jilala.

Jilala

Jilala are another brotherhood – the devotees of **Moulay Abdelkader Jilal**. Their music is perhaps even more hypnotic and mysterious than that of the Gnaoua and sometimes seems to come from a different plane of existence. The plaintive cycling flute (*qsbah*) and mesmeric beats of the *bendir* (frame drums) carry you forward unconsciously. While in a trance, Jilala devotees can withstand the touch of burning coals or the deep slashes of a Moroccan dagger, afterwards showing no injury or pain.

Hamadja and Aissaoua

Other Sufi brotherhoods still practising their own brand of psychic-musical healing in various parts of Morocco include the **Hamadja**, followers of Sidi Ben Ali Hamduj and Sidi Ahmed Dghughi, two saints who lived at the end of the eighteenth century, and the **Aissaoua** from Meknes, who venerate the sixteenth century holy man Sidi Mohamed Ben Aïssa. The boundaries between these different brotherhoods are often quite blurred, and they tend to hold a common veneration for many saints and spirits, prominent amongst whom is the fiendish female *djinn* Aisha Kandisha.

Folk instruments

Folk instruments are very rudimentary and fairly easy to make, and this, combined with the fact that many music cafés keep their own, allows for a genuinely amateur development. Many of the instruments mentioned below are also to be found under the same or similar names (and with slight variations) in Algeria, Tunisia, Libya and even Egypt.

Morocco has a great many stringed and percussion instruments, mostly fairly basic in design. There are also a few **wind instruments**. The **Arab flute**, known by different tribes as the *nai*, *talawat*, *nira* or *gasba*, is made of a straight piece of cane open at both ends, with no mouthpiece and between five and seven holes, one at the back. It requires a great deal of skill to play it properly, by blowing at a slight angle. The **ghaita** or *rhaita*, a type of oboe popular under various names throughout the Muslim world, is a conical pipe made of hardwood, ending in a bell often made of metal. Its double-reeded mouthpiece is encircled by a broad ring on which the player rests his lips in order to produce the circular breathing needed to obtain a continuous note. It has between seven and nine holes, one at the back. The **aghanin** is a double clarinet, identical to the Arab *arghoul*. It consists of two parallel pipes of wood or cane, each with a single-reed mouthpiece, five holes and a horn at the end for amplification.

The most common **stringed instrument** is the **ginbri**. This is an African lute, very similar to the west African *ngoni*, whose soundbox is covered in front by a piece of hide. The rounded, fretless stem has two or three strings. The body of the smaller treble *ginbri* is pear-shaped, that of the bass *ginbri* (*hadjuj* or *sentir*) rectangular. The Gnaoui often put a resonator at the end of the stem to produce the buzz typical of Black African music. The **lotar** is another type of lute, used exclusively by the Chleuh Berbers. It has a circular body, also closed with a piece of skin, and three or four strings which are plucked with a plectrum.

The classic Arab lute, the **oud**, is used in classical orchestras and the traditional Arab orchestras known as *takhts*. Its pear-shaped body is covered by a piece of wood with two or three rosette-shaped openings. It has a short, fretless stem and six strings, five double and one single. The most popular stringed instruments played with a bow are the **kamanjeh** and the **rabab**. The former is an Iranian violin which was adopted by the Arabs. Its present Moroccan character owes a lot to the Western violin, though it is held vertically, supported on the knees. The *rabab* is a spike fiddle, rather like a viol. The bottom half of its long, curved body is covered in hide, the top in wood with a rosette-shaped opening. It has two strings. The Chleuh Berbers use an archaic single-stringed *rabab* with a square stem and soundbox covered entirely in skin. Lastly, there is the **kanum**, a trapezoidal Arab zither with over seventy strings, grouped in threes and plucked with plectra attached to the fingernails. It is used almost exclusively in classical music.

Rapid hand-clapping and the clashes of bells and cymbals are only part of the vast repertoire of Moroccan **percussion**. Like most Moroccan drums the **darbuka** is made of clay, shaped into a cylinder swelling out slightly at the top. The single skin is beaten with both hands. It is used in both folk and classical music. The **taarija**, a smaller version of the *darbuka*, is held in one hand and beaten with the other. Then there are treble and bass **tan-tan** bongos, and the Moorish **guedra**, a large drum which rests on the ground. There is also a round wooden drum with skins on both sides called a **tabl**, which is beaten with a stick on one side and by hand on the other. This is used only in folk music.

As for **tambourines**, the ever-popular **bendir** is round and wooden, 40 or 50cm across, with two strings stretched under its single skin to produce a buzzing sound. The **tar** is smaller, with two rings of metal discs round the frame and no strings under its skin. The **duff** is a double-sided tambourine, often square in shape, which has to be supported so that it can be beaten with both hands. Only two percussion instruments are made of metal: **karkabat**, also known as *krakesh* or *karakab*, double castanets used by the Gnaoui, and the **nakous**, a small cymbal played with two rods.

Chaabi – Morocco's pop music

Chaabi simply means "popular" music – which covers a huge mix of styles, just as it does in the west.

Arabic song

More or less since the advent of radio, the whole Arab world has listened to **Egyptian popular songs** – the tradition epitomized by Umm Kulthum (Oum Khalsoum) and Mohammed Abdalwahab. Morocco has provided some names of its own to this tradition, in particular **Houcine Slaoui** (in the 1940s), and in the following decades, **Ahmed Bidaoui, Abdelhadi Belkhoyat** and **Abdelwahab Doukkali**. These stars tended to record in Cairo or Beirut, and their music – and language – is essentially Egyptian. The most recent star in this vein is the singer **Samira Said**, who is hugely popular around the Arab world, and has recorded with raï singer Cheb Khaled.

Al'aïta

The oldest of Morocco's more individual *chaabi* styles is **al'aïta**, the music of the Arabic-speaking rural populations of Morocco's Atlantic coast. It is performed at private and public celebrations, as well as in concert, and is usually sung in Darija (Moroccan colloquial Arabic). Its songs tell of love, loss, lust and the realities of daily life. They begin with a *lafrash*, a slow instrumental prelude (usually played on the violin), then move into free rhythm verses before shifting gear for the finale or *leseb*, which is often twice the speed of the song and forms a background for syncopated clapping, shouting and dancing.

An al'aïta ensemble usually consists of a male or female vocalist, a violinist, and several percussionists and backing singers, though some groups add a *lotar*. Stars over the years have included the singers **Bouchaïb el Bidaoui** and **Fatna bent Lhoucine**, and the (literally) six-fingered violinist, **Abdelaziz Staati**.

Sephardic music

Moroccan Jews, many of whom have now emigrated to Israel, left an important legacy in the north of the country, where their songs and ballads continued to be sung in the medieval Spanish spoken at the time of their expulsion from Spain five centuries ago. Apart from the narrative ballads, these were mainly songs of courtly love, as well as lullabies and biblical songs, usually accompanied on a *tar*. Rounder Records released a two-CD set of Paul Bowles' rousing recordings of Moroccan Jewish liturgy, which transport you into the heart of what was once a vibrant subculture but is now, sadly, almost extinct in Morocco.

Moroccan Jewry also produced a great classical Arabic singer, Samy el Maghribi, who was born in Safi in 1922. Inspired by the Algerian singer Say el Hilali, he was one of the most appreciated Arabic singers of the 1950s. In 1960 he moved to Canada and in later years devoted himself to a liturgical repertoire.

Moroccan Sephardic traditions and music continue to thrive in Israel, the best known names including Albert Bouhadanna and Rabat-born Emil Zrihan, whose music mixes Arab and Andalusian influences with the Hebrew liturgy.

In the 1990s, an electric style of al'aïta developed, adding keyboards, electric guitars and drum machines. This is still very popular and is the music you most often hear blasting out of stalls in Casablanca or Rabat. Top artists include **Orchestre Jedouane**, **Orchestre Senhaji**, **Khalid Bennani** and **Moustapha Bourgogne**.

Chaabi groups and Berber power

During the 1970s, a more sophisticated Moroccan *chaabi* began to emerge, with groups setting themselves up in competition with the Egyptian and Lebanese pop scene. Using *hadjuj* (bass *ginbri*), lute and *bendir* percussion, along with bouzoukis and electric guitars, they combined Berber music with elements of Arab *milhûn*, Sufi and Gnaoua ritual music, western rock and reggae. More recently, rap has had a huge influence. The songs were often political, dealing with social issues, and the vocals were dominant, with the whole group tending to sing, either in chorus or backing a lead soloist. Lyrics occasionally carried messages that got their authors into trouble with the authorities – even jailed.

The leading lights in this movement were **Nass el Ghiwane**, **Jil Jilala** and **Lemchaheb**. It's almost impossible to exaggerate the impact of this trio of groups, not only on Moroccan music but on Moroccan culture as a whole. After decades of subservience to Egypt, Lebanon and Syria, Morocco suddenly discovered that it had its own indigenous musical culture which was every bit as vibrant and exciting as that of the Middle East. The music was also hugely influential in the development of **raï music** in neighbouring Algeria, where *raï* singers like Khaled, Cheb Mami, Chaba Fadela and Chaba Sahraoui emerged in the 1980s.

Nass el Ghiwane, the most politicized of all the *chaabi*-fusion groups, laid great emphasis on the words of its songs, which lambasted lazy government officials and bemoaned social injustice. The band was originally a five-piece (banjo, *hadjuj*, *bendir*, *tan-tan* and *darbuka*), fronted by the powerfully melodic voice of **Boujemaa Hagour**. After his death in the mid-1970s (some said by the shady hand of the secret service), the group continued as a four-piece, led by the charismatic **Omar Sayid**. They are still touring and giving fiery energetic performances, although no new recorded material has appeared for some time. Here is Boujemaa's song *The Table*, which first made them famous:

Where are they now?
The friends who sat at my table
Where are they now?
All the friends that I loved
Where are the glasses?
Where are the glasses we drank from?
Friendship can be bitter
But it was also sweet to sit at my table

Jil Jilala was formed in 1972 as a Sufi theatre group devoted to their leader, Jilali. Their music is based on the *milhûn* style, using poetry as a starting point. More recently they have worked with Gnaoua rhythms. The group's central figures are the conga-player and lyricist **Mohammed Darhem**, and **Hassan Mista**, who plays an amplified, fretless *buzuk*. They are rhythmically accompanied by two *bendir* players – Moulai Tahar and Abdel Krim Al-Kasbaji – and have recorded with a variety of *hadjuj* players, including **Mustapha Baqbou**.

Lemchaheb is probably the Moroccan group best known abroad, through its work with the German band **Dissidenten** (two of whose members play and record with them). Featuring the virtuoso figure of guitarist and *buzuk* player Lamrani Moulay Cherif, they are also the most Westernized of the three big names in electric *chaabi*. A fourth important *chaabi* group who began in the 1970s – and are still very active – is **Tagada.** They were formed by the Gnaoua *ma'alem* **Chérif Regragui** from Essaouira, and their popularity almost rivalled that of Nass el Ghiwane at one time.

These pioneering *chaabi* groups also inspired a new generation of **Berber musicians,** foremost among them the group **Izanzaren** from Agadir. Formed in 1974, this was the first of the "Berber power" groups to sing – in the Tachel-häit language – about the discrimination suffered by Morocco's Berber popula-tion. Musically, they sounded rather like Nass el Ghiwane, though with a bit more rhythmic punch. Another significant Berber group, **Usman,** was formed by the singer **Ammouri M'barek,** who started out singing French and American rock'n'roll in a covers band. He went on to Arabic and Berber, and has created some of the most innovative Berber music of recent decades.

In the 1980s, another wave of groups emerged, based in Marrakesh and employing Gnaoua rhythms. One of the most successful of these has been **Muluk El Hwa** (Demon of Love), a group of Berbers who used to play in the Djemaa El Fna in Marrakesh. Their line-up is totally acoustic: *bendir, tan-tan, sentir, buzuk, garagab* and hand claps. They have recorded with the Spanish group **Al Tall,** creating an album that fused medieval Valencian music and Arabic poetry from Andalusia – songs about the whims of rulers, exile, love and wine that are still relevant today. Their contemporaries, **Nass el Hal,** formed in 1986, offer two shows – one using a traditional acoustic line-up with *buzuk* and violin, the other with drum kit and electric guitar. Their repertoire includes peasant harvest and hunting songs, and religious dances.

By far the most popular of the Berber *chaabi* singers, however, is singer **Najat Aatabou,** whose sensational debut, *J'en ai marre* (I am sick of it), sold 450,000 copies – many of them in France. Each of her subsequent recordings have sold more than half-a-million copies, and she is now a huge star throughout the Maghreb and can fill large venues in Europe. She is proud of her Berber heritage and uses traditional Berber rhythms – though she crossed over to sing in Arabic and French – and is very outspoken in her lyrics, which address the inequality between men and women and the injustice of tradi-tional family rules. She is equally capable of writing beautiful love songs. When her ensemble uses electric instruments they blend beautifully with more traditional *oud* and *bendir.*

Another Berber from the Middle Atlas who has crossed over to appeal to Moroccan Arabic audiences is **Mohammed Rouicha,** a moving player of the *outar* – an instrument similar to the *lotar* but with a bigger body. Accompanied by driving percussion and strident backing vocals, he sings of the plight of Morocco's rural poor, and is about as roots as you can get.

By contrast, in the current decade, a much more hedonistic and poppy breed of *chaabi* artist has come to the fore, to whom good times are as important as social or political commentary. Pre-eminent amongst this younger generation of popsters is the singer and violinist **Mustapha Bourgogne.**

Fusion

Morocco is an ideal starting point for all kinds of fusion experiments. From the 1960s on, such disparate figures as Brian Jones, Ornette Coleman, Jimi Hendrix,

Robin Williamson, John Renbourn and Pharaoh Sanders have been attracted by its rhythms, and in recent decades collaborations have come thick and fast.

One of the earliest attempts to combine Moroccan music with European electronic sounds was made by the German group **Dissidenten**. Before their collaboration with Lemchaheb (see p.750) they had worked with **Mohammed Zain**, a star player of the *nai* (flute) from Tangier, and a number of Gnaoua *ginbri* players. It was their albums with Lemchaheb, however, that placed a genuine Moroccan element into a rock context.

Since then all manner of Moroccan sounds have been successfully blended with reggae, funk, hip hop, house and drum and bass by groups like **Gnawa Diffusion** and **Gnawa N'joum Experience** from France, **Gnawa Impulse** from Germany, and **MoMo** from London. UK-based Moroccan-born producer **U-cef** has also been a pioneer in this field, while in Belgium the madcap Flemish globetrotters **Think Of One** have recorded enjoyable, accessible and authentic Moroccan music with a number of Moroccan musicians, notably the Marrakesh-based female trio, **Bnet Houaryet**.

Other names to look out for include **Yosefa Dahari**, who has worked (singing in Maghrebi and English) with David Rosenthal and Gil Freeman on the Worldly Dance Music label; **Hassan Hakmoun** – a New York-based Gnaoua musician who mixes it in the city with all manner of ideas and musicians; and **Bachir Attar**, leader of the **Jajouka** troupe (see box, p.747), and again New York-based these days, who has recorded with jazz saxophonist Maceo Parker under the direction of avant-garde funk producer **Bill Laswell**, and with the UK Asian tabla and electronic beats guru **Talvin Singh**.

Laswell has also been involved in production work with the group **Aisha Kandisha's Jarring Effects** (or AKJE), who mix Moroccan trance sounds with rock, hip hop and techno. They released an amazing debut CD, *Buya*, in 1991 on the Swiss Barbarity label, and followed up with a techno-driven, Laswell production, *Shabeesation*. They are only known on a subterranean level in Morocco and are yet to perform or release a cassette at home. They have an attitude as radical as their music – akin to, say, Cypress Hill or Ice Cube. Their name refers to a female spirit, whose very mention is taboo, and their lyrics question Moroccan social and religious norms. The **Barbarity label** has now released about a dozen titles by AKJE and other like-minded bands such as **Amira Saqati**, **Ahlam** and **Argan**, all of which feature AKJE musicians.

Some other Moroccan fusionistas of note are: the long-haired rocker **Houssaine Kili**, who is based in Germany; blues fanatic **Majid Bekkas;** the accomplished and outward-looking **Nass Marrakech**, who seem to be able to mix all manner of sounds in their Gnaoui-influenced pot; and the blind *oud* player **Hassan Erraji**, now living in Wales.

In **Spain** there have been a couple of notable collaborations between flamenco musicians and Andalusian orchestras, such as that of **José Heredia Maya and Enrique Morente** with the **Tetouan Orchestra** (Ariola, Spain), and **Juan Peña Lebrijano** with the **Tangier Orchestra** (GlobeStyle, UK). The Tetouan orchestra have also collaborated in concert with the British composer **Michael Nyman**.

Moroccan raï

Raï – the word means "opinion", "outlook" or "point of view" – originated in the western Algerian region around the port of Oran. It has traditional roots in Bedouin music, with its distinctive refrain (*ha-ya-raï*), but as a modern phenomenon has more in common with Western music. The backing is now solidly electric, with rhythm guitars, synthesizers and usually a rock drum kit as well as traditional drums. Its lyrics reflect highly contemporary concerns – cars, sex, sometimes alcohol – which have created some friction with the authorities.

Moroccans have taken easily to the music, especially in the northeastern part of the country around the towns of Oujda and Al Hoceima, an area that shares the same cultural roots as the province of Oran over the border in Algeria, where *raï* was born. Home-grown *raï* stars include **Cheb Khader, Cheb Mimoun** and the superb **Cheb Djellal,** a pop-*raï* legend from Oujda whose recordings are well worth seeking out. **Sawt El Atlas** have also made huge strides with a poppy *raï*-flavoured sound and have sold handsome amounts of CDs in their adopted home of France. *Raï* influence can also be heard in the sound of folk artists like **Rachid Briha** and **Hamid M'Rabati**, from the Oujda region.

Rap, dance and metal

Rap is immensely popular in Morocco, as it is throughout the African continent, and you're likely to see a fair amount of Eminem, Sean Paul and 50 Cent graffiti daubed on the ancient walls of the country's Medinas. The homegrown scene is still largely underground, though the most popular crews – **H-Kayne** from Meknes and **Fuaïre** from Marrakesh – have got some national visibility. The young urban hipsters of modern cities like Casablanca, Rabat and Agadir have also become fond of **House, R&B and funk.** The Casablanca scene has produced artists such as Hoba Hoba Spirit – who blend rock, funk, reggae and Gnaoua – and Barry, who combines bossa nova with reggae and Gnaoua influences. Huge New Year raves have been organized near Ouarzazate in the last few years.

Heavy metal is also a burgeoning fashion. However, in 2003 the Moroccan authorities showed the limits of their tolerance for the wayward antics of young rock fans when they (briefly) imprisoned members of the heavy metal bands **Nekros, Infected Brain** and **Reborn,** along with five of their fans, on charges of moral depravity and playing "anti-Islamic" music. Clearly not all of Morocco is ready just yet for full on head-banging and satanic T-shirts.

Discography

There has been quite a boom in CDs of Moroccan music in recent years. Most record stores in Britain or the US with a decent World Music section should yield at least a few discs of ethnic, folk and andalous music, or fusion with European groups. In Morocco itself, cassettes are still dominant.

Compilations

Various *Morocco: Crossroads of Time* (Ellipsis Arts, US). An excellent introduction to Moroccan music that comes with a well-designed and informative book. The disc includes everything from ambient sounds in the Fes Medina, to powerful Jilala and Gnaoua music, andalous, *rwai*, Berber, and some good contemporary pop from Nouamane Lahlou.

Various *The Rough Guide to the Music of Morocco* (World Music Network, UK). This Rough Guide's release focuses on contemporary Moroccan sounds, featuring selections from the Amenzou Ensemble,

Nass El Ghiwane, Nass Marrakech, Jil Jilala, Mustapha Bourgogne, Bnet Marrakech and U-cef. It is backed up by fulsome liner notes.

Various *Anthologie de la Musique Marocaine* (Ministère de la Culture, Morocco). These four boxed sets (with a total of 31 CDs) cover most bases in Moroccan folk and traditional music. All include liner notes in French and Arabic and can be purchased at the Ministry of Culture in Rabat.

Classical/andalous

Ensemble Amenzou *Le malhûn à Marrakech* (Institut du Monde Arabe, France). The Amenzou brothers belong to a revered dynasty of *milhûn* singers and their energetic, youthful approach to the genre is much admired.

El Hadj Houcine Toulali *Le malhûn de Meknes* (Institut du Monde Arabe, France). A fine live recording of the great *milhûn* master on top form.

Ihsan Rmiki *Al-Samâa: Ecstatic Spiritual Audition* (Institut du Monde Arabe, France). Rmiki is the new voice of andalous music – and this is a moving set, her voice leading a six-person ensemble.

Orchestre Moulay Ahmed Loukili de Rabat *Nuba Al-'Ushshâq* (Inédit, France). This expensive six-CD box is not for the casual – but quite an experience, finely presented with informative notes.

Ustad Massano Tazi *Musique Classique Andalouse de Fes* (Ocora, France). Again, beautifully recorded and presented. Includes Nuba Hijaz Al-Kabir and Nuba Istihilal.

Various *Maroc: Anthologie d'Al-Melhûn* (Maison des Cultures du Monde, France). A three-CD set containing performances from many of Morocco's finest *milhûn* singers. An excellent introduction.

Berber music

Compagnies musicales du Tafilalet *The Call of the Oasis* (Institut du Monde Arabe, France). Sublime recordings from the edge of the Sahara, showcasing four groups recorded live at a festival in Erfoud.

Hmaoui Abd El-Hamid *La Flûte de l'Atlas* (Arion, France). Hypnotic and haunting flute-like ney, backed by percussion, *oud* and zither.

Les Imazighen *Chants du Moyen-Atlas* (Institut du Monde Arabe, France). A fantastic live recording of musicians from the Middle Atlas, full of power and extravagant emotion.

Muluk el Hwa *Xara Al-Andalus* (Erde Records, Germany). A collaboration between this acoustic Berber band and the Spanish group Al Tall, fusing medieval Valencian music and Arabic poetry from Andalusia.

Gnaoua and trance

Les Aissawa de Fes *Trance Ritual* (L'Institut du Monde Arabe, France). Entrancing and intricate music from the Aissawa brotherhood of Fes.

Gnawa Njoum Experience (Night and Day, France) One the most successful fusions of trad Gnaoua with modern day electronica. Sounds especially majestic in a club setting.

Maleem Mahmoud Ghania with Pharaoh Sanders *The Trance of the Seven Colours* (Axiom/Island, US) Gnaoua-jazz crossover, featuring the great sax player from Coltrane's band.

The Master Musicians of Jajouka *Apocalypse Across the Sky* (Axiom, UK). The power and clarity of these remarkable performers stands out on this Bill Laswell production.

Various *Gnawa Night – Music of the Marrakesh Spirit Masters* (Axiom, UK). Gnaoua music at its evocative best, again recorded by Bill Laswell.

Various *Moroccan Trance Music* (Sub Rosa, Belgium). Not for the faint-hearted, this is intense Gnaoua and Jilala music, combined on the disc with some of Paul Bowles' personal recordings.

Chaabi

Najat Aatabou *The Voice of the Atlas* (GlobeStyle, UK). A superb collection of some of Najat's best-loved songs, including "Shouffi Rhirou" which has been covered brilliantly by the 3Mustaphas3.

Bnet Marrakech *Chama'a* (L'empreinte Digitale, France). A legendary women's group from Houara in their favoured unstoppable freight-train mode. Powerful to say the least.

Jil Jilala *Chama'a* (Blue Silver, France). A classic early recording of the seminal *chaabi* rockers, which

was only available on cassette until very recently. The title track "Chama'a" ("candle") is an old *milhûn* song, which is given a very moody and edgy modern makeover.

Nass el Ghiwane *Maroc: Chants d'Espoir* (Créon Music, France). Many recordings by the "Rolling Stones of North Africa" are marred by atrocious sound quality. This set however captures them razor sharp and passionate and it includes their moving nine-minute long tribute to victims of the Sabra and Chatila massacres in Lebanon.

Contemporary and fusion

Aisha Kandisha's Jarring Effects *El Buya* (Barbarity, Switzerland). An intoxicating mix of Moroccan melodies and traditional string instruments with scratching reverb and rushes of industrial noise.

Yosefa Dahari *Yosefa* (Worldly Dance, UK). Just what the label says: dance music with English and Maghrebi songs. A bit of an exotica product but one with promise.

Houssaine Kili *Mountain to Mohammed* (Tropical Music, France). How Morrocan music sounds when reworked by an inveterate Neil Young fan... some great contemporary Maghrebi rock.

Nass Marrakech *Bouderbala* (World Village, USA). A curious mix of styles on a vaguely gnaoui foundation, with some excellent songs and innovative arrangements.

Juan Peña Lebrijano and the Orquesta Andalusi de Tanger *Encuentros* (GlobeStyle, UK). A stunning cross-cultural blend that combines the passion of flamenco with the beauty and grace of andalous music.

MoMo *The Birth Of Dar* (Apartment 22, UK). House-flavoured Moroccan madness with a heavy dance beat. *Dar* means "house" in Arabic...you get the picture.

Despite a considerable increase in CD reissues in recent years, some of the best Moroccan music is still only available on cassette. In Morocco itself, cassettes of all kinds are readily available in any market – and you can buy videos of many artists, too (though keep in mind that these are French format – not playable on many UK/US machines), and even a few DVDs. Don't hesitate to ask the shopkeeper if you can listen to any cassette that takes your fancy. More often than not they'll only be too willing to oblige and to recommend items that might interest you.

This is a selection of artists who are still primarily only available on cassette, and who deserve a much wider international audience.

Archach Featuring Gnaoua ginbri, banjo and terrific singing, the band's early cassettes are great.

Bnet el Ghiwane An all-female troupe of modern troubadours, with a nice line in unison singing to bass, *bendir* and banjo backing.

Fatima Chebbai A great Berber pop singer from the Marrakesh area. Her cassette *Adouaa Al Madina* is a killer.

Cheb Djallel The *raï* prince from Oujda is an absolute must. His cassette *Le Prince de la Chanson Maghrébine* is the one to ask for.

Essiham A fine *chaabi* outfit from the 1980s who never saw the light of day on CD.

Mahmoud Guinea and Mustapha Baqbou Although they have both collaborated with countless musicians and producers both in Morocco and on the international circuit, these two great Gnaoua *ma'alem* still sound best on their early cassettes.

Hajja Hamdaouia One of the queens of al'aïta. Her four cassettes are all excellent – lots of percussion, violin, funky keyboards and her very expressive voice.

Raïs Ajmaa Lahcen and Raïs Ilhya The great masters of *ahouache* have a dozen or so cassettes on the market – stark and powerful music.

Fatima Taabamrant The queen of Berber music from the Souss – she sounds almost Malian and keeps getting better with each release.

Tagada One of the greatest ever "new" *chaabi* bands of the 1970s, who are still going strong. Look out for any of their early releases on the Hassaniya label.

Sawt El Atlas *Donia* (Small/Sony Music, France). Unapologetically pop and *raï*-flavoured tunes from one of the most popular contemporary Moroccan groups in France.

Think of One *Marrakech Emballages Ensemble* (De Beek, Belgium). This remarkable Belgian band collaborated with a Marrakesh-based group, Bnet Houaryet, to produce one of the most accessible and authentic Moroccan crossover albums.

U-cef *Halalium* (Apartment 22, UK). A Moroccan producer based in London who fuses the roughneck sounds of the English capital with traditional *chaabi* and Gnaoua, often to wondrous effect.

Jewish Moroccan music

Samy el Maghribi (Club du Disque Arabe, France) A collection of old recordings by this legendary Jewish musician whose pride of place in the annals of Moroccan music proves what a big influence Jews once had on urban music.

Various *Sacred music of the Moroccan Jews* (Rounder Select, USA). Haunting recordings from 1959 of Jewish liturgies from Essaouira and Meknes made by Paul Bowles.

Moroccan storytelling

Storytelling is an age-old Moroccan tradition – and an active one, as any visit to a weekly souk will reveal. In print, however, it exists largely through the oral translations by the American novelist Paul Bowles (1910–99; see p.778). Bowles became interested in such tales in the 1950s, and began tape-recording and transcribing examples told by various Moroccan friends – Ahmed Yacoubi, Larbi Layachi, Abdeslam Boulaich and, in particular, Mohammed Mrabet, with whom he collaborated on more than a dozen books.

The stories below are from Bowles' 1979 collection, *Five Eyes*. The piece by **Mohammed Mrabet** (born 1940) shows his masterful handling of a deeply traditional theme of Moroccan storytelling, the casting of spells. **Abdeslam Boulaich** (born 1943), who is better known as a painter, reveals a similar interest in folk humour. **Mohamed Choukri** (1935–2003), by contrast, was a more literary figure, with a novel and books on Tennessee Williams and Jean Genet to his name. Alone among the three authors here, he wrote his text (in Classical Arabic), with Bowles translating from an oral reading in Maghrebi.

Mohammed Mrabet: The Lute

A young man named Omar got onto his mare one day and rode over his father's land for many miles, looking for the right place to build a small house of his own. He came to a hill between the forest and the olive groves. This is the spot, he said, here I can play my lute all day.

Little by little he built a cottage, bringing the materials from his father's house, and doing all the work himself. When it was done he furnished it with everything he needed for the pleasant life he intended to lead. His most important possession was his lute, which he had trained so that when anyone was coming it sounded its strings in warning. Then Omar would look into the opening under the strings and watch the person as he approached.

Outside the house he built an arbor of canes where he could lie back and drink his tea. And he would sit out there in the shade of the arbor with the green trees all around him, smoking *kif* and drinking tea. At length he would take down his lute and begin to play.

Farther down the valley lived two sisters whose father and mother had died, leaving them alone in a big house. The younger sister was still only a girl, and there was a handsome village lad with whom she was friendly. The older sister, who desired the boy for herself, caught sight of him talking to the girl under a tree. Later she questioned her.

Who was that you were talking to?

The boy from the village.

What did he say to you?

The girl smiled and looked very happy. He said beautiful words and wonderful things. Because I love him and he loves me.

What? cried the woman. And you're not ashamed to say such a thing?

Why should I be? We're going to be married.

The older sister jumped up and rushed out. She began to burn powders and to chant, and it was not long before she burst into the room with a scream and flung a handful of black powder over the girl. At that instant her sister no longer stood in front of her – only a camel, which she chained outside.

A few days later the village boy came to see the younger sister. The woman greeted him from the doorway and invited him into the house. He sat down and looked around, and then through the window he saw the camel.

Why have you got that camel chained to the ground with its legs tied together? he asked her.

She's a bad animal, the woman said. I have to keep her chained up so she won't get into trouble.

Let the poor thing loose so it can graze, he told her. It has no life at all this way. Unfasten the chain and untie the ropes.

No, no. I can't do that.

The boy waited a moment. Then he said: The girl who lives here. Where is she?

That girl? She's getting married tomorrow.

What? he cried. But she was going to marry me!

No. She never mentioned anything about that to me, she told him. Anyway, that's the way it is.

Then she laughed. And what about me? Don't you like me?

Yes, he said. Of course I like you.

Why don't you and I get married, then?

The boy looked at her, and then he looked out at the camel. All right, he said at length. I'll marry you. But only if you set that camel free.

Without saying anything the woman went outside and undid the chain and ropes, and the camel walked away. Then she came in and said she would see him that evening.

As the boy went along the path to the village he came upon the camel waiting for him. He was horrified to hear it speak with the voice of the girl.

Don't trust my sister, it said. You see what she's done to me. I'm the one you were going to marry. Go as far away from here as you can, and stay away. I've got to try and get back my body somehow.

Then the camel walked away, and the boy was too downcast to call after it. He left the village the same afternoon.

One day not long afterward as Omar lay under his arbor on a mat drinking tea, the cords of his lute suddenly sounded. When he peered inside it he saw a camel. He watched it come nearer, and then he hung up the lute and went out into the orchard. The camel walked straight to him and said: Good afternoon.

Omar was startled. You can speak?

I said good afternoon. Yes, I can speak.

I've never seen a talking camel, he said.

But I'm not a camel. That's the trouble. And she told him what her sister had done to her. Then she said: I have a favor to ask of you. Let me stay here with you for a while.

Omar looked thoughtfully at the animal, and said: Ouakha. You can stay with me.

The camel lay down beside the arbor, and Omar began to play the lute. It was the hour when the birds sang and flew from tree to tree. When the birds became quiet, he glanced at the camel and saw that tears were falling from its eyes. He put the lute aside.

The next day as Omar sat in the arbor talking with the camel, he heard the strings of the lute. When he looked inside, he saw a woman walking through the wilderness, over the rocks and between the trees. He watched for a while, but she did not come any closer. Finally she disappeared. He sat down.

Tell me, he said to the camel. What was your sister doing at the moment you felt yourself becoming a camel?

The camel thought for a while. Then it said: She sprinkled some powder over my head, and she had a piece of green cloth in her hand. I saw her fold it three times and then throw it on top of a chest.

I have a friend who might be able to help, Omar told her. He often comes by around this hour.

As they sat there a large crow came flying over the trees, and alighted on the ground beside the arbor. After they had greeted each other, Omar said: You're an expert thief, aren't you?

The crow was embarrassed. It's true I've stolen things. But all that is in the past.

Omar smiled. Good, he said. But you've still got to steal one more time. Do you know Tchar Flanflani?

Yes.

You've got to get into that big house there and look around until you find a green cloth. Don't unfold it. Bring it to me.

Quickly, said the crow, and it flew off.

They did not have to wait long for it to return, carrying the green cloth in its claws. As Omar took the cloth in his hands and let it unfold, instead of a camel lying on the ground beside the arbor, it was a girl.

He stared at her first in amazement and then with delight, for she was beautiful. Then she jumped up and threw her arms around him, and he embraced her. Together they went into the house.

The following day when the sister looked to see if the green cloth was safe in its place, she did not find it. She searched for it inside the house and out, but without success. As Omar and the girl sat in the shade of the arbor, the strings of the lute began to vibrate. He peered into it and saw the woman walking in the forest.

Here, he said to the girl. Look in here and see if you know who that is.

She looked inside the lute and drew back. It's my sister! she whispered. She's looking for me.

Omar hung up the lute and walked out to the orchard to meet the woman. When he came up to her she looked at him and said: Who are you?

That's what I want to ask you, he said. Who are you and where have you come from and what do you want here? This is my land you're on, and the edge of it is a long way from here.

I'm looking for a camel, she said. A camel I've lost.

I have your camel, he told her.

What! Where is it? What have you done with it?

It's over there, he said, pointing to the arbor where the girl stood. And she came out and walked toward them.

The woman looked at Omar. You won't win! she cried. Then she turned and went back the way she had come.

A few days after this, Omar put the girl onto the mare and rode with her to his father's house, where they celebrated their marriage with a wedding feast that lasted for three days. Then the married couple rode back to the little house. The two were very happy together, and the days passed swiftly.

But one moonlit night as they lay asleep in bed, the lute hanging on the wall twanged its strings. Omar sprang up and put his eye to the hole. A woman dressed all in white walked in the brilliant moonlight. He pulled the lute down and played softly for a while. The next time he looked in, a dense white cloud had formed around the figure of the woman in the orchard, and the cloud was so thick that she could not move one way or the other. Omar hung the lute on the wall and got back into bed.

What was it?

It was your sister. She's down there in the orchard now, dressed all in white. I've got her shut in. She can't go forward or backward.

Let her go! the girl begged him. We mustn't be cruel to her. I can't bear to think of her suffering.

Omar paid no attention to her pleas, but turned over and went to sleep. In the morning after he had bathed and had his breakfast, he sat down under the arbor, smoked a few pipes of *kif*, and said to the girl: Come here and look.

Inside the lute she saw the swirling cloud among the olive trees. Omar took the lute and played on it for a moment. Then he handed it back, and she looked again. The cloud had disappeared, and the woman stood there shouting up at them from the orchard.

I'll be back! she screamed.

Another night as they slept, the lute again sounded a warning, and Omar seized it and put his eye to the hole. Seeing the woman, he played a loud fast melody for a while. When he peered in the next time, he saw that once again a cloud had formed around the woman, but this time it had risen high into the air with her, where it remained, as still as a rock. He got into bed and said nothing about it.

But the next morning when the girl looked outside she called to Omar. There's something hanging in the air above the orchard!

It's your sister, he said.

Forgive her this time, and she'll never come back to bother us any more, his wife said, and she went on pleading with him.

Your sister will never change, Omar told her. She ought not to be pardoned and turned loose to do harm in the world.

But the girl sobbed and begged him to let her sister down, and finally he got up and plucked on the lute. The cloud slowly settled onto the ground and blew away. This time the woman did not stay to say anything, but ran off as soon as she felt the earth beneath her feet.

When she got back to her house, she shut herself in and fasted for four days. At the end of this time she had a vision of two trees whose trunks stood very close one to the other. She forced herself between them and knew that something great had happened. When she turned, she saw eight strings of gut stretched from a crosspiece between the tree trunks, and she knew that this was the way to get into Omar's house without alerting the lute. From then on she spent all her time preparing the strips of gut and the other things she would need when she found the two trees. When she had everything ready, she began to go regularly to the forest below the little house, in search of the place she had seen in her vision. She found it one night. It was in a dense part of the woods, just below the house. Quickly she squeezed in between the two tree trunks.

The moment she had pushed through, a wall formed around her body and over her head, so that she was encased in a shell of rock between the two trees. The lute by Omar's bed made a loud sound as though it had been hurled to the floor, and then it began to play a strange, halting melody, a thing Omar had never heard it do before. He waited until it had stopped, and then he took it down and looked into it.

Your sister! he cried. There's nothing I can do! She's dying. The lute did it by itself. I didn't touch it.

The girl seized the lute and held it close to her face. Beyond the strings she saw the two trees and the boulder between them. And then through the casing of the stone she saw her sister's face. Her mouth was open and her eyes rolled from side to side as she gasped.

Then the wall of stone around her body became smoke and blew away through the trees, and she fell forward onto the ground.

The next morning Omar and his wife went to the spot and found her body lying there between the two arar trees.

We must bury her, said the girl.

Not on my land, Omar told her. On her own land, if you like, but not here.

And each afternoon when he sat with his wife under the arbor playing the lute, the crow came and sat with them, and listened.

1977

Abdeslam Boulaich: Three Hekayas

Cowardice

A Moslem, a Jew, and a Christian were sitting in a cafe talking about Heaven. They agreed that it was a difficult place to get into, but each one thought he would have a better chance than the others.

You have to have the right clothes, the Christian told them. I always wear a jacket and a tie.

Let's go and see, said the other two.

They started out, and when they got close to Heaven, the Moslem and the Jew stopped walking, and the Christian kept going until he reached the door of Heaven.

Our Lord Solomon, who guards the door, said to him: Where are you going?

Inside, the Nazarene answered.

Who are you?

My name is John.

Stand back, said Our Lord Solomon.

Then the Jew and the Moslem spoke together. The Moslem said: He didn't get in. But we will.

I'll go first, said the Jew.

That's right. You go, the Moslem told him.

So the Jew walked up to the door of Heaven. And Our Lord Solomon said to him: Where are you going?

Inside.

Who are you?

Yaqoub, said the Jew.

Stand back!

The Moslem saw this and said to himself: That's that. Neither one of them got in. Now I'll try.

He walked until he got to the door of Heaven. Then he pulled the hood of his djellaba down over his face. And Our Lord Solomon said to him: Where are you going?

Inside.

Who are you? Our Lord Solomon asked him.

I am the Prophet Mohammed, he said. And he went in. The Jew was watching. He said to himself: If he can get in there, so can I.

And he took a sack and filled it with sticks of wood and slung it over his shoulder. Then he walked up to the door.

Where are you going? asked Our Lord Solomon.

The Jew stuck his foot in the door.

Who are you?

The Prophet Mohammed's manservant, he said. And the Jew went in.

The Christian had been watching. He was afraid to try to get in by lying, and so he went back to his country and told everyone that Heaven did not exist.

Stupidity

In a small mountain village lived a man who could not talk very well because he had no roof to his mouth. When it came time for him to marry, his family chose him a girl who had the same trouble. But since the man had never seen her, nor had the girl seen him, neither one knew how the other one spoke.

The day of the wedding, the man went into the girl's room. The servant brought in the taifor with a pot of couscous on it, and then she went home, leaving the front door unlatched.

The man sat with his hands folded in front of him, and so did the girl. Each one was looking at the other, waiting for the other to speak. She was waiting for the man to say: Eat. And he was waiting for her to say: Eat. He was afraid to speak for fear she would hear his voice and not be able to love him. And the girl was afraid he would hear hers and not want her for a wife. Each one looked at the other, and the door of the house was unlatched.

A beggar was passing through the street, crying: For the love of Allah, a little bread! And no one paid him any attention. When he came to the house of the bridegroom he saw the door ajar, and he pushed it open and walked in. He went through the courtyard and came to the room where the two were sitting. Then he saw the man and the girl looking at one another, with the food in front of them on the taifor, and neither one saying anything. The bridegroom saw the beggar standing there. He wanted to tell him to get out. But he would not speak, and so he shook his head up and down at him. But the beggar thought he meant: Go on and eat. He sat down and began to eat the couscous, and he went on eating until there was only a little left. Then he ate the meat, and when he had finished, he took the bone and hung it around the man's neck on a string, because he thought the man was simple-minded. And he went out.

A dog was running through the street. When it came to the house of the bridegroom it caught the smell of food coming through the open door, and it went into the courtyard. It ran to the door of the room where they were sitting, and went in. The man and the girl sat still and said nothing. The dog put its feet up on the taifor and licked up the rest of the couscous. It was still hungry. Then it saw the bone that hung around the bridegroom's neck, and it seized it between its jaws and tried to run. The man fell over onto the floor, and the dog dragged him to the door. The dog kept pulling, and the man's head hit the wall.

Then the man cried out: Help me untie the string!

The girl heard his words, and she was no longer afraid to speak.

The beggar was right! she said. I can't live with such a man!

But you speak the same way! he cried.

I'm the only one who wouldn't have minded that, she told him. And she went out of the house, and left the man on the floor with the dog pulling at the bone.

Greed

A sickly man who lived in the city married a girl from the country. He was never very hungry, but the girl was healthy and ate a great deal. One day the man went to the market and bought many vegetables and four cow's feet.

When he took the food home to his wife, he told her: Make me a stew so I can have it when I come home for lunch.

Yes, she said.

But wait for me, he said. Don't eat anything until I get back.

I won't, she said.

When he had gone she made the stew. And then she waited. He ought to be here soon, she said to herself. He'll be here any minute.

After he had finished working, the man went to a café and began to play cards. He stayed there in the café a long time, and his wife went on waiting. Soon she was very hungry. She took one of the cow's feet out of the stew and ate it. And she said to herself: It doesn't matter. When he comes I'll make up something to tell him.

The man came home and sat down. Where's the stew? he said. You haven't eaten anything, have you?

Not yet, she told him. She went to the stove and began to ladle it out. Then the man noticed that there were only three feet in the pot. He began to shout: And the other foot? Where is it?

I haven't got it, she said. You brought three and I cooked three. I hate cow's feet anyway.

The man was very unhappy. Do you want to kill me? he cried. Bring me the other foot, or I may die right here.

Die, if that's what you want, she told him. Why are you waiting?

The man rolled over onto the floor and began to moan.

Get up! said his wife. But he only told her to fetch the fqih and make him wash him so he could be buried.

When she came in with the fqih, the girl said to her husband again: Get up off the floor!

Have you got the cow's foot? he asked her.

The fqih began to wash him.

Get up! she said. Don't you want to have your burial clothes put on you?

Have you brought the cow's foot?

She did not answer. The people came in and dressed the man in his kfin, ready to be buried. And then they laid him on the litter.

You're off to the cemetery, his wife told him.

They carried him through the doorway into the street.

Where's the cow's foot? he cried. His wife shut the door.

The people walked through the streets carrying him on the litter. When they passed in front of the market, the butcher saw the procession. Who's that who has died? he asked. They told him.

And to think that only this morning he was here in my shop, the poor man, and he bought four cow's feet!

When the dead man heard this, he sat up on his litter. How many did you say? he called to the butcher.

Four!

Ah, you see? he said. And my wife told me I'd bought only three.

No. It was four, said the butcher.

The man lay down again. And the men carrying him were talking and did not notice anything. They went on their way to the cemetery. When they got there they lifted him off the litter and started to lower him into the ground. But at that moment he sat up again.

Wait! he told the fqih. I've got three cow's feet at home that I still haven't eaten. It's not good to be hungry when you arrive in Heaven. I'm going to run back and eat them now. If I do get to Heaven then, at least I'll have some food inside me.

The people let go of him, and he ran home. When he went into the house his wife said: You came back? You're still alive?

Give me the three cow's feet, he told her. She gave them to him. He ate one. But then he was no longer hungry, and his wife ate the other two.

1961

Mohamed Choukri: The Prophet's Slippers

More pleasure and fantasy. More money, more ways of getting hold of it. I was tired of enjoying myself, and yet I was not satisfied. Fatin walked toward me, white as snow in the blood-red light of the bar. She took one of my notebooks, looked at it, and grinned.

She muttered something unintelligible and moved away again, disappearing among those who were kicking the air. It was three o'clock in the morning, and I was bored and nervous. Om Kalsoum was singing: "Sleep never made life seem too long, nor long waiting shortened life."

A black man appeared, white on black. He took one of my books and began to read aloud: "This total liberty has its tragic and pessimistic side." He put it down. "What's that book about?" he demanded.

"It's about a man who doesn't understand this world," I said. "He hurts himself and everybody who comes near him."

He nodded, lifted his glass, and drank. When he had finished, he said: "You're crazy."

I saw Fatin writing in a notebook. Meanwhile I smoked, drank, and thought about the matter of the slippers. The lights went off. Women cried out. When they came on again, both men and women murmured. I bought another drink for Khemou, and she gave me a kiss that left a sweet taste in my mouth. Her brown tongue tickled. She was eating chocolate, and her laugh was red in the light from the bar. Khemou walked off and Fatin came up to me. She handed me a slip of blue paper. On it she had written: Rachid. What do you know about love? You spend more time writing about love than you do making love. The one who has never studied love enjoys it more than the one who knows all about it. Love is not a science. Love is feeling, feeling, feeling.

Miriam Makeba went into "Malaysia." She has a white voice. I began to write on the same piece of blue paper. Fatin, you are my red bed, and I'm your black blanket. I'm beginning to see it that way.

I looked around for Fatin. Her mouth was a wound in her face, and a foreign sailor was sucking on it. She had her right arm around him and was pouring her drink onto the floor with her left hand. Khemou came by and offered me her lips, like a mulberry. I bought her another drink. I was so pleased with the effect of her kiss that I began to think once more about selling the slippers. How much ought I to ask for them? A million francs, the Englishman ought to pay, if he wants the Prophet's slippers. He's an idiot in any case, or he couldn't be taken in by such a tale. But how can I tell just how stupid he is? It was he who first brought it up, the black-market story.

Fatin appeared, black, blonde, white. I handed her the slip of blue paper. She looked at me and smiled. I was thinking that girls like her only made trouble. Her little mouth now looked like a scar that had healed. I thought of the Indian poet Mirzah Asad Allah Ghalef:

For those who are thirsty
I am the dry lip.

She wants a kind of love that will make her unhappy. What I like about her is that she still believes the world ought to be changed.

Khemou and Latifa began to scream at each other like two cats fighting, while Miriam Makeba's white voice continued to sing. Khemou pulled Latifa's black hair, knocked her down, and kicked her face. Latifa screamed and the blood ran from her nose. The colors all came together in my head. Leaving the blue paper with me, Fatin ran to separate the two. I read on it: You're right. I serve them my flesh, but I don't feel it when they eat me.

Vigon is singing in his white voice. "Outside the Window." Vigon is singing, and I think of the almond trees in flower, and of snow, which I love.

Khemou and Latifa came out of the rest room. They had made up, like two little girls. They began to laugh and dance as if nothing had happened. I sat there smoking, while in my imagination I attacked each man in the bar whose face I didn't like. A kick for this one, a slap in the face for that one, a punch in the jaw for that one over there. Watching myself do as I pleased with them put me into a better frame of mind.

Tomorrow I'll sell the slippers. Fatin came past again, and I asked her why Khemou and Latifa had been quarrelling. She said it was because Khemou had told the man Latifa was drinking with that she had tuberculosis.

Is it true? I asked her.

Yes, she said. But she says she's cured now.

The Englishman and I were at my house, eating couscous. He turned to me and said: "This is the best couscous I've ever tasted."

From time to time he looked toward the corner where my grandmother sat, her head bent over. I told him the couscous had been sent from Mecca. "My aunt sends a lot of it each month."

He looked at me with amazement. "It's fantastic!"

So that he would get the idea, I added: "Everything in the house was brought from Mecca. Even that incense burning is sent each month."

We finished the couscous and started on another dish of meat baked with raisins and hot spices. "It's called mrozeya," I told him.

He muttered a few words, and then said: "Ah, nice. Very nice." My grandmother's head was still bent over. I saw that the Englishman was looking at her, sitting there in her white robes. The incense and the silence in the room made her seem more impressive. She was playing her part very well. Our demure little servant brought the tea in a silver teapot. She too was dressed in immaculate white, and she too kept her face hidden. Her fingers were painted with elaborate designs in henna, and her black hair shone above her enormous earrings. She made no false moves. She greeted the Englishman without smiling, as I had instructed her to do. It became her to look grave. I had never seen her so pretty.

The mint tea with ambergris in it seemed to please the Englishman. "Do you like the tea?" I asked him.

"Oh, yes! It's very good!"

There was silence for a while. I thought: The time has come to rub Aladdin's lamp. I got up and went to whisper in my grandmother's ear. I did not even form words; I merely made sounds. She nodded her head slowly, without looking up. Then I lifted the white cushion and removed the piece of gold-embroidered green silk that covered it.

The Englishman looked at the slippers, made colourless by age. His hand slowly advanced to touch the leather. Then he glanced at me, and understood that I did not want him to touch them.

"My God! They're marvellous!"

I covered the slippers as I stood there, in order to let him observe them through the veil of green silk. Slowly and with great care I turned and put the cushion back into its place, as if I were applying a bandage to an injury. He glanced at me, and then stared for a long time in the direction of the slippers. Understanding that it was time to leave, he stood up.

We were sitting at the Café Central. For the third time since we had left the house, he said: "Then it's impossible?"

"A thing like that is so difficult," I said. "I wouldn't know how to do it. It was hard enough to get her to let you even look at them. You can be sure you're the only Christian ever to have seen them. And no other is going to, either."

"I understand," he said. "But perhaps we can come to an agreement."

"I understand too. But what can I do? Those slippers are my grandmother's very life. If she should find them missing, she might lose her mind, or have a heart attack. I'm very fond of her, naturally, and I respect her feelings about the slippers."

"I'll give you time to think about it," he said. "But try and persuade her."

"Yes. But when you think of how hard it was to get her to allow you to look at them, you can see how much harder it would be to persuade her."

"Do what you can," he said.

I said I would. but that I thought it was out of the question. Then I said: "Listen. I have an idea. But only on one condition."

"What's that?"

I hesitated for an instant.

"Tell me. Perhaps we can find a way."

"You'd have to leave Tangier the minute you got the slippers."

"That would be all right," he said, understanding. "It's an excellent tactic."

"And I'd have to get out of Tangier myself and stay somewhere else. And I couldn't come back as long as my grandmother was still alive."

"No."

"I couldn't stay on here once they were gone."

"I quite understand."

"It's those slippers that keep her alive, you might say."

"Yes, yes. How much do you want for them?"

I stared at him, and my voice said: "A million francs."

"Oh !" he cried. "No! That's very high!"

"But you'll have something extremely rare. No museum has anything like them. And I'll regret what I've done for the rest of my life."

"I know, I know. But that's a great deal of money. I'll give you half a million. I can't pay any more than that."

"You'd have to pay more than that," I told him.

"No, no. I can't. I haven't got it."

"You give me your address, and I'll write you from wherever I go, and you can send me the rest later."

We looked at each other for a few seconds. In my mind I was thinking: Go on, say the word, Mister Stewart.

"Very well," he finally said.

Wonderful, Mister Stewart, I thought.

"Where shall we meet tomorrow?" I asked him.

He reflected for a moment, and said: "I'll wait for you in the lobby at the Hotel Minzah."

"No," I said. "Outside the hotel. In the street. And you must have your ticket with you, so you can leave the minute I give you the slippers."

"Of course."

"What time will that be?"

While he hesitated I was thinking: Come on, Mister Stewart. Make up your mind.

"At three o'clock in the afternoon."

I got up, shook hands with him, and said: "Keep it to yourself."

"I shan't breathe a word."

"It's not only my grandmother who's going to be upset, but everybody who knows she has the slippers."

I walked away. A moment later I turned and saw him leaving the café.

I found him waiting for me in front of the hotel. He seemed nervous, and he looked wide-eyed at the bag I was carrying. I saw that he had a packet in his hand. Half a million, I thought. More pleasure, more time to think of other such tricks later. The colors in the bar.

I motioned to him to follow me, and stopped walking only when we were a good distance from the entrance to the hotel. We stood facing one another. We shook hands. He looked down at my bag, and I glanced at the packet he held in his hand.

I opened the bag, and he touched the slippers for a second. Then he took it out of my hands, and I took the packet from him. Pointing to a parked car, he said: "There's the car that's going to take me to the airport."

I thought to myself. And tonight I'll be at the Messalina Bar.

I sat down in the corner the same as always. I smoked, drank, and bought kisses without haggling over their price. I'm fed up with pleasure. Fed up, but not satisfied. One woman is not enough.

"Khemou's in the hospital," Fatin told me. "And Latifa's at the police station. She got drunk and hit Khemou on the head with a bottle."

I asked Fatin who the girls were who were sitting in the corner opposite me. She said they were both from Dar El Beida. She picked up one of my notebooks and walked away with it. I waved at the younger of the two. She spoke for a while with her friend. And I drank and smoked and waited for the first kiss of a girl I had never yet touched.

She got up and came over, and I saw the small face relax. Her mouth was like a strawberry. She began to sip the drink I bought her. Her lips shone. Her mouth opened inside mine. A strawberry soaked in gin and tonic. Eve eating mulberries. Adam approaches her, but she puts the last berry into her mouth before he can get to her. Then he seizes the last berry from between her teeth. The mulberry showed Eve how to kiss. Adam knows all the names of things, but Eve had to teach him how to kiss.

Two men had begun to fight over one of the girls. The shorter of the two lost his balance. The other kicked until someone seized him from behind.

Fatin put a piece of blue paper in front of me. I was drinking, smoking, and eating mulberries from the new small mouth. I read what was written on the piece of blue paper. I'm not the same person I was yesterday. I know it but I can't say it clearly. You must try and understand me.

The new face held up her empty glass. I looked again at the mulberries. The barman was busy drawing squares on a small piece of white paper. "Give her another drink," I told him. The friend who had been sitting with her came over. "Give her a drink too," I said.

I thought: More mulberries and human flesh. More tricks and money. I began to write on Fatin's slip of blue paper: I must not try to understand you.

1973

Books

here is a real wealth of books about Morocco, set in Morocco, or (increasingly) by Moroccans – and you won't regret having one or two along on a trip. Personal favourites include Paul Bowles' Fes novel, *The Spider's House*, a brilliant political novel, whose concerns seem utterly modern; Esther Freud's *Hideous Kinky*, a magic evocation of a childhood hippy trip to Marrakesh; Walter Harris's account of the last days of feudal Morocco in the 1920s, *Morocco That Was*; and the various story collections of Mohammed Mrabet, impeccably rendered by Paul Bowles. Books or authors that are especially recommended are indicated with the symbol ⚘.

The main Internet bookstores – **Amazon** in particular (try both US and UK sites) – are likely to yield the highest returns on the more esoteric recommendations below, while **abebooks.com** is good for those out of print (o/p in our listings). You might also want to try the UK-based **Maghreb Bookshop**, 45 Burton St, London WC1 (☎020 7388 1840, ⊛www.maghrebbookshop.com), which supplies current, out-of-print and rare books on all aspects of North Africa, and will ship worldwide.

General and travel

There are huge numbers of travel books about Morocco, so the most interesting (and they are real classics) are indicated by ⚘

Leo Africanus *History and Description of Africa* (no recent edition but available in major libraries). Written in the mid-sixteenth century, this was the book Budgett Meakin followed, "astounded at the confirmation [of its accuracy] received from natives of remote and almost inaccessible districts". Leo, who was Moroccan by birth, was captured as a young man by Christian pirates. He subsequently converted and lived in Italy; the book was suggested to him by the pope, and so there's more than a hint of propaganda about his accounts. (See also Amin Malouf in "Other Fiction".)

Edmondo de Amicis *Morocco: Its People and Places* (1882; reprinted by Darf Publishers, UK). Intrepid journeying through Morocco in an era when few Europeans travelled beyond Tangier or the coast. Illustrated with copious line drawings.

Ibn Battuta *The Travels of Ibn Battutah* (ed. Tim Mackintosh-Smith; Picador, UK). Ibn Battuta is often called Morocco's Marco Polo – though he was probably a more reliable witness to the medieval world. He set out in 1325 from his native Tangier, aged just 21, on a pilgrimage to Mecca, and did not return to Morocco for another 29 years, travelling instead through more than forty countries on the modern map, covering 75,000 miles and getting as far north as the Volga, as far east as China and as far south as Tanzania. He wrote of his travels, and comes across as a superb ethnographer, biographer, anecdotal historian and occasional botanist and gastronome. Tim Mackintosh-Smith, who edited this volume, has also written a superb biography retracing many of the original journeys – *Travels with a Tangerine: A Journey in the Footnotes of Ibn Battutah* (Picador, UK; Random House, US).

Margaret and Robin Bidwell (eds) *Morocco: The Traveller's Companion* (IB Tauris, UK; o/p). A good if rather traditional anthology from the mid-1990s, with excerpts from key writers of the past five centuries, including many translated by the editors from the French.

Paul Bowles *Points in Time* (Peter Owen, UK; Harper, US), *Their Heads Are Green* (Peter Owen, UK; Harper, US). Novelist, poet and composer Paul Bowles (1910–99) lived in Tangier for half a century and, more or less singlehandedly, brought translations of local writers to Western attention (see p.776). These two books of his own are superb. *Points* is a series of tales and short pieces inspired by episodes and sources from earliest times to the present day. *Heads* includes a couple of travel essays on Morocco and a terrific piece on the psychology of desert travel.

Elias Canetti *The Voices of Marrakesh* (Marion Boyars, UK). A small, compelling volume of impressions of Marrakesh in the last years of French rule, by the Nobel prize winning author. The atmosphere of many pieces still holds

R.B. Cunninghame Graham *Mogreb-El-Acksa: A Journey in Morocco* (1898; reprinted by Northwestern University Press, US). Fin-de-siècle adventuring and anecdotes, the most interesting of which is an enforced stay in a caidal kasbah in the High Atlas (Graham's host did not understand the motive of "curiosity").

Nina Epton *Saints and Sorcerers* (1958, o/p). A very readable – and inquiring – travelogue, concentrating on folk customs and religious sects and confraternities in the 1950s.

Walter Harris *Morocco That Was* (Eland Books, UK). Harris, *Times* correspondent in Tangier from the 1890s until his death in 1933,

saw the country at probably the strangest ever stage in its history – the last years of "Old Morocco" in its feudal isolation and the first of French occupation. *Morocco That Was*, first published in 1921, is a masterpiece – alternately sharp, melodramatic and very funny. It incorporates, to some extent, the anecdotes in his earlier *Land of an African Sultan* (1889, o/p) and *Tafilet* (1895, o/p).

Orin Hargraves *Culture Shock! Morocco* (Kuperard, UK; Graphic Arts Center, US), Hargraves worked in Morocco in the 1980s as a Peace Corps volunteer and this valuable paperback, revised in 2007, is a distillation of his experience, supported by an impressive range of research and, clearly, a lot of conversations throughout the country. He offers perceptive accounts of almost every aspect of contemporary Moroccan life, along with a good overview of history and religion, and an instructive section of dos and don'ts.

J.D. Hooker and J. Ball *A Tour in Morocco and the Great Atlas* (1878, o/p). A weighty tome, as befits this duo – the director of Kew Gardens and the first president of the Alpine Club. Together with G. Mawr, they made the first ever sortie by Westerners in the Atlas.

John Hopkins *Tangier Journals 1962–79* (1997; Arcadia, UK; Cadmus Editions, US). Highly entertaining journals of Tangier life – and travels across Morocco – from an American novelist, resident in Tangier during the Beat years. Paul and Jane Bowles and William Burroughs all figure large in the diary entries.

Barrie Kerper (ed.) *Morocco – The Collected Traveler* (Three Rivers Press, US; o/p). This is a wonderful anthology of all things Moroccan – perfect café reading that delivers on its promise of "like being accompanied by a group of savvy and observant friends". The book begins with an A to Z of practical and cultural information, then moves into essays and writerly extracts on everything from carpets to movies to time. Featured authors include Paul Bowles, Patricia Storace and Jeffrey Tayler – among many others. Well worth tracking down.

Wyndham Lewis *Journey into Barbary* (1932; Black Sparrow Press, US). You'll learn more about Lewis than Morocco from this obscure, eccentric and rambling text – but the drawings are wonderful.

Peter Mayne *A Year in Marrakesh* (Eland Books, UK). Mayne went to Marrakesh in the early 1950s, found a house in an ordinary district of the Medina, and tried to live like a Moroccan. He couldn't, but wrote an unusually perceptive account explaining why.

Budgett Meakin *The Land of the Moors* (1900; reprinted by Darf Publishers, UK), *The Moors: A Comprehensive Description* (1902, o/p). These wonderful encyclopedic volumes were the first really detailed books on Morocco and Moroccan life. Many of Meakin's "Comprehensive Descriptions" remain accurate and the sheer breadth of his knowledge – from "Berber Feuds" to "Specimen Recipes" and musical notations of "Calls to Prayer" – is fascinating in itself. Highly recommended library browsing.

Barnaby Rogerson (ed.) *Marrakech Through Writers' Eyes* (Eland Books, UK). A feast of an anthology, ranging from the earliest accounts, through eighteenth- and nineteenth-century explorers and envoys, to contemporary writers such as Esther Freud and Juan Goytisolo.

Antoine de Saint-Exupéry *Wind, Sand and Stars and Southern Mail* (Penguin, UK; Harcourt Brace, US). Accounts by the French aviator (and

author of the children's classic, *The Little Prince*) of his postal flights down to West Africa, by way of Cap Juby in the then Spanish Sahara. Stacy Shiff's biography, *Saint-Exupéry* (Pimlico, UK) is, if anything, even more gripping, taking the story through to Saint-Exupéry's disappearance flying for the Free French in 1944.

Tahir Shah *The Caliph's House* (Doubleday, UK; Bantam, US). This is a terrific read, good for anyone's holiday: a funny, eccentric and insightful look at Casablanca, and Morocco as a whole, through the narrative of buying and restoring a house in the city.

Jeffrey Tayler *Valley of the Casbahs* (Abacus, UK). Tayler set out, in 2001, on a journey to trace the Drâa valley from source to sea, on foot and by camel. His chief objective was to try to meet and understand the "Ruhhal" – the remaining desert nomads. The journey – one of the most compelling of modern accounts – left him by turns appalled and inspired.

Joseph Thomson *Travels in the Atlas and Southern Morocco* (1889, o/p). The most wide-ranging and daring of the early explorers, Thomson was the first to pinpoint Toubkal as the highest Atlas summit. A lively read – his only companion was badly stung by a scorpion while hiking in his pyjamas.

Gordon West *By Bus to the Sahara* (1932, Black Swan, UK; o/p). This fascinating travelogue, reprinted in the 1990s but again out of print, describes a journey from Tangier to Rissani, as undertaken by the author and his wife, an amateur artist, coyly referred to as "the spirit". As a touristic insight into prewar Morocco, it is unique.

Edith Wharton *In Morocco* (1920, Ecco Press, US). Wharton dedicated her book of travels in Morocco to

General Lyautey, resident general of the Protectorate, whose modernizing efforts she greatly admired. By no

means a classic, it is nonetheless worth reading for glimpses of harem life in the early years of the twentieth century.

History

General

Barnaby Rogerson *A Traveller's History of North Africa* (Windrush, UK; Interlink, US) Rogerson takes on a daunting task here, covering the history not just of Morocco, but Tunisia, Algeria and Libya, but he pulls it off with style. This is an authoritative but very readable book, establishing a surprisingly clear vision of North African history from Carthage to the present. Rogerson sees his chosen area as a kind of island, isolated by sea and desert, and thus set apart from Europe and sub-Saharan Africa. Written in the 1990s, this a good, up-to-date, general history.

Specific periods

J.M. Abun-Nasr *History of the Maghreb in the Islamic Period* (Cambridge University Press, UK & US). Morocco in the wider context of North Africa by a distinguished Arab historian.

E.V. Bovill *The Golden Trade of the Moors* (Oxford University Press, UK). An account of the historic trans-Saharan caravan trade, and especially the routes between Morocco and Mali, and the influences of those countries on each other.

Fergus Fleming *The Sword and the Cross* (Granta, UK). This is a superb read: the story of two adventurers – Charles de Foucauld and Henri Laperrine – who, in the first decade of the twentieth century, forged the French imperial conquest of the Sahara. Each of them found his vocation in the desert: Foucauld in a religious asceticism; Laperrine in forming a legendary camel corps to pursue the Touareg nomads. Both were to pay a terrible price, in self-sacrifice and utter self-delusion.

Moshe Gershovich *French Military Rule in Morocco: Colonialism and its Consequences* (Frank Cass, UK & US). A detailed but not overly academic study of the French colonial period. The reputation of General Lyautey, still seen in France as the embodiment of "enlightened colonialism", is severely reassessed.

Marvine Howe *Morocco: The Islamist Awakening and Other Challenges* (Oxford University Press, UK & US). This is a highly readable book by a former *New York Times* correspondent who had known the country since the 1950s but returns to live – and get inside the country – in 1999. Her return coincides with the new king, Mohammed VI, and the rise of Islamic radicalism in the Arab world. She takes the story through to 2005.

Roger Le Tourneau *Fez in the Age of the Marinides* (University of Oklahoma Press, US; o/p). Interesting scholarly study of the Merenid capital of Morocco. Tourneau has also

written on *The Almohad Movement*
(1981, Princeton University Press,
US; o/p).

🏃 **Gavin Maxwell** *Lords of the
Atlas* (Cassell, UK). Drawing
heavily on Walter Harris's accounts of
the Moorish court (see p.769), this is
the story of the Glaoui family –
literally the "Lords" of the High
Atlas, where they exercised almost
complete control from the turn of
the nineteenth century right through
to Moroccan independence in 1956.
Not an attractive tale but a compelling one, and superbly told. Originally published in 1966, it was
republished in a superbly illustrated
edition in 2000.

Giles Milton *White Gold – The
Extraordinary Story of Thomas Pellow
and North Africa's One Million
European Slaves* (Hodder, UK).
Milton tells a story as well as any
popular historian – and this is quite a
tale. Pellow was captured by Barbary
pirates in 1715, aged eleven, and
spent the next 23 years in Morocco,
converting to Islam and becoming a
commander in Sultan Moulay
Ismail's slave army. Milton postulates
that Pellow was one of a million

Europeans enslaved in North Africa
– a figure much higher than other
historians have suggested.

C.R. Pennell *Morocco from Empire to
Independence* (Oneworld, UK; New
York University Press, US). This is
the first general history of modern
Morocco. It covers the major strands
of power but also the social and
cultural life of ordinary Moroccans
and is strong on the country's
pressing contemporary concerns of
poverty, drought, and worsening
agricultural land.

Douglas Porch *The Conquest of
Morocco* (Forward Movement, US).
Accessible and fascinating account of
the extraordinary manoeuvrings and
characters in Morocco at the turn of
the twentieth century.

Susan Raven *Rome in Africa*
(Routledge, UK & US). A well-illus-
trated survey of Roman (and
Carthaginian) North Africa.

David Woolman *Rebels in the Rif*
(Stanford University Press, US; o/p).
An academic but fascinating study of
the Riffian war in the 1920s and of
the tribes' uprising against the
Moroccan government in 1956.

Anthropology

There are many anthropology books about Morocco; below are just a selection
of the more popular, not overly academic titles.

**Michael Brett and Elizabeth
Fentress** *The Berbers* (1997, Black-
wells, UK). A valuable recent
overview of the Berber peoples of
Morocco, Algeria and beyond,
ranging through anthropology,
history and literature.

Shlomo Deshen *The Mellah
Society: Jewish Community Life in
Sherifian Morocco* (University of
Chicago Press, US). A study of
economic activity and political

organization in the Mellahs prior to
the Protectorate.

Elizabeth Fernea *A Street in
Marrakesh* (Waveland Press, US). A
nicely written account of a woman
anthropologist's study of and experiences in Marrakesh in the 1980s.

David Hart *Tribe and Society in
Rural Morocco* (Frank Cass, UK &
US). A collection of essays, dating
from 1985 to 2000, around the

CONTEXTS | Books

themes of tribalism and Berberism in Morocco. More accessible than it sounds, with titles such as *Scratch a Moroccan, Find a Berber*.

David A. McMurray *In and Out of Morocco* (University of Minnesota Press, US). McMurray is an American who based himself in Nador to study the phenomenon of migrants and smugglers in this frontier boomtown. He unearths some fascinating material.

Fatima Mernissi *Doing Daily Battle: Interviews with Moroccan Women* (The Women's Press, UK, Rutgers University Press US). Here women – carpet weavers, rural and factory workers, teachers – talk about all aspects of their lives, from work and housing to marriage. A fascinating insight into a resolutely private world by one of Morocco's foremost academics.

Malika Oufkir and Michele Fitoussi *Stolen Lives: Twenty Years in a Desert Jail* (Miramax, US). The bestselling account by the daughter of General Oufkir He was executed for his role in the attempted coup and assassination of Hassan II in 1973 and Malika and her family were subsequently imprisoned in a desert prison for the next fifteen years. Published in 2001, it was an Oprah Book Club choice; it is arguably more relevant these days to the US government than to Morocco.

Islam

The Koran (Oxford University Press, UK & US). The Word of God as handed down to the Prophet is the basis of all Islam, so essential reading for anyone interested. There are dozens of editions but the Oxford edition is probably the clearest and liveliest translation.

S.H. Nasr *Ideas and Realities of Islam* (Collins, UK & US). A good general introduction.

Barnaby Rogerson *The Prophet Muhammad – A Biography* and *The Heirs to the Prophet* (Abacus, UK; Warner, US). Rogerson's gripping, modern biography of the Prophet could hardly be more timely. He captures a real sense of Muhammad's time and his struggles, as well as his historical and spiritual significance. The "sequel" carries the story forward to the split in Islam between Sunni and Shia.

Art, architecture and crafts

In addition to the recommendations below, a number of large, glossy books on Moroccan jewellery, gardens, paintings, manuscripts, carpets and buildings, usually with French texts, are to be found in most of the larger bookshops in Morocco – notably at the excellent bookshop of the Marrakesh Museum.

Pierre Bergé and Madison Cox *Majorelle, A Moroccan Oasis* (Thames & Hudson, UK). This is one of a series of "small books on great gardens": a superbly photographed volume on the Marrakesh garden created by French designer Jacques Majorelle and now maintained by Yves Saint Laurent.

Michael Brett *The Moors* (Orbis; o/p). A fine illustrated survey of the Moorish medieval world, well thought out and with a thoughtful text.

Titus Burckhardt *Fes: City of Islam* (Islamic Texts Society, UK); *Moorish Culture in Spain* (o/p). Burckhardt's *Moorish Culture* is a classic study of architecture, history, Islamic city-design and the mystical significance of its art – and as such entirely relevant to medieval Morocco. *City of Islam* is worth dipping into for the photos, though its conceptual approach is hard going.

Salma Damluji *Zillij: the Art of Moroccan Ceramics* (Garnet, UK). An expensive but beautifully illustrated study of the art of ceramic mosaic-work.

🏃 **Lisl and Landt Dennis** *Living in Morocco* (Thames & Hudson, UK). An entrancing picture study of Moroccan craft and domestic design, both traditional and modern.

James F. Jereb *Arts and Crafts of Morocco* (Thames & Hudson, UK; Chronicle Books, US; o/p). The arts and crafts of Morocco express the kaleidoscope of influences from Black Africa and Islam to the cultural alliance of the Moors and Spaniards. This book, with over 150 colour photographs, is a fine introduction.

Jack Cowart et al *Matisse in Morocco* (Thames & Hudson, UK; Abrams, US; o/p). A gorgeous book of the paintings and drawings from the artist's stay in 1912–13.

🏃 **Lisa Lovatt-Smith** *Moroccan Interiors* (Taschen, UK). This coffee-table tome may be aimed at the interior design market but it goes beyond that in its coverage of traditional crafts, and traditional and modern architecture. Given the mass of colour photography and high production values, it is also amazing value.

Mark Luscombe-Whyte and Dominic Bradbury *Morocco: Decorations, Interior, Design* (Conran, UK). An elegant (if pricey) book of photo spreads of rural, traditional, palace and colonial buildings and decoration, with an emphasis on the new riad hotels.

Andre Paccard *Traditional Islamic Craft in Moroccan Architecture* (2 vols; Editions Atelier, France). This hugely expensive coffee-table book was written by an architect much favoured by King Hassan. The text is none too engaging but it is massively illustrated and – uniquely – includes photographs of Moroccan Royal Palaces currently in use.

Brook Pickering et al *Moroccan Carpets* (Laurence King, UK). Edited by a New York collector and dealer, this is the best book on Moroccan carpets – a large format, fully illustrated guide, showing examples region by region.

🏃 **Herbert Ypma** *Morocco Modern* (Thames & Hudson, UK; Stewart, Tabori & Chang, US). A superbly illustrated book that traces the origins of the great artisan traditions of Morocco (weavers, woodworkers, potters, zellij-makers) and looks at the way contemporary designers and architects reinterpret these influences to create surprisingly modern work.

Photographs

🏃 **Ann and Yann Arthus-Bertrand** *Morocco Seen From The Air* (Vendome Press, UK & US). Seek out this stunning, large-format book published in 1994 – and be amazed at Moroccan cities, valleys, kasbahs, carpet souks captured from the air. Browse after a trip and odd, apparently impenetrable pockets of cities that you've walked through will begin to fall into place. Other photos simply have the appearance of abstract paintings.

Margaret Courtney-Clarke *Imazighen: The Vanishing Traditions of Berber Women* (Thames & Hudson, UK). The photographs here are of Berber communities across Morocco, Algeria and Tunisia. They are intimate portraits of communities at home and show the harsh nature of life and its constant work, as well as the beauty of the crafts and landscape.

🏃 **Hugues Demeude, Jacques Bravo, Xavier Richer** *Morocco* (Taschen, Germany). A magnificent assembly of photographs, published in 1998, and hard to beat (in quality and price) if you want a photo book to browse before or after a trip.

Alan Keohane *Berbers of the Atlas* (Hamish Hamilton, UK; o/p). A marvellous collection of colour photos of daily life in the Atlas.

Published in the mid-1990s, it is well worth tracking down.

Abderrahman Slaoui *The Orientalist Poster* (Slaoui Foundation, Marrakesh). A fascinating selection from the Marrakesh Museum, depicting travel to and throughout Morocco in the early twentieth century.

Jean-Marc Tingaud and Tahar Ben Jelloun *Medinas: Morocco's Hidden Cities* (Assouline, France; Thames & Hudson, UK & US). Wonderful photos of the mansions and palaces of Fes, Marrakesh and other cities, whose existence you could hardly imagine from the street outside. Tingaud's photos are accompanied by poems from the Moroccan novelist Ben Jelloun.

Albert Watson *Maroc* (Rizzoli, US; o/p). A large-format, exquisite collection of duotone shots by this renowned US fashion photographer, from his travels across Morocco in 1998.

Food

Robert Carrier *Taste of Morocco* (Arrow, UK; o/p). Robert Carrier lived in Marrakesh for several months of each year and this beautifully illustrated cookbook reflects his love of Morocco and its distinctive cuisine – particularly the grand dishes of the south. Carrier considered Morocco to have (with France and China) one of the three greatest cuisines in the world. His focus is on wealthy kitchen dishes rather than anything very rustic.

Zette Guinaudeau *Traditional Moroccan Cooking: Recipes from Fez* (Interlink, US). Madame Guinaudeau lived in Fes for over thirty years and first published her recipes in French in 1964. Now translated into English, they redress the imbalance of Robert Carrier's focus on Marrakesh cuisine. Some of her recipes echo Mrs

Beeton's catering, for at least eight people and sometimes as many as twenty, but they can be adapted.

🏃 **Anissa Helou** *Café Morocco* (Conran Octopus, UK & US). This sumptuous book is the best of the many recent Moroccan cookery guides. It combines good recipe writing with colourful background – and stunning photography – on the food (from street snacks to haute cuisine) and its origins.

Paula Wolfert *Couscous and Other Good Foods from Morocco* (HarperCollins, US). This is a new edition of a book originally published in the 1960s, which at the time was groundbreaking in its emphasis on ordinary, rural cooking. Its recipes work and there's a nice line in anthropological background.

Moroccan fiction/biography

By far the largest (and finest) body of Moroccan fiction/biography published in English is the translations by the American writer Paul Bowles, who lived in Tangier from the 1940s until his death in 1999. Many of the small press editions duck in and out of print but they are reasonably available if you do an Internet search; prices are now very high for first editions but reprints are reasonable.

Translations by Paul Bowles

All of the books below are taped and translated from the Maghrebi by Paul Bowles. It's hard to generalize about them, except to say that they are mostly "tales" (even the biographies, which seem little different from the fiction), share a common fixation with intrigue and unexpected narrative twists, and are often punctuated by episodes of violence. None have particular characterization, though this hardly seems relevant as they have such a strong, vigorous narrative style – brilliantly matched by Bowles' sharp, economic language. For a taste of the stories, see "Moroccan Storytelling" on pp.757–767.

Mohamed Choukri *For Bread Alone* (Telegram Books, UK). Now translated into more than ten languages, this first volume of Mohammed Choukri's autobiography (see opposite) spoke for an entire generation of North Africans. Born in the Rif, he moved with his family to Tangier at a time of great famine, spending his childhood in abject poverty. During his adolescence he worked for a time for a French family. He then returned to Tangier, where he experienced the violence of the 1952 independence riots. At the age of twenty, and still illiterate, he took the decision to read and write classical Arabic – a decision which transformed his life.

Driss Ben Hamed Charhadi *A Life Full of Holes* (Grove Press, US). This was Bowles' first Moroccan translation – in 1964 – a direct narrative of street life in Tangier. It was published under a pseudonym, the author being Larbi Layachi who, two decades later, published *Yesterday and Today* (Black Sparrow Press, US),

a kind of sequel, describing in semi-fictionalized (and not very sympathetic) form his time with Paul and Jane Bowles.

Mohammed Mrabet *Love with a Few Hairs* (City Lights, US); *The Boy Who Set the Fire & Other Stories* (City Lights, US); *The Lemon* (Peter Owen, UK; City Lights, US); *M'Hashish* (City Lights, US); *The Chest* (Tombouctou, US); *Marriage With Papers* (Tombouctou, US); *The Big Mirror* (Black Sparrow Press, US); *Harmless Poisons, Blameless Sins* (Black Sparrow Press, US); *The Beach Café and The Voice* (Black Sparrow Press, US); *Look and Move On: An Autobiography* (Peter Owen, UK; Black Sparrow Press, US). Mohammed Mrabet's stories – *The Beach Café* is perhaps his best – are often *kif*-inspired, and this gives them a slightly paranoid quality, as Mrabet himself explained: "Give me twenty or thirty pipes . . . and an empty room can fill up with wonderful things, or terrible things. And the stories come from these things."

Other translations

Abdelkader Benali *Wedding by the Sea* (Phoenix House, UK; Arcade Publishing, US). Moroccan magic realism? This is an impressive debut novel by a Moroccan-born author who has lived in the Netherlands since childhood. The story is about a young man who returns (from Holland) to his seaside village in Morocco for his sister's wedding, and during the festivities finds the bridegroom has made off to the local brothel. Sweet revenge lies in store from his sister.

Mahi Binebine *Welcome to Paradise* (Granta, UK). Binebine grew up in Morocco, lived in America and has now settled in France, where he has become a significant novelist. This is his first book to be published in English and it is utterly engaging: a tale of life in the poorest areas of contemporary Morocco and the motivations that drive the country's boat people (and migrants from West Africa) to hand over all their savings to a trafficker to cross the Straits of Gibraltar, and then take their chances as illegals in Europe. Superbly translated, it is hugely evocative and should be required reading for anyone who cares to pronounce on – or cares about – Africa's "economic" refugees.

Mohamed Choukri *Streetwise* (Telegram Books, UK). The second volume of Choukri's autobiography (translated by Ed Emery) spans the 1960s and 1970s and ranks among the best works of contemporary Arabic literature. Throughout his adversities, two things shine through: Choukri's determination to use literacy to surmount his desperate circumstances; and his compassion for the normally despised human beings who share this life of "the lowest of the low".

Driss Chraibi *Heirs to the Past* (Heinemann, UK & US; o/p). A benchmark novel, written in French, this takes the crisis of Moroccans' post-colonial identity as its theme; it is semi-autobiographical as the author-narrator (who has lived in France since the war) returns to Morocco for the funeral of his father. A number of other Chraibi novels are also available in translation.

Fatima Mernissi *Dreams of Trespass: Tales of a Harem Girlhood* (Perseus Press, US) Part fairy tale, part feminist manifesto, this is a mix of biographical narrative, stories and fantasies from the renowned Moroccan sociologist, who was born in a harem in Fes in 1940.

Tahar Ben Jelloun *The Sand Child* (Johns Hopkins University Press, US) and *Corruption* (New Press, US). Ben Jelloun, long resident in Paris, and writing in French, is Morocco's most acclaimed writer. His is a deserved reputation and he has getting on for a dozen books translated into English. These two are probably the best. *The Sand Child*, which won the prestigious Prix Goncourt, is the tale of a girl brought up in southern Morocco as a boy in order to thwart Morocco's inheritance laws. *Corruption*, as its title suggests, explores the endemic corruption in contemporary Morocco, through the story of Mourad, the last honest man in the country, who attempts to stay clear of brown envelopes in Casablanca and Tangier.

Anouar Majid *Si Yussef* (Quartet, UK). An interesting if somewhat tortuous narrative: the author writes as Lamin, a student in Fes, who presents the life story of an old man, born in Tangier in 1908, and his tales of the city.

Brick Ousaïd *Mountains Forgotten by God* (Lynn Rienner, UK; Three

Continents Press, US). Autobiographical narrative of an Atlas Berber family, which gives an impressive sense of the harshness of mountain life. As the author describes it, it is "not an exercise in literary style [but] a cry from the bottom of my heart, of despair and revolt".

Foreign fiction set in Morocco

Once again, the late Paul Bowles is the outstanding figure in American and European fiction set in Morocco, so no apologies for splitting this section into "Bowles" and "Others". Though the "Others" do include a couple of gems.

Paul Bowles

NOVELS: *The Sheltering Sky* (Penguin, UK; Ecco Press, US); *Let It Come Down* (Penguin, UK; Black Sparrow Press, US); *The Spider's House* (Arrow, UK; Black Sparrow Press, US).

STORIES: *Collected Stories of Paul Bowles* 1939–76 (Black Sparrow Press, US) gathers together work from numerous editions, as does the more selective *Collected Stories* (Penguin, UK). Post-1976 collections include *Midnight Mass* (Peter Owen, UK; Black Sparrow Press, US) and *Unwelcome Words* (Tombouctou, US).

Paul Bowles stands out as the most interesting and the most prolific writer using North African themes – and following Bertolucci's film of *The Sheltering Sky* he at last regained some of the recognition he was due (the novel had been a US bestseller on publication in 1955). Many of his stories are similar in vein to those of Mohammed Mrabet (see p.776), employing the same sparse forms, bizarre twists and interjections of violence. The novels are something different, exploring both Morocco (or, in *The Sheltering Sky*, the Algerian desert) and the ways in which Europeans and Americans react to it and are affected by it. If you read nothing else on the country, at least get hold of *The Spider's House* – one of the best political novels ever

written, its backdrop the traditional daily life of Fes, its theme the conflicts and transformation at the last stages of the French occupation of the country.

The last few years have seen a flurry of biographies and memoirs of Bowles and his literary friends and acquaintances in Tangier. The best of these are:

Iain Finlayson *Tangier: City of the Dreams* (HarperCollins, UK; o/p). Good on the Moroccans whom Bowles has translated.

Michelle Green *The Dream at the End of the World: Paul Bowles and the Literary Renegades of Tangier* (Bloomsbury, UK). A strong narrative, compulsively peopled: the best read if you're looking for one book on Tangier literary life.

Paul Bowles *Without Stopping* (Peter Owen, UK; Ecco Press, US). Bowles' autobiography is of interest for its Moroccan episodes (though William Burroughs wryly dubbed it "Without Telling"), as is his *Two Years Beside the Strait* (Peter Owen, UK; published in US as *Days: A Tangier Journal, 1987–89*, Ecco Press). *In Touch: the Letters of Paul Bowles*, edited by **Daniel Halpern** (HarperCollins, US; o/p), spans sixty years and reveals a little more, with letters (predominantly from Tangier) to intimates such as Burroughs and Aaron Copland.

Other fiction

Arturo Barea *The Forging of a Rebel* (Granta, UK). This is an autobiographical trilogy of the key Spanish events of the 1930s. The second part, *The Track*, concerns the war and colonization of the Rif, the Spanish entry into Chefchaouen and life in Tetouan.

Jane Bowles *My Sister's Hand in Mine: The Collected Works of Jane Bowles* (Farrar Straus Giroux, US). Jane Bowles was resident in Morocco, on and off, with her husband Paul, from the 1940s until her tragic death in 1973. Her work is strange and unique, and she set a handful of stories (such as *Everything is Nice*) in Morocco. Millicent Dillon's biography, *A Little Original Sin: the Life of Jane Bowles* (University of California Press, US), includes some fascinating material.

Anthony Burgess *Earthly Powers* (Penguin, UK; Carroll & Graf, US), *The Complete Enderby* (Carroll & Graf, US). Both these Enderby novels feature sporadic scenes in 1950s-decadent Tangier.

William Burroughs *Naked Lunch* (Flamingo, UK; Grove Press, US). This iconic Beat novel was written in a Tangier hotel room in 1954–57, and published in France in 1959, though its brazen obscenity prevented publication in the US until 1962 and in the UK until 1964. The book is a confused series of nightmarish sex-and-drugs-obsessed tableaux dreamed up by Burroughs while withdrawing from a heroin habit. It isn't especially about Morocco, but Tangier features as "Interzone", and is undoubtedly the place to read it.

Aldo Busi *Sodomies in Eleven Point* (Faber, UK). A (highly) picaresque tour of Morocco by the Italian novelist.

Elisa Chimenti *Tales and Legends of Morocco* (Astor-Honor, US). Travelling in the 1930s and 1940s with her father, personal physician to Sultan Moulay Hassan, Chimenti learned many of these simple, fable-like tales from Berber tribesmen whose guest she was.

Rafael Chirbes *Mimoun* (Serpent's Tail, UK & US). Compelling tale of a Spanish teacher based south of Fes, amid sexual adventures and bizarre local life and antagonisms.

Esther Freud *Hideous Kinky* (Penguin, UK; WW Norton, US). You've seen the film? Well read the book – it's even better. An English hippy takes her two daughters to Marrakesh, where they live simply, as locals. The narrative – funny, sad, and full of informed insights – is told through the persona of the 5-year-old.

Brion Gysin *The Process* (The Overlook Press, US). Beat novel by ex-Tangier resident and friend of Paul Bowles and William Burroughs. Fun, if a little caught in its zany 1960s epoch.

John Haylock *Body of Contention* (Arcadia, UK). An enjoyable romp set amid the expat community of Tangier in the months following Independence in 1957.

John Hopkins *All I Wanted Was Company* (Arcadia, UK). Another Tangier novel – this time a gossipy tale about an American and his lovers, one of whom disappears to the Sahara.

Richard Hughes *In the Lap of Atlas* (Chatto, UK; o/p). Traditional Moroccan stories – cunning, humorous and ironic – reworked by the author of *A High Wind In Jamaica*. Also includes a narrative of Hughes' visit to Telouet and the Atlas in 1928.

Jane Kramer *Honor to the Bride Like the Pigeon that Guards its Grain Under the Clove Tree* (1970, Farrar, Straus & Giroux, US; o/p). Fictional narrative based on the true story of a Berber woman's kidnap in Meknes.

Amin Malouf *Leo the African* (Abacus, UK); published as *Leo Africanus* (New Amsterdam, US). Superb historical novel, re-creating the life of Leo Africanus, the fifteenth-century Moorish geographer, in Granada and Fes and on later travels.

Umberto Pasti *Age of Flowers* (Pushkin Press, UK). An Italian novel, once again set in Tangier, with a decadent scene of writers and artists counterposed with the Islamicists taking control of the city.

Glossary

ADHAN the call to prayer

AGADIR fortified granary

AGDAL garden or park containing a pool

AGUELMANE lake

AÏN spring

AÏT tribe (literally, "sons of")

ALAOUITE ruling Moroccan dynasty from the seventeenth century to the present king, Mohammed VI

ALMOHAD the greatest of the medieval dynasties ruled Morocco (and much of Spain) from c.1147 until the rise to power of the Merenids c.1224

ALMORAVIDS dynasty that preceded the Almohads, from c.1060 to c.1147

AMAZIGH Berber

ANDALOUS Muslim Spain (a territory that centred on modern Andalusia)

ARABESQUE geometrical decoration or calligraphy

ASSIF river (often seasonal) in Berber

BAB gate or door

BABOUCHES slippers (usually yellow)

BALADIYA town hall or local council

BALI old

BARAKA sanctity or blessing, obtained through saints or *marabouts*

BARBARY European term for North Africa in the sixteenth to nineteenth centuries

BENI tribe (literally, "sons of")

BERBERS native inhabitants of Morocco, particularly those whose first language is Berber (though most Moroccans claim to be at least partly Berber)

BILDI country-style (of the bled)

BLED countryside, or, literally "land"; BLED ES MAKHZEN – governed lands; BLED ES SIBA – land outside government control

BORDJ fort

CAID district administrator; CADI is an Islamic judge

CHLEUH southern Berber from the High or Anti-Atlas or plains

COL mountain pass (French)

DAR house or palace; DAR EL MAKHZEN, royal palace

DARJ W KTARF literally "cheek and shoulder", an Almohad architectural motif resembling a fleur-de-lis

DAYA, DEYET lake

DJEBEL mountain peak or ridge, a DJEBALI is someone from the mountains; the DJEBALA are the main tribe of the Western Rif

DJEDID new

DJELLABA wool or cotton hooded outer garment

DJEMAA, JAMAA mosque, or Friday (the main day of worship)

DJINN nature spirits (genies)

ERG sand dune

FAKIR Koranic schoolteacher or lawyer, or just an educated man

FANTASIA display of horsemanship performed at larger festivals or moussems

FASSI inhabitant of Fes

FILALI alternative name for the Alaouite dynasty – from the southern Tafilalt region

FIRDAOUS Paradise

FONDOUK inn and storehouse, known as a caravanserai in the eastern part of the Arab world

GANDOURA man's cotton garment (male equivalent of a kaftan); also known as a *fokia*

GHARB coastal plain between Larache and Kenitra

GNAOUA itinerant musician belonging to a Sufi brotherhood of West African origin (the name is from the same root as "Guinea")

HABBOUS religious foundation

or bequest of property for religious charities

HADJ pilgrimage to Mecca

HAMMADA stony desert of the sub-Sahara

HAMMAM Turkish-style steam bath

HARKA "burning" raid undertaken by sultans in order to raise taxes and assert authority

IDRISSID first Arab dynasty of Morocco – named after its founder, Moulay Idriss

IMAM prayer leader and elder of mosque

ISTIQLAL nationalist party founded during the struggle for independence

JEDID, JDID, DJEDID old

JEBEL, JBEL, DJEBEL mountain

JOUTIA flea market

KASBAH palace centre and/or fortress of an Arab town; also used to mean a walled residential quarter around the Medina (eg Fes), or the citadel (eg Tangier and in Tunisia), or the whole Medina (eg Algiers). In the south of Morocco, it is a feudal family castle – and it's the root of the Spanish *alcazar*

KHETTARA underground irrigation canal

KEDIM old

KIF marijuana, cannabis

KOUBBA dome; small *marabout* tomb

KSAR, KSOUR (pl.) village or tribal stronghold in the south

LALLA "madam", also a saint

LITHAM veil

MAGHREB "West" in Arabic, used for Morocco and the North African countries

MAISON D'HÔTE guesthouse, usually upmarket

MAKHZEN government

MARABOUT holy man, and by extension his place of burial. These tombs, usually whitewashed domes, play an important (and heterodox) role in the religion of country areas

MECHOUAR assembly place, court of judgment

MEDERSA student residence and, in part, a teaching annexe, for the old mosque universities

MEDINA literally, "city", now used for the original Arab part of any Moroccan town

MELLAH Jewish quarter

MERENIDS dynasty from eastern plains who ruled from the thirteenth to fifteenth century

MIHRAB niche indicating the direction of Mecca (and for prayer)

MINARET tower attached to a mosque, used for call to prayer

MINBAR the pulpit, usually placed next to the mihrab, from which the imam delivers his sermon at the midday Friday service in the mosque

MINZAH pavilion in a (usually palace) garden

MOULAY descendant of the Prophet Muhammad, a claim and title adopted by most Moroccan sultans

MOULOUD festival and birthday of the Prophet

MOUSSEM pilgrimage festival

MSALLA prayer area

MUEZZIN, MUEDDIN singer who calls the faithful to prayer

NAZARENE, NSRANI Christian, or, more loosely, a European

OUED (wadi in its anglicized form) river, but particularly a seasonal river or creek

PISÉ mud and rubble building material

PISTE unsurfaced road or track

PROTECTORATE period of French and Spanish colonial occupation (1912– 56)

QAHWA coffee or café

QAHOUAJI café *patron*

RAMADAN month of fasting

RAS source or head

RAS EL MA water source

RIAD patio garden, and by extension a house built around a

patio garden; now also used to signify
an upmarket guesthouse
RIBAT monastic fortress
ROMI urban, sophisticated – the
opposite of *bildi* (see p.781)
SAADIAN southern dynasty from
Drâa Valley, who ruled Morocco
during the fifteenth century
SEBGHA lake or lagoon
SEBSI pipe for smoking *kif*
SEGUIA irrigation canal
SHEIKH leader of religious
brotherhood
SHEREEF descendant of the
Prophet
SIDI, SI respectful title used for any
man, like "Sir" or "Mister", also a
saint
SOUK market, or market quarter
SUFI religious mystic; philosophy
behind most of the religious
brotherhoods

TABIA mud building material, as *pisé*
TIGHREMT similar to an agadir
– fortified Berber home and storage
place
TOUAREG nomadic Berber
tribesmen of the disputed Western
Sahara, fancifully known as "Blue
Men" because of the blue dye of
their cloaks (which gives a slight
tinge to their skin)
TIZI mountain pass
UMA (Union du Maghreb Arabe)
regional association whose members
are Morocco, Algeria, Tunisia, Libya
and Mauritania
WATTASID fifteenth-century
dynasty who replaced their cousins,
the Merenids
ZAOUIA sanctuary established
around a *marabout* tomb; seminary-
type base for religious brotherhood
ZELLIJ geometrical mosaic tilework

Glossary of Moroccan street names

Moroccan streets are often named after well-known historical figures, events and dates, and in recent years there has been a concerted drive to replace the old panoply of French and Spanish colonial names. As they're revealing of Moroccan interests and historical figures, a glossary follows of some of the most common.

Transliteration from Arabic into the Roman alphabet means that there are often many variations of the same name.

ABDELKRIM EL KATTABI
Leader of the Rif war against the Spanish. In 1921, his Berber warriors defeated a Spanish army of 60,000 at Annoual. He formed the independent republic of the Rif, but was defeated by Spanish/French forces in 1926.

ALLAL BEN ABDALLAH On September 11, 1953, he tried to kill Sultan Ibn Aaraf who had been appointed by the French to succeed Mohammed V when he was sent into exile. Allal Ben Abdallah crashed an open car into the royal procession on its way to the mosque in Rabat and attacked the sultan with a knife.

EL FARABI Born in Farab, now in Uzbekistan, he studied in Baghdad and taught as a Sufi in Aleppo, now in Syria. He lived from 870 to 950 and was one of the greatest Islamic philosophers; he harmonized Greek philosophy and Islamic thinking. He studied Aristotle, and was known as second only to him. Thus, he was known as Al Muallim Al Thani (the second teacher).

FERHAT HACHAD Tunisian trade union leader and Arab nationalist murdered in 1952 by extremist French settlers.

HASSAN II The previous monarch and elder son of Mohammed V, whom he succeeded on March 3, 1961. He launched the Green March (see p.684) on November, 6 1975. He died in July 1999.

IBN BATOUTA Fourteenth-century Tanjawi traveller who visited China and India, returning to Fes where he dictated his discoveries to a student. At the time, he was regarded as a romancer, but his reports turned out to be true.

IBN KHALDOUN Highly influential philosopher and historian from Tunis (born 1322), who first proposed a cyclical view of history in which civilizations rise, decline and are superseded.

IBN ROCHD Also known as Averroes, another of Islam's greatest philosophers. He was born in Cordoba (1126) and died in Marrakesh (1198). He introduced Christian monks to the works of Aristotle, but worked principally on astronomy, theology, mathematics and, particularly, medicine. Based in Marrakesh, he was doctor to Yacoub el Mansour.

IBN TACHFINE/YOUSSEF IBN TACHFINE A devout Muslim Berber from Adrar, now in Mauritania, and the first sultan of the Almoravid dynasty. He founded Marrakesh in 1060, captured Fes in 1069, fought against Alphonse IV and ruled Muslim Spain and the Maghreb as far east as Algiers.

IBN TOUMERT/MEHDI IBN TOUMERT Learned theologian, radical reformer and revolutionary leader, known as "The Torch". He was born around 1080, travelled to the Middle East in 1107, returned to Marrakesh in 1121, was expelled from there and took refuge with his warrior monks in the mountain stronghold of Tin Mal in 1124, where he died around 1130. He was believed by his followers to be the Mahdi – the "sinless one".

IBN ZAIDOUN Leading Andalusian poet of the eleventh century; like others, he followed the traditions of the east.

IBN ZIAD/TARIK BEN ZIAD/TARIK IBN ZIAD/ Berber chieftain who led the troops of Moussa Ibn Noussar across the Straits of Gibraltar. He defeated the Visigoths, near Tarifa, in 711, to bring seven centuries of civilization when the rest of Europe lived in the Dark Ages. He gave his name to Gibraltar – Djebel (mount) Tarik.

EL MANSOUR EDDAHBI Saadian sultan who inherited the throne in 1578 following the Battle of the Three Kings (see p.709) and ruled until 1603. Mansour means "victorious"; Eddahbi means "golden".

MOHAMMED V Born in Fes in 1909, the third son of Sultan Moulay Youssef, he was chosen by the French to succeed his father on November 18, 1927. He was unprepared for his role, but gained strength with experience. He supported the joint manifesto of January 11, 1944, arguing for independence; he spoke openly for independence in Tangier, then in the International Zone, on April 9, 1947, and was deposed by the French on August 20, 1953. He returned from exile on November 16, 1955, to a hero's welcome and secured independence on March 2, 1956. He died in 1961 and was succeeded by his elder son, Hassan II.

MOHAMMED VI The current king, born in Rabat on August 21,

1963. He came to the throne on the death of his father, Hassan II, in 1999.

MOHAMMED BEN ABDALLAH/SIDI MOHAMMED BEN ABDALLAH Grandson of Moulay Ismail and sultan 1757–1790. He established Essaouira, drove the Portuguese from El Jadida, armed the port of Larache and developed Tangier.

MOHAMMED ZERKTOUNI The most famous Moroccan freedom fighter. On December 24, 1953, in Casablanca's central market he placed a bomb in a shopping basket which killed twenty people and injured twenty-eight.

MOKHTAR SOUSSI Poet and nationalist figure during the French occupation. On independence, he became the government minister of *habous* (religious foundations which fund mosques, hospitals and schools). He also wrote a twelve-volume history of the Souss, his native province.

MOULAY ABDALLAH/ PRINCE MOULAY ABDALLAH Younger son of Mohammed V. He married a Lebanese princess, Lamia Sohl, and often deputized for his brother, Hassan II. He died in 1984.

MOULAY EL CHERIF/ MOULAY RACHID First sultan (1666–1672) of the Alaouite dynasty – originally an Arab family which settled in the Tafilalt in the twelfth century, where they lived modestly for centuries before seizing power. Er Rachidia (and its main street) are named after Moulay Rachid.

MOULAY HASSAN/HASSAN I The last notable Alaouite sultan (1873–1894) before the French Protectorate. He strived to damp down European-sponsored rebellion, attempting to reform his army with the help of a Scot, *Caïd* Harry

MacLean. He died suddenly and was succeeded by his son, Abd el Aziz, a profligate dreamer.

MOULAY IDRISS/MOULAY IDRISS I/ MOULAY IDRISS II Father and his posthumous son by a Berber mother. Moulay Idriss I (788–91) founded the first orthodox Muslim dynasty, ruling the northern Maghreb from Tlemcen (now in Algeria) to the Atlantic. After a regency, his son, Moulay Idriss II (804–28), came to the throne; he founded Fes and is regarded as the father of the Moroccan state.

MOULAY ISMAIL The second sultan of the Alaouite dynasty (1672–1727), but the first to establish complete rule over Morocco. His 55-year reign was one of the longest, and said to be the most brutal, in Moroccan history. He chose, and developed, Meknes as his capital. After his death, his sons fought over the succession and chaos ensued.

MOULAY YOUSSEF Appointed by the French as sultan (1912–27); he was the father of Mohammed V and grandfather of Hassan II.

MOUSSA IBN NOUSSAR Followed Oqba Ibn Nafi (see next column) and converted many Berbers to Islam. He conquered all the territory as far south as the Tafilalt, and launched Tarik Ibn Zaid across the Straits of Gibraltar.

OQBA IBN NAFI Military general and missionary who led the first Arab expedition westwards to convert the Berbers to Islam. He left Arabia in 666; founded Kairouan in present-day Tunisia in 670; and moved on into Morocco, reaching the Atlantic in 682. He was ambushed and killed by Berbers in (present-day) Algeria on his return to the east.

SALAH EDDINE EL AYOUBI (1137–90) Better known in the West as Saladin (Salah al-Din), a Kurdish-born Islamic leader who ruled Egypt and Syria 1171–93. He recaptured Jerusalem from the Crusaders in 1187.

YACOUB EL MANSOUR/ YACOUB EL MANSOUR AL MOUAHIDI Powerful sultan (1184–99) who created an empire comprising Muslim Spain and most of North Africa. He won the title "Mansour" (Victorious) when he defeated the Christians under Alfonso VIII of Castile at the battle of Alarcos on July 18, 1195. He was a generous patron of poets and philosophers.

Dates

Numerous dates, particularly those associated with Mohammed V and Hassan II, have been commemorated as street names. The most common include:

January 11, 1944 Mohammed V backed the nationalist cause when the Istiqlal party issued its manifesto on January 11, 1944, demanding, for the first time, not just reform but independence.

February 29, 1960 The Agadir earthquake struck thirteen minutes before midnight, lasting fifteen seconds.

March 2, 1956 France renounced the Protectorate and, in a formal treaty, recognized Moroccan independence. It was the 45th anniversary of the entry of French troops into Fes.

July 5, 1999 Aïd el Arch (Festival of the Throne) is celebrated on the anniversary of the accession of the king.

August 16, 1953 Over three days (August 16–18, 1953) there were anti-French riots in Casablanca, Rabat, Marrakesh and Oujda. Over 45 people were killed and more than eighty injured in Oujda alone on August 16.

August 20, 1953 On this day, the eve of Aïd el Kebir, Mohammed V was deposed by the French and was exiled first in Corsica, then Madagascar. Mayhem followed.
November 6, 1975 The date of the Green March – el Massira el Khadra (see below).
November 16, 1955 Mohammed V returned from exile to a hero's welcome. He told crowds around the Rabat Palace that the Protectorate was over and independence would follow.

November 18, 1927/November 18, 1955 Mohammed V ascended the throne on November 18, 1927 and thus, during his reign, this was celebrated as Aïd el Arch (see July 5). In 1955, it was also celebrated as Independence Day and has been celebrated subsequently as such. The three days (November 16, 17 & 18) are taken as a holiday and are known as Les Trois Glorieuses.

Parties/Organizations

AL JAMIA AL ARABI The Arab League: formed in Egypt in 1945 and moved to Tunisia in 1979 following the Camp David peace accord between Egypt and Israel.
AL MASSIRA AL KHADRA/ MARCHE VERTE The Green March into then Spanish Sahara was led by Ahmed Osman, prime minister at the time and brother-in-law to Hassan II. It began on November 6, 1975, and on November 14 Spain transferred administration of the territory to Morocco and Mauritania.
BIR ANZARANE Town in the Western Sahara and site of fierce battle between Moroccan and Polisario forces in 1979.
EL HOURIA Houria means freedom/*liberté*.

F.A.R./FORCES ARMÉES ROYALES After Mohammed V and Hassan II, the Armed Forces is the most popular name for avenues/ boulevards, and their motto "God, Country and King" is to be found prominently displayed on many a hillside.
ISTIQLAL Istiqlal means "independence" and was adopted as its name by the nationalist party formed in Fes in 1943, with Allal al Fasi as its first president. By 1951, the party had 100,000 members.
OUED EL MAKHAZINE Site of the Battle of the Three Kings (see El Mansour Eddahbi). The Portuguese found themselves trapped in a fork between the river Loukis and its tributary, the Oued El Makhazine. In European histories it is more often referred to as the battle of Ksar el Kebir.

Language

Language

Language

Very few people who come to Morocco learn to speak a word of Arabic, let alone anything of the country's three distinct Berber dialects. This is a pity – you'll be treated in a very different way if you make even a small effort to master basic phrases – though not really surprising. Moroccans are superb linguists: much of the country is bilingual in French, and anyone who has significant dealings with tourists will know some English and similar other languages too.

If you can speak French, you'll be able to get by almost anywhere you care to go; it is worth refreshing your knowledge before coming – and, if you're not too confident, bringing a good English–French phrasebook. Spanish is also useful, and widely understood in the old Spanish colonial zones around Tetouan and the Rif, and in the Deep South.

Moroccan Arabic

Moroccan Arabic, the country's official language, is substantially different from classical Arabic, or from the modern Arabic spoken in Egypt and the Gulf States. If you speak any form of Arabic, however, you will be able to make yourself understood. Egyptian Arabic, in particular, is familiar to most Moroccans, through soap operas on TV, and many will adapt their speech accordingly.

Pronunciation

There are no silent letters – you pronounce everything that's written including double vowels. Letters and syllables **in bold** should be stressed.

Here are some keys to follow:

kh	like the "ch" in Scottish loch
gh	like the French "r" (a slight gargling sound)
ai	as in "eye"
ay	as in "say"
ou/oua	w/wa (Essaouria is pronounced Essa-weera)
q	like "k" but further back in throat
j	like "s" in pleasure

Arabic and French Glossary

English	Arabic	French

Basics and everyday phrases

yes	**eyeh, na**am	oui
no	la	non

I	ena	moi
you (m/f)	enta/entee	vous
he	hoowa	lui
she	heeya	elle
we	nehnoo	nous
they	hoom	ils/elles
(very) good	mezyen (bzef)	(très) bon
big	kebeer	grand
small	segheer	petit
old	kedeem	vieux
new	jedeed	nouveau
a little	shweeya	un peu
a lot	bzef	beaucoup
open	mahlul	ouvert
closed	masdud	fermé
hello/how's it going?	le bes?	ça va?
good morning	sbah l'kheer	bonjour
good evening	msa l'kheer	bon soir
good night	leila saeeda	bonne nuit
goodbye	biselama	au revoir
who...?	shkoon...?	qui...?
when...?	imta...?	quand...?
why...?	alash...?	pourquoi...?
how...?	kifesh...?	comment...?
which/ what...?	shnoo...?	quel...?
is there...?	kayn...?	est-ce qu'il y a...?
do you have...?	andak...? /kayn...	avez-vous...?
please	afak/minfadlak to a man or afik/minfadlik to a woman	s'il vous plaît
thank you	shukran	merci
ok/agreed	wakha	d'accord
that's enough/that's all	safee	ça suffit
excuse me	ismahlee	excusez-moi
sorry/ I'm very sorry	ismahlee/ana asif	pardon/je suis désolé
let's go	nimsheeyoo	on y va
go away	imshee	va t'en
I don't understand	mafahemsh	je ne comprends pas
do you (m/f) speak English?	takelem/takelmna ingleesi?	parlez-vous anglais?

Directions

where's...?	fayn...?	où est...?
the airport	el matar	l'aeroport
the train	mahattat	la gare de

station	el tren	train
bus station	mahattat el car	la gare routière
the bank	el bank	le banque
the hospital	el mostashfa	l'hôpital
near/far	qurayab/baeed	près/loin
(from here)	(min huna)	(d'ici)
left	liseer	à gauche
right	limeen	à droit
straight ahead	neeshan	tout droit
here	hina	ici
there	hinak	là

Accommodation

hotel	funduq	hôtel
do you have a room?	kayn beet?	avez-vous une chambre?
two beds	jooj tlik	deux lits
one big bed	wahad tlik keblr	un grand lit
shower	doosh	douche
hot water	maa skhoona	eau chaud
can I see?	Mumkin ashoofha?	je peux le voir?
key	sarut	clé

Shopping

I (don't) want...	ena (mish) bgheel...	je (ne) veux (pas)...
how much	shahal	combien
(money)?	(flooss)?	(d'argent)?
(that's)	(hada)	(c'est) cher
expensive	ghalee	

Numbers

0	·	sifr	zéro
1	١	wahad	un
2	٢	jooj	deux
3	٣	tlata	trois
4	٤	arbaa	quatre
5	٥	khamsa	cinq
6	٦	sitta	six
7	٧	sebaa	sept
8	٨	temanya	huit
9	٩	tisaoud	neuf
10	١٠	ashra	dix
11	١١	hadashar	onze
12	١٢	etnashar	douze
13	١٣	talatashar	treize
14	١٤	arbatashar	quatorze

15	١٥	kham**tashar**	quinze
16	١٦	sit**tashar**	seize
17	١٨	seba**tashar**	dix-sept
18	١٩	taman**tashar**	dix-huit
19	١٩	tisa**tashar**	dix-neuf
20	٢٠	ash**reen**	vingt
21	٢١	**wah**ad wa ash**reen**	vingt-et-un
22	٢٢	jooj wa ash**reen**	vingt-deux
30	٣٠	tala**teen**	trente
40	٤٠	arba**een**	quarante
50	٥٠	kham**seen**	cinqante
60	٦٠	sit**teen**	soixante
70	٧٠	saba**een**	soixante-dix
80	٨٠	taman**een**	quatre vingts
90	٩٠	tısa**een**	quatre-vingt-dix
100	١٠٠	mia	cent
121	١٢١	mia wa **wah**ad wa ash**reen**	cent vingt-et-un
200	٢٠٠	mia**teen**	deux cents
300	٣٠٠	**tol**ta mia	trois cents
1000	١٠٠٠	alf	mille
a half		nuss	demi
a quarter		**rob**a	quart

Days and times

Monday	na**har** el it **neen**	lundi
Tuesday	na**har** et te**lat**	mardi
Wednesday	na**har** el **ar**baa	mercredi
Thursday	na**har** el khe**mis**	jeudi
Friday	na**har** el je**ma**a	vendredi
Saturday	na**har** es sabt	samedi
Sunday	na**har** el had	dimanche
yesterday	im**bar**ih	hier
today	el yoom	aujourd'hui
tomorrow	**ghe**da	demain
what time is it?	sha**hal** fisa'a?	quelle heure est-il?
one o'clock	sa'a **wah**da	une heure
2.15	jooj wa **ro**ba	deux heures et quart
3.30	t**lat**a wa nuss	trois heures et demi
4.45	**ar**baa ila **ro**ba	quatre heures moins quart

Food and drink

Basics

| restaurant | **mat**aam | restaurant |
| breakfast | if**tar** | petit déjeuner |

egg	beyd	ouef
butter	**zib**da	beurre
jam	marma**lad**	confiture
cheese	**jib**na	fromage
yoghurt	**ra**yeb	yaourt
salad	sa**lat**a	salade
olives	zi**toun**	olives
oil	zit	huile
bread	khobz	pain
salt	**mel**ha	sel
pepper	har**oor**	piment
(without)	(bi**lesh**)	(sans)
sugar	sukkar	sucre
the bill	el hisab	l'addition
fork	for**shaat**	fourchette
knife	mooss	couteau
spoon	malka	cuillère
plate	tab**seel**	assiete
glass	**kess**	verre
What do you have . . .	**Ash**noo **kane** . . .	Qu'est ce que vous avez. . .
. . . to eat?	. . . f'l-**mak**la?	. . . pour manger?
. . . to drink?	. . . f'l-mucha**roubat?**	. . .pour boire?
What is this?	Shnoo **hada?**	Qu'est ce que c'est?
I'm a vegetarian	ana na**bati** wa la a**kulu** lehoum **wala** hout	Je suis vegetarien/ vegetarienne
This is not what I asked for!	Hedea **meshee heea li tlubt!**	Ceci n'est pas ce que j'ai demande
The bill, please.	L'**h'seb** minfa**dlik**	L'addition s'il vous plaît
Please write it down.	Mɪnfadlik, k'**tib'h**	Est-ce que vous pouvez l'écrite s'il vous plaît?

Meat, poultry and fish

meat	**lah**em	viande
beef	**baq**ri	boeuf
chicken	djaj	poulet
lamb	**hou**li	mouton
liver	**kib**da	foie
pigeon	**ham**am	pigeon
fish	hout	poisson
prawns	**qam**bri	crevettes

Vegetables

vegetables	khadra**wat**	légumes
artichoke	qoq	artichaut
aubergine	badin**jan**	aubergine
beans	**loo**bia	haricots
onions	**ba**sal	oignons

potatoes	batata	patates
tomatoes	mateesha	tomates

Fruits and nuts

almonds	looz	amandes
apple	tufah	pomme
banana	banan	banane
dates	tmer	dattes
figs	kermooss	figues
grapes	ainab	raisins
lemon	limoon	limon
melon	battikh	melon
orange	limoon	orange
pomegranate	rooman	granade
prickly pear (cactus fruit)	hendiya	figues de Barbarie
strawberry	frowla	fraise
watermelon	dellah	pastèque

Beverages

water	maa	de l'eau
mineral water	Sidi Ali/Sidi Harazem (brand names)	eau minérale
ice	jeleedi	glace
ice cream	glace	glace
milk	haleeb	lait
coffee	qahwa	café
coffee with a little milk	nuss nuss	café cassé
coffee with plenty of milk	qahwa bi haleeb	café au lait/café crème
tea (with mint/with wormwood)	atay (bi nana/ bi sheeba)	thé (à la menthe/ à l'absinthe)
juice	aseer	jus
beer	birra	bière
wine	sharab	vin
almond milk	aseer looz	jus d'amande
apple milkshake	aseer tufah	jus de pomme
banana milkshake	aseer banan	jus des bananes
orange juice	aseer limoon	jus d'orange
mixed fruit milkshake		jus panache

Common dishes and foods

bisara	thick pea soup, usually served with olive oil and cumin		though sometimes containing meat or eggs
chakchouka	a vegetable stew not unlike ratatouille,	couscous aux sept legumes	seven-vegetable couscous (sometimes

	vegetarian, though often made with meat stock)		pastry; a speciality of Fes
		(pommes) frites	French fries
harira	bean soup, usually also containing pasta and meat	salade Marocaine	salad of tomato and cucumber, finely chopped
kefta	minced meat (usually lamb)	tajine	a Moroccan casserole cooked over charcoal in a thick ceramic bowl (which is what the word really refers to) with a conical lid
loobia	bean stew		
mechoui	roast lamb		
merguez	small, spicy dark red sausages – typically lamb, though sometimes of beef – usually grilled over charcoal		
		tajine aux olives et citron	tajine of chicken with olive and preserved lemon
pastilla	sweet pigeon or chicken pie with cinnamon and filo	tanjia	a Marrakshi speciality, jugged beef – the term in fact refers to the jug

Breads and pastries

briouats/ doits de Fatima	sweet filo pastry with a savoury filling, a bit like a miniature pastilla	harsha	flat, leavened griddle bread with a gritty crust, served at cafés for breakfast
briouats au miel	sweet filo pastry envelopes filed with nuts and honey	millefeuille	custard slice
		msammen	flat griddle bread made from dough sprinkled with oil, rolled out and folded over several times, rather like an Indian paratha
cornes de gazelles (Fr.)/ kab l-ghazl (Ar.)	marzipan-filled, banana-shaped pastry horns		

Berber words and phrases in Tashelhaït

There are three Berber dialects which encompass roughly geographical areas. They are known by several names, of which these are the most common:

Riffi – The Rif mountains and Northern Morocco
Zaian, **Tamazight** – The Middle Atlas and Central Morocco
Tashelhaït, **Soussi**, **Chleuh** – The High and Anti-Atlas and the South

As the most popular Berber areas for visitors are the High Atlas and South, the following is a very brief guide to **Tashelhaït words and phrases**.

Basics

Yes, no	Eyeh, Oho	Good	Eefulkee/Eeshwa
Thank you, please	Barakalaufik	Bad	Khaib

Today	Ghasad	Excuse me	Semhee
Tomorrow	Sbah	Berbers	Shleuh
Yesterday	Eegdam		

Greetings and farewells (All Arabic greetings understood)

Hello	La bes darik (man)	See you later	Akrawes dah inshallah
(response – la bes)	La bes darim (woman)	Goodbye	Akayaoon Arbee
How are you?	Meneek antgeet?	Say hello to	Sellum flfamilenik
	(response – la bes	your family	
	lmamdulah)		

Directions and names on maps

Where is. . . ?	Mani heela . . . ?	I want to go to . . .	Reeh . . .
. . . the road to . . .	. . . aghares s . . .		(literally, "I want")
. . . the village . . .	. . . doowar . . .	On survey maps you'll find these names:	
. . . the river . . .	. . . aseet . . .	Mountain	Adrar, Djebel
. . . the mountain . . .	. . . adrar . . .	River	Assif, Oued
. . . the pass . . .	. . . tizee . . .	Pass (of)	Tizi (n.)
. . . your house	. . . teegimeenik	Shepherd's hut	Azib
Is it far/close?	Ees yagoog/eeqareb?	Hill, small mountain	Aourir
Straight	Neeshan	Ravine	Talat
To the right/left	Fofaseenik/fozelmad	Rock	Azrou
Where are	Manee treet? (s.)	("n" between words indicates the	
you going?	Manee drem? (pl.)	possessive, "of")	

Buying and numbers

1	yen	30	Ashreent d mrawet
2	seen	40	Snet id ashreent
3	krad	50	Snet id ashreent
4	koz		d mrawet
5	smoos	100	Smoost id ashreent/
6	sddes		meeya
7	sa	How much is it?	Minshk aysker?
8	tem	No good	oor eefulkee
9	tza	Too expensive	Eeghula bzef
10	mrawet	Come down a	Nuqs emeek
11	yen d mrawet	little (in price)	
12	seen d mrawet	Give me . . .	Feeyee . . .
20	Ashreent	I want . . .	Reeh . . .
21	Ashreent d yen d	Big/Small	Mqorn/Eemzee
	mrawet	A lot/little	Bzef/eemeek
22	Ashreent d seen	Do you have . . . ?	Ees daroon . . . ?
	d mrawet	Is there . . . ?	Ees eela . . . ?

... food	... teeremt	... a place to sleep	... kra lblast
... a mule	... aserdon		mahengwen
		... water	... amen

Sit	Gawer, Skoos	Here	Rede (when handing
Drink	Soo		something to
Eat	Shta		someone)

Arabic/Berber phrasebooks & learning materials

Arabic phrasebooks

Moroccan Arabic Phrasebook (Lonely Planet, Australia). The most functional English–Moroccan Arabic phrasebook.

In Moroccan bookshops, you can pick up a *Guide de Conversation/Conversation Guide*, which covers basic phrases of English–French–Moroccan Arabic–Berber.

Arabic coursebooks

Ernest T. Abdel Massih, *An Introduction to Moroccan Arabic; Advanced Moroccan Arabic*. Both of these are published by University of Michigan Press, with accompanying tapes

Richard S. Harris and Mohammed Abn Tald, *Basic Course in Moroccan Arabic* (Georgetown UP).

Berber coursebooks

Ernest T. Abdel Massih, *A Course in Spoken Tamazight: Berber Dialects of the Middle Atlas; A Reference Grammar of Tamazight, Plus An Introduction to the Berber Language*. Again, both of these are published by University of Michigan Press, with accompanying tapes.

Arabic lessons in Morocco

Contact the American Language Centre (head office: 1 Pl de la Fraternité, Casablanca).

University of Michigan Publications

For books write to: The Publications Secretary, Centre for Near Eastern and North African Studies, 144 Lane Hall, University of Michigan, Ann Arbor, Michigan 48109. For tapes write to: Michigan Media Resource Centre (Tape Duplication Service), University of Michigan, 400 S. Fourth Street, Ann Arbor, Michigan 48103.

Bookshops

The following bookshops usually have language reference material:

Librairie des Colonnes, Boulevard Pasteur, Tangier.

American Language Centre Bookstore, 1 Pl de la Fraternité, just off Boulevard Moulay Youssef, Casablanca.

American Bookstore, Rue Tanger, Rabat.

The Maghreb Review and Bookshop, 45 Burton St, London WC1, England.

Travel store

D: Rough Guide
DIRECTIONS for
short breaks

Available from all good bookstores

enya
arrakesh **D**
orocco
outh Africa, Lesotho
  & Swaziland
yria
anzania
unisia
West Africa
Zanzibar

Travel Specials
First-Time Africa
First-Time Around
  the World
First-Time Asia
First-Time Europe
First-Time Latin
  America
Travel Health
Travel Online
Travel Survival
Walks in London
  & SE England
Women Travel
World Party

Maps
Algarve
Amsterdam
Andalucia
  & Costa del Sol
Argentina
Athens
Australia
Barcelona
Berlin
Boston & Cambridge
Brittany
Brussels
California
Chicago
Chile
Corsica
Costa Rica
  & Panama
Crete
Croatia
Cuba
Cyprus
Czech Republic
Dominican Republic
Dubai & UAE
Dublin
Egypt

Florence & Siena
Florida
France
Frankfurt
Germany
Greece
Guatemala & Belize
Iceland
India
Ireland
Italy
Kenya & Northern
  Tanzania
Lisbon
London
Los Angeles
Madrid
Malaysia
Mallorca
Marrakesh
Mexico
Miami & Key West
Morocco
New England
New York City
New Zealand
Northern Spain
Paris
Peru
Portugal
Prague
Pyrenees & Andorra
Rome
San Francisco
Sicily
South Africa
South India
Spain & Portugal
Sri Lanka
Tenerife
Thailand
Toronto
Trinidad & Tobago
Tunisia
Turkey
Tuscany
Venice
Vietnam, Laos
  & Cambodia
Washington DC
Yucatán Peninsula

**Dictionary
Phrasebooks**
Croatian
Czech
Dutch
Egyptian Arabic
French
German
Greek
Hindi & Urdu
Italian
Japanese
Latin American
  Spanish
Mandarin Chinese
Mexican Spanish
Polish
Portuguese
Russian
Spanish
Swahili
Thai
Turkish
Vietnamese

Computers
Blogging
eBay
iPhone
iPods, iTunes
  & music online
The Internet
Macs & OS X
MySpace
PCs and Windows
PlayStation Portable
Website Directory

Film & TV
American
  Independent Film
British Cult Comedy
Chick Flicks
Comedy Movies
Cult Movies
Film
Film Musicals
Film Noir
Gangster Movies
Horror Movies
Kids' Movies
Sci-Fi Movies
Westerns

Lifestyle
Babies
Ethical Living
Pregnancy & Birth
Running

Music Guides
The Beatles
Blues
Bob Dylan
Book of Playlists
Classical Music
Elvis
Frank Sinatra
Heavy Metal
Hip-Hop
Jazz
Led Zeppelin
Opera
Pink Floyd
Punk
Reggae
Rock
The Rolling Stones
Soul and R&B
Velvet Underground
World Music
  (2 vols)

Popular Culture
Books for Teenagers
Children's Books,
  5-11
Conspiracy Theories
Crime Fiction
Cult Fiction
The Da Vinci Code
His Dark Materials
Lord of the Rings
Shakespeare
Superheroes
The Templars
Unexplained
  Phenomena

Science
The Brain
Climate Change
The Earth
Genes & Cloning
The Universe
Weather

For more information go to www.roughguides.com

ROUGH GUIDES

The most accurate maps in the world"

For **flying visits**, check out Rough Guide **DIRECTIONS**

It's like having a local friend plan your trip.

"A guide as *direct* as DIRECTIONS is exactly what I need when I'm visiting a city for the first time"
The Independent, UK

Focusing on cities, islands and resort regions, Rough Guides **DIRECTIONS** are richly illustrated in full-colour throughout. US$10.99, CAN$15.99, £6.99

Choose from dozens of worldwide titles, from London to Las Vegas.

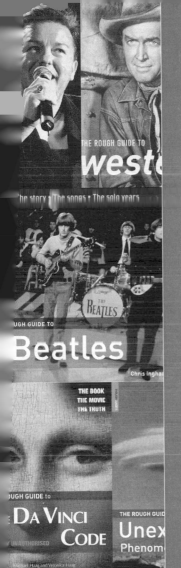

Avoid Guilt Trips

Buy fair trade coffee + bananas ✓

Save energy – use low energy bulbs ✓

    – don't leave tv on standby ✓

Offset carbon emissions from flight to Madric

Send goat to Africa ✓

Join Tourism Concern today ✓

Slowly, the world is changing
Together we can, and will, make a difference

Tourism Concern is the only UK registered charity fighting exploitation in one of the largest industries on earth: people forced from their homes in order that holiday resorts can be built, sweatshop labour conditions in hotels and destruction of the environment are just some of the issues that we tackle.

Sending people on a guilt trip is not something we do. We know as well as anyone that holidays are precious. But you can help us to ensure that tourism always benefits the local communities involved.

Call 020 7133 3330
or visit **tourismconcern.org.uk** to find out how.

A year's membership of Tourism Concern costs just £20 (£12 unwaged) – that's 38 pence a week, less than the cost of a pint of milk, organic of course.

Fighting Exploitation in Tourism

TourismConcern

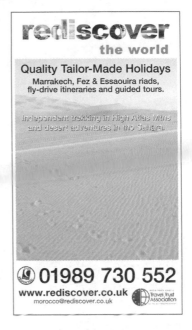

NOTES

NOTES

NOTES

Small print and

Index

A Rough Guide to Rough Guides

Published in 1982, the first Rough Guide – to Greece – was a student scheme
that became a publishing phenomenon. Mark Ellingham, a recent graduate in
English from Bristol University, had been travelling in Greece the previous summer
and couldn't find the right guidebook. With a small group of friends he wrote his
own guide, combining a highly contemporary, journalistic style with a thoroughly
practical approach to travellers' needs.

The immediate success of the book spawned a series that rapidly covered dozens
of destinations. And, in addition to impecunious backpackers, Rough Guides
soon acquired a much broader and older readership that relished the guides' wit
and inquisitiveness as much as their enthusiastic, critical approach and value-for-
money ethos.

These days, Rough Guides include recommendations from shoestring to luxury
and cover more than 200 destinations around the globe, including almost every
country in the Americas and Europe, more than half of Africa and most of Asia and
Australasia. Our ever-growing team of authors and photographers is spread all
over the world, particularly in Europe, the USA and Australia.

In the early 1990s, Rough Guides branched out of travel, with the publication of
Rough Guides to World Music, Classical Music and the Internet. All three have
become benchmark titles in their fields, spearheading the publication of a wide
range of books under the Rough Guide name.

Including the travel series, Rough Guides now number more than 350 titles,
covering: phrasebooks, waterproof maps, music guides from Opera to Heavy
Metal, reference works as diverse as Conspiracy Theories and Shakespeare, and
popular culture books from iPods to Poker. Rough Guides also produce a series of
more than 120 World Music CDs in partnership with World Music Network.

Visit www.roughguides.com to see our latest publications.

Rough Guide travel images are available for commercial licensing at
www.roughguidespictures.com

Rough Guide credits

Text editors: Alice Park, Alison Murchie, Helena Smith, Sarah Eno, Lucy White
Layout: Pradeep Thapliyal
Cartography: Rajesh Mishra
Picture editor: Nicole Newman
Production: Rebecca Short
Proofreader: Anita Sach
Cover design: Chloë Roberts
Photographer: Suzanne Porter
Editorial: **London** Kate Berens, Claire Saunders, Ruth Blackmore, Polly Thomas,Suzanne Porter, Karoline Densley, Andy Turner, Keith Drew, Edward Aves, Nikki Birrell, Jo Kirby, Samantha Cook, James Smart, Natasha Foges, Róisín Cameron, Emma Traynor, Emma Gibbs, Joe Staines, Duncan Clark, Peter Buckley, Matthew Milton, Tracy Hopkins, Ruth Tidball; **New York** Andrew Rosenberg, Steven Horak, AnneLise Sorensen, Amy Hegarty, April Isaacs, Ella Steim, Anna Owens, Joseph Petta, Sean Mahoney; **Delhi** Madhavi Singh, Karen D'Souza
Design & Pictures: **London** Scott Stickland, Dan May, Diana Jarvis, Mark Thomas, Jj Luck, Chloë Roberts, Sarah Cummins; **Delhi** Umesh Aggarwal, Ajay Verma, Jessica Subramanian,
Ankur Guha, Sachin Tanwar, Anita Singh, Nikhil Agarwal
Production: Aimee Hampson, Vicky Baldwin
Cartography: **London** Maxine Repath, Ed Wright, Katie Lloyd-Jones; **Delhi** Jai Prakash Mishra, Rajesh Chhibber, Ashutosh Bharti, Animesh Pathak, Jasbir Sandhu, Karobi Gogoi, Amod Singh, Alakananda Bhattacharya, Swati Handoo
Online: **New York** Jennifer Gold, Kristin Mingrone; **Delhi** Manik Chauhan, Narender Kumar, Rakesh Kumar, Amit Verma, Rahul Kumar, Ganesh Sharma, Debojit Borah
Marketing & Publicity: **London** Liz Statham, Niki Hanmer, Louise Maher, Jess Carter, Vanessa Godden, Vivienne Watton, Anna Paynton, Rachel Sprackett, Lenalisa Fornberg; **New York** Geoff Colquitt, Megan Kennedy, Katy Ball; **Delhi** Reem Khokhar
Manager India: Punita Singh
Series Editor: Mark Fllingham
Reference Director: Andrew Lockett
Publishing Coordinator: Helen Phillips
Publishing Director: Martin Dunford
Commercial Manager: Gino Magnotta
Managing Director: John Duhigg

Publishing information

This eighth edition published October 2007 by **Rough Guides Ltd**,
80 Strand, London WC2R 0RL
345 Hudson St, 4th Floor,
New York, NY 10014, USA
14 Local Shopping Centre, Panchsheel Park, New Delhi 110017, India
Distributed by the Penguin Group
Penguin Books Ltd,
80 Strand, London WC2R 0RL
Penguin Group (USA)
375 Hudson Street, NY 10014, USA
Penguin Group (Australia)
250 Camberwell Road, Camberwell, Victoria 3124, Australia
Penguin Books Canada Ltd,
10 Alcorn Avenue, Toronto, Ontario, Canada M4V 1E4
Penguin Group (NZ)
67 Apollo Drive, Mairangi Bay, Auckland 1310, New Zealand

Cover concept by Peter Dyer.
Typeset in Bembo and Helvetica to an original design by Henry Iles.
Printed in Italy by Legoprint S.p.A.
© Mark Fllingham 2007
No part of this book may be reproduced in any form without permission from the publisher except for the quotation of brief passages in reviews.
840pp includes index
A catalogue record for this book is available from the British Library
ISBN: 978-1-84353-861-5

The publishers and authors have done their best to ensure the accuracy and currency of all the information in **The Rough Guide to Morocco**, however, they can accept no responsibility for any loss, injury, or inconvenience sustained by any traveler as a result of information or advice contained in the guide.

1 3 5 7 9 8 6 4 2

Help us update

We've gone to a lot of effort to ensure that the eighth edition of **The Rough Guide to Morocco** is accurate and up to date. However, things change – places get "discovered", opening hours are notoriously fickle, restaurants and rooms raise prices or lower standards. If you feel we've got it wrong or left something out, we'd like to know, and if you can remember the address, the price, the time, the phone number, so much the better. We'll credit all contributions, and send a copy of the next edition (or any other Rough Guide if you prefer) for the best letters. Everyone who writes
to us and isn't already a subscriber will receive a copy of our full-color thrice-yearly newsletter. Please mark letters: "**Rough Guide Morocco Update**" and send to: Rough Guides, 80 Strand, London WC2R 0RL, or Rough Guides, 345 Hudson St, 4th Floor, New York, NY 10014. Or send an email to **mail@roughguides.com**
Have your questions answered and tell others about your trip at
www.roughguides.atinfopop.com

Acknowledgements

Daniel Jacobs would like to thank Jan Piebe, Martin Davies, Roger Norum, Houssine Laroussi, Mohammed Ouhammou Sahnoun, Richard Lim, Abdelillah Alami, Tony Howard and special thanks to Hamish Brown for his copious notes on chapters other than his own, and to James Stewart for his information on surfing.

Daniel Lund would like to thank Abdelghani Znati, Said Naceur, Ibriham Kamal and Jennifer Condell.

Readers' letters

Thanks to all the readers who have taken the time to write in with comments and suggestions (and apologies if we've inadvertently omitted or misspelt anyone's name):

Lola Reid Allin and Jeffrey Allin, Kathy Anderson, Kamal Arji, Abdenbi Bahrouch, Rose Balfour, Gianfranco Ballardin, Tom Barrance, Jane Bayley, Mike Beasley, Abdelkhalek Benalila, Souad Benzakour, Simon Birkenhead and Chris McIntosh, Rachel Blech, Jane Borges, Mohamed Bouinbaden, Jim and Margie Campbell, Ian Cantwell, Helene Caron, Des and Nathalie Clark, Sophia Cheema, Charles Clarke, Jethro Clunies-Ross, Laura "Luraah", Loc Dao, Jean Dunleavy, Dietmar Dzieyk, Emma Fellows, Rokos Frangos, Adrian Gatton, Philippe Charlie Gillett, V. Greaves, Guiguet-Bologne, Sarah Hill, Elsa Holmes, Rachid Imerhane, Philip Jones, Eddie Joseph, Jasmin Jouhar, Helen Kilner-MacPhee, Justine Kirby, David L. Kleinman, Moulay Abdellah Lahrizi, Tony Lear, George Lewis, Tiny and Riana Ligthart, Peter Lilley, Alison Macdonald, Charlotte Marceau, George May, Anna Mietta, Shukwai Milner, Sally O' Halloran, Mhamed Oukhouya, Bruno Ouvrard, Graham Otter, Mary Pease, Susan Phillips, Aliisa Piskonen, Guy Poirier, Barry Powney, Kieth [sic] Primental, Christian Raun, Caroline Redrup, Hilary Rees, Arnold Reijndorp, Joyce Rice, George Ricketts, Tim and Rowan Roberts, Dan Robertson and Clare Clewer, Malcolm Sandall, Dietrich Scheiter, Erik Schmollinger, Carrie Schaffner, Marvin and Trish Scott, Jim and Elaine Scullion, Chris Skeaping, Ingvar Skobba, Mary Snelling, Mohammed Souidi, Graham Solo and Anne Stone, Matt Summers, Ellen Tasker and Neil Gatward, Paul Tasker, Molly and Robin Taylor, Laurel Teo, Valerie Thoen and Marc Droessaert, Barbara u. Tobi, Dominique Tolbert, Jan van Ingen Schenau and Marleen Rolie, Christian Vesin and Soukkani Imane, Meg Ward and Wayne Griffiths, Tina Weiss, C.G. Welburn, Christopher Wright, Matthias Wüstefeld, Andrew Youngson

Photo credits

All photos © Rough Guides except the following:

Introduction
Souks, Marrakesh © Nicole Newman

Things not to miss
01 Ruins of Glaoui kasbah at Telouet © Robert Harding/Getty
02 Chefchaouen © Olivier Asselin/Alamy
03 Majorelle garden, Marrakesh © Nicole Newman
05 Windsurfing, Agadir Beach © Jon Arnold images/ Corbis
07 Berber marhaya © Thodor Marchante Wholograph/Gotti
08 Tizi n'Tichka Pass © Darren Humphrys
10 Snowboarding, Djebel Toubkal © Stefan Schuetz/zefa/Corbis
11 Musicians, Marrakesh © Neil Emmerson/ Robert Harding
15 Cascades d'Ouzoud © Jason Friend/Alamy
18 Tin Mal mosque © John & Lisa Merrill/Getty
20 Unfastened track through the Sahara © Guenter Rossenbach/zefa/Corbis
22 Asilah © Aliki image library/Alamy
23 Berber transport © Hamish Brown
24 Imilchil Wedding Ceremony © Bruno Morandi/ Robert Harding
26 Hikers in High Atlas Mountains © David Samuel Robbins/Corbis
27 Tangier © Jean du Boisberranger/ImageBank/ Getty
28 Riad Al Moussika © Riad Al Moussika
32 Djemaa el-Fna © Gavin Hellier/Robert Harding
34 Woman applying a henna tattoo, Djemaa el Fna © Martin Norris / Alamy

Festivals and music colour section
Djemma el Fna, Gnaoua musician © Darren Humphrys

Meknes Gnaoua © Neil van der Linden
Fes, Sufi nights © Neil van der Linden
Moulay Idriss © Neil van der Linden
Berber music © Neil van der Linden
Berber music © Neil van der Linden

Black and whites
p.98 Asilah © Aliki image library/Alamy
p.113 Main beach at Tangier © Robert Harding Library/Alamy
p.117 Tangier © Roger Viollet Collection/Getty
p.129 Hercules Caves © Greg Balfour Evans / Alamy
p.161 Old town houses Chefchaouen © The Photolibrary Wales/Alamy
p.176 Rif mountains © Sean Burke / Alamy
p.172 Melilla Art Nouveau © Jose Navarro
p.200 Oued Moulouya © Darren Humphrys
p.311 Barbary monkey © Abdelhak Senna /AFP/Getty
p.484 Berber village, Ouarikt Valley, High Atlas mountains © David C Poole/Robert Harding
p.507 Weekly market, Tahanoute, High Atlas Mountains © Ethel Davies/Robert Harding
p.515 Kasbah of Telouet Atlas Mountains in background © Robert Frerck/Getty
p.672 Laayoune, Colonial architecture © Worldwide Picture Library/Alamy
p.675 Nomad riders on their camels during a parade in Tan-Tan © Jack Dabaghian /Reuters/Corbis
p.686 Fish market, Tarfaya © Worldwide Picture Library / Alamy
p.738 Elephant shrew © Anthony Bannister/ Corbis

SMALL PRINT

Index

Map entries are in colour.

INDEX

O

INDEX

W

X

Y

Z

Map symbols

maps are listed in the full index using coloured text

▪▪▪▪▪	International boundary	⬆	Refuge hut
▪▪▪	Chapter division boundary	☼	Viewpoint
▪▪▪	Historic boundary	ⵜ	Gardens
▬▬	Motorway	🅢	Swimming pool
═══	Major road	▫	Restaurant
▬▬	Minor road	◉	Accommodation
▬▬	Pedestrianised road	@	Internet
▪▪▪▪▪	Piste (unpaved road)	ⓘ	Tourist office
▥▥▥	Steps	♟	Fort & Fortress
▪▪▪▪	Path	ⵏ	Lighthouse
⋯⋯	Trail	∴	Ruin
▬▬	Railway	▮	Tower
▬ ▬	Ferry route	✈	Airport
——	River	⌒	Arch
——	Wall	🕌	Mosque
↑	One way arrow	🏛	Monument
/|\	Hill	✕	Battle site
《	Dune	✡	Synagogue
	Saltpan	✉	Post office
	Rocks	◉	Picturesque village
	Cliff	⊓	Ksar
	Mountain range	★	Bus/taxi stop
	Gorge	⊞	Hospital
▲	Peak	🅿	Parking
⇗	Mountain pass	▮	Building
	Cave	⊞	Church (town maps)
	Waterfall	⌣	Mosque
⋎⋎	Spring	◯	Stadium
ⵉⵉ	Oasis	▭	Market
△	Campsite	⊹	Christian cemetery
⊠	Gate	⋮	Jewish cemetery
♦	Place of interest	ⵉ	Muslim cemetery
●	Barracks and engravings	⬚	Park
⌣	Bridge	⬚	Beach

MAP SYMBOLS